Queer Cultures

D0145289

Deborah Carlin, Editor
Jennifer DiGrazia, Associate Editor

PEARSON
Prentice
Hall

Upper Saddle River, New Jersey 07458

Library of Congress Cataloging-in-Publication Data
Queer cultures / Deborah Carlin, editor ;
Jennifer DiGrazia, associate editor.
    p. cm.
  ISBN 0-13-041653-3
  1. Homosexuality—Philosophy. 2. Gays—Identity. I. Carlin, Deborah
II. DiGrazia, Jennifer.
HQ76.25 .Q363 2004
306.76'6'01—dc22

                                            2003016036

Editor-in-Chief: Leah Jewell
Acquisitions Editor: Vivian Garcia
Marketing Assistant: Adam Laitmen
Editorial Assistant: Jennifer Migueis
Production Liaison: Fran Russello
Director of Marketing: Beth Gillette Mejia
Senior Marketing Manager: Rachel Falk
Manufacturing Buyer: Brian Mackey
Cover Design: Robert Farrar-Wagner
Composition/Full-Service Project Management: Pine Tree Composition
Printer/Binder: Courier Companies, Inc.
Cover Printer: Phoenix Color Corp.

Credits and acknowledgments borrowed from other sources and reproduced, with permission, in this textbook appear on page 780.

Pearson Prentice Hall™ is a trademark of Pearson Education, Inc.
Pearson® is a registered trademark of Pearson plc
Prentice Hall® is a registered trademark of Pearson Education, Inc.

Pearson Education, Ltd., London
Pearson Education Singapore Pte. Ltd.
Pearson Education Canada, Ltd.
Pearson Education—Japan
Pearson Education Australia Pty. Limited
Pearson Education North Asia Ltd.

Pearson Educación de Mexico,
  S.A. de C.V.
Pearson Education Malaysia, Pte. Ltd.
Pearson Education, Upper Saddle River,
  New Jersey

10 9 8 7 6 5 4 3 2 1
ISBN 0-13-041653-3

In loving memory of Chris Norris,
teacher, mentor, friend

Contents

Acknowledgments

This book never would have come into being had not Carrie Brandon and Ed Weisman from Prentice-Hall come into my office one afternoon and broached the subject of a Queer Theory anthology and textbook. Carrie Brandon's imagination about what this book could be, her open-mindedness, and her incredible patience have been inspirational, while Ed Weisman's enthusiasm, support, and encouragement humble me in their generosity and professionalism. Mary Dalton-Hoffman also deserves many thanks for all of her work with manuscript permissions; it is much appreciated. I would also like to extend a sincere thanks to Patty Donovan of Pine Tree Composition, for her patience and her support during trying times, as well as to Leah Jewell and Vivian Garcia, who helped shepherd this project through at its end.

Jennifer DiGrazia, the Associate Editor of *Queer Cultures*, is responsible for many of the best aspects of this work: Its chapter questions, its writing assignments, a pedagogy bibliography, and for both writing and feedback on the introductions to each section. Her intelligence, energy, patience, dedication, good humor, and composition expertise have been a steady source of inspiration and motivation in the completion of this project. My most profound thanks to this valued colleague and extraordinary person.

The undergraduate and graduate students in the Queer Cultures and Queer Theory courses I have taught at the University of Massachusetts, Amherst have been the imaginative audience for me throughout this work. Their questions, their insights, and their challenges have contributed to this work in countless ways. I would especially like to recognize the graduate students with whom I have read, discussed, and explored queer theory in the classroom and in independent studies; our intellectual exchange informs this book at its core: James Allan, Tricia Asklar, John Bickford, Michel Boucher, Pamela Burdack, Adrianne Bushey, Kim Costino, Carl Cyr, Athena Devlin, Jennifer DiGrazia, Vincent Doyle, Alex Fleck, Carlos Gonzalez, Neil Hartlen, Monika

Hogan, Jenny Kurtz, Pamela Lawrence, Sara Lewis, Warren Longmire, Christine Monahan, Don Operario, Angelo Robinson, Cynthia Roderick, Jennifer Rogers, Katy Ryan, Andrew Schiffer, Katherine Sender, Karen Skoifield, Dan Smith, Kenneth Smith, Lori Walk and Mary Wilson.

The incredibly knowledgeable and cool staff of Pleasant Street Video in Northampton fielded all my queries for film information with their characteristic grace and good humor; thanks to Dana Gentes, Bill Dwight, Gene Kane, Chris St. George, and Jen Lassig. I am very grateful for the support of Stephen Clingman and Anne Herrington, the former and current chairs of English at the University of Massachusetts, Amherst, who made it possible for me to extend my sabbatical with department leave, without which I would not have finished this book. Thanks also to my friends and colleagues, too numerous to list, who turned a kind ear and sharp intelligence to some of the personal and theoretical challenges posed by this book.

And finally, how can I begin to thank Deborah Fairman, who is as necessary to my life as air, as vital as poetry, as trustworthy as the sun's rising? I can't, so this will, I hope, in its small way, begin that process.

Introduction

To describe this collection as a "textbook" of queer theory is to venture into dangerous territory indeed, for one of our common assumptions about textbooks is that they codify a body of material and, as a consequence, reify the subject of the text into something coherent, material, whole, and unified. Such, I am happy to report, is neither the goal nor the effect of this collection. On the contrary, *Queer Cultures* is organized in such a way that readers are invited to examine the range of arguments (as well as their underlying assumptions) that have been instrumental in the intellectual amalgamation that is sexuality studies, Gay, Bisexual, Lesbian, and Transgender (GBLT) studies, and queer theory combined. The essays in this anthology have been chosen because they present various, sometimes opposing, always intellectually challenging points-of-view across the disciplines of philosophy, literature, history, film, political science, anthropology, economics, and sociology. They represent nothing less, and indeed, nothing more, than the continuously evolving dialogue that constitutes any arena of academic investigation.

There are several fine anthologies already on the market in the field of GBLT/Queer Studies, and this anthology not only shares some essays in common with them, but is intellectually indebted to their evolving vision of what issues and authors characterize this field. *The Lesbian and Gay Studies Reader* (NY: Routledge, 1993), edited by Henry Abelove, Michèle Aina Barale, and David M. Halperin, was the first comprehensive anthology of theory wide enough to serve as the text for a graduate or highly advanced undergraduate course. It was followed by two later anthologies, each of which incorporated a broad range of essays, articles, and personal narratives: *A Queer World: The Center for Lesbian and Gay Studies Reader* (NY: NYUP, 1997), edited by Martin Duberman, and *The Columbia Reader on Lesbians & Gay Men in Media, Society, & Politics* (NY: Columbia UP, 1999), edited by Larry Gross and James D. Woods. Donald R. Morton's, *The Material Queer: A LesBiGay Cultural Studies Reader* (Boulder, CO: Westview Press, 1996) has been enormously influential on the scheme of this collection in its self-conscious design as an anthology that is also a course text appropriate for advanced undergraduate and graduate students. Several other brilliant and formative collections of essays have been published throughout the 1990s and now into the beginning of the twenty-first century, and the reader will see many of their influential essays listed throughout the RE-LATED READING bibliographies located at the end of each chapter in *Queer Cultures*. Instructors seeking an appropriate textbook for high school and early college students should examine *Becoming Visible: A Reader in Gay and Lesbian History for High School and College Students* (Boston, MA: Alyson Publications, 1994), edited by Kevin Jennings.

Queer Cultures is an anthology of some of the most important and influential articles written in GBLT and Queer Studies in the past twenty years, ones that will be engaging and comprehensible to both an undergraduate and a graduate student audience. In addition to being a compilation of essays and personal narratives, *Queer Cultures* has been designed as textbook for a GBLT and Queer Studies, Gender and Sexuality Studies, and Writing Across the Curriculum courses. Introductory essays to each of its seven sections provide a conceptual framework for the issues raised throughout the chapters. Each chapter is followed by QUESTIONS FOR REFLECTION, DISCUSSION AND WRITING, and by a RELATED READING bibliography organized chronologically from least to most recently published, so readers can sample some of the evolving thinking and dialogue on specific issues. When applicable, FILM, WEB RESOURCES, WRITING ASSIGNMENTS, AND SOCIAL ACTIVISM components appear in each chapter as well. Several of the chapters also feature SPECIAL TOPIC sections which present readings, films, and writing activities that constitute a separate, related unit in themselves. This text has been designed to be expansive, multifaceted, and comprehensive enough to encompass several different kinds of courses. As such, the essays collected in this book do not constitute any fixed (and implicitly normative) conception of queer theory. Rather they, like the abundance of other texts that are referenced in this collection, should be considered contributions to the ongoing, energetic, exploratory, boundary-breaking dialogue that is queer theory today.

To the Student

F. Scott Fitzgerald wrote in 1936 that "The test of a first-rate intelligence is the ability to hold two opposed ideas in the mind at the same time, and still retain the ability to function." This book, *Queer Cultures*, will require you to exercise precisely this ability, to hold oppositions, contradictions, and sometimes ideological conflicts in your mind as you undertake to study the ever evolving discipline known as "queer theory."

For queer theory is not *a* theory. It constitutes no singular or collectively agreed upon definition or perspective. It possesses no canonical texts. In other words, what you will read throughout this anthology is never the last word on the subject. None of these essays are prescriptive, none absolute. In fact, what you will discover as you read is that many of these writers are in dialogue with one another; note parallel lines of thinking, intersections, shared assumptions, as well as disagreements. The task before you as a student and a reader is to hold, as Fitzgerald wisely counsels, multiple ideas in your mind as you struggle to articulate what it is that you think and feel about the many issues raised throughout *Queer Cultures*. Many of these essays will challenge and perhaps ever disrupt your established ideas about what is "natural" and "normative." This disruption is one of the essential attributes of queer theory, and it will help you enormously if you are able to keep an open and inquisitive mind as you are grappling with the essays and their wide-ranging viewpoints. You do not have to believe everything that you read in here, but you should be able to explain cogently why you disagree and develop a counter-argument that speaks both from your experience and your analysis of the material. Such a reading perspective can be thought of as skeptical or critical. You might also be attuned to those ideas that resonate strongly with you and pursue their effects in your own thinking and feeling through journal writing. Learn what you can from this material but never regard it as gospel. Also remember that reaching agreement with an idea or position doesn't mean that one can cease thinking; there are always social, personal, and political consequences for the stances we adopt. Ask questions. Consider contradictions. Probe. Amplify. Refuse to be easily satisfied. The material in this anthology is designed for such an intellectual engagement, and your learning experience will be successful in proportion to the degree of critical awareness you bring to the texts.

One word of caution: theoretical texts can be difficult, sometimes even headache-inducing. Though we have self-consciously chosen essays that we believe are accessible to undergraduate and graduate students alike, some of the most influential essays in the discipline of queer theory (Butler, Sedgwick, Hennessy) are by no means easy. Our suggestion is that you read the most challenging of these essays when you are fully awake (i.e., not late at night or right before your class). Read slowly and with deliberation. Take notes and ask questions about sentences you do not understand. If you find yourself lost, consult the questions at the end of each essay and read with them in mind; it might help you to sort through what is unintelligible and to focus instead on the central points of each text. Above all, don't despair! Keep in mind that theory is *just thinking*; it is not information you must fully comprehend and commit to memory like a mathematical formula or a series of historical events. And some thinking is more difficult than others. The truth is that no one, really, grasps the totality of any theoretical argument. We all select pieces which resonate with us for whatever reason and we try to get at the core points. If this modest success is your goal, you will be able to attain it with patience, diligence, and hard work.

Following the questions after each essay is a bibliography of RELATED READING. Any research or group project you begin should start with your attention to this selected bibliography. Graduate students will doubtless wish to augment their reading of specific chapters with texts from this source. Keep in mind too that these suggested readings only begin to scratch the surface of what is out there. Follow footnotes, research data bases, surf the web, investigate scholarly journals, and keep abreast of current ideas and arguments in the field. See what connections you can foster between texts and among ideas. You might well find unusual juxtapositions and original paper topics or course projects that arise from your investigation. The SPECIAL TOPIC sections at the end of selected chapters feature projects that can be undertaken and investigated during the semester, as do the SOCIAL ACTIVISM sections.

To the Instructor

Our intent is that this book have sufficient intellectual breadth and diversity of perspectives to make it truly representative of the evolving discipline that is queer and GBLT studies. Though we have organized it into seven sections that we would teach in numerical order, other instructors may prefer differing approaches. A chronological strategy, for instance, might begin with the historical chapters contained in Section Six, followed by the D'Emilio essay "After Stonewall" in Section One and the chapters on the 1980s in Section Two. Other instructors may wish to select chapters across the sections and reformulate them into an order they adduce is most useful for their student population and their own intellectual interests.

For undergraduate populations, the questions that succeed each chapter may be assigned as study guides, as journal prompts, or as individual writing assignments. They can also be employed as jumping-off points for classroom discussion. SPECIAL TOPIC items and SOCIAL ACTIVISM suggestions are ideal for group work. Graduate course coverage can be extended through the RELATED READINGS, and for this student population, some of the SPECIAL TOPIC items could form the germ of a conference paper or the first draft of a potentially publishable article.

Film suggestions have been referenced throughout this collection. They include title, date, director, and running time. Many of the films listed are first-run features and may be available at local video stores. Others are documentaries and independent and experimental short films. Descriptions of these films and ordering information can be obtained by requesting catalogues from individual distributors. The primary distributors consulted to compile the films mentioned in *Queer Cultures* are:

The Cinema Guild
1697 Broadway, Suite 506
New York, NY 10019-5904
246-5522

Facets Video
1517 West Fullerton Avenue
Chicago, IL 60614
(312) 281-9075

Frameline
346 Ninth Street
San Francisco, CA 94103
703-8654.

Women Make Movies
462 Broadway, Suite 500-C
New York, NY 10013
(212) 925-0606

Another invaluable resource is Chris Holmlund's and Cynthia *Fuchs's Between the Sheets, In the Streets: Queer, Lesbian, Gay Documentary* (Minneapolis: U of Minnesota P, 1997), which contains an Annotated Film and Videography (241–261), as well as the address and telephone lists of over forty video distributors (261–263).

Selected web resources are also listed throughout the chapters. For further web listings, please consult Jeff Dawson's *Gay & Lesbian Online* (Los Angeles, CA: Alyson, 1999) and "The Lavender Web: LGBT Resources on the Internet" by David C. Barnett and Ronni L. Sanlo in *Working With Lesbian, Gay, Bisexual, and Transgender College Students* (Greenwood Press, 1998).

Teaching a course that includes or is about sexuality, especially non-heteronormative sexualities, can be both a rewarding and a challenging experience. Such courses tend to self-select, resulting in an enthusiastic and committed group of students. It is also frequently a population that is actively questioning itself about sexual identities and feelings, as well as about social and familial norms. This can often create a high degree of intensity in classroom discussions and in journal entries. Instructors should expect and be prepared to ride out tides of emotion on occasion throughout the semester. The following bibliography (compiled by Jennifer DiGrazia), highlighting queer pedagogy and writing articles, will prove especially helpful in thinking through the various issues, approaches and successes in queer classroom and writing practices.

Related Reading

Adams, Kate and Kim Emery. "Classroom Coming Out Stories: Practical Strategies for Productive Self-Disclosure" in *Tilting the Tower*. Linda Garber Ed. NY: Routledge. 1994. 25–34.

Barnard, Ian. "Anti-Homophobic Pedagogy: Some Suggestions for Teachers." *Radical Teacher 45* (Winter 1994): 26–28.

Barale, Michèle Aina. "The Romance of Class and Queers: Academic Erotic Zones" in *Tilting the Tower*. Linda Garber Ed. NY: Routledge. 1994. 16–24.

Bredbeck, Gregory W. "Anal/yzing the Classroom: On the Impossibility of a Queer Pedagogy" in *Professions of Desire: Lesbian and Gay Studies in Litera-*

ture. George E. Haggerty and Bonnie Zimmerman, Eds. NY: MLA. 1995. 169–180.

Breen, Margaret Soenser. "Professor Petcock, or How the Academy Turns on Queer Studies." *Journal of Gay, Lesbian and Bisexual Identity 4.3* (July 1999): 257–264.

Britzman, Deborah. "Is There a Queer Pedagogy? Or, Stop, Reading Straight." *Educational Theory* 45 (1995): 151–165.

———. "Queer Pedagogy and Its Strange Techniques" in *Inside the Academy and Out: Lesbian/Gay/Queer Studies and Social Action*. Janice L. Ristock and Catherine Taylor, Eds. U.Toronto Press, 1998. 49–71.

Bryson, M. and S. de Castell. "Queer Pedagogy: Praxis Makes Im/Perfect." *Canadian Journal of Education 18.3* (1993): 285–305.

Chadwick, Joseph. "Toward An Antihomophobic Pedagogy" in *Professions of Desire: Gay and Lesbian Studies in Literature*. George E. Haggerty and Bonnie Zimmerman, Eds. NY: MLA. 1995. 31–37.

Chinn, Sarah. "Queering the Profession, or, Just Professionalizing the Queer?" in *Tilting the Tower*. Linda Garber, Ed. NY: Routledge. 1994. 243–250.

Clarke, Cheryl. "'Out' Outside the Classroom: The Co-curricular Challenge." *Radical Teacher 45* (Winter 1994): 23–25.

Cotton-Huston, Annie L. and Bradley M. Walte. "Anti-Homosexual Attitudes in College Students: Predictors and Classroom Interventions." *Journal of Homosexuality 38.3* (2000): 117–133.

De Castell, Suzanne and Mary Bryson. "Queer Ethnography: Identity, Authority, Narrativity and a Geopolitics of Text" in *Inside the Academy and Out: Lesbian/Gay/Queer Studies and Social Action*. Janice L. Ristock and Catherine Taylor, Eds. U.Toronto Press. 1998. 97–110.

Evans, Nancy J. and Vernon A. Wall, Eds., *Beyond Tolerance: Gays, Lesbians, and Bisexuals on Campus*. Alexandria, VA: American College Personnel Association, 1991.

Francis, Margot. "On the Myth of Sexual Orientation: Field Notes from the Personal, Pedagogical, and Historical Discourses of Identity" in *Inside the Academy and Out: Lesbian/Gay/Queer Studies and Social Action*. Janice L. Ristock and Catherine Taylor, Eds. U. Toronto Press. 1998. 72–96.

Gibson, M. and D. Meem. "Teaching, Typecasting and Butch-Femme Identity." *Feminist Teacher 10.1* (1996): 12–16.

Goldstein, Lynda. "Queer Theory: The Monster that is Destroying Lesbianville" in *Lesbians in Academia*. Beth Mintz and Esther Rothblum, Eds. NY: Routledge. 1997. 261–268.

Gonzalez, Maria. "Cultural Conflict: Introducing the Queer in Mexican-American Literature Classes" in *Tilting the Tower*. Linda Garber, Ed. NY: Routledge. 1994. 56–62.

Green, Herb and Nancy Ordover. "Out of these Silences: Voicing Race, Gender, and Sexuality in Ethnic Studies." *Radical Teacher 45* (Winter 1994): 42–45.

Halberstam Judith. "Queering Lesbian Studies" in *The New Lesbian Studies: Into the Twenty-first Century.* Bonnie Zimmerman and Toni A.H. McNaron, Eds. NY: The Feminist Press. 1996. 256–261.

Jackson, Jr., Earl. "Explicit Instruction: Teaching Gay Male Sexuality in Literature Classes." *Professions of Desire: Lesbian and Gay Studies in Literature.* George E. Haggerty and Bonnie Zimmerman, Eds. NY: MLA. 1995. 136–155.

Jeffreys, Sheila. "The Queer Disappearance of Lesbians" in *Lesbians in Academia.* Beth Mintz and Esther Rothblum, Eds. NY: Routledge, 1997. 269–278.

Jenkins, Mercilee. "Ways of Coming Out in the Classroom" in *Queer Words, Queer Images.* R. Jeffrey Ringer, Ed. NY: NYU Press. 1994. 332–334.

Klages, Mary. "The Ins and Outs of a Lesbian Academic" in *Tilting the Tower.* Linda Garber, Ed. NY: Routledge. 1994. 235–242.

Keating, AnnLouise. "Heterosexual Teacher, Lesbian/Gay/Bisexual Text: Teaching the Sexual Other(s)" in *Tilting the Tower.* Linda Garber, Ed. NY: Routledge. 1994. 96–107.

Knopp, L. "Queer Theory, Queer Pedagogy: New Spaces and New Challenges in Teaching Geography." *Journal of Geography in Higher Education 23.1* (March 1999): 77–79.

Koski, Fran F. "Queer Theory in the Undergraduate Writing Course" Paper presented at the Annual Meeting of the Conference on College Composition and Communication. March 23–25. 1995.

Lee, Ntanya, Don Murphy and Lisa North. "Sexuality, Multicultural Education and the New York City Public Schools." *Radical Teacher 45* (Winter 1994): 12–16.

Malinowitz, Harriet. "Lesbian Studies and Postmodern Queer Theory" in *The New Lesbian Studies: Into the Twenty-First Century.* Bonnie Zimmerman and Toni A.H. McNaran, Eds. NY: The Feminist Press. 1996. 262–268.

Malinowitz, Harriet. *Textual Orientations: Lesbian and Gay Students and the Making of Discourse Communities.* Portsmouth, NH: Boynton/Cook. 1995.

Monifa, Akilah. "Of African Descent: A Three-fers Story" in *Lesbians in Academia.* Beth Mintz and Esther Rothblum, Eds. New York: Routledge. 1997. 134–140.

Murdy, Anne-Elizabeth, Scott Mendel and Elizabeth Freeman. "Teaching Outside the Curriculum: Guerilla Sex Education and the Public Schools." *Radical Teacher 45* (Winter 1994): 17–19.

Myrick, Roger and Mary Helen Brown. "Out of the Closet and into the Classroom: A Survey of Lesbian, Gay, and Bisexual Educators' Strategies and

Experiences in Colleges and Universities." *Journal of Gay, Lesbian and Bisexual Identity* 3.4 (October 1998): 295–317.

Namaste, Ki. "The Everyday Bisexual as Problematic: Research Methods Beyond Monosexism" in *Inside the Academy and Out: Lesbian/Gay/Queer Studies and Social Action.* Janice L. Ristock and Catherine Taylor, Eds. U. Toronto Press. 1998. 111–136.

Nelson, C. "Sexual Identities in ESL: Queer Theory and Classroom Inquiry." *TESOL Quarterly 33.1* (1999): 371–391.

Pelligrini, Ann and Paul B. Franklin. "Queer Collaborations: Feminist Pedagogy" in *The New Lesbian Studies: Into the Twenty-First Century.* Bonnie Zimmerman and Toni A.H. McNaron, Eds. NY: The Feminist Press. 1996. 120–126.

Phillips, David. "Pedagogy, Theory and the Scene of Resistance." *Radical Teacher 45* (Winter 1994): 38–41.

Pollak, Janet. "Lesbian/Gay Role Models in the Classroom: Where Are They When You Need Them?" in *Tilting the Tower.* Linda Garber, Ed. New York: Routledge. 1994. 131–134.

Price-Spratlen, T. "Negotiating Legacies: Audre Lorde, W.E.B DuBois, Marlon Riggs, and Me" in *Harvard Educational Review, Special issue: Lesbian, Gay, Bisexual and Transgender People in Education 66.2* (Summer 1996): 216–230.

Rand, Erica. "Doing it in Class: On the Payoffs and Perils of Teaching Sexually Explicit Queer Images." *Radical Teacher 45* (Winter 1994): 29–32.

Regan, Alison. "'Type Normal Like the Rest of Us': Writing, Power and Homophobia in the Networked Composition Classroom" in *Tilting the Tower.* Linda Garber, Ed. NY: Routledge. 1994. 117–127.

Resenbrink, C.W. "What Difference Does It Make?: The Story of a Lesbian Teacher." *Harvard Educational Review, Special Issue: Lesbian, Gay, Bisexual and Transgender People in Education* 66–2 (Summer 1996): 257–270.

Ristock, Janice L. "Community-Based Research: Lesbian Abuse and Other Telling Tales" in *Inside the Academy and Out: Lesbian/Gay/Queer Studies and Social Action.* Janice L. Ristock and Catherine Taylor, Eds. U. Toronto Press. 1998. 137–154.

Seidman, Steven. "Queer Pedagogy: Queer-ing Sociology." *Critical Sociology 20.3* (1994): 169–176.

Silin, Johnathan G. "Teaching As a Gay Man: Pedagogical Resistance or Public Spectacle?" *GLQ 5.2* (1999): 95–107.

Stoller, Nancy. "Creating a Nonhomophobic Atmosphere on a College Campus" in *Tilting the Tower.* Linda Garber, Ed. NY: Routledge. 1994. 198–207.

Sumara D. and B. Davis. "Interrupting Heteronormativity: Toward a Queer Curriculum Theory." *Curriculum Inquiry 29.* 1–2 (1999): 191–208.

Taylor, Catherine. "Teaching For A Freer Future In Troubled Times" in *Inside the Academy and Out: Lesbian/Gay/Queer Studies and Social Action*. Janice L. Ristock and Catherine Taylor, Eds. U. Toronto Press. 1998. 15–30.

Turley, Hans. "Queer in the Classroom: Authority and Space in Computer-Assisted Instruction." *Radical Teacher 45* (Winter 1994): 33–37.

Wells, Joel W. "What Makes a Difference?: Various Teaching Strategies to Reduce Homophobia in University Students." *Journal of Interpersonal Violence 7.3* (September 1992): 383–395.

Working With Lesbian, Gay, Bisexual, and Transgender College Students: A Handbook for Faculty and Administrators. Ronnie Sanlo, Ed. Connecticut: Greenwood Press. 1998.

Film

Reaching Out to Lesbian, Gay and Bisexual Youth. (1996). Sylvie Rokab.

SECTION ONE

What is Queer Theory?

The *Oxford English Dictionary* notes that the word "queer" is "of doubtful origin" and did not make its way into common parlance until the beginning of the eighteenth century. As an adjective, it most commonly refers to something that is strange, odd, or peculiar, something that deviates from the expected or from the norm. When applied to a person it frequently suggests a character that is questionable, dubious, or suspicious, or a behavior that is odd, eccentric, unconventional. To feel queer has meant, through the ages, to feel ill or queasy, sometimes even mentally unbalanced. Webster's *Third New International Dictionary* records that as a verb, "to queer" something means to spoil its success, to interfere, to ruin, and to thwart, as well as to put into an embarrassing or disadvantageous situation. And as slang, "queer" has carried the connotations of being false and counterfeit, and finally, of being homosexual.

With such a litany of derogation in its etymological history, why has this word been resuscitated at the end of the twentieth century, and to what purpose? To begin to formulate a provisional answer, it is necessary to return to the swirl of meanings engendered by the word queer itself. For in late-twentieth and early twenty-first century Western societies, queer is often deployed as a replacement term, a kind of umbrella category, for gay, lesbian, bisexual, and transgendered people Queer, in other words, is shorthand for sexualities and gender presentations which dominant thinking characterizes as deviant and as non-normative. The use of this word, too, it should be noted, is more often than not generationally specific, preferred by younger scholars and activists who did not grow up during times when it was hurled as an insult, the legacy of its history as a term of social opprobrium. Queer is now embraced by many as a term that proudly flouts its deviance from the norm, its ability to interfere with and to thwart established social, political, and philosophical conventions which privilege heterosexuality and all it stands for (otherwise known as heteronormativity) over all other forms and practices of sexuality, including, though not limited to, homosexuality. Queer then not only refuses to be shamed by its origins, but it espouses them avidly as markers of difference, of resistance, of refusal to capitulate to norms which compress and potentially distort expressions of human experience and behavior in all their confusing complexity.

1

Though queer theory shares a history with gay and lesbian studies, the two projects do differ in important ways. Lesbian and gay studies began with the recuperation and the recovery of gay and lesbian subjects, texts, experiences, and histories as legitimate fields of inquiry in a homophobic society. Moreover, lesbian and gay studies orients itself toward and organizes its tenets through the *politics of identity*, the belief that there exist discrete categories of gay and lesbian identities that share similar concerns, understandings, and experiences, regardless of whether those identities are fixed at birth or socially constructed. Queer theory, on the other hand, denies the existence of any fixed or stable notion of identity and, like postmodernism generally, disputes the notion that there exist universal, absolute truths in or across cultures. Rather, it asserts that identities are permeable and provisional, that they can and do often change over time. Eve Sedgwick, one of queer theory's most important advocates, refers to the belief in discrete categories of identity defined through sexual orientation and object choice as the "heterosexual/homosexual binary," a formulation which has become central to queer theoretical concerns. Segdwick argues that the gender of one's object choice in western civilizations throughout the twentieth century has been the crucial factor in the organization of social relations within cultures. Rather than accept this master plot of identity construction, Sedgwick proposes that we deconstruct its totalizing power through: a) an analysis of the historical process through which this binary was created; b) an analysis of how this binarism operates throughout representation; and c) the creation of interventions that disrupt and challenge this binary. As a literary critic, Sedgwick's interventions have taken place within the field of textual studies, and much of her focus is localized through and within how language (rhetoric, discourse) shapes power relations within cultures. For her, homosexuality is not so much an identity as it is a *cultural category* which reinforces specific hierarchies and power relations throughout western cultures in the modern era.

■

After Stonewall

John D'Emilio

The Homophile Years[1]

A movement first formed in the post–World War II decade, at a critical moment in our history, a moment of tension and conflict. As Allan Bérubé has ably shown in his book *Coming Out Under Fire: The History of Gay Men and Women in World War Two*, the 1940s opened a larger cultural and social space in which to be gay.[2] The war years led to a sharpened sense of sexual identity, dramatically expanded the opportunities for a collective life to develop, and saw a significant growth in the urban subculture of gay men and lesbians. Yet just as the wartime generation was shaping this new world, the political currents associated with the Cold War and McCarthyism widened the dangers associated with gay life. The homosexual emerged from the shadows, but in the image of a menace to the nation. Various branches and agencies of the national government in Washington investigated, exposed, excluded, harassed, purged, and spied upon gay Americans. Irrational witch-hunts swept through communities. Across the country, urban police forces harassed gays and lesbians with impunity.

World War II, the Cold War, and McCarthyism provided the context in which a gay freedom struggle initially formed and did its work. In the course of the 1950s and 1960s, the politics of the movement underwent many twists and turns, and throughout this era the movement itself remained small and relatively marginal to the social forces shaping the life of the nation. Nonetheless, by the end of the 1960s, there existed a core of activists who spoke in crisply articulate ways of injustice, projected a firm sense of moral righteousness in presenting their cause, and put themselves squarely on the line as proponents of an unpopular cause. By the time of Stonewall, some limited but important gains had been made:

- The Supreme Court had affirmed the right to publish gay and lesbian magazines;
- The first employment discrimination cases had been won in federal court;
- In a number of states, court rulings had given gay bars a more secure existence, and in cities like New York and San Francisco, the movement had placed constraints on police harassment of the subculture;
- A dialogue had opened with segments of the scientific community about the classification of homosexuality as mental illness, and with the religious community about the categorization of homosexuality as sin;

- Because of the shift to direct action tactics of public protest, the movement was now achieving some occasional media visibility;
- The organizational impulse had spread from its place of origin in Southern California and, on the eve of Stonewall, about fifty lesbian and gay movement organizations existed;
- Finally, through the persistent work of activists, the idea that gays and lesbians were a mistreated, persecuted minority had begun to infiltrate American society and the gay subculture.

The birth of gay liberation has so overshadowed this earlier activism that it has been easy to overlook the continuities between the pre- and post-Stonewall eras. The slogan "Gay is good," an empowering rejection of cultural norms, was adopted by homophile activists a year before Stonewall. In Southern California, Troy Perry had formed the first Metropolitan Community Church, and the *Advocate* was being hawked in gay bars in Los Angeles. Gays and lesbians staged "visibility actions," to borrow a term from Queer Nation in the 1990s, outside the California State Fair; activists "came out" in the press and on television. In many ways, the movement was straining to reach new heights.

As the 1960s ended, the homophile movement could accurately be described as a reform movement solidly implanted in the American liberal tradition. It had isolated a problem, the mistreatment of homosexuals, and identified the configuration of laws, policies, and beliefs that sustained a caste-like status for gay women and men. It proposed a solution: decriminalization of homosexual acts, equal treatment and equal rights under the law, and the dissemination of accurate, "unbiased" information about homosexuality. Activists had formed organizations, were mobilizing support, and were petitioning through a variety of means for the redress of grievances.

The problem was not an absence of gay politics. Rather, pre-Stonewall activists were employing ordinary means to attack an extraordinary situation. The hostility to homosexuality was so deeply embedded in American society and culture, and the penalties attached to exposure were so great in the 1950s and 1960s, that few gay men and lesbians were willing to affiliate with the movement. The enticements of the closet were far more alluring than anything activists could offer. Oppression posed a seemingly insuperable barrier to recruitment.

It was this problem—how to challenge the regime of the closet—that the Stonewall Riot and its aftermath appeared to solve. The Stonewall generation of gay liberationists crashed through the recruitment barrier and landed in a wide sunlit space that, for many, proved far more attractive than the closet.

Stonewall and the Emergence of Radical Gay Liberation[3]

The Stonewall Riot has come to assume mythic proportions among gay men and lesbians. The image of drag queens rioting in the streets and engaging in combat with the helmeted officers of New York City's tactical police inverted the stereotype of meek, limp-wristed fairies. It was a wonderful moment of explosive rage in which a few transvestites and young gay men of color reshaped gay life forever.

The story of the Stonewall Riot has been told many times. Here I want to explore more closely its genesis. It would be a mistake, I think, to describe it, as is so often done, as a spontaneous outpouring of anger that changed the course of history. Yes, the riot was unplanned, impulsive, and unrehearsed—three common meanings of "spontaneous"—but it was also rooted in a specific context that shaped the experience and consciousness of the participants. To wrench the riot from its moorings in time and place impoverishes our understanding of it.

On the most immediate level, a memorial service for Judy Garland had taken place earlier in the day, just a few miles uptown on the West Side. Garland was *the* cultural icon for gay men of the 1950s and 1960s. Through her music, her movies, and her life, a generation of gay men bonded with each other. Her death was a shared tragedy, a loss that rippled through the gay world and that crossed class and race boundaries. Something precious had been taken away, and one can imagine that sensibility coursing through the psyches of those at the Stonewall as the police attempted to seize another symbol of community.

The raid on the Stonewall provoked outrage for another reason. By 1969, bar raids were no longer commonplace in New York City. A few years earlier, the homophile movement had successfully pressed the liberal Lindsay administration to rein in the police. Though harassment did not stop entirely—some forms of public cruising still made one especially vulnerable to arrest—the bars were for the most part left alone, and they flourished. With less harassment, bars had longer lifespans, patrons could become "regulars" and form stronger ties to one another, and particular bars might become community centers of sorts. But 1969 was also an election year in municipal politics. That spring, police raids recommenced. When the cops arrived at the Stonewall, they were invading a space that patrons had come to see as rightfully theirs.

Finally, the outburst took place in a larger nongay context. Put most simply, a riot was not an unusual event in 1969. Martha Shelley, who was an antiwar activist and former officer of the Daughters of Bilitis, and who would become a key activist in early gay and lesbian liberation, was in the Village with a friend the night of the raid on the Stonewall. She remembered approaching Sheridan Square and noticing all the turmoil. Rather than investigate, she simply looked at her friend and said, "Oh, another riot," and continued on her way.[4]

The unruly social practices that the 1960s had made into a norm had to have been absorbed by the patrons of the Stonewall. Young gay men of color as many of them were, they could not have been immune to the rhetoric and politics of groups such as the Black Panthers and the Young Lords, whose cachet ran especially high among young, dispossessed African–Americans and Puerto Ricans in New York. The Stonewall Riot may very well have been the first of its kind in history, but when the patrons confronted the police they were extending to gay turf familiar modes of action.

The larger political context also explains the aftermath of Stonewall. In the days and weeks that followed, lesbians and gay men in New York City kept talking. Before long, some of them had coalesced into a new organization, the Gay Liberation Front, fundamentally different from its homophile predecessors. A radical mass movement was aborning.

How could this happen? In the 1960s, many strands of radicalism were exerting their influence on a generation of young Americans. And, in one way or another, every major movement of the decade spoke to the condition of gays and lesbians. The civil rights movement had proven that ordinary folk, people brutally oppressed and without access to the resources of money and influence that typically defined power in our society, could shake the nation. Its metamorphosis into a militant nationalist politics in the late 1960s only made the parallels more striking. Black Power, Black Is Beautiful: the conjoining of words that in the lexicon of American English were always meant to be separate. Could gay come to embody power, too? Might gay be as good as black was now beautiful?

The white student movement and the antiwar movement also spoke to young gays. Children of privilege were challenging the system, engaging with ferocious abandon in pitched battles with armed police and, in some cases, with troops. The counterculture—that diffuse cultural impulse reflected in music, styles of hair and dress, and drug use, which contrasted being "true to one's self" and "doing your own thing" with the obscene materialism of consumer capitalism—scoffed at the hypocrisy of middle-class sexual mores. Finally, feminism, only recently reborn when the Stonewall Riot occurred, was articulating a new language of gender and sexuality that was transforming personal tribulation into political grievance. In this setting, how could a gay liberation movement *not* be born?

I said that the movements of the 1960s "spoke to" young lesbians and gays. That is not quite accurate. That phrase implies that they were not in the stream of radical protest, when in fact many participated with vigor. Just as women's liberation exploded into existence because a generation of young women had already been radicalized in other movements, so too could gay liberation erupt onto the landscape because many of us were part of the turmoil of the decade. Once those queens rioted outside the Stonewall, the political connections were unmistakable.

In contrast to the reform orientation of homophile politics, the phase of gay and lesbian activism that Stonewall initiated was radical. A number of characteristics marked it in this way. The name these new activists took, the Gay Liberation Front, was the queer version of the National Liberation Front in Vietnam, whose flag was often brandished in demonstrations of the late 1960s. GLFers identified the problem they were attacking—the mistreatment of gay men and lesbians—not as a narrow, discrete issue, but as systemic. Echoing the rhetoric of the radicalism around them, the founding document of GLF in New

York denounced the "dirty, vile, fucked-up capitalist conspiracy" which it placed at the heart of the matter.[5]

GLFers began to construct a rudimentary analysis of gay *oppression*. It was not a matter of simple prejudice, misinformation, or outmoded beliefs. Rather, the oppression of homosexuals was woven into the fabric of sexism. Institutionalized heterosexuality reinforced a patriarchal nuclear family that socialized men and women into narrow roles and placed homosexuality beyond the pale. These gender dichotomies also reinforced other divisions based on race and class, and thus allowed an imperial American capitalism to exploit the population and make war around the globe.

Finally, the liberation of lesbians and gay men would come not by waging a separate, self-contained struggle but by making common cause with "all the oppressed: the Vietnamese struggle, the Third World, the blacks, the workers."[6] Many of GLF's early actions were not gay events at all, but rather displays of commitment to a much larger project of political change. With eye-catching banners designed for everyone to see, they appeared at rallies in support of the Black Panther Party and at the massive antiwar mobilizations held in Washington and in other cities around the country.

The men and women of GLF made these choices for reasons that were not simply "political." As Toby Marotta has pointed out in his study of gay and lesbian politics in New York, most of these radicals were young. Many of them were still struggling to come to terms with their sexual identity, and they lacked roots in the traditional gay world. Instead, much of their time was spent in the milieu of "the Movement." The New Left and countercultural values about community and human relationships that they had imbibed made them recoil from the subculture of Mafia-run bars, seedy bathhouses, butch-femme roles, and anonymous sex. The people they knew and the people with whom they felt an affinity were to be found among the ranks of radicalized youth at antiwar, Black Panther, and campus demonstrations. Where better, then, to propagate the message of gay liberation than among the already radical, in an environment that felt to them like home?

Their instincts proved accurate. Over the next year or two, as GLFers appeared at Movement events, word of this new liberation struggle spread very rapidly. The process was closely akin to what Sara Evans has described in her study of the origins of women's liberation.[7] The networks that the black, student, and antiwar movements provided allowed the first wave of radical feminists to reach hordes of politicized young women in short order. Similarly, these new lesbian and gay radicals could also tap the Movement in order to find converts. GLFs, or kindred groups, formed in city after city and on many college campuses; the speed with which gay liberation spread seemed to accelerate with each passing month.[8]

When it came to planning a strategy to achieve the liberation of homosexuals, GLFers stumbled. One option was to align with the Movement and thus add to the forces of radical change. But, since most GLFers were already enmeshed in that world, simply changing banners would hardly expand the number of radicals in America. Another was to convince radical leaders that gays and lesbians were oppressed, and therefore an integral part of the struggle, so that when the revolution came, it would liberate homosexuals as well. Although this strategy did win new allies, no revolutionary clouds appeared on the horizon. As for destroying sex roles and "smashing the nuclear family," how was a movement to do that?

The inability of radical gay liberationists to devise a strategy commensurate with their political vision should not lead us to dismiss the significance of this political impulse. Across the country, for the three or four years after Stonewall, this new breed of radicals participated in an almost continuous round of flashy, dramatic public demonstrations. Their most common targets were the media, the police, and the medical profession, all of whom were seriously implicated in the maintenance of gay oppression. GLFers rioted in the streets, and spoke in high school civics classes. In everything they did and everywhere they went, they sought to create visibility, to give substance to a new image of lesbians and gays.

The achievements of radical gay liberation were great, even if they are not best measured by reference to changes in institutional practices, public policies, or legal codes. GLF and similar groups operated on the terrain of culture and everyday life, and here their accomplishments were profound. Let me suggest three:

1. Radical GLFers fashioned a new language and style of homosexuality. The accent was on pride and affirmation; they were blatant, outrageous, and flamboyant. Discarding notions of sickness and sin, they represented homosexuality as a revolutionary path toward freedom, as a step out of the constricted, stultifying gender roles of middle-class America. They engaged in public displays of affection, violated gender conventions, and gloried in the discomfort they deliberately provoked in others.

2. These radicals unleashed a mania for organization. On the eve of Stonewall, some fifty gay and lesbian movement groups existed; by the end of 1973, there were upwards of a thousand. These organizations published newspapers, sponsored speakers' bureaus, planned dances, staffed crisis lines, and engaged in many other kinds of activities as well, some overtly political, others more broadly social or cultural. But whatever their purpose or goal, the impulse to join together, which radical gay liberation so visibly embodied, proved irresistible. The organizational results were the essential building blocks of both a movement and a community.

3. Most significantly of all, radical gay liberation transformed the meaning of "coming out." Before Stonewall, the phrase had signified the acknowledgment of one's sexuality to others in the gay world; after Stonewall, it meant the public affirmation of homosexual identity. This revised form of coming out became, I believe, the quintessential expression of sixties cultural radicalism. It was "doing your own thing" with a vengeance; it em-

bodied the insight that "The personal is political" as no other single act could.

It was also a tactical stroke of great genius. Here was a decision that any gay person could make. The results were personally transformative, and the consequences socially significant. People who came out were relinquishing the one protection that gays had against stigmatization. They therefore required new forms of self-defense, which is precisely what a gay liberation movement was. Once out of the closet, a gay man or lesbian was heavily invested in the success of the movement. Coming out created an army of permanent recruits.

These young radicals were ideally, perhaps even uniquely, suited to scout what must have felt like unknown territory. Because they were already converts to a radical critique of American society, the usual penalties that kept gays and lesbians in line failed to intimidate them. To declare one's homosexuality disqualified one from the draft, but GLF men were already opposed to the war. Lesbians and gays were excluded from federal civil service jobs and many other kinds of employment, but these counterculturalists believed in dropping out of a materialistic, straight rat race. Flaunting one's homosexuality might subject one to arrest, but in the New Left, getting arrested was a mark of commitment. They called the system's bluff in a way that most gay men and lesbians of the time would not. And, although it took a cohort of young radicals to challenge the regime of the closet, their example proved irresistible to others.

The new generation of gay liberationists saved the Stonewall Riot from being simply "an event." They fleshed out the implications of the riot, and ensured that they would become the symbol of a new militance. GLF broke through the barriers that had constrained the reform-oriented homophile movement. It transformed forever the shape of lesbian and gay activism in this country. It was radicalism, theirs and the times, that made these achievements possible.

By the mid-1970s, the version of gay politics which I have been describing as "radical gay liberation" was clearly in retreat. Many GLFs had died, and were being replaced by other kinds of gay and lesbian organizations. Radical gay liberation had ceased to be the leading edge, or the defining tendency, of the movement.

This rapid dissolution of radical gay liberation in the face of the powerful influence that GLF exerted on the lives of gay men and lesbians requires explanation. Certainly one reason is that the soil that fertilized GLF, the radicalism of the 1960s, was drying up rapidly. The belief that a revolution was imminent and that gays and lesbians should get on board, was fast losing whatever momentary plausibility it had. By the early 1970s, the nation was entering a long period of political conservatism and economic retrenchment. With every new proclamation of revolutionary intentions, radicals compromised their credibility.

Another serious problem was organizational. GLF was, quite frankly, chaotic. It was more of an impulse, or a mood, than an organization. Its distrust of leadership and its lack of structure made things infuriatingly difficult to get done. Small subsets of like-minded people could unite behind a short-term project or a particular action, but GLF was not well suited for the long march through institutions that a sustained movement would have to undertake. As time went on, the endless talking and the empty rhetoric generated impatience and estranged more and more recruits until most GLFs simply faded away.

Finally, GLF ran aground on the rocks of identity politics. It had been born just at the moment when identity had pressed to the foreground in the configuration of social movements in this country. This attention to identity, both as the organizing framework for oppression and as the basis for collective mobilization, simultaneously expanded and fractured the forces campaigning for change. As people came to see the many ways they were targeted because of who they were, their newly discovered anger brought many into grass-roots social activism.

But the politics of identity also proved to be a centrifugal force pulling that world apart. In the case of GLF, it worked in two conflicting ways. For many white lesbians and for people of color, GLF offered too little: it could not adequately address their needs as individuals who experienced not only gay oppression, but also sexism, or racism, or both. For many white gay men, GLF demanded too much. Just as they were awakening to a political consciousness of their oppression and beginning to fashion an agenda for action, GLF was calling for a commitment to fight all forms of oppression. The insistence on solidarity with the struggles of others too easily sounded like self-abnegation.

No single form of movement politics rose to preeminence in place of radical gay liberation; instead, the gay and lesbian freedom struggle spun out in many different directions. Here and there, the GLF impulse remained alive, though it was far overshadowed by the multiplicity of new political tendencies. I want to follow two of those tendencies as they developed in the 1970s; a gay rights movement, largely male in composition and reformist in its political orientation; and lesbian-feminism, an initially radical movement that became increasingly utopian with the passage of time.

The Gendered Seventies, I: A Gay Rights Movement[9]

By the beginning of the 1970s, gay activism—most particularly its white, middle-class male variant—was quickly reconfiguring itself. Already in December 1969, some GLF members in New York, disgruntled by the agenda and the procedures of the organization, had seceded to form the Gay Activists Alliance. This development was not unique to New York, not a product of its fractious politics. Rather, in city after city, a similar process took place, reflected in a change of nomenclature from liberation to activist. As the 1970s wore on, many gay communities new to the movement skipped the GLF phase entirely and launched their organizations in the gay activist mold.

Peering in from the outside, one would have initially been hard-pressed to notice the differences between radical gay liberation and what I'm choosing to call gay rights. Gay rights activists retained a central emphasis on coming out; they engaged in militant, angry protests; they adopted the language of pride and self-affirmation that radical gay liberation constructed.

Nonetheless, there were differences beyond the not-insignificant change in name. The newer gay activist groups tended to share a number of characteristics that sharply separated them from the radical GLF impulse. For one, they were single-issue organizations, completely gay-focused in their concerns. Their agendas might be large—civil rights legislation, media responsiveness, social activities, publishing, hot lines, and the like—but everything was defined by its overriding gay content. They also were *organizations*, with clearly specified structures and processes. Constitutions were written, bylaws adopted, officers elected, committees formed, meetings held, and membership requirements specified. Votes were taken and meetings conduced by *Robert's Rules of Order*. Gay activist groups also occupied a relationship to the political system different from that of GLF. Rather than try to destroy the old in order to build something new, they saw themselves as unjustly excluded from full participation in American society and wanted recognition and a place inside. This perspective helped to shape an agenda that diverged from that of GLF. Thus a GAA would work for changes in municipal civil rights codes to include sexual orientation; the groups sought the endorsement of elected officials and candidates for political office.

The shift to a single-issue politics encouraged the further proliferation of organizations. It made sense for new groups to form in order to reflect a particular need or to focus on a particular issue within the framework of gay rights. Gay and lesbian Episcopalians formed Integrity, an organization devoted to winning acceptance within their church. Gay and lesbian academics created the Gay Academic Union to fight for visibility and an end to discrimination within higher education. These examples could be multiplied.

What the complex of changes meant is that by the middle of the 1970s the bulk of gay male activism—and some lesbian activism as well—had returned to the reform-oriented perspective of the pre-Stonewall homophile movement. Rather than a struggle for liberation, the movement had become, once again, a quest for "rights." Rather than trying to reconstruct American society and its institutions from top to bottom, the movement sought gay inclusion into the system as it stood, with only the adjustments necessary to ensure equal treatment. Once again, the gay movement was riding the track of liberal reform: it had identified a particular problem, proposed a limited solution, formed organizations to work for change, and employed a range of tactics to win redress of grievances.

Reformist though it was, the gay rights movement of the mid-1970s did not mimic homophile politics. Reform-oriented activists could not erase—indeed, were not interested in erasing—the entire legacy of lesbian and gay liberation. Certain key changes effected by gay liberation were enthusiastically incorporated into the outlook, the style, and the program of these newer groups. Among these, the imperative to come out publicly, with all that implied about pride, self-affirmation, and the rejection of mainstream cultural views of homosexuality, stands out. Many gay activists remained as bold and brazen as their GLF predecessors had been. They expected and demanded acceptance for who they were, without apology.

The assimilation of pride into the very marrow of the movement also meant that, even as reformers campaigned for inclusion, activists were willing to absorb unruly tactics into their repertoire of methods to achieve their goals. GAA in New York City, for instance, can be credited with perfecting the "zap." When Mayor John Lindsay proved unwilling to support unequivocally the gay rights bill before the City Council, GAA felt no compunction about declaring "total war" against Lindsay. For a time, wherever he went in the city, Lindsay faced angry gays who disrupted cultural events, chained themselves to offices, and threw themselves in front of TV cameras to embarrass the mayor. A gay rights perspective did not necessarily translate into a suit-and-tie, dress-and-stockings style of political mobilization. Finally, whether fighting for rights or fighting for liberation, the gay and lesbian movement was forever transformed by the huge infusion of numbers wrought by Stonewall and radical gay liberation.

Taken together, the living legacies of gay liberation served to mask troubling contradictions that inhered in single-issue politics. The movement had grown larger in size, yet its political framework, and hence its possibilities, had contracted. The goals of activists had narrowed, yet activists in the mid-1970s almost uniformly displayed an élan that made them feel as if they were mounting the barricades. Activists increasingly engaged in routinized and mundane organizational tasks, yet they believed they were remaking the world.

My own experience in New York City in the Gay Academic Union between 1973 and 1975 illustrates what I mean.[10] During these years an ever-expanding group of gay men and lesbians associated with colleges and universities came together to translate the new post-Stonewall zeitgeist into an agenda for higher education. Some of the participants might be described as mainstream liberals or even conservatives; others of us positioned ourselves as radicals. Some already had a background in the movement; many, like me, were new to it. No other experience in my life up to that point matched the intensity of those endless meetings and monstrously large conferences. And, to judge by the commitment and excitement of the people around me, most of the others felt the same way. We believed, as I said, that we were remaking the world, yet our program—an end to discrimination; encouraging academics to come out; support for gay research and the teaching of gay studies—was a textbook example of a reform agenda.

What accounts, then, for the disparity between our goals and the way many of us, including the radicals, interpreted what we were doing? How could so modest a program, in the grand scheme of things, provoke among us such an inflated sense of its meaning? The answer lies, I think, in the magic of coming out. No matter what one's personal or political aspirations were—to be a chaired professor at Harvard, to win a seat on the New York Stock Exchange, or to build a revolutionary socialist state—coming out in the 1970s profoundly reshaped one's life. The anxiety one experienced in anticipating it, the exhilaration of surviving it, and the cheers and strokes from peers in the movement after the fact, made it a step of profound significance. For a gay man or lesbian of that time, I don't think that it was possible to experience anything of comparable intensity. In a psychological sense it was an act of "revolutionary" import. No manner of political analysis could convince someone who had come out that he or she wasn't turning the world inside out and upside down. Only later, as the movement matured, would it become clear that coming out was a first step only. An openly gay banker is still a banker.

Critical though this analysis of a gay reform perspective sounds, it is also true that reformers were able to provoke important, ground-breaking change. Unlike GLFers, who were long on rhetoric and had a flair for the dramatic action, reformers began to target in a sustained way the range of institutions implicated in lesbian and gay oppression. In late 1973, they won a major victory when the American Psychiatric Association voted to eliminate homosexuality from its list of mental disorders. In 1975, the federal Civil Service Commission dropped its ban on the employment of gays and lesbians.

Activists began to burrow their way into the churches of America, demanding a reconsideration of Christian teaching and calling for the ordination of openly gay and lesbian ministers. The National Council of Churches issued a strong statement condemning discrimination against homosexuals. In some denominations, such as the United Church of Christ and the Episcopal Church, insurgents brought forward test cases of the ban on ordination.

Some elements of the print media, particularly in those cities where the movement was most in evidence, began to cover its activities, breaking the invisibility and the silence that hampered its growth. Through sustained lobbying by the National Gay Task Force, a gay rights bill was introduced into Congress in 1975. By 1976, seventeen states had repealed their sodomy statutes, and thirty-six cities, including some of the largest, had enacted legislation banning discrimination.

Activists also worked to draw others into the movement enterprise. Lesbians won a statement of support at the annual conference of the National Organization for Women in 1971; four years later, NOW committed itself programmatically to supporting lesbian rights. Ties with organizations such as the American Civil Liberties Union, which even before Stonewall had backed some test cases for the homophile movement, grew stronger, and gay activists in a number of states could count on the legal resources and skill of ACLU lawyers. In 1977, as activities for International Women's Year geared up, lesbian staffers and board members of the National Gay Task Force fashioned a major campaign to promote lesbian visibility and to make lesbian rights a key issue embraced by feminists around the country. At thirty of the state conferences held in the summer of 1977, lesbian rights resolutions were adopted, and at the national conference in Houston, a high-water mark of feminist solidarity in the 1970s, a sexual preference resolution was accepted by an overwhelming margin.[11]

One other change of great import occurred during these years: in cities where a visible movement coalesced, law enforcement practices shifted dramatically. Throughout the 1950s and 1960s, police harassment of the subculture—not only in public spaces where gay men had sex, but in gay male bathhouses, in lesbian and gay bars, and even in the privacy of homes—was like a cancer raging out of control. Even if an individual managed to elude arrest, he or she would know of others less fortunate—men and women taken away in vans, forced to appear in night court, and sometimes confronted by the next day's newspaper revealing their names, addresses, and places of employment. The effects were devastating. To whatever joys or satisfactions the collective gay world brought, police persecution inevitably fused emotions of terror, humiliation, and shame.

Police harassment certainly hadn't disappeared by the mid-1970s, but the pattern had altered and new boundaries were drawn. In many large cities change came in two forms: 1) a major reduction in the sheer quantity of incidents, so that harassment was no longer ubiquitous; and 2) something of a "hands off" policy toward the less public manifestations of gay male life (bathhouses rather than public sex) and toward the gay neighborhoods that partook of middle-class "respectability" (the Castro and Greenwich Village rather than the Tenderloin and Times Square). In other words, the benefits of the movement were unevenly distributed.

This renegotiation of relations between the police and a newly mobilized community had important effects. When the police did overstep the new boundaries that the movement had drawn, their actions stimulated resistance and could be used effectively by activists to mobilize support. For middle-class white gay men especially, the change in law enforcement practices also meant that the texture of daily experience was thoroughly reshaped. Institutions of a public commercialized subculture proliferated. The pre-Stonewall pattern of control by the criminal underworld was replaced by legitimate small-time entrepreneurs, typically gay themselves, venturing into a new world of economic opportunity. Bars, bathhouses, sex clubs, restaurants, and discos seemed to appear everywhere, sustaining a thick network of social connections.[12]

This world bore little resemblance to what only recently had seemed the divine order of things. A vignette from my own experience in New York: I was taken to a gay bar for the first time in 1968. We descended a few steps below street level to enter. There was a small window with blackened glass, and a thick wooden door. The inside looked and felt like a dank, unfinished basement. It was dark, some men were dancing near the back, and the smell of tobacco, beer, and men's cologne combined in less than sweet ways. I didn't return. Six years later the bar of preference for me and my friends was the

Roadhouse. Located on a busy corner of Hudson Street in the West Village, it was light and airy, with a large plate glass window occupying most of one wall and a door that, in late spring and summer, was always open. On Sundays, the management offered a simple buffet-style dinner at a nominal price. The crowd of men moved easily between bar and street; the line dividing inside from out dissolved. Knots of men engaging in jovial conversation stood on the street, some with plates of food, some with a beer in one hand and the other resting on the shoulder, or curled around the waist, of a friend.

Most of the men who participated in this public world of sociability and sexual exchange were not activists. They did not belong to movement organizations. But they were the beneficiaries of what the movement had already wrought. The message of gay pride wafted through the air; it altered the way they lived and the way they understood their lives and identity. Gay male activists also enthusiastically participated in this world, at the same time that they—we—experienced no end of frustration with the seemingly apolitical stance of these "new" gay men. Though it was not apparent at the time, the commercialized subculture was, however, the seedbed for a consciousness that would be susceptible to political mobilization.

Ironically, the absence of overt politicization can be attributed in part to the success, in its own narrow terms, of reformist politics. Reformers fought for the right to be gay, free from harassment and punishment. Since the sexual subculture had been the location where gay men most acutely experienced both their gayness and their vulnerability, the fading police presence seemed incontrovertible evidence that they were free. As far as they could tell, gay liberation had succeeded. They could be open about their "lifestyle" on the streets of the burgeoning gay neighborhoods suddenly visible in large American cities after the mid-1970s. Activist harangues about the persistence of job discrimination, about media invisibility, about the role of the churches and the military in excluding homosexuals from equal participation in American life, seemed like the ravings of grim politicos who just didn't know how to have fun.

The Gendered Seventies, II: Lesbian-Feminism[13]

I have described the gay rights movement as male in its composition and emphasis, and I believe this is accurate as a generalized statement of its orientation. Yet it is also true that throughout the 1970s lesbians were a part of it. Lesbians who framed their identity primarily through their homosexuality, lesbians whose personal ties to gay men were stronger than their ties to heterosexual women, and those who were more attracted to the reform politics of gay rights, all struggled to make a home for themselves in a male-dominated movement. It wasn't easy. The new consciousness of sexism in interpersonal relationships, spawned by feminism, meant that everyday encounters with men bristled with tension. And most gay men's lack of understanding of institutionalized sexism forced lesbians repeatedly to fight for political formulations and action agendas that recognized their needs. Gender-mixed organizations in the 1970s were a minefield in which a single misstep could shatter the enterprise. They worked best in those rare situations where gender parity was incorporated into organizational structure, where sufficient numbers of women were involved to counter isolation, and where the organization's potential seemed promising enough to warrant continuing participation. In the seventies, such organizations were rare.

The main action of lesbian politics in the decade took place not in mixed organizations but in autonomous lesbian-feminist groups. In the early 1970s, a separate lesbian-feminist movement coalesced and declared itself heir of the "revolutionary" politics of the 1960s. Initially radical in its aspirations and self-conception, it would become in time ever more utopian as separatism traveled the long distance from political tactic to social vision.

The lesbian-feminist movement owed its existence to the convergence of two clusters of activists: lesbians with experience in women's liberation, and women with experience in gay liberation. Of the two movements, women's liberation proved most critical in birthing lesbian-feminism. Feminism was constructing a framework for interpreting the dissatisfaction women experienced in GLF, while the rhetoric of sisterhood was inducing many previously heterosexual women in the radical wing of the feminist movement to come out as lesbians. The sense of betrayal that these new lesbians experienced in feeling silenced and dismissed by those who had only recently been their comrades would propel them into a lesbian-feminist movement of their own; once there, a feminist consciousness would draw sharp lines between them and the men of the gay rights movement.

As a collective movement, lesbian-feminism embarked on two distinct projects. The first was an effort to fashion an ideology of lesbianism and its political significance free of the corrosive implications of the dominant rhetoric. The second was organizational, the building of institutions and the creation of lesbian-only spaces where a culture and a community could flourish.

In constructing a new discourse of lesbianism, these young radicals had several goals. One was to overcome what has been described as the "historical denial of lesbianism."[14] Within the traditional domains of science, religion, and law, lesbianism appeared as little more than a footnote to theories and discussions that revolved around male homosexuality. Another was to counter the new rhetoric of gay liberation, which often framed its purpose in terms of a model of sexual freedom shaped by male experience. Finally, radical lesbians sought to contest the views of feminists who, at best, relegated lesbianism to the private sphere and, at worst, dismissed it as evidence of male conditioning, as a preoccupation with sex from which feminists were trying to disentangle themselves.

A radically new formulation of lesbianism made its debut in May 1970 in New York City at the Congress to Unite Women, a conference of women's liberationists from the East Coast. A consciousness-raising group initiated by Rita Mae Brown and bringing together lesbians from the women's movement and the gay movement organized a "lavender menace" zap of the gathering. There they presented a carefully crafted document, "The Woman-Identified Woman," which would rapidly achieve canonical status among lesbian activists in the 1970s.

The opening lines of the essay staked out the ground on which radical lesbians would make their claims. "What is a lesbian?" it began. "A lesbian is the rage of all women condensed to the point of explosion." Here was a formulation that, as Alice Echols has pointed out, stripped lesbianism of its sexual content, and in which lesbianism was defined as the very essence of female anger.[15] To be a lesbian was to make a political statement about gender. The authors identified lesbians as the vanguard of the feminist revolution. Over the next few years, the most often-repeated assertion of lesbian-feminists would be that feminism was impossible without lesbianism. The two were so conflated that to be one was necessarily to be the other; conversely, the failure to identify as a lesbian was to have one's feminist loyalties disputed.

Lesbian-feminists also elaborated a political critique of heterosexuality. No longer simply a statement of behavior, or an expression of deep-rooted drives, it became an institution through which male supremacy was enforced and through which some women achieved limited privileges. As Charlotte Bunch, one of the key figures in this emergent movement, argued, virtually every institution that feminists had identified as oppressive to women was also premised on the naturalness of women's ties to men through marriage.[16] The failure to question the assumption of heterosexuality would forever inhibit women's quest for autonomy.

Although the analysis of heterosexism would eventually be picked up and incorporated into feminist and gay politics, the definition of lesbianism as a political vanguard always remained highly charged. With heterosexual feminists, the assertion of a vanguard role led to emotionally scarring combat and the rupture of the women's liberation movement in many cities as the "gay-straight split" became an impassable divide. Within gay liberation organizations the insistence that lesbians always put women first left no ground for common action: men, as much as male supremacy, were defined as the enemy.

Among a new generation of lesbians, however, the "Woman-Identified Woman" quickly came to define their lives and served to plot their course of action. Since all institutions were corrupted by patriarchal assumptions, to counter the invisibility of lesbians they applied themselves to creating an institutional world of their own. The 1970s witnessed an extraordinarily vital drive to build a self-sufficient lesbian community. Lesbians set up crisis lines and community centers. They founded magazines and newspapers, established publishing companies to print the steady flow of novels, poetry, and nonfiction that lesbian-feminists were composing, and bookstores to sell them. Theater groups performed the work of lesbian writers, record companies and concert producers ensured that lesbian musicians would reach an audience of eager listeners, and film collectives gave visual representation to lesbian lives. Lesbians formed archives and libraries to gather and preserve their culture; they bought land in common for rural separatist retreats; they opened food co-ops and restaurants and coffeehouses and self-defense schools and shelters for battered women. Groups of women created collectives to teach skills ranging from carpentry and plumbing to auto mechanics. In a few short years, a thriving lesbian-feminist community flowered around the country. The energy, creativity, and sheer will that went into sustaining it at times made Amazon Nation seem closer to literal truth than to metaphor.

Liberating as this new lesbian world was, in time it generated problems and tensions of its own. One concerned the balance between institution-building and political action. Hard as lesbian-feminists tried, they were never able to formulate a distinctively *lesbian* political agenda. With the exception of the rights of lesbian mothers, it proved impossible to identify a goal that wasn't either feminist (that is, about gender) or gay (that is, about sexual orientation). And since their ideology kept lesbian-feminists from working in coalition with men and insisted on their vanguard status within feminism, many found themselves withdrawing into a separate institutional world as much through inexorable political logic as out of choice. Community-building, in other words, had eclipsed political engagement.

This narrowing of vision did not go unchallenged. Some radical lesbians commented on the substitution of "community" for "movement" in the lesbian-feminist lexicon. "Somewhere along the way," declared one, "we stopped calling ourselves a movement and now call ourselves a community. . . . Communities may be groovy things to belong to . . . but communities don't make a revolution."[17] Charlotte Bunch, one of the fashioners of lesbian-separatist ideology, had by the mid-1970s moved away from a separatist politics because it had left her "too isolated." Instead of defining separatism as a permanent condition, she came to see it as a "dynamic strategy to be moved in and out of."[18] Bunch was not alone in this analysis. Some lesbian activists, having nurtured their identity and having internalized a lesbian-feminist analysis of heterosexism, plunged into other social movements, such as the campaigns against nuclear power and the nuclear arms race. For them, the lesbian community was a place to return to in order to find sustenance.

A second set of tensions was spawned by the continuing effort to shape a new lesbian identity. As the energies of many lesbian-feminists focused ever more intently on building a separate community, the power of the woman-identified-woman model accomplished a strange sleight of hand. Women's music, women's culture, the women's community, the women's coffeehouse: "lesbian" was becoming as invisible in the representation of this new universe as it was in the world at large. Did this betray, as some critics suggested, an uneasiness with the stigma attached to the label? Was it a tactical effort to weaken the heterosexual-homosexual division among women, to welcome all women into this inchoate community? Or did it signal the triumph of a lesbian-feminist ideology that erased, without a trace, the distinction between woman and lesbian?

Whatever the complex of motives, the conviction that lesbianism was fundamentally a matter of political consciousness was hardening for many into dogma. As it did so, it proved a source of stress to the very survival of the community. The patriarchy was powerful; consciousness was malleable. A lifetime of socialization, the fragility of female autonomy in a sexist society, and the threat of male violence meant not only that most women faced insuperable obstacles before they could achieve woman-identification, but also that this consciousness, once attained, was precarious. It had to be protected and defended. Thus at the very source of the lesbian-feminist movement were the elements that would lead it from a radical political stance into a utopian, perfectionist impulse. For many, separatism became not a tactic, not a temporary oasis, not a means of elaborating an ideology untainted by sexist and homophobic assumptions, not a prelude to a politics of engagement, but a way of life.

Dogma breeds both heresy and inquisition. To counter the external threats to this unstable identity and to protect this slippery consciousness led some to specify ever more precisely the elusive content of "lesbian." But the drive toward correctness, in lifestyle, political commitment, relationships, and sexuality, generated conflict. The "separatist wars" of the mid-1970s found not only separatists and nonseparatists clashing over what constituted true women-identification but also separatists themselves fighting to determine who best embodied separatist philosophy. Even in locales where separatism was not the dominant tendency, it seemed to shape the political dialogue: one had to defend or justify one's choices in relation to the purest expression of the idea. In this fragile, newly created, and beleaguered community, deviance was as dangerous as in the world at large.

Challenges

By the second half of the 1970s, each of these gendered movements was confronted by a paradox. On one hand, each had accomplished a lot. The gay rights movement could congratulate itself for the significant institutional changes it had effected in a mere handful of years. Life was clearly better than it had been in the previous decade. There was less discrimination and harassment, greater visibility, and a much larger and more congenial gay world. Lesbian-feminists had succeeded in building a multiplicity of institutions in which lesbians could flourish. In particular, the movement had created a range of woman-identified cultural products that affirmed the choice these women had made to focus their energy on women.

On the other hand, each of these political impulses was defining itself in ways that sharply limited its capacity for recruiting an expanding constituency.

For the gay rights movement, a huge gulf had opened between activists and the men who populated the urban subculture. Activists had defined the goal of the movement as the freedom to be gay. They had accomplished enough for white middle-class gay men in the cities to experience unprecedented freedom. The movement, in other words, was succeeding according to its own lights. Moreover, as gay rights advocates became more and more wedded to working within institutions, and as institutions proved just flexible enough to initiate dialogue and adjust some of their practices, activists fell back on techniques—lobbying, negotiation, and the like—that made their work invisible to the men of the subculture. Movement participants might cry "false consciousness," but it was a consciousness they had helped to shape through their political rhetoric and tactics.

Meanwhile, as the leading edge of lesbian feminism became ever more identified with a separatist philosophy, it too progressively narrowed its appeal. Reform-minded women were put off by what they considered the glorification of marginality. Many of them struggled to work within largely male gay rights groups of within mainstream feminist organizations; others built lesbian reform organizations committed to working in coalition with both the gay movement and the women's movement. Some lesbians with allegiance to a broad radical vision of social transformation dispersed into a range of other political causes where they provided tough, incisive leadership. Women who were "old gay" identified, who had an allegiance to the traditional lesbian and gay world of the pre-Stonewall era and for whom lesbianism was a sexual identity, not simply an expression of feminism, were alienated by the prescriptive lifestyle politics of separatists. Finally, the relentless celebration of sameness, the emphasis on femaleness as the overarching definition of self, kept away lesbians with conflicting loyalties. Especially among women whose identity bound them to racial and ethnic home communities, lesbian separatism demanded choices they were unwilling to make. Like gay rights activists, separatists might attribute the failure of all women to flock to their banner as a sign of false consciousness, as evidence of an identity corrupted by the patriarchy. But such an explanation only dramatized the inability of separatists to speak to the needs of most lesbians.

Both movements also tended drastically to misapprehend their strength. The fact is that by the end of the 1960s, the oppression of homosexuals was increasingly out of step with contemporary culture. With the "sexual revolution" of the sixties, two generations of change had coalesced into a substantially new sexual order. In a society in which heterosexuality was only tenuously attached to procreative intent, and in which sexual pleasure was championed in the media of mass and popular culture, the prohibitions on homosexual expression seemed increasingly anachronistic. This profound cultural shift seemed to accelerate in the 1970s. As the birth rate plummeted and the age of marriage rose, as divorce rates skyrocketed and cohabitation among heterosexuals spread, as the number of households diverging from the nuclear family ideal grew dramatically, the boundaries separating gay and lesbian experience from that of heterosexuals blurred.

Moreover, the upheavals of the 1960s had, for a brief historical moment, seriously weakened those very institutions that enforced gay oppression. Years of urban riots and antiwar agitation left municipal authorities shaken; one can imagine them easily abandoning age-worn policies of harassing gay meeting places, once those policies were vigorously challenged. The psychiatric profession, buffeted by ideological assaults ranging from the work of Thomas Szasz to that of R. D. Laing, meekly reversed generations of pronouncements about the pathology of homosexuality.[19] Religion, too, was in ferment, with liberation theology and issues of social justice displacing doctrine and ritual in the concerns of many churches.

I am not suggesting that the gains associated with gay liberation in the 1970s came through the beneficence of a responsive system. Without a social movement agitating for change, without collective action persistently applying pressure on a range of institutions, and without masses of gay people willing to force the issue by coming out, the pace of progress in the seventies might well have resembled the snail-like inching forward of the homophile movement in the 1960s. But the achievements of gay liberation and its successor movements owed at least as much to the broad crisis of authority that existed by the end of the 1960s as they did to the power of the movement. To be sure, in absolute terms the movement was larger and stronger. But our opponents were also temporarily enfeebled. By the latter part of the 1970s the crisis was over; its passing would make new demands of gay and lesbian politics.

Misapprehension played itself out in another way. At the time, most activists of each of these gendered movements were acutely aware of how different the trajectories of gay and lesbian life were. Depending on conviction or experience, one might evaluate these differences in any one of a variety of ways. I know that I, and some of my gay male friends, tended to look with envy at the solidarity, the sense of community, and the commitment to radical transformation that we associated with lesbian-feminism, including its separatist form. Later I would learn that many lesbian-feminists were fascinated and, to some degree, attracted by the richness of our sexual subculture. But most would have agreed that the points of convergence between gay men and lesbians were few and far between.

As I look retrospectively at these two political impulses, I am now struck by their surprisingly similar outcomes. Take, for instance, what may very well be the quintessential product of each: the elaborate, glitzy, high-tech gay male discos found in many cities, and the self-sufficient, rural communes of lesbian separatists. Here were men, in a public space, spending money, focused on themselves, and searching for sex. And here were women, in a private retreat, financially marginal, focused on group process, and nurturing loving relationships. For all our talk about a brave new world of sexual freedom, or the building of an Amazon Nation, what I now see is how thoroughly enmeshed such institutions remained in gender conventions. A cynic might argue that, unencumbered by the constraints imposed by the "opposite sex," stereotypical gender roles reached their full flowering. A more accurate view, I believe, would acknowledge that some scrambling of gender characteristics did occur, while still conceding that gender dichotomies continued to be reproduced by those who claimed little allegiance to them.

During the flush times of new freedoms in the early and mid-1970s, it was possible to brush aside uncertainties and revel in the adventure of remaking our worlds. But as the decade neared its end, challenges erupted on a variety of fronts. These challenges exposed both strengths and weaknesses in the gendered movements that replaced radical gay liberation.

The first of these challenges came in the form of the New Right's crusade against homosexuality, a crusade that testified to the gains the movement had achieved.[20] After 1977, activists faced not the garden-variety homophobia that had come to seem familiar, but a more truculent, militant variety. Two disparate forces—a religious fundamentalism only recently politicized, and an aggressive new conservatism burrowing into the Republican Party and looking for a winning strategy—began to make common cause. Sharing a revulsion at the effects of the upheavals of the 1960s and fashioning a rhetoric of moral renewal and national resuscitation, they formed a potent coalition that shaped the politics of the 1980s.

The New Right initially targeted the gay movement in Dade County, Florida. In January 1977 the county commissioners, with little public debate or fanfare, added sexual orientation to the local civil rights ordinance. Fundamentalists countered very quickly, forming as their vehicle an organization with the emotionally explosive name of "Save Our Children" and with the popular singer Anita Bryant as its spokesperson. Bryant's involvement guaranteed that the repeal campaign would draw national media attention—the first such sustained exposure for issues of gay rights—and New Right luminaries such as Jerry Falwell made repeated appearances in south Florida. Activists attempted to respond, but their efforts at reasoned presentation of the issues and the sparse resources they could muster on their behalf proved sorely inadequate. When voters cast their ballot in June, the gay rights clause was overwhelmingly defeated.

The Dade County drive was the first of several referenda and initiative campaigns that were waged over the next eighteen months. In St. Paul, in Wichita, and in Eugene, Oregon, voters resoundingly rejected gay rights. In Seattle and in California, the gay community emerged victorious. The California campaign against the Briggs initiative was especially significant because of its statewide scope. In particular, it offered a favorable portent of things to come as many gay men and lesbians for the first time found themselves working together against a common enemy. But even this victory turned sour when Harvey Milk, the openly gay supervisor in San Francisco, was assassinated three weeks after the November balloting.

The rise of the New Right sent tremors of fear through the gay and lesbian community across the country. Its press increasingly offered analogies with McCarthy's America and Nazi Germany. The movement seemed to lack the financial resources, the numbers, the influence, and the political sophistication to counter the threat. The placid politics of gay rights lobbying was helpless before the emotional onslaught of fundamentalist rhetoric. The single-issue orientation of gay rights activists made effective coalitions difficult to construct, or even to conceive; the separate community-building strategy of lesbian-feminism left little room for fierce political engagement. A collective crisis of faith seemed to paralyze the movement. The dazed leadership of national organizations expended more energy in internecine warfare and mutual recrimination than in attending to the crisis at hand.

A second challenge came in the form of the collapse of the lesbian-separatist utopia. In part this could be blamed on the changing economic times. High inflation in the Carter years and high unemployment in the early Reagan years pressed marginal institutions to the wall. Organizations fully dependent on volunteer labor struggled to survive, and the accumulated stress of years of subsistence living took their toll on women who, by virtue of their class position and educational background, in fact had other options. Downward mobility became less and less liberating and more and more painful.

But the shattering of utopian dreams stemmed from internal tensions as well. Toward the end of the 1970s, the effort to enforce standards of "political correctness" turned toward sexual issues. Some radical feminists, enraged by images of sexual violence, campaigned for restrictions on the distribution and sale of pornography. Using emotionally volatile slogans—"Pornography is the theory; rape is the practice"—they seemed to be making common cause with the New Right. In fact, they were encouraging an assault on elements of the sexual revolution that, by permitting discussion of previously forbidden topics, had opened a space for the representation of lesbian and gay life.[21]

The pornography issue sparked an acrimonious debate within the lesbian community—and among feminists more generally—about a broad spectrum of sexual matters. As some lesbians expressed reservations about the pornography crusade, they found their "credentials" as lesbian-feminists questioned. Soon lesbian-feminists with roots in the pre-Stonewall world, such as Joan Nestle, began to deconstruct the rhetorical strategem of "The Woman-Identified Woman," which had conflated lesbianism with feminism and eliminated the erotic component of lesbian identity.[22] Discussions of butch-femme roles, a style of sexual interaction that had predominated in pre-Stonewall bar life, of sexual fantasy, and of sadomasochism coursed through the lesbian-feminist community. At the 1982 Scholar and the Feminist Conference, "Towards a Politics of Sexuality," held at Barnard College, the tensions exploded into view as some of the lesbians present were attacked publicly because of their sexuality.[23]

The eruption of the "sex wars," as these controversies came to be known, exposed divisions within the lesbian community. In the long run, the woman-identified-woman model of lesbianism, so powerful in creating a lesbian-feminist movement, lost its hegemony, slowly to be replaced by a more fluid discourse that acknowledged and affirmed sexual differences. In the short run, however, the emotionally searing conflicts soured the utopian dreams of the 1970s.

A third challenge emanated from the autonomous organizing efforts of lesbians and gays of color, which by the end of the 1970s had reached a critical mass.[24] One characteristic that gay rights and lesbian separatism shared was that each, in some sense, was a "single identity" movement. In the former case, sexual "orientation" was the focal point for organizing; in the latter, it was gender. Neither left much room for a broader, more complex vision of social change; neither easily tolerated competing claims or loyalties.

Separate organizing by people of color began within a year or so after Stonewall. In some GLFs, Third World caucuses formed; in a few cities, distinct groups were started. Like GLF, these early organizations were deeply affected by the changing political climate. The demoralization that by the early 1970s infected communities of color hastened their decline. As government repression hit radical organizations with special force, many groups collapsed under the pressure.

In the ensuing years, some people managed to navigate the currents of a gendered politics. Some women of color could be found in lesbian-feminist organizations, including the most separatist-oriented, although evidence abounds from this era of tensions around race. A few individuals—I think of Betty Powell and Mel Boozer, for instance, both of whom worked with the National Gay Task Force in the 1970s and early 1980s—maintained a presence in the gay rights movement. Others joined forces in organizations that were explicitly interracial in their focus, such as Black and White Men Together, which had chapters in many cities by the end of the 1970s. But increasingly the preferred option was to establish a political space of their own. Organizations such as Salsa Soul Sisters in New York, the collective that published the magazine *Azalea*, and the multi-chaptered National Coalition of Black Gays sought to define a political agenda and to create a collective identity true to their own experience.

A major step forward came in 1979, when a call was issued for a national conference of Third World gays, to be held in Washington in October. Initiated by African-American groups, which at that point were the most solidly established, the conference provided the opportunity for intensive mobilizing in an effort to gather a large, nationally representative body of people. The significance of the conference was magnified when other grass-roots activists called for a national march on Washington the same weekend. The march guaranteed that large numbers of white lesbians and gay men would learn of the work and the demands of people of color.

Autonomous organization-building would continue and, indeed, accelerate in the 1980s, but after 1979 activists of color self-consciously confronted white organizations with ever greater insistence. (During these years a similar process was under way within the women's movement.) They demanded inclusion in both representation and setting of agendas. Their demands rested on an analysis of oppression and identity fundamentally different from that of the gendered politics of the 1970s. Rather than the single-issue orientation of the gay rights movement, or the vanguard cry of "We are the most oppressed" emanating from some lesbian separatists, lesbians and gays of color argued for what Barbara Smith has called "the simultaneity of oppression." The many layers of identity inscribed in each person made individuals the target of multiple vectors of oppression. White activists were challenged to expand their vision to include whole human beings instead of just slices of the self.

By the early 1980s the clamor for recognition and inclusiveness had become ever present. There were few significant movement gatherings where the demands of people of color were not raised. Although the response of white organizations was limited, the level of discomfort was rising dramatically.

We can never know what response this combination of challenges might have generated: Would it have led in the 1980s to dynamic growth, strategic innovation, and increased effectiveness? Or would it have led to fracturing, demoralization, and disarray? Local community studies may someday tell us a variety of conflicting stories. Certainly the massive organizing that occurred in California around the Briggs initiative evinced creative, constructive possibilities. But, at this stage of my own research, I am more impressed by the signs of danger. The New Right, not the gay and lesbian movement, was setting the terms of the debate. Lesbian-feminists were engaged in bruising, destructive battles with one another. White activists and activists of color were locked in what Torie Osborn has called "the guilt-rage dance."

I have said that "we can never know" what might have happened. The reason is probably obvious to many readers. As the 1980s began, yet another challenge, life-threatening in nature, made its appearance. The AIDS epidemic mapped the terrain on which resolutions of these other challenges would get worked through.

The Impact of AIDS[25]

It is not my task here to recount the history of the AIDS epidemic. AIDS has already found a number of able chroniclers and, as the epidemic goes on and reaches ever more deeply into American life, it will produce many more. But I do want to look at the ways that the virus, which struck the gay male community with special force, has thoroughly reshaped lesbian and gay politics. Through the imperative of mounting an effective response to the epidemic, the movement has achieved a level of sophistication, influence, and permanence that activists of the 1970s could only dream about.

Among white middle-class gay men, AIDS has bridged the gulf that divided the movement from the subculture. The epidemic elucidated, in a manner that movement rhetoric could not, the continuing strength of gay oppression. Men with a firm sense of gay identity, but who had eschewed activism, were forced to acknowledge that only a deeply rooted, systemic homophobia could explain the callous, even murderous, neglect by the government and the mass media of an epidemic that was killing them and their loved ones. Many had to admit how marginal and despised they were, despite the class or race or gender privileges they enjoyed. The epidemic provoked some extraordinary transformations: who would have predicted that Wall Street stockbrokers would become street militants and advocates of massive civil disobedience?

The impact on the movement has likewise been profound. The dense and extensive social networks that developed in the 1970s but that remained resistant to political mobilization now could be tapped. The movement gained access to new reservoirs of money, of skills, and of recruits. Much of this, of course, went toward building AIDS service and advocacy organizations, but much of it was also directed toward the broader agenda of gay politics.

For gays and lesbians of color, the epidemic sounded a clarion call to escalate their organizing efforts. From the beginning of the epidemic, African–American and Latino communities were disproportionately struck by the disease. Not only gay and bisexual men, but intravenous drug users, their sexual partners, and their children were at risk. Because drug users lacked the organizational infrastructure of the gay community, and because they and their communities were resource-poor, they were not easily able to mount a response of their own. And because of the homophobia within communities of color, the established leadership was often unwilling to concede the severity of the problem in their midst.

Gay and lesbian activists of color thus found themselves in a strategically unique position. In relation to gay-focused AIDS organizations, their demands for entry, access, and power took on added urgency. Without exaggerating or romanticizing the openness of AIDS organizations, the fact is that many of them proved more responsive to calls for inclusion than gay organizations had previously been. In relation to their racial and ethnic communities, gays and lesbians of color were among the first to perceive the significance of the epidemic; through it, they have been able to initiate—or extend—a dialogue about homophobia and gay oppression. And, as the epidemic spread and funds were pried loose from government agencies to target minority communities, it was often gays and lesbians who had the experience and the willingness to staff these new organizations. The result has been a dramatic increase in the level of organization and visibility of gays of color.

Two examples can illustrate the scope of change. In February 1990, I helped facilitate a leadership retreat for paid executive directors of gay and lesbian organizations. The planners had made a commitment to assemble a diverse group, but our criteria for invitations were leading to a very white list. By expanding our reach to include gay directors of AIDS organizations, we ended up with 29 participants, of whom forty percent were of color. The AIDS service bureaucracy has become a vehicle for placing gays and lesbians of color in formal leadership roles.

Later that year another retreat was designed for activist leaders in New York City. Here the specifications for attendance were broad enough to make it relatively easy to have half the attendees be white and half be of color. The participants included an assistant to the mayor, two city commissioners, a deputy commissioner, and an elected Democratic Party district leader; all five were people of color. It is difficult to imagine a similar scenario from ten, or even five, years ago.

As the 1990s begin, the turn toward racial and ethnic inclusion is growing. Conferences are less likely to be virtually all-white gatherings; some of the national gay and lesbian organizations are acting on firm commitments to diversify staffs and boards; and in some cities, the movement is taking on rainbow hues.

For many white lesbians, the AIDS epidemic propelled them into political work with gay men. Two of the more widely remarked gay-related phenomena of the 1980s were the depth of lesbian involvement in the fight against AIDS and the assumption by lesbians of key leadership roles in what had been male-dominated organizations. Too often the explanations for this change have been framed in ways that cynically impugn its significance or that make it sound like a temporary accommodation during a crisis. Lesbians have flocked to AIDS work, the story goes, because they embody qualities of generosity, self-sacrifice, or nurturance—in other words, for the stereotypically female reason of putting the needs of others first. Or lesbians are now leading the movement because gay men are dying off—our variation on the heterosexual theme of women's skills being valued in wartime.

I don't buy these explanations as sufficient to account for the seismic shift in gender relations that has occurred in the movement. Something deeper and more complex is going on. There is, it seems to me, both a political and a cultural component to the rapprochement between women and men. Politically, lesbian-feminism offered sharper analytical tools for comprehending the full significance of the AIDS epidemic from its earliest years. The confrontation with sexism that was at the heart of feminism made most lesbian activists—whether separatist, reformist, or somewhere in between—acutely conscious of the systemic nature of oppression. Few had ever bought the notion, common in gay rights politics, that minor adjustments in law and public policy would bring freedom. Health issues, moreover, had been a key component of feminist organizing since the late 1960s. Much consciousness raising had been done, for instance, around fights to expose the dangers of the birth-control pill and the IUD. One result of these and other battles was that lesbians were less likely than gay men initially were to frame the epidemic as a simple issue of medicine and public health.

That this understanding of the politics of health might play itself out in the choices of lesbian activists was brought home to me in a particular conversation of a few years ago. Katy Taylor was working as an investigator in the AIDS discrimination unit of the New York City Human Rights Commission. Her previous history of activism stretched back to the civil rights and antiwar movements; in the 1970s, she had focused on union organizing among women and on issues of sexual violence. She had never before worked with gay men, or on gay-related issues. When I asked Taylor why in 1983 she had chosen, when AIDS was still barely spoken about outside big-city gay male circles, to apply for the job, her answer was direct: "I didn't just apply for the job—I pursued it. Because of the work I had done," she said, "I *knew* that AIDS was going to bring together all of the issues I cared about. Right away I could see that AIDS was about class, and race, and sexuality, and homophobia, and gender—it was about everything. And I wanted to be there." I suspect that many other lesbian-feminists thought in similar ways.

Once the lesbian presence was established in the world of AIDS service and politics, it struck a deep vein of gratitude among gay men. But the bonds that have developed between men and women could become strong and sturdy because of changes in the sexual culture of *both genders*. The modifications of gay male sexuality that the epidemic provoked—the new emphasis on dating, on intimacy, on relationships—were occurring at the very moment that the sex wars had incited explorations of sexuality within the lesbian community. In other words, the gender gap that had yawned so widely in the 1970s was narrowing. A new culture of sexuality was taking shape, in which some men and women could meet on ground that, if not common, was at least in the same neighborhood.

Finally, the AIDS epidemic helped dissolve the political marginalization and social isolation that had hampered the movement's ability to counter the New Right. AIDS forced many mainstream institutions into sustained negotiation with the gay and lesbian community. As the epidemic spread, churches, mental health professionals, the medical and public health establishment, the social and human service bureaucracies, corporations, municipal, state, and federal officials, congressional staffers, and many more eventually had no choice but to deal with AIDS. When gays had approached these institutions for a cause that smacked of sexual freedom, it was relatively easy to turn the other way. When these same activists arrived wearing the hat of AIDS service provider or educator and addressing a menace to the public health of the nation, at least some doors opened. And doors that opened because of AIDS remained access points for dealing later on with a range of other lesbian and gay issues. The relationships that formed, the bonds of respect that were forged, and the knowledge of how institutions worked and how decisions were made became valuable resources for the gay community.

The AIDS epidemic may not have been the sole motivator of change in the 1980s, but it certainly shaped the field on which other challenges and problems were played out. Through it, the gay and lesbian movement has been so thoroughly reconstructed that it scarcely resembles the creature of a decade ago. Some of the differences between 1980 and 1990 are as follows:

1. Many groups have access to vastly expanded resources and have become permanent fixtures. In 1980, there were few gay and lesbian organizations

whose future seemed assured. Most depended on volunteer labor. Their funding base was insecure and the life cycle of most was short.

The situation of New York City gives some sense of the scope of change. In 1981, on the eve of the epidemic, the city where the Stonewall Riot occurred and with the largest population of gay men and lesbians in the country, sustained fewer than a dozen activists in paid staff positions. In 1990, if one includes AIDS organizations with a gay focus and AIDS workers who are gay-identified, the number is pushing two hundred.

The growth is not simply confined to AIDS organizations. The resource pie has grown. The budgets of many gay and lesbian groups in cities across the country have expanded. These groups have become sophisticated in the use of fund-raising techniques pioneered by the New Right in the 1970s. Incorporation and boards of directors give some measure of stability. Activists with years of grass-roots experience behind them are now able to have "careers" in the movement, instead of retreating to private pursuits when the burden of volunteerism becomes too great. Experience and sophistication are accumulating within the ranks of the movement, replacing the revolving-door pattern characteristic of volunteer-based efforts.

2. The 1980s have witnessed the reinvigoration of grass-roots local activism and the spread of the movement to parts of the country that had barely been touched by it in the 1970s.

Maybe these changes would have occurred without AIDS, but I'm not persuaded. The conservatism of the Reagan years and the vitriolic campaigns of the New Right were inhibiting the spread of activism beyond large metropolitan areas, especially in parts of the country where political conservatism and religious fundamentalism were strongest. But, whereas many people might have been reluctant to fight for gay liberation, they were unwilling to turn their backs on the casualties of the epidemic. AIDS added altruism, compassion, and kindness to the bag of possible motivations for activism, and it overcame constraints against mobilization.

Participation in AIDS service work, which was often the initial path toward involvement, could not easily remain sequestered in an apolitical world. AIDS service organizations found their efforts threatened by state legislative proposals to make HIV status reportable and to forbid the use of tax dollars for certain kinds of educational material, and by other, more draconian measures. Service providers also needed levels of funding that only municipal, state, or federal officials could provide. Caretaking work, especially when it stretched for months or years, provoked anger, reshaped consciousness, and forged unexpected commitments. In short, the lines dividing service and politics blurred. So, too, did the boundaries between AIDS organizing and gay and lesbian organizing.

The 1987 March on Washington to demand a national response to AIDS and attention to lesbian and gay rights marked a critical moment in this process. In 1979, the first national march had attracted perhaps 100,000; eight years later the crowd surpassed half a million. The turnout was a sign of the density of organizational networks and community ties. And in some states, like my own of North Carolina, where ad hoc groups had coalesced to bring people to Washington (a "safe" activity that did not threaten exposure at home), the weekend in Washington proved uncontainable. The display of the Names Project Quilt, the massive wedding ceremony at the National Cathedral, and the impressive parade of contingents from every state in the nation, struck a chord of self-respect so deep that it could not be ignored. People returned to their home communities transformed, ready to do what seemed unimaginable a few days before.

3. AIDS has stimulated a return to tactics of direct action and civil disobedience on a scale not seen since the early 1970s.

    Most closely associated with ACT UP, direct action has been reincorporated among the spectrum of tactics considered permissible even by the reform wing of the movement. Indeed, the most notable feature of the growing militance of the last few years has been the approval of it even by those organizations and activists who do not engage in such tactics themselves. The movement seems willing to tolerate both insider and outsider strategies, recognizing the necessity of both in order to reach common goals. The deliberate manipulation of a spectrum of protest techniques bespeaks a political sophistication absent a decade earlier in the Dade County repeal campaign.

4. The stubborn resistance of the nation's top leadership, political and otherwise, to address some fundamental—and simple—issues posed by the epidemic has sparked the revival of a radical political analysis and a broad strategic vision within the movement.

The AIDS epidemic has once again given plausibility to understandings of gay and lesbian oppression as systemic; it has exposed the complex ways in which it is tied to a host of other injustices. The observation that most victims of the disease are either gay or of color, or both; the fact that the media and the federal health bureaucracy could be instantly mobilized by a disease that struck a few score members of the American Legion, but could look the other way as tens of thousands of gay men and IV drug users wasted away; the ability of the government to transport half a million personnel across the globe, and then provide for their food, shelter, clothing, *and* health care, while scarcely blinking an eye: all this and more has made AIDS an extraordinarily effective primer in politics.

One concrete result has been the initiative taken by the movement to break out of its ghettoized politics. Fighting AIDS effectively has made this a necessity, and the broad-based NORA coalition (National Organizations Responding to AIDS), conceived and shaped by gay activists, is the most obvious example. But movement leaders are not simply engaged in an unavoidable effort to draw others to their cause. They have effectively reached out to participate in coalition with other movements around issues of common concern. The passage in 1990 of the Hate Crimes Statistics Act and the Americans with Disabilities Act signify a coming of age of lesbian and gay activism.

A Few Final Thoughts

The good news is that the movement is stronger and more vital now than at any time in the past, a statement which could not have been made ten years ago. The sobering view is that it has taken a deadly epidemic to lead us to this point. And a cautious assessment requires me to acknowledge that the resolution of the crises of a decade ago is still incomplete and unstable.

Of the many changes that occurred in the 1980s, I am most confident of the continuing ability of men and women to work together. There are good reasons for optimism. Many of our organizations have built gender parity into their structure. Lesbians in large numbers have important leadership roles, nationally and locally, in the movement. Far more consciousness raising has occurred around sexism than around other issues of identity and oppression. The institutional legacy of lesbian-feminism remains strong enough that lesbians have a secure base from which to bargain. Without question, conflict and tension will continue to assert themselves, but I suspect that the progressive changes of the last ten years in this area are irreversible.

The issue of resources—particularly financial—is more troubling. Movement organizations, despite the growth in the budgets of many of them and despite greater sophistication in techniques of fund-raising, still groan under the burden of work loads swollen, paradoxically, by the movement's success: our agenda grows with each new victory. Any number of scenarios could restrict the growth, or even shrink the size, of the resource pie. What if a dramatic scientific breakthrough occurs in the treatment or prevention of AIDS? What if the budgetary crunch that state and local governments are facing deepens, and public money for AIDS dries up? Will contributions going to our political organizations be diverted to AIDS service work? If the movement wins a significant national victory in the next few years—rescinding the military's exclusion policy or passage of a federal civil rights bill, neither of which is beyond imagination—will donors grow complacent and think that the movement can close up shop?

On the question of racial and ethnic inclusion, there is cause for both optimism and caution. In some organizations and in some cities, commitments to inclusion have been made and are being acted upon. The impulse toward organization among lesbians and gays of color is so dynamic that their base for negotiation and dialogue is becoming stronger and stronger. Counterbalancing this is the simple fact that identity politics is always explosive: Will white organizations move fast enough to satisfy the expectations of people of color? Will some activists of color prove willing to absorb the inevitable frustrations, or will their autonomous organizing be transformed into a new separatism?

So far, most of the discussion about race and ethnicity has revolved around the issue of inclusion. Yet to be considered in any sustained way is the question of setting agendas. It's one thing to open the doors of organizations so that they encompass racial, ethnic, and class differences. It is quite another to reshape an organization's or a movement's agenda so that it incorporates the goals of these new constituencies. Profound change will occur when inclusion begins to affect the goals and direction of the movement. I suspect that the process, if we get far enough to engage in it seriously, will be tumultuous.

Already, it seems to me, the movement is taking small steps in this direction. Two issues that have risen to prominence in the last handful of years—the military's exclusion policy and family benefits—speak directly to the needs of working-class people, whatever their color. Can the movement go further? Is it willing, and able, to frame its agenda in ways that create broad coalitions for social change? Will the quest for domestic partnership rights be transformed into a drive for an inclusive national family policy? Will the organizing for access to drugs and medical care be redefined as a campaign for a system of national health care?

A final issue that bears watching is whether the movement can continue the elaborately choreographed dance in which "outsiders" and "insiders," local grassroots activists and national lobbyists, paid professional staffers and volunteer laborers, all stay in step with one another. The history of social movements suggests that it will not be easy: the various places that people occupy in the spectrum of activities and functions are not simply different roles that they have taken. Often they represent sharply divergent visions of both the process of social change and the society one hopes to create. How do we negotiate the conflicts that always threaten to disrupt the movement?

One hopeful sign is that many key leadership roles in the movement, at both the national and local level, are held by activists who represent themselves as "progressive." As an identifying label, the word came into vogue in the late 1970s and early 1980s after a long dormancy. It seems to describe heirs of sixties radicalism who are willing to work for change "within the system" yet without abandoning a long-term vision of social transformation. Or, to adapt the language of gay emancipationists of a century ago, they are radical souls residing in the bodies of reformers. Many are able to speak with credibility and authority to both reformers and radicals, to local grass-roots militants as well as wealthy donors, to those comfortable in legislative corridors and to those at home in a picket line. Their flexible leadership has helped to move us closer to our goals over the last few years.

This sketch of the gay and lesbian movement has been a partial one: partial in that it is not based on exhaustive research and partial in that it is meant to give coherence to what has often seemed ornery and confusing. There are topics that I haven't attended to with the depth they deserve, such as the complex relationship between culture and politics, between communities and movements. I have also ignored the many crosscurrents of the 1970s and 1980s—for instance, the persistent thread of gay male radicalism, even at the height of the gay rights movement, or the continuing allegiance of some lesbians to a separatist vision, even in the era of AIDS. I am aware, too, that the experience of some cities (San Francisco, Boston, and Houston come to mind), at least on the surface, defies the construction I have given to events. Nonetheless, as I have rehearsed this overall analysis with groups of activists, it elicits nods of recognition.

I would love—of course—to believe that these signs of approval are evidence of the insightful accuracy of my inquiry. Though I suspect that at least some of what I have written will withstand closer scrutiny, I know that the affirmations I've received are testimony to something else. The vast majority of us who are active in the gay and lesbian movement are saddled with a heavy burden of ignorance about our history of political struggle. The frenzy of activity that envelops us leaves little room for thoughtful reflection; the past vanishes before the image of the next task or crisis.

Community historians need to undertake the task of researching the history of lesbian and gay politics. We need studies of organizations, former and current. We need careful examination of issues—how have gays and lesbians worked with the churches, or the federal bureaucracy, or the Democratic Party? We need studies of geographic communities—from Boston to Seattle to San Diego to Atlanta—as well as studies of identity communities. The list is long. But only then will we have the richly textured history of emancipatory struggle that will preserve a collective memory of the past and serve as resource to meet today's—and tomorrow's—challenges.

Notes

1. Useful works on the homophile years include John D'Emilio, *Sexual Politics, Sexual Communities: The Making of a Homosexual Minority in the United States, 1940–1970* (Chicago: University of Chicago Press, 1983); Today Marotta, *The Politics of Homosexuality* (Boston: Houghton Mifflin, 1981); and Stuart Timmons, *The Trouble with Harry Hay: Founder of the Modern Gay Movement* (Boston: Alyson, 1990).
2. Allan Bérubé, *Coming Out Under Fire: The History of Gay Men and Women in World War Two* (New York: Free Press, 1990).
3. Useful works on radical gay liberation include Dennis Altman, *Homosexual: Oppression and Liberation* (New York: Avon, 1971); Karla Jay and Allen Young, *Out of the Closets: Voices of Gay Liberation* (New York: Douglas/Links, 1972); Donn Teal, *The Gay Militants* (New York: Stein and Day, 1971); Len Richmond and Gary Noguera, eds., *The Gay Liberation Book* (San Francisco: Ramparts Press, 1973); and Marotta, *The Politics of Homosexuality*.
4. The information on Shelley is drawn from an interview conducted by Jonathan Katz. I am grateful to Katz for allowing me access to the tape.
5. Quoted in Marotta, *The Politics of Homosexuality*, 88.
6. Ibid.

7. See Sara Evans, *Personal Politics: The Roots of Women's Liberation in the Civil Rights Movement and the New Left* (New York: Alfred A. Knopf, 1979).

8. For a partial list of GLF groups see the list of organizations at the end of Jay and Young, *Out of the Closets*, 375–403.

9. Useful works on gay rights activism include Teal, *The Gay Militants*, Marotta, *The Politics of Homosexuality*, and Arthur Bell, *Dancing the Gay Lib Blues* (New York: Simon & Schuster, 1971). All of these works focus on gay activism in New York City and thus highlight the need for historians and sociologists to study the evolution of activism in other cities in the 1970s.

10. On the Gay Academic Union see *The Universities and the Gay Experience: Proceedings of the Conference Sponsored by the Women and Men of the Gay Academic Union*, November 23 and 24, 1973 (New York, 1974).

11. The events and victories mentioned in this and the preceding paragraphs all deserve more detailed study and analysis by researchers.

12. A good description of this new public subculture can be found in Edmund White, *States of Desire: Travels in Gay America* (New York: Dutton, 1980).

13. Useful works on the evolution of lesbian feminism include Jay and Young, *Out of the Closets;* Marotta, *The Politics of Homosexuality;* Sidney Abbott and Barbara Love, *Sappho Was a Right-On Woman: A Liberated View of Lesbianism* (New York: Stein and Day, 1972); Nancy Myron and Charlotte Bunch, eds., *Lesbianism and the Women's Movement* (Baltimore: Diana Press, 1975); Michal Brody, ed., *Are We There Yet?: A Continuing History of Lavender Woman* (Iowa City: Aunt Lute, 1985); Alice Echols, *Daring to Be Bad: Radical Feminism in America, 1967–75* (Minneapolis: University of Minnesota Press, 1989); Sarah Lucia Hoagland and Julia Penelope, eds., *For Lesbians Only: A Separatist Anthology* (London: Onlywomen Press, 1988); and Ginny Vida, ed., *Our Right to Love: A Lesbian Resource Book* (Englewood Cliffs, N.J.: Prentice-Hall, 1978).

14. See Blanche Wiesen Cook, "The Historical Denial of Lesbianism," *Radical History Review* 20 (Spring/Summer 1979): 60–65.

15. Alice Echols has written extensively on the evolution of lesbian-feminist ideology and politics. See, especially, *Daring to Be Bad*, 210–241; "The Taming of the Id: Feminist Sexual Politics, 1968–1983," in Carole S. Vance, ed., *Pleasure and Danger: Exploring Female Sexuality* (Boston: Routledge and Kegan Paul, 1984), pp. 50–72; and "The New Feminism of Yin and Yang," in Snitow, Stansell, and Thompson, eds., *Powers of Desire: The Politics of Sexuality* (New York: Monthly Review Press, 1983), 439–459. "The Woman-Identified Woman" has been reprinted in many places. See Jay and Young, *Out of the Closets*, 172–177.

16. See Charlotte Bunch, "Learning from Lesbian Separatism," in Karla Jay and Allen Young, eds., *Lavender Culture* (New York: Jove/HBJ Publications, 1979), 433–444.

17. Women's Press Collective, *Lesbians Speak Out*, 2nd ed. (Berkeley, 1974), 139–140.

18. Charlotte Bunch, "Learning from Lesbian Separatism," in Jay and Young, *Lavender Culture*, 441.

19. See, for example, Thomas S. Szasz, *The Manufacture of Madness* (New York: Harper & Row, 1970); and R. D. Laing, *The Politics of Experience* (New York: Pantheon, 1967). The story of the American Psychiatric Association's reversal can be found in Ronald Bayer, *Homosexuality and American Psychiatry: The Politics of Diagnosis* (New York: Basic Books, 1981).

20. On the New Right and the gay movement, see Randy Shilts, *The Mayor of Castro Street: The Life and Times of Harvey Milk* (New York: St. Martin's Press, 1982); Gay Rights Writer's Group, *It Could Happen To You: An Account of the Gay Civil Rights Campaign in Eugene, Oregon* (Boston: Alyson, 1983); and Perry Deane Young, *God's Bullies: Native Reflections on Preachers and Politics* (New York: Holt, Rinehart and Winston, 1982).

21. For feminist statements against pornography see Laura Lederer, ed., *Take Back the Night* (New York: William Morrow, 1980), and Andrea Dworkin, *Pornography: Men Possessing Women* (New York: Perigee, 1981).

22. See "Butch-Femme Relationships: Sexual Courage in the 1950s," in Joan Nestle, *A Restricted Country* (Ithaca, N.Y.: Firebrand Books, 1987), 100–109.

23. On the Barnard Conference, see Carole S. Vance, ed., *Pleasure and Danger*.

24. On the experience and organizing efforts of gays and lesbians of color, see Cherrie Moraga and Gloria Anzaldua, eds., *This Bridge Called My Back: Writings by Radical Women of Color* (New York: Kitchen Table Press, 1983); Joseph Beam, ed., *In the Life: A Black Gay Anthology* (Boston: Alyson, 1986); and Barbara Smith, ed., *Home Girls: A Black Feminist Anthology* (New York: Kitchen Table Press, 1983).

25. The literature on the AIDS epidemic is vast. Useful works include Dennis Altman, *AIDS in the Mind of America* (Garden City, N.Y.: Anchor/Doubleday, 1986); Cindy Patton, *Sex and Germs: The Politics of AIDS* (Boston: South End Press, 1985); Simon Watney, *Policing Desire: Pornography, AIDS, and the Media* (Minneapolis: University of Minnesota Press, 1987); Randy Shilts, *And the Band Played On: Politics, People, and the AIDS Epidemic* (New York: St. Martin's Press, 1987); Larry Kramer, *Reports from the Holocaust: The Making of an AIDS Activist* (New York: St. Martin's Press, 1989); Douglas Crimp, ed., *AIDS: Cultural Analysis, Cultural Activism* (Cambridge: MIT Press, 1988); and Douglas Crimp with Adam Ralston, *AIDS demo graphics* (Seattle: Bay Press, 1990).

Questions for Reflection, Discussion, and Writing

1. D'Emilio identifies the Gay Liberation Front of the 1960s as being fundamentally concerned with the ways in which "institutionalized heterosexuality reinforced a patriarchal nuclear family that socialized men and women into narrow roles and placed homosexuality beyond the pale. These gender dichotomies," he continues, "also reinforced other divisions based on race and class." Forty years later, are societal attitudes and prescriptions different from this characterization? What has changed and what hasn't?

2. D'Emilio distinguishes Gay Liberation of the 1960s from Gay Activism of the 1970s by characterizing the former as "a struggle for liberation" and the latter as "a quest for 'rights.'" Do either of these categories shed light on where we are now? What do you think D'Emilio means when he suggests that there is a difference between liberation and rights?

3. On which groups (racial, gendered, activist) does D'Emilio focus his efforts? In what ways have those groups divided, and according to D'Emilio, in what ways have they formed alliances and coalitions over the years? What prompted those alliances? Those divisions? What does he think the present environment reflects about gay and lesbian communities, coalitions, alliances and divisions?

4. Toward the end of his essay, D'Emilio documents the impact of AIDS and its connection to community. What issues surrounding community and sexuality does D'Emilio claim the specter of AIDS raises?

5. What are the issues and concerns D'Emilio raises in "A Few Final Thoughts" that have a direct relation to challenges facing a GLBT or queer movement today? In what direction do you think a movement ought to head and why?

Writing Assignment

Research and write a brief history of a gay, lesbian, or GBLT organization on your campus or in your immediate area. Interview staff and founding members in order to learn what hurdles they had to overcome in terms of organization, administration, space and funding. How do they see the evolution and history of their organization? Where do they hope to lead it in the future?

Related Reading

On Gay Liberation:

Dennis Altman, *Homosexual Oppression and Liberation.* New York: Avon. 1971.

Donn Teal, *The Gay Militants.* NY: Stein and Day. 1971.

Karla Jay and Allen Young, Eds. *Out of the Closets: Voices of Gay Liberation.* London: Gay Men's Press. 1972.

Karla Jay and Allen Young, Eds. *Lavender Culture.* NY: Harcourt Brace. 1978.

Karen A. Foss, "The Logic of Folly in the Political Campaigns of Harvey Milk" in *Queer Words, Queer Images: Communication and the Construction of Homosexuality.* R. Jeffrey Ringer, Ed. NY: NYUP. 1994. 7–29.

Terence Kissack, "Freaking Fag Revolutionaries: New York's Gay Liberation Front, 1969-1971." *Radical History Review 62* (Spring 1995): 104–134.

Martin Duberman. *Midlife Queer: Autobiography of a Decade, 1971-1981.* Madison: University of Wisconsin Press. 1998.

Vern L. Bullough, Ed. *Before Stonewall: Activists for Gay and Lesbian Rights in Historical Context.* Binghamton, NY: Haworth Press. 2002.

Film

The Times of Harvey Milk (1984). Robert Epstein and Richard Schmiechen. 90 m.

The Cockettes (2002). David Weissman and Bill Weber. 100 m.

On Lesbian Feminism:

Radicalesbians, "The Woman-Identified Woman" (1970) in *We Are Everywhere: A Historical Sourcebook of Gay and Lesbian Politics.* Mark Blasius and Shane Phelan, Eds. NY: Routledge. 1997. 396–399.

Adrienne Rich, "Compulsory Heterosexuality and Lesbian Existence" (1980) in *The Lesbian and Gay Studies Reader*. H. Abelove, et.al., Eds. NY: Routledge. 1993. 227–254.

Tania Abdulahad, et. al., "Black Lesbians/Feminist Organizing: A Conversation" in *Home Girls: A Black Feminist Anthology*. Barbara Smith, Ed. NY: Kitchen Table: Women of Color Press. 1983. 293–319.

Cheryl Clarke, "Lesbianism: An Act of Resistance" in *This Bridge Called My Back: Writings by Radical Women of Color*. Cherríe Moraga and Gloria Anzaldúa, Eds. Watertown, MA.: Persephone Press. 1981. 128–137.

Mary Daly, *Gyn/Ecology: The Methods of Radical Feminism*. Boston: Beacon. 1978.

Marilyn Frye, "Some Reflections on Separatism and Power" (1978) in *The Lesbian and Gay Studies Reader*. H. Abelove, et.al., Eds. NY: Routledge. 1993. 91–98.

Lillian Faderman, "Lesbian Nation: Creating a Woman-Identified Women Community in the 1970s" in *Odd Girls and Twilight Lovers*. NY: Penguin. 1991. 215–245.

On the Lesbian "Sex Wars" of the 1980s:

Ann Snitow, et.al., Eds. *Powers of Desire: The Politics of Sexuality*. NY: Monthly Review Press. 1983.

Carol S. Vance, Ed. *Pleasure and Danger: Exploring Female Sexuality*. NY: Routledge. 1984.

Varda Burstyn, Ed. *Women Against Censorship*. Vancouver: Douglas & Mclntyre. 1985

Janice G. Raymond and Dorchen Leidholdt, Eds. *The Sexual Liberals and the Attack On Feminism*. NY: Pergammon Press. 1990.

Sheila Jeffreys, "The Lesbian Sexual Revolution" in *The Lesbian Heresy*. Melbourne: Spinifex Press. 1993. 17–46.

Lillian Faderman, "Lesbian Sex Wars in the 1980s" in *Odd Girls and Twilight Lovers*. NY: Penguin. 1991. 246–270.

Susie Bright, *Susie Sexpert's Lesbian Sex World*. Pittsburgh: Cleis Press. 1990.

Lisa Duggan and Nan D. Hunter, Eds. *Sex Wars: Sexual Dissent and Political Culture*. NY: Routledge. 1995.

Special Topics

In conjunction with a viewing of any of the films below, read Thomas Waugh's "Walking on Tippy Toes: Lesbian and Gay Liberation Documentary of the Post-Stonewall Period 1969–84" in *The Fruit Machine: Twenty Years of Writing on Queer Cinema*. Durham, N.C.: Duke UP. 2000. 246–271. Be prepared to discuss the representational strategies of your chosen film in light of its historical and political contexts.

Film

Lesbian Sexuality: Four Films by Barbara Hammer (1974–76). Barbara Hammer. 57m. [*Dyketactics, Multiple Orgasm, Double Strength, Women I Love*]

Lesbian Humor: Six Films by Barbara Hammer (1975–87). Barbara Hammer. 59 m. [*Menses, Superdyke, Our Trip, Sync Touch, Doll House, No No Nooky*]

Word Is Out: Stories of Some of Our Lives (1977). Peter Adair. 130 m.

Gay USA. (1977). Arthur Bressan. 78 m.

In the Best Interests of the Children (1977). Frances Reid, Elizabeth Stevens, and Cathy Zheutilin. 53 m.

■

Excerpt from *Lesbians Talk Queer Notions*

Cherry Smyth

The insistence on "queer"—a term defined against "normal" and generated precisely in the context of terror—has the effect of pointing out a wide field of normalisation, rather than simple tolerance, as the site of violence.
                                        Michael Warner, "Fear of a Queer Planet"

The language of sexualities informs and transforms the cultural, social, political and historical contexts we inhabit. And no naming has been so vociferously contested in recent years as the word 'queer.' In several cities in the US, queer politics has been constituted in movements such as Queer Nation, while Britain has witnessed the birth of the direct action against homophobia group OutRage, with branches in London and other cities with high gay and lesbian populations such as Manchester. But queer identification exists beyond the membership of campaigning groups and signals a more general dissatisfaction with former lesbian and gay politics. The AIDS epidemic triggered anger, disbelief and a renewed sense of disenfranchisement among younger lesbians and gay men, who saw the meek acceptance of marginalisation as leading to a dangerous complacency within the community and victimisation from without. SILENCE = DEATH became the motto of a new generation who refused to be silenced, not only by government neglect in the face of AIDS, but by new homophobic legislation and a dramatic rise in the incidence of queer-bashing. The cry for safer sex information, research and drugs to fight the AIDS epidemic expanded into a campaign against all homophobic oppression. An urgent sense of mortality inspired the rejection of respectability and discretion.

We feel angry and disgusted, not gay. Using 'queer' is a way of reminding us how we are perceived by the rest of the world. It's a way of telling ourselves we don't have to be witty, charming people who keep our lives marginalised and discreet in the straight world. 'Queer' can be a rough word, but it is also a sly and ironic weapon we can steal from the homophobe's hand and use against him. 'NYQ', January 1992

What Is This Thing Called Queer?

Queer means to fuck with gender. There are straight queers, biqueers, tranny queers, lez queers, fag queers, SM queers, fisting queers in every single street in this apathetic country of ours.

Anonymous leaflet: "Queer Power Now," London 1991

Queer is a symptom, not a movement, a symptom of a desire for radical change.

Keith Alcom, "Pink Paper," issue 208

In April 1990 a group met in New York to discuss the frequent bashings of gays and lesbians in the East Village. Queer Nation was born with the slogan, 'Queers Bash Back' and stencils were drawn on the pavements: 'My beloved was queerbashed here. Queers fight back.' In classic postmodern fashion, Queer Nation borrowed styles and tactics from popular culture, black liberation struggles, hippies, AIDS activists, feminists and the peace movement to build its confrontational identity.

Queer Nationals are torn between affirming a new identity—'I am queer'—and rejecting restrictive identities—'I reject your categories'; between rejecting assimilation—'I don't need your approval, just get out of my face'—and wanting to be recognised by mainstream society—'we queers are gonna get in your face'. 'Outlook', No 11, Winter 1991

In London, OutRage was formed a few weeks later, with a similar 'in your face' agenda. It was time.

OutRage defines itself as:

A broad-based group of lesbians and gay men committed to radical non-violent direct action and civil disobedience to:
* assert the dignity, pride and human rights of lesbians and gay men
* fight homophobia, discrimination and violence against lesbians and gay men
* affirm the rights of lesbians and gay men to sexual freedom, choice and self-determination.

OutRage's first year produced a mass KISS-IN in Piccadilly Circus and a Queer Wedding in Trafalgar Square and provided plenty of sexy copy for a British press that had increasingly ignored or trivialised gay and lesbian politics.

Meanwhile, the legal system was introducing plenty of new challenges around which to rally disaffected queers. In December 1990, fifteen gay men were convicted on a series of charges for having **consensual** SM sex—a case that became known as Operation Spanner after the police code-name. In February 1992 their appeals were quashed. And in early 1991 the government introduced Clause 25 (now Section 27) of the Criminal Justice Act, which imposes stiffer sentences for certain sexual offences, including gay male procuring, solicitation and indecency, as well as child abuse, incest, rape, murder and sexual assault. The Clause was seen as the most serious move in over a century to increase the sentences for consenting homosexual behaviour and OutRage demonstrated outside Bow Street police station (chosen because it was where Oscar Wilde was charged almost 100 years ago), where activists 'turned themselves in' for crimes of importuning, indecency (kissing in the street) and procuring.

Legislation aimed at preventing lesbians from reproducing and lesbians and gay men from parenting also came to light. Paragraph 16 of the guidance notes to the 1989 Children Act contained an invidious little statement: ' "Equal rights" and "gay rights" have no place in fostering,' which was later amended, largely thanks to pressure from lesbian and gay campaigners. This followed closely on the Embryology Bill, which attempted to prevent lesbians using public A.I.D. services. The implication that only white, het, middle-class couples were fit parents had wide-reaching consequences for lesbian, gay, black and disabled parents, childcare workers, teachers and social services employees.

In March 1991, during the hysterical 'virgin births' furore about whether a woman who had not had penetrative sex with a man should be allowed artificial insemination, even the *Independent* newspaper supported the idea of dysfunctional lesbians:

> How far is it reasonable to assume, on the basis of what we know of human psychology, that a woman who's been unable to establish a relationship with a man, will relate any better to a child?

For many woman, lesbian or not, it has often amounted to the same thing. OutRage rallied against all three threats and over 10,000 marched to Hyde Park in protest. In covering the event, an allegedly liberal, quality newspaper wrote:

> Not unexpectedly, the rally was addressed by a lesbian woman [sic] from Australia with a daughter produced by artificial insemination. The mother now faces deportation as an illegal immigrant. People do go to the ends of the earth in order to land up in the most extraordinary fixes. *'Observer', 10 March 1991*

This sort of reporting reinforces the insidious moral code in Britain which suggests that:

- lesbians choose to fall in love with the wrong object choice in the wrong country (and that we certainly don't want to encourage any more of them pouring in from foreign places and getting away with it)

- the only healthy way to reproduce is by good old-fashioned 'planned' hetero-fucking and only then if both people are the same colour, race, class and age—note the frenzy when older women mate younger men
- people get arrested on peaceful demos because they choose to get in the policeman's way
- people die of AIDS because they have chosen to contract the disease

> You just have to look at the way the press has been condoning the attacks on the transsexual hookers in the Bois de Boulogne. It is being talked about as if transsexuals from the Third World come to Paris out of sheer bloody-mindedness, and that somehow they are, of their nature, 'infected,' and the punters are 'innocent victims' of these terrible people. Roz Kaveney

By mid-1991, OutRage had sprouted several affinity groups including the Whores of Babylon (Queers Fighting Religious Intolerance); SISSY (Schools Information Services on Sexuality); and PUSSY (Perverts Undermining State Scrutiny). Their often extravagant actions signalled the emergence of a highly ironic, camp, theatrical politics of direct action which bullied its way to the heart of the complacent media and put fun back into a wearied lesbian and gay movement. 'We've lobbied our tits off,' said Anna-Marie Smith, a founder member of PUSSY, 'and it didn't get us anywhere.'

Action vs Assimilation

Tired of the gentlemanly approach, queer activists saw OutRage as distinctly anti-assimilationist compared to the parliamentary reform group, Stonewall, which had been established as a response to Clause 28 in 1989. The Stonewall agenda is described as:

> To work for equality under the law and full social acceptance for lesbians and gay men. Our approach is an innovatory one for lesbian and gay rights—professional, strategic, tightly managed, able and willing to communicate with decision-makers in a constructive and informed way. 'Interim Report,' The Stonewall Group, 1990

This much-criticised, self-elected group of twenty lesbians and gay men has never professed to be representative:

> There really is no gay community. Most of us devise ways of keeping ourselves invisible. One feels one is on one's own. Sir Ian McKellen, 'Independent on Sunday', 10 November 1991

But Stonewall has been perceived as the legitimate voice of the 'lesbian and gay community' by government ministers, though it did not succeed in using the fame or prestige of Sir Ian McKellen and many 'poofs with privilege' to resist Clause 28, or as yet to obtain an equal age of consent.

Assimilationist strategies have nonetheless worked in other European countries. In the Netherlands and Scandinavia, for example, the lesbian and gay community has achieved greater access to the state and has been able to push though an impressive range of legal and social rights. Legalised gay and lesbian weddings (as in Denmark) are far from my own reading of what constitutes equality, whether queer or not, but the acknowledgement of gay and lesbian sexuality in sex education signals the possibility of building a society with a greater tolerance of diversity. Will the fact that legal reforms are being achieved mean that there will not be the same need for queer politics in these countries?

OutRage activists are not interested in seeking acceptance within an unchanged social system, but are setting out to 'fuck up the mainstream' as visibly as possible. It can also be argued that the extremism of OutRage actually facilitates the gains of Stonewall, who are seen as 'rational' and 'civilised' in comparison.

> In reality today, the main conflict is not simply between older 'gay' assimilationists. . . and 'queers' asserting their 'queerness.' Rather it is between those who think of the politics of sexuality as a matter of securing minority rights and those who are contesting the overall validity and authenticity of the epistemology of sexuality itself. Simon Watney

What's in a Name?

Each time the word 'queer' is used it defines a strategy, an attitude, a reference to other identities and a new self-understanding. (And queer can be qualified as 'more queer,' 'queerer' or 'queerest' as the naming develops into a more complex process of identification.) For many, the term marks a growing lack of faith in the institutions of the state, in political procedures, in the press, the education system, policing and the law. Both in culture and politics, queer articulates a radical questioning of social and cultural norms, notions of gender, reproductive sexuality and the family. We are beginning to realise how much of our history and ideologies operate on a homo-hetero opposition, constantly privileging the hetero perspective as normative, positing the homo perspective as bad and annihilating the spectrum of sexualities that exists.

> I love queer. Queer is a homosexual of either sex. It's more convenient than saying 'gays' which has to be qualified, or 'lesbians and gay men.' It's an extremely useful polemic term because it is who we say we are, which is, 'Fuck You.' *Spike Pittsberg*
>
> I use queer to describe my particular brand of lesbian feminism, which has not much to do with the radical feminism I was involved with in the early 80s.
>
> I also use it externally to describe a political inclusivity—a new move towards a celebration of difference across sexualities, across genders, across sexual preference and across object choice. The two link. *Linda Semple*
>
> I define myself as gay mostly. I will not use queer because it is not part of my vernacular—but I have nothing against its use. The same debates around naming occur in the 'black community.' Naming is powerful. Black people and gay people

constantly renaming ourselves is a way to shift power from whites and hets respectively. *Inge Blackman*

What's in queer, for X, Y, Z, is mostly what people decide to make it. I like dyke and TS. *Roz Kaveney*

I don't use that term. I associate it with gay men and I'm dubious about reclaiming derogatory terms. The 'queer agenda,' as you call it, isn't my struggle. I put my feminism before my lesbianism. *Harriet Wistrich*

I've got a badge that says QUEER BISEXUAL. *Alison Thomas*

I say 'I'm KHUSH,' and that's from talking to Indian gay men and lesbians and finding that we want to find another word for ourselves that comes from our own culture. But I have used queer in the context of other queers. *Pratibha Parmar*

I'm more inclined to use the words 'black lesbian,' because when I hear the word queer I think of white, gay men. *Isling Mack-Nataf*

Queer gives me politics for things I've always been interested in—like how I feel as a woman who's mistaken for a man, who's intrigued by men and gay male sexuality and as a lesbian and a feminist, connecting to my affinities with men's struggles around sexuality. *Tori Smith*

I do have problems with it, but I use queer in the sense that I'M FUCKED OFF, like 'faggots with attitude.' My anger has come from the work I've done around policing. I had no idea how outrageous it was. *Paul Burston*

I describe myself as a queer dyke. I never identified with the word lesbian because it seemed quite medical, it was the word I used to come out to my mother and it seemed to have negative connotations. Queer was one of the ways of identifying with a mixed movement and challenging both separatism and misogyny at the same time. *Tessa Boffin*

While there is resistance to the word queer, it is useful to remember that there were also battles over 'gay,' which was not a term without contradictions. In the early 70s, gay too was characterised as radical and oppositional. By the 80s, lesbians felt the term had rendered them invisible and the addition of 'lesbians and' became a necessary part of naming. For some people who have come out since the beginning of the AIDS epidemic, there is a tendency to associate 'gay' with AIDS and to fail to identify with its happy subtext. However, criticism of the term is hardly new.

> I never liked the word 'gay' (although I never said so), because it exuded a false optimism. It wasn't my word. I was in the party of miserabilists. *Derek Jarman*

While some older gay liberationists claim that gay is the only way to be, their earnest defence of the term fails to acknowledge either the evolution of self-naming, or the experiences of a younger generation. One of the most vehement members of the anti-queer lobby is Chris White, whose 'Inrage' mounts a one-man picket, complete with a placard claiming 'Homosexuals Are Not Queer,' outside the London Lesbian and Gay Centre to discourage people from attending OutRage meetings.

> I shall continue to fight for as long as OutRage and their ilk believe it is part of
> their role to oppress us, split us and do our enemies' work for us. *Chris White,*
> *'Capital Gay', 24 January 1991*

The debate has certainly produced lively political exchanges in the letters' pages
of the gay press. Yet although for some of the older generation, the term
'queer' painfully the recalls the homophobic abuse of a former era, for others it
is merely a return to a word they used in a positive, self-parodying sense many
years ago.

> Back in the 60s when I was trying to figure out whether I was 'gay' or transsexual or
> what, the people I got to know in the TS/drag queen network in the north would
> use 'queer' in a 'what of it?' way. They'd sometimes use it in a self-deprecating
> manner and the two uses would shade into each other. 'Gay' was useful, but it
> changed nothing. The average homophobe uses it as derogatively as 'poofter' or
> 'homo.' It's just another word, it doesn't have intrinsic power for good. *Roz Kaveney*

Lesbians Fight Back

Queer politics is renowned for its sex-positive reclamation of words that have
been used negatively against women and lesbians and gays, as well as for its outlandish acronyms. The OutRage affinity group, PUSSY (Perverts Undermining
State Scrutiny) is a mixed gay and lesbian group set up to fight censorship, sexism and 'promote queer sex.' PUSSY's aim is to work actively to gain acknowledgement of lesbian sexual practices, both within and beyond the lesbian and
gay community, rather than simply to campaign against prohibitive measures.

However, many of PUSSY's campaigns to date have been reactions to
censorship from within the community—as in its organisation of protests when
London gay and feminist bookshops Gay's the Word, Silver Moon and Sister-
write refused to carry Della Grace's book *Love Bites* (although West & Wilde,
the gay and lesbian bookshop in Edinburgh, and major bookshop chains
stocked the title). PUSSY also worked to support the distribution of *Quim*
(Britain's first lesbian sex mag), which encountered similar restrictions.

Other campaigns include defending the Terrence Higgins Trust's safer
sex material and drawing attention to the Jenny White case. In 1991, White, a
fifty-seven-year-old member of the London Older Lesbian Network, had ordered several porn tapes made by lesbians (Blush Productions and Fatale
Videos) and sold through a lesbian sex shop in San Francisco. The tapes were
seized by Customs and Excise and declared obscene, under the nineteenth-
century law that prohibits the importation of 'obscene material.' With the support of FAC (Feminists Against Censorship) and PUSSY, White took the case
to court, on point of principle, knowing that she would lose, but keen to highlight the inequality in the law. In court she explained that the videos were for
private use and the depictions of safer sex and sexuality were less violent and
'obscene' than much of what is available through heterosexual outlets. The

judge proceeded to view the most 'depraved, lewd and filthy' extracts and in a bizarre venture in voyeurism, lesbians in the gallery watched men watching lesbians. White's defence argued that it was absurd that these materials could be imported through the EC, but not from the US. It also seemed strange that this material was being banned, since many women had viewed at least two of the videos in screenings at the Rio cinema and National Film Theatre. Although the tapes were ordered to be destroyed, White did not have to pay costs and felt that this was a minor victory and could be claimed as a queer intervention into the anomalies of the law.

> *Your sexuality is yours. It's not the state's, the Customs Officer's, or your husband's. It's yours and its exploration with another person is the only way to claim your birthright.* *Jenny White*

In November of the same year a legal precedent was established concerning lesbian sexual practices which could be seen as a measure of the virulent hostility the threat of queer sex invokes. Jennifer Saunders, an eighteen-year-old, was sentenced to six years' imprisonment for dressing as a man and seducing two seventeen-year-old women. The age of consent laws could not be used against her—again revealing the anomaly whereby lesbians remain invisible—and so she was charged with indecent assault. In court, the two women said they would not have consented to sex if they had been aware of Saunders' true gender; in her defence, Saunders insisted that she had dressed as a boy at the women's request, to conceal the fact that they were having a lesbian relationship. Passing sentence in Doncaster, Judge Crabtree summed up:

> I suppose that both girls would rather have been raped by some young man . . . I assume you must have some sort of bisexual feelings and I suspect that you have contested the case in the hope of getting some ghastly fame from it. I feel you may be a menace to young girls.

Saunders allegedly had sex with one of the women several times a week, using a strap-on dildo, in the course of a five-month affair. A new OutRage affinity group, LABIA (Lesbians Answer Back in Anger) took up the case and picketed the office of the Lord Chancellor to demand the dismissal of Judge Crabtree from the bench. In a letter to LABIA from prison, Saunders reiterated that the affairs were entirely consensual:

> She told her family I was a man to make herself clear, if you know what I mean. . . I couldn't believe it when I was arrested. I went along with all the stupid things she was saying as I loved her more than anything in the world. I couldn't hurt her. So I promised to say nothing.

Without LABIA, the press would have ignored the fact that the case had anything to do with lesbians. And indeed there was a distinct failure of other lesbian feminist groups to rally to Saunders' defence—was this due to moral disapproval of the dildo or of the ultra-butch (ie perceived as het male) persona Saunders chose? In the same month as the case came to trial, there was a huge International Women's Day to End Violence Against Women march which focused on legal injustices to women. It highlighted the cases of Sara Thornton, Kiranjit Ahwalia and Amelia Rossiter, all of whom were given life sentences for killing their husbands. There was no mention of the Saunders' case in the publicity.

On the press front, the *Sun* not unexpectedly ran a headline: '6 Years for blonde who posed as boy to bed girls' (21 September 1991), while the *Guardian* ran a coy little piece on cross-dressing entitled 'Girls will be boys,' in which Julie Wheelwright, author of *Amazons and Military Maids: Women Who Dressed as Men in Pursuit of Life, Liberty and Happiness*, opined that cross-dressing was a 'forgotten historical phenomenon,' and concluded:

> *In the end, cross-dressing proves to be an unsatisfying alternative since it forces women to caricature male virility and fear their feminine self.* 'Guardian', 24 September 1991

With moralising reactionary analysis like that, all butch women should forget it. The article omitted the 'L word' and made no attempt to discuss why teenagers had been forced to use such subterfuge in England in the late twentieth century: **homophobia**. Saunders' six-year sentence was longer than most rape sentences and it was clear that she was being punished for being a woman who dared to step out of line. At the time of writing Saunders is in Styal prison, awaiting appeal.

Whose Agenda Is It?

> *By building an identity exclusively around one sexuality and developing a political agenda that either excludes or subordinates other forms of oppression, the lesbian and gay movement has narrowly defined its subject.*
>
>   Charles Fernandez, "Outlook," Spring 1991

Queer is welcomed as breaking up lesbian and gay orthodoxies and making possible new alliances across gender and other disparate identities; it is claimed by some as neutral in terms of race and gender. But is the umbrella as all-embracing as queer claims? Are we in danger of denying our heterogeneity in favour of a false 'queer nationalism'?

> I think that too much emphasis on 'queer nation' is itself a new kind of separatism and can lead in the direction of an equally narrow politics in which queers become the new 'most of all oppressed' group. I'm opposed to separatism of any kind, whether it's lesbian, black, Muslim or anything else. *Elizabeth Wilson*

One of the challenges that each new generation of lesbians and gay men faces is how to build on the gains and experience of previous movements. Queer rhetoric often gives the impression that direct action politics was invented in 1987, that the Black and Women's Liberation Movements haven't happened, that the campaigns for or against nuclear weapons, abortion, reproductive rights and violence against women have not occurred and have had no influence on the way queer activism manifests itself. But despite the inevitable frustration experienced by more seasoned campaigners, there is also a celebration of the fact that a new generation of gay and lesbian activists is resurrecting old debates in new contexts and formulating new debates in old contexts they believe to be new.

> It's infuriating to re-invent the wheel, to see people make the same mistakes we made fifteen years ago. We don't have a proper way of passing on skills. Lisa Power

Working with Men

Queer has enabled many of the discussions that were happening in single-sex spaces to be continued in mixed public contexts for the first time in many years. (This had, of course, been happening in private all along, as dykes and faggots swopped cruising disasters with cottaging tales and was a feature of groups of the 70s which sound remarkably familiar—for example, DAFT: Dykes And Faggots Together.) But many lesbians who worked with men in the years before the AIDS crisis were branded as 'bad' lesbians by their peers.

> I had worked with gay men on 'Ecstatic Antibodies' and there was a lot of unease about it. People didn't say anything to my face, but I heard of comments that I was getting where I was because I was arse-licking men. *Tessa Boffin*

Of course, ridding men of misogyny and creating a mutual confidence whereby lesbians no longer need to separate from men to define their own agendas is a difficult process. Are gay men in mixed queer settings willing to listen and be challenged?

> Gay men can learn from dykes what it's like to be a woman, the reality, not the fantasy. They can listen and learn that being a man means they are automatically given many privileges which are not open to women. They should learn how lesbophobic they are. It's not just as simple as being misogynistic, which a lot of them are, but their active fear, dislike and loathing of LESBIANS. *Inge Blackman*

> There's a brand of boy around at the moment who reckon that just because you're a pro-sex dyke, maybe don a bit of leather. . . you have forgotten your feminism and they can get away with sexist put downs, anti-women jokes and all the rest. It's as if they think there are two kinds of dykes the 'old kind' who got on their nerves with their 'excuse me that's the third time you've interrupted me' and some new kind which they reckon is me. I've been. . . with gay men who assumed, until set straight, that they could get snide about the 'feminist kind of lesbian' and I'd laugh along. *'Quim', Winter 1991*

Other women members of OutRage have complained about the 'faggot cringe' response, whereby gay men seem to assume that anything a dyke says should be accepted without criticism. Overall, however, it seems that many of the white gay men drawn to OutRage because of the increased levels of queer-bashing have only recently become aware of the street violence and harassment that women and black men and women have always suffered. A 'Condom Patrol' organised to give out safer sex materials on Hampstead Heath pointed up some of the differences in perspective. When lesbians bemoaned the lack of cottaging for lesbians, men suggested they went to the Heath too.

> I said to them, 'What about safety?' and they said, 'oh yeah.' It was pretty remarkable to be in a park after midnight and not feel scared for the first time in my life. *Tori Smith*

For many gay men who felt constructed as the enemy or simply irrelevant to previous feminist discourses, working with dykes on queer issues has been a valuable process. Lesbians who've been involved with feminism are more familiar with making links between theories of representation and practice, and are offering a broad experience of political organising to queer campaigns.

> I've gained a broader overview of political structures and the ways that our sexuality is oppressed. I can recognise now that it isn't simply to do with gay male issues, like getting arrested for wanking in a public toilet. *Paul Burston*

> One of the things that could emerge from queer is gay men seeing their own practices, styles and culture taken over by dykes and then reflected back with inflections and criticisms. The danger being that reciprocity won't operate in quite this way, and at worst, gay men will glory in the fact that at last 'lesbians have seen the light, owned up to their mistakes and come back to what are considered correct queer political and cultural practices.' *Philip Derbyshire*

Despite the initial idea of queer politics as a movement in which men and women would work together and learn from each other, groups such as DAM (Dyke Action Machine) in New York and the LABIA groups in San Francisco and London have been set up to focus on women's issues. Isn't setting up a lesbian caucus within OutRage admitting that the agenda is controlled by men's concerns? There seemed a danger in 1991 that campaigns about sex (Clause 25) were perceived as men's and campaigns about parenting (Paragraph 16) as women's. And on a practical level, the group's failure to organise a crèche attracted widespread, justified criticism. But is it also the case that lesbians have yet to initiate a queer agenda that is proactive rather than a reaction to feelings of exclusion?

> It's how to be involved in a movement that makes you invisible and ignores you. We want to be in the queer movement, but it's still on the level of having to ask men to include us. *Della Grace*

> Oppression infantalises people. There's been a tradition in the past few years of women telling other women not to do things, like work with men, but people are not starting activist groups based on women's issues. They're only starting them in response to men not fulfilling their needs and that's because people haven't figured

out what a lesbian agenda is. Last year I called a meeting for lesbians to start a direct action group and I got 150 women. Half of them were ready to go to work and the other half had come to stop the first half from doing it. It was that fear of action (as opposed to being reactive) and the destructive critical tradition. *Sarah Schulman*

I get annoyed when OutRage says 'this is a lesbian action' because queer actions should cross both sexes. The lesbian action was the most boring one they had. *Tessa Boffin*

But whatever its short-term (or longer-term) failures, queer does signal that discussions between lesbians and gay men—until recently marked by their absence, hostility or accusatory approach—are now beginning to be framed by mutual curiosity and responsibility. There is still a lot we don't know or understand about our distinct sexual, political and cultural histories. Queer presents the possibility and challenge to find out.

Questions for Reflection, Discussion, and Writing

1. After having read Smyth's essay, how would you define "queer"? Why?
2. Look at the epigraphs with which Smyth opens her essay. What are the various definitions of "queer" she offers? Are there any connections between these various epigraphs? What do those definitions suggest about the various appropriations of queer and the context in which it might be used?
3. Smyth documents the trial and sentencing of Jennifer Saunders. According to Smyth, what was Saunders' sentence based on? Which groups mobilized in support of Saunders? On what grounds? What tactics did they use to expose the issues on which Smyth claims Saunders' sentencing was based? How did other activist groups react, according to Smyth? What legal, social, and cultural issues does the Saunders trial raise?
4. What are some of the objections to the term queer, according to Smyth? Who voices them? Why?
5. What are some reasons, according to Smyth, that some people might be more likely than others to use the term "queer"?
6. What are some of the tensions that arise, according to quotes Smyth includes, when women and men work together in queer alliances?

Related Reading

Allan Bérubé and Jeffery Escoffier, "Queer/Nation," *Outlook* 11 (Winter 1991). 14–23.

Maria Maggenti, "Women as Queer Nationals." *Out/Look* 3.3 (Winter 1991): 20–23.

Michael Cunningham, "If You're Queer and You're Not Angry in 1992, You're Not Paying Attention." *Mother Jones* 17 (May/June 1991): 60–68.

Anna Marie Smith, "Resisting the Erasure of Lesbian Sexuality" in *Modern Homosexualities: Fragments of Lesbian and Gay Experience*. Ken Plummer, Ed. London: Routledge. 1992. 200–213.

Vicki Carter, "Abseil Makes the Heart Grow Fonder: Lesbian and Gay Campaigning Tactics and Section 28" in *Modern Homosexualities: Fragments of Lesbian and Gay Experience*. Ken Plummer, Ed. London: Routledge. 1992. 217–226.

Peter Tatchell, "Equal Rights For All: Strategies for Lesbian and Gay Equality in Britain" in *Modern Homosexualities: Fragments of Lesbian and Gay Experience*. Ken Plummer, Ed. London: Routledge. 1992. 237–247.

Lauren Berlant and Elizabeth Freeman, "Queer Nationality" in *Fear of a Queer Planet*. Michael Warner, Ed. Minneapolis, MN: U of Minnesota P. 1993. 193–229.

Phillip Brian Harper, E. Frances White and Margaret Cerullo. "Multi/Queer/Culture." *Radical America 24*.4 (1993): 27–37.

Mary McIntosh, "Queer Theory and the War of the Sexes" in *Activating Theory: Lesbian, Gay, Bisexual Politics*. Joseph Bristow and Angelia R. Wilson, Eds. London: Lawrence & Wishart. 1993. 30–52.

Simon Watney, "Queer Epistemology: Activism, 'Outing', and the Politics of Sexual Identities." *Critical Quarterly 36*.1 (Spring 1994): 13–27.

Philip Derbyshire, "A Measure of Queer." *Critical Quarterly 36*.1 (Spring 1994): 39–45.

Anthony Slagle, "In Defense of Queer Nation: From Identity Politics to a Politics of Difference." *Western Journal of Communication* 59.2 (Spring 1995): 85–102.

Michael R. Fraser, "Identity and Representation As Challenges to Social Movement Theory: A Case Study of Queer Nation" in *Mainstream(s) and Margins: Cultural Politics in the 90s*. Michael Morgan and Susan Leggett, Eds. Westport, CN: Greenwood Press. 1996. 32–44.

Brian Walker, "On the Very Idea of a Queer Nation" in *Rethinking Nationalism*. Jocelyne Couture, Kai Nelson and Michel Seymour, Eds. *Canadian Journal of Philosophy 22* (1996): 505–547.

Carrie Mayer and Dyke Action Machine, "Do You Love the Dyke in Your Face?" in *Queers in Space: Communities/Public Places/Sites of Resistance*. Gordon Brent Ingram, Anne-Marie Bouthillette and Yolanda Retter, Eds. Seattle: Bay Press. 1997. 436–446.

Angelina R. Wilson, "Somewhere Over the Rainbow: Queer Translating," in *Playing With Fire: Queer Politics, Queer Theories*. Ed., Shane Phelan. NY: Routledge. 1997. 99–111.

Ian Lucas, *Outrage! An Oral History*. London: Cassel. 1998.

Carl F. Stychin, *A Nation by Rights: National Cultures, Sexual Identity Politics, and the Discourse of Rights*. Philadelphia: Temple UP. 1998.

Pauline L. Rankin, "Sexualities and National Identities: Re-Imagining Queer Nationalism." *Journal of Canadian Studies* 35.2 (2000): 176–196.

Linda Garber, *Identity Politics: Race, Class, and the Lesbian-Feminist Roots of Queer Theory*. NY: Columbia UP. 2001.

Film

Passion of Remembrance (1986). Maureen Blackwood and Isaac Julien. 80 m.

Alfalfa (1987). Richard Kwietniowski. 9 m.

Generation Q (1995). Robert Byrd. 60 m.

Web Resource

http://www.cs.cmu.edu/Web/People/mjw/Queer/Mainpage:html

Special Topics

Using any of the quotes in Smyth's essay under the section "Working With Men" as a jumping off point, and after reading one or more of the essays below, begin meditating on points of commonality and points of difference between and among gay men and lesbians. How does the inclusion of bisexuality and/or transgenderism complicate this discussion in terms of gender, behavior, and politics?

Reading

Julia Creet, "Lesbian Sex/Gay Sex: What's the Difference?" *Out/Look* 3.3 (Winter 1991): 29–34.

Karla Jay, "Ties That Bind: Friendship Between Lesbians and Gay Men." *The Harvard Gay & Lesbian Review* 4.1 (Winter 1997): 9–12.

Jill C. Humphrey, "Cracks in the Feminist Mirror? Research and Reflections on Lesbians and Gay Men Working Together." *Feminist Review 66* (2000): 95–130.

Writing

Compose a brief narrative in which you relate something you learned in an interaction with someone of a different gender, however you might want to construe and construct that term.

Making It Perfectly Queer

Lisa Duggan

During the past few years, the new designation "queer" has emerged from within lesbian, gay, and bisexual politics and theory. "Queer Nation" and "Queer Theory," now widely familiar locations for activists and academics, are more than just new labels for old boxes. They carry with them the promise of new meanings, new ways of thinking and acting politically—a promise sometimes realized, sometimes not. In this essay I want to elucidate and advocate this new potential within politics and theory.

Because I am a Southern girl, I want to arrive at my discussion of these new meanings through a process of storytelling. From an account of concrete events—recent events that gripped and provoked me personally—I will construct a certain political history, and from that history raise certain theoretical questions. Because the position "queer" has arisen most proximately from developments in lesbian and gay politics, the trajectory I follow here reflects my own passage through those politics. Were I to follow another trajectory—through feminist or socialist politics, for example—I would arrive at a similar position, with many of the same questions and suggestions. But the stories would be different, and the "work" of those stories would be differently constructed. Here, I want to take up the position of "queer" largely in order to criticize (but not completely displace) the liberal and nationalist strategies in gay politics and to advocate the constructionist turn in lesbian and gay theories and practices.

Scene #1: New York City, March 1991. The St. Patrick's Day Parade.

The Irish Lesbian and Gay Organization (ILGO) has been denied permission to march. After much public protest of this exclusion, a deal has been struck with the march organizers. ILGO members will be permitted to march as the guests of a contingent of the Ancient Order of Hibernians, but they have had to agree not to carry any identifying banners or signs. Mayor David Dinkins, who helped to broker the deal, has decided to walk with the lesbian and gay group. On the day of the parade, this group, marked out for the curious by the presence of Dinkins, becomes the target of repeated outbursts of intense hostility on the part of spectators, parade organizers, and officials of the Catholic Church.

These events received extensive nationwide news coverage, which focused largely on the spectacle of the Mayor under attack. Dinkins himself used this spectacle to frame an analogy between the treatment of the lesbian and gay marchers in the St. Patrick's Day parade and the hostile treatment of civil rights marchers in the South decades earlier. In an op-ed published in *The New York Times* several days after the parade, he extended and elaborated on this analogy:

> On Saturday, despite our taking great care to see that the parade rules were observed, a fearful rage erupted—a rage of intolerance. The anger hurled at the gay and lesbian Irish Americans and me was so fierce that one man threw a filled beer can at us. Perhaps the anger from those watching the parade stemmed from a fear of a lifestyle unlike their own; perhaps it was the violent call of people frightened by a future that seems unlike the past.
>
> It is strange that what is now my most vivid experience of mob hatred came not in the South but in New York—and was directed against me, not because I was defending the rights of African Americans but of gay and lesbian Americans.
>
> Yet, the hostility I saw was not unfamiliar. It was the same anger that led a bus driver to tell me back in 1915, when I was en route to North Carolina in Marine uniform, that there was no place for me: "Two more white seats," he said. It was the same anger that I am sure Montgomery marchers and Birmingham demonstrators experienced when they fought for racial tolerance. It is the fury of people who want the right to deny another's identity.

We cannot flinch from our responsibility to widen the circle of tolerance. For the true evil of discrimination is not in the choice of groups to hate but in the fact that a group is chosen at all. Not only does our Bill of Rights protect us all equally, but every religious tradition I know affirms that, in the words of Dr. Martin Luther King, Jr., "Every man is somebody because he is a child of God."[1]

I quote the Dinkins op-ed extensively here even though it is in most respects formulaic and unsurprising, an invocation of the themes and images of a familiar brand of liberal politics, with its limited call for "tolerance" and an end to "discrimination." I quote it because even my most radical and cynical lesbian and gay friends found it deeply moving, because it was in one important respect quite rare. Dinkins' analogy to the civil rights movement, an analogy liberal gay organizations have outlined and pursued for decades, is still seldom heard outside lesbian and gay circles. In the hands of David Dinkins, a political figure with national visibility and a well-known record of civil rights activism, this analogy mobilizes images of noble suffering in the face of naked hatred. It invokes the culturally resonant figure of Martin Luther King, Jr. on behalf of lesbians and gay men, thereby endowing our struggle for equality with a precious and, for us, elusive political resource—moral authority.

Appeals to Liberalism

For nearly fifty years now, lesbian and gay organizations have worked to forge a politically active and effective lesbian and gay "minority" group, and to claim the liberal "rights" of privacy and formal equality on its behalf. As a rhetorical strategy, this positioning has aimed to align lesbian and gay populations with racial, ethnic, and religious minority groups and women in a quest for full economic, political, and cultural participation in U.S. life. This rhetorical move, when successful, opens up avenues of political and legal recourse forged by the civil rights and feminist movements to lesbian and gay action: support for group-specific anti-discrimination statutes, participation in political coalitions to design, pass, and enforce broad civil rights provisions; application to the courts for equal protection under various constitutional provisions; organization to elect and pressure public officials; lobbying of media organizations for fair and equitable representation, etc.

But this rhetorical overture to the logic of liberal tolerance has generally met with very limited success. The inclusion of lesbians and gay men in the pantheon of unjustly persecuted groups is everywhere unstable and contested. Political coalitions risk their legitimacy when they include lesbian and gay groups or issues. Group-specific municipal anti-discrimination ordinances are constantly subject to repeal attempts. Cultural groups from the National Endowment for the Arts to the Modern Language Association are attacked or ridiculed for the presence of lesbian and gay topics on their agendas. And the legal climate for lesbian and gay organizations has been poisoned for the rest of this century (at least) by the nasty, brutish, and short 1986 decision of the U.S. Supreme Court in *Bowers* vs. *Hardwick* (upholding the state of Georgia's statute criminalizing consensual sodomy).

The spectacle of the suffering Mayor walking with downcast gays and lesbians in the St. Patrick's Day parade brings both these failures and the important achievements of liberal gay politics into vivid relief. The hostility of the spectators, the parade organizers, and the Roman Catholic Cardinal underscored the precarious position of the ILGO, and by extension of gay communities more generally. Inclusion could be negotiated only on humiliating terms, and even then public civility could not be enforced.

But as the subsequent press coverage and the Dinkins op-ed show, the parade was also a moment of highly visible achievement for the rhetoric of liberal gay politics. The circulation of images from the parade evoked a response supportive of Dinkins and the ILGO from non-gay politicians and pundits, a response which frequently framed the issues in language that liberal gay organizations have proposed, appropriating the American Dream for the "minority" that seems to reside permanently at the bottom of the list.

At this historical moment, marked by the precarious and contested achievements illustrated by the example of the St. Patrick's Day parade, the liberal strategy has also come under increasing attack from within lesbian and gay communities. Of course, this strategy has never occupied the field of gay politics unopposed. Challenges to it have appeared from the overlapping yet distinguishable positions of militant nationalism and radical constructionism. In the 1990s, both of these positions appear to be gaining ground.

The Call to Militant Nationalism

Scene #2: New York City, Spring 1991.

Posters of celebrities labeled "Absolutely Queer" appear on Manhattan walls. One, featuring an image of actress Jodie Foster, is captioned "Actress, Yalie, Dyke." These posters have not been produced by homophobic conservatives, but by gay militants engaged in the practice of "outing."

"Outing" is a political tactic inaugurated by New York City's now defunct gay weekly newspaper *Outweek* (though the term for it was coined by *Time*), and associated most closely with the paper's "lifestyle" columnist, Michelangelo Signorile. As a practice, it is an extension of the early gay liberationist appeal to lesbians and gay men to "come out of the closet," reveal their hidden lives, and reject the fear and stigma attached to their identities. In "outing," this appeal is transformed from an invitation into a command. Journalists and activists expose "closeted" lesbians or gay men in public life, especially those deemed hypocritical in their approach to gay issues. Their goal is to end the secrecy and hypocrisy surrounding homosexuality, to challenge the notion that gay life is somehow shameful, and to show the world that many widely admired and respected men and women are gay.

Both "outing" and *Outweek* sprang from the efflorescence of militance surrounding the rhetoric and politics of ACT UP and its spinoff, Queer Nation. Many of these new gay militants reject the liberal value of privacy and the appeal to tolerance which dominate the agendas of more mainstream gay organizations. Instead, they emphasize publicity and self-assertion; confrontation and direct action top their list of tactical options; the rhetoric of difference replaces the more assimilationist liberal emphasis on similarity to other groups.

But the challenge that the new politics poses to the liberal strategy is not only the challenge of militance—the familiar counterposing of anger to civility, of flamboyance to respectability, often symbolized through "style"—but also the challenge of nationalism.*

Nationalisms have a long history in gay and lesbian politics and culture. From turn-of-the-century German homosexual emancipationist Magnus Hirschfeld to contemporary radical feminist philosopher Mary Daly, the "nation" and its interests have been defined in varying ways. With no geographical base or kinship ties to provide boundaries, gay and lesbian nationalists have offered biological characteristics (as in the "Third Sex"), or shared experience (whether of sexual desire or gender solidarity) as common ground. Of these various nationalisms, two broadly distinguishable competing forms have appeared and reappeared since the mid 19th century: 1) the ethnic model of a fixed minority of both sexes defined by biology and/or the experience of desire (most often estimated at 10 percent)[2] and 2) the single-sex union of gender loyalists, the no-fixed-percentage model associated with lesbian separatism (theoretically, all women could belong to the Lesbian Nation).[3]

The ethnic model also underpins the liberal strategy, of course. The argument for "rights" is made on behalf of a relatively fixed minority constituency. It becomes the basis for a more militant nationalism when the "ethnic" group is represented as monolithic, its interests primary and utterly clear to a political vanguard. The example of "outing" serves as an illustration of this brand of gay politics. Outers generally not only believe in the existence of a gay nation, but are confident of their ability to identify its members and of their authority to do so. They have no doubts about definitions or boundaries, and do not hesitate to override the welfare and autonomy of individuals "in the national interest."[4]

Outers present their version of gay nationalism as radical, but like other nationalisms its political implications are complex, and often actually reactionary. These new nationalists define the nation and its interests as unitary; they suppress internal difference and political conflict. Self-appointed ayatollahs explain it all.

This reactionary potential was especially apparent in the pages of *Outweek* in 1990, when Malcolm Forbes, then recently deceased, was "outed" and pre-

---

*The ideas in this discussion of gay nationalism were generated in conversations with Jenny Terry, Jackie Urla, and Jeff Escoffier. It was Urla who first suggested to me that certain strains in gay politics could be considered nationalist discourses.

sented as a role model for gay youth. The same magazine had earlier reviled Tim Sweeney, a longtime gay activist and executive director of Gay Men's Health Crisis in New York City, for compromising the gay national interests by negotiating with African-American groups over the conditions for appointment of a New York City health commissioner.[5] *Outweek's* "nation," it appears, is white, values wealth and celebrity for their own sake, and pursues self-interest in the narrowest possible terms.

This particularly virulent strain of gay nationalism has been criticized with increasing vehemence by those excluded, misrepresented, or terrorized by it. C. Carr, writing in *The Village Voice* under the banner headline, "Why Outing Must Stop," called it "the most absurd excuse for political thinking I have ever encountered," and commented:

> Anyone who thinks . . . that a lesbian can proclaim her sexuality in an industry as male-centered as Hollywood, where even straight women have trouble getting work . . . has to be out of his fucking mind.

Voicing the sentiments of many, Carr also noted that "I'm still waiting for the news of Malcolm Forbes' homosexuality to improve my life."[6]

Carr's critique of "outing" takes up the liberal defense of "privacy"—emphasizing the continuing strategic value of a "right to privacy" for lesbians and gay men threatened with everyday persecution. But her column also echoes the criticisms of gay political discourses that women and people of color (especially, though not exclusively) have forged and developed over the past two decades.

Whose Identity?

Both the liberal assimilationist and the militant nationalist strands of gay politics posit gay identity as a unitary, unproblematic given—the political project revolves around its public articulation. But for people with multiple "marked" identities, the political project begins at the level of the very problematic construction of identities and their relation to different communities and different political projects. In Audre Lorde's much quoted words: "It was a while before we came to realize that our place was the very house of difference rather than the security of any one particular difference.[7]

Thus Carr hypothesizes that, for Jodie Foster, being a woman defines her relationship to Hollywood in a way that shifts the meaning of being "gay," and the consequences of "coming out." From this perspective, advocacy of "outing" is colonizing. Foster's situation is appropriated by a single-issue politics that cannot honor the complexity of her differences.

The charge I want to make here against both the liberal and nationalist strategies, but especially against the latter, is this: *Any* gay politics based on the primacy of sexual identity defined as unitary and "essential," residing clearly, intelligibly and unalterably in the body or psyche, and fixing desire in a gendered direction, ultimately represents the view from the subject position "20th-century Western white gay male."

Scene #3: San Francisco, February 1991. The 2nd Annual Lesbian and Gay Writers' Conference.

The designation of this conference as simply "lesbian and gay" is contested everywhere I look. An organized bisexual lobby is highly visible and voluble. The designation "Queer" is ubiquitous, sometimes used in the "in-your-face" manner of the many "Faggot" and "Dyke" buttons that I see, but also used to designate a more broadly inclusive "community."

Louise Sloan, reporting on this conference in the *San Francisco Bay Guardian*, wrote that it constructed a "community"

> of men, women, transsexuals, gay males, lesbians, bisexuals, straight men and women, African Americans, Chicanos, Asian Americans, Native Americans, people who can see and/or walk and people who cannot, welfare recipients, trust fund recipients, wage earners, Democrats, Republicans, and anarchists—to name a few. . . . Indeed, since difference from the "norm" is about all that many people in the "gay community" have in common with each other, these sorts of "gay and lesbian" gatherings, at their best and worst and most radical, seem to be spaces where cross-sections of the human multiverse can gather to thrash out differences and perhaps to lay the groundwork for peaceful and productive futures. . . . In my most naively hopeful moments, I often imagine it will be the "queer community"—the oxymoronic community of difference—that might be able to teach the world how to get along.[8]

Sloan's description of the "oxymoronic community of difference" at the writers' conference challenges the oversimplified notion that the essentialist versus social constructionist debate, now saturating the gay press, is a controversy of activist politics versus academic theory.

In its most clichéd formulations, this controversy is presented in one of two ways: Valiant and dedicated activists working to get civil rights for gay and lesbian people are being undermined by a bunch of obscure, arcane, jargon-ridden academics bent on "deconstructing" the gay community before it even comes into full visibility, or: Theoretically informed writers at the cutting edge of the political horizon are being bashed by anti-intellectual activists who cling naively to the discursive categories of their oppressors.[9] Both these formulations fail to acknowledge the vigor and longevity of the constructionist strand in lesbian and gay politics, a strand which theorists have taken up, not produced.

From the first appearance of the homosexual/heterosexual polarity just over 100 years ago, "essentialist" theories, both homophile and homophobic, have had to account for the observed malleability of sexual desire. Each theoretical assertion of the fixity of desire has had attached to it a residual category—a catch-all explanation for those formations of pleasure that defy the proffered etiologies. In Havelock Ellis' scheme, flexible "acquired" sexual inversion accompanied the more permanent "congenital" type. In the lexicon of contemporary sociology, "situational" homosexuality occurs among "heterosexual" persons under special circumstances—in prisons or other single-sex institutions, for example. ("Situational" heterosexuality is seldom discussed.)[10] In each theoretical paradigm, the "essential" nature and truth of the homo/hetero dyad is shored up with a rhetoric of authenticity. The "real" is distinguished from the "copy," the "true inverts" from those merely susceptible to seduction.

Such constructionist branches on the tree of essentialism grew up on their own during the heady days of early gay liberation. Drawing on the more constructionist versions of psychoanalytic theories of sexuality, visionaries painted a utopia in which everyone was potentially polymorphously sexual with everyone else.[11] During the 1970s, lesbian feminists outlined a somewhat more ambivalent position, with a sharper political edge. They aggressively denaturalized heterosexuality and presented it as a central apparatus in the perpetuation of patriarchy. But these same women often presented lesbianism as the naturalized alternative. When Alix Dobkin sang that "Any Woman Can Be a Lesbian," the implication was that any woman not suffering from false consciousness *would be.*[12]

The current revival of constructionist rhetoric in activist discourses is, like its constructionist predecessors, also partial and ambivalent—but in a very different sense. The new political currency of the term "bisexual," for instance, which has been added to the titles of lesbian/gay organizations from coast to coast in the United States, has had contradictory effects. Activists have used the term "bisexual" to disrupt the natural status of the dualism heterosexual/homosexual. But they have then paradoxically reinstated sexual polarity through the addition of a third naturalized term, as rigidly gendered as the original two, only doubled. The tendency of bisexual writers and organizations to appropriate wholesale the rhetoric of the lesbian and gay rights movement reinforces the latter effect.[13]

Defining A Queer Community

The notion of a "queer community" can work somewhat differently. It is often used to construct a collectivity no longer defined solely by the gender of its members' sexual partners. This new community is unified only by a shared dissent from the dominant organization of sex and gender. But not every individual or group that adopts the name "queer" means to invoke these altered boundaries. Many members of Queer Nation, a highly decentralized militant organization, use the term "queer" only as a synonym for lesbian or gay. Queer Nation, for some, is quite simply a gay nationalist organization. For others, the "queer" nation is a newly defined political entity, better able to cross boundaries and construct more fluid identities. In many other instances, various contradictory definitions coexist—in a single group, or in an individual's mind. This ambivalent mixture is illustrated in a series of interviews with Queer Nation activists published in *OUT/LOOK:*

Miguel Gutierrez: Queerness means nonassimilationist to me.

Rebecca Hensler: A lot of what the "queer generation" is arguing for is the same stuff that was being fought for by gay liberation.

Alexander Chee: The operant dream is of a community united in diversity, queerly ourselves. . . . [The facilitators] took great care to explain that everyone was welcome under the word *queer*.

Laura Thomas: I don't see the queer movement as being organized to do anything beyond issues of anti-assimilation and being who we want to be.

Adele Morrison: Queer is not an "instead of," it's an "inclusive of." . . . It's like the whole issue of "people of color".

Gerard Koskovich: I think *queer* has been adopted here in San Francisco by people who are using their experience of marginalization to produce an aggressive critique of the prevailing social system. . . . I think we're seeing in its early stages a reorganization of some of those forces into a new community of people where the range of defining factors is rather fluid. People's limits have shifted significantly from the traditional urban gay community of the 1970s.[14]

Or, as former *Outweek* editor Gabriel Rotello explained to a *New York Times* reporter,

> When you're trying to describe the community, and you have to list gays, lesbians, bisexuals, drag queens, transsexuals (post-op and pre), it gets unwieldy. Queer says it all.[15]

In addition to the appearance of organizations for "bisexuals" and "queers," the boundaries of community have also been altered by a new elasticity in the meanings of "lesbian" and "gay." When Pat Califia announced that sex between lesbians and gay men is "gay sex," and *Outweek* published a cover story on "Lesbians Who Sleep With Men," the notion of a fixed sexual identity determined by a firmly gendered desire began to slip quietly away.[16]

Queer Theory on the Move

The constructionist perspective began to generate theoretical writing beginning in the 1970s. British historical sociologist Jeffrey Weeks, influenced by the earlier work of Mary McIntosh, appropriated and reworked the sociological theories known as "symbolic interactionism" or "labeling theory" to underpin his account of the emergence of a homosexual identity in Western societies during the 19th century. Other British writers associated with the Gay Left Collective produced work from within this same field of influence. U.S. historians Jonathan Ned Katz and John D'Emilio, influenced primarily by feminist theory and the work of Marxists such as E.P. Thompson, began to produce "social construction" theories of homosexuality by the early 1980s.[17]

This theory, though rich with implications for theoretical investigations of identity and subjectivity generally, remained severely ghettoized until relatively recently. Gay authors and gay topics, stigmatized and tabooed in the academy, have found audiences and sources of support elsewhere. But lesbian and gay history and theory have suffered from this ghettoization, as have history and theory more broadly.[18]

The figure who most clearly marks the recent movement of this theory out of the ghetto is Michel Foucault. His reputation and influence placed his investigations of the emergence of homosexual identity within a theoretical context, embedded in a body of work, that legitimated it—and ultimately served to legitimate the work of other, more stigmatized and marginalized theorists. The history of sexuality ultimately became a subject, a disciplinary location, largely as an effect of the circulation of Foucault's work through the work of (predominantly) lesbian and gay authors.[19]

Since the publication of Foucault's *History of Sexuality*, the cultural work of lesbian and gay theory has shifted. After a couple of decades of staking out a position, a territory, a locate, our theories are now preparing to travel. After defining a viewpoint, articulating a set of questions, and producing a body of knowledges, we are determined now to transport these resources across cultural boundaries. Theory is now working—finally—to get us out of the academic ghetto.

"Constructionist" theories accomplish this in a way "essentialist" theories never could. Lesbian and gay identities, theorized as fixed and borne by a minority, place certain limits on the horizon of theory as well as politics. They contain desire and naturalize gender through the operations of their very definitions. Constructionist theories, on the other hand, recognize the (constrained) mobility of desire and support a critical relation to gender. They stake out a new stance of opposition, which many theorists now call "queer." This stance is constituted through its dissent from the hegemonic, structured relations and meanings of sexuality and gender, but its actual historical forms and positions are open, constantly subject to negotiation and renegotiation.

Queer theories do their ghetto-busting work by placing the production and circulation of sexualities at the core of Western cultures, defining the emergence of the homosexual/heterosexual dyad as an issue that *no* cultural theory can afford to ignore. As Eve Sedgwick put it in the first paragraph of her new book *The Epistemology of the Closet*:

> This book will argue that an understanding of virtually any aspect of modern Western culture must be, not merely incomplete, but damaged in its central substance to the degree that it does not incorporate a critical analysis of modern homo/heterosexual definition.[20]

This project works in at least two directions—taking queer questions and knowledges into the domain of mainstream theoretical paradigms, and bringing the formulations of feminist, Marxist, postmodernist, and poststructuralist theories to bear on issues of queer culture and politics.

In the case of a major figure such as Foucault, the project involved the smuggling of queer questions into the very foundations of contemporary theory. Without being *completely* crude and reductive, it is possible to ask: From what subject position do prisons, mental asylums, confessionals, and sexuality seem connected and central to the operations of power? Foucault's own queerness, seldom stated but widely known, may have shaped his questions and his work in ways that endowed it with its current legitimating power.[21]

In the area of literary studies, Eve Sedgwick's work is now performing the work of legitimation and de-ghettoization. She is importing "queer readings" into the house of critical theory. She's able to accomplish this effectively in part because, as the "Judy Garland" of gay studies, she doesn't bear the stigma of homosexuality herself. She can be perceived (however wrongly) as in some sense "disinterested," and therefore as a more "credible" standard bearer for theoretical queerness. (This is not a criticism of Sedgwick, but of the conditions of reception for her work.)

Sedgwick's work performs its magic primarily for the benefit of gay male readers and readings, and on the texts of the traditional white male "canon."[22] Within the field defined by queer literary theory, lesbian visions remain profoundly ghettoized, though they are gaining ground from within feminist theory (which is itself only newly emerging from its own ghetto). Only a few literary theorists have embarked on queer readings of the texts of lesbians, especially those from less privileged class backgrounds or from communities of color.[23]

It is precisely from within feminist theory, however, that a "queer" critique of the dominant categories of sexuality and gender is emerging most imaginatively and persuasively. The work of film theorist Teresa de Lauretis, especially, has effected the de-ghettoization of a queer perspective in feminist theory. As she wrote in *Technologies of Gender* in 1987:

> The problem, which is a problem for all feminist scholars and teachers, is one we face almost daily in our work, namely, that most of the available theories of reading, writing, sexuality, ideology, or any other cultural production are built on male narratives of gender, whether oedipal or anti-oedipal, bound by the heterosexual contract; narratives which persistently tend to re-produce themselves in feminist theories. They *tend* to, and will do so unless one constantly resists, suspicious of their drift.[24]

We can surmise who is the "one" who is most likely to become and remain so relentlessly suspicious.

Following on the work of de Lauretis, feminist philosopher Judith Butler has hacked away at the heterosexual assumptions built into the foundations of theories of gender, whether feminist, non-feminist, or anti-feminist. Her *Gender Trouble: Feminism and the Subversion of Identity*, draws upon the queer practices of drag and cross-dressing (treated in the earlier work of anthropologist Esther Newton) and the queer "styles" of lesbian butch-femme to build her own conception of gender as performance, and of gender parodies as subversive bodily acts.[25]

Though neither de Lauretis nor Butler has staked out a position named specifically as "queer," the elaboration of such a locale within feminist theory could work a radical magic similar to that of the category "women of color." As many feminists have argued, the category "women of color" as proposed in such ground-breaking anthologies as *This Bridge Called My Back*, is a significant conceptual and political innovation.[26] As Donna Haraway wrote in 1985:

> This identity marks out a self-consciously constructed space that cannot affirm the capacity to act on the basis of natural identification, but only on the basis of conscious coalition, of affinity, of political kinship. Unlike the "woman" of some streams of the white women's movement in the United States, there is no naturalization of the matrix, or at least this is what [Chela] Sandoval argues is uniquely available through the power of oppositional consciousness.[27]

This description (I would argue) applies equally well to the political community and theoretical standpoint constructed by the designation "queer."

Activism Versus Academia?

The challenge for queer theory as it emerges from the academic ghetto is to engage intellectually with the political project in the best sense of "theory," while avoiding jargon and obscurantism in the worst sense of "academic." The record to date is at best uneven. On the down side, there is a tendency among some queer theorists to engage in academic debates at a high level of intellectual sophistication, while erasing the political and activist roots of their theoretical insights and concerns. Such theorists cite, modify, or dispute Foucault, Lacan, and Derrida, while feminist, lesbian, and gay innovations and political figures disappear from sight. They use formal languages to exclude all but the most specialized from the audience for theory.

On the up side, some queer theorists work in a way that disrupts the activist/theorist opposition, combining sophisticated thinking, accessible language, and an address to a broadly imagined audience. Writer/activists such as Gloria Anzaldúa, Kobena Mercer, Douglas Crimp, and Gayle Rubin offer us the possibility of escape from the twin pitfalls of anti-intellectual posturing among some activists *and* the functional elitism of some would-be radical theorists.[28]

The continuing work of queer politics and theory is to open up possibilities for coalition across barriers of class, race, and gender, and to somehow satisfy the paradoxical necessity of recognizing differences, while producing (provisional) unity. Can we avoid the dead end of various nationalisms and separatisms, without producing a bankrupt universalism?

I think queer politics and theory offer us promising new directions for intervention in U.S. life—though in different ways in differing arenas. In the arena of academic cultural theory, queer theory is breaking into the mainstream, making a difference and providing (some, limited) material support in the form of careers. This is possible because queer theory shares with much academic cultural theory a critique of U.S. liberalism and a focus on the process of political marginalization. But in the arena of political activism—the kind that takes place in mass institutions from mainstream media to Congress—queer politics occupies the critical margins. This is because the language and logic of liberalism still occupy the progressive edge of the possible in mainstream U.S. politics. Lesbian and gay liberal politics offer us the best opportunities we have to make gains in courtrooms, legislatures, and TV sit-coms. Queer politics, with its critique of the categories and strategies of liberal gay politics, keeps the possibility of radical change alive at the margins. It also infuses a remarkable efflorescence of off-center cultural production—art, music, dance, theater, film and video, and more.

Jeffrey Escoffier and Allan Bérubé describe this paradoxical reality in the special *OUT/LOOK* section on Queer Nation:

> The new generation calls itself *queer*, not *lesbian, gay, and bisexual*—awkward, narrow, and perhaps compromised words. *Queer* is meant to be confrontational—opposed to gay assimilationists and straight oppressors while inclusive of people who have been marginalized by anyone in power. Queer Nationals are undertaking an awesome task. They are trying to combine contradictory impulses: to bring together people who have been made to feel perverse, queer, odd, outcast, different, and deviant, and to affirm sameness by defining a common identity on the fringes.
>
> Queer Nationals are torn between affirming a new identity—"I am queer"—and rejecting restrictive identities—"I reject your categories," between rejecting assimilation—"I don't need your approval, just get out of my face"—and wanting to be recognized by mainstream society—"We queers are gonna get in your face."
>
> These queers are constructing a new culture by combining elements that usually don't go together. They may be the first wave of activists to embrace the retrofuture/classic contemporary styles of postmodernism. They are building their own identity from old and new elements—borrowing styles and tactics from popular culture, communities of color, hippies, AIDS activists, the antinuclear movement, MTV, feminists, and early gay liberationists. Their new culture is slick, quick, anarchic, transgressive, ironic. They are dead serious, but they also just wanna have fun. If they manage not to blow up in contradiction or get bogged down in process, they may lead the way into new forms of activism for the 1990s.[29]

For the foreseeable future, we need both our liberal and radical fronts. But queer politics and theory, in their best guises and combinations, offer us a possible future full of provocations and possibilities.

Notes

This essay was first presented at the University of Illinois at Champaign-Urbana's Unit for Criticism and Interpretive Theory Colloquium in April, 1991, then at the 5th Annual Lesbian and Gay Studies Conference at Rutgers University in November, 1991. I would like to thank Alan Hance and Lee Furey for their comments in Urbana, and Kathleen McHugh, Carole Vance, Cindy Patton, Jeff Escoffier, Jonathan Ned Katz, and especially Nan D. Hunter, for their invaluable contributions to my thinking. I would also like to thank Gayle Rubin and Larry Gross for providing me with copies of important but obscure articles from their voluminous files, and the *SR* Bay Area collective for their helpful editorial suggestions.

1. David N. Dinkins, "Keep Marching for Equality," *The New York Times*, March 21, 1991.

2. For a description and defense of the "ethnic model" see Steven Epstein, "Gay Politics, Ethnic Identity: The Limits of Social Constructionism," *Socialist Review*, vol. 17, no. 3/4 (May-August 1987).

3. For an account of a 1970s incarnation of this form of nationalism—based on gender rather than sexuality per se—see Charlotte Bunch, "Learning from Lesbian Separatism," in her *Passionate Politics: Feminist Theory in Action* (New York: St. Martin's Press, 1987).

4. See for example Michelangelo Signorile, "Gossip Watch," *Outweek*, April 18, 1990, pp. 55–57. For an extended discussion of these issues see Steve Beery et. al., "Smashing the Closet: The Pros and Cons of Outing," *Outweek*, May 16, 1990, pp. 40–53. The many opinions expressed in this issue indicate that not all editors of *Outweek* agreed with Signorile—though the editor-in-chief Gabriel Rotello was in complete agreement.

5. See Michelangelo Signorile, "The Other Side of Malcolm," *Outweek*, March 18, 1990, pp. 40–45. The Tim Sweeney controversy continued in the pages of the magazine for several months.

6. C. Carr, "Why Outing Must Stop," *The Village Voice*, March 19, 1991, p. 37. She was later joined in the letters column of the *Voice* by B. Ruby Rich, who announced the formation of DAO—Dykes Against Outing.

7. Audre Lorde, *Zami: A New Spelling of My Name* (Watertown, MA: Persephone Press, 1982), p. 226.

8. Louise Sloan, "Beyond Dialogue," *San Francisco Bay Guardian Literary Supplement*, March 1991, p. 3.

9. For an excellent account of the political ramifications of this debate, see Jeffrey Escoffier, "Inside the Ivory Closet: The Challenges Facing Lesbian and Gay Studies," *OUT/LOOK: National Lesbian and Gay Quarterly*, no. 10 (Fall 1990), pp. 40–48. For a theoretical discussion, see Diana Fuss, "Lesbian and Gay Theory: The Question of Identity Politics" in her *Essentially Speaking: Feminism, Nature and Difference* (New York: Routledge, 1989), pp. 97–112. (Neither of these writers offers the clichéd version of the debate that I have caricatured.)

10. For discussions of the emergence of the homosexual/heterosexual dyad and its representations in various medical-scientific discourses, see Jeffrey Weeks, *Coming Out: Homosexual Politics in Britain From the Nineteenth Century to the Present* (London: Quarter Books, 1977) and his *Sex, Politics and Society: The Regulation of Sexuality Since 1800* (London: Longman, 1981). See also Jonathan Katz, "The Invention of the Homosexual, 1880–1950," in his *Gay/Lesbian Almanac* (New York: Harper & Row, 1983), pp. 137–174.

11. See Dennis Altman, *Homosexual Oppression and Liberation* (New York: Avon Books, 1971), especially Chapter 3, "Liberation: Toward the Polymorphous Whole."

12. Alix Dobkin, "Any Woman Can Be a Lesbian," from the album *Lavender Jane Loves Women*. The best known example of this move—the denaturalization of heterosexuality, and the naturalization of lesbianism—is Adrienne Rich, "Compulsory Heterosexuality and Lesbian Existence," reprinted in *Powers of Desire: The Politics of Sexuality*, A. Snitow, C. Stansell, and S. Thompson, eds. (New York: Monthly Review Press, 1983), pp. 177–205. It is important to note that male-dominated gay politics has seldom supported a critique of the convention of heterosexuality for most people (the 90 percent or so seen as "naturally" heterosexual). Lesbian feminists *always* regarded heterosexuality as an oppressive institution, which any woman (potentially all women) might escape through lesbianism.

13. See for example the anthology edited by Loraine Hutchins and Lani Kaahumani, *Bi Any Other Name: Bisexual People Speak Out* (Boston: Alyson Publications, 1991).

14. "Birth of A Queer Nation," *OUT/LOOK: National Lesbian and Gay Quarterly*, no. 11 (Winter 1991), pp. 14–23. The interviews and articles in this special section were collected from New York and San Francisco, though there are other groups all over the country. My account of Queer Nation is drawn from my own (limited) knowledge of the New York and Chicago groups, and from articles and interviews in the gay and lesbian press. Because Queer Nation has no central "organization," I'm not attempting to describe it exhaustively; I am pointing to several tendencies and possibilities within it.

15. " 'Gay' Fades as Militants Pick 'Queer,' " *The New York Times*, April 6, 1991.

16. Pat Califia, "Gay Men, Lesbians and Sex: Doing It Together," *The Advocate*, July 7, 1983, pp. 24–27; Jorjet Harper, "Lesbians Who Sleep With Men," *Outweek*, February 11, 1990, pp. 46–52.

17. These developments are summarized by Jeffrey Escoffier in "Inside the Ivory Closet." See note 9.

18. See Lisa Duggan, "History's Gay Ghetto: The Contradictions of Growth in Lesbian and Gay History," in *Presenting the Past: Essays on History and the Public*, Susan Porter Benson et. al., eds. (Philadelphia: Temple University Press), 1986, pp. 281–290; and John D'Emilio, "Not A Simple Matter: Gay History and Gay Historians," *Journal of American History*, vol. 76, no. 2 (Sept. 1989), pp. 435–442.

19. The most influential single text in the United States was the English translation of *The History of Sexuality Volume I* (New York: Pantheon, 1978). My point about the ubiquity of lesbian and gay authors in the field of "history of sexuality" can be confirmed with a glance at the list of editors for the new journal, *Journal of the History of Sexuality*. All but a few are known to be lesbian or gay.

20. Eve Kosofsky Sedgwick. *Epistemology of the Closet* (Berkeley: University of California Press, 1990), p. 1.

21. In a fascinating interview with Foucault published in the gay periodical *The Advocate* just after his death from AIDS in 1984, he comments: "Sexuality is something that we ourselves create. . . . We have to understand that with our desires, through our desires, go new forms of relationships, new forms of love, new forms of creation." Bob Gallagher and Alexander Wilson, "Foucault and the Politics of Identity," *The Advocate*, Aug. 7, 1984, pp. 27–30, 58.

22. See Julie Abraham's review of Sedgwick's *Epistemology of the Closet* in *The Women's Review of Books*, vol. 8, no. 7 (April 1991), pp. 17–18. Abraham concludes provoca-

tively that "*Epistemology of the Closet* is an extraordinary book. The questions Sedgwick addresses, and those her work provokes, together create a great deal of theoretical space. But all the women are straight, all the gays are male (and all the males are, potentially, gay). The sisters are still doing it for themselves."

23. See especially Biddy Martin, "Lesbian Identity and Autobiographical Difference(s)," in *Life/lines: Theorizing Women's Autobiography*, Bella Brodzky and Celeste Schenck, eds. (Ithaca, NY: Cornell University Press, 1988), pp. 77–103. The texts of privileged lesbians such as Gertrude Stein, Radclyffe Hall, and Willa Cather have received relatively more attention, of course.

24. Teresa de Lauretis, *Technologies of Gender* (Bloomington: Indiana University Press, 1987), p. 25.

25. Judith Butler, *Gender Trouble: Feminism and the Subversion of Identity* (New York: Routledge, 1990). See especially pp. 136–139.

26. Cherríe Moraga and Gloría Anzaldúa, *This Bridge Called My Back: Writings by Radical Women of Color* (Watertown, MA: Persephone Press, 1981).

27. Donna Haraway, "A Manifesto for Cyborgs: Science, Technology, and Socialist Feminism in the 1980s," *Socialist Review*, vol. 15, no. 2 (March-April, 1985), p. 73–74. Haraway is citing Chela Sandoval, "Dis-Illusionment and the Poetry of the Future: The Making of Oppositional Consciousness," Ph.D. qualifying essay, University of California, Santa Cruz, 1984.

28. Gloria Anzaldúa, *Borderlands/La Frontera: The New Mestiza* (San Francisco: Spinsters/Aunt Lute, 1987); Kobena Mercer, "Skin Head Sex Thing: Racial Difference and the Homoerotic Imaginary," in *How Do I Look? Queer Film and Video*, Bad Objects Collective, ed. (Seattle: Bay Press, 1991), pp. 169–210; Douglas Crimp with Adam Rolston, *AIDS DemoGraphics* (Seattle: Bay Press, 1990); Gayle Rubin, "Thinking Sex: Notes for a Radical Theory of the Politics of Sexuality," in *Pleasure and Danger: Explorations in Female Sexuality*, Carole S. Vance, ed. (New York: Routledge, 1984), pp. 267–319.

29. Jeffrey Escoffier and Allan Bérubé, "Queer/Nation," *OUT/LOOK: National Lesbian and Gay Quarterly*, no. 11 (Winter 1991), pp. 14–16.

Questions for Reflection, Discussion, and Writing

1. Duggan presents three "stories" or scenes that form the backdrop for her essay. What are those three scenes and what issues does she use them to raise?

2. Discuss the ways Duggan traces the prevalence of constructionist thought and behavior throughout gay and lesbian history.

3. Duggan presents queer as a means of moving beyond the "academic ghetto." According to her, what are the contributions of theorists like Michel Foucault, Eve Sedgewick, Teresa deLauretis, and Judith Butler in constructing queer theory and ideologies of power? What role does feminist theory play?

4. Currently, what is the central challenge that queer theory needs to address, according to Duggan? What are the implications for that challenge to her claim that queer carries "the promise of new meanings, new ways of thinking and acting politically—a promise sometimes realized and sometimes not?" How does her essay develop and support that claim?

Related Reading

Teresa deLauretis, "Queer Theory: Lesbian and Gay Sexualities, An Introduction." *differences: A Journal of Feminist Cultural Studies 3.2* (1991): iii–xviii.

Michael Warner, "Introduction" in *Fear of A Queer Planet.* NY: Routledge. 1993. vii–xxxi.

Barbara Smith, "Queer Politics: Where's the Revolution?" *Nation,* July 5, 1993. 12–16.

Lee Edelman, "Queer Theory: Unstating Desire." *GLQ 2* (1995): 343–346.

Annamarie Jagose, "Queer" and and "Contestations of Queer" in *Queer Theory: An Introduction.* NY: NYUP. 1996. 72–126.

Sally O'Driscoll, "Outlaw Readings: Beyond Queer Theory." *Signs 22.1* 1996): 30–51.

Simon Gage, Lisa Richards and Howard Wilmot, *Queer.* New York: Thunder's Mouth Press. 2002.

Web Resource

http://www.queertheory.com/

Axiomatic

Eve Kosofsky Sedgwick

Epistemology of the Closet proposes that many of the major nodes of thought and knowledge in twentieth-century Western culture as a whole are structured—indeed, fractured—by a chronic, now endemic crisis of homo/heterosexual definition, indicatively male, dating from the end of the nineteenth century. The book will argue that an understanding of virtually any aspect of modern Western culture must be, not merely incomplete, but damaged in its central substance to the degree that it does not incorporate a critical analysis of modern homo/heterosexual definition; and it will assume that the appropriate place for that critical analysis to begin is from the relatively decentered perspective of modern gay and antihomophobic theory.

The passage of time, the bestowal of thought and necessary political struggle since the turn of the century have only spread and deepened the long crisis of modern sexual definition, dramatizing, often violently, the internal incoherence and mutual contradiction of each of the forms of discursive and institutional "common sense" on this subject inherited from the architects of our present culture. The contradictions I will be discussing are not in the first place those between prohomosexual and antihomosexual people or ideologies, although the book's strongest motivation is indeed the gay-affirmative one. Rather, the contradictions that seem most active are the ones internal to all the important twentieth-century understandings of homo/heterosexual definition, both heterosexist and antihomophobic. Their outlines and something of their history are sketched in Chapter 1. Briefly, they are two. The first is the contradiction between seeing homo/heterosexual definition on the one hand as an issue of active importance primarily for a small, distinct, relatively fixed homosexual minority (what I refer to as a minoritizing view), and seeing it on the other hand as an issue of continuing, determinative importance in the lives of people across the spectrum of sexualities (what I refer to as a universalizing view). The second is the contradiction between seeing same-sex object choice on the one hand as a matter of liminality or transitivity between genders, and seeing it on the other hand as reflecting an impulse of separatism—though by no means necessarily political separatism—within each gender. The purpose of this book is not to adjudicate between the two poles of either of these contradictions, for, if its argument is right, no epistemological grounding now exists from which to do so. Instead, I am trying to make the strongest possible introductory case for a hypothesis about the centrality of this nominally marginal, conceptually intractable set of definitional issues to the important knowledges and understandings of twentieth-century Western culture as a whole.

The word "homosexual" entered Euro-American discourse during the last third of the nineteenth century—its popularization preceding, as it happens, even that of the word "heterosexual."[1] It seems clear that the sexual behaviors, and even for some people the conscious identities, denoted by the new term "homosexual" and its contemporary variants already had a long, rich history. So, indeed, did a wide range of other sexual behaviors and behavioral clusters. What *was* new from the turn of the century was the world-mapping by which every given person, just as he or she was necessarily assignable to a male or a female gender, was now considered necessarily assignable as well to a homo- or a hetero-sexuality, a binarized identity that was full of implications, however confusing, for even the ostensibly least sexual aspects of personal existence. It was this new development that left no space in the culture exempt from the potent incoherences of homo/heterosexual definition.

New, institutionalized taxonomic discourses—medical, legal, literary, psychological—centering on homo/heterosexual definition proliferated and crystallized with exceptional rapidity in the decades around the turn of the century, decades in which so many of the other critical nodes of the culture were being, if less suddenly and newly, nonetheless also definitively reshaped. Both the power relations between the genders and the relations of nationalism and imperialism,

---

[1]On this, see Jonathan Katz, *Gay/Lesbian Almanac: A New Documentary* (New York: Harper & Row, 1983), pp. 147–50; for more discussion, David M. Halperin, *One Hundred Years of Homosexuality* (New York: Routledge, 1989), p. 155*n*.1 and pp. 158–59*n*.17.

for instance, were in highly visible crisis. For this reason, and because the structuring of same-sex bonds can't, in any historical situation marked by inequality and contest *between* genders, fail to be a site of intensive regulation that intersects virtually every issue of power and gender,[2] lines can never be drawn to circumscribe within some proper domain of sexuality (whatever that might be) the consequences of a shift in sexual discourse. Furthermore, in accord with Foucault's demonstration, whose results I will take to be axiomatic, that modern Western culture has placed what it calls sexuality in a more and more distinctively privileged relation to our most prized constructs of individual identity, truth, and knowledge, it becomes truer and truer that the language of sexuality not only intersects with but transforms the other languages and relations by which we know.

Accordingly, one characteristic of the readings in this book is to attend to performative aspects of texts, and to what are often blandly called their "reader relations," as sites of definitional creation, violence, and rupture in relation to particular readers, particular institutional circumstances. An assumption underlying the book is that the relations of the closet—the relations of the known and the unknown, the explicit and the inexplicit around homo/heterosexual definition—have the potential for being peculiarly revealing, in fact, about speech acts more generally. It has felt throughout this work as though the density of their social meaning lends any speech act concerning these issues—and the outlines of that "concern," it turns out, are broad indeed—the exaggerated propulsiveness of wearing flippers in a swimming pool: the force of various rhetorical effects has seemed uniquely difficult to calibrate.

But, in the vicinity of the closet, even what *counts* as a speech act is problematized on a perfectly routine basis. As Foucault says: "there is no binary division to be made between what one says and what one does not say; we must try to determine the different ways of not saying such things. . . . There is not one but many silences, and they are an integral part of the strategies that underlie and permeate discourses."[3] "Closetedness" itself is a performance initiated as such by the speech act of a silence—not a particular silence, but a silence that accrues particularity by fits and starts, in relation to the discourse that surrounds and differentially constitutes it. The speech acts that coming out, in turn, can comprise are as strangely specific. And they may have nothing to do with the acquisition of new information. I think of a man and a woman I know, best friends, who for years canvassed freely the emotional complications of each other's erotic lives—the man's eroticism happening to focus exclusively on men. But it was only after one particular conversational moment, fully a decade into this relationship, that it seemed to either of these friends that permission had been given to the woman to refer to the man, in their conversation to-

---

[2]This is an argument of my *Between Men: English Literature and Male Homosocial Desire* (New York: Columbia University Press, 1985).

[3]Michel Foucault, *The History of Sexuality*. Volume I: *An Introduction*, trans. Robert Hurley (New York: Pantheon, 1978), p. 27.

gether, as *a gay man*. Discussing it much later, both agreed they had felt at the time that this one moment had constituted a clear-cut act of coming out, even in the context of years and years beforehand of exchange predicated on the man's *being* gay. What was said to make this difference? Not a version of "I am gay," which could only have been bathetic between them. What constituted coming out for this man, in this situation, was to use about himself the phrase "coming out"—to mention, as if casually, having come out to someone else. (Similarly, a T-shirt that ACT UP sells in New York bearing the text, "I am out, therefore I am," is meant to do for the wearer, not the constative work of reporting that s/he *is* out, but the performative work of coming out in the first place.) And as Chapter 1 will discuss, the fact that silence is rendered as pointed and performative as speech, in relations around the closet, depends on and highlights more broadly the fact that ignorance is as potent and as multiple a thing there as is knowledge . . . .

As several of the formulations above would suggest, one main strand of argument in this book is deconstructive, in a fairly specific sense. The analytic move it makes is to demonstrate that categories presented in a culture as symmetrical binary oppositions—heterosexual/homosexual, in this case—actually subsist in a more unsettled and dynamic tacit relation according to which, first, term B is not symmetrical with but subordinated to term A; but, second, the ontologically valorized term A actually depends for its meaning on the simultaneous subsumption and exclusion of term B; hence, third, the question of priority between the supposed central and the supposed marginal category of each dyad is irresolvably unstable, an instability caused by the fact that term B is constituted as at once internal and external to term A. Harold Beaver, for instance, in an influential 1981 essay sketched the outlines of such a deconstructive strategy:

> The aim must be to reverse the rhetorical opposition of what is "transparent" or "natural" and what is "derivative" or "contrived" by demonstrating that the qualities predicated of "homosexuality" (as a dependent term) are in fact a condition of "heterosexuality"; that "heterosexuality," far from possessing a privileged status, must itself be treated as a dependent term.[4]

To understand these conceptual relations as irresolvably unstable is not, however, to understand them as inefficacious or innocuous. It is at least premature when Roland Barthes prophesies that "once the paradigm is blurred, utopia begins: meaning and sex become the objects of free play, at the heart of which the (polysemant) forms and the (sensual) practices, liberated from the binary prison, will achieve a state of infinite expansion."[5] To the contrary, a deconstructive understanding of these binarisms makes it possible to identify them as sites that are *peculiarly* densely charged with lasting potentials for pow-

---

[4]Harold Beaver, "Homosexual Signs," *Critical Inquiry* 8 (Autumn 1981): 115.

[5]*Roland Barthes by Roland Barthes*, trans. Richard Howard (New York: Hill and Wang, 1977), p. 133.

erful manipulation—through precisely the mechanisms of self-contradictory definition or, more succinctly, the double bind. Nor is a deconstructive analysis of such definitional knots, however necessary, at all sufficient to disable them. Quite the opposite: I would suggest that an understanding of their irresolvable instability has been continually available, and has continually lent discursive authority, to antigay as well as to gay cultural forces of this century. Beaver makes an optimistic prediction that "by disqualifying the autonomy of what was deemed spontaneously immanent, the whole sexual system is fundamentally decentred and exposed."[6] But there is reason to believe that the oppressive sexual system of the past hundred years was if anything born and bred (if I may rely on the pith of a fable whose value doesn't, I must hope, stand or fall with its history of racist uses) in the briar patch of the most notorious and repeated decenterings and exposures.

These deconstructive contestations can occur, moreover, only in the context of an entire cultural network of normative definitions, definitions themselves equally unstable but responding to different sets of contiguities and often at a different rate. The master terms of a particular historical moment will be those that are so situated as to entangle most inextricably and at the same time most differentially the filaments of other important definitional nexuses. In arguing that homo/heterosexual definition has been a presiding master term of the past century, one that has the same, primary importance for all modern Western identity and social organization (and not merely for homosexual identity and culture) as do the more traditionally visible cruxes of gender, class, and race, I'll argue that the now chronic modern crisis of homo/heterosexual definition has affected our culture through its ineffaceable marking particularly of the categories secrecy/disclosure, knowledge/ignorance, private/public, masculine/feminine, majority/minority, innocence/initiation, natural/artificial, new/old, discipline/terrorism, canonic/noncanonic, wholeness/decadence, urbane/provincial, domestic/foreign, health/illness, same/different, active/passive, in/out, cognition/paranoia, art/kitsch, utopia/apocalypse, sincerity/sentimentality, and voluntarity/addiction.[7] And rather than embrace an idealist faith in the necessarily, immanently self-corrosive efficacy of the contradictions inherent to these definitional binarisms, I will suggest instead that contests for discursive power can be specified as competitions for the material or rhetorical leverage required to set the terms of, and to profit in some way from, the operations of such an incoherence of definition . . . .

Gender has increasingly become a problem for this area of terminology, and one to which I have, again, no consistent solution. "Homosexual" was a rel-

---

[6]Beaver, "Homosexual Signs," pp. 115–16.

[7]My casting of all these definitional nodes in the form of binarisms, I should make explicit, has to do not with a mystical faith in the number two but, rather, with the felt need to schematize in some consistent way the treatment of social vectors so exceedingly various. The kind of falsification necessarily performed on each by this reduction cannot, unfortunately, itself be consistent. But the scope of the kind of hypothesis I want to pose does seem to require a drastic reductiveness, at least in its initial formulations.

atively gender-neutral term and I use it as such, though it has always seemed to have at least some male bias—whether because of the pun on Latin *homo* = man latent in its etymological macaronic, or simply because of the greater attention to men in the discourse surrounding it (as in so many others). "Gay" is more complicated since it makes a claim to refer to both genders but is routinely yoked with "lesbian" in actual usage, as if it did not—as increasingly it does not—itself refer to women. As I suggest in Axiom 3, this terminological complication is closely responsive to real ambiguities and struggles of gay/lesbian politics and identities: e.g., there are women-loving women who think of themselves as lesbians but not as gay, and others who think of themselves as gay women but not as lesbians. Since the premises of this study make it impossible to presuppose either the unity or the distinctness of women's and men's changing, and indeed synchronically various, homosexual identities, and since its primary though not exclusive focus is in fact on male identities, I sometimes use "gay and lesbian" but more often simply "gay," the latter in the oddly precise sense of a phenomenon of same-sex desire that is being treated as indicatively but not exclusively male. When I mean to suggest a more fully, equitably two-sexed phenomenon I refer to "gay men and women," or "lesbians and gay men"; when a more exclusive one, to "gay men." . . .

Let me give an example. There is reason to believe that gay-bashing is the most common and most rapidly increasing among what are becoming legally known as bias-related or hate-related crimes in the United States. There is no question that the threat of this violent, degrading, and often fatal extrajudicial sanction works even more powerfully than, and in intimately enforcing concert with, more respectably institutionalized sanctions against gay choice, expression, and being. The endemic intimacy of the link between extrajudicial and judicial punishment of homosexuality is clear, for instance, from the argument of legislators who, in state after state, have fought to exclude antigay violence from coverage under bills that would specifically criminalize bias-related crime—on the grounds that to specify a condemnation of *individual* violence against persons perceived as gay would vitiate the *state*'s condemnation of homosexuality. These arguments have so far been successful in most of the states where the question has arisen; in fact, in some states (such as New York) where coverage of antigay violence was not dropped from hate-crimes bills, apparently solid racial/ethnic coalitions have fractured so badly over the issue that otherwise overwhelmingly popular bills have been repeatedly defeated. The state's treatment of nonstate antigay violence, then, is an increasingly contested definitional interface of terms that impact critically but nonexclusively on gay people.

In this highly charged context, the treatment of gay-bashers who do wind up in court is also very likely to involve a plunge into a thicket of difficult and contested definitions. One of the thorniest of these has to do with "homosexual panic," a defense strategy that is commonly used to prevent conviction or to lighten sentencing of gay-bashers—a term, as well, that names a key analytic tool in the present study. Judicially, a "homosexual panic" defense for a person (typically a man) accused of antigay violence implies that his responsibility for the crime was diminished by a pathological psychological condition, perhaps brought on by an unwanted sexual advance from the man whom he then attacked. In addition to the unwarranted assumptions that all gay men may plausibly be accused of making sexual advances to strangers and, worse, that violence, often to the point of homicide, is a legitimate response to any sexual advance whether welcome or not, the "homosexual panic" defense rests on the falsely individualizing and pathologizing assumption that hatred of homosexuals is so private and so atypical a phenomenon in this culture as to be classifiable as an accountability-reducing illness. The widespread acceptance of this defense really seems to show, to the contrary, that hatred of homosexuals is even more public, more typical, hence harder to find any leverage against than hatred of other disadvantaged groups. "Race panic" or "gender panic," for instance, is not accepted as a defense for violence against people of color or against women; as for "heterosexual panic," David Wertheimer, executive director of the New York City Gay and Lesbian Anti-Violence Project, remarks, "If every heterosexual woman who had a sexual advance made to her by a male had the right to murder the man, the streets of this city would be littered with the bodies of heterosexual men.[8] A lawyer for the National Gay Rights Advocates makes explicit the contrast with legal treatment of other biasrelated crimes: "There is no factual or legal justification for the use of this [homosexual panic] defense. Just as our society will not allow a defendant to use racial or gender-based prejudices as an excuse for his violent acts, a defendant's homophobia is no defense to a violent crime.[9]

Thus, a lot of the popularity of the "homosexual panic" defense seems to come simply from its ability to permit and "place," by pathologizing, the enactment of a socially sanctioned prejudice against one stigmatized minority, a particularly demeaned one among many. Its special plausibility, however, seems also to depend on a difference between antigay crime and other bias-related antiminority crime: the difference of how much less clear, perhaps finally how impossible, is the boundary circumscription of a minoritizing gay identity. After all, the reason why this defense borrows the name of the (formerly rather obscure and little-diagnosed) psychiatric classification "*homosexual* panic" is that it refers to the supposed uncertainty about his own sexual identity of the perpetrator of the antigay violence. That this should be the typifying scenario of defenses of gay-bashers (as uncertainty about one's own race, religion, ethnicity, or gender is not in other cases of bias-related violence) shows once again how the overlapping aegises of minoritizing and universalizing understandings of

---

[8] Peter Freiberg, "Blaming the Victim: New Life for the 'Gay Panic' Defense," *The Advocate*, May 24, 1988, p. 12. For a more thorough discussion of the homosexual panic defense, see "Burdens on Gay Litigants and Bias in the Court System: Homosexual Panic, Child Custody, and Anonymous Parties," *Harvard Civil Rights—Civil Liberties Law Review* 19 (1984): 498–515.

[9] Quoted from Joyce Norcini, in "NGRA Discredits 'Homosexual Panic' Defense," *New York Native*, no. 322 (June 19, 1989): 12.

male homo/heterosexual definition can tend to redouble the victimization of gay people. In effect, the homosexual panic defense performs a double act of minoritizing taxonomy: there is, it asserts, one distinct minority of gay people, and a second minority, equally distinguishable from the population at large, of "latent homosexuals" whose "insecurity about their own masculinity" is so anomalous as to permit a plea based on diminution of normal moral responsibility. At the same time, the efficacy of the plea depends on its universalizing force, on whether, as Wertheimer says, it can "create a climate in which the jurors are able to identify with the perpetrator by saying, 'My goodness, maybe *I* would have reacted the same way.'"[10] The reliance of the homosexual panic plea on the fact that this male definitional crisis is systemic and endemic is enabled only, and precisely, by its denial of the same fact.

When in my work on *Between Men,* knowing nothing about this judicial use of "homosexual panic" (at that time a less common and publicized defense), I needed a name for "a structural residue of terrorist potential, of *blackmailability,* of Western maleness through the leverage of homophobia," I found myself attracted to just the same phrase, borrowed from the same relatively rare psychiatric diagnosis. Through a linguistic theft whose violence I trusted would be legible in every usage of the phrase, I tried to turn what had been a taxonomic, minoritizing medical category into a structural principle applicable to the definitional work of an entire gender, hence of an entire culture. I used it to denominate "the most private, psychologized form in which many twentieth-century Western men experience their vulnerability to the social pressure of homophobic blackmail"—as, specifically, "only one path of control, complementary to public sanctions through the institutions described by Foucault and others as defining and regulating the amorphous territory of 'the sexual.'"[11]

The forensic use of the "homosexual panic" defense for gay-bashers depends on the medically mediated ability of the phrase to obscure an overlap between individual pathology and systemic function. The reason I found the phrase attractive for my purposes was quite the opposite: I thought it could dramatize, render visible, even render scandalous the same space of overlap. The set of perceptions condensed in that usage of "male homosexual panic" proved, I think, a productive feature of *Between Men* for other critics, especially those doing gay theory, and I have continued my explorations of the same phrase, used in the same sense, in *Epistemology of the Closet.* Yet I feel, as well, with increasing dismay, in the increasingly homophobic atmosphere of public discourse since 1985, that work done to accentuate and clarify the explanatory power of this difficult nexus may not be able to be reliably insulated from uses that ought to be diametrically opposed to it. For instance, it would not require a willfully homophobic reader to understand these discussions of the centrality and power of male homosexual panic as actually contributing to the credibility

[10]Freiberg, "Blaming the Victim," p. 11.
[11]Sedgwick, *Between Men,* p. 89.

of the pathologizing "homosexual panic" legal defense of gay-bashers. All it would require would be a failure or refusal to understand how necessarily the discussions are embedded within their context—the context, that is, of an analysis based on systemwide skepticism about the positivist taxonomic neutrality of psychiatry, about the classificatory coherence (e.g., concerning "individual responsibility") of the law. If, foreseeing the possibility of this particular misuse, I have, as I hope, been able to take the explanatory measures necessary to guard against it, still there may be too many others unforeseen.

Of course, silence on these issues performs the enforcing work of the status quo more predictably and inexorably than any attempt at analysis. Yet the tensions and pleasures that, even ideally, make it possible for a writer to invest such a project with her best thought may be so different from those that might enable a given reader to. . . .

. . . In the particular area of sexuality, for instance, I assume that most of us know the following things that can differentiate even people of identical gender, race, nationality, class, and "sexual orientation"—each one of which, however, if taken seriously as pure *difference*, retains the unaccounted-for potential to disrupt many forms of the available thinking about sexuality.

- Even identical genital acts mean very different things to different people.
- To some people, the nimbus of "the sexual" seems scarcely to extend beyond the boundaries of discrete genital acts; to others, it enfolds them loosely or floats virtually free of them.
- Sexuality makes up a large share of the self-perceived identity of some people, a small share of others'.
- Some people spend a lot of time thinking about sex, others little.
- Some people like to have a lot of sex, others little or none.
- Many people have their richest mental/emotional involvement with sexual acts that they don't do, or even don't *want* to do.
- For some people, it is important that sex be embedded in contexts resonant with meaning, narrative, and connectedness with other aspects of their life; for other people, it is important that they not be; to others it doesn't occur that they might be.
- For some people, the preference for a certain sexual object, act, role, zone, or scenario is so immemorial and durable that it can only be experienced as innate; for others, it appears to come late or to feel aleatory or discretionary.
- For some people, the possibility of bad sex is aversive enough that their lives are strongly marked by its avoidance; for others, it isn't.
- For some people, sexuality provides a needed space of heightened discovery and cognitive hyperstimulation. For others, sexuality provides a needed space of routinized habituation and cognitive hiatus.
- Some people like spontaneous sexual scenes, others like highly scripted ones, others like spontaneous-sounding ones that are nonetheless totally predictable.

- Some people's sexual orientation is intensely marked by autoerotic pleasures and histories—sometimes more so than by any aspect of alloerotic object choice. For others the autoerotic possibility seems secondary or fragile, if it exists at all.
- Some people, homo-, hetero-, and bisexual, experience their sexuality as deeply embedded in a matrix of gender meanings and gender differentials. Others of each sexuality do not.

The list of individual differences could easily be extended. That many of them could differentiate one from another period of the same person's life as well as one person's totality from another's, or that many of them record differentia that can circulate from one person to another, does not, I believe, lessen their authority to demarcate; they demarcate at more than one site and on more than one scale. The impact of such a list may seem to depend radically on a trust in the self-perception, self-knowledge, or self-report of individuals, in an area that is if anything notoriously resistant to the claims of common sense and introspection: where would the whole, astonishing and metamorphic Western romance tradition (I include psychoanalysis) be if people's sexual desire, of all things, were even momentarily assumed to be transparent to themselves? Yet I am even more impressed by the leap of presumptuousness necessary to dismiss such a list of differences than by the leap of faith necessary to entertain it. To alienate conclusively, *definitionally*, from anyone on any theoretical ground the authority to describe and name their own sexual desire is a terribly consequential seizure. In this century, in which sexuality has been made expressive of the essence of both identity and knowledge, it may represent the most intimate violence possible. It is also an act replete with the most disempowering mundane institutional effects and potentials. It is, of course, central to the modern history of homophobic oppression. . . .

Sex, gender, sexuality: three terms whose usage relations and analytical relations are almost irremediably slippery. The charting of a space between something called "sex" and something called "gender" has been one of the most influential and successful undertakings of feminist thought. For the purposes of that undertaking, "sex" has had the meaning of a certain group of irreducible, biological differentiations between members of the species Homo sapiens who have XX and those who have XY chromosomes. These include (or are ordinarily thought to include) more or less marked dimorphisms of genital formation, hair growth (in populations that have body hair), fat distribution, hormonal function, and reproductive capacity. "Sex" in this sense—what I'll demarcate as "chromosomal sex"—is seen as the relatively minimal raw material on which is then based the social construction of *gender*. Gender, then, is the far more elaborated, more fully and rigidly dichotomized social production and reproduction of male and female identities and behaviors—of male and female *persons*—in a cultural system for which "male/female" functions as a primary and perhaps model binarism affecting the structure and meaning of many, many other binarisms whose apparent connection to chromosomal sex will often be exiguous or nonexistent. Compared to chromosomal sex, which is seen (by these definitions) as tending to be immutable, immanent in the individual, and biologically based, the meaning of gender is seen as culturally mutable and variable, highly relational (in the sense that each of the binarized genders is defined primarily by its relation to the other), and inextricable from a history of power differentials between genders. This feminist charting of what Gayle Rubin refers to as a "sex/gender system,"[12] the system by which chromosomal sex is turned into, and processed as, cultural gender, has tended to minimize the attribution of people's various behaviors and identities to chromosomal sex and to maximize their attribution to socialized gender constructs. The purpose of that strategy has been to gain analytic and critical leverage on the female-disadvantaging social arrangements that prevail at a given time in a given society, by throwing into question their legitimative ideological grounding in biologically based narratives of the "natural."

"Sex" is, however, a term that extends indefinitely beyond chromosomal sex. That its history of usage often overlaps with what might, now, more properly be called "gender" is only one problem. ("I can only love someone of my own sex." Shouldn't "sex" be "gender" in such a sentence? "M. saw that the person who approached was of the opposite sex." Genders—insofar as there are two and they are defined in contradistinction to one another—may be said to be opposite; but in what sense is XX the opposite of XY?) Beyond chromosomes, however, the association of "sex," precisely through the physical body, with reproduction and with genital activity and sensation keeps offering new challenges to the conceptual clarity or even possibility of sex/gender differentiation. There is a powerful argument to be made that a primary (or *the* primary) issue in gender differentiation and gender struggle is the question of who is to have control of women's (biologically) distinctive reproductive capability. Indeed, the intimacy of the association between several of the most signal forms of gender oppression and "the facts" of women's bodies and women's reproductive activity has led some radical feminists to question, more or less explicitly, the usefulness of insisting on a sex/gender distinction. For these reasons, even usages involving the "sex/gender system" within feminist theory are able to use "sex/gender" only to delineate a problematical *space* rather than a crisp distinction. My own loose usage in this book will be to denominate that problematized space of the sex/gender system, the whole package of physical and cultural distinctions between women and men, more simply under the rubric "gender." I do this in order to reduce the likelihood of confusion between "sex" in the sense of "the space of differences between male and female" (what I'll be grouping under "gender") and "sex" in the sense of sexuality.

---

[12]Gayle Rubin, "The Traffic in Women: Notes on the 'Political Economy' of Sex," in Rayna R. Reiter, ed., *Toward an Anthropology of Women* (New York: Monthly Review Press, 1975), pp. 157–210.

For meanwhile the whole realm of what modern culture refers to as "sexuality" and *also* calls "sex"—the array of acts, expectations, narratives, pleasures, identity-formations, and knowledges, in both women and men, that tends to cluster most densely around certain genital sensations but is not adequately defined by them—that realm is virtually impossible to situate on a map delimited by the feminist-defined sex/gender distinction. To the degree that it has a center or starting point in certain physical sites, acts, and rhythms associated (however contingently) with procreation or the potential for it, "sexuality" in this sense may seem to be of a piece with "chromosomal sex": biologically necessary to species survival, tending toward the individually immanent, the socially immutable, the given. But to the extent that, as Freud argued and Foucault assumed, the distinctively sexual nature of human sexuality has to do precisely with its excess over or potential difference from the bare choreographies of procreation, "sexuality" might be the very opposite of what we originally referred to as (chromosomal-based) sex: it could occupy, instead, even more than "gender" the polar position of the relational, the social/symbolic, the constructed, the variable, the representational (see Figure I). To note that, according to these different findings, *something* legitimately called sex or sexuality is all over the experiential and conceptual map is to record a problem less resolvable than a necessary choice of analytic paradigms or a determinate slippage of semantic meaning; it is rather, I would say, true to quite a range of contemporary worldviews and intuitions to find that sex/sexuality *does* tend to represent the full spectrum of positions between the most intimate and the most social, the most predetermined and the most aleatory, the most physically rooted and the most symbolically infused, the most innate and the most learned, the most autonomous and the most relational traits of being.

Biological	Cultural
Essential	Constructed
Individually immanent	Relational

Constructivist Feminist Analysis

chromosomal sex ———————————————— gender
gender inequality

Radical Feminist Analysis

chromosomal sex
reproductive relations ———————————————— reproductive relations
sexual inequality   sexual inequality

Foucault-influenced Analysis

chromosomal sex ——————— reproduction——————— sexuality

Figure I. Some Mappings of Sex, Gender, and Sexuality

If all this is true of the definitional nexus between sex and sexuality, how much less simple, even, must be that between sexuality and gender. It will be an assumption of this study that there is always at least the potential for an analytic distance between gender and sexuality, even if particular manifestations or features of particular sexualities are among the things that plunge women and men most ineluctably into the discursive, institutional, and bodily enmeshments of gender definition, gender relation, and gender inequality. This, too, has been posed by Gayle Rubin:

> I want to challenge the assumption that feminism is or should be the privileged site of a theory of sexuality. Feminism is the theory of gender oppression. . . . Gender affects the operation of the sexual system, and the sexual system has had gender-specific manifestations. But although sex and gender are related, they are not the same thing.[13]

This book will hypothesize, with Rubin, that the question of gender and the question of sexuality, inextricable from one another though they are in that each can be expressed only in the terms of the other, are nonetheless not the same question, that in twentieth-century Western culture gender and sexuality represent two analytic axes that may productively be imagined as being as distinct from one another as, say, gender and class, or class and race. Distinct, that is to say, no more than minimally, but nonetheless usefully.

Under this hypothesis, then, just as one has learned to assume that every issue of racial meaning must be embodied through the specificity of a particular class position—and every issue of class, for instance, through the specificity of a particular gender position—so every issue of gender would necessarily be embodied through the specificity of a particular sexuality, and vice versa; but nonetheless there could be use in keeping the analytic axes distinct. . . .

From the point of view of this relatively new and inchoate academic presence, then, the gay studies movement, what distinctive soundings are to be reached by posing the question our way—and staying for an answer? Let's see how it sounds.

Has there ever been a gay Socrates?
Has there ever been a gay Shakespeare?
Has there ever been a gay Proust?

Does the Pope wear a dress? If these questions startle, it is not least as tautologies. A short answer, though a very incomplete one, might be that not only have there been a gay Socrates, Shakespeare, and Proust but that their

---

[13]Rubin, "Thinking Sex," pp. 307–8.

names are Socrates, Shakespeare, Proust; and, beyond that, legion—dozens or hundreds of the most centrally canonic figures in what the monoculturalists are pleased to consider "our" culture, as indeed, always in different forms and senses, in every other.

What's now in place, in contrast, in most scholarship and most curricula is an even briefer response to questions like these: Don't ask. Or, less laconically: You shouldn't know. The vast preponderance of scholarship and teaching, accordingly, even among liberal academics, does simply neither ask nor know. At the most expansive, there is a series of dismissals of such questions on the grounds that:

1. Passionate language of same-sex attraction was extremely common during whatever period is under discussion—and therefore must have been completely meaningless. Or
2. Same-sex genital relations may have been perfectly common during the period under discussion—but since there was no language about them, *they* must have been completely meaningless. Or
3. Attitudes about homosexuality were intolerant back then, unlike now—so people probably didn't do anything. Or
4. Prohibitions against homosexuality didn't exist back then, unlike now—so if people did anything, it was completely meaningless. Or
5. The word "homosexuality" wasn't coined until 1869—so everyone before then was heterosexual. (Of course, heterosexuality has always existed.) Or
6. The author under discussion is certified or rumored to have had an attachment to someone of the other sex—so their feelings about people of their own sex must have been completely meaningless. Or (under a perhaps somewhat different rule of admissible evidence)
7. There is no actual proof of homosexuality, such as sperm taken from the body of another man or a nude photograph with another woman—so the author may be assumed to have been ardently and exclusively heterosexual. Or (as a last resort)
8. The author or the author's important attachments may very well have been homosexual—but it would be provincial to let so insignificant a fact make any difference at all to our understanding of any serious project of life, writing, or thought.

These responses reflect, as we have already seen, some real questions of sexual definition and historicity. But they only reflect them and don't reflect *on* them: the family resemblance among this group of extremely common responses comes from their closeness to the core grammar of *Don't ask; You shouldn't know.* It didn't happen; it doesn't make any difference; it didn't mean anything; it doesn't have interpretive consequences. Stop asking just here; stop asking just now; we know in advance the kind of difference that could be made by the invocation of *this* difference; it makes no difference; it doesn't mean. The

most openly repressive projects of censorship, such as William Bennett's literally murderous opposition to serious AIDS education in schools on the grounds
that it would communicate a tolerance for the lives of homosexuals, are,
through this mobilization of the powerful mechanism of the open secret, made
perfectly congruent with the smooth, dismissive knowingness of the urbane and
the pseudo-urbane.

And yet the absolute canonical centrality of the list of authors about
whom one might think to ask these questions—What was the structure, func-
tion, historical surround of same-sex love in and for Homer or Plato or Sap-
pho? What, then, about Euripides or Virgil? If a gay Marlowe, what about
Spenser or Milton? Shakespeare? Byron? But what about Shelley? Montaigne,
Leopardi . . .? Leonardo, Michelangelo, but . . .? Beethoven? Whitman,
Thoreau, Dickinson (Dickinson?), Tennyson, Wilde, Woolf, Hopkins, but
Brontë? Wittgenstein, but . . . Nietzsche? Proust, Musil, Kafka, Cather, but . . .
Mann? James, but . . . Lawrence? Eliot? but . . . Joyce? The very centrality of
this list and its seemingly almost infinite elasticity suggest that no one *can* know
in advance where the limits of a gay-centered inquiry are to be drawn, or where
a gay theorizing of and through even the hegemonic high culture of the Euro-
American tradition may need or be able to lead. The emergence, even within
the last year or two, of nascent but ambitious programs and courses in gay and
lesbian studies, at schools including those of the Ivy League, may now make it
possible for the first time to ask these difficult questions from within the very
heart of the empowered cultural institutions to which they pertain, as well as
from the marginal and endangered institutional positions from which, for so
long, the most courageous work in this area has emanated.

Furthermore, as I have been suggesting, the violently contradictory and
volatile energies that every morning's newspaper proves to us are circulating even
at this moment, in our society, around the issues of homo/heterosexual definition
show over and over again how pre-posterous is anybody's urbane pretense at having a clear, simple story to tell about the outlines and meanings of what and who
are homosexual and heterosexual. To be gay, or to be potentially classifiable as
gay—that is to say, *to be sexed or gendered*—in this system is to come under the radically overlapping aegises of a universalizing discourse of acts or bonds and at the
same time of a minoritizing discourse of kinds of persons. Because of the double
binds implicit in the space overlapped by universalizing and minoritizing models,
the stakes in matters of definitional control are extremely high.

Obviously, this analysis suggests as one indispensable approach to the traditional Euro-American canon a pedagogy that could treat it neither as something quite exploded nor as something quite stable. A canon seen to be
genuinely unified by the maintenance of a particular tension of homo/hetero-
sexual definition can scarcely be dismantled; but neither can it ever be treated as
the repository of reassuring "traditional" truths that could be made matter for
any settled consolidation or congratulation. Insofar as the problematics of
homo/heterosexual definition, in an intensely homophobic culture, are seen to

be precisely internal to the central nexuses of that culture, this canon must always be treated as a loaded one. . . .

Questions for Reflection, Discussion, and Writing

1. What are some of the implications (medical, cultural, historical, rhetorical) of the word "homosexual" in Euro-American discourse?
2. How are silence and the closet dependent terms, according to Sedgwick? What does Sedgwick's use of the example of the man and woman illustrate?
3. What is "homosexual panic"? How is it used, and what premises and belief systems support it, according to Sedgwick? What argument does she present against it?
4. Sedgwick offers a list that "retains the unaccounted-for potential to disrupt many forms of the available thinking about sex." The list is not conclusive, and doesn't account for all points in an individual's lifetime. What, according to Sedgwick, are the implications and importance of the list? What does it help identify?
5. What arguments are often used to dismiss homosexuals and discussion of homosexuality from historical and literary canons? What are the implications of such erasure?
6. What is the difference between sex, gender and sexuality? In what ways can they/do they intersect? In what ways are they mutually dependent as they are currently constructed and understood, according to Sedgwick?

Related Reading

Donald Morton, "The Politics of Queer Theory in the (Post) Modern Moment." *Genders 17* (Fall 1993): 121–150.

Elizabeth Weed, "The More Things Change." *differences: A Journal of Feminist Cultural Studies* 6.2+3 (1994): 249–259.

David Van Leer, "The Beast of the Closet: Sedgwick and the Knowledge of Homosexuality" in *The Queening of America*. NY: Routledge. 1995. 99–132.

Biddy Martin, "Sexualities Without Genders and Other Queer Utopias" in *Femininity Played Straight*. NY: Routledge. 1996. 71–94.

Michael Bacchus, "Eating Eve's Plums: On Citation and Hero-Worship" in *Queer Frontiers*. Ed., Joseph A. Boone, et al. Madison: U of Wisconsin P. 2000. 278–297.

David Clark and Stephen Barber, Ed. *Regarding Sedgwick: Essays on Queer Culture and Critical Theory*. New York: Routledge. 2002.

■

Who Is That *Queer* Queer? Exploring Norms around Sexuality, Race, and Class in Queer Theory

Ruth Goldman

Several years ago, when I came across the term "queer theory," I thought I had finally found my academic home, a theoretical space in which my voice would be welcome. Because I understood the term "queer" to represent any number of intersecting anti-normative identities, I expected queer theory to provide an appropriate framework in which to continue my explorations of the intersections between representations of race, sexuality, and gender (with an emphasis on bisexuality) in popular culture. However, I found that it was very difficult to apply existing queer theory to popular culture without collapsing some of the very nuances that I was trying to highlight. This led me to begin to consider some of the existing tensions and contradictions within and without queer theory, and in this article, I intend to explore the roots of some of these tensions and contradictions as well as to suggest some possible resolutions.[1] I am particularly interested in examining the ways in which rhetoric operates to produce a normative discourse within queer theory, which in turn serves to limit, in the words of Gloria Anzaldúa, "the ways in which we think about being queer."[2]

Although queer theory scholars have taken great pains to differentiate their work from lesbian and gay studies, lesbian and gay studies is now often referred to as queer studies (in order, theoretically, to make space for diversity), and both of these fields are frequently conflated with queer theory. But, while lesbian and gay studies and queer studies are primarily concerned with documenting past and current manifestations and implications of same-sex attractions, queer theory operates from the perspective that heterosexuality, or "normative" sexuality, could not exist without queer, or "anti-normative," sexualities. That is, that which is not normal works to define the normal. The fact that such very different approaches to scholarship are often lumped into the same category indicates that queer theory has many, sometimes conflicting, interpretations. To some people, queer theory represents simply another nebulous, abstract form of academic discourse, understood only through the signifier of "queer": a complex term which itself allows for many, sometimes contradictory, interpretations. Thus, depending on one's position and knowledge, queer theory lends itself to a variety of definitions, including: a theoretical perspective from which to challenge the normative; another term for lesbian and gay studies; another term for queer studies; a theory about queerness and queers (intentionally vague); another way that queer academics waste their time and taxpayers' money; or, at worst, judging simply from article titles like Eve Sedgwick's, "How to Bring Your Kids Up Gay," a plot by sexually perverted academics to recruit and indoctrinate unsuspecting young undergraduates.

In order to explore and clarify some of the conflicting ideas associated with queer theory, I decided to turn to the theory itself. I chose to examine a number of articles that address the subject of queer theory, as well as several articles and books that claim to be applying queer theory to various topics. I was interested in looking at both early and ongoing goals of queer theory, which include a strong commitment to creating/maintaining a theoretical space for polyphonic and diverse discourses that challenge heteronormativity.

At the core of any discussion of queer theory lies the question of rhetoric: the significance of the term "queer." Although queer theorists distanced themselves from the queer power movement, specifically Queer Nation, from the start,[3] I will be considering the evolution of the term "queer" along with the evolution of the field of queer theory, because of the way in which the two are inextricably linked in so many people's minds.

The term "queer" emphasizes the blurring of identities, and as a young bisexual activist who had encountered a great deal of resistance to the concept of bisexuality within lesbian and gay communities, it didn't take me long to embrace all that I perceived "queer" as representing. In fact, the queer movement/community was founded on principles of inclusivity and flexibility, summed up quite nicely by Elisabeth Daümer: "In the queer universe, to be queer implies that not everybody is queer in the same way. It implies a willingness to articulate their own queerness."[4]

As Daümer indicates, the signifier "queer" goes further than simply signaling an alternative sexuality; it offers a way in which to express many intersecting queer selves—in my case, to name just a few, as a bisexual,[5] a Jew, a feminist, an anti-capitalist, an anti-racist—all of which stand in opposition to powerful societal norms. And finally, as a strident reminder of difference, perversity, and a willingness to position oneself outside of the norm, the term "queer" simply makes many people uncomfortable. It is something most often uttered behind people's backs or yelled out of car windows, and thus its recuperative powers cannot be underestimated.

According to Jeffrey Escoffier, "Queer politics offers a way of cutting across race and gender lines. It implies the rejection of a minoritarian logic of toleration or simple interest-representation. Instead, queer politics represents an expansive impulse of inclusion; specifically, it requires a resistance to regimes of the normal."[6] However, we all must be aware of the risks inherent in embracing the term "queer" as a signifier of community, identity, politics, or theory. Gloria Anzaldúa argues that "queer" can be used/understood to disappear the very diversity which we are trying to highlight: "Queer is used as a false unifying umbrella which all 'queers' of all races, ethnicities and classes are shoved under. At times we need this umbrella to solidify our ranks against outsiders. But even when we seek shelter under it we must not forget that it homogenizes, erases our differences."[7] Although many people employ the term "queer" in part because it blurs—and some would argue erases—boundaries, Anzaldúa's point must be carefully considered. She herself chooses to identify as queer rather than as lesbian because of lesbian's Anglo-European roots and associations, but as "queer" gains currency, it is increasingly being appropriated and commodified, and thus increasingly risks collapsing into another term for white lesbians and gays, and ultimately white gay men. This is due to the fact that we live in a society in which the hegemonic discourses center around whites, men, and monosexuals, and so as "queer" becomes more popular *amongst* these "dominant" groups, it will increasingly come to *represent* these "dominant" groups.

Thus many lesbian feminists resist the term because they feel that it threatens to collapse gender and, in doing so, risks erasing awareness of gender-based oppression.[8] However, we are left with the fact that for many individuals like Anzaldúa and myself, who claim any number of anti-normative identities, the term "queer" best encompasses these identities. Additionally, "queer" provides an acceptable alternative for the many people who wish to try to avoid essentializing identities.

Contemporary queer theory embodies similar contradictions/tensions in relation to the term "queer." In his introduction to *Fear of a Queer Planet: Queer Politics and Social Theory*, Michael Warner gives queer theory the potential to engage in a radical polyphonic discourse: "For both academics and activists, 'queer' gets a critical edge by defining itself against the normal rather than the heterosexual and normal includes normal business in the academy."[9] However, as I shall illustrate, in many ways queer theory does tend to support the normal business of the academy.

In 1990, Jeffrey Escoffier wrote an article for *OUT/LOOK* that warned of a growing gap in lesbian and gay studies between "the field's 'new historicists' and the lesbians and gays of communities." According to Escoffier, these "new historicists" "emphasize[d] sophisticated interpretation of texts rather than the social history or the sociology of gay life." Additionally, Escoffier pointed out that this new field had thus far failed "to incorporate women and people of color into its ranks and analyses" and warned that the utilization of theoretical concepts from French postmodernists like Michel Foucault and Jacques Derrida "make the work of the new generation difficult and obscure to those outside of the academy."[10]

In 1991, Teresa de Lauretis introduced the term "queer theory" to encompass the work of these "new historicists" in the introduction to a special issue of *differences* entitled "Queer Theory: Lesbian and Gay Sexualities." Es-coffier's criticisms are especially interesting in light of the fact that de Lauretis chose to differentiate queer theory from Queer Nation by stating in an endnote to the issue's introduction that: "My 'queer,' had no relation to the Queer Na-tion group of whose existence I was ignorant at the time."[11] This serves to dis-tance *her* "queer"—and thus queer theory—from the version of "queer" widely circulating in lesbian, gay, bisexual, and transgender non-academic communi-ties. However, the fact that the term "queer" was chosen at a time when Queer Nation was active and getting frequent coverage in the lesbian, gay, and bisex-ual media, as well as in the mainstream media, has served to link queer theory in many people's minds with a growing queer power movement.

De Lauretis explains that the term "queer" was suggested to her by a 1989 conference whose proceedings were subsequently published in the book *How Do I Look? Queer Film and Video*. Interestingly enough, in the introduction to this book, the editorial collective freely exchange the term "queer film theory" with the term "lesbian and gay film theory." And nowhere is there an explana-tion as to why they chose the word "queer" for the title, implying that by then it had become an accepted and convenient terminology that allowed space for dif-ferences among lesbians and gays, while still maintaining the exclusivity of those identities.

How Do I Look? Queer Film and Video does contain several articles by and about "queer" people of color, but Gloria Anzaldúa argues that from the field's inception, it has been white middle-class lesbians and gay men "who have pro-duced queer theory and for the most part their theories make abstractions of us colored queers. They control the production of queer knowledge in the acad-emy and in the activist communities. . . . They police the queer person of color with theory. . . . Their theories limit the ways we think about being queer."[12] Part of the problem here lies in the fact that, as Anzaldúa herself points out, "queer" can serve as a term that erases difference. So that unless we strive to elaborate its meaning whenever we use it in our theories, it becomes like theo-retical tofu: it will simply absorb the meaning of whatever particular aspect or aspects of queerness we are addressing. However, Oscar Montero, in his article "Latino Queers and National Identity" considers this characteristic of queer theory to be a positive one:

> "Queer" (from the German quer: oblique) puts the spectacle back in "theory" (theorema = spectacle); in other words, it puts a number of slants into any reading, and these slants are not always clearly defined. . . . Queer theory skirts identity, sometimes literally and brings other identities, ethnic, racial, and national into play.[13]

I would argue that while queer theory certainly has the potential for such an impact, it fails to do so at present, because it is being generated mainly by white academics. Just as the academy has been structured around heterosexual-ity in such a way as to limit discourses on other sexualities, it has been similarly structured around whiteness. Thus scholars of color, by virtue of the fact that they are not white, find themselves in an oppositional stance to the academy itself. And, as a result, many lesbian, bisexual, queer, and gay scholars of color choose to focus on issues of race and not issues of gender and sexuality. All the anthologies on queer theory include work by lesbians and gays of color, but we rarely find white lesbian or gay theorists discussing how intersections between anti-normative identities inform or affect one's queer perspective. If queer theory were to promote these types of discourses, it might then provide a more welcoming space for lesbian, gay, bisexual, and queer scholars of color.

Teresa de Lauretis calls for contributions to queer theory by other than white lesbians and gays:

> The difference made by race in self-representation and identity argue for the necessity to examine, question, or contest the usefulness and/or the limitations of current discourses on lesbian and gay sexualities. . . . These differences urge the reframing of the question of queer theory from different perspectives, histories, experiences, and in different terms.[14]

The fundamental problem with this line of reasoning is that it leaves the burden of dealing with difference on the people who are themselves different, while simultaneously allowing white academics to continue to construct a discourse of silence around race and other queer perspectives. Thus those of us who write from such "other" queer perspectives must set ourselves up in opposition to the norm within queer theory. We are forced to essentialize our identities by drawing attention to the ways in which certain parts of ourselves are consistently being left out of the discourse.

As I have indicated, one of the major problems lies in the use of rhetoric. The term "queer" has now been so wholeheartedly embraced by lesbian and gay academic and non-academic communities alike that, in many cases, it has simply become an abbreviated way of saying "lesbian and gay" or, less often, "lesbian, gay, and bisexual." However, as Montero, Escoffier, and de Lauretis all point out, queer theory is theoretically structured around the concept of intersecting identities. And, in fact, as Judith Butler explains, all of us take-on or "perform" many different identities in any given day.[15]

Relying heavily on postmodernist theorists such as Foucault and Derrida, queer theory aims to transform power structures by altering discourses about sexuality and gender or, in Butler's terms, "disrupting" "performances" of heterosexuality,[16] and thus disrupting the hegemony of heteropatriarchy. For example, when we choose to view (or "queer") an advertisement with two women as representing a lesbian couple, we disrupt the flow of the notoriously heterosexist world of advertising. However, these disruptions also have the potential to be significantly undermined or even collapsed when undertaken from a queer perspective that brings into play notions of more than just gender and sexuality. In Gloria Anzaldúa's words, "Identity is not a bunch of little cubbyholes stuffed respectively with intellect, race, sex, class, vocation, gender. Identity flows between, over, aspects of a person. Identity is a river—a process."[17] Even though the concept might get lost in individual queer theory scholarship, definitions of queer theory do consider identity to be multivalent.

Thus we must ask ourselves why, in a theory that intends to problematize identity and challenge the normative, we often foreground sexuality and gender (and the latter only as a theoretical concept—the experiences of transgendered people are rarely discussed) to the exclusion of all other notions of identity. For example, those of us who are white tend not to dwell on our race, perhaps because this would only serve to normalize us—reduce our queerness, if you will. However, by failing to consider the ways in which such aspects of our identity inform our queer perspectives, we also fail to disrupt the hegemonic discourses around race and other anti-normative categories/identities. And, despite claims to the contrary, this is one of the ways in which queer theory continues to practice normal business in the academy.

At present, queer theory is sufficiently narrow to almost prohibit a discourse that allows for considerations of the multiplicity of identities possible within the term "queer." Alexander Doty's work *Making Things Perfectly Queer: Interpreting Mass Culture* provides an excellent example of this phenomenon. Doty's book serves as a ground-breaking text in its convincing use of queer theory to destabilize—or queer—texts produced within the very heterosexist medium of television. However, in his introduction, Doty states that "[u]ltimately, queerness should challenge and confuse our understanding and uses of sexual and gender categories."[18] By defining the progressive potential of queerness as such, he participates in imposing the type of limitations on queerness that, as Anzaldúa points out, characterize most of the work of white queer theorists. In fact, when Doty does examine television shows like *The Jack Benny Show* or *Peewee's Playhouse*, he mentions their racist and/or misogynist aspects without undertaking a truly critical analysis of them.[19] He does this because these aspects of television are neither on his main agenda in writing this book, nor on the main agenda of queer theory in general.

One book cannot, of course, cover everything, and Doty's book does provide some excellent groundwork, but if queer theory is to truly challenge the "normal," it must provide a framework in which to challenge racist, misogynist, and other oppressive discourses/norms, as well as those that are heterosexist and homophobic. We must not simply challenge heteronormativity but must instead question the very system that sustains heteronormativity.

By examining a performance by Madonna which took place at the 1993 MTV Music Video awards, I intend to provide an example which illuminates the complexity that queer theory allows when the queer discourse is broadened. Madonna performed a piece entitled "This Is Not a Love Song," which featured Madonna and two other women wearing top hats and tails performing opposite three women wearing only bathing suits. In casting women opposite one another in such "traditional" male/female garb, Madonna was obviously playing with lesbian butch/femme roles. And if we were to apply a queer reading which centered only around gender and sexuality to this performance, we would certainly find it a queer performance, in the sense of being positively oppositional.

We could then argue, as Doty does, that such a performance would have the effect of queering the audience, however temporarily. We could also argue that, as queers, the portrayal of same-sex couples is important for our own well-being; that is, any kind of visibility provides us with reassurance that there are others out there like us. And finally, we might argue that watching such queer couplings would provide pleasure to many lesbians and bisexual women. In all of these ways, Madonna's performance would be operating to disrupt the heteronormative discourse within popular culture.

However, when we examine the performance from a more complex queer perspective that includes issues of race and class, we get entirely different readings. The butches are played by Madonna, another white woman, and an African-American woman, and all of the femmes are played by Asian-American women. In addition, the actions and lyrics within the performance consistently set the Asian-American women up as bad and deserving of punishment. The refrain is: "You're never going to see me cry again . . . Bye-bye, baby, bye-bye" and includes Madonna chanting, "This is not a love song." At one point, Madonna and the other butches grab the femmes' faces and at another, simulate rough sexual penetration. The butches physically control the femmes, and, since Madonna sings the lyrics, they control the language and the story as well. The fact that Madonna chose Asian-American women as the femmes reinforces stereotypes of Asian women as the passive, exotic, and feminine "other." It also mocks the fact that Asian women have been economically exploited as "comfort girls" for American servicemen for many years now.

That Madonna would "do" lesbian butch/femme in this nationally televised performance at a time when "lesbian chic" was all the rage—around the same time that lesbians appeared on the cover of *Newsweek* and k.d. lang and Cindy Crawford did the famous *Vanity Fair* spread—might seem a victory to anyone who champions visibility and the idea of queering popular culture (and having pop culture queer society). However, since Madonna has insisted on labeling herself as heterosexual, it can also be viewed as another of Madonna's cultural commodification efforts—what bell hooks refers to as "eating the other."[20] This same type of commodification would apply to the use of Asian-American women in her performance. Thus, were we to claim this performance as queer without qualifying it, we would be complicit in allowing racist, classist, and misogynistic discourses to continue uninterrupted. This performance may be queer in its use of same-sex couples and female- to-male cross-dressing, but it is normalized in its use of classism, sexual racism, and commodification, and any disruption of the heteronormative discourse would be mitigated by these factors. As Donald Morton argues:

> The emancipation of the word "queer" cannot be achieved without a radical transformation of the regimes of labor, family, . . . and other social structures that pro-

duce homophobia in the first place. . . . [H]omophobia is . . . a structure of exploitation linked—not eccentrically, locally, or contingently, but systemically—to other social practices.[21]

If we truly want to create theories that will enable us to eradicate homophobia and heterosexism, we must understand the ways in which they are linked to all systems of oppression and undertake discourses that seek to undermine/expose that entire system.

Another way in which existing queer theory serves to limit the ways in which we conceptualize queerness is in its preservation of binary notions of sexuality. In the introduction to the special issue of *differences* referred to above, de Lauretis calls for queer theory to undertake "the necessary critical work of deconstructing our own discourses and their constructed silences."[22] However, bisexuality, along with race, continues to be one of the "constructed silences" within queer theory, as it is within lesbian and gay studies. Although queer theory indicates a significant ideological shift from lesbian and gay studies, it has carried with it the essentializing categories of "lesbian" and "gay," and although queer theory scholarship sometimes includes superficial mentions of bisexuality, it is often disappeared at best and disarticulated at worst. Thus, in some ways, bisexuality has become the contemporary version of "the love that dare not speak its name."

Michael Warner's anthology, *Fear of a Queer Planet*, is notable for its emphasis on community politics and social theory, but for the most part, it fails to incorporate understandings of diversity. There are articles written by and about lesbians and gays of color, but bisexuality is mentioned in only one essay. For example, in his introduction, Warner states that "queers live as queers, as lesbians, as gays, as homosexuals, in contexts other than sex."[23] Although some might argue that "queer" could include bisexual and, as I will illustrate, there are many bisexuals who identify as queer, the fact that Warner uses other essentializing categories, such as "lesbian" and "gay," renders bisexuality noticeably absent from his equation. This exclusion of bisexuality from discussions concerning issues of sexuality and gender has been typical of queer theory, unless the theory is being written by bisexuals themselves.

This is especially disturbing in light of the fact that early queer theorists like Teresa de Lauretis claimed that queer theory intended "to both transgress and transcend . . . or at the very least problematize" monolithic categories like "lesbian" and "gay."[24] In pointing out the necessity of finding new ways to conceptualize our alternative sexualities, de Lauretis was primarily referring to the fact that the terms "lesbian" and "gay" (because of their Anglo-European roots) are considered to be white terms, but in employing the term "queer," she was also bringing into question the whole notion of identity. Interestingly enough, bisexuals, especially feminist bisexuals, have been using the concept of bisexuality to pose similar questions and challenges for a number of years now. For instance, Elisabeth Daümer argues that bisexuality offers a unique "epistemological as well as ethical vantage point from which we can examine and deconstruct the bipolar framework of gender and sexuality."[25] She goes on to argue that the "ambiguous position" of bisexuals "can also lead to a deep appreciation of the differences among people—whether cultural, sexual, gendered—since any attempt to construct a coherent identity in opposition to another would flounder on the multiplicity of at times conflicting identifications generated by the bisexual point of view."[26]

Compare Daümer's comments about the concept of bisexuality to Rosemary Hennessy's definition of queer theory:

> Queer theory calls into question obvious categories (man, woman, latina, jew, butch, femme), oppositions (man vs. woman, heterosexual vs. homosexual), or equations (gender = sex) upon which conventional notions of sexuality and identity rely.[27]

Theoretically then, queer theory and bisexual feminist theory seem to have much in common. Thus I was surprised to find that queer theory—except that written by bisexuals themselves—consistently ignored bisexuality and rarely quoted bisexual theorists.

The notable exception is Alexander Doty, who includes a lengthy endnote on bisexuality in *Making Things Perfectly Queer.*

> Looking through this book, I realize I have given rather cursory attention to specifically bisexual positions. Since examining bisexuality seems crucial in many ways to theorizing nongay and nonlesbian queerness—indeed, some see bisexuality as queerness—I consider the absence of any extended discussion of bisexuality and mass culture a major omission.[28]

He goes on to quite provocatively suggest that we might consider texts that contain both opposite-sex and same-sex narratives as bisexual texts. When I questioned him as to why he initially ignored bisexuality, he explained that, because there was so little existing scholarly work on bisexuality, he wasn't quite sure how to theorize about it in relation to popular culture.[29] The fact that Doty's discussion of bisexuality is contained in an endnote further emphasizes the fact that bisexuality has not been a central part of discourses within queer theory. However, the fact that Doty does choose to broaden his own discourse on queerness to include bisexuality can serve as an example/foundation for other queer theorists to build upon.

Bisexuality is sometimes mentioned as an identity within queer theory, but it remains relatively invisible, in part because of resistance to viewing bisexuality as an identity on its own, separate from both heterosexuality and homosexuality. In fact, in a discussion on lesbian and gay spectatorship, Judith Mayne, one of the contributors to *How Do I Look? Queer Film and Video*, characterizes bisexuality as " 'wishy-washy' in the sense that such a subject-object position carries very little political impact in our present society."[30] In contrast, bisexual sociologist Paula Rust proclaims that bisexuals have the potential "to radically alter the way we think about not only gender and sexuality, but also the nature of power itself."[31] In other words, since a belief in monosexuality and binary notions of gender are built into the very foundations of this society, the concept of bisexuality threatens the very structure of heteropatriarchy. Thus I would argue that bisexuality actually carries a phenomenal amount of political impact, and this is one reason why it encounters so much resistance as a concept and an identity.

One of the few discussions that I came across which actually considered bisexuality as a political concept was an exchange that took place on the e-mail list "Queer Studies." In the course of this discussion, Eve Sedgwick claimed that bisexuality as a political concept, while providing a place for "the many people who are not fixed or exclusive in gender-of-object choice," ultimately fails to adequately challenge existing models of sexuality, because these paradigms are structured around gender-of-object choice.[32] Sedgwick argued that using bisexuality, as currently conceived, would simply function as an addition to, or completion of, the existing paradigm, so that what is now a dichotomy would become a trichotomy. What Sedgwick fails to consider, though, is that the concept of bisexuality could function to disrupt and further open a paradigm that depends on binary oppositions. Indeed, Gilbert Herdt argues that "the third is emblematic of other possible combinations that transcend dimorphism."[33] Thus, in the case of bisexuality, the third becomes significant, not in and of itself, but as a reminder that there are more than just two ways to conceptualize sexuality.

Sedgwick goes on to argue that, in posing the questions of "the relation of bisexual to gay/lesbian" and "the relation of bisexual to queer, . . . bisexuality as a political concept could function to break boundaries in the first context and yet to preserve them in the second." This is based on the premise that the meaning behind the utilization of "queer" as a political concept is to challenge "the decisiveness of gender-of-object choice as a way of understanding sexuality."[34] Certainly part of this argument revolves around the question of terminology—that is, the "bi" in "bisexuality" points us directly to binary notions of gender and sexuality. Rebecca Kaplan explains that:

> The very existence of the word "bisexual" is based on a false belief in sexual dichotomy. . . . The word implies that there are two (and only two) groups, groups that are discrete, discontinuous and mutually exclusive. . . . It also indicates that this particular method of grouping people is the single most important form of categorization.[35]

Many bisexuals and bisexual theorists have expressed discomfort with the term for these very reasons. Paula Rust suggests that "what we need to do . . . is to remove the characteristic of partner sex from its privileged position altogether so that we are free to choose our own ways of defining ourselves and choosing our partners." She goes on to suggest that bisexuals rename themselves "pansensuals," in order to avoid emphasizing "biological sex as the basis for sexual identification," as well as to avoid the term "bi," which suggests binary attraction and returns us to the notion that we need to be either/or or both. The term "pansensuals" also allows us to conceptualize a broader notion of sexuality and creates a category exclusively for those of us who reject binary notions of gender and sexuality.[36]

Many of Rust's arguments for the use of the term "pansensual" could be made for the term "queer," but, as with any group, self-identified queers encompass a wide range of people, who do not necessarily share the same ideological beliefs. And, as I have been arguing, the term "queer" has its own set of limitations, most significantly the power to collapse difference, compounded by its current interchangeability with the categories of lesbian and gay, or lesbian, gay, and bisexual. In my own experience, I have found that to argue from a queer perspective, as opposed to a bisexual perspective, lends added weight by eliminating the troublesome word "bisexual," while also enabling me to argue from a perspective that does not carry the kind of negative stereotypes and misunderstandings that bisexuality does.[37] Additionally, many bisexuals believe that bisexuality and queerness are fundamentally linked. As Carol Queen observes, "It is the queer in me that . . . lets me question the lies we were all told about who women are, who men are. . . . The queer in all of us clamors for pleasure or change, will not be tamed or regulated, wants a say in the creation of a new reality."[38]

Since many bisexuals, like myself, are attracted to people in spite of their gender and not because of it,[39] and the gender of object choice (based on binary notions of gender and sexuality) is what informs the sexual identity of lesbians, gays, and heterosexuals, then bisexuality is nothing *but* queer, odd, different— *existing in opposition to and challenging the norm*. And, if we understand "queer" to represent an identity/community/theoretical space that is fluid and specifically defined only through its opposition/resistance to heteronormativity, then bisexuals and bisexuality would certainly be included within such a framework. However, if we understand "queer" to mean only lesbian and gay, then bisexuals become *queer* queers, standing outside the norms of queerness. Similarly, if we simply define queerness as anti-normative modes of gender and sexuality, then claiming other anti-normative identities besides sexual preference, such as race, ethnicity, or class—to name a few—would also render one a *queer* queer. This is not to fall into reductive arguments about the hierarchy of oppression, but simply to point out the ways in which we manage to establish norms even when we are struggling to resist and challenge them.

The focus on lesbian and gay sexualities and a constructed silence around race operate to establish part of the norm within queer theory. Another part of the norm that needs to be addressed involves class. Here I mean class to encompass those of us who position ourselves within the academy, thus occupying a certain intellectual, if not economic, class. In a discussion about queer theory as it is presented in *Fear of a Queer Planet*, Jeffrey Escoffier points out that: "[t]o identify the problem of queer politics as *normalization* rather than *intolerance* suggests that, overwhelmingly, the power of homophobia resides not in the power of repression and physical violence, but in normalizing moral and scientific discourses."[40]

And this is where queer theory has consistently failed to make its case outside of a rather narrow academic community—largely because the "norm" in queer theory is also about privilege. As academics, we often write theories onto the bodies of "others," and while we are certainly at risk of suffering discrimination and violence based on our sexual orientation, the academy is in many ways a protected and insular environment. A large number of academic institutions have anti-discrimination clauses that include sexual orientation, and more and more are instituting domestic partnership benefits for same-sex couples. Unfortunately, such basic rights are not found within many other working environments. Because of the relative safety of our surroundings, some of us are able to direct our energies to theorizing our sexualities and in doing so, many of us focus on texts, and not actual lived experience.[41]

The threat of violence combined with the fact that anti-lesbian, -gay, and -bisexual legislation is appearing all over the country leads many queer community activists to resent academicians' persistence in working on theories that have no obvious practical applications. While extremely important, our efforts to "counteract dominant discourses"[42] are centered within the academy and seem at odds with the political activism that takes place outside it. As Jeffrey Escoffier notes, "Queer theory and the cultural studies paradigm are mapping the discursive regimes of power/knowledge that constitute the queer, the homosexual and the sexual pervert. These regimes of cultural hegemony are immensely powerful, but the performative character of discourse does not exhaust the forms of domination that shape the lives of homosexuals and other sexual perverts."[43] In order to be a truly progressive field, to be what Rosemary Hennessy calls "an in-your-face rejection of the proper response to heteronormativity, a version of acting up,"[44] queer theory has to include theories that we queers, in our multiplicity of identities, can use in more than just our academic lives.

By expanding the ways that we think about queerness, we will also be opening up our theories to a wider audience. If one of the inherent goals of queer theory is to undermine heteronormative hegemonic discourses—to reconceptualize the ways that we think about the relationships between power and the heteropatriarchal norm—then it behooves us to create and utilize theories that will pass through the doors of the ivory tower and spill into the streets and minds of queers everywhere.

As I have illustrated in this essay, existing queer theory, despite attempts to avoid normativity, harbors a normative discourse around race, sexuality, and class. Those of us who fall outside of this normativity are thus rendered *queer* queers and must position ourselves and our work in opposition to it. However, I want to make clear that I believe that the work that is being done within queer theory is quite significant, and I am by no means suggesting that it should be dismissed because of its limitations. What I am suggesting is that we strive to continuously problematize that which we have created—that we identify the constructed silences within our work and transform them into meaningful discourses.

Notes

1. This chapter was supported in part by a grant from the Student Research Allocations Committee of the Graduate Student Association at the University of New
   Mexico.
2. Gloria Anzaldúa, "To(o) Queer the Writer: Loca, escrita y chicana," *In Versions:
   Writing by Dykes, Queers and Lesbians*, ed. Betsy Warland (Vancouver: Press Gang,
   1991), 251.
3. See Teresa de Lauretis, Introduction to *differences* 3 (Summer 1991): xvii.
4. Elisabeth Daümer, "Queer Ethics, or the Challenge of Bisexuality to Lesbian
   Ethics," *Hypatia* 7 (Fall 1992): 100.
5. I use "bisexuality" because, as an identity, it best represents my dissatisfaction with
   the narrow confines of binary notions of sexuality and gender. Throughout this
   chapter, I find myself falling back into essentialist notions of identity in order to
   make my points clear, but because of the language currently available with which
   to discuss sexuality, I felt that I had no choice.
6. Jeffrey Escoffier, "Under the Sign of the Queer," *Found Object* (Fall 1994): 135.
7. Anzaldúa, "To(o) Queer the Writer," 250.
8. The term "queer" is intended by many to challenge binary notions of gender. But
   because women as a socially constructed category are still subject to both sexism
   and misogyny, many lesbian feminists quite understandably feel that it is important to recognize that gender categories remain an enforced reality.
9. Michael Warner, Introduction to *Fear of a Queer Planet: Queer Politics and Social
   Theory* (Minneapolis: University of Minnesota Press, 1993), xxvi.
10. Jeffrey Escoffier, "Inside the Ivory Closet: The Challenges Facing Lesbian and
    Gay Studies," *OUT/LOOK* 3 (Fall 1990): 40–48.
11. de Lauretis, Introduction, xvii.
12. Anzaldúa, "To(o) Queer the Writer," 251.
13. Oscar Montero, "Latino Queers and National Identity," *Radical America* 24, no. 4
    (April 1993): 16–17.
14. de Lauretis, Introduction, x.
15. Judith Butler, "Imitation and Gender Insubordination," *The Lesbian and Gay Stud-
    ies Reader*, ed. Henry Abelove, Michèle Aina Barale, and David M. Halperin (New
    York: Routledge, 1993), 308.
16. Ibid., 315.
17. Anzaldúa, "To(o) Queer the Writer," 252–53.
18. Alexander Doty, *Making Things Perfectly Queer: Interpreting Mass Culture* (Min-
    neapolis: University of Minnesota Press, 1993), xvii.
19. Doty does condemn misogyny and includes a lengthy endnote in which he asserts
    the importance of differentiating between straight male misogyny and gay male
    misogyny, but he does not consider just how misogyny (in any form) might affect
    the transformative powers of a queer(ed) text.
20. bell hooks, "Eating the Other," *Black Looks: Race and Representation* (Boston: South
    End Press, 1992), 21.
21. Donald Morton, "The Politics of Queer Theory in the (Post)Modern Moment,"
    Genders 17 (Fall 1993): 122.
22. de Lauretis, Introduction, iv.
23. Warner, *Fear of a Queer Planet*, vii.

24. de Lauretis, Introduction, v. De Lauretis uses words like "transgress" and "transcend" as part of an ongoing debate about the usefulness and truthfulness of identities, but it seems ridiculous to suggest that we can transcend/transgress terms that inform our identities, as well as endanger our lives/families/careers, in that they are foisted upon us by a heterosexist society whenever we act queerly. Despite arguments that we should do away with identities/labels, the fact remains that many of us structure our lives around these concepts and will continue to use them, whatever theorists say. This is not intended as an argument against the term "queer" (which is itself understood/claimed by some as an identity), but simply a cautionary note that we need to continuously problematize it.
25. Daümer, "Queer Ethics," 98.
26. Ibid., 98.
27. Rosemary Hennessy, "Queer Theory: A Review of the *differences* Special Issue and Wittig's *The Straight Mind*," *Signs* 18 (Summer 1993): 964.
28. Doty, *Making Things Perfectly Queer*, 105.
29. I spoke with Doty about this in April 1994 at the "Console-ing Passions" conference in Tucson, Arizona. Interestingly enough, at the same conference, Maria Pramaggiore presented a paper entitled "Double Crossing Identities: Constructing Queerness in Contemporary Television and Film," in which she used Doty's idea of bisexuality as the mediating force in homoerotic "straight" texts to analyze *Singing in the Rain* and other movies. The only published work that I'm aware of that deals with bisexuality and popular culture is Robin Wood's *Hollywood from Vietnam to Reagan* (1986), which considers bisexuality more as a concept (derived from Freud) than as a viable identity.
30. Judith Mayne, discussion following "Dorothy Azner and Female Authorship," *How Do I Look? Queer Film and Video*, ed. Bad Object Choices (Seattle: Bay Press, 1992), 137.
31. Paula Rust, "Who Are We and Where Do We Go from Here? Conceptualizing Bisexuality," *Closer to Home: Bisexuality and Feminism*, ed. Elizabeth Reba Weise (Seattle: Seal Press, 1992), 306.
32. Eve Sedgwick, "Queer Studies List," August 17, 1994.
33. Gilbert Herdt, *Third Sex, Third Gender: Beyond Sexual Dimorphism in Culture and History* (New York: Zone, 1994), 20. Thanks to Rebecca Kaplan for bringing my attention to Herdt's ideas by starting a discussion on the topic on the "Bisexual Theory" e-mail list.
34. Ibid., 20, emphasis in original text.
35. Rebecca Kaplan, "Compulsory Heterosexuality and the Bisexual Existence: Toward a Bisexual Feminist Understanding of Heterosexism," *Closer to Home*, 274.
36. Rust, "Who Are We and Where Do We Go from Here?," 299–304.
37. However, I realize that the term "queer" is rapidly losing such a status, for as it gains a wider circulation, it becomes more problematic, especially as it is increasingly being understood as a "male" term.
38. Carol Queen, "The Queer in Me," *Bi Any Other Name: Bisexual People Speak Out*, ed. Loraine Hutchins and Lani Kaahumanu (Boston: Alyson, 1991), 20–21.
39. I realize that I am once again encountering a terminology problem. To say that one is attracted to someone in spite of, but not because of, their gender is infinitely problematic in a society that organizes itself around gender. However, what

I am trying to express here is that for many bisexuals, gender is not the primary organizational concept in their attractions to people.

40. Escoffier, "Under the Sign of the Queer," 135.
41. I realize that the academy is in fact structured in such a way as to promote these types of scholarship: it is what many of us are paid to do, and to shift our focus away from such "traditional" scholarship could mean jeopardizing one's career. That notwithstanding, we must consider why it is that the academy promotes such scholarship; our exclusive language alone often serves to effectively limit the message that we are trying to disseminate.
42. de Lauretis, Introduction, iii.
43. Escoffier, "Under the Sign of the Queer," 141.
44. Hennessy, "Queer Theory," 967.

Questions for Reflection, Discussion, and Writing

1. How does Goldman understand "the significance of the term 'queer'"? What multiple perspectives operate in her analysis of this word?
2. Along what lines and why does Ruth Goldman think we should expand our ideas of queer theory?
3. What critique of the Madonna music video does Goldman present? In what ways does she claim Madonna might be queering norms about sexuality and gender? What other lenses or viewpoints does Goldman offer, and why does she offer the Madonna video as a microcosm of her argument/point?
4. Why does Goldman think bisexuality presents a unique opportunity to queer other systems? What issues, problems, and sexual conceptualizations does she think bisexuality presents and represents? Why does she think "pansexual" might be a more useful word?
5. What does Goldman identify as the major problems in the ways which the academy has understood and produced queer theory?

Related Reading

Lisa Duggan, "Scholars and Sense," *Village Voice Literary Supplement*, June 1992. 27.

Jeffrey Escoffier, "Under the Sign of the Queer: Cultural Studies and Social Theory" in *American Homo*. Berkeley: University of California Press. 1998. 173–185.

Joane Nagel, "Ethnicity and Sexuality." *Annual Review of Sociology* 26 (2000): 107–133.

Judith Raiskin, "Inverts and Hybrids: Lesbian Rewritings of Sexual and Racial Identities" in *The Lesbian Postmodern*. Laura Doan, Ed. NY: Columbia UP. 1994. 156–172.

Janice L. Ristock and Catherine G. Taylor, Eds. *Inside the Academy and Out: Lesbian/Gay/Queer Studies and Social Action*. Toronto: U of Toronto Press. 1998.

William G. Tierney, "Queer Theory as Cultural Politics" in *Academic Outlaws: Queer Theory and Cultural Studies in the Academy*. Thousand Oaks, CA.: Sage Publications. 1997. 19–44.

Robyn Wiegman, "Queering the Academy" in *The Gay '90s: Disciplinary and Interdisciplinary Formations in Queer Studies*. Eds., Thomas Foster, Carol Siegel and Ellen E. Berry. NY: NYUP. 1997. 3–22.

SECTION TWO

The Sociopolitical Origins of Queer

Though the preponderance of queer theory is currently housed within the halls of academia as an emerging field of inquiry concerned with sexuality, gender, performance, and representational strategies, many of its most radical premises were developed by young activists in the 1980s who designed strategies of public theater as political protest. One could point to the 1978 murder of San Francisco selectman Harvey Milk and to the acquittal in the following year of his assassin, State Senator Dan White, as a catalyzing event in the consciousness of queers about the viability of hope for assimilation and social acceptance in the United States. But it was truly the initial diagnosis of AIDS in 1982 and the subsequent governmental policies of denial, neglect, and demonization of people with AIDS (PWAs) that galvanized young queers into political strategies that foregrounded public confrontation, a refusal to accede to the status quo, and an uncompromising rejection of all the subtle and pervasive pressures of normativity throughout culture.

Throughout the 1980s, lesbians and gay men watched as their friends, lovers, business and life partners began to die wasting, agonizing deaths. At first there was no name for the disease that was clearly ravaging queer communities; it was known initially as "gay cancer" and then as GRID, (Gay-Related-Immune Deficiency). In 1983, the virus was identified as HIV (Human Immunodeficiency Virus) and AIDS became a fixture of media and public attention. In the middle of the decade, some statisticians were convinced that over 50 percent of the gay male population had been infected with the virus. The death tolls began to mount, decimating the cultural enclaves of theater, art, dance, and fashion. And yet the administration of Ronald Reagan purposely ignored the health crisis within its midst, refusing to provide funding for research and education as the years of the decade rolled on. Though the gay and lesbian community took immediate measures to attend to its own needs—beginning hospice care, like the Shanti program in San Francisco, instituting its own educational outreach efforts to promote safe sex, and memorializing its dead in the Names Quilt Project—by 1987 the situation was so grim and unrelenting that three hundred young activists in New York City decided to create a new organization to fight for queer human rights, the AIDS Coalition to Unleash

Power, or ACT UP. The strategies of ACT UP were theatrical and media-savvy, rooted in the tradition of peaceful civil disobedience. Yet their outrage at the genocide perpetrated by government inaction, their clearly articulated analysis of discrimination in both the medical profession and in civic life, and their refusal to accept the status quo galvanized an entire generation of queer youth. SILENCE = DEATH became a logo of the movement, announcing to the world at large that U.S. queers would never relinquish their strong voices or their active presence in the nation's landscape.

ACT UP groups proliferated and spawned other loose collections of protest groups such as the Lavender Menace, the Lesbian Avengers, and, near the end of the 1980s, Queer Nation. No longer content to persuade heterosexual culture to recognize the humanity of gay and lesbian people, young activists rallied around the cry, "We're here, we're queer, get used to it!" Embracing and flaunting their sexual difference, activists staged kiss-ins at malls and neighborhood bars, protested outside of public schools whose homophobic curriculum damaged the development of healthy and self-affirming queer children, printed broadsides proclaiming "I Hate Straights" and warned in rallies that "Queers Bash Back!" Profoundly dissatisfied with and divorced from an increasingly hostile mainstream culture, Queer Nation underscored the psychic and social separation of a sexual subgroup from its (dis)inclusion within the nation at large. Clearly, remaining in, or retreating to, the closet was no longer an option in this changed political climate.

Nowhere was this clearer than in the practice of "outing." First introduced by Michaelangelo Signorile in his column in the glossy gay monthly, *The Advocate*, the outing of queer individuals in politics and in the entertainment industry occurred when activists and self-proclaimed watchdogs like Signorile made the judgment that certain individuals were promoting policy or engaged in activities that harmed queers. Thus Jodie Foster was outed as a lesbian because of her participation in what many queers felt was the homophobic nature of Jonathan Demme's 1990 film, *The Silence of the Lambs*. So, too, Pentagon spokesman Pete Williams, who hid his own homosexuality while promoting anti-gay policy in the military. Signorile defended outing from critics who complained about the violation of personal privacy by insisting that hypocrisy was the organizing principle of outing, and that those queers who closeted themselves and then participated in anti-gay activities deserved to have their covers blown, and in both a dramatic and public fashion.

The religious right responded to these new developments with a sustained backlash that is still evident in the spate of anti-gay legislation that continues well into the twenty-first century. Yet the openness about sexual orientation and life choices, the absolute refusal to feel shame about being queer, and the mocking disregard for the ignorance and prejudice that underlies homophobia have all had a powerful and even a profound effect on the ways queers are represented in the media and in educational curricula some two decades later. There is no going back. Queers are here to stay, and we have the courageous activists of the 1980s and 1990s to thank for it.

■

AIDS, Homophobia, and Biomedical Discourse: An Epidemic of Signification*

Paula A. Treichler

An Epidemic of Signification

In multiple, fragmentary, and often contradictory ways we struggle to achieve some sort of understanding of AIDS, a reality that is frightening, widely publicized, and yet finally neither directly nor fully knowable. AIDS is no different in this respect from other linguistic constructions, which, in the commonsense view of language, are thought to transmit preexisting ideas and represent real-world entities and yet, in fact, do neither. For the nature of the relationship between language and reality is highly problematic; and *AIDS* is not merely an invented label, provided to us by science and scientific naming practices, for a clear-cut disease entity caused by a virus. Rather, the very nature of AIDS is constructed through language and in particular through the discourses of medicine and science; this construction is "true" or "real" only in certain specific ways—for example, insofar as it successfully guides research or facilitates clinical control over the illness.[2] The name *AIDS* in part *constructs* the disease and helps make it intelligible. We cannot therefore look "through" language to determine what AIDS "really" is. Rather we must explore the site where such determinations *really* occur and intervene at the point where meaning is created: in language.

*Reprinted from *Cultural Studies*, vol. 1, no. 3 (October 1987), pp. 263–305; minor changes and corrections have been made for the present publication; information and references have not been updated. Research for this essay was funded in part by grants from the National Council of Teachers of English and the University of Illinois Graduate College Research Board. My thanks to Teresa Mangum, research assistant on this project; to Stephen J. Kaufman, M. Kerry O'Banion, Eve Kosofsky Sedgwick, and Michael Witkovsky for guidance and insight; and to those who have kept me in touch with AIDS developments in diverse fields. An earlier version of this essay was presented at the annual meeting of the Modern Language Association, New York, December 1986.

[2]Discussing the validity of their interpretation of everyday life in a science laboratory, Bruno Latour and Steve Woolgar claim, similarly, that the "value and status of any text (construction, fact, claim, story, this account) depend on more than its supposedly 'inherent' qualities. . . . The degree of accuracy (or fiction) of an account depends on what is subsequently made of the story, not on the story itself" (*Laboratory Life: The Construction of Scientific Facts*, Cambridge, England, Cambridge University Press, 1985, p. 284).

Of course, AIDS is a real disease syndrome, damaging and killing real human beings. Because of this, it is tempting—perhaps in some instances imperative—to view science and medicine as providing a discourse about AIDS closer to its "reality" than what we can provide ourselves. Yet the AIDS epidemic—with its genuine potential for global devastation—is simultaneously an epidemic of a transmissible lethal disease and an epidemic of meanings or signification.[3] Both epidemics are equally crucial for us to understand, for, try as we may to treat AIDS as "an infectious disease" and nothing more, meanings continue to multiply wildly and at an extraordinary rate.[4] This epidemic of meanings is readily apparent in the chaotic assemblage of understandings of AIDS that by now exists. The mere enumeration of some of the ways AIDS has been characterized suggests its enormous power to generate meanings:

1. An irreversible, untreatable, and invariably fatal infectious disease that threatens to wipe out the whole world.
2. A creation of the media, which has sensationalized a minor health problem for its own profit and pleasure.
3. A creation of the state to legitimize widespread invasion of people's lives and sexual practices.
4. A creation of biomedical scientists and the Centers for Disease Control to generate funding for their activities.
5. A gay plague, probably emanating from San Francisco.
6. The crucible in which the field of immunology will be tested.
7. The most extraordinary medical chronicle of our times.
8. A condemnation to celibacy or death.
9. An Andromeda strain with the transmission efficiency of the common cold.
10. An imperialist plot to destroy the Third World.
11. A fascist plot to destroy homosexuals.
12. A CIA plot to destroy subversives.
13. A capitalist plot to create new markets for pharmaceutical products.
14. A Soviet plot to destroy capitalists.

---

[3] I use the term *epidemic* to refer to the exponential compounding of meanings as opposed to the simpler spread of a term through a population.

[4] The term *signification*, derived from the linguistic work of Ferdinand de Saussure, calls attention to the way in which language (or any other "signifying system") organizes rather than labels experience (or the world). Linking signifiers (phonetic segments or, more loosely, words) and signifieds (concepts, meanings) in ways that come to seem "natural" to us, language creates the illusion of "transparency," as though we could look through it to "facts" and "realities" that are unproblematic. Many scientists and physicians, even those sensitive to the complexities of AIDS, believe that "the facts" (or "science" or "reason") will resolve contradiction and supplant speculation; they express impatience with social interpretations, which they perceive as superfluous or incorrect. (See, for example, Richard Restak, "AIDS Virus Has No Civil Rights," *Chicago Sun-Times*, September 15, 1985, pp. 1, 57–58.) Even Jacques Leibowitch writes that, with the discovery of the virus, AIDS loses its "metaphysical resonances" and becomes "now no more than one infectious disease among many" (*A Strange Virus of Unknown Origin*, trans. Richard Howard, intro. by Robert C. Gallo, New York, Ballantine, 1985, p. xiv). The position of this essay is that signification processes are not the handmaidens of "the facts"; rather, "the facts" themselves arise out of the signifying practices of biomedical discourse.

15. The result of experiments on the immunological system of men not likely to reproduce.
16. The result of genetic mutations caused by "mixed marriages."
17. The result of moral decay and a major force destroying the Boy Scouts.
18. A plague stored in King Tut's tomb and unleashed when the Tut exhibit toured the US in 1976.
19. The perfect emblem of twentieth-century decadence, of fin-de-siècle decadence, of postmodern decadence.
20. A disease that turns fruits into vegetables.
21. A disease introduced by aliens to weaken us before the takeover.
22. Nature's way of cleaning house.
23. America's *Ideal Death Sentence.*
24. An infectious agent that has suppressed our immunity from guilt.
25. A spiritual force that is creatively disrupting civilization.
26. A sign that the end of the world is at hand.
27. God's punishment of our weaknesses.
28. God's test of our strengths.
29. The price paid for the sixties.
30. The price paid for anal intercourse.
31. The price paid for genetic inferiority and male aggression.
32. An absolutely unique disease for which there is no precedent.
33. Just another venereal disease.
34. The most urgent and complex public health problem facing the world today.
35. A golden opportunity for science and medicine.
36. Science fiction.
37. Stranger than science fiction.
38. A terrible and expensive way to die.[5]

---

[5]These conceptualizations of AIDS come chiefly from printed sources (journals, news stories, letters to the editor, tracts) published since 1981. Many are common and discussed in the course of this essay; the more idiosyncratic readings of AIDS (e.g., as a force destroying the Boy Scouts) are cited to suggest the dramatic symbol-inducing power of this illness as well as our continuing lack of social consensus about its meaning. Sources for the more idiosyncratic views are as follows: (2) Senator Jesse Helms; (6) Gallo's introduction to Leibowitch, *A Strange Virus,* pp. xvi–xvii; (8) gay rights activist on Channel 5 television broadcast, Cincinnati, October 18, 1985 (compare the French joke that the acronym for AIDS, SIDA in French, stands for Syndrome Imaginaire pour Décourager les Amoureux [*Newsweek,* November 24, 1986, p. 47]); (9) one science writer's characterization of the popular view (John Langone, "AIDS: The Latest Scientific Facts," *Discover,* December 1985, pp. 27–52); (10) GRIA (Haitian Revolutionary Internationalist Group), "AIDS: Syndrome of an Imperialist Era," undated flyer distributed in New York City, Fall 1982 (and see Marcia Pally, "AIDS and the Politics of Despair: Lighting Our Own Funeral Pyre," *The Advocate,* no. 436, December 24, 1985, p. 8); (12) Gary Lee, "AIDS in Moscow: It Comes from the CIA, or Maybe Africa," *Washington Post National Weekly Edition,* December 30, 1985, p. 16; (13) Langone, in *Discover,* citing a story in a Kenyan newspaper; (14) *National Inquirer* story cited in Brian Becher, "AIDS and the Media: A Case Study of How the Press Influences Public Opinion," unpublished research paper, College of Medicine, University of Illinois at Urbana-Champaign, 1983; (15) John Rechy, "An Exchange on AIDS," Letter to the Editor, with reply by Jonathan Lieberson, *New York Review of Books,* October 13, 1983, pp. 43–45; (16) Soviet view cited in Jonathan Lieberson, "The Reality of AIDS," *New York Review of Books,* January 16, 1986, p. 45; (17) Jonathan Gathorne-Hardy, Letter to the Editor, *New York Times Book Review,* June 29, 1986, p. 35; (18) cited in William Check, "Public Education on AIDS: Not Only the Media's Responsibility," *Hastings Center Report,* Special Supplement, vol. 15, no. 4 (August 1985), p. 28; (19) Toby Johnson, "AIDS and Moral Issues," *The*

Such diverse conceptualizations of AIDS are coupled with fragmentary interpretations of its specific elements. Confusion about transmission now causes approximately half the US population to refuse to *give* blood. Many believe you can "catch" AIDS through casual contact, such as sitting beside an infected person on a bus. Many believe that lesbians—a population relatively free of sexually transmitted diseases in general—are as likely to be infected as gay men. Other stereotypes about homosexuals generate startling deductions about the illness: "I thought AIDS was a gay disease," said a man interviewed by *USA Today* in October 1985, "but if Rock Hudson's dead it can kill anyone."

We cannot effectively analyze AIDS or develop intelligent social policy if we dismiss such conceptions as irrational myths and homophobic fantasies that deliberately ignore the "real scientific facts." Rather they are part of the necessary work people do in attempting to understand—however imperfectly—the complex, puzzling, and quite terrifying phenomenon of AIDS. No matter how much we may desire, with Susan Sontag, to resist treating illness as metaphor, illness *is* metaphor, and this semantic work—this effort to "make sense of" AIDS—has to be done. Further, this work is as necessary and often as difficult and imperfect for physicians and scientists as it is for "the rest of us."[6]

I am arguing, then, not that we must take both the social and the biological dimensions of AIDS into account, but rather that the social dimension is far more pervasive and central than we are accustomed to believing. Science is not the true material base generating our merely symbolic superstructure. Our social constructions of AIDS (in terms of global devastation, threat to civil rights, emblem of sex and death, the "gay plague," the postmodern condition, whatever) are based not upon objective, scientifically determined "reality" but upon what we are told about this reality: that is, upon *prior* social constructions

---

Advocate, no. 379, October 27, 1983, pp. 24–26: "Perhaps AIDS is just the first of a whole new class of diseases resulting from the tremendous changes human technology has wrought in the earth's ecology"; (20) example of AIDS "humor" cited in David Black, *The Plague Years: A Chronicle of AIDS, The Epidemic of Our Times*, New York, Simon & Schuster, 1986; (23) acronym cited in Lindsy Van Gelder and Pam Brandt, "AIDS on Campus," *Rolling Stone*, no. 483, 1986, p. 89; (24) Richard Goldstein, "Heartsick: Fear and Loving in the Gay Community," *Village Voice*, June 28, 1983; (25) Black, *The Plague Years*, citing one view of plagues; (31) cited in Pally, "AIDS and the Politics of Despair"; (37) Robert C. Gallo, "The AIDS Virus," *Scientific American*, January 1987, pp. 47–56.

[6]Sontag, in *Illness as Metaphor*, New York, Farrar, Strauss & Giroux, 1978, argues that the confusion of illness with metaphor damages people who are ill, and certainly with AIDS there is ample evidence for this argument. Laurence R. Tancredi and Nora D. Volkow, for example, in "AIDS: Its Symbolism and Ethical Implications," *Medical Heritage*, vol. 2, no. 1 (January-February 1986), pp. 12–18, arguing that "the metaphor essentially creates the framework for the individual's experience of the disease," cite studies indicating that many people with AIDS experience a variety of psychological difficulties as a result of its symbolic (as opposed to its prognostic) message. But metaphor cannot simply be mandated away. Goldstein, in "Heartsick," writes: "Since we are so vulnerable to the erotic potential of metaphor, how can we hope to be less susceptible when illness intersects with sex and death?" Sontag argues that once the cause and cure of a disease are known it ceases to be the kind of mystery that generates metaphors. Her view that biomedical discourse has a special claim on the representation of "reality" implies as well that the entities it identifies and describes are themselves free from social construction (metaphor). But as Stephen Durham and Susan Williams insist, in "AIDS Hysteria: A Marxist Analysis," presented at the Pacific Northwest Marxist Scholars Conference, University of Washington, Seattle, April 11–13, 1986 (Freedom Socialist Publications, 5018 Rainier Ave. South, Seattle, WA 98118), despite the origins of the AIDS crisis in the domain of microbiology, the "greatest obstacles to establishing a cure for AIDS and a rational, humane approach to its ravages do not flow from the organic qualities of the [virus]."

routinely produced within the discourses of biomedical science.[7] (AIDS as infectious disease is one such construction.) There is a continuum, then, not a dichotomy, between popular and biomedical discourses (and, as Latour and Woolgar put it, "a continuum between controversies in daily life and those occurring in the laboratory"),[8] and these play out in language. Consider, for example, the ambiguities embedded within this statement by an AIDS "expert" (an immunologist) on a television documentary in October 1985 designed to *dispel* misconceptions about AIDS:

> The biggest misconception that we have encountered and that most cities throughout the United States have seen is that many people feel that casual contact—being in the same room with an AIDS victim—will transmit the virus and may infect them. This has not been substantiated by any evidence whatsoever. . . . [This misconception lingers because] this is an extremely emotional issue. I think that when there are such strong emotions associated with a medical problem such as this it's very difficult for facts to sink in. I think also there's the problem that we cannot give any 100 percent assurances one way or the other about these factors. There may always be some exception to the rule. Anything we may say, someone could come up with an exception. But as far as most of the medical–scientific community is concerned, this is a virus that is actually very *difficult* to transmit and therefore the general public should really not worry about casual contact—not even using the same silverware and dishes would probably be a problem.[9]

Would you buy a scientific fact from this man? Can we expect to understand AIDS transmission when this is part of what we have to work with? The point is not merely that this particular scientist has not yet learned to "talk to the media," but that ambiguity and uncertainty are features of scientific inquiry

---

[7]Allan M. Brandt, in *No Magic Bullet: A Social History of Venereal Disease in the United States since 1880*, New York, Oxford University Press, 1987 (expanded version of 1985 edition), p. 199, summarizes the ways in which AIDS thus far recapitulates the social history of other sexually transmitted diseases: the pervasive fear of contagion, concerns about casual transmission, stigmatization of victims, conflict between the protection of public health and the protection of civil liberties, increasing public control over definition and management, and the search for a "magic bullet." Despite the supposed sexual revolution, Brandt writes, we continue through these social constructions "to define the sexually transmitted diseases as uniquely sinful." This definition is inaccurate but pervasive, and as long as disease is equated with sin "there can be no magic bullet" (p. 202).

[8]Latour and Woolgar, *Laboratory Life*, p. 281.

[9]Allan Sollinger, PhD, Department of Immunology, University of Cincinnati Medical Center, speaking as an expert guest on a television documentary, Cincinnati, October 1985. By this time a number of leading authorities on AIDS had come to believe that scientists had to begin communicating to the public with greater clarity and certainty. The Centers for Disease Control issued a "definitive statement" in October 1985 that AIDS *cannot* be spread by casual contact. Mathilde Krim, PhD, director of the American Foundation for AIDS Research, discussed transmission with emphatic clarity on the *MacNeil-Lehrer Newshour*, September 4, 1985: "AIDS is contagious strictly through the transmission of a virus which passes from one person to another during sexual intercourse or with contaminated blood. It is not contagious *at all* through casual interaction with people, in normal social conditions such as living in a household with a patient or meeting patients on the bus or in the working place or in school." Interestingly, as Deborah Jones Merritt's comprehensive review makes clear, constitutional precedents for addressing public health problems give broad latitude to the state; strong scientific "evidence" is essentially not required as a basis for interventions ("Communicable Disease and Constitutional Law: Controlling AIDS," *New York University Law Review*, no. 61 [November 1986], pp. 739–799).

that must be socially and linguistically managed.[10] What is at issue here is a fatal infectious disease that is simply not fully understood; questions remain about the nature of the disease, its etiology, its transmission, and what individuals can do about it. It does not seem unreasonable that in the face of these uncertainties people give birth to many different conceptions; to label them "*mis*conceptions" implies what? Wrongful birth? That only "facts" can give birth to proper conceptions and only science can give birth to facts? In that case, we may wish to avert our eyes from some of the "scientific" conceptions that have been born in the course of the AIDS crisis:

> AIDS could be *anything*, considering what homosexual men do to each other in gay baths.
> Heroin addicts won't use clean needles because they would rather get AIDS than give up the ritual of sharing them.
> Prostitutes do not routinely keep themselves clean and are therefore "reservoirs" of disease.
> AIDS is homosexual; it can only be transmitted by males to males.
> AIDS in Africa is heterosexual but uni-directional; it can only be transmitted from males to females.
> AIDS in Africa is heterosexual because anal intercourse is a common form of birth control.[11]

The point here is that no clear line can be drawn between the facticity of scientific and nonscientific (mis)conceptions. Ambiguity, homophobia, stereotyping, confusion, doublethink, them-versus-us, blame-the-victim, wishful thinking: none of these popular forms of semantic legerdemain about AIDS is absent from biomedical communication. But scientific and medical discourses have traditions through which the semantic epidemic as well as the biological one is controlled, and these may disguise contradiction and irrationality. In writing about AIDS, these traditions typically include characterizing ambiguity and contradiction as "nonscientific" (a no-nonsense, lets-get-the-facts-on-the-table-and-clear-up-this-muddle approach), invoking faith in scientific inquiry, taking for granted the reality of quantitative and/or biomedical data, deducing social and behavioral reality from quantitative and/or biomedical data, setting forth fantasies and speculations as though they were logical deductions, using technical euphemisms for sensitive sexual or political realities, and revising both past and future to conform to present thinking.

---

[10]Nathan Fain and Check discuss turning points in AIDS-related communications as scientists gained skill in reducing ambiguity. See Nathan Fain, "AIDS: An Antidote to Fear," *Village Voice*, October 1, 1985, p. 35, and Check, "Public Education on AIDS."

[11]These conceptions and others are widespread. For specific citations and discussion, see, for example, Leibowitch, *A Strange Virus*; Langone, "AIDS: The Latest Scientific Facts"; Wayne Barrett, "Straight Shooters: AIDS Targets Another Lifestyle," *Village Voice*, October 26, 1985, pp. 14–18; Lawrence K. Altman, "Linking AIDS to Africa Provokes Bitter Debate," *New York Times*, November 21, 1985, pp. 1, 8.

Many of these traditions are illustrated in an article by John Langone in the December 1985 general science journal *Discover*.[12] In this lengthy review of research to date, entitled "AIDS: The Latest Scientific Facts," Langone suggests that the virus enters the bloodstream by way of the "vulnerable anus" and the "fragile urethra"; in contrast, the "rugged vagina" (built to be abused by such blunt instruments as penises and small babies) provides too tough a barrier for the AIDS virus to penetrate.[13] "Contrary to what you've heard," Langone concludes—and his conclusion echoes a fair amount of medical and scientific writing at the time—"AIDS isn't a threat to the vast majority of heterosexuals. . . . It is now—and is likely to remain—largely the fatal price one can pay for anal intercourse."[14] (This excerpt from the article also ran as the cover blurb.) It sounded plausible; and detailed illustrations demonstrated the article's conclusion.[15]

But by December 1986 the big news—what the major US news magazines were running cover stories on—was the grave danger of AIDS to heterosexuals.[16] No dramatic discoveries during the intervening year had changed the fundamental scientific conception of AIDS.[17] What had changed was not "the facts" but the way in which they were now used to construct the AIDS text and

---

[12]Langone, "AIDS: The Latest Scientific Facts."

[13]*Ibid.*, pp. 40–41.

[14]*Ibid.*, p. 52.

[15]Visual representations of AIDS are not the subject of this essay, yet it is worth noting that they have been a source of continuing controversy. In Watney and Gupta's textual and visual "dossier" on the rhetoric of AIDS, one writer calls the magnified electron micrograph of the HTLV-III virus "the spectre of the decade" (Simon Watney and Sunil Gupta, "The Rhetoric of AIDS: A Dossier Compiled by Simon Watney, with Photographs by Sunil Gupta," *Screen*, vol. 27, no. 1 [January–February 1986], pp. 72–85). The cover of *Time*, August 12, 1985, also treats a photograph of the virus as proof of its reality; "magnified 135,000 times," the virus is pictured "destroying T-cell"—cf. Roberta McGrath's analysis of the cultural and political role of photography in naturalizing the biomedical model ("Medical Police," *Ten*, no. 8 [1984], p. 14). Some members of the San Francisco gay community complained early that public health warnings used euphemistic language ("avoid exchange of bodily fluids") and through innocuous pictures subverted the message that AIDS was a deadly and physically ravaging disease (Frances FitzGerald, *Cities on a Hill*, New York, Simon & Schuster/Touchstone, 1987, p. 93. First published as "A Reporter at Large: The Castro-II," *The New Yorker*, July 28, 1986). On other aspects of media coverage of AIDS, see Becher, "AIDS and the Media"; Black, *The Plague Years*; Check, "Public Education on AIDS"; Barbara O'Dair, "Anatomy of a Media Epidemic," *Alternative Media*, vol. 14, no. 3 (Fall 1983), pp. 10–13; Harry Schwartz, "AIDS in the Media," in *Science in the Streets: A Report to the Twentieth Century Task Force on the Communication of Scientific Risk*, New York, Priority Press, 1984. Controversies over graphics were not limited to popular journals: a photo published in *Science* purporting to be an isolated strain of Gallo's "AIDS virus" figured in the international dispute over its discovery (Robert C. Gallo, *et al.*, "HTLV-III Legend Correction," Letter to the Editor, *Science*, no. 232 [April 18, 1986], p. 307; Colin Norman, "A New Twist in AIDS Patent Fight," News and Comment, *Science*, no. 232 [April 18, 1986], pp. 308–309).

[16]See, for example, *Newsweek*, November 3, 1986, pp. 66–67, and November 24, 1986, pp. 30–47; Erik Eckholm, "Broad Alert on AIDS: Social Battle Is Shifting," *New York Times*, June 17, 1986, pp. 19–20; Kathleen McAuliffe, *et al.* "AIDS: At the Dawn of Fear," *US News and World Report*, January 12, 1987, pp. 60–69; Mortimer B. Zuckerman, "AIDS: A Crisis Ignored," Editorial, *US News and World Report*, January 12, 1987, p. 76; Katie Leishman, "Heterosexuals and AIDS: The Second Stage of the Epidemic," *The Atlantic*, February 1987, pp. 39–58; "Science and the Citizen," *Scientific American*, January 1987, pp. 58–59.

[17]The 2nd International Conference on AIDS, held in Paris in June 1986, revealed no major scientific breakthroughs (Deborah M. Barnes, "AIDS Research in New Phase," *Science*, no. 233 [July 18, 1986], p. 282); rather, answers to several crucial questions were clarified or strengthened. Check notes that, as health and science reporting on AIDS has evolved, "articles about the spread of AIDS to the so-called general public do not have to be pegged to any specific new data" ("Public Education on AIDS," p. 31).

the meanings we were now allowed—indeed, at last encouraged—to read from that text.[18] The AIDS story, in other words, is not merely the familiar story of heroic scientific discovery. And until we understand AIDS as both a material and a linguistic reality—a duality inherent in all linguistic entities but extraordinarily exaggerated and potentially deadly in the case of AIDS—we cannot begin to read the story of this illness accurately or formulate intelligent interventions.

Intelligent interventions from outside biomedical science have helped shape the discourse on AIDS. Almost from the beginning, members of the gay community, through intense interest and informed political activism, have repeatedly contested the terminology, meanings, and interpretations produced by scientific inquiry. Such contestations had occurred a decade earlier in the struggle over whether homosexuality was to be officially classified as an illness by the American Psychiatric Association.[19] Gay men and lesbians in the succeeding period had achieved considerable success in political organizing. AIDS, then, first struck members of a relatively seasoned and politically sophisticated community. The importance of not relinquishing authority to medicine was articulated early in the AIDS crisis by Michael Lynch:

> Another crisis exists with the medical one. It has gone largely unexamined, even by the gay press. Like helpless mice we have peremptorily, almost inexplicably, relinquished the one power we so long fought for in constructing our modern gay community: the power to determine our own identity. And to whom have we relinquished it? The very authority we wrested it from in a struggle that occupied us for more than a hundred years: the medical profession.[20]

To challenge biomedical authority—whose meanings are part of powerful and deeply entrenched social and historical codes—has required considerable tenacity and courage from people dependent in the AIDS crisis upon science and medicine for protection, care, and the possibility of cure. These contestations provide the model for a broader social analysis, which moves away from AIDS as a "life-style" issue and examines its significance for this country, at this time, with the cultural and material resources available to us. This, in turn, requires us to acknowledge and examine the multiple ways in which our social constructions guide our visions of material reality.

---

[18]The Paris conference was one of several fact-pooling and consensus-building events in 1986 that influenced new readings of existing evidence. Also influential were the *US Surgeon General's Report on Acquired Immune Deficiency Syndrome*, Washington, D.C., Public Health Service, 1986, which advocated intensified sex education in the schools; an investigation by the National Institute of Medicine and the National Academy of Sciences (David Baltimore and Sheldon M. Wolff, *Confronting AIDS: Directions for Public Health, Health Care, and Research*, Washington, D.C., National Academy Press, 1986), which emphasized the dangers of heterosexual transmission; and a World Health Organization conference that concluded that AIDS must now be considered a pandemic of catastrophic proportions. (An epidemic disease is prevalent within a specific community, geographical area, or population at a particular time, usually originating elsewhere; a pandemic disease is present over the whole of a country, a continent, or the world.) See also "AIDS: Public Health and Civil Liberties," *Hastings Center Report*, Special Supplement, vol. 16, no. 6 (December 1986); "AIDS: Science, Ethics, Policy," Forum, *Issues in Science and Technology*, vol. 2, no. 2 (Winter 1986), pp. 39–73.

[19]See Ronald Bayer, *Homosexuality and American Psychiatry: The Politics of Diagnosis*, New York, Basic Books, 1981.

[20]Michael Lynch, "Living with Kaposi's," *Body Politic*, no. 88 (November 1982).

AIDS and Homophobia: Constructing the Text of the Gay Male Body

Whatever else it may be, AIDS is a story, or multiple stories, read to a surprising extent from a text that does not exist: the body of the male homosexual. It is a text people so want—need—to read that they have gone so far as to write it themselves. AIDS is a nexus where multiple meanings, stories, and discourses intersect and overlap, reinforce, and subvert one another. Yet clearly this mysterious male homosexual text has figured centrally in generating what I call here an epidemic of signification. Of course "the virus," with mysteries of its own, has been a crucial influence. But we may recall Camus's novel: "The word 'plague' . . . conjured up in the doctor's mind not only what science chose to put into it, but a whole series of fantastic possibilities utterly out of keeping" with the bourgeois town of Oran, where the plague struck.[21] How could a disease so extraordinary as *plague* happen in a place so ordinary and dull? AIDS, initially striking people perceived as alien and exotic by scientists, physicians, journalists, and much of the US population, did not pose such a paradox. The "promiscuous" gay male body—early reports noted that AIDS "victims" reported having had as many as 1,000 sexual partners—made clear that even if AIDS turned out to be a sexually transmitted disease it would not be a commonplace one. The connections between sex, death, and homosexuality made the AIDS story inevitably, as David Black notes, able to be read as "the story of a metaphor."[22]

---

[21]Albert Camus, *The Plague*, trans. Stuart Gilbert, New York, Modern Library, 1948 (first published Paris, Gallimard, 1947).

[22]"I realized . . . that any account of AIDS was not just a medical story and not just a story about the gay community, but also a story about the straight community's reaction to the disease. More than that: it's a story about how the straight community has used and is using AIDS as a mask for its feelings about gayness. It is a story about the ramifications of a metaphor" (Black, *The Plague Years*, p. 30). AIDS is typically characterized as a "story," but whose? For AIDS as a story of scientific progress, see Gallo, "The AIDS Virus"; Arnold Relman, "Introduction," *Hastings Center Report*, Special Supplement, vol. 15, no. 4 (August 1985), p. 1; Eve K. Nichols, *Mobilizing Against AIDS: The Unfinished Story of a Virus* (Conference of the Institute of Medicine/National Academy of Sciences), Cambridge, Massachusetts, Harvard University Press, 1986; Jonathan Lieberson, "Anatomy of an Epidemic," *New York Review of Books*, August 18, 1983, pp. 17–22. But for Lynch ("Living with Kaposi's"), Goldstein ("Heartsick"), FitzGerald (*Cities on a Hill*), Larry Kramer ("1,112 and Counting," *New York Native*, March 1983, pp. 14–27), D. W. McLeod and Alan V. Miller ("Medical, Social, and Political Aspects of the AIDS Case: A Bibliography," *Canadian Gay Archives*, no. 10), Thom Gunn (*Lament*, Champaign, Illinois, Doe Press, 1985), Steve Ault ("AIDS: The Facts of Life," *Guardian*, March 26, 1986, pp. 1, 8), Dennis Altman (*AIDS in the Mind of America*, New York, Doubleday, 1986), the San Francisco *A.I.D.S. Show—Artists Involved with Death and Survival* (documentary video produced by Peter Adair and Rob Epstein, directed by Leland Moss; based on theater production at Theatre Rhinoceros, San Francisco; aired on PBS, November 1986), and others, AIDS is the story of crisis and heroism in the gay community. In the tabloids, AIDS has become the story of Rock Hudson (ROCK IS DEAD, ran the headlines in the [London] *Sun* on October 3, 1985, THE HUNK WHO LIVED A LIE), Liberace, and other individuals. A documentary film about the Fabian Bridges case, a young man with AIDS in Houston, is called *Fabian's Story* (see J. Ostrow, "AIDS Documentary Addresses Agonizing Issues," *Denver Post*, March 24, 1986). For Geoff Mains (*Urban Aboriginals: A Celebration of Leathersexuality*, San Francisco, Gay Sunshine Press, 1985), AIDS interrupts the adventure story of leather sex, a "unique and valuable cultural excursion" (p. 178). And in Thom Gunn's poem, *Lament*, AIDS is a story of change and the death of friends. The stories we tell help us determine what our own place in the story is to be. FitzGerald writes that the "new mythology" about AIDS in the San Francisco gay community—that many gay men are changing their lives for the better—was "an antidote to the notion that AIDS was a punishment—a notion that . . . lay so deep as to be unavailable to reason. And it helped people act against the threat of AIDS" (*Cities on a Hill*, p. 116). But for Richard Mohr ("Of Deathbeds and

Ironically, a major turning point in US consciousness came when Rock Hudson acknowledged that he was being treated for AIDS. Through an extraordinary conflation of texts, the Rock Hudson case dramatized the possibility that the disease could spread to the "general population."[23] In fact this possibility had been evident for some time to anyone who wished to find it: as Jean Marx summarized the evidence in *Science* in 1984, "Sexual intercourse both of the heterosexual and homosexual varieties is a major pathway of trans-

---

Quarantines: AIDS Funding, Gay Life and State Coercion," *Raritan*, vol. 6, no. 1 [Summer 1986], pp. 38–62), this new mythology—in which the loving relationship replaces anonymous sex—is a dangerous one: "The relation typically is asked to bear more than is reasonable. The burden on the simple dyad is further weighed down by the myth, both romantic and religious, that one finds one's completion in a single other. White knights and messiahs never come in clusters" (p. 56). For discussion of AIDS as a public drama, see "AIDS: Public Health and Civil Liberties"; Ronald Bayer, "AIDS: The Public Context of an Epidemic," *Millbank Quarterly*, no. 64, Supplement 1, pp. 168–182; and McLeod and Miller, "Medical, Social, and Political Aspects."

[23]Articulate voices had taken issue with the CDC position from the beginning, warning against the public health consequences of treating AIDS as a "gay disease" and separating "those at risk" from the so-called "general population." See, for example, comments by Gary MacDonald, executive director of an AIDS action organization in Washington: "I think the moment may have arrived to desexualize the disease. AIDS is *not* a 'gay disease,' despite its epidemiology. . . . AIDS is not transmitted because of who you *are*, but because of what you *do*. . . . By concentrating on gay and bisexual men, people are able to ignore the fact that this disease has been present in what has charmingly come to be called 'the general population' *from the beginning*. It was not spread from one of the other groups. It was *there* ("AIDS: What Is to Be Done?" Forum, *Harper's Magazine*, October 1985, p. 43).

One can extrapolate from Ruth Bleier's observation that questions shape answers (*Science and Gender*, London, Pergamon, 1986, p. 4), and suggest that the question "Why are all people with AIDS sexually active homosexual males?" might more appropriately have been *"Are* all people with AIDS sexually active homosexual males?" It is widely believed (not without evidence) that federal funding for AIDS research was long in coming because its chief victims were gay or otherwise socially undesirable. Black describes a researcher who made jokes about *fagocytes* (phagocytes), cells designed "to kill off fags" (*The Plague Years*, pp. 81–82). Secretary of Health and Human Services Margaret Heckler was only one of many officials who expressed concern not about existing people with AIDS but about the potential spread of AIDS to "the community at large" (with the result that Heckler was called "the Secretary of Health and Heterosexual Services" by some gay activists; see "AIDS: What Is to Be Done?" p. 51).

There is evidence that the "gay disease" myth interferes with diagnosis and treatment. Many believe that AIDS may be underdetected and underreported in part because people outside the "classic" high-risk groups are often not asked the right questions (physicians typically take longer to diagnose AIDS in women, for example). Health professionals and AIDS counselors sometimes avoid the word *gay* because for many people this implies an identity or life-style; even *bisexual* may mean a life-style. Although "homosexually active" is officially defined as including even a single same-sex sexual contact over the past five years, many who have had such contact do not identify themselves as "homosexual" and therefore as being at risk for AIDS. Nancy Shaw ("California Models for Women's AIDS Education and Services," report, San Francisco AIDS Foundation [333 Valencia St., 4th Floor, San Francisco, CA 94103], and "Women and AIDS: Theory and Politics," presented at the annual meeting of the National Women's Studies Association, University of Illinois, Urbana, June 1986) suggests that for women as well the homosexual/heterosexual dichotomy confuses diagnosis and treatment as well as the perception of risk. Pally ("AIDS and the Politics of Despair"), Marea Murray ("Too Little AIDS Coverage," Letter to the Editors, *Sojourner*, July 1985, p. 3), and Cindy Patton ("Feminists Have Avoided the Issue of AIDS," *Sojourner*, October 1985, pp. 19–20) all argue that AIDS is a "women's issue" and should receive more attention in feminist publications (and see COYOTE, Background Paper, 1985 COYOTE Convention Summary, May 30–June 2, 1985, San Francisco; Ellen Switzer, "AIDS: What Women Can Do," *Vogue*, January 1986, pp. 222–223, 264–265; Jane Sprague Zones, "AIDS: What Women Need to Know," *The [National Women's Health] Network News*, vol. 11, no. 6 [November–December 1986], pp. 1, 3). The persistence and consequences of the perception that AIDS is a disease of gay men and IV drug users are documented in a number of recent publications, notably Leishman, "Heterosexuals and AIDS." CDC interviews with members of two heterosexual singles clubs in Minneapolis documented that as of late 1986 this already infected population had made virtually no modifications in their sexual practices ("Positive HTLV-III/LAV Antibody Results for Sexually Active Female Members of Social/Sexual Clubs—Minnesota," *Morbidity and Mortality Weekly Report*, no. 35 [1986], pp. 697–699). Ralph J. DiClemente, Jim Zorn, and Lydia Temoshok ("Adolescents and AIDS: A Survey of Knowledge, Attitudes, and Beliefs about AIDS in San Francisco," *American Journal of Public Health*, vol. 76, no. 12 [1986], pp. 1443–1445) found that many adolescents in San Francisco, a city where public health information about AIDS has been extensive, were not well informed about the seriousness of the disease, its causes, or preventive measures.

mission."[24] But only in late 1986 (and somewhat reluctantly at that) did the Centers for Disease Control expand upon their early "4-H list" of high-risk categories: HOMOSEXUALS, HEMOPHILIACS, HEROIN ADDICTS, and HAITIANS, and the sexual partners of people within these groups.[25] The original list, developed during 1981 and 1982, has structured evidence collection in the intervening years and contributed to a view that the major risk factor in acquiring AIDS is being a particular kind of person rather than doing particular things.[26] Ann Giudici Fettner pointed out in 1985 that "the CDC admits that at least 10 percent of AIDS sufferers are gay *and* use IV drugs. Yet they are automatically counted in the homosexual and bisexual men category, regardless of what might be known—or not known—about how they became infected."[27] So the "gay" nature of AIDS was in part an artifact of the way in which data was collected and reported. Though almost from the beginning scientific papers have cited AIDS cases that appeared to fall outside the high-risk groups, it has been generally hypothesized that these cases, assigned to the categories of UNKNOWN, UNCLASSIFIED, or OTHER, would ultimately turn out to be one of the four H's.[28] This commitment to categories based on stereotyped identity filters out information. Nancy Shaw argues that when women are asked in CDC protocols "Are you heterosexual?" "this loses the diversity of behaviors that may have a bearing on infection."[29] Even now, with established evidence that transmission can be heterosexual (which begins with the letter *H* after all), scientific discourse continues to construct women as "inefficient" and "incompetent" transmitters of HIV, passive receptacles without the projectile capacity of a penis or syringe—stolid, uninteresting barriers that impede the unrestrained passage of the virus from brother to brother.[30] Exceptions include prostitutes, whose

[24]Jean L. Marx, "Strong New Candidate for AIDS Agent," Research News, *Science*, May 4, 1984, p. 147.

[25]Centers for Disease Control, "Update: Acquired Immunodeficiency Syndrome—United States," *Morbidity and Mortality Weekly Report*, no. 35 (1986), pp. 757–760, 765–766.

[26]Jeff Minson, "The Assertion of Homosexuality," *m/f*, nos. 5–6 (1981), pp. 19–39, and Jeffrey Weeks, *Sexuality and Its Discontents: Meanings, Myths, and Modern Sexualities*, London, Routledge & Kegan Paul, 1985, analyze the evolution of homosexuality as a coherent identity. Bayer, *Homosexuality and American Psychiatry*, and Ronald Bayer and Robert L. Spitzer, "Edited Correspondence on the Status of Homosexuality in DSM-III," *Journal of the History of the Behavioral Sciences*, no. 18 (1982), pp. 32–52, document the intense and acrimonious "contests for meaning" during the American Psychiatric Association's 1970s debates over the official classification of homosexuality.

[27]Fettner, in "AIDS: What Is to Be Done?" p. 43.

[28]See Nichols, *Mobilizing Against AIDS*, and Associated Press, "571 AIDS Cases Tied to Heterosexual Causes," *Champaign-Urbana News-Gazette*, December 12, 1986, p. A-7, on the reclassification in 1986 of the CDC's 571 previously "unexplained cases"; formerly classified as "none of the above" (i.e., outside the known high-risk categories), some of these cases were reclassified as heterosexually transmitted.

[29]Shaw, "Women and AIDS."

[30]Even after consensus in 1984 that AIDS was caused by a virus, there continued to be conflicting views on transmission and different explanations for the epidemiological finding that AIDS and HIV infection in the US were appearing predominantly in gay males. One view holds that this is essentially an artifact ("simple mathematics") created because the virus (for whatever reason) infected gay men first and gay men tend to have sex with each other. The second is that biomedical/physiological factors make gay men and/or the "passive receiver" more infectable. A third view is that the virus can be transmitted to anyone but that certain cofactors facilitate the development of infection and/or clinical symptoms. For more information, see Leibowitch, *A Strange Virus*, pp. 72–73, Leishman, "Heterosexuals and AIDS," and Mathilde Krim, "AIDS: The Challenge to Science and Medicine," in

discursive legacy—despite their longstanding professional knowledge and continued activism about AIDS—is to be seen as so contaminated that their bodies are virtual laboratory cultures for viral replication.[31] Other exceptions are African women, whose exotic bodies, sexual practices, or who knows what are seen to be so radically different from those of women in the US that anything can happen in them.[32] The term *exotic*, sometimes used to describe a virus that appears to have originated "elsewhere" (but "elsewhere," like "other" is not a fixed category), is an important theme running through AIDS literature.[33] The fact that one of the more extensive and visually elegant analyses of AIDS appeared recently in *National Geographic* is perhaps further evidence of its life on an idealized "exotic" terrain.[34]

The early hypotheses about AIDS, when the first cases appeared in New York, Los Angeles, and Paris, were sociological, relating it directly to the supposed "gay male life-style." In February 1982, for example, it was thought that a particular supply of amyl nitrate (poppers) might be contaminated. "The poppers fable," writes Jacques Leibowitch, becomes

---

AIDS: The Emerging Ethical Dilemmas: A Hastings Center Report, Special Supplement, vol. 15, no. 4 (August 1985), p. 4. Many scientists suggest that, whatever sex the partners may be, infection, as Fain ("AIDS: An Antidote to Fear") put it, "requires a jolt injected into the bloodstream, likely several jolts over time, such as would occur with infected needles or semen. In both cases, needle and penis are the instruments of contagion." Women, having no penises, are therefore "inefficient" transmitters. For more detailed discussion, see my essay on women and AIDS, forthcoming in *AIDS: The Burdens of History*, ed. Elizabeth Fee and Daniel M. Fox, Berkeley, University of California Press.

Evidence of heterosexual transmission was at first explained away. When R. R. Redfield, *et al.* ("Heterosexually Acquired HTLV-III/LAV Disease [AIDS-Related Complex and AIDS]: Epidemiological Evidence for Female-to-Male Transmission," *Journal of the American Medical Association*, no. 254 [1985], pp. 2094–2096; "Female-to-Male Transmission of HTLV-III," *Journal of the American Medical Association*, no. 255 [1986], pp. 1705–1706) identified infection in US servicemen who claimed sexual contact only with female prostitutes, some hypothesized "quasi-homosexual contact" or called the data into question on the grounds that servicemen would be likely to withhold information about homosexuality or drug use (some evidence for this is offered by John J. Potterat, *et al.*, "Lying to Military Physicians about Risk Factors for HIV Infections," Letter to *Journal of the American Medical Association*, vol. 257, no. 13 [April 3, 1987], p. 1727). For discussion of the relation of transmission to funding, see Barnes, "AIDS Research in New Phase," p. 283, and "AIDS Funding Boost Requested," *Daily Illini*, September 27, 1985, p. 7.

[31]Brandt, *No Magic Bullet*, and Judith Walkowitz, *Prostitution and Victorian Society: Women, Class, and the State*, New York, Cambridge University Press, 1983, review the longstanding equation of prostitutes with disease, and the conceptual separation of infected prostitutes (and other voluntarily sexually active women) from "innocent victims" (see also COYOTE, "Background Paper"; Shaw, "Women and AIDS"; Colin Douglas, *The Intern's Tale*, New York, Grove, 1975, repr. 1982; Erik Eckholm, "Prostitutes' Impact on Spread of AIDS Debated," *New York Times*, November 5, 1985, pp. 15, 18; and Nancy Shaw and Lyn Paleo, "Women and AIDS," in *What to Do about AIDS*, ed. Leon McKusick, Berkeley, University of California Press, 1986, pp. 142–154).

[32]Discussions of AIDS and heterosexual transmission in Africa include Lieberson, "The Reality of AIDS"; Treichler, forthcoming in *AIDS: The Burdens of History*; Cindy Patton, *Sex and Germs: The Politics of AIDS*, Boston, South End Press, 1985; June E. Osborn, "The AIDS Epidemic: An Overview of the Science," *Issues in Science and Technology*, vol. 2, no. 2 (Winter 1986), pp. 40–55; Jean L. Marx, "New Relatives of AIDS Virus Found," *Research News, Science*, no. 232 (April 11, 1986), p. 157; Fran P. Hosken, "Why AIDS Pattern Is Different in Africa," Letter to the *New York Times*, December 15, 1986; Douglas A. Feldman, "Role of African Mutilations in AIDS Discounted," Letter to the *New York Times*, January 7, 1987; Lawrence K. Altman, "Heterosexuals and AIDS: New Data Examined," *New York Times*, January 22, 1985, pp. 19–20; and "New Human Retroviruses: One Causes AIDS . . . and the Other Does Not," *Nature*, no. 320 (April 3, 1986), p. 385.

[33]Leibowitch, *A Strange Virus*, p. 73.

[34]Peter Jaret, "Our Immune System: The Wars Within," *National Geographic*, June 1986, pp. 702–735.

a Grimm fairy tale when the first cases of AIDS-without-poppers are discovered among homosexuals absolutely repelled by the smell of the product and among heterosexuals unfamiliar with even the words *amyl nitrate* or *poppers*. But, as will be habitual in the history of AIDS, rumors last longer than either common sense or the facts would warrant. The odor of AIDS-poppers will hover in the air a long time—long enough for dozens of mice in the Atlanta epidemiology labs to be kept in restricted cages on an obligatory sniffed diet of poppers 8 to 12 hours a day for several months, until, nauseated but still healthy, without a trace of AIDS, the wretched rodents were released—provisionally—upon the announcement of a new hypothesis: *promiscuity*.[35]

This new perspective generated numerous possibilities. One was that sperm itself could destroy the immune system. "God's plan for man," after all, "was for Adam and Eve and not Adam and Steve."[36] Women, the "natural" receptacles for male sperm, have evolved over the millennia so that their bodies can deal with these foreign invaders; men, not thus blessed by nature, become vulnerable to the "killer sperm" of other men. AIDS in the lay press became known as the "toxic cock syndrome."[37] While scientists and physicians tended initially to define AIDS as a gay sociological problem, gay men, for other reasons, also tended to reject the possibility that AIDS was a new contagious disease. Not only could this make them sexual lepers, it didn't make sense: "How could a disease pick out just gays? That had to be medical homophobia."[38] Important to note here is a profound ambivalence about the origins of illness. Does one prefer an illness caused by who one is and therefore perhaps preventable, curable, or containable through "self-control"—or an illness caused by some external "disease" which has a respectable medical name and can be addressed strictly as a medical problem, beyond individual control? The townspeople of Oran in *The Plague* experience relief when the plague bacillus is identified: the odd happenings—the dying rats, the mysterious human illnesses—are caused by something that has originated elsewhere, something external, something "objective," something medicine can name, even if not cure. The tension between self and not-self becomes important as we try to understand the particular role of viruses and origin stories in AIDS.

But this anticipates the next chapter in the AIDS story. Another favored possibility in the early 1980s (still not universally discarded, for it is plausible so long as the cases of AIDS among monogamous homebodies are ignored) was

---

[35]Leibowitch, *A Strange Virus*, p. 5.

[36]Congressman William Dannemeyer, October 1985, during a debate on a homosexual rights bill (quoted in Langone, "AIDS: The Latest Scientific Facts," p. 29).

[37]Black, *The Plague Years*, p. 29.

[38]*Ibid.*, p. 40. In the gay community, the first reaction to AIDS was disbelief. FitzGerald quotes a gay physician in San Francisco: "A disease that killed only gay white men? It seemed unbelievable. I used to teach epidemiology, and I had never heard of a disease that selective. I thought, They are making this up. It can't be true. Or if there is such a disease it must be the work of some government agency—the F.B.I. or the C.I.A.—trying to kill us all" (*Cities on a Hill*, p. 98). In the San Francisco *A.I.D.S. Show*, one man is said to have learned of his diagnosis and at once wired the CIA: "I HAVE AIDS. DO YOU HAVE AN ANTIDOTE?"

the notion of "cofactors": no *single* infectious agent causes the disease; rather, someone who is sexually active with multiple partners is exposed to a kind of bacterial/viral tidal wave that can crush the immune system.[39] Gay men on the sexual "fast-track" would be particularly susceptible because of the prevalence of specific practices that would maximize exposure to pathogenic microbes. What were considered potentially relevant data came to be routinely included in scientific papers and presentations, with the result that the terminology of these reports was increasingly scrutinized by gay activists.[40] Examples from *Science* from June 1981 through December 1985 include "homosexual and bi-sexual men who are extremely active sexually," "admitted homosexuals," "ho-mosexual males with multiple partners," "homosexual men with multiple partners," "highly sexually active homosexual men," and "promiscuous" versus "nonpromiscuous" homosexual males.[41] Also documented (examples are also from the *Science* collection) are exotic travels or practices: "a Caucasian who had visited Haiti," "persons born in Haiti," "a favorite vacation spot for US homo-sexuals," rectal insemination, "bisexual men," "increased frequency of use of ni-trite inhalants," and "receptive anal intercourse."[42]

Out of this dense discursive jungle came the "fragile anus" hypothesis (tested by Richards and his colleagues, who rectally inseminated laboratory rab-bits) as well as the vision of "multiple partners."[43] Even after sociological expla-nations for AIDS gave way to biomedical ones involving a transmissible virus, these various images of AIDS as a "gay disease" proved too alluring to abandon.

---

[39]See Lieberson, "The Reality of AIDS," p. 43, for an example of the view that, although the virus is the "sine qua non" for AIDS, the syndrome actually develops "chiefly in those whose immune systems are already weak or de-fective." For broader discussion of public health issues in relation to scientific uncertainties and questions of civil liberties, see Ronald Bayer, "AIDS and the Gay Community: Between the Specter and the Promise of Medicine," *Social Research*, vol. 52, no. 3 (Autumn 1985), pp. 581–606; Mervyn F. Silverman and Deborah B. Silverman, "AIDS and the Threat to Public Health," *Hastings Center Report*, Special Supplement, vol. 15, no. 4 (August 1985), pp. 19–22; and Gene W. Matthews and Verla S. Neslund, "The Initial Impact of AIDS on Public Health Law in the United States—1986," *Journal of the American Medical Association*, vol. 257, no. 3 (January 16, 1987), pp. 344–352.

[40]L. Altman, "Heterosexuals and AIDS," and Black, *The Plague Years*, discuss changes in specific terminology as a result of gays' objections; "sexually promiscuous" generally shifted, for example, to "sexually active" or "contact with multiple sex partners." A new classification system for AIDS and AIDS/HIV-related symptoms (adopted at the 2nd International AIDS Conference in Paris, June 1986) is based on the diverse clinical manifestations of the syndrome and its documented natural history; it avoids presumptive terminology like "pre-AIDS." J. Z. Grover's useful review of Nichols's *Mobilizing Against AIDS* ("The 'Scientific' Regime of Truth," *In These Times*, Decem-ber 10–16, 1986, pp. 18–19) points out a number of problematic terms and assumptions that occur repeatedly in this book and other scientific writing on AIDS: (1) the term *AIDS victim* presupposes helplessness (the term *person with AIDS* or PWA was created to avoid this), prevention and cure are linked with a conservative agenda of "indi-vidual responsibility," sex with multiple partners and/or strangers is equated with "promiscuity," and "safe" sexual practices are conflated with the cultural practice of monogamy; (2) it differentiates "caregivers" from "victims," scientific/medical expertise from other kinds of knowledge, and "those at risk" from "the rest of us"; and (3) it notes but fails to challenge existing inequities in the health-care system. Julie Dobrow, "The Symbolism of AIDS: Perspectives on the Use of Language in the Popular Press," presented at the International Communication Asso-ciation annual meeting, Chicago, May 1986, notes the dramatic and commercial appeal of common "cultural im-ages" in popular press scenarios of AIDS.

[41]Terms are quoted from the collection *AIDS: Papers from Science 1982–1985*, ed. Ruth Kulstad, Washington, D.C., American Association for the Advancement of Science, 1986, pp. 22, 40, 49, 65, 142 and 160, respectively.

[42]*Ibid.*, pp. 47, 130, 73, 142–146, 130, 611, 611, respectively.

[43]*Ibid.*, pp. 142–146.

It is easy to see both the scientific and the popular appeal of the "fragile anus" hypothesis: scientifically, it confines the public health dimensions of AIDS to an infected population in the millons—merely mind-boggling, that is—enabling us to stop short of the impossible, the unthinkable billions that widespread hetero-sexual transmission might infect. Another appeal of thinking of AIDS as a "gay disease" is that it protects not only the sexual practices of heterosexuality but also its ideological superiority. In the service of this hypothesis, both homopho-bia and sexism are folded imperturbably into the language of the scientific text. Women, as I noted above, are characterized in the scholarly literature as "inef-ficient" transmitters of AIDS; Leibowitch refers to the "refractory imperme-ability of the vaginal mucous membrane."[44] A study of German prostitutes that appeared to demonstrate female-to-male transmission of AIDS, reported in the *Journal of the American Medical Association*, was interpreted by one reader as ac-tually representing "quasi-homosexual" transmission: Man A, infected with HIV, has vaginal intercourse with Prostitute; she, "[performing] no more than perfunctory external cleansing between customers," then has intercourse with Man B; Man B is infected with the virus via the semen of Man A.[45] The prosti-tute's vagina thus functions merely as a reservoir, a passive holding tank for semen that becomes infectious only when another penis is dipped into it—like a swamp where mosquitoes come to breed.

But the conception and the conclusion are inaccurate. It is not monogamy or abstention per se that protects one from AIDS infection but practices and protections that prevent the virus from entering one's bloodstream. Evidence suggests that prostitutes are at greater risk not because they have multiple sex partners, but because some of them use intravenous drugs; at this point "they may be better protected than the typical woman who is just going to a bar or a woman who thinks of herself as not sexually active but who 'just happens to have this relationship.' They may be more aware than women who are involved in serial monogamy or those whose self-image is 'I'm not at risk so I'm not going to learn more about it.'"[46] Indeed, COYOTE and other organizations of prostitutes have addressed the issue of AIDS rather aggressively for several years.[47]

---

[44]Leibowitch, *A Strange Virus*, p. 36.

[45]Data on female-to-male transmission presented at the 1985 International Conference on AIDS in Atlanta are summarized by Marsha F. Goldsmith, "More Heterosexual Spread of HTLV-III Virus Seen," *Journal of the American Medical Association*, no. 253 (1985), pp. 3377–3379. The hypothesis that such data reflect "quasi-homosexual contact" is suggested by Harold Sanford Kant, "The Transmission of HTLV-III," Letter to the Editor, *Journal of the American Medical Association*, no. 254 (1985), p. 1901.

[46]Shaw and Paleo, "Women and AIDS," p. 144.

[47]Kant's hypothesis in *JAMA* is quoted by Langone, "AIDS: The Latest Scientific Facts," p. 49, to support his own "vulnerable anus" hypothesis: "It is not unlikely that these prostitutes had multiple partners during a very short time, and performed no more than perfunctory external cleansing between customers." Langone does not note that the source is a Letter to the Editor. Meanwhile, reports from prostitutes in many countries, summarized in the June 1986 *World Wide Whores' News* (published by the International Committee for Prostitutes' Rights), in-dicate familiarity with AIDS as well as concern with obtaining better protection from infection and better health care. See also COYOTE, "Background Paper."

Donald Mager discusses the proliferation among heterosexuals of visions about homosexuality and their status as fantasy:

> Institutions of privilege and power disenfranchise lesbians and gay men because of stereotypic negative categorizations of them—stereotypes which engage a societal fantasy of the illicit, the subversive, and the taboo, particularly due to assumptions of radical sex role parodies and inversions. This fantasy in turn becomes both the object of fear and of obsessed fascination, while its status as fantasy is never acknowledged; instead, the reality it pretends to signify becomes the justification of suppression both of the fantasy itself and of those actual persons who would seem to embody it. Homophobia as a critique of societal sexual fantasy, in turn, enforces its primary location as a gay discourse, separate and outside the site of the fantasy which is normative male heterosexuality.[48]

Leibowitch comments as follows on AIDS, fantasy, and "the reality it pretends to signify":

> When they come to write the history of AIDS, socio-ethnologists will have to decide whether the "practitioners" of homosexuality or its heterosexual "onlookers" have been the more spectacular in their extravagance. The homosexual "life style" is so blatantly on display to the general public, so closely scrutinized, that it is likely we never will have been informed with such technicophantasmal complacency as to how "other people" live their lives.[49]

It was widely believed in the gay community that the connection of AIDS to homosexuality delayed and problematized virtually every aspect of the country's response to the crisis. That the response *was* delayed and problematic is the conclusion of various investigators.[50] Attempting to assess the degree to which prejudice, fear, or ignorance of homosexuality may have affected public policy and research efforts, Panem concluded that homosexuality per se would not have deterred scientists from selecting interesting and rewarding research projects. But "the argument of ignorance appears to have more credibility."[51] She quotes James Curran's 1984 judgment that policy, funding, and communication were all delayed because only people in New York and California had any real sense of crisis or comprehension of the gay male community. "Scientists avoid issues that relate to sex," he said, "and there is not much understanding of homosexuality." This was an understatement: according to Curran, many eminent scientists during this period rejected the possibility that AIDS was an

---

[48]Donald Mager, "The Discourse about Homophobia, Male and Female Contexts," presented at the annual meeting of the Modern Language Association, New York, December 1986.

[49]Leibowitch, *A Strange Virus*, p. 3.

[50]See, for example, Schwartz, "AIDS in the Media"; Baltimore and Wolff, *Confronting AIDS*; "AIDS Hearing," Committee on Energy and Commerce, Subcommittee on Health and the Environment, US House of Representatives, September 17, 1984 (Serial No. 98–105, Washington, D.C., US Government Printing Office); and Office of Technology Assessment, *Review of the Public Health Service's Response to AIDS: A Technical Memorandum*, OTA-TM-H-24, Congress of the US, Washington, D.C., US Government Printing Office, February 1985.

[51]Sandra Panem, "AIDS: Public Policy and Biomedical Research," *Hastings Center Report*, Special Supplement, vol. 15, no. 4 (August 1985), p. 24.

infectious disease because they had no idea how a man could transmit an infectious agent to another man.[52] Other instances of ignorance are reported by Patton and Black.[53] Physician and scientist Joseph Sonnabend attributes this ignorance to the sequestered ivory towers that many AIDS investigators (particularly those who do straight laboratory research as opposed to clinical work) inhabit and argues instead that AIDS needs to be studied in its cultural totality. Gay male sexual practices should not be dismissed out of hand because they seem "unnatural" to the straight (in both senses) scientist: "the rectum is a sexual organ, and it deserves the respect that a penis gets and a vagina gets. Anal intercourse is a central sexual activity, and it should be supported, it should be celebrated."[54] A National Academy of Sciences panel studying the AIDS crisis in 1986 cited an urgent need for accurate and *current* information about sex and sexual practices in the US, noting that no comprehensive research had been carried out since Kinsey's studies in the 1940s; they recommended, as well, social science research on a range of social behaviors relevant to the transmission and control of AIDS.[55]

It has been argued that the perceived *gayness* of AIDS was ultimately a crucial political factor in obtaining funding. Dennis Altman observes that the principle of providing adequate funding for AIDS research was institutionalized within the federal appropriations process as a result of the 1983 Congressional hearings chaired by Representatives Henry Waxman and Theodore Weiss, members of Congress representing large and visible gay communities.

> Here one sees the effect of the mobilization and organization of gays . . . it is salutary to imagine the tardiness of the response had IV users and Haitians been the only victims of AIDS, had Republicans controlled the House of Representatives as well as the Senate (and hence chaired the relevant oversight and appropriations committees) or, indeed, had AIDS struck ten years earlier, before the existence of an organized gay movement, openly gay professionals who could testify before the relevant committees and openly gay congressional staff.[56]

But these social and political issues were felt by many to be essentially irrelevant. From the beginning, the hypothesis that AIDS was caused by an infectious agent was favored within the US scientific community. The hypothesis was strengthened when the syndrome began to be identified in a diversity of populations and found to cause apparently identical damage to the underlying immune system. By May 1984 a viral etiology for AIDS had been generally accepted, and the real question became precisely what kind of viral agent this could be.

---

[52] *Ibid.*

[53] Patton, *Sex and Germs*; Patton, "Feminists Have Avoided the Issue of AIDS"; Black, *The Plague Years.*

[54] Joseph Sonnabend, "Looking at AIDS in Totality: A Conversation," *New York Native*, 129 (October 7–13, 1985).

[55] Baltimore and Wolff, *Confronting AIDS.*

[56] D. Altman, *AIDS in the Mind of America*, pp. 116–117.

Rendezvous with 007

"Interpretations," write Bruno Latour and Steve Woolgar in *Laboratory Life*, their analysis of the construction of facts in science, "do not so much *in*form as *per*form.[57] And nowhere do we see interpretation shaped toward performance so clearly as in the issues and controversies surrounding the identification and naming of "the AIDS virus."

As early as 1979, gay men in New York and California were coming down with and dying from illnesses unusual in young healthy people. One of the actors who helped create the San Francisco *A.I.D.S. Show* recalled that early period:

> I had a friend who died way way back in New York in 1981. He was one of the first to go. We didn't know what AIDS was, there was no name for it. We didn't know it was contagious—we had no idea it was sexually transmitted—we didn't know it was anything. We just thought that he—alone—was ill. He was 26 years old and just had one thing after another wrong with him. . . . He was still coming to work—'cause he didn't *know* he had a terminal disease.[58]

The oddness of these nameless isolated events gave way to an even more terrifying period in which gay men on both coasts gradually began to realize that too many friends and acquaintances were dying. As the numbers mounted, the deaths became "cases" of what was informally called in New York hospitals WOGS: the Wrath of God Syndrome.[59] It all became official in 1981, when five deaths in Los Angeles from *Pneumocystis* pneumonia were described in the June 5 issue of the CDC's bulletin *Morbidity and Mortality Weekly Report* with an editorial note explaining that

> the occurrence of pneumocystosis in these 5 previously healthy individuals without a clinically apparent underlying immunodeficiency is unusual. The fact that these patients were all homosexuals suggests an association between some aspect of a homosexual lifestyle or disease acquired through sexual contact and *Pneumocystis* pneumonia in this population.[60]

Gottlieb's 1981 paper in the *New England Journal of Medicine* described the deaths of young, previously healthy gay men from another rare but rarely fatal

---

[57]Latour and Woolgar, *Laboratory Life*.

[58]From *The A.I.D.S. Show*.

[59]See Sontag, *Illness as Metaphor*.

[60]Centers for Disease Control, "*Pneumocystis* Pneumonia—Los Angeles," *Morbidity and Mortality Weekly Report*, vol. 30, no. 21 (June 5, 1981), pp. 250–252.

disease.[61] The deaths were attributed to a breakdown of the immune system that left the body utterly unable to defend itself against infections not normally fatal. The syndrome was provisionally called GRID: gay-related immunodeficiency. These published reports drew similar information from physicians in other cities, and before too long these rare diseases had been diagnosed in nongay people (for example, hemophiliacs and people who had recently had blood transfusions).[62] Epidemiological follow-up interviews over the next several months confirmed that the problem—whatever it was—was growing at epidemic rates, and a CDC task force was accordingly established to coordinate data collection, communication, and research. The name *AIDS* was selected at a 1982 conference in Washington (*GRID* was no longer applicable now that nongays were also getting sick): acquired immune deficiency syndrome ("reasonably descriptive," said Curran, "without being pejorative").[63]

Over the next two years, epidemiological and clinical evidence increasingly pointed toward the role of some infectious agent in AIDS. Researchers divided over this, with some searching for a single agent, others positing a "multifactorial cause." Most scientists affiliated with federal scientific agencies (primarily the National Institutes of Health and Centers for Disease Control) have tended toward the single-agent theory (as though "cofactors" were a kind of deuces-wild element that vulgarized serious investigation), and this view has tended to dominate scientific reporting. Although some independent researchers, clinicians, and non-US scientists protested the increasingly rigid party line of what has been called "the AIDS Mafia," multifactorial and environmental theories were subordinated to the quest for the single agent.[64] The National Cancer Institute (NCI), for example, developed a research strategy that focused on retroviruses, essentially to the exclusion of other lines of research, while other US virology and immunology laboratories put forward their own favored possibilities.[65] By 1983 the "leading candidate" for the AIDS virus seemed to be a member of the human T-cell leukemia family of viruses (HTLV), so called because they typically infect a particular kind of cell, the T-helper cells. But these were *retroviruses*, and there was doubt that a retrovirus

---

[61]M. S. Gottlieb, R. Schroff, H. M. Schanker, *et al.*, "Pneumocystis Carinii Pneumonia and Mucosal Candidiasis in Previously Healthy Homosexual Men," *New England Journal of Medicine*, 305 (1981), pp. 1425–1431.

[62]See Centers for Disease Control, "Kaposi's Sarcoma and *Pneumocystis* Pneumonia among Homosexual Men— New York City and California," *Morbidity and Mortality Weekly Report*, vol. 30, no. 25 (July 3, 1981), pp. 305–308, and Keewhan Choi, "Assembling the AIDS Puzzle: Epidemiology," in *AIDS: Facts and Issues*, ed. Victor Gong and Norman Rudnick, New Brunswick, New Jersey, Rutgers University Press, 1986.

[63]Quoted in Black, *The Plague Years.*

[64]Some scientists outside the federal health care network charge that the US government—"the AIDS Mafia"— dictates a party line on AIDS. Joseph Sonnabend, MD, former scientific director of the AIDS Medical Foundation, began the *Journal of AIDS Research* to print scientific articles he believed were being suppressed because they argued for a multifactorial cause rather than a single virus. See Black, *The Plague Years*, pp. 112–118, for discussion.

[65]Panem, "AIDS: Public Policy and Biomedical Research," p. 25.

could cause immunosuppression in humans.[66] Yet by this time it was widely agreed that AIDS was, indeed, a "new" disease—neither a statistical fluke nor a feature of the gay life-style. This generated excitement in the medical and scientific community not only because truly new diseases are rare, but also because its *cause* might be new as well. In 1983 Luc Montagnier at the Pasteur Institute in Paris identified what he called LAV, lymphadenopathy-associated virus.[67] In 1984 Robert Gallo, at NCI, identified what *he* called HTLV-III, human T-cell lymphotropic virus type III (the third type identified by his laboratory).[68] In accordance with Koch's postulates, both viruses were isolated in the blood and semen of AIDS patients; no trace was found in the healthy control population.[69]

These powerful findings—disputed and contentious though they were to be—narrowed almost at once the basic biomedical science agenda with regard to AIDS. In the construction of scientific facts, the existence of a name plays a crucial role in providing a coherent and unified signifier—a shorthand way of signifying what may be a complex, inchoate, or little-understood concept. Latour and Woolgar divide the research they studied into the long and uncer-

---

[66]The scientific account of retroviruses goes something like this: A virus (from Latin *virus*, "poison") cannot reproduce outside living cells: it enters into another organism's "host" cell and uses that cell's biochemical machinery to replicate itself. These replicant virus particles then infect other cells; this process is repeated until the infection is either brought under control by the host's immune system or the infection overwhelms and kills or debilitates the host, making it susceptible to other infections (as HIV does). Alternatively, virus and host may reach a state of equilibrium in which both coexist for years. The virus's initial entry into the host cell may cause symptoms of viral infections. Certain viruses can remain inactive, or latent, inside the host cell for long periods without causing problems; they can remain integrated with the cell's DNA (genetic material) until triggered to replicate (typically when the organism is compromised by old age, immunosuppressive drug therapy, or infection by another virus or bacteria); at this point the DNA is transcribed to RNA, which in turn becomes protein.

A retrovirus replicates "backward," transferring genetic information from viral RNA into DNA, the opposite of previously known viral actions. The retrovirus carries RNA (instead of DNA) as its genetic material along with a unique enzyme, reverse transcriptase (from which the name *retro* comes); this uses the RNA as a template to generate (transcribe) a DNA copy. This viral DNA inserts itself among the cell's own chromosomes; thus positioned to function as a "new gene" for the infected host, it can immediately start producing viral RNAs (new viruses) or remain latent until activated. In the case of HIV the latency period can be as long as fourteen years (as of this writing) followed by a very sudden explosion of replication activity that may directly kill the host's cell—chiefly the T4-lymphocyte, a white blood cell that regulates the body's immune response. The rapid depletion of T4-cells, characteristic of AIDS, leaves the human host vulnerable to many infections that a normal immune system would repel. The HTLV isolated by Gallo in 1980 was the first identified retrovirus associated with human disease (see Osborn, "The AIDS Epidemic," p. 47).

[67]F. Barre-Sinoussi, J. C. Chernann, F. Rey, *et al.*, "Isolation of a T-Lymphotropic Retrovirus from a Patient at Risk for Acquired Immune Deficiency Syndrome," *Science*, no. 220 (1983), pp. 868–871; L. Montagnier, J. C. Chernann, F. Barre-Sinoussi, *et al.*, "A New Human T-Lymphotropic Retrovirus: Characterization and Possible Role in Lymphadenopathy and Acquired Immune Deficiency Syndromes," in *Human T-Cell Leukemia/Lymphoma Virus*, ed. R. C. Gallo, M.E. Essex, and L. Gross, Cold Spring Harbor, New York, Cold Spring Harbor Laboratory, 1984, pp. 363–379.

[68]Gallo and his colleagues published four papers on the isolation of HTLV-III in *Science*, no. 224 (1984), pp. 497–508.

[69]Koch's postulates, developed by bacteriologist Robert Koch, would require that, in order to establish a specific virus as the "cause" of the AIDS syndrome, the virus would have to be present in all cases of the disease; antibody to the virus must be shown to develop in constant temporal relation to the development of AIDS; and transmission of the same virus to a previously uninfected animal or human must be demonstrated with subsequent development of the disease and reisolation of the infective agent. With AIDS, a lethal disease, this last requirement cannot be tested on humans, but a demonstration that the virus could be used to produce an effective vaccine would more or less fulfill this requirement. See Marx, "Strong New Candidate for AIDS Agent," p. 151, and P. M. Feorino, *et al.*, "Lymphadenopathy Associated Virus Infection of a Blood Donor-Recipient Pair with Acquired Immunodeficiency Syndrome," in Kulstad, ed., *AIDS: Papers from Science*, p. 216.

tain phase that led up to the identification, synthesis, and naming of TRF (H) (the thyrotropin-releasing factor [hormone], a substance involved in neuroendocrine hormone regulation) and the subsequent narrower and more routine phase in which the concept's status as "a fact" was taken for granted (the dispute over naming is relevant to the tussle over the names LAV and HTLV).[70] So too with AIDS: before the isolation of the virus, there were considerably more universes of inquiry and open-ended speculations. Evidence for a virus as agent intensified scientific control over signification and enabled scientists to rule out less relevant hypotheses and lines of research. Of course, the existence of *two* names—LAV and HTLV-III—complicated the signification process: did two signifiers entail two distinct signifieds? Despite the wrangling over this point between the involved parties, a clearer consensus nevertheless emerged that basic research should now relate directly to the hypothesis that a single virus was "the culprit" responsible for AIDS. Important issues included (1) etiology, (2) the identification of the virus's genetic structure and precise shape, (3) clinical and other information about transmission, (4) information about the clinical expression of the disease (discovery that the virus infected brain cells encouraged its renaming, since the names LAV and HTLV both presupposed an attack on lymph cells), (5) the scope and natural history of the disease, (6) differences among "risk groups," and (7) epidemiological information including the long-term picture (circumstantial evidence but important nevertheless).

To most scientists this process of narrowing inquiry and relinquishing peripheral lines of thought is simply the way science is done, the procedural sine qua non for establishing anything that can be called a "fact." But "a statement always has borders peopled by other statements,"[71] and it is important for us to keep in mind the provisional and consensual nature of this US AIDS research agenda, each area of which exists within a heavily populated social, cultural, and ideological territory. Consider the hypothesis that AIDS originated in Africa, for example (a view supported by the research of Gallo's colleague Myron Essex, whose African viruses are genetically similar to the virus Gallo's lab identified). Not surprisingly, some "geographic buck-passing" took place among the African countries themselves (Rwanda and Zambia say AIDS originated in Zaire, Uganda says it came from Tanzania, and so on). Beneath such public maneuvering, however, many Africans privately believe AIDS may have originated somewhere else. And, despite Gallo's assertion that he cannot "conceive of AIDS coming from elsewhere into Africa," the view is by no means universal, especially among non-US researchers.[72] Further, Americans refuse to acknowledge the possibility that exports of American blood products may have spread the disease to people elsewhere. In the Soviet Union, AIDS is considered a

---

[70]Latour and Woolgar, *Laboratory Life*, pp. 105–150, esp. pp. 108–112.

[71]Michel Foucault, *The Archaeology of Knowledge*, trans. A. M. Sheridan Smith, New York, Pantheon, 1972, p. 97.

[72]African data are reviewed in L. Altman, "Linking AIDS to Africa," p. 8.

"foreign problem," attributable to the CIA or to tribes in Central Africa.[73] In the Caribbean, and even within the US, AIDS is widely believed to come from US biological testing.[74] The French first believed AIDS was introduced by way of an "American pollutant," probably contaminated amyl nitrate (they also believed AIDS came from Morocco).[75] The Soviet Union, Israel, Africa, Haiti, and the US Armed Forces deny the existence of indigenous homosexuality and thus claim that AIDS must always have originated "elsewhere."[76]

By 1986, five years after the initial article in the *Morbidity and Mortality Weekly Report*, a Human Retrovirus Subcommittee empowered by the International Committee on the Taxonomy of Viruses was at work "to propose an appropriate name for the retrovirus isolates recently implicated as the causative agents of the acquired immune deficiency syndrome (AIDS)"—to consider, that is, what "the AIDS virus" should officially be named. After more than a year of deliberation, the nomenclature subcommittee published its recommendations in the form of a letter to scientific journals.[77] Their task has been made crucial, they note, by the widespread interest in AIDS and the multiplicity of names now in use:

LAV:	lymphadenopathy-associated virus (1983—Montagnier, Pasteur)
HTLV-III:	human T-cell lymphotropic virus type III (1984—Gallo, NCI)
IDAV:	immunodeficiency-associated virus
ARV:	AIDS-associated retrovirus (1984—Levy, UCSF)
HTLV-III/LAV and LAV/HTLV-III:	compound names used to keep peace (the CDC's use was perhaps a reprimand to the NCI for its perceived uncooperativeness in sharing data)
AIDS virus:	popular press

The subcommittee proposes HIV, "human immunodeficiency viruses." They reason that this conforms to the nomenclature of other viruses in which the first slot signals the host species (human), the second slot the major pathogenic property (immunodeficiency), and the last slot V for virus. (For some viruses, though not HIV, individual strains are distinguished by the initials of the thus "immortalized" patient from whom they originally came and in whose "daughter cells" they are perpetuated.) The multiple names of "the AIDS virus"

---

[73]Lee, "AIDS in Moscow."

[74]See Rechy, "An Exchange on AIDS."

[75]Leibowitch documents French views in *A Strange Virus*.

[76]For a fuller analysis of the theory and politics of these origin and alibi stories, see Patton, *Sex and Germs*; Weeks, *Sexuality and Its Discontents*; D. Altman, *AIDS in the Mind of America*; Ann Guidici Fettner and William Check, *The Truth About AIDS: Evolution of an Epidemic*, New York, Holt, Rinehart & Winston, 1985; and Leibowitch, *A Strange Virus*.

[77]The letter appeared in *Science*, no. 232, (May 9, 1986), p. 697.

point toward a succession of identities and offer a fragmented sense indeed of what this virus, or family of viruses, "really" is. The new name, in contrast, promises to unify the political fragmentations of the scientific establishment and to certify the health of the single-virus hypothesis. The subcommittee argues in favor of its proposed name that it does not incorporate the term AIDS, on the advice of many clinicians; it is distinct from all existing names and "has been chosen without regard to priority of discovery" (not insignificantly, Montagnier and Levy signed the subcommittee letter but Gallo and Essex did not); and it distinguishes the HI viruses from those with distinctly different biological properties, for example, the HTLV line (HTLV-I and HTLV-II), which this subcommittee calls "human t-cell leukemia viruses," perhaps to chastise Gallo for changing the *L* in the nomenclature of the HTLVs from *leukemia* to *lymphotropic* so that HTLV-III (the AIDS virus) would appear to fit generically into the same series (and bear the stamp of his lab). In the same issue of *Science*, the editors chose to discuss this letter in their "News and Comment" column: "Disputes over viral nomenclature do not ordinarily command much attention beyond the individuals immediately involved in the fray"; but the current dissension, part of the continuing controversy over who should get credit for discovering the virus, "could provide 6 months of scripts for the television series 'Dallas.'"[78]

Why such struggles over naming and interpretation? Because, as the *Science* editors point out, there are high stakes where this performance is concerned—not only patent rights to the lucrative test kits for the "AIDS virus" (Gallo fears that loss of the HTLV-III designation will weaken his claims) but the future and honor of immunology. Modern immunology, as Donna Haraway observes, moved into the realm of high science when it reworked the military combat metaphors of World War II (battles, struggle, territory, enemy, truces) into the language of postmodern warfare: communication command control—coding, transmission, messages—interceptions, spies, lies.[79] Scientific descriptions for general readers, like this one from the *National Geographic* article on the immune system, accentuate this shift from combat to code:

> Many of these enemies [of the body, or self] have evolved devious methods to escape detection. The viruses that cause influenza and the common cold, for example, constantly mutate, changing their fingerprints. The AIDS virus, most insidious of all, employs a range of strategies, including hiding out in healthy cells. What makes it fatal is its ability to invade and kill helper T cells, thereby short-circuiting the entire immune response.[80]

---

[78]Jean L. Marx, "AIDS Virus Has New Name—Perhaps," News and Comment, *Science*, no. 232 (May 9, 1986), pp. 699–700.

[79]Donna J. Haraway, "The Biological Enterprise: Sex, Mind, and Profit from Human Engineering to Sociobiology," *Radical History Review*, no. 20 (Spring–Summer 1979), pp. 206–237, and "A Manifesto for Cyborgs: Science, Technology, and Socialist Feminism in the 1980s," *Socialist Review*, no. 80 (March–April 1985), pp. 65–108.

[80]Jaret, "Our Immune System," p. 709.

No ground troops here, no combat, not even generals: we see here the evolution of a conception of the "AIDS virus" as a top-flight secret agent—a James Bond of secret agents, armed with "a range of strategies" and licensed to kill. "Like Greeks hidden inside the Trojan horse," 007 enters the body concealed inside a helper T-cell from an infected host,[81] but "the virus is not an innocent passenger in the body of its victims."[82]

> In the invaded victim, helper T's immediately detect the foreign T cell. But as the two T's meet, the virus slips through the cell membrane into the defending cell. Before the defending T cell can mobilize the troops, the virus disables it. . . . Once inside an inactive T cell, the virus may lie dormant for months, even years. Then, perhaps when another, unrelated infection triggers the invaded T cells to divide, the AIDS virus also begins to multiply. One by one, its clones emerge to infect nearby T cells. Slowly but inexorably the body loses the very sentinels that should be alerting the rest of the immune system. Phagocytes and killer cells receive no call to arms. B cells are not alerted to produce antibodies. The enemy can run free.[83]

But on no mundane battlefield. The January 1987 *Scientific American* column "Science and the Citizen" warns of the mutability—the "protean nature of the AIDS virus"—that will make very difficult the development of a vaccine, as well as the perfect screening of blood. "It is also possible," the column concludes, "that a more virulent strain could emerge"; even now "the envelope of the virus seems to be changing."[84] Clearly, 007 is a spy's spy, capable of any deception: evading the "fluid patrol officers" is child's play. Indeed, it is so shifting and uncertain we might even acknowledge our own historical moment more specifically by giving the AIDS virus a postmodern identity: a terrorist's terrorist, an Abu Nidal of viruses.[85]

---

[81]*Ibid.*, p. 723; and see D. J. Anderson and E. J. Yunis, "'Trojan Horse' Leukocytes in AIDS," *New England Journal of Medicine*, no. 309 (1983), pp. 984–985.

[82]Krim, "AIDS: The Challenge to Science and Medicine."

[83]Jaret, "Our Immune System," pp. 723–724.

[84]"Science and the Citizen," pp. 58–59.

[85]Leibowitch, in *A Strange Virus*, describes the scientific effort to identify the AIDS virus as a "medico-biological Interpol" on the trail of an international "criminal" charged with "breaking and entering" (pp. 41–42), and asks "Who is HTLV?" (p. 48). Mervyn B. Silverman, describing the mechanism of AIDS transmission at the Congressional AIDS hearing in 1983, testified in comparable language that "many believe that the virus does not act alone" ("AIDS Hearing," p. 125). In an article on a related finding in immunological research, Jos Van ("Cell Researchers Aim to Flush Out Body's Terrorists," *Chicago Tribune*, October 5, 1986) refers to cells called "free radicals," which serve as the body's "terrorists." A *Consumer Reports* article entitled "AIDS: Deadly but Hard to Catch" inadvertently invokes the structural ambiguity of "catching" the virus (who is the catcher; who is the catchee?). The policing metaphor (and the connection between *policy* and *police* has not gone unnoticed) carries over to efforts to control the spread of the virus. Lieberson ("The Reality of AIDS," p. 47) reports that some gay clubs have created "fluid patrol officers" who try to ensure that no "unsafe sex" takes place. Mohr argues that such attempts to promote "safe" sexual behavior, like recommendations for celibacy, seem "remote from reality and quite oblivious to the cussedness of sex and culture." Further, Mohr argues, "though in midcrisis it is politically injudicious to say so, safe-sex is poor sex" ("Of Deathbeds and Quarantines," p. 52); as an epigram for his essay he quotes a former gay "reprobate," now reformed: "Who wants to suck a dick with a rubber on it?" (See also Richard Goldstein, "The New Sobriety," *Village Voice*, December 30, 1986, pp. 23–28.)

So long as AIDS was seen as a battle for the body of the gay male—a battle linked to "sociological" factors at that—the biomedical establishment was not tremendously interested in it. The first professionals involved tended to be clinicians in the large urban hospitals where men with AIDS first turned up, epidemiologists (AIDS, writes Black, is an "epidemiologist's dream"; a mystery disease that is fatal),[86] and scientists and clinicians who were gay themselves. Although from the beginning some saw the theoretical implications of AIDS, the possibility that AIDS was "merely" some unanticipated side-effect of gay male sexual practices (about which, as I've noted above, there was considerable ignorance) limited its appeal for basic scientists. But with the discovery that the agent associated with AIDS appeared to be a virus—indeed, a *novel retrovirus*— what had seemed predominantly a public health phenomenon (clinical and service-oriented) suddenly could be rewritten in terms of high theory and high science. The performance moved from off-off Broadway to the heart of the theater district and the price of the tickets went way up. Among other things, identifying the viral agent made possible the development of a "definitive test" for its presence; not only did this open new scientific avenues (for example, in enabling researchers to map precise relationships among diverse AIDS and AIDS-like clinical manifestations), it also created opportunities for monetary rewards (for example, in revenue from patents on the testing kits). For these reasons, AIDS research became a highly competitive professional field.[87] Less-established assistant professors who had been working on the AIDS problem out of commitment suddenly found senior scientists peering at their data, while in the public arena the triumphs of pure basic science research were proclaimed. "Biomedical science is going brilliantly well," was how Dr. June Osborn summarized AIDS progress in mid-1986.[88] "Indeed," writes one science reporter, "had AIDS struck 20 years ago, we would have been utterly baffled by it."[89] Ten years ago we had not even confirmed the *existence* of human retroviruses, notes *Scientific American*. Asked whether NCI's strategy of focusing exclusively on retrovirus research was appropriate (considering that it might not have paid off), an official said this wouldn't have mattered: basic retroviral research was NCI's priority in any case.[90] Because it *did* pay off, it can now be said (as it could not have been said before 1984) that "AIDS may be a disease that has arrived at the right time."[91] In the words of one biomedical scientist,

[86]Black, *The Plague Years.*

[87]For discussion and analysis of the growing competition in AIDS research as the funding increased, see D. Altman, *AIDS in the Mind of America*; Black, *The Plague Years*; Patton, *Sex and Germs*; Panem, "AIDS: Public Policy and Biomedical Research"; Schwartz, "AIDS in the Media"; Office of Technology Assessment, *Review*; *Hastings Center Report*, Special Supplements. For an account of the case of French physician Willy Rozenbaum, see Paul Raeburn, "Doctor Faces Politics of AIDS Research," *Champaign-Urbana News-Gazette*, January 25, 1986, p. A-8.

[88]Cited in Eckholm, "Broad Alert on AIDS," p. 19.

[89]Jaret, "Our Immune System," p. 23.

[90]Panem, "AIDS: Public Policy and Biomedical Research," p. 25.

[91]"Science and the Citizen," p. 59.

we face "an impending Armageddon of AIDS, and the salvation of the world through molecular genetics."[92]

Reconstructing the AIDS Text: Rewriting the Body

There is now broad consensus that AIDS—"plague of the millennium," "health disaster of pandemic proportions"—is the greatest public health problem of our era.[93] The epidemic of signification that surrounds AIDS is neither simple nor under control. AIDS exists at a point where many entrenched narratives intersect, each with its own problematic and context in which AIDS acquires meaning. It is extremely difficult to resist the lure, familiarity, and ubiquitousness of these discourses. The AIDS virus enters the cell and integrates with its genetic code, establishing a disinformation campaign at the highest level and ensuring that replication and dissemination will be systemic. We inherit a series of discursive dichotomies; the discourse of AIDS attaches itself to these other systems of difference and plays itself out there:

---

[92]Quoted in Morton Hunt, "Teaming Up against AIDS," *New York Times Magazine*, March 2, 1986, p. 78. Despite whatever criticisms biomedical scientists may have had about AIDS research, an ideology of heroism, progress, and faith in ultimate scientific conquest pervades discussions. Examples include Choi, "Assembling the AIDS Puzzle"; Relman, "Introduction"; Gallo, "The AIDS Virus"; Donald S. Frederickson, "Where Do We Go from Here?" in *The AIDS Epidemic*, ed. Kevin M. Cahill, New York, St. Martin's Press, 1983, pp. 151–161; Donald P. Francis, "The Search for the Cause," in *The AIDS Epidemic*; American Medical Association Council on Scientific Affairs, "The Acquired Immunodeficiency Syndrome: Commentary," *Journal of the American Medical Association*, vol. 252, no. 15 (October 19, 1984), pp. 2037–2043; Sheldon H. Landesman, Harold M. Ginzburg, and Stanley H. Weiss, "The AIDS Epidemic," *New England Journal of Medicine*, vol. 312, no. 8 (February 21, 1985), pp. 521–525; and Merle A. Sande, "Transmission of AIDS: The Case against Casual Contagion," *New England Journal of Medicine*, vol. 314, no. 6 (February 6, 1986), pp. 380–382. Sonnabend ("Looking at AIDS in Totality") criticizes the assumptions of heroic science, while Leibowitch (*A Strange Virus*) is distinctive in his irony and political self-consciousness about the nature of the scientific enterprise.

[93]As of December 1986, ten million people were estimated to carry the virus worldwide; at least a quarter of these people are expected to develop AIDS within the next five years and many more to develop illnesses ranging from mildly disabling to lethal. By the end of 1986, almost 30,000 people in the US had been diagnosed with AIDS, and half of them had already died. The number of diagnosed cases is expected to reach 270,000 by the end of 1991, with a cumulative death toll of 179,000. There will be a heavy financial toll. With repeated hospitalizations, a person with AIDS may have medical costs of up to $500,000. The cases of AIDS diagnosed in 1986 alone will eventually cost the nation $2.25 billion in health care costs and $7 billion in lost lifetime earnings. Its expenses are seventy-five times what we are currently spending on it. (Costs vary greatly from city to city: the CDC estimated in 1986 that each case would average $147,000; the US Army estimated that a case could cost as much as $500,000 to treat; but in San Francisco, use of nonphysician caretakers, home care, and nursing home services can bring the cost of a comparable case down to $42,000. See "AIDS Hearing"; Patton, *Sex and Germs*; D. Altman, *AIDS in the Mind of America*; David L. Wheeler, "More Research Is Urged in Fight against AIDS," *Chronicle of Higher Education*, November 5, 1986, pp. 7, 10; and David Tuller, "Trying to Avoid an Insurance Debacle," *New York Times*, February 22, 1987, sec. 3, pp. 1, 8, for discussion of the politics of AIDS funding. The National Academy of Sciences Report [Baltimore and Wolff, *Confronting AIDS*] judges recent federal allocations to be "greatly improved" but still "woefully inadequate" and calls for spending $2 billion per year by 1990 for education and the development of drugs and vaccines.) See American Medical Association Council on Scientific Affairs, "Commentary," Centers for Disease Control, "Update"; Edward S. Johnson and Jeffrey Vieira, "Cause of AIDS: Etiology," in *AIDS: Facts and Issues*, ed. Victor Gong and Norman Rudnick, New Brunswick, New Jersey, Rutgers University Press, 1986, pp. 25–33; Redfield *et al.*, "Heterosexually Acquired HTLV-III/LAV," and "Female-to-Male Transmission"; Katie Leishman, "Two Million Americans and Still Counting," review of Black, *The Plague Years*, and Nichols, *Mobilizing Against AIDS*, *New York Times Book Review*, July 27, 1986, p. 12; Gong and Rudnick, eds., *AIDS: Facts and Issues*; and Warren Winkelstein, Jr., *et al.*, "Sexual Practices and Risk of Infection by the Human Immunodeficiency Virus: The San Francisco Men's Health Study," *Journal of the American Medical Association*, vol. 257, no. 3 (January 16, 1987), pp. 321–325, for predictions based on current distribution of HIV antibodies.

self and not-self
the one and the other
homosexual and heterosexual
homosexual and "the general population"
active and passive, guilty and innocent, perpetrator and victim
vice and virtue, us and them, anus and vagina
sins of the parent and innocence of the child
love and death, sex and death, sex and money, death and money
science and not-science, knowledge and ignorance
doctor and patient, expert and patient, doctor and expert
addiction and abstention, contamination and cleanliness
contagion and containment, life and death
injection and reception, instrument and receptacle
normal and abnormal, natural and alien
prostitute and paragon, whore and wife
safe sex and bad sex, safe sex and good sex
First World and Third World, free world and iron curtain
capitalists and communists
certainty and uncertainty
virus and victim, guest and host

As Christine Brooke-Rose demonstrates, one must pay close attention to the way in which these apparently fundamental and natural semantic oppositions are put to work.[94] What is self and what is not-self? Who wears the white and who the black hat? (Or, in her discussion, perhaps, who wears the pants and who the skirt?) As Bryan Turner observes with regard to sexually transmitted diseases in general, the diseased are seen not as "victims" but as "agents" of biological disaster. If Koch's postulates must be fulfilled to identify a given microbe with a given disease, perhaps it would be helpful, in rewriting the AIDS text, to take "Turner's postulates" into account: (1) disease is a language; (2) the body is a representation; and (3) medicine is a political practice.[95]

There is little doubt that for some people the AIDS crisis lends force to their fear and hatred of gays; AIDS appears, for example, to be a significant factor in the increasing violence against them, and other homophobic acts in the US.[96] But to talk of "homophobia" as though it were a simple and rather easily recognized phenomenon is impossible. When we review the various conceptions of the gay male body produced within scientific research by the signifier

---

[94]Christine Brooke-Rose, "Woman as a Semiotic Object," in *The Female Body in Western Culture: Contemporary Perspectives*, ed. Susan Rubin Suleiman, Cambridge, Massachusetts, Harvard University Press, 1986, pp. 305–316. See also Teresa de Lauretis, *Alice Doesn't: Feminism, Semiotics, Cinema*, Bloomington, Indiana University Press, 1984.

[95]Bryan A. Turner, *The Body and Society*, New York, Basil Blackwell, 1984, pp. 221, 209.

[96]William R. Greer, "Violence against Homosexuals Rising, Groups Say in Seeking Protections," *New York Times*, November 23, 1986, p. 15.

AIDS, we find a discourse rich in signification as to what AIDS "means." At first, some scientists doubted that AIDS could be an infectious disease because they could not imagine what gay men could do to each other to transmit infection. But intimate knowledge generated quite different conceptions:

> AIDS is caused by multiple and violent gay sexual encounters: exposure to countless infections and pathogenic agents overwhelms the immune system.
>
> AIDS is caused by killer sperm, shooting from one man's penis to the anus of another.
>
> Gay men are as sexually driven as alcoholics or drug addicts.
>
> AIDS cannot infect females because the virus can't penetrate the tough mucous membranes of the vagina.
>
> Women cannot transmit AIDS because their bodies do not have the strong projectile capacity of a penis or syringe.
>
> Prostitutes can transmit the virus because their contaminated bodies harbor massive quantities of killer microbes.

Repeated hints that the male body is sexually potent and adventurous suggest that homophobia in biomedical discourse might play out as a literal "fear of the same." The text constructed around the gay male body—the epidemic of signification so evident in the conceptions cited above and elsewhere in this essay—is driven in part by the need for constant flight from sites of potential identity and thus the successive construction of new oppositions that will barricade self from not-self. The homophobic meanings associated with AIDS continue to be layered into existing discourse: analysis demonstrates ways in which the AIDS virus is linguistically identified with those it strikes: the penis is "fragile," the urethra is "fragile," the virus is "fragile"; the African woman's body is "exotic," the virus is "exotic." The virus "penetrates" its victims; a carrier of death, it wears an "innocent" disguise. AIDS is "caused" by homosexuals; AIDS is "caused" by a virus. Homosexuality exists on a border between male and female, the virus between life and nonlife. This cross-cannibalization of language is unsurprising. What greater relief than to find a final refuge from the specter of gay sexuality where the language that has obsessively accumulated around the body can attach to its substitute: the virus. This is a signifier that can be embraced forever.

The question is how to disrupt and renegotiate the powerful cultural narratives surrounding AIDS. Homophobia is inscribed within other discourses at a high level, and it is at a high level that they must be interrupted and challenged. Why? The following scenario for Armageddon (believed by some, desired by many) makes clear why: AIDS will remain confined to the original high-risk groups (primarily gay males and IV drug users) because of their specific practices (like anal intercourse and sharing needles). At the Paris International AIDS Conference in June 1986, the ultimate spread of the disease was posed in terms of "containment" and "saturation." "Only" gay males and drug addicts will get infected—the virus will use them up and then have nowhere to go—the "general population" (who are also in epidemiological parlance a "virgin" population) will remain untouched. Even if this view is correct (which seems doubtful, given growing evidence of transmission through plain old everyday heterosexual intercourse), and the virus stops spreading once it has "saturated" the high-risk population, we would still be talking about a significant number of US citizens: 2.5 million gay men, 7 million additional men who have at some time in the last ten years engaged in homosexual activity, 750,000 habitual IV drug users, 750,000 occasional drug users, 10,000 hemophiliacs already infected, the sex partners of these people and the children of infected women—in other words, a total of more than 10 million people (the figures are from the June 1986 Paris conference). And "saturation" is currently considered a *best*-case scenario by the public health authorities.

The fact is that any separation of not-self ("AIDS victims") from self (the "general population") is no longer possible. The US Surgeon General and National Academy reports make clear that "that security blanket has now been stripped away."[97] Yet the familiar signifying practices that exercise control over meaning continue. The *Scientific American* column goes on to note fears that the one-to-one African ratio of females with AIDS to males may foreshadow US statistics: "Experts point out, however, that such factors as the prevalence of other venereal diseases that cause genital sores, the use of unsterilized needles in clinics, and the lack of blood-screening tests may explain the different epidemiology of AIDS in Africa."[98] Thus the African data are reinterpreted to reinstate the "us"/"them" dichotomy and project a rosier scenario for "us" (well, maybe it improves on comic Richard Belzer's narrative: "A monkey bites some guy on the ass in Africa and *he* balls some guy in Haiti and now we're all gonna fuckin' die. THANKS A LOT!").[99]

Meanwhile on the home front monogamy is coming back into its own, along with abstention, the safest sex of all. The virus in itself—by whatever name—has come to represent the moment of truth for the sexual revolution: as though God has once again sent his only beloved son to save us from our

---

[97]"Science and the Citizen," p. 58.

[98]*Ibid.*, p. 59.

[99]Though Lieberson insists that a "heterosexual pandemic [comparable to Africa's] has not occurred in the United States" and criticizes those who suggest it is going to ("The Reality of AIDS," p. 44), current data based on tests for antibodies to HIV among 1986 army recruits (nongay, non-drug-using, so far as researchers could determine) argue for increasing heterosexual transmission (Redfield, *et al.*, "Female to Male Transmission"). For discussion and analysis, see L. Altman, "Heterosexuals and AIDS"; D. Altman, *AIDS in the Mind of America*; Marx, "New Relatives of AIDS Virus Found"; Osborn, "The AIDS Epidemic"; Patton, *Sex and Germs*; Hosken, "Why AIDS Pattern Is Different in Africa"; Feldman, "Role of African Mutilations in AIDS Discounted"; and Robert Pear, "Ten-Fold Increase in AIDS Death Toll Is Expected by '91," *New York Times*, June 13, 1986, pp. A-1, A-17. See also Potterat, *et al.*, "Lying to Military Physicians." It has been suggested that malnutrition plays an important role in the rapid spread of AIDS in Africa (worldwide, malnutrition is the most common cause of acquired immune deficiency).

high-risk behavior. Who would have thought He would take the form of a virus: a viral Terminator ready to die for our sins.[100]

The contestations pioneered by the gay community over the past decade offer models for resistance. As old-fashioned morality increasingly infects the twentieth-century scenario, whether masquerading as "preventive health" or spiritual transformation, a new sampler can be stitched to hang on the bedroom wall: BETTER WED THAN DEAD. "It's just like the fifties," complains a gay man in San Francisco. "People are getting married again for all the wrong reasons."[101] One disruption of this narrative occurs in the San Francisco *A.I.D.S. Show:* "I *like* sex; I like to get drunk and smoke grass and use poppers and sleep with strangers: Call me old-fashioned, but that's what I like!" A gay pastor in San Francisco tells Frances FitzGerald that the moral transformation being forced upon the gay community reminds him of the days before Stonewall: "If I had to go back to living in the closet, I'd have to think very clearly about whether or not I'd rather be dead."[102] For Michel Foucault, the "tragedy" of AIDS was not intrinsically its lethal character, but rather that a group that has risked so much—gays—are looking to standard authorities—doctors, the church—for guidance in a time of crisis. "How can I be scared of AIDS when I could die in a car?" Foucault asked a year or so before he died. "If sex with a boy gives me pleasure. . . . " And he added: "Don't cry for me if I die."[103]

For AIDS, where meanings are overwhelming in their sheer volume and often explicitly linked to extreme political agendas, we do not know whose meanings will become "the official story." We need an epidemiology of signification—a comprehensive mapping and analysis of these multiple meanings—to form the basis for an official definition that will in turn constitute the policies, regulations, rules, and practices that will govern our behavior for some time to come. As we have seen, these may rest upon "facts," which in turn may rest

---

[100]We must even, perhaps, identify with the virus, an extraordinarily successful structure that has been comfortably making the acquaintance of living organisms for many more millions of years than we have. A virus that enters the human bloodstream and circulates through the body may ultimately negotiate with the host some mutually livable equilibrium. The relationship may be a close one: it is difficult to separate the effects of the virus from those of the body's defenses; and any poison intended for the guest may kill the host as well. Any given species, including human beings, may sometimes prove to be an inhospitable, even unnatural host. To speak teleologically for a moment, it is obvious that to kill the host is not in the microorganism's best interests; this sometimes happens, however, when a virus adapted to a nonhuman host shifts, through some untoward turn of events, to the human body. For the human immunodeficiency virus, believed to be a relative newcomer on earth (the presence of antibodies in stored blood now goes back to 1959 samples collected in Africa, to 1973 in US blood) and to have first inhabited African monkeys, we might have turned out to be inhospitable. But though from our perspective the virus is indeed virulent, killing quickly, in fact the long latency between infection and the appearance of clinical damage provides plenty of time—often years—for the virus to replicate and infect a new host. For the time being we are sufficiently hospitable for this virus to live off us relatively "successfully"; if mutation occurs, our relationship to the AIDS virus could evolve into something relatively benign or mutually disastrous.

[101]FitzGerald, *Cities on a Hill,* p. 115.

[102]*Ibid.,* p. 104.

[103]Philip Horvitz, "Don't Cry for Me, Academia," Interview with Michel Foucault, *Jimmy and Lucy's House of K* (Berkeley), no. 2 (August 1985), pp. 78–80. This interview, conducted in Berkeley (and scrutinized, it's said, like the Watergate transcripts, to find out what did he know and when did he know it), concludes as Foucault enters the BART station: "Good luck," he tells Horvitz. "And don't be scared!"

upon the deeply entrenched cultural narratives I have been describing. For this reason, what AIDS signifies must be democratically determined: we cannot afford to let scientists or any other group of "experts" dismiss our meanings as "misconceptions" and our alternative views as noise that interferes with the pure processes of scientific inquiry. Rather, we need to insist that many voices contribute to the construction of official definitions—and specifically certain voices that need urgently to be heard. Although the signification process for AIDS is by now very broad—just about everyone, seemingly, has offered "readings" of what AIDS means—one excluded group continues to be users of illegal intravenous drugs. Caught between the "first wave" (gay men) and the "second wave" (heterosexuals), drug users at high risk for AIDS remain silent and invisible. One public health official recently challenged the rush to educate heterosexuals about their risk when what is needed (and has been from the beginning) is "a massive effort directed at intravenous-drug abusers and their sex partners. This means treatment for a disease—chemical dependence on drugs. We have to prevent and treat one disease, drug addiction, to prevent another, AIDS."[104]

If AIDS's dual life as both a material and linguistic entity is important, the emphasis on *dual* is critical. Symbolic and social reconceptualizations of AIDS are necessary but not sufficient to address the massive social questions AIDS raises. The recognition that AIDS is heterosexually as well as homosexually transmitted certainly represents progress, but it does not interrupt fantasy. It is fantasy, for example, to believe that "safer sex" will protect us from AIDS; it may save us from becoming infected with the virus—New York City has instituted Singles Night at the Blood Bank, where people can meet and share their seropositivity status before they even exchange names.[105] But AIDS is to be a fundamental force of twentieth-century life, and no barrier in the world can make us "safe" from its complex material realities. Malnutrition, poverty, and hunger are unacceptable, in our own country and in the rest of the world; the need for universal health care is urgent. Ultimately, we cannot distinguish self from not-self: for "plague is life," and each of us has the plague within us; "no one, no one on earth is free from it."[106]

The discursive structures I have discussed in this essay are familiar to those of us in "the human sciences." We have learned that there is a disjunction between historical subjects and constructed scientific objects. There is still

---

[104]See also Barrett, "Straight Shooters"; Stephen C. Joseph, "Intravenous-Drug Abuse Is the Front Line in the War on AIDS," Letter to the Editor, *New York Times*, December 22, 1986, p. 18. Though Check writes that "it sometimes appears that the only risk group that hasn't raised a ruckus is the IV drug users, who are not organized" ("Public Education on AIDS," p. 28), a few commentators are beginning to draw attention to this critical problem: Barrett, "Straight Shooters"; Joseph, "Intravenous Drug Abuse"; Shaw and Paleo, "Women and AIDS"; Peg Byron, "Women with AIDS: Untold Stories," *Village Voice*, September 24, 1985, pp. 16–19; and Francis X. Clines, "Via Addicts' Needles, AIDS Spreads in Edinburgh," *New York Times*, January 4, 1987, p. 8. In the last year, the Gay Men's Health Crisis in New York, aware that many drug users may avoid information centers as well as medical authorities, has taken responsibility for going to "shooting galleries," clinics, and drug treatment centers to provide AIDS education and training to these people so that they can in turn work with other drug users.

[105]"A 'Social Card' to Reassure Sex Partners," *San Francisco Chronicle*, October 17, 1985, p. 30.

[106]Camus, *The Plague*, p. 229.

debate about whether, or to what extent, scientific discourse can be privileged—and relied upon to transcend contradiction. My own view is unequivocal: it cannot be privileged in this way. Of course, where AIDS is concerned, science can usefully perform its interpretive part: we can learn to live—indeed, *must* learn to live—as though there are such things as viruses. The virus—a constructed scientific object—is also a historical subject, a "human immunodeficiency virus," a real source of illness and death that can be passed from one person to another under certain conditions that we can apparently—individually and collectively—influence. The trick is to learn to live with this disjunction, but the lesson is imperative. Dr. Rieux, the physician-narrator of Camus's novel, acknowledges that by dealing medically with the plague he is allowing himself the luxury of "living in a world of abstractions." But not indefinitely; for "when abstraction sets to killing you, you've got to get busy with it."

But getting busy with it may require us to relinquish some luxuries of our own: the luxury of accepting without reflection the "findings" science seems effortlessly able to provide us, the luxury of avoiding vigilance, the luxury of hoping it will all go away. Rather, we need to use what science gives us in ways that are selective, self-conscious, and pragmatic ("as though" they were true). We need to understand that AIDS is and will remain a provisional and deeply problematic signifier. Above all, we need to resist, at all costs, the luxury of listening to the thousands of language tapes playing in our heads, laden with prior discourse, that tell us with compelling certainty and dizzying contradiction what AIDS "really" means.

Questions for Reflection, Discussion, and Writing

1. According to Treichler, in what ways does dualistic thinking contribute to the cultural construction of AIDS as a "complex, puzzling, and quite terrifying phenomenon"? In what ways does ambiguity help to counteract those dualisms, according to Treichler? What do you think?

2. What links does Treichler establish between the words used by the medical community in constructing AIDS discourse and our current understanding of AIDS? How is medical discourse used to sanction AIDS discourse? In what ways have the medical community and media supported each other?

3. What is the role of language in signifying our understanding of facts and ideological constructions? More specifically, in what ways does language signify our understanding of AIDS discourse? According to Treichler, AIDS discourse has been authorized by our faith in science's ability to present us with objective "facts." Treichler suggests that these "facts" have been interpreted by a community of people. Given such a distinction, how might "facts" work to reproduce social and cultural inequalities?

4. In her examination and analysis of the ways AIDS has been presented historically, Treichler investigates the ways various groups have been positioned in media, medical and cultural constructions of what has caused the AIDS epidemic. Trace the

ways she calls into question these (re)presentations, perhaps by focusing on one group (racial, social, national, sexual) and examine the forces Treichler identifies as working to reproduce social beliefs. What is the role of power and authority in reproducing such social and cultural "truths"?

Writing Assignment

Locate a current article from a news, health or science magazine about HIV-AIDS and perform an analysis of its language about AIDS in an essay. Use the methods of observation and analysis Treichler employs in your close reading of how the article's discourse presents, and represents, HIV-AIDS.

Related Reading

Cindy Patton, *Sex & Germs: The Politics of AIDS*. Boston: South End Press. 1985.

David Black, *The Plague Years: A Chronicle of AIDS, the Epidemic of Our Times*. NY: Simon and Schuster. 1985.

Dennis Altman, *AIDS in the Mind of America: The Social, Political, and Psychological Impact of a New Epidemic*. NY: Doubleday. 1986.

Edward Albert, "Illness and Deviance: The Response of the Press to AIDS" in *Social Dimensions of AIDS*. Douglas A. Feldman and Thomas M. Johnson, Eds. Westport, CT: Praeger. 1986. 163–178.

Simon Watney. *Policing Desire: Pornography, AIDS, and the Media*. Minneapolis: U of Minnesota P. 1987.

Randy Shilts, *And the Band Played On*. NY: St. Martin's Press. 1987.

Paul Monette, *Borrowed Time: An AIDS Memoir*. NY: Harcourt Brace. 1988.

"PWA Coalition Portfolio" in *AIDS: Cultural Analysis: Cultural Activism*. Douglas Crimp, Ed. Cambridge, MA: MIT Press. 1988. 147–168.

Susan Sontag, *AIDS and Its Metaphors*. NY: Farrar Straus Giroux. 1989.

Erica Carter and Simon Watney, *Taking Liberties: AIDS and Cultural Politics*. London: Serpent's Tail and ICA. 1989.

Billy Howard, *Epitaphs for the Living: Words and Images in the Time of AIDS*. Dallas, TX: Southern Methodist UP. 1989.

Joshua Gamson, "Silence, Death, and the Invisible Enemy: AIDS Activism and Social Movement 'Newness.' " *Social Problems 38*.4 (October 1989): 351–367.

John Preston, *Personal Dispatches*. NY: St. Martin's. 1989.

James Kinsella, *Covering the Plague: AIDS and the American Media*. New Brunswick, N.J.: Rutgers UP. 1989.

Lee Edelman, "The Plague of Discourse: Politics, Literary Theory, and AIDS." *South Atlantic Quarterly 88*.1 (1989): 301–316.

Douglas Crimp, *AIDS Demo Graphics*. Seattle, WA: Bay Press. 1990.

Mike Hippler, *So Little Time: Essays on Gay Life*. Berkeley, CA: Celestial Arts. 1990.

Michael Callen, *Surviving AIDS.* NY: Harper/Collins. 1990.

Michael Adams, "The House That Brenda Built: A Transvestite Response to AIDS." *Out/Look 2*.4 (Spring 1990): 22–26.

Douglas Crimp, "Art Acts Up: A Graphic Response to AIDS." *Out/Look 3*.1 (Summer 1990): 22–30.

Cindy Patton. *Inventing AIDS.* NY: Routledge, Chapman, and Hall. 1990.

Stephen Schecter, *The AIDS Notebooks.* Albany: State University of NYP. 1990.

Samuel R. Delany, "Street Talk/Straight Talk." *Differences: A Journal of Feminist Cultural Criticism 3*.2 (1991): 21–38.

Nicholas Nixon and Bebe, Nixon, *People With AIDS.* NY: David R. Godine. 1991.

Timothy F. Murphy, "Testimony" in *Writing AIDS.* Timothy F. Murphy and Suzanne Poirier, Eds. NY: Columbia UP. 1993. 306–320.

Michael S. Sherry, "The Language of War in AIDS Discourse" in *Writing AIDS.* Timothy F.Murphy and Suzanne Poirier, Eds. NY: Columbia UP. 1993. 39–53.

David Román, "*Fierce Love* and Fierce Response: Intervening in the Cultural Politics of Race, Sexuality, and AIDS" in *Critical Essays: Gay and Lesbian Writers of Color.* Emmanuel S. Nelson, Ed. NY: Haworth Press. 1993. 195–219.

Martha Gever, "Pictures of Sickness: Stuart Marshall's Bright Eyes" in *Queer Looks.* Martha Gever, John Greyson and Pratibha Parmar, Eds. NY: Routledge. 1993. 186–203.

David Feinberg, *Queer and Loathing: Rants and Raves of a Raging AIDS Clone.* NY: Viking. 1994.

Peggy Phelan, "Dying Man With A Movie Camera: *Silverlake Life: The View From Here.*" *GLQ 2*.4 (1995): 379–398.

Simon Watney, "These Waves of Dying Friends: Gay Men, AIDS and Multiple Loss" in *Outlooks: Lesbian and Gay Sexualities and Visual Cultures.* Peter Horne and Reina Lewis, Eds. London: Routledge. 1996. 159–169.

Joseph P. Stokes, Kittiwut Taywaditep, Peter Vanable, and Daniel J. McKirnan, "Bisexual Men, Sexual Behavior and HIV/AIDS" in *Bisexuality: The Psychology and Politics of an Invisible Minority.* Beth A. Firestein, Ed. Thousand Oaks, CA: Sage Publications. 1996. 149–168.

G. Thomas Couser, "Family Plot: AIDS Memoirs and the Narrative of Reaffiliation." *Southwest Review 81*.3 (Summer 1996): 404–422.

Jewelle Gomez, "Silence Equals Forgetting." *The Harvard Gay & Lesbian Review 4*.2 (Spring 1997): 25–27.

Michael Denneny, "Bearing Witness in the Age of Aids." *The Harvard Gay & Lesbian Review* 4.2 (Spring 1997): 27–28.

Mark Doty, *Heaven's Coast: A Memoir.* NY: Perennial. 1997.

Beverly Seckinger and Janet Jakobsen, "Love, Death and Videotape: *Silverlake Life*" in *Between the Sheets, In the Streets: Queer, Lesbian, Gay Documentary.* Chris Holmlund and Cynthia Fuchs, Eds. Minneapolis: U of Minnesota P. 1997. 144–157.

Dion Dennis, "AIDS and the New Medical Gaze: Bio-Politics, AIDS, and Homosexuality." *Journal of Homosexuality 32*.3/4 (1997): 169–184.

Eric Rofes, *Dry Bones Breathe: Gay Men Creating Post-AIDS Identities and Cultures.* Binghamton, NY: Haworth Press. 1998.

Michael R. Botnick, Part 1, HIV as "The Line in the Sand," 39–76; Part 2, "Fear of Contagion: Fear of Intimacy," 77–101; Part 3, "A Community Divided," 103–132. *Journal of Homosexuality* 38.4 (2000).

Jacqueline Foertsch, *The Cold War and the AIDS Crisis in Literature, Film, and Culture.* Chicago, IL: U of Illinois P. 2001.

Walter O. Bockting, Ed. *Transgender and HIV: Risks, Prevention, Care.* Binghamton, NY: 2001.

Film

Snow Job: The Media Hysteria of AIDS (1986). Barbara Hammer. 10 m.

This Is Not an AIDS Advertisement (1988). Isaac Julien. 10 m.

Reframing AIDS (1988). Pratibha Parmar. 36 m.

AIDS in the Barrio (1989). Peter Biella and Frances Negrón. 29 m.

They Are Lost To Vision Altogether (1989). Tom Kalin. 10 m.

Positive (1991). Rosa von Praunheim. 80 m.

Non, je ne regrette rien (1992). Marlon Riggs. 38 m.

And the Band Played On (1993). Roger Spottiswoode. 140 m.

Silverlake Life: The View From Here (1993). Tom Joslin and Peter Friedman. 99 m.

Fast Trip, Long Drop (1993). Gregg Bordowitz. 54 m.

Living Proof (1993). Kermit Cole. 72 m.

Both (1993). Vic De La Rosa. 8 m.

Sometimes My Feet Go Numb (1996). Lourdes Portillo. 2 m.

Paul Monette: The Brink of Summer's End (1997). Monte Bramer. 90 m.

Web Resource

http://www.aegis.com
http://www.aids.org

Social Activism

Volunteer at a local AIDS services organization. Find out what the current issues are in your community regarding health care and People With Aids. What specific steps can you take to a) raise awareness? b) help increase funding? c) improve services?

Special Topics

Writing

Using the Clum (1993) and/or Waugh articles as a model, choose either a novel or a film from the sources below and compose an essay about how and in what ways the text in question deploys specific strategies of representation in its narrative about AIDS.

Reading

John M. Clum, " 'The Time Before the War': AIDS, Memory, and Desire." *American Literature* 62.4 (December 1990): 648–667.

John M. Clum, " 'And Once I Had It All': AIDS Narratives and Memories of an American Dream" in *Writing AIDS.* Timothy F. Murphy and Suzanne Poirier, Eds. NY: Columbia UP. 1993. 200–224.

Sarah Schulman, "Fiction and Action in the Age of Aids." *The Harvard Gay & Lesbian Review* 4.2 (Spring 1997): 1, 23–24.

Franklin Brooks and Timothy F. Murphy, "Annotated Bibliography of AIDS Literature, 1982-91" in *Writing AIDS.* Timothy F. Murphy and Suzanne Poirier, Eds. NY: Columbia UP. 1993. 32–339.

Douglas Eisner, "Liberating Narrative: AIDS and the Limits of Melodrama in Monette and Weir." *College Literature* 24.1 (February 1997): 213–226.

Robert Burns Neveldine, "Skeletons in the Closet: Paradox, Resistance, and The Undead Body of the PWA." *College Literature* 24.1 (February 1997): 263–279.

Thomas Waugh, "Erotic Self-Images in the Gay Male AIDS Melodrama" in *The Fruit Machine: Twenty Years of Writing on Queer Cinema.* Durham, N.C.: Duke UP. 2000. 218–234.

Kylo-Patrick R. Hart, *The AIDS Movies: Representing a Pandemic in Film and Television.* Binghamton, NY: 2000.

Film

Parting Glances (1986). Bill Sherwood. 90 m.

Longtime Companion (1990). Norman Rene. 100 m.

It's My Party (1995). Randal Kleiser. 110m.

Love! Valour! Compassion! (1997). Jeff Dupre. 70m.

Special Topics

Lesbians played a crucial role in the AIDS movement, thus changing the relations between gay men and lesbians in ways that have affected the social and sexual politics of both.

Reading

Ines Rider and Patricia Ruppelt, Eds. *AIDS: The Women.* San Francisco, CA: Cleis Press. 1988.

Jackie Winnow, "Lesbians Working on AIDS: Assessing the Impact on Health Care for Women." *Out/Look* 2.1 (Summer 1989): 10–18.

Marion Banzhaf, and the ACT UP New York Women and AIDS Book Group, Eds. *Women, AIDS, and Activism.* Boston: South End Press. 1990.

Related Reading

Dennis Cooper, "QUEERCORE: Johnny Noxzema to the Gay Community: 'You Are the Enemy,'" *Village Voice*, June 30, 1992. 31–33.

Arnie Kantrowitz, "Letter to the Queer Generation" (1992) in *We Are Everywhere: A Historical Sourcebook of Gay and Lesbian Politics.* Mark Blaius and Shane Phelan, Eds. NY: Routledge. 1997. 812–817.

Dennis Cooper, Ed., *Discontents: New Queer Writers.* NY: Amethyst Press. 1992.

Richard Smith, "Preaching to the Perverted: Homocore and Queercore" in *Seduced and Abandoned: Gay Men and Popular Music.* London: Cassell. 1995. 172–179.

Michael du Plessis and Kathleen Chapman, "Queercore: The Distinct Identities of Sub-culture." *College Literature* 24.1 (February 1997): 45–58.

Film

Chocolate Babies (1996). Stephen Winter. 83 m.

This Is about People Dying: The Tactics of Early ACT UP and Lesbian Avengers in New York City

An Interview with Maxine Wolfe by Laraine Sommella

The following is a compilation of excerpts from telephone interviews recorded in 1995 by Laraine Sommella. In 1994 informal discussions with Brent Ingram in Maxine Wolfe's garden in Park Slope, Brooklyn, on the early tactics of ACT UP New York City[1] led to these interviews with lesbian scholar Laraine Sommella. Passages that function as background are included in the notes for this essay.

LARAINE SOMMELLA: I was just reading a review of Sarah Schulman's *My American History*[2] in the *Nation.* It was by Jan Clausen,[3] and she makes reference to "the [Lesbian] Avengers' particular brand of organizing." Have you seen that?

MAXINE WOLFE: No. How does she [Clausen] know anything about it?

LS: Well, she doesn't really say. She's talking about the Avengers' "energetic protests" but wonders "really how far can we go in the current climate?" Some interesting issues that she raises.

MW: She certainly doesn't come to Avenger meetings. One of the Avengers confronted Tory Osborne at the National Creating Change Conference of the National Lesbian and Gay Task Force (NLGTF). Never having spoken to any one of us or done anything with us, saying how our entire strategy was totally wrong in the *Advocate*,[4] which has never seriously covered the group. She actually apologized. Everyone just wants to bash anyone who is doing anything. I've never seen such negativism. Recently, at a women's studies conference, someone who none of us had ever heard of gave a paper, and she had had nothing to do with the Avengers and totally bashed the Avengers. Who is this person? Did she ever talk to anybody? No. You know what I'm saying? Like, don't be an Avenger. . . . If you're not part of it, you're not doing anything else, you come to an academic conference, and you tear some group apart when you have absolutely done nothing about the issue yourself . . . and haven't even spoken to anyone. Many people basically assume that anyone who does visible creative public actions that are "energetic"—what a condescending word—and "catchy" are empty-headed idiots with no political strategy. They think that we don't think. Apparently the only people who think—in their view—are those who lobby, who are not "energetic." The U.S. left has always been suspicious of anyone who gets mainstream coverage or who looks and acts "nonintellectual."

LS: Before we talk about your more current work in the Avengers and the evolution of tactics for taking and remaking of public space, I would like to ask you about the activism that lead up to ACT UP New York. What was the chronology that foreshadowed the formation of ACT UP New York[5] and what other groups were involved in direct action that perhaps you were involved in or knew about?

MW: Everyone sort of thinks that ACT UP came out of the blue and in fact, there's a certain mythology that Larry Kramer gave this talk one night at the Lesbian and Gay Community Center and everyone went "Oh my God" and then they formed ACT UP and nothing had been there. As usual, that's not true. That's a discontinuous history.

LS: Yes, people don't necessarily think in terms of development.

MW: In 1986 I was at the first public meeting of what was called the Lesbian and Gay Antidefamation League, which became GLAAD, and which was held in the New York City Community Center. I went with a lesbian friend, and we were in this room with about three hundred gay men and four lesbians, and we were sitting next to these two guys and one turned to the other and said, "Wow, this is the first thing that's happened in fifteen years." And I turned to her and said, "Where have these people been?"

A brief overview—with the last two years leading up to the formation of ACT UP New York being the most important. After the first few years of the Gay Activist Alliance (GAA) and especially after the firehouse was arsoned in 1974, most of the gay male community in New York and a few Democratic Party dykes focused on getting the gay rights bill passed in New York City and New York State. Basically they became part of the Democratic Party organization, whether formally or informally, and attempted to orchestrate passage of bills behind the scenes. At the same time, in the gay male mainstream, "the community," certain professional, business, and religious groups formed. While those organizations and networks were totally reformist, if political at all, they enabled the Gay Men's Health Crisis (GMHC) to form in the early 1980s. There was a new basis to get money, to know where people were, to create an infrastructure. That was not there before. But for a lot of that period, from the mid-1970s to the early 1980s, that is what gay men were doing. Most lesbians were not involved with gay men in activism and were basically either in the antirape or anti-violence movement or lesbian-feminist groups, forming their own organizations and doing political work. But this work was not necessarily focused on lesbians and gay men and rather much more on women.[6] Activism was focused on either women's issues, generically defined, or other global ones against racism and nuclear technology. For example, there was the Women's Pentagon Action, which did not have an analysis of homophobia nor a focus on lesbians. But in New York City, in 1984 and 1985, when the whole issue of closing the bathhouses came up, there were a lot of spontaneous actions. These had similarities to actions in 1981 and 1982 when there were raids on black and Latino transvestite bars and the demonstrations against the viciously homophobic film, *Cruising*.

In terms of a specific AIDS focus early in the 1980s, there were the People With AIDS Coalition (PWA) and the GMHC. Right away, people in GMHC got more and more pissed because the organization was unwilling to take political stands. Part of it was that they were looking for money and government funding, and so, as it happens in those kinds of formalized institutions, GMHC became less and less political. They did not want to alienate the people who are going to give them money. But the PWA Coalition formed in 1982 in Denver with principles that focused on empowerment, which really came out of the feminist health movement.

LS: There's a link.

MW: In New York City, there was a huge uproar over the closing of the bathhouses and many people went to hearings at the City Council. They showed up on the steps of City Council, almost spontaneously I would say, and started chanting when David Summers, who was there to testify and who was a person with AIDS, was arrested when he tried to go in to testify. The police were so crazed. People nearly rioted outside, shouting, "We won't go until you let him go." That is where GLAAD started, the Gay and Lesbian Alliance Against

Defamation. They called a community meeting and I went to it. It was pretty tame, as far as I was concerned, and very much in the image of earlier kinds of generally progressive organizations. There was already a board. They already had an idea about what they were doing. And basically, they wanted an army of soldiers. It was a very hierarchical organization. The first meeting that I went to was the marshaling committee. One of the guys who was running it, Marty Robinson, was one of the founders of GAA and basically told all of the men sitting there that they did not have to worry and that they had talked to the cops already, and they were doing an action against the *New York Post* because of its homophobic coverage of AIDS. He basically told them that the marshals were a kind of barrier between the police and the protesters, which is certainly not my idea of what a marshal does; and the idea of wanting to get a permit from the cops to demonstrate—quite amazing.

There was a group of us in 1983 at the City Council hearings on the gay rights bill, including a lesbian-feminist group that I was in at that time called Women For Women, along with some women from Women's Pentagon Action, and two gay men. After years of trying to negotiate the bill through the back doors of the Democratic Party and having it never even getting out of committee for a vote, we decided that when the bill was coming up to that committee for a vote on whether it should even come out of committee that it was time to "fuck the people who are telling everybody to be nice, we weren't gonna be nice." We formed this very ad hoc group that ended up at the end of the council meeting when they did not vote it out of committee that year, sitting in at the City Council and having to be dragged out and arrested. Our banner said "Lesbian liberation, we won't go away."

GLAAD soon formed and immediately became a bone of contention because it started doing these very orchestrated demonstrations. By "orchestrated," I mean they negotiated with the cops, they basically told you when to show up, when to go home, and there was absolutely no input from anybody into what was going to be done. The board of directors made the decisions. Women coming to their meetings eventually just stopped because they were huge meetings and no one would even get a chance to get up and speak.

At that point, I just decided there wasn't anything I was going to be able to do about this shit because coming from the lesbian community, I wasn't a gay man. Most of the gay men with whom I had worked in the left were not around, and nobody was doing anything very much. Who was I to tell gay men how to do stuff about AIDS? So I just sort of kept looking for stuff to do. I helped form a group of faculty and students at City University of New York (CUNY) just to keep my hand in. I worked at the Lesbian Herstory Archives, "The Archives," and then one day a friend of mine said, "There's this new group that's meeting. Do you want to go to their meeting the Monday after Gay Pride Day?" and I said "Yes" and we went to ACT UP.

LS: When was this?

MW: ACT UP started in March of 1987, and I started going in June of 1987. The people who came to the first meeting of ACT UP included individuals from GMHC who had become totally disaffected by its unwillingness to do any political stuff. There were people from the PWA Coalition who wanted to get out on the streets, and they already had this image of a feminist take on the health establishment because of Michael Callen who was very much influenced by the feminist health movement. There was also the SILENCE = DEATH Project, which was a group of men who had started meeting a year and half before, including Avram Finklestein, Oliver Smith, and Chris Lione. They were a whole group of men who needed to talk to each other and others about what the fuck were they going to do, being gay men in the age of AIDS?! Several of them were designers of various sorts—graphic designers—and they ended up deciding that they had to start doing wheat-pasting on the streets, to get the message out to people: "Why aren't you doing something?" So they created the SILENCE = DEATH logo well before ACT UP ever existed, and they made posters before ACT UP ever existed, and the posters at the bottom said something like, "What's really happening in Washington? What's happening with Reagan and Bush and the Food and Drug Administration?" It ended with this statement: "Turn anger, fear, grief into action." Several of these graphic designers were at that first evening that Larry spoke.

The other group that was represented at the first meeting of ACT UP in March 1987 was the Lavender Hill Mob. The Lavender Hill Mob included Marty Robinson, who had left GLAAD because the organization had become much more focused on not holding public meetings and not wanting to do big actions. Marty had run their "Swift and Terrible Retribution Committee" and was one of the founders of GAA. He felt totally strangulated by GLAAD's agenda. Marty got together a few friends including Bill Balhman, who was also from GAA, Henry Yaeger, and a young dyke who was seventeen at the time, Jean Elizabeth Glass, along with a couple of other people. They formed this thing called the Lavender Hill Mob. Not only did they start doing zaps[7] but they also started meeting with government officials around AIDS policy issues. They had been going to government conferences, had started leafletting, their message being: "What the fuck are you doing in Washington?" and "Why aren't you finding treatments?" etcetera. The first article that was in the *New York Native* about ACT UP, that everyone thinks was the first public presence of ACT UP, the Wall Street Action in March 1987, had the headline "Kramer, Mob, and others call for traffic blockade."[8]

So the night when Larry came to speak, in March of 1987, there was a very particular audience in that room. The person who was originally supposed to read was Nora Ephron. Now, I would never go to hear Nora Ephron read. It's definitely more a gay male focus. But she couldn't come and Larry Kramer spoke instead. When I came into ACT UP, I did not even know who the fuck Larry Kramer was. He was irrelevant in my life. I had vaguely heard people say that he had written a book called *Faggots*,[9] but why would I ever read that? For me, he was not an icon at all. But for the people in that room, he spoke to them. He had been screaming for years and nobody had done anything. From my point of view, there was a whole group of people there ready to do something. They were looking for a kick in the ass and needed an event to be at together, that would lead to that, and that was it. At some point he yelled, "What are you gonna do?" and somebody in the audience said, "Why don't we revive the AIDS Action Network?"[10] Then people said, "Let's have a meeting and let's do something." They called a meeting and about seventy people showed up. Soon after, they did their first Wall Street Action. They did not have a lot of people coming to their meetings until after Gay Pride that June and the March on Washington in the fall of 1987. If you did not read the *New York Native*, you wouldn't know that they existed.

LS: Was the Wall Street action covered in the mainstream press?

MW: I think the April one they did about taxes might have been because they were charged by horses. But I do not remember ever seeing it. When someone said to me, "We should go meet this group," I had no idea who they were except that I had marched behind them at the Gay Pride March and saw this incredible "thing," which was a concentration camp with wire all around and people inside. There were people outside the wire dressed in masks and military gear and handing out flyers and people were selling ACT UP T-shirts with the SILENCE = DEATH logo,[11] which the SILENCE = DEATH project had given them permission to use. I went up to this guy and I said, "Are there any lesbians in your group?" and he said, "Yeah," and the next day I showed up and there were four visible women and two of them were straight. It had that kind of impact. If you can imagine, there is always this tension in the Gay Pride March in New York because the majority come to it for a celebration and they do not want it to be anything political at all. And this was 1987: We're already five years into the crisis, loads of people had died, the community was in a state of shock, and Gay Pride was supposed to be a way to get away from all of this. And ACT UP had the *chutzpah* to build a concentration camp float.

LS: It was an "in-your-face" move and very dramatic.

MW: When I came to the meeting the next night, there were three hundred people in that room.

LS: And you directly connect that parade presence with that turnout?

MW: Absolutely.

LS: This was what people needed. They saw something that they were enthused about.

MW: Yes. AIDS really knocked people for a loop. It's hard for people to understand if they aren't part of it. Larry Kramer and I disagree on almost everything, especially on his use of holocaust imagery, but he lost an entire life network. He would say that he had five hundred friends and acquaintances who had died. If you think about it, that's the size of a small town in Germany. For gay people who did not have close relationships with their families, and especially if they were Larry's age, in their late fifties, they had to go through finding themselves and new friends. There was no one around to form this new group of people, your village, and so many were dead—suddenly, in a very short time. At the beginning of the epidemic, you would go into the hospital on Monday and be dead on Tuesday. People were dying left and right, horrible deaths, and nobody knew why. The shock was incredible. People were trying to figure out so hard how to take care of the people they cared about, how to take care of themselves, how not to get sick, how to prevent people from dying, how to get services to people in every way, shape, and form. The idea of doing anything else was overwhelming. ACT UP took that leadership role in that Gay Pride march and marched in the middle of a "space" that is apolitical and often commercial. The political groups are usually in the back, and nobody pays any attention to them. Instead, ACT UP marched up there, basically in your face, saying people want to quarantine us and tattoo us and saying, "Get with it folks, we have to do something." The imagery was so stark that people said, "Got It." The same thing happened in the fall of 1987 at the March on Washington.

LS: What happened in Washington?

MW: ACT UP got there late. The SILENCE = DEATH Project[12] had made incredible posters. One was a Ronald Reagan poster in dayglo green that said "AIDSGATE." We had another poster that said "SILENCE = DEATH." ACT UP member Michael Miles was a stage designer, and he designed an incredible contraption with these posters—a snake formation. Each poster was held by an individual person but was connected and we used those in Washington and they went way up above your head and we all wore SILENCE = DEATH T-shirts. We also had these huge banners that were of the late eighties order of things— black with huge white letters—very stark, very black. ACT UP had become very well known for these banners. Everyone else had purple banners with flourishing letters but our posters were very striking, very stark, with very clean lines. This was very graphic-design-oriented kind of stuff and had a tremendous impact. Many ACT UP groups started after that march.

The New York ACT UP style was wonderful—writing leaflets that you could read and I think, more importantly, not relying only on the written word but also visual media. Although the ages of people in ACT UP have always been quite diverse, there were a lot of young people. ACT UP people were always "classified" as young sexy people. The friends I had in ACT UP tended to be older and more literate. But they were visual: people in theater and art. Other younger men and women, who were not part of that scene, were totally willing to go with it. They were media generation people who had grown up with television and multimedia. They were well aware, any time we did a demo, that there would be TV cameras present and what these cameras would be looking at.

LS: How do you utilize that?

MW: We focused on what would stand out, what would show up. This was in a way that no one I ever knew had done before. It was easy to learn stuff. What color do you make banners when you use them at night as opposed to day? And what size does something have to be to show up? How will this move through space? And I think that was very important because in fact that's exactly what caught the media's attention. Not just that we did things that other people did not do, but that the way that we did them, we were very present. We did not just picket around the front of a building, which is totally boring; we broke into the building [laughter]. We dressed up in costume. Half the time we would go to dinners that were held by Republicans, we'd go in drag to get in. And we would pretend to be most anything if we could to get in somewhere. There was this whole idea that you would do what you had to do to get in somewhere, and that you would get into it; you wouldn't be on the outside looking in, asking people to take your leaflet but you would be demanding that people pay attention to what you had to say and taking over spaces where people would not expect that you could get in.

LS: You said that a group of AIDS activists came together in Washington, D.C., during the 1987 March on Washington? Who were they? Were they both newcomers to political action and others with a history or herstory of activist tactics?

MW: That meeting had been arranged mostly by gay men, and some lesbians. They had been working on the left for years and obviously wanted to do something about the AIDS crisis. They called ACT UP and said they wanted to hold this meeting and they called themselves ACT NOW. So on the Monday after the march, some of us stayed in D.C. and went to the meeting. It was horrifying. These people had arranged the whole day—the agenda had been planned. There were various "lefty" groups involved, who of course had already come with proposals and started putting them out. Several proposals were in opposition to each other. One was The Nine Days of Action (or Nine Days of Rage)—to do actions for nine days in a row that spring, all over the country, and each day would deal with a different AIDS issue. But they were stuck in a rut. They said things about doing a day on "AIDS in the Barrio and the Ghetto," a sort of "lefty version" of politics that was outdated in language and style. They had no day for AIDS and homophobia! I was with a lot of men from ACT UP who had been very excited about the idea that there would actually be a national network of activist AIDS groups.

Forget even imagining that it would be ACT UP groups; just people who were willing to do something about this crisis in a grassroots way. They were freaked by the ACT UP approach. They couldn't believe that this is what people were doing. I got up to the microphone and I said, "I don't get why you don't have a day on AIDS and homophobia," and one of the guys said to me, "Well, you know, I mean, gay men aren't gonna come out for anybody else." I said, "Fuck that; they're dying, they'll come out for themselves and then you can worry about getting them out for somebody else." This is an example of the homophobia of the left. Other issues such as those of "poor people or people of color" were always more important and there were still some very chauvinist illusions, on the part of some people, that none of the people in these "more oppressed groups" were gay or vulnerable to AIDS, and that they, the "lefties," were the "unusual" gay men who were progressive, while every other white gay man was horrible.

The people affected by the crisis, at that point, were overwhelmingly gay males. People were dead and dying and the majority of them were, and still are, gay males. But if they knew the statistics, even then, they would have seen that a lot of them were gay men of color. But many of the lefty white gay men, even as late as 1987, had completely divorced those categories from one another and wanted people to do actions only about people of color and not about gay men. Although groups did start after that, they weren't necessarily the groups that came to those early meetings. They were people who had come to the March on Washington and had seen ACT UP and we had made twenty thousand leaflets to hand out. That is the other thing that ACT UP used to do. We would go to a Gay Pride march even in New York with twenty thousand leaflets and hand them all out. They would be very straightforward leaflets. It wouldn't take you three days to read them. And these leaflets were very political, very clear, and to the point. They would say something like "Racism and Homophobia started the AIDS crisis." But they wouldn't go on and on. They would always be in a very catchy kind of style and comprehensible. So the impact of ACT UP was from the combination of the visual imagery and the accessibility of everything that was produced in terms of language, and the fact that we were out on the streets in places where people did not want us and without asking their permission. In terms of going to places where people did not expect us, one of the first things of course was the Wall Street Action where people blocked traffic and got arrested, and it had been many years in the gay male community since they had seen anybody do that. To explain the evolution of ACT UP's particular orientation around direct action, it is necessary to go back a few years.

Soon after GLAAD New York was formed, they had the "Swift and Terrible Retribution" Committee. This was right around the time of the *Hardwick* decision. The U.S. Supreme Court upheld the Georgia sodomy law.[13] Everyone headed down to Sheridan Square.[14] The word gets around, and people just show up. A huge mob congregated at Sheridan Square spontaneously that night. It was, by the way, the night after the Gay Pride March. The decision was well timed in Washington not to be on the day of the Gay Pride March. But it was four days before the Statue of Liberty Centennial in 1986, July 4th, and they were expecting a million visitors to New York City, and so a couple of thousand people gathered in Sheridan Square. The people from GLAAD came, and they were trying to get everybody to go home. "Go home, go home, go home, you're gonna get into trouble." But nobody would go home and people ended up spontaneously blocking traffic on Sixth Avenue and 8th Street in the heart of the Village for hours, and then finally people said, "Let's meet tomorrow night at the church near the community center, and let's figure out what we're gonna do."

A dyke that I know showed up there with a flyer already made that said "Storm the Statue of Liberty; Meet at Sheridan Square on July 4th," and the people from GLAAD were horrified. They really did not want this to happen. They did not want anyone to fuck up this party. They said things like "People are coming here and it's a big holiday, and you don't want to fuck it up for people; you're gonna ruin their party; you're not gonna get your point across." Nobody listened to them. People put out these flyers. And it's the beginning of the summer. . . . On the 4th of July weekend, five thousand showed up with a couple of day's notice! When I got there everyone was whispering "Battery Park, Battery Park." GLAAD had negotiated with the cops for a permit to march to Federal Plaza, about ten blocks north of where the Centennial Celebration was happening and to rally there. But people were determined to go down to Battery Park—to be a presence in the midst of the tourists at the Centennial. After the rally at Federal Plaza, GLAAD stationed marshals to block the demonstration from going downtown. This was just a totally spontaneous act of about five thousand people, who were communicating by passing the word back; these people broke through the marshal line. The cops formed a barricade around Trinity Place with cars and horses and were basically telling people that they weren't gonna let them go through. There were some people from GLAAD who were standing up and saying, "Break it up now, you don't want to do this stuff." So everybody basically decided that we would split up and then meet in Battery Park; we would break up and go to Battery Park and in twos and threes. About two thousand people showed up in Battery Park, right in the middle of Middle America visiting the Statue of Liberty Centennial, and people gave speeches and took over statues and marched again to the New York Post, and this thing went on for seven hours. It was making a statement that people were not going to stay contained in the area of the city that everyone said you had to be in. One of the things that I always felt in my years in the left in New York is that people always stayed where they were supposed to. People would hand out leaflets in Greenwich Village; what's the big deal? Who are you talking to? And I remember having huge fights when I was doing abortion stuff because the group of lesbians that I was working with in CARASA New York wanted to go and give out stuff in Fordham Road in the Bronx, and Flatbush Avenue in Brooklyn—to go to various ethnic and cultural neighborhoods. Everyone panicked. The difference between ACT UP and those earlier groups was twofold. First, ACT UP was about organizing the unorganized. It wasn't a lefty coalition where there's one person from this group and one person from that group and one person for the other group and you claim you have a coalition but you really have three people. It was about mobilizing a community that had not been organized to do this kind of direct action in at least twelve or fourteen years. Secondly, ACT UP was about people doing stuff for themselves. We weren't being philanthropists. We weren't a vanguard. We were trying to save our own lives and the lives of people we knew. We were very materially affected.

LS: That material-interest issue reminds me of the stake early antiwar activists had in their political work.

MW: ACT UP definitely draws from that kind of perspective. It works. ACT UP has always been called a gay white male group, and I once gave a talk that everyone calls gay white males rich *"bougie,"*[15] worse than *"bougie,"* upper middle class. ACT UP, the group of people who started ACT UP initially, included women and people of color. There have always been people—lesbians and gay men of color and straight women. About the only group not really represented in ACT UP were straight men, and there have been a couple of those too.

LS: And the lesbians were a significant force?

MW: Even though we were a small group, we were the people who had done politics. We were the people who did the civil disobedience training. We have always been the marshals. We have always been the logistics people because we came out of that kind of background. The men have always been the graphic artists and we do the xeroxing and typesetting. There are things that everyone has access to. Gay men have access to graphics; we have access to reproduction.

LS: They utilize the male gaze. [laughter]

MW: The group of lesbians who were in ACT UP, from early on, were grown-up in a way because we had come through the lesbian-feminist wars and because we knew we were in a gay male group. We knew we wanted to work on AIDS issues; we did not come in there to work on women and AIDS. Because we had learned a few things, thankfully, from the years previous, someone could get up and say, "We need people to man this table," and we wouldn't stand up and say, "You sexist, chauvinist pig." We would say, "Staff the table," and they would go, "Oh, staff the table," and then people would go on.

LS: You did not have to walk out. You had maturity.

MW: Well, there were a couple of reasons. The truth is that we were not in the raw state of pain in which you should never be if you are in a mixed group like that. And the men were, most of them, badly trained but not ill intentioned. There were some misogynists who never could be trained, some men who were incredibly feminist, and some—the majority—were just badly trained like we all are. And we women who were there were grown-up enough to understand being badly trained. We weren't in the state of rawness where we thought everyone was a misogynist to the core or thought to ourselves, "Kill them, get rid of them." It actually worked out very well, and I think that the women became a very strong force because we were also very gutsy about the kinds of things we did. The first huge action was at Shea Stadium, and it really scared the men in the group.[16]

In the spring of 1988, activist AIDS groups across the country called for the Nine Days of Action. In New York we actually called them the "Nine Days of Rain" because it rained on almost every one of the days. The only two days it did not rain was for the women's action, which was at Shea Stadium, and an action that we did at the Harlem Office Building, about prisoners and AIDS. Afterwards we decided that God must be a Black Lesbian.

As a women's committee, we were trying to figure out what we were gonna do because it was supposed to be a day on women and AIDS. We were sitting around one night trying to figure out what to do, and we threw out all these ideas like driving up to some big political event in a horse-drawn carriage that looked like part of a wedding. We were just drawing out the craziest ideas we could think of, and one of the women asked, "What is the goal of what we want to do?" Part of this was about the difference in status between women and men at the very beginning of the AIDS crisis, even though they were both sick. Women were erased totally and also pictured as vectors to men getting infected, and all the advertising on the subways in New York was about women taking condoms with them in their purse. It would say "Don't forget *these* when you go out," as if women wore condoms. It sort of reminded me of my own growing up, and it was the woman who always had to be the one responsible. We said that we wanted to get the message out that heterosexual men are responsible; that they're the only people being let off the hook in this epidemic by the media. Gay men are being put down; prostitutes and women are being told they have to take condoms along. What is anyone asking from straight men in the world? Nothing. So we decided that we wanted to go to a venue that in people's minds was heterosexual, and male heterosexual, to the core. And the Nine Days of Action were in the spring—May 4th—and we were trying to figure out what venue would fit this, and all of a sudden, one of the women said, "Baseball games! The Mets game!" and everyone in the room just went crazy.

We began to throw around crazy ideas like jumping on the field, wearing hats with two frankfurters sticking out and so on. One woman was absolutely panicked. She had absolutely never had anything to do with sports. But everybody else in the room was taking off on it. Two of the women were baseball nuts, so we finally decided this was the best idea we ever had, and we sat down and really worked out a plan. We were gonna get tickets in blocks. Shea Stadium is U-shaped. We planned to get seating in blocks in the three different areas of the "U" and that we would do "call-and-response" like you do at college football games. Originally we were gonna have each person hold a card and the cards would spell out messages. And then we called up Shea Stadium and found out that in fact there was a ball game that night and that we could get blocks of seats and that if you bought sixty seats, you could even get a message on the message board! And we thought, "Wow, this is fucking amazing!"

And then we really got into it; we made up leaflets that used baseball terminology: "AIDS is not a ball game," "Here's the score," and then it had a scorecard. And it said: "Single: There's not a single woman in a clinical treatment trial in the United States of America," "Double: The number of cases of women with AIDS has doubled since x years ago," and at the bottom it said, "No glove, no love." Our idea was that we would get there before the game started. We'd make up ten thousand flyers and bring condoms, and we'd stand at every entrance at the ball park and we'd give a condom and a flyer to any man we saw coming by. And then we would go inside with these banners and do this call-and-response thing. We came up with these banners that said things like "Don't balk at safer sex," "Strike out AIDS," and "No glove, no love," and in between we had "Aids kills women—Men use condoms." And in the center we had "SILENCE = DEATH" and this huge triangle.

So we come to the floor of ACT UP and we presented it as our Nine Days of Action thing and the room becomes like dead silent. Panic is in the air, absolute panic. So people start standing up and speaking. First, we got the "class" stuff. "We're gonna get beaten to death there," and we're standing there very calmly saying, "Do you know who goes to Shea Stadium? We go to Shea Stadium. Kids go to Shea Stadium on Friday nights to pick each other up. Queers go to Shea Stadium." And in the room all of a sudden the closet baseball queers start standing up. All these gay men who wouldn't tell anyone they were baseball nuts because it's not the "thing to be," and they started saying, "Yeah! I go to Shea Stadium." So we finally got people to go.

So we went and it was really funny how we even knew how big to make things because, for example, we had to measure the seats to know how big to make the banner. A woman, Debbie, and I went to buy the first sixty seats, and we had to get people to pay for them because we did not have that much money in ACT UP then, and what we decided to do was to buy sixty at a time and sell them and then get sixty more. Our goal was to get sixty in each section. At that point one of the guys from the SILENCE = DEATH Project, Chris Lione, correctly assessed that we should not make up individual cards because if people did not show up, we wouldn't have the letters. So we went to Shea Stadium to measure the seats so we could make the banners. All you needed was a person at each end. So we went to make banners. We bought the first sixty. We asked this woman if we could go and see where the seats were located exactly and she said, oh, they were constructing in Shea Stadium that day and we couldn't go in. We said, "Oh, really?" and she said, "Really, you really can't." We said okay, but as we were walking out we saw an entrance into the park and decided that we'd try to go through. We started to walk through it and this guy comes, a security guard comes from the office, and he says, "Excuse me, girls, what are you doing?" But it was really easy. If you're a woman, especially a "femmy" woman, you can get away with so much. We just said, "Oh, you know, this is our very first baseball game and we're coming here with a whole bunch of friends and they sent us to get the tickets and we don't know anything about it and now we wanted to go see the seats and they won't let us do it and we're so worried because we don't know anything about it and don't you think we could go inside and just look?" and he said, "What I don't see, I don't know."

We went in, found the seats we had just bought, measured them all out. We had rulers so that we could make banners that were exactly the right length. We also went to a night game to check out the lighting and to figure out how big the letters would have to be to be seen.

Word of this got out. In the beginning we could hardly get anybody to buy seats. By the last day, I was getting phone calls from people I hadn't heard from in years from the left because the word had gotten out that this was gonna be the most amazing thing that had ever happened, and people were acting like I was their connection for a seat in the orchestra. They'd say, "Do you have seats at Shea Stadium?" and I'd say, "No, I don't." So it actually turned out to be quite amazing because we ended up selling around 400 tickets.

At Shea Stadium we had people spread in three different sections and there was also a whole big issue about standing outside and handing out these leaflets. Because Shea Stadium is owned by the City of New York, but the Mets rent it. Anything that happens *in* Shea Stadium is in relationship to the Mets. The parking lot is owned by Kenny or was then. That's private property. They can decide what happens in the parking lot. But there's a whole space that is not really either publicly or privately owned or leased—almost like a street or plaza that goes around the entrances to the stadium, that looks like a sidewalk but a big sidewalk and that is not the parking lot and is not the stadium. We could not find out for weeks who it belonged to. We wanted to know, if we were going to get arrested, what it was we would be getting arrested for. Were we on private property or public property? Who knew? And we kept trying to get in touch with Shea Stadium. We also wanted to get in touch with them because we wanted the Mets to declare this National Woman and AIDS Day, and we left them many messages and they never called us back. And by that time, ACT UP had a reputation for doing things. Especially the women, because we had just done another demonstration in January, and the police nearly went crazy because we did not ask the city and the police for permits.

We had coming up on the LED screen a message that said "Welcome the National Women and AIDS Day Committee," and we did not think we'd have any trouble getting in because we had tickets. But giving out these flyers outside, that we thought we would end up getting arrested for. About a week and a half before this whole thing was going to happen, some guy wrote a story in the *Village Voice* about ACT UP that mentioned we were going to Shea Stadium. A friend of mine who was actually working with Shea Stadium on a totally different thing—she was working with them on a performance art thing that was going to be happening in their parking lot, and they did not know that she had anything to do with ACT UP—was there one day when the guy she was working with was talking to the community/police liaison. The officer was saying, "Did you hear? These crazy people are coming to the ballpark next week— these ACT UP people—and they're going to rip up the turf and they're going to do this and we're going to do that." And we thought, "Holy Shit, we're going to show up, and they're going to be in riot gear!" And we weren't even doing anything that provocative, from our point of view. I mean we saw this as an educational action. There was nothing we wanted from Shea Stadium. So we actually thought of this as a lighthearted but hard-hitting educational action because it would be in a place where no one would ever expect us to be.

So we got one of the women to call up the cops—not to ask for a permit. She said, "You know, we've been trying to get in touch with Shea Stadium for three and a half months and nobody has called us back. We just wanted to let you know that we're going to be out there on Wednesday night, and we just did not want you to maybe get freaked that we were coming." And of course, when he started asking questions like "How many?" she just said, "Well, I don't know, but we just wanted you to know." So it wouldn't be this kind of riot gear kind of thing. When we got there, they had spoken to the people at Shea Stadium, and the head of their public relations department came out and put our leaflets in every one of their press packets, and he made sure that we could stand at every single doorway and give out all of our stuff. It was great, but we hadn't negotiated; we just went.

It was the most amazing thing because we had made these banners with a black background and white lettering. We had six long rows in each area and each row had a set of banners, and we only opened them up when the visiting team was up because we did not want to upset the New York Mets fans. At a certain point, I do not remember what inning it was, the first banners opened up. They started at the top of the group and they were always three lines. And the first one opened up and it said "Don't balk at safe sex." And then across the stadium, opposite them, in the seats above the other field, three banners rolled open and they said "Aids kills women," and then in the center, behind home plate, the next three opened up and they said "Men! Use condoms."

And then, people in ACT UP got so into having these banners that people started swaying back and forth, up and down, and the visual effect was incredible. Because it was at night, totally dark, and the lighting from the ballpark totally reflected the white letters of the banners. An inning and a half later, we opened the next set of banners. They said "Strike out Aids," "No glove, no love," and the final one said "SILENCE = DEATH" and it had a huge triangle and ACT UP! This was on C-Span. We not only got to the twenty thousand people who were in the ballpark, but it was televised around the country and we gave out leaflets. We reached an incredible number of people in an audience that we'd otherwise never have been able to get to. Most of the people came from ACT UP, but many people from other groups got wind of it and thought it was the most exciting thing. So there was one whole section of non-ACT UP people.

LS: In early ACT UP New York, what was the attitude toward conventional rather than alternative science or AIDS treatment? What role did the women play in moving ACT UP beyond framings of treatment solutions in terms of conventional medicine? Was there a switch in emphasis at some point from conventional to alternative treatments?

MW: The switch to the more alternative treatment wasn't just a women-versus-men thing. I think that's the one thing that people shared initially or that the men got that the women already had was that the health care system was political and the research system was political and it wasn't just a matter of good and bad science. It was a matter of who did they care about and what were they going to do and that you couldn't separate politics and science.

LS: So this was a feminist perspective that had already been developed by the women's movement.

MW: Yes, it was from the women's health movement. And many gay men in ACT UP knew firsthand already because the initial ravages of the epidemic were happening to them. But gradually a particular set or subset of people in ACT UP starting thinking that the problem was not the structure of science. Rather, it was a problem of who was doing it. A major issue was that the people doing the research were kind of divorced from the people who were being affected by the research.

LS: Which is a political issue and not a science issue?

MW: Right. But they did not have any critique of the way that science gets done in any other sense. In effect, they moved to a point where they did not have an analysis of the fact that the government only tests drugs that drug companies can make money from, and those decisions in science are being determined by profit and advancement through the university system and not by what will save people's lives. At that point there was a very decided split, with people leaving ACT UP to form the Treatment Advocacy Group (TAG). They told everyone that they represented the people who had AIDS and that everybody else in ACT UP was seronegative, which was a total lie. If you were talking about women, it was a social thing, while if you were talking about treatment, it was a male issue. You could not talk about women's stuff with that group of people without them believing that it was a social issue associated with AIDS instead of a treatment issue. In that way they were no different from the government people that we were confronting. If science does not include everyone, it's not really science; it's white male science, and that's a very specific kind of science. A lot of the people who left to form TAG were more allopathically oriented, like traditional U.S. medicine, and they had far more faith in the capitalist system of profit. They even thought it was going to work for them. Eventually.

LS: It sounds like most of the people who eventually became involved with ACT UP were not politicized in terms of their gay identity.

MW: Not originally; no, not at all.

LS: That was something that developed over time, then.

MW: Right. They were . . . some of the people were very strong from the beginning. But the majority of gay men coming to ACT UP, really I would describe it as "hiding their gayness behind AIDS." In other words, they were coming out only to fight the AIDS crisis. And then they discovered the kind of experience of working with the gay community when you're gay and being able to be out in that place and the electricity of it and of people feeling good about themselves—really experiencing it firsthand—and became totally out. People changed their career paths; people dropped corporate jobs.

LS: Their consciousness got raised.

MW: Yes. And there's no way to go back.

LS: In light of this issue we've just been discussing, how did Lesbian Avengers develop out of ACT UP?

MW: It did not develop out of ACT UP. In a couple of instances I've tried to correct this impression. Actually, there were six lesbians who started the Avengers.

LS: When was that?

MW: Our first public meeting was in July 1992, but our first meeting to talk about the Avengers was in May 1992. In 1982, when we were kicked out of CARASA,[17] Sarah Schulman and myself and some other women started a group called Women For Women, which was a lesbian-feminist group. We called it "a lesbian-feminist group fighting for women's liberation with warmth and a sense of humor." And we told everybody they could spell Women For Women anyway they wanted to. So it was incredible, because some people spelled it Wimmin and some people would spell it Womyn and some would spell it Women.

LS: Pure anarchy.

MW: Yes. We wanted to say, "Why are we operating on that level?" Anyway, we were the people who sat in at that gay-rights hearing that had the big banner that said "Lesbian liberation, we won't go away." Then that group kind of fell apart, around antiporn versus anticensorship, and people began getting panicked about being lesbians out on the street. It was okay when we did stuff about reproductive rights, but when it was about lesbians there was a whole bunch of younger women who just panicked to be out on the street. It began to devolve into them discussing coming out and what not. Anyway, it died. And then also, about a year before we started Lesbian Avengers, Sarah Schulman and I always used to talk about how are we going to get more lesbians out on the street. And then with the resurgence of the stuff around abortion we said, "Come on, all these dykes are going to be fighting for abortion again, and none of these people have ever come out to do anything for us. Still. Yet. Never." And we were over the top on abortion stuff because we'd done it for so many years and had gotten thrown out as soon as we'd mentioned lesbians.

So Sarah said she was going to call a community meeting to get together whatever lesbian groups there were, just to come together to talk about what they were doing and what things we could do together. But I said to her, "Sarah, this is the wrong time." And she said, "Well, I'm going to try it." And I said, "Well, go ahead. I don't feel like it's the right time." So she went ahead and she called every single group up in New York personally and said, "You don't have to agree with each other, you don't have to come to agree with each other." Over one hundred women showed up at this meeting. Some of them were younger dykes from ACT UP and Dyke Action Machine! (DAM!), which was originally part of Queer Nation/New York, and some had been doing organizing for years. But it dissolved into a parody of why people stopped doing stuff years ago. While going around the room, one woman stood up and claimed that we should be doing work on animal rights, and somebody else got up saying we should do something else. As this is happening, Sarah was getting more and more crazed because she has this style which is that she wants things to go the way she wants them to go. And she was there to find out what actions we could do, and people weren't talking about that. At one point, as this was starting to happen, it got to me and I stood up and I said "I can't believe that I'm sitting here and there's not one person in this room who is talking about what a lesbian issue is. Are you all out at your workplaces? Are you all getting decent health care?" I mean, they were living in another world, and the only person who had spoken about this was June Chan, who we had worked with in Women for Women who had started Asian Lesbians of the East Coast. She was organizing with this whole other group a protest against Lambda Legal Defense, who refused to stop their fundraiser at *Miss Saigon*.[18] I said, "Now, do you want to know why *that's* a lesbian and gay issue? Because an organization that says "lesbian" in its title is holding a fundraiser there. Otherwise, I don't hear anybody doing anything." Sarah was desperately trying to rein these people in and I said, "Sarah, let it go because if you keep trying to tell them they can't argue about this, you're going to get massacred."

LS: In fact, it wasn't the time, as you said.

MW: It wasn't the time, and it wasn't the way to go about it. So, I kept wanting to do this but I was very tied into ACT UP stuff, and Sarah is friends with Ana Simo, who is a lesbian who ran the first lesbian performance space in New York called "Medusa's Revenge." She's a writer and translator, a Cuban dyke, and she was very upset about what was going on in New York around the AIDS curriculum and the Rainbow curriculum. Sarah told Ana that she should talk to me because my idea was that we should just arbitrarily, without asking anybody, make up leaflets that said "Are you being harassed at work?" and other examples and then to say "Call the Lesbian Direct Action Hotline. We'll do an action for you." And she thought that was a great idea. She and I went out to have a drink and she said she really wanted to do something and this was January and I said, "Ana, I can't do anything until May," and she said, "OK, in May I'm going to invite people to my house for dinner." I said, "OK, you do that in May and I'll come." And damned if she did not remember. In May she called me and said, "OK, it's time to do something."

We ended up calling a lot of different women who we had worked with in different ways over the years. The people who ended up at that meeting included Marie Honan and Anne Maguire, who were two of the lesbians who started the Irish Lesbian and Gay Organization, Sarah, Ana, Anne D'Adetsky and myself.[19] And we sat and had dinner and talked about whether starting a lesbian group was a possibility. In forty minutes we had a name. The group had to be a fait accompli, and no one could have a say in whether or not the group could exist because then it would never exist. We had to have a name and a group and an action and, basically, we had to figure out a way for lesbians to come to this action and to become part of planning for it. Ana had noticed what was in the newspapers at the time about the AIDS curriculum and the Rainbow curriculum and the right-wingers on the New York City School Board. After about two days, the issue of the Rainbow curriculum had disappeared and all the focus was on AIDS and not on lesbian and gay issues.

So we decided that night that our first action would be in September of 1992 against one of the school boards that refused to implement the Rainbow curriculum. We decided on Lesbian Avengers[20] as a name. We decided that we would give out club cards at Gay Pride, which was coming up in June. We each chipped in thirty-three dollars to pay for the making of eight thousand club cards. Sarah and someone else wrote the original text of the club card, which said something like "Lesbians, dykes, gay women: Cold-blooded liars like George Bush in the White House—what did they ever do for us? Religion. The State. Who cares. We want revenge and we want it now. What have you got to lose?" And then we put down the phone number of the telephone in the up-stairs part of my house and set up a tape machine. When you called the number, the tape said "You have reached the Lesbian Avengers. We're planning our first action for the first day of school in September against the community school boards that have refused to accept the Rainbow curriculum. If you want to be part of the planning, come to our first meeting on July 6th." Ana was looking for a logo, and she went into the graphics file in her computer and her son said, "What about this funny bomb logo?" And she loved it—we all loved it, so we took the bomb. And then we gave the cards out only to lesbians who were not in the March. We did not want women who were already committed to nine thousand other groups. We wanted to reach women who were new. Seventy lesbians showed up for the first meeting.[21]

LS: Where was this?

MW: Our first action was in Queens, in a totally almost suburban area of Queens, which was almost totally white. Middle Village. There's never been a public demonstration in Middle Village. Basically, we decided that the only way to do anything about this was to do something that nobody else would do.[22] The women who came to the first meeting were all willing to do this. They were risk-takers. They had called a number they knew nothing about that they got from a card handed to them by someone they did not know. They knew that they were coming to a meeting about doing something on the first day of school about the Rainbow curriculum. Then word-of-mouth kicked in, and every week new women would show up. And what were their biggest issues? Their biggest issues were, "Aren't we using children, who are going to school on the first day, when it's already so chaotic and so upsetting to them already, and isn't this going to be terrible for kids?" And I said, "As someone who has two kids, this is what's going to happen. The first day of school is going to be great. The first day of school, these kids are going to get balloons and marching bands. They're going to think, 'Wow! This is fantastic!' And then the second day of school we're not going to be there and they're going to think, 'Oh my God. This is so boring. I can't believe it.'"

LS: "Where are those women?" [laughter]

MW: The other issue was that we had come up with this idea to make balloons that said "Ask about lesbian lives." People were really upset about that—these new women who would come in later weeks to the planning meeting. And we would have to go through the same argument again and again. They said "How can you give those balloons to children? That's really manipulating them." And I would then say, "What if the balloons said 'Save the Whales'?" The trademark of what the Avengers wanted to do was to be in a place and confront the issue that is the "no-no." Gay people connected to kids. That's where everyone falls apart—especially in Queens suburbs where no one ever goes. So we ended up doing it. We had seventy women show up on the first day of school. We had to go to the end of the train line, and then we marched. We were lucky when we picked out the school district that it ended up being the district of this totally right-wing woman who then gave us a lot of publicity. We wheat-pasted the neighborhood for weeks beforehand saying we were coming. And the Queens police showed up panicked but very nice because they have never ever had this happen to them. And we marched down this main street and then went over to the school. And when we got to the school, the police tried to tell us that we couldn't walk in front of the school. And we said, "That's not the law; the law says that if there's voting here, we can't give out literature within fifty feet of the voting site, but this is a city street and we're allowed to walk here." So we actually marched around the school and the kids were coming in for the first day of school and we handed out balloons and we had a marching band and sang songs like "We Are Family."

LS: How did the children and the parents respond?

MW: Well, there were a couple of parents who took the balloons and gave them to the kids, and there were other parents who were just horrified. They said things like "Let that balloon go! Don't you take that balloon!" And we thought that was fine, too, because then the kid is going to ask "Why? Why can't we say the word 'lesbian'?" So in the end none of us got arrested. We got a good amount of publicity for the issue, for ourselves, and that became our trademark—to do cutting-edge kind of stuff—out in places where people do not want us to be out. I think that a lot of that kind of attitude is not just a direct descendent from ACT UP because ACT UP's tactics were already an appropriation of those tactics from Gay Activist Alliance and feminists. Sarah Schulman had been arrested in 1991 for busting up the East hearings in Congress. It is not as if these tactics had directly evolved from ACT UP. Not everyone originally in the Avengers had anything to do with ACT UP. Nor were the

Avengers even in opposition to ACT UP. It was simply that, and this is the way several of us have felt for many years, lesbians have always been at the forefront of all movements for social change and most often in the leadership, especially in the women's movement, but they've been closeted. We wanted to be out, and we wanted to do something for ourselves because no one ever does anything about lesbians. No one.

LS: Were the Avengers formed as a reaction to political differences with "the boys"?

MW: No. Not at all.

LS: So that it wasn't because of political differences with the men in ACT UP?

MW: No. In fact Anne and Marie started the Irish Gay and Lesbian Organization and have and still do work in ILGO, the International Lesbian and Gay Organization. Anne D'Adetsky has worked in ACT UP and in TAG. I've worked in mixed groups all my life. We did want to be able to be in a group where we did not have to deal with either the homophobia of straight women or the sexism of gay men. But that's not because we don't work with men. *We wanted to work on lesbian issues.* It was proactive. It became clear to us that nobody could even articulate what that was anymore. We wanted to work with women, with lesbians, around those issues and not have to worry about that other stuff. And I still work in ACT UP, for example, and Anne and Marie are still in the Irish Lesbian and Gay Organization, and the Avengers have done the marshaling and logistics strategy for the Irish Lesbian and Gay Organization for the last two years.

LS: So there's lots of crossover between and among the memberships.

MW: Yes. Going back to what Jan Clausen said about "energetic" . . . somehow people think that if you are visible and do media-grabbing events, then all it is about is frivolity. For example, our "signature," so to speak, is the fact that we eat fire. Lots of people think that this is a circus stunt to open or close events. But eating fire has great significance for the Avengers, as does the frequent use of fire, and we refuse to simply go somewhere and do it as a stunt. We started fire-eating as part of our actions against the Oregon antilesbian and gay amendment.[23] In September 1992 an African-American lesbian and a disabled white gay man, Hattie Cohens and Brian Mock, were burned to death in their apartment in Salem when neo-Nazi skinheads threw a molotov cocktail through their window. This was in the middle of the Citizen Alliance's first (unsuccessful) campaign, which was filled with hate, to pass the amendment. There had been no national media attention paid to the murders. And even our side in Oregon had not made the murders widely known. When we heard about it, we decided that we could focus on making it known widely, both within New York City and nationally. We sent press releases around the country, held a press conference at City Hall. Eventually, Anna Quindlan picked it up in the *New York Times*.[24] Quindlan's article was photocopied and put in mailboxes in Oregon. When the Anti-Violence Project in New York asked us to be one of the groups doing "something" on a street corner during the annual Take Back the Night March, which took place on the night before Hallowe'en, when there is the highest level of antilesbian and gay violence in New York City, we came up with the idea to focus on the Oregon murders. We were ambitious—not only did we plan something for the march but something we could do leading up to the day of the vote three days later. We created a huge shrine to Hattie and Brian—a triptych—with their photos and the words—"Burned to Death for Being Who They Are." We took the corner of Sixth Avenue and Bleecker Street as our place. This is where two dykes had been badly bashed a few months earlier. We camped out there for three days and nights and handed out leaflets about the murders and about the antilesbian and gay initiatives around the country. Our kickoff was the antiviolence Take Back the Night March. Jennifer Monson, who had been a fire-eater in Jennifer Miller's Circus Amok, came up with the idea of us eating fire and taught everyone to eat fire who wanted to learn. Lysander Puccio, who was studying theology, wrote a eulogy. When the March got to our corner, she gave her eulogy—it sounds corny but it was incredibly moving because she spoke about our fears and about the real hatred against us, using as an example not only Hattie and Brian but about the two dykes who had been bashed on that corner. Then, she basically said that we could not let their fire consume us; instead we had to take it and make it our own, letting it give us the energy to fight back. At that point about ten dykes got into a circle in front of the crowd and lit their torches from one another's tongues and then ate the fire while the rest of us chanted "Their fire will not consume us; we take it and make it our own." The crowd roared! We stayed on that corner for three days and nights; it was freezing and raining. Passersby started bringing us food and blankets. People came and lit candles in front of the shrine and brought mementos of friends who had died of physical violence, from AIDS. And so fire-eating and the use of fire became a way of expressing our purpose and still is. And we refuse to do it unless we can tell the story. A couple of weeks later, after the votes in Oregon and Colorado were in, we staged a march down Fifth Avenue during rush hour. A group of women had made torches to light the way down from the Plaza Hotel to Rockefeller Center, our symbol of the major media that had not covered the murders nor other violence against us. To march without a permit was against the law. But the women with the torches persisted, and when the flames were lit and they wrestled them away from the cops, everyone was empowered. We ended that demo by burning replicas of the Oregon and Colorado amendments there, in front of Rockefeller Center, while everyone chanted "Their fire will not consume us; we take it and make it our own." We also ate fire in front of the White House during the dyke march we organized, again without a permit, the night before the 1993 Lesbian/Gay March on Washington.[25]

The Dyke Marches are another example of taking over public space for our own ends. It began in October 1992, when we realized that lesbians would blend invisibly into the massive numbers of gay men who would come to the

1993 March on Washington, and the message would be all about assimilation and the military. We sent an announcement to the *Lesbian Connection*, a newsletter that goes to thousands of lesbians around the country, saying there would be a dyke march. Lesbians from Los Angeles and Philadelphia, from ACT UP New York and the Avengers, had conference phone calls during January and solidified plans. The New York Avengers came down to D.C. and handed out eight thousand palm cards on Friday in the day and at night, and on Saturday during the day. First we thought no one would show up. Then we realized that thousands would and that there was no way that we could actually marshal this, except to trust that enough dykes in the crowd had done it and would take care of each other. As the time approached, hundreds of dykes started to show up at Dupont Circle. It was overwhelming, and the excitement was extraordinary. There were about twenty thousand dykes at the "nonpermitted" march and we marched past the White House, where the Avengers ate fire, and onto a grassy part of the mall for a closing ceremony. Amazingly, the gay press hardly covered it. There was an article in the *Nation*, which said that all of the media except the *Washington Post* had not covered the most important event of the weekend that was not assimilationist and not about the military, the Dyke March.[26] We always have that problem, even with the gay media, and it happened again during Stonewall 25 when we organized the International Dyke March. All the papers covered was the Stonewall Committee's arguments with Guiliani about whether they could march down Fifth Avenue, which they did not, and ACT UP saying they would anyway, which they did. Meanwhile, we organized a nonpermitted International Dyke March for Saturday evening. It began at Bryant Park, on 42nd Street, between Fifth and Sixth Avenues, and marched downtown on Fifth Avenue all the way to Washington Square Park, where we had a rally. Although the March was not slated to begin until 5:30, by 3:30 dykes were already showing up at the park, and by 5 P.M., it was totally a dyke space—dykes chatting in groups, sitting on benches reading, a dyke saxophone quartet playing music. And then the drum rolls began at 5:30, and the banner went up in the air. The effect was electrifying. There were thousands of dykes marching down 42nd Street to Fifth Avenue, they were willing to risk arrest, and *boom* we were on Fifth Avenue, and a huge roar went up, not only from the marchers but from a couple of thousand dykes and fags sitting and waiting for us on the main library steps on Fifth. The cops kept trying to keep us to two lanes, and then they started to push on us and tried to have vehicles drive on the side of us. We just stood there chanting—not moving—and told them it would get worse if they did not let us march. We had two or three standoffs like this, and then they just gave up.

    Again, the gay media hardly covered this but the straight media did. But the lesbian grapevine still exists and now there are dyke marches all over the country and in some places they are seen as *the* alternative marches in the Stonewall celebrations in late June. Because there are no contingents, you do not have to be in a group to have a place in the march; you do not have to dress or act in a certain way. Fag friends stand on the sidelines and cheer us on. In some cities gay men march along. Lots of dykes feel that this is the real event of the weekend.

LS: What are the Lesbian Avengers doing now? What kinds of actions are you involved in, and what kinds of missions are you undertaking?

MW: Well, we're still going where no one wants us to go. I'll give you two examples. The first is that we have a Lesbian Avengers civil-rights organizing project. This is our second year of doing it. This year we sent eight full-time organizers and ten part-time organizers to live and work in rural northern Idaho to do "out" organizing against Proposition One there[27]—much to the chagrin of the mainstream lesbian and gay campaign there, who were once again going to do a campaign that did not mention lesbians and gay men, even though the right wing mentions us all the time. We were incredibly successful in every place that we worked, including extreme right-wing areas where the Aryan Nation shows up at Human Rights Tasks Force events in Nazi regalia. We actually won by far larger percentages in every area in which we worked than the mainstream campaign or in comparison to the statewide vote.

LS: What kinds of actions did you do?

MW: We did everything from wrapping a ribbon around a Unitarian Church to help the minister declare it a "hate-free zone" to going to the Latah County Fair and holding a Lesbian and Gay Freedom Picnic and handing out Hershey's Kisses, with a little card that said "Last year at this Fair fifteen lesbians and gay men were harassed. Wouldn't you like a kiss instead?" We did door-to-door out canvassing. We wrote literature that was about lesbians and gay men. There were some independent northern campaigns like Voices for Human Rights which, while they weren't as radical as we were, were perfectly willing to not use the closeted literature of the mainstream lesbian and gay campaign in Boise and used ours instead. We made lawn signs that, instead of saying "No on One," said "No lesbian bashing, No on One" and "No Gay Teen Suicide, No on One." We actually worked with some people in Lewiston, Idaho, and we helped them to form the Lewiston Lesbian and Gay Society, and they held a public town meeting at which five lesbians and gay men who had grown up in that town came out. That's the kind of stuff that we've been doing there. And in that campaign, people went out and lived there for four months, and I was out there for ten days in November.

In New York City, we just did a series of coalition actions Ana organized with Las Buenas Amigas, which is a Latina lesbian group, and African-American Women United for Societal Change about this radio station called "Mega K Q," which is one of only two radio stations in New York and the only one on AM that does Spanish music and programming. Their major morning program is also in Los Angeles and several other parts of the country and is the most racist homophobic sexist dialogue you've ever heard—like "Women want to be raped" and "Latina lesbians and gay men should be eliminated." It's horrifying. So we started out a few months ago with an Avenger action in which we did a small picket outside the station calling it "hate radio," and six women got inside and actually took over their microphones and said "Enough. Stop this. Stop the Hate. Hate isn't funny," and then walked out without getting arrested. Then we came back and did another action. In that one we wheat-pasted in Latin neighborhoods saying "Stop the Hate. Call Mega K Q." We called their advertisers and got them to put pressure on them. Then, last week, we did this joint action with Las Buenas Amigas and African Ancestral Lesbians for a march that went down 57th Street and across Sixth Avenue and down 56th Street to their building, chanting. We had a huge piñata that was made like a radio, and it had two monster heads coming out of it. We had a drum corps drumming Latin music, and we had made up songs. We do a lot of stuff like that.

We also do very visual actions, and we go to places where no one wants us to be. We did an action on Staten Island. We went to the Alice Austin House, which is a National Historic Landmark. Alice Austin was a dyke photographer at the turn of the century, who actually produced one of the most incredible collections of photographs of lesbians and gay men. But the people who run the House refuse to admit that she was a lesbian and that she lived in it for thirty-three years with her lover. Everyone knows this. We went out there when they had a "Nautical Day" dressed as turn-of-the-century lifeguards and carrying big life preservers that said "Dyke Preserver" on them. And we had rewritten songs like "Ho Ho Homosex Homosexual/Alice and Gertrude were lesbians and we are as well." We did a whole performance thing out there—in Staten Island.

LS: That's a scary thing to do, Maxine. I know people on Staten Island. [laughter]

MW: We do serious politics. For example, when we worked in Idaho, we lived out there for four months—eight organizers living in northern Idaho and really getting to know the people and working with the people and being part of what was going on there and just helping people express it in ways that are unusual.

This Is About People Dying

1. *Editors' note:* For articles in the mainstream media that often contradict Wolfe's experience at the actual events and that convey the concern on the part of the state about ACT UP activism, see Cynthia Crossen, Shock troops: AIDS activist group harasses and provokes to make its point, *Wall Street Journal* (December 7, 1989): A1; Jason DeParle, Rash, rude, and effective. ACT UP helps change AIDS policy, *New York Times* 139 (January 3, 1990): A12, B1; Editorial, AIDS and misdirected rage (ACT UP disrupts sixth annual International AIDS Conference), *New York Times* 139 (June 26, 1990): A18, A22; James Barron, Prosecutor's appeal dropped on police beating of protester, *New York Times* 141 (October 17, 1991): B4; Debbi

Wilgoren, 74 AIDS activists arrested in Capitol protests, *Washington Post* 114 (October 2, 1991): A24; David W. Dunlap, FBI kept file on Act Up in protest years; dossier appears to be mainly news clippings, *New York Times* 144 (May 16, 1995): A15, B3.

2. Schulman, *My American History*.

3. Jan Clausen, Review, *My American History*, 583.

4. In a one-page opinion at the back of an issue of *The Advocate*, Tory Osborne stated that "some of our vibrant activist groups need to get real: Sending the Lesbian Avengers into Lewiston, Me., last fall during the city's ballot struggle was about as effective as it would be to send the '60s group the Yippies into factories to organize against the Vietnamese War." (Up against the wall, 80).

5. The discussion in this interview augments a more structured chronology of ACT UP NY already published. See Maxine Wolfe, The AIDS Coalition to unleash power, in *AIDS Prevention and Services*, 217–47.

6. I worked in a lesbian and gay male leftist coalition in the early 80s called CRASH—Committee against Racism, Sexism, Antisemitism, and Heterosexism. There was a group called DARE—Dykes Against Racism Everywhere. There was a group called DONT—Dykes Opposed to Nuclear Technology. But a lot of that stuff was not necessarily focused, especially after the early years, on lesbian issues.

7. They dressed up and then busted up a dinner that Cardinal O'Connor was at, the Alfred E. Smith Memorial Dinner, which the Catholic Church holds in New York every year.

8. Kramer, Mob, others call for traffic blockade, *New York Native* (March 30, 1987): 1.

9. Kramer, *Faggots*.

10. The AIDS Action Network was basically a group of the Democratic Party made up of politically oriented people who had started meeting early on, in 1981 and 1982 Vivian Shapiro was part of it. They wanted to see if they could do anything in Albany about getting money for AIDS treatment. But it really fizzled.

11. Patton, *Inventing AIDS*, 126–31.

12. The SILENCE = DEATH Project may have renamed itself Gran Fury by then, but I think that it was still referred to as the SILENCE = DEATH Project.

13. For two discussions of the implications of the *Hardwick* decision, see Lisa Duggan, Banned in the U.S.A, 80–84 and Nan D. Hunter, Life after *Hardwick*, in *Sex Wars*, 84–100.

14. Sheridan Square is in the "West Village" and was the site of the 1969 Stonewall riots.

15. "*Bougie*" was a New Left adjective roughly equivalent to "bourgeois," when used in the same way.

16. For a background overview on the work of ACT UP NY, leading up to the 1988 Shea Stadium action, see David France, ACT UP fires up, *Village Voice* (May 3, 1988): 36.

17. CARASA stood for Coalition for Abortion Rights and Against Sterilization Abuse.

18. A coalition of Asian American groups protested against the performance of Miss Saigon. There were different organizational responses. The Asian Lesbians of the East Coast (ALOEC) tried to pressure two community groups who were holding fundraisers with that show. They successfully pressured the Lesbian and Gay Community Center to drop their plans. Lambda Legal Defense refused to drop it

saying it was their major fundraiser of the year. So on the night of their fundraiser ALOEC organized a picket at the theater and handed out flyers—lots of community people came to that demonstration.

19. Anne D'Adetsky often came to ACT UP meetings, but I would not say that she was a central person in ACT UP. But she had never been in the Women's Caucus.

20. Some of the early history of the Lesbian Avengers in New York City is recounted on their homepage: *www.cc.columbia.edu/vk20/lesbian/avenger.html* (as of June 1996).

21. See the description of the September 9, 1992 action on the New York City Lesbian Avengers homepage (see n. 20).

22. Faye Penn, Avenging angels or diabolical dykes? Lesbian direct-action group is targeting school kids. *QW* (September 2, 1992): 26 and Gary Terracino, When dykes met Queens—Gary Terracino on the Lesbian Avengers' first day at school, *QW* (September 20, 1992): 26–27.

23. Jennifer Monson, Moving dyke bodies, 8.

24. Anne Quindlan, Putting hatred to a vote, Presidential candidates should decry Oregon's antihomosexual Ballot Measure 9, *New York Times* 142 (October 28, 1992): A19, A21.

25. Some of these events are also recounted on New York City Lesbian Avengers homepage (see n. 20).

26. Andrew Kopkind, Editorial, Paint it pink, March on Washington, *The Nation* 256(19) (May 17, 1993): 652–53.

27. Sara Pursley, With the Lesbian Avengers in Idaho, *The Nation* (January 23, 1995): 90–94.

Works Cited

Clausen, J. 1994. Review of *My American History: Lesbian and gay life during the Reagan/Bush years*. *The Nation* 259(16) (November 14).

Duggan, L. 1995. Banned in the U.S.A: What the *Hardwick* ruling will mean. In *Sex Wars: Sexual dissent and political culture*. New York: Routledge.

Hunter, N. D. 1995. Life after Hardwick. In *Sex Wars: Sexual dissent and political culture*. New York: Routledge.

Kramer, L. 1978. *Faggots*. New York: Routledge.

Monson, J. 1995. Moving dyke bodies. *Movement Research* 10.

Osborne, T. 1994. Up against the wall. *The Advocate* 652 (April 5).

Patton, C. 1990. *Inventing AIDS*. New York: Routledge.

Schulman, S. 1994. *My American History: Lesbian and gay life during the Reagan/Bush years*. New York: Routledge.

Wolfe, M. 1994. The AIDS Coalition to unleash power, New York (ACT UP NY): A direct action political model of community research for AIDS prevention. In *AIDS Prevention and Services: Community-based research*. Edited by Johannes P. Van Vugt. Westport, Connecticut: Bergin and Garvey.

Questions for Reflection, Discussion, and Writing

1. What are some of the strategies that Wolf describes among early 1980s gay and lesbian organizations that frustrated her sense of political action? What were her perceptions about gender in these groups? About assimilationist strategies?
2. According to Wolf, how did early ACT UP events utilize a youthful generation's increasing sophistication with visual imagery? Why and how was this effective?
3. What were the components that went into making the ACT UP event at Shea stadium so successful?
4. What wisdom and strategies did the feminist movement contribute to ACT UP?
5. Wolf advocates, both in ACT UP and Lesbian Avenger political actions, an approach that is more confrontational and, she perceives, more radical than assimilationist strategies. Do you agree with her that radical tactics are equally, if not more, effective than more conventional ones? Why and how?

Related Reading

ACT UP and WHAM, "Action Update, Letter to Parishioners of St. Patrick's Cathedral, post-action Position Statement and Media Report" (1989) in *We Are Everywhere: A Historical Sourcebook of Gay and Lesbian Politics*. Mark Blasius and Shane Phelan, Eds. NY: Routledge. 1997. 622–627.

Lation/a AIDS Activists of ACT UP, "Silence = Death" (1989) in *We Are Everywhere: A Historical Sourcebook of Gay and Lesbian Politics*. Mark Blasius and Shane Phelan, Eds. NY: Routledge. 1997. 635–636.

Caucus of Asian and Pacific Islander AIDS Activists, "Manifesto" (1989) in *We Are Everywhere: A Historical Sourcebook of Gay and Lesbian Politics*. Mark Blasius and Shane Phelan, Eds. NY: Routledge. 1997. 636–637.

Joshua Gamson, "Silence, Death, and the Invisible Enemy: AIDS Activism and Social Movement 'Newness'" (1989) in *Social Perspectives in Lesbian and Gay Studies*. Peter M. Nardi and Beth E. Schneider, Eds. NY: Routledge. 1989. 334–348.

Donna Minkowitz, "ACT UP at a Crossroads" (1990) in *We Are Everywhere: A Historical Sourcebook of Gay and Lesbian Politics*. Mark Blasius and Shane Phelan, Eds. NY: Routledge. 1997. 655–651.

Vito Russo, "A Test of Who We Are As a People: ACT UP Rally, Albany, New York, May 7, 1988" in *Democracy: Discussions in Contemporary Culture*. Brian Wallis, Ed. Seattle: Bay Press. 1990. 299–302.

Catherine Saalfield and Ray Navarro, "Shocking Pink Praxis: Race and Gender on the ACT UP Frontlines" in *Inside/Out: Lesbian Theories, Gay Theories*. Diana Fuss, Ed. NY: Routledge. 1991. 341–369.

Gregg Bordowitz, "The AIDS Crisis Is Ridiculous" in *Queer Looks: Perspectives on Lesbian and Gay Film and Video*. Martha Gever, John Greyson and Pratibha Parmar, Eds. NY: Routledge. 1993. 209–224.

Stanley Aronowitz, "Against the Liberal State: Act-Up and the Emergence of Postmodern Politics" in *Social Postmodernism: Beyond Identity Politics*. Linda Nicholson and Steven Seidman, Eds. Cambridge: Cambridge UP. 1995. 357–383.

Mary Patten, "The Thrill Is Gone: An Act Up Post-Mortem (Confessions of a Former AIDS Activist" in *The Passionate Camera: Photography and Bodies of Desire*. Deborah Bright, Ed. NY: Routledge. 1998. 385–406.

Film

Laura, Ingrid, and Rebecca (1990). Philippe Roques. 7 m.
Lesbian Avengers Eat Fire Too (1993). Janet Baus and Su Friedrich. 55 m.
Voices From the Front (1991). Sandra Elgear, Robyn Hutt and David Meleran. 90 m.

Web Resource

http://www.actupny.org

Social Activism

Using some of your classmates as a political base, plan a political action on your campus or in your community. Think through carefully what you want your goal(s) to be, how best to make this happen, and how to involve members of other constituencies in this action. Make a written plan that outlines your strategies and your goals, and get feedback from people who have experience in political organizing. Think about how you will engage the media in order to reach as many people as possible.

Right On, Girlfriend!

Douglas Crimp

At Vito Russo's memorial service in December of 1990, the first speaker was New York's mayor David Dinkins. It had been reported in the gay press that Dinkins paid a hospital visit a few days before Vito died, and that Vito had mustered the strength to sit up and say, "In 1776, Edmund Burke of the British Parliament said about the slavery clause, 'A politician owes the people not only his industry but his judgment, and if he sacrifices his judgment to their opinions, he betrays them.'"[1] Those of us who are queer and/or AIDS activists knew very well what Vito was alluding to, because Mayor Dinkins had by then already sacrificed what we took to be his judgment when we voted for him. He

failed to make a public issue of the rising tide of violence against gays and lesbians, refusing to march with us in Staten Island to protest the homophobically
motivated murder of a disabled gay man, and unwilling to press for labeling as
bias-related the murder of a gay Latino in a Jackson Heights cruising area.[2] He
appointed Woodrow Myers health commissioner over the vehement objections
of AIDS activists; he canceled New York's pilot needle-exchange program, initiated by Myers's predecessor but opposed by the city's conservative black leadership; he allowed thousands of homeless people with HIV infection to remain
in warehouse shelters, where they are vulnerable to opportunistic diseases, especially to the terrifying new epidemic of multi–drug-resistant strains of tuberculosis; and he drastically cut funding for health services even as the city's
health-care system faced collapse from underfinancing. Still, when Dinkins eu-
logized Vito Russo, he quoted what Vito had said to him in the hospital and,
with no apparent sense of irony, professed that he would always remember it.

As soon as he had delivered his short speech, the mayor and his entourage
left the memorial service, accompanied by a small chorus of boos. The next
speaker was Vito's old friend Arnie Kantrowitz, who began by saying that, just
in case we thought we had learned something new about Vito—that he was a
student of American history—we should know that the lines he'd quoted to
Dinkins came from the movie version of the Broadway musical *1776*. Our
laughter at Arnie's remark brought back the Vito we knew and loved, the fierce
activist who was very funny and very queer, a very funny queer who knew and
loved movies, who knew better than anybody how badly the movies treated
queers, but still loved them. Those qualities were captured yet again in another
of Arnie's remarks. Reminiscing about Vito's pleasure in showing movies at
home to his friends and about his unashamed worship of Judy Garland, Arnie
summed up Vito's brand of gay militancy (or perhaps I should say, his gay
brand of militancy): "In Vito's house," Arnie quipped, "either you respected
Judy . . . or you left."

A very different chord was struck later in the service by Larry Kramer.
"The Vito who was my friend was different from the one I've heard about
today," the Hollywood screenwriter said. "Since I hate old movies, I wasn't in
his home-screening crowd." Kramer went on to ask, rhetorically, "Who killed
Vito?" And his answer? "As sure as any virus killed him, we killed him. Everyone in this room killed him. Twenty-five million people outside this room
killed him. Vito was killed by 25 million gay men and lesbians who for ten long
years of this plague have refused to get our act together. Can't you see that?"

The "can't you see that?" was the refrain of Kramer's speech, which went
on to name names—mostly those of closeted gay men and lesbians in the entertainment industry. The last names mentioned were those associated with an
AIDS fundraiser:

> There's going to be a benefit screening of a movie called *Silence of the Lambs*. The
> villain is a gay man who mass-murders people. AmFAR is holding the benefit.
> Thanks a lot, Mathilde Krim [Mathilde Krim is, as is well known, the chairperson

of the American Foundation for AIDS Research]. Thanks a lot, Arthur Krim, for financing the film [Arthur Krim, Mathilde's husband, is the founder of Orion Pictures]. Thanks a lot, Jodie Foster, for starring in it [Jodie Foster is . . . well, we know who Jodie Foster is . . .].[3]

Some other people at the memorial service disagreed with Larry about who killed Vito. As several hundred of Vito's friends and admirers arrived at the service, we were handed a xeroxed flier signed "Three Anonymous Queers." "On the same night last month," it began,

> Vito Russo died from AIDS and Jesse Helms was reelected to another six years of power. . . . I believe with all my heart that Jesse Helms killed Vito Russo. And I believe without question that when I was queer-bashed, Helms was as responsible for my injuries as if he had inflicted the wounds with his own hands. I fully imagine in a meeting with Helms, he would have the blood and flesh of dead dykes and fags dripping from his hands and mouth. And I hate him and I believe he is a threat to my very existence and I have every right to defend myself against him with any amount of force I choose.

The flier closed with two questions: "If I am ever brave enough to murder Jesse Helms, will you hand me the gun to carry out the deed? Will you hide me from the law once it is done?"

Most queers will recognize, in these two rhetorical answers to the question, Who killed Vito?, positions taken on debates in contemporary queer politics, debates about "outing" and "bashing back." My interest here is not so much to take sides in these debates as to describe both the political conjuncture within which they take place and some of the cultural interventions within them. I also want to attend to their relevance for AIDS activism, the movement that to some degree brought them to the fore and in which they are sometimes played out. It is not coincidental that they surfaced at Vito Russo's memorial service, for in many ways Vito was the quintessential gay activist turned AIDS activist.

Vito's death was more than a personal loss to his friends and admirers. It was also a great symbolic loss to ACT UP. The Three Anonymous Queers put it this way: "Vito is dead and everything remains the same. I thought I might go to sleep the night after his death and wake up to find the city burned to the ground." Such a fantasy, which recalls spontaneous riots in the wake of murdered civil rights leaders of the 1960s, arises, I think, not only because Vito was a cherished leader, but because he held out hope in a very particular way, hope that he voiced in his famous Albany speech from ACT NOW's Nine Days of Protest in the spring of 1988.[4] The speech began:

> A friend of mine has a half-fare transit card which he uses on busses and subways. The other day when he showed his card, the token attendant asked what his disability was. He said, "I have AIDS," and the attendant said, "No you don't. If you had AIDS, you'd be home, dying." I'm here to speak out today as a PWA [Person

with AIDS] who is not dying from, but for the last three years quite successfully living with, AIDS.

Vito ended the speech by saying, "After we kick the shit out of this disease, I intend to be alive to kick the shit out of this system, so that this will never happen again."

Vito's death painfully demonstrated to many AIDS activists that the rhetoric of hope we invented and depended upon—a rhetoric of "living with AIDS," in which "AIDS is not a death sentence," but rather "a chronic manageable illness"—was becoming difficult to sustain. I don't want to minimize the possibility that anyone's death might result in such a loss of hope for someone, and, moreover, within a two-week period of Vito's death, four other highly visible members of ACT UP New York also died, a cumulative loss for us that was all but unbearable. But I think many of us had a special investment in Vito's survival, not only because he was so beloved, but because, as a long-term survivor, as a resolute believer in his own survival, and as a highly visible and articulate fighter for his and others' survival, he fully embodied that hope.

Vito's death coincided with the waning not only of our optimism but also of a period of limited but concrete successes for the AIDS activist movement. During that period—roughly, the first two and one-half years after the founding of ACT UP in the spring of 1987—we had succeeded in focusing greater public attention on AIDS, in shifting the discussion of AIDS from one dominated by a punitive moralism to one directed toward combating a public health emergency, and in affecting policy in concrete ways, particularly drug development policy.

During the past two years, however, we have experienced only disappointments and setbacks. We have seen almost no new drugs to combat AIDS, whether antivirals or treatments for, or prophylaxes against, opportunistic infections (OIs). The results of ddI and ddC studies have been less than encouraging, and the few potentially effective treatments for OIs are either held up in the FDA's approval process or, when granted marketing approval, subject to record-breaking price gouging. We have had to return to other battles we had thought were behind us, such as the call for mandatory testing of health-care professionals in the wake of hysteria caused by the possible transmission of HIV from a dentist to his patients; after having worked tirelessly to get the voices of people with AIDS heard, the media and Congress finally listened sympathetically to one, that of Kimberly Bergalis, who in fact spoke not as a person with AIDS ("I didn't do anything wrong," she protested), but as the "victim" of people with AIDS ("My life has been taken away").[5] We have seen the leveling off or shrinking of spending on AIDS at local, state, and federal levels, a particularly disheartening example of which was the passage, with great fanfare, of the Ryan White Emergency CARE bill providing disaster relief to the hardest hit cities, and then, at budget time, the failure to provide most of the funding for it. At the same time, case loads continue to spiral upwards, new HIV infections continue to multiply, and the epidemic becomes more entrenched in populations already burdened with other poverty-related problems, populations with no primary health care, no health insurance, often no housing.

Perhaps even more demoralizing than the cumulative effects of these setbacks, we are faced with a new kind of indifference, an indifference that has been called the "normalization of AIDS." If, for the first eight years of the epidemic—the term of Ronald Reagan's presidency—indifference took the form of callously ignoring the crisis, under George Bush, AIDS was "normalized" as just one item on a long list of supposedly intractable social problems. How often do we hear the list recited?—poverty, crime, drugs, homelessness, and AIDS. AIDS is no longer an emergency. It's merely a permanent disaster. One effect of this normalization process is the growing credence granted the claim that AIDS has received a disproportionate amount of federal funding for medical research. This claim overlooks the fact that AIDS is a new disease syndrome, that it primarily threatens the lives of the young, that it is not merely an illness but a bewildering array of illnesses, and, most importantly, that it is an epidemic still out of control. The saddest irony is that, now that our optimism has turned to grim realism, our old rhetoric is appropriated to abet the process of normalization and defunding. Hence our ambivalence at Magic Johnson's powerful example of "living with HIV," since we now know that, particularly among people of color, Johnson's ability to "fight the virus," as he puts it, will be exceptional, and that the sense that AIDS is already manageable will only relax efforts to make it so.

This is a very sketchy background against which new tactics have been embraced by queers. More importantly, it is the background against which AIDS activism is being painfully transformed. The interrelation between the two—queer activism and AIDS activism—is complex, shifting, sometimes divisive. As a means of analyzing the transformations and the divisions, I want to return to Larry Kramer's finger-pointing at Vito Russo's memorial service.

Before coming to Jodie Foster and *The Silence of the Lambs*, a short archaeology of "outing."[6] All queers have extensive experience with the closet, no matter how much of a sissy or tomboy we were as children, no matter how early we declared our sexual preferences, no matter how determined we are to be openly gay or lesbian. The closet is not a function of homosexuality in our culture, but of compulsory and presumptive heterosexuality. I may be publicly identified as gay, but in order for that identity to be acknowledged, I have to declare it on each new occasion. By "occasion," I mean something as simple as asking a cab driver to take me to a bar like the Spike, or kissing my friend Jeff good-bye on a crowded subway when he gets off two stops before me on our way home from the gym. Fearing for my safety, I might choose not to kiss Jeff, thereby hiding behind our fellow riders' presumption that we're straight.[7]

As part of our experience with the closet, which was for most of us the only safe place to be as adolescents, we also know what it's like to keep the closet door firmly shut by pretending not only to be heterosexual but also to be homophobic—since in many circumstances the mark of one's heterosexuality is the open expression of hatred toward queers. Thus most of us have the experience, usually from our youth, of oppressing other queers in order to elude that same oppression. Eve Sedgwick writes in *Epistemology of the Closet* that "it is entirely within the experience of gay people to find that a homophobic figure in power has . . . a disproportionate likelihood of being gay and closeted."[8] I'm not so sure. I don't think there is much likelihood at all that Jesse Helms or Cardinal O'Connor or Patrick Buchanan, for example, are gay and closeted. We do have experience with homophobia dictated by the closet, but that experience is as much of ourselves as of others. And it is often the projection of that experience that makes us suspicious of the homophobic figure in power.

Such suspicions, enhanced by rumors, have sometimes lead us to impugn the heterosexuality of our oppressors. A celebrated case is that of former New York City mayor Ed Koch. A confirmed bachelor, Koch required a former beauty queen for a "beard" to win his first mayoral primary, since the opposition's slogan was "Vote for Cuomo, not the homo." The "homo" won the election, and thereby gained control of the city that would soon have the highest number of AIDS cases of any city in the world. During the time when attention to AIDS implied attention to a gay disease, Koch paid no attention, and many interpreted his need to dissociate himself as a form of self-defense, the defense of his closet. The spectacular conclusion, some years later, was Koch's open admission on a radio talk show of his *hetero*sexuality, which, after many years of insisting that his sexuality was nobody's business, made the front page of *New York Newsday*. For ACT UP's Target City Hall demonstration in March 1989, an affinity group pasted that *Newsday* cover to placards. Its banner headline— "KOCH: I'M HETEROSEXUAL"—answered with "Yeah, and I'm Carmen Miranda." The *Newsday* headline also inspired a tongue-twister chant for the day: "Why's New York AIDS care ineffectual? Ask Ed Koch, the heterosexual." Target City Hall was an outing with a queer sense of humor.

The tendency to suspect a closeted homosexual behind a lack of commitment to fighting AIDS migrated, in the figure of Michelangelo Signorile, from ACT UP to *Outweek*, New York's short-lived gay and lesbian weekly. In charge of ACT UP's media committee during Target City Hall and later *Outweek*'s features editor, Signorile also wrote a column called "Gossip Watch," a queer variation on media watches that restricted its purview to gossip columns. Using the blunt instruments of all-caps, four-letter-word invective and the AIDS crisis as an excuse for righteous indignation, "Gossip Watch" chastised gossip columnists—often themselves closeted homosexuals—for, among other things, inventing beards for closeted celebrities who had done nothing publicly about the AIDS crisis.

This circumscribed context of what came to be called outing has important bearing on the ensuing debate. Signorile appeared initially to want to say something about the privileged position of gossip in our culture's management of *the* open secret. Outing is not (at least not at first) the revelation of that secret, but the revelation that the secret was no secret at all. That was the scandal of *Outweek*'s Malcolm Forbes cover story, for which *Time* and *Newsweek*—not *Outweek*—invented the term "outing."[9] The dominant media heaped fear and loathing upon Signorile, *Outweek*, and queers generally, not because Forbes's homosexuality had been revealed, but because their own complicity in concealing it had been revealed. Forbes was not "outed," the media's homophobia was.

From the moment "outing" was named, however, the straight media set the terms of debate, and we queers foolishly accepted those terms by seeking to justify an act of which we had not been guilty. We resorted then to our two, mutually contradictory excuses: that our oppressors are disproportionately likely to be gay and closeted and that we need them as role models. In adopting our paradoxical defense, we ignored the ways in which both of these positions are turned against us, especially in the context of AIDS.

AIDS has often resulted in a peculiarly public and unarguable means of outing. Day after day, as we read the obituary section of the *New York Times*, we are faced with incontrovertible proof—in their survival by "long-time companions" (a term invented by the *Times*)—of the homosexuality of artists, actors, and dancers; of fashion designers, models, and interior decorators; of doctors, lawyers, and stockbrokers. The tragic irony is that it has taken AIDS to prove our Stonewall slogan: "We are everywhere."[10]

But the two most notorious outings by AIDS should give us pause about the benefits of such revelations. Responses to the deaths of Rock Hudson and Roy Cohn have a perverse symmetry. Hudson was locked in Hollywood's 1950s closet, hiding from, among other things, a McCarthyism that equated commies and queers. Cohn was the closeted McCarthyite. Hudson personified decency to a majority of Americans, and his homosexuality was seen as a betrayal. He became "the hunk who lived a lie."[11] Roy Cohn came belatedly to represent indecency to most Americans; *his* homosexuality was seen as fidelity to his very being. He was the McCarthyite queer, the evil homosexual who lied about everything.[12] The revelation of the secret—the secret that was, of course, no secret in either case—became in both cases the revelation that homosexuals are liars and traitors. Nothing new about that.

In this scenario, who is the oppressor and who the role model? As I read the homophobic press accounts, Hudson is the oppressor (guilty of oppressing himself and all the innocent fans who believed him) and Cohn the role model (absolutely faithful to the truth of homosexuality in his duplicity and cowardice). Our outing fantasy—that the revelation of homosexuality would have a transformative effect on homophobic discourse—was only a fantasy after all, and a dangerous one at that. As Sedgwick counsels in *Epistemology of the Closet*:

> We have too much cause to know how limited a leverage any individual revelation can exercise over collectively scaled and institutionally embodied oppressions. Acknowledgment of this disproportion does not mean that the consequences of such acts as coming out can be circumscribed within *predetermined* boundaries, as if be-

tween "personal" and "political" realms, nor does it require us to deny how disproportionately powerful and disruptive such acts can be. But the brute incom-
mensurability has nonetheless to be acknowledged. In the theatrical display of an
already institutionalized ignorance no transformative potential is to be looked for.[13]

Signorile's initial impulse was perhaps, then, more productive: not to "out" supposedly closeted gay men and lesbians, but to "out" enforcers of the closet, not
to reveal the "secret" of homosexuality, but to reveal the "secret" of homophobia. For it is only the latter that is truly a secret, and a truly *dirty* secret. As for
the former, the speculation about the sexuality of celebrities, gossip is a privileged activity for queers, too.

Which brings us to Jodie Foster . . . and *The Silence of the Lambs*. Larry
Kramer, who claimed in his speech that Vito Russo "was the only person who
agreed with me unequivocally on everything I said and did," added, after his
thank you to Jodie Foster for starring in *Silence*: "Vito would really have
screamed about that one." But Vito can speak for himself. In his introduction to
The Celluloid Closet, entitled "On the Closet Mentality," Vito wrote:

> The public should . . . be aware of the sexuality of gay actors just as it is aware of
> the heterosexuality of the majority. I do not believe that such a discussion is no-
> body's business, nor do I believe that it is one of a sexual and therefore private na-
> ture. Discussing such things in a book without the knowledge or consent of the
> people in question is, alas, immoral and libelous. It is immoral because unless peo-
> ple by their own choice come out of the closet, the announcement is valueless; it is
> libelous because such information has been known to destroy people's lives. Some
> of us will change that in time.[14]

The last sentence is characteristic of Vito, of his fighting spirit, his optimism,
and his understanding of what needed changing. Among the things we need to
change is the fact that calling someone homosexual is, to this day, considered by
our legal system to be libelous per se. Malicious intent does *not* have to be
proved.

One thing Vito would surely have disagreed with Larry about is whom to
blame for his own death. Vito pointed his finger at queers only to tell us how
much he loved us and to praise our courage. As for *The Silence of the Lambs*, Vito
would have been the best equipped among us to show just how careless
Jonathan Demme was in his characterization of serial killer Buffalo Bill, aka
Jame Gumb, with his miniature poodle named Precious, his chiffon scarves, his
made-up face, his nipple ring, and his murdered boyfriend. Maybe these features don't have to add up to a homophobic stereotype within the complex
alignments of sexuality and pathology represented in *The Silence of the Lambs*,
but they most certainly do within the history of their deployment by Hollywood, the history Vito Russo wrote.

Up to a point, Demme was careful about his portrayals in *Silence*—of both
Clarice Starling and the men around her. Feminist approval of the film derives,
I think, not only from the strength and intelligence of Foster's character,

Clarice, but also from her independence from an array of alternately annoying or sinister patriarchal figures, although just *how* independent is a matter of contention. But Clarice does reject every attempt to put the make on her; her commitment is to the captured woman. Demme ultimately failed, though, to follow through on his film's antipatriarchal logic. He let patriarchy off the hook by homosexualizing the psychopaths—Buffalo Bill, obviously, but Hannibal Lecter as well, whose disturbing appeal can hardly be divorced from his camp, effete intelligence. What straight man would get off a line like, "Oh, Senator, . . . love your suit!"? Demme's homophobia is thus a matter not only of underwriting the tradition of Hollywood's stereotyping of gay men as psychopathic killers, but also of his displacement of the most horrifying consequences of patriarchy onto men who are far from straight.

In Thomas Harris's novel, Jame Gumb is not homosexual—the boyfriend he murdered was not his, but Hannibal Lecter's patient's. On the contrary, Gumb is explicitly referred to in the book as a fagbasher.[15] He was refused the sex-change operation he applied for at Johns Hopkins not only because he failed the requisite psychological tests, but also because he had a police record for two assaults on gay men. One has to wonder why Demme decided to leave out this information in a film that otherwise follows the novel very precisely. Would the fact that the killer was a homophobe have brought yet another murderous consequence of patriarchy too close to home?

The displacement of patriarchy's most serious consequences can also be seen in the film's illustration of another mode of feminist analysis, one that moves beyond positive-versus-negative images to the enforcement of sexual difference through psychic processes provoked in the spectator by cinematic codes. Laura Mulvey might well have written the climactic scene.[16] Deprived of agency by being the object rather than the subject of vision, Clarice Starling is stalked by the voyeuristic gaze of the spectator, who, unseen in the darkness, just like the serial killer, sees her through infrared glasses worn by Jame Gumb. There is no question where spectatorial identification ought to lie, and how it ought to be gendered: what the killer male's gaze sees is all the camera shows, and the image of the woman is trapped by the cinematic apparatus, represented in the prosthetic device the killer wears. But something unexpected happens. The tension of the scene is broken not by Clarice's gunshots, but by an often-remarked male spectator's shout in the dark: "Shoot the fucking faggot!" Homophobia breaks the power of cinema, "proper" interpellation fails, and only then is Clarice restored to agency.

The film is thus perhaps feminist, though insufficiently, and certainly homophobic, quite sufficiently. Acknowledging these two different positions should not be impossible; although they are interdependent in the film's mapping of them, they do not have to be mutually exclusive in our reading of the film. What makes the debate about *The Silence of the Lambs* troubling, however, is its polarization along gender lines. Women, including lesbians, have tended to defend the film, while gay men usually decry it. And Jodie Foster gets caught in the middle. As B. Ruby Rich, an "out" lesbian, put it in the *Village Voice*, "Male and female desires, fears, and pleasures in the cinema have rarely coincided, so it should come as no surprise that dyke and faggot reactions to this movie are likely to diverge as well."[17] For gay men, Foster lends her prestige to the film's homophobic portrayal; for women, including lesbians, she lends her skill to a feminist one. For gay men, Foster is a closeted oppressor; for lesbians, she's a role model.

The division is a double one, for it entails, on the one hand, the identity of Foster and, on the other, the conception of identity itself. Castigating Foster as oppressor both presumes her (closeted) lesbian identity and presumes that identity precedes and determines political enactment. Praising Foster as role model, by contrast, accepts her feminism as itself constitutive of her identity. Rich insists, "I'm not willing to give up the immense satisfactions of a heroine with whom women can identify. Not willing to reduce all the intricate components of this movie down to the pass/fail score of one character. Please excuse me if my attention is focused not on the killer, but on the women he kills." And her defense concludes, "Guess I'm just a girl." Which is to say that in this debate, Rich's identification, her politics, emphasizes gender identity over sexual identity. As we know from her writing, in debates *within* feminism, Rich is perfectly capable of reversing the emphasis. Rich's identity is not fixed, does not determine her political identifications; rather her political identification momentarily fixes her identity: "Guess I'm just a girl." But where is the lesbian in this picture? Hasn't she again been rendered invisible? And what, if not outing, will make her visible?

Videomaker Jean Carlomusto's video *L Is for the Way You Look* provides one answer. In the central section of the tape, nine women, speaking singly or in groups, tell the story of an evening at the Lower East Side performance space PS 122 when lesbian comedian Reno was performing. What made the occasion worth talking about was that someone special was in the audience. First Zoe tells us that halfway through Reno's performance, Nancy leaned over to say, "Fran Liebowitz is over there"; Zoe adds, "We're both, you know, we both kinda have a thing for Fran." Nancy then says she had more fun watching Fran laughing at Reno than she did laughing at Reno herself, after which Cynthia, sitting with her friend Bea, describes a commotion on the stairway as the audience was leaving. "Finally," Cynthia says, "the crowd parted a little bit and . . . ," cut back to Nancy in midsentence, ". . . and all I see is this giant hair. It's almost like it could've been hair on a stick passing by, this platinum huge thing on this little black spandex." In case we haven't yet figured out what the commotion is about, Zoe adds another clue: "I turned around, and I saw her breasts, I saw this cleavage, I saw this endowment, and, oh my God, I saw the hair, and it was . . . Dolly Parton." It turns out that Hilery was there, too, and though Emily, Polly, and Gerri weren't, the news has traveled, and, after joking around about it, they decide to say they *were* there, and that Dolly had a crew cut like Nancy's, and that she was making out with Fran.

This sequence of *L Is for the Way You Look* (which was initially titled *The Invisible Woman*) is, as Carlomusto told me, not really about Dolly Parton; it's about gossip. Dolly Parton may be the subject of the gossip, but the subjectivity represented in the video is that of the lesbians who gossip among themselves about Dolly. What matters is *their* visibility. Dolly is the absence around which a representation of lesbianism is constituted. But this is no simple structuralist lesson about representation founded on absence; rather it is meant to tell us something about the identifications we make and the communities we form through these identifications.

I don't mean to suggest that the focus of gossip on Dolly Parton doesn't matter at all. Of course it matters that Dolly's lesbianism has long been rumored and that her attendance at a lesbian performance in the company of another well-known closeted lesbian seems to confirm the rumors. But the emphasis on signifiers of Dolly's feminine masquerade—huge hair, huge cleavage, tiny spandex miniskirt—by a group of women whose masquerade differs so significantly from hers implicates their identifications and their desire in difference. None of the lesbians visible in *L Is for the Way You Look* looks femme like Dolly; compared with her absent image, they are in fact a pretty butch bunch.

Identification is, of course, identification with an other, which means that identity is never identical to itself. This alienation of identity from the self it constructs, which is a constant replay of a primary psychic self-alienation, does not mean simply that any proclamation of identity will be only partial, that it will be exceeded by other *aspects* of identity, but rather that identity is always a relation, never simply a positivity. As Teresa de Lauretis put it so concisely in her essay on lesbian spectatorship in Sheila McLaughlin's *She Must Be Seeing Things*, "It takes two women, not one, to make a lesbian.[18] And if identity is relational, then perhaps we can begin to rethink identity politics as a politics of relational identities, of identities formed through political identifications that constantly remake those identities. As Zoe says in *L Is for the Way You Look*, "We decided to milk this for all it was worth, in terms of a female bonding experience."

Again in *Epistemology of the Closet*, Sedgwick writes:

> I take the precious, devalued arts of gossip, immemorially associated in European thought with servants, with effeminate and gay men, with all women, to have to do not even so much with the transmission of necessary news as with the refinement of necessary skills for making, testing, and using unrationalized and provisional hypotheses about what *kinds of people* there are to be found in one's world. . . . I don't assume that all gay men or all women are very skilled at the nonce-taxonomic work represented by gossip, but it does make sense to suppose that our distinctive needs are peculiarly disserved by its devaluation.[19]

The most fundamental need gossip has served for queers is that of the construction—and reconstruction—of our identities. Most of us can remember the first time we heard someone called a queer or a fag or a dyke, and—that someone *not* being ourselves—nevertheless responding, within, "So that's what I am." Because the name-calling is most often a derogation, our identifications are also self-derogations. We painstakingly emerge from these self-derogations through new identifications, a process that often depends on gossip among ourselves: "Really, *he's* gay? *She's* a dyke? Jodie's a dyke? Then maybe I'm fabulous, too." From this, we go on to deduce the role-model defense. "If little tomboys growing up today knew about Jodie, they'd be spared the self-derogation." But the deduction misses two crucial points: first, what Sedgwick means by "an already institutionalized ignorance," and second, our conception of identity.

Little tomboys won't be told about an openly lesbian actress, whose career will in any case probably be cut short the moment she comes out. As Vito Russo famously quipped about coming out, "The truth will set you free . . . but first it will make you miserable." The eradication of the homophobia that constructs the celebrity's closet does not depend on the individual celebrity's avowal, the limitations of which we have seen again and again: Did the exemplary midshipman's confession of his homosexuality change the rules at Annapolis or the Pentagon? Did the Olympic medal winner's founding of the Gay Olympics persuade the U.S. Olympics committee or the Supreme Court to let us use that rubric? No, the eradication of homophobia—of this already institutionalized ignorance—depends on our collective political struggle, on our identity politics.

Identity politics has most often been understood, and is now denigrated, as essentialist (denigrated in certain quarters, in fact, as *essentially* essentialist; this is what Diana Fuss recognizes as the essentialism of antiessentialism).[20] We were gay, and upon our gayness, we built a political movement. But is this really what happened? Wasn't it an emerging political movement that enabled the enunciation of a gay—rather than homosexual or homophile—identity? And wasn't that political movement formed through identifications with other political movements—Black Power and feminism, most particularly? Remember, the Gay Liberation Front, named in identification with third-world liberation struggles, came apart over two issues: whether to support the Black Panthers and whether women would have an equal voice. It was our inability to form alliances with those movements identifications with which secured our own identities, as well as our inability to acknowledge those very same differences of race and gender within our own ranks, that caused the gay and lesbian movements to shift, on the one hand, to an essentialist separatism and, on the other, to a liberal politics of minority rights. The AIDS crisis brought us face-to-face with the consequences of both our separatism and our liberalism. And it is in this new political conjuncture that the word "queer" has been reclaimed to designate new political identities.

The setbacks for the AIDS activist movement that I mentioned above avoided one of the most difficult of them: troubles within the movement itself. Our political unity has been badly shaken by our constantly increasing knowledge of both the breadth and depth of the crisis—breadth, in the sense of the many different kinds of people affected by HIV disease; depth, in the sense of the extent of social change that will be required to improve all these different people's chances of survival. It is impossible here to describe fully either the scope of the crisis or the factionalism it has caused. But consider just this: whereas at first the structure of ACT UP in New York consisted of six committees—Actions, Coordinating, Fundraising, Issues, Media, and Outreach—by 1991, when our internal difficulties emerged most damagingly, we had fourteen committees, twenty-one working groups, and ten caucuses: forty-five different subgroups in all. Apart from a few remaining committees that are still essentially organizational and several working groups centered on actions-in-progress, these various committees, working groups, and caucuses are mostly oriented either toward specific issues (Addicts' Rights, Alternative and Holistic Treatment, Insurance and Access, Health-care Action, Medicaid Task Force, Needle Exchange, Pediatric Caucus, Police Violence, Prison Issues, PWA Housing, Treatment and Data, YELL [Youth Education Life Line]) or toward identities (Asian and Pacific Islanders, Black AIDS Mobilization, Foreign Nationals, Latina/o AIDS Activists, Lesbian Caucus, PISD [People with Immune System Disorders], and Women's Action). This level of specialization does not, in and of itself, necessarily result in factionalism; it merely suggests something of the complexity of issues raised by the epidemic and of the make-up of the AIDS activist movement. But conflict does exist, and much of it concerns competing identities and contradictory identifications *across* identities. There are conflicts between men and women, between lesbians and straight women, between white people and people of color, between those who are HIV-positive or have AIDS and those who are HIV-negative. There are also conflicts between those who think we should devote all our energies to militant direct action and those who favor meeting with government officials and pharmaceutical company executives as well; between those who want to concentrate on a narrowly defined AIDS agenda and those who feel we must confront the wider systemic ills that AIDS exacerbates; between those who see ACT UP as the vanguard in the struggle against AIDS and those who see direct action as only one of many forms of AIDS activism, which also includes advocacy, fundraising, legal action, and providing services. Negotiating these conflicts is painful and perilous; it has even resulted in splits or dissolutions of ACT UP chapters in some cities.

These conflicts are not new to ACT UP, but their intensity is. Earlier in our history, they were mitigated by a queer hegemony. Most of us were gay and lesbian, and ACT UP meant for us not only fighting AIDS, but fighting AIDS as queers, fighting homophobia, and rejuvenating a moribund queer activism. In New York, we met at the Lesbian and Gay Community Services Center; you had to confront your homophobia just to cross the threshold. Our meetings and actions, our fact sheets and chants, our T-shirts and placards, our videos and even our acronyms—everything about us was queer. We camped a lot, laughed a lot, kissed each other, partied together. ACT UP fundraisers at nightclubs were the hot ticket in queer social life.

But that hegemony didn't last. Attacks on queers escalated, both officially, with the congressional assault on government support of our culture, and unofficially, on the streets. As queers became more and more visible, more and more of us were getting bashed. Overburdened by the battles AIDS required us to take on, ACT UP couldn't fight the homophobia anymore. That, too, was a full-time struggle, a struggle taken on by the newly formed Queer Nation. I don't want to oversimplify this capsule history. Queer Nation didn't take either the queers or the queerness out of ACT UP. But it made possible, at least symbolically, a shift of our attention to the nonqueer, or the more-than-queer, problems of AIDS.

It was then that new political identifications began to be made, as I said, across identities. I have already mentioned a number of identities-in-conflict in ACT UP: men and women, whites and people of color, and so forth. In spite of the linguistic necessity of specifying identities with positive terms, I want to make clear that I am not speaking of identity as nonrelational. Because of the complexities of the movement, there is no predicting what identifications will be made and which side of an argument anyone might take. A white, middle-class, HIV-negative lesbian might form an identification with a poor, black mother with AIDS, and through that identification might be inclined to work on pediatric health-care issues; or, outraged by attention to the needs of babies at the expense of the needs of the women who bear them, she might decide to fight against clinical trials whose sole purpose is to examine the effects of an antiviral drug on perinatal transmission and thus ignores effects on the mother's body. She might form an identification with a gay male friend with AIDS and work for faster testing of new treatments for opportunistic infections, but then, through her understanding that her friend would be able to afford such treatments while others would not, she might shift her attention to health-care access issues. An HIV-positive, gay Latino might fight homophobia in the Latin community and racism in ACT UP; he might speak Spanish at Latina/o AIDS Activist meetings and English everywhere else.

Political identifications remaking identities are, of course, productive of collective political struggle, but only if they result in a broadening of alliances rather than an exacerbation of antagonisms. And the latter seems often to result when, from within a development toward a politics of alliance based on relational identities, old antagonisms based on fixed identities reemerge. Activist politics then faces the impasse of ranking oppressions, moralism, and self-righteousness. This is the current plight of AIDS activism, but it is not the whole story.

During the very time that ACT UP's internal antagonisms began to tear us apart, we won a crucial victory. Arrested for taking to the streets of New York to distribute—openly and illegally—clean IV needles to injecting drug

users, a group of ACT UP queers stood trial, eloquently argued a necessity defense, and won a landmark ruling that called into question the state's laws
against possession of hypodermic needles and eventually forced Mayor Dinkins
to relent on his opposition to needle exchange. AIDS activists are still—I'm
sorry and angry to have to say—mostly a bunch of queers. But what does *queer*
mean now? Who, for example, were those queers in the courtroom, on trial for
attempting to save the lives of drug addicts? They were perhaps queers whose
sexual practices resulted in HIV infection, or placed them at high risk of infection, or made them members of gay communities devastated by the epidemic,
and for any of these reasons brought them to AIDS activism. But once engaged
in the struggle to end the crisis, these queers' identities were no longer the
same. It's not that "queer" doesn't any longer encompass their sexual practices;
it does, but it also entails a *relation* between those practices and other circumstances that make very different people vulnerable both to HIV infection and to
the stigma, discrimination, and neglect that have characterized the societal and
governmental response to the constituencies most affected by the AIDS epidemic.

ABSOLUTELY QUEER: that was the anonymous group OUTpost's
headline claim about Jodie Foster on the poster that appeared around New
York about the time *The Silence of the Lambs* was released. "Jodie Foster," the
caption beneath her photograph read, "Oscar winner. Yale graduate. Ex-Disney
Moppet. Dyke." Well yes, . . . but queer? Absolutely queer? Through what
identification? Interviewed about queer protests at the 1992 Academy Awards
ceremony, where she won her second best-actress Oscar for her performance in
The Silence of the Lambs, Foster declared, "Protesting is constitutional. You can
learn from it. Anything beyond that falls into the category of being undigni-
fied."[21] Confronted with such a statement, I'm forced to agree with Larry
Kramer: "Vito would really have screamed about that one." For Vito's was a
feistier kind of dignity, not Jodie's idea of dignity but Judy's, a survivor's dignity. If we really want to honor Vito's memory—as a film scholar and movie
buff, as a queer, an activist, and a friend—we shouldn't forget that he loved
Judy, and that his identification with her made *him* queer, not her.

Notes

1. Arnie Kantrowitz, "Milestones: Vito Russo," *Outweek* 73, 21 November 1990, 37.
2. Several months later, however, Dinkins took a courageous stand against antigay
   and antilesbian prejudice by marching with the Irish Gay and Lesbian Organization (IGLO) in New York's St. Patrick's Day parade. He did this in order to broker a compromise between IGLO and the Ancient Order of Hibernians, the
   parade organizers who had refused IGLO's application to participate. The result
   was that Dinkins was subjected to torrents of abuse from the crowd and a cold
   shoulder from Cardinal O'Connor, which led the mayor to compare his experience to civil rights marches in the South in the 1960s. See Duncan Osborne, "The
   Cardinal, the Mayor and the Balance of Power," *Outweek* 92, 3 April 1990, 30–37.

3. Larry Kramer, "Who killed Vito Russo?" *Outweek* 86, 20 February 1990, 26.
4. See Douglas Crimp, with Adam Rolston, *AIDS Demo Graphics* (Seattle: Bay Press, 1990), 53–69.
5. Quoted in *The New York Times*, 27 September 1991, sec. A, p. 12.
6. For a detailed account of outing, including historical background and analysis of the contemporary debates as well as an appendix of essential articles from the media, see Larry Gross, *The Contested Closet: The Politics and Ethics of Outing* (Minneapolis: University of Minnesota Press, 1993).
7. It's not that Jeff and I are so butch as to be unreadable as gay; indeed many people might presume that we *are* gay, but our not behaving "overtly" allows them to act precisely as if the operative presumption is that everyone is straight unless openly declaring themselves not to be.
8. Eve Kosofsky Sedgwick, *Epistemology of the Closet* (Berkeley and Los Angeles: University of California Press, 1990), 81.
9. William Henry III, "Forcing Gays Out of the Closet," *Time*, 29 January 1990, 67; David Gelman, "'Outing': An Unexpected Assault on Sexual Privacy," *Newsweek*, 30 April 1990, 66. See also Michelangelo Signorile, *Queer in America* (New York: Random House, 1993).
10. This was not always the case. It took intense pressure from queers and AIDS activists to force the *Times* to list surviving lovers of gay men. Even now, the *Times* only mentions a "companion" in the course of an obituary story, not as one of the survivors, who are still limited to blood relatives and legal spouses.
11. See Richard Meyer, "Rock Hudson's Body," in Diana Fuss, ed., *Inside/Out: Lesbian Theories, Gay Theories* (New York and London: Routledge, 1991), 259–88.
12. See, for example, Robert Sherrill, "King Cohn," *The Nation*, 21 May 1988, 719–25. Beginning with the sentence, "Cohn was a particularly nasty homosexual," Sherrill recounts stories of Cohn's extreme promiscuity and his supposed relations with other duplicitous right-wing homosexuals, then ends his account with the following paragraph: "Typically disloyal, Cohn gave no support to homosexuals who were trying to win public acceptance. He called them 'fags,' did all he could to make their lives miserable, lectured against them, berated politicians for any display of tolerance toward homosexuals and urged laws to restrict their freedom. To his death he denied that he was homosexual, but the Dorian Gray scene of his dying of AIDS said it all: 'Roy . . . lay in bed, unheeding, his flesh cracking open, sores on his body, his faculties waning' and with a one-inch 'slit-like wound above [his] anus.'" The final quotations, indicative for Sherrill not of disease but of homosexuality (or perhaps the two are not to be differentiated), are uncredited, but are taken from one of the two books under review in the article, *Citizen Cohn* by Nicholas von Hoffman.
13. Sedgwick, *Epistemology*, 78.
14. Vito Russo, *The Celluloid Closet: Homosexuality in the Movies* (New York: Harper & Row, 1987), xi.
15. In the novel, Dr. Danielson of Johns Hopkins reports to Jack Crawford: "The Harrisburg police were after [Gumb] for two assaults on homosexual men. The last one nearly died" (Thomas Harris, *The Silence of the Lambs* [New York: St. Martin's, 1989], 312). And Crawford reports to Clarice Starling about Gumb: "He's a fag-basher" (322). This is not to say that Harris's portrayal of Gumb is

free of homophobic stereotyping. Most of the details of Gumb's characterization in the film are taken directly from the novel. Demme added one (the nipple ring) and omitted one (Gumb's obsession with his mother). But it is important to add that stereotyping functions differently in the two media and that their respective histories of homophobic portrayals differ even more significantly.

16. I have in mind, of course, Mulvey's classic and often-reprinted essay "Visual Pleasure and Narrative Cinema" (1975), now in her collected essays, *Visual and Other Pleasures* (Bloomington and Indianapolis: Indiana University Press, 1989), 14–26.

17. B. Ruby Rich, contribution to "Writers on the *Lamb:* Sorting Out the Sexual Politics of a Controversial Film," *Village Voice,* 5 March 1991, 59. This series of short pieces on the film was partially in response to questions raised about the film's homophobic stereotyping and the threat of "outing" Jodie Foster by Michelangelo Signorile in *Outweek.*

18. Teresa de Lauretis, "Film and the Visible," in Bad Object Choices, ed., *How Do I Look? Queer Film and Video* (Seattle: Bay Press, 1991), 232.

19. Sedgwick, *Epistemology,* 23.

20. See Diana Fuss, *Essentially Speaking: Feminism, Nature, and Difference* (New York: Routledge, 1989).

21. See John Gallagher, "Protest Threats Raise Visibility at Academy Awards," *The Advocate,* 5 May 1992, 15. In this same issue of *The Advocate,* the "etcetera" column contains a photo of Jodie Foster whose caption reads, "A first-rate actress with a third-rate consciousness we hope is straight" (88).

Questions for Reflection, Discussion, and Writing

1. Crimp begins with a scene depicting the funeral of author Vito Russo, and uses that scene to offer a context for understanding issues of identity and community as they relate to various intersections of our "selves" as gendered, raced and classed beings. What are the qualities in Vito Russo that Crimp eulogizes? According to Crimp, what does Russo stand for? What attributes does Crimp identify in Russo as "queer"? What is it about his identification with Judy Garland that makes him "queer"?

2. How does Crimp define "the closet"? Are there ways you would refine and/or expand his definition? What sorts of issues about public and private lives does the closet raise? What ideas do you have about the closet? Do you consider yourself out about your sexuality? In what ways? In what contexts?

3. According to Crimp, what is the role AIDS activism and outing may have played in perpetuating the split from a seemingly unified group of activists to a more fractured group of queer nationalists? What are some of the issues?

4. Crimp supports Signorile's belief that, by outing public and political figures, he was outing homophobia as an institution and claims that gossip plays a large role in both sustaining and challenging that institution. What proof does he offer to support that claim? What does the release and reception of *Silence of the Lambs* suggest, according to Crimp?

Writing Assignment

Choose any one of the feature films, 1968–1980, under the **FILM** section. View it at least twice, taking notes during the second viewing about specific lines, camera shots, narrative perspective, scene juxtaposition, and character representation. What was happening historically during the film's release? What was the social, cultural and political milieu? What kinds of connections can you make between history and representation?

A. Research the reviews written about the film when it premiered, and summarize their arguments and interpretations. Which points do you find especially compelling and accurate about the film? What assumptions are made about sexuality, identity, and behavior in the reviews?

B. Analyze and discuss what you see as the film's portrayal of its queer characters. Do you see this representation as more positive? More negative? Ambivalent? Ambiguous? Use specific examples from the film in your discussion.

Related Reading

Vitto Russo, "Struggle: fear and loathing in gay Hollywood" in *The Celluloid Closet: Homosexuality in the Movies.* NY: Harper & Row, 1981, 180–246.

David Ehrenstein, *Open Secret: Gay Hollywood 1928–1998.* NY: William Morrow. 1998.

Thomas Waugh, "In Memoriam: Vito Russo, 1946–1990" in *The Fruit Machine: Twenty Years of Writing on Queer Cinema.* Durham, N.C.: Duke UP. 2000. 235–236.

Film

The Celluloid Closet (1995). Rob Epstein and Jeffrey Friedman. 102 m.

The Killing of Sister George (1968). Robert Aldrich. 138 m.

The Boys in the Band (1970). William Friedkin. 119 m.

Sunday, Bloody Sunday (1971). John Schlesinger. 110 m.

Dog Day Afternoon (1975). Sidney Lumet. 130 m.

Outrageous! (1977). Richard Benner. 100 m.

Cruising (1980). William Friedkin. 106 m.

The Naked Civil Servant (1980). Jack Gold. 80 m.

Special Topics

Jonathan Demme's 1990 film *The Silence of the Lambs* created incredible controversy that the publication of Harris's novel two years earlier did not. Activists blamed Jodie Foster for appearing in a homophobic film and picketed the Academy Awards that year. This assignment asks you to look closely at both the film and the novel on which it is based. Discuss the crucial differences between Harris's portrayal of Jame Gumb and Jonathan Demme's refashioning of that same character. Do you agree that one or both portrayals are homophobic? What are the responsibilities of representation raised by the novel and the film? Do such responsibilities curtail freedom of creative expression? Should Foster be blamed for being queer and for starring in this film?

Film

The Silence of the Lambs (1990). Jonathan Demme. 118 m.

Reading

Thomas Harris, *The Silence of the Lambs*. NY: Saint Martin's Press. 1988.

"Writers on the Lamb: Sorting Out the Sexual Politics of a Controversial Film," *Village Voice*, March 5, 1991. 49, 54, 58–59.

Diana Fuss, "Monsters of Perversion: Jeffrey Dahmer and *The Silence of the Lambs*" in *Media Spectacles*. Marjorie Garber, Jann Matlock and Rebecca Walkowitz, Eds. NY: Routledge. 1993. 181–205.

Terry Brown, "The Butch Femme Fatale" in *The Lesbian Postmodern*. Laura Doan, Ed. NY: Columbia UP. 1994. 229–243.

Clare Whatling, "Fostering the Illusion: Stepping Out With Jodie" in *The Good, The Bad and the Gorgeous: Popular Culture's Romance With Lesbianism*. Diane Hamer and Belinda Budge, Eds. London: Pandora. 1994. 184–195.

Special Topics

1. After examining at least *five* of the essays below, compose an editorial stating your position on outing.

Reading

Richard D. Mohr, "The Outing Controversy: Privacy and Dignity in Gay Ethics" (c. 1) in *Gay Ideas: Outing and Other Controversies*. Boston: Beacon. 1992. 11–48.

Michelangelo Signorile, "Outing, Part I" (c. 5) in *Queer in America: Sex, the Media, and the Closets of Power*. NY: Anchor Doubleday. 1993. 69–93.

Larry Gross, Ed. "The Insider's Debate: Gay and Alternate Press" in *Contested Closets: The Politics and Ethics of Outing*. Minneapolis: U of Minnesota P. 1993. 231–281. Essays:
- Stuart Bryon, "Naming names"
- Michelangelo Signorile, "Smashing the Closet: The Pros and Cons of Outing"
- Hunter Madsen, "Tattle Tale Traps"
- Steve Beery, "Liz Smith Mon Amour"

- Ayofemi Folayan, "Whose Life Is It, Anyway?"
- Vicoria A. Brownworth, "Campus Queer Query"
- Andrew Miller, "Malcolm Forbes, Malcolm X and Me"
- Sarah Petit, "On Glamour and Parochialism"
- Gabriel Rotello, "Tactical Considerations"
- Michael Bronski, "Outing: The Power of the Closet"
- C. Carr, "Why Outing Must Stop"
- Gabriel Rotello, "Why I Oppose Outing"

Warren Johansson and William A. Percy, Eds., *Outing: Shattering the Conspiracy of Silence*. NY: The Haworth Press. 1994.

Jeremiah McCarthy, "The Closet and the Ethics of Outing." *Journal of Homosexuality* 27.3/4 (1994): 27–45.

David J. Mayo and Martin Gunderson, "Privacy and the Ethics of Outing." *Journal of Homosexuality* 27.3/4 (1994): 47–65.

Mark Chekola, "Outing, Truth-Telling, and the Shame of the Closet." *Journal of Homosexuality* 27.3/4 (1994): 67–90.

Victoria A. Brownworth, "Lesbians, Outing, and the Politics of the Closet" in *Too Queer: Essays From A Radical Life*. Ithaca, NY: Firebrand Books. 1996. 59–73.

"Naming names: Outing" in *The Columbia Reader on Lesbians and Gay Men in Media, Society, & Politics*. Larry Gross & James D. Woods, Eds. NY: Columbia UP. 1999. 417–420.

2. Analyze and discuss the ways in which the film, *In and Out*, depoliticizes the concept of outing some years after its initial controversy. What are the political ramifications of making a comedy about outing? Are any of the ideas present in the debates during the 1980s relevant for this 1990s text?

Film

In and Out (1997). Frank Oz. 92 m.

Reading

James Keller and William Glass, "In and Out: Self-Referentiality and Hollywood's 'Queer' Politics." *Journal of Popular Film & Television* 26.3 (1998 Fall): 136–143.

SECTION THREE

Queer Formulations and the Politics of Identity

The United States, in particular, seems to conceive of identity as a marker of individualism, a self-conception that is unique, idiosyncratic, and expressive of a person's most deeply felt beliefs about some amorphous, essential self. In its etymology, identity, from the Latin *idem*, signifies sameness, a unity and persistence of personality that remains fixed in differing circumstances and instances. And it is this sameness, this essentialism, that has made identity into such a fraught and contested subject within queer studies and queer theory. Influenced by French poststructuralist thought, queer theory, as Annamarie Jagose argues, is "less an identity than a *critique* of identity" (131). One of its projects, accordingly, has been to deconstruct norms that surround and maintain identity markers, in the realm of gender and sexuality, as well as in the arena of race and class. Because identity markers like race and class intersect and operate in conjunction with conceptions of gender and sexuality, some advocates of queer theory contend that placing undue emphasis on one identity marker over another sustains and upholds binary belief systems, the very antithesis of the polymorphous spectrum of self constructions queer espouses. Such an approach, for example, could conceivably have alleviated the agony of Marlon Riggs who, in his 1985 documentary *Tongues Untied*, articulated his frustration about how, because of homophobia and racism, his two primary communities were trying to force him to choose between being gay and black, as if these identities could not exist together in his person and in his conception of self. By recognizing and complicating ideas of identity, queer theorists have begun the difficult work of disrupting the primacy of unproblematized sexual, gender, sociocultural, economic, and racial norms that sustain and privilege the few and exclude many.

Yet many contemporary activists and theorists maintain deep skepticism about the perhaps too easy conjunction of queerness with ethnicity, gender, race, and class. They point first to the problem of assuming that the disruption of sexual and gender norms contained within queer theory necessarily includes an anti-racist and anti-sexist agenda, something, they argue correctly, which simply cannot be taken for granted. Nor can we forget, they counsel wisely, that many of the strides western societies have made in the past half century regarding racial and gender equality have arisen directly out of an identity politics based on pride, self-affirmation, and political organizing through the identity markers of race, ethnicity, and gender. Identity, it seems, is not so easy or so advantageous to dislodge, especially given its strong ties to liberation movements that have shaped our contemporary social landscape so profoundly and progressively.

Since many would agree, however cautiously, that queer is in itself an unstable term, one whose effectiveness depends upon it remaining unstable, it is safe to say that positing a "queer identity" is neither possible nor desirable. The utility of a queer theoretical perspective when investigating identity may, in fact, lie in its very instability, its function as a tool that interrogates identity categories not to render them obsolete or politically ineffectual, but rather to explore the often unrecognized intersections between gender, sexuality, race, and class, and the ways these identity markers inform one another in pluralistic and heterogeneous ways.

The essays in this section of the anthology all explore the ways that queer theory has impacted upon conceptions of identity. African American, Chicano/a, South Asian, and regional identity markers are critiqued, explored, and even interpolated through a queer theoretical framework. Many of the theorists contained in this section express their reservations and their skepticism about the conjunction of queer and identity, and Gamson's essay delineates how the impulse to deconstruct identity categories conflicts with the urge to consolidate them in social-movement theory and research. This section, in other words, offers no easy answers about identity formulation. Rather, it, like queer theory generally, seeks to open up more questions, to examine common assumptions and to encourage that which has been unrecognized and unexplored to be given utterance. It is intended to stimulate new thinking and to spark debate about what heretofore, we may have too easily taken for granted.

Works Cited

Jagose, Annamarie (1996). *Queer Theory: An introduction*. New York: NYUP.

Some Queer Notions
About Race

Samuel R. Delany

Race is a fracturing trauma in the body politic of the nation—and in the mortal bodies of its people. Race kills, liberally and unequally; and race privileges, unspeakably and abundantly. Like nature, race has much to answer for; and the tab is still running for both categories. Race, like nature, is at the heart of stories about the origins and purposes of the nation. Race, at once an uncanny unreality and an inescapable presence, frightens me; and I am not alone in this paralyzing historical pathology of body and soul. Like nature, race is the kind of category about which no one is neutral, no one unscathed, no one sure of their ground, if there is a ground. Race is a peculiar kind of object of knowledge and practice. The meanings of the word are unstable and protean; the status of the word's referent has wobbled—and still wobbles—from being considered real and rooted in the natural, physical body to being considered illusory and utterly socially constructed. In the United States, race immediately evokes the grammars of purity and mixing, compounding and differentiating, segregating and bonding, lynching and marrying. Race, like nature and sex, is replete with all the rituals of guilt and innocence in the stories of nation, family, and species. Race, like nature, is about roots, pollution, and origins. An inherently dubious notion, race, like sex, is about the purity of lineage, the legitimacy of passage; the drama of inheritance of bodies, property, and stories.
—Donna Haraway, Modest Witness@Second Millennium

I

I don't remember ever being unaware of racial injustice as a major problem in America. My family talked about it constantly. My Uncle Hubert, a New York judge and a crusading politician, fought it passionately. My Uncle Myles, my mother's brother-in-law and another judge in Brooklyn, fought it, too. In 1950, when I was eight, our Park Avenue school sent my whole, largely white third-grade class on a week-long trip up to an Otis, Massachusetts, farmhouse owned by a friendly white couple, George and Lois. Our first night in the country, Lois proposed to entertain us by reading us some Joel Chandler Harris's Uncle Remus tales in dialect. When she was about three sentences into the story of "Brer Rabbit an' the Tar Baby," I raised my hand vigorously. Surprised, she called on me, and I stood up from the rug where we sat listening and announced, "My father says that those stories are insulting to Negroes and are just a white writer making fun of Negro speech so that white people can laugh at us. And you shouldn't do that." Then, among Robert and Wendy and Johnny and Pricilla and Nancy, I dropped back down, cross-legged on the rug.

I'm not sure what response I expected. What shocked me, however, as Lois sat there on a stolid wood-framed chair in her heavy sweater and long winter skirt, was her sudden embarrassment, her quick agreement ("You're perfectly right. I know that . . . I just wasn't . . . Really, I didn't mean to offend any of you—any of you at all." Besides me, there were three black students in my class of twenty-three: Linda, Peggy, and Mary.), and the speed with which she jumped up and turned to go to the wall bookshelf—while, on the rug in the sprawling farmhouse library, among my equally surprised classmates, black and white, I was struck by the presence of extraordinary power, suddenly and surprisingly.

For a third grader, such power is *hugely* uncomfortable.

The discomfort was enough to make me mumble now, with embarrassment, "Of course, *I* don't really care. I mean, it's just my parents . . ." But, with me as their mediator, my parents had already won.

Understand, I knew those stories. My father had read me the "Brer Rabbit" tales and had often laughed out loud in spite of himself. Years before, my mother had read me "Lil' Black Sambo." Both had explained why their racial humor was a problem—still, Sambo's tigers melting into a pool of butter around the palm tree had remained with me as a delicious bit of fantasy. If Lois had been prepared to read them, even enjoy them with provisos, caveats, and explanations, I would not have objected. Instead she was doing precisely what my parents had warned me white people did with those tales: present them as language to laugh at and be surprised that such funny speech could actually yield a maxim that made sense, wholly detachable from the human experiences that had taught it. Now Lois slid the orange-covered volume back into the book case and, a moment later, returned to the chair with another book.

The memory of my power, and the strangeness with which it sat—the part of it now mine—in my body for the rest of the evening, blots out all recollection of what Lois finally read that night.

II

Strongly aware of my own homosexual feelings by the time I was nine, ten, eleven, I learned with the feelings themselves, however, that I must keep them secret. About my sexual feelings I couldn't possibly have stood up for myself against another unthinking child's comments, much less an adult's. A couple of times during my adolescence, I had one or another experience when, believing I was discovered, I learned only how anxious and even determined the straight world was not to see or acknowledge such feelings in anyone—and I felt as if I were being given a boon, a gift, another sort of power to aid me in my secrecy.

In 1961, at nineteen I married—a white woman of eighteen, a poet, with whom I had gone to high school. Paradoxically, she was the person with whom I would share these feelings the most. But it wasn't until I was twenty-two, when I'd had what at that point was called a "nervous breakdown," brought on largely by the pressure of having written and sold five novels in three years, and exacerbated by the added pressures of trying to negotiate a heterosexual relationship along with whatever homosexual outlets were available to me, that I began to realize, more than half a dozen years before Stonewall, that the oppression all women in our society in general and gay men in particular suffered was something other than the psychological *Sturm und Drang* Lillian Hellman had portrayed in *The Children's Hour,* but was a centrally political problem.

Since then, both problems have focused a great deal of my thinking and my writing. In June 1998, in Texas, a black man, James Byrd, was chained to a truck and dragged to his death by a group of white men for the crime of being black. Four months later, an openly gay student in Wyoming, Matthew Shepherd, was beaten, burned, roped to a fence on a cold Wyoming road and left to die for the crime of being gay. And the murder of pediatrician Barnett Schlepian in his own upper New York state home by an antiabortionist—made clear how threatening the notion of any structural change in the status of women is to many.

Yet, I have always felt a difficulty in discussing the problems together. The ability to be clear and logical about any one of them at any one time has always come to me as a feeling of power. But the others have tended to stay silent within, a discomfort whose articulation might subvert that power, reveal flaws in its logic, and ultimately negate the socially beneficial authority of my position. The distance between New York, Texas, and Wyoming is, if anything, the allegorical marker informed by the difficulty of bridging the topics throughout my own articulation.

To speak of gay oppression in the context of racial oppression always seemed an embarrassment. Somehow it was to speak of the personal and the mechanics of desire in the face of material deprivation and vast political and imperialist and nationalist systemics.

I remember clearly when to speak of women's oppression in the context of racial oppression seemed to be speaking of something selfish, personal, not large-hearted enough. After all, men took care of women. If you improved the lot of one group of men, wouldn't you of necessity be improving the lot of their women, their children? Pointing out that the very discursive structure embedded in such an argument, such a perception, *was* the locus of rampant abuse to women because it denied them full autonomy in the family, the society, the race—and because it occasioned all manner of abuse to women in all the country's races—seemed like moving a millstone up a hill with your shoulder.

Similarly, to speak of racial oppression in the midst of discussing gay liberation was to confront an embarrassing reminder of the huge amount of homophobia that manifested itself most forcefully right at the strongest areas of black nationalism and the fight to end racial power imbalances.

How, then, was one supposed to negotiate, as it were, the road from New York to Texas to Wyoming? How could we look at the highways between them, their intricate and connecting side paths, their main lanes and alternate routes, their service roads, much less their ecological interdependencies?

III

Functioning as a kind of momentary historical vision of the fall of some never-experienced utopia, a childhood story I grew up with, told and retold a dozen times, came from my Aunt Amaza Reed—a woman on my mother's side of the family who, among my black and brown cousins, was blond and had green eyes.

Actually, Aunt Ameza, a second or third cousin, fifteen years or so older than my mother was from a small town near Salem, North Carolina, and her story centered on a town meeting of the then much smaller city, a meeting she attended with her parents when *she* was a little girl of seven or eight—a meeting that must have occurred around 1904, when the subway system opened in New York City and the Jim Crow laws mandating separate-but-equal schooling were first instituted throughout the South. As Aunt Ameza described it, "Salem was one of those little southern towns where everybody was related to everybody else. At the town meeting in the church where they announced that, by law from now on, they would have "separate but equal" facilities, after the mayor explained the 'one drop of Negro blood makes you Negro' rule, he added, 'But we'd go crazy here if we all try to figure *that* one out.' So he told the eighty or so people gathered that night: 'All right, what we'll do is: everybody who wants to be Negro get on this side of the room and everybody who wants to be white get on that side.' Now—" my Aunt Ameza continued—"if cousin Henry was not speaking to Aunt Clem that month, and if Aunt Clem had decided she was white, then cousin Henry was fit to be tied if he was going to be the same race as *that* hard-headed woman—and went over to the Negro side. People went with their friends—and saw it as a fine opportunity to get away from their enemies, their nuisance relatives. That's pretty much how the decisions on who was which race were made. And I'll tell you, by the end of the evening, there were an awful lot of pretty dark people on the white side of the room, and an awful lot of pretty light people on the Negro side. And don't *talk* to me about families! But they took all the names down in a book." Here my aunt grew pensive. "They didn't know, back then, what it was all going to mean, you see. They just didn't know."

By the time I was nine or ten, I had heard the story several times. I'm sure I was not more than ten or eleven when I began to realize that the "single drop of blood" rule, while its intentions were strictly prophylactic, also managed legally to fix the vector of racial pollution in one direction alone. Black contaminates white—but not the other way around. Over the long durrée, then, this seemed certainly a legal mandate that eventually the nation *must* be all black.

IV

I was nowhere near as lucky in my political education about gay oppression. I had no early vision of a prelapserian utopia to fall back on. The topic would have bewildered my otherwise politically liberal parents. What my early education in that matter actually was, was only brought home to me not a full year back at the February '98 Out/Right Conference of Lesbian and Gay Writers in Boston, Massachusetts. One of the Sunday morning programs began with the two questions:

"Why is there homophobia?" and "What makes us gay?"

As I listened to the discussion over the next hour and a half, I found myself troubled: Rather than attack both questions head on, the discussants tended to veer away from them, as if those questions were somehow logically congruent to the two great philosophical conundrums, ontological and epistemological, that grounded Western philosophy—"Why is there something rather than nothing?" and, "How can we know it?"—and, as such, could only be approached by elaborate indirection.

It seems to me there are pointed answers to be given to both the questions—Why is there homophobia? and What makes us gay?—answers it is imperative that we know, historify, and contextualize if gay men and lesbians are to make any progress in passing from what Urvashi Vaid has called, so tellingly, "virtual equality" (the appearance of equality with few or none of the material benefits) to a material and legal-based equality.

By the time I was ten or eleven, I knew why "prostitutes and perverts" were to be hated, if not feared. My Uncle Myles—Judge Paige, a black man who had graduated from Tuskegee, a Republican, a Catholic, and who, as I've said, was a respected judge in the Brooklyn Domestic Relations Court—told us the reason repeatedly throughout the '40s and '50s, during a dozen family dinners, over the roast lamb, the macaroni and cheese, the creamed onions, and the kale (this was *how* I knew I had to hide those sexual feelings; this is what I had to hide them from), from the head of the family dinner table.

"Prostitutes and perverts," he explained, "destroy, undermine, and rot the foundations of society." I remember his saying, again and again, that, if he had his way, "I would take all those people out and shoot 'em!" while his more liberal wife—my mother's sister—protested futilely. "Well," my uncle grumbled, "*would* . . ." The implication was that he had some arcane and secret information about "prostitutes and perverts" that, although it justified the ferocity of his position, could not be shared at the dinner table with women and children. But I entered adolescence knowing the law alone, and my uncle's judicial position in it, kept his anger, and by extension the anger of all right-thinking men like him, in check—kept it from breaking out in a concerted attack on "those people," who were destroying, undermining, and rotting the foundations of society—which meant, as far as I understood it, they were menacing my right to sit there in the dining room in the Brooklyn row house on Macdonnah Street and eat our generous, even lavish Sunday dinner, that my aunt and grand-mother had fixed over the afternoon . . .

These were the years between, say, 1949 and 1953, that I—and I'm sure, many, many others—heard this repeatedly as the general social judgment on sex workers and/or homosexuals. That is to say, it was about half a dozen years after the end of World War II. Besides being a judge, my Uncle Myles had also been a captain in the U.S. Army.

What homosexuality and prostitution represented for my uncle was the untrammeled pursuit of pleasure; and the untrammeled pursuit of pleasure was the opposite of social responsibility. Nor was this simply some abstract princi-pal to the generation so recently home from European military combat. Many had begun to wake, however uncomfortably, to a fact that problematizes much of the discourse around sadomasochism today. In the words of Bruce Bender-son, writing in the *Lambda Book Report 12:* "The true Eden where all desires are satisfied is red, not green. It is a blood bath of instincts, a gaping maw of orality, and a basin of gushing bodily fluids." Too many had seen "nice ordinary Amer-ican boys" let loose in some tiny French or German or Italian town where, with the failure of the social contract, there was no longer any law—and there had seen all too much of that red "Eden." Nor—in World War II—were these situ-ations officially interrogated, with attempts to tame them for the public with images such as Lt. Calley and My Lai, as they would be a decade-and-a-half later in Vietnam. Rather they circulated as an unstated and inarticulate horror whose lessons were supposed to be brought back to the States while their speci-ficity was, in any collective narrativity, unspeakable, left in the foreign outside, safely beyond the pale, a purely masculine knowledge of an asocial horror which was somehow at once presumed to be both in the American male and what American males had to save civil American society (that is, an abstraction that contained both women as bodies, capable of reproduction, and all institu-tions as systems) from.

The clear and obvious answer (*especially* to a Catholic Republican army of-ficer and judge) was that pleasure must be socially doled out in minuscule amounts, tied by rigorous contracts to responsibility. Good people were people who accepted this contractual system. Anyone who rebelled *was* a prostitute or a pervert—or both. (And he was painfully aware that prostitutes and pimps—if not perverts—were strongly associated in the minds of many in those years, black and white, with blacks.) Anyone who actively pursued prostitution or per-version was working, whether knowingly or not, to unleash precisely those red Edenic forces of desire that could only topple society, destroy all responsibility, and produce a nation without families, without soldiers, without workers—in-deed, a crazed, drunken, libertine chaos that was itself no state, for clearly no such space of social turbulence could maintain any but the most feudal state apparatus.

That was and will remain the answer to the question, "Why is there ha-tred and fear of homosexuals (homophobia)?" as long as this is the systematic relation between pleasure and responsibility in which "prostitution and perversion" are seen to be caught up. The herd of teenage boys who stalk the street with their clubs looking for a faggot to beat bloody and senseless, or the employer who fires the worker who is revealed to be gay or the landlord who turns the gay tenant out of his or her apartment, or the social circle who refuses to associate with someone who is found out to be gay, or the young murderers of Wyoming, are simply the Valkyries—the *Wunchmaids*—to my Uncle's legally constrained Woton.

What I saw in the conversation at Out/Right was that the argument exists today largely at the level of discourse, and that younger gay activists find it hard to articulate the greater discursive structure they are fighting to dismantle. And discourses in such condition tend to remain at their most stable.

The overall principal that must be appealed to in order to dismantle such a discourse is the principal that claims desire is *never*—outside all social constraint. Desire may be outside one set of constraints or another; but social constraints are what engender desire; and, one way or another, even at its most apparently catastrophic, they contour desire's expression.

V

The fall 1993 cover of *Time* magazine ("The New Face of America") most recently morphed that softly brown face of the future, which Donna Haraway, in the same chapter from which I've taken my epigraph, has reread as the face of SimEve. ("Never has there been a better toy for playing out sexualized racial fantasies, anxieties, and dreams.") That face, as Haraway points out, allows us to see the results of myriad micropollutions as it cajoles us into forgetting the bloody history of miscegenation that brings it about.

If one of the reasons I am black was because my grandfather, Henry Beard Delany, was born a slave in Georgia (as were six out of eight of my great grandparents), another reason was because black members of my family had been lynched by white people for looking like my Aunt Ameza—even like me.

Two qualities among its many make the concept of race theoretically problematic—and I mean theoretically in the sense of something to be theorized.

First, of the three races of mankind—Caucasian, Mongoloid, and Negroid as they were once known: white, black, and yellow—the black race among them, at least within the bounds of the white United States (thanks to that one-drop rule), at the level of the law functions entirely as a hereditary pollutant.

Second, race is a concept that has no opposite. It has no negative. The word "race" comes from the Spanish "raza"— a large, old family of many generations. By the beginning of sixteenth century, it had spread around the northern rim of the Mediterranean, so that in Italy one spoke of "the Sforza race" or "the Medici race," while on the back of his pen-and-ink drawing with wash over traces of black and red chalk, done between 1510 and 1512, "The Fetus in the Womb," Leonardo da Vinci could write:

> The black races of Ethiopia are not the product of the sun; for if black gets black with child in Scythia, the offspring is black; but if a black gets a white woman with child, the offspring is gray.

Here, the term "races"— and note the plural—simply means the great old families that comprise Ethiopia. That such an observation about racial mixing appears, even before, historically, the term means race, endorses an image of conception, hereditary, and birth that is not without significance.

Not until the eighteenth century was the term, however, "racialized," when writers, Oliver Goldsmith for example, began to use phrases such as "Tarter race" (in *The Natural History of Animals* [1774]). It is not without significance that, along with *The Vicar of Wakefield, She Stoops to Conquer*, and *The Deserted Village*, the works by which we are likely to know him today, Goldsmith also wrote a series of travel letters, presumably from China, that were republished under the title "The Citizen of the World," in 1762. The eighteenth century's totalization of the world begins to pull forward the modern concept of race, that is, "The major divisions of mankind" (as the OED characterizes section "d" of definition 2).

But compare this notion of "race" (a major division of humanity) to the earlier notion, race as family, whether progenitors or progeny. Race as family allows an opposite.

"He has no family . . . All his family are dead . . . She is without family." All these are rational sentences. But once the term becomes racialized, that rationality is precisely what the negative looses: "He has no race . . . All his race is dead . . . She is without race." These sentences are irrational, meaningless. At best (in the case, say, of "his race is dead") they throw us back to the specifically *pre*-racial, family meaning of the term. This is a semantic sign, I would hazard, that race has now become something—an essence—that suffuses the body of the subject and deeply affects the mind, rather than remains caught solely in the process (as with the concept of family) by which the subject is reproduced or reproduces itself.

It would appear, then, that the concept of race develops to assuage the anxiety at the absence of a term for a group larger than a single family, that is specifically not coextensive with the idea of a nation but is nevertheless mediated by heredity rather than by geography.

At this point, the relation of sex to race becomes self evident: You can't very well have heredity *without* sex.

But here we are at the verge of the polluting powers of race. For if family is taken to be the form of the process by which heredity occurs, then race is the thing in the body that is inherited—but the "thing inherited" always turns out to be its own pollutability, which is sometimes called purity. Indeed, even without appealing to the "drop" rule (the United States's historical, if inanely

Pyrrhic, method for policing racial borders), we can see that the inescapable imbrication of race and sex via the concept of heredity makes race itself nothing more than a field of potential pollutions.

The polluting power of race is simply another name for the inclusionary power of a great family. One cannot marry out of such families. One can only marry into them. The concept of race arises, however, when the great family becomes so large that it looses locatable boundaries and the relation between members becomes purely sexual—natural, transcendental, essential—rather than contractual; as a corollary to the same transformation, inclusion everts into pollution.

Is it a paradox, then, that in so many narratives of racial impurity, the sign of pollution actualized is the emergence of homosexuality? In the conceptual field of race, a field that has no necessary existence apart from the threat of pollution, of sexual infiltration, the dramatic proof that pollution has occurred is the emergence of men and women whose commitment to heredity, to preserving the threat of pollution to other races (marked or unmarked) that maintains the racial field in its stable/unstable existence, is, at least in the popular imagination where much of my narrative calculus takes place, radically in question?

The difficulty of speaking of racism and homophobia together is precisely this: Although the machinery of oppression to both races and sexual orientations is distressingly the same, the underlying desire to end racism is seen as the desire to lift the proscription on pollution itself, allowing it to run wild, even self-destruct, into the micro-pollutions represented by the grid of constitutive photographs behind SimEve's benign (as a vampire's expression is benign, as homosexual Pater noted of the Giaconda, the Renaissance model of all-woman) smile. The desire to end homophobia is seen, however, as the desire to remove the stigma on opting out of the pollution game entirely.

Black men coupling with white women—in this country—extend the black race. Black women coupling with white men weaken, pollute, dilute the black race. The difficulty of speaking about the relationship between the oppression of one sex by the other and the oppression of one race by the other is the fear that the oscillating system of exploitation of women, white and black, by black men and by white, that alone is what allows race to be, will be revealed.

Race exists through potential pollution/procreation.

Same-sex relations threaten to bring pollution/procreation to a halt.

Woman is the cherished/guarded/enslaved ground on which this game of pollution/procreation is played out.

What I am doing, is tracing out the negative calculus of desire underlying the positive arithmetics of the discourse falling out of patriarchal inheritances. This sense of a contradiction at the level of desire is what paralyzes so many of us in speaking about both oppressions at the same time and relating them in any rational hierarchy. What we can be certain of is that, in any discussion of any one field, however forward looking we believe our statements and position to be, if any discomfort lingers about either of the other two, however silent, then some aspect or other of our articulated positions are, in some manner, acceding to this spurious, fatal calculus.

The power of race is that it grows, strengthens, spreads, reproduces itself, takes all into itself, revels in its ability to include—which, again, is its ability to pollute given another name. (Quite probably for certain white slaveholders, what now and again went on in their black breeding pens, sequestered from the main house, across the fields, played the same discursive role for them as what went on in the European theater did for my uncle, the judge.) To believe that race exists is to believe that its energy—specifically, its sexual energy as a potential for procreation—is a real and potent force, for good or ill. But by the same uncritical calculus, homosexuality is seen as the element that is at once within it but that which, at the same time, denies procreation its all-important outlet. Breeding is, after all, what white slaveowners in the early years of slavery *wanted* their slaves to do. Presumably, having same-sex relationships is what they *didn't* want them to do.

VI

From some time in the '70s comes one of my most vivid memories of this paralysis—well after I had come out—in this case while I was sitting at the blond wood tables of the Schomberg Library on 135th Street. A brother, who had come into the library to read, soon engaged me in a heated and pressing conversation, where I felt I could do nothing but listen: "Don't you realize," he declared, leaning forward and taking my forearm, "homosexuality is the white man's evil—that he has inflicted on us, to help destroy us. Black men ain't gay—unless they've been paying too much attention and listening to white men. There ain't no gay people in Africa . . .!"

Ten years later, again in the Schomberg, I'd been invited to give a reading with Octavia Butler. In the Q-and-A session afterwards, the responses of our community audience were upset by a young man in dashiki and batiked cap presenting the same set of concepts, that evoked mumblings both of disapproval and approval all throughout.

Mumblings, yes—but no one said anything clear and articulate. And the moderator chose that moment to bring the session to a close.

Today, anyone interested can go to the 42nd Street area today (October '98) and listen to the street preaching of a black sect, decked out in leather, turbans, and metal studs, calling itself the Nation of Zion whose preachers stand, flanked by two or more guards. Although their rhetoric begins with a historically reasoned critique of the image of a "white" Christ, they soon move on to exhort openly, as they have almost daily for more than a decade now, the extermination of all mixed-blooded blacks, all homosexuals, black and white, and all blacks with vitiligo (the disease where the pigment producing cells break down and white blotches appear on the face and hands and eventually over most of the skin) because they are seen as unclean and polluted.

Wherever we find it, the hidden calculus supporting this argument remains invariants. Homosexuality pollutes the family, the race, the nation *precisely because* it appears to reduce the threat or menace of pollution *to others*—the mutual menace that holds the boundaries of a given family, race, or nation in tense stability. And "woman" is an undifferentiated, wholly invaginated ground of reparation/procreation that, as it pervades all as an essence, is simply absent on any other level: material, bodily, intellectual, economic, political, an absence often designated in a false positivity by the "social."

VII

Interestingly, the first time I encountered these ideas, and the paralysis they sometimes engender, was, of all places, in Greece—a location that, through the rest of European culture, is historically associated with homosexuality as much as it is, so inextricably, with the origins of European culture through its literature and art.

During the months I lived in Greece, during the mid-'60s (I was twenty-three), one of the places I visited regularly in Athens was a pair of movie theaters, one right next to the other, about three or four blocks off Oimoinia Square. Both screened Steve Reeves-style Italian muscle epics, alternating with American Westerns. To say that one was slightly rougher than the other simply meant there were more young Greek men there, often from the army or the navy, actively hustling the procession of middle-aged Greek business men, in and out. One day I noticed a young man sitting on the balcony in—for that place and time—an uncharacteristic suit and tie—rare among the work clothes, military uniforms, and slouch jackets most of the patrons wore. He seemed a bit too proper for this milieu. But, after observing him for twenty minutes, I saw he knew a number of the people moving about from seat to seat in the balcony—and a bit later, once we had passed each other on the narrow stairway up to the balcony, he came over to talk to me! Petros was a student (was he nineteen? was he twenty?) and turned out to be extraordinarily intelligent. Committed to being a doctor, he was nevertheless a lover of literature. At the movies—and, later, back at the Boltetziou Street room that my three (straight) traveling companions (an Englishman, a Canadian, and another American) and I were sharing—while my roommates were out exploring the city, over four or five days Petros and I had sex some three or four times. "Are you really black?" he wanted to know.

I explained as best I could that, according to American law and culture, I was. His response was to leap on me for another session of love making, which merely confirmed what I'd already learned, really, in France and Italy: that the racial myths of sexuality were, if anything, even more alive in European urban centers than they were in the cities of the United States.

Almost as soon as we finished, Petros asked me would I give him English lessons—though he already spoke the language fairly well. In return, he said, he would help me with my Greek.

Could he take one of the novels I had written home with him to try to read? Certainly, I said. The four or five sessions over which I helped Petros unscramble the syntax of various paragraphs in my fifth novel, *City of a Thousand Suns*, were some of the most useful lessons in the writing of English *I* have ever had.

And for my first Greek lesson, a day or two later, Petros came over to my room after his university classes with a chapbook of Yanis Ritsos's 1956 *'O Sonata Selinophotos* (The Moonlight Sonata). In that high-ceilinged room, with its four cot beds and tall, shuttered windows, we sat down to begin.

"If you are going to learn Greek, you start with very good Greek—very great Greek poetry," Petros explained. "You know Ritsos? A great modern poet."

In some ways reminiscent in both tone and matter of Eliot's "Portrait of a Lady," *'O Sonata Selinophotos* is a good deal longer and, finally, more complex. The speaker, an old woman in a house (which may, after all, be empty), keeps looking out the French windows, wanting to go with someone in the moonlight as far as "the bend in the road—"*'o streve tou dromou.*" No literary slouch, Petros spent an hour and a half explicating the phrase "let me come with you," which tolls repeatedly through the poem, each time modulated in its nuance—the phrase with which, as he reminded me with a grin, he'd first invited himself to my room.

By the end of two weeks, sex had fallen out of our relationship: poetry had taken its place. Then, with a burst of warm weather, now at my excuse, now at his, even the language lessons dropped off. But the friendship endured.

One evening, some weeks on in our now platonic friendship, Petros and I decided to go for dinner down to the Piraeus—a few stops out on the subway that began at Oimoineia Square, with its dozens of lottery salesmen with their sticks and streaming ticket strips, strolling around the underground concourse.

Along the docks, as the clouds striped the east with evening, we hunted out the smallest and most pleasant of places we could find: a wooden structure, it was built out over the dock boards. Inside, it was painted green, with screening at the windows rather than glass. At places you could look down between the floorboards and see water flicker.

At a picnic-style, or perhaps barracks-style, bench, we got beer and a plate of *mezie*—hors d'oeuvres. As we sat, talking, jabbing toothpicks into oily bits of octopus, artichokes, and stuffed grape leaves, somehow we got into the politics of Greek-American relations.

What pushed up across the transition from the amiable converse of two young gay men out in the purple evening to something entirely other, I've never been able to reconstruct (though it must have been some uniformed, or insensitive statement, or even argument, of mine), but suddenly Petros was leaning across the table toward me, both his fists on the boards. "Even this place—" he was saying. "What could be more Greek than this place—eh? You think, yes? Here on the Piraeus docks? Eh? Well, I tell you—everything you see here is American? The paint on the walls—American! The screening in the windows—American! The nails in the boards—American! The fixtures on the sink over there—American! Even the calendar on the wall, there—even you can see *that's* American!" He pointed to a pin-up calendar, in Greek, advertising Coca-Cola. "The blades that cut the paper mats we're eating on! The machinery that puts the electro-plaiting on this knife and fork. None of that is Greek. Look out the windows at the boats in the harbor. Even if some of them are Italian-built, their hull-paint is American. Everything, the floor, the ceiling, everything you look at, every surface that you see—in this Greekest of Greek places—is American! I *have* no country! You—you Americans—have it all!"

To say I was taken aback just does not cover my response.

Somehow, incensed as he was, Petros, then I, recovered. Soon, we were more or less amiable. We finished eating, then we went for a walk outside by the water. But it was, indeed, as if I had come so far along an evening road, only to round a certain bend and to discover a waterfall or an ocean or a mountain beyond, that I had never seen before, so that, even on the return trip, nothing looked quite the same.

As we walked back to the Piraeus subway station, I told Petros where I had to go the next afternoon—a street that made him raise an eyebrow, then laugh.

It was famous in the city for its cross-dressers. But, I explained to Petros, "No—that's not why I'm going. There's an English-language school down there, where a British friend of mine teaches. Because I write books, he's asked me to come and visit his class. He wants me to read them something of mine. And to talk about writing English with them."

"Will you talk to them about some of the things you spoke to me about, in your book that we read?"

"Probably," I told him.

"Good!" Petros pronounced.

On the dark, ill-lit platform, with wedges of light from above, we caught the subway back to Athens, and I hiked up steep 'Ippocratou to 'Odos Boltetziou, trying to keep hold of the fact that what I was seeing—much of it at any rate—was not what I had thought I was seeing when I'd left to go to dinner.

The next afternoon at twenty to four, I threaded my way out from Oimoineia Square to the glass door with the venetian blinds inside it, hurried up to the second floor of what was called something very like the Panipistemiou Ethnike Anglike; and my British friend John let me into the room, where his fourteen pupils—two girls and twelve boys, all about seventeen or so—had been in session for twenty minutes of their hour-and-a-half English lesson.

The pages I read, from one of my science fiction novels and our discussion of them were nowhere near as interesting as Petros's exegesis of Ritsos. But the students made a brave attempt to question me intelligently. ("How much money you make from writing of a book in America?" At the time, I made a thousand dollars a novel seven hundred fifty if it was under sixty thousand words. "Are writers very rich in America—they are no so rich in Greece, I think.") Then my part of the lesson was more or less over, and John turned to other material.

One of the students or John, I don't remember, at some point made a joke about the cross-dressers who would soon be strolling up and down the evening street outside. Then one thick-set, dark-eyed youngster leaned forward. "I must say . . ." he began three times: "I must say . . . I must say, because we have a guest today, I must say—must explain: there is no homosexuality in Greece!" In concentration, his fists knotted on the school-desk table before him, as he leaned with an intensity that mirrored Petros's from the night before—though this young man was a year younger, a head taller, and weighed, I'm sure, half again as much. "There is *no* homosexuality in Greece! The Greeks must not *cannot* do that. It is dirty. It is bad. It is bad and disgusting they who do that. The Greeks do not *do* that. There is homosexuality only from foreigners! It is all the bad and dirty tourists that make—that bring homosexuality in Greece. The Englishmen. The Americans. The Germans. The tourists! Not Greeks—you know, now!"

John knew that I was gay—though I doubt the students did. Perhaps, as someone who had invited me to his class, he felt he had to defend me, though I would have been perfectly happy to let it ride. "That just doesn't make sense to me, Costa. When you all go home from here, the people you see down on the street, most of them are pretty obviously Greek. You hear them talking with one another, joking. That's Greek I hear, downstairs."

"You don't *see* that!" Costa insisted "you don't *see* that! Not Greeks. Not Greeks! If Greeks do that, it is only because of the foreigners. They do it, sometimes, maybe for need money—maybe, that the foreigners pay them. But Greeks not do that. It is bad. It is very bad, Why would Greeks do that? It—how you say—doesn't make sense!"

I watched this impassioned young man. I looked at the other youngsters around the room: one girl in a dark sweater rubbed the edge of a book with a foreknuckle. A boy with a bush of light hair slouched back, one hand forward over the front edge of his desk. Some smiled. Some just looked uncomfortable without smiling. The room's walls were gray. A ceiling fan hung from the center, not turned on. Blinds were raised halfway up the windows. Costa's white shirt was open at the neck; his sleeves were rolled up his forearms. Beneath his desk, he wore dark socks beneath broad-strapped sandals, which now he slid back under his chair. I wondered what surfaces of Greece, if any, I was seeing.

After the class, I walked home with English John—who was rather breezy about it all, though even he seemed troubled. "You know, he manages to make that speech to us almost every other week. I wasn't expecting it today though, but, like he said, we had a guest."

Over the next days, I found myself thinking about both experiences. What was particularly bothersome to me was the way the second seemed posed to obliterate the first—to impugn the very social conduit by which my new vision had been gained. If, indeed, as Costa insisted, I "didn't see that," what was I to make of what I did see?

At any rate, this is certainly the young man I remembered when my table-mate at the Schomberg seized my forearm to insist, so passionately: "Homosexuality is the white man's evil. Black men ain't gay—unless they've been paying too much attention to white men. They ain't no gay people in Africa"; just as, when America takes so much pride in pointing out the influences of black culture on its music, fashion, and language, it was Petros who first alerted me to all the white surfaces that already make up so much of black, melanist culture, even to its most virulent homophobic protestations—by teaching me to see the American surfaces of Greece.

VIII

Because, at the level of cultural myth, in terms of the calculus of desire, within the silent space of discourse, homosexuality represents an opting out of the pollution game altogether, because as far as I can see, the only *uniquely* racial power that exists is specifically the power to pollute (all others can be reread in terms of class, culture, sociality); because the only power to be seized by women is that which directly or indirectly holds stable "the race" (black or white or Asian, it makes no difference), I think that gay liberation is, in its very small way, privileged—in that there can be no advance on that front until there have been advances, changes, and material shifts on the fronts of both racism and sexism. I think this is the explanation of why the gay rights movement followed the civil rights movement and the feminist movement in time as it emerged into postmodern consciousness—even though, as a movement itself, it goes back to the very nineteenth century coinage of the terms homosexual and heterosexual; from here on in, advances on this front cannot proceed much further without advances on the other two fronts.

Conceptually, they are inextricably linked.

On the particular level where the argument must proceed case by case, incident by incident, before it reaches discursive (or counter-discursive) mass, we must look at how that principal operates in the answer to our second question: What makes us gay?

The question, What makes us gay? has at least three different levels where an answer can be posed.

First, the question, What makes us gay? might be interpreted to mean, What do we do, what qualities do we possess, that signal the fact that we partake of the preexisting essence of "gayness" that gives us our gay "identity" and that, in most folks' minds, means that we belong to the category of "those who are gay"? This is, ultimately, the semiotic or epistemological level: How do we—or other people—know we are gay?

There is a second level, however, on which the question, What makes us gay? might be interpreted: What forces or conditions in the world take the potentially "normal" and "ordinary" person—a child, a fetus, the egg and sperm before they even conjoin as a zygote—and "pervert" them (that is, turn them away) from that "normal" condition so that now we have someone who does some or many or all of the things we call gay—or at least wants to, or feels compelled to, even if she or he would rather not? This is, finally, the ontological level: What makes these odd, statistically unusual, but ever-present, gay people exist in the first place?

The confusion between questions one and two, the epistemological and the ontological, is already enough to muddle many arguments. People who think they are asking question two are often given (very frustrating) answers to question one, and vice versa.

But there is a third level where this question, What makes us gay? can be interpreted that is often associated with queer theory and academics of a post-structuralist bent. Many such academics have claimed that their answer to (and thus their interpretation of) the question is the most important one, and that this answer absorbs and explains what is really going on at the first two levels.

This last is not, incidentally, a claim that I make. But I do think that this third level of interpretation (which, yes, is an aspect of the epistemological, but might be more intelligibly designated today as the theoretical) is imperative if we are to explain to a significant number of people what is wrong with a discourse that places pleasure and the body in fundamental opposition to some notion of a legally constrained social responsibility, even as the same view is reduced, under conditions of oppression, to seeing homosexuality as an abnegation of the racial imperative to produce and multiply, rather than a discourse that sees that pleasure and the body are constitutive elements of the social as much as the law and responsibility themselves, and the racial as a remnant of the most hidden, violent, and ruthless class division, between genders and families:

". . . everybody who wants to be Negro get on this side of the room and everybody who wants to be white . . ."

One problem with this third level of interpretation of What makes us gay? that many of us academic folk have come up with is that it puts considerable strain in such a question on the ordinary meaning of "makes."

The argument with our interpretation might start along these lines (I begin here because, after first seeing the polemic against it, the reader may have an easier time recognizing the interpretation when it arrives in its positive form): "To make" is an active verb. You seem to be describing a much more passive process. It sounds like you're describing some answer to the question What allows us to be gay? or What facilitates our being gay? or even What allows people to speak about people as gay? Indeed, the answer you propose doesn't seem to have anything to do with "making" at all. It seems to be all about language and social habit.

To which, if we're lucky enough for the opposition to take its objection to this point, we can answer back: "You're right! That's *exactly* our point. We now believe that language and social habit are much more important than heretofore, historically, they have been assumed to be. Both language and social habit perform many more jobs, intricately, efficiently, and powerfully, shaping not only what we call social reality, but also what we call reality itself (against which we used to set social reality in order to look at it as a separate situation *from* material reality). Language and social habit don't produce only the appearance of social categories—rich, poor, educated, uneducated, well mannered, ill bred—those signs that, according to Professor Henry Higgins in *My Fair Lady*, can be learned and therefore faked. They produce as well what heretofore were considered ontological categories: male, female, black, white, Asian, straight, gay, normal, and abnormal, as well as trees, books, dogs, wars, rainstorms, and mosquitoes. And they empower us to put all those ironizing quotation marks around words such as "normal," "ordinary," and "pervert" in our paragraph describing the ontological level.

Because we realize just how powerful the sociolinguistic process is, we *insist* on coupling it to those active verbs, to make, to produce, to create. Early in the dialogue, however, there was another common verb for this particular meaning of "make" that paid its due to the slow, sedentary, and passive (as well as to the inexorable and adamantine) quality of the process: 'to sediment'—a verb which fell away because it did not suit the polemical nature of the argument, but which at this point it might be well to retrieve: What makes us gay? in the sense of, What produces us as gay? What creates us as gay? What sediments us as gay?

The level where these last four questions overlap is where our interpretation of the question—and our answer to it—falls.

Consider a large ballroom full of people.

At various places around the walls there are doors. If one of the doors is open, and the ballroom is crowded enough, after a certain amount of time there will be a certain number of people in the other room on the far side of the open door (assuming the lights are on and nothing is going on in there to keep them out). The third-level theoretical answer to the question, What makes us gay? troubles the ordinary man or woman on the street for much the same reason it would trouble him or her if you said, of the ballroom and the room beside it, "The open door is what makes people go into the other room."

Most folks are likely to respond, "Isn't it really the density of the ballroom's crowd, the heat, the noise, the bustle in the ballroom that drives (that is, that *makes*) people go into the adjoining room? I'm sure you could come up with experiments, where, if, on successive nights, you raised or lowered the temperature and/or the noise level, you could even correlate that to how much faster or slower people were driven out of the ballroom and into the adjoining room—thus proving crowd, heat, and noise were the causative factors, rather than the door, which is finally just a facilitator, *n'est pas?*"

The answer to this objection is: "You're answering the question as though it were being asked at level two. And for level two, your answer is fine. The question *I* am asking, however, on level three, is: What makes the people go into *that* room rather than any number of other possible rooms that they might have entered, behind any of the other *closed* doors around the ballroom? And the actual answer to *that* question really *is*, That, particular *open* door.

Keep this in mind for a moment, while I turn to the actual and troubling answer that we have come up with to the newly interpreted question, What makes us gay? The answer is usually some version of the concept: We are made gay because that is how we have been interpellated.

"Interpellate" is a term that was revived by Louis Althuser in his 1969 essay, "Ideology and Ideological State Apparatuses."[1] The word once meant "to interrupt with a petition." Prior to the modern era, the aristocrats who comprised many of the royal courtiers could be presented with petitions by members of the *haute bourgeoisie*. These aristocrats fulfilled their tasks as subjects to the king by reading over the petitions presented to them, judging them, and acting on them in accord with the petitions' perceived merit. Althuser's point is that "we become subjects when we are interpellated." In the same paragraph, he offers the word "hailed" as a synonym, and goes on to give what has become a rather notorious example of a policeman calling out or hailing, "Hey, you!" on the street. Says Althuser, in the process of saying, "he must mean me," we cohere into a self—rather than being, presumably, simply a point of view drifting down the street.

That awareness of "he must mean me," is the constitutive *sine qua non* of the subject. It is the mental door through which we pass into subjectivity and selfhood. And (maintains Althuser) this cannot be a spontaneous process, but is always a response to some hailing, some interpellation, by some aspect of the social.

In that sense, it doesn't really matter whether someone catches you in the bathroom, looking at a same-sex nude, and then blurts out, "Hey, you're gay!" and you look up and realize "you" ("He means me!") have been caught, or if you're reading a description of homosexuality in a text book and "you" think, "Hey, they're describing me!" The point is, rather, that anyone who self-identifies as gay must have been interpellated, at some point, as gay by some individual or social speech or text to which he or she responded, "He/she/it/they must mean me." That is the door opening. Without it, nobody can say, proudly, "I *am* gay!" Without it, nobody can think guiltily and in horror, "Oh, my God, I'm *gay* . . . !" Without it, one cannot remember idly or in passing, "Well, I'm gay."

Because interpellation only talks about one aspect of the meaning of "making"/"producing"/"creating"/"sedimenting," it does not tell the whole story. It is simply one of the more important things that happens to subjects at the level of discourse. And in general discourse constitutes and is constituted by what Walter Pater once called, in the "Conclusion" to *The Renaissance*, "a roughness of the eye." Thus, without a great deal more elaboration the notion of interpellation is as reductive as any other theoretical move. But it locates a powerful and pivotal point in the process. And it makes it clear that the process is, as are all the creative powers of discourse, irrevocably anchored within the social, rather than somehow involved with some fancied breaking out of the social into an uncharted and unmapped beyond, that only awaits the release of police surveillance to erupt into that red Eden of total unconstraint. What the priority of the social says about those times in war where that vision of hell was first encountered by people like my uncle, possibly among our own soldiers, is: Look, if you spend six months socializing young men to "kill, kill, kill," it's naive to be surprised when some of them, in the course of pursuing their pleasure, do. It is not because of some essentialist factor in "perversion" or "prostitution" (or sexuality in general) that always struggles to break loose.

It is language (and/as social habit) that cuts the world up into the elements, objects, and categories we so glibly call reality—a reality that includes the varieties of desire. It is a reality where what is real *is* what must be dealt with, which is one with the political: the world *is* what it is cut up into. All else is metaphysics. That is all that is meant by that troubling poststructuralist assertion that the world is constituted of and by language and nothing more that we have any direct access to.

The problem with this assertion is that one of the easiest things to understand about it is that if language social habit makes/produces/sediments anything, it makes/produces/sediments the meanings of words. Thus, the meaning of "makes" on the semiological/epistemological level is a socio linguistic sedimentation. The meaning of "makes" on the ontological level is a socio linguistic sedimentation. And, finally, the meaning of "makes" on the theoretical (that is, socio linguistic) level is also a socio linguistic sedimentation. This is what those who claim the third meaning encompasses and explains the other two are saying. When I said above I do not make that claim, what *I* was saying in effect was: I am not convinced this is an important observation telling us something truly interesting about ontology or epistemology. It may just be an empty tautology that can be set aside and paid no more attention to. Personally, I think the decision as to whether it is or is not interesting is to be found *in* ontology and epistemology themselves, rather than in theory—that is to say, if the observation emboldens us to explore the world, cut it up into new and different ways, and learn what new and useful relationships can result, then the observation is of use and interest, but it is not interesting to the extent it leads only to materially unattended theoretical restatements of itself.

I hope, that without having to go through the same argument again, we can see that at this theoretical level it is the same process of interpellation that "makes us gay" that also "makes us black." Such a process *is* the social construction that everyone so often speaks of and no one seems ever to do anything about. And when race is cut up ontologically—specifically by the science of genetics—we simply find nothing there: the genes for dark skin, full lips, broad noses, and kinky hair are, irrevocably tied neither to each other nor to anything else. They are merely physical traits. They fall together in the people they do merely because, historically, people with those traits have been sexually segregated—so do blond hair and blue eyes, or epicanthic folds and straight black hair. When the sexual segregation is lifted, they flow and disseminate through the population, and reconvene when a few generations of natural selection bring them back together.

IX

Homophobia is not a natural distaste. It is learned. It is supported by lack of familiarity, yes. But, even more, it is supported by a structure of logic. It occupies a place on a conceptual map. That is to say, it is part of a discourse. Such discursive elements are transcendentalized—attached to nature or religion—only when the larger discursive logic is lost sight of. To dismantle such discourses, as a step toward remapping them, requires that we begin by retrieving precisely that overall discursive logic—by showing precisely how it relates to images of man and woman in their functional definitions; of how it relates to the tribe, to the race, to the state, to the nation. However, what is difficult to internalize is that, for the same reasons and on the same theoretical level, homosexuality is no more natural than the homophobia that counters it.

The natural in our rhetorical gallery is directly connected to the good.

If homophobia is "natural," then what it counters—homosexuality—must be bad.

If homosexuality is "natural," then *it* must be good, and attempts to counter it must be bad.

But this, of course, *is* the system that we are fundamentally trying to dismantle—and must dismantle—if we are to institute a more functional conceptual mapping: One that sees homosexuality as pleasurable and useful to a number of people, some of them gay, some of them not, and of no particular consequence to anyone else—though "pleasurable," "useful," "indifferent," just as much as "harmful" and "dangerous," are also all socially constructed categories. The larger social job—which, slowly but surely is coming about—is to demonstrate that in the greater world today, such libertarian ideas leave the whole nation better off and closer to is a more functional and efficient national model. Given our current level of technology (where, indeed, war becomes a far smaller profession of a much more specialized sub group than anything close to the standing armies of the nineteenth century)—and the world's population problem—it seems self-evident that the nations that divorce sex from procreation (and distance themselves from the nineteenth-century discourse in which the country with the largest and the most violent male population of necessity wins out over its neighbors) are the most likely to endure. I also think, by the bye, that a level of international cooperation and assistance must also and of necessity replace the nineteenth-century imperialistic logic that even makes such a statement as the above comprehensible today. But that is an elaboration and we have to start somewhere.

Let me end, however, with another tale, then, from a few months ago.

In Michigan, where I taught last term, a traveling gay discussion seminar came to the women's dorm where the administration had housed my partner Dennis and me. The evening's topic was "coming out." At the beginning of the seminar, a black freshman woman in the audience got up and announced, clearly and strongly, that she felt homosexuality was wrong—contravening the laws of God and nature. If, however, we all understood that she felt that way, she would consent to sit there and listen.

And she did.

I do not know what she made of the discussion from the four young people in the seminar, all within a year or two of her own age, who told of their own fears and moments of bravery in the course of coming to terms with their own homosexuality; of the problems dealing with parents, school mates, friends at home; of the moments of frightening hostility; of the times of unexpected support and understanding. There was one Asian young man on the panel. There was a Mexican woman. One white boy was the son of a minister. There were no blacks. As I sat there, a gay black man of fifty-five, who had spent half of his life before Stonewall and the other half since, listening to them talk, I found much of what they said moving. I found much of it—yes—naive. Some of it I thought was insightful. (I thought, I must confess, one of the women on the panel had all the political sophistication of a clam.) Some of what they said I agreed with. Some of what they said I felt could be further thought through.

But what was probably clear both to me and to the young woman who'd made her initial statement, is that these were sincere young people saying how they'd felt, how the world looked to them. They were clearly people of goodwill who clearly wanted the world to be better for themselves and for those around them.

When we actually change our political ideas, most of us change them fairly slowly. Exposure is as much a factor as logic.

In a democracy, the respect the young woman asked for must be granted if she is ever to change her thinking. That is as much a democratic right as the right of the brave youngsters in the seminar to be heard.

Somewhere, in Michigan then, as it does here and has done before, as it has so many times now, sedimentation continues, sedimentation begins.

Notes

1. (*Lenin and Philosophy*, by Louis Althuser, [Monthly Review Press, New York: 1971]).

Questions for Reflection, Discussion and Writing

1. The idea of multiple oppressions points to "patriarchal inheritances," according to Delany. What are the types of oppressions and social, racial, gendered "inheritances" Delany identifies? In what ways do they intersect?

2. How do the stories and vignettes Delany narrates about his childhood and life as a gay Black man illustrate the multiple oppressions he experiences and identifies? In what ways do those stories offer a framework for understanding his theories of oppression?

3. Delany's title contains the word "queer." Given your understanding of the word queer, what queer notions about race does he present?

4. Delany claims that the question: "What makes us gay?" should be changed to: "What produces us as gay? What creates us as gay? What sediments us as gay?" How are those different questions? What is the function of "interpellation" in Delany's answer to those questions? How does it intersect with issues of race?

Related Reading

Joseph Beam, Ed. *In the Life: A Black Gay Anthology.* Boston: Alyson. 1986.

Jackie Goldsby, "What It Means To Be Colored Me." *Out/Look 3.*1 (Summer 1990): 8–17.

Jewelle Gomez and Barabara Smith, "Taking the Home Out of Homophobia." *Out/Look 2.*4 (Spring 1990): 32–37.

Essex Hemphill, Ed. *Brother to Brother: New Writings By Black Gay Men.* Boston: Alyson. 1991.

Ekua Omosupe, "Black/Lesbian/Bulldagger." *differences 3.*2 (1991): 112–134.

Barbara Smith, "Blacks and Gays: Healing the Great Divide" (1993) in The *Columbia Reader on Lesbians & Gay Men in Media, Society, & Politics.* Larry Gross and James D. Woods, Eds. NY: Columbia UP. 1999. 649–652.

Kobena Mercer, "Dark and Lovely Too: Black Gay Men in Independent Film" in *Queer Looks.* Martha Gever, John Greyson and Partibha Parmar, Eds. NY: Routledge. 1993. 238–256.

Evelyn Hammonds, "Black (W)holes and the Geometry of Black Female Sexuality" in differences: *A Journal of Feminist Cultural Studies 6.* 2–3 (1994): 126–145.

Kobena Mercer, "Black Masculinity and the Sexual Politics of Race" in *Welcome to the Jungle: New Positions in Black Cultural Studies.* NY: Routledge. 1994. 131–170.

Gideon Ferebee Jr., *Out! To Lead.* Newport Beach, CA: Brownell & Carroll. 1994.

Z. Isiling Nataf, "Black Spectatorship and Pleasure in Popular Cinema" in *A Queer Romance: Lesbians, Gay Men and Popular Culture.* Paul Burston and Colin Richardson, Eds. NY: Routledge. 1995. 57–80.

Catherine E. McKinley & Joyce DeLaney, Eds. *Afrekete: An Anthology of Black Lesbian Writing.* NY: Anchor Books. 1995.

Keith Boykin, *One More River to Cross: Black and Gay in America.* NY: Anchor Doubleday. 1996.

Cathy J. Cohen, "Contested Membership: Black Gay Identities and the Politics of AIDS" in *Queer Theory/Sociology*. Steven Seidman, Ed. Cambridge, MA: Blackwell. 1996. 362–394.

Gregory Conerly, "The Politics of Black Lesbian, Gay, and Bisexual Identity" in *Queer Studies: A Lesbian, Gay, Bisexual, and Transgender Anthology*. Brett Beemyn and Mickey Eliason, Eds. NY: NYUP. 1996. 133–145.

Shawn Stewart Ruff, *Go the Way Your Blood Beats: An Anthology of Lesbian and Gay Fiction By African-American Writers*. NY: Henry Holt. 1996.

Robert F. Reid-Pharr, "Tearing the Goat's Flesh: Homosexuality, Abjection and the Production of a Late Twentieth-Century Black Masculinity." *Studies in the Novel* 28.3 (Fall 1996): 372–394.

Gary Fisher, *Gary In Your Pocket*. Eve Sedgwick, Ed. Durham, N.C.: Duke UP. 1996.

Amy Abugo Ongiri, "We Are Family: Black Nationalism, Black Masculinity, and the Black Gay Cultural Imagination." *College Literature* 24.1 (1997): 280–294.

Lisa C. Moore, Ed., *Does Your Mama Know? An Anthology of Black Lesbian Coming-Out Stories*. Decatur, GA: Red Bone Press. 1997.

David Bergman, "Race and the Violet Quill." *American Literary History* 9.1 (Spring 1997): 79–102.

Lyle Ashton Harris and Thomas Allen Harris, "Black Widow: A Conversation" in *The Passionate Camera: Photography and Bodies of Desire*. Deborah Bright, Ed. NY: Routledge. 1998. 248–262.

Jewelle Gomez, "Representations of Black Lesbians." *The Harvard Gay & Lesbian Review* 6.3 (Summer 1999): 32–35.

Cheryl Clarke, "The Failure To Transform: Homophobia in the Black Community" in *Dangerous Liaisons: Blacks, Gays, and the Struggle for Equality*. Eric Brandt, Ed. NY: The New Press. 1999. 31–44.

Cathy J. Cohen and Tamara Jones, "Fighting Homophobia versus Challenging Heterosexism: 'The Failure to Transform' Revisited" in *Dangerous Liaisons: Blacks, Gays, and the Struggle for Equality*. Eric Brandt, Ed. NY: The New Press. 1999. 80–101.

Darieck Scott, "More Man Than You'll Ever Be: Antonio Fargas, Eldridge Cleaver, and Toni Morrison's *Beloved*" in *Dangerous Liaisons: Blacks, Gays, and the Struggle for Equality*. Eric Brandt, Ed. NY: The New Press. 1999. 217–242.

Robert F. Reid-Pharr, "The Shock of Gary Fisher" in *Dangerous Liaisons: Blacks, Gays, and the Struggle for Equality*. Eric Brandt, Ed. NY: The New Press. 1999. 243–255.

Rhonda M. Williams, "Being Queer, Being Black: Living Out in Afro-American Studies" in *Is Academic Feminism Dead?: Theory in Practice*. The Social Justice Group at The Center for Advanced Feminist Studies, Ed. NY: NYUP. 2000. 266–282.

Sapphrodykie, "The Iconoclast" in *Out & About On Campus: Personal Accounts by Lesbian, Gay, Bisexual & Transgendered Students*. Kim Howard and Annie Stevens, Eds. Los Angeles, CA: Alyson Publications. 2000. 131–141.

Phillip Brian Harper, "The Evidence of Felt Intuition: Minority Experience, Everyday Life, and Critical Speculative Knowledge." *GLQ* 6.4 (2000): 641–657.

Callaloo Special Issue 23.1 (2000). "'In the Family': Creative Work by Lesbian, Gay, Bisexual and Transgender Writers of Color" and "'Plum Nelly': New Essays in Black Queer Studies."

Jennifer DeVere Brody, "Theory in Motion: A Review of the Black Queer Studies in the Millennium Conference (University of North Carolina, Chapel Hill, April 7–9, 2000)." *Callaloo 23*.4 (2000): 1274–1277.

Vincent Woodard, "Just As Quare As They Want To Be: A Review of the Black Queer Studies in the Millennium Conference (University of North Carolina, Chapel Hill, April 7–9, 2000)." *Callaloo 23*.4 (2000): 1278–1284.

Bryant Keith Alexander, "Reflections, Riffs and Remembrances: The Black Queer Studies in the Millennium Conference (University of North Carolina, Chapel Hill, April 7–9, 2000)." *Callaloo 23*.4 (2000): 1285–1305.

Laura L. Sullivan, "Chasing Fae: *The Watermelon Woman* and Black Lesbian Possibility." *Callaloo 23*.1 (2000): 448–460.

Delroy Constantine-Simms, Ed. *The Greatest Taboo: Homosexuality in Black Communities.* Los Angeles, CA: Alyson Books. 2001.

Film

If She Grows Up Gay (1983). Karen Sloe Goodman. 23 m.

Nocturne (1990). Joy Chamberlain. 58m.

Splash (1991). Thomas Harris. 10 m.

Young Soul Rebels (1991). Isaac Julien. 105m.

Among Good Christian Peoples (1991). Jacqueline Woodson and Catherine Gund (Saalfield). 30 m.

Long Time Comin' (1993). Dionne Brand. 52 m.

Intro to Cultural Skit-Zo-Frenia (1993). Jamika Ajalon. 10 m.

Born in Flames (1993). Lizzie Borden. 90m.

Heaven Earth & Hell (1993). Thomas Allen Harris. 25 m.

B.D. Women (1994). Inge Blackman. 20 m.

Black Nations/Queer Nations?: Lesbian and Gay Sexualities in the African Diaspora (1996). Shari Frilot. 52 m.

All God's Children (1996). Dee Mosbacher. 26 m.

The Watermelon Woman (1997). Cheryl Dunye. 85m.

Web Resource

http://www.pridelinks.com/Ethnic_Groups/African_American
http://www.nblglf.org
http://demeter.hampshire.edu/~sistah

Special Topics

Marlon Rigg's 1989 documentary *Tongues Untied* (55 minutes) articulated his experience of liminal positionality between and among both the gay and the black communities, examined the complexities of race and sexual desire, and argued for positive self-love

———, "Latina Performance and Queer Worldmaking; or, Chusmería at the End of the Twentieth Century" in *Disidentifications: Queers of Color and the Performance of Politics.* Minneapolis: U of Minnesota P. 1999. 181–200.

Cherríe Moraga with Rosemary Weatherston, "An Interview with Cherríe Moraga: Queer Reservations; or, Art, Identity, and Politics in the 1990s" in *Queer Frontiers: Millennial Geographies, Genders, and Generations.* Joseph A. Boone, et al, Eds. Madison: U of Wisconsin P. 2000. 64–83.

Susana Chávez-Silverman and Librada Hernández, Eds. *Reading and Writing the Ambiente: Queer Sexualities in Latino, Latin American, and Spanish Culture.* Madison: U of Wisconsin P. 2000.

Juanita Diaz-Cotto, "Lesbian Feminism Activism and Latin American Feminist *Encuentros*" in *Sexual Identities: Queer Politics.* Mark Blasius, Ed. Princeton, NJ: Princeton UP. 2001. 73–95.

Film

Tampon Thieves (Ladronas de Tampones) (1996). Jorge Lozano. 22 m.
Mama . . . I Have Something To Tell You (1996). Calogero Salvo. 41m.

Web Resource

http://www.pridelinks.com/Ethnic_Groups/Latino

Special Topics

Gloria Anzaldúa's influential 1987 work of essays, *Borderlands/La Frontera: The New Mestiza*, introduced ground-breaking concepts of multiple identities and of liminality, of identities that cannot be categorized because they are neither simply one thing or another, but combinations of several affiliations and identities. Her work has been enormously influential on gay, lesbian and queer theory, feminist studies, Chicano/a Studies, and Ethnic Studies in general.

Reading

Gloria Anzaldúa, *Borderlands/La Frontera: The New Mestiza.* San Francisco, CA: Aunt Lute Books. 1987.

———, "Bridge, Drawbridge, Sandbar or Island: Lesbians of Color *Haciendo Alianzas*" in *Bridges of Power: Women's Multicultural Alliances.* Philadelphia: New Society. 1990. 216–231.

———, *Interviews: Entrevistas.* AnaLouise Keating, Ed. NY: Routledge. 2000.

Shane Phelan, "Lesbians and Mestizas: Appropriation and Equivalence" in *Playing With Fire: Queer Politics, Queer Theories.* Shane Phelan, Ed. NY: Routledge. 1997. 75–95.

Ian Barnard, "Gloria Anzaldua's Queer Mestisaje." *MELUS 22*.1 (Spring 1997): 35–43.

Lynda Hall, "Writing Selves Home at the Crossroads: Anzaldúa and Crystos (Re)Configure Lesbian Bodies." *Ariel 30*.2 (April 1999): 99–117.

Special Topics

The complex construction of both gender and sexual identities in indigenous native populations in the Americas, and their resistance to easy categorization, may be explored in the readings and films listed below.

Reading

Walter Williams, *The Spirit and the Flesh: Sexual Diversity in American Indian Culture.* Boston: Beacon Press. 1986.

Will Roscoe, Ed. *Living the Spirit: A Gay American Indian Anthology.* NY: St. Martin's Press. 1988.

Ramón A. Gutiérrez, "Must We Deracinate Indians To Find Gay Roots?" *Out/Look* (Winter 1989).

Paula Gunn Allen, "Lesbians in American Indian Cultures" in *Hidden From History: Reclaiming the Gay & Lesbian Past.* Martin Duberman, Martha Vicinus and George Chauncey, Eds. NY: NAL. 1989: 106–117.

Jonathan Goldberg, "Sodomy in the New World: Anthropologies Old and New." *Social Text 9* (1991): 46–56.

Harriet Whitehead, "The Bow and the Burden Strap: A New Look at Institutionalized Homosexuality in Native North America"" in *The Lesbian and Gay Studies Reader.* Henry Abelove, Michèle Aina Barale and David M. Halperin, Eds. NY: Routledge. 1993. 498–527.

Will Roscoe, "How to Become a Berdache: Toward a Unified Analysis of Gender" in *Third Sex, Third Gender: Beyond Sexual Dimorphism in Culture and History.* Gilbert Herdt, Ed. NY: Zone Books. 1994. 329–372.

———, "Was We'Wha a Homosexual? Native American Surveillance and the Two-Spirit Migration." *GLQ 2*.3 (1995): 193–235.

Film

Long Eyes of Earth (1990). Lawrence Brose. 10 m.

Honored by the Moon (1990). Mona Smith. 15 m.

Two-Spirit People (1991). Michel Beauchemin, Lori Levy & Gretchen Vogel. 20 m.

Yukiko Hanawa, "inciting sites of political interventions: queen 'n asian." *positions: east asia cultures critique 4*.3 (Winter 1996): 459–489.

David L. Eng, "Out Here and Over There: Queerness and Diaspora in Asian American Studies." *Social Text 52–53 15*. 3–4(Fall/Winter 1997): 31–52.

David L. Eng and Alice Y. Hom, Eds. *Q & A: Queer in Asian America*. Philadelphia: Temple UP. 1998.

Paul B. Franklin, "Orienting the Asian Male Body in the Photographs of Yasumasa Morimura" in *The Passionate Camera: Photography and Bodies of Desire*. Deborah Bright, Ed. NY: Routledge. 1998. 233–247.

Sandip Roy, "Curry Queens and Other Spices" in *Q & A: Queer in Asian America*. David L. Eng and Alice Y. Hom, Eds. Philadelphia: Temple UP. 1998. 256–262.

Jasbir K. Puar, "Transnational Sexualities: South Asian (Trans)nation(alism)s and Queer Diasporas" in *Q & A: Queer in Asian America*. David L. Eng and Alice Y. Hom, Eds. Philadelphia: Temple UP. 1998. 405–423.

Nayan Shah, "Sexuality, Identity, and the Uses of History" in *Q & A: Queer in Asian America*. David L. Eng and Alice Y. Hom, Eds. Philadelphia: Temple UP. 1998. 141–156.

Surabhi Kukke and Svati Shah, "Reflections on Queer South Asian Progressive Activism in the US." *Amerasia Journal 25*.3 (1999): 129–137.

Walter Penrose, "Hidden in History: Female Homoeroticism and Women of a 'Third Nature' in the South Asian Past. *Journal of the History of Sexuality 10*.1 (January 2001): 3–39.

Eric C. Wat, *The Making of a Gay Asian Community: An Oral History of Pre-AIDS Los Angeles*. Lanham, MD: Rowman and Littlefield. 2001.

Film

Orientations (1984). Richard Fung. 56 m.

Chinese Characters (1985). Richard Fung. 22 m.

Ten Cents a Dance (1985). Midi Onodera. 30 m.

The Displaced View (1988). Midi Onodera. 52 m.

Memory Pictures (1989). Pratibha Parmar. 24 m.

Flesh and Paper (1990). Pratibha Parmar. 26 m.

Women of Gold (1990). Eileen Lee and Marilyn Abbink. 30 m.

Khush (1991). Pratibha Parmar. 24 m.

Fated To Be Queer (1992). Pablo Bautista. 25 m.

Toc Storee (1992). Ming-Yuen S. Ma. 22 m.

The Wedding Banquet (1993). Ang Lee. 111 m.

Dream Girls (1993). Kim Longinotto and Jano Williams. 50 m.

Love Thang Trilogy (1994). Mari Keiko Gonzalez. 12 m.

Surviving Sabu (1997). Ian Iqbal Rashid. 15 m.

Sambal Belacan in San Francisco (1997). Madeline Lim. 25 m.

Yellow Fever (1998). Raymond Yeung. 26 m.
A Seeker (1998). Kian H. Kuan. 6 m.

Web Resource

http://trikone.org
http://www.khushnet.com
http://www.angelfire.com/ca2/queermuslims
http://www.pridelinks.com/Ethnic-Groups/Asian/
http://www.geocities.com/WestHollywood/Heights/5010/resources.html

■

Lost in Space

Queer Geography and the Politics of Location

Sherrie A. Inness

Imagine that a mischievous fairy disrupted our space–time continuum and threw us all into an alternate reality in which Cincinnati, instead of San Francisco, were the queer capital of the United States. How would queer culture, queer studies, and queer theory in that new universe compare to how we know them in this familiar one? Would they be identical, similar, or radically divergent? Perhaps the differences would be minor. If Cincinnati were the queer mecca instead of San Francisco, there might be an explosion of gay and lesbian chefs coast to coast concocting Cincinnati's renowned "Cincinnati chili," which seems to be sold on every block, rather than cooking the Pacific Rim dishes so trendy in the city of our world. Possibly Cincinnati's Northside neighborhood would have the fame that the Castro has achieved. But perhaps the differences would be far more dramatic. The Cincinnati of our universe is a very conservative city. What impact would that fact have on gay and lesbian cultural evolution? How farreaching would be the effects? Would Stonewall still have occurred in New York City? Would ACT UP ever have come into being?

    These musings are designed in part to highlight the preeminence of San Francisco in the queer cultural imagination. Cincinnati will not soon eclipse

San Francisco as the most prominent city in the United States' queer geography, nor will any other city. It seems a trifle sacrilegious—like the idea of painting a moustache on the Mona Lisa—even to suggest that another city or town could replace the fabled City by the Bay. San Francisco, after all, does have a large, flourishing gay culture and a long history of providing refuge to lesbians and gay men, particularly after the end of World War II when the city's gay and lesbian community expanded rapidly as veterans of the armed forces moved to the city rather than move back to the more conservative cities and towns where they grew up. This sense of uneasiness about displacing San Francisco as the "queer capital" points out how taken for granted queer geography has become in the United States. It is this fixity that this chapter seeks to destabilize. I wish to reinspect queer geography to study the margins that queer studies—an area that is very much in the margins already—is creating within itself, whether intentionally or unintentionally.

I am turning my attention not only to San Francisco, although that city does play a significant role in my argument, but to the entire "queer geography" of the United States to make four points: (1) The geography of the United States, particularly what I identify as its "queer" geography, shapes queer studies in ways that might be harmful as well as beneficial. (2) The dominance of gay and lesbian culture in San Francisco, Los Angeles, New York and a few other enclaves (Northampton, Provincetown, Fire Island, Key West) overshadows the true multiplicity of lesbian/gay culture in the United States today. (3) Geography helps to constitute the queer subject in such a way that the queer subject par excellence becomes a lesbian or gay man from a major urban city on one of the coasts, particularly someone from New York City or San Francisco. (4) Geography shapes, in part, a person's understanding of his or her homosexuality.

Although this chapter draws much from recent work in post-modern and feminist geography, it should not be categorized solely as a geographical analysis.[1] Geographers traditionally have been the scholars most concerned with space, but there is growing interest among other social and cultural theorists in the study of space, spatial relationships, and the processes of space. This chapter has been influenced not only by researchers interested primarily in geography, such as Alison Blunt, J. Nicholas Entrikin, Gillian Rose, and Edward H. Soja, but also by scholars, such as Gloria Anzaldúa and María Lugones, who are interested in how minority communities construct their identities in relationship to the mainstream, as well as by theorists, such as Mark Blasius, Judith Butler, and Michael Foucault, whose main focus of research lies elsewhere. This interdisciplinary approach is necessary to bridge the gap between geography and queer studies and to demonstrate the importance of place for gay and lesbian theory.

Since a person's locatedness in space inevitably influences his/her perceptions of the world, there are limitations to my approach in this chapter. I am white, middle-class, highly educated, and female; thus my view of the United

States' queer geography will be colored accordingly. In addition, my subject position as a lesbian who has experienced life in a variety of locations in the United States, including San Francisco, Boston, Cincinnati, San Diego, and Northampton, creates an unavoidable bias to this chapter, a geographical bias that no person can escape. A working-class African American man living in the South or an upper-class Asian American woman working in the Northwest might have completely different stories to tell about how they perceive the queer geography of the United States. I hope, however, that this chapter will be a starting point for a larger discussion of the way queer geography is constituted both by individual lesbians and gay men and by much larger cultural forces.[2]

Standard geographical descriptions of the United States typically fail to allow a space for the lives and experiences of gays and lesbians. As a result, we have to create our own worlds and words to describe our spaces; only in this way can we maintain existence where existence is denied. As lesbian philosopher Joyce Trebilcot writes, "Dykes *especially* cannot be expected to live in worlds made by others. A commitment to being a dyke is partly a commitment to invention—a commitment to making up one's own world, or parts of it, anyway" (138). Lesbians and gays need not only to create a new, inclusive geography but also to analyze the dominant, exclusive geography around them. This is a difficult task. Since people tend to normalize their surroundings, unraveling the network of relationships that constitute a place can be an arduous task. We are used to seeing space as no more than a void to be filled. Yet geography is socially constructed, though it takes on the appearance of naturalness and the authority of reality, just as do constructs of gender, sexuality, race, and ethnicity.

Scholars and theorists need to recognize and acknowledge the biases implicit or explicit in queer cultures and queer scholarship today and guard against the creation of a queer version of what Donna Haraway calls the "master subject," which she defines as "an autonomous subject who observes social conflicts from a privileged and unconflicted place" and whose claim to pure objectivity "can be converted from fantasy into reality only by denying the relational character of subjectivity and by relegating other viewpoints—different subjectivities—to invisible, subordinate, or competing positions" (qtd. in Blunt and Rose 5). Variations on the "master subject" already exist in the gay and lesbian world; although "[c]ontemporary lesbian and gay male cultures evidence a heightened sensitivity to issues of difference and the social formation of desire, sexuality, and identity" (Seidman 105), this sensitivity, as Steven Seidman points out, has its limitations, and lesbian and gay research still tends to privilege Anglo-American accounts. The elision of differing subjectivities that constitute gayness is based not only on factors such as race, ethnicity, age, gender, and class but also on geographic region. A regional bias exists in contemporary research on gays and lesbians, with a large amount of work concentrating on a relative paucity of locations. The opening of new, prestigious lesbian/gay research centers in Los Angeles and New York, the creation of the Harvey Milk Institute in San Francisco, or the production of books such as George Chauncey's *Gay New*

York: Gender, Urban Culture, and the Making of the Gay Male World, 1890–1940
(1994), Martin Duberman's *Stonewall* (1993), Esther Newton's *Cherry Grove,
Fire Island: Sixty Years in America's First Gay and Lesbian Town* (1993), and Kath
Weston's *Families We Choose: Lesbians, Gays, Kinship* (1991) all demonstrate a
tendency toward privileging specific geographical locations, notably on the East
or West Coast, particularly San Francisco, New York, and, to a lesser extent,
Key West, Provincetown, or Fire Island.[3]

To avoid simply giving status or attention to the cities and towns with the
highest concentration of gays and lesbians, scholars need to construct a new
queer geography. This is not to suggest that there is no value in studying pre-
eminently gay areas. To the contrary, much valuable information can be gained
about how gay people formulate identity and create institutions in areas where
they are numerous, visible, and relatively powerful. As Weston points out in
Families We Choose, which is based on fieldwork conducted in the San Francisco
bay area, "With its unique history and reputation as a gay city, San Francisco
hardly presents a 'typical' lesbian and gay population for study. Yet the Bay
Area proved to be a valuable field site because it brought together gay men and
lesbians from very different colors and classes, identities and backgrounds" (8).
Further, large cities are a "hotbed" of diversity and "fringe" activity—this is the
case for everyone, not just gays. This element of diversity means that newer
movements, such as queer politics, are more likely to emerge in locations like
San Francisco, Los Angeles, or New York before moving inland to the more
conservative areas of the country where they might eventually be assimilated
even into the mainstream. As Denyse Lockard writes, "the East and West
Coasts are at the forefront of cultural innovation" (88) for many lesbians.

But, as exciting and important as studying new behaviors and trends is,
scholars should not lose sight of the fact that the majority of lesbians and gay
men in the United States are not in the vanguard of the movement and do not
live in the cradles of gay civilization. Many gays and lesbians live in areas with
small gay communities or no discernible gay presence; they are trying to survive
in what are often inhospitable, conservative environments. In some ways their
situation is akin to that of gays and lesbians before Stonewall, but it is not identical. The antagonism they face is similar, but the gay culture has changed.
Gays and lesbians today are much more visible and vocal in demanding rights
and recognition than ever before and have managed to change a number of institutionalized homophobias including the classification of homosexuality as a
psychiatric disorder. Gays and lesbians are also creating a national culture by
disseminating a multitude of cultural artifacts, including travel books, magazines, comics, clothing, postcards, and a host of other commodities that are accessible to nearly every gay person in the United States (sometimes travel to a
gay cultural center is required, sometimes items must be borrowed from well-
traveled friends). Though these cultural artifacts and signs travel across spatial
geographies and engender a sense of cohesive gay culture, they never entirely
negate the differences that are produced by living in places that have disparate

perceptions about what it means to be queer. Overall, the United States remains hostile to gays and lesbians—the *Bowers* v. *Hardwick* Supreme Court case and the debate over whether homosexuals should be allowed to serve in the military are perfect examples of America's unwillingness to accept homosexuality—though some areas are more welcoming than others. In effect, most gays are living in a curious mixture of pre- and post-Stonewall gay/lesbian culture. So while some of the writings that center on gay/lesbian cultural centers are outstanding and deserve high praise, this intense concentration on only a few sites of gay/lesbian culture provides a distorted glass through which to view the gay/lesbian "hinterlands."

This is not to suggest, of course, that *no* work has been done on smaller gay and lesbian communities across the United States. A great deal of such work has been accomplished, and this scholarship continues to grow, as do calls for recognition of the diversity of gay cultures.[4] Elizabeth Kennedy and Madeline Davis, Susan Krieger, James T. Sears, Edmund White, and numerous other writers have looked at lesbian and gay experience in a variety of different regions. This chapter is concerned, however, with the damaging effects of universalizing certain types of gay experiences while relegating others to a marginalized position. Studies of gay men and lesbians in San Francisco and New York are often universalized, whereas the work of those concentrating on other locations is particularized. Simply because the experiences of gay men and women in certain areas, such as San Francisco and New York, are so visible, it is all too easy for writers, both academic and nonacademic, to assume that the experiences of such gays reflect the experiences of other gays in the rest of the United States. Lesbian/gay studies should be wary of creating universal theories from looking at only a small number of locations. Shane Phelan's words about how grand theories operate are useful here: "Grand theories work by subsuming all struggles under a single rubric, delaying or denying the importance of other categories" ("(Be)coming" 784). It is important to avoid creating grand theories about lesbian/gay studies that do not account for regional differences in gay/lesbian identity and culture. Gays and lesbians may acknowledge that obvious superficial differences exist among communities in various regions, but there is an expectation of a universal "gayness" that denies the profound differences between gay cultures in different regions. I shall explore some of these differences, particularly for lesbians, in the following section.

Queer Culture Shock

> In the South industrialization and the end of segregation reoriented all values. In the West the frontier spirit, no matter how faint, can still be sensed. In the East, wave after wave of social change has made everything seem transient.
>
> Only in the Midwest has so little changed over such a long period. Only here can people sneer at the antics of less stable populations. (White 192)

I first became interested in queer geography when I moved with my girlfriend from California to Hamilton, Ohio, a small working-class city located about twenty miles north of Cincinnati. As transplants from San Francisco and Northampton, Massachusetts (dubbed "Lesbianville, USA" by the *National Enquirer*), who had lived in Boston and San Diego, we were disconcerted by what constituted gay/lesbian culture and community in the Cincinnati area. The semiotics of lesbian identity in Cincinnati was unfamiliar; the social institutions were different; the backgrounds and values of most lesbians we met were unlike our own; the diversity of cultural institutions was minuscule compared to what had been available in our previous home regions. Our profound sense of dislocation was more than geographic; we suffered a dislocation of identity as well. What did it mean for us to identify as lesbian when what constituted "lesbian," as reflected in the culture and community, had apparently shifted under our feet? This rupture in our sense of lesbian selves made it clear that our subjectivities as lesbians were constructed in relation to a specific culture in a particular place.[5]

The recognition that place affects one's sense of identity is not new, yet what became clear to us was how place operated specifically on our lesbian identities, creating a universalizing perception of lesbian identity and lifestyle based on where we had learned what it meant to be homosexual. This experience echoes the work of Mark Blasius, who argues that "coming out is a lifelong process of *becoming* lesbian or gay" (654–55), which involves the feedback of one's community. A number of other theorists, including Judith Butler in *Gender Trouble: Feminism and the Subversion of Identity* (1990) and Cindy Patton in her essay "Tremble, Hetero Swine!" (1993), concur with Blasius: Gay identity is not constituted in a singular moment of "coming out"; rather, it is a lifelong process that is influenced by one's community. Butler, for instance, writes about gender identities: "gender intersects with racial, class, ethnic, sexual, and regional modalities of discursively constituted identities. As a result, it becomes impossible to separate 'gender' from the political and cultural intersections in which it is invariably produced and maintained" (3). According to her, numerous factors shape a lesbian's gender display, including the region of the nation where she lives, and if one accepts that gay identity is similarly constructed, then it follows that *where* one comes out has a profound effect on how one perceives one's gay identity. Michele, a thirty-four-year-old computer systems analyst, who spent ten formative years in San Francisco, comments:

> In San Francisco, part of my sense of dyke identity lay in being on the fringe. I relied on markers such as a leather jacket and extensive tattoos to anchor my sense of self as different from the mainstream, and I moved within a community of others who utilized similar symbols. But in Ohio, in an area where I saw few lesbians, and even fewer who looked like me, I experienced a disruption in my sense of identity. Surrounded by conservative heterosexuals, with little "lesbian feedback," I found that the meaning of the concept "being a lesbian" as I had conceived it in San Francisco was growing increasingly fuzzy.

When a person leaves a familiar community and enters another that has unfamiliar norms and values, the resulting sense of internal disruption is commonly known as culture shock. Gays and lesbians experience a culture shock related specifically to their experience of gay community and identity. As Blasius notes, "one enters into a specific discourse and practice about what it means to be lesbian or gay that the existence of community has made possible and through which one voluntarily forms oneself as an ethical subject *in relation to the values of that community*" (657; emphasis added). Because gay communities are influenced by the character of the larger region in which they are found, there can be enormous variance in norms and values among gay communities, despite a relatively high cultural congruence at a more superficial level. Members of one gay or lesbian community might be surprised at the values of another: The rainbow flag could be the same as the one at home, but other differences might surface that surprise and confound the unwary.[6]

An excellent example of the subtleties of difference among places is the reaction to the film *Go Fish*. This full-length feature film is the first one about lesbian life that I had viewed that reflected my own experiences in the gay community. All of my friends whose gay communities of origin were big coastal cities like San Francisco, New York, or Boston loved the film for similar reasons. Yet reactions from lesbians in other parts of the country were not always as favorable. One woman, Susan, who recently moved to Austin, Texas, from San Francisco, reported her experience at a party where Austin lesbians were discussing the film. None of the Austin lesbians liked the film, not because they thought it was poorly made or too arty but rather because they could not "relate" to the characters and their lifestyles. As one woman put it, she could not understand why the characters were living "as if they were poor or something," a reference to the communal households portrayed in the film. Some lesbians found the depiction of communal living to be an authentic and endearing representation of lesbian life, while others could not recognize themselves in that picture. Nor was this response unique to Austin—another San Francisco transplant, in North Carolina, reported the same reaction to the movie there. Although it is obvious that not all lesbians live or have lived in communal households, what was surprising to me was that some lesbians could not even *conceive* of the possibility of living in such a household: Communal households are not a part of their experience or of their conception of lesbian community. This may be because they live in areas where the American Dream of owning one's own home is still realizable by the average working person, including most lesbians. Cities like Austin and many midwestern cities, including Cincinnati, are also influenced by the strong religious and "family values" attitudes of the surrounding area, which insist upon households based on couple relationships. The economic and cultural values of Texas, in this case, had a strong influence on how lesbians constructed their identities, an influence that, in the case of *Go Fish*, took precedence over a common bond of lesbianism.

Hence, "being a lesbian" in suburban Cincinnati means something different from "being a lesbian" in San Francisco. Judith Butler tells an anecdote about being a lesbian in her essay "Imitation and Gender Insubordination": "When I spoke at the conference on homosexuality in 1989, I found myself telling my friends beforehand that I was off to Yale to be a lesbian, which of course didn't mean that I wasn't one before, but that somehow then, as I spoke in that context, I was one in some more thorough and totalizing way, at least for the time being. . . . To say that I 'play' at being [a lesbian] is not to say that I am not one 'really'; rather, how and where I play at being one is the way in which that 'being' gets established, instituted, circulated, and confirmed" (18). Here, Butler's ideas echo those of Blasius, acknowledging the crucial role of the arena in which gay identity is enacted. One can interpret Butler's words as describing the difference between simply living as a lesbian in a more or less nonreflective manner and *being* a lesbian as that distinction was highlighted by her recognition that being a lesbian publicly, for an audience, connoted something different from the being of daily life. Blasius and Butler agree that audience matters in the formation and enactment of gay identity: The actor is shaped in part by the audience for which she is performing. I apply this idea to geography, using it to explain why my experience of myself as a lesbian in San Francisco was different from my experience in Cincinnati.

In moving from queer-saturated areas to the Cincinnati suburbs, my girlfriend and I felt the shock of moving from a very public community to a very private one. Having coastal-big-city aesthetics, we had both come to expect certain signifiers and a certain level of visibility from other members of the gay community. One such signifier is what I call "the look"—eye contact between lesbians on the street that extends just a few seconds longer than between casual passers-by.[7] It's a look that is meant to say "I see you," a secret sign in a society where overt recognition of lesbianism is not done. "The look" was a common feature of life in urban areas, but where I live in the suburbs it does not exist. To the trained observer, my girlfriend and I are obviously lesbian, yet we have passed other lesbian couples in the local mall who give no indication of any kind of having seen us.

Another important identifier of lesbians is clothing style. In Cincinnati, we found a city where the dress codes that identified lesbians were notably toned down from what we were used to in San Francisco and Northampton, areas where lesbians enjoy a public community and culture. That element of public-versus-private culture makes it easy to focus on the "gay cities" when writing about gay cultural expressions such as fashion. For instance, Inge Blackman and Kathryn Perry write: "Today's lesbian 'self' is a thoroughly urban creature who interprets fashion as something to be worn and discarded. Nothing is sacred for very long. Constantly changing, she dabbles in fashion, constructing one self after another, expressing her desires in a continual process of experimentation" (77). Blackman and Perry are concentrating on English lesbian culture, but their words are equally applicable in the United States where many lesbians assume that the "real" lesbian is the urban one, particularly the woman who lives in Los Angeles, San Francisco, New York, or, to a lesser extent, Chicago, Boston, or Seattle. Northampton and Provincetown are special cases because, despite their small size, they have large proportions of lesbians and gays. Another description of lesbian fashion appears in Lisa Duggan's essay "The Anguished Cry of an 80s Fem: 'I Want to Be a Drag Queen,'" which focuses chiefly on San Francisco, New York, and Cherry Grove. She remarks: "Dykes in their 20s in the major urban centers are looking less like nuns and more like motorcycle club members and their molls" (63). Duggan's words might describe lesbian fashion in San Francisco but have little to do with Cincinnati, where the fashions are apt to be far more conservative. This example shows the tendency of writers to focus on what is happening to lesbians in San Francisco or New York, while intentionally or unintentionally overlooking other areas.[8] The emphasis on lesbian fashions in these cities tends to promote the idea that *all* lesbians have the same lifestyle as a few East or West Coast urban-chic dykes.

But you cannot always identify a lesbian by her style. I sometimes wish that lesbians had some universal, cross-cultural signal of identity, because not only are the lesbian codes and fashions in this part of Ohio different from those in San Francisco, but so are codes for heterosexual women. I frequently mistake straight women for lesbians because they use many of the signifiers I associate with lesbians, including short hair, no makeup, and comfortable, androgynous clothing. This constant misinterpretation of my environment has, at times, led to serious feelings of disorientation and a sense of "not belonging." I am missing what John Jackson identifies as a sense of place, which he associates with "a lively awareness of the familiar environment, a ritual repetition, a sense of fellowship based on shared experience" (159). I am missing that sense of place, and I find myself longing for the familiar forms of lesbian culture with which I was "raised." I long for "home."

Slowly, my girlfriend and I are learning how to "read" mid-western lesbian culture, and we are finding that it is profoundly influenced by the social geography in which it is located, as is the lesbian culture of any other region. The Cincinnati area differs in some fundamental aspects from San Francisco and Northampton. Cincinnati is a conservative city in the part of the country known as the Bible Belt. A strong fundamentalist Christian presence exists here, with the attendant homophobia. Cincinnati voters overwhelmingly passed Issue 3, which struck gays, lesbians, and bisexuals from the city's human rights amendment. Do not forget the attempt to close down the Robert Mapplethorpe exhibit here in 1992; that fiasco is a quintessential example of Cincinnati's obsession with what it calls "decency." This conservative backdrop inevitably affects the form gay and lesbian culture takes.

Where I live, just north of Cincinnati, I can go for weeks without meeting with another obvious lesbian.[9] Contrast this with a recent trip my girlfriend made back to Northampton, where she counted twenty lesbians during a half-hour walk along Main Street. The Cincinnati area is not a very hospitable environment for gays and lesbians, yet, in my research on the area before moving there, I was told more than once that there was a large and thriving lesbian community. There is, but it does not look like what I, having had my gay identity shaped in "queer hotbeds," think a lesbian community should look like.

Cincinnati proper, as a fairly large city, does have a more visible gay presence than the outlying suburbs, including a gay ghetto located in an area called Northside. Many lesbians and gay men own property there, and rainbow flags are not an uncommon sight. The women's bookstore, considered by many to be the center of lesbian activity, is in that neighborhood, along with a new lesbian-owned cafe and a new lesbian bar. But there is simply no comparison between Northside and San Francisco's gay ghetto, the Castro. That lesbians and gay men are not as visible here as in San Francisco or Northampton makes sense in an area like Cincinnati (and much of the rest of the United States). Lesbianism is less of a public identity here; the trendy urban dyke styles of San Francisco or Los Angeles are seldom visible. Lesbians are far more likely to wear clothing that allows them to blend in with heterosexual society. While this serves as a protection against potential threats, it has the side effect of making it difficult for lesbians to identify each other, weakening or inhibiting the sense of public community that is such a marked feature of the Castro.

Perhaps I can best describe my current experiences by referring to Gloria Anzaldúa's discussion of what she calls *"mestiza* consciousness." In her influential book *Borderlands/La Frontera: The New Mestiza* (1987), she writes: "Living on borders and in margins, keeping intact one's shifting and multiple identity and integrity, is like trying to swim in a new element, an 'alien' element" (preface). She describes borderlands as being "physically present wherever two or more cultures edge each other, where people of different races occupy the same territory, where under, lower, middle and upper classes touch" (preface). Although Anzaldúa is writing about her experiences living on the Texas/Mexico border, her words are equally germane to our experiences in Ohio where we straddle the border between homosexual and heterosexual communities. A form of *mestiza* consciousness arises for lesbians and gays in the Midwest. They need to circulate in a variety of different cultures, always negotiating their way between cultural systems that share little in common and may even be diametrically opposed.[10] They must learn how to negotiate in those different cultures to survive—their "straight" jobs are frequently necessary for their economic well-being. But living in different cultures can carry a price—a heavy one. Sometimes I feel as if my lesbianism were being diminished—becoming almost ghostlike—because there are so few times when it is acceptable to show it.

Place helps constitute my lesbianism far more than I realized before moving to Cincinnati. Place is always shaping people, just as people are always shaping it. This is why queer theorists need to gain a better understanding of how place functions, particularly for queers, and how queer geography influences our interactions in queer communities across the United States.

Lost in Space

The space in which we live, which draws us out of ourselves, in which the erosion of our lives, our time and our history occurs, the space that claws and knaws [*sic*] at us, is . . . , in itself, a heterogeneous space. In other words, we do not live in a kind

of void, inside of which we could place individuals and things. We do not live inside a void that could be colored with different shades of light, we live inside a set
of relations that delineates sites which are irreducible to one another and absolutely not superimposable on one another. (Foucault, "Other Spaces" 23)

Geography is, in the most basic sense, the study of space. The above quotation
from Foucault presents an evocative description of what it feels like to live in
space, the human condition none of us can escape. Space, as he points out, is more
than measured volumes of air molecules that we displace by our presence. It is also
constituted by the relationships between the things "inside" of it—including relationships between people. Hence, it makes sense to say that queer people inhabit
and create a different kind of space than do heterosexuals, and the terrain of queer
space needs to be explored and mapped to understand more fully its multivalent
nature. But queer space is equally defined by its relationship to power and its relationship to the heterosexual spaces into which it is woven, and for that reason
queer studies cannot afford to overlook the impact of geography on its turf.

I am using the term "queer geography" to refer to the particular geography that is uniquely significant to the lesbian/gay community. For instance, in
thinking about queer geography, it is evident that San Francisco would be
equivalent to the capital of the United States. Similarly, Provincetown and
Northampton would be far more important than their small sizes would seem
to suggest. Obviously, queer geography creates a map that shares similarities
with the "real" United States but also varies widely in places. To better conceptualize queer geography, consider one of those maps of the United States that
graphic artists create using the world view of a particular city or town. For instance, a New York inhabitant views New York as taking up much of the map,
with the entire Midwest taking up very little room. For a lesbian, San Francisco
and Northampton might have room on a queer map that is far disproportionate
to their actual size. When looking at the United States from a lesbian or gay
perspective, what emerges is a map that bears little resemblance to the more
traditional map found hanging in a geography classroom.

Though the term "queer geography" initially elicits images of physical
space, geophysical terrain, and mapping strategies, geography as a discipline
and space as its subject encompass more than our eighth-grade geography
teachers let on. Space, in its most rudimentary and recognizable form, is conceived of as a static, concrete backdrop to human endeavors as humanity
marches forward through time; it is the arena in which people play out their social lives. Such a view emphasizes the ways that space can be measured and
described and assumes that these accounts of space serve as mimetic representations achieved through objective observation.

Yet, increasingly, theorists have been disputing this perception of space,
arguing that space is actually dynamic and "constituted through struggles over
power/knowledge" (Blunt and Rose 5). Maps are a good example of these differing perceptions of geography. Under the first view, a map is a truthful representation of the space it describes. From this perspective, the "queer" map of

the United States 1 described earlier would be considered a parodic distortion of reality. But under the second view, mapping is inherently political, creating "a spatial image that directly addresses the politics of representation as they are bound into the politics of location" (Blunt and Rose 8). For example, many of the popular maps of the world that were manufactured in the United States or Europe have been shown to be politically influenced: Europe and North America appear larger than they actually are in relation to other countries and continents and tend to be centrally located in the map's image.

Space is more than terrain; space is socially produced as "a set of relations between individuals and groups" (Soja 120), and social life is both the producer and the product of spatiality (Soja 129). Every space becomes imbued with political meaning: The bathroom, the closet, the cemetery, the body, all are sites that are simultaneously constituted within a sociopolitical schema and shape it as well. For example, in *Gender Trouble*, Butler describes the impact of social constructions on the female body (a physical space) as being "constituted through discursively constrained performative acts that produce the body through and with the categories of sex" (viii). She goes on to note that acts of parody and gender rebellion highlight the constructedness of hegemonic categories of sex; she postulates that such acts are effective strategies for destabilizing the established order. Her argument demonstrates that not only does space influence the social world but the social world in turn affects space.

Because space is imbued with many meanings, its study is crucial in order to understand the workings of the world and the operations of power. As Foucault wrote, "A whole history remains to be written of *spaces*—which would at the same time be the history of *powers* (both of these terms in the plural)—from the great strategies of geopolitics to the little tactics of the habitat" (qtd. in Soja 21). Feminists and feminist geographers, in their critiques of masculine-dominated geographies, have already begun this project, focusing on the diversity of experience and what Adrienne Rich termed "the politics of location." Much of this scholarship has consisted of breaking down earlier essentializing and universalizing feminisms, which tended to homogenize the female experience without regard for the variations in women's lives due to the effects of racism, classism, colonialism, and religion on their lives, and of bringing multicultural voices into feminism. I am pursuing one small fragment of such a project as I explore the significance of geographical location in the United States for queers.

If space consists of both concrete spatialities *and* networks of relationships, queer geography can be seen to be constituted, in part, by the relations between queers and nonqueers within different spatial regions. By this argument, areas that tend toward liberal politics, for example, will shape the gay communities that exist within them differently than will more conservative parts of the country. Queer geography can then be used to discuss how gay identity is influenced by traditional geographical divisions of the United States. The Bureau of the Census recognizes four regions and nine divisions of the United States—the West (Pacific and Mountain), the Midwest (West North Central and East North

Central), the Northeast (Middle Atlantic and New England), and the South (West South Central, East South Central, and South Atlantic)[11]—each of which is commonly considered to have a unique "character," manifested in the personalities of its inhabitants. For instance, a popular stereotype of southern people portrays them as friendly and welcoming on the surface but likely to stab a person in the back. They are also depicted as suffering still over their defeat in the Civil War. New Englanders, on the other hand, are spoken of as initially cold and difficult to get to know but also as intensely loyal to trusted friends. These stereotypes about regions and their inhabitants have an overwhelming influence. "We recognize upon reflection that such place references are often based on stereotypes and misconceptions," J. Nicholas Entrikin writes, "but they are nonetheless a real and an important part of everyday discourse" (12).

Among geographers, the word "place" is often used to describe these spatial "personalities." Gillian Rose discusses how places are unique: "Places differ one from another in that each is a specific set of interrelationships between environmental, economic, social, political and cultural processes" (41). These forces act upon the inhabitants of a given region, and the inhabitants, in turn, act upon each other and the processes around them. Hence, geography is never static; human experience is intimately intertwined with spatial relationships and connections. As Entrikin writes, "Place presents itself to us as a condition of human experience. As agents in the world we are always 'in place,' much as we are always 'in culture.' For this reason our relations to place and culture become elements in the construction of our individual and collective identities" (1). The meaning and enactment of "queer," as a collective identity, are shaped, altered, molded, and created through the interactions of queers with the places that make up the United States and the world.

Because of its overwhelming influence in our lives, space is as vital to our sense of self as is history, although frequently history is understood to be more significant. Foucault discusses the prevalent privileging of time and history over space in "Questions on Geography" (1976): "A critique could be carried out of this devaluation of space that has prevailed for generations. . . . Space was treated as the dead, the fixed, the undialectical, the immobile. Time, on the contrary, was richness, fecundity, life, dialectic. . . . [T]he use of spatial terms seems to have the air of an anti-history. If one started to talk in terms of space that meant one was hostile to time. . . . They didn't understand that to trace the forms of implantation, delimitation and demarcation of objects, the modes of tabulation, the organisation of domains meant the throwing into relief of processes—historical ones, needless to say—of power" (70). Foucault's words help to articulate my project in this chapter. History, of course, is not inconsequential, but I wish to highlight the ways in which the operations and functions of space can grant us a better understanding of historical forces and of how time and space interact in forming queer communities.

Space is too frequently conflated with history by scholars and theorists. It is important to remember that events occur in a temporalspatial moment, not simply a historical one. Edward H. Soja provides an intelligent summation of historical bias: "An already made geography sets the stage, while the willful making of history dictates the action and defines the story line" (14). If one assumes, as Foucault commented that many people do, that space is the static background against which the "true" story of human affairs, history, plays itself out, then the geographical will seem less important or even unimportant in comparison to the historical. The privilege frequently given to the historical is described by Claudie Lesselier: "The narrative of the past obeys its own codes and is inscribed in the existing structures of narrative and description. In itself it produces meaning, establishes a code and ends, and transforms lived experience by pouring it into molds" (91). These molds eclipse the spatial in favor of the temporal. Lesselier's words reflect the current predilection for the historical over the spatial, but this is changing as more scholars recognize that "spatial relations are . . . no less complex and contradictory than historical processes" (Hebdige, "Subjects" vii). I do not mean that analyzing, studying, and surveying history should be disregarded. In fact, much of my own scholarship is informed by historical understandings. The role of space, however, needs to be scrutinized with greater care; exploring spatial differences can enrich and deepen scholars' understanding of queer studies, showing the ways that space inescapably interacts with history, as Foucault points out.

Foucault considered geography crucial to understanding the present age. He wrote that "The present epoch will perhaps be above all the epoch of space" ("Other Spaces" 22) and that "the anxiety of our era has to do fundamentally with space, no doubt a great deal more than with time" (23). He may have been referring to the phenomenon of the "shrinking world," where transportation and communication technologies are transforming our conceptions of space and distance, causing an increasing homogenization within and between cultures, along with the inevitable reaction of cultural resistance to assimilation. This tension between homogenization and heterogeneity is playing itself out within America in numerous ways. Describing the homogenization of the United States, Michael Bradshaw writes that there "has been a convergence of values, economies and experiences for individuals" (57). He points out that personal mobility is far more feasible today than even thirty years ago, creating something of an internal "melting pot" of American cultures. He also notes that the differences in regional average per capita income have become narrower than at any time throughout this century (57). Though much of the nation's physical terrain remains unique from region to region, the human landscape is becoming more undifferentiated as national chain stores and restaurants proliferate. Anyone who has driven a long distance on the interstate highways will be familiar with the increasing uniformity of the American gastronomic landscape. No matter what medium-sized town you pull into, you have your choice of the same restaurants: Burger King, McDonald's, Wendy's, Taco Bell, Hardee's, and a host of similar restaurants serving similar food for similar prices in similar surroundings. It is possible for a person to travel across the vast expanse of the

United States and *never* be exposed to a different culture than that of the fast-food, Wal-Mart world. All across the country, people see the same advertisements, watch the same television shows, eat in the same restaurants, buy the same brands of food, and sleep in the same motels. This confluence of space, this crowding of cultures, is the source of Foucault's anxiety. It is the anxiety of a people losing a sense of unique cultural identity. Identity movements, such as the queer movement, are in part a response to this anxiety, and queer geography becomes a place from which to examine from a new perspective not only queers but the entire field of queer studies as well.

All of this homogenization has helped to create a nation that appears far less diverse than even twenty years ago. These similarities, however, do not fully conceal the countless differences that exist in the United States from region to region, differences that need to be considered when developing the queer studies agenda. Lesbian/gay cultures, and hence lesbians and gays coming out within them, are tremendously influenced by the external "straight" geography. Further, queer geography contains unique elements that do not occur within straight geography; for instance, queer geography is plagued by gaps and holes in places where gays find life so unbearable that they never come out to themselves at all or, if they do, they flee at the earliest opportunity to more accepting locales.

Queer geography, like traditional geography, is not unitary. Multiple differences, such as race, ethnicity, and socioeconomic background, affect how queer geography is constituted. For instance, a Hispanic lesbian might see Los Angeles as more culturally significant than an Anglo lesbian would, perhaps as even more central to her world view than New York, Provincetown, or San Francisco. The lesbian earning $10,000, and living in the Western Addition, a poor section of San Francisco, is going to have a different experience of gay life in the city than a lesbian making $100,000 and living in a remodeled Victorian in the Castro.

As with all theoretical frameworks, queer geography is made up of a series of concentric rings, emanating from the individual to the general. Geography, as a network of relationships, is in an endless state of flux for the individual. To understand geography and the many ways in which it functions, one must scrutinize it on a macroscopic and microscopic level, recognizing that change can occur on one level and not another. One can live in San Francisco, for instance, and be marked by its metaphors, but moving within the city from the Castro to Hunter's Point, say, will create an entirely new personal environment and a new perception of one's place in the world. The lesbian separatist living on a farm in Oregon is likely to have a different understanding of queer culture than the lesbian ACT UP activist living in New York City.[12] Inexorably, both of these people are shaped to a large extent by their immediate surroundings, a relationship that helps to create an image of what lesbian culture is truly about. However, these two women, one on her farm and another in her Greenwich Village loft, are not only influenced, affected, and altered by their relationships to two distinct places. These women, and all others, are shaped by their relationships to a myriad of places, a process that continues throughout their lives. People never stop being molded by their contacts with different places. Even a temporary geography, such as the Michigan Women's Festival or the "space" of an on-line lesbian/gay e-mail conference, can alter one's experience of queerness.

Queer geography, however, is not created merely through the perceptions of lone individuals. Institutions such as gay/lesbian/heterosexual media, historical accounts, academic discourse, and word-of-mouth dissemination all manufacture and perpetuate geography. One manner in which queer geography is created is what Barbara Ponse terms "gay referencing": "the practice of specifying people, places, and events as gay or straight in conversations among gay people," where "[g]ayness becomes a lens through which the rest of experience is focused. Through reiteration, gay referencing effects a normalization of gayness and simultaneously increases the relevance of gayness as a standard against which experience is measured" (94). In other words, gay referencing, a kind of "gay gaze," actively helps to create gay space. When a place is labeled gay, it becomes part of a common language and enters into the gay discourse. Places that do not receive the label do not become part of the "lens." They are not used in the process of creating a standard against which gay and lesbian experiences are measured. Some places, such as San Francisco, Provincetown, Northampton, and, to a lesser extent, New York and Los Angeles, become imbued with a certain mystique and are elevated in the cultural imagination to queer "utopias" that begin to seem more truly "gay" to queers than the countless other cities, towns, and suburban or rural regions that fill the United States. These areas come to be regarded as the "norm" against which all other places are judged and, often, come up lacking in some respects. San Francisco, in particular, has become identified as the lesbian/gay utopia, a vision that does not always mesh with the reality of living there. Such a view frequently elides the all too real queer bashing and overlooks the city's social problems, such as expensive housing, crime, overcrowding, traffic congestion, poverty, and drugs. In addition, San Francisco is plagued by problems within the lesbian and gay communities, such as divisions between lesbians and gay men with different backgrounds. But the "dream" of San Francisco still fills the imagination of nearly every lesbian or gay man in the United States, as well as much of the world.

San Francisco: The Queer Mecca

The symbolic location of San Francisco in the gay/lesbian community can be better understood if it is compared to the spiritual home of another group: Israel, which many Jews perceive to be their homeland. In a similar way, lesbians and gay men understand San Francisco to be their homeland, a city that offers the alluring possibility of a better life, whether they currently live in Anchorage, Alaska; Fresno, California; Topeka, Kansas; Tucson, Arizona; or Cincinnati,

Ohio. Both Israel and San Francisco are far more than mere geographical locations; they shape the very being of the Jews and gays who live in those locales. Seven days a week, a person can be immersed in a culture that represents his or her singular identity position. Even if a woman chooses to avoid a complete immersion in such a culture, just knowing that culture is there changes the way she views the world. If she lives in a world that is largely inimical to her lived experience, finding a geographical place where she can "be herself" can have a dramatic effect on her being. But there is a negative side to San Francisco and Israel and their unique identities. Whenever an "authentic," "true" culture is postulated, other cultures and regions seem inferior, even "wrong."

Because lesbians and gay men see San Francisco as a semimythical homeland, its position has received little theoretical scrutiny. Why is it such a special place, and how has that shaped the field of queer studies?

San Francisco holds a dual position in my mind: It is the very real city less than thirty miles from where I grew up. This San Francisco has clear geographical areas—the Haight-Ashbury, Chinatown, Fisherman's Wharf, Nob Hill, the Mission District—places I visited with my parents. I saw different areas later in my life as a high school and college student: the Castro, Valencia Street—the gay/lesbian neighborhoods I visited with lesbian friends and lovers. But there is a different San Francisco that has little in common with the actual city that I knew. This version, which is far more idealized than the real city, comes into being only in my mind. It is a city that I imagine as full of gays and lesbians, so full that the heterosexuals do not even appear, at least in my imagination. It is this imaginary city I yearn to move to, conveniently forgetting the real problems of the actual City by the Bay. This dream city is such a potent image in my mind that it thoroughly obscures the actual city, just as the real city is sometimes obscured by dense fog.

Other lesbians share this experience of imagining San Francisco as a semimythical site. For instance, a professor at a small liberal arts college on the East Coast comments, "When I imagine San Francisco, I imagine the light bathing the Victorians, always cast in improbable sun rather than fog. And the Golden Gate stands out sharply (even if it is painted orange rather than the golden yellow of my dreams). As a lesbian, it seems so appropriate to head for a city with a golden gate, a gate that brings up images of Dorothy in *The Wizard of Oz* as well as San Francisco." Another woman, an engineer in New York, writes:

> San Francisco conjures up the same sort of imagery as the first Ann Bannon novel that I read some years before "coming out"—bars full of smoke and women, unfamiliar social codes, and cues and rules to learn—an illicit excitement of being a lesbian in a group of lesbians. I always imagine the streets to be full of gay folks—a perpetual Pride fest with leather and bikes and optional clothing.
>
> I think the most important part of San Francisco for me is the knowledge that it does exist in some form (albeit most likely not as I imagine it to be)—the knowledge that there is some safe place that I could go to if I wanted to. It plays the same sort of role as P-town for me in that it provides an emotional escape hatch

just by existing in my imagination. I can tell myself: Well, if things get really bad, I can always move to San Francisco/Provincetown where I can relax, be myself, and truly live.

For many lesbians and gay men, San Francisco is the equivalent of Shangri-la, part of that larger myth of California as paradise, the promised land that has been such a powerful image throughout the twentieth century. Only recently is this image starting to change, as socioeconomic problems turn the California dream into a nightmare. The specter of AIDS has also colored gay and lesbian views of San Francisco, creating a deathly pall that darkens our visions of San Francisco's promise. AIDS has irrevocably changed the queer landscape in San Francisco; it is a potent force that demonstrates how queer geography, like racial or ethnic geography, is always in the process of alteration as diverse social forces reshape the spaces that make up queer societies. For instance, as more and more gay men die of AIDS, their property in the Castro district goes on the market and can be bought by heterosexuals. Could AIDS force the gay mecca out of San Francisco to another, less stricken, location?

Queer Geography in Queer Studies

Axiom 1: "People are different from each other" (Sedgwick 22). Though generalization is an important, perhaps even necessary, tool of theoretical musings, it always fails to encompass the true diversity of life itself. There is a growing trend, especially in postmodern scholarship, to break down generalities, to attempt to be as specific as possible. As Dick Hebdige writes, "Renouncing generalities means concentrating on the material effects of *specific* organisations of space. . . . It means concentrating on what is at stake in representations of particular places. It means exploring, as openly as possible, the myriad defiles which connect the intermeshing architectures not just of *the* City and the Psyche, but of individual cities, individual psyches" ("Subjects" vii). Queer studies is itself part of a larger movement that challenges globalizing representations, and in this chapter I have sought to challenge queer studies to ferret out its own tendencies toward exclusionary representations, in this case in the spatial arena.

What is evident is that no singular gay/lesbian/queer community exists in the United States, although, in the lesbian community at least, the idea of building a unified community, one that stretches from coast to coast, has a long history. In its most famous appearance, this notion was discussed by Jill Johnston in her book *Lesbian Nation* (1973), which argued that a distinct lesbian community should develop in order to give a home to lesbians across the country. Lesbian Nation depended on women's music, festivals, and literature to build a sense of community among diverse women. But, as Lillian Faderman writes, "Lesbian Nation was doomed finally to failure because of youthful inexperience and inability to compromise unbridled enthusiasms" (*Odd Girls* 220). Efforts to build a single community to represent the needs of lesbians across the

United States are always doomed to failure not only because of the class, socioeconomic, racial, ethnic, and age differences that fissure any large group but also because of the differences in community caused by differences in geography. My task in this chapter has been to explain how queer geography affects the lives of all queers in the United States, who cannot help but be influenced by their relationships to places. Only by recognizing that place is as crucial an element in shaping queer identities as is history can lesbians and gay men hope to create a queer studies that more fully understands the various perspectives of the people for whom it claims to speak. Studying space and spatial differences, I hope, will help to ensure that queers, in all their guises, are given equal voices to express their own particular visions about what it means to be queer in the United States.

I would like to add that this inspection of the United States' queer geography has been an intensely personal trip for me, as well as a theoretic one. Debates about the concepts and theories contained in this chapter have followed my girlfriend and me to the dinner table, the bookstore, our local bagel shop, our favorite pizzeria—named "No Anchovies"— where we invariably order the "groovy pizza" (spinach, feta cheese, and garlic). At the same time that we were arguing about how place functions, all of these places were defining us; we continually recognized how caught up in space we were. The personal questions that this chapter has inspired are many. I have debated what queer geography actually means to my friends and me and thought in new ways about how my lesbianism is changed or altered due to place. I have thought about the many ways in which I engage with places on a daily basis and how those encounters shape my identity as a lesbian. I have considered how I "do" lesbianism differently in Cincinnati than in San Francisco and the reasons this is true. I have scrutinized the mestiza consciousness I have developed, circulating as I do between heterosexual and homosexual worlds, and have considered how this form of consciousness, paradoxically, can both imprison and set free. In some ways, writing this chapter has done what all academic work should strive to do: It has destabilized my subject position. It has also called for me to look anew at the way space is constructed for queers. One of my goals in writing this essay will be satisfied if my words have the same destabilizing effect on my readers, who, I hope, will rethink their own relationships to the places that help to constitute them as subjects.

But let us return now, for a moment, to that hypothetical scenario with which I began: Cincinnati as Queen City for the Queers. This picture, however, is not the one with which I wish to close. Instead, I would imagine no city or town as being the "capital" of queer culture, as suggesting by its very location and pride of place that other places lack a queer culture that is equally as significant. Instead, let us imagine a world in which each place, small or large, has a role to play in our creation of queer studies. This idea is crucial in order to understand more fully the multiplicity that makes up queer communities throughout the United States and the rest of the world.

Lost in Space

1. Recent geography studies shaped by postmodernism and feminism have influenced my thinking about queer geography. See, e.g., John A. Agnew and James S. Duncan, eds., *The Power of Place: Bringing Together Geographical and Sociological Imaginations;* James Duncan and David Ley, eds., *Place/Culture/Representation;* J. Nicholas Entrikin, *The Betweenness of Place: Towards a Geography of Modernity;* Derek Gregory, *Geographical Imaginations;* Susan Hanson and Geraldine Pratt, *Gender, Work, and Space;* Michael Keith and Steve Pile, eds., *Place and the Politics of Identity;* Gillian Rose's feminist critique of traditional geography studies, *Feminism and Geography: The Limits of Geographical Knowledge;* Edward H. Soja, *Postmodern Geographies: The Reassertion of Space in Critical Social Theory;* and Women and Geography Study Group of the IBG, *Geography and Gender: An Introduction to Feminist Geography.*

     For information specifically about lesbians and gay men and their relationship to space, see Sy Adler and Johanna Brenner, "Gender and Space: Lesbians and Gay Men in the City"; many of the essays in the outstanding collection edited by David Bell and Gill Valentine, *Mapping Desire: Geographies of Sexualities;* Gill Valentine, "Toward a Geography of the Lesbian Community"; Barbara Weightman, "Commentary: Towards a Geography of the Gay Community"; and Maxine Wolfe, "Invisible Women in Invisible Places: Lesbians, Lesbian Bars, and the Social Production of People/Environment Relationships."

2. I decided to vary terminology in this chapter to show that many of the topics addressed are applicable to *all* queers, however they might define that term. In some places, I refer to "queers"; in other places, my preferred terminology is "lesbians and gays." Sometimes, I use "gays" to refer to both gay men and lesbians. Elsewhere "gay" or "lesbian" is used when the issues discussed apply specifically to one group or the other. In yet other places I speak from a subject position that is particularly coded as "lesbian" to ensure that lesbians are not subsumed by the generic word "gay." These variations in terminology, I believe, are important in order to understand the slippage and confusion of identities that constitute queer communities.

3. A text that analyzes the cultural focus on the East and West Coasts and the reasons behind it is Patrick Douglas, *East Coast/West Coast.*

4. Studies of lesbian/gay experiences outside of New York, San Francisco, and Los Angeles include Martha Barron Barrett, *Invisible Lives: The Truth about Millions of Women-Loving-Women;* Frank Browning, *The Culture of Desire: Paradox and Perversity in Gay Lives Today,* and *A Queer Geography: Journeys toward a Sexual Self;* Joseph P. Goodwin, *More Man Than You'll Ever Be: Gay Folklore and Acculturation in Middle America;* Elizabeth Lapovsky Kennedy and Madeline Davis, *Boots of Leather, Slippers of Gold: The History of a Lesbian Community;* Susan Krieger, *The Mirror Dance: Identity in a Women's Community;* Neil Miller, *In Search of Gay America: Women and Men in a Time of Change;* James T. Sears, "The Impact of Gender and Race on Growing Up Lesbian and Gay in the South"; and Edmund White, *States of Desire: Travels in Gay America.* A number of these works, however, including those by Barrett, Browning, Miller, and White, devote significant space to life in New York, San Francisco, and Los Angeles.

5. There have been numerous studies of the influence of environment on people's sense of well-being and feeling of belonging. See Barbara Allen and Thomas J.

Schlereth, eds., *Sense of Place: American Regional Cultures*; Winifred Gallagher, *The Power of Place: How Our Surroundings Shape Our Thoughts, Emotions, and Actions*; John Brinckerhoff Jackson, *A Sense of Place, a Sense of Time*; and Simon Schama, *Landscape and Memory*.

6. Studies that focus on different forms of lesbian community include Marilyn Frye, "The Possibility of Lesbian Community"; Denyse Lockard, "The Lesbian Community: An Anthropological Approach"; Barbara Ponse, *Identities in the Lesbian World: The Social Construction of Self*; Kath Weston, *Families We Choose: Lesbians, Gays, Kinship*; and Deborah Golman Wolf, *The Lesbian Community*.

7. My thanks to Michele Lloyd for suggesting this idea.

8. Similarly, in her essay, "Do Clothes Make the Woman? Gender, Performance Theory, and Lesbian Eroticism," Kath Weston concentrates solely on the lesbian fashions found in San Francisco at a lesbian prom night sponsored by a local women's center. Some of the articles that emphasize the high-fashion lesbian styles found in such urban centers as New York or San Francisco include Lisa Duggan, "The Anguished Cry of an 80s Fem: 'I Want to Be a Drag Queen'"; Esther Kaplan, "All Dressed Up, No Place to Go?"; and Arlene Stein, "All Dressed Up, but No Place to Go? Style Wars and the New Lesbianism."

9. In Cincinnati, I do not have the same access to lesbian friends that I had in San Francisco, and therefore I make a different political statement, whether I wish to or not. Queer friends make one visible; they provide support and a sense of community. Peter M. Nardi writes about how friendship functions in gay communities: "[G]ay friendship can be seen as a political statement, since at the core of the concept of friendship is the idea of 'being oneself' in a cultural context that may not approve of that self. For many people, the need to belong with others in dissent and out of the mainstream is central to the maintenance of self and identity" (115).

10. Maria Lugones calls such movement between different cultures and communities "world traveling": "I think that most of us who are outside the mainstream of, for example, the U.S. dominant construction or organization of life, are 'world travelers' as a matter of necessity and of survival. It seems to me that inhabiting more than one 'world' at the same time and 'traveling' between 'worlds' is part and parcel of our experience and our situation" (282).

11. Numerous sources are available on the distinct regional identities of the United States. Geographical studies include Michael Bradshaw, *Regions and Regionalism in the United States*; and Raymond D. Gastil, "Cultural Regions of America." For an economic study, see Ann Markusen, *Regions: The Economics and Politics of Territory*.

12. For a collection that addresses rural lesbians and their perception of the importance of place, see Joyce Cheney, ed., *Lesbian Land*.

Works Cited

Adler, Sy, and Johanna Brenner. "Gender and Space: Lesbians and Gay Men in the City." *International Journal of Urban and Regional Research* 16.1 (1992): 24–34.

Agnew, John A., and James S. Duncan, eds. *The Power of Place: Bringing Together Geographical and Sociological Imaginations*. Boston: Unwin Hyman, 1989.

Allen, Barbara, and Thomas J. Schlereth, eds. *Sense of Place: American Regional Cultures*. Lexington: UP of Kentucky, 1990.

Anzaldúa, Gloria. *Borderlands/La Frontera: The New Mestiza.* San Francisco: Spinsters, 1987.

Barrett, Martha Barron. "Double Lives: What It's Like to Be Lesbian Today." *Glamour* 87.9 (Sept. 1989): 316–17; 352; 356; 358–59.

Bell, David, and Gill Valentine, eds. *Mapping Desire: Geographies of Sexualities.* New York: Routledge, 1995.

Blackman, Inge, and Kathryn Perry. "Skirting the Issue: Lesbian Fashion for the 1990s." *Feminist Review* 34 (1990): 67–78.

Blasius, Mark. "An Ethos of Lesbian and Gay Existence." *Political Theory* 20.4 (1992): 642–71.

Blunt, Alison, and Gillian Rose. Introduction. *Writing Women and Space: Colonial and Postcolonial Geographies.* Ed. Alison Blunt and Gillian Rose. New York: Guilford, 1994. 1–25.

Bradshaw, Michael. *Regions and Regionalism in the United States.* Jackson: UP of Mississippi, 1988.

Browning, Frank. *The Culture of Desire: Paradox and Perversity in Gay Lives Today.* New York: Crown, 1993.

———. *A Queer Geography: Journeys toward a Sexual Self.* New York: Crown, 1996.

Butler, Judith. *Bodies that Matter: On the Discursive Limits of 'Sex.'* New York: Routledge, 1993.

———. *Gender Trouble: Feminism and the Subversion of Identity.* New York: Routledge, 1990.

———. "Imitation and Gender Insubordination." *Inside/Out: Lesbian Theories, Gay Theories.* Ed. Diana Fuss. New York: Routledge, 1991. 13–31.

Chauncey, George, Jr. *Gay New York: Gender, Urban Culture, and the Making of the Gay Male World, 1890–1940.* New York: Basic, 1994.

Cheney, Joyce, ed. *Lesbian Land.* Minneapolis: Word Weavers, 1985.

Douglas, Patrick. *East Coast/West Coast.* New York: D. I. Fine, 1989.

Duberman, Martin. *Stonewall.* New York: Dutton, 1993.

Duggan, Lisa. "The Anguished Cry of an 80s Fem: 'I Want to Be a Drag Queen.'" *Out/Look* 1.1 (1988): 62–65.

Duncan, James, and David Ley, eds. *Place/Culture/Representation.* New York: Routledge, 1993.

Faderman, Lillian. *Odd Girls and Twilight Lovers: A History of Lesbian Life in Twentieth-Century America.* New York: Columbia UP, 1991.

Foucault, Michel. "Of Other Spaces." *Diacritics* 16 (1986): 22–27.

———. "Questions on Geography." *Power/Knowledge: Selected Interviews and Other Writings, 1972–1977.* Ed. Colin Gordon. New York: Pantheon, 1980. 63–77.

Frye, Marilyn. "The Possibility of Lesbian Community." *Lesbian Ethics* 4.1 (1990): 84–87.

Gallagher, Winifred. *The Power of Place: How Our Surroundings Shape Our Thoughts, Emotions, and Actions.* New York: Poseidon, 1993.

Gastil, Raymond D. "Cultural Regions of America." *Making America: The Society and Culture of the United States.* Ed. Luther S. Luedtke. Chapel Hill: U of North Carolina P, 1992. 129–43.

Goodwin, Joseph P. *More Man Than You'll Ever Be: Gay Folklore and Acculturation in Middle America.* Bloomington: Indiana UP, 1989.

Gregory, Derek. *Geographical Imaginations.* Cambridge: Blackwell, 1994.

Hanson, Susan, and Geraldine Pratt. *Gender, Work, and Space.* New York, Routledge, 1995.

Hebdige, Dick. "Subjects in Space." *New Formations* 11 (1990): v–x.

Jackson, John Brinckerhoff. *A Sense of Place, a Sense of Time.* New Haven: Yale UP, 1994.

Johnston, Jill. *Lesbian Nation: The Feminist Solution.* New York: Simon and Schuster, 1973.

Kaplan, Esther. "All Dressed Up, No Place to Go?" *Village Voice* 34.26 (27 June 1989): 29; 36.

Keith, Michael, and Steve Pile, eds. *Place and the Politics of Identity.* New York: Routledge, 1993.

Kennedy, Elizabeth Lapovsky, and Madeline Davis. *Boots of Leather, Slippers of Gold: The History of a Lesbian Community.* New York: Routledge, 1993.

Krieger, Susan. *The Mirror Dance: Identity in a Woman's Community.* Philadelphia: Temple UP, 1983.

Lesselier, Claudie. "Social Categorizations and Construction of a Lesbian Subject." Trans. Mary Jo Lakeland. *Feminist Issues* 7 (Spring 1987): 89–94.

Lockard, Denyse. "The Lesbian Community: An Anthropological Approach." *Journal of Homosexuality* 11.3–4 (1985): 83–95.

Lugones, María. "Playfulness, 'World'-Traveling, and Loving Perception." *Women, Knowledge, and Reality: Explorations in Feminist Philosophy.* Ed. Ann Garry and Marilyn Pearsall. Boston: Unwin Hyman, 1989. 275–90.

Markusen, Ann. *Regions: The Economics and Politics of Territory.* Totowa, N.J.: Rowman and Littlefield, 1987.

Miller, Neil. *In Search of Gay America: Women and Men in a Time of Change.* New York: Atlantic Monthly P, 1989.

Nardi, Peter M. "That's What Friends Are For: Friends as Family in the Gay and Lesbian Community." *Modern Homosexualities: Fragments of Lesbian and Gay Experience.* Ed. Ken Plummer. New York: Routledge, 1992. 108–20.

Newton, Esther. *Cherry Grove, Fire Island: Sixty Years in America's First Gay and Lesbian Town.* Boston: Beacon, 1993.

Patton, Cindy. "Tremble, Hetero Swine!" *Fear of a Queer Planet: Queer Politics and Social Theory.* Ed. Michael Warner. Minneapolis: U of Minnesota P, 1993. 143–77.

Phelan, Shane. "(Be)coming Out: Lesbian Identity and Politics." *Signs* 18.4 (1993): 765–90.

Ponse, Barbara. *Identities in the Lesbian World: The Social Construction of Self.* Westport, Conn.: Greenwood, 1978.

Rose, Gillian. *Feminism and Geography: The Limits of Geographical Knowledge.* Minneapolis: U of Minnesota P, 1993.

Sears, James T. "The Impact of Gender and Race on Growing Up Lesbian and Gay in the South." *NWSA Journal* 1.3 (1989): 422–57.

Sedgwick, Eve Kosofsky. *Epistemology of the Closet.* Berkeley: U of California P, 1990.

Soja, Edward H. *Postmodern Geographies: The Reassertion of Space in Critical Social Theory.* New York: Verso, 1989.

Stein, Arlene. "All Dressed Up, but No Place to Go? Style Wars and the New Lesbianism." *Out/Look* 1.4 (1989): 34–42.

Trebilcot, Joyce. *Dyke Ideas: Process, Politics, Daily Life.* Albany: State U of New York P, 1994.

Weightman, Barbara. "Commentary: Towards a Geography of the Gay Community." *Journal of Cultural Geography* 1 (1981): 106–12.

Weston, Kath. "Do Clothes Make the Woman?: Gender Performance, Theory, and Lesbian Eroticism." *Genders* 17 (Fall 1993): 1–21.

———. *Families We Choose: Lesbians, Gays, Kinship.* New York: Columbia UP, 1991.

White, Edmund. *States of Desire: Travels in Gay America.* 1980. New York: Plume, 1991.

Wolf, Deborah Goleman. *The Lesbian Community.* Berkeley: U of California P, 1979.

Wolfe, Maxine. "Invisible Women in Invisible Places: Lesbians, Lesbian Bars, and the Social Production of People/Environment Relationships." *Architecture and Behaviour* 8 (1992): 137–58.

Women and Geography Study Group of the Institute of British Geographers. *Geography and Gender: An Introduction to Feminist Geography.* London: Hutchinson, 1984.

Questions For Reflection, Discussion, and Writing

1. What are some of the conceptions about urban queer life that Inness believes have become "normative" in queer theory?

2. Because queers and queer experiences are vastly under represented in "mainstream" culture, we both create our own culture and are created by the signifiers that surround us. Relating her experiences and using quotes from other lesbians, Inness discusses the ways *Go Fish* was understood by lesbians in various geographic locations. What differences does she note? On what factors are those differences based?

3. What constitute, for Inness, "the semiotics of lesbianism" in Cincinnati, Ohio? What did Inness claim that she and her girlfriend had to learn about queer signifiers when they moved from San Francisco to Cincinnati? On what were some of the differences between queer cultures based, according to Inness?

4. Inness discusses some stereotypes about lesbian fashion that are clearly urban based (London, New York, San Francisco). What would you characterize as lesbian, gay, or queer fashion on your campus? In your town or city of origin?

5. Because San Francisco is often seen as a "queer homeland," Inness argues that queers (including herself) tend to idealize it. What does such idealization obscure?

6. What are some of the ways Inness conceptualizes a "queer geography?"

Writing Assignment

Inness contends that place is formative in the construction of a queer (or any other kind of) identity. Compose an essay that discusses how the specific place/region you grew up in shaped your understanding and social presentation of a sexual self. Think carefully about how norms around gender may also factor into your analysis.

Related Reading

Neil Miller, *In Search of Gay America*. NY: The Atlantic Monthly Press. 1989.

Michael J. Clark, *Diary of a Southern Queen*. Dallas, TX: Monument Press. 1990.

James T. Sears, Ed. *Growing Up Gay in the South: Race, Gender, and Journeys of the Spirit.* NY: Haworth Press. 1991.

Frederick Lynch, "Nonghetto Gays: An Ethnography of Suburban Homosexuals" in *Gay Culture in America: Essays From the Field*. Gilbert Herdt, Ed. Boston: Beacon Press. 1992. 165–201.

William Poole, "Bringing it Back Home." *Out/Look 4*.4 (Spring 1992): 36–44.

Robert McRuer, "A Visitation of Difference: Randall Kenan and Black Queer Theory" in *Critical Essays: Gay and Lesbian Writers of Color*. Emmanuel S. Nelson, Ed. NY: Haworth Press. 1993. 221–232.

Jerry Lee Kramer, "Bachelor Farmers and Spinsters: Gay and Lesbian Identities and Communities in Rural North Dakota" in *Mapping Desire: Geographies of Sexualities*. David Bell and Gill Valentine, Eds. NY: Routledge. 1995.

Will Fellows, Ed. *Farm Boys: Lives of Gay Men From the Rural Midwest*. Madison: U of Wisconsin P. 1996.

Elizabeth Lapovsky Kennedy, "'But we would never talk about it': The Structures of Lesbian Discretion in South Dakota, 1928–1933" in *Inventing Lesbian Cultures in America*. Ellen Lewin, Ed. Boston: Beacon Press. 1996. 15–39.

Michael Riordan, *Out Our Way: Gay and Lesbian Life in the Country*. Toronto: Between the Lines. 1996.

John Howard, Ed. *Carryin' On in the Lesbian and Gay South*. NY: NYUP. 1997.

Chris Cagle, "Imaging the Queer South: Southern Lesbian and Gay Documentary" in *Between the Sheets, in the Streets. Queer, Lesbian, Gay Documentary*. Chris Holmlund and Cynthia Fuchs, Eds. Minneapolis: U of Minnesota P. 1997. 30–45.

Gordon Brent Ingram, Anne-Marie Bouthillette and Yolanda Retter, Eds. *Queers in Space: Communities/Public Places/Sites of Resistance*. Seattle: Bay Press. 1997.

Steven F. Philipp, "Gay and Lesbian Tourists at a Southern U.S.A. Beach Event." *Journal of Homosexuality 37*.3 (1999): 69–86.

John Howard, *Men Life That: A Southern Queer History*. Chicago: University of Chicago Press. 1999.

Gill Valentine, Ed. *From Nowhere to Everywhere: Lesbian Geographies*. Binghamton, NY: 2000.

Linda McCarthy, "Poppies in a Wheat Field: Exploring the Lives of Rural Lesbians." *Journal of Homosexuality 39*.1 (2000): 75–94.

Richard Phillips, Diane Watt and David Shuttleton, Eds. *De-Centering Sexualities: Politics and Representations Beyond the Metropolis*. NY: Routledge. 2000.

Michael P. Brown, *Closet Space: Geographies of Metaphor From the Body to the Globe*. NY: Routledge. 2000.

Carlos L. Dews and Carolyn Leste Law, Eds. *Out in the South*. Philadelphia: Temple
UP. 2001.
Clare Hemmings, *Bisexual Spaces: A Geography of Sexuality and Gender*. NY: Routledge.
2002.

Film

Out in Suburbia (1989). Pam Walton. 28 m.
Fighting in Southwest Louisiana (1991). Peter Friedman and Jean-Francois Brunet. 27 m.
Where Are We? (1992). Robert Epstein and Jeffrey Friedman. 73 m.
American Fabulous (1992). Reno Dakota. 105 m.
Greetings From Out Here (1993). Ellen Spiro. 58 m.
Horse Dreams in BBQ Country (1996). Daniel Baer. 20 m.
Bayou (1997). Dina Ciraulo. 7 m.

■

Must Identity Movements Self-Destruct?: A Queer Dilemma

Joshua Gamson

Focused passion and vitriol erupt periodically in the letters columns of San
Francisco's lesbian and gay newspapers. When the *San Francisco Bay Times* announced to "the community" that the 1993 Freedom Day Parade would be
called "The Year of the Queer," missives fired for weeks. The parade was what
it always is: a huge empowerment party. But the letters continue to be telling.
"Queer" elicits familiar arguments: over assimilation, over generational differences, over who is considered "us" and who gets to decide.

   On this level, it resembles similar arguments in ethnic communities in
which "boundaries, identities, and cultures, are negotiated, defined, and produced" (Nagel 1994: 152). Dig deeper into debates over queerness, however,
and something more interesting and significant emerges. Queerness in its most
distinctive forms shakes the ground on which gay and lesbian politics have been
built, taking apart the ideas of a "sexual minority" and a "gay community," indeed of "gay" and "lesbian" and even "man" and "woman."[1] It builds on central
difficulties of identity-based organizing: the instability of identities both individual and collective, their made-up yet necessary character. It exaggerates and
explodes these troubles, haphazardly attempting to build a politics from the

rubble of deconstructed collective categories. This debate, and other related debates in lesbian and gay politics, are not only over the *content* of collective identity (whose definition of "gay" counts?), but over the everyday *viability* and political *usefulness* of sexual identities (is there and should there be such a thing as "gay," "lesbian," "man," "woman"?).

This paper, using internal debates from lesbian and gay politics as illustration, brings to the fore a key dilemma in contemporary identity politics, and traces out its implications for social-movement theory and research.[2] As I will show in greater detail, in these sorts of debates—which crop up in other communities as well—two different political impulses, and two different forms of organizing, can be seen facing off. The logic and political utility of deconstructing collective categories vies with that of shoring them up; each logic is true, and neither is fully tenable.

On the one hand, lesbians and gay men have made themselves an effective force in this country over the past several decades largely by giving themselves what civil-rights movements had: a public collective identity. Gay and lesbian social movements have built a quasi-ethnicity, complete with its own political and cultural institutions, festivals, neighborhoods, even its own flag. Underlying that ethnicity is typically the notion that what gays and lesbians share—the anchor of minority status and minority rights claims—is the same fixed, natural essence, a self with same-sex desires. The shared oppression, these movements have forcefully claimed, is the denial of the freedoms and opportunities to actualize this self. In this *ethnic/essentialist* politic,[3] clear categories of collective identity are necessary for successful resistance and political gain.

Yet this impulse to build a collective identity with distinct group boundaries has been met by a directly opposing logic, often contained in queer activism (and in the newly anointed "queer theory"): to take apart the identity categories and blur group boundaries. This alternative angle, influenced by academic "constructionist" thinking, holds that sexual identities are historical and social products, not natural or intrapsychic ones. It is socially produced binaries (gay/straight, man/woman) that are the basis of oppression; fluid, unstable experiences of self become fixed primarily in the service of social control. Disrupting those categories, refusing rather than embracing ethnic minority status, is the key to liberation. In this *deconstructionist* politic, clear collective categories are an obstacle to resistance and change.

The challenge for analysts, I will argue, is not to determine which position is accurate, but to cope with the fact that both logics make sense. Queerness spotlights a dilemma shared by other identity movements (racial, ethnic, and gender movements, for example):[4] fixed identity categories are both the basis for oppression and the basis for political power. This raises questions for political strategizing and, more importantly for the purposes here, for social-movement analysis. If identities are indeed much more unstable, fluid, and constructed than movements have tended to assume—if one takes the queer challenge seriously, that is—what happens to identity-based social movements such as gay and lesbian rights? Must socio-political struggles articulated through identity eventually undermine themselves? Social-movement theory, a logical place to turn for help in working through the impasse between deconstructive cultural strategies and category-supportive political strategies, is hard pressed in its current state to cope with these questions. The case of queerness, I will argue, calls for a more developed theory of collective identity formation and its relationship to both institutions and meanings, an understanding which *includes the impulse to take apart that identity from within.*

In explicating the queer dilemma and its implications for social-movement theory, I first briefly summarize the current state of relevant literature on collective identity. Then, zeroing in on the dilemma itself, I make use of internal debates, largely as they took place in the letters column of the weekly *San Francisco Bay Times* in 1991, 1992, and 1993. I turn initially to debates within lesbian and gay communities over the use of the word "queer," using them to highlight the emergence of queer activism, its continuities with earlier lesbian and gay activism, and its links with and parallels to queer theory. Next, I take up debates over the inclusion of transgender and bisexual people, the two groups brought in under an expanded queer umbrella, in lesbian and gay politics. Here I point to a distinctive (although not entirely new) element of queerness, a politic of boundary disruption and category deconstruction, and to the resistance to that politic, made especially visible by the gendered nature of these debates. Finally, in drawing out ramifications for social-movement theory, I briefly demonstrate affinities between the queer debates and debates over multiracialism in African-American politics, arguing that queerness illuminates the core dilemma for identity movements more generally. I conclude by suggesting ways in which social-movement literature can be pushed forward by taking seriously, both as theoretical and empirical fact, the predicament of identity movements.

Social Movements and Collective Identity

Social-movements researchers have only recently begun treating collective identity construction[5] as an important and problematic movement activity and a significant subject of study. Before the late 1980s, when rational-actor models began to come under increased critical scrutiny, "not much direct thought [had] been given to the general sociological problem of what collective identity is and how it is constituted" (Schlesinger 1987: 236). As Alberto Melucci (1989: 73) has argued, social-movement models focusing on instrumental action tend to treat collective identity as the nonrational expressive residue of the individual, rational pursuit of political gain. And "even in more sophisticated rational actor models that postulate a *collective* actor making strategic judgments of cost and benefit about collective action," William Gamson points out, "the existence of an *established* collective identity is assumed" (1992: 58; emphasis in original). Identities, in such models, were (and continue to be) typically conceived as existing prior to movements, which then make them visible through organizing and deploy them politically.

Melucci and other theorists of "new social movements" argue more strongly that collective identity is not only necessary for successful collective action, but that it is often an end in itself, as the self-conscious reflexivity of many contemporary movements seems to demonstrate.[6] Collective identity, in this model, is conceptualized as "a continual process of recomposition rather than a given," and "as a dynamic, *emergent* aspect of collective action" (Schlesinger 1987: 237; emphasis in original; see also Cohen 1985; Mueller 1992; Kauffman 1990). Research on ethnicity has developed along similar lines, emphasizing, for example, the degree to which "people's conceptions of themselves along ethnic lines, especially their ethnic identity, [are] situational and changeable" (Nagel 1994: 154). "An American Indian might be 'mixed-blood' on the reservation," as Joane Nagel describes one example, "'Pine Ridge' when speaking to someone from another reservation, a 'Sioux' or 'Lakota' when responding to the US census and 'Native American' when interacting with non-Indians" (1994: 155; see also Padilla 1985; Alba 1990; Waters 1990; Espiritu 1992).

How exactly collective identities emerge and change has been the subject of a growing body of work in the study of social movements. For example, Verta Taylor and Nancy Whittier, analyzing lesbian-feminist communities, point to the creation of politicized identity communities through boundary-construction (establishing "differences between a challenging group and dominant groups"), the development of consciousness (or "interpretive frameworks"), and negotiation ("symbols and everyday actions subordinate groups use to resist and restructure existing systems of domination") (1992: 100–11; see also Franzen 1993). Other researchers, working from the similar notion that "the location and meaning of particular ethnic boundaries are continuously negotiated, revised, and revitalized," demonstrate the ways in which collective identity is constructed not only from within but is also shaped and limited by "political policies and institutions immigration policies, by ethnically linked resource policies, and by political access structured along ethnic lines" (Nagel 1994: 152, 157; see also Omi and Winant 1986).

When we turn to the disputes over queerness, it is useful to see them in light of this recent work. We are certainly witnessing a process of boundary-construction and identity negotiation: as contests over membership and over naming, these debates are part of an ongoing project of delineating the "we" whose rights and freedoms are at stake in the movements. Yet as I track through the queer debates, I will demonstrate a movement propensity that current work on collective identity fails to take into account: the drive to blur and deconstruct group categories, and to keep them forever unstable. It is that tendency that poses a significant new push to social-movement analysis.

Queer Politics and Queer Theory

Since the late 1980s, "queer" has served to mark first a loose but distinguishable set of political movements and mobilizations, and second a somewhat parallel set of academy-bound intellectual endeavors (now calling itself "queer theory").

Queer politics, although given organized body in the activist group Queer Nation, operates largely through the decentralized, local, and often anti-organizational cultural activism of street postering, parodic and non-conformist self-presentation, and underground alternative magazines ("zines") (Berlant and Freeman 1993; Duggan 1992; Williams 1993);[7] it has defined itself largely against conventional lesbian and gay politics. The emergence of queer politics, although it cannot be treated here in detail, can be traced to the early 1980s backlash against gay and lesbian movement gains, which "punctured illusions of a coming era of tolerance and sexual pluralism"; to the AIDS crisis, which "underscored the limits of a politics of minority rights and inclusion"; and to the eruption of "long-simmering internal differences" around race and sex, and criticism of political organizing as "reflecting a white, middle-class experience or standpoint" (Seidman 1994: 172).[8]

Queer theory, with roots in constructionist history and sociology, feminist theory, and poststructuralist philosophy, took shape through several late-1980s academic conferences, and continues to operate primarily in elite academic institutions through highly abstract language; it has defined itself largely against conventional lesbian and gay studies (Stein and Plummer 1994).[9] Stein and Plummer have recently delineated the major theoretical departures of queer theory: a conceptualization of sexual power as embodied "in different levels of social life, expressed discursively and enforced through boundaries and binary divides"; a problematization of sexual and gender categories, and identities in general; a rejection of civil rights strategies "in favor of a politics of carnival, transgression, and parody, which leads to deconstruction, decentering, revisionist readings, and an anti-assimilationist politics"; and a "willingness to interrogate areas which would not normally be seen as the terrain of sexuality, and conduct queer 'readings' of ostensibly heterosexual or non-sexualized texts" (1994: 181–2).

Through these simultaneous and tenuously linked actions, then, the word "queer," as Steven Epstein puts it, has recently "escaped the bounds of quotation marks" (Epstein 1994: 189; see also Duggan 1992; Warner 1993). Its escape has been marked by quite wrenching controversy within sexual identity-based communities. To understand the uses of "queer," and its links to and departures from lesbian and gay activism, it helps to hear these controversies, here presented primarily through the letters-column debates over "The Year of the Queer."

My discussion of this and the two debates that follow is based on an analysis of some 75 letters in the weekly *San Francisco Bay Times*, supplemented by related editorials from national lesbian and gay publications. The letters were clustered: the debates on the word "queer" ran in the *San Francisco Bay Times* beginning in December 1992 and continued through April 1993; the disputes over bisexuality began in April 1991 and continued through May 1991; clashes over transsexual inclusion began in October 1992 and continued through December 1992. Although anecdotal evidence suggests that these disputes are widespread, it should be noted that I use them here not to provide conclusive data, but to provide a grounded means for conceptualizing the queer challenge.

The Controversy Over Queerness: Continuities with Existing Lesbian and Gay Activism

In the discussion of the "Year of the Queer" theme for the 1993 lesbian and gay pride celebration, the venom hits first. "All those dumb closeted people who don't like the Q-word," the *Bay Times* quotes Peggy Sue suggesting, "can go fuck themselves and go to somebody else's parade." A man named Patrick argues along the same lines, asserting that the men opposing the theme are "not particularly thrilled with their attraction to other men," are "cranky and upset" yet willing to benefit "from the stuff queer activists do." A few weeks later, a letter writer shoots back that "this new generation assumes we were too busy in the '70s lining up at Macy's to purchase sweaters to find time for the revolution—as if their piercings and tattoos were any cheaper." Another sarcastically asks, "How did you ever miss out on 'Faggot' or 'Cocksucker'?" On this level, the dispute reads like a sibling sandbox spat.

Although the curses fly sometimes within generations, many letter-writers frame the differences as generational. The queer linguistic tactic, the attempt to defang, embrace, and resignify a stigma term, is loudly rejected by many older gay men and lesbians.[10] "I am sure he isn't old enough to have experienced that feeling of cringing when the word 'queer' was said," says Roy of an earlier letter-writer. Another writer asserts that 35 is the age that marks off those accepting the queer label from those rejecting it. Younger people, many point out, can "reclaim" the word only because they have not felt as strongly the sting, ostracism, police batons, and baseball bats that accompanied it one generation earlier. For older people, its oppressive meaning can never be lifted, can never be turned from overpowering to empowering.

Consider "old" as code for "conservative," and the dispute takes on another familiar, overlapping frame: the debate between assimilationists and separatists, with a long history in American homophile, homosexual, lesbian, and gay politics. Internal political struggle over agendas of assimilation (emphasizing sameness) and separation (emphasizing difference) have been present since the inception of these movements, as they are in other movements. The "homophile" movement of the 1950s, for example, began with a Marxist-influenced agenda of sex-class struggle, and was quickly overtaken by accommodationist tactics: gaining expert support; men demonstrating in suits, women in dresses.[11] Queer marks a contemporary anti-assimilationist stance, in opposition to the mainstream inclusionary goals of the dominant gay-rights movement.

"They want to work from within," says Peggy Sue elsewhere (Bérubé and Escoffier 1991), "and I just want to crash in from the outside and say, 'Hey! Hello, I'm queer. I can make out with my girlfriend. Ha ha. Live with it. Deal with it.' That kind of stuff." In a zine called *Rant & Rave*, co-editor Miss Rant argues that "I don't want to be gay, which means assimilationist, normal, homosexual. . . . I don't want my personality, behavior, beliefs, and desires to be cut up like a pie into neat little categories from which I'm not supposed to stray" (1993: 15). Queer politics, as Michael Warner puts it, "opposes society itself," protesting "not just the normal behavior of the social but the *idea* of normal behavior" (1993: xxvii). It embraces the label of perversity, using it to call attention to the "norm" in "normal," be it hetero or homo.

Queer thus asserts in-your-face difference, with an edge of defiant separatism: "We're here, we're queer, get used to it," goes the chant. We are different, that is, free from convention, odd and out there and proud of it, and your response is either your problem or your wake-up call. Queer does not so much rebel against outsider status as revel in it.[12] Queer confrontational difference, moreover, is scary, writes Alex Chee (1991), and thus politically useful: "Now that I call myself queer, know myself as a queer, nothing will keep [queer-haters] safe. If I tell them I am queer, they give me room. Politically, I can think of little better. I do not want to be one of them. They only need to give me room."

This goes against the grain of civil-rights strategists, of course, for whom at least the appearance of normality is central to gaining political "room." Rights are gained, according to this logic, by demonstrating similarity (to heterosexual people, to other minority groups) in a non-threatening manner. "We are everywhere," goes the refrain from here. We are your sons and daughters and coworkers and soldiers, and once you see that lesbians and gays are just like you, you will recognize the injustices to which we are subject. "I am not queer," writes a letter-writer named Tony. "I am normal, and if tomorrow I choose to run down the middle of Market Street in a big floppy hat and skirt I will still be normal." In the national gay weekly *10 Percent*—for which *Rant & Rave* can be seen as a proudly evil twin—Eric Marcus (1993: 14) writes that "I'd rather emphasize what I have in common with other people than focus on the differences," and "the last thing I want to do is institutionalize that difference by defining myself with a word and a political philosophy that set me outside the mainstream." The point is to be not-different, not-odd, not-scary. "We have a lot going for us," Phyllis Lyon puts it simply in the *Bay Times*. "Let's not blow it"—blow it, that is, by alienating each other and our straight allies with words like "queer."

Debates over assimilation are hardly new, however; but neither do they exhaust the letters-column disputes. The metaphors in queerness are striking. Queer is a "psychic tattoo," says writer Alex Chee, shared by outsiders; those similarly tattooed make up the Queer Nation. "It's the land of lost boys and lost girls," says historian Gerard Koskovich (in Bérubé and Escoffier 1991), "who woke up one day and realized that not to have heterosexual privilege was in fact the highest privilege." A mark on the skin, a land, a nation: these are the metaphors of tribe and family. Queer is being used not just to connote and glorify differentness, but to revise the criteria of membership in the family, "to affirm sameness by defining a common identity on the fringes" (Bérubé and Escoffier 1991; see also Duggan 1992).[13]

In the hands of many letter-writers, in fact, queer becomes simply a short-hand for "gay, lesbian, bisexual, and transgender," much like "people of color" becomes an inclusive and difference-erasing shorthand for a long list of ethnic and racial groups. And as some letter-writers point out, as a quasi-national shorthand "queer" is just a slight shift in the boundaries of tribal membership with no attendant shifts in power; as some lesbian writers point out, it is as likely to become synonymous with "white gay male" (perhaps now with a nose ring and tatoos) as it is to describe a new community formation. Even in its less nationalist versions, queer can easily be difference without change, can subsume and hide the internal differences it attempts to incorporate. The queer tribe attempts to be a multicultural, multigendered, multisexual, hodge-podge of outsiders; as Steven Seidman points out, it ironically ends up "denying differences by either submerging them in an undifferentiated oppositional mass or by blocking the development of individual and social differences through the disciplining compulsory imperative to remain undifferentiated" (1993: 133). Queer as an identity category often restates tensions between sameness and difference in a different language.

Debates Over Bisexuality and Transgender: Queer Deconstructionist Politics

Despite the aura of newness, then, not much appears new in queerness: debates and fault lines are familiar from gay and lesbian (and other identity-based) movements. Yet letter-writers agree on one puzzling point: right now, it matters what we are called and what we call ourselves. That a word takes so prominent a place is a clue that this is more than another in an ongoing series of tired assimilationist-liberationist debates. The controversy of queerness is not just strategic (what works), nor even only a power struggle (who gets to call the shots); it is those, but not only those. At their most basic, queer controversies are battles over identity and naming (who I am, who we are). Which words capture us and when do words fail us? Words, and the "us" they name, seem to be in critical flux.

But even identity battles are not especially new. In fact, within lesbian-feminist and gay male organizing, the meanings of "lesbian" and "gay" were contested almost as soon as they began to have political currency as quasi-ethnic statuses. Women of color and sex radicals loudly challenged lesbian feminism of the late 1970s, for example, pointing out that the "womansculture" being advocated (and actively created) was based in white, middle-class experience and promoted a bland, desexualized lesbianism. Lesbians of many colors and gay men of color have consistently challenged "gay" as a term reflecting the middle-class, white homosexual men who established its usage (Stein 1992; Phelan 1993; Seidman 1993; Seidman 1994; Clarke 1983; Moraga 1983; Reid-Pharr 1993; Hemphill 1991). They challenged, that is, the definitions.

The ultimate challenge of queerness, however, is not just the questioning of the content of collective identities, but the *questioning of the unity, stability, viability and political utility of sexual identities*—even as they are used and assumed.[14] The radical provocation from queer politics, one which many pushing queerness seem only remotely aware of, is not to resolve that difficulty, not to take us out of flux, but to exaggerate and build on it. It is an odd endeavor, much like pulling the rug out from under one's own feet, not knowing how and where one will land. To zero in on the distinctive deconstructionist politics of queerness, turn again to the letters columns. It is no coincidence that two other major *Bay Times* letters-column controversies of the early 1990s concerned bisexual and transgender people, the two groups included in the revised queer category. Indeed, in his anti-queer polemic in the magazine *10 Percent* (a title firmly ethnic/essentialist in its reference to a fixed homosexual population), it is precisely these sorts of people, along with some "queer straights,"[15] from whom Eric Marcus seeks to distinguish himself:

> Queer is not my word because it does not define who I am or represent what I believe in. . . . I'm a man who feels sexually attracted to people of the same gender. I don't feel attracted to both genders. I'm not a woman trapped in a man's body, nor a man trapped in a woman's body. I'm not someone who enjoys or feels compelled to dress up in clothing of the opposite gender. And I'm not a "queer straight," a heterosexual who feels confined by the conventions of straight sexual expression. . . . I don't want to be grouped under the all-encompassing umbrella of queer . . . because we have different lives, face different challenges, and don't necessarily share the same aspirations. (1993: 14)

The letters columns, written usually from a different political angle (by lesbian separatists, for example), cover similar terrain. "It is not empowering to go to a Queer Nation meeting and see men and women slamming their tongues down each others' throats," says one letter arguing over bisexuals. "Men expect access to women," asserts one from the transgender debate. "Some men decide that they want access to lesbians any way they can and decide they will become lesbians."

Strikingly, nearly all the letters are written by, to, and about women—a point to which I will later return. "A woman's willingness to sleep with men allows her access to jobs, money, power, status," writes one group of women. "This access does not disappear just because a woman sleeps with women 'too'. . . . That's not bisexuality, that's compulsory heterosexuality." You are not invited; you will leave and betray us. We are already here, other women respond, and it is you who betray us with your back-stabbing and your silencing. "Why have so many bisexual women felt compelled to call themselves lesbians for so long? Do you think biphobic attitudes like yours might have something to do with it?" asks a woman named Kristen. "It is our community, too; we've worked in it, we've suffered for it, we belong in it. We will not accept the role of the poor relation." Kristen ends her letter tellingly, deploying a familiar phrase: "We're here. We're queer. Get used to it."[16]

The letters run back and forth similarly over transgender issues, in particular over transsexual lesbians who want to participate in lesbian organizing. "'Transsexuals' don't want to just be lesbians," Bev Jo writes, triggering a massive round of letters, "but insist, with all the arrogance and presumption of power that men have, on going where they are not wanted and trying to destroy lesbian gatherings." There are surely easier ways to oppress a woman, other women shoot back, than to risk physical pain and social isolation. You are doing exactly what anti-female and anti-gay oppressors do to us, others add. "Must we all bring our birth certificates and two witnesses to women's events in the future?" asks a woman named Karen. "If you feel threatened by the mere existence of a type of person, and wish to exclude them for your comfort, you are a bigot, by every definition of the term."

These "border skirmishes" over membership conditions and group boundaries have histories preceding the letters (Stein 1992; see also Taylor and Whittier 1992), and also reflect the growing power of transgender and bisexual organizing.[17] Although they are partly battles of position, more fundamentally the debates make concrete the anxiety queerness can provoke. They spotlight the possibility that sexual and gender identities are not the solid political ground they have been thought to be—which perhaps accounts for the particularly frantic tone of the letters.

Many arguing for exclusion write like a besieged border patrol. "Live your lives the way you want and spread your hatred of women while you're at it, if you must," writes a participant in the transgender letter spree, "but the fact is we're here, we're dykes and you're not. Deal with it." The Revolting Lesbians argue similarly in their contribution to the *Bay Times* bisexuality debate: "Bisexuals are not lesbians—they are bisexuals. Why isn't that obvious to everyone? Sleeping with women 'too' does not make you a lesbian. We must hang onto the identity and visibility we've struggled so hard to obtain." A letter from a woman named Caryatis sums up the perceived danger of queerness:

> This whole transsexual/bisexual assault on lesbian identity has only one end, to render lesbians completely invisible and obsolete. If a woman who sleeps with both females and males is a lesbian; and if a man who submits to surgical procedure to bring his body in line with his acceptance of sex role stereotypes is a lesbian; and if a straight woman whose spiritual bond is with other females is a lesbian, then what is a female-born female who loves only other females? Soon there will be no logical answer to that question.

Exactly: in lesbian (and gay) politics, as in other identity movements, a logical answer is crucial. An inclusive queerness threatens to turn identity to nonsense, messing with the idea that identities (man, woman, gay, straight) are fixed, natural, core phenomena, and therefore solid political ground. Many arguments in the letters columns, in fact, echo the critiques of identity politics found in queer theory. "There is a growing consciousness that a person's sexual identity (and gender identity) need not be etched in stone," write Andy and Selena in the bisexuality debate, "that it can be fluid rather than static, that one has the right to PLAY with whomever one wishes to play with (as long as it is consensual), that the either/or dichotomy ('you're either gay or straight' is only one example of this) is oppressive no matter who's pushing it." Identities are fluid and changing; binary categories (man/woman, gay/straight) are distortions. "Humans are not organized by nature into distinct groups," Cris writes. "We are placed in any number of continuums. Few people are 100 percent gay or straight, or totally masculine or feminine." Differences are not distinct, categories are social and historical rather than natural phenomena, selves are ambiguous. "Perhaps it is time the lesbian community reexamined its criteria of what constitutes a woman (or man)," writes Francis. "And does it really matter?" Transsexual performer and writer Kate Bornstein, in a *Bay Times* column triggered by the letters, voices the same basic challenge. Are a woman and a man distinguished by anatomy? "I know several women in San Francisco who have penises," she says. "Many wonderful men in my life have vaginas" (1992: 4). Gender chromosomes, she continues, are known to come in more than two sets ("could this mean there are more than two genders?"), testosterone and estrogen don't answer it ("you could buy your gender over the counter"); neither child-bearing nor sperm capacities nail down the difference ("does a necessary hysterectomy equal a sex change?"). Gender is socially assigned; binary categories (man/woman, gay/straight) are inaccurate and oppressive; nature provides no rock-bottom definitions. The opposite sex, Bornstein proposes, is neither.[18]

Indeed, it is no coincidence that bisexuality, transsexualism, and gender crossing are exactly the kind of boundary-disrupting phenomena embraced by much poststructuralist sexual theory. Sandy Stone, for example, argues that "the transsexual currently occupies a position which is nowhere, which is outside the binary oppositions of gendered discourse" (1991: 295).[19] Steven Seidman suggests that bisexual critiques challenge "sexual object-choice as a master category of sexual and social identity" (1993: 123). Judith Butler argues that butch and femme, far from being "copies" of heterosexual roles, put the "very notion of an original or natural identity" into question (1990: 123). Marjorie Garber writes that "the cultural effect of transvestism is to destabilize all such binaries: not only 'male' and 'female,' but also 'gay' and 'straight,' and 'sex' and 'gender.' This is the sense—the radical sense—in which transvestism is a 'third'" (1992: 133).

The point, often buried in over-abstracted jargon, is well taken: the presence of visibly transgendered people, people who do not quite fit, potentially subverts the notion of two naturally fixed genders; the presence of people with ambiguous sexual desires potentially subverts the notion of naturally fixed sexual orientations. (I say "potentially" because the more common route has continued to be in the other direction: the reification of bisexuality into a third orientation, or the retention of male-female boundaries through the notion of transgendered people as "trapped in the wrong body," which is then fixed.) Genuine inclusion of transgender and bisexual people can require not simply an expansion of an identity, but a subversion of it. This is the deepest difficulty queerness raises, and the heat behind the letters: if gay (and man) and lesbian (and woman) are unstable categories, "simultaneously possible and impossible" (Fuss 1989: 102), what happens to sexuality-based politics?

The question is easily answered by those securely on either side of these debates. On the one side, activists and theorists suggest that collective identities with exclusive and secure boundaries are politically effective. Even those agreeing that identities are mainly fictions may take this position, advocating what Gayatri Spivak has called an "operational essentialism" (cited in Butler 1990; see also Vance 1988). On the other side, activists and theorists suggest that identity production "is purchased at the price of hierarchy, normalization, and exclusion" and therefore advocate "the deconstruction of a hetero/homo code that structures the 'social text' of daily life" (Seidman 1993: 130).

The Queer Dilemma

The problem, of course, is that both the boundary-strippers and the boundary-defenders are right. The gay and lesbian civil-rights strategy, for all its gains, does little to attack the political culture that itself makes the denial of and struggle for civil rights necessary and possible. Marches on Washington, equal protection pursuits, media-image monitoring, and so on, are guided by the attempt to build and prove quasi-national and quasi-ethnic claims. As such, they do not interrogate the ways in which the construction of gays and lesbians as a singular community united by fixed erotic fates distorts complex internal differences and complex sexual identities. Nor do they challenge the system of meanings that underlie the political oppression: the division of the world into man/woman and gay/straight. On the contrary, they ratify and reinforce these categories. They therefore build distorted and incomplete political challenges, neglecting the political impact of cultural meanings, and do not do justice to the subversive and liberating aspects of loosened collective boundaries.

Thus the strong claims of queer politics and theory: that this is not how it must be, that political and social organization can and should be more true to the inessential, fluid, and multiply sited character of sexuality; and that gay-ethnic movements make a serious error in challenging only the idea that homosexuality is unnatural, affirming rather than exposing the root cultural system.

Yet queer theory and politics tend to run past a critique of the particular, concrete forces that make sexual identity, in stabilized and binary form, a basis for discipline, regulation, pleasure, and political empowerment. In the hurry to deconstruct identity, they tend to "slide into viewing identity itself as the fulcrum of domination and its subversion as the center of an anti-identity politic" (Seidman 1993: 132); the politic becomes overwhelmingly cultural, textual, and subjectless. Deconstructive strategies remain quite deaf and blind to the very concrete and violent institutional forms to which the most logical answer is resistance in and through a particular collective identity.

The overarching strategy of cultural deconstruction, the attack on the idea of the normal, does little to touch the institutions that make embracing normality (or building a collective around inverted abnormality) both sensible and dangerous. Mall kiss-ins by San Francisco's Suburban Homosexual Outreach Program (SHOP) and other actions that "mime the privileges of normality" (Berlant and Freeman 1993: 196), "Queer Bart" (Simpson, the popular cartoon character) t-shirts and other actions that "reveal to the consumer desires he/she didn't know he/she had, to make his/her identification with the product 'homosexuality' both an unsettling and a pleasurable experience" (Berlant and Freeman 1993: 208), do very little to take on the more directly political: regulatory institutions such as law and medicine, for example, which continue to create and enforce gay/straight and male/female divisions, often with great physical and psychic violence. They do not do justice to the degree to which closing group boundaries is both a necessary and fulfilling survival strategy.

Interest-group politics on the ethnic model is, quite simply but not without contradictory effects, how the American socio-political environment is structured. Official ethnic categories provide "incentives for ethnic group formation and mobilization by designating particular ethnic subpopulations as targets for special treatment"; politically controlled resources are "distributed along ethnic lines"; ethnic groups mean larger voting blocs and greater influence in electoral systems (Nagel 1994: 157–9). Ethnic categories serve, moreover, as the basis for discrimination and repression, both official and informal, and thus as a logical basis for resistance. This is the buried insight of the border-patrolling separatists and the anti-queer pragmatists: that here, in this place, at this time, we need, for our safety and for potential political gains, to construct ourselves as a group whose membership criteria are clear.

The overwhelmingly female participation in the *Bay Times* disputes over bisexuality and transgender inclusion underscores this point. Lesbians are especially threatened by the muddying of male/female and gay/straight categorizations exactly because it is by keeping sexual and gender categories hard and clear that gains are made. Lesbian visibility is more recent and hard-won; in struggles against patriarchal control, moreover, lesbianism and feminism have often been strongly linked.[20] Gay men react with less vehemence because of the stronger political position from which they encounter the queer challenge: as men, as gay men with a more established public identity. Just as they are gaining political ground *as lesbians*, lesbians are asked not only to share it but to subvert it, by declaring "woman" and "lesbian" to be unstable, permeable, fluid categories.

Similar pitfalls were evident in the 1993 fight over Colorado's Amendment 2, which prohibits "the state or any of its subdivisions from outlawing discrimination against gay men, lesbians, or bisexuals" (Minkowitz 1993). The Colorado solicitor general, as reporter Donna Minkowitz put it, made arguments "that could have appeared in a queercore rant," promoting "a remarkably Foucaultian view of queerness as a contingent category, whose members can slip in and out of its boundaries like subversive fish" (1993: 27). "We don't have a group that is easily confinable," he argued. Here, the fluidity of group boundaries and the provisional nature of collective identity was used to argue that no one should receive legal benefits or state protection—because there is no discernible group to be protected. Although the solicitor-general-as-queer-theorist is a strange twist, the lesson is familiar: as long as membership in this group is unclear, minority status, and therefore rights and protection, is unavailable. Built into the queer debates, then, is a fundamental quandary: in the contemporary American political environment, clear identity categories are both necessary and dangerous distortions, and moves to both fix and unfix them are reasonable. Although it comes most visibly to the fore in them, this dynamic is hardly unique to lesbian and gay movements. The conflict between a politics of identity-building and identity-blurring has erupted, for example, in recent debates in African-American movements over multiracialism. When a group lobbied the Office of Management and Budget (whose 1977 Statistical Directive recognizes four racial groups), proposing the addition of a "multiracial" classification, they were met with tremendous opposition from those who "see the Multiracial box as a wrecking ball aimed at affirmative action," since it threatens to "undermine the concept of racial classification altogether" (Wright 1994: 47; see also Omi and Winant 1986; Webster 1992; Davis 1991).

As one advocate put it, "Multiracialism has the potential for undermining the very basis for racism, which is its categories" (G. Reginald Daniel, quoted in Wright 1994: 48); as one observer put it, "multiracial people, because they are both unable and unwilling to be ignored, and because many of them refuse to be confined to traditional racial categories, inevitably undermine the entire concept of race as an irreducible difference between peoples" (Wright 1994: 49). Opponents respond vehemently to multiracial organizing, in part because civil-rights laws are monitored and enforced through the existing categories. In a debate in *The Black Scholar*, African and Afro-American Studies professor Jon Michael Spencer attacked "the postmodern conspiracy to explode racial identity," arguing that "to relinquish the notion of race—even though it's a cruel hoax—at this particular time is to relinquish our fortress against the powers and principalities that still try to undermine us" (in Wright 1994: 55). Here, in a different form, is the same queer predicament.

Conclusion: Collective Identity, Social-Movement Theory and the Queer Dilemma

Buried in the letters-column controversies over a queer parade theme, and over bisexual and transsexual involvement in lesbian organizations, are fights not only over who belongs, but over the possibility and desirability of clear criteria of belonging. Sexuality-based politics thus contain a more general predicament of identity politics, whose workings and implications are not well understood: it is as liberating and sensible to demolish a collective identity as it is to establish one. Honoring both sets of insights from the queer debates is a tall order. It calls for recognizing that undermining identities is politically damaging in the current time and place, and that promoting them furthers the major cultural support for continued damage. It means reconnecting a critique of identity to the embodied political forces that make collective identity necessary and meaningful, and reconnecting a critique of regulatory institutions to the less tangible categories of meaning that maintain and reproduce them.[21]

The neatest, and most true to life means for doing so, the theoretical recognition of paradoxes and dialectics, can satisfy intellectually. Certainly a political structure that directs action towards ethnic interest-group claims, and requires therefore solid proofs of authentic ethnic membership (the immutability of sexual orientation, for example), creates paradoxical forms of action for stigmatized groups. In the case of lesbians and gays, for example, gender stereotypes used to stigmatize actors (the gay man as woman, the lesbian as man) have been emphasized in order to undermine them; pejorative labels are emphasized in an effort to get rid of them.[22] But the recognition of paradox, while a significant step, is too often a stopping point of analysis. I want to suggest potentially fruitful paths forward, through research and theorizing that take the queer dilemma to heart.

The recent revival of sociological interest in collective identity has brought important challenges to earlier assumptions that identities were either irrational (and irrelevant) or antecedents to action. Yet, even as theorizing has recognized that collective identities are achieved in and through movement activity, the assumption has remained that the impetus to solidify, mobilize, and deploy an identity is the only rational one. The suggestion of most social-movement theory, sometimes assumed and sometimes explicit, is that secure boundaries and a clear group identity are achievable, and even more importantly, that "if a group fails in [these], it cannot accomplish any collective action" (Klandermans 1992: 81); without a solid group identity, no claims can be made. These theories cannot have little to say about the queer impulse to blur, deconstruct, and destabilize group categories. Current theories take hold of only one horn of the dilemma: the political utility of solid collective categories.

Serious consideration of queerness as a logic of action can force important revisions in approaches to collective identity formation and deployment, and their relationship to political gains. First, it calls attention to the fact that *secure boundaries and stabilized identities are necessary not in general, but in the specific*—a point current social-movement theory largely misses. The link between the two logics, the ways in which the American political environment makes stable collective identities both necessary and damaging, is sorely undertheorized and underexamined.

More importantly, accommodating the complexity of queer activism and theory requires sociology to revisit the claim that social movements are engaged in simply constructing collective identities. Queer movements pose the challenge of a form of organizing in which, far from inhibiting accomplishments, the *destabilization of collective identity is itself a goal and accomplishment of collective action*. When this dynamic is taken into account, new questions arise. The question of how collective identities are negotiated, constructed, and stabilized, for example, becomes transformed into a somewhat livelier one: for whom, when, and how are stable collective identities *necessary* for social action and social change? Do some identity movements in fact avoid the tendency to take themselves apart?

Investigating social movements with the queer predicament in mind, moreover, brings attention to repertoires and forms of action that work with the dilemma in different ways. At the heart of the dilemma is the simultaneity of cultural sources of oppression (which make loosening categories a smart strategy) and institutional sources of oppression (which make tightening categories a smart strategy). Are some movements or movement repertoires more able to work with, rather than against, the simultaneity of these systems of oppression? When and how might deconstructive strategies take aim at institutional forms, and when and how can ethnic strategies take aim at cultural categories? Are there times when the strategies are effectively linked, when an ethnic maneuver loosens cultural categories,[23] or when a deconstructionist tactic simultaneously takes aim at regulatory institutions?[24]

Such questions can point the way towards novel understandings and evaluations of social movements in which collective identity is both pillaged and deployed. They are not a path out of the dilemma, but a path in. The fact that the predicament may be inescapable is, after all, the point: first to clearly see the horns of the dilemma, and then to search out ways for understanding political actions taking place poised, and sometimes skewered, on those horns.

Notes

My thanks to Steven Epstein, William Gamson, Arlene Stein, Verta Taylor, Jeffrey Escoffier, Cathy Cohen, Mark Blasius, Roger Lancaster and Matthew Rottnek.

1. Although I am discussing them together because of their joint struggle against the "sex/gender system" (Rubin 1975) on the basis of same-sex desire, lesbians and gay men have long histories of autonomous organizing (Adam 1987; D'Emilio 1983). Gender has been the strongest division historically in movements for gay and lesbian rights and liberation, not surprisingly, given the very different ways in which male homosexuality and lesbianism have been constructed and penalized. This division is taken up explicitly later in the discussion.

2. In this discussion, I am heeding recent calls to bring sociology into contact with queer theory and politics (Seidman 1994). It has taken a bit of time for sociologists and other social scientists to join queer theoretical discussions, which although they emerged primarily from and through humanities scholars, could hardly be "imagined in their present forms, absent the contributions of sociological theory" (Epstein 1994: 2). On the relationship between sociology of sexuality and queer theory, see also Stein and Plummer (1994); Namaste (1994).

3. I borrow this term from Seidman (1993).

4. See, for example, Di Stefano (1990); Bordo (1990); Davis (1991).

5. Collective identity is variously defined. I am using it here to designate not only a "status—a set of attitudes, commitments, and rules for behavior—that those who assume the identity can be expected to subscribe to," but also "an individual pronouncement of affiliation, of connection with others" (Friedman and McAdam 1992: 157). See also Schlesinger (1987).

6. There is no reason to limit this claim to "identity-based" movements, although identity construction is more visible and salient in such movements. As Taylor and Whittier argue in reviewing existing scholarship, "identity construction processes are crucial to grievance interpretation in all forms of collective action, not just in the so-called new movements" (1992: 105).

7. Queer Nation, formed in 1990, is an offshoot of the AIDS activist organization ACT UP. Queer Nation owes much to ACT UP, in its emergence, its personnel, and its tactics, which are often to "cross borders, to occupy spaces, and to mime the privileges of normality" (Berlant and Freeman 1993: 195). On similar tactics within ACT UP, see Gamson (1989). On Queer Nation specifically, and queer politics more generally, see Bérubé and Escoffier (1991); Duggan (1992); Stein (1992); Cunningham (1992); Patton (1993); Browning (1993; esp. chs 2, 3, and 5).

8. See e.g. Rich (1980); Moraga (1983); Hemphill (1991); Clarke (1983); Reid-Pharr (1993).

9. Although social-constructionist thought generally informs queer theory, it is important to distinguish different strands of constructionist work and their varying contributions to the development of sexual theory. Much constructionist history and sociology, which concerned "the origin, social meaning, and changing forms of the modern homosexual" and challenged essentialist notions of homosexuality, was also "often tied to a politics of the making of a homosexual minority" (Seidman 1994: 171; see e.g. D'Emilio 1983; Faderman 1981). Poststructuralist writing on gender and sexuality, although often looking quite similar, tends to "shift the debate somewhat away from explaining the modern homosexual to questions of the operation of the hetero/homosexual binary, from an exclusive preoccupation with homosexuality to a focus on heterosexuality as a social and political organizing principle, and from a politics of minority interest to a politics of knowledge and difference" (Seidman 1994: 192; see also Epstein 1994; Namaste 1994; Warner 1993; Hennessy 1993).

It is this latter strand that has most strongly informed queer theory. Eve Kosofsky Sedgwick's *Epistemology of the Closet*, with its famous assertion that "an understanding of virtually any aspect of modern Western culture must be, not merely incomplete, but damaged in its central substance to the degree that it does not incorporate a critical analysis of modern homo/heterosexual definition" (1990: 1), is now often taken as the founding moment of queer theory; Judith Butler's *Gender Trouble* (1989) also made a tremendous impact in the field. For further examples of queer-theoretical work, see Fuss (1991); de Lauretis (1991); Butler (1993). These theoretical and political developments in the field of lesbian and gay studies also draw from and overlap with similar ones in feminism. See Ingraham (1994), and the essays in Nicholson (1990).

10. Although its most familiar recent usage has been as an anti-gay epithet, the word actually has a long and complex history. Along with "fairy," for example, "queer"

was one of the most common terms used before World War II, "by 'queer' and 'normal' people alike to refer to 'homosexuals.'" In the 1920s and 1930s, "the men who identified themselves as part of a distinct category of men primarily on the basis of their homosexual interest rather than their womanlike gender status usually called themselves queer" (Chauncey 1994: 14, 16). Whether as chosen marker or as epithet, the word has always retained its general connotation of abnormality (Chauncey 1994).

11. On assimilation–separation before Stonewall, see D'Emilio (1983); Adam (1987). On assimilation–separation after Stonewall, see Epstein (1987).

12. Indeed, the "outlaw" stance may help explain why gender differences are (somewhat) less salient in queer organizing (Duggan 1992). Whereas in ethnic/essentialist lesbian and gay organizations participants are recruited as gay men and lesbian women, in queer organizations they are recruited largely as *gender outlaws*.

13. There is no question that part of what has happened with queer activism is simply the construction of a new, if contentious, collective identity: Queer Nation, with its nationalist rhetoric, is one clear example. My point, however (developed below), is not that queer indicates a group with no boundaries, but that it indicates a strategy of identity destabilization. This logic is not confined to a particular group formation; although it is considerably stronger in groups identifying as queer, many of which are loose associations that are very intentionally decentralized (Williams 1993), it is also often present in more mainstream organizing, albeit in more occasional and muted form. Queer is more useful, I am suggesting, as a description of a particular action logic than as a description of an empirically distinguishable movement form.

14. This questioning is not entirely unique to recent queer politics, but has historical ties to early gay-liberation calls to "liberate the homosexual in everyone" (Epstein 1987). That the current queer formulations have such affinities with earlier political activity underlines that queerness is less a new historical development than an action impulse that comes to the fore at certain historical moments. There is certainly a difference in degree, however, between the strength of a queer-style politic now and in earlier decades: with a few exceptions, earlier lesbian-feminist and gay-liberationist discourses rarely questioned "the notion of homosexuality as a universal category of the self and a sexual identity" (Seidman 1994: 170).

15. On "queer straights," self-identifying heterosexuals who seek out and participate in lesbian and gay subcultures, see Powers (1993).

16. For more bisexuality debate, see Wilson (1992) and Queen (1992).

17. For articulations of these young movements see, on bisexual organizing, Hutchins and Kaahumanu (1991), and on transgender organizing, Stone (1991).

18. For a more developed version of these arguments, see Bornstein (1994).

19. See also Shapiro (1991) on the ways in which transsexualism is simultaneously conservative of sex and gender organization.

20. On lesbian feminism, see Phelan (1989); Taylor and Whittier (1992); Taylor and Rupp (1993).

21. I am indebted here to Steven Seidman's discussion and critique of queer theory and politics, which makes some of the same points from different directions (Seidman 1993; see also Patton 1993; Vance 1988). I want to push the discussion towards the ground, however, to open up questions for political action and empirical research.

22. On this dynamic, see Weeks (1985; esp. ch. 8); Epstein (1987); Gamson (1989).
23. The public pursuit of same-sex marriage and parenting may be an example of this. On the one hand, the call for institutions of "family" to include lesbians and gays—as a recognizably separate species—is quite conservative of existing gender and sexual categories. It often appears as mimicry, and its proponents typically appear as close to "normal" as possible: Bob and Rod Jackson-Paris, for example, a former body-builder/model married couple who have been the most publicly available symbol of gay marriage, are both conventionally masculine, "traded vows in a commitment ceremony, share a house in Seattle, and plan to raise children" (Bull 1993: 42).

      Yet gay families, in attacking the gender requirements of family forms, attack the cultural grounding of normality at its heart (as the religious right fully recognizes). If and when family institutions, pushed by ethnic/essentialist identity movements, shift to integrate gays and lesbians, the very markers of gay/straight difference start to disintegrate (see Weston 1991). If bodily erotic desire implies nothing in particular about the use of one's body for reproduction, its usefulness as a basis of social categories is largely gutted. In this, the gay family strategy may also be a queer one. To the degree that it succeeds, to the degree that the institution of the family changes, the categories must also lose much of their sense—and their power. This may not be true of all ethnic/essentialist actions.

24. The AIDS activist group ACT UP provides a promising starting point from this direction. Much of ACT UP's tactics have been discursive: meaning deconstruction, boundary crossing, and label disruption (Gamson 1989). Yet, for reasons obviously related to the immediacy of AIDS and the visible involvement of medical and state institutions, it has rarely been possible to make the argument that AIDS politics should have as its goal the deconstruction of meanings of sex, sexual identity, and disease. In much queer AIDS activism, the disruption of these meanings takes place through direct targeting of their institutional purveyors: not only media and other cultural institutions, but science, medicine, and government (Epstein 1991).

      For example, interventions into some spaces (medical conferences as opposed to opera houses) put queerness, its sometimes scary confrontation, its refusal to identify itself as a fixed gay or lesbian subject, its disruption of sex and gender boundaries, to use in ways that clearly mark the dangers of institutional control of sexual categories. Refusing the categories for itself, this strategy names and confronts the agents that fix the categories in dangerous, violent, and deadly ways. To the degree that the strategy succeeds, to the degree that cultural categories become frightening and nonsensical, institutional actors—and not just the vague and ubiquitous purveyors of "normality"—must also be called upon to justify their use of the categories.

References

Adam, Barry. 1987. *The Rise of a Gay and Lesbian Movement*. Boston: Twayne.

Alba, Richard. 1990. *Ethnic Identity: The Transformation of White America*. New Haven: Yale University Press.

Berlant, Lauren and Elizabeth Freeman. 1993. "Queer Nationality." In M. Warner, Ed., *Fear of a Queer Planet*. Minneapolis: University of Minnesota Press.

Bérubé, Allan and Jeffrey Escoffier. 1991. "Queer/Nation." *Out/Look* (winter).

Bordo, Susan. 1990. "Feminism, Postmodernism, and Gender-Scepticism." In L. Nicholson, ed., *Feminism/Postmodernism*. New York: Routledge.

Bornstein, Kate. 1994. *Gender Outlaw*. New York: Routledge.

———. 1992. "A Plan for Peace." *San Francisco Bay Times*, Dec. 3, p. 4.

Browning, Frank. 1993. *The Culture of Desire*. New York: Vintage.

Bull, Chris. 1993. "Till Death Do Us Part." *The Advocate* (Nov. 30), pp. 40–7.

Butler, Judith. 1993. "Critically Queer." *GLO*, 1: 17–32.

———. 1990. "Gender Trouble, Feminist Theory, and Psychoanalytic Discourse." In L. Nicholson, ed., *Feminism/Postmodernism*. New York: Routledge.

———. 1989. *Gender Trouble: Feminism and the Subversion of Identity*. New York: Routledge.

Chauncey, George. 1994. *Gay New York*. New York: Basic.

Chee, Alexander. 1991. "A Queer Nationalism." *Out/Look* (winter): 15–19.

Clarke, Cheryl. 1983. "Lesbianism: An Act of Resistance." In G. Anzaldua and C. Moraga, eds, *The Bridge Called My Back*. New York: Kitchen Table Press.

Cohen, Jean. 1985. "Strategy or Identity: New Theoretical Paradigms and Contemporary Social Movements." *Social Research*, 52: 663–716.

Cunningham, Michael. 1992. "If You're Queer and You're Not Angry in 1992, You're Not Paying Attention." *Mother Jones* (May/June).

Davis, F. James. 1991. *Who Is Black? One Nation's Definition*. University Park, Penn.: Pennsylvania State University Press.

D'Emilio, John. 1983. *Sexual Politics, Sexual Communities: The Making of a Homosexual Minority in the United States, 1940–1970*. Chicago: University of Chicago Press.

de Lauretis, Teresa (ed.) 1991. *Queer Theory*. Special Issue of *differences* (summer).

Di Stefano, Christine. 1990. "Dilemmas of Difference: Feminism, Modernity, and Postmodernism." In L. Nicholson, ed., *Feminism/Postmodernism*. New York: Routledge.

Duggan, Lisa. 1992. "Making It Perfectly Queer." *Socialist Review* (Jan.–Mar.).

Epstein, Steven. 1994. "A Queer Encounter: Sociology and the Study of Sexuality." *Sociological Theory*, 12 (2) (July): 188–202.

———. 1991. "Democratic Science? AIDS Activism and the Contested Construction of Knowledge." *Socialist Review*, 21 (2) (April–June): 35–64.

———. 1987. "Gay Politics, Ethnic Identity: The Limits of Social Constructionism." *Socialist Review*, 93/94: 9–54.

Espiritu, Yen. 1992. *Asian American Panethnicity: Bridging Institutions and Identities*. Philadelphia: Temple University Press.

Faderman, Lillian. 1981. *Surpassing the Love of Men*. New York: Morrow.

Franzen, Trisha. 1993. "Differences and Identities: Feminism in the Albuquerque Lesbian Community." *Signs*, 18 (4) (summer): 891–906.

Friedman, Debra and Doug McAdam. 1992. "Collective Identity and Activism." In A. Morris and C. M. Mueller, eds, *Frontiers in Social Movement Theory*. New Haven: Yale University Press.

Fuss, Diana (ed.) 1991. *Inside/Out*. New York: Routledge.

———. 1989. *Essentially Speaking: Feminism, Nature, and Difference*. New York: Routledge.

Gamson, Josh. 1989. "Silence, Death, and the Invisible Enemy: AIDS Activism and Social Movement 'Newness.'" *Social Problems*, 36 (4) (Oct.): 351–67.

Gamson, William. 1992. "The Social Psychology of Collective Action." In A. Morris and C. M. Mueller, eds, *Frontiers in Social Movement Theory*. New Haven: Yale University Press.

Garber, Marjorie. 1992. *Vested Interests: Cross-Dressing and Cultural Anxiety*. New York: Routledge.

Hemphill, Essex (ed.) 1991. *Brother to Brother*. Boston: Alyson.

Hennessy, Rosemary. 1993. "Queer Theory: A Review of the *differences* Special Issue and Wittig's *The Straight Mind.*" *Signs*, 18 (4) (summer): 964–73.

Hutchins, Loraine and Lani Kaahumanu (eds) 1991. *Bi Any Other Name*. Boston: Alyson.

Ingraham, Chrys. 1994. "The Heterosexual Imaginary: Feminist Sociology and Theories of Gender." *Sociological Theory*, 12 (2) (July): 203–19.

Kauffman, L. A. 1990. "The Anti-Politics of Identity." *Socialist Review*, 20 (1) (Jan.–Mar.): 67–80.

Klandermans, Bert. 1992. "The Social Construction of Protest and Multiorganizational Fields." In A. Morris and C. M. Mueller, eds, *Frontiers in Social Movement Theory*. New Haven: Yale University Press.

Marcus, Eric. 1993. "What's In a Name." *10 Percent* (winter): 14–15.

Melucci, Alberto. 1989. *Nomads of the Present: Social Movements and Individual Needs in Contemporary Society*. Philadelphia: Temple University Press.

Minkowitz, Donna. 1993. "Trial By Science." *Village Voice* (Nov. 30): 27–9.

Moraga, Cherrie. 1983. *Loving in the War Years*. Boston: South End Press.

Mueller, Carol McClurg. 1992. "Building Social Movement Theory." In A. Morris and C. M. Mueller, eds, *Frontiers in Social Movement Theory*. New Haven: Yale University Press.

Nagel, Joane. 1994. "Constructing Ethnicity: Creating and Recreating Ethnic Identity and Culture." *Social Problems*, 41 (1) (Feb.): 152–76.

Namaste, Ki. 1994. "The Politics of Inside/Out: Queer Theory, Poststructuralism, and a Sociological Approach to Sexuality." *Sociological Theory*, 12 (2) (July): 220–31.

Nicholson, Linda (ed.) 1990. *Feminism/Postmodernism*. New York: Routledge.

Omi, Michael and Howard Winant. 1986. *Racial Formation in the United States*. New York: Routledge and Kegan Paul.

Padilla, Felix. 1985. *Latino Ethnic Consciousness: The Case of Mexican Americans and Puerto Ricans in Chicago*. Notre Dame: University of Notre Dame Press.

Patton, Cindy. 1993. "Tremble, Hetero Swine!" In M. Warner, ed., *Fear of a Queer Planet*. Minneapolis: University of Minnesota Press.

Phelan, Shane. 1993. "(Be)Coming Out: Lesbian Identity and Politics." *Signs*, 18 (4): 765–90.

———. 1989. *Identity Politics: Lesbian Feminism and the Limits of Community*. Philadelphia: Temple University Press.

Powers, Ann. 1993. "Queer in the Streets, Straight in the Sheets: Notes on Passing." *Utne Reader* (Nov./Dec.).

Queen, Carol. 1992. "Strangers at Home: Bisexuals in the Queer Movement." *Out/Look* (spring).

Rant, Miss. 1993. "Queer Is Not a Substitute for Gay." *Rant & Rave*, 1 (1) (autumn): 15.

Reid-Pharr, Robert. 1993. "The Spectacle of Blackness." *Radical America*, 24(4) (April): 57–66.

Rich, Adrienne. 1980. "Compulsory Heterosexuality and Lesbian Existence." *Signs*, 5(4): 631–60.

Rubin, Gayle. 1975. "The Traffic in Women." In R. Reiter, ed., *Toward an Anthropology of Women*. New York: Monthly Review Press.

Schlesinger, Philip. 1987. "On National Identity: Some Conceptions and Misconceptions Criticized." *Social Science Information*, 26(2): 219–64.

Sedgwick, Eve Kosofsky. 1990. *Epistemology of the Closet*. Berkeley: University of California Press.

Seidman, Steven. 1994. "Symposium: Queer Theory/Sociology: A Dialogue." *Sociological Theory*, 12(2) (July): 166–77.

———. 1993. "Identity Politics in a 'Postmodern' Gay Culture: Some Historical and Conceptual Notes." In M. Warner, ed., *Fear of a Queer Planet*. Minneapolis: University of Minnesota Press.

Shapiro, Judith. 1991. "Transsexualism: Reflections on the Persistence of Gender and the Mutability of Sex." In J. Epstein and K. Straub, eds, *Body Guards*. New York: Routledge.

Stein, Arlene. 1992. "Sisters and Queers: The Decentering of Lesbian Feminism." *Socialist Review* (Jan.–Mar.).

——— and Ken Plummer. 1994. " 'I Can't Even Think Straight': 'Queer' Theory and the Missing Sexual Revolution in Sociology." *Sociological Theory*, 12 (2) (July): 178–87.

Stone, Sandy. 1991. "The *Empire* Strikes Back: A Posttranssexual Manifesto." In J. Epstein and K. Straub, eds, *Body Guards*. New York: Routledge.

Taylor, Verta and Leila Rupp. 1993. "Women's Culture and Lesbian Feminist Activism: A Reconsideration of Cultural Feminism." *Signs*, 19 (1) (Autumn): 32–61.

——— and Nancy Whittier. 1992. "Collective Identity in Social Movement Communities." In A. Morris and C. M. Mueller, eds, *Frontiers in Social Movement Theory*. New Haven: Yale University Press.

Vance, Carole S. 1988. "Social Construction Theory: Problems in the History of Sexuality." In D. Altman et al., *Homosexuality, Which Homosexuality?* London: GMP Publishers.

Warner, Michael (ed.) 1993. *Fear of a Queer Planet: Queer Politics and Social Theory*. Minneapolis: University of Minnesota Press, 1993.

Waters, Mary. 1990. *Ethnic Options: Choosing Identities in America*. Berkeley: University of California Press.

Webster, Yehudi. 1992. *The Racialization of America*. New York: St. Martin's Press.

Weeks, Jeffrey. 1985. *Sexuality and Its Discontents*. New York: Routledge.

Weston, Kath. 1991. *Families We Choose: Lesbians, Gays, Kinship*. New York: Columbia University Press.

Williams, Andrea. 1993. "Queers in the Castro." Unpublished paper, Dept of Anthropology, Yale University.

Wilson, Ara. 1992. "Just Add Water: Searching for the Bisexual Politic." *Out/Look* (spring).

Wright, Lawrence. 1994. "One Drop of Blood." *The New Yorker*, July 25, pp. 46–55.

Questions for Reflection, Discussion, and Writing

1. Gamson identifies two ways of understanding lesbian and gay identity: ethnic/essentialist and deconstructionist. Who tends to voice arguments both for and against these categories? On what are those arguments based? According to Gamson, what is at stake?

2. Groups who identify as lesbian, bisexual, transgender, transsexual are all imbricated in the debate over the appropriation of the term "queer." As evidenced by the editorials Gamson references, what are the arguments members of each group raise, and what stake does each group have in the debate?

3. What do identity politics enable, politically, and socially? What are some of their limitations and omissions?

4. According to Gamson, what are some of the structural fault lines in queer theory's deconstruction of sexual identity?

5. According to Gamson, what is "the queer dilemma" about identity politics?

Writing Assignment

Most of us do not identify one single characteristic that constitutes our "self." Instead, many of us belong to several organizations and we sometimes embody seemingly contradictory identities. We select some of our beliefs, friends, likes, dislikes and identities from multiple sources. We are born or "placed" into other categories by virtue of biological sex, sexuality, skin color, ethnicity, geographic location, economic status, and family of origin. Sometimes, we can choose to reject or change these; other times we accept or modify them. As you work through this series of prompts, pay attention to those seeming contradictions, for they often contain "rich" material; they are the intersections of belief systems and parts of our identities.

Who are you? Begin by brainstorming a series of lists. Start each list with a different prompt:

1. I am ....
2. I do ....
3. I have ....
4. I own ....
5. I believe ....
6. I hope ....
7. I like ....

8. I dislike ....
9. I used to think .... but now I think .... because ....
10. I want. .. ..
11. I belong to .... because ....

Choose two seemingly contradictory beliefs, ideas, or identities from the list you have generated. Explain how these two elements are or aren't contradictory. How do you reconcile these two elements of your self? When is each present? Do you call upon certain aspects of self under particular circumstances? When and where?

Related Reading

Alisa Solomon, "Breaking Out" and "Identity Crisis: Queer Politics in the Age of Possibilities." [Interview with Marcellus Blount, Gregg Bordowitz, Holly Hughes, Jeff Nunokawa and Eve Sedgwick] *Village Voice*, June 30, 1992. 27–29, 33.

Steven Seidman, "Identity and Politics in a 'Postmodern' Gay Culture: Some Historical and Conceptual Notes" in *Fear of a Queer Planet*. Michael Warner, Ed. NY: Routledge. 1993. 105–142.

Marylynne Diggs, "Surveying the Intersection: Pathology, Secrecy, and the Discourses of Racial and Sexual Identity." *Journal of Homosexuality 26*.2–3 (August–September 1993): 1–18.

Kobena Mercer, "Welcome to the Jungle: Identity and Diversity in Postmodern Politics" in *Welcome to the Jungle: New Positions in Black Cultural Studies*. NY: Routledge. 1994. 259–285.

Ki Namaste, "The Politics of Inside/Out: Queer Theory, Poststructuralism, and a Sociological Approach to Sexuality." *Sociological Theory 12*.2 (July 1994): 220–231.

Sharon Smith, "Mistaken Identity—Or Can Identity Politics Liberate the Oppressed?" *International Socialism* (Spring 1994): 12–21.

Arlene Stein and Ken Plummer, "'I Can't Even Think Straight': 'Queer' Theory and the Missing Sexual Revolution in Sociology" in *Queer Theory/Sociology*. Steven Seidman, Ed. Cambridge, MA: Blackwell. 1996. 129–144.

Steven Epstein, "A Queer Encounter: Sociology and the Study of Sexuality" in *Queer Theory/Sociology*. Steven Seidman, Ed. Cambridge, MA: Blackwell. 1996. 145–167.

Frank Browning, "Do Gays Exist" in *A Queer Geography: Journeys Toward A Sexual Self*. New York: Crown, 1996. 11–48.

Lance Selfa, "What's Wrong With 'Identity Politics'" in *The Material Queer*. Donald Morten, Ed. Boulder, CO: Westview Press. 1996. 46–48.

Jewell L. Gomez, "The Event of Becoming" in *A Queer World*. Martin Duberman, Ed. NY: NYUP. 1997. 17–23.

Phililip Brian Harper. "Gay Male Identities, Personal Privacy and Relations of Public Exchange: Notes on Directions for Queer Critique." *Social Text* 52–53 (Fall/Winter 1997): 5–29.

Carla Trujillo, "Sexual Identity and the Discontents of Difference" in *Ethnic and Cultural Diversity Among Lesbians and Gay Men*. Beverly Greene, Ed. Thousand Oaks, CA: Sage Publications. 1997. 266–278.

D. Travers Scott, "Le Freak, C'est Chic! Le Fag, Quelle Drag!: Celebrating the Collapse of Homosexual Identity" in *PoMoSexuals: Challenging Assumptions About Gender and Sexuality*. Carol Queen and Lawrence Schimel, Eds. San Francisco, CA: Cleis Press. 1997. 62–68.

Kath Weston, *Long Slow Burn: Sexuality and Social Science*. NY: Routledge. 1998.

Baden Offord and Leon Cantrell, "Unfixed in a Fixated World: Identity, Sexuality, Race and Culture." *Journal of Homosexuality* 36.3/4 (1999): 207–220.

Sean P. O'Connell, *Outspeak: Narrating Identities That Matter*. Albany: SUNY Press. 2000.

M.N. Lance and A. Tanesini, "Identity Judgments, Queer Politics." *Radical Philosophy* 100 (2000): 42–51.

Web Resource

http://alexia.Lis.uiuc.edu/~Kroberto/queer

SECTION FOUR

(De)/(Re)Gendering Sexualities

Gayle Rubin's groundbreaking 1984 essay "Thinking Sex" brought into stark relief many of the social and political divisions about sexuality and gender that had festered under the surface of the gay and lesbian community for quite some time. Rubin's essential argument—that there exists a hierarchy of acceptable sexual behavior subject to historical change and social reinterpretation—had the effect of highlighting sexual hierarchies of normative and non-normative behaviors both in society at large, and especially within the gay and lesbian community itself. In examining this sexual stratification, Rubin looked critically at the taboos and the prejudices that swirled around transvestites, transsexuals, fetishists, sadomasochists, and sex workers in particular. Her interrogation of sexual norms mirrored a debate that arose throughout the United States whenever gay pride parades were held: whether or not bisexuals, drag queens, and transgendered people should be included in the planning and promotion of the event and, in some cases, whether or not they should march at all.

One of the more positive effects of queer theory has been the way it has helped to open up an ongoing dialogue about discrimination based on some unnamed conception of what is normative. For years, bisexuals have felt excluded from and rejected by the gay and lesbian community, treated as dabblers in same-sex relationships who will return to sanctioned heterosexual relationships when the going gets rough, as "wannabes," and even as "hasbians," a term applied to women who have left lesbian relationships to be with men. Drag queens and transgendered people have also been the objects of discrimination both in a heteronormative society and in the gay and lesbian community as well, challenging, as they inevitably do, the conventions of what is the "proper" expression of gender or, in the case of transgendered people, whether categories of gender adequately suffice any longer to encompass the range of human expressivity. As Judith Butler argues in her important 1991 essay, "Imitation and Gender Insubordination," *all gender is performative*, and all manifestations of gender across the spectrum are imitations for which there is *no* original. Butler's insight has had a profound effect on queer theory, helping to foster a climate in which there is a regard for and an embrace of differences beyond the tight boundary of what is, and is not, "gay" and "lesbian." We have,

it seems, finally begun to understand that homonormativity can be as dangerously distorting and destructive a social force as heteronormativity.

Gender and sexuality are inextricably intertwined in queer theory for, of
course, homosexuality itself is based on the notion of a sexual preference for a
gender that deviates from the norm. The essays throughout this section all address, to some degree, the rich and varied continuum of sexual and gender expression in a queer world today. Female masculinity, male femininity, intersex,
drag, and transgender all push the boundaries of how we understand gender,
and about how desires are organized around attractions that may sometimes
seem familiar and may, in some instances, startle and discomfit. Queer theory
has made its most politically powerful impact in the arena of gender and sexuality, deconstructing the walls of normativity that we have been taught to erect as
a barrier in what Rubin would define as our sex negative society. As these walls
weaken and perhaps even collapse, as we begin to struggle with what expansion
and greater inclusion might mean, as we grow increasingly unafraid of the difference that manifests itself in human self-representation and sexual attraction,
we will begin to dismantle the legacy of discrimination, criminalization, and
pain that has for so long ostracized too many members of our human family.
There is indeed room enough for all of us in the parade.

Thinking Sex: Notes
for a Radical Theory
of the Politics of Sexuality

Gayle Rubin

Gayle S. Rubin, "Thinking Sex: Notes for a Radical Theory of the Politics of Sexuality" in *Pleasure
And Danger: Exploring Female Sexuality*. Carole S. Vance, Ed. Boston: Routledge & Kegan Paul,
1984, 267–319. Reprinted by permission of the author.

I   The Sex Wars

> *Asked his advice, Dr. J. Guerin affirmed that, after all other treatments had
> failed, he had succeeded in curing young girls affected by the vice of onanism by
> burning the clitoris with a hot iron. . . . I apply the hot point three times to each of
> the large labia and another on the clitoris. . . . After the first operation, from forty
> to fifty times a day, the number of voluptuous spasms was reduced to three or
> four. . . . We believe, then, that in cases similar to those submitted to your consider-*

ation, one should not hesitate to resort to the hot iron, and at an early hour, in order to combat clitoral and vaginal onanism in little girls.

Demetrius Zambaco[1]

The time has come to think about sex. To some, sexuality may seem to be an unimportant topic, a frivolous diversion from the more critical problems of poverty, war, disease, racism, famine, or nuclear annihilation. But it is precisely at times such as these, when we live with the possibility of unthinkable destruction, that people are likely to become dangerously crazy about sexuality. Contemporary conflicts over sexual values and erotic conduct have much in common with the religious disputes of earlier centuries. They acquire immense symbolic weight. Disputes over sexual behavior often become the vehicles for displacing social anxieties, and discharging their attendant emotional intensity. Consequently, sexuality should be treated with special respect in times of great social stress.

The realm of sexuality also has its own internal politics, inequities, and modes of oppression. As with other aspects of human behavior, the concrete institutional forms of sexuality at any given time and place are products of human activity. They are imbued with conflicts of interest and political maneuvering, both deliberate and incidental. In that sense, sex is always political. But there are also historical periods in which sexuality is more sharply contested and more overtly politicized. In such periods, the domain of erotic life is, in effect, renegotiated.

In England and the United States, the late nineteenth century was one such era. During that time, powerful social movements focused on "vices" of all sorts. There were educational and political campaigns to encourage chastity, to eliminate prostitution, and to discourage masturbation, especially among the young. Morality crusaders attacked obscene literature, nude paintings, music halls, abortion, birth control information, and public dancing.[2] The consolidation of Victorian morality, and its apparatus of social, medical, and legal enforcement, was the outcome of a long period of struggle whose results have been bitterly contested ever since.

The consequences of these great nineteenth-century moral paroxysms are still with us. They have left a deep imprint on attitudes about sex, medical practice, child-rearing, parental anxieties, police conduct, and sex law.

The idea that masturbation is an unhealthy practice is part of that heritage. During the nineteenth century, it was commonly thought that "premature" interest in sex, sexual excitement, and, above all, sexual release, would impair the health and maturation of a child. Theorists differed on the actual consequences of sexual precocity. Some thought it led to insanity, while others merely predicted stunted growth. To protect the young from premature arousal, parents tied children down at night so they would not touch themselves; doctors excised the clitorises of onanistic little girls.[3] Although the more gruesome techniques have been abandoned, the attitudes that produced them persist. The notion that sex *per se* is harmful to the young has been chiseled into extensive social and legal structures designed to insulate minors from sexual knowledge and experience.

Much of the sex law currently on the books also dates from the nineteenth-century morality crusades. The first federal anti-obscenity law in the United States was passed in 1873. The Comstock Act—named for Anthony Comstock, an ancestral anti-porn activist and the founder of the New York Society for the Suppression of Vice—made it a federal crime to make, advertise, sell, possess, send through the mails, or import books or pictures deemed obscene. The law also banned contraceptive or abortifacient drugs and devices and information about them.[4] In the wake of the federal statute, most states passed their own anti-obscenity laws.

The Supreme Court began to whittle down both federal and state Comstock laws during the 1950s. By 1975, the prohibition of materials used for, and information about, contraception and abortion had been ruled unconstitutional. However, although the obscenity provisions have been modified, their fundamental constitutionality has been upheld. Thus it remains a crime to make, sell, mail, or import material which has no purpose other than sexual arousal.[5]

Although sodomy statutes date from older strata of the law, when elements of canon law were adopted into civil codes, most of the laws used to arrest homosexuals and prostitutes come out of the Victorian campaigns against "white slavery." These campaigns produced myriad prohibitions against solicitation, lewd behavior, loitering for immoral purposes, age offenses, and brothels and bawdy houses.

In her discussion of the British "white slave" scare, historian Judith Walkowitz observes that: "Recent research delineates the vast discrepancy between lurid journalistic accounts and the reality of prostitution. Evidence of widespread entrapment of British girls in London and abroad is slim."[6] However, public furor over this ostensible problem

> forced the passage of the Criminal Law Amendment Act of 1885, a particularly nasty and pernicious piece of omnibus legislation. The 1885 Act raised the age of consent for girls from 13 to 16, but it also gave police far greater summary jurisdiction over poor working-class women and children . . . it contained a clause making indecent acts between consenting male adults a crime, thus forming the basis of legal prosecution of male homosexuals in Britain until 1967 . . . the clauses of the new bill were mainly enforced against working-class women, and regulated adult rather than youthful sexual behaviour.[7]

In the United States, the Mann Act, also known as the White Slave Traffic Act, was passed in 1910. Subsequently, every state in the union passed anti-prostitution legislation.[8]

In the 1950s, in the United States, major shifts in the organization of sexuality took place. Instead of focusing on prostitution or masturbation, the anxieties of the 1950s condensed most specifically around the image of the "homosexual menace" and the dubious specter of the "sex offender." Just before and after World War II, the "sex offender" became an object of public fear and scrutiny. Many states and cities, including Massachusetts, New Hampshire, New Jersey, New York State, New York City and Michigan, launched investigations to gather information about this menace to public safety.[9] The term "sex offender" sometimes applied to rapists, sometimes to "child molesters," and eventually functioned as a code for homosexuals. In its bureaucratic, medical, and popular versions, the sex offender discourse tended to blur distinctions between violent sexual assault and illegal but consensual acts such as sodomy. The criminal justice system incorporated these concepts when an epidemic of sexual psychopath laws swept through state legislatures.[10] These laws gave the psychological professions increased police powers over homosexuals and other sexual "deviants."

From the late 1940s until the early 1960s, erotic communities whose activities did not fit the postwar American dream drew intense persecution. Homosexuals were, along with communists, the objects of federal witch hunts and purges. Congressional investigations, executive orders, and sensational exposés in the media aimed to root out homosexuals employed by the government. Thousands lost their jobs, and restrictions on federal employment of homosexuals persist to this day.[11] The FBI began systematic surveillance and harassment of homosexuals which lasted at least into the 1970s.[12]

Many states and large cities conducted their own investigations, and the federal witch-hunts were reflected in a variety of local crackdowns. In Boise, Idaho, in 1955, a schoolteacher sat down to breakfast with his morning paper and read that the vice-president of the Idaho First National Bank had been arrested on felony sodomy charges; the local prosecutor said that he intended to eliminate all homosexuality from the community. The teacher never finished his breakfast. "He jumped up from his seat, pulled out his suitcases, packed as fast as he could, got into his car, and drove straight to San Francisco. . . . The cold eggs, coffee, and toast remained on his table for two days before someone from his school came by to see what had happened."[13]

In San Francisco, police and media waged war on homosexuals throughout the 1950s. Police raided bars, patrolled cruising areas, conducted street sweeps, and trumpeted their intention of driving the queers out of San Francisco.[14] Crackdowns against gay individuals, bars, and social areas occurred throughout the country. Although anti-homosexual crusades are the best-documented examples of erotic repression in the 1950s, future research should reveal similar patterns of increased harassment against pornographic materials, prostitutes, and erotic deviants of all sorts. Research is needed to determine the full scope of both police persecution and regulatory reform.[15]

The current period bears some uncomfortable similarities to the 1880s and the 1950s. The 1977 campaign to repeal the Dade County, Florida, gay rights ordinance inaugurated a new wave of violence, state persecution, and legal initiatives directed against minority sexual populations and the commercial sex industry. For the last six years, the United States and Canada have undergone an extensive sexual repression in the political, not the psycho-logical, sense. In the spring of 1977, a few weeks before the Dade County vote, the news media were suddenly full of reports of raids on gay cruising areas, ar-rests for prostitution, and investigations into the manufacture and distribution of pornographic materials. Since then, police activity against the gay commu-nity has increased exponentially. The gay press has documented hundreds of ar-rests, from the libraries of Boston to the streets of Houston and the beaches of San Francisco. Even the large, organized, and relatively powerful urban gay communities have been unable to stop these depredations. Gay bars and bath houses have been busted with alarming frequency, and police have gotten bolder. In one especially dramatic incident, police, in Toronto raided all four of the city's gay baths. They broke into cubicles with crowbars and hauled almost 300 men out into the winter streets, clad in their bath towels. Even "liberated" San Francisco has not been immune. There have been proceedings against sev-eral bars, countless arrests in the parks, and, in the fall of 1981, police arrested over 400 people in a series of sweeps of Polk Street, one of the thoroughfares of local gay nightlife. Queerbashing has become a significant recreational activity for young urban males. They come into gay neighborhoods armed with base-ball bats and looking for trouble, knowing that the adults in their lives either se-cretly approve or will look the other way.

The police crackdown has not been limited to homosexuals. Since 1977, enforcement of existing laws against prostitution and obscenity has been stepped up. Moreover, states and municipalities have been passing new and tighter regulations on commercial sex. Restrictive ordinances have been passed, zoning laws altered, licensing and safety codes amended, sentences increased, and evidentiary requirements relaxed. This subtle legal codification of more stringent controls over adult sexual behavior has gone largely unnoticed outside of the gay press.

For over a century, no tactic for stirring up erotic hysteria has been as re-liable as the appeal to protect children. The current wave of erotic terror has reached deepest into those areas bordered in some way, if only symbolically, by the sexuality of the young. The motto of the Dade County repeal campaign was "Save Our Children" from alleged homosexual recruitment. In February 1977, shortly before the Dade County vote, a sudden concern with "child pornogra-phy" swept the national media. In May, the *Chicago Tribune* ran a lurid four-day series with three-inch headlines, which claimed to expose a national vice ring organized to lure young boys into prostitution and pornography.[16] Newspapers across the country ran similar stories, most of them worthy of the *National En-quirer*. By the end of May, a congressional investigation was underway. Within weeks, the federal government had enacted a sweeping bill against "child pornography" and many of the states followed with bills of their own. These laws have reestablished restrictions on sexual materials that had been relaxed by some of the important Supreme Court decisions. For instance, the Court ruled that neither nudity nor sexual activity *per se* were obscene. But the child pornography laws define as obscene any depiction of minors who are nude or engaged in sexual activity. This means that photographs of naked children in anthropology textbooks and many of the ethnographic movies shown in college classes are technically illegal in several states. In fact, the instructors are liable to an additional felony charge for showing such images to each student under the age of 18. Although the Supreme Court has also ruled that it is a constitutional right to possess obscene material for private use, the child pornography laws prohibit even the private possession of any sexual material involving minors.

The laws produced by the child porn panic are ill-conceived and misdirected. They represent far-reaching alterations in the regulation of sexual behavior and abrogate important sexual civil liberties. But hardly anyone noticed as they swept through Congress and state legislatures. With the exception of the North American Man/Boy Love Association and the American Civil Liberties Union, no one raised a peep of protest.[17]

A new and even tougher federal child pornography bill has just reached House-Senate conference. It removes any requirement that prosecutors must prove that alleged child pornography was distributed for commercial sale. Once this bill becomes law, a person merely possessing a nude snapshot of a 17-year-old lover or friend may go to jail for fifteen years, and be fined $100,000. This bill passed the House 400 to 1.[18]

The experiences of art photographer Jacqueline Livingston exemplify the climate created by the child porn panic. An assistant professor of photography at Cornell University, Livingston was fired in 1978 after exhibiting pictures of male nudes which included photographs of her seven-year-old son masturbating. *Ms. Magazine*, *Chrysalis*, and *Art News* all refused to run ads for Livingston's posters of male nudes. At one point, Kodak confiscated some of her film, and for several months, Livingston lived with the threat of prosecution under the child pornography laws. The Tompkins County Department of Social Services investigated her fitness as a parent. Livingston's posters have been collected by the Museum of Modern Art, the Metropolitan, and other major museums. But she has paid a high cost in harassment and anxiety for her efforts to capture on film the uncensored male body at different ages.[19]

It is easy to see someone like Livingston as a victim of the child porn wars. It is harder for most people to sympathize with actual boy-lovers. Like communists and homosexuals in the 1950s, boy-lovers are so stigmatized that it is difficult to find defenders for their civil liberties, let alone for their erotic orientation. Consequently, the police have feasted on them. Local police, the FBI, and watchdog postal inspectors have joined to build a huge apparatus whose sole aim is to wipe out the community of men who love underaged youth. In twenty years or so, when some of the smoke has cleared, it will be much easier to show that these men have been the victims of a savage and undeserved witch-hunt. A lot of people will be embarrassed by their collaboration with this persecution, but it will be too late to do much good for those men who have spent their lives in prison.

While the misery of the boy-lovers affects very few, the other long-term legacy of the Dade County repeal affects almost everyone. The success of the anti-gay campaign ignited long-simmering passions of the American right, and sparked an extensive movement to compress the boundaries of acceptable sexual behavior.

Right-wing ideology linking non-familial sex with communism and political weakness is nothing new. During the McCarthy period, Alfred Kinsey and his Institute for Sex Research were attacked for weakening the moral fiber of Americans and rendering them more vulnerable to communist influence. After congressional investigations and bad publicity, Kinsey's Rockefeller grant was terminated in 1954.[20]

Around 1969, the extreme right discovered the Sex Information and Education Council of the United States (SIECUS). In books and pamphlets, such as *The Sex Education Racket: Pornography in the Schools and SIECUS: Corrupter of Youth*, the right attacked SIECUS and sex education as communist plots to destroy the family and sap the national will.[21] Another pamphlet, *Pavlov's Children (They May Be Yours)*, claims that the United Nations Educational, Scientific and Cultural Organization (UNESCO) is in cahoots with SIECUS to undermine religious taboos, to promote the acceptance of abnormal sexual relations, to downgrade absolute moral standards, and to "destroy racial cohesion," by exposing white people (especially white women) to the alleged "lower" sexual standards of black people.[22]

New Right and neo-conservative ideology has updated these themes, and leans heavily on linking "immoral" sexual behavior to putative declines in American power. In 1977, Norman Podhoretz wrote an essay blaming homosexuals for the alleged inability of the United States to stand up to the Russians.[23] He thus neatly linked "the anti-gay fight in the domestic arena and the anti-communist battles in foreign policy."[24]

Right-wing opposition to sex education, homosexuality, pornography, abortion, and pre-marital sex moved from the extreme fringes to the political center stage after 1977, when right-wing strategists and fundamentalist religious crusaders discovered that these issues had mass appeal. Sexual reaction played a significant role in the right's electoral success in 1980.[25] Organizations like the Moral Majority and Citizens for Decency have acquired mass followings, immense financial resources, and unanticipated clout. The Equal Rights Amendment has been defeated, legislation has been passed that mandates new restrictions on abortion, and funding for programs like Planned Parenthood and sex education has been slashed. Laws and regulations making it more difficult for teenage girls to obtain contraceptives or abortions have been promulgated. Sexual backlash was exploited in successful attacks on the Women's Studies Program at California State University at Long Beach.

The most ambitious right-wing legislative initiative has been the Family Protection Act (FPA), introduced in Congress in 1979. The Family Protection Act is a broad assault on feminism, homosexuals, non-traditional families, and teenage sexual privacy.[26] The Family Protection Act has not and probably will not pass, but conservative members of Congress continue to pursue its agenda in a more piecemeal fashion. Perhaps the most glaring sign of the times is the Adolescent Family Life Program. Also known as the Teen Chastity Program, it gets some 15 million federal dollars to encourage teenagers to refrain from sexual intercourse, and to discourage them from using contraceptives if they do have sex, and from having abortions if they get pregnant. In the last few years, there have been countless local confrontations over gay rights, sex education, abortion rights, adult bookstores, and public school curricula. It is unlikely that the anti-sex backlash is over, or that it has even peaked. Unless something changes dramatically, it is likely that the next few years will bring more of the same.

Periods such as the 1880s in England, and the 1950s in the United States, recodify the relations of sexuality. The struggles that were fought leave a residue in the form of laws, social practices, and ideologies which then affect the way in which sexuality is experienced long after the immediate conflicts have faded. All the signs indicate that the present era is another of those watersheds in the politics of sex. The settlements that emerge from the 1980s will have an impact far into the future. It is therefore imperative to understand what is going on and what is at stake in order to make informed decisions about what policies to support and oppose.

It is difficult to make such decisions in the absence of a coherent and intelligent body of radical thought about sex. Unfortunately, progressive political analysis of sexuality is relatively underdeveloped. Much of what is available from the feminist movement has simply added to the mystification that shrouds the subject. There is an urgent need to develop radical perspectives on sexuality.

Paradoxically, an explosion of exciting scholarship and political writing about sex has been generated in these bleak years. In the 1950s, the early gay rights movement began and prospered while the bars were being raided and anti-gay laws were being passed. In the last six years, new erotic communities, political alliances, and analyses have been developed in the midst of the repression. In this essay, I will propose elements of a descriptive and conceptual framework for thinking about sex and its politics. I hope to contribute to the pressing task of creating an accurate, humane, and genuinely liberatory body of thought about sexuality.

II Sexual Thoughts

"You see, Tim," Phillip said suddenly, "your argument isn't reasonable. Suppose I granted your first point that homosexuality is justifiable in certain instances and under certain controls. Then there is the catch: where does justification end and degeneracy begin? Society must condemn to protect. Permit even the intellectual homosexual a place of respect and the first bar is down. Then comes the next and the next until the sadist, the flagellist, the criminally insane demand their places, and society ceases to exist. So I ask again: where is the line drawn? Where does degeneracy begin if not at the beginning of individual freedom in such matters?"

(Fragment from a discussion between two gay men trying to decide if they may love each other, from a novel published in 1950.[27])

A radical theory of sex must identify, describe, explain, and denounce erotic injustice and sexual oppression. Such a theory needs refined conceptual tools which can grasp the subject and hold it in view. It must build rich descriptions of sexuality as it exists in society and history. It requires a convincing critical language that can convey the barbarity of sexual persecution.

Several persistent features of thought about sex inhibit the development of such a theory. These assumptions are so pervasive in Western culture that they are rarely questioned. Thus, they tend to reappear in different political contexts, acquiring new rhetorical expressions but reproducing fundamental axioms.

One such axiom is sexual essentialism—the idea that sex is a natural force that exists prior to social life and shapes institutions. Sexual essentialism is embedded in the folk wisdoms of Western societies, which consider sex to be eternally unchanging, asocial, and transhistorical. Dominated for over a century by medicine, psychiatry, and psychology, the academic study of sex has reproduced essentialism. These fields classify sex as a property of individuals. It may reside in their hormones or their psyches. It may be construed as physiological or psychological. But within these ethnoscientific categories, sexuality has no history and no significant social determinants.

During the last five years, a sophisticated historical and theoretical scholarship has challenged sexual essentialism both explicitly and implicitly. Gay history, particularly the work of Jeffrey Weeks, has led this assault by showing that homosexuality as we know it is a relatively modern institutional complex.[28] Many historians have come to see the contemporary institutional forms of heterosexuality as an even more recent development.[29] An important contributor to the new scholarship is Judith Walkowitz, whose research has demonstrated the extent to which prostitution was transformed around the turn of the century. She provides meticulous descriptions of how the interplay of social forces such as ideology, fear, political agitation, legal reform, and medical practice can change the structure of sexual behavior and alter its consequences.[30]

Michel Foucault's *The History of Sexuality* has been the most influential and emblematic text of the new scholarship on sex. Foucault criticizes the traditional understanding of sexuality as a natural libido yearning to break free of social constraint. He argues that desires are not preexisting biological entities, but rather, that they are constituted in the course of historically specific social practices. He emphasizes the generative aspects of the social organization of sex rather than its repressive elements by pointing out that new sexualities are constantly produced. And he points to a major discontinuity between kinship–based systems of sexuality and more modern forms.[31]

The new scholarship on sexual behavior has given sex a history and created a constructivist alternative to sexual essentialism. Underlying this body of work is an assumption that sexuality is constituted in society and history, not biologically ordained.[32] This does not mean the biological capacities are not prerequisites for human sexuality. It does mean that human sexuality is not comprehensible in purely biological terms. Human organisms with human brains are necessary for human cultures, but no examination of the body or its parts can explain the nature and variety of human social systems. The belly's hunger gives no clues as to the complexities of cuisine. The body, the brain, the genitalia, and the capacity for language are all necessary for human sexuality. But they do not determine its content, its experiences, or its institutional forms. Moreover, we never encounter the body unmediated by the meanings that cultures give to it. To paraphrase Lévi-Strauss, my position on the relationship between biology and sexuality is a "Kantianism without a transcendental libido."[33]

It is impossible to think with any clarity about the politics of race or gender as long as these are thought of as biological entities rather than as social constructs. Similarly, sexuality is impervious to political analysis as long as it is primarily conceived as a biological phenomenon or an aspect of individual psychology. Sexuality is as much a human product as are diets, methods of transportation, systems of etiquette, forms of labor, types of entertainment, processes of production, and modes of oppression. Once sex is understood in terms of social analysis and historical understanding, a more realistic politics of sex becomes possible. One may then think of sexual politics in terms of such phenomena as populations, neighborhoods, settlement patterns, migration, urban conflict, epidemiology, and police technology. These are more fruitful categories of thought than the more traditional ones of sin, disease, neurosis, pathology, decadence, pollution, or the decline and fall of empires.

By detailing the relationships between stigmatized erotic populations and the social forces which regulate them, work such as that of Allan Bérubé, John D'Emilio, Jeffrey Weeks, and Judith Walkowitz contains implicit categories of political analysis and criticism. Nevertheless, the constructivist perspective has displayed some political weaknesses. This has been most evident in misconstructions of Foucault's position.

Because of his emphasis on the ways that sexuality is produced, Foucault has been vulnerable to interpretations that deny or minimize the reality of sexual repression in the more political sense. Foucault makes it abundantly clear that he is not denying the existence of sexual repression so much as inscribing it within a large dynamic.[34] Sexuality in Western societies has been structured within an extremely punitive social framework, and has been subjected to very real formal and informal controls. It is necessary to recognize repressive phenomena without resorting to the essentialist assumptions of the language of libido. It is important to hold repressive sexual practices in focus, even while situating them within a different totality and a more refined terminology.[35]

Most radical thought about sex has been embedded within a model of the instincts and their restraints. Concepts of sexual oppression have been lodged within that more biological understanding of sexuality. It is often easier to fall back on the notion of a natural libido subjected to inhumane repression than to reformulate concepts of sexual injustice within a more constructivist framework. But it is essential that we do so. We need a radical critique of sexual arrangements that has the conceptual elegance of Foucault and the evocative passion of Reich.

The new scholarship on sex has brought a welcome insistence that sexual terms be restricted to their proper historical and social contexts, and a cautionary scepticism towards sweeping generalizations. But it is important to be able to indicate groupings of erotic behavior and general trends within erotic discourse. In addition to sexual essentialism, there are at least five other ideological formations whose grip on sexual thought is so strong that to fail to discuss them is to remain enmeshed within them. These are sex negativity, the fallacy of misplaced scale, the hierarchical valuation of sex acts, the domino theory of sexual peril, and the lack of a concept of benign sexual variation.

Of these five, the most important is sex negativity. Western cultures generally consider sex to be a dangerous, destructive, negative force.[36] Most Christian tradition, following Paul, holds that sex is inherently sinful. It may be redeemed if performed within marriage for procreative purposes and if the pleasurable aspects are not enjoyed too much. In turn, this idea rests on the assumption that the genitalia are an intrinsically inferior part of the body, much lower and less holy than the mind, the "soul," the "heart," or even the upper part of the digestive system (the status of the excretory organs is close to that of the genitalia).[37] Such notions have by now acquired a life of their own and no longer depend solely on religion for their perseverance.

This culture always treats sex with suspicion. It construes and judges almost any sexual practice in terms of its worst possible expression. Sex is presumed guilty until proven innocent. Virtually all erotic behavior is considered bad unless a specific reason to exempt it has been established. The most acceptable excuses are marriage, reproduction, and love. Sometimes scientific curiosity, aesthetic experience, or a long-term intimate relationship may serve. But the exercise of erotic capacity, intelligence, curiosity, or creativity all require pretexts that are unnecessary for other pleasures, such as the enjoyment of food, fiction, or astronomy.

What I call the fallacy of misplaced scale is a corollary of sex negativity. Susan Sontag once commented that since Christianity focused "on sexual behavior as the root of virtue, everything pertaining to sex has been a 'special case' in our culture."[38] Sex law has incorporated the religious attitude that heretical sex is an especially heinous sin that deserves the harshest punishments.

Throughout much of European and American history, a single act of consensual anal penetration was grounds for execution. In some states, sodomy still carries twenty-year prison sentences. Outside the law, sex is also a marked category. Small differences in value or behavior are often experienced as cosmic threats. Although people can be intolerant, silly, or pushy about what constitutes proper diet, differences in menu rarely provoke the kinds of rage, anxiety, and sheer terror that routinely accompany differences in erotic taste. Sexual acts are burdened with an excess of significance.

Modern Western societies appraise sex acts according to a hierarchical system of sexual value. Marital, reproductive heterosexuals are alone at the top of the erotic pyramid. Clamoring below are unmarried monogamous heterosexuals in couples, followed by most other heterosexuals. Solitary sex floats ambiguously. The powerful nineteenth-century stigma on masturbation lingers in less potent, modified forms, such as the idea that masturbation is an inferior substitute for partnered encounters. Stable, long-term lesbian and gay male couples are verging on respectability, but bar dykes and promiscuous gay men are hovering just above the groups at the very bottom of the pyramid. The most despised sexual castes currently include transsexuals, transvestites, fetishists, sadomasochists, sex workers such as prostitutes and porn models, and the lowliest of all, those whose eroticism transgresses generational boundaries.

Individuals whose behavior stands high in this hierarchy are rewarded with certified mental health, respectability, legality, social and physical mobility, institutional support, and material benefits. As sexual behaviors or occupations fall lower on the scale, the individuals who practice them are subjected to a presumption of mental illness, disreputability, criminality, restricted social and physical mobility, loss of institutional support, and economic sanctions.

Extreme and punitive stigma maintains some sexual behaviors as low status and is an effective sanction against those who engage in them. The intensity of this stigma is rooted in Western religious traditions. But most of its contemporary content derives from medical and psychiatric opprobrium.

The old religious taboos were primarily based on kinship forms of social organization. They were meant to deter inappropriate unions and to provide proper kin. Sex laws derived from Biblical pronouncements were aimed at preventing the acquisition of the wrong kinds of affinal partners: consanguineous kin (incest), the same gender (homosexuality), or the wrong species (bestiality). When medicine and psychiatry acquired extensive powers over sexuality, they were less concerned with unsuitable mates than with unfit forms of desire. If taboos against incest best characterized kinship systems of sexual organization, then the shift to an emphasis on taboos against masturbation was more apposite to the newer systems organized around qualities of erotic experience.[39]

Medicine and psychiatry multiplied the categories of sexual misconduct. The section on psychosexual disorders in the *Diagnostic and Statistical Manual of Mental Disorders (DSM)* of the American Psychiatric Association (APA) is a fairly reliable map of the current moral hierarchy of sexual activities. The APA list is much more elaborate than the traditional condemnations of whoring, sodomy, and adultery. The most recent edition, *DSM-III*, removed homosexuality from the roster of mental disorders after a long political struggle. But fetishism, sadism, masochism, transsexuality, transvestism, exhibitionism, voyeurism, and pedophilia are quite firmly entrenched as psychological malfunctions.[40] Books are still being written about the genesis, etiology, treatment, and cure of these assorted "pathologies."

Psychiatric condemnation of sexual behaviors invokes concepts of mental and emotional inferiority rather than categories of sexual sin. Low status sex practices are vilified as mental diseases or symptoms of defective personality integration. In addition, psychological terms conflate difficulties of psychodynamic functioning with modes of erotic conduct. They equate sexual masochism with self-destructive personality patterns, sexual sadism with emotional aggression, and homoeroticism with immaturity. These terminological muddles have become powerful stereotypes that are indiscriminately applied to individuals on the basis of their sexual orientations.

Popular culture is permeated with ideas that erotic variety is dangerous, unhealthy, depraved, and a menace to everything from small children to national security. Popular sexual ideology is a noxious stew made up of ideas of sexual sin, concepts of psychological inferiority, anti-communism, mob hysteria, accusations of witchcraft, and xenophobia. The mass media nourish these attitudes with relentless propaganda. I would call this system of erotic stigma the last socially respectable form of prejudice if the old forms did not show such obstinate vitality, and new ones did not continually become apparent.

All these hierarchies of sexual value—religious, psychiatric, and popular—function in much the same ways as do ideological systems of racism, ethnocentrism, and religious chauvinism. They rationalize the well-being of the sexually privileged and the adversity of the sexual rabble.

Figure 1 diagrams a general version of the sexual value system. According to this system, sexuality that is "good," "normal" and "natural" should ideally be heterosexual, marital, monogamous reproductive, and non-commercial. It should be coupled, relational, within the same generation, and occur at home. It should not involve pornography, fetish objects, sex toys of any sort, or roles other than male and female. Any sex that violates these rules is "bad," "abnormal," or "unnatural." Bad sex may be homosexual, unmarried, promiscuous, non-procreative, or commercial. It may be masturbatory or take place at orgies, may be casual, may cross generational lines, and may take place in "public," or at least in the bushes or the baths. It may involve the use of pornography, fetish objects, sex toys, or unusual roles (see Figure 1).

Figure 2 diagrams another aspect of the sexual hierarchy: the need to draw and maintain an imaginary line between good and bad sex. Most of the discourses on sex, be they religious, psychiatric, popular, or political, delimit a very small portion of human sexual capacity as sanctifiable, safe, healthy, mature, legal, or politically correct. The "line" distinguishes these from all other

The charmed circle:
Good, Normal, Natural, Blessed Sexuality
Heterosexual
Married
Monogamous
Procreative
Non-commercial
In pairs
In a relationship
Same generation
In private
No pornography
Bodies only
Vanilla

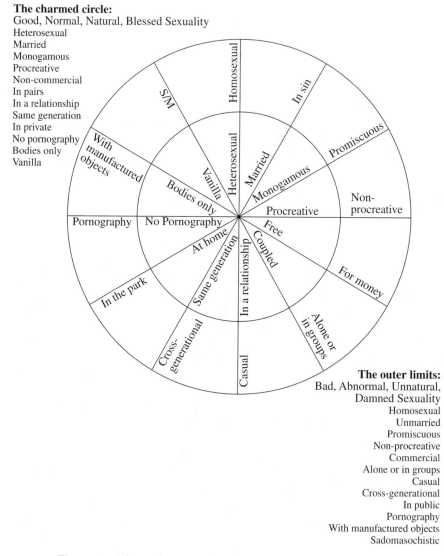

The outer limits:
Bad, Abnormal, Unnatural,
Damned Sexuality
Homosexual
Unmarried
Promiscuous
Non-procreative
Commercial
Alone or in groups
Casual
Cross-generational
In public
Pornography
With manufactured objects
Sadomasochistic

Figure 1.   The sex hierarchy: the charmed circle vs. the outer limits

erotic behaviors, which are understood to be the work of the devil, dangerous, psychopathological, infantile, or politically reprehensible. Arguments are then conducted over "where to draw the line," and to determine what other activities, if any, may be permitted to cross over into acceptability.

All these models assume a domino theory of sexual peril. The line appears to stand between sexual order and chaos. It expresses the fear that if anything is permitted to cross this erotic DMZ, the barrier against scary sex will crumble and something unspeakable will skitter across.

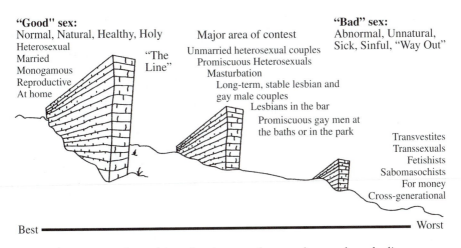

"Good" sex:
Normal, Natural, Healthy, Holy
Heterosexual
Married
Monogamous
Reproductive
At home

Major area of contest

"The Line"

Unmarried heterosexual couples
Promiscuous Heterosexuals
Masturbation
Long-term, stable lesbian and
gay male couples
Lesbians in the bar
Promiscuous gay men at
the baths or in the park

"Bad" sex:
Abnormal, Unnatural,
Sick, Sinful, "Way Out"

Transvestites
Transsexuals
Fetishists
Sabomasochists
For money
Cross-generational

Best ━━━━━━━━━━━━━━━━━━━━━━━━━━━━━━━━━━ Worst

Figure 2. The sex hierarchy: the struggle over where to draw the line

Most systems of sexual judgment—religious, psychological, feminist, or socialist—attempt to determine on which side of the line a particular act falls. Only sex acts on the good side of the line are accorded moral complexity. For instance, heterosexual encounters may be sublime or disgusting, free or forced, healing or destructive, romantic or mercenary. As long as it does not violate other rules, heterosexuality is acknowledged to exhibit the full range of human experience. In contrast, all sex acts on the bad side of the line are considered utterly repulsive and devoid of all emotional nuance. The further from the line a sex act is, the more it is depicted as a uniformly bad experience.

As a result of the sex conflicts of the last decade, some behavior near the border is inching across it. Unmarried couples living together, masturbation, and some forms of homosexuality are moving in the direction of respectability (see Figure 2). Most homosexuality is still on the bad side of the line. But if it is coupled and monogamous, the society is beginning to recognize that it includes the full range of human interaction. Promiscuous homosexuality, sadomasochism, fetishism, transsexuality, and cross-generational encounters are still viewed as unmodulated horrors incapable of involving affection, love, free choice, kindness, or transcendence.

This kind of sexual morality has more in common with ideologies of racism than with true ethics. It grants virtue to the dominant groups, and relegates vice to the underprivileged. A democratic morality should judge sexual acts by the way partners treat one another, the level of mutual consideration, the presence or absence of coercion, and the quantity and quality of the pleasures they provide. Whether sex acts are gay or straight, coupled or in groups, naked or in underwear, commercial or free, with or without video, should not be ethical concerns.

It is difficult to develop a pluralistic sexual ethics without a concept of benign sexual variation. Variation is a fundamental property of all life, from the simplest biological organisms to the most complex human social formations. Yet sexuality is supposed to conform to a single standard. One of the most tenacious ideas about sex is that there is one best way to do it, and that everyone should do it that way.

Most people find it difficult to grasp that whatever they like to do sexually will be thoroughly repulsive to someone else, and that whatever repels them sexually will be the most treasured delight of someone, somewhere. One need not like or perform a particular sex act in order to recognize that someone else will, and that this difference does not indicate a lack of good taste, mental health, or intelligence in either party. Most people mistake their sexual preferences for a universal system that will or should work for everyone.

This notion of a single ideal sexuality characterizes most systems of thought about sex. For religion, the ideal is procreative marriage. For psychology, it is mature heterosexuality. Although its content varies, the format of a single sexual standard is continually reconstituted within other rhetorical frameworks, including feminism and socialism. It is just as objectionable to insist that everyone should be lesbian, nonmonogamous, or kinky, as to believe that everyone should be heterosexual, married, or vanilla—though the latter set of opinions are backed by considerably more coercive power than the former.

Progressives who would be ashamed to display cultural chauvinism in other areas routinely exhibit it towards sexual differences. We have learned to cherish different cultures as unique expressions of human inventiveness rather than as the inferior or disgusting habits of savages. We need a similarly anthropological understanding of different sexual cultures.

Empirical sex research is the one field that does incorporate a positive concept of sexual variation. Alfred Kinsey approached the study of sex with the same uninhibited curiosity he had previously applied to examining a species of wasp. His scientific detachment gave his work a refreshing neutrality that enraged moralists and caused immense controversy.[41] Among Kinsey's successors, John Gagnon and William Simon have pioneered the application of sociological understandings to erotic variety.[42] Even some of the older sexology is useful. Although his work is imbued with unappetizing eugenic beliefs, Havelock Ellis was an acute and sympathetic observer. His monumental *Studies in the Psychology of Sex* is resplendent with detail.[43]

Much political writing on sexuality reveals complete ignorance of both classical sexology and modern sex research. Perhaps this is because so few colleges and universities bother to teach human sexuality, and because so much stigma adheres even to scholarly investigation of sex. Neither sexology nor sex research has been immune to the prevailing sexual value system. Both contain assumptions and information which should not be accepted uncritically. But sexology and sex research provide abundant detail, a welcome posture of calm, and a well developed ability to treat sexual variety as something that exists rather than as something to be exterminated. These fields can provide an empirical grounding for a radical theory of sexuality more useful than the combination of psychoanalysis and feminist first principles to which so many texts resort.

III   Sexual Transformation

> As defined by the ancient civil or canonical codes, sodomy was a category of forbidden acts; their perpetrator was nothing more than the juridical subject of them. The nineteenth-century homosexual became a personage, a past, a case history, and a childhood, in addition to being a type of life, a life form, and a morphology, with an indiscreet anatomy and possibly a mysterious physiology.... The sodomite had been a temporary aberration; the homosexual was now a species.
>
> Michel Foucault[44]

In spite of many continuities with ancestral forms, modern sexual arrangements have a distinctive character which sets them apart from preexisting systems. In Western Europe and the United States, industrialization and urbanization reshaped the traditional rural and peasant populations into a new urban industrial and service workforce. It generated new forms of state apparatus, reorganized family relations, altered gender roles, made possible new forms of identity, produced new varieties of social inequality, and created new formats for political and ideological conflict. It also gave rise to a new sexual system characterized by distinct types of sexual persons, populations, stratification, and political conflict.

The writings of nineteenth-century sexology suggest the appearance of a kind of erotic speciation. However outlandish their explanations, the early sexologists were witnessing the emergence of new kinds of erotic individuals and their aggregation into rudimentary communities. The modern sexual system contains sets of these sexual populations, stratified by the operation of an ideological and social hierarchy. Differences in social value create friction among these groups, who engage in political contests to alter or maintain their place in the ranking. Contemporary sexual politics should be reconceptualized in terms of the emergence and on-going development of this system, its social relations, the ideologies which interpret it, and its characteristic modes of conflict.

Homosexuality is the best example of this process of erotic speciation. Homosexual behavior is always present among humans. But in different societies and epochs it may be rewarded or punished, required or forbidden, a temporary experience or a life-long vocation. In some New Guinea societies, for example, homosexual activities are obligatory for all males. Homosexual acts are considered utterly masculine, roles are based on age, and partners are determined by kinship status.[45] Although these men engage in extensive homosexual and pedophile behavior, they are neither homosexuals nor pederasts.

Nor was the sixteenth-century sodomite a homosexual. In 1631, Mervyn Touchet, Earl of Castlehaven, was tried and executed for sodomy. It is clear from the proceedings that the earl was not understood by himself or anyone else to be a particular kind of sexual individual. "While from the twentieth-century viewpoint Lord Castlehaven obviously suffered from psychosexual problems requiring the services of an analyst, from the seventeenth century viewpoint he had deliberately broken the Law of God and the Laws of England, and required the simpler services of an executioner."[46] The earl did not slip into his tightest doublet and waltz down to the nearest gay tavern to mingle with his fellow sodomists. He stayed in his manor house and buggered his servants. Gay self-awareness, gay pubs, the sense of group commonality, and even the term homosexual were not part of the earl's universe.

The New Guinea bachelor and the sodomite nobleman are only tangentially related to a modern gay man, who may migrate from rural Colorado to San Francisco in order to live in a gay neighborhood, work in a gay business, and participate in an elaborate experience that includes a self-conscious identity, group solidarity, a literature, a press and a high level of political activity. In modern, Western, industrial societies, homosexuality has acquired much of the institutional structure of an ethnic group.[47]

The relocation of homoeroticism into these quasi-ethnic, nucleated, sexually constituted communities is to some extent a consequence of the transfers of population brought about by industrialization. As laborers migrated to work in cities, there were increased opportunities for voluntary communities to form. Homosexually inclined women and men, who would have been vulnerable and isolated in most pre-industrial villages, began to congregate in small corners of the big cities. Most large nineteenth-century cities in Western Europe and North America had areas where men could cruise for other men. Lesbian communities seem to have coalesced more slowly and on a smaller scale. Nevertheless, by the 1890s, there were several cafes in Paris near the Place Pigalle which catered to a lesbian clientele, and it is likely that there were similar places in the other major capitals of Western Europe.

Areas like these acquired bad reputations, which alerted other interested individuals of their existence and location. In the United States, lesbian and gay male territories were well established in New York, Chicago, San Francisco, and Los Angeles in the 1950s. Sexually motivated migration to places such as Greenwich Village had become a sizable sociological phenomenon. By the late 1970s, sexual migration was occurring on a scale so significant that it began to have a recognizable impact on urban politics in the United States, with San Francisco being the most notable and notorious example.[48]

Prostitution has undergone a similar metamorphosis. Prostitution began to change from a temporary job to a more permanent occupation as a result of nineteenth-century agitation legal reform, and police persecution. Prostitutes, who had been part of the general working-class population, became increasingly isolated as members of an outcast group.[49] Prostitutes and other sex workers differ from homosexuals and other sexual minorities. Sex work is an occupation, while sexual deviation is an erotic preference. Nevertheless, they share some common features of social organization. Like homosexuals, prostitutes are a criminal sexual population stigmatized on the basis of sexual activity. Prostitutes and male homosexuals are the primary prey of vice police everywhere.[50] Like gay men, prostitutes occupy well demarcated urban territories and battle with police to defend and maintain those territories. The legal persecution of both populations is justified by an elaborate ideology which classifies them as dangerous and inferior undesirables who are not entitled to be left in peace.

Besides organizing homosexuals and prostitutes into localized populations, the "modernization of sex" has generated a system of continual sexual ethnogenesis. Other populations of erotic dissidents—commonly known as the "perversions" or the "paraphilias"—also began to coalesce. Sexualities keep marching out of the *Diagnostic and Statistical Manual* and on to the pages of social history. At present, several other groups are trying to emulate the successes of homosexuals. Bisexuals, sadomasochists, individuals who prefer cross-generational encounters, transsexuals, and transvestites are all in various states of community formation and identity acquisition. The perversions are not proliferating as much as they are attempting to acquire social space, small businesses, political resources, and a measure of relief from the penalties for sexual heresy.

IV   Sexual Stratification

An entire sub-race was born, different—despite certain kinship ties—from the libertines of the past. From the end of the eighteenth century to our own, they circulated through the pores of society; they were always hounded, but not always by laws; were often locked up, but not always in prisons; were sick perhaps, but scandalous, dangerous victims, prey to a strange evil that also bore the name of vice and sometimes crime. They were children wise beyond their years, precocious little girls, ambiguous schoolboys, dubious servants and educators, cruel or maniacal husbands, solitary collectors, ramblers with bizarre impulses; they haunted the houses of correction, the penal colonies, the tribunals, and the asylums; they carried their infamy to the doctors and their sickness to the judges. This was the numberless family of perverts who were on friendly terms with delinquents and akin to madmen.

Michel Foucault[51]

The industrial transformation of Western Europe and North America brought about new forms of social stratification. The resultant inequalities of class are well known and have been explored in detail by a century of scholarship. The construction of modern systems of racism and ethnic injustice has been well documented and critically assessed. Feminist thought has analyzed the prevailing organization of gender oppression. But although specific erotic groups, such as militant homosexuals and sex workers, have agitated against their own mistreatment, there has been no equivalent attempt to locate particular varieties of sexual persecution within a more general system of sexual stratification. Nevertheless, such a system exists, and in its contemporary form it is a consequence of Western industrialization.

Sex law is the most adamantine instrument of sexual stratification and erotic persecution. The state routinely intervenes in sexual behavior at a level that would not be tolerated in other areas of social life. Most people are unaware of the extent of sex law, the quantity and qualities of illegal sexual behavior, and the punitive character of legal sanctions. Although federal agencies may be involved in obscenity and prostitution cases, most sex laws are enacted at the state and municipal level, and enforcement is largely in the hands of local police. Thus, there is a tremendous amount of variation in the laws applicable to any given locale. Moreover, enforcement of sex laws varies dramatically with the local political climate. In spite of this legal thicket, one can make some tentative and qualified generalizations. My discussion of sex law does not apply to laws against sexual coercion, sexual assault, or rape. It does pertain to the myriad prohibitions on consensual sex and the "status" offenses such as statutory rape.

Sex law is harsh. The penalties for violating sex statutes are universally out of proportion to any social or individual harm. A single act of consensual but illicit sex, such as placing one's lips upon the genitalia of an enthusiastic partner, is punished in most states with more severity than rape, battery, or murder. Each such genital kiss, each lewd caress, is a separate crime. It is therefore painfully easy to commit multiple felonies in the course of a single evening of illegal passion. Once someone is convicted of a sex violation, a second performance of the same act is grounds for prosecution as a repeat offender, in which case penalties will be even more severe. In some states, individuals have become repeat felons for having engaged in homosexual love-making on two separate occasions. Once an erotic activity has been proscribed by sex law, the full power of the state enforces conformity to the values embodied in those laws. Sex laws are notoriously easy to pass, as legislators are loath to be soft on vice. Once on the books, they are extremely difficult to dislodge.

Sex law is not a perfect reflection of the prevailing moral evaluations of sexual conduct. Sexual variation *per se* is more specifically policed by the mental-health professions, popular ideology, and extra-legal social practice. Some of the most detested erotic behaviors, such as fetishism and sadomasochism, are not as closely or completely regulated by the criminal justice system as somewhat less stigmatized practices, such as homosexuality. Areas of sexual behavior come under the purview of the law when they become objects of social concern and political uproar. Each sex scare or morality campaign deposits new regulations as a kind of fossil record of its passage. The legal sediment is thickest—and sex law has its greatest potency—in areas involving obscenity, money, minors, and homosexuality.

Obscenity laws enforce a powerful taboo against direct representation of erotic activities. Current emphasis on the ways in which sexuality has become a focus of social attention should not be misused to undermine a critique of this prohibition. It is one thing to create sexual discourse in the form of psycho-analysis, or in the course of a morality crusade. It is quite another to graphically depict sex acts or genitalia. The first is socially permissible in a way the second is not. Sexual speech is forced into reticence, euphemism, and indirection. Freedom of speech about sex is a glaring exception to the protections of the First Amendment, which is not even considered applicable to purely sexual statements.

The anti-obscenity laws also form part of a group of statutes that make al-most all sexual commerce illegal. Sex law incorporates a very strong prohibition against mixing sex and money, except via marriage. In addition to the obscenity statutes, other laws impinging on sexual commerce include anti-prostitution laws, alcoholic beverage regulations, and ordinances governing the location and operation of "adult" businesses. The sex industry and the gay economy have both managed to circumvent some of this legislation, but that process has not been easy or simple. The underlying criminality of sex-oriented business keeps it marginal, underdeveloped, and distorted. Sex businesses can only operate in legal loopholes. This tends to keep investment down and to divert commercial activity towards the goal of staying out of jail rather than the delivery of goods and services. It also renders sex workers more vulnerable to exploitation and bad working conditions. If sex commerce were legal, sex workers would be more able to organize and agitate for higher pay, better conditions, greater con-trol, and less stigma.

Whatever one thinks of the limitations of capitalist commerce, such an extreme exclusion from the market process would hardly be socially acceptable in other areas of activity. Imagine, for example, that the exchange of money for medical care, pharmacological advice, or psychological counseling were illegal. Medical practice would take place in a much less satisfactory fashion if doctors, nurses, druggists, and therapists could be hauled off to jail at the whim of the local "health squad." But that is essentially the situation of prostitutes, sex workers, and sex entrepreneurs.

Marx himself considered the capitalist market a revolutionary, if limited, force. He argued that capitalism was progressive in its dissolution of pre-capitalist superstition, prejudice, and the bonds of traditional modes of life. "Hence the great civilizing influence of capital, its production of a state of soci-ety compared with which all earlier stages appear to be merely local progress and idolatry of nature."[52] Keeping sex from realizing the positive effects of the market economy hardly makes it socialist.

The law is especially ferocious in maintaining the boundary between childhood "innocence" and "adult" sexuality. Rather than recognizing the sexu-ality of the young, and attempting to provide for it in a caring and responsible manner, our culture denies and punishes erotic interest and activity by anyone under the local age of consent. The amount of law devoted to protecting young people from premature exposure to sexuality is breathtaking.

The primary mechanism for insuring the separation of sexual generations is age of consent laws. These laws make no distinction between the most brutal rape and the most gentle romance. A 20-year-old convicted of sexual contact with a 17-year-old will face a severe sentence in virtually every state, regardless of the nature of the relationship.[53] Nor are minors permitted access to "adult" sexuality in other forms. They are forbidden to see books, movies, or television in which sexuality is "too" graphically portrayed. It is legal for young people to see hideous depictions of violence, but not to see explicit pictures of genitalia. Sexually active young people are frequently incarcerated in juvenile homes, or otherwise punished for their "precocity."

Adults who deviate too much from conventional standards of sexual conduct are often denied contact with the young, even their own. Custody laws permit the state to steal the children of anyone whose erotic activities appear questionable to a judge presiding over family court matters. Countless lesbians, gay men, prostitutes, swingers, sex workers, and "promiscuous" women have been declared unfit parents under such provisions. Members of the teaching professions are closely monitored for signs of sexual misconduct. In most states, certification laws require that teachers arrested for sex offenses lose their jobs and credentials. In some cases, a teacher may be fired merely because an unconventional lifestyle becomes known to school officials. Moral turpitude is one of the few legal grounds for revoking academic tenure.[54] The more influence one has over the next generation, the less latitude one is permitted in behavior and opinion. The coercive power of the law ensures the transmission of conservative sexual values with these kinds of controls over parenting and teaching.

The only adult sexual behavior that is legal in every state is the placement of the penis in the vagina in wedlock. Consenting adults statutes ameliorate this situation in fewer than half the states. Most states impose severe criminal penalties on consensual sodomy, homosexual contact short of sodomy, adultery, seduction, and adult incest. Sodomy laws vary a great deal. In some states, they apply equally to homosexual and heterosexual partners and regardless of marital status. Some state courts have ruled that married couples have the right to commit sodomy in private. Only homosexual sodomy is illegal in some states. Some sodomy statutes prohibit both anal sex and oral-genital contact. In other states, sodomy applies only to anal penetration, and oral sex is covered under separate statutes.[55]

Laws like these criminalize sexual behavior that is freely chosen and avidly sought. The ideology embodied in them reflects the value hierarchies discussed above. That is, some sex acts are considered to be so intrinsically vile that no one should be allowed under any circumstance to perform them. The fact that individuals consent to or even prefer them is taken to be additional evidence of depravity. This system of sex law is similar to legalized racism. State prohibition of same sex contact, anal penetration, and oral sex make homosexuals a criminal group denied the privileges of full citizenship. With such laws, prosecution is persecution. Even when they are not strictly enforced, as is usually the case, the members of criminalized sexual communities remain vulnerable to the possibility of arbitrary arrest, or to periods in which they become the objects of social panic. When those occur, the laws are in place and police action is swift. Even sporadic enforcement serves to remind individuals that they are members of a subject population. The occasional arrest for sodomy, lewd behavior, solicitation, or oral sex keeps everyone else afraid, nervous, and circumspect.

The state also upholds the sexual hierarchy through bureaucratic regulation. Immigration policy still prohibits the admission of homosexuals (and other sexual "deviates") into the United States. Military regulations bar homosexuals from serving in the armed forces. The fact that gay people cannot legally marry means that they cannot enjoy the same legal rights as heterosexuals in many matters, including inheritance, taxation, protection from testimony in court, and the acquisition of citizenship for foreign partners. These are but a few of the ways that the state reflects and maintains the social relations of sexuality. The law buttresses structures of power, codes of behavior, and forms of prejudice. At their worst, sex law and sex regulation are simply sexual apartheid.

Although the legal apparatus of sex is staggering, most everyday social control is extra-legal. Less formal, but very effective social sanctions are imposed on members of "inferior" sexual populations.

In her marvelous ethnographic study of gay life in the 1960s, Esther Newton observed that the homosexual population was divided into what she called the "overts" and the "coverts." "The overts live their *entire* working lives within the context of the [gay] community; the coverts live their entire *nonworking* lives within it."[56] At the time of Newton's study, the gay community provided far fewer jobs than it does now, and the non-gay work world was almost completely intolerant of homosexuality. There were some fortunate individuals who could be openly gay and earn decent salaries. But the vast majority of homosexuals had to choose between honest poverty and the strain of maintaining a false identity.

Though this situation has changed a great deal, discrimination against gay people is still rampant. For the bulk of the gay population, being out on the job is still impossible. Generally, the more important and higher paid the job, the less the society will tolerate overt erotic deviance. If it is difficult for gay people to find employment where they do not have to pretend, it is doubly and triply so for more exotically sexed individuals. Sadomasochists leave their fetish clothes at home, and know that they must be especially careful to conceal their real identities. An exposed pedophile would probably be stoned out of the office. Having to maintain such absolute secrecy is a considerable burden. Even those who are content to be secretive may be exposed by some accidental event. Individuals who are erotically unconventional risk being unemployable or unable to pursue their chosen careers.

Public officials and anyone who occupies a position of social consequence are especially vulnerable. A sex scandal is the surest method for hounding someone out of office or destroying a political career. The fact that important people are expected to conform to the strictest standards of erotic conduct discourages sex perverts of all kinds from seeking such positions. Instead, erotic dissidents are channeled into positions that have less impact on the mainstream of social activity and opinion.

The expansion of the gay economy in the last decade has provided some employment alternatives and some relief from job discrimination against homosexuals. But most of the jobs provided by the gay economy are low-status and low-paying. Bartenders, bathhouse attendants, and disc jockeys are not bank officers or corporate executives. Many of the sexual migrants who flock to places like San Francisco are downwardly mobile. They face intense competition for choice positions. The influx of sexual migrants provides a pool of cheap and exploitable labor for many of the city's businesses, both gay and straight.

Families play a crucial role in enforcing sexual conformity. Much social pressure is brought to bear to deny erotic dissidents the comforts and resources that families provide. Popular ideology holds that families are not supposed to produce or harbor erotic non-conformity. Many families respond by trying to reform, punish, or exile sexually offending members. Many sexual migrants have been thrown out by their families, and many others are fleeing from the threat of institutionalization. Any random collection of homosexuals, sex workers, or miscellaneous perverts can provide heart-stopping stories of rejection and mistreatment by horrified families. Christmas is the great family holiday in the United States and consequently it is a time of considerable tension in the gay community. Half the inhabitants go off to their families of origin; many of those who remain in the gay ghettoes cannot do so, and relive their anger and grief.

In addition to economic penalties and strain on family relations, the stigma of erotic dissidence creates friction at all other levels of everyday life. The general public helps to penalize erotic nonconformity when, according to the values they have been taught, landlords refuse housing, neighbors call in the police, and hoodlums commit sanctioned battery. The ideologies of erotic inferiority and sexual danger decrease the power of sex perverts and sex workers in social encounters of all kinds. They have less protection from unscrupulous or criminal behavior, less access to police protection, and less recourse to the courts. Dealings with institutions and bureaucracies—hospitals, police, coroners, banks, public officials—are more difficult.

Sex is a vector of oppression. The system of sexual oppression cuts across other modes of social inequality, sorting out individuals and groups according to its own intrinsic dynamics. It is not reducible to, or understandable in terms of, class, race, ethnicity, or gender. Wealth, white skin, male gender, and ethnic privileges can mitigate the effects of sexual stratification. A rich, white male pervert will generally be less affected than a poor, black, female pervert. But even the most privileged are not immune to sexual oppression. Some of the consequences of the system of sexual hierarchy are mere nuisances. Others are quite grave. In its most serious manifestations, the sexual system is a Kafkaesque nightmare in which unlucky victims become herds of human cattle whose identification, surveillance, apprehension, treatment, incarceration, and punishment produce jobs and self-satisfaction for thousands of vice police, prison officials, psychiatrists, and social workers.[57]

V Sexual Conflicts

> The moral panic crystallizes widespread fears and anxieties, and often deals with them not by seeking the real causes of the problems and conditions which they demonstrate but by displacing them on to 'Folk Devils' in an identified social group (often the 'immoral' or 'degenerate'). Sexuality has had a peculiar centrality in such panics, and sexual 'deviants' have been omnipresent scapegoats.
>
> Jeffrey Weeks[58]

The sexual system is not a monolithic, omnipotent structure. There are continuous battles over the definitions, evaluations, arrangements, privileges, and costs of sexual behavior. Political struggle over sex assumes characteristic forms.

Sexual ideology plays a crucial role in sexual experience. Consequently, definitions and evaluations of sexual conduct are objects of bitter contest. The confrontations between early gay liberation and the psychiatric establishment are the best example of this kind of fight, but there are constant skirmishes. Recurrent battles take place between the primary producers of sexual ideology—the churches, the family, the shrinks, and the media—and the groups whose experience they name, distort, and endanger.

The legal regulation of sexual conduct is another battleground. Lysander Spooner dissected the system of state sanctioned moral coercion over a century ago in a text inspired primarily by the temperance campaigns. In *Vices Are Not Crimes: A Vindication of Moral Liberty*, Spooner argued that government should protect its citizens against crime, but that it is foolish, unjust, and tyrannical to legislate against vice. He discusses rationalizations still heard today in defense of legalized moralism—that "vices" (Spooner is referring to drink, but homosexuality, prostitution, or recreational drug use may be substituted) lead to crimes, and should therefore be prevented; that those who practice "vice" are *non compos mentis* and should therefore be protected from their self-destruction by state-accomplished ruin; and that children must be protected from supposedly harmful knowledge.[59] The discourse on victimless crimes has not changed much. Legal struggle over sex law will continue until basic freedoms of sexual action and expression are guaranteed. This requires the repeal of all sex laws except those few that deal with actual, not statutory, coercion; and it entails the abolition of vice squads, whose job it is to enforce legislated morality.

In addition to the definitional and legal wars, there are less obvious forms of sexual political conflict which I call the territorial and border wars. The processes by which erotic minorities form communities and the forces that seek to inhibit them lead to struggles over the nature and boundaries of sexual zones.

Dissident sexuality is rarer and more closely monitored in small towns and rural areas. Consequently, metropolitan life continually beckons to young perverts. Sexual migration creates concentrated pools of potential partners, friends, and associates. It enables individuals to create adult, kin-like networks in which to live. But there are many barriers which sexual migrants have to overcome.

According to the mainstream media and popular prejudice, the marginal sexual worlds are bleak and dangerous. They are portrayed as impoverished, ugly, and inhabited by psychopaths and criminals. New migrants must be sufficiently motivated to resist the impact of such discouraging images. Attempts to counter negative propaganda with more realistic information generally meet with censorship, and there are continuous ideological struggles over which representations of sexual communities make it into the popular media.

Information on how to find, occupy, and live in the marginal sexual worlds is also suppressed. Navigational guides are scarce and inaccurate. In the past, fragments of rumor, distorted gossip, and bad publicity were the most available clues to the location of underground erotic communities. During the late 1960s and early 1970s, better information became available. Now groups like the Moral Majority want to rebuild the ideological walls around the sexual undergrounds and make transit in and out of them as difficult as possible.

Migration is expensive. Transportation costs, moving expenses, and the necessity of finding new jobs and housing are economic difficulties that sexual migrants must overcome. These are especially imposing barriers to the young, who are often the most desperate to move. There are, however, routes into the erotic communities which mark trails through the propaganda thicket and provide some economic shelter along the way. Higher education can be a route for young people from affluent backgrounds. In spite of serious limitations, the information on sexual behavior at most colleges and universities is better than elsewhere, and most colleges and universities shelter small erotic networks of all sorts.

For poorer kids, the military is often the easiest way to get the hell out of wherever they are. Military prohibitions against homosexuality make this a perilous route. Although young queers continually attempt to use the armed forces to get out of intolerable hometown situations and closer to functional gay communities, they face the hazards of exposure, court martial, and dishonorable discharge.

Once in the cities, erotic populations tend to nucleate and to occupy some regular, visible territory. Churches and other anti-vice forces constantly put pressure on local authorities to contain such areas, reduce their visibility, or to drive their inhabitants out of town. There are periodic crackdowns in which local vice squads are unleashed on the populations they control. Gay men, prostitutes, and sometimes transvestites are sufficiently territorial and numerous to engage in intense battles with the cops over particular streets, parks, and alleys. Such border wars are usually inconclusive, but they result in many casualties.

For most of this century, the sexual underworlds have been marginal and impoverished, their residents subjected to stress and exploitation. The spectacular success of gay entrepreneurs in creating a variegated gay economy has altered the quality of life within the gay ghetto. The level of material comfort and social elaboration achieved by the gay community in the last fifteen years is unprecedented. But it is important to recall what happened to similar miracles. The growth of the black population in New York in the early part of the twentieth century led to the Harlem Renaissance, but that period of creativity was doused by the Depression. The relative prosperity and cultural florescence of the gay ghetto may be equally fragile. Like blacks who fled the South for the metropolitan North, homosexuals may have merely traded rural problems for urban ones.

Gay pioneers occupied neighborhoods that were centrally located but run down. Consequently, they border poor neighborhoods. Gays, especially low-income gays, end up competing with other low-income groups for the limited supply of cheap and moderate housing. In San Francisco, competition for low-cost housing has exacerbated both racism and homophobia, and is one source of the epidemic of street violence against homosexuals. Instead of being isolated and invisible in rural settings, city gays are now numerous and obvious targets for urban frustrations.

In San Francisco, unbridled construction of downtown skyscrapers and high-cost condominiums is causing affordable housing to evaporate. Megabuck construction is creating pressure on all city residents. Poor gay renters are visible in low-income neighborhoods; multimillionaire contracters are not. The specter of the "homosexual invasion" is a convenient scapegoat which deflects attention from the banks, the planning commission, the political establishment, and the big developers. In San Francisco, the well-being of the gay community has become embroiled in the high-stakes politics of urban real estate.

Downtown expansion affects all the territorial erotic underworlds. In both San Francisco and New York, high investment construction and urban renewal have intruded on the main areas of prostitution, pornography, and leather bars. Developers are salivating over Times Square, the Tenderloin, what is left of North Beach, and South of Market. Anti-sex ideology, obscenity law, prostitution regulations, and the alcoholic beverage codes are all being used to dislodge seedy adult businesses, sex workers, and leathermen. Within ten years, most of these areas will have been bulldozed and made safe for convention centers, international hotels, corporate headquarters, and housing for the rich.

The most important and consequential kind of sex conflict is what Jeffrey Weeks has termed the "moral panic." Moral panics are the "political moment" of sex, in which diffuse attitudes are channeled into political action and from there into social change.[60] The white slavery hysteria of the 1880s, the anti-homosexual campaigns of the 1950s, and the child pornography panic of the late 1970s were typical moral panics.

Because sexuality in Western societies is so mystified, the wars over it are often fought at oblique angles, aimed at phony targets, conducted with misplaced passions, and are highly, intensely symbolic. Sexual activities often function as signifiers for personal and social apprehensions to which they have no intrinsic connection. During a moral panic, such fears attach to some unfortunate sexual activity or population. The media become ablaze with indignation, the public behaves like a rabid mob, the police are activated, and the state enacts new laws and regulations. When the furor has passed, some innocent erotic group has been decimated, and the state has extended its power into new areas of erotic behavior.

The system of sexual stratification provides easy victims who lack the power to defend themselves, and a preexisting apparatus for controlling their movements and curtailing their freedoms. The stigma against sexual dissidents renders them morally defenseless. Every moral panic has consequences on two levels. The target population suffers most, but everyone is affected by the social and legal changes.

Moral panics rarely alleviate any real problem, because they are aimed at chimeras and signifiers. They draw on the pre-existing discursive structure which invents victims in order to justify treating "vices" as crimes. The criminalization of innocuous behaviors such as homosexuality, prostitution, obscenity, or recreational drug use, is rationalized by portraying them as menaces to health and safety, women and children, national security, the family, or civilization itself. Even when activity is acknowledged to be harmless, it may be banned because it is alleged to "lead" to something ostensibly worse (another manifestation of the domino theory).[61] Great and mighty edifices have been built on the basis of such phantasms. Generally, the outbreak of a moral panic is preceded by an intensification of such scapegoating.

It is always risky to prophesy. But it does not take much prescience to detect potential moral panics in two current developments: the attacks on sadomasochists by a segment of the feminist movement, and the right's increasing use of AIDS to incite virulent homophobia.

Feminist anti-pornography ideology has always contained an implied, and sometimes overt, indictment of sadomasochism. The pictures of sucking and fucking that comprise the bulk of pornography may be unnerving to those who are not familiar with them. But it is hard to make a convincing case that such images are violent. All of the early anti-porn slide shows used a highly selective sample of S/M imagery to sell a very flimsy analysis. Taken out of context, such images are often shocking. This shock value was mercilessly exploited to scare audiences into accepting the anti-porn perspective.

A great deal of anti-porn propaganda implies that sadomasochism is the underlying and essential "truth" towards which all pornography tends. Porn is thought to lead to S/M porn which in turn is alleged to lead to rape. This is a just-so story that revitalizes the notion that sex perverts commit sex crimes, not normal people. There is no evidence that the readers of S/M erotica or practicing sadomasochists commit a disproportionate number of sex crimes. Anti-porn literature scapegoats an unpopular sexual minority and its reading material for social problems they do not create.

The use of S/M imagery in anti-porn discourse is inflammatory. It implies that the way to make the world safe for women is to get rid of sadomasochism. The use of S/M images in the movie *Not a Love Story* was on a moral par with the use of depictions of black men raping white women, or of drooling old Jews pawing young Aryan girls, to incite racist or anti-Semitic frenzy.

Feminist rhetoric has a distressing tendency to reappear in reactionary contexts. For example, in 1980 and 1981, Pope John Paul II delivered a series of pronouncements reaffirming his commitment to the most conservative and Pauline understandings of human sexuality. In condemning divorce, abortion, trial marriage, pornography, prostitution, birth control, unbridled hedonism, and lust, the pope employed a great deal of feminist rhetoric about sexual objectification. Sounding like lesbian feminist polemicist Julia Penelope, His Holiness explained that "considering anyone in a lustful way makes that person a sexual object rather than a human being worthy of dignity."[62]

The right wing opposes pornography and has already adopted elements of feminist anti-porn rhetoric. The anti-S/M discourse developed in the women's movement could easily become a vehicle for a moral witch hunt. It provides a ready-made defenseless target population. It provides a rationale for the re-criminalization of sexual materials which have escaped the reach of current obscenity laws. It would be especially easy to pass laws against S/M erotica resembling the child pornography laws. The ostensible purpose of such laws would be to reduce violence by banning so-called violent porn. A focused campaign against the leather menace might also result in the passage of laws to criminalize S/M behavior that is not currently illegal. The ultimate result of such a moral panic would be the legalized violation of a community of harmless perverts. It is dubious that such a sexual witch-hunt would make any appreciable contribution towards reducing violence against women.

An AIDS panic is even more probable. When fears of incurable disease mingle with sexual terror, the resulting brew is extremely volatile. A century ago, attempts to control syphilis led to the passage of the Contagious Diseases Acts in England. The Acts were based on erroneous medical theories and did nothing to halt the spread of the disease. But they did make life miserable for the hundreds of women who were incarcerated, subjected to forcible vaginal examination, and stigmatized for life as prostitutes.[63]

Whatever happens, AIDS will have far-reaching consequences on sex in general, and on homosexuality in particular. The disease will have a significant impact on the choices gay people make. Fewer will migrate to the gay meccas out of fear of the disease. Those who already reside in the ghettos will avoid situations they fear will expose them. The gay economy, and the political apparatus it supports, may prove to be evanescent. Fear of AIDS has already affected sexual ideology. Just when homosexuals have had some success in throwing off the taint of mental disease, gay people find themselves metaphorically welded to an image of lethal physical deterioration. The syndrome, its peculiar qualities, and its transmissibility are being used to reinforce old fears that sexual activity, homosexuality, and promiscuity led to disease and death.

AIDS is both a personal tragedy for those who contract the syndrome and a calamity for the gay community. Homophobes have gleefully hastened to turn this tragedy against its victims. One columnist has suggested that AIDS has

always existed, that the Biblical prohibitions on sodomy were designed to protect people from AIDS, and that AIDS is therefore an appropriate punishment
for violating the Levitical codes. Using fear of infection as a rationale, local
right-wingers attempted to ban the gay rodeo from Reno, Nevada. A recent
issue of the *Moral Majority Report* featured a picture of a "typical" white family
of four wearing surgical masks. The headline read: "AIDS: HOMOSEXUAL
DISEASES THREATEN AMERICAN FAMILIES."[64] Phyllis Schlafly has recently issued a pamphlet arguing that passage of the Equal Rights Amendment
would make it impossible to "legally protect ourselves against AIDS and other
diseases carried by homosexuals."[65] Current right-wing literature calls for
shutting down the gay baths, for a legal ban on homosexual employment in
food-handling occupations, and for state-mandated prohibitions on blood do-
nations by gay people. Such policies would require the government to identify
all homosexuals and impose easily recognizable legal and social markers on
them.

It is bad enough that the gay community must deal with the medical mis-
fortune of having been the population in which a deadly disease first became
widespread and visible. It is worse to have to deal with the social consequences
as well. Even before the AIDS scare, Greece passed a law that enabled police to
arrest suspected homosexuals and force them to submit to an examination for
veneral disease. It is likely that until AIDS and its methods of transmission are
understood, there will be all sorts of proposals to control it by punishing the
gay community and by attacking its institutions. When the cause of Legion-
naires' Disease was unknown, there were no calls to quarantine members of the
American Legion or to shut down their meeting halls. The Contagious Diseases Acts in England did little to control syphilis, but they caused a great deal
of suffering for the women who came under their purview. The history of panic
that has accompanied new epidemics, and of the casualties incurred by their
scapegoats, should make everyone pause and consider with extreme scepticism
any attempts to justify anti-gay policy initiatives on the basis of AIDS.

VI   The Limits of Feminism

> We know that in an overwhelmingly large number of cases, sex crime is associated
> with pornography. We know that sex criminals read it, are clearly influenced by it.
> I believe that, if we can eliminate the distribution of such items among impres-
> sionable children, we shall greatly reduce our frightening sex-crime rate.
>
> J. Edgar Hoover[66]

In the absence of a more articulated radical theory of sex, most progressives
have turned to feminism for guidance. But the relationship between feminism
and sex is complex. Because sexuality is a nexus of the relationships between
genders, much of the oppression of women is borne by, mediated through, and
constituted within, sexuality. Feminism has always been vitally interested in sex.
But there have been two strains of feminist thought on the subject. One

tendency has criticized the restrictions on women's sexual behavior and denounced the high costs imposed on women for being sexually active. This tradition of feminist sexual thought has called for a sexual liberation that would work for women as well as for men. The second tendency has considered sexual liberalization to be inherently a mere extension of male privilege. This tradition resonates with conservative, anti-sexual discourse. With the advent of the anti-pornography movement, it achieved temporary hegemony over feminist analysis.

The anti-pornography movement and its texts have been the most extensive expression of this discourse.[67] In addition, proponents of this viewpoint have condemned virtually every variant of sexual expression as anti-feminist. Within this framework, monogamous lesbianism that occurs within long-term, intimate relationships and which does not involve playing with polarized roles, has replaced married, procreative heterosexuality at the top of the value hierarchy. Heterosexuality has been demoted to somewhere in the middle. Apart from this change, everything else looks more or less familiar. The lower depths are occupied by the usual groups and behaviors: prostitution, transsexuality, sadomasochism, and cross-generational activities.[68] Most gay male conduct, all casual sex, promiscuity, and lesbian behavior that does involve roles or kink or non-monogamy are also censured.[69] Even sexual fantasy during masturbation is denounced as a phallocentric holdover.[70]

This discourse on sexuality is less a sexology than a demonology. It presents most sexual behavior in the worst possible light. Its descriptions of erotic conduct always use the worst available example as if it were representative. It presents the most disgusting pornography, the most exploited forms of prostitution, and the least palatable or most shocking manifestations of sexual variation. This rhetorical tactic consistently misrepresents human sexuality in all its forms. The picture of human sexuality that emerges from this literature is unremittingly ugly.

In addition, this anti-porn rhetoric is a massive exercise in scapegoating. It criticizes non-routine acts of love rather than routine acts of oppression, exploitation, or violence. This demon sexology directs legitimate anger at women's lack of personal safety against innocent individuals, practices, and communities. Anti-porn propaganda often implies that sexism originates within the commercial sex industry and subsequently infects the rest of society. This is sociologically nonsensical. The sex industry is hardly a feminist utopia. It reflects the sexism that exists in the society as a whole. We need to analyze and oppose the manifestations of gender inequality specific to the sex industry. But this is not the same as attempting to wipe out commercial sex.

Similarly, erotic minorities such as sadomasochists and transsexuals are as likely to exhibit sexist attitudes or behavior as any other politically random social grouping. But to claim that they are inherently anti-feminist is sheer fantasy. A good deal of current feminist literature attributes the oppression of women to graphic representations of sex, prostitution, sex education, sadomasochism, male homosexuality, and transsexualism. Whatever happened to the family, religion, education, child-rearing practices, the media, the state, psychiatry, job discrimination, and unequal pay?

Finally, this so-called feminist discourse recreates a very conservative sexual morality. For over a century, battles have been waged over just how much shame, distress, and punishment should be incurred by sexual activity. The conservative tradition has promoted opposition to pornography, prostitution, homosexuality, all erotic variation, sex education, sex research, abortion, and contraception. The opposing, pro-sex tradition has included individuals like Havelock Ellis, Magnus Hirshfeld, Alfred Kinsey, and Victoria Woodhull, as well as the sex education movement, organizations of militant prostitutes and homosexuals, the reproductive rights movement, and organizations such as the Sexual Reform League of the 1960s. This motley collection of sex reformers, sex educators, and sexual militants has mixed records on both sexual and feminist issues. But surely they are closer to the spirit of modern feminism than are moral crusaders, the social purity movement, and anti-vice organizations. Nevertheless, the current feminist sexual demonology generally elevates the anti-vice crusaders to positions of ancestral honor, while condemning the more liberatory tradition as anti-feminist. In an essay that exemplifies some of these trends, Sheila Jeffreys blames Havelock Ellis, Edward Carpenter, Alexandra Kollantai, "believers in the joy of sex of every possible political persuasion," and the 1929 congress of the World League for Sex Reform for making "a great contribution to the defeat of militant feminism."[71]

The anti-pornography movement and its avatars have claimed to speak for all feminism. Fortunately, they do not. Sexual liberation has been and continues to be a feminist goal. The women's movement may have produced some of the most retrogressive sexual thinking this side of the Vatican. But it has also produced an exciting, innovative, and articulate defense of sexual pleasure and erotic justice. This "pro-sex" feminism has been spearheaded by lesbians whose sexuality does not conform to movement standards of purity (primarily lesbian sadomasochists and butch/femme dykes), by unapologetic heterosexuals, and by women who adhere to classic radical feminism rather than to the revisionist celebrations of femininity which have become so common.[72] Although the anti-porn forces have attempted to weed anyone who disgrees with them out of the movement, the fact remains that feminist thought about sex is profoundly polarized.[73]

Whenever there is polarization, there is an unhappy tendency to think the truth lies somewhere in between. Ellen Willis has commented sarcastically that "the feminist bias is that women are equal to men and the male chauvinist bias is that women are inferior. The unbiased view is that the truth lies somewhere in between."[74] The most recent development in the feminist sex wars is the emergence of a "middle" that seeks to evade the dangers of anti-porn fascism, on the one hand and a supposed "anything goes" libertarianism, on the other.[75] Although it is hard to criticize a position that is not yet fully formed, I want to draw attention to some incipient problems.

The emergent middle is based on a false characterization of the poles of the debate, construing both sides as equally extremist. According to B. Ruby Rich, "the desire for a language of sexuality has led feminists into locations (pornography, sadomasochism) too narrow or overdetermined for a fruitful discussion. Debate has collapsed into a rumble."[76] True, the fights between Women Against Pornography (WAP) and lesbian sadomasochists have resembled gang warfare. But the responsibility for this lies primarily with the anti-porn movement, and its refusal to engage in principled discussion. S/M lesbians have been forced into a struggle to maintain their membership in the movement, and to defend themselves against slander. No major spokeswoman for lesbian S/M has argued for any kind of S/M supremacy, or advocated that everyone should be a sadomasochist. In addition to self-defense, S/M lesbians have called for appreciation for erotic diversity and more open discussion of sexuality.[77] Trying to find a middle course between WAP and Samois is a bit like saying that the truth about homosexuality lies somewhere between the positions of the Moral Majority and those of the gay movement.

In political life, it is all too easy to marginalize radicals, and to attempt to buy acceptance for a moderate position by portraying others as extremists. Liberals have done this for years to communists. Sexual radicals have opened up the sex debates. It is shameful to deny their contribution, misrepresent their positions, and further their stigmatization.

In contrast to cultural feminists, who simply want to purge sexual dissidents, the sexual moderates are willing to defend the rights of erotic nonconformists to political participation. Yet this defense of political rights is linked to an implicit system of ideological condescension. The argument has two major parts. The first is an accusation that sexual dissidents have not paid close enough attention to the meaning, sources, or historical construction of their sexuality. This emphasis on meaning appears to function in much the same way that the question of etiology has functioned in discussions of homosexuality. That is, homosexuality, sadomasochism, prostitution, or boy-love are taken to be mysterious and problematic in some way that more respectable sexualities are not. The search for a cause is a search for something that could change so that these "problematic" eroticisms would simply not occur. Sexual militants have replied to such exercises that although the question of etiology or cause is of intellectual interest, it is not high on the political agenda and that, moreover, the privileging of such questions is itself a regressive political choice.

The second part of the "moderate" position focuses on questions of consent. Sexual radicals of all varieties have demanded the legal and social legitimation of consenting sexual behavior. Feminists have criticized them for ostensibly finessing questions about "the limits of consent" and "structural constraints" on consent.[78] Although there are deep problems with the political discourse of consent, and although there are certainly structural constraints on sexual choice, this criticism has been consistently misapplied in the sex debates. It does not take into account the very specific semantic content that consent has in sex law and sex practice.

As I mentioned earlier, a great deal of sex law does not distinguish between consensual and coercive behavior. Only rape law contains such a distinction. Rape law is based on the assumption, correct in my view, that heterosexual activity may be freely chosen or forcibly coerced. One has the legal right to engage in heterosexual behavior as long as it does not fall under the purview of other statutes and as long as it is agreeable to both parties.

This is not the case for most other sexual acts. Sodomy laws, as I mentioned above, are based on the assumption that the forbidden acts are an "abominable and detestable crime against nature." Criminality is intrinsic to the acts themselves, no matter what the desires of the participants. "Unlike rape, sodomy or an unnatural or perverted sexual act may be committed between two persons both of whom consent, and regardless of which is the aggressor, both may be prosecuted."[79] Before the consenting adults statute was passed in California in 1976, lesbian lovers could have been prosecuted for committing oral copulation. If both participants were capable of consent, both were equally guilty.[80]

Adult incest statutes operate in a similar fashion. Contrary to popular mythology, the incest statutes have little to do with protecting children from rape by close relatives. The incest statutes themselves prohibit marriage or sexual intercourse between adults who are closely related. Prosecutions are rare, but two were reported recently. In 1979, a 19-year-old Marine met his 42-year-old mother, from whom he had been separated at birth. The two fell in love and got married. They were charged and found guilty of incest, which under Virginia law carries a maximum ten-year sentence. During their trial, the Marine testified, "I love her very much. I feel that two people who love each other should be able to live together."[81] In another case, a brother and sister who had been raised separately met and decided to get married. They were arrested and pleaded guilty to felony incest in return for probation. A condition of probation was that they not live together as husband and wife. Had they not accepted, they would have faced twenty years in prison.[82]

In a famous S/M case, a man was convicted of aggravated assault for a whipping administered in an S/M scene. There was no complaining victim. The session had been filmed and he was prosecuted on the basis of the film. The man appealed his conviction by arguing that he had been involved in a consensual sexual encounter and had assaulted no one. In rejecting his appeal, the court ruled that one may not consent to an assault or battery "except in a situation involving ordinary physical contact or blows incident to sports such as football, boxing, or wrestling."[83] The court went on to note that the "consent of a person without legal capacity to give consent, such as a child or insane person, is ineffective," and that "It is a matter of common knowledge that a normal person in full possession of his mental faculties does not freely consent to the use, upon himself, of force likely to produce great bodily injury."[84] Therefore, anyone who would consent to a whipping would be presumed *non compos mentis* and legally incapable of consenting. S/M sex generally involves a much lower level of force than the average football game, and results in far fewer injuries than most sports. But the court ruled that football players are sane, whereas masochists are not.

Sodomy laws, adult incest laws, and legal interpretations such as the one above clearly interfere with consensual behavior and impose criminal penalties on it. Within the law, consent is a privilege enjoyed only by those who engage in the highest-status sexual behavior. Those who enjoy low-status sexual behavior do not have the legal right to engage in it. In addition, economic sanctions, family pressures, erotic stigma, social discrimination, negative ideology, and the paucity of information about erotic behavior, all serve to make it difficult for people to make unconventional sexual choices. There certainly are structural constraints that impede free sexual choice, but they hardly operate to coerce anyone into being a pervert. On the contrary, they operate to coerce everyone toward normality.

The "brainwash theory" explains erotic diversity by assuming that some sexual acts are so disgusting that no one would willingly perform them. Therefore, the reasoning goes, anyone who does so must have been forced or fooled. Even constructivist sexual theory has been pressed into the service of explaining away why otherwise rational individuals might engage in variant sexual behavior. Another position that is not yet fully formed uses the ideas of Foucault and Weeks to imply that the "perversions" are an especially unsavory or problematic aspect of the construction of modern sexuality.[85] This is yet another version of the notion that sexual dissidents are victims of the subtle machinations of the social system. Weeks and Foucault would not accept such an interpretation, since they consider all sexuality to be constructed, the conventional no less than the deviant.

Psychology is the last resort of those who refuse to acknowledge that sexual dissidents are as conscious and free as any other group of sexual actors. If deviants are not responding to the manipulations of the social system, then perhaps the source of their incomprehensible choices can be found in a bad childhood, unsuccessful socialization, or inadequate identity formation. In her essay on erotic domination, Jessica Benjamin draws upon psychoanalysis and philosophy to explain why what she calls "sadomasochism" is alienated, distorted, unsatisfactory, numb, purposeless, and an attempt to "relieve an original effort at differentiation that failed."[86] This essay substitutes a psychophilosophical inferiority for the more usual means of devaluing dissident eroticism. One reviewer has already construed Benjamin's argument as showing that sadomasochism is merely an "obsessive replay of the infant power struggle."[87]

The position which defends the political rights of perverts but which seeks to understand their "alienated" sexuality is certainly preferable to the WAP-style bloodbaths. But for the most part, the sexual moderates have not confronted their discomfort with erotic choices that differ from their own. Erotic chauvinism cannot be redeemed by tarting it up in Marxist drag, sophisticated constructivist theory, or retro-psychobabble.

Whichever feminist position on sexuality—right, left, or center—eventually attains dominance, the existence of such a rich discussion is evidence that the feminist movement will always be a source of interesting thought about sex. Nevertheless, I want to challenge the assumption that feminism is or should be the privileged site of a theory of sexuality. Feminism is the theory of gender oppression. To automatically assume that this makes it the theory of sexual oppression is to fail to distinguish between gender, on the one hand, and erotic desire, on the other.

In the English language, the word "sex" has two very different meanings. It means gender and gender identity, as in "the female sex" or "the male sex." But sex also refers to sexual activity, lust, intercourse, and arousal, as in "to have sex." This semantic merging reflects a cultural assumption that sexuality is reducible to sexual intercourse and that it is a function of the relations between women and men. The cultural fusion of gender with sexuality has given rise to the idea that a theory of sexuality may be derived directly out of a theory of gender.

In an earlier essay, "The Traffic in Women," I used the concept of a sex/gender system, defined as a "set of arrangements by which a society transforms biological sexuality into products of human activity."[88] I went on to argue that "Sex as we know it—gender identity, sexual desire and fantasy, concepts of childhood—is itself a social product."[89] In that essay, I did not distinguish between lust and gender, treating both as modalities of the same underlying social process.

"The Traffic in Women" was inspired by the literature on kin-based systems of social organization. It appeared to me at the time that gender and desire were systemically intertwined in such social formations. This may or may not be an accurate assessment of the relationship between sex and gender in tribal organizations. But it is surely not an adequate formulation for sexuality in Western industrial societies. As Foucault has pointed out, a system of sexuality has emerged out of earlier kinship forms and has acquired significant autonomy.

> Particularly from the eighteenth century onward, Western societies created and deployed a new apparatus which was superimposed on the previous one, and which, without completely supplanting the latter, helped to reduce its importance. I am speaking of the deployment of *sexuality*. . . . For the first [kinship], what is pertinent is the link between partners and definite statutes; the second [sexuality] is concerned with the sensations of the body, the quality of pleasures, and the nature of impressions.[90]

The development of this sexual system has taken place in the context of gender relations. Part of the modern ideology of sex is that lust is the province of men, purity that of women. Women have been to some extent excluded from the modern sexual system. It is no accident that pornography and the perversions have been considered part of the male domain. In the sex industry, women have been excluded from most production and consumption, and allowed to participate primarily as workers. In order to participate in the "perversions," women have had to overcome serious limitations on their social mobility, their economic resources, and their sexual freedoms. Gender affects the operation of the sexual system, and the sexual system has had gender-specific manifestations. But although sex and gender are related, they are not the same thing, and they form the basis of two distinct arenas of social practice.

In contrast to my perspective in "The Traffic in Women," I am now arguing that it is essential to separate gender and sexuality analytically to more accurately reflect their separate social existence. This goes against the grain of much contemporary feminist thought, which treats sexuality as a derivation of gender. For instance, lesbian feminist ideology has mostly analyzed the oppression of lesbians in terms of the oppression of women. However, lesbians are also oppressed as queers and perverts, by the operation of sexual, not gender, stratification. Although it pains many lesbians to think about it, the fact is that lesbians have shared many of the sociological features and suffered from many of the same social penalties as have gay men, sadomasochists, transvestites, and prostitutes.

Catherine MacKinnon has made the most explicit theoretical attempt to subsume sexuality under feminist thought. According to MacKinnon, "Sexuality is to feminism what work is to marxism . . . the molding, direction, and expression of sexuality organizes society into two sexes, women and men."[91] This analytic strategy in turn rests on a decision to "use sex and gender relatively interchangeably."[92] It is this definitional fusion that I want to challenge.

There is an instructive analogy in the history of the differentiation of contemporary feminist thought from Marxism. Marxism is probably the most supple and powerful conceptual system extant for analyzing social inequality. But attempts to make Marxism the sole explanatory system for all social inequalities have been dismal exercises. Marxism is most successful in the areas of social life for which it was originally developed—class relations under capitalism.

In the early days of the contemporary women's movement, a theoretical conflict took place over the applicability of Marxism to gender stratification. Since Marxist theory is relatively powerful, it does in fact detect important and interesting aspects of gender oppression. It works best for those issues of gender most closely related to issues of class and the organization of labor. The issues more specific to the social structure of gender were not amenable to Marxist analysis.

The relationship between feminism and a radical theory of sexual oppression is similar. Feminist conceptual tools were developed to detect and analyze gender-based hierarchies. To the extent that these overlap with erotic stratifications, feminist theory has some explanatory power. But as issues become less those of gender and more those of sexuality, feminist analysis becomes irrelevant and often misleading. Feminist thought simply lacks angles of vision which can encompass the social organization of sexuality. The criteria of relevance in feminist thought do not allow it to see or assess critical power relations in the area of sexuality.

In the long run, feminism's critique of gender hierarchy must be incorporated into a radical theory of sex, and the critique of sexual oppression should enrich feminism. But an autonomous theory and politics specific to sexuality must be developed.

It is a mistake to substitute feminism for Marxism as the last word in social theory. Feminism is no more capable than Marxism of being the ultimate and complete account of all social inequality. Nor is feminism the residual theory which can take care of everything to which Marx did not attend. These critical tools were fashioned to handle very specific areas of social activity. Other areas of social life, their forms of power, and their characteristic modes of oppression, need their own conceptual implements. In this essay, I have argued for theoretical as well as sexual pluralism.

VII Conclusion

> . . . these pleasures which we lightly call physical . . .
>
> Colette[93]

Like gender, sexuality is political. It is organized into systems of power, which reward and encourage some individuals and activities, while punishing and suppressing others. Like the capitalist organization of labor and its distribution of rewards and powers, the modern sexual system has been the object of political struggle since it emerged and as it has evolved. But if the disputes between labor and capital are mystified, sexual conflicts are completely camouflaged.

The legislative restructuring that took place at the end of the nineteenth century and in the early decades of the twentieth was a refracted response to the emergence of the modern erotic system. During that period, new erotic communities formed. It became possible to be a male homosexual or a lesbian in a way it had not been previously. Mass-produced erotica became available, and the possibilities for sexual commerce expanded. The first homosexual rights organizations were formed, and the first analyses of sexual oppression were articulated.[94]

The repression of the 1950s was in part a backlash to the expansion of sexual communities and possibilities which took place during World War II.[95] During the 1950s, gay rights organizations were established, the Kinsey reports were published, and lesbian literature flourished. The 1950s were a formative as well as a repressive era.

The current right-wing sexual counter-offensive is in part a reaction to the sexual liberalization of the 1960s and early 1970s. Moreover, it has brought about a unified and self-conscious coalition of sexual radicals. In one sense, what is now occurring is the emergence of a new sexual movement, aware of new issues and seeking a new theoretical basis. The sex wars out on the streets have been partly responsible for provoking a new intellectual focus on sexuality. The sexual system is shifting once again, and we are seeing many symptoms of its change.

In Western culture, sex is taken all too seriously. A person is not considered immoral, is not sent to prison, and is not expelled from her or his family, for enjoying spicy cuisine. But an individual may go through all this and more for enjoying shoe leather. Ultimately, of what possible social significance is it if a person likes to masturbate over a shoe? It may even be non-consensual, but since we do not ask permission of our shoes to wear them, it hardly seems necessary to obtain dispensation to come on them.

If sex is taken too seriously, sexual persecution is not taken seriously enough. There is systematic mistreatment of individuals and communities on the basis of erotic taste or behavior. There are serious penalties for belonging to the various sexual occupational castes. The sexuality of the young is denied, adult sexuality is often treated like a variety of nuclear waste, and the graphic representation of sex takes place in a mire of legal and social circumlocution. Specific populations bear the brunt of the current system of erotic power, but their persecution upholds a system that affects everyone.

The 1980s have already been a time of great sexual suffering. They have also been a time of ferment and new possibility. It is up to all of us to try to prevent more barbarism and to encourage erotic creativity. Those who consider themselves progressive need to examine their preconceptions, update their sexual educations, and acquaint themselves with the existence and operation of sexual hierarchy. It is time to recognize the political dimensions of erotic life.

Acknowledgments

It is always a treat to get to the point in a paper when I can thank those who contributed to its realization. Many of my ideas about the formation of sexual communities first occurred to me during a course given by Charles Tilly on "The Urbanization of Europe from 1500–1900." Few courses could ever provide as much excitement, stimulation, and conceptual richness as did that one. Daniel Tsang alerted me to the significance of the events of 1977 and taught me to pay attention to sex law. Pat Califia deepened my appreciation for human sexual variety and taught me to respect the much-maligned fields of sex research and sex education. Jeff Escoffier shared his powerful grasp of gay history and sociology, and I have especially benefited from his insights into the gay economy. Allan Bérubé's work in progress on gay history has enabled me to think with more clarity about the dynamics of sexual oppression. Conversations with Ellen Dubois, Amber Hollibaugh, Mary Ryan, Judy Stacey, Kay Trimberger, and Martha Vicinus have influenced the direction of my thinking.

I am very grateful to Cynthia Astuto for advice and research on legal matters, and to David Sachs, book-dealer extraordinaire, for pointing out the right-wing pamphlet literature on sex. I am grateful to Allan Bérubé, Ralph Bruno, Estelle Freedman, Kent Gerard, Barbara Kerr, Michael Shively, Carole Vance, Bill Walker, and Judy Walkowitz for miscellaneous references and factual information. I cannot begin to express my gratitude to those who read and commented on versions of this paper: Jeanne Bergman, Sally Binford, Lynn Eden, Laura Engelstein, Jeff Escoffier, Carole Vance and Ellen Willis. Mark Leger both edited and performed acts of secretarial heroism in preparing the manuscript. Marybeth Nelson provided emergency graphics assistance.

I owe special thanks to two friends whose care mitigated the strains of writing. E.S. kept my back operational and guided me firmly through some monumental bouts of writer's block. Cynthia Astuto's many kindnesses and unwavering support enabled me to keep working at an absurd pace for many weeks.

None of these individuals should be held responsible for my opinions, but I am grateful to them all for inspiration, information, and assistance.

A Note on Definitions

Throughout this essay, I use terms such as homosexual, sex worker, and pervert. I use "homosexual" to refer to both women and men. If I want to be more specific, I use terms such as "lesbian" or "gay male." "Sex worker" is intended to be more inclusive than "prostitute," in order to encompass the many jobs of the sex industry. Sex worker includes erotic dancers, strippers, porn models, nude women who will talk to a customer via telephone hook-up and can be seen but not touched, phone partners, and the various other employees of sex businesses such as receptionists, janitors, and barkers. Obviously, it also includes prostitutes, hustlers, and "male models." I use the term "pervert" as a shorthand for all the stigmatized sexual orientations. It used to cover male and female homosexuality as well but as these become less disreputable, the term has increasingly referred to the other "deviations." Terms such as "pervert" and "deviant" have, in general use, a connotation of disapproval, disgust, and dislike. I am using these terms in a denotative fashion, and do not intend them to convey any disapproval on my part.

Notes

1. Demetrius Zambaco, "Onanism and Nervous Disorders in Two Little Girls," in Francois Peraldi (ed.), *Polysexuality, Semiotext(e)*, vol. IV, no. 1, 1981, pp. 31, 36.
2. Linda Gordon and Ellen Dubois, "Seeking Ecstasy on the Battlefield: Danger and Pleasure in Nineteenth Century Feminist Sexual Thought," *Feminist Studies*, vol. 9, no. 1, Spring 1983; Steven Marcus, *The Other Victorians*, New York, New American Library, 1974; Mary Ryan, "The Power of Women's Networks: A Case

Study of Female Moral Reform in America," *Feminist Studies*, vol. 5, no. 1, 1979; Judith R. Walkowitz, *Prostitution and Victorian Society*, Cambridge, Cambridge University Press, 1980; Judith R. Walkowitz, "Male Vice and Feminist Virtue: Feminism and the Politics of Prostitution in Nineteenth-Century Britain," *History Workshop Journal*, no. 13, Spring 1982; Jeffrey Weeks, *Sex, Politics and Society: The Regulation of Sexuality Since 1800*, New York, Longman, 1981.

3. G.J. Barker-Benfield, *The Horrors of the Half-Known Life*, New York, Harper Colophon, 1976; Marcus, op. cit.; Weeks, op. cit., especially pages 48–52; Zambaco, op. cit.

4. Sarah Senefield Beserra, Sterling G. Franklin, and Norma Clevenger (eds), *Sex Code of California*, Sacramento, Planned Parenthood Affiliates of California, 1977, p. 113.

5. Ibid., pp. 113–17.

6. Walkowitz, "Male Vice and Feminist Virtue," op. cit., p. 83. Walkowitz's entire discussion of the *Maiden Tribute of Modern Babylon* and its aftermath (pp. 83–5) is illuminating.

7. Walkowitz, "Male Vice and Feminist Virtue," op. cit., p. 85.

8. Beserra et al, op. cit., pp. 106–7.

9. Commonwealth of Massachusetts, *Preliminary Report of the Special Commission Investigating the Prevalence of Sex Crimes*, 1947; State of New Hampshire. *Report of the Interim Commission of the State of New Hampshire to Study the Cause and Prevention of Serious Sex Crimes*, 1949; City of New York, *Report of the Mayor's Committee for the Study of Sex Offences*, 1939; State of New York, *Report to the Governor on a Study of 102 Sex Offenders at Sing Sing Prison*, 1950; Samuel Hartwell, *A Citizen's Handbook of Sexual Abnormalities and the Mental Hygiene Approach to Their Prevention*, State of Michigan, 1950; State of Michigan, *Report of the Governor's Study Commission on the Deviated Criminal Sex Offender*, 1951. This is merely a sampler.

10. Estelle B. Freedman, "'Uncontrolled Desire': The Threat of the Sexual Psychopath in America, 1935–1960," paper presented at the Annual Meeting of the American Historical Association, San Francisco, December 1983.

11. Allan Bérubé, "Behind the Spectre of San Francisco," *Body Politic*, April 1981; Allan Bérubé, "Marching to a Different Drummer," *Advocate*, October 15, 1981; John D'Emilio, *Sexual Politics, Sexual Communities: The Making of the Homosexual Minority in the United States, 1940–1970*, Chicago, University of Chicago Press, 1983; Jonathan Katz, *Gay American History*, New York, Thomas Y. Crowell, 1976.

12. D'Emilio, op. cit., pp. 46–7; Allan Bérubé, personal communication.

13. John Gerassi, *The Boys of Boise*, New York, Collier, 1968, p. 14. I am indebted to Allan Bérubé for calling my attention to this incident.

14. Allan Bérubé, personal communication; D'Emilio, op. cit.; John D'Emilio, "Gay Politics, Gay Community: San Francisco's Experience," *Socialist Review*, no. 55, January–February 1981.

15. The following examples suggest avenues for additional research. A local crackdown at the University of Michigan is documented in Daniel Tsang, "Gay Ann Arbor Purges," *Midwest Gay Academic Journal*, vol. 1, no. 1, 1977: and Daniel Tsang, "Ann Arbor Gay Purges," part 2, *Midwest Gay Academic Journal*, vol. 1, no. 2, 1977. At the University of Michigan, the number of faculty dismissed for alleged homosexuality appears to rival the number fired for alleged communist tendencies. It would be interesting to have figures comparing the number of

professors who lost their positions during this period due to sexual and political offenses. On regulatory reform, many states passed laws during this period prohibiting the sale of alcoholic beverages to "known sex perverts" or providing that bars which catered to "sex perverts" be closed. Such a law was passed in California in 1955, and declared unconstitutional by the state Supreme Court in 1959 (Allan Bérubé, personal communication). It would be of great interest to know exactly which states passed such statutes, the dates of their enactment, the discussion that preceded them, and how many are still on the books. On the persecution of other erotic populations, evidence indicates that John Willie and Irving Klaw, the two premier producers and distributors of bondage erotica in the United States from the late 1940s through the early 1960s, encountered frequent police harassment and that Klaw, at least, was affected by a congressional investigation conducted by the Kefauver Committee. I am indebted to personal communication from J.B. Rund for information on the careers of Willie and Klaw. Published sources are scarce, but see John Willie, *The Adventures of Sweet Gwendoline*, New York, Belier Press, 1974; J.B. Rund, "Preface," *Bizarre Comix*, vol. 8, New York, Belier Press, 1977; J.B. Rund, "Preface," *Bizarre Fotos*, vol. 1, New York, Belier Press, 1978; and J.B. Rund, "Preface," *Bizarre Katalogs*, vol. 1, New York. Belier Press, 1979. It would be useful to have more systematic information on legal shifts and police activity affecting non-gay erotic dissidence.

16. "Chicago is Center of National Child Porno Ring: The Child Predators," "Child Sex: Square in New Town Tells it All," "U.S. Orders Hearings On Child Pornography: Rodino Calls Sex Racket an 'Outrage,'" "Hunt Six Men, Twenty Boys in Crackdown," *Chicago Tribune*, May 16, 1977; "Dentist Seized in Child Sex Raid: Carey to Open Probe," "How Ruses Lure Victims to Child Pornographers," *Chicago Tribune*, May 17, 1977; "Child Pornographers Thrive on Legal Confusion," "U.S. Raids Hit Porn Sellers," *Chicago Tribune*, May 18, 1977.

17. For more information on the "kiddie porn panic" see Pat Califia, "The Great Kiddy Porn Scare of '77 and Its Aftermath," *Advocate*, October 16, 1980; Pat Califia, "A Thorny Issue Splits a Movement," *Advocate*, October 30, 1980; Mitzel, *The Boston Sex Scandal*, Boston, Glad Day Books, 1980; Gayle Rubin, "Sexual Politics, the New Right, and the Sexual Fringe," in Daniel Tsang (ed.), *The Age Taboo*, Boston, Alyson Publications, 1981; on the issue of cross-generational relationships, see also Roger Moody, *Indecent Assault*, London, Word Is Out Press, 1980; Tom O'Carroll, *Paedophilia: The Radical Case*, London, Peter Owen, 1980; Tsang, *The Age Taboo*, op. cit., and Paul Wilson, *The Man They Called A Monster*, New South Wales, Cassell Australia, 1981.

18. "House Passes Tough Bill on Child Porn," *San Francisco Chronicle*, November 15, 1983, p. 14.

19. George Stambolian, "Creating the New Man: A Conversation with Jacqueline Livingston," *Christopher Street*, May 1980; "Jacqueline Livingston," *Clothed With the Sun*, vol. 3, no. 1, May 1983.

20. Paul H. Gebhard, "The Institute," in Martin S. Weinberg (ed.), *Sex Research: Studies from the Kinsey Institute*, New York, Oxford University Press, 1976.

21. Phoebe Courtney, *The Sex Education Racket: Pornography in the Schools (An Exposé)*, New Orleans, Free Men Speak, 1969; Dr Gordon V. Drake, *SIECUS: Corrupter of Youth*, Tulsa, Oklahoma, Christian Crusade Publications, 1969.

22. *Pavlov's Children (They May Be Yours)*, Impact Publishers, Los Angeles, California, 1969.

23. Norman Podhoretz, "The Culture of Appeasement," *Harper's*, October 1977.

24. Alan Wolfe and Jerry Sanders, "Resurgent Cold War Ideology: The Case of the Committee on the Present Danger," in Richard Fagen (ed.), *Capitalism and the State in U.S.-Latin American Relations*, Stanford, Stanford University Press, 1979.

25. Jimmy Breslin, "The Moral Majority in Your Motel Room," *San Francisco Chronicle*, January 22, 1981, p. 41; Linda Gordon and Allen Hunter, "Sex, Family, and the New Right," *Radical America*, winter 1977–8; Sasha Gregory-Lewis, "The Neo-Right Political Apparatus," *Advocate*, February 8, 1977; Sasha Gregory-Lewis, "Right Wing Finds New Organizing Tactic," *Advocate*, June 23, 1977; Sasha Gregory-Lewis, "Unravelling the Anti-Gay Network," *Advocate*, September 7, 1977; Andrew Kopkind, "America's New Right," *New Times*, September 30, 1977; Rosalind Pollack Petchesky, "Anti-abortion, Anti-feminism, and the Rise of the New Right," *Feminist Studies*, vol. 7, no. 2, summer 1981.

26. Rhonda Brown, "Blueprint for a Moral America," *Nation*, May 23, 1981.

27. James Barr, *Quatrefoil*, New York, Greenberg, 1950, p. 310.

28. This insight was first articulated by Mary McIntosh, "The Homosexual Role," *Social Problems*, vol. 16, no. 2, fall 1968; the idea has been developed in Jeffrey Weeks, *Coming Out: Homosexual Politics in Britain from the Nineteenth Century to the Present*, New York, Quartet, 1977, and in Weeks, *Sex, Politics and Society*, op. cit.; see also D'Emilio, *Sexual Politics, Sexual Communities*, op. cit.; and Gayle Rubin, "Introduction" to Renée Vivien, *A Woman Appeared to Me*, Weatherby Lake, Mo., Naiad Press, 1979.

29. Bert Hansen, "The Historical Construction of Homosexuality," *Radical History Review*, no. 20, Spring/Summer 1979.

30. Walkowitz, *Prostitution and Victorian Society*, op. cit.; and Walkowitz, "Male Vice and Female Virtue," op. cit.

31. Michael Foucault, *The History of Sexuality*, New York, Pantheon, 1978.

32. A very useful discussion of these issues can be found in Robert Padgug, "Sexual Matters: On Conceptualizing Sexuality in History," *Radical History Review*, no. 20, spring/summer 1979.

33. Claude Lévi-Strauss, "A Confrontation," *New Left Review*, no. 62, July–August 1970. In this conversation, Lévi-Strauss calls his position "a Kantianism without a transcendental subject."

34. Foucault, op. cit., p. 11.

35. See the discussion in Weeks, *Sex, Politics and Society*, op. cit., p. 9.

36. See Weeks, *Sex, Politics and Society*, op. cit., p. 22.

37. See, for example, "Pope Praises Couples for Self-Control," *San Francisco Chronicle*, October 13, 1980, p. 5; "Pope Says Sexual Arousal Isn't a Sin If It's Ethical," *San Francisco Chronicle*, November 6, 1980, p. 33; "Pope Condemns 'Carnal Lust' As Abuse of Human Freedom," *San Francisco Chronicle*, January 15, 1981, p. 2; "Pope Again Hits Abortion, Birth Control," *San Francisco Chronicle*, January 16, 1981, p. 13; and "Sexuality, Not Sex in Heaven," *San Francisco Chronicle*, December 3, 1981, p. 50. See also footnote 62 below.

38. Susan Sontag, *Styles of Radical Will*, New York, Farrar, Strauss, & Giroux, 1969, p.46.

39. See Foucault, op. cit., pp. 106–7.

40. American Psychiatric Association, *Diagnostic and Statistical Manual of Mental and Physical Disorders*, 3rd edn, Washington, DC, American Psychiatric Association.

41. Alfred Kinsey, Wardell Pomeroy, and Clyde Martin, *Sexual Behavior in the Human Male*, Philadelphia, W.B. Saunders, 1948; Alfred Kinsey, Wardell Pomeroy, Clyde Martin, and Paul Gebhard, *Sexual Behavior in the Human Female*, Philadelphia, W.B. Saunders, 1953.

42. John Gagnon and William Simon, *Sexual Deviance*, New York, Harper & Row, 1967; John Gagnon and William Simon, *The Sexual Scene*, Chicago, Transaction Books, Aldine, 1970; John Gagnon, *Human Sexualities*, Glenview, Illinois, Scott, Foresman, 1977.

43. Havelock Ellis, *Studies in the Psychology of Sex* (two volumes), New York, Random House, 1936.

44. Foucault, op. cit., p. 43.

45. Gilbert Herdt, *Guardians of the Flutes*, New York, McGraw-Hill, 1981; Raymond Kelly, "Witchcraft and Sexual Relations," in Paula Brown and Georgeda Buchbinder (eds), *Man and Woman in the New Guinea Highlands*, Washington, DC, American Anthropological Association, 1976; Gayle Rubin, "Coconuts: Aspects of Male/Female Relationships in New Guinea," unpublished ms., 1974; Gayle Rubin, review of *Guardians of the Flutes*, *Advocate*, December 23, 1982; J. Van Baal, *Dema*, The Hague, Nijhoff, 1966; F.E. Williams, *Papuans of the Trans-Fly*, Oxford, Clarendon, 1936.

46. Caroline Bingham, "Seventeenth-Century Attitudes Toward Deviant Sex," *Journal of Interdisciplinary History*, spring 1971, p. 465.

47. Stephen O. Murray, "The Institutional Elaboration of a Quasi-Ethnic Community," *International Review of Modern Sociology*, July–December 1979.

48. For further elaboration of these processes, see: Bérubé, "Behind the Spectre of San Francisco," op. cit.; Bérubé, "Marching to a Different Drummer," op. cit.; D'Emilio, "Gay Politics, Gay Community," op. cit.; D'Emilio, *Sexual Politics, Sexual Communities*, op. cit.; Foucault, op. cit.; Hansen, op. cit.; Katz, op.cit.; Weeks, *Coming Out*, op. cit.; and Weeks, *Sex, Politics and Society*, op. cit.

49. Walkowitz, *Prostitution and Victorian Society*, op. cit.

50. Vice cops also harass all sex businesses, be these gay bars, gay baths, adult book stores, the producers and distributors of commercial erotica, or swing clubs.

51. Foucault, op. cit., p. 40.

52. Karl Marx, in David McLellan (ed.), *The Grundrisse*, New York, Harper & Row, 1971, p. 94.

53. Clark Norton, "Sex in America," *Inquiry*, October 5, 1981. This article is a superb summary of much current sex law and should be required reading for anyone interested in sex.

54. Bessera et al., *op. cit.*, pp. 165–7.

55. Sarah Senefeld Beserra, Nancy M. Jewel, Melody West Matthews, and Elizabeth R. Gatov (eds), *Sex Code of California*, Public Education and Research Committee of California, 1973, pp. 163–8. This earlier edition of the *Sex Code of California* preceeded the 1976 consenting adults statute and consequently gives a better overview of sodomy laws.

56. Esther Newton, *Mother Camp: Female Impersonators in America*, Englewood Cliffs, New Jersey, Prentice-Hall, 1972, p. 21, emphasis in the original.

57. D'Emilio, *Sexual Politics, Sexual Communities*, op. cit., pp. 40–53, has an excellent discussion of gay oppression in the 1950s which covers many of the areas I have mentioned. The dynamics he describes, however, are operative in modified forms for other erotic populations, and in other periods. The specific model of gay oppression needs to be generalized to apply, with appropriate modifications, to other sexual groups.

58. Weeks, *Sex, Politics and Society*, op. cit., p. 14.

59. Lysander Spooner, *Vices Are Not Crimes: A Vindication of Moral Liberty*, Cupertino, CA, Tanstaafl Press, 1977.

60. I have adopted this terminology from the very useful discussion in Weeks, *Sex, Politics and Society*, op. cit., pp. 14–15.

61. See Spooner, op. cit., pp. 25-9. Feminist anti-porn discourse fits right into the tradition of justifying attempts at moral control by claiming that such action will protect women and children from violence.

62. "Pope's Talk on Sexual Spontaneity," *San Francisco Chronicle*. November 13, 1980, p. 8; see also footnote 37 above. Julia Penelope argues that "we do not need anything that labels itself purely sexual" and that "fantasy, as an aspect of sexuality, may be a phallocentric 'need' from which we are not yet free." in "And Now For the Really Hard Questions," *Sinister Wisdom*, no. 15, fall 1980, p. 103.

63. See especially Walkowitz, *Prostitution and Victorian Society*, op. cit., and Weeks, *Sex, Politics and Society*, op. cit.

64. *Moral Majority Report*, July 1983. I am indebted to Allan Bérubé for calling my attention to this image.

65. Cited in Larry Bush, "Capitol Report," *Advocate*, December 8, 1983, p. 60.

66. Cited in H. Montgomery Hyde, *A History of Pornography*, New York, Dell, 1965, p. 31.

67. See for example Laura Lederer (ed.), *Take Back the Night*, New York, William Morrow, 1980; Andrea Dworkin, *Pornography*, New York, Perigee, 1981. The *Newspage* of San Francisco's Women Against Violence in Pornography and Media and the *Newsreport* of New York Women Against Pornography are excellent sources.

68. Kathleen Barry, *Female Sexual Slavery*, Englewood Cliffs, New Jersey, Prentice-Hall, 1979; Janice Raymond, *The Transsexual Empire*, Boston, Beacon, 1979; Kathleen Barry, "Sadomasochism: The New Backlash to Feminism," *Trivia*, no. 1, fall 1982; Robin Ruth Linden, Darlene R. Pagano, Diana E. H. Russell, and Susan Leigh Starr (eds), *Against Sadomasochism*, East Palo Alto, CA, Frog in the Well, 1982; and Florence Rush, *The Best Kept Secret*, New York, McGraw-Hill, 1980.

69. Sally Gearhart, "An Open Letter to the Voters in District 5 and San Francisco's Gay Community," 1979; Adrienne Rich, *On Lies, Secrets, and Silence*, New York, W.W. Norton, 1979, p. 225. ("On the other hand, there is homosexual patriarchal culture, a culture created by homosexual men, reflecting such male stereotypes as dominance and submission as modes of relationship, and the separation of sex from emotional involvement—a culture tainted by profound hatred for women. The male 'gay' culture has offered lesbians the imitation role-stereotypes of 'butch' and 'femme', 'active' and 'passive,' cruising, sado-masochism, and the violent, self-destructive world of 'gay' bars."); Judith Pasternak, "The Strangest Bedfellows: Lesbian Feminism and the Sexual Revolution," *WomanNews*, October 1983; Adrienne Rich, "Compulsory Heterosexuality and Lesbian Existence," in

Ann Snitow, Christine Stansell, and Sharon Thompson (eds), *Powers of Desire: The Politics of Sexuality*, New York, Monthly Review Press, 1983.

70. Julia Penlope, op. cit.

71. Sheila Jeffreys, "The Spinster and Her Enemies: Sexuality and the Last Wave of Feminism," *Scarlet Woman*, no. 13, part 2, July 1981, p. 26; a further elaboration of this tendency can be found in Judith Pasternak, op. cit.

72. Pat Califia, "Feminism vs. Sex: A New Conservative Wave," *Advocate*, February 21, 1980; Pat Califia, "Among Us, Against Us—The New Puritans," *Advocate*, April 17, 1980; Califia, "The Great Kiddy Porn Scare of '77 and Its Aftermath," op. cit.; Califia, "A Thorny Issue Splits a Movement," op. cit.; Pat Califia, *Sapphistry*, Tallahassee, Florida, Naiad, 1980; Pat Califia, "What Is Gay Liberation," *Advocate*, June 25, 1981; Pat Califia, "Feminism and Sadomasochism," *Co-Evolution Quarterly*, no. 33, spring 1981; Pat Califia, "Response to Dorchen Leidholdt," *New Women's Times*, October 1982; Pat Califia, "Public Sex," *Advocate*, September 30, 1982; Pat Califia, "Doing It Together: Gay Men, Lesbians, and Sex," *Advocate*, July 7, 1983; Pat Califia, "Gender-Bending," *Advocate*, September 15, 1983; Pat Califia, "The Sex Industry," *Advocate*, October 13, 1983; Deirdre English, Amber Hollibaugh, and Gayle Rubin, "Talking Sex," *Socialist Review*, July-August 1981; "Sex Issue," *Heresies*, no. 12, 1981; Amber Hollibaugh, "The Erotophobic Voice of Women: Building a Movement for the Nineteenth Century," *New York Native*, September 26-October 9, 1983; Maxine Holz, "Porn: Turn On or Put Down, Some Thoughts on Sexuality," *Processed World*, no. 7, spring 1983; Barbara O'Dair, "Sex, Love, and Desire: Feminists Struggle Over the Portrayal of Sex," *Alternative Media*, spring 1983; Lisa Orlando, "Bad Girls and 'Good' Politics," *Village Voice*, Literary Supplement, December 1982; Joanna Russ, "Being Against Pornography," *Thirteenth Moon*, vol. VI, nos 1 and 2, 1982; Samois, *What Color Is Your Handkerchief*, Berkeley, Samois, 1979; Samois, *Coming to Power*, Boston, Alyson, 1982; Deborah Sundahl, "Stripping For a Living," *Advocate*, October 13, 1983; Nancy Wechsler, "Interview with Pat Califia and Gayle Rubin," part I, *Gay Community News*, Book Review, July 18, 1981, and part II, *Gay Community News*, August 15, 1981; Ellen Willis, *Beginning to See the Light*, New York, Knopf, 1981; for an excellent overview of the history of the ideological shifts in feminism which have affected the sex debates, see Alice Echols, "Cultural Feminism: Feminist Capitalism and the Anti-Pornography Movement," *Social Text*, no. 7, spring and summer 1983.

73. Lisa Orlando, "Lust at Last! Spandex Invades the Academy," *Gay Community News*, May 15, 1982; Ellen Willis, "Who Is a Feminist? An Open Letter to Robin Morgan," *Village Voice*, Literary Supplement, December 1982.

74. Ellen Willis, *Beginning to See the Light*, op. cit., p. 146. I am indebted to Jeanne Bergman for calling my attention to this quote.

75. See, for example, Jessica Benjamin, "Master and Slave: The Fantasy of Erotic Domination," in Snitow et al., op. cit., p. 297; and B. Ruby Rich, review of *Powers of Desire*, *In These Times*, November 16–22, 1983.

76. B. Ruby Rich, op. cit., p. 76.

77. Samois, *What Color Is Your Handkerchief*, op. cit.; Samois, *Coming To Power*, op. cit.; Pat Califia, "Feminism and Sadomasochism," op. cit.; Pat Califia, *Sapphistry*, op. cit.

78. Lisa Orlando, "Power Plays: Coming To Terms With Lesbian S/M," *Village Voice*, July 26, 1983; Elizabeth Wilson, "*The Context of 'Between Pleasure and*

Danger': *The Barnard Conference on Sexuality*," *Feminist Review*, no. 13, spring 1983, especially pp. 35–41.

79. *Taylor* v. *State*, 214 Md. 156, 165, 133 A. 2d 414, 418. This quote is from a dissenting opinion, but it is a statement of prevailing law.
80. Bessera, Jewel, Matthew, and Gatov, op. cit., pp. 163–5. See note 55 above.
81. "Marine and Mom Guilty of Incest," *San Francisco Chronicle*, November 16, 1979, p. 16.
82. Norton, op. cit., p. 18.
83. *People* v. *Samuels*, 250 Cal. App. 2d 501, 513, 58 Cal. Rptr. 439, 447 (1967).
84. *People* v. *Samuels*, 250 Cal. App. 2d. at 513–514, 58 Cal. Rptr. at 447.
85. Mariana Valverde, "Feminism Meets Fist-Fucking: Getting Lost in Lesbian S & M," *Body Politic*, February 1980; Wilson, op. cit., p. 38.
86. Benjamin, op. cit. p. 292, but see also pp. 286, 291–7.
87. Barbara Ehrenreich, "What Is This Thing Called Sex," *Nation*, September 24, 1983, p. 247.
88. Gayle Rubin, "The Traffic in Women," in Rayna R. Reiter (ed.), *Toward an Anthropology of Women*, New York, Monthly Review Press, 1975, p. 159.
89. Rubin, "The Traffic in Women," op. cit., p. 166.
90. Foucault, op. cit., p. 106.
91. Catherine MacKinnon, "Feminism, Marxism, Method and the State: An Agenda for Theory," *Signs*, vol. 7, no. 3, spring 1982, pp. 515-16.
92. Catherine MacKinnon, "Feminism, Marxism, Method, and the State: Toward Feminist Jurisprudence," *Signs*, vol. 8, no. 4, summer 1983, p. 635.
93. Colette, *The Ripening Seed*, translated and cited in Hannah Alderfer, Beth Jaker, and Marybeth Nelson, *Diary of a Conference on Sexuality*, New York, Faculty Press, 1982, p. 72.
94. John Lauritsen and David Thorstad, *The Early Homosexual Rights Movement in Germany*, New York, Times Change Press, 1974.
95. D'Emilio, *Sexual Politics, Sexual Communities*, op. cit.; Bérubé "Behind the Spectre of San Francisco," op. cit.; Bérubé, "Marching to a Different Drummer," op. cit.

Questions for Reflection, Discussion, and Writing

1. There are times, or eras in our history when the politics of sex and sexuality come under scrutiny and attack, according to Gayle Rubin. What social, cultural and political scenarios tend to characterize those times? What evidence does Rubin cite to suggest that the 1980s and 1990s constitute such a time?
2. How does the religious right use children to draw attention to (homo)sexuality, and what form does the resulting legislation tend to take? What are some of the most public groups, and what arguments do they present in support of their legislation?
3. What is Rubin's "radical theory of sex"? On what premises and beliefs is it based? In what ways does it tend to challenge "normative" and "essentialist" notions of sexuality?
4. What sexual hierarchy does Rubin claim characterizes current "sexual values"? What lines exist? How does she represent those lines and that hierarchy? What institutions (social, legal, cultural) sustain the hierarchy and the divides between these lines?

5. Aside from homosexuality and prostitution, what other practices tend to come under scrutiny? What arguments (like moral panic) does Rubin offer to explain why this scrutiny and resulting legislation is often misplaced? What are the "underlying" issues, and how are they obscured? What tactics does the media use to help obscure those issues?

6. While feminism has helped to start a discourse about sexuality, Rubin claims that "the relationship between feminism and sex is complex". What tensions and debates about sex within feminist thought and scholarship does Rubin identify? Who is arguing about it, and what are their positions, according to Rubin? How does she position herself?

Related Reading

Dennis Altman, "Sex: The New Front Line for Gay Politics" (1982) in *We Are Everywhere: A Historical Sourcebook of Gay and Lesbian Politics.* Mark Blasius and Shane Phelan, Eds. NY: Routledge. 1997.529–534.

Jan Browne and Victor Minichiello, "Research Directions in Male Sex Work." *Journal of Homosexuality 31*.4 (1996): 29–56.

Pat Califia, "Feminism and Sadomasochism." *Heresies* 12 (1981): 30–34.

Pat Califia, "The Limits of the S/M Relationship." *Out/Look* 4.3 (Winter 1992): 16–21.

Pat Califia, *Public Sex: The Culture of Radical Sex.* San Francisco: Cleis Press. 2000.

R.W. Connell, "Democracies of Pleasure: Thoughts on the Goals of Radical Sexual Politics" in *Social Postmodernism: Beyond Identity Politics.* Linda Nicholson and Steven Seidman, Eds. Cambridge: Cambridge UP. 1995. 384–397.

Julia Creet, "Daughter of the Movement: The Psychodynamics of Lesbian S/M Fantasy." *differences* 3.2 (1991): 135–159.

Patricia L. Duncan, "Identity, Power, and Difference: Negotiating Conflict in an S/M Dyke Community" in *Queer Studies: A Lesbian, Gay, Bisexual, and Transgender Anthology.* Brett Beemyn and Mickey Eliason, Eds. NY: NYUP. 1996. 87–114.

John Nguyet Emi, "Queer Figurations in the Media: Critical Reflections on the Michael Jackson Sex Scandal." *Critical Studies in Mass Communication 15* (2 June 1998): 158–180.

Jeffrey Escoffier, "Sexual Revolution and the Politics of Gay Identity" in *American Homo.* Berkeley: University of California Press. 1998. 33-33–64.

Lynda Hart, *Between the Body and the Flesh: Performing Sadomasochism.* NY: Columbia UP. 1998.

Lisa Henderson, "Lesbian Pornography: Cultural Transgression and Sexual Demystification" in *New Lesbian Criticism.* Sally Munt, Ed. NY: Columbia UP. 1991. 173–191.

Marti Holman, "Leatherdykes Under the Skin." *The Harvard Gay & Lesbian Review* 4.2 (Spring 1997): 37–40.

Jackie James, "Excuse Me Madam, Are You Looking For A Good Time?" in *Assaults on Convention: Essays on Lesbian Transgressors.* Nicola Godwin, Belinda Hollows and Sheridan Nye, Eds. London: Cassell. 1996. 146–155.

Eva Pendleton and Jane Goldschmidt, "Sex Panic!—Make the Connections." *The Harvard Gay & Lesbian Review 5.3* (Summer 1998): 30–33.

John Preston, "What Happened?" *Out/Look* 4.3 (Winter 1992): 8–14.

Mark Pritchard, "Liberating Pornography" in *Bisexual Politics: Theories, Queries, and Visions.* Naomi Tucker, Ed. Binghamton, NY: Harrington Park Press. 1995. 171–178.

Wieland Speck, "Porno?" in *Queer Looks.* Martha Gever, John Greyson and Pratibha Parmar, Eds. NY: Routledge. 1993. 348–354.

Wickle Stamps, "Fine Lines" in *Queer View Mirror: Lesbian and Gay Short Short Fiction.* James C. Johnson and Karen X. Tulchinsky, Eds. Vancouver, BC: Arsenal Pulp Press. 1995. 253.

Jeffrey Weeks, "The Meaning of Diversity" in *Social Perspectives in Lesbian and Gay Studies.* Peter M. Nardi and Beth E. Schneider, Eds. NY: Routledge. 1998. 312–333.

Film

Leather (1995). Hardy Haberman. 10 m.

The Attendant (1992). Isaac Julien. 8 m.

S & M In the Hood (1998). Al Lujan. 5 m.

Malaysian Series 1–6 (1986–1987). Azian Nurudin. 15 m.

Wicked Radiance (1992). Azian Nurudin. 5 m.

Female Misbehavior (1983–92). Monika Treut. 80 m.

Special Topics

Many people have strong reactions to the idea of intergenerational sex. Of course, pedophilia has long been used by the right and by conservative Christian America as a propaganda tool to make the idea of queer (queer = child abuse) profoundly threatening to mainstream, heteronormative America. So it is hard to *want* to claim it as an issue; the sexual abuse of children *is* a reality in a society that accords patriarchal power, privilege and entitlement both within and outside of the home. Yet the issue *is* a complex one. What is the age of consent? Is it different for genders; however those genders are configured? Does age difference always and already signal a dangerous difference of power in a relationship? What if the young person initiates the sex? If Rubin challenges us to examine where our lines are drawn about sexual morality and the law, as well as the sexual acts we will accept being outlawed in our society, where do you draw your own line on this issue, and why?

Helmut Graupner, "Love versus Abuse: Crossgenerational Sexual Relations of Minors: A Gay Rights Issue." *Journal of Homosexuality* 37.4 (1999): 23–56.

Gerald P. Jones, "The Study of Intergenerational Intimacy in North America: Beyond Politics and Pedophilia." *Journal of Homosexuality* 20.1/2 (1990): 275–295.

North American Man-Boy Love Association, "The Case for Abolishing the Age of Consent Laws" (1980) in *We Are Everywhere: A Historical Sourcebook of Gay and Lesbian Politics.* Mark Blasius and Shane Phelan, Eds. NY: Routledge. 1997. 459–468.

Imitation and Gender Insubordination[1]

Judith Butler

So what is this divided being introduced into language through gender? It is an impossible being, it is a being that does not exist, an ontological joke.

Monique Wittig[2]

Beyond physical repetition and the psychical or metaphysical repetition, is there an ontological *repetition? . . . This ultimate repetition, this ultimate theatre, gathers everything in a certain way; and in another way, it destroys everything; and in yet another way, it selects from everything.*

Gilles Deleuze[3]

To Theorize as a Lesbian?

At first I considered writing a different sort of essay, one with a philosophical tone: the "being" of being homosexual. The prospect of *being* anything, even for pay, has always produced in me a certain anxiety, for "to be" gay, "to be" lesbian seems to be more than a simple injunction to become who or what I already am. And in no way does it settle the anxiety for me to say that this is "part" of what I am. To write or speak *as a lesbian* appears a paradoxical appearance of this "I," one which feels neither true nor false. For it is a production, usually in response to a request, to come out or write in the name of an identity which, once produced, sometimes functions as a politically efficacious phantasm. I'm not at ease with "lesbian theories, gay theories," for as I've argued elsewhere,[4] identity categories tend to be instruments of regulatory regimes, whether as the normalizing categories of oppressive structures or as the rallying points for a liberatory contestation of that very oppression. This is not to say that I will not appear at political occasions under the sign of lesbian, but that I would like to have it permanently unclear what precisely that sign signifies. So it is unclear how it is that I can contribute to this book and appear under its title, for it announces a set of terms that I propose to contest. One risk I take is to be recolonized by the sign under which I write, and so it is this risk that I seek to thematize. To propose that the invocation of identity is always a risk does not imply that resistance to it is always or only symptomatic of a self-inflicted homophobia. Indeed, a Foucaultian perspective might argue that the affirmation of "homosexuality" is itself an extension of a homophobic discourse. And yet "discourse," he writes on the same page, "can be both an instrument and an effect of power, but also a hindrance, a stumbling-block, a point of resistance and a starting point for an opposing strategy."[5]

So I am skeptical about how the "I" is determined as it operates under the title of the lesbian sign, and I am no more comfortable with its homophobic determination than with those normative definitions offered by other members of the "gay or lesbian community." I'm permanently troubled by identity categories, consider them to be invariable stumbling-blocks, and understand them, even promote them, as sites of necessary trouble. In fact, if the category were to offer no trouble, it would cease to be interesting to me: it is precisely the *pleasure* produced by the instability of those categories which sustains the various erotic practices that make me a candidate for the category to begin with. To install myself within the terms of an identity category would be to turn against the sexuality that the category purports to describe; and this might be true for any identity category which seeks to control the very eroticism that it claims to describe and authorize, much less "liberate."

And what's worse, I do not understand the notion of "theory," and am hardly interested in being cast as its defender, much less in being signified as part of an elite gay/lesbian theory crowd that seeks to establish the legitimacy and domestication of gay/lesbian studies within the academy. Is there a pre-given distinction between theory, politics, culture, media? How do those divisions operate to quell a certain intertextual writing that might well generate wholly different epistemic maps? But I am writing here now: is it too late? Can this writing, can any writing, refuse the terms by which it is appropriated even as, to some extent, that very colonizing discourse enables or produces this stumbling block, this resistance? How do I relate the paradoxical situation of this dependency and refusal?

If the political task is to show that theory is never merely *theoria*, in the sense of disengaged contemplation, and to insist that it is fully political (*phronesis* or even *praxis*), then why not simply call this operation *politics*, or some necessary permutation of it?

I have begun with confessions of trepidation and a series of disclaimers, but perhaps it will become clear that *disclaiming*, which is no simple activity, will be what I have to offer as a form of affirmative resistance to a certain regulatory operation of homophobia. The discourse of "coming out" has clearly served its purposes, but what are its risks? And here I am not speaking of unemployment or public attack or violence, which are quite clearly and widely on the increase against those who are perceived as "out" whether or not of their own design. Is the "subject" who is "out" free of its subjection and finally in the clear? Or could it be that the subjection that subjectivates the gay or lesbian subject in some ways continues to oppress, or oppresses most insidiously, once "outness" is claimed? What or who is it that is "out," made manifest and fully disclosed, when and if I reveal myself as lesbian? What is it that is now known, anything? What remains permanently concealed by the very linguistic act that offers up the promise of a transparent revelation of sexuality? Can sexuality even remain sexuality once it submits to a criterion of transparency and disclosure, or does it perhaps cease to be sexuality precisely when the semblance of full explicitness is achieved? Is sexuality of any kind even possible without that opacity designated by the unconscious, which means simply that the conscious "I" who would reveal its sexuality is perhaps the last to know the meaning of what it says?

To claim that this is what I *am* is to suggest a provisional totalization of this "I." But if the I can so determine itself, then that which it excludes in order to make that determination remains constitutive of the determination itself. In other words, such a statement presupposes that the "I" exceeds its determination, and even produces that very excess in and by the act which seeks to exhaust the semantic field of that "I." In the act which would disclose the true and full content of that "I," a certain radical *concealment* is thereby produced. For it is always finally unclear what is meant by invoking the lesbian-signifier, since its signification is always to some degree out of one's control, but also because its *specificity* can only be demarcated by exclusions that return to disrupt its claim to coherence. What, if anything, can lesbians be said to share? And who will decide this question, and in the name of whom? If I claim to be a lesbian, I "come out" only to produce a new and different "closet." The "you" to whom I come out now has access to a different region of opacity. Indeed, the locus of opacity has simply shifted: before, you did not know whether I "am," but now you do not know what that means, which is to say that the copula is empty, that it cannot be substituted for with a set of descriptions.[7] And perhaps that is a situation to be valued. Conventionally, one comes out *of* the closet (and yet, how often is it the case that we are "outed" when we are young and without resources?); so we are out of the closet, but into what? what new unbounded spatiality? the room, the den, the attic, the basement, the house, the bar, the university, some new enclosure whose door, like Kafka's door, produces the expectation of a fresh air and a light of illumination that never arrives? Curiously, it is the figure of the closet that produces this expectation, and which guarantees its dissatisfaction. For being "out" always depends to some extent on being "in"; it gains its meaning only within that polarity. Hence, being "out" must produce the closet again and again in order to maintain itself as "out." In this sense, *outness* can only produce a new opacity; and *the closet* produces the promise of a disclosure that can, by definition, never come. Is this infinite postponement of the disclosure of "gayness," produced by the very act of "coming out," to be lamented? Or is this very deferral of the signified *to be valued*, a site for the production of values, precisely because the term now takes on a life that cannot be, can never be, permanently controlled?

It is possible to argue that whereas no transparent or full revelation is afforded by "lesbian" and "gay," there remains a political imperative to use these necessary errors or category mistakes, as it were (what Gayatri Spivak might call "catachrestic" operations: to use a proper name improperly[8]), to rally and represent an oppressed political constituency. Clearly, I am not legislating against the use of the term. My question is simply: which use will be legislated, and what play will there be between legislation and use such that the instrumental uses of "identity" do not become regulatory imperatives? If it is already true that "lesbians" and "gay men" have been traditionally designated as impossible identities, errors of classification, unnatural disasters within juridico-medical discourses, or, what perhaps amounts to the same, the very paradigm of what calls to be classified, regulated, and controlled, then perhaps these sites of disruption, error, confusion, and trouble can be the very rallying points for a certain resistance to classification and to identity as such.

The question is not one of *avowing* or *disavowing* the category of lesbian or gay, but, rather, why it is that the category becomes the site of this "ethical" choice? What does it mean to *avow* a category that can only maintain its specificity and coherence by performing a prior set of *disavowals?* Does this make "coming out" into the avowal of disavowal, that is, a return to the closet under the guise of an escape? And it is not something like heterosexuality or bisexuality that is disavowed by the category, but a set of identificatory and practical crossings between these categories that renders the discreteness of each equally suspect. Is it not possible to maintain and pursue heterosexual identifications and aims within homosexual practice, and homosexual identifications and aims within heterosexual practices? If a sexuality is to be disclosed, what will be taken as the true determinant of its meaning: the phantasy structure, the act, the orifice, the gender, the anatomy? And if the practice engages a complex interplay of all of those, which one of this erotic dimensions will come to stand for the sexuality that requires them all? Is it the *specificity* of a lesbian experience or lesbian desire or lesbian sexuality that lesbian theory needs to elucidate? Those efforts have only and always produced a set of contests and refusals which should by now make it clear that there is no necessarily common element among lesbians, except perhaps that we all know something about how homophobia works against women—although, even then, the language and the analysis we use will differ.

To argue that there might be a *specificity* to lesbian sexuality has seemed a necessary counterpoint to the claim that lesbian sexuality is just heterosexuality once removed, or that it is derived, or that it does not exist. But perhaps the claim of specificity, on the one hand, and the claim of derivativeness or nonexistence, on the other, are not as contradictory as they seem. Is it not possible that lesbian sexuality is a process that reinscribes the power domains that it resists, that it is constituted in part from the very heterosexual matrix that it seeks to displace, and that its specificity is to be established, not *outside* or *beyond* that reinscription or reiteration, but in the very modality and effects of that reinscription? In other words, the negative constructions of lesbianism as a fake or a bad copy can be occupied and reworked to call into question the claims of heterosexual priority. In a sense I hope to make clear in what follows, lesbian sexuality can be understood to redeploy its 'derivativeness' in the service of displacing hegemonic heterosexual norms. Understood in this way, the political problem is not to establish the specificity of lesbian sexuality over and against its derivativeness, but to turn the homophobic construction of the bad copy against the framework that privileges heterosexuality as origin, and so 'derive' the former from the latter. This description requires a reconsideration of imitation, drag, and other forms of sexual crossing that affirm the internal complexity of a lesbian sexuality constituted in part within the very matrix of power that it is compelled both to reiterate and to oppose.

On the Being of Gayness as Necessary Drag

The professionalization of gayness requires a certain performance and production of a "self" which is the *constituted effect* of a discourse that nevertheless claims to "represent" that self as a prior truth. When I spoke at the conference on homosexuality in 1989,[9] I found myself telling my friends beforehand that I was off to Yale to be a lesbian, which of course didn't mean that I wasn't one before, but that somehow then, as I spoke in that context, I *was* one in some more thorough and totalizing way, at least for the time being. So I *am* one, and my qualifications are even fairly unambiguous. Since I was sixteen, being a lesbian is what I've been. So what's the anxiety, the discomfort? Well, it has something to do with that redoubling, the way I can say, I'm going to Yale to be a lesbian; a lesbian is what I've been being for so long. How is it that I can both "be" one, and yet endeavor to be one at the same time? When and where does my being a lesbian come into play, when and where does this playing a lesbian constitute something like what I am? To say that I "play" at being one is not to say that I am not one "really"; rather, how and where I play at being one is the way in which that "being" gets established, instituted, circulated, and confirmed. This is not a performance from which I can take radical distance, for this is deep-seated play, psychically entrenched play, *and this "I" does not play its lesbianism as a role.* Rather, it is through the repeated play of this sexuality that the "I" is insistently reconstituted as a lesbian "I"; paradoxically, it is precisely the *repetition* of that play that establishes as well the *instability* of the very category that it constitutes. For if the "I" is a site of repetition, that is, if the "I" only achieves the semblance of identity through a certain repetition of itself, then the I is always displaced by the very repetition that sustains it. In other words, does or can the "I" ever repeat itself, cite itself, faithfully, or is there always a displacement from its former moment that establishes the permanently non-self-identical status of that "I" or its "being lesbian"? What "performs" does not exhaust the "I"; it does not lay out in visible terms the comprehensive content of that "I," for if the performance is "repeated," there is always the question of what differentiates from each other the moments of identity that are repeated. And if the "I" is the effect of a certain repetition, one which produces the semblance of a continuity or coherence, then there is no "I" that precedes the gender that it is said to perform; the repetition, and the failure to repeat, produce a string of performances that constitute and contest the coherence of that "I."

But *politically*, we might argue, isn't it quite crucial to insist on lesbian and gay identities precisely because they are being threatened with erasure and obliteration from homophobic quarters? Isn't the above theory *complicitous* with those political forces that would obliterate the possibility of gay and lesbian identity? Isn't it "no accident" that such theoretical contestations of identity emerge within a political climate that is performing a set of similar obliterations of homosexual identities through legal and political means?

The question I want to raise in return is this: ought such threats of obliteration dictate the terms of the political resistance to them, and if they do, do such homophobic efforts to that extent win the battle from the start? There is no question that gays and lesbians are threatened by the violence of public erasure, but the decision to counter that violence must be careful not to reinstall another in its place. Which version of lesbian or gay ought to be rendered visible, and which internal exclusions will that rendering visible institute? Can the visibility of identity *suffice* as a political strategy, or can it only be the starting point for a strategic intervention which calls for a transformation of policy? Is it not a sign of despair over public politics when identity becomes its own policy, bringing with it those who would 'police' it from various sides? And this is not a call to return to silence or invisibility, but, rather, to make use of a category that can be called into question, made to account for what it excludes. That any consolidation of identity requires some set of differentiations and exclusions seems clear. But which ones ought to be valorized? That the identity-sign I use now has its purposes seems right, but there is no way to predict or control the political uses to which that sign will be put in the future. And perhaps this is a kind of openness, regardless of its risks, that ought to be safeguarded for political reasons. If the rendering visible of lesbian/gay identity now presupposes a set of exclusions, then perhaps part of what is necessarily excluded is *the future uses of the sign*. There is a political necessity to use some sign now, and we do, but how to use it in such a way that its futural significations are not *foreclosed?* How to use the sign and avow its temporal contingency at once?

In avowing the sign's strategic provisionality (rather than its strategic essentialism), that identity can become a site of contest and revision, indeed, take on a future set of significations that those of us who use it now may not be able to foresee. It is in the safeguarding of the future of the political signifiers-preserving the signifier as a site of rearticulation-that Laclau and Mouffe discern its democratic promise.

Within contemporary U.S. politics, there are a vast number of ways in which lesbianism in particular is understood as precisely that which cannot or dare not *be*. In a sense, Jesse Helms's attack on the NEA for sanctioning representations of "homoeroticism" focuses various homophobic fantasies of what gay men are and do on the work of Robert Mapplethorpe.[10] In a sense, for

Helms, gay men exist as objects of prohibition; they are, in his twisted fantasy, sadomasochistic exploiters of children, the paradigmatic exemplars of "obscenity"; in a sense, the lesbian is not even produced within this discourse as a prohibited object. Here it becomes important to recognize that oppression works not merely through acts of overt prohibition, but covertly, through the constitution of viable subjects and through the corollary constitution of a domain of unviable (un)subjects—*abjects*, we might call them—who are neither named nor prohibited within the economy of the law. Here oppression works through the production of a domain of unthinkability and unnameability. Lesbianism is not explicitly prohibited in part because it has not even made its way into the thinkable, the imaginable, that grid of cultural intelligibility that regulates the real and the nameable. How, then, to "be" a lesbian in a political context in which the lesbian does not exist? That is, in a political discourse that wages its violence against lesbianism in part by excluding lesbianism from discourse itself? To be prohibited explicitly is to occupy a discursive site from which something like a reverse-discourse can be articulated; to be implicitly proscribed is not even to qualify as an object of prohibition.[11] And though homosexualities of all kinds in this present climate are being erased, reduced, and (then) reconstituted as sites of radical homophobic fantasy, it is important to retrace the different routes by which the unthinkability of homosexuality is being constituted time and again.

It is one thing to be erased from discourse, and yet another to be present within discourse as an abiding falsehood. Hence, there is a political imperative to render lesbianism visible, but how is that to be done outside or through existing regulatory regimes? Can the exclusion from ontology itself become a rallying point for resistance?

Here is something like a confession which is meant merely to thematize the impossibility of confession: As a young person, I suffered for a long time, and I suspect many people have, from being told, explicitly or implicitly, that what I "am" is a copy, an imitation, a derivative example, a shadow of the real. Compulsory heterosexuality sets itself up as the original, the true, the authentic; the norm that determines the real implies that "being" lesbian is always a kind of miming, a vain effort to participate in the phantasmatic plenitude of naturalized heterosexuality which will always and only fail.[12] And yet, I remember quite distinctly when I first read in Esther Newton's *Mother Camp: Female Impersonators in America*[13] that drag is not an imitation or a copy of some prior and true gender; according to Newton, drag enacts the very structure of impersonation by which *any gender* is assumed. Drag is not the putting on of a gender that belongs properly to some other group, i.e. an act of *ex*propriation or *ap*propriation that assumes that gender is the rightful property of sex, that "masculine" belongs to "male" and "feminine" belongs to "female." There is no "proper" gender, a gender proper to one sex rather than another, which is in some sense that sex's cultural property. Where that notion of the "proper" operates, it is always

and only *improperly* installed as the effect of a compulsory system. Drag constitutes the mundane way in which genders are appropriated, theatricalized, worn,
and done; it implies that all gendering is a kind of impersonation and approxi-
mation. If this is true, it seems, there is no original or primary gender that drag
imitates, but *gender is a kind of imitation for which there is no original*; in fact, it is a
kind of imitation that produces the very notion of the original as an *effect* and
consequence of the imitation itself. In other words, the naturalistic effects of
heterosexualized genders are produced through imitative strategies; what they
imitate is a phantasmatic ideal of heterosexual identity, one that is produced by
the imitation as its effect. In this sense, the "reality" of heterosexual identities is
performatively constituted through an imitation that sets itself up as the origin
and the ground of all imitations. In other words, heterosexuality is always in the
process of imitating and approximating its own phantasmatic idealization of itself—*and failing*. Precisely because it is bound to fail, and yet endeavors to succeed, the project of heterosexual identity is propelled into an endless repetition
of itself. Indeed, in its efforts to naturalize itself as the original, heterosexuality
must be understood as a compulsive and compulsory repetition that can only
produce the *effect* of its own originality; in other words, compulsory heterosexual identities, those ontologically consolidated phantasms of "man" and
"woman," are theatrically produced effects that posture as grounds, origins, the
normative measure of the real.[14]

Reconsider then the homophobic charge that queens and butches and
femmes are imitations of the heterosexual real. Here "imitation" carries the
meaning of "derivative" or "secondary," a copy of an origin which is itself the
ground of all copies, but which is itself a copy of nothing. Logically, this notion
of an "origin" is suspect, for how can something operate as an origin if there are
no secondary consequences which retrospectively confirm the originality of
that origin? The origin requires its derivations in order to affirm itself as an origin, for origins only make sense to the extent that they are differentiated from
that which they produce as derivatives. Hence, if it were not for the notion of
the homosexual *as* copy, there would be no construct of heterosexuality *as* origin. Heterosexuality here presupposes homosexuality. And if the homosexual *as*
copy *precedes* the heterosexual as *origin*, then it seems only fair to concede that
the copy comes before the origin, and that homosexuality is thus the origin, and
heterosexuality the copy.

But simple inversions are not really possible. For it is only *as* a copy that
homosexuality can be argued to *precede* heterosexuality as the origin. In other
words, the entire framework of copy and origin proves radically unstable as
each position inverts into the other and confounds the possibility of any stable
way to locate the temporal or logical priority of either term.

But let us then consider this problematic inversion from a psychic/
political perspective. If the structure of gender imitation is such that the
imita*ted* is to some degree produced—or, rather, *re*produced—by imitation (see

Section Four: (De)/(Re)Gendering Sexualities

again Derrida's inversion and displacement of mimesis in "The Double Session"), then to claim that gay and lesbian identities are implicated in heterosexual norms or in hegemonic culture generally is not to *derive* gayness from straightness. On the contrary, *imitation* does not copy that which is prior, but produces and *inverts* the very terms of priority and derivativeness. Hence, if gay identities are implicated in heterosexuality, that is not the same as claiming that they are determined or derived from heterosexuality, and it is not the same as claiming that that heterosexuality is the only cultural network in which they are implicated. These are, quite literally, *inverted* imitations, ones which invert the order of imitated and imitation, and which, in the process, expose the fundamental dependency of "the origin" on that which it claims to produce as its secondary effect.

What follows if we concede from the start that gay identities as derivative inversions are in part defined in terms of the very heterosexual identities from which they are differentiated? If heterosexuality is an impossible imitation of itself, an imitation that performatively constitutes itself as the original, then the imitative parody of "heterosexuality"—when and where it exists in gay cultures—is always and only an imitation of an imitation, a copy of a copy, for which there is no original. Put in yet a different way, the parodic or imitative effect of gay identities works neither to copy nor to emulate heterosexuality, but rather, to expose heterosexuality as an incessant and *panicked* imitation of its own naturalized idealization. That heterosexuality is always in the act of elaborating itself is evidence that it is perpetually at risk, that is, that it "knows" its own possibility of becoming undone: hence, its compulsion to repeat which is at once a foreclosure of that which threatens its coherence. That it can never eradicate that risk attests to its profound dependency upon the homosexuality that it seeks fully to eradicate and never can or that it seeks to make second, but which is always already there as a prior possibility.[15] Although this failure of naturalized heterosexuality might constitute a source of pathos for heterosexuality itself—what its theorists often refer to as its constitutive malaise—it can become an occasion for a subversive and proliferating parody of gender norms in which the very claim to originality and to the real is shown to be the effect of a certain kind of naturalized gender mime.

It is important to recognize the ways in which heterosexual norms reappear within gay identities, to affirm that gay and lesbian identities are not only structured in part by dominant heterosexual frames, but that they are *not* for that reason *determined* by them. They are running commentaries on those naturalized positions as well, parodic replays and resignifications of precisely those heterosexual structures that would consign gay life to discursive domains of unreality and unthinkability. But to be constituted or structured in part by the very heterosexual norms by which gay people are oppressed is not, I repeat, to be claimed or determined by those structures. And it is not necessary to think of such heterosexual constructs as the pernicious intrusion of "the straight mind," one that must be rooted out in its entirety. In a way, the presence of heterosexual constructs and positionalities in whatever form in gay and lesbian identities presupposes that there is a gay and lesbian repetition of straightness, a recapitulation of straightness—which is itself a repetition and recapitulation of its own ideality—within its own terms, a site in which all sorts of resignifying and parodic repetitions become possible. The parodic replication and resignification of heterosexual constructs within non-heterosexual frames brings into relief the utterly constructed status of the so-called original, but it shows that heterosexuality only constitutes itself as the original through a convincing act of repetition. The more that "act" is expropriated, the more the heterosexual claim to originality is exposed as illusory.

Although I have concentrated in the above on the reality-effects of gender practices, performances, repetitions, and mimes, I do not mean to suggest that drag is a "role" that can be taken on or taken off at will. There is no volitional subject behind the mime who decides, as it were, which gender it will be today. On the contrary, the very possibility of becoming a viable subject requires that a certain gender mime be already underway. The "being" of the subject is no more self-identical than the "being" of any gender; in fact, coherent gender, achieved through an apparent repetition of the same, produces as its *effect* the illusion of a prior and volitional subject. In this sense, gender is not a performance that a prior subject elects to do, but gender is *performative* in the sense that it constitutes as an effect the very subject it appears to express. It is a *compulsory* performance in the sense that acting out of line with heterosexual norms brings with it ostracism, punishment, and violence, not to mention the transgressive pleasures produced by those very prohibitions.

To claim that there is no performer prior to the performed, that the performance is performative, that the performance constitutes the appearance of a "subject" as its effect is difficult to accept. This difficulty is the result of a predisposition to think of sexuality and gender as "expressing" in some indirect or direct way a psychic reality that precedes it. The denial of the *priority* of the subject, however, is not the denial of the subject; in fact, the refusal to conflate the subject with the psyche marks the psychic as that which exceeds the domain of the conscious subject. This psychic excess is precisely what is being systematically denied by the notion of a volitional "subject" who elects at will which gender and/or sexuality to be at any given time and place. It is this excess which erupts within the intervals of those repeated gestures and acts that construct the apparent uniformity of heterosexual positionalities, indeed which compels the repetition itself, and which guarantees its perpetual failure. In this sense, it is this excess which, within the heterosexual economy, implicitly includes homosexuality, that perpetual threat of a disruption which is quelled through a reenforced repetition of the same. And yet, if repetition is the way in which power works to construct the illusion of a seamless heterosexual identity, if heterosexuality is compelled to *repeat itself* in order to establish the illusion of its own uniformity and identity, then this is an identity permanently at risk, for what if it fails to repeat, or if the very exercise of repetition is redeployed for a very different performative purpose? If there is, as it were, always a compulsion to repeat, repetition never fully accomplishes identity. That there is a need for a repetition at all is a sign that identity is not self-identical. It requires to be instituted again and again, which is to say that it runs the risk of becoming de-instituted at every interval.

So what is this psychic excess, and what will constitute a subversive or de-instituting repetition? First, it is necessary to consider that sexuality always exceeds any given performance, presentation, or narrative which is why it is not possible to derive or read off a sexuality from any given gender presentation. And sexuality may be said to exceed any definitive narrativization. Sexuality is never fully "expressed" in a performance or practice; there will be passive and butchy femmes, femmy and aggressive butches, and both of those, and more, will turn out to describe more or less anatomically stable "males" and "females." There are no direct expressive or causal lines between sex, gender, gender presentation, sexual practice, fantasy and sexuality. None of those terms captures or determines the rest. Part of what constitutes sexuality is precisely that which does not appear and that which, to some degree, can never appear. This is perhaps the most fundamental reason why sexuality is to some degree always closeted, especially to the one who would express it through acts of self-disclosure. That which is excluded for a given gender presentation to "succeed" may be precisely what is played out sexually, that is, an "inverted" relation, as it were, between gender and gender presentation, and gender presentation and sexuality. On the other hand, both gender presentation and sexual practices may corollate such that it appears that the former "expresses" the latter, and yet both are jointly constituted by the very sexual possibilities that they exclude.

This logic of inversion gets played out interestingly in versions of lesbian butch and femme gender stylization. For a butch can present herself as capable, forceful, and all-providing, and a stone butch may well seek to constitute her lover as the exclusive site of erotic attention and pleasure. And yet, this "providing" butch who seems *at first* to replicate a certain husband-like role, can find herself caught in a logic of inversion whereby that "providingness" turns to a self-sacrifice, which implicates her in the most ancient trap of feminine self-abnegation. She may well find herself in a situation of radical need, which is precisely what she sought to locate, find, and fulfill in her femme lover. In effect, the butch inverts into the femme or remains caught up in the specter of that inversion, or takes pleasure in it. On the other hand, the femme who, as Amber Hollibaugh has argued, "orchestrates" sexual exchange,[16] may well eroticize a certain dependency only to learn that the very power to orchestrate that dependency exposes her own incontrovertible power, at which point she inverts into a butch or becomes caught up in the specter of that inversion, or perhaps delights in it.

Psychic Mimesis

What stylizes or forms an erotic style and/or a gender presentation—and that which makes such categories inherently unstable—is a set of *psychic identifications* that are not simple to describe. Some psychoanalytic theories tend to construe identification and desire as two mutually exclusive relations to love objects that have been lost through prohibition and/or separation. Any intense emotional attachment thus divides into either wanting to have someone or wanting to be that someone, but never both at once. It is important to consider that identification and desire can coexist, and that their formulation in terms of mutually exclusive oppositions serves a heterosexual matrix. But I would like to focus attention on yet a different construal of that scenario, namely, that "wanting to be" and "wanting to have" can operate to differentiate mutually exclusive positionalities internal to lesbian erotic exchange. Consider that identifications are always made in response to loss of some kind, and that they involve a certain *mimetic practice* that seeks to incorporate the lost love within the very "identity" of the one who remains. This was Freud's thesis in "Mourning and Melancholia" in 1917 and continues to inform contemporary psychoanalytic discussions of identification.[17]

For psychoanalytic theorists Mikkel Borch-Jacobsen and Ruth Leys, however, identification and, in particular, identificatory mimetism, *precedes* "identity" and constitutes identity as that which is fundamentally "other to itself." The notion of this Other *in* the self, as it were, implies that the self/Other distinction is *not* primarily external (a powerful critique of ego psychology follows from this); the self is from the start radically implicated in the "Other." This theory of primary mimetism differs from Freud's account of melancholic incorporation. In Freud's view, which I continue to find useful, incorporation—a kind of psychic miming—is a response to, and refusal of, *loss*. Gender as the site of such psychic mimes is thus constituted by the variously gendered Others who have been loved and lost, where the loss is suspended through a melancholic and imaginary incorporation (and preservation) of those Others into the psyche. Over and against this account of psychic mimesis by way of incorporation and melancholy, the theory of primary mimetism argues an even stronger position in favor of the non-self-identity of the psychic subject. Mimetism is not motivated by a drama of loss and wishful recovery, but appears to precede and constitute desire (and motivation) itself; in this sense, mimetism would be prior to the possibility of loss and the disappointments of love.

Whether loss or mimetism is primary (perhaps an undecidable problem), the psychic subject is nevertheless constituted internally by differentially gendered Others and is, therefore, never, as a gender, self-identical.

In my view, the self only becomes a self on the condition that it has suffered a separation (grammar fails us here, for the "it" only becomes differentiated through that separation), a loss which is suspended and provisionally resolved through a melancholic incorporation of some "Other." That "Other" installed in the self thus establishes the permanent incapacity of that "self" to achieve self-identity; it is as it were always already disrupted by that Other; the disruption of the Other at the heart of the self is the very condition of that self's possibility.[18]

Such a consideration of psychic identification would vitiate the possibility of any stable set of typologies that explain or describe something like gay or lesbian identities. And any effort to supply one—as evidenced in Kaja Silverman's recent inquiries into male homosexuality—suffer from simplification, and conform, with alarming ease, to the regulatory requirements of diagnostic epistemic regimes. If incorporation in Freud's sense in 1914 is an effort to *preserve* a lost and loved object and to refuse or postpone the recognition of loss and, hence, of grief, then to become *like* one's mother or father or sibling or other early "lovers" may be an act of love and/or a hateful effort to replace or displace. How would we "typologize" the ambivalence at the heart of mimetic incorporations such as these?[19]

How does this consideration of psychic identification return us to the question, what constitutes a subversive repetition? How are troublesome identifications apparent in cultural practices? Well, consider the way in which heterosexuality naturalizes itself through setting up certain illusions of continuity between sex, gender, and desire. When Aretha Franklin sings, "you make me feel like a natural woman," she seems at first to suggest that some natural potential of her biological sex is actualized by her participation in the cultural position of "woman" as object of heterosexual recognition. Something in her "sex" is thus expressed by her "gender" which is then fully known and consecrated within the heterosexual scene. There is no breakage, no discontinuity between "sex" as biological facticity and essence, or between gender and sexuality. Although Aretha appears to be all too glad to have her naturalness confirmed, she also seems fully and paradoxically mindful that that confirmation is never guaranteed, that the effect of naturalness is only achieved as a consequence of that moment of heterosexual recognition. After all, Aretha sings, you make me feel *like* a natural woman, suggesting that this is a kind of metaphorical substitution, an act of imposture, a kind of sublime and momentary participation in an ontological illusion produced by the mundane operation of heterosexual drag.

But what if Aretha were singing to me? Or what if she were singing to a drag queen whose performance somehow confirmed her own?

How do we take account of these kinds of identifications? It's not that there is some kind of *sex* that exists in hazy biological form that is somehow *expressed* in the gait, the posture, the gesture; and that some sexuality then expresses both that apparent gender or that more or less magical sex. If gender is drag, and if it is an imitation that regularly produces the ideal it attempts to approximate, then gender is a performance that *produces* the illusion of an inner sex or essence or psychic gender core; it *produces* on the skin, through the gesture, the move, the gait (that array of corporeal theatrics understood as gender presentation), the illusion of an inner depth. In effect, one way that gender gets naturalized is through being constructed as an inner psychic or physical *necessity*. And yet, it is always a surface sign, a signification on and with the public body that produces this illusion of an inner depth, necessity or essence that is somehow magically, causally expressed.

To dispute the psyche as *inner depth*, however, is not to refuse the psyche altogether. On the contrary, the psyche calls to be rethought precisely as a compulsive repetition, as that which conditions and disables the repetitive performance of identity. If every performance repeats itself to institute the effect of identity, then every repetition requires an interval between the acts, as it were, in which risk and excess threaten to disrupt the identity being constituted. The unconscious is this excess that enables and contests every performance, and which never fully appears within the performance itself. The psyche is not "in" the body, but in the very signifying process through which that body comes to appear; it is the lapse in repetition as well as its compulsion, precisely what the performance seeks to deny, and that which compels it from the start.

To locate the psyche within this signifying chain as the instability of all it-erability is not the same as claiming that it is inner core that is awaiting its full and liberatory expression. On the contrary, the psyche is the permanent failure of expression, a failure that has its values, for it impels repetition and so rein-states the possibility of disruption. What then does it mean to pursue disruptive repetition within compulsory heterosexuality?

Although compulsory heterosexuality often presumes that there is first a sex that is expressed through a gender and then through a sexuality, it may now be necessary fully to invert and displace that operation of thought. If a regime of sexuality mandates a compulsory performance of sex, then it may be only through that performance that the binary system of gender and the binary sys-tem of sex come to have intelligibility at all. It may be that the very categories of sex, of sexual identity, of gender are produced or maintained in the *effects* of this compulsory performance, effects which are disingenuously renamed as causes, origins, disingenuously lined up within a causal or expressive sequence that the heterosexual norm produces to legitimate itself as the origin of all sex. How then to expose the causal lines as retrospectively and performatively pro-duced fabrications, and to engage gender itself as an inevitable fabrication, to fabricate gender in terms which reveal every claim to the origin, the inner, the true, and the real as nothing other than the effects of *drag*, whose subversive possibilities ought to be played and replayed to make the "sex" of gender into a site of insistent political play? Perhaps this will be a matter of working sexuality *against* identity, even against gender, and of letting that which cannot fully ap-pear in any performance persist in its disruptive promise.

Notes

1. Parts of this essay were given as a presentation at the Conference on Homosexual-ity at Yale University in October, 1989.
2. "The Mark of Gender," *Feminist Issues* 5 no. 2 (1985): 6.
3. *Différence et répétition* (Paris: PUF, 1968), 374; my translation.
4. *Gender Trouble: Feminism and the Subversion of Identity* (New York and London: Routledge, 1990).
5. Michel Foucault, *The History of Sexuality, Vol. I*, trans. John Hurley (New York: Random House, 1980), 101.
6. Here I would doubtless differ from the very fine analysis of Hitchcock's *Rope* of-fered by D. A. Miller in this volume.

7. For an example of "coming out" that is strictly unconfessional and which, finally, offers no content for the category of lesbian, see Barbara Johnson's deftly constructed "Sula Passing: No Passing" presentation at UCLA, May 1990.

8. Gayatri Chakravorty Spivak, "Displacement and the Discourse of Woman." In *Displacement: Derrida and After*, ed. Mark Krupnick (Bloomington: Indiana University Press, 1983).

9. Let me take this occasion to apologize to the social worker at that conference who asked a question about how to deal with those clients with AIDS who turned to Bernie Segal and others for the purposes of psychic healing. At the time, I understood this questioner to be suggesting that such clients were full of self-hatred because they were trying to find the causes of AIDS in their own selves. The questioner and I appear to agree that any effort to locate the responsibility for AIDS in those who suffer from it is politically and ethically wrong. I thought the questioner, however, was prepared to tell his clients that they were self-hating, and I reacted strongly (too strongly) to the paternalistic prospect that this person was going to pass judgment on someone who was clearly not only suffering, but already passing judgment on him or herself. To call another person self-hating is itself an act of power that calls for some kind of scrutiny, and I think in response to someone who is already dealing with AIDS, that is perhaps the last thing one needs to hear. I also happened to have a friend who sought out advice from Bernie Segal, not with the belief that there is an exclusive or even primary psychic cause or solution for AIDS, but that there might be a psychic contribution to be made to surviving with AIDS. Unfortunately, I reacted quickly to this questioner, and with some anger. And I regret now that I didn't have my wits about me to discuss the distinctions with him that I have just laid out.

    Curiously, this incident was invoked at a CLAGS (Center for Lesbian and Gay Studies) meeting at CUNY sometime in December of 1989 and, according to those who told me about it, my angry denunciation of the social worker was taken to be symptomatic of the political insensitivity of a "theorist" in dealing with someone who is actively engaged in AIDS work. That attribution implies that I do not do AIDS work, that I am not politically engaged, and that the social worker in question does not read theory. Needless to say, I was reacting angrily on behalf of an absent friend with AIDS who sought out Bernie Segal and company. So as I offer this apology to the social worker, I wait expectantly that the CLAGS member who misunderstood me will offer me one in turn.

10. See my "The Force of Fantasy: Feminism, Mapplethorpe, and Discursive Excess," *differences* 2, no. 2 (Summer 1990). Since the writing of this essay, lesbian artists and representations have also come under attack.

11. It is this particular ruse of erasure which Foucault for the most part fails to take account of in his analysis of power. He almost always presumes that power takes place through discourse as its instrument, and that oppression is linked with subjection and subjectivation, that is, that it is installed as the formative principle of the identity of subjects.

12. Although miming suggests that there is a prior model which is being copied, it can have the effect of exposing that prior model as purely phantasmatic. In Jacques Derrida's "The Double Session" in *Dissemination*, trans. Barbara Johnson (Chicago: University of Chicago Press, 1981), he considers the textual effect of the mime in Mallarmé's "Mimique." There Derrida argues that the mime does

not imitate or copy some prior phenomenon, idea, or figure, but constitutes—
some might say *performatively*—the phantasm of the original in and through the
mime:

> He represents nothing, imitates nothing, does not have to conform to any prior
> referent with the aim of achieving adequation or verisimilitude. One can here
> foresee an objection: since the mime imitates nothing, reproduces nothing,
> opens up in its origin the very thing he is tracing out, presenting, or producing,
> he must be the very movement of truth. Not, of course, truth in the form of ad-
> equation between the representation and the present of the thing itself, or be-
> tween the imitator and the imitated, but truth as the present unveiling of the
> present. . . . But this is not the case. . . . We are faced then with mimicry imi-
> tating nothing: faced, so to speak, with a double that couples no simple, a
> double that nothing anticipates, nothing at least that is not itself already dou-
> ble. There is no simple reference. . . . This speculum reflects no reality: it pro-
> duces mere "reality-effects". . . . In this speculum with no reality, in this mirror
> of a mirror, a difference or dyad does exist, since there are mimes and phan-
> toms. But it is a difference without reference, or rather reference without a
> referent, without any first or last unit, a ghost that is the phantom of no
> flesh . . . (206)

13. Esther Newton, *Mother Camp: Female Impersonators in America* (Chicago: University of Chicago Press, 1972).

14. In a sense, one might offer a redescription of the above in Lacanian terms. The
sexual "positions" of heterosexually differentiated "man" and "woman" are part of
the *Symbolic*, that is, an ideal embodiment of the Law of sexual difference which
constitutes the object of imaginary pursuits, but which is always thwarted by the
"real." These symbolic positions for Lacan are by definition impossible to occupy
even as they are impossible to resist as the structuring telos of desire. I accept the
former point, and reject the latter one. The imputation of universal necessity to
such positions simply encodes compulsory heterosexuality at the level of the Symbolic, and the "failure" to achieve it is implicitly lamented as a source of heterosexual pathos.

15. Of course, it is Eve Kosofsky Sedgwick's *Epistemology of the Closet* (Berkeley: University of California Press, 1990) which traces the subleties of this kind of panic in
Western heterosexual epistemes.

16. Amber Hollibaugh and Cherrie Moraga, "What We're Rollin Around in Bed
With: Sexual Silences in Feminism," in *Powers of Desire: The Politics of Sexuality*,
ed. Ann Snitow, Christine Stansell, and Sharon Thompson (New York: Monthly
Review Press, 1983), 394–405.

17. Mikkel Borch-Jacobsen, *The Freudian Subject* (Stanford: Stanford University Press,
1988); for citations of Ruth Leys's work, see the following two endnotes.

18. For a very fine analysis of primary mimetism with direct implications for gender
formation, see Ruth Leys, "The Real Miss Beauchamp: The History and Sexual
Politics of the Multiple Personality Concept," in *Feminists Theorize the Political*,
eds. Judith Butler and Joan W. Scott (New York and London: Routledge, forthcoming 1991). For Leys, a primary mimetism or suggestibility requires that the
"self" from the start is constituted by its incorporations; the effort to differentiate
oneself from that by which one is constituted is, of course, impossible, but it
does entail a certain "incorporative violence," to use her term. The violence of

identification is in this way in the service of an effort at differentiation, to take the place of the Other who is, as it were, installed at the foundation of the self. That this replacement, which seeks to be a displacement, fails, and must repeat itself endlessly, becomes the trajectory of one's psychic career.

19. Here again, I think it is the work of Ruth Leys which will clarify some of the complex questions of gender constitution that emerge from a close psychoanalytic consideration of imitation and identification. Her forthcoming book manuscript will doubtless galvanize this field: *The Subject of Imitation.*

Questions for Reflection, Discussion, and Writing

1. In what ways does Butler claim that it is paradoxical to "write or speak as a lesbian"? What central tension does this raise for her? In what ways does she resist theorizing this tension?

2. In suggesting that the "I" is provisional, what sexual identity issues does Butler articulate? How does "the closet" function to maintain that "I"?

3. According to Butler, why is it necessary to identify a lesbian and gay specificity? What is at stake?

4. What is the problem, as Butler sees it, with gay and lesbian signification? Why does she claim it needs to be provisional?

5. How does drag act as a form of gender insubordination? Why isn't it strictly imitation of heterosexual gender norms?

6. Butler claims that homosexuality as a category preceded heterosexuality and that heterosexuality depends on imitation to sustain it. What does Butler claim this says about identity, performance, gender and sexuality?

7. What connection does Butler make between "otherness," Aretha Franklin, identity, and compulsory heterosexuality?

Related Reading

Judith Butler, "Critically Queer." *GLQ 1* (1993): 17–32.

Mariam Fraser, "Classing Queer: Politics in Competition." *Theory, Culture & Society* 16.2 (April 1999): 107–131.

Elizabeth Freeman, "Packing History, Count(er)ing Generations." *New Literary History* 31.4 (Autumn 2000): 727–744.

Max H. Kirsch, "Meta-identity, performativity, and internalized homophibia" in *Queer Theory and Social Change.* NY: Routledge. 2000. 79–93.

Brett Levinson, "Sex Without Sex, Queering the Market, the Collapse of the Political, the Death of Difference, and AIDS: Hailing Judith Butler." *Diacritics* 29.3 (1999): 81–101.

Moya Lloyd, "Performativity, Parody, Politics." *Theory, Culture & Society* 16.2 (April 1999): 195–214.

Joyce McCarl Nielsen, Glenda Walton and Charlotte A. Kunkel, "Gendered Heteronormativity: Empirical Illustrations in Everyday Life." *Sociological Quarterly* 41.2
(2000): 283–296.

Jay Prosser, "Judith Butler: Queer Feminism, Transgender, and the Transubstantiation
of Sex" in *Second Skins: The Body Narratives of Transsexuality*. NY: Columbia UP.
1998. 21–60.

Joseph Valente, "Performative Chic: The Fantasy of a Performative Politics." *College
Literature* 24.1 (February 1997): 295–304.

Michael Warner, "From Queer to Eternity: An Army of Theorists Cannot Fail." *Village
Voice Literary Supplement*. June 1992. 18–19.

My Dangerous Desires

Falling in Love with Stone Butches; Passing Women and Girls (Who Are Guys) Who Catch My Eye

Amber Hollibaugh

> She said, *"When the door opens, of sensuality, then you will understand it too. The
> struggle begins . . ."*
>
> —Muriel Rukeyser, *"Kathe Kollwitz"*

In 1969 this is the dream I most feared, the dream I denied, dreamed, denied,
dreamed, again and again:

> I have on a negligee. Its fabric skims my body, drapes my breasts, curves against
> my hips, catches the shape of my cunt beneath its silky folds. It holds and captures
> the female shape of me, makes absolutely clear the contours of my expectations.
>
> In the dream, I walk slowly across the room toward the bed, pause, move
> again, then stay in place for my lover's gaze. As I reach the edge of the bed and
> drop down, I am urged in against the yearning I have created, coaxed in and down
> until I blister the darkness. As I am undressed, my body scalds the palms of my
> lover's hands, pulling her fierce desire inside me, giving it shape, pulling her cock
> unrelentingly into my body, drawing it deep, holding it there, riding it, molding
> it, liquefying it inside my cunt. I am overtaken by a woman's hands, a man's cock,
> a lover's fever. I am possessed.

This is what I wanted. This is what filled me with horror.

My dream lover was no customary female, no "normal" lesbian of 1969, or of today. She was not a woman who is primarily a girl but a person who is a man that is a woman. This is an identity incompatible with girl/guy biology or its specifics, someone whose body conjures both authority and its subversion, who situates her autonomy through a transgressive gender strategy, who does not dread the outline of her masculine differences or shrink from her desire for my woman's form. This was and is a person who does not exist in the domain of the purely female.

I have desired this kind of woman, women who are men that are women, since I first came out as a lesbian and saw a butch. It was the first time in my sexual life that I understood the focus of my precise yearnings, felt my own longing answered, knew for certain that I required this kind of woman with a hunger that would not quiet down—knew that, with her, I could finally be had. And the only time in my life that I tried to kill myself because of my erotic cravings was over a butch lover—though by that time I had been a lesbian for many years. I was filled with the terror of it, as I was filled with its hunger.

I am not sure now which I believed was worse: the fantasy of myself in the negligee or my fantasy about the kind of a woman I wanted to remove it! I was horrified to find within myself the kind of rapturous longing I attributed to straight women. Yes, it was terrifying to recognize my need to be possessed and, furthermore, to be possessed by a person who had the affect of a man but whom I knew to be—whom I needed to be—biologically female. I had no idea how to begin to understand my own complex desires. I had no one to ask.

I'd been having the dream constantly since breaking up with my first butch lover, a woman who often passed as a man. Together we brought each other fully inside the erotic and emotional landscape of queer working-class life as butch and femme dykes. I bought her her first tuxedo; she picked me up for our first date on her Harley. We were a powerful butch/femme couple in the bars and in the working-class social world of UPS drivers and hookers. But I was also a part of the independent revolutionary Left and a member of a radical Communist collective.

The questions that that dream corroborated—and which I lived but could not answer—were about which world I would be a part of, which world represented what I believed, which world I would live within, which world I would authenticate and fight for. The world of submachine guns, anti-Vietnam War demonstrations, running in the streets from tear gas and police, joining the newly forming women's liberation consciousness-raising groups? Or a world of nighttime negligees, of living unconditionally for the passion I experienced with women the world saw as men, lovers who rode me on the backs of their bikes to the local lesbian bar? I bought ties and BVDS for them, like I had for the men in my poor white- and Gypsy-trash family. These women who weren't interested in building a leftist political movement, they wanted to join the Roller Derby.

I could not square it.

The entire world seemed, in those days, to be irretrievably dangerous. Not that it had ever seemed safe. But the apparent contradictions in my life were more than I could tolerate or understand. Especially after my first butch lover and I had broken up and I could no longer believe that loving her had been an aberration or an accident. I could not forget her hands, the ways she had touched me, brought me fully alive within my own desire. I already lived on the edge as a political organizer and a sex worker, and I told no one but her about my work as a dancer and a whore. Even back then, I knew that my silence was about class, that I was in a political movement that had never understood my kind of background or its violence and poverty. But the particular meaning of my own passionate erotic need and my resulting queer, high femme, old-gay lesbian identity—this looked suspiciously deviant, even to me.

Facing my profound longings after the breakup meant facing the truth that, erotically and emotionally, I needed to be with lovers who were butch. I required that world, that way of coming together, that environment, in order to sustain my own femme erotic identity. This meant to me that I was a femme.

I knew no other women who claimed that sexuality, that identity, that life. At best, I saw them out of the corner of my eye at the bar on Saturday nights, as my lover and I left the dance floor to reclaim our table. There were other femmes in that universe, sure. But we didn't talk with each other about our femme-ness, didn't speak to each other directly about our identities or the meaning we attached to our perilous relationships with the butch women we desired, slept with, committed our hopes to, betrayed, and adored. We didn't talk much to each other at all. We would look one another over, evaluate the other as threat or friend, then separate to be alone or with individual butch lovers.

At that time femmes were at a premium in the bars, a very desired object in a world dominated by an overflow of butches. But I could find no women there who were like me, who crossed into and out of the worlds I traversed daily, women who lived fiercely as a high femme lesbian hooker and a Commie dyke organizer. Politically radical lesbians or women's liberationists lived in one stratosphere; working-class femmes and hookers lived in another. I appeared to be the only person around straddling both environments. And I feared that, in ways I could hardly imagine but which I dreaded, exploring and living out my femme identity meant going further away from the movements I ardently identified as my own, meant turning my back on the political work that had saved my mind and my life and given me vision, context, hope. It was, at the same time, a confrontation with class, with the very background I had tried so hard to escape. For many years I remained in a state of crisis about which world would define my human life.

Gay liberation was the most passionately personal movement I belonged to. Betraying its values, or disputing its implicit sexual codes, seemed to me then to act against myself, to transgress—and, in that transgression, to become even more marginalized as a lesbian. I had already lived outside my own desires

in the heterosexual world and then again in the closet of my first lesbian love affair. I could not go back. But there was no way I could see to go forward either.
I knew I could never return to the ways in which I'd existed before that first relationship with a butch lover crystallized my lust. My own desires seemed to me
too dangerous to live with. But I already knew what it would mean to live without them.

It was 1978. The Gay Pride March that year in San Francisco was a passionate testament against Anita Bryant and the loss of an important gay rights
initiative in Dade County, Florida. It was a reply to the frightening wave of
antigay politics sweeping the country. People were at that march in defiance,
protest, mobilization. It galvanized gay resistance. I was proud to be part of it
that year, angry and defiant about all the homophobia surrounding us. I was
also full of inarticulate grief. The fundamental importance of gay liberation was
unequivocally clear to me. But my desires, the ways I felt and expressed my own
queer femme sexuality, now positioned me outside the rights I was marching to
defend. My internal erotic identity made me an alien to the politics of my own
movement—a movement I had helped start, a movement whose survival and
growth I was committed to.

It was obvious to me that butch/femme sexuality, and my own particular
high femme variation, had no place in the sexual politics of the time (as it barely
has today). Then, the old-gay lesbian images and historical narratives, sepia-
toned photographs from the past depicting femmes alone or with their partners, depicting butch dandies and their female lovers, were presented as
larger-than-life icons representing a long-ago era that the lesbian movement
was hesitantly willing to acknowledge and affirm. But, to the upper-middle-
class voices of the movement, butch and femme now, in the present, current
universe of lesbian and gay liberation descended from the Stonewall rebellions,
was not seen as a vigorous living system, a powerful way of being, existing, and
desiring. The movement in which I found myself viewed butch/femme desire
and methods of social interaction as dangerous, odd, ridiculous, shameful, a ru-
inous erotic system which was considered antithetical to the goals and ambitions of that movement. Femme and butch eloquence was reduced, in the
movement's eyes, to stereotypical masculine/feminine "roles". The lesbian and
gay liberation movement of those days thought of itself as representing fluidity,
androgyny, freedom. The battleground was established. There was no apparent
way out.

I marched all that day, then left the march late in the afternoon and
rented a motel room just outside the Castro. There I cried for hours, pacing between the bathroom and the bed. Finally, I took every pill I had managed to
buy, steal, or collect, snorted large quantities of coke, drank a quart of something that was eighty proof, ran hot water in the sink, and held my wrists under
it one by one until I had finished cutting them with a razor. I passed out.

To this day, I don't know why it didn't kill me.

When a cleaning woman found me the next morning, I was taken to the
hospital by ambulance, questioned, treated, and released that afternoon. I re-

turned to my commune; there was nowhere else for me to go. Though much of it is a blur, I remember swearing that day that, if I could somehow find a way to live through this sexual terror and come out the other side, I would never let anyone go to that place alone again. No movement, no community that I was a part of would ever again create a politics of sexual exclusion and rigid sexual judgment without me protesting loudly, publicly, insistently, until things changed. Then I started the hard work of unraveling my own sexual skeletons and investigating what moved them around inside me.

I know that, for some people, gay rights and gay liberation do not hinge on the particulars of sexual desire. I have heard for the last twenty-five years that we aren't *just* our erotic identities; the current movement is thick with it. But, for many of us, it *does* begin there, does revolve around the ways we organize our erotic choices. And erotic identities are not just behaviors or individual sexual actions; they reflect a much broader fabric that is the weave and crux of our very personhood, a way of mediating and measuring all that we experience, all that we can interpret through the language of our bodies, our histories, our eyes, our hips, our intelligence, our willful, desiring selves. However we've gotten there, erotic identity is not simply a specific activity or "lifestyle," a set of heels or ties that dress up the quirk. It is as deep and rich, as dangerous, explosive, and unique as each of us dares to be or become.

What I believe now, after all these years, is that it doesn't really matter what the erotic violation is. For some people, the forbidden may be any feelings of homosexual attraction at all; for others, it may be S/M—whether queer or straight—or it may be the specifics of butch/femme, top/bottom, dominance and submission, etc., etc. But, when individual desire rides that fiercely through a person's intrinsic, intimate set of principles, there can be no resolution of the crisis without an extraordinary self-confrontation, a coming to terms.

Because of that, this story is important to tell and remember.

By the time I tried to kill myself I had already survived incest at the hands of my father and violence—and silence—at the hands of my mother. I had worked for years as a hooker and a stripper. I had left my husband for a woman, then lived five years with her in the closet. I had found and joined and helped build the exploding gay liberation struggle in its first years. I had navigated all that sexual terrain while also participating openly in the effort to build the Left. I had every reason to believe I was skillful in handling issues of sexual conflict and identity, difference, politics. I had always traveled in a world of sexual appetites and sexual needs, a world charted by its passions, its hungers, and its sexual opposition, a world sketched by expression and resistance. I had the experience of choosing sex and setting its terms; I had experienced having no say in the face of violence and violation. I knew of all the reasons people turned to sex: for release, revenge, tenderness, aggression, to satisfy their own hunger or their need for power. I thought all this had given me the skills and seasoning necessary to survive the challenge that butch desire and femme identity had created for me. I thought I could ride out that storm and invent a bridge for it into the new movement I had helped establish. I was wrong.

It was insidious, really, how I had become worn down by the fear and shame, the ceaseless scrutiny and interrogation that flowed poisonously through the lesbian wing of the early gay liberation movement. Sometimes when I was with my lover we were treated like a joke: a frozen, fixed, antiquated, irrational vestige of comic buffoonery. We were deluded, they said; we were foolish, absurd. Sometimes it was more brittle, more hostile, more derogatory. At meetings I attended, marches I participated in, dances my lover and I showed up to attend, I was asked why we had bothered to come or told we were not welcome: "No femme women with he/she men." How I looked, how I acted with a lover, how I acted by myself, how I walked, spoke, dressed, expressed my passion, all were constantly called into question. I was told I should find myself a "real" man if that's what I was into. I often had to escort and then remain with my butch lovers so they could use the women's bathroom at movement institutions. That was in 1973. In 1995, I and my stone butch lover of the time were refused entrance to a lesbian feminist women's dance at the New York City Lesbian and Gay Community Center during Gay Pride Week. We were told the same things I'd been told twenty-five years before: It—butch/femme—was a dangerous heterosexist trap. I was parroting heterosexuality because I was "into traditional male and female roles."

The hostility and ridicule we faced inside the lesbian movement paralleled and overlapped our lives in the broader straight world—where we were often treated as criminals. My first butch lover and I began to fear coming home after we found our cat murdered in front of our apartment, with a note pinned to the door saying we'd be next. We regularly fought with men who waited outside the bar for the most obvious bull daggers and their "faggot girlfriends," or we turned away and hated ourselves for giving in. We lived constantly with the rude looks and loud, bitterly spoken comments—in the restaurants where we ate, the stores where we bought our clothes and groceries. Insults could be flung at us as we walked along any street, at any time. Strolling together as a butch/femme couple, we were an erotic, magnetic, moving target for all the sexual fear, envy, and ignorance of this culture. Our movements and our decisions were fraught with potential danger: unexpected visits to the emergency room, how to rent a motel room when we traveled, crossing a border between the United States and Canada or Mexico, being busted at bars when the cops came for their weekly payoffs, getting an apartment. None of these acts were simple or could ever be taken for granted. I have always had to laugh whenever I hear that femmes are not as tough, capable, or rugged as our butch lovers. We fought together, we carried ourselves with our heads high, we protected the women we loved when we could—as they tried to protect us—we held each other when we didn't win, and we held each other when we did. We tried to make the world normal and predictable. Mostly, that meant being alone together, creating a little home somewhere that might provide a haven from the omnipresent hostility and ridicule. We also tried to create a smaller world that included others like ourselves, a world we could relax and function in. We were scared all the time about who we loved. We were often afraid about who we were. We lived each day in a hostile and volatile universe.

It is terrifying to live out your desire in a haunted system of ridicule and attack. The interior world of identity and desire becomes a place of fear and doubt, even as you actively give it expression. Whatever is difficult about being queer becomes a hundred times more provocative and full of menace when you struggle to understand a way of wanting and being which you know is held in contempt, even by other queers, which balances your selfhood and your erotic identity on the edge of continual humiliation. When my lover looks both male and female, wants a cock and wears one, thinks of herself as a faggot or a guy, is she a man? If I want a woman who looks like a man who is a woman who has a cock, what kind of hybrid gender does that make of me? Since my sexual land-scape of desire always moves between variants on the butch spectrum and my own shades of femme self-construction, there is no escaping the issue. All these categories and states of being are full of strife.

In this internal struggle, you become "different" not just in terms of the gender you are or of the person you desire but in your own imagination as well—inside the treasured illusion and sexual invention of your own erotic self—although you struggle, you resist becoming paralyzed. To this day, the question of something apparently so simple as what to wear is fraught with po-litical and sexual decision making; it is weighted down with considerations about who I will see and who I will be and of how to modify, soften, exaggerate, or edge out the worst of what might happen or of how to survive if I just go as I am. If I am with a lover who passes and refuses to hide, my partnering will be taken as a flamboyant challenge, a defiant statement of difference. If I am with a woman who is a softer butch, the challenge will be less confrontational—but it will remain. If, as a femme or a high femme, I am open about the centrality of that system to my world, I am always quickly reduceable to erotic trash in the eye of the beholder.

I had already entered butch/femme life with a preexisting set of sexual scars that permanently marked me. I wasn't a fool. I knew the cost of my own sexual history. But much of that sexual story had been shaped by my own inter-nal anger and resistance—and by my ability to differentiate sex as desire from sex as a job, a violation, a paying event. My history was a part of me, but it was also me with a defiant face, a spit-at-you-if-you-don't-like-it persona. And, though sexual histories may prepare us for some things, they also serve to make us cautious, wary of being questioned. The doubts that people around me had about femme/butch life were most often not my own, were not at all where my own fear and worry centered. But, regardless of whether the questions being asked were my own or not, I was afraid to respond. And I knew that I neverthe-less intended to go ahead with what I was doing—whatever the answers.

When I found butch/femme, it was like rediscovering my heart through my cunt. It signified myself, my most naked feelings and desires; it defined and reflected the spirit living at the center of me. Here, in this place, I was vulnerable. I had no armor at first to battle the assumptions of movement feminists that femme/butch was a gag, a perversion. I was in isolation as I faced all the accusations and silences made by those very people I trusted and valued inside my own gay political world, people I still needed in order to survive. And I knew where these interrogations could lead, even though I didn't have a clue, then, about how to respond.

I also knew deep down in my femme bones that the uncertainties and fears raised by an erotic identity can be answered only by living it, experiencing and learning about your own personal intersections with passionate singularity. And your own understanding of love and desire is traced and changed by the women you love, by the women you want and need. You will also discover who you are alone and to yourself, regardless of who you are partnering or sleeping with. You will begin to understand who you are in your own imagination. To see, through time, what really does or doesn't work. To determine what is absolutely necessary and what is changeable, what depends on you alone, what depends on a partner. It takes years. It takes a lifetime. And sometimes there is nothing as simple as one single answer. There is only the rich, multilayered understanding that the living of desire gleans.

In myself, over the years, I continued to face questions for which I had no immediate answers. What kind of woman did my desires make me? What in God's name was a femme lesbian—a high femme lesbian? Why did I continue to dream my dream? I needed to begin to comprehend my own strategy of desire in order to defend it. I have struggled to understand what fuels my own desires, what propels my feelings for the women I desire, for the last twenty-five years. This struggle has led me to study the larger worlds of sexual cravings and currencies as they swirl around me, around us all. I still have few things as simple as an answer.

So I have gone back to how it was for me in the beginning: first when I discovered women, later when I found butch women, and again when I fell in love with my first passing woman. Since I've loved women, it has always been those specific types of women I've wanted. Women the world refuses to acknowledge as female, women who turn people's heads toward us and then away in a single continuous motion. I have wanted these particular women whom the world often sees as men, and I have been seduced by women who are faggots with the eyes and the hopes of boys. Tricksters and she-guys and diesel dykes and bull daggers and softer butches. I have been given a gift of wonder by living alongside these other gay women's self-constructed truths.

Before there is thought, there is sensation and desire. Always the miracle appears when there are no expectations left for its arrival. Sex has always been that way for me. Explosive sex I mean—sex that is momentous enough or relentless enough to suck me totally into its savage, beautiful whirlpool. Sex that is so compelling, so necessary, so absolutely fundamental that it cannot be denied. That kind of sex—and my craving for it—has configured and reconfigured my life. It has branded me, punished me, and given me gifts unlike any others I've received or been able to create. Finally, it has proved to be, for me, a precarious and a life-transforming gift. Sex is the method I've used to search for wonder and awe. It is ecstasy I've craved and sought, nothing less. Sex is one of the few realms where my need for ecstasy was realizable, conceivable, resting on no resource save my own body and imagination. But miracles are usually double-edged swords. They open up worlds and catalyze unimaginable dreams, but they also fashion particular requirements and extract specific bounties, shaping and necessitating engagement with another. This is as it was for me: my longing for a woman's mouth or cock, the hunger, the search, and the completion I found through a butch lover's body thrusting forward.

I have also looked to other femmes for a powerful reflection and confirmation of myself and my own longings. I've tried to walk across the defenses that often separate women who desire similar partners and create friendships there. Sometimes I succeeded. It is here, late at night, on phones held in rage or tears or fiercely felt pleasure, leaning toward each other over restaurant tables, where I have finally talked with other femme women (and men) about our self-created femme identities, our search for erotic capability and fulfillment. Across generations and genders, through differences in color and class, I have listened with ongoing fascination and respect to other femmes' stories and survival strategies. I've been honored by the gift of those tales, and I've been challenged by these women in ways that no one else has ever managed to do.

The others I've most looked to, in order to understand and construct my own identity, have been drag queens. Drag queens are familiar to me in the way I feel about my own sense of femininity, and drag queens often have a physical affect very similar to mine when they enter a room. Being femme, for me, is a conscious way to be female—it does not mean merely accepting and existing within the preconstructed boundaries of "natural" womanhood. Daily I construct it and remove it, live it totally, betray it, reconstruct it from dust and fear, find it again. So do they. Like butches, drag queens make obvious what is usually masked, unquestioned, and assumed about gender. Gender is mutable and vibrant and not dependent on the biological body for its breath or its truth. Drag queens build women over their masculine bodies. I understand this. I am a woman whose femininity rests on a parental foundation far more like my father's than my mother's. I am my father's drag queen daughter.

I consider myself a feminist. I don't believe in "natural" womanhood or "normal" genders—of any category. Not for men, and not for women. No gender system is natural, no system of desire organic or removed from the way culture creates human experience. We are raised to become "masculine" or "feminine," and any rebellion against that still takes place within a constructed system of gender and erotic binaries—at least in white America. The expression and meanings of desire ride through our cultural body, leaving us intertwined with the roots of thousands of years of indoctrination that have sought to cement sexual identity, to point all erotic choice toward procreation, within the context of a purely male/female set of oppositions.

Our religions, our languages, our political theories, our family trees, our wars, our sciences, our work, and our categories of study have been bent to the task of creating and sustaining a gendered world of biologically specific people who we agree to call women or men. Sexual orientation is one of the pillars of that gender system, one of its most useful and necessary limbs. Heterosexuality is the core. To begin to question this complex set of systems is to begin a journey away from all the concepts used to structure the universe of common human existence we have developed as a nation. This is one of the reasons why the early women's liberation and gay liberation movements were seen as such a profound challenge to "normal" life and to the existence of family in this country. And it is why, to this day, the question of who is "normal"—and who determines it—is so fundamentally a political issue.

As our struggle developed over the years and those fundamental systems were challenged, something else happened. Some gay people began to represent normalcy, while some of us were left to stand at the outer edge of the homosexual circle. An internal hierarchy of deviance was instituted, by gay people, about each other. In the beginning, whether dressed as conservatively as possible or wearing drag, any gay person was queer in a collectively queer movement. But, through the years, the radical sexual politics of that early movement became more and more tempered, and the kinds of gay people considered important or central to the movement began to shift. Nowadays, all gay people are not seen as the same, and we are not all considered equal threats to the body politic of the nation. Some gay people are perceived to be "normal homosexuals," while some of us continue to represent a dangerous *otherness*, an ongoing threat of queer menace and deviance.

In the last twenty-five years of struggle, we have moved from gay liberation as a freedom struggle—a struggle for sexual, economic, and social justice—to a movement for gay legal rights. This struggle now parodies and duplicates a heterosexual middle-class/upper-class agenda based on re-creating the rights of heterosexuals for gay people, with all the implicit and explicit pieces of class and race prejudice that go with it. The freedom struggle of our movement, once committed to sexual liberation, has become, instead, a movement for gay nuclear family rights and for serial monogamy. It represents the entire movement as a sort of tame civil rights challenge: one of judicial battles in the courts and referenda in the towns, cities, and states. The gains have been significant. But, looking at the bigger picture, we have gone from a movement that was full of sensibility and humor, powerful difference and sexual contrast, a world of camp and butch and femme, of leather communities, drag queens and kings, flamboyant girls and effeminate gay boys, a movement full of our sexual cultures and creative, erotic dreams, to a movement that chooses only those representatives who may sit politely in the president's office, gender-appropriate gay representatives who work for gay inclusion and try very hard to show everyone else that "we are just like them."

This has also led to the creation of a group of assimilationist, power-hungry lesbian and gay male power brokers, negotiating their way back into class privilege—a privilege they feared they had once lost by being queer or coming out. For lesbians, the overwhelming sexual androgyny of this group of women deflects fear that they might appear to be too butch or too femme, too working class, too erotic. I have been asked to stand around in so many rooms, through the years, in some vain attempt to reassure straight people that I wasn't "too" gay—while knowing all along that I was. I believe that gay people are different, uniquely gifted with the insights and brilliance that stepping outside the heterosexual norm has given us. *That is exactly the source of our power.*

These last twenty years we have also had to fight an incurable, fatal epidemic. We have had to comfort and sustain each other in the terrible grief and loss which became our daily experience, to struggle, adapt, and change our sexuality because of that crisis. We have needed to find a way to give voice to new and challenging definitions of gayness—which is the birthright of each new gay generation. And in these twenty years of work we have become a movement even more divided by sexual politics, even more stratified by gender, class, and race. In that stratification and the struggle to articulate a common agenda, it has become necessary to vilify and marginalize many sexual and erotic communities and all the "differences" they have come to represent.

Sex is difficult to want, intricate to defend. To have our lives and our rights reduced to who we slept with was infuriating. But, in trying to respond, we gave up the fight for desire and sexual difference—as we gave up a more radical vision of the world we want to create. Homosexuality has always stood in for desire in this country—while heterosexuality has always been allowed to represent everything else. No matter where we speak and on what topic, sex, our sex, is always a current running through or below the discussion. Our civil rights struggle has had to give away desire in order to seem reasonable and legitimate. Only by not fucking, not sweating and feeling and wanting and possessing each other, will we be allowed to enter the Big House. Like Clinton's "don't ask, don't tell" military policy, so it goes with sex—now even we are expected "not to see" and "not to tell." Those of us who embody and expose the queerness of our still-existing and explicit sexual desires are kept at a distance or given no voice in a continually more straight-appearing gay movement. Because of that, though, the movement itself has also become a struggle full of dirty little secrets.

And it is the secrets we keep within our own communities that are killing us. We keep those secrets about sex and desire and the erotic as we have kept other secrets like class and color and addiction—because they seem too dangerous or too explosive, or we are too powerless, to have them acknowledged inside our communities or in the larger heterosexual world. And it is here that the tragedy of not being able to claim or struggle with our desires becomes obvious. Gay men cannot admit that they long for the taste of their male partners' semen or want anal sex without a condom, and they cannot say openly that they do not want to be monogamous. Lesbians and gay men of color are asked to choose between their communities of birth and their desires for other men or women. Gay women are not considered "real lesbians" if they fuck men, love dildos, believe their HIV infection came as a result of unprotected sex with an

HIV-positive female partner, love a butch or a femme, or shoot drugs or are alcoholics. The warnings to not tell, not talk, not reveal, are like huge flashing neon signs that go off when any of these things are mentioned. For transsexual and transgender people, and for bisexual women and men caught between these very different communities, behaviors, and identities, the "secrets" which they are forced to carry in order to survive socially are brutal—and sometimes physically fatal.

I have always believed that it is secrets which propel homophobia and the fear of sex through every community, in every setting. What cannot be named, admitted to, or claimed delineates the geography of our risks, becomes the slippery slope of our needs and desires. The end result of keeping these secrets—and maintaining all the lies it takes to support them—will be the crisis this movement needs to break through. Silence and denial—such popular feminist, lesbian, and AIDS community code words—are what have to be dismantled here if we are to truly understand our own stake in those silences, our own stake in denial itself.

I do not say these things without being aware of the political context of erotiphobia, homophobia, racism, sexism, and class oppression or to let the government or our society off the hook. So many communities continue to struggle, in relative isolation, with the crisis of homophobia and HIV with sexism and racism. But I fervently believe that the tragedy of our secrets and our lies is what we will have to confront and change, regardless of who is in power—this year or next. We are the leaders and activists in our own communities, and it is we who must challenge ourselves to speak—haltingly at first, perhaps, or with great fear—of a deeper set of truths in order for all of us to survive.

I believe that, as lesbians, gay men, bisexuals, and transgendered people, we share many collective bonds as well as some bitter commonalities, and it is around those commonalities that our struggle to affirm and demand sexual liberation must be built. We must, as a community, affirm desire. But we cannot take on sexual and erotic desire without also addressing the violence that happens internally in our communities and the daily violence, mandated by fear and hatred, that is visited on us from the outside. We cannot affirm butch and femme identities without seeing and valuing the contexts where it is most alive: in working-class communities, often in working-class communities of color. We cannot fight for sex shops staying open without addressing capitalism's relentless consumption of our cities, without addressing issues such as the workfare programs that serve to underwrite Wall Street's unbelievable profits. Unions, too, are seen as representing "somebody else," and the sexual scapegoating of women on our nation's welfare rolls is something we cannot continue to ignore. But our queerness, our desire, our otherness, cannot be removed from place and context. We are queer at the tables we eat at and at the tables we serve. Queer: femme, butch, trans, bisexual, wanting. Needed. Necessary.

There is one thing I've seen clearly from my earliest life: people will risk their most precious possessions to fulfill desire, no matter how dangerous the end result. No matter how awkward, damaging, or ill advised, sexual desire may spur people to leap off the cliff and go for broke. The key to organizing around sexual issues, its incredible power, lies precisely here: erotic desire, whether couched as romantic or ferocious, is what will make most people risk everything. This is precisely because sexual fulfillment is where most people hope to find true ecstasy. And there is no human hope without the promise of ecstasy. Organizers are confounded by this phenomenon, left dazed in the face of all the workplace affairs, wrecked marriages, unexpected pregnancies, queer liaisons, and sexual cover-ups that constitute the underbelly and folk fables of modern culture. But, instead of being confounded, organizers for true social and political change must learn how to use it—must learn how to incorporate the human yearning for ecstasy into the structure of struggle itself. Because this yearning, this search, is also the source of tremendous human energy, power, life.

I live in a world that makes wanting sex, actualizing and realizing desire, a thing of danger. But this is what I want: To be my own idiom and my own voice. To call the shots—even when what I most want is a lover who calls the shots. To love butch women without apology or fear. To be acclaimed in my own flagrant femme-girl body and high femme attitude. To be a warrior against shame of the erotic and for the right to taste and smell passion's will. To finally be at peace in my own body, my own desires, my experiences and most secret dreams. To give my children the right to their own sexual beauty, as they discover it. To fight for a world which values human sexual possibility without extracting a terrible human price. To battle human greed and human fear in any of its forms. To create a movement willing to live the politics of sexual danger in order to create a culture of human hope.

This is my dream today. These are my most dangerous desires.

In gratitude to Paula

Questions for Reflection, Discussion, and Writing

1. Beginning her essay by recounting a dream that "filled her with horror," what does Hollibaugh suggests that the dream has come to signify for her? What worlds does she suggest she has had to learn to mediate between?

2. In what ways does Hollibaugh suggest that her desires and femme identify placed her outside of the gay liberation movement, a movement she claims "I had helped to start, a movement whose survival and growth I was committed to"?

3. In what ways does Hollibaugh suggest that her position, identity, and background have prepared her to negotiate terrains of desire, sexuality, difference, politics?

4. According to Hollibaugh, what kind of shift has taken place within the gay liberation movement? Within what larger systems does she suggest such a shift is "assimilation-

ist"? What sources of power are currently being ignored or undermined by that assimilation, according to Hollibaugh?

5. What desires and needs does Hollibaugh list? In order to attain them, what does she believe needs to happen? To what other social, political, sexual constructs does she link those desires?

Related Reading

Joan Nestle, "The Femme Question" in *The Persistent Desire: A Femme-Butch Reader.* Joan Nestle, Ed. Boston: Alyson Publications. 1992. 138–146.

Amber Hollibaugh & Cherríe Moraga, "What We're Rollin' around in Bed With: Sexual Silences in Feminism: A Conversation Toward Ending Them" in *The Persistent Desire: A Femme-Butch Reader.* Joan Nestle, Ed. Boston: Alyson Publications. 1992. 243–253.

Madeline Davis, Amber Hollibaugh, & Joan Nestle, "The Femme Tapes" in *The Persistent Desire: A Femme-Butch Reader.* Joan Nestle, Ed. Boston: Alyson Publications. 1992. 254–267.

Elizabeth Lapovsky Kennedy and Madeline Davis, "'They Was No One to Mess With': The Construction of a Butch Identity in the 1940s and 1950s" in *The Persistent Desire: A Femme-Butch Reader.* Joan Nestle, Ed. Boston: Alyson Publications. 1992. 62–80.

Gayle Rubin, "Of Catamites and Kings: Reflections on Butch, Gender, and Boundaries" in *The Persistent Desire: A Femme-Butch Reader.* Joan Nestle, Ed. Boston: Alyson Publications. 1992. 466–482.

Judith Halberstam, "F2M: The Making of Female Masculinity" in *The Lesbian Postmodern.* Laura Doan, Ed. NY: Columbia UP. 1994. 210–218.

Robin Sweeney, "Too Butch to Be Bi (or You Can't Judge a Boy by Her Lover)" in *Bisexual Politics: Theories, Queries, and Visions.* Naomi Tucker, Ed. Binghamton, NY: Harrington Park Press. 1995. 179–187.

Sherrie A. Inness and Michele E. Lloyd, "G.I. Joes in Barbie Land: Recontextualizing Butch in Twentieth-Century Lesbian Culture" in *Queer Studies: A Lesbian, Gay, Bisexual, and Transgender Anthology.* Brett Beemyn and Mickey Eliason, Eds. NY: NYUP. 1996. 9–34.

JeeYeun Lee, "Why Suzie Wong Is Not A Lesbian: Asian and Asian American Lesbian and Bisexual Women and Femme/Butch/Gender Identities" in *Queer Studies.* Brett Beemyn and Mickey Eliason, Eds. NY: NYUP. 1996. 115–132.

Laura Harris and Liz Crocker, "Bad Girls: Sex, Class, and Feminist Agency" in *Femme: Feminists, Lesbians, and Bad Girls.* Laura Harris and Elizabeth Crocker, Eds. NY: Routledge. 1997. 93–102.

Joan Nestle and Barbara Cruikshank, "I'll Be The Girl: Generations of Fem" in *Femme: Feminists, Lesbians, and Bad Girls.* Laura Harris and Elizabeth Crocker, Eds. NY: Routledge. 1997. 105–118.

Leah Lilith Albrecht-Samarasinha, "Gender Warriors: An Interview With Amber Hollibaugh" in *Femme: Feminists, Lesbians, and Bad Girls.* Laura Harris and Elizabeth Crocker, Eds. NY: Routledge. 1997. 210–222.

Leah Lilith Albrecht-Samarasinha, "On Being a Bisexual Femme" in *Femme: Feminists, Lesbians, and Bad Girls.* Laura Harris and Elizabeth Crocker, Eds. NY: Routledge. 1997. 138–144.

Judith Halberstam, "Transgender Butch: Butch/FTM Border Wars and the Masculine Continuum." *GLQ: 4.2* (1998): 287–301.

Alisa Solomon, "Not Just A Passing Fancy: Notes on Butch" in *The Passionate Camera: Photography and Bodies of Desire.* Deborah Bright, Ed. NY: Routledge. 1998. 263275.

Sandra Lee Golvin, "Passage" in *Opposite Sex: Gay Men on Lesbians, Lesbians on Gay Men.* Sara Miles and Eric Rofes, Eds. NY:NYUP. 1998. 37–43.

Peggy Shaw, "You're Just Like My Father" in *O Solo Homo: the New Queer Performance.* Holly Hughes and David Roman, Eds. NY: Grove Press. 1998.

Pat Califia, "Genderbending: Playing With Roles and Reversals" in *Public Sex: The Culture of Radical Sex.* San Francisco: Cleis Press. 2000. 181–190.

Film

Tomboy (1994). Dawn Logsdon. 17 m.

Scent uVa Butch (1998). Shoshona Rosenfeld. 35m.

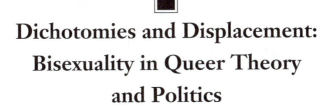

Dichotomies and Displacement: Bisexuality in Queer Theory and Politics

Stacey Young

Queer theory and queer politics continue to exhibit a marked silence around bisexuality. This silence is perhaps more complete in theory than in politics, given the nature of the theoretical enterprise. The solitude in which theory, in the final instance, is produced—despite its being shaped fundamentally through the collective processes of reading, teaching, studying, attending conferences, and so on—gives the author greater control than the activist over what issues make it onto her agenda.

In queer politics, the silence has occasionally been interrupted by vocal skirmishes, sometimes initiated by bisexuals, sometimes not. Until recently, these skirmishes have typically involved a swift conquest and subsequent banishment of the topic of bisexuality and, on occasion, of bisexuals.[1] This scenario has, in many cases, given way to another, in which "bisexual" is added to the title of an organization or event. In some cases, that addition has then been overturned: the word has been added only to be removed (and, sometimes, added again later). Very occasionally, the addition of "bisexual" has been followed by the addition of "transgendered."[2]

Silence can take many forms, however, and for all the name changes, queer politics has yet to reflect any real transformation in analyses or agendas: "queer" is usually used interchangeably with "lesbian/gay;" challenges to AIDS-related homophobia remain silent about the demonization of bisexual men ("stealth killers") in mainstream/heterosexist AIDS discourses; calls for civil rights are typically framed in terms of "lesbian and gay" rights; biphobia continues to find crude expression among some lesbians and gay men; and—in part, but not entirely, because of these factors, lesbian/gay political organizations and bisexual ones still operate largely in isolation from one another. By and large, bisexuality continues to be avoided or dismissed.

On paper, we see a similar phenomenon: when bisexuality is mentioned at all in writings about queerness that aren't specifically about bisexuality, it is often in the form of being tacked on to one or more of the innumerable iterations of "lesbian and gay" one finds in a given book or article—and then not mentioned again. Very rarely is it actually discussed, explored, or articulated as a queer identity alongside "lesbian" and "gay."

These silences are extremely curious; the critical stance that leads us to investigate other sexualities should, it would seem, lead us to investigate this one, but this has not been the case. Figuring out why can certainly aid us in our understanding of bisexuality. Such an enterprise is necessary: bisexuals, like lesbians and gay men, are queer, are part of queer movements and communities, and are subject to oppression on the basis of their sexuality. They make conscious choices about their sexuality that lie beyond those acceptable within the institution of heterosexuality. Investigations of queer politics and queer realities are incomplete without looking at bisexuality, in terms both of its consonance with lesbianism and male homosexuality and its difference from them.

But discerning the reasons for so much silence around bisexuality can do more than simply begin to fill those silences; it can assist us in our interrogations of other sexualities as well. This is because attention to bisexuality—and, in particular, to what the silences surrounding it can tell us—can reveal the costs to queer theory and politics of these lacunae, and can prod our thinking about sexuality in general in new directions—specifically, those suggested by what we discover when we look at bisexuality.

Bisexuality's heuristic value in the analysis of other sexualities stems not from any status it enjoys as a "universal" or "more complete" sexuality than lesbianism, male homosexuality, or heterosexuality. Ironically, its value has to do with the fact that it has been only marginal to the process by which other queer identities have been constructed. Queer identity politics has necessarily involved constructing definitions of queer identities whose content is characterized by the reversal of constructions of heterosexuality. While this has facilitated coherence among queers and an oppositional stance toward heterosexism, it has also had the effect of closing off certain avenues of inquiry into queer sexuality—avenues which, should we wander them, may expand our understanding of the consequences of narrowing our focus. These consequences are costly not only to bisexuals but to lesbians and gay men as well.

To put this another way: lesbian and gay identity and experience are coming to be the subject of intense and insightful scrutiny in the burgeoning field of queer theory. This produces both insight and restriction, for, as certain "truths," experiences, and realities begin to be articulated, others, not having been explored, recede to the margins and become eclipsed, while an accepted body of knowledge (and an accepted body of questions and unknowns) comes to govern discourse—and to preclude other questions, acknowledgment of other unknowns, and construction of other knowledges.

This paper begins to examine, through the lens of bisexuality, how the requisites of identity politics and the binarisms at the center of those requisites structure (and limit) queer theories and politics. It argues that beginning the work of theorizing bisexuality can assist us in articulating bisexual realities and bisexual politics, in theorizing lesbianism and male homosexuality, and in constructing political practices that can more effectively subvert existing power structures.

Reasons for "Bisexual Avoidance"

One reason some people avoid or dismiss bisexuality has to do with the garden variety (which is not to say simple) revulsion of prejudice. Some people, queer and heterosexual, respond to bisexuals directly through the phobic filter of stereotypes. They want nothing to do with people who are cast, variously, as indiscriminate, disease-ridden, unwilling to commit, promiscuous, opportunistic, apolitical, in a phase, cowardly, and deceitful.

Another factor in queer silence around bisexuality is the fact that silence tends to breed silence, and the relative lack of bisexual theory no doubt impedes those who don't think much about bisexuality from acknowledging it as an important analytic category. The phenomenon is somewhat circular, of course: queer institutions, milieux, collectivities, and intellectual enterprises have certainly reduced the costs to bisexuals, along with other queers, of pursuing same-sex desire, and have assisted efforts to analyze that pursuit in terms of homophobia and heterosexism. However, they have not been particularly conducive to the development of specifically *bisexual* political and theoretical analyses—nor in helping queers of any orientation (including bisexuals) to identify what might be gained from such analyses. Publishing and other forms of communication are mediated through highly politicized institutions. Editors of queer publications sometimes reject manuscripts about bisexuality on the grounds that it lies beyond their publication's scope, or because "we haven't decided yet what we want to do about covering this issue."[3] Conference organizers often ghettoize all papers on bisexuality into a few panels on the subject, rather than adopting a more integrative approach.[4] And so on.

This relative lack of theoretical work on bisexuality is compounded by a general lack of attention among queer theorists to the bisexual theory and writing that does exist—which is in turn compounded by the fact that most of this work has been published in collections specifically of work on bisexuality. Collections of this sort are often overlooked in queer studies, given the equation, in most instances, of "queer" with "lesbian and gay."

A fourth consideration contributing to lesbian and gay resistance to taking bisexuality seriously is the propensity on the part of some bisexual activists and writers to posit bisexuality as somehow superior to all other sexualities, claiming that it is "universal," that it transcends boundaries between genders and between sexualities, that it escapes the "limitations" of "monosexuality." These grandiose and patronizing claims, though by no means common to all bisexuals, have augmented existing antipathies toward bisexuals and have fueled resistance among lesbians and gay men to viewing bisexuals as part of queer communities and bisexuality as a legitimate and necessary subject of inquiry for queer theorists.

Beyond stereotypes, the relative paucity of work on bisexuality, the lack of attention to the work that has been done, and condescension on the part of some bisexuals, there are more complex reasons for lesbians' and gay men's silences around bisexuality—reasons that have to do with identity politics and its requisites, as well as with the intransigence of the homo/hetero dichotomy, its importance to identity politics, and its force in structuring our theorizing about sexuality. When we look at the status of bisexuality in queer politics in light of the exigencies of identity politics in general, we begin to see how these factors combine in certain strategies (dismissal, avoidance, displacement) that ultimately obscure not just bisexuality, but also a host of other identities that differentiate queers from one another, as well as a range of lesbian and gay experience.

Identity Politics

The question of what one calls oneself, how one identifies one's sexuality—and why it matters—is bound up in identity politics as it has been practiced by various social movements in this country since the 1960s (including the Civil Rights, Black Power, women's, homophile, and gay movements). Despite these movements' differences—in goals, targets, participants, and tactics—and despite increasingly sophisticated analyses of identity, identity-based political movements have generally shared a common set of assumptions about the relationships between identity, ideology and behavior, political commitment and trustworthiness. These assumptions include the notions that

- people who belong to the same identity group have more or less the same political analysis of (at least) the oppression they share (e.g., that all women share a feminist analysis of women's status);
- that form of oppression supersedes all others for all members of the group (e.g., that people of color are primarily concerned with racism, queers are primarily concerned with homophobia and heterosexism—the overlap between the categories gets lost behind this assumption);
- identity group members are always each other's natural allies, and can be trusted politically simply because they share an identity (e.g., all women are "sisters," all queers can be counted upon to resist homophobic practices);
- those in the "oppressor" group all benefit directly, consciously, and equally from their subordination of the "oppressed" group, and thus are rarely or never allies of the oppressed (e.g., all men, regardless of race, class, etc, enjoy higher status and more power than do all women; there's no such thing as a heterosexual ally to queer movements); and so forth.

These assumptions in turn originate from two grounding binary constructions:

1. The binary split between "us" and "them"

    - Identity politics movements represent people who share a common identity and who are oppressed as a group on the basis of that identity by people who share a different, "opposite" identity. There are only two main groups, for all practical purposes, and they are easily distinguishable from each other: we know who belongs in which group (e.g., blacks and whites, women and men, homosexuals and heterosexuals).

2. The binary split between active oppressors and active resisters

    - Members of the privileged group are complicit with those power structures, and will work actively to maintain them should they be threatened. Members of the oppressed identity group naturally resist the power structures that facilitate their oppression and that confer privileges upon those who belong to the other, opposite, oppressing identity group; unless they are suffering from extreme self-hatred, they feel solidarity with others who share their identity and they act accordingly. Hence, oppressed people need only mobilize "our own kind" in order to strengthen our movements and achieve our goals.

    On the basis of these dichotomies, identity politics has freighted the question of identity with the baggage of legitimacy: one's claim to being a member of a given identity category is gauged by one's political analysis and political commitments, which in turn are assumed to be evident in one's personal practices. Identity is seen as preceding the individual: individuals base their claims to membership in a particular identity category on the content of that category as it has been constructed.

Lived reality, though, inevitably exceeds identity categories. Where the political stakes of the constructions of those identity categories are highest, this excess can sometimes be perceived as a form of treason, expressed in such terms as "Uncle Tom" or "oreo cookie," "male-identified" or "closety"; explained as "false consciousness," "internalized oppression," or "self-hatred"; or rejoined with expressions of doubt about the legitimacy of an individual's claim to inclusion in a given category. In some cases, individuals find themselves called upon to prove the legitimacy of their claims to a certain identity by others within the identity category who doubt that legitimacy; most often, they defend their claims to legitimacy in a way that upholds the fiction that identity categories are discrete, their membership self-evident (a fiction belied, of course, by the need to prove membership in the first place). That is, they are likely to formulate their claims to legitimacy in terms of their congruity with the established discursive content of the identity in question.

But not always. Theory and practical politics increasingly seek to problematize these very assumptions, challenge these binarisms, and call into question the assumed links between what one practices, what one calls oneself, how one views the world, and what political commitments one makes. Particularly strong within feminist movements, these challenges to established notions about what characterizes the subjects of a particular movement have also emerged within queer movements. Some queer or queer-inspired organizations (such as Queer Nation and ACT UP) have reflected these challenges in some of their actions and agendas. ACT UP New York, for example, has had active Women's Issues and Majority Outreach caucuses that were able to steer substantial portions of the organization's activity in the direction of addressing the concerns of women and people of color—pressuring the Centers for Disease Control to base its definition of AIDS on clinical factors that are more relevant to women's experience of the disease, for example, and setting up needle exchange programs to meet the HIV-prevention needs of injection drug users, who disproportionately come from communities of color.

But these actions did not come about without significant struggle—nor do they reflect the end of that struggle. And there are certainly many more examples of activists and intellectuals presuming to speak on behalf of whole categories of subjects but doing so from a limited—and usually dominant—perspective that represents the experiences and interests of only a relatively privileged few. Thus, for example, we hear white queer activists say that racism isn't their issue, while male activists complain, when called upon to explain the mostly male membership of their organizations, that "women can come—they just won't; it's not like we keep them out." Or we read political theory that paints a two-dimensional, homogenizing portrait of queers:

for lesbians and gay men, [sexuality] is *the* principle [of identity]. It is on the basis of their sexuality that they are subjected to domination . . .

thus

the part of themselves that [lesbian and gay people] have had to pay most attention to ethically, and that hence centers the way they live their lives, is their sexuality and their erotic relationships.[5]

The fact is that no matter how compelling are the challenges to homogenizing constructions of "lesbians and gay men"—constructions that reduce them to a unitary group with identical interests—the impact of these challenges is often startlingly limited, even among those most receptive to them. Those who have worked politically within identity politics movements will recognize the tenacity of reductive, homogenizing binary notions of who a movement's constituents are, even among people who are intellectually persuaded by challenges to them. (One of the most common—and most devastating—manifestations of these assumptions is an unwillingness to work sincerely to establish coalitions with people who share political goals even as they inhabit different subcultures.) These notions are difficult to uproot not because they are "true" or compelling on a rational level: candid observation turns up many counterexamples, more than enough to call those assumptions into question. Rather, as Derrida and so many others have argued, they are difficult to uproot because the binary structures of thought they represent are so ingrained, and are constantly reinforced. (Consider, for example, the widespread, automatic acceptance enjoyed in our society by such commonsense pronouncements as "There are two sides [read: only two] to every story," and that those two are necessarily each other's opposite.)

In a way, the continued theoretical and practical efforts to complicate categories of identity that so often get figured homogeneously testify to the resilience of the homogeneous constructions of identity categories. That is, the challenges are continually made necessary by the strength and resilience of constructions that (inevitably) fail to take account of a range of experience, and that exert some disciplinary force over individuals' lives. The challenges continue precisely because the governing binarisms are so intransigent.

Identity Categories: Uses and Limitations

Challenges to identity politics-based assumptions of homogeneity among those represented by a given identity category have resulted in the proliferation of terms of difference. For example, the category "homosexuals"—the subjects on whose behalf queer movements have sought to pursue progressive change—has been complicated both by historical and political shifts (which brought the terms "gays" and "queers" into use); and by the articulation of the ways that a queer person's interests are shaped not only by her/his position vis-à-vis the social organization of sexuality, but also by her/his position vis-à-vis the social organization of race, class, gender, ethnicity, nationality, and so forth. In political practice, this complication has enhanced, in particular, the visibility of women in queer collectivities. It has also spawned an abundance of terms that seek, in ever-increasing degrees of specificity, to define the totality of people's (salient) identities. Thus we get terms like "white, heterosexual, middle-class women," "Jewish lesbian," and "working-class gay men of color." These terms reflect what Eve Sedgwick calls the "tiny number of inconceivably coarse axes of categorization" that we have available to us and that, in the end, still leave us mired in descriptions that obscure their variable content and relevance, such that "even people who share all or most of our own positionings along these crude axes may still be different enough from us, and from each other, to seem like all but different species."[6]

One of the political consequences of this proliferation can be seen in one form of dismissal or avoidance of bisexuality: In debates over whether to add "bisexual" to the titles of "lesbian and gay" organizations and events, a common response is "Why stop at adding 'bisexual' to the title of this event?" In other words, why not be all-inclusive? And yet, it is at this point that so many people balk, sometimes because they recognize, when faced with the task of making language more accurately reflect the diversity of social reality, that that diversity is impossible to capture fully in language. This impossibility of being truly representative, however, seems contrary to the stated premises of so much recent important activity directed at expanding rights and representation to "include everyone": even as we might recognize the impossibility of representing "everyone," we still feel that we must represent "someone."

A dilemma thus takes shape: identity categories (including "bisexual") seem to be simultaneously indispensable to and restricting of our political projects. When these and other identity categories are invoked to represent the subjects in whose names political movements are launched, the implicit or explicit demarcations that serve to distinguish these subjects as a group (and to identify what might be the project of a movement advanced in their name) automatically work to secure exclusion at the very moment that they appear to facilitate inclusion. The dilemma centers around the paradoxical relationship between the desire to represent categories of subjects as such for political purposes, and the desire to avoid the exclusions that seem inevitably to take place when one seeks to identify and define the content of such categories. In practice, it is not uncommon for people to opt for the status quo—that is, "lesbian and gay"—as a way to deal with the conflicting demands of inclusiveness and expediency.

Challenges to identity politics' assumptions have sought to move the debate to a different level by contesting the ostensible content of established identity categories. Sometimes the critique is that they are over- or under-inclusive, as in Greta Christina's effort to define "lesbian":

Is a lesbian: a woman who only fucks other women? That would include bi women who're monogamously involved with other women. A woman who doesn't fuck men? That would include celibate straight women. A woman who would never get seriously involved with men? Rules out lesbians who've been married in the past. A woman who never has sexual thoughts about men? That excludes dykes who are into heavy and complex gender play, who get off on gay men's porn, or who are maybe just curious.

Christina goes on to make the point that the category "bisexual women" includes desires, behaviors, and identifications that are so disparate as to defy any coherent representation:

For me, being bi means I mostly like to fuck women, and I also like to fuck men. For Joan, it means that she's attracted to both men and women, regardless of who she is or isn't humping. For Sandra, it means that she only gets serious about women, but is willing to fuck men for fun as well. Marta, who's been monogamously married to a man for some time, says she's bi because she's been involved with women in the past and is still attracted to them. Rachel, on the other hand, is sexual almost entirely with women, but occasionally likes to tie men up and dominate them—she also calls herself bi. The key factor can be who you're attracted to, who you're willing to sleep with, who you're actually screwing, who you fall in love with. And the key factor is different for each woman. It's very hard to pin down.[7]

Moreover, there's a certain amount of overlap in sexual practices between the categories "lesbians" and "bisexual women"; this overlap might be represented by the examples of a lesbian who sleeps with men on occasion and a bisexual woman who is monogamous with her woman lover. All of these examples illustrate the impossibility of defining all the possible meanings that can attach to a particular identity category.

Yet the categories' limitations have to do not simply with their content being over- or under-inclusive, but with the ways that their content shifts depending on who employs them, in what contexts, and so on. Critics of identity categories argue persuasively that these categories, far from signifying discrete and coherent groupings of individuals, in fact function as representational fictions that do violence to differences between people, as well as to individuals' own internal complexities, in order to secure an appearance of coherence among all those who "belong" to a given category. Biddy Martin discusses this phenomenon when she writes of efforts at "boundary control," those explicit attempts to impose a stable content that is supposed to describe or define all members of a given category. Specifically with regard to efforts from within to control the boundaries around the category "lesbian," Martin writes:

A friend of mine recently referred to these efforts at boundary control as "purification rituals," and they do seem to involve efforts to rid the category "lesbian" of anything messy, anything like its inevitable internal differences or our own irreducible heterogeneities. . . . The amount of work required to keep the category intact exposes its ultimate instability and its lack of fixed foundations.[8]

These "rituals" themselves, Martin notes, when they are conducted from within the category, are part and parcel of the intense high-stake struggles that characterize the construction of identities.[9]

Purification rituals take many forms, including the more subtle form of insisting that we retain for political purposes constructions of subjects—lesbians, women, and so forth—that, through their denial of internal instability, retain and impose meanings that work to marginalize certain kinds of individuals those subject categories are supposed to represent. This is a political strategy that is destined to fail, according to Martin:

> The question is whether the perceived need for uniformity, complete autonomy and authenticity is the best way to challenge heterosexism and misogyny, or an effective strategy to defend against annihilation. . . . Whatever the intent of these efforts to render lesbianism internally coherent and stable, discipline and control are the effects. Unruly sexual fantasies, desires, pleasures and practices, *but also more complex analyses of social realities, are sacrificed to investments in identity.*[10] [emphasis added]

Often, of course, explicit efforts to control boundaries are not even necessary, because the process by which individuals group themselves and articulate their supposed shared identity is one that involves suppressing the possibility of internal contradictions. Sometimes this process takes place consciously: people will discipline their own desires and behaviors in order to fit acceptable categories, rather than place themselves outside of them or have to challenge them—like one gay man who told me that he called himself bisexual for a while, and had lovers of both sexes, but then decided that he had to choose, and that he did so because "nobody likes bisexuals." Biphobia rendered bisexuality an inviable choice for him.

Judith Butler describes this process as the "juridical definition" of subjects:

> The question of "the subject" is crucial for politics . . . because juridical subjects are invariably produced through certain exclusionary practices that do not "show" once the juridical structure of politics has been established. In other words, the political construction of the subject proceeds with certain legitimating and exclusionary aims, and these political operations are effectively concealed and naturalized by a political analysis that takes juridical structures as their foundation. *Juridical power inevitably "produces" what it claims merely to represent . . .*[11] (emphasis added)

In other words, while categories such as "lesbian" or "bisexual" are often employed as ontological givens—as if their "truth" lay beneath their cultural construction and need only be revealed and mobilized—the categories themselves make sense only within a paradigm that emphasizes some behaviors, desires, or analyses, reduces others, and ignores still others altogether in order to appear natural and self-evident.

Complexity, Instability, and the Status of Bisexuality

What's so interesting about this, of course, is that *while lesbianism, male homosexuality, and male and (especially) female heterosexuality may have been explored and theorized at greater length than bisexuality thus far has been, those other sexualities are by no means less complex or more stable than bisexuality, not even in terms of object choice.* Certainly there are many lesbians and heterosexual men who sleep only with women, many gay men and heterosexual women who sleep only with men. However, as categories, these identities also include, for example, gay men who occasionally sleep with women; lesbians who are in long-term relationships with men; and countless heterosexuals who form short- or long-term sexual relationships with people of the same sex. The stability that these categories seem to represent with regard to object choice is, in many cases, a fiction. Likewise, while some bisexuals have multiple male and female partners, others are fairly constant in the gender of their partners, or are in long-term, monogamous relationships—and thus may have less variability in the gender of their partners than some people expect when they hear the term "bisexual," with all that it seems to connote.

This is not to imply that identity categories are empty or useless (even as descriptive terms) simply because they don't mean the same thing to everyone, or because their content is unstable. But I do want to challenge both the notion that identity categories represent epistemological certainties, and the notion that the uncertainties that do exist are located primarily at what we think of as the boundaries that demarcate one category from another. This view of sexual object choice among members of identity categories—the view of a stable center with flux relegated to the margins—obscures the degree to which uncertainty and variability may be closer to a rule than an exception. It also does a great deal to maintain the homosexual/heterosexual binarism.

If variability is as prevalent in most or all categories as it seems to be when we investigate those categories typically associated, in discourses on sexuality, with stability and certainty (i.e., lesbianism and male homosexuality), *why, then, does the mention of bisexuality in particular raise the specter of unrepresentability in ways that the mention of other identities does not?*

If we begin to investigate this phenomenon, I believe we will learn a great deal about some of the ways that homosexual/heterosexual dichotomies function at the levels of discourse and identity construction, and specifically how bisexuality is made to stand in for multiplicity and complexity, and is then banished together with all of that multiplicity in order to restore the appearance of a stable, binary world.

The example of the title of recent national queer studies conferences is a good place to begin this investigation.

*****

"Pleasure/Politics: 4th Annual Lesbian, Bisexual and Gay Studies Conference," held at Rutgers in the fall of 1991, was the first time that "bisexual" was included in the conference title.[12] When the organizing committee for the fifth annual conference decided to remove bisexual from the title, changing it back to "Lesbian and Gay Studies" after "Bisexual" had been included only once, even they seemed unable to articulate what was at stake. Even at the moment of enacting this change, the organizing committee stated, "We have decided that we are not ready to change the title at this point." This statement came in a form letter the organizing committee sent to those who wrote to protest the removal of "bisexual" from the conference title. It was also the gist of one of the organizers' discussions, at the fouth annual conference, of the fifth annual conference's title—a discussion that accompanied the circulation of a flyer announcing, "Lesbian and Gay Studies Conference #5: Untitled. (ca. 1991)" The flyer included three columns of nouns and adjectives organized under the headings, "titles," "subtitles," and "entitlements." The terms "lesbian," "gay," and "bisexual" all appeared in the "subtitles" column but only "lesbian" and "gay" appeared in what was, in fact, the title of the conference—contrary to what the word "untitled" might be meant to suggest. (In later correspondence, the word "untitled" was dropped altogether, and along with it the pretense that "Fifth Annual Lesbian and Gay Studies Conference" was not, in fact, the title of the conference.)

Several events took place simultaneously with the appearance of "bisexual" in the conference title. These simultaneous events included: the claim on the part of the organizing committee that they were choosing not to change the conference title even as they were changing it back to what it had been before; the claim that the conference was untitled, even as the title was the subject both of change and of claims that it was not the subject of change; the compilation and circulation of an extensive list of nouns and adjectives representing a number of potential differences within queer collectivities; and, finally, the distribution (to those who wrote to protest the change) of a form letter from the organizing committee expressing the sentiment that "this question about the conference and bisexuality itself should be important areas of discussion at the conference."

It is striking that the organizing committee represented their actions as a decision not to change when, in fact, they were changing the title, claiming not to be changing it, and claiming that there was no title. It is equally striking that the issue of whether "bisexual" should appear in the conference title, and the sentiment that "bisexuality itself" (whatever that might mean) should be an important area of discussion at the conference, first inaugurated, and then came to stand in for, a discussion of a whole range of identities, practices, and differences (represented on the flyer) that, if taken into account, would have a profoundly destabilizing effect on the categories "lesbian" and "gay"—categories that have been retained, one can only conclude, as signifiers of the stability that is so much in question at the moment. In other words, *the destabilizing effects of all these points of difference were displaced onto bisexuality* by the committee's call for a discussion of bisexuality specifically, rather than of all the sexualities and other identifications represented by the terms listed on the flyer. In this way, not only is the homosexual/heterosexual dichotomy sustained; but also, crucial questions of race, ethnicity, class, and gender are suppressed. That is, as long as queer studies and other queer entities marginalize or suppress questions of, for example, race, then the terms "lesbian" and "gay" will continue to carry racialized connotations that implicitly reinforce the hegemony of whiteness in queer collectivities.

The message of the committee's actions seems to be that there is something uniquely destabilizing about bisexuality, whereas the categories "lesbian" and "gay" are more stable; and that once you throw bisexuality in, everything is up in the air: too complicated, unstable, impossible to define. But these conclusions make sense only if the heterosexual/homosexual binarism and the resistance to multiplicity go unchallenged. The fact is, of course, that everything is already complicated and unstable; definitions are always partial and provisional. The removal of "bisexual" while lesbian and gay remain, and the suppression of the other terms on the conference flyer from this call for discussion, are symptomatic of the way that the heterosexual/homosexual binarism is still so central to how we think, and of an abiding, generalized resistance to grapple with multiplicity and resist boiling several things down to two. This dogged adherence to binarisms arises from the apparent stability they seem to represent.[13]

And stability—or rather, its appearance—seems to be what is at stake when bisexuality is made to stand in for complexity in general, and when both bisexuality and complexity are then dismissed.

*****

This phenomenon of displacement and avoidance is clearly evident in other recent debates surrounding the question of what to call queer collectivities (such as communities and movements, organizations, pride marches, and academic conferences).[14] Many queer collectivities are choosing to add "bisexual" alongside "lesbian and gay" to their titles. This addition is double edged. On the one hand, it represents a long-overdue recognition of the presence of bisexuals in queer communities and queer political struggles, and of a burgeoning bisexual movement. On the other hand, adding "bisexual" alongside "lesbian and gay" can perpetuate the notion that the titles we give our organizations are inclusive—that they define the full spectrum of possible sexualities. That is, the addition somehow ratifies the notion that, by coming up with the right string of subject signifiers, we can reach a full solution to the problem of exclusion in representation. (That the term "queer" is less susceptible to this interpretation is one of its most appealing aspects.) Despite being double edged, however, the addition of "bisexual" to the names of queer organizations and events does signal an important step both toward addressing biphobia and, potentially, toward opening up our thinking beyond the homo/hetero binarism.

But we're also seeing another phenomenon: the removal of "bisexual" soon after it has been added to the titles of certain queer entities. The national queer studies conference is one example. The Northampton Pride March is another: "bisexual" was added to the march title one year, only to be voted out the following year by members of the local lesbian communities who organized precisely for that purpose, arguing that the presence of "bisexuality" in the march title rendered lesbians invisible. (They also voted bisexuals off the march steering committee.)[15]

Again, what is so interesting about this series of events is the particular capacity that acknowledgements of bisexuality seem to have for unsettling things, and the fact that that capacity seems to revolve around the anxiety of not knowing with which term in a binary opposition someone is aligned.[16] Moreover, bisexuality becomes the magnet for problems—in this case, the relative invisibility of lesbians within queer communities—that certainly stem from sources other than the assertion of a bisexual presence, and that would certainly persist even if bisexuals took the suggestion of some lesbians in this case to "go off to form their own community."

*****

These practical examples of displacement and avoidance surrounding bisexuality find parallels in the emerging field of queer theory. This field's otherwise careful and insightful projects are nonetheless practically uniform in leaving the homosexual/heterosexual binarism undisturbed—to the detriment of our understanding of sexuality and power. Two works will serve as brief examples here.

At the end of her groundbreaking study *Epistemology of the Closet*, Eve Sedgwick points out that, thus far, discussions of bisexuality don't "signal any movement at all on two analytic blockages as old as the century: the transitive/separatist question about gender identity, and the minoritizing/universalizing question about sexual definition" (251). This is because, in her examples, these discussions figure bisexual men as both effeminate and masculine, and as both a tiny minority and a potentially vast cross section of the population.

It seems more than a little odd that Sedgwick begins and abruptly ends her discussion of bisexuality in the last three pages of her study. Her virtual silence on bisexuality and the shortcomings of discussions of it begs explanation, given her laser-like attention to ambiguities and shortcomings in homosexual and ostensibly heterosexual representation. While it is true that most, if not all, discussions of bisexuality to date are in fact characterized by precisely the blockages she identifies, it may also be the case that further probing will reveal bisexuality to be not only an important subject of inquiry in itself but also a useful heuristic when it comes to looking at the general phenomenon of sexuality and its structuring within hetero/homo binarisms. For example, one way to expand on Sedgwick's work would be to turn her critique of the heterosexual/homosexual binarism to questions of its disciplining effects on people who would choose partners of either or both sexes, in addition to the effects on those who would choose partners only of their own sex.

There are no doubt other insights to be gleaned by addressing what Sedgwick's silences around bisexuality mean for her work in terms of some of the holes those silences produce, some of the subjects the silences allow to be glossed over. But what does it mean that after she tirelessly (and splendidly) interrogates queerness in representations of heterosexuality and homosexuality, for hundreds of pages, she then tacks bisexuality literally onto the end of her study, concluding (apparently without the need to demonstrate, as she does so thoroughly throughout the rest of her discussions) that what she has said about homosexuality in these portrayals applies to bisexuality as well? After plumbing the depths of matters overlooked to tease out insightful readings of queerness in canonical texts, is she simply "overlooking" bisexuality? And, if so, can this be due to anything more or less than the paralysis that takes hold when we try to contemplate more than two (binary) terms at one time?

Similar obfuscations operate in Mark Blasius's *Gay and Lesbian Politics: Sexuality and the Emergence of a New Ethic*. In his book, Blasius claims to articulate an experience universal among queers—the coming out process—from a perspective that is

> not primarily that of a category of subjective identity (the author's lived experience as a gay man of middle-class European American ancestry—although it has obviously been informed by it). Rather, I have tried to *create* perspective from the analytical category of *sexuality:* one that applies to all lesbians and gay men regardless of other differences. (6)

Blasius goes on to argue for an "ethic of reciprocity," which he says characterizes not only queer sexual relationships, but political ones as well. Lesbians and gay men, he says, have developed

> an erotics that integrates the pleasure of the other into one's own pleasure, an ethic of erotic reciprocity. As such, it is the creation of equality within and by means of sexual relationships. This can lead toward social equality (as it has to some degree with lesbian and gay communities—that is not to say there is no class, racial or ethnic, and age stratification there, merely that erotics offers a bridge across these divisions). . . . (125)

Replete with galloping generalizations and totalizing constructions of lesbianism and male homosexuality, Blasius's book manages to avoid engaging with the whole range of complicated and often painful differences that sometimes divide queers. The passage above represents a rare nod to those

differences—one that he declines to follow with any real focused discussion of
the implications of those differences for queer politics.

Blasius makes another nod that he does not follow up—this time to bisexuality and the homosexual/heterosexual binarism:

> the contemporary lesbian and gay movement, *to the extent that it incorporates bisex-
> uals and transgendered people*, de-essentializes the sexual binary (male/female) itself,
> the "keeper" of heterosexuality.[17] (emphasis added)

Elsewhere, he asserts:

> The March on Washington document: (1) through the inclusion of bisexuals,
> challenges the teleological grounding of sexuality as an instinct; . . . [and] by the
> inclusion of transgender and cross-gender as a component of the freedom of ex-
> pression of sexual identity, eliminates dimorphic biological sex or gender as the
> ground of what sexuality is at all.[18]

At first glance, these textual moments may seem to be unrelated. However, Blasius's project in this book is to limn that which is unique to lesbian and
gay experience, and universal to lesbians and gay men, and to set that against
heterosexuality. Given this project, and given his momentary acknowledgment
of the potential for attention to bisexuality and transgenderism to upset sexual
and gender binarisms, it may well be the case that he retains his own binary
construction of queer and heterosexual experience only by failing to follow his
own vague assertions about bisexuality and transgenderism to their logical conclusions.

In other words, Blasius's argument, which is an enthusiastic capitulation
to the heterosexual/homosexual binary, can barely contain itself. If Blasius were
to look fully at the challenges he claims bisexuality poses for that binary, it is
unlikely that he could retain it intact. And once the homosexual/heterosexual
binary raveled, he would no longer have any need to construct a homogenizing
account of queers or to suppress the racial, class, gendered, or ethnic—let alone
sexual—differences that often divide us from one another.

This is not to say that bisexuality is the "magic bullet" for totalizing constructions of sexuality. It is simply to say that bisexuality, brought into theoretical play, might exert enough pressure on those constructions to disrupt,
irreparably, *sexually homogenized* accounts of queers. Doing so might in turn
make way for disrupting the homogenization that takes place around race, gender, class, and other sources of difference that are so often suppressed in the
service of constructing a coherent subject of queer theory and politics.

What Is to be Done?

I have argued here that queer theory and politics can gain from paying greater
attention to bisexuality and its relation to the binarisms embedded in queer
identity politics. This is true both in terms of exploring the largely uncharted

territory of bisexual identity, bisexual theory and other bisexual writings, and bisexual politics; and in terms of using bisexuality heuristically, to find out what it can tell us about other queer identities, experiences, theories, and politics. What follows is a brief discussion of what these enterprises might entail.

Theorizing about bisexuality

Examining the ways the heterosexual/homosexual binarism structures theories about bisexual lives will entail, first of all, moving beyond the tendency in some bisexual theory to claim that bisexuality transcends this opposition. We should certainly examine the potential for some manifestations of bisexuality to *subvert* this opposition, just as we should examine the potential for various manifestations of lesbianism, male homosexuality, and male and female heterosexuality to subvert it. We should not, however, claim that the very existence of bisexuality—or of anything—*transcends* this opposition. We also need to look at how some of the theoretical work on bisexuality makes the mistake of accepting the premise that bisexuality embodies complexity and other sexual identities do not—a premise whose implications are both homophobic and biphobic. Just as we have come to recognize that lesbian relationships are in some way structured by the same gender divisions that structure the rest of society—they don't transcend those divisions, though they may in some cases work to subvert them—we need to recognize that bisexuality is imbricated in the homo/hetero binarism that structures the rest of society—it does not transcend that dichotomy, though it may in some cases work to subvert it. Our task should be to interrogate this imbrication with an eye to how it might be transformed—not to circumvent that difficult work as if by fiat.

A good way to begin theorizing about this imbrication of bisexuality in the heterosexual/homosexual binarism is by looking at examples of how that opposition gets mapped onto bisexuality in ways that construct bisexuality as a combination of heterosexuality and homosexuality, rather than as an identity unto itself; and the related phenomenon of some bisexuals referring to their "straight side" and their "lesbian/gay side." We need to explore the consequences of labels that identify, where bisexuals are concerned, the genders of the people in the relationship but not their sexualities, whereas the terms "lesbian," "gay," and "heterosexual" can signify both. That is, what are the consequences of the erasure of bisexual identity that takes place when bisexuals' relationships are labeled "lesbian" or "gay" if our partners are the same sex as us, or "heterosexual" if they are not?

For example, common among bisexuals is the experience of seeing our relationships to queer communities shift according to whether our lovers are the same sex as us. The pressures that bring about these shifts can take many forms and issue from many sources, but many of them certainly stem from a homosexual/heterosexual dichotomy that breaks people into respective "camps," assigns individuals to one or the other depending on how the gender of one's partner compares with one's own, and, on the same basis, derives conclusions about one's complicity with or resistance to homophobic oppression. The disciplining effects of such an arrangement are complex and extensive, not only for bisexuals but for lesbians, gay men, and heterosexuals as well (as in the example, above, of the gay man who chose not to identify as bisexual and to restrict himself to male partners because "nobody likes bisexuals"; or when bisexuals stay in the closet as such in queer contexts; or when lesbians and gay men feel discomfort, guilt, or fear at being found out for having sexual feelings toward members of the other sex; etc.). While they are not as calamitous, perhaps, as societal exhortations to heterosexuality, the disciplining effects of an enforced appearance of uncomplicated homosexuality need to be investigated to a much greater extent than they have been thus far in queer theory.

A second undertaking of bisexual theory, and of queer theory in general, should be to examine how projects celebrated by some bisexuals, such as the Kinsey Scale and Fritz Klein's Sexual Orientation Grid, reinscribe the heterosexual/homosexual opposition by continuing to characterize sexual orientation and identity solely in terms of gender. The Kinsey Scale places individuals on a continuum from zero (exclusively heterosexual) to six (exclusively homosexual), based on their sexual behavior (conceived narrowly as genital sexual encounters leading to orgasm) as adults. Klein's taxonomy is a step up from conceptualizations like Kinsey's and others that hinge completely on sexual *behavior* with respect to the gender of one's partner. In Klein's method, one maps one's sexuality using Kinsey's numbers (zero to six) on a grid that charts gender preference in the past, present (defined as "in the past year"), and "ideal future goal," with respect to sexual and social attraction, sexual fantasies, and self-identification, along with sexual behavior (which nonetheless remains unspecified).[19] While both these taxonomies accommodate the possibility of bisexuality, they retain an approach to sexuality that focuses exclusively on gender in object choice. Theoretical work on any sexual identity is more likely to gain from an approach that takes into account the sort of wide-ranging array of sexual differences, some relating to gender and some not, that Eve Sedgwick advances in *Epistemology of the Closet*. In her study, Sedgwick proposes a number of other differences to be considered as a way to refine our theoretical inquiries into sexuality. These factors include, among others, the different meanings to different people of identical "genital acts"; the different degrees of importance different people attach to the psychic and/or physical aspects of sex; and the degree to which different people feel that their response to a sexual act, object, context, or role is innate or chosen.

Third, it will be theoretically useful to explore instances in queer praxis in which the homo/hetero binarism seems to enable lesbians and gay men to operate under a double standard, denouncing bisexuality in the very terms to which they strenuously object when used by homophobes to denounce lesbians and gay men. For example, it bears investigating the discursive relationship that emerged in debates surrounding the title of the "1993 March on Washington for Lesbian, Gay and Bi Rights." In these debates, "bisexual" was constructed as carrying sexual connotations that were too overt, and much more so than "lesbian" or "gay"; hence, the representation of bisexuals in the title of the march was made conditional upon bisexuals accepting the designation "bi" over "bisexual."[20] What does it mean for the sexual liberation of lesbians and gay men, as well as that of bisexuals, that this kind of internalized sex-phobia—so frequently and devastatingly marshaled against all queers—was in this instance, at least, mobilized against bisexuals from within a queer movement? What can this discursive incident reveal about the status and function of bisexuality in queer movement politics?

Theorizing through bisexuality

Any theoretical work on sexuality in general would be greatly enhanced by an examination not only of what bisexuality means for bisexuals, but of how it functions in larger discourses around sexuality as well. Besides the function I have identified here—that of standing in for complexity and instability—what other functions does bisexuality perform in discourses on sexuality? When does it get invoked, and how? When and why does it disappear, and with what effects? What other issues seem to attach to it, what questions does it perennially raise? What complications that appear when we theorize bisexuality actually exist for, but are obscured in theories about, lesbianism, male homosexuality, and male and female heterosexuality?

For example: how can theorizing the multiple closets bisexuals inhabit complicate a discussion of the closets gay men and lesbians inhabit? One of the closets bisexuals occupy is that which homophobia creates—that is, the closet produced by the need of some bisexuals to conceal same-sex desire, behavior, etc., in relation to heterosexist institutions and individuals, for the same reasons that some lesbians and gay men also need to do so. Another closet bisexuals inhabit is created specifically by biphobia within queer communities, such that bisexuals sometimes "pass" as gay or lesbian, concealing their bisexuality, in ways that are similar to the imperative some lesbians and gay men feel to conceal, in relation to queer communities, sexual interaction with or desire for members of the other sex.

Additionally, bisexuals sometimes "pass" as lesbians or gay men among heterosexuals for a number of reasons, including the sense that, in some situations, correcting a straight person's assumption that one is lesbian or gay with the statement, "I'm not lesbian/gay, I'm bisexual" is more likely to fuel homophobia than to combat it (because of the heterosexist construction of bisexuality in some discourses). Like the ways in which many lesbians and gay men feel the need in queer contexts to "closet" sexual desire for members of the other sex, they may also inhabit this closet—for reasons similar to bisexuals'—among heterosexuals, that is, to combat the heterosexist assumption that even queers are really straight at heart.

In some arguments against including bisexuals in queer collectivities, these closets are constructed as being primarily the province of bisexuals—a construction that works to isolate bisexuals, characterizing them as untrustworthy; and that also works to flatten the experiences of some lesbians and gay men, to keep them in these closets, and to simplify the complex negotiations they must make with regard to sexuality, identity, and power.

Theorizing bisexuals' multiple and complex relationships to the closet could begin to clarify bisexual realities. But it could also illuminate some of the hidden aspects of lesbian/gay experience, identity construction, and politicization, by looking at how lesbians and gay men feel they need to represent themselves—to other queers and to heterosexuals—and to what extent that coincides with their views of themselves, their own experiences, their identities.

Related to discourses about closets is the issue of heterosexual privilege: thus, another fruitful area of investigation would be the discursive relationship between bisexuality and heterosexual privilege, and what that relationship reveals or obscures (and with what effects) about important realities in the lives of bisexuals, as well as those of lesbians and gay men, who also, of course, can occupy myriad positions in relation to heterosexual privilege.

These are just some of the questions that emerge from a strategy of theorizing *from* bisexuality—that is, theorizing bisexual lives—and theorizing *through* bisexuality to gain insights into the construction and deployment of other sexualities as well. This strategy has a great deal to offer queer theory and politics.

Notes

My thanks to Linda Nicholson, Trevor Hope, and Kim Christensen for helping me to clarify some of the ideas I present here, and to Shane Phelan for her comments on earlier versions of this article.

1. For example, the 1990 pride march in Northampton, Massachusetts, was preceded by a bitter struggle in which members of the lesbian community organized to remove "bisexual" from the march title and bisexuals from the steering committee.
2. One example is a students' organization at Cornell University that over the past decade has gone from being called the Cornell Lesbian and Gay Coalition to the Cornell Lesbian, Gay and Bisexual Coalition to the Cornell Lesbian, Gay, Bisexual and Transgendered Coalition.
3. I encountered the latter response from the editorial board of *OUT/LOOK: National Lesbian & Gay Quarterly* when I submitted a piece on bisexuality to that journal in 1991. OUT/LOOK's Spring 1992 issue featured its first and only article on bisexuality, whose inauspicious title, "What do Bisexuals Want?" was followed by a "debate" between Ara Wilson and Carol A. Queen (the latter a bisexual woman) over the legitimacy of bisexuals' claims to inclusion in queer movements.
4. The Fourth Annual Lesbian, Bisexual and Gay Studies (Harvard, 1990) and the Fifth Annual Lesbian and Gay Studies (Rutgers, 1991) conferences are cases in point: at these conferences, papers concerning bisexuality were clustered in two or three panels, regardless of their topic, while bisexuality went unrepresented—even

unmentioned—in more general panels on such topics as "new directions in queer theory." Moreover, conference organizers sometimes neglect to ensure at least a nominally bi-positive setting even for these panels. For example, organizers for the Fifth Annual conference assigned the job of moderator of a panel on bisexuality to Martin Duberman, who, at the beginning of the session, felt compelled to inform the audience, "I'm not bisexual. I've never had a bisexual impulse in my life."

5. Mark Blasius, *Gay and Lesbian Politics: Sexuality and the Emergence of a New Ethic* (Philadelphia: Temple University Press, 1994), 82, 204.

6. Eve Kosofsky Sedgwick, *Epistemology of the Closet* (Berkeley/Los Angeles: University of California Press, 1990), 22.

7. Greta Christina, "Drawing the Line: Bisexual Women in the Lesbian Community," in *On Our Backs: the magazine for adventurous lesbians* (May-June 1990), 14–15.

8. Biddy Martin, "Sexual Practice and Changing Lesbian Identities," in Michele Barrett and Anne Phillips, eds., *Destabilizing Theory: Contemporary Feminist Debates* (Stanford: Stanford University Press, 1991), 97–9

9. Ibid., 99.

10. Ibid., 98. Moreover, as Martin points out, these rituals reflect the relatively disadvantaged positions of those who conduct them. She writes: "I would suggest that they are also ritualistic efforts to deal with what is experienced as loss, and exhibit all the forms of denial that accompany unresolved losses. Surely the perceived need for uniformity, authenticity and firm, separate foundations in a world outside of heterosexuality operates as a defence against the continued marginalization, denial and prohibition of women's love and desire for other women".

11. Judith Butler, *Gender Trouble: Feminism and the Subversion of Identity* (New York: Routledge, 1990), 2.

12. "Bisexual" reappeared in the title of the national queer studies conference held in Iowa in November 1994.

13. Eve Sedgwick argues (in *Epistemology of the Closet*) that it is the appearance of a secure boundary demarcating the terms in the homo/hetero binarism that is at stake in the physical and symbolic violence directed at queers so routinely in our culture. Leslie Feinberg's novel, *Stone Butch Blues* (Ithaca, NY: Firebrand Books, 1992), painfully illustrates the violence with which this appearance of stable binarisms is relentlessly enforced with respect to lines of gender and sexuality in the lives of butch lesbians.

14. Calling them "queer" is, of course, one option, and a good one. Some people balk at this, both out of concern that the term might not be the most intelligible and effective one for intervening in certain institutional settings, and out of a sense that there has been too much homophobic hatred and violence associated with the term for it to be reclaimed, for its meanings to be sufficiently transfigurable. My own view is that "queer" can be a very useful term, both because of its association with the reemergence of radical, antihomophobic direct action activism; and because its meaning is both sufficiently intelligible and sufficiently ambiguous to encompass a wide range of nonhegemonic sexualities without needing to impose rigid definitions on them, or to mark fixed boundaries that determine what is and isn't queer.

Of course, as with any term, "queer" lends itself to multiple and sometimes contradictory interpretations and uses. All too often, "queer" is used interchangeably with "lesbian" and "gay." In these cases, the use of "queer" doesn't seem to result in the articulation of sexualities other than "lesbian" and "gay." "Queer" 's potential to articulate and advance an expanded view of what constitutes a non-hegemonic and potentially subversive sexuality depends on how it is used. Certainly, when it is implicitly equated only with "lesbian/gay," it doesn't expand much of anything. When it is explicitly equated with "lesbian/gay" only, as in the case of a few Queer Nation chapters in the United States and Canada that reportedly exclude self-identified bisexuals, its use can be simply reactionary. There are, however, many examples of the term "queer" initiating or representing a progressive expansion of how we think about sexuality, politics, and the subversion of sexual hegemony and repression.

15. For an in-depth discussion of these events, see Stacey Young, "Bisexuality, Lesbian and Gay Communities, and the Limits of Identity Politics," in *Bisexual Politics: Queries, Theories, and Visions*, edited by Naomi Tucker (Binghamton, NY: Haworth Press, 1995).

16. Of course, it comes up when people raise the issue of other sexual minorities within the queer community as well, particularly when the sexual minorities in question explicitly blur the lines of the male/female binarism—transgenderists, transsexuals, cross-dressers. Just as bisexuals blur the lines of (homo/hetero) sexual binarisms, those who blur the lines of gender binarisms evoke the anxiety of not knowing.

17. Blasius, *Gay and Lesbian Politics*, 125–26.

18. Ibid., 174.

19. For a discussion of Kinsey and Klein, see Amanda Udis-Kessler, "Appendix: Notes on the Kinsey Scale and Other Measures of Sexuality" in *Closer to Home: Bisexuality and Feminism*, edited by Elizabeth Reba Weise (Seattle: Seal Press, 1992), 311–18.

20. This debate was covered in *Gay Community News* in the spring of 1992.

Questions for Reflection, Discussion, and Writing

1. What can be learned or understood by examining bisexuality in relation to homosexuality and heterosexuality, according to Young?

2. What are some ways bisexuality is understood in both homosexual and mainstream contexts? According to Young, what are some reasons for the silence surrounding and refusal to acknowledge bisexuality?

3. How does Young characterize bisexuality, and what underlying binaries does her theory about homosexual identity politics expose?

4. What political "dilemma" springs from identity politics, according to Young?

5. What debate took place among the "Lesbian and Gay Studies Conference" organizers at Rutgers, and how does Young present that debate as a microcosm of the issues surrounding queer theory and bisexuality as a category within it?

6. What solutions does Young offer to the displacement of bisexuality in queer theory? Do you think these solutions are viable? Why or why not? What issues remain, according to Young?

Related Reading

Jan Clausen, "My Interesting Condition." *Out/Look* 2.3 (Winter 1990): 10–21.

Amanda Udis-Kessler, "Present Tense: Biphobia As A Crisis of Meaning" in *Bi Any Other Name: Bisexual People Speak Out*. Loraine Hutchins and Lani Ka'ahumanu, Eds. Boston: Alyson Publications. 1991. 350–358.

Annie Sprinkle, "Beyond Bisexual" in *Bi Any Other Name: Bisexual People Speak Out*. Loraine Hutchins and Lani Ka'ahumanu, Eds. Boston: Alyson Publications. 1991. 103–107.

Carol A. Queen, "The Queer In Me," in *Bi Any Other Name: Bisexual People Speak Out*. Loraine Hutchins and Lani Ka'ahumanu, Eds. Boston: Alyson Publications. 1991. 17–21.

Leonard Tirado, "Reclaiming Heart and Mind," in *Bi Any Other Name: Bisexual People Speak Out*. Loraine Hutchins and Lani Ka'ahumanu, Eds. Boston: Alyson Publications. 1991. 117–123.

Dave Matteson, "Bisexual Feminist Man" in *Bi Any Other Name: Bisexual People Speak Out*. Loraine Hutchins and Lani Ka'ahumanu, Eds. Boston: Alyson Publications. 1991. 43–50.

Carol A. Queen, "Strangers at Home: Bisexuals in the Queer Movement." *Out/Look* 4.4 (Spring 1992): 23, 29–33.

Ara Wilson, "Just Add Water: Searching for the Bisexual Politic." *Out/Look* 4.4 (Spring 1992): 22, 24–28.

Elizabeth Reba Weise, *Closer To Home: Bisexuality and Feminism*. Seattle, WA: Seal Press. 1992.

Elizabeth D. Däumer, "Queer Ethics; or, The Challenge of Bisexuality to Lesbian Ethics." *Hypatia* 7.4 (1992): 91–105.

Gabriel Rotello. "Bi Any Means Necessary." *Village Voice*. June 30, 1992. 37–38.

Jo Eadie, "Activating Bisexuality: Towards a Bi/Sexual Politics" in *Activating Theory: Lesbian, Gay, Bisexual Politics*. Joseph Bristow and Angelia R. Wilson, Eds. London: Lawrence & Wishart. 1993. 139–170.

Clare Hemmings, "Resituating the Bisexual Body: From Identity to Difference" in *Activating Theory: Lesbian, Gay, Bisexual Politics*. Joseph Bristow and Angelia R. Wilson, Eds. London: Lawrence & Wishart. 1993. 118–138.

Martin S, Weinberg, Colin J, Williams and Douglas W. Pryor, *Dual Attraction: Understanding Bisexuality*. New York: Oxford UP. 1994.

Rebecca Kaplan, "Your Fence Is Sitting on Me: The Hazards of Binary Thinking" in *Bisexual Politics: Theories, Queries, and Visions*. Naomi Tucker, Ed. Binghamton, NY: Harrington Park Press. 1995. 267–279.

Marjorie Garber, *Vice Versa: Bisexuality and the Eroticism of Everyday Life*. NY: Simon and Schuster. 1995.

Paula C. Rust, *Bisexuality and the Challenge to Lesbian Politics: Sex, Loyalty and Revolution.* NY: NYUP. 1995.

Liz A. Highleyman, "Identity and Ideas: Strategies for Bisexuals" in *Bisexual Politics: Theories, Queries, and Visions.* Naomi Tucker, Ed. Binghamton, NY: Harrington Park Press. 1995. 73–92.

Nicola Field, "Bisexuality" in *Over the Rainbow: Money, Class and Homophobia.* London: Pluto Press. 1995. 133–150.

Loraine Hutchins, "Bisexuality: Politics and Community" in *Bisexuality: The Psychology and Politics of an Invisible Minority.* Beth A. Firestein, Ed. Thousand Oaks, CA: Sage Publications. 1996. 240–259.

Indigo Sam, "The Queer Kitchen" in *Surface Tension.* Meg Dely, Ed. NY: Touchstone. 1996. 169–174.

Michelle T. Clinton, "Almost a Dyke: In Search of the Perfect Bisexual" in *Surface Tension.* Meg Daly, Ed. NY: Touchstone. 1996. 160–165.

Amber Ault, "The Dilemma of Identity: Bi Women's Negotiations" in *Queer Theory/Sociology.* Steven Seidman, Ed. Cambridge, MA: Blackwell. 1996. 311–330.

Meg Clarion, "The Hasbians" in *Bisexual Horizons: Politics, Histories, Lives.* Sharon Rose, Cris Stevens, et al., Eds. London: Lawrence & Wishart. 1996. 122–126.

Christopher James, "Denying Complexity: The Dismissal and Appropriation of Bisexuality in Queer, Lesbian, and Gay Theory" in *Queer Studies: A Lesbian, Gay, Bisexual and Transgender Anthology.* Brett Beemyn and Mickey Eliason, Eds. NY: NYUP. 1996. 217–240.

Michael du Plessis, "Blatantly Bisexual; or, Unthinking Queer Theory" in *Representing BiSexualities Subjects and Cultures of Fluid Desire.* Donald Hall and Maria Pramaggiore, Eds. NY: NYUP. 1996. 19–54.

Paul Chandler, "Coming in From the Cold: Bisexuality and the Politics of Diversity" in *Bisexual Horizons: Politics, Histories, Lives.* Sharon Rose, Cris Stevens, et al., Eds. London: Lawrence & Wishart. 1996. 227–235.

Amber Ault, "Hegemonic Discourse in an Oppositional Community: Lesbian Feminist Stigmatization of Bisexual Women" in *Queer Studies: A Lesbian, Gay, Bisexual, and Transgender Anthology.* Brett Beemyn and Mickey Eliason, Eds. NY: NYUP. 1996. 204–216.

Guy Chapman, "Roots of a Male Bisexual Nature" in *Bisexual Horizons: Politics, Histories, Lives.* Sharon Rose, Cris Stevens, et al., Eds. London: Lawrence & Wishart. 1996. 62–69.

Brian Loftus, "*Biopia*: Bisexuality and the Crisis of Visibility in a Queer Symbolic" in *RePresenting BiSexualities Subjects and Cultures of Fluid Desire.* Donald Hall and Maria Pramaggiore, Eds. NY: NYUP. 1996. 207–233.

Paula C. Rust, "Managing Multiple Identities: Diversity Among Bisexual Women and Men" in *Bisexuality: The Psychology and Politics of an Invisible Minority.* Beth A. Firestein, Ed. Thousand Oaks, CA: Sage Publications. 1996. 53–83.

Carol Queen, "Beyond the Valley of the Fag Hags" in *PoMoSexuals: Challenging Assumptions About Gender and Sexuality.* Carol Queen and Lawrence Schimel, Eds. San Francisco, CA: Cleis Press. 1997. 76–84.

Merl Storr, Ed. *Bisexuality: A Critical Reader.* NY: Routledge. 1999.

Related Reading

Sue Ellen Jacobs and Jason Cromwell, "Visions and Revisions of Reality: Reflections on Sex, Sexuality, Gender, and Gender Variance." *Journal of Homosexuality* 23.4 (1992): 43–69.

Kory Martin-Damon, "Essay for the inclusion of Transsexuals" in *Bisexual Politics: Theories, Queries, and Visions.* Naomi Tucker, Ed. Binghamton, NY: Harrington Park Press. 1995. 241–249.

David Harrison, "Becoming A Man: The Transition From Female to Male" in *Assaults on Convention: Essays on Lesbian Transgressors.* Nicola Godwin, Belinda Hollows and Sheridan Nye, Eds. London: Cassell. 1996. 24–37.

Loren Cameron, *Body Alchemy: Transsexual Portraits.* Pittsburgh: Cleiss Press. 1996.

Vernon Rosario III, "Trans (Homo) Sexuality? Double Inversion, Psychiatric Confusion, and Hetero-Hegemony" in *Queer Studies: A Lesbian, Gay, Bisexual, and Transgender Anthology.* Brett Beemyn and Mickey Eliason, Eds. NY: NYUP. 1996. 35–51.

Holly Devor, *FTM: Female-To-Male Transsexuals in Society.* Bloomington, IN: Indiana UP. 1997.

———, "More Than Manly Women: How Female-to-Male Transsexuals Reject Lesbian Identities" in *Gender Blending.* Bonnie Bollough, Vern Bullough, and James Elias, Eds. Amherst, NY: Prometheus Books. 1997. 87–102.

Pat Califia, *Sex Changes: The Politics of Transgenderism.* San Francisco: Cleis Press. 1997.

Nan Alamilla Boyd, "Bodies in Motion: Lesbian and Transsexual Histories" in *A Queer World.* Martin Duberman, Ed. 1997. 134–152.

David Harrison, "The Personals" in *PoMoSexuals: Challenging Assumptions About Gender and Sexuality.* Carol Queen and Lawrence Schimel, Eds. San Francisco, CA: Cleis Press. 1997. 129–137.

Henry S. Rubin, "Phenomenology As Method in Trans Studies." *GLQ 4.2* (1998): 263–281.

C. Jacob Hale, "Consuming the Living, Dis(Re)Membering the Dead in the Butch/FTM Borderlands." *GLQ 4.2* (1998): 311–348.

Taran Rabideau, "Finding My Place in the World, or Which Bathroom Should I Use Today?" in *Out & About On Campus: Personal Accounts by Lesbian, Gay, Bisexual & Transgendered Students.* Kim Howard and Annie Stevens, Eds. Los Angeles, CA: Alyson Publications. 2000. 172–179.

Vernon Rosario, "Transgenderism Comes of Age." *The Harvard Gay & Lesbian Review* 7.4 (Fall 2000): 31–33.

Pat Califia-Rice, "Family Values." *Village Voice.* 27 June 2000. 46–48.

Film

P(l)ain Truth (1993). llpo Pohjola. 15 m.

The Brandon Teena Story (1998). Susa Muska & Greta Olafsdottir. 88 m.

Boys Don't Cry (1999). Kimberly Pierce. 118 m.

A Boy Named Sue (2000). Julie Wyman. 57m.

Web Resource

http://www.ftm-intl.org/
http://web.ukonline.co.uk/agitor/ftm
Kimberly Peirce's 1999 *Boys Don't Cry* (119m) earned a best actress Academy Award for Hilary Swank and a nomination for Chloë Sevigny. Some viewers were confused and discomfited when the transgender identity Brandon Teena has created morphs into a gendered lesbian identity, seemingly without complications. Judith Halberstam's continuum of masculinity may help in thinking through the representational politics of this film. Students may want to compare its representational strategy with the Muska and Olafsdótter documentary below.

Film

The Brandon Teena Story (1998). Susan Muska and Gréta Olafsdótter. 88m.

Reading

Michele Aaron, The *Boys Don't Cry* Debate: "Pass/Fail." *Screen 42.1* (2001): 92–96.

C. Jacob Hale, "Consuming the Living, Dis(Re)Membering the Dead in the Butch/FTM Borderlands." *GLQ 4.2* (1998): 311–348.

Francesca Miller, "Putting Teena Brandon's Story on Film," An interview with Kimberly Peirce. *The Harvard Gay & Lesbian Review 7.4* (Fall 2000): 37–?

Julianna Pidduck, The *Boys Don't Cry* Debate: "Risk and Queer Spectatorship." *Screen 42.1* (2001): 97–102.

John M. Sloop, "Disciplining the Transgendered: Brandon Teena, Public Representation, and Normativity." *Western Journal of Communication 64.2* (Spring 2000): 165–189.

Special Topics

Leslie Feinberg pioneered transgender studies with the publication of *Stone Butch Blues, Transgender Warriors and Transliberation: Beyond Pink or Blue*. In particular, his 1993 novel, *Stone Butch Blues*, illustrates engagingly and movingly the story of one person's transgender journey through several different manifestations of self-definition and self-representation.

Reading

Leslie Feinerg, *Stone Butch Blues*. Ithaca, NY: Cornell UP. 1993.

Minnie Bruce Pratt, *S/He*. Ithaca, NY: Firebrand Books. 1995.

Jay Prosser, "No Place Like Home: The Transgendered Narrative of Leslie Feinberg's Stone Butch Blues." *Modern Fiction Studies 41* (1995): 483–514.

Judith Halberstam, "Lesbian Masculinity; or, Even Stone Butch Gets the Blues." *Women & Performance: a Journal of Feminist Theory 8.2* (1996): 61–73.

Film

Outlaw (994). Alisa Lebow. 26 m.

SECTION FIVE

Cinema Queerité and Queer Pop Culture

R ob Epstein's 1995 documentary, *The Celluloid Closet*, opens with a montage of classic film clips that both startles and amazes. One has seen many of these images before, yet, abstracted and condensed into clips, it is impossible not recognize how many queer moments there are and have been throughout twentieth-century cinema, and how easy it has been not to actually register them as *queer* unless one looks attentively, so seamlessly are they interwoven into film as jokes or as ribald gags. In other words, queer representations are often in our view, but we need to train ourselves to become aware of them. It is also essential that one do the research and be aware of the historical context in which queer representations occur, for they will vary enormously across time and place. Learning to look queerly at film, television, art, advertisements, and the web can involve any variation and/or combination of the following perspectives:

- Identifying in media readable or identifiable markers that denote gay, lesbian, bisexual or transgender identity. In what context(s) are they used? To what purpose? What is the historical context of their production? What are the political overtones of this representation? Are stereotypes involved? To what degree? What are their effects?
- A focus on author studies or on the biography of an actor or director who is thought to be gay, lesbian, bisexual, or transgender. Does this knowledge of either the author's, the director's, or the actor's sexual orientation or identity facilitate a queer reading of his or her texts/paintings/photographs/movies? How and why?
- Attention to representations beyond heterosexuality. Because we are so accustomed to ubiquitous representations of heteronormativity, sexual ambiguity, or ambivalence, can often be read as queer. Actors and characters who flout the conventions of gender and masculinity (like Pee-Wee Herman) or gender and femininity (like Agnes Moorehead) are frequently read as queer. Are there texts (literature, painting, photography, advertisements, television, film) in which you see this happening? Are there

particular authors, directors, or actors to whom sexual ambiguity also applies? What kinds of queer readings do deviations from heteronormativity open up for readers and viewers?

- The role(s) that race, ethnicity, gender, and class play in queer representations. What are the axes and lines of connection and of contrast we can draw between these categories and representations? What happens when queer is *not* synonymous with white or with male? What happens when it is? What insider and outsider positions in society do queers occupy?

- The queer readings that are engendered through audience reception. What happens when a viewer is queer? What kinds of readings become possible? Are there ways in which sexual desires and cross-gender identifications can reinterpret and/or revise heteronormative narratives? If you are watching *The Sound of Music* and are a queer viewer, for example, how do you solve a problem like Maria? In what ways can we chart such a dynamic interplay between audience and text?

There's Something Queer Here

Alexander Doty

But standing before the work of art requires you to act too.
The tension you bring to the work of art is an action.

Jean Genet[1]

I'm gonna take you to queer bars
I'm gonna drive you in queer cars
You're gonna meet all of my queer friends
Our queer, queer fun it never ends.
"The Queer Song," Gretchen Phillips, Two Nice Girls[2]

The most slippery and elusive terrain for mass culture studies continues to be negotiated within audience and reception theory. Perhaps this is because within cultural studies, "audience" is now always already acknowledged to be fragmented, polymorphous, contradictory, and "nomadic," whether in the form of individual or group subjects. Given this, it seems an almost impossible task to conduct reception studies that capture the complexity of those moments in which audiences meet mass culture texts. As Janice Radway puts it:

No wonder we find it so difficult to theorize the dispersed, anonymous, unpredictable nature of the use of mass-produced, mass-mediated cultural forms. If the receivers of such forms are never assembled fixedly on a site or even in an easily identifiable space, if they are frequently not uniformly or even attentively disposed to systems of cultural production or to the messages they issue, how can we theorize, not to mention examine, the ever-shifting kaleidoscope of cultural circulation and consumption?[3]

In confronting this complexity, Radway suggests that mass culture studies begin to analyze reception more ethnographically by focusing upon the dense patterns and practices "of daily life and the way in which the media are integrated and implicated within it," rather than starting with already established audience categories.[4] Clearly the danger of making essentializing statements about both audiences and their reception practices lurks behind any uncritical use of categories such as "women," "teenagers," "lesbians," "housewives," "blue-collar workers," "blacks," or "gay men." Further, conducting reception studies on the basis of conventional audience categories can also lead to critical blindness about how certain reception strategies are shared by otherwise disparate individuals and groups.

I would like to propose "queerness" as a mass culture reception practice that is shared by all sorts of people in varying degrees of consistency and intensity.[5] Before proceeding, however, I will need to discuss—even defend—my use of "queer" in such phrases as "queer positions," "queer readers," "queer readings," and "queer discourses." In working through my thoughts on gay and lesbian cultural history, I found that while I used "gay" to describe particulars of men's culture, and "lesbian" to describe particulars of women's culture, I was hard-pressed to find a term to describe a cultural common ground between lesbians and gays as well as other nonstraights—a term representing unity as well as suggesting diversity. For certain historical and political reasons, "queer" suggested itself as such a term. As Adele Morrison said in an OUT/LOOK interview: "Queer is not an 'instead of,' it's an 'inclusive of.' I'd never want to lose the terms that specifically identify me."[6]

Currently, the word "gay" doesn't consistently have the same gender-unifying quality it may once have possessed. And since I'm interested in discussing aspects of cultural identification as well as of sexual desire, "homosexual" will not do either. I agree with those who do not find the word "homosexual" an appropriate synonym for both "gay" and "lesbian," as these latter terms are constructions that concern more than who you sleep with—although the objects of sexual desires are certainly central to expressions of lesbian and gay cultural identities. I also wanted to find a term with some ambiguity, a term that would describe a wide range of impulses and cultural expressions, including space for describing and expressing bisexual, transsexual, and straight queerness. While we acknowledge that homosexuals as well as heterosexuals can operate or mediate from within straight cultural spaces and positions—after all, most of us grew up learning the rules of straight culture—we have paid less attention to the proposition that basically heterocentrist texts can contain queer elements, and basically heterosexual, straight-identifying people can experience queer moments. And these people should be encouraged to examine and express these moments as queer, not as moments of "homosexual panic," or temporary confusion, or as unfortunate, shameful, or sinful lapses in judgment or taste to be ignored, repressed, condemned, or somehow explained away within and by straight cultural politics—or even within and by gay or lesbian discourses.

My uses of the terms "queer readings," "queer discourses," and "queer positions," then, are attempts to account for the existence and expression of a wide range of positions within culture that are "queer" or non-, anti-, or contra-straight.[7] I am using the term "queer" to mark a flexible space for the expression of all aspects of non- (anti-, contra-) straight cultural production and reception.[8] As such, this cultural "queer space" recognizes the possibility that various and fluctuating queer positions might be occupied whenever *anyone* produces or responds to culture. In this sense, the use of the term "queer" to discuss reception takes up the standard binary opposition of "queer" and "nonqueer" (or "straight") while questioning its viability, at least in cultural studies, because, as noted earlier, the queer often operates within the nonqueer, as the nonqueer does within the queer (whether in reception, texts, or producers). The queer readings of mass culture I am concerned with in this essay will be those readings articulating positions *within* queer discourses. That is, these readings seem to be expressions of queer perspectives on mass culture from the inside, rather than descriptions of how "they" (gays and/or lesbians, usually) respond to, use, or are depicted in mass culture.

When a colleague heard I had begun using the word "queer" in my cultural studies work, she asked if I did so in order to "nostalgically" recapture and reassert the "romance" of the culturally marginal in the face of trends within straight capitalist societies to co-opt or contain aspects of queer cultures. I had, in fact, intended something quite different. By using "queer," I want to recapture and reassert a militant sense of difference that views the erotically "marginal" as both (in bell hook's words) a consciously chosen "site of resistance" and a "location of radical openness and possibility."[9] And I want to suggest that within cultural production and reception, queer erotics are already part of culture's erotic center, both as a necessary construct by which to define the heterosexual and the straight (as "not queer"), and as a position that can be and is occupied in various ways by otherwise heterosexual and straight-identifying people.

But in another sense recapturing and reasserting a certain nostalgia and romance is part of my project here. For through playfully occupying various queer positions in relation to the fantasy/dream elements involved in cultural production and reception, we (whether straight-, gay-, lesbian-, or bi-identifying) are offered spaces to express a range of erotic desire frequently linked in Western cultures to nostalgic and romantic adult conceptions of childhood. Unfortunately, these moments of erotic complexity are usually explained away as part of the "regressive" work of mass media, whereby we are tricked into certain "unacceptable" and "immature" responses as passive subjects. But when cultural texts encourage straight-identified audience members to express a less-censored range of queer desire and pleasure than is possible in daily life, this "regression" has positive gender- and sexuality-destabilizing effects.[10]

I am aware of the current political controversy surrounding the word "queer." Some gays, lesbians, and bisexuals have expressed their inability to also identify with "queerness," as they feel the term has too long and too painful a history as a weapon of oppression and self-hate. These nonqueer lesbians, gays, and bisexuals find the attempts of radical forces in gay and lesbian communities (such as Queer Nation) to recover and positively redefine the term "queer" successful only within these communities—and unevenly successful at that. Preferring current or freshly created terms, non-queer-identifying lesbians, gays, and bisexuals often feel that any positive effects resulting from reappropriating "queer" are more theoretical than real.

But the history of gay and lesbian cultures and politics has shown that there are many times and places where the theoretical can have real social impact. Enough lesbians, gays, bisexuals, and other queers taking and making enough of these moments can create a more consistent awareness within the general public of queer cultural and political spaces, as these theory-in-the-flesh moments are concerned with making what has been for the most part publicly invisible and silent visible and vocal. In terms of mass culture reception, there are frequent theory-in-the-flesh opportunities in the course of everyday life. For example, how many times do we get the chance to inform people about our particular queer perspectives on film, television, literature, or music during conversations (or to engage someone else's perhaps unacknowledged queer perspective)? And how often, even if we are openly lesbian, gay, or bisexual, have we kept silent, or edited our conversations, deciding that our queer opinions are really only interesting to other queers, or that these opinions would make people uncomfortable—even while we think family, friends, and strangers should, of course, feel free to articulate various heterosexual or straight opinions in detail at any time?

Of course, queer positions aren't the only ones from which queers read and produce mass culture. As with nonqueers, factors such as class, ethnicity, gender, occupation, education, and religious, national, and regional allegiances influence our identity construction, and therefore are important to the positions we take as cultural producers and reader-consumers. These other cultural factors can exert influences difficult to separate from the development of our identities as queers, and as a result, difficult to discuss apart from our engagement in culture as queers. For example, most people find it next to impossible to articulate their sexual identities (queer or non-queer) without some reference to gender. Generally, lesbian- and gay-specific forms of queer identities involve some degree of same-gender identification and desire or a cross-gender identification linked to same-gender desire. The understanding of what "gender" is in these cases can range from accepting conventional straight forms, which naturalize "feminine" and "masculine" by conflating them with essentializing, biology-based conceptions of "woman" and "man"; to imitating the outward forms and behaviors of one gender or the other while not fully subscribing to the straight ideological imperatives that define that gender; to combining or ignoring traditional gender codes in order to reflect attitudes that have little or nothing to do with straight ideas about femininity/women or masculinity/men. These last two positions are the places where queerly reconfigured gender identities begin to be worked out.[11]

"Begin to be," because most radically, as Sue-Ellen Case points out, "queer theory, unlike lesbian theory or gay male theory, is not gender specific."[12] Believing that "both gay and lesbian theory reinscribe sexual difference, to some extent, in their gender-specific constructions," Case calls for a queer theory that "works not at the site of gender, but at the site of ontology."[13] But while a nongendered notion of queerness makes sense, articulating this queer theory fully apart from gendered straight feminist, gay, and lesbian theorizing becomes difficult within languages and cultures that make gender and gender difference so crucial to their discursive practices. Through her discussions of vampire myths, Case works hard to establish a discourse that avoids gendered terms, yet she finds it necessary to resort to them every so often in order to suggest the queerness of certain things: placing "she" in quotation marks at one point, or discussing R. W. Fassbinder's film character Petra von Kant as "a truly queer creature who flickers somewhere between haute couture butch lesbian and male drag queen."[14]

Since I'm working with a conception of queerness that includes gay- and lesbian-specific positions as well as Case's nonlesbian and nongay queerness, gender definitions and uses here remain important to examining the ways in which queerness influences mass culture production and reception. For example, gay men who identify with some conception of "the feminine"[15] through processes that could stem from conscious personal choice, or from internalizing long-standing straight imperatives that encourage gay men to think of themselves as "not men" (and therefore, by implication or by direct attribution, as being like "women"), or from some degree of negotiation between these two processes, are at the center of the gay culture cults built around the imposing, spectacular women stars of opera (Maria Callas, Joan Sutherland, Beverly Sills, Renata Scotto, Teresa Stratas, Leontyne Price), theater (Lynn Fontanne, Katharine Cornell, Gertrude Lawrence, Maggie Smith, Angela Lansbury, Ethel Merman, Tallulah Bankhead), film (Bette Davis, Joan Crawford, Judy Garland, Marlene Dietrich, Vivien Leigh, Bette Midler, Glenda Jackson), popular music (Midler, Garland, Eartha Kitt, Edith Piaf, Barbra Streisand, Billie Holiday, Donna Summer, Diana Ross, Debbie Harry, Madonna), and television (Carol Burnett, the casts of *Designing Women* and *The Golden Girls*, Candice Bergen in *Murphy Brown*, Mary Tyler Moore and the supporting cast of women on *The*

Mary Tyler Moore Show).[16] For the past two decades in the gay popular press, book chapters and articles on the connections between gay men and women stars have been a commonplace, but only occasionally do these works go beyond the monolithic audience label "gay men" to suggest the potential for discussing reception in a manner attuned to more specific definitions of sexual identity, such as those constructed to some degree within the dynamics of gender and sexuality.[17]

Given this situation, one strand of queer mass culture reception studies might be more precisely focused upon these networks of women performers who were, and are, meaningful at different times and places and for different reasons to feminine-identified gay men. One of most extended analytic pieces on feminine gay men's reception of women stars is the "Homosexuals' Girls" chapter of Julie Burchill's *Girls on Film*. But Burchill is clearly writing critically *about* a particular queer reception position; she is not queerly positioned herself. Indeed, Burchill's analysis of how "queens" respond to women stars seems written to conform to very narrow-minded ideas about audience and reception. For Burchill, all "feminine homosexual" men's investment in women stars is rooted in envy, jealousy, misogyny, and cruelty—and she concludes this even as she relates a comment by one of her gay friends: "You may have a flaming faggot's taste in movies, kid, but your perspective is pure Puritan."[18]

Clearly we need more popular and academic mass culture work that carefully considers feminine gay and other gendered queer reception practices, as well as those of even less-analyzed queer readership positions formed around the nexus of race and sexuality, or class and sexuality, or ethnicity and sexuality, or some combination of gender/race/class/ethnicity and sexuality.[19] These studies would offer valuable evidence of precisely how and where specific complex constructions of queerness can and do reveal themselves in the uses of mass culture, as well as revealing how and where that mass culture comes to influence and reinforce the process of queer identity formation.

One of the earliest attempts at such a study of queers and mass culture was a series of interviews with nine lesbians conducted by Judy Whitaker in 1981 for *Jump Cut*. "Hollywood Transformed." These interviews touched upon a number of issues surrounding lesbian identity, including gender identification. Although careful to label these interviews "biographical sketches, not sociological or psychological studies," Whitaker does make some comments suggesting the potential for such studies:

> Of the nine women who were interviewed, at least six said they identified at some time with male characters. Often the explanation is that men had the interesting active roles. Does this mean that these lesbians want to be like men? That would be a specious conclusion. None of the women who identified with male characters were "in love" with the characters' girl friends. All of the interviewees were "in love" at some time with actresses, but they did not identify with or want to be the male suitors of those actresses. While the context of the discussion is film, what

these women are really talking about is their lives. . . . Transformation and positive self-image are dominant themes in what they have to say. Hollywood is transcended.[20]

After reading these interviews, there might be some question about how fully
the straight ideologies Hollywood narratives encourage are "transcended" by
these lesbian readers' uses of mainstream films, for as two of the interviewees
remark, "We're so starved, we go see anything because something is better than
nothing," and "It's a compromise. It's a given degree of alienation."[21] This
sense of queer readings of mass culture as involving a measure of "compromise"
and "alienation" contributes to the complexity of queer articulations of mass
culture reception. For the pathos of feeling like a mass culture hanger-on is
often related to the processes by which queers (and straights who find themselves queerly positioned) internalize straight culture's homophobic and heterocentrist attitudes and later reproduce them in their own queer responses to film
and other mass culture forms.

Even so, traditional narrative films such as *Sylvia Scarlett, Gentlemen Prefer
Blondes, Trapeze, To Live and Die in L.A., Internal Affairs,* and *Thelma and Louise,*
which are ostensibly addressed to straight audiences, often have greater potential for encouraging a wider range of queer responses than such clearly lesbian-
and gay-addressed films as *Scorpio Rising, Home Movies, Women I Love,* and
Loads.[22] The intense tensions and pleasures generated by the woman-woman
and man-man aspects within the narratives of the former group of films create a
space of sexual instability that already queerly positioned viewers can connect
with in various ways, and within which straights might be likely to recognize
and express their queer impulses. For example, gays might find a form of queer
pleasure in the alternately tender and boisterous rapport between Lorelei/
Marilyn Monroe and Dorothy/Jane Russell in *Gentlemen Prefer Blondes,* or in
the exhilarating woman-bonding of the title characters in *Thelma and Louise.* Or
lesbians and straights could queerly respond to the erotic elements in the relationships between the major male characters in *Trapeze, To Live and Die in L.A.,*
or *Internal Affairs.* And any viewer might feel a sexually ambiguous attraction—
is it gay, lesbian, bisexual, or straight?—to the image of Katharine Hepburn
dressed as a young man in *Sylvia Scarlett.*

Of course, these queer positions and readings can become modified or can
change over time, as people, cultures, and politics change. In my own case, as a
white gay male who internalized dominant culture's definitions of myself as "like
a woman" in a traditional 1950s and 1960s understanding of who "a woman" and
what "femininity" was supposed to be, my pleasure in *Gentlemen Prefer Blondes* initially worked itself out through a classic gay process of identifying, alternately,
with Monroe and Russell; thereby experiencing vicarious if temporary empowerment through their use of sexual allure to attract men—including the entire
American Olympic team. Reassessing the feminine aspects of my gay sexual identity sometime in the 1970s (after Stonewall and my coming out), I returned to the

film and discovered my response was now less rooted in the fantasy of being Monroe or Russell and gaining sexual access to men, than in the pleasure of Russell being the "gentleman" who preferred blonde Monroe, who looked out for her best interests, who protected her against men, and who enjoyed performing with her. This queer pleasure in a lesbian text has been abetted by extratextual information I have read, or was told, about Russell's solicitous and supportive offscreen behavior toward Monroe while making the film.[23] But along with these elements of queer reading that developed from the interaction of my feminine gay identity, my knowledge of extratextual behind-the-scenes gossip, and the text itself, I also take a great deal of direct gay erotic pleasure in the "Is There Anyone Here for Love?" number, enjoying its blatantly homo-historic and erotic ancient Greek Olympics mise-en-scène (including Russell's large column earrings), while admiring Russell's panache and good humor as she sings, strides, and strokes her way through a sea of half-naked male dancer-athletes. I no longer feel the need to mediate my sexual desires through her.

In 1985, Al La Valley suggested that this type of movement—from negotiating gay sexual desire through strong women stars to directly expressing desire for male images on screen—was becoming increasingly evident in gay culture, although certain forms of identification with women through gay connections with "the feminine" continue:

> One might have expected Stonewall to make star cults outmoded among gays. In a sense it did: The natural-man discourse, with its strong political and social vision and its sense of a fulfilled and open self, has supplanted both the aesthetic and campy discourses. . . . A delirious absorption in the stars is now something associated with pre-Stonewall gays or drag queens, yet neither gay openness nor the new machismo has completely abolished the cults. New figures are added regularly: Diana Ross, Donna Summer, Jennifer Holliday from the world of music, for example. There's a newer, more open gay following for male stars: Richard Gere, Christopher Reeve [and, to update, Mel Gibson], even teen hunks like Matt Dillon [Christopher Atkins, Johnny Depp, Jason Priestley, and Luke Perry].[24]

One could also add performers such as Bette Midler, Patti LaBelle, and Madonna to La Valley's list of women performers. While ambivalent about her motives ("Is she the Queen of Queers. . . . Or is she just milking us for shock value?"), Michael Musto's *Outweek* article "Immaculate Connection" suggests that Madonna is queer culture's post-Stonewall Judy Garland:

> By now, we finally seem willing to release Judy Garland from her afterlife responsibility of being our quintessential icon. And in the land of the living, career stagnation has robbed Diana [Ross], Liza [Minnelli], and Barbra [Streisand] of their chances, while Donna [Summer] thumped the bible on our heads in a way that made it bounce back into her face. That leaves Madonna as Queer Queen, and she merits the title as someone who isn't afraid to offend straight America if it does the rest of us some good.[25]

Musto finds Madonna "unlike past icons" as she's "not a vulnerable toy"; this indicates to him the need to reexamine gay culture's enthusiasms for women stars with greater attention to how shifting historic (and perhaps generational) contexts alter the meanings and uses of these stars for particular groups of gay men.[26]

Examining how and where these gay cults of women stars work in relation to what La Valley saw in the mid-1980s as the "newer, more openly gay following for male stars" would also make for fascinating cultural history. Certainly there have been "homosexual" followings for male personalities in mass culture since the late nineteenth century, with performers and actors—Sandow the muscleman, Edwin Booth—vying with gay enthusiasms for opera divas and actresses such as Jenny Lind and Lillian Russell. Along these lines, one could queerly combine star studies with genre studies in order to analyze the gay appreciation of women musical performers, and the musical's "feminine" or "effeminized" aesthetic, camp, and emotive genre characteristics (spectacularized decor and costuming, intricate choreography, and singing about romantic yearning and fulfillment), with reference to the more hidden cultural history of gay erotics centered around men in musicals.[27]

In film, this erotic history would perhaps begin with Ramon Navarro (himself gay) stripped down to sing "Pagan Love Song" in *The Pagan*. Beyond this, a gay beefcake musical history would include Gene Kelly (whose ass was always on display in carefully tailored pants); numbers like "Is There Anyone Here for Love?" (*Gentlemen Prefer Blondes*) and "Y.M.C.A." (*Can't Stop the Music*) that feature men in gym shorts, swimsuits (Esther Williams musicals are especially spectacular in this regard), military (especially sailor) uniforms, and pseudo-native or pseudo-classical (Greek and Roman) outfits; films such as *Athena* (bodybuilders), *Seven Brides for Seven Brothers* (Western Levis, flannel, and leather men), *West Side Story* (Hispanic and Anglo t-shirted and blue-jeaned delinquents, including a butch girl); Elvis Presley films (and those of other "teen girl" pop and rock music idols—Frank Sinatra, Ricky Nelson, Fabian, Cliff Richard, the Beatles, and so on); and the films of John Travolta (*Saturday Night Fever*, *Grease*, *Staying Alive*), Patrick Swayze (*Dirty Dancing*), and Mikhail Baryshnikov, who in *The Turning Point and White Nights* provided the impetus for many gays to be more vocal about their "lowbrow" sexual pleasure in supposedly high-cultural male bodies. If television, music video, and concert performers and texts were added to this hardly exhaustive list, it would include David Bowie, Morrissey, David Cassidy, Tom Jones, and Marky Mark, among many others, and videos such as *Cherish*, *Express Yourself*, and *Justify My Love* (all performed by Madonna), *Being Boring* (The Pet Shop Boys), *Love Will Never Do Without You* (Janet Jackson), *Just Tell Me That You Want Me* (Kim Wilde), and *Rico Suave* (Gerardo), along with a number of heavy-metal videos featuring long-haired lead singers in a variety of skintight and artfully opened or ripped clothes.[28]

I can't leave this discussion of gay erotics and musicals without a few more words about Gene Kelly's "male trio" musicals, such as *On the Town, Take Me Out to the Ball Game,* and *It's Always Fair Weather.*[29] Clad in sailor uniforms, baseball uniforms, and Army uniforms, the male trios in these films are composed of two conventionally sexy men (Kelly and Frank Sinatra in the first two films, Kelly and Dan Dailey in the last) and a comic, less attractive "buffer" (Jules Munshin in the first two, Michael Kidd in the last) who is meant to diffuse the sexual energy generated between the two male leads when they sing and dance together. Other Kelly films—*Singin' in the Rain, An American in Paris,* and *Anchors Aweigh*—resort to the more conventional heterosexual(izing) narrative device of using a woman to mediate and diffuse male-male erotics.[30] But whether in the form of a third man or an ingenue, these devices fail to fully heterosexualize the relationship between Kelly and his male costars. In *Singin' in the Rain,* for example, I can't help but read Donald O'Connor maniacally unleashing his physical energy to entertain Kelly during the "Make 'Em Laugh" number as anything but a case of overwrought, displaced gay desire.[31]

Kelly himself jokingly refers to the queer erotics of his image and his many buddy musicals in *That's Entertainment!,* when he reveals the answer to the often-asked question, "Who was your favorite dancing partner . . . Cyd Charisse, Leslie Caron, Rita Hayworth, Vera-Ellen?," by showing a clip of the dance he did with Fred Astaire ("The Babbit and the Bromide") in *Ziegfeld Follies.* "It's the only time we danced together," Kelly remarks over the clip, "but I'd change my name to Ginger if we could do it again." As it turned out, Kelly and Astaire did "do it again" in *That's Entertainment 2,* and their reunion as a dancing couple became the focus of much of the film's publicity campaign, as had been the case when Astaire reunited with Ginger Rogers in *The Barkleys of Broadway.*[32]

While there has been at the very least a general, if often clichéd, cultural connection made between gays and musicals, lesbian work within the genre has been less acknowledged. However, the evidence of lesbian viewing practices—in articles such as "Hollywood Transformed," in videos such as *Dry Kisses Only* (1990, Jane Cottis and Kaucyila Brooke) and *Grapefruit* (1989, Cecilia Dougherty), and in informal discussions (mention *Calamity Jane* to a group of thirty- to forty-something American lesbians)—suggests that lesbian viewers have always negotiated their own culturally specific readings and pleasures within the genre.[33] Although it never uses the word "lesbian," Lucie Arbuthnot and Gail Seneca's 1982 article "Pre-text and Text in *Gentlemen Prefer Blondes*" is perhaps the best-known lesbian-positioned piece on the musical. While couched in homosocial rhetoric, this analysis of the authors' pleasures in the film focuses upon Lorelei/Monroe's and Dorothy/Russell's connection to each other through looks, touch, and words ("lovey," "honey," "sister," "dear"). Noting that a "typical characteristic of [the] movie musical genre is that there are two leads, a man and a woman, who sing and dance together, and eventually become romantically involved," Seneca and Arbuthnot recognize that in *Gentlemen Prefer Blondes* "it is

Monroe and Russell who sing—and even harmonize, adding another layer to the metaphor—and dance as a team."[34] Since the men in the film are "never given a musical role," the authors conclude "the pretext of heterosexual romance is so thin that it scarcely threatens the text of female friendship."[35]

One note hints at a possible butch-femme reading of the Russell/Monroe relationship, centered upon Russell's forthright stride and stance: "The Russell character also adopts a 'masculine' stride and stance. More often, Monroe plays the 'lady' to Russell's manly moves. For example, Russell opens doors for Monroe; Monroe sinks into Russell's strong frame, allowing Russell to hold her protectively."[36] Released in 1953, during the height of traditional butch-femme role-playing in American urban lesbian culture, *Gentlemen Prefer Blondes* could well have been read and enjoyed by lesbians at the time with reference to this particular social-psychological paradigm for understanding and expressing their sexual identity.[37] The film continues to be read along these lines by some lesbians as well as by other queerly positioned viewers. Overall, Seneca and Arbuthnot's analysis of *Gentlemen Prefer Blondes* qualifies as a lesbian reading, as it discusses the film and the musical genre so as to "re-vision . . . connections with women" by focusing upon the pleasures of and between women on the screen and women in the audience, rather than on "the ways in which the film affords pleasure, or denies pleasure, to men."[38]

Working with the various suggestive comments in this article and considering actual and potential lesbian readings of other musicals can lead to a consideration of other pairs and trios of song-and-dance women performers (often related as sisters in the narratives), certain strong solo women film and video musical stars (Eleanor Powell, Esther Williams, Carmen Miranda, Lena Horne, Eartha Kitt, Doris Day, Julie Andrews, Tina Turner, Madonna), and musical numbers performed by groups of women, with little or no participation by men.[39] Of particular interest in this latter category are those often-reviled Busby Berkeley musical spectacles, which appear in a different light if one considers lesbians (and other queers) as spectators, rather than straight men. I'm thinking here especially of numbers like "The Lady in the Tutti-Frutti Hat" in *The Gang's All Here*, where Carmen Miranda triggers an all-woman group masturbation fantasia involving banana dildos and foot fetishism; "Dames" in *Dames*, where women sleep, bathe, dress, and seek employment together— some pause to acknowledge the camera as bearer of the voyeuristic (straight) male gaze, only to prohibit this gaze by using powder puffs, atomizer sprays, and other objects to cover the lens; "The Polka-Dot Ballet" in *The Gang's All Here*, where androgynized women in tights rhythmically move neon hoops and large dots in unison, then melt into a vivid, hallucinogenically colored vaginal opening initially inhabited by Alice Faye's head surrounded by shiny cloth; "Spin a Little Web of Dreams" in *Fashions of 1934*, where a seamstress falls asleep and "spins a little web of dreams" about a group of seminude women amid giant undulating ostrich-feather fans who, at one point, create a tableau called "Venus with Her Galley Slaves"; and parts of many other numbers (the two women sharing an upper berth on the Niagara Limited who cynically comment upon marriage in *42nd Street*'s "Shuffle Off to Buffalo," for example).[40]

Since this discussion of queer positions and queer readings seems to have worked itself out so far largely as a discussion of musical stars and the musical genre, I might add here that of the articles and books written about film musicals only the revised edition of Jane Feuer's *Hollywood Musicals* goes beyond a passing remark in considering the ways in which this genre has been the product of gay film workers, or how the ways in which musicals are viewed and later talked about have been influenced by gay and lesbian reception practices.[41] From most accounts of the musical, it is a genre whose celebration of heterosexual romance must always be read straight. The same seems to be the case with those other film genres typically linked to gays, lesbians, and bisexuals: the horror/fantasy film and the melodrama. While there has been a rich history of queers producing and reading these genres, surprisingly little has been done to formally express this cultural history. There has been more queer work done in and on the horror film: vampire pieces by Richard Dyer, Bonnie Zimmerman, and Sue-Ellen Case; Bruna Fionda, Polly Gladwin, Isiling Mack-Nataf's lesbian vampire film *The Mark of Lilith* (1986); Amy Goldstein's vampire musical film *Because the Dawn* (1988); a sequence in *Dry Kisses Only* that provides a lesbian take on vampire films; an article by Martin F. Norden on sexuality in *The Bride of Frankenstein*; and some pieces on *The Rocky Horror Picture Show* (although most are not written from a queer position), to cite a few examples.[42]

But there is still much left unexamined beyond the level of conversation. Carl Dreyer's lesbophobic "classic" *Vampyr* could use a thorough queer reading, as could Tod Browning's *Dracula*—which opens with a coach ride through Transylvania in the company of a superstitious Christian straight couple, a suit-and-tie lesbian couple, and a feminine gay man, who will quickly become the bisexual Count Dracula's vampirized servant. Subsequent events in the film include a straight woman who becomes a child molester known as "The Woman in White" after the count vampirizes her. It is also amazing that gay horror director James Whale has yet to receive full-scale queer auteurist consideration for films such as *Frankenstein* (the idea of men making the "perfect" man), *The Bride of Frankenstein* (gay Dr. Praetorius; queer Henry Frankenstein; the erotics between the blind man, the monster, and Jesus on the cross; the overall campy atmosphere), *The Old Dark House* (a gay and lesbian brother and sister; a 103-year-old man in the attic who is actually a woman), and *The Invisible Man* (effete, mad genius Claude Rains spurns his fiancée, becomes invisible, tries to find a male partner in crime, and becomes *visible* only after he is killed by the police).[43] Beyond queer readings of specific films and directors, it would also be important to consider how the central conventions of horror and melodrama actually encourage queer positioning as they exploit the spectacle of heterosexual romance, straight domesticity, and traditional gender roles gone awry. In a sense, then, *everyone's* pleasure in these genres is "perverse," is queer, as much of it takes place within the space of the contra-heterosexual and the contra-straight.

Just how much everyone's pleasures in mass culture are part of this contra-straight, rather than strictly antistraight, space—just how *queer* our responses to cultural texts are so much of the time—is what I'd finally like this chapter to suggest. Queer positions, queer readings, and queer pleasures are part of a reception space that stands simultaneously beside and within that created by heterosexual and straight positions. These positions, readings, and pleasures also suggest that what happens in cultural reception goes beyond the traditional opposition of homo and hetero, as queer reception is often a place beyond the audience's conscious "real-life" definition of their sexual identities and cultural positions—often, but not always, beyond such sexual identities and identity politics, that is. For in all my enthusiasm for breaking down rigid concepts of sexuality through the example of mass culture reception, I don't want to suggest that there is a queer utopia that unproblematically and apolitically unites straights and queers (or even all queers) in some mass culture reception area in the sky. Queer reception doesn't stand outside personal and cultural histories; it is part of the articulation of these histories. This is why, politically, queer reception (and production) practices can include everything from the reactionary to the radical to the indeterminate, as with the audience for (as well as the producers of) "queercore" publications, who individually and collectively often seem to combine reactionary and radical attitudes.

What queer reception often does, however, is stand outside the relatively clear-cut and essentializing categories of sexual identity under which most people function. You might identify yourself as a lesbian or a straight woman yet queerly experience the gay erotics of male buddy films such as *Red River* and *Butch Cassidy and the Sundance Kid*; or maybe as a gay man your cultlike devotion to *Laverne and Shirley*, *Kate and Allie*, or *The Golden Girls* has less to do with straight-defined cross-gender identification than with your queer enjoyment in how these series are crucially concerned with articulating the loving relationships between women.[44] Queer readings aren't "alternative" readings, wishful or willful misreadings, or "reading too much into things" readings. They result from the recognition and articulation of the complex range of queerness that has been in popular culture texts and their audiences all along.

Notes

1. Jean Genet, *Gay Sunshine Interviews*, ed. Winston Leyland (San Francisco: Gay Sunshine Press, 1978), 73.
2. Gretchen Phillips, "The Queer Song," performed by Two Nice Girls, *Chloe Likes Olivia* (Rough Trade Records, 1991). Lyrics quoted by permission.
3. Janice Radway, "Reception Study: Ethnography and the Problems of Dispersed Audiences and Nomadic Subjects," *Cultural Studies* 2, no. 3 (October 1988): 361.
4. Ibid., 366.
5. Stuart Hall's article "Encoding/Decoding" informs much of my general approach to queer cultural readings of mass culture. This important essay is in *Culture, Media, Language*, ed. Stuart Hall, Andrew Lowe, and Paul Willis (Birmingham: Center for Contemporary Cultural Studies, 1980), 128–38.

6. Adele Morrison as quoted in "Queer," Steve Cosson, *OUT/LOOK* 11 (Winter 1991): 21.

7. Although the ideas that comprise "straightness" and "heterosexuality" are actually flexible and changeable over time and across cultures, these concepts have been—and still are—generally understood within Western public discourses as rather clearly defined around rigid gender roles, exclusive opposite sex desires, and such social and ideological institutions as patriarchy, marriage, "legitimate" childbearing and -rearing, and the nuclear, patrilineal family. And all of this has been/is placed in binary opposition to "homosexuality" or "queerness." However, if we consider the notion of "queerness" in relation to the terms of the still commonly evoked utopian binary of sexuality (with its implicit dynamics of heterosexual gender stability versus homosexual [cross-]gender instability), it becomes clear that queerness, not straightness, describes an enormous space of cultural production and reception. For it is *deviance* from the demands of strict straight/heterosexual paradigms (however they are defined in a given time and place) that most often defines and describes our sexualized and/or gendered pleasures and positions in relation to movies, television, videos, and popular music. Indeed, many so-called straight mass culture texts encourage "deviant" erotic and/or gendered responses and pleasures in straight viewers.

8. These thoughts about queer spaces in mass culture are most immediately indebted to Robin Wood's "Responsibilities of a Gay Film Critic," *Movies and Methods II*, ed. Bill Nichols (Berkeley: University of California Press, 1985), 649–60, and Marilyn R. Farwell's "Heterosexual Plots and Lesbian Subtexts: Toward a Theory of Lesbian Narrative Space," *Lesbian Texts and Contexts: Radical Revisions*, ed. Karla Jay and Joanne Glasgow (New York: New York University Press, 1990), 91–103. Concerned with the politics of film critics/theorists (Wood) and the creation of uniquely lesbian narrative spaces for characters in literature (Farwell), these articles lucidly combine academic theory with gay- and lesbian-specific cultural concerns to suggest how and where being gay or lesbian makes a difference in cultural production and reception.

9. bell hooks, "Choosing the Margins as a Space of Radical Openness," *Yearning: Race, Gender, and Cultural Politics* (Boston: South End Press, 1990), 153.

10. While I use the term "regression" here in relation to queerness and mass culture, I don't want to invoke conventional psychoanalytic and popular ideas about queerness as a permanently infantilized stage past which heterosexuals somehow progress.

11. In "On Becoming a Lesbian Reader," *Sweet Dreams: Sexuality, Gender and Popular Fiction*, ed. Susannah Radstone (London: Lawrence and Wishart, 1988), Alison Hennegan offers many incisive examples of the complex workings of gender in the construction of queer identities and cultural reading practices, as well as indicating the reciprocity between sexual identity formation and reading cultural texts. Speaking of her adolescence, Hennegan states: "That I turned to ancient Greece need come as no surprise. If there's one thing everyone knows about the Greeks it's that they were all That Way. . . . That women's own voices were virtually silent, bar a few precious scraps of lyric poetry and the occasional verbatim transcript from a court hearing, did not then worry me. What I was looking for were strong and passionate emotions which bound human beings to members of their own sex rather than to the other. That the bonds depicted existed primarily between men didn't matter. In part this was because I spent at least half my adolescence 'being male' inside my own head: 'gender identity confusion' in today's

terminology, or 'male identified,' but neither phrase is right or adequate. I never for one moment thought I was a man nor wished to be. But somehow I had to find a way of thinking of myself which included the possibility of desiring women. And those who desire women are men" (p. 170).

12. Sue-Ellen Case, "Tracking the Vampire," *differences* 3, no. 2 (Summer 1991): 2.

13. Ibid., 3.

14. Ibid., 8, 12.

15. Some gay men will prefer the terms "effeminate" or "woman-identified" where I use "feminine" in this section, and throughout the text. I find the former term still too closely connected to straight uses that simultaneously trivialize and trash women and gay men, while the latter term might appear to place gay men in the position of essentializing theoretical transsexuals. Where I use "effeminate" in this book, it should be understood as describing culturally dictated heterosexist ideas about gays and gender (which queers might also employ).

16. Although most of these performers have an international gay following, this list is rather Anglo-American. To begin to expand it, one would add names like Zarah Leander (Germany), Isa Miranda (Italy), Dolores del Rio, Maria Felix, Sara Montiel (Latin America and Spain), and Josephine Baker (France). As is the case in the United States and Great Britain, while some national and regional queer cultural work has been done regarding (feminine) gays and women stars, much more needs to be done. Television series cited in this section: *Designing Women* (1986–present, CBS), *The Golden Girls* (1985–92, NBC), *Murphy Brown* (1989-present, CBS), *The Mary Tyler Moore Show* (1970–77, CBS).

17. Among the work on women stars that concerns feminine gay reception (with the "feminine" aspects usually implied) are: Parker Tyler, "Mother Superior of the Faggots and Some Rival Queens," *Screening the Sexes: Homosexuality in the Movies* (Garden City, N.Y.: Anchor Books, 1973), 1–15 [on Mae West]; Quentin Crisp, "Stardom and Stars," *How to Go to the Movies* (New York: St. Martin's Press, 1989), 11–30; Gregg Howe, "On Identifying with Judy Garland" and "A Dozen Women We Adore," *Gay Life*, ed. Eric E. Rofes (New York: Doubleday, 1986), 178–86; Seymour Kleinberg, "Finer Clay: The World Eroticized," *Alienated Affections: Being Gay in America* (New York: St. Martin's, 1980), 38–69; Michael Bronski, "Hollywood Homo-sense," *Culture Clash: The Making of Gay Sensibility* (Boston: South End Press, 1984), 134–43; Jack Smith. "The Perfect Filmic Appositeness of Maria Montez," *Film Culture* 27 (1962–1963): 28–32. I might also include critic John Simon's *Private Screenings* (New York: Macmillan, 1967) on this list, for its Wildean bitchy-witty critiques of stars such as Elizabeth Taylor, Barbra Streisand, Anna Karina, and Monica Vitti, which are embedded in film reviews. Simon may be a self-declared straight, but his style and sensibility, in this collection at least, are pure scathing urban queen—which works itself out here, unfortunately, to include a heavy dose of misogyny.

18. Julie Burchill, *Girls on Film* (New York: Pantheon Books, 1986), 109.

19. More work is being done in these areas all the time. Some of the more recent essays include: Richard Fung, "Looking for My Penis: The Eroticized Asian in Gay Porn Video," *How Do I Look? Queer Film and Video*, ed. Bad Object-Choices (Seattle: Bay Press, 1991), 145–60; Kobena Mercer, "Skin Head Sex Thing: Racial Differences and the Homoerotic," ibid., 169–210; Mark A. Reid, "The Photography of Rotimi Fani-Kayode," *Wide Angle* 14, no. 2 (April 1992): 38–51; Essex Hemphill, "*In Living Color*: Toms, Coons, Mammies, Faggots and Bucks,"

Outweek 78 (December 26, 1990): 32–40; Marlon Riggs, "Black Macho Revisited: Reflections on a Snap! Queen," *The Independent* 14, no. 3 (April 1991): 32–34; Manthia Diawara, "The Absent One: The Avant-Garde and the Black Imaginary in *Looking for Langston,*" *Wide Angle* 13, nos. 3/4 (July-October 1991): 96–109; Anthony Thomas, "The House the Kids Built: The Gay Imprint on American Dance Music," OUT/LOOK 2, no. 1 (Summer 1989): 24–33; Jackie Goldsby, "What It Means to Be Colored Me," OUT/LOOK 3, no. 1 (Summer 1990): 8–17; Kobena Mercer and Isaac Julien, "Race, Sexual Politics and Black Masculinity: A Dossier," *Unwrapping Masculinity*, ed. Rowena Chapman and Jonathan Rutherford (London: Lawrence and Wishart, 1988), 97–164.

20. Judy Whitaker, "Hollywood Transformed," *Jump Cut* 24/25 (1981): 33. Gail Sausser's "Movie and T.V. Heart-Throbs" chapter of *Lesbian Etiquette* (Trumansburg, N.Y.: Crossing Press, 1986) offers another expression of lesbian reception practices, their connection to gender identity, and the evolution of both through time: "I loved romantic movies when I was a teenager. I unconsciously identified with all the heroes who got the girl. Since I came out, however, my identifications have changed. Now I yell, 'No, no, not him!' at the heroine and root for her female roommate. What a difference a decade (or two) makes" (p. 57).

21. Whitaker, "Hollywood," 34.

22. Films mentioned in this section: *Sylvia Scarlett* (1936, RKO, George Cukor), *Gentlemen Prefer Blondes* (1953, Twentieth Century-Fox, Howard Hawks), *Trapeze* (1956, United Artists, Carol Reed), *To Live and Die in L.A.* (1985, New Century, William Friedkin), *Internal Affairs* (1990, Paramount, Mike Figgis), *Thelma and Louise* (1991, MGM, Ridley Scott), *Scorpio Rising* (1962–63, Kenneth Anger), *Home Movies* (1972, Jan Oxenberg), *Women I Love* (1976, Barbara Hammer), *Loads* (1980, Curt McDowell).

    When I say certain mainstream films elicit a "wider range of queer responses" than films made by, for, or about lesbians, gays, and bisexuals. I am not commenting upon the politics of these films or their reception, only about the multiplicity of queer responses. And while the lesbian and gay films listed here are much more direct and explicit about the sex in them being homo, the sexual politics of these films are not necessarily more progressive or radical than that of the mainstream films.

23. The strength of the Monroe-Lorelei/Russell-Dorothy pairing on and off screen was publicly acknowledged shortly after the film's release when, as a team, the two stars went through the ceremony of putting prints of their hands and feet in the fore-court of Grauman's Chinese Theatre in Hollywood.

24. Al LaValley, "The Great Escape," *American Film* 10, no. 6 (April 1985): 71.

25. Michael Musto, "Immaculate Connection," *Outweek* 90 (March 20, 1991): 35–36.

26. Ibid., 36.

27. In the revised edition of *The Hollywood Musical* (London: BFI/Macmillan, forthcoming), Jane Feuer has added a brief section focusing on MGM's Freed Unit and Judy Garland that suggests ways of developing gay readings of musicals with reference to both production and queer cultural contexts. Mentioned in Feuer's discussions, Richard Dyer's chapter "Judy Garland and Gay Men," in *Heavenly Bodies: Film Stars and Society* (New York: St. Martin's Press, 1986), 141–94, is an exemplary analysis of how and why queers and queer cultures read and, in certain ways, help to create star personas.

28. Films mentioned in this section: *The Pagan* (1929, MGM, W. S. Van Dyke), *Athena* (1954, MGM, Richard Thorpe), *Seven Brides for Seven Brothers* (1954, MGM, Stanley Donen), *West Side Story* (1961, United Artists, Robert Wise and Jerome Robbins), *Saturday Night Fever* (1977, Paramount, John Badham), *Grease* (1980, Paramount, Randall Kleiser), *Staying Alive* (1984, Paramount, Sylvester Stallone), *Dirty Dancing* (1987, Vestron, Emile Ardolino), *The Turning Point* (1977, Twentieth Century-Fox, Herbert Ross), *White Nights* (1987, Paramount, Taylor Hackford).

29. Films cited: *On the Town* (1950, MGM, Gene Kelly and Stanley Donen), *Take Me Out to the Ball Game* (1949, MGM, Busby Berkeley), *It's Always Fair Weather* (1955, MGM, Gene Kelly and Stanley Donen). For a more extended discussion of Gene Kelly and the "buddy" musical, see Steven Cohan's chapter, "Les Boys," in *Masked Men: American Masculinity and the Movies in the Fifties* (Indianapolis and Bloomington: Indiana University Press, forthcoming).

30. Films cited: *Singin' in the Rain* (1952, MGM, Gene Kelly and Stanley Donen), *An American in Paris* (1951, MGM, Vincente Minnelli), *Anchors Aweigh* (1945, MGM, George Sidney).

31. In *The Celluloid Closet: Homosexuality in the Movies*, rev. ed. (New York: Harper and Row, 1987), Vito Russo uncovers material on *Singin' in the Rain's* production history that reveals that the erotics between Kelly and O'Connor were referred to in the original script: "One line of dialogue in Betty Comden and Adolph Green's screenplay for *Singin' in the Rain* (1952) was penciled out by the censors because it gave 'a hint of sexual perversion' between Donald O'Connor and Gene Kelly. When O'Connor gets the idea of dubbing the voice of Debbie Reynolds for the high-pitched, tinny voice of Jean Hagen in a proposed musical, *The Dancing Cavalier*, he illustrates his idea for Kelly by standing in front of Reynolds and mouthing the words to "Good Morning" while she sings behind him. When the song is over, O'Connor turns to Kelly and asks 'Well? Convincing?' Kelly, not yet catching on, takes it as a joke and replies, 'Enchanting! What are you doing later?' The joke was eliminated" (pp. 98–99).

32. Films cited: *That's Entertainment!* (1974, MGM, Jack Haley, Jr.), *Ziegfeld Follies* (1946, MGM, Vincente Minnelli), *That's Entertainment 2* (1976, MGM, Gene Kelly), *The Barkleys of Broadway* (1949, MGM, Charles Walters).

33. Film cited: *Calamity Jane* (1953, Warners, David Butler). Some lesbians also take what they would describe as a gay pleasure in musicals, and perform readings of individual films and of the genre in terms they identify as being influenced by their understanding of the ways gay men appreciate musicals. These kinds of gay approaches might take the form of specific star cult enthusiasms (for Judy Garland, Barbra Streisand, or Bette Midler, for example) that individual lesbian readers feel aren't important in lesbian culture, or of an appreciation for certain aesthetic or critical approaches (camp, for example) which seem unpopular, inoperative, or not "politically correct" in the lesbian culture(s) within which the individual reader places herself.

34. Lucie Arbuthnot and Gail Seneca, "Pre-text and Text in *Gentlemen Prefer Blondes*," *Film Reader* 5 (1982): 20. This essay is reprinted in *Issues in Feminist Film Criticism*, ed. Patricia Erens (Bloomington and Indianapolis: Indiana University Press, 1990), 112–25.

35. Arbuthnot and Seneca, "Pre-text and Text," 21.

36. Ibid., 23.

37. Alix Stanton's "Blondes, Brunettes, Butches and Femmes" (unpublished seminar paper, Cornell University, 1991) offers a more extended consideration of butch-femme roles and cultures in relation to readings of *Gentlemen Prefer Blondes* (and *How to Marry a Millionaire* [1953, Twentieth Century-Fox, Jean Negulesco]).

38. Arbuthnot and Seneca, "Pre-text and Text," 21. For another approach to the lesbian aspects of this film, see Maureen Turim's "Gentlemen Consume Blondes," in *Issues in Feminist Film Criticism*, ed. Erens, 101–11; originally in *Wide Angle* 1, no. 1 (1979), also reprinted in *Movies and Methods, Volume II*, ed. Bill Nichols (Berkeley and Los Angeles: University of California Press, 1985): 369–78. As part of an addendum to the original article, Turim considers lesbianism and *Gentlemen Prefer Blondes* in light of certain feminist film theories about straight male spectatorship. Turim sees the main characters as male constructed "pseudo-lesbians," and the film's use of them as being related to "how lesbianism has served in male-oriented pornography to increase visual stimulation and to ultimately give twice as much power to the eye, which can penetrate even the liaisons which would appear to deny male entry" (pp. 110–11).

39. While not a lesbian-specific reading, Shari Roberts's "You Are My Lucky Star: Eleanor Powell's Brief Dance with Fame" (from an unpublished Ph.D. dissertation, "Seeing Stars: Female WWII Hollywood Musical Stars," University of Chicago, 1993) is suggestive of how and where such a reading might begin, with its discussion of Powell's (autoerotic) strength as a solo performer and its threatening qualities: "If. . .Powell represents a recognition of women as independent, working women, her films also reflect society's related fear of this 'new' woman, and potential gender confusion. . . . This anxiety is demonstrated with homophobic and cross-dressing jokes in the Powell films" (p. 7).

40. Films mentioned in this section: *The Gang's All Here* (1943, Twentieth Century-Fox, Busby Berkeley), *Dames* (1934. Warners, Ray Enright), *Fashions of 1934* (1934, Warners, William Dieterle), *42nd Street* (1933, Warners, Lloyd Bacon).

41. Feuer's "Gay Readings of Musicals" section in *Hollywood Musicals* (cited in note 27) concentrates on gay male production and reception of musicals.

42. Articles mentioned in this section: Richard Dyer, "Children of the Night: Vampirism as Homosexuality, Homosexuality as Vampirism," *Sweet Dreams: Sexuality, Gender and Popular Fiction*, ed, Susannah Radstone (London: Lawrence and Wishart, 1988), 47–72; Bonnie Zimmerman, "*Daughters of Darkness:* Lesbian Vampires," *Jump Cut* 24/25 (1981): 23–24; Sue-Ellen Case, "Tracking the Vampire," *differences* 3, no. 2 (Summer 1991): 1–20; Martin F. Norden, "Sexual References in James Whale's *Bride of Frankenstein,*" *Eros in the Mind's Eye: Sexuality and the Fantastic in Art and Film*, ed. Donald Palumbo (New York: Greenwood Press, 1986), 141–50; Elizabeth Reba Weise, "Bisexuality, *The Rocky Horror Picture Show*, and Me," *Bi Any Other Name: Bisexual People Speak Out*, ed. Loraine Hutchins and Lani Kaahumanu (Boston: Alyson, 1991), 134–39.

43. Films mentioned in this section: *Vampyr* (1931, Gloria Film, Carl Theodore Dryer), *Dracula* (1931, Universal, Tod Browning), *Frankenstein* (1931, Universal, James Whale), *The Bride of Frankenstein* (1935, Universal, James Whale), *The Old Dark House* (1932, Universal, James Whale), *The Invisible Man* (1933, Universal, James Whale). In light of the discussion of musicals in this essay, it is interesting to recall here that Whale's biggest success apart from his horror films was directing Universal's 1936 version of *Show Boat*.

44. Films and television series mentioned in this section: *Red River* (1948, United Artists, Howard Hawks), *Butch Cassidy and the Sundance Kid* (1969, Twentieth Century-Fox, George Roy Hill), *Laverne and Shirley* (1976–83, ABC), *Kate and Allie* (1984–90, CBS), *The Golden Girls* (1985–92, NBC).

Questions for Reflection, Discussion, and Writing

1. What argument does Doty offer to justify his use of "queer"? In choosing the term "queer" what difficulties does he acknowledge? What benefits? What other terms does he reject as a result? What and who does he claim his use of queer encompasses?

2. Why, according to Doty, do we need more scholarship on the ways queer, gays, lesbians, and "the less-analyzed queer readership positions formed around the nexus of race and sexuality, or class and sexuality, or some combination of gender/race/ class/ethnicity and sexuality" have been understood and represented?

3. Doty reviews the ways lesbians and gays have interpreted films differently from those who comprise "the norm." What are some examples he offers? Using the two ways he has interpreted and positioned himself when viewing *Gentlemen Prefer Blondes*, what argument is he demonstrating about audience and queer subjectivity?

4. In what ways, according to Doty, does queer reception stand within "personal and cultural histories?" Why is this important? Yet, Doty argues that queer reception also remains outside of the "clear-cut and essentializing categories of sexual identity under which most straight people function"? How do these seemingly contradictory effects happen?

Related Reading

Robin Wood, "Responsibilities of A Gay Film Critic" in *Movies and Methods II*. Bill Nichols, Ed. Berkeley: U of California P. 1985. 649–660.

Al LaValley, "The Great Escape." *American Film 10.6* (April 1985): 28–34, 70–71.

Richard Dyer, "Judy Garland and Gay Men" in *Heavenly Bodies: Film Stars and Society*. NY: St. Martin's Press. 1986. 141–193.

————. "Believing in Fairies: The Author and The Homosexual" in *Inside/Out: Lesbian Theories, Gay Theories*. Diana Fuss, Ed. NY: Routledge. 1991. 185–201.

Parker Tyler, *Screening the Sexes: Homosexuality in the Movies*. NY: Da Capo Press. 1993.

Thomas Waugh, "The Third Body: Patterns in the Construction of the Subject in Gay Male Narrative Film" in *Queer Looks*. Martha Gever, John Greyson and Pratibha Parmar, Eds. NY: Routledge. 1993. 141–161.

Douglas Crimp, "Fassbinder, Franz, Fox, Elvira, Erwin, Armin, and All the Others" in *Queer Looks*. Martha Gever, John Greyson and Pratibha Parmar, Eds. NY: Routledge. 1993. 257–274.

James R. Parrish, *Gays and Lesbians in Mainstream Cinema*. Jefferson, NC: McFarland & Co. 1993.

John Champagne, "Psychoanalysis and Cinema Studies: A 'Queer' Perspective." *Post Script: Essays in Film & the Humanities 14.1–2* (1994–95): 33–44.

Caroline Evans and Lorraine Gamman, "The Gaze Revisited, or Reviewing Queer Viewing" in *A Queer Romance: Lesbians, Gay Men and Popular Culture.* Paul Burston and Colin Richardson, Eds. NY: Routledge. 1995. 13–56.

Honey Glass, "Q For Queer." *Sight & Sound* 7.10 (1997 October): 36–39.

Harry M. Benshoff, *Monsters in the Closet: Homosexuality and the Horror Film.* Manchester, England: Manchester UP. 1997.

Michael Moon, "Outlaw Sex and the 'Search for America': Representing Male Prostitution and Perverse Desire in Sixties Film (*My Hustler* and *Midnight Cowboy*" in *A Small Boy and Others: Imitation and Initiation in American Culture from Henry James to Andy Warhol.* Durham, NC: Duke UP. 1998. 117–132.

Allen Ellenzweig, "The Movies Made Me Homo." *The Harvard Gay & Lesbian Review* 5.1 (Winter 1998): 28–29.

Gary Devore, " 'I'M **Queer!**' 'No, I'M **Queer!**': Hollywood Homosexuality and Roman Epic Films." *Popular Culture Review 10.1* (1999 February): 127–138.

Blake Allmendinger, "The Queer Frontier" in *The Queer Sixties.* Patricia Juliana Smith, Ed. NY: Routledge. 1999. 223–236.

D.A. Miller, "Visual Pleasure in 1959" in *Out Takes: Essays on Queer Theory and Film."* Ellis Hanson, Ed. Durham: Duke UP. 1999. 97–125.

George F. Custen, "Where Is the Life That Late He Led? Hollywood's Construction of Sexuality in the Life of Cole Porter" in *The Columbia Reader on Lesbians & Gay Men in Media, Society & Politics.* Larry Gross and James D. Woods, Eds. NY: Columbia UP. 1999. 307–316.

Alexander Doty, *Flaming Classics: Queering the Film Canon.* NY: Routledge. 2000.

Richard Dyer, *The Culture of Queers.* NY: Routledge. 2002.

John M. Clum, *"He's All Man": Learning Masculinity, Gayness, and Love From American Movies.* New York: Palgrave. 2002.

Film

Homo Pomo (1956–1976). Jenni Olson. 62 m.

Dry Kisses Only (1990). Jane Cortis and Kaucyila Brooke. 75m.

The Celluloid Closet (1995). Rob Epstein and Jeffrey Friedman. 102 m.

Lavender Limelight: Lesbians in Film (1997). Marc Mauceri. 57 m.

Web Resource

http://www.queertheory.com/arts/media/queer_hollywood.htm

Special Topics

Alfred Hitchcock's films have inspired a host of queer readings, both *auteur* studies and interpretations of individual films. The readings in this section may be paired with films cited below.

Reading

Tania Modleski, *The Women Who Knew Too Much: Hitchcock and Feminist Theory*. NY: Routledge. 1988.

D.A. Miller, Anal *Rope*" in *Inside/Out: Lesbian Theories, Gay Theories*. Diana Fuss, Ed. NY: Routledge. 1991. 119–141.

John Hepworth, "Hitchcock's Homophobia" in *Out in Culture: Gay, Lesbian and Queer Essays on Popular Culture*. Corey E. Creekmur and Alexander Doty, Eds. Durham: Duke UP. 1995. 186–196.

Robin Wood, "The Murderous Gays: Hitchcock's Homophobia" in *Out in Culture: Gay, Lesbian and Queer Essays on Popular Culture*. Corey E. Creekmur and Alexander Doty, Eds. Durham: Duke UP. 1995. 197–215.

Sabrina Barton, "'Criscross': Paranoia and Projection in *Strangers on a Train*" in *Out in Culture: Gay, Lesbian and Queer Essays on Popular Culture*. Corey E. Creekmur and Alexander Doty, Eds. Durham: Duke UP. 1995. 216–238.

Rhona J. Berenstein, "'I'm not the sort of person men marry': Monsters, Queers, and Hitchcock's *Rebecca*" in *Out in Culture: Gay, Lesbian and Queer Essays on Popular Culture*. Corey E. Creekmur and Alexander Doty, Eds. Durham: Duke UP. 1995. 239–261.

Lucretia Knapp, "The Queer Voice in *Marnie*" in *Out in Culture: Gay, Lesbian and Queer Essays on Popular Culture*. Corey E. Creekmur and Alexander Doty, Eds. Durham: Duke UP. 1995. 262–281.

Lee Edelman, "Piss Elegant: Freud, Hitchcock, and the Micturating Penis." *GLQ 2*. 1/2 (1995): 149–177.

———, "*Rear Window's* Glasshole" in *Out Takes: Essays on Queer Theory and Film*." Ellis Hanson, Ed. Durham, N.C.: Duke UP. 1999. 72–96.

Thomas Waugh, "Hauling an Old Corpse Out of Hitchcock's Trunk: *Rope*" in *The Fruit Machine: Twenty Years of Writing on Queer Cinema*. Durham, N.C.: Duke UP. 2000. 148–150.

Alexander Doty, "'He's a transvestite!' 'Ah, not exactly.' How Queer Is My *Psycho*" in *Flaming Classics*. NY: Routledge. 2000. 155–187.

Film

Rebecca (1940). 130 m.

Notorious (1946). 101 m.

Rope (1948). 80 m.

Strangers on a Train (1951). 101 m.

Rear Window (1954). 112 m.

Psycho (1960). 109 m.

Marnie (1964). 129 m.

Special Topics

"Queer New Wave Cinema" is the name applied to any number of films released in the 1990s that broke with older humanist approaches to the subject of sexuality. They embody a heady combination of socially constructed identities, doomed romanticism, irreverence, excess, and minimalism.

Reading

José Arroyo, "Death Desire and Identity: The Political Unconscious of 'New Queer Cinema' " in *Activating Theory: Lesbian, Gay, Bisexual Politics*. Joseph Bristow and Angelia R. Wilson, Eds. London: Lawrence & Wishart. 1993. 70–96.

B. Ruby Rich, "Homo Pomo: The New Queer Cinema" in *Women and Film: A Sight and Sound Reader*. Pam Cook and Philip Dodd, Eds. Philadelphia: Temple UP. 1993. 164–175.

Daryl Chin, "Girlfriend in a Coma: Notes on the Films of Gregg Araki" in *Queer Looks*. Martha Gever, John Greyson and Pratibha Parmar, Eds. NY: Routledge. 1993. 103–107.

Kimberly Yutani, "Gregg Araki and the Queer New Wave." *Amerasia Journal 20*.1 (1994): 85–91.

David Román, "Shakespeare Out in Portland: Gus Van Sant's *My Own Private Idaho*, Homoerotics, and Boy Actors" in *Eroticism and Containment: Notes From the Flood Plain*. Carol Siegel and Ann Kibbey, Eds. NY: NYUP. 1994. 311–333.

Babara Reumuller, "Whatever Happened to New Queer Cinema?" *Blimp: Film Magazine 35* (1996): 27–32.

Rhona J. Berenstein, "Where the Girls Are: Riding the New Wave of Lesbian Feature Films." *GLQ 3* (1996): 125–137.

James M. Moran, "Gregg Araki: Guerrilla Film-Maker for a Queer Generation." *Film Quarterly 50*.1 (1996 Fall): 18–26.

Katie Mills, "Revitalizing the Road Genre: *The Living End* as an AIDS Road Film" in *The Road Movie Book*. Steven Cohan and Ina Rae Hark, Eds. NY: Routledge. 1997. 307–329.

Maria Pramaggiore, "Fishing for Girls: Romancing Lesbians in New Queer Cinema." *College Literature 24*.1 (1997): 59–75.

Robert Lang, "*My Own Private Idaho* and the New Queer Road Movies" in *The Road Movie Book*. Steven Cohan and Ina Rae Hark, Eds. NY: Routledge. 1997. 330–348.

K. Burdette, "Queer Readings/Queer Cinema: An Examination of the Early Work of Todd Haynes." *Velvet Light Trap 41*(1998): 68–80.

José Esteban Muñoz, "Dead White: Notes on the Whiteness of the New Queer Cinema." *GLQ 4*.1 (1998): 127–138.

Jim Ellis, "Queer Period: Derek Jarman's Renaissance" in *Out Takes: Essays on Queer Theory and Film*." Ellis Hanson, Ed. Durham: Duke UP. 1999. 288–315.

B. Ruby Rich, "Queer and Present Danger: What's Happened to Queer Cinema Since *Poison, Swoon, Edward II, The Living End* and Others Made it 'New' in 1992?" *Sight and Sound 10*.3 (2000): 22–25.

Film

My Own Private Idaho (1991). Gus Van Sant. 102 m.

Edward II (1991). Derek Jarman. 91 m.

Poison (1991). Todd Haynes. 85 m.
Swoon (1992). Tom Kalin. 92 m.
The Living End (1992). Gregg Araki. 93 m.
Zero Budget (1996). Emma Hindley. 25 m.

Just A Gigolo?

Narcissism, Nellyism
and the 'New Man' Theme

Paul Burston

Oh he wears such a thin disguise
Look a little closer and unmask his eyes
See right through him, see him oozing with lies . . .
(Hazel O'Connor, Gigolo Albion Music, 1980)

There is nothing about gay people's physiognomy that declares them gay, no equiva-
lents to the biological markers of sex and race. There are signs of gayness, a reper-
toire of gestures, expressions, stances, clothing *and* even environments.[1]
(Richard Dyer [my italics])

This essay is the story of a gay man's obsession with gigolos, in particular
with those men Hollywood paid to drop their pants during the 1980s. The
Collins English Dictionary defines 'gigolo' as 'a man who is kept by a woman, especially an older woman; a man who is paid to dance with or escort women'. I take
it for granted that the men who signed the cheques for Richard Gere's exhibitionism in *American Gigolo* (1980) and Tom Cruise's posturing in *Top Gun*
(1986) would insist that the stars' bodies were put on display for the sole purpose
of pleasuring women. But as Yvonne Tasker recently pointed out, 'the meaning
of the body on the screen is not secure, but shifting, inscribed with meaning in

different ways at different points.[2] And as I intend to show, both films relied heavily on a tradition of homoerotic textual codes which, though hardly securing the male body as the exclusive object of homosexual desire, certainly invited gay men as well as heterosexual women to grab their share of visual pleasure.

Historically, popular cinema has shied away from presenting sexually explicit images of its male stars. Of course this is no accident. Socially and cinematically, male authority is bound up with the act of looking. Any representation of masculinity denoting 'to-be-looked-at-ness' is therefore perceived as a threat to dominant notions of what it means to be a 'real' (i.e. rigidly heterosexual) man. Still Hollywood has always had its share of male narcissists, from Valentino to Schwarzenegger, actors whose bankability was (and is) dependent precisely on an audience's desire to look at them. And cinema audiences, as we all know, are not composed entirely of swooning heterosexual women. The knowledge that male viewers might enjoy the spectacle of the male body is a constant source of anxiety: men are not supposed to function as objects for one another's erotic gaze. Which is why displays of male flesh are usually given an alibi (e.g. 'this man isn't posing for our pleasure, he's demonstrating his brute strength'), and accompanied by acts of sadism and/or punishment. As Steve Neale observes, 'Were this not the case, mainstream cinema would have openly to come to terms with the male homosexuality it so assiduously seeks to denigrate or deny.[3]

If the look of the male viewer is cause for concern, the look between men on the screen can provoke all kinds of hysterical reactions. Yet many of the film genres targeted specifically at male audiences, from the traditional Western to the modern buddy cop movie, invite us to inhabit a man's world where the 'innocent' pleasures of the homosocial are constantly under threat from the homosexual. Discussing the buddy movies of the late 1960s and early 1970s, Cynthia J. Fuchs describes how 'the exclusion of women compelled overt condemnation of implicit and even explicit homoeroticism, as the texts worked precisely to keep such frightening feelings "below the surface."'[4]

Fast forward to 1980. Westerns are out, wardrobes are in. Richard Gere's well-dressed portrayal of a male narcissist in *American Gigolo* signalled the dawn of a decade in which pleasures previously branded taboo or feminine would be sold to men on a grand scale. A full five years before Nick Kamen dropped his Levi's in that launderette, Richard Gere offered us a tantalising peek at what the so-called 'New Man' might look like under his designer clothes. A marketing phenomenon analysed by media commentators and advertising executives, the New Man has, for the most part, been spared the scrutiny of film theorists.[5] Newspapers and women's magazines may have devoted considerable copy-space to discussion of where the New Man's priorities lay (in the bed or in the bathroom?); surprisingly little has been written about how the images of 'New' masculinity presented to us at the cinema might relate to questions of homosexuality.

Yet on the face of it, the rise of Richard Gere, Tom Cruise, and all the brazen young dudes who followed in their footsteps appeared to signal a measure of acceptance of the male body as an object of desire, a challenge to tradition through a redefining of masculinity which created space for homoerotic desire. Suzanne Moore, writing about the New Man advertising phenomenon in 1988, observed that many of the images used to denote the New Man were 'culled in both form and technique from a long tradition of soft-core homoerotica'.[6] This is hardly a surprise. Historically-speaking, women have been denied the social power to examine, let alone market erotic images of masculinity. Gay men, on the other hand, have enjoyed the economic strength necessary to articulate their erotic pleasures through the celebration and marketing of the male physique, from the coy *Athletic Models' Guild* studio shots of the 1950s to the booming gay porn industry we see in the present day. Rowena Chapman, in a stimulating discussion of 'Variations on the New Man Theme', agrees that the increased availability and acceptability of nude male images in advertising during the 1980s was due largely to a thriving gay economy which 'had an influence on heterosexual men, enabling them to treat other men as objects of desire and to give vent to suppressed homoeroticism'.[7]

But as she also takes care to point out, the manipulation of recognisably homoerotic imagery was usually accompanied by 'moves to ensure that male models [are] presented as images of desire for women alone'.[8] This comment not only serves as a timely reminder of the obvious (but often neglected) fact that gay men do not automatically respond to the same erotic stimuli as heterosexual women; it also challenges us to expose the 'moves' applied to protect the boundaries of heterosexual viewing, and to examine the film industry's attempts to incorporate the forms and techniques of gay erotica into the presentation of its male stars and still deny, if not a homoerotic, then certainly a queer reading of the film text.

American Gigolos Don't Do Fags

Nowhere is this tension between the employment of homoeroticism and the denial of homosexuality more clearly illustrated than in *American Gigolo*. Paul Schrader's visually stylish, emotionally sterile thriller ushered in the new decade with a false promise of available male sexuality—pampered, preened, and (herein lies the crux) on offer exclusively to those who can afford it.

Richard Gere plays a high-class male prostitute, Julian Kay, who is framed for the murder of a client. The detective assigned to the case, while displaying an over-active interest in the nature of Julian's employment, decides that he is 'guilty as sin' (of murder?). Our poor hero finds himself in the unfortunate position of being unable to come up with an alibi, since the woman he was with at the time of the murder refuses to put her marriage on the line. On the level of narrative alone Schrader's film functions as a warning of the dangers inherent in the male body being eroticised. Julian is taught the error of his ways, and undergoes a remarkable conversion just in time for the closing titles. In the film's final scene, Michelle (Lauren Hutton) visits him in prison. The wife of a senator, she has been in love with our hero since their first encounter, following him around by day and turning up at his apartment in the middle of the night.

Throwing caution and reputation to the wind, she announces that she is willing to provide Julian with an alibi. She places her hand against the glass that separates them. He leans his head against it, whimpering poignantly 'My God, Michelle! It's taken me so long to come to you.'

Within this cautionary narrative, a paranoid fear of homosexuality is expressed in a variety of ways, most overtly in Julian's repeated assertion that 'I don't do fags'. The first disclaimer is issued within the first few minutes of the film—indicative, surely, of the depth of anxiety provoked by the subject. From here on in, the denials fly thick and fast. Not wishing to be sidetracked into a debate on 'positive' and 'negative images', it is still worth pointing out, as Vito Russo does, that the only gay characters to appear in the film are 'a lesbian pimp, a black pimp, and a closet case who hates women and has his wife beaten while he watches'.[9]

Russo neglects to mention also the blond boy who appears towards the end of the film, and is supposedly guilty of the murder for which Julian stands accused. Moreover, Russo contents himself with the suggestion that the deployment of such stereotypes is simply another example of the sort of Hollywood homophobia he is committed to cataloguing. Not wanting to defend *American Gigolo* against such charges, it none the less seems to me that, within the scheme of the film as a whole, the presentation of a series of stereotyped images of gay men serves as more than simply an excuse to vent a prejudice.

This should become clearer if we consider for a moment the scene where Julian escorts one of his regular clients to an auction. Catching sight of another, older woman, who has a reputation for being something of a gossip, his client warns Julian that he is about to become subject to unsolicited advances. Our hero's immediate response to the problem is to adopt an exaggerated German accent and camp manner, complete with limp wrist and mincing gait, and to rush up to the woman, kissing her ostentatiously on both cheeks and remarking on her 'beautiful dress'.

The comic appeal of Richard Gere 'acting the fag' is, to say the least, limited, and the scene serves little other purpose. Certainly, it has no part to play in the forwarding of the narrative. What it does provide, however, is an alibi, an opportunity to remind the audience of what a 'real fag' is. In a film which ostensibly sets out to challenge familiar models of masculinity, it should hardly come as a surprise to discover such comforting clichés strategically positioned along the way. 'Don't worry,' the film is saying, 'this is what fags are like. Our gigolo is nothing like this.' Within the precarious framework of gender relations (which the eroticised male threatens to disturb), stereotyped images of gay men serve to reassure the audience of what Gere's character is *not*. The film's construction of overt, exaggerated homosexuality acts as a decoy, directing us away from the conclusion that this gentleman protesteth too much, and towards the preferred (i.e., heterosexual) reading of the text.

Of course Richard Gere wasn't the first or last screen idol to 'act the fag' in order to maintain a straight face.[10] Still *American Gigolo* is noteworthy (if not exactly unique) for the extent to which it actively courts that which it also seeks to deny. For as I have already suggested, the film's reconstruction of a purport-edly heterosexual man as a source of erotic spectacle borrows extensively from a catalogue of textual codes which have their roots in gay male culture. Inevitably this presents a problem: how to transpose the technique and form of homo-erotica into a convincingly heterosexual context? I would argue that Schrader employs two main tactics: tacit denial and autoeroticism.

Before discussing these, it would be useful to establish the fact that Schrader's protagonist exists in what was in 1980 an identifiably gay world. It is a world of sun-kissed bodies and swimming pools, of pastel interiors and micro-blinds. It is the world revealed in the paintings of gay artist David Hockney. Of course Hollywood has always exploited the attraction of exotic, unfamiliar loca-tions. Still there is something very specific riding on Schrader's choice of set-tings. The deployment of late 1970s gay iconography is part of a wider strategy to establish a context which makes it possible, if not imperative, to view the male as erotic spectacle. Framed within this world, Julian is coded as an object-to-be-looked-at.

As if to underline the fact of his object-ivity, the first glimpse of his naked torso is directly preceded by a series of establishing shots which do more than simply alert us to the particulars of time and place. The camera focuses on a pile of paintings, then a collection of vases, a sofa, a pair of dumb-bells, a pair of feet, hands gripping a bar, feet locking on the bar and finally the torso extended downward. The fetishisation of Gere's body—the way in which he is set up as a commodity, the fragmentary quality of the camerawork—suggests a reworking of traditional film strategies for viewing women. At the same time, the precise way in which he is coded for visual pleasure borrows heavily from a long tradi-tion of homoerotica. The shot of his fully extended naked torso is a classic ex-ample of gay soft-porn posturing. Artfully lit, with a glistening coat of sweat highlighting his straining pectorals, he hangs upside down, arms outstretched, a dumb-bell clutched in either hand.[11]

Having established a scene charged with ambiguous eroticism, Schrader then has the object of desire issue a statement of intent, designed to remove any sexual ambiguity. 'I am not interested in that,' Gere says, ostensibly as part of his Teach Yourself Swedish home-cassette course. Issued at the time it is, pre-ceded by a titillating survey of his musculature (complete with standard gay iconography), and immediately followed by a phone call from Leon (the black pimp who is constantly pressurising Julian to do 'fag tricks'), such a declaration functions as a tacit denial of homosexuality and an attempt to reaffirm the fron-tiers of heterosexual viewing.

And yet to what extent is Gere's sexuality really on offer to anyone? He may be stripped and fetishised, but would it be true to say that he was disempowered? An invitation to feast our eyes upon his well-oiled torso hardly constitutes a sur-render of all will and autonomy. It is clear from the way in which the scene is framed that the pleasure is not exclusively, or even predominantly, ours. As Rowena Chapman comments, when discussing the erotification of the male form in calendar-shots, 'The images presented are peopled by paragons of male aesthetics . . . expressive of action, power and control. Everyone knows you don't get a body like that just by whistling, it requires effort, patience and commitment. Even in passivity it articulates action and potential, identifying the participants as active subjects.[12] In Gere's case, the overall impression is of some kind of superman, capable of stretching both his physical and mental limits simultaneously.

Evidently, the erotic potential of the scene is conditioned as much by Gere's character as by our voyeuristic position to him. He is clearly depicted as deriving autoerotic pleasure from his activity, and certainly not as relinquishing all power to the spectator. Faced with the 'threat' of homoeroticism, Schrader struggles to deliver Gere from the hungry eyes of the proverbial predatory gay male viewer by overstating the narcissistic side to Julian's nature. Since there is no female character present in the scene to provide the much-coveted proof of heterosexuality, the male subject himself takes control of the gaze, pre-empting our erotic interest and claiming the pleasure as his own. In a peculiar sense, the gaze becomes self-centred. Autoeroticism is offered as the last safeguard against homoerotica.

Throughout *Gigolo*, Schrader takes pains to regulate the male spectator's reading of the film-text. Attention is repeatedly drawn to the distinction between Gere as the male viewer's ego-ideal and the female viewer's source of erotic visual pleasure, most explicitly in the scene at the Ryman's house. When Julian arrives he is greeted by Mr. Ryman, to whom he trots off the by-now-familiar line, 'I don't do fags'. Ryman, whom we are led to believe is a repressed homosexual, responds by insisting that he watch while Julian has intercourse with his wife. It is hardly surprising that Ryman (who in some sense embodies the active, gay male gaze within the subsequent scene) is portrayed as a nasty piece of work. Why would any self-respecting gay male viewer want to identify with him?

Still Ryman's plaintive 'I can still look' serves as a reminder that neither the queer gaze nor the processes of queer identification are fixed. As Kobena Mercer points out, 'The gendered hierarchy of seeing/being seen is not so rigidly coded in homoerotic representations, since sexual sameness liquidates the associative opposition between active subject and passive object'.[13] It may be possible, in fact, for the gay male viewer to identify with the gigolo while at the same time adopting the spectator position represented by Ryman, or else to oscillate between the two positions, enjoying the various pleasures offered by each.

A simple extension of the denial strategies outlined above explains why mirrors figure so consistently throughout *American Gigolo*, and brings us to a consideration of one of the film's most self-conscious (and, I believe, revealing) scenes. Suspecting Julian of the Ryman murder, Detective Sunday turns up at a hotel lobby where Julian is discovered having his shoes shined in preparation for meeting a 'special' client. They settle into a conversation, Julian offering the detective 'a few pointers to picking up women', Sunday responding by questioning the ethics of Julian's occupation. Their relative social, sexual and legal positions are made abundantly clear. 'Doesn't it bother you, Julian, what you do?' asks Sunday. 'Giving pleasure to women?' retorts Julian. 'I'm supposed to feel guilty about that?'

Throughout the exchange, the camera is centred on Julian's face, with the detective's face reflected in the mirror behind him. Sunday is clearly intended to represent what we would have to call the 'Old Man'. Uncultured and unkempt, he lacks dress-sense and pays little attention to the finer details of his appearance, as Julian is quick to point out. The composition of the scene—Julian in the foreground, the detective reflected behind him—invites us to compare the two, the Old with the New Man. We are also clearly asked to identify with Julian, since it is he who expresses the views with which the 'modern', 'liberal' male spectator would surely align himself. 'Legal is not always right,' Julian says. 'Men make laws. Sometimes they're wrong. Stupid. Or jealous.'

Stupid? Perhaps. Jealous? Possibly. One thing we are left in no doubt about is the threat Julian's lifestyle poses to patriarchal norms. Condemned by the senator as 'a whore', he represents the antithesis to the whole concept of family, the promotion of which has provided the basis of the politician's election campaign. Such is the threat embodied by the male sex-object that no man will come near him (with the notable exception of a criminally motivated black gay pimp). Julian's only real friends in the film are women, and these relationships are, to say the least, fraught. His salvation lies in the fact that he recognises the error of his ways and forges a commitment to a woman we know to be 'good wife material', a woman who is prepared to forsake her reputation for her man, a woman who fulfills her role as one half of the traditional gender equation. Any pretence at exploring a new, liberated version of masculinity is dropped. Male-bonding—the stock theme of 1980s Hollywood—could find no place in the turn-of-the-decade, autonomous, autoerotic world of the all-American gigolo.

The Iceman Cometh?

Top Gun, Tony Scott's 1986 *Boy's Own* story, was memorable on two accounts. It established Tom Cruise (an aspiring brat-packer whose previous experience included dropping his trousers at regular intervals throughout 1983's *Risky Business*) as a major box office attraction, effectively eclipsing the more mature Gere in the heart-throb stakes. And it brought the fetishisation of flying jackets out of the gay clubs and onto the high street.

Cruise plays Maverick, a new recruit at Fighter Weapons school (referred to by the recruits as 'Top Gun'), whose tempestuous temperament makes him a hazard to all around him. 'I'm dangerous,' he boasts to rival recruit Iceman (Val Kilmer), whose frigid demeanour and blond-boy good looks confirm him as Maverick's polar opposite. If the Iceman is impressed, he doesn't let it show, but an intense and intimate rivalry between the two is established from the point at which they look each other in the eye and issue challenges across a crowded room.

Like every good *Boy's Own* story, *Top Gun* has its share of heterosexual love interest, provided here in the shape of Charlotte (Kelly McGillis), who goes by the name of 'Charlie' and gradually falls for Maverick's cheeky-boy charms after overcoming her reservations at being his instructor. True to her name, Charlie spends half the film dressed in unisex naval uniform, complete with peaked cap, though she does have the courtesy to let her hair down and put on a frock for her big love scenes. Her first conversation with Maverick, which starts in the bar and ends in the ladies' room, serves to underline the fact that flying fighter planes isn't all that different from having a good fuck. 'So, are you a good pilot?' asks Charlie. 'I can hold my own,' replies Maverick with a lecherous grin. On this occasion, Charlie holds her own. She would have been well advised to do so on each subsequent occasion, too, though this would have made things a bit difficult for poor Tony Scott, whose valiant attempts to defend the frontiers of heterosexual viewing against the onslaught of homoerotica are already failing hopelessly. The romance may be firmly on the ground, but the passion is anchored in the cockpit.

The coding of the young fighter pilots as erotic spectacle relies heavily on cockpit to locker room editing techniques and the camera's lingering looks over torsos and precariously held towels. In the first locker-room scene, one man is laid out on a bench next to Iceman, who appears to be contending with an erection through his towel. As the scene changes, a senior officer's voice is heard shouting 'I want somebody's butt and I want it now!' Mere coincidence? A later scene, in which Maverick and Iceman compete in a game of volleyball, is lifted straight out of the homoerotic portfolio of Herb Ritts. Stripped to the waist, the men jump in the sunlight, their torsos glistening under the customary coat of sweat, their pleasures heightened by a rock rendition of *Playing with the Boys*. The homoerotic charge between the pilots is exemplified by the language used whenever they are together, whether it is in the air, the locker room or the instruction room. Iceman's first words in the film, offered as an aside to his buddy Slider during an instruction on flying technique, are, 'This gives me a hard-on'—to which Slider replies: Don't tease me.' Once we're up in the air, the *double entendres* fly thick and fast, borne by phrases like 'this guy's hot on my tail', 'this boy's all over me', 'I've given him the finger' and 'my dick, my ass'. (With all this testosterone flying about, Charlie's sexually coded advice to Maverick—it takes a lot more than just fancy flying'—seems oddly out of place in a heterosexual context.)

Generically, *Top Gun* has all the trimmings of the male action movie, including the traditional buddy scenario, though here the homoeroticism is more pronounced. Maverick's buddy throughout the film is Goose, who is prepared to be Maverick's wing-man in spite of his hot-head reputation. 'You're the only family I've got and I'm not going to let you down,' promises Maverick. Ten minutes later he's apologising to Goose for losing his cool and coming within an inch of securing their joint dismissal. 'It'll never happen again', says Maverick solemnly in the locker room. 'I know,' says Goose, barely audible over a swell of harp strings.

But it does happen again, and Goose is killed, leaving poor old Maverick to stand around in his jockey-shorts, look deep into his troubled soul and wonder about his dear old pop (whose death in action is surrounded by rumours of misconduct and whose memory prompts his son to behave as though 'he's up there flying against a ghost'). Charlie's efforts to talk him out of quitting the force are unsuccessful. After dismissing her, Maverick rides off into the night, finally showing up at Commander Metcalfe's house on Sunday morning, where it is revealed that Maverick's daddy was Metcalfe's sidekick and 'a fine pilot'. One ghost thus laid to rest Maverick returns to the locker room, where Iceman extends the hand of friendship. Following a half-hearted return handshake at the graduation ceremony, where Iceman is honoured as 'the best of the best', fire and ice are finally joined in symbolic union during a real-life battle situation, during which Maverick rescues Iceman from possible death. The two land side by side, are met by a crowd of emotionally charged men, and indulge in the kind of physical male-bonding normally reserved for the football pitch. 'You can be my wingman anytime,' offers Iceman, 'Bullshit! You can be mine,' replies Maverick, before wandering off and throwing his last token reminder of Goose into the ocean.

As Cynthia J. Fuchs has observed, the paradox of homosexual attraction between men claiming to be heterosexual is 'rehearsed in the buddy film's movement from conflict to resolution (between the two men or between them and a hostile environment)'.[14] In *Top Gun*, the sexual tensions already implicit in the male-to-male bond are further exacerbated by the order of the narrative, which implies that emotional ties between men are both (a) exclusive and (b) reproductive. Just as Commander Metcalfe becomes, in a sense, Maverick's father figure, so Ice replaces Goose in the young pilot's affections. This transference of intimacy between men is so powerfully inscribed that any relationship not subject to its thematic conditions lacks credibility.

In the film's penultimate scene, Maverick heads off for a romantic reunion with Charlie. Determined to reaffirm his hero's heterosexuality, the director throws in every known romantic cliché. Framed against a blood-red sky, the couple repeat their first-ever conversation, only this time with the roles reversed—the suggestion being, presumably, that any tension between them has now been successfully negotiated. But even as the scene fades (to the strains of *You've Lost That Loving Feeling*), there is no indication of the kind of emotional physicality we witnessed when Maverick and Ice 'made up'. The final shot is of two fighter planes soaring together into the sky. Love is very clearly in the air. But where on earth is Charlie?[15]

Conclusion: 'All in this Together'?

Jane Fonda apologised, but not Barbarella.

(Sandra Bernhard)

Queer readings of popular culture can take many shapes, drawing as they do from a wide range of disciplines (psychoanalysis, constructionism, reception theory, considerations of authorship, stars, etc.). What they all share is the understanding that cultural texts do not have single meanings, that what is denied at the level of narrative (i.e., queerness) can often be deciphered through closer inspection of the textual codes.

A critic who adopts this kind of approach is often accused of 'reading against the text', of taking an 'oppositional' or (better yet) an 'alternative' view. Such allegations are founded on the assumption that all cultural production is, by its very nature, straight, unless it proclaims itself otherwise (and sometimes even then its queerness is passed over, played down, or called into question—a heterosexist response Eve Kosofsky Sedgewick characterises as 'Don't ask; You shouldn't know. It didn't happen; it doesn't make any difference; it didn't mean anything; it doesn't have interpretative consequences.'[16]) A similar thing happens whenever a lesbian or gay man dares to suggest that another (closeted) person might be lesbian or gay. 'How could you possibly know that?' the heterosexual interrogator demands. The answer, more often than not, is desperately (and unhelpfully) simple: some things you just know.

Another way to argue this would be to point out that queerness (precisely because of its 'invisibility') has managed to pervade popular culture to such a degree that it hardly makes sense to draw distinctions between what is 'mass culture' and what is 'queer subculture'. Or as the British playwright and author Neil Bartlett recently put it: 'The history of mainstream entertainment is the history of gay culture.'[17] Considered in this light, queer readings are hardly 'oppositional'. Rather, they represent an attempt to point out what really ought to have been clear to everybody from the start.

The pleasures of such readings are simple: what better revenge on a culture which seeks to exclude you than to demonstrate how you were there all along? The problems—by which I really mean the politics—are rather more complex: if queers devote their time and energies to the interpretation of popular texts (texts which, however queer they may be, still represent the interests and ideologies of a heterosexist society), where will the support come from for openly queer cultural production by and about queers? Isn't all this 'textual fetishism' simply an excuse to shrug the responsibilities of *Realpolitik?*

The answer depends on whether or not you regard pleasure and politics as mutually exclusive — depends, in fact, on whether you accept that criticism is itself a form of activism, with its own activist strategies and political goals. My readings of *American Gigolo* and *Top Gun* concentrate far more on the potentially queer pleasures of the texts than on the politics of their production. Still this isn't to say that such readings aren't political.

In *The Celluloid Closet*, Vito Russo expressed his fears that 'reality will never be profitable until our society overcomes its fear and hatred of difference and begins to see that we're all in this together'.[18] It seems to me that queer readings are part of a wider project to prove that we are 'all in this together' precisely by demonstrating the presence of that 'difference'. It is only by declaring our position in relation to popular cultural texts that we can ever hope to expose the myth that the only profitable forms of cultural production are those which express a uniform straightness. Then, perhaps, we can hope for a bit of 'reality'.

Notes

1. Richard Dyer, *The Matter of Images*, Routledge, London, 1993, p.19.
2. Yvonne Tasker, *Spectacular Bodies: Gender, Genre and the Action Cinema*. Routledge, London, 1993. p.165.
3. Steve Neale, 'Masculinity as Spectacle: Reflections on Men and Mainstream Cinema', *Screen* vol.24, no.6, November–December 1983, p.15.
4. Cynthia J. Fuchs, 'The Buddy Politic', in *Screening the Male*, Routledge, London. 1993, p.196.
5. Steve Neale's ground-breaking essay concentrates on images of masculinity prior to the period under discussion.
6. Suzanne Moore, 'Here's Looking at You, Kid!', in Lorraine Gamman and Margaret Marshment (eds), *The Female Gaze*, The Women's Press, London, 1988, p.51.
7. Rowena Chapman, 'Variations on the New Man Theme', in *Male Order: Unwrapping Masculinity*, Lawrence & Wishart, London, 1988, p.236.
8. Ibid.
9. Vito Russo, *The Celluloid Closet*, Harper & Row, New York. 1987, p.238.
10. Rumours surrounding Gere's own sexual orientation were rife as early as 1979, when he played one of the two homosexual prisoners in the Broadway production of Martin Sherman's *Bent*. Given the potentially catastrophic effect of such speculation on a young actor's career in Hollywood, we oughtn't to underestimate the degree to which *Gigolo* might have served as a cinematic 'right to reply', providing Gere with the perfect opportunity to set the record 'straight'.

   In an interview in *Vanity Fair* (January 1994), Gere refused to confirm or deny rumours that he is gay. 'The accusation is meaningless', he was quoted as saying, 'and whether it's true or false is nobody's business. I know who I am; what difference does it make what anyone thinks, if I live truthfully and honestly and with as open a heart as I can?' Shortly afterwards, he and his wife, Cindy Crawford, took out a full page advertisement in *The Times* newspaper, reassuring the world of their heterosexuality.
11. Interviewed in the US lesbian and gay magazine *The Advocate* (issue 609, 13 August 1992), Schrader confirmed that the employment of homoerotic images had been 'a kind of current in my life'.
12. Chapman, op. cit., p.237.
13. Kobena Mercer, 'Skin Head Sex Thing: Racial Difference and the Homoerotic Imaginary', in Bad Object-Choices (ed.), *How Do I Look? Queer Film and Video*, Bay Press, Seattle, 1991, p.182.
14. Fuchs, op. cit., p.195.
15. For further discussion of homoeroticism in *Top Gun*, see Mark Simpson, *Male Impersonators*, Cassell, London and New York, 1994. For an example of how openly queer cultures appropriate the effects of mass culture, it's worth noting how *Top Gun* provided the scenario for a gay porn flick released within a year of the film's release. Matt Sterling's 1987 best-seller *Big Guns* picks up on Maverick's first meeting with Iceman in the bar. Rejected by 'Charlie', Maverick follows Iceman outside for some serious horseplay.
16. Eve Kosofsky Sedgwick, *Epistemology of the Closet*, University of California Press, California, 1990, p.53.
17. Neil Bartlett, interview with the author, published in *Time Out*, 24 November 1993.
18. Russo, op. cit., p.323.

Questions for Reflection, Discussion, and Writing

1. For what reasons has Hollywood historically been reluctant to display explicit images of its male stars, according to Burston? Under what premises has masculine virility been used in films? Through what techniques have charges and "readings" of homoeroticism been denied in Hollywood films?

2. Richard Gere, as the character of Julian, "doesn't do fags." According to Burston, how does the film's producer use narcissism and the theme of the "new man" to both reinforce and undermine this message?

3. Julian's body is fetishized, according to Burston. Does Gere's own "gaze" save him from objectification?

4. In what ways does Burston's analysis of Maverick's relationships with "Charlie" and with "IceMan" suggest that they are meant to be read as not solely heterosexual?

5. Ultimately, what argument does Burston offer to suggest that "queerness" has infiltrated modern culture? He suggests that queer readings reaffirm queerness by "demonstrating the presence of that 'difference'" which Vito Russo expressed as evidence of fear. Do you agree?

Writing Assignment

Using the Burston essay and any of the related readings as models, choose a seemingly "straight" film in which you see sexual representations and politics being queered and queried in some interesting ways. Research the film to see what other interpretations have been published, and add your own queer reading to the critical conversation on that film.

Related Reading

Ellis Hanson, "Technology, Paranoia and the Queer Voice." *Screen* 34.2 (1993 Summer): 137–161.

Corey K. Creekmur, "Acting Like A Man: Masculine Performance in *My Darling Clementine*" in *Out in Culture: Gay, Lesbian and Queer Essays on Popular Culture*. Corey E. Creekmur and Alexander Doty, Eds. Durham: Duke UP. 1995. 167–182.

Scott D. Paulin, "Sex and the Singled Girl: Queer Representation and Containment in *Single White Female*." *Camera Obscura* 37 (1996): 33–68.

Ed Sikov, "Laughing Hysterically: Sex, Repression, and American Film Comedy" in *Queer Representations: Reading Lives, Reading Cultures*. Martin Duberman, Ed. NY: NYUP. 1997. 85–104.

George F. Custen, "Strange Brew: Hollywood and the Fabrication of Homosexuality in Tea and Sympathy" in *Queer Representations: Reading Lives: Reading Cultures*. Martin Duberman, Ed. NY: NYUP. 1997. 116–138.

Wahneema Lubiano, "Don't Talk With Your Eyes Closed: Caught in the Hollywood Gun Sights" in *Queer Representations: Reading Lives, Reading Cultures*. Martin Duberman, Ed. NY: NYUP. 1997. 139–145.

Steven Cohan, "On the Road With Hope and Crosby" in *Out Takes: Essays on Queer Theory and Film*." Ellis Hanson, Ed. Durham: Duke UP. 1999. 23–45.

Ann Shillinglaw, "'Give Us A Kiss': Queer Codes, Male Partnering and the Beatles" in *The Queer Sixties*. Patricia Juliana Smith, Ed. NY: Routledge. 1999. 127–143.

Liora Moriel, "Erasure and Taboo: A Queer Reading of *Bonnie and Clyde*" in Arthur Penn's *Bonnie and Clyde*. Cambridge, England: Cambridge UP. 2000. 148–176.

Film

American Gigolo (1980). Paul Schrader. 117 m.
Top Gun (1986). Tony Scott. 110 m.

Special Topics

Bob Rafelson's 1987 film *Black Widow* (103 m.), starring Debra Winger and Theresa Russell, is, like the films mentioned in this chapter and in the related reading, an ostensibly "straight" film whose sexual politics invite a queer reading. Both of the essays listed below offer nuanced and provocative readings of this film.

Readings

Cherry Symth, "The Transgressive Sexual Subject" in *A Queer Romance: Lesbians, Gay Men and Popular Culture*. Paul Burston and Colin Richardson, Eds. NY: Routledge. 1995. 123–143.

Valerie Traub, "The Ambiguities of 'Lesbian' Viewing Pleasure: The (Dis)articulations of Black Widow" in *Body Guards: The Cultural Politics of Gender Ambiguity*. Julia Epstein and Kristina Straub, Eds. NY: Routledge. 1991. 305–328.

■

Supporting Character

The Queer Career of Agnes Moorehead

Patricia White

The main character of Robert Aldrich's *The Killing of Sister George* is a role-playing lesbian in more than one sense. In "real life" June Buckridge (Beryl Reid) is "George," a bawdy, domineering, cigar-smoking butch, whose younger lover Childie keeps house and collects dolls. As the country nurse "Sister George" on a television soap opera, she is a character actress beloved by the public. Produced in 1968, on the verge of Stonewall and just in time to receive an X under the ratings system that finally replaced the Production Code, *The Killing of Sister George* is one of the first Hollywood films to represent lesbianism openly. But, in making its main character a character actress, the film suggests that lesbians may always have been present in popular culture, accepted and loved by audiences in genres that never admitted of the existence of homosexuality.

The film thematizes the continuity between the off-screen "masculine," tweed-suited dyke type and the on-screen "asexual," tweed-suited nurse type—thus George is able to appropriate her lesbian moniker from her television character—and demonstrates that the very construction of the "asexual" is, of course, a heterosexist one. At one point the drunken George makes a pass at a group of nuns in a taxicab—a scene that at once demonstrates her butch sexual courage and visibility and wittily restates the theme of covert and overt types. George ought to be able to recognize a sister when she sees one. In the film's lesbian bar scene, filmed on location and thus with extraordinary subcultural verisimilitude at London's Gateways Club—George and Childie dress up as Laurel and Hardy. This additional level of role-playing makes reference to a practice of comic typing that conceals homoerotic logic within a wildly popular mass cultural form.

When chic BBC executive Mercy Croft takes a fancy to Childie and has the Sister George character killed off the soap, following a familiar script of homophobic narrative exigency, the question of the actress's visibility as a lesbian is preempted. The supporting actress is offered instead the leading role in her very own series—as Clarabell the Cow. In Frank Marcus's play from which the film was adapted, Sister George was a character on a radio soap opera; the movie parallels the demotion from human to animal with the step down from on-camera ham to voice-over cow. Yet the role, however demeaning and misogynist, affords a certain finesse of George's disguise. At the end of the film, George, who had at first scornfully turned down the role of Clarabell, begins to practice her "moos." But even in her humiliation lies a certain triumph—her "unrepresentable" butch persona will still enter the homes of countless television viewers, her voice recognizable to her fans.

Agnes Moorehead was a familiar and popular television personality in the role of Endora on "Bewitched" when in one of the last of some sixty film roles she provided the voice of the goose in the animated feature *Charlotte's Web*. It was not a degrading part, as Clarabell Cow was meant to be—she co-starred with her "beloved friend" Debbie Reynolds, and Paul Lynde contributed to the barnyard fun. The role drew on her roots in radio—what one reviewer described as her trademark "crackling, snapping, sinister, paranoic, paralyzing voice."[1] And, before her stardom as television's preeminent witch, Moorehead reigned as one of the most widely recognized and highly regarded supporting actresses in Hollywood cinema. Like George, she played "types"; she was the

silver screen's definitive spinster aunt. In accounting for the adaptability of her
persona across a range of popular media, I believe that another element of
Moorehead's star image must be considered. In an interview with Boze
Hadleigh, "A Hollywood Square Comes Out," Lynde, a special guest star on
"Bewitched" who played an "uncle" as aptly and as memorably as Moorehead
played an "aunt," remarks, "Well, the whole world knows Agnes was a lesbian—I mean classy as hell, but one of the all-time Hollywood dykes."[2]

Regardless of whether the lady really was a lesbian, the characterization
complements her persona. It represents a gendered node within what Eve
Sedgwick has described as the modern Western "epistemology of the closet."[3]
If the "whole world" knows about Agnes, the so-called general audience may
exercise what Sedgwick calls "the privilege of unknowing"—after all, it's only
entertainment. I would like to argue that it is no mere queer coincidence that
Agnes Moorehead can be dubbed both one of the all-time Hollywood supporting actresses and one of the all-time Hollywood dykes. Moorehead is a prime
candidate for gay hagiography. Her best known incarnation, Endora, is a camp
icon; she passes even the cinephile test, having been featured in films by auteurs
such as Welles, Sirk, Ray, and Aldrich. But, more important, Moorehead's
ubiquity and longevity as a character actress are such that she can be identified
with the very media in which she triumphed, with the regime of popular entertainment itself, and with the continuities and ruptures in gender and sexual
ideology that can be read off from it. At once essential to classical realism
and marginal to its narrative goals, the supporting character is a site for the
encoding of the threat and the promise of female deviance. As New York lesbian performance artist Lisa Kron writes in a biographical note, reflecting on
the animal and grandmother roles she was asked to play in college, "It begins to
dawn on her that 'character actress' is really a code word for lesbian."[4] The negative valence of many of Moorehead's roles is marked—Endora herself is the
butt of a constant barrage of mother-in-law jokes. Her persona is less "heart-
warming" than many a golden age supporting actress—from Anne Revere to
Mary Wickes to Marjorie Main. Although the ideological stake in subordinating female difference is apparent, this negativity may also be Moorehead's most
subversive edge.

My discussion of Moorehead takes up three overlapping areas of inquiry:
the narrative function of supporting characters in the heterosexual Hollywood
regime (as well as the ideological weight that they carry in television's world of
family values); the importance of typification in these roles and in lesbian recognizability more generally; and the understanding of star images as complex,
contradictory signs, as exemplified in the work of gay film theorist Richard
Dyer as well as in the reception practices of gay culture.

What is it that supporting characters are meant to "support" if not the
imbricated ideologies of heterosexual romance and white American hegemony
permeating Hollywood cinema? They prop up a very particular representational order. As Stephen Heath describes the operation of narrativity, "The film
picks up . . . the notable elements (to be noted in and for the progress of the

narrative which in return defines their notability) without for all that giving up what is thus left aside and which it seeks to retain—something of an available reserve of insignificant material—in order precisely to ring 'true,' true to *reality.*" Retained to speak a social "truth," the supporting character represents "an available reserve of insignificant," if "realistic," types of women—workers, older women, nonwhite women. Lacking a love interest—Hollywood deems only one type of love of interest—she doesn't get "picked up" by the story: in the most basic narratological terms, she is the witch, not the princess. By film's end she has literally been left aside, just as she is compositionally marginal in the frame. For, as Heath economically puts it, "Narrative contains a film's multiple articulations as a single articulation, its images as a single image (the 'narrative image,' which is a film's presence, how it can be talked about, what it can be sold and bought on—in the production stills displayed outside a cinema, for example)."[5] Supporting characters are sacrificed to the narrative image of heterosexual closure; their names rarely appear in the television-guide blurbs about old movies, nor are their photographs included on the videotape box that delivers a "picture" to a potential viewer.

Yet attention to the function of certain types of female characters can throw into relief the single-mindedness with which the Hollywood system represents heterosexuality. For example, the discourse of lesbian desire introduced by housekeeper Mrs. Danvers (Judith Anderson) in Hitchcock's *Rebecca* significantly undercuts the film's conventional romantic "resolution." And, while melodramatic pathos depends on Jane Wyman's long separation from Rock Hudson in Sirk's *Magnificent Obsession,* an alternative reading—or a different focus of spectatorial regard—might note that she spends this off-screen time in the company of her devoted nurse/companion, played by Agnes Moorehead, who offered Wyman support in four films besides. A film may be dismissive of a minor player, portray her fate as gratuitous, but it may take less time and care to assimilate her to its ideological project than it would in the case of the female protagonist. In Hedda Hopper's column "Bit Player Outshines the Stars," Moorehead remarks, "I sort of look at myself sideways on the screen."[6] While this comment indicates a failure of narcissistic identification, even, perhaps, a cringing at the conservatism to which her image is often harnessed, it also suggests an astute reading of her liminal, and at times disruptive, narrative function. It replicates, too, the oblique sightline traced on Hollywood cinema by many queer spectators.

Nurses, secretaries, career women, nuns, companions, and housekeepers connote, not lesbian identity, but a deviation from heterosexualized femininity. Gay male critics often register an affinity with such characters. Inasmuch as character actresses are enjoyed, admired, or pressed into camp service by a queer mode of reading, it is apparently character itself that is supported. Thelma Ritter, a great ironic interpreter of this type of role, was a particular favorite of gay film historian Vito Russo, for example. In his book on the gay sensibility, Michael Bronski singles out the woman friend that "many top female stars were paired off with . . . before they ended up getting the leading man" as a cinematic type with particular appeal. Portrayed by the likes of Joan Blondell and Eve Arden, "the sidekick's role was generally to act as a confidante and to give the audience a pungent analysis of the plot. Sidekicks were sarcastic, unromantic, and sensible. They were cleverly self-deprecating . . . but could also turn the wit on men. Too smart ever to get the man, sidekicks had to settle for being funnier than everybody else. For gay men who would never walk off into the sunset with a leading man, the sidekick was a dose of real life." Bronski attributes a sort of metacritical role to confidante characters and a self-conscious reading practice to their fans, but he reads these images in relation only to male characters and spectators. He goes on to cite Russo's work on sissy roles and the actors who specialized in their portrayal in Hollywood films of the thirties and forties. Bronski asserts, "Woman sidekicks were never played as lesbians, just 'old maids,' but the non-romantic male was always implicitly gay."[7]

Given the virtual conceptual blank that is lesbianism in the culture at large, it is no accident that the social types standing in for lesbians in Hollywood cinema are misogynistically coded as "asexual." They are trivialized and rendered comical rather than threatening. Although sex and ideology certainly mark the stereotypes of sissy and old maid differently, in particular in relation to tropes of gender inversion, Bronski's statement limits the operation of the connotative in the female images and thus compounds the invisibility to which lesbians are already consigned.

In contrast, one lesbian writer confidently attributes sexuality to a much later incarnation of the "old maid" type. In a cover article for *Lesbian News* entitled "The Truth about Miss Hathaway," Marion Garbo Todd defends the spinster secretary character played by Nancy Kulp on the sixties American sitcom "The Beverly Hillbillies" from the following assessment in the fan magazine *Television Collector:* "Miss Jane Hathaway could have been the prototype for the term 'Plain Jane.' Tall and lanky, with an asexual manner, the epitome of a spinster." Todd retorts, "Where does this 'plain Jane' stuff come from? How can the word plain be used to describe the handsome Miss Hathaway? 'Tall and lanky' is not the right phrase for her body; 'long and sensuous' is much more accurate. Her long neck, aquiline nose, wavy hair, and large bright eyes made her very beautiful. She had smile lines to swoon over, and her voice was a delight. . . . In her tasteful skirt suit, short hairdo, and horn-rimmed glasses, she could have been the lead character in any lesbian pulp novel."[8]

Visual codes are recognized, enumerated, and deployed to cast Kulp in a leading role in a different genre. In her groundbreaking work on studio-era lesbian director Dorothy Arzner, Judith Mayne notes that, in her films, secondary women characters can be seen sporting the dapper dress and masculine manner that Arzner herself affected. Lesbianism is made visible within the text through ironic inflection of an "asexual" type.[9]

As Richard Dyer writes, in an essay on "typical" lesbian and gay representations, "A major fact about being gay is that it doesn't show. . . . There are signs of gayness, a repertoire of gestures, expressions, stances, clothing, and even environments that bespeak gayness, but these are cultural forms designed to show what the person's person alone does not show: that he or she is gay. Such a repertoire of signs, making visible the invisible, is the basis of any representation of gay people involving visual recognition, the requirement of recognizability in turn entailing that of typicality."[10] Thus, historically and culturally specific codes in lesbian and gay communities function similarly to the codes of recognition in popular cultural forms. In this light, the often-heard demand for nonstereotypical, "well-rounded" gay and lesbian characters in film may go against the very conditions of our visibility. Dyer detects the prevalence of the sexological discourse of "in-betweenism"—the notion that homosexuals betray characteristics of the opposite gender—in a range of typical visual representations, including self-representations, of effeminate men and mannish women. Citing *The Killing of Sister George*, he sees both George's tweeds and her rival Mercy Croft's chic and tailored predatory look as variations on this "dyke" type.[11] The vexed question of lesbian stereotyping can be related to the potentially subversive implications of more general practices of visual typing in female supporting characters.

The widespread apprehension of the Sister Georges or Miss Jane Hathaways as asexual or, worse, man starved—precisely invisible as lesbian—has to do, perhaps paradoxically, with the visual overdetermination of "woman" as sexual in film. The supporting character necessarily diverges from this ideal—not incidentally, a white one—of woman in film. The cinematic system of the look constructs the singular female star as image and guarantee of masculine desire and spectatorial fascination. As images of a different version of femininity than that of female stars, supporting characters may not ultimately be so supportive of the status quo, for they can inflect with female desire the image of woman embodied in the leading lady, with whom they are narratively paired and icono-graphically contrasted, often within the same frame.

One of the most consequential operations of Hollywood's containment and social enforcement of difference is the near-exclusive restriction of non-white and visually and audibly recognizable ethnic types precisely to supporting roles. Mary Ann Doane remarks that the "woman's film" genre is really the "white woman's film": "When black women are present, they are the ground rather than the figure; often they are made to merge with the diegesis. They inhabit the textual sidelines, primarily as servants."[12] The complexity, code crossing, and incoherence of racialized sexual and gender ideology is performed by the onscreen conjunction of, and contrast between, black and white women. The mammy stereotype, often denounced as "asexual," may be inflected as "lesbian" in its close articulation with the presentation of the white heroine's desire. Such a character, or a known performer such as Ethel Waters in a mammy role, might not merge altogether with the diegesis for African American, lesbian, and gay viewers.

A process of erotic doubling between a woman of color and the white star may also serve to figure lesbianism—for example, between Anna May Wong and Marlene Dietrich as traveling companions in *Shanghai Express*, in which the signifier *prostitution* sexualizes the contiguity of the two women. Or the racist projection of sexuality onto the "other woman" may indicate erotic tension between the stereotyped woman of color and the "repressed" and only presumptively heterosexual white heroine. Bette Davis's character performs two passionate acts in *The Letter*—she kills her lover in the opening sequence and goes into the night to meet her death at the hands of his Asian widow at the end. While the man in the triangle is never shown, the "other" woman's body is insistently present, bizarrely underscored by the excessive makeup and costuming used to transform white supporting actress Gale Sondergaard. This common casting practice foregrounds the way in which the representation of racial difference turns on the attributes of whiteness in the classical Hollywood cinema. In *Beyond the Forest*, the Davis character's long, center-parted black hair is uncannily mirrored in the background by that of her mocking Latina maid, played by Mexican actress Dona Drake. At a crucial point in the story, the heroine disguises herself in the jeans and flannel shirt worn by her servant. That the masquerade involves an element of gender transgression ironically makes visible the irreducible difference between women—race, class, and power—that appears to give such doubling its frisson.

Judith Mayne goes on to discuss how images of Dorothy Arzner—often two-shots of her looking at a conventionally feminine actress—have been used to illustrate feminist critical texts that emphatically do not mention her lesbianism. When these lesbian looks, these exchanges of the gaze between contrasting female types—generally between supporting and lead actresses—are echoed in Arzner's films, Mayne argues, they can be read as her authorial signature. In a two-shot from Raoul Walsh's *The Revolt of Mamie Stover*, the look of Agnes Moorehead in her bathrobe prevents Jane Russell's sexuality from being perceived as intended for the male spectator alone. Yet the early feminist analysis of this film, too, ignored its lesbian visual economy. In another two-shot, Agnes Moorehead and Debbie Reynolds embody the visual relation between a supporting actress "type" and a bona fide female star. On-screen and off, the couple conforms to the stereotype of older, sapphic sophisticate who preys on innocent younger woman, in this case the singing nun.

While great Hollywood supporting actresses such as Thelma Ritter or Mercedes McCambridge could perhaps be read as working-class butch or fifties in-betweenist types, Agnes Moorehead's persona fits a more upper-class sapphic stereotype.[13] As a promotional item describes her, "Rated as one of the best dressed stars of screen and radio, her preference runs to tailored suits"—to recall Lynde's words, she was "classy as hell." On-screen, the spinster type refuses both the masculine signifiers that make lesbianism visible in heterosexual terms and the hyperbolization of the feminine that is the very definition of *womanliness*. The type is a product of a misogynist and heterosexist imagination—yet within it the spinster can at once "pass" as straight and be recognizable as lesbian.

It is impossible to unpack the ambivalent character of the narrative category of *support* and the negotiable aspects of visual typification apart from a consideration of the performer as text. Donald Bogle, in *Toms, Coons, Mulattos, Mammies and Bucks*, his influential book on African American stereotypes, presents the most sustained argument for how particular performers become visible in these roles and transform types. As he states in an interview, "There was another life and point of view that was being suggested to me by Hattie Mc-Daniel's rather hostile edge."[14] It is Ritter's nurses, Arden's sidekicks, Franklin Pangborn's sissies, and McDaniel's maids that capture the imagination. The more roles an actress appears in, the more unforeseen the effects that are introduced in a particular text by her casting. Star texts are ongoing, modified by shifting ideological imperatives, shaped by audience response. On series television, the weekly appearance of the performer works like typecasting in studio films. It is in this sense that I want to speak of Moorehead's *queer career*.

In his work on stars, Dyer argues that, in narrative films, novelistic conceptions of character are articulated with stars as already signifying images—which essentially function within the same bourgeois ideology of the self-consistent individual. How might this approach apply to Moorehead, who, as a character actress, however familiar, is not strictly a "star"? As Dyer notes, "Type characters are acknowledged to have a place . . . but only to enable the proper elaboration of the central, individuated character(s). In this respect, no star could be just a type, since all stars play central characters."[15] Moorehead does not have a fully individuated star image (at least not before "Bewitched"), yet neither can her onscreen type be considered merely an extension of her off-screen "self" (which would reintroduce the category of the individual in another way). She has a subversive edge that does not get "rounded off." What was distinct was the fact of her *acting*, which allowed her to represent and to "quote" a type at the same time.

Agnes Moorehead's long career encompassed a gallery of types connoting female difference. Her early success was achieved on radio as, among other things, a stooge to male comics. After she went to Hollywood with Orson Welles and the Mercury Theater, she continued her radio work as an all-purpose female voice, impersonating Eleanor Roosevelt and scores of other women on the "March of Time." Outside the Hollywood regime of the gaze, it seems that a deviant version of femininity could represent the norm. Onscreen, she never portrayed a central character, receiving top billing only in the posthumously released horror flick *Dear Dead Delilah*. Instead, she played second fiddle, variations on the unmarried woman: nurses (*Magnificent Obsession*), nuns (*The Singing Nun, Scandal at Scourie*), governesses (*The Youngest Profession, The Untamed*), ladies' companions (*Mrs. Parkington, Her Highness and the Bellboy*), busybodies (*Since You Went Away, All That Heaven Allows*), hypochondriacs (*Pollyanna*), maids (*Hush, Hush, Sweet Charlotte*), and, of course, aunts.

In *The Magnificent Ambersons*, Jack Amberson rebukes his nephew for tormenting the Moorehead character: "You know George, just being an aunt isn't really the great career it may sometimes seem to be." But this, her second film, launched the actress on a trajectory that proved otherwise. Despite her fifth billing, she was named best actress by the New York Film Critics and went on to play aunts again in *Jane Eyre, Tomorrow the World, The Lost Moment, Summer Holiday, Johnny Belinda,* and *The Story of Three Loves,* and on Broadway in *Gigi* just before her death. For variety, she portrayed women in professions that lesbians might suitably pursue: a WAC commander (*Keep Your Powder Dry*), a prison superintendent (*Caged*), a literary agent (*From Main Street to Broadway*), a drama teacher (*Jeanne Eagels*), a mystery writer (*The Bat*), a judge (*Bachelor in Paradise*), and, in a blond wig, a "sort of school marm and madam rolled into one," offering firm support to Jane Russell's Mamie Stover.[16] When she played married women, she was generally a nagging wife, most notably in the radio play *Sorry, Wrong Number,* written expressly for her talents. Critics note the "waspish and neurotic," "mean-spirited, shrewish," "possessive, puritanical, and vitriolic," "bitter, nasty, frustrated," and "meddlesome" traits of her "old crones," "harridans, spinsters and bitches," "termagants and passionate viragos." Her many mother parts did not always evince maternal qualities. Besides Samantha, her screen offspring included Citizen Kane, Jesse James, and Genghis Khan. Her role in *The Story of Mankind* was a brief appearance as Queen Elizabeth I; she commissioned a portrait of herself costumed as the red-haired virgin queen.

The Agnes Moorehead of the "Bewitched" era (the show ran on ABC from 1964 to 1972) can aptly be described with the title of her one-woman show, in which she toured extensively in the fifties—"The Fabulous Redhead." On "Bewitched," she was a flippant, vividly costumed, outrageously madeup, impeccably coiffed, castrating witch with a mortal hatred for her daughter's husband, whose name she somehow could not recall. This is the Moorehead-as-"character" association that the contemporary viewer brings to her earlier film roles. Moorehead turned her Actress-with-a-capital-A stage image—regal bearing, exaggerated gestures and enunciation, and taste for high fashion—to high camp effect in her interpretation of Endora, flagrantly foregrounding "performance." Offscreen, she was nicknamed "Madame Mauve" because of her inordinate fondness for lavender, which she insisted on having everything "done" in—from her luggage and Thunderbird to her dressing room lightbulbs and maids' uniforms.[17]

Before the fifties stage and sixties television brought color to her roles, Agnes Moorehead was considered an actress of "character." Her Victorian-sounding name (her father was a minister), aristocratic profile, penchant for accents and other vocal trademarks, her manners, even manneredness, contributed to the public perception of Moorehead as a "serious" actress. As one critic notes, she is associated with "heavy dramatics on the grand scale. For many, Agnes's performances represent the near epitome of screen theatrics."[18] Although she was "typecast," versatility was regarded as part of her artistry.[19] A studio publicity item raved, "The accomplished character actress of stage, screen and radio is given here one of her rare opportunities to bid for romantic interest. The result is a revelation of a new facet of the versatile actress's many-sided repertory, strikingly effective."[20] The implication is that her ability to portray a heterosexual is a true sign of talent.

Moorehead was distinguished by four Academy Award nominations for best actress in a supporting role, although she never won the Oscar. As six-time loser Thelma Ritter cracked, "Always the bridesmaid and never the bride."[21] A profile in a nostalgia magazine muses about the fact that Moorehead never snagged the award: "It is an interesting speculation that one of the reasons she always lost was that she played neurotic aunts, stepmothers, spinsters who reflected the dark side of the human condition."[22] That the old maid should evoke such a grandiose conception as the dark side of the human condition attests to Moorehead's considerable achievement—she makes the spinster positively sinister. In an essay on the functions of feminist criticism, Tania Modleski chastises a male literary critic who, "casting about for an example of the trivial, strikes irresistibly upon the image of the spinster." "From a feminist point of view," Modleski argues, "nothing could be *more* 'historically and ideologically significant' than the existence of the single woman in patriarchy, her (frequently caricatured) representation in patriarchal art, and the relationship between the reality and the representation."[23] Moorehead's image captured some of this, perhaps lesbian, significance, if only in the mirror image of anxiety. The profile goes on to suggest how closely the spinster image was identified with the actress: "Never married, she, nevertheless, had an adopted son; a close friendship with Debbie Reynolds, with whom she co-starred in several of her last pictures; and a religious faith as a Methodist." This "nevertheless" means to blur over a logical relation between spinster and lesbian that the syntax sets up: "Never married, she had a close friendship with Debbie Reynolds." The statement is interesting for another reason: its blatant, symptomatic contradiction of fact, for Agnes Moorehead was married at least twice (Reynolds mentions three unions). I presume that the actress's much-vaunted privacy and cultivated "mystery" were not intended to conceal this facet of her "many-side repertory."

Moorehead's image reconciles the serious with the trivial—having "character" with being "a character"—and thus occupies the domain of camp. As Susan Sontag notes, "Camp is the glorification of 'character.' . . . Character is understood as a state of continual incandescence—a person being one, very intense thing. . . . Wherever there is development of character, Camp is reduced."[24] Camp is a crucial and far from trivial dimension of Moorehead's reception, but, with its emphasis on style, it is an insufficient analytic category for a feminist consideration of what is at stake in the "content" of her image. Looking at how that image was articulated in and utilized by certain of her films can illuminate the contradiction that she embodies, as a figure simultaneously necessary to the Hollywood system and suppressed by it. She is taken seriously, featured in so many films as to seem ubiquitous. At the same time, her parts are marginal ones, the characters she portrays trivialized or vilified. If her roles as written often smack of misogyny, as performed they suggest a different negativity—a negativity that cannot be represented within the terms of classical cinema and that shares the semiotic field of lesbianism.

Fanny Minnafer in Orson Welles's *The Magnificent Ambersons* is the role that established at once Moorehead's reviled spinster image *and* the difficulty of reconciling that image with the Hollywood plot. Lacking economic independence, Aunt Fanny lives with the fading Amberson clan as an observer rather than as a participant. *The Magnificent Ambersons* is a self-conscious film, and her restlessness and discontent contribute greatly to its mood. She accuses her nephew George, "You wouldn't treat anybody in the world like this, except old Fanny. 'Old Fanny,' you say, 'it's nobody but old Fanny so I'll kick her. Nobody'll resent it, I'll kick her all I want to.' " But the film inscribes Fanny's position on the periphery—lurking in the shadows to whisper her suspicions to George, looking on from the edge of the frame or the background of the composition—as a vantage point for the spectator. She actually prevents the formation of two heterosexual couples by her interference. In material excised from the film's release version, Fanny is shown at the end among a veritable colony of spinsters at the boarding house. Her discourse pervades the film, even if she triumphs only as the representative of its themes of frustration and barrenness.

One commentator characterizes the challenge for Moorehead as an actress, "to channel her tremendous energy so that it would emerge in accord with the film rather than as an intriguing distraction."[25] Elements of her tour-de-force characterization of Aunt Fanny erupt as fascinating "distractions" in such later roles as Mrs. Reed in *Jane Eyre* and Countess Fosco in *The Woman in White*. The question of Moorehead's discordant difference and of her relation to the fulfillment of the romance plot is marked in another literary film, *The Lost Moment* (1947). In this adaptation of Henry James's *The Aspern Papers*, Moorehead plays the elderly aunt who in her youth was the recipient of love letters from a famous poet. A mere octogenarian in the novella becomes a hideously madeup 105-year-old in the film. It is as if the plausibility of Moorehead's participation in such a romance even in the past demands extremes of disguise.

Moorehead thoroughly embraced that inexplicable quality of her characters that prompted others to react with dislike, even phobia. In *Since You Went Away* (directed by John Cromwell, 1944), David O. Selznick's sentimental story of women on the homefront during World War II, Agnes portrays a local busybody, a character who embodies a displaced anxiety about the unheroic activities in which women might become involved while the menfolk are away at war. Joseph Cotten's character repeatedly insults her, joking that the sound of her voice grates on him even when he's far away from her. The penetrating, persecuting female voice signifies here not only as a quality of Moorehead's character, Emily Hawkins, but as Moorehead as an actress, who often worked with Cotten. Ultimately, the disparate desires of the women in the film are rallied into patriotic solidarity when they castigate the Moorehead character for petty war profiteering. The film scapegoats her to consolidate both nationalist and gender ideology, a project that could be seen as operating across the forties, the period in which Moorehead's image was established.

In *Good Dames,* his book on five female "character stars" (supporting actresses rarely receive individual biographies), James Robert Parish comments on Moorehead's performance in this film:

> The role itself was a variation of the cinema type portrayed throughout the 1940s by the very adept Eve Arden. The difference in these two actresses' approach to such a part is that whenever Agnes is required to make a flip remark on the screen, it comes across in total seriousness as a reflection of her character's basic, unregenerate meanness. Her piercing eyes and overall body movements provide the viewer with no other interpretation. In contrast, Arden can toss off the most devastating remark, and it emerges as a pert observation, juicy and smart, but essentially nonvicious.[26]

Although Moorehead did play essentially nonvicious roles, she was more convincing—and less recuperable—in her moments of unregenerate meanness. The subversiveness of the best character stars, such as Arden and Ritter, can be neutralized by their being enthusiastically adopted as cuddly curmudgeons. Moorehead's unlikableness, on the razor-thin edge of misogynist dismissal, contravenes this tendency. It is hard to embrace Moorehead without being spattered with acid.

Madge Rapf in the Bogart/Bacall vehicle *Dark Passage* (1947), directed by Delmar Daves, is a curious sort of femme fatale, whose fate is a telling example of the retribution that the Moorehead character could bring down. Moorehead's being cast against character in a "sexual" role is in part responsible for the film's surreal effects.[27] As Dana Polan comments in an important analysis, "The narrative of *Dark Passage* is one in which dramatic coincidences occur so often as to break down any question of plausibility."[28] When Madge happens to knock at the door of the apartment where, through an unlikely chain of circumstances, escaped convict Vincent Parry (Bogart) is hiding, he instantly recognizes the voice of his nemesis. Madge had testified against him at his murder trial. As he observes, "She's the type that comes back, and back again." This not only indicates how she functions in the film as the return of the repressed but is a fitting comment on Moorehead's career.

Madge's character is attributed with the evil, inconsistency, and unintelligibility of motive of an ordinary femme fatale, without the movie conceding that sexuality is her tool for leading men to destruction. Instead, her fatal quality seems to be the simple fact of her existence, rendered as "interference" through Moorehead's "nagging" connotations. As Vincent describes her, "Madge knows everybody, pesters everybody." Her ex-fiancé, Bob, snaps at her, "You're not satisfied unless you're bothering people. I'm annoyed whenever I see you." Responding to her concern that Parry will try to kill her, Bob remarks, with an extraordinary mixture of outright malignance and contemptuous dismissal, "You're the last person he wants to see, let alone kill. . . . You're not the type that makes people hate." Her insignificance is thus marked in rather significant terms. It is as if the other characters recognize the difficulty of integrating her in the plot. Vincent muses, "Maybe she'll get run over or something." And his wish is granted.

In this profoundly illogical film, the logic of misogyny works with classic simplicity; it can be placated only by Madge's abjection, by the spectacle of her death. When Vincent comes to her apartment to accuse *her* of murdering his wife, she defies him to prove it. At her crowning moment of Moorehead histrionics, she "accidently" and quite improbably falls through a picture window, with a flounce of floor-length drapes. The camera dwells on her body's descent, a markedly excessive cinematic flourish. Polan has commented on the ambiguity and threat embodied in domestic space in forties films: "Significantly, in several films, murder, suicide, and accidental death through windows blur (and not only for the characters but also for the spectator), thereby suggesting the ambivalence of sense." He captures something of the spectator's bewilderment in this instance: "In *Dark Passage*, for example, it is never clear (even with motion-analyzing equipment and freeze-framing) how Madge manages to fall through her apartment window to her death."[29]

Dark Passage plays out the film noir's generic fear of feminine difference. The hero is vindicated, and woman is both criminal and victim. However, here it is not the alluring but the annoying woman who is punished, an extreme case of the anxiety that the Moorehead character could provoke. Madge, as a "bad," superfluous woman, is marked for death from the beginning. But for all that it is an almost mundane exigency of plot, her killing seems to require a supernatural force, thereby foregrounding the ideology that demands it. And Madge's fall doesn't immediately benefit the hero; it has something of the quality of a self-willed disappearance. Madge threatens, "You will never be able to prove anything because I won't be there."

Here, I would like to quote the late, legendary underground gay filmmaker and Hollywood camp tastemaker Jack Smith:

> I'm being haunted now by a performance in a movie. It was in *Dark Passage*. Agnes Moorehead plays this pest. . . . In a huge close-up you see the twitch of her little purse of a mouth. [Movies] can reveal a certain personality type—a certain kind of pest or what have you—and then you have something to remember when you see a person in life. . . . That happened to me just recently. This raging pest from the Gay Men's Health Crisis just called and said she'd be right over. . . . The poor creature, her life was so empty that she had to join the Gay movement to pester AIDS victims in order to have a social life. Right away I looked at her and thought of Madge in *Dark Passage*."[30]

Smith relates the star and the practice of cinematic typification to real life and to a gay context, using her quality of "intensity" to make sense of some aspect of the tragically implausible but all too real and very dark passage that is living with AIDS.

John Cromwell's *Caged* (1950) features Moorehead as Mrs. Benton, the efficient and smartly tailored head of a woman's prison, but here her philanthropic impulse is benevolent and welcome. In such an environment, among female deviates, Moorehead's persona is not pitted against other women but appears at its most benign. This is also the most overtly lesbian of her films—it establishes a genuine genre—and Moorehead receives second billing. Like *The Killing of Sister George* or the lesbian classic *Maedchen in Uniform* with its conflict between stern headmistress and compassionate teacher, this feminist drama opposes two "dyke" types in a struggle for control over the young heroine (Eleanor Parker). The sympathetic, reform-minded prison superintendent tries to protect innocent Marie Allen from the corruptions of life inside. "You'll find all kinds of women in here, just as you would outside," Benton promises. Hope Emerson portrays Evelyn Harper, the sadistic matron in uniform who provides small comforts for her girls in exchange for payment. Of this remarkable six-foot, two-inch, 230-pound character actress (who, incidentally, provided the voice of Elsie the Borden cow), gay porn editor and film critic Boyd MacDonald writes, "Perhaps only members of a sexual elite—that is, outlaws—can instinctively appreciate the grandeur of an Emerson."[31] In one scene, Harper, grotesquely dressed up for her night off, describes in detail her upcoming "date" in order to taunt the imprisoned women. This attribution of heterosexuality, like the photograph of a "husband" displayed on Moorehead's desk, can easily be read as an out-and-out charade.

When Benton attempts to fire Harper, the latter leaks a scandalous tale to the press: "Matron charges immorality," headlines blare. "Blames superintendent." The article is accompanied by a singularly apt sketch of Benton/Moorehead's face encircled by a huge question mark. The unspoken questions dogging Moorehead's persona are here explicitly tied to a story full of "filthy lies" that euphemistically signify lesbianism.

In this classic struggle between good and evil, Harper is finally stabbed by a prisoner. But, in the meantime, Marie has gone bad—the beginning of her defiance marked when her kitten is crushed in a riot provoked by Harper's attempt to snatch Fluff away from her. Marie finally accepts the attentions of the vice queen Kitty, who arranges for her parole. Forced to relinquish her wedding ring when she went to prison, Marie tosses it away when it is returned on her release. Benton tells her devoted secretary to keep Marie's file active: "She'll be back." Ultimately, different tropes of lesbian seduction—nurturance and dominance—represented by different types of character actresses, Moorehead and Emerson, work in consort to keep the female community intact. In *Caged*, Moorehead's character can represent the film's moral center because here she presides over a homosocial world and, fittingly, over an extraordinarily talented female supporting cast.

While the pleasures of reading Moorehead's ornery forties persona are obviously augmented by her syndication canonization in "Bewitched," both her situation and its comedy on that show are made possible by the character of her prior Hollywood career. Writing on the popularization of camp taste in the sixties and on *Whatever Happened to Baby Jane?* in particular, Andrew Ross claims, "The camp effect. . . . is created. . . . when the products (stars, in this case) of a much earlier mode of production, which has lost its power to dominate cultural meanings, become available.... for redefinition to contemporary codes of taste."[32] Of Robert Aldrich's follow-up to *Baby Jane*, *Hush, Hush Sweet Charlotte*, produced the year "Bewitched" debuted, Bosley Crowther ranted, "Agnes Moorehead as [Bette Davis's] weird and crone like servant is allowed to get away with some of the broadest mugging and snarling ever done by a respectable actress on the screen. If she gets an Academy Award for this performance . . . the Academy should close up shop!"[33] The slatternly Velma Cruther significantly reverses an important element of Moorehead's image—her fastidiousness. In a cycle in which the biggest female stars travestied their former images, it is appropriate for one of the great supporting actresses to play a classic supporting role, the loyal servant, in a spectacularly unsupportive manner—to indulge in upstaging and scenery chewing that puts Davis herself to shame. Velma may be killed off for her snooping by a fall nearly as dramatic as that in *Dark Passage*, but icons never die.

One of Moorehead's last films, scripted by Henry Farrell, who wrote *Baby Jane*, continues this self-conscious exploitation of her image. Set in the thirties, *What's the Matter with Helen?* (directed by Curtis Harrington, 1971) features Debbie Reynolds and Shelley Winters as the mothers of two convicted thrill killers in the Leopold and Loeb mode, who move to Hollywood to escape their past. Reynolds, intrigued by the story, which was originally titled *Best of Friends*, persuaded her friend Agnes Moorehead to play powerful radio evangelist Sister Alma. The "matter" with Helen concerns not only her psychopathic murderous tendencies but her fanatical devotion to the evangelist's message and, surprise, her lesbian love for her best friend. The role and the project thus summed up a number of strong components of the Moorehead persona: radio, religion, the famous personality, lesbianism, the relationship with Reynolds.

Endora represents the culmination of Moorehead meddlesomeness. In the premiere episode of "Bewitched," she repeatedly evicts Samantha's husband from the honeymoon suite, and she literally casts a dark shadow over heterosexual relations each week when her credit "and Agnes Moorehead as Endora" appears on a black cloud of smoke blotting out "Derwood" and Samantha's embrace. What's-his-name's anxiety about his wife's powers are well founded: she belongs to a matriarchal order of superior beings. "Bewitched" supported a veritable gay subculture among its "funny" witch and warlock character actors. A recent "Bewitched"-kitsch revival attests to the show's influence on the queer nation generation. In a recent interview with the Los Angeles lesbian and gay newsweekly the *Advocate*, star Elizabeth Montgomery even agreed that the show's premise was "the ultimate closet story."[34]

If Moorehead's earlier characters were outside the central action, Endora is transcendently ex-centric. As Pat Mellencamp writes, in the situation comedy, "expectation of pleasurable performance. . . . rather than narrative suspense [is the] currency of audience exchange."[35] Endora has an enunciative role in the series. Casting spells on small-minded mortals, she disrupts the couple's petty suburban lives and generates the weekly plot. She appears and disappears with a flutter of the wrist—her ability to materialize when least expected or to drop out of the picture altogether is almost a commentary on the disappearing act that "incidental" characters performed in countless Hollywood films.

From stern spinster to fabulous redhead to silly goose, Agnes Moorehead's queer career attests to the ideological, narratological, and iconographic congruence among old maid, witch, and lesbian. Her star image also appeals to lesbian and gay audiences because it connotes acting itself—artifice, impersonation, and exaggeration. I do not wish to suggest that the characters that Moorehead portrayed "really were" lesbians, nor to imply that lesbians can simply recover our presence in Hollywood cinema by identifying actresses who really were lesbians, although gossip in its many forms is a legitimate text to be read. Rather, the peculiarities of Moorehead's image and the enthusiasms that it has generated illustrate how supporting characters were essential but also potentially disruptive to the construction of sexual difference in classical cinema. They were the types who were meant to remain invisible so that the codes of Hollywood's heterosexual contract would also remain invisible. By resituating such performers in patriarchal domesticity, American television often ended up broadcasting forms of queer performativity. Gay criticism and culture have been alert to the pleasures and resistances embodied in star signs. Feminist film theory has explicated the patriarchal construction of woman *as* image—and demonstrated the difficulty of articulating female desire and difference in relation to that construction. An exploration of the paradoxical conditions of lesbian representability in popular culture might fruitfully draw on both approaches. Whether playing it straight or camping it up, Agnes Moorehead is quite a character, "the type that comes back, and back again," as an insistent reminder of the price of heterosexual presumption.

Postscript

The television "personality" remains a privileged locus of lesbian and gay iconic signification, as a recent, metatextual example shows. On the top-rated ABC sitcom "Roseanne," Nancy, a supporting character played by Sandra Bernhard—a notorious real-life, role-playing queer—declared that she is a lesbian. Yet, in putting forward an overt lesbian characterization, in this age of outing and the representational politics of acting up, the show draws on a covert one. At first surprised by her friend's announcement, Roseanne then recalls a code in which the coming-out message is intelligible: "Nancy always did like that Miss Jane Hathaway on 'The Beverly Hillbillies.' That about says it all."

Notes

For Montana Silkwood. Thanks to Lisa Cohen and Cynthia Schneider for their helpful comments.

1. Quoted in Warren Sherk, *Agnes Moorehead: A Very Private Person* (Philadelphia: Dorrance, 1976), 73.

2. While filming *How Sweet It Is* on an ocean liner, Lynde recounts, "At night, we'd sit around and dish. [Director] Jerry [Paris] told me those rumors that everybody's heard about Debbie [Reynolds] and her *close friend* Agnes Moorehead. . . . I'd heard those rumors, but Jerry filled in some details that. . . . Oh, I'd better not, I'm not even sure if the story's really true" (*Outlook* 6 [Fall 1989]: 26). Hadleigh claims that Reynolds threatened to sue Eddie Fisher if he included the story in his autobiography.

Reynolds herself reports the "innuendo" that she and Moorehead were lovers without explicitly denying it (see Debbie Reynolds with David Patrick Columbia, *My Life* [New York: Pocket, 1988], 388). Moorehead repeatedly discussed "why I adore Debbie Reynolds" (interview with Sidney Skolsky, *New York Post*, 2 August 1964), avowing, "It's really the loneliest sort of life. . . . I did become good friends with Debbie Reynolds" (*New York Post*, 11 January 1969). The friendship is generally considered a salient fact about Moorehead. The two women "became close friends, in a mother-daughter type relationship" (James Robert Parish, *Good Dames* [New Brunswick, N.J.: Barnes, 1974], 122).

As corroboration goes, there is no more than ample documentation of the *rumor* in the gay press: "Hollywood knew her as its reigning lesbian, queen of Sapphic love. ('Who was Carrie Fisher's mother?' the old joke went. 'Debbie Reynolds. Who was her father? Agnes Moorehead')" (*NYQ*, 22 December 1991, 4I). Dick Sargent, the second actor to play Samantha's mortal husband on "Bewitched," who recently came out in *People* and on "Entertainment Tonight" as well as in the gay press, was unable to confirm the tales about Moorehead's lesbianism. The knowledge that Darrin, the show's representative of put-upon normalcy, was played by a gay actor literalizes what the *Advocate* calls the "gay allegory" of "Bewitched" (30 July 1992, 69). In a gracious interview with the lesbian and gay news weekly on the occasion of her serving with Sargent as grand marshall of the Los Angeles lesbian and gay pride parade, star Elizabeth Montgomery notes, "Don't think that didn't enter our minds at the time. We talked about it on the set . . . that this was about people not being allowed to be what they really are . . . and all the frustration and trouble it can cause. It was a neat message to get across" (ibid., 69). Asked about Moorehead's lesbianism, Montgomery replies, "I've heard the rumors, but I never talked with her about them. . . . It was never anything she felt free enough to talk to me about. I wish . . . that Agnes felt she could trust me. . . . We were very fond of one another, but it never got personal." In characteristically grande dame fashion, Moorehead herself wrote, "I have played so many authoritative and strong characters that some people are nervous at the prospect of meeting me. . . . There is a certain amount of aloofness on my part at times, because an actor can so easily be hurt by unfair criticism. I think an artist should be kept separated to maintain glamour and a kind of mystery. . . . I don't believe in the girl-next-door image. What the actor has to sell to the public is fantasy, a magic kind of ingredient that should not be analyzed" (quoted in the *New York Times* obituary, I May 1974, 48).

Outside of gay publications, what often appears in place of any remarks about Moorehead's sexuality is an emphasis on her religious beliefs (see Herbie J. Pilato, *The Bewitched Book* [New York: Delta, 1992], 24–26). That Moorehead was devout is not in question. But religion seems to appear as a defense against a homosexual reading, as the very emblem and safeguard of spinsterishness. Ann B. Davis, who played Alice, the housekeeper who resembled a physical education teacher, on

"The Brady Bunch" (and before portrayed Schultzy on "The Bob Cummings Show"), has also enjoyed a surge in appreciation. In a recent update, she is reported as having shared a home since 1976 with an Episcopal bishop and his wife. "The three are dedicated to prayer and Bible study." She "never married" and admits, "I basically don't do that well with children, although my sister [identical twin Harriet] says I'm a great aunt" (*People*, 1 June 1992, 86).

Material on Moorehead cited throughout this essay was found in clippings files at the New York Public Library for the Performing Arts and the Museum of Modern Art Film Study Center.

3. Eve Kosofsky Sedgwick, *Epistemology of the Closet* (Berkeley: University of California Press, 1990).

4. Lisa Kron, *Program*, "101 Humiliating Stories," performed at P.S. 122, New York City, January 7–31, 1993.

5. Stephen Heath, *Questions of Cinema* (Bloomington: Indiana University Press, 1981), 135, 121.

6. Agnes Moorehead clippings file, New York Public Library for the Performing Arts.

7. Michael Bronski, *Culture Clash: The Making of Gay Sensibility* (Boston: South End, 1984), 102. See also chapter 1, "Who's a Sissy?" of Vito Russo, *The Celluloid Closet* (New York: Harper & Row, 1981).

8. Marion Garbo Todd, "The Truth about Miss Hathaway: The Fascination of Television's Perennial Spinster," *Lesbian News* 16, no. 10 (May 1991): 40.

9. See Sarah Halprin, "Writing in the Margins" (review of E. Ann Kaplan, *Women and Film: Both Sides of the Camera*), *Jump Cut* 29 (February 1984): 32, cited in Judith Mayne, "Lesbian Looks: Dorothy Arzner and Female Authorship," in *How Do I Look?* ed. Bad Object Choices (Seattle: Bay, 1991), 115. Mayne's argument about Arzner also appears in chapter 3, "Female Authorship Reconsidered," of her book *Woman at the Keyhole* (Bloomington: Indiana University Press, 1990).

10. Richard Dyer, "Seen to Be Believed: Some Problems in the Representation of Gay People as Typical," *Visual Communication* 9, no. 2 (Spring 1983): 2. See also his "Stereotyping" in *Gays in Film*, ed. Richard Dyer (London: BFI, 1978; rev., 1984), 27–39; and T.E. Perkins, "Rethinking Stereotypes," in *Ideology and Cultural Production*, ed. Michèle Barrett et al. (New York: St. Martin's, 1979), 135–59.

11. Dyer, "Seen to Be Believed," 8.

12. Mary Ann Doane, "Dark Continents: Epistemologies of Racial and Sexual Difference in Psychoanalysis and the Cinema," in *Femmes Fatales: Feminism, Film Theory, Psycho-analysis* (New York: Routledge, 1991), 233.

13. Ritter was a member of the early lesbian community on Fire Island documented in Esther Newton's study *Cherry Grove, Fire Island: Sixty Years in America's First Gay and Lesbian Town* (Boston: Beacon, 1993). McCambridge's career encompasses a series of telling roles: the unforgettable Emma Small in *Johnny Guitar*, an uncredited bit in Welles's *Touch of Evil* as a leather-jacketed onlooker at Janet Leigh's rape, a guest spot as mom to an effeminate warlock on "Bewitched," another as the woman who wanted to marry Dr. Smith on "Lost in Space," and the voice of the devil in *The Exorcist*.

That Ritter and McCambridge were radio performers like Moorehead suggests an interesting dialectic between lesbian representability and literal visibility.

14. Lisa Jones, "The Defiant Ones: A Talk with Film Historian Donald Bogle," *Village Voice* (June 1991): 69. See Donald Bogle, *Toms, Coons, Mulattoes, Mammies*

    and Bucks: An Interpretive History of Blacks in American Films (1973; New York: Continuum, 1992).

15. Richard Dyer, *Stars* (London: BFI, 1979), 117; see also 109–10.

16. The comment that character actors are a "brassiere for the star, literally holding him or her up," is difficult to resist quoting in this case (Hortense Powdermaker, *Hollywood: The Dream Factory* [New York: Little, Brown, 1950], 206, quoted in Barry King, "Articulating Stardom," in *Stardom: Industry of Desire*, ed. Christine Gledhill [New York: Routledge, 1991], 179).

17. See Sherk, *Agnes Moorehead*, 70. In Charles Laughton's bio of Moorehead for *Don Juan in Hell*, in which they toured extensively in the early fifties, he writes about her days as a drama student in New York: "She was kind of mad around this time, not because she had to pull in her belt notches, but because she hadn't enough money to buy mauve lace, and mauve taffeta and mauve velvet and mauve feathers and geegaws which are a necessity to Agnes Moorehead's breathing."

18. James Robert Parish, *Good Dames*, 78.

19. The Agnes Moorehead fan club's publication was originally entitled "Versatility," as noted in an issue of "Moorehead Memos," a later incarnation of the club's newsletter.

20. Unidentified clipping, Agnes Moorehead Clipping File, Museum of Modern Art Film Study Center, n.p.

21. Quoted in Mason Wiley and Damien Bona, *Inside Oscar* (New York: Ballantine, 1986), 241.

22. *Classic Images* 136 (October 1986): 18.

23. Tania Modleski, *Feminism without Women* (New York: Routledge, 1991), 50.

24. Susan Sontag, "Notes on Camp," in *Against Interpretation* (New York: Farrar, Straus, Giroux, 1975), 283.

25. James Robert Parish, *Good Dames*, 84.

26. James Robert Parish, *Good Dames*, 90.

27. In another revealing comparison, Parish notes that *Dark Passage* gave Moorehead an "opportunity to portray . . . a woman close to her own age without disguising costumes, makeup or foreign accents. . . . Here was a jealous, sex-starved characterization that the electric Dame Judith Anderson would have been proud to play in her heyday" (ibid., 94). Charles Higham and Joel Greenberg acknowledge that "Agnes Moorehead's prying, vicious Madge Rapf is a definitive portrait of bitchery" (*Hollywood in the Forties* [New York: Barnes, 1968], 39).

28. Dana Polan, *Power and Paranoia: History, Narrative, and the American Cinema, 1940–1950* (New York: Columbia University Press, 1986), 195.

29. Ibid., 274.

30. Jack Smith, "Remarks on Art and the Theatre," in *Jack Smith*, ed. Ira Cohen, Historical Treasures no. 33 (New York: Haumann, 1993), 133–35.

31. Boyd MacDonald, *Cruising the Movies: A Sexual Guide to Oldies on TV* (New York: Gay Press, 1988), 21.

32. Andrew Ross, *No Respect: Intellectuals and Popular Culture* (New York: Routledge, 1989), 139.

33. Bosley Crowther, *The New York Times*, 4 March 1965, section 1, 36.

34. *Advocate*, no. 608 (30 July 1990): 69.

35. Patricia Mellencamp, "Situation Comedy, Feminism, and Freud: Discourses of Gracie and Lucy," in *Studies in Entertainment*, ed. Tania Modleski (Bloomington: Indiana University Press, 1986), 91.

Questions for Reflection, Discussion, and Writing

1. What "types" were available to Agnes Moorehead as a supporting actress, according to White?
2. Using Agnes Moorehead's career as an example, what social and cultural parallels does White draw between "supporting actress" and "lesbian"?
3. What "norms" and characters does White argue supporting actresses are meant to support? In what ways can supporting actresses subvert the "status quo"? What examples from the career of Agnes Moorehead does she offer as evidence?
4. In what ways might we read what Hollywood critics characterize as "asexual" as "lesbian"? According to White, in what ways can race be used as "a process of erotic doubling" in conjunction with "lesbian" to suggest an alternative narrative or subtext?
5. What is "camp" according to White, and in what ways is it an inadequate lens with which to understand Moorehead"s career?

Related Reading

Claire Whitaker, "Hollywood Transformed: Interviews With Lesbian Viewers" in *Jump Cut: Hollywood, Politics, and Counter Cinema.* Peter Stevens, Ed. NY: Praeger. 1981. 106–118.

Patricia White: Female Spectator, Lesbian Specter: *The Haunting*" in *Inside/Out: Lesbian Theories, Gay Theories.* Diana Fuss, Ed. NY: Routledge. 1991. 142–172.

Judith Mayne, "Lesbian Looks: Dorothy Arzner and Female Authorship" *in How Do I Look? Queer Film and Video.* Bad Object-Choices. Seattle: Bay Press. 1991. 105–143.

Andrea Weiss, "'A Queer Feeling When I Look at You': Hollywood Stars and Lesbian Spectatorship in the 1930s" in *Stardom: Industry of Desire.* Christine Gledhill, Ed. NY: Routledge. 1991. 283–299.

Andrea Weiss, "Transgressive Cinema: Lesbian Independent Film" in *Vampires and Violets: Lesbians in Film.* NY: Penguin. 1992. 137–161.

Amy Taubin, "Queer Male Cinema and Feminism" in *Women and Film: A Sight and Sound Reader.* Pam Cook and Philip Dodd, Eds. Philadelphia: Temple UP. 1993. 176–179.

Liz Kotz, "Anything But Idyllic: Lesbian Filmmaking in the 1980s and 1990s" in *Sisters, Sexperts, Queers.* Arlene Stein, Ed. NY: Penguin. 1993. 67–80.

———. "An Unrequitred Desire for the Sublime: Looking at Lesbian Representation Across the Works of Abagail Child, Cecelia Dougherty, and Su Friedrich" in *Queer Looks.* Martha Gever, John Greyson and Pratibha Parmar, Eds. NY: Routledge. 1993. 86–102.

Teresa de Lauretis, "Recasting the Primal Scene: Film and Lesbian Representation" in *The Practice of Love: Lesbian Sexuality and Perverse Desire.* Bloomington, Indiana UP. 1994. 81–148.

Edith Becker, Michelle Citron, Julia Lesage, and B. Ruby Rich, "Lesbians and Film" in *Out in Culture: Gay, Lesbian and Queer Essays on Popular Culture.* Corey E. Creekmur and Alexander Doty, Eds. Durham: Duke UP. 1995. 25–43.

Mary Desjardins, "Meeting Two Queens: Feminist Film-Making, Identity Politics, and the Melodramatic Fantasy." *Film Quarterly 48.3* (1995 Spring): 26–33.

Axel Madsen, *The Sewing Circle: Female Stars Who Loved Other Women.* NY: Carol Publishing Group. 1995.

Eric Savoy, "'That Ain't *All* She Ain't': Doris Day and Queer Performativity" in *Out Takes: Essays on Queer Theory and Film.*" Ellis Hanson, Ed. Durham: Duke UP. 1999. 151–182.

Jennifer A. Rich, "'(W)Right in the Faultlines': The Problematic of Identity in William Wyler's *The Children's Hour*" *The Queer Sixties.* Patricia Juliana Smith, Ed. NY: Routledge. 1999. 187–200.

Film

Citizen Kane (1941). Orson Welles. 119 m.

The Magnificent Ambersons (1942). Orson Welles. 88 m.

Since You Went Away (1944). John Cromwell. 172 m.

Dark Passage (1947). Delmer Daves. 106 m.

Caged (1950). John Cromwell. 96 m.

Magnificent Obsession (1954). Douglas Sirk. 108 m.

The Revolt of Mamie Stover (1956). Raoul Walsh. 92 m.

The Singing Nun (1966). Henry Koster. 98 m.

The Killing of Sister George (1968). Robert Aldrich. 138 m.

What's The Matter With Helen (1971). Curtis Harrington. 101 m.

Special Topics

A flurry of lesbian films featuring biracial romances came out in the 1990s; they all exhibit varying degrees of self consciousness regarding their own racial politics. What strategies of representation are at work in each film? What's important about what is, and is not said regarding race in these films? What is the construction of whiteness in each film? Of blackness? Where are the intersections of queerness, sexuality and race in each? How do class politics manifest themselves? How are they constructed? How do they figure in the representation of race?

Film

When Night Is Falling (1995). Patricia Rozema. 96 m.

The Incredibly True Adventures of Two Girls in Love (1995). Maria Maggenti. 94 m.

She Must be Seeing Things (1988). Shelia McLaughlin. 85 m.

Reading

Alison Bulter, "She Must be Seeing Things: An Interview With Sheila McLaughlin" in *Queer Looks*. Martha Gever, John Greyson and Pratibha Parmar, Eds. NY: Routledge. 1993. 368–376.

Special Topics

As in White's essay, in which queerness is read through the actor's life and through representations in a film *oeuvre*, the closeted life, film career and death from AIDS of actor Rock Hudson has provoked similar approaches. Mark Rappaport's 1992 *Rock Hudson's Home Movies* (63 m.), features Rappaport performing Hudson narrating his own home movie of a queer career in Hollywood viewed through the notable sexual ambiguity of many of his starring roles. This film, combined with Richard Meyer's "Rock Hudson's Body" in *Inside/Out: Lesbian Theories, Gay Theories*. Diana Fuss, Ed. NY: Routledge, 1991, 259–288, provides another model for reading performers as queer and queerly, similar to the reading of Agnes Moorehead by Patricia White.

Reading

David Ehrenstein, *Open Secret: Gay Hollywood, 1928–1998*. NY: William Morrow. 1998.
William J. Mann, *Wisecracker: The Life and Times of William Haines, Hollywood's First Openly Gay Star*. NY: Viking. 1998.

Straddling the Screen: Bisexual Spectatorship and Contemporary Narrative Film

Maria Pramaggiore

Bisexual characters have been popping up all over the screen, usually in the midst of romantic triangles, scenarios that highlight the inevitability of choosing between "same" and "opposite" sex desire[1] In her recent account of the lesbian vampire film in *Vampires and Violets: Lesbians in Film*, Andrea Weiss examines bisexual romantic triangles and argues that "[t]he degree of narrative closure largely determines what meanings the lesbian vampire films can generate, and the extent to which lesbians can find alternative or oppositional meanings. In the conclusion of a typical bisexual triangle film—*Personal Best, The Bostonians*—given an even fight between a heterosexual man and a lesbian, the man will win out every time, thereby restoring the 'natural order.' "[2] The natural order Weiss refers to is, of course, the narratively and socially "natural" resolution heterosexual coupling provides. Weiss's observation is insightful, because it acknowledges that a textual element—the degree of narrative closure—plays a role in generating viewer resistance. In other words, audience members, in this case lesbian spectators, do not produce oppositional readings of films solely on the basis of their sexual identities; the text itself must in some manner invite alternative readings.

Weiss's comments on lesbian vampire films are important in another regard. She mentions the bisexual triangle as a common trope in films that deal with lesbian relationships but considers the triangle only insofar as it functions as an impediment to lesbian desire, as an obstacle that sets the stage for the ultimate and inevitable conflict between a lesbian vampire and a mortal man. By treating the bisexual triangle only as a means through which a lesbian narrative is recuperated by heteronormative coupling, Weiss neglects to examine how bisexual triangles might complicate, rather than enable, hetero- and homosexuality. Thus, she perpetuates the notion of bisexual desire as an intermediate or transitory developmental phase.[3]

In *Making Things Perfectly Queer: Interpreting Mass Culture*, Alexander Doty raises the issue of bisexual triangles in the context of another film genre—the Hollywood musical—and characterizes triangulated erotics as instruments of heterosexual recuperation of gay male sexuality.[4] Gene Kelly's "male trio" musicals, for example, feature two "conventionally sexy" actors who are teamed (tripled?) with a "comic, less attractive buffer who is meant to diffuse the sexual energy generated between the two male leads when they sing and dance together" (11). Another group of Kelly's films—which includes *Singin' In the Rain*—"resort[s] to the more conventional heterosexual(izing) narrative device of using a woman to mediate and diffuse male-male erotics" (11). According to Doty, neither strategy is successful: ultimately the triangulated narratives fail to "fully heterosexualize" Kelly and his male costars (11). Like Weiss, Doty does not explore how the bisexual triangle may be responsible for the narrative's failure to fully heterosexualize these characters and acknowledges in a footnote that he has given rather cursory attention to "specifically bisexual [reading] positions" (105).

The comments of Weiss and Doty regarding the bisexual triangle offer a useful starting point from which to examine contemporary films that feature triangulation and to ask whether they invite specifically bisexual readings. Analyzing triangulation as more than merely a weapon in the heterosexual narrative arsenal offers a more complex understanding of the way films depict sexuality than the "either/or" imperative offered by many feminist, gay, and lesbian analyses of film. Reading contemporary films from the bisexual "fence" involves a reconsideration of both narrative structure and spectatorial identification. The fence is a position from which "same" and "opposite" sex desires of particular characters can be explored rather than viewed as mutually exclusive and is a location from which spectators may be expected to form multiple identifications among variously sexed and gendered characters. Reading from the fence also calls into question the foreclosure of bisexual desire by monosexual, coupled resolutions. As a bisexual spectator, necessarily straddling a screen constructed for heterosexual couples.[5] I question the monosexual imperative that characters within film narratives must and do choose between identification and desire and that spectators must do so in relation to the screen. I therefore seek to eroticize identification as well as to explore the fluidity of desire.[6]

Bisexual reading practices may be invited by recent mainstream films that depict fluid eroticisms and nonheterosexual desires; in other words, these film texts may construct a "fence-sitting" spectator. It is important, therefore, to briefly examine how mainstream studios and independent producers have found representing sexual alternatives a lucrative business practice, and how the new economics of sexual deviance informs the texts produced within this context.

Contemporary Queer Film: Industrial Fences

The historical circumstances which have given rise to explicitly gay and lesbian films are numerous and complex, involving film production, marketing, distribution, viewing practices, research and criticism. Film critic/theorist Robin Wood, for example, identifies the "steadily growing force of the gay liberation movement, no longer content with a plea for tolerance of homosexuals, but in close alliance with radical feminism, calling into question the very construction of sexuality within our culture" as a force motivating his avowedly political perspective.[7] Film scholarcritics such as Vito Russo and Parker Tyler have surveyed the representations of gays and lesbians from the vantage points of politics and aesthetics. Tyler, who in 1973 claimed that "sexual integrity is omnisexed," wanted to "free the sexual body and all its behavior from the straitjacket of conventional ideas that limit them for serious contemplation and cripple them on the open ground of the imagination." In order to do so, he argued that we must consider the "basic genders . . . irrelevant."[8] Mainstream and avant garde films have represented a variety of genders and sexualities since before the feminist and gay liberation movements gained prominence in the early 1970s, yet few popular writers or academics have acknowledged mainstream films' representations of alternatives to heterosexuality prior to the "sexual revolution" of the late 1960s. Criticism in the 1980s and 1990s has only just begun to address celluloid sexualities in a more comprehensive manner, informed by feminist, gay and lesbian film, cultural theory, and political activism.

During the 1980s, partially in response to the AIDS crisis, the popular press and academia have focused attention on the cultural presumption of heterosexuality and its attendant circumscription—political, legal, and cultural—of "deviant" sexualities. "Queer theory," made visible during the late 1980s and early 1990s with the publication of Eve Kosofsky Sedgwick's *Epistemology of the Closet*, is the academic counterpart of the activism outside academia which increased visibility of gay and lesbian political and representational issues.

The "in your face" politics of ACT UP and the widespread commitment to "outness" and identity politics have made certain economic opportunities obvious to creators and purveyors of mass culture. As Danae Clark explicates in "Commodity Lesbianism," the capitalist practice of product differentiation and the increased visibility of gays and lesbians have given rise to "gay window advertising" practices.[9] Advertisers and their clients adopt this dual ("both/and") representational strategy in order to make inroads into gay and lesbian markets while not offending "traditional" audiences.

This strategy, double-edged in its conception and execution, is also at work in contemporary cinema. Films that depict alternatives to heterosexuality have found profitable markets, a situation which calls to mind (yet another) fence: that straddled by film producers seeking a wider audience than that comprising lesbians, gay men, bisexuals, and transgendered people. The economic imperative of the mass market informs even the most well-intentioned attempts to move beyond compulsory heterosexuality, however, and subtends recent film narratives that attempt to have their sex both ways. In her review of *Three of Hearts*, for example, Lucy Richer notes that an unconvincing action subplot only serves to further the romance narrative, a structural flaw which "is a sure sign that the film is protesting too much, an over-compensation typical of Hollywood movies which are genuinely trying to work sexual roles into new stories, but are nervous of trampling on too many traditions at once."[10] Independent films with gay, lesbian, and bisexual themes, such as *The Crying Game*, *Priscilla: Queen of the Desert*, and *The Wedding Banquet* have been successful at the box office, relative to production costs and relative to mainstream products such as *Three of Hearts* and *Threesome* (perhaps because as independents they are able to take more risks), suggesting that their appeal is not limited to gay, lesbian, and bisexual consumers. If Hollywood, and the plethora of independent producers whose work dominates the contemporary film industry, need to "cheat" their representations of homosexualities for mass audience appeal—making them legible to those on both sides of the fence—it may be the case that the ambiguities, doubleness, and "both/and" of bisexual desire are encoded in contemporary films and may, in part, make bisexual reading practices possible and necessary.

Bisexual reading practices, theoretically, need not be limited to spectators who identify as bisexual persons.[11] I share Doty's position in this regard: "[U]nless the text is about queers . . . the queerness of most mass cultural texts is less an essential waiting-to-be-discovered property than the result of acts of production or reception. . . . [Q]ueerness [is] a mass culture reception practice that is shared by all sorts of people in varying degrees of consistency and intensity" (xi, 2). I would add, however, that even when texts are "about" queers or queerness, textual elements can repress or express possibilities for bisexual desires, that is, nonsingular desires that may be detached from strict sex and/or gender oppositions. Furthermore, bisexual readings may be available to anyone reading cultural texts, but they are also a specific product of historical and cultural circumstances which authorize these readings.

If reading bisexually is conceived of as a cultural practice that requires for its existence a formal apparatus as well as a readership motivated to perform such readings, then identifying as a bisexual person is neither necessary nor sufficient for reading bisexually. However, an understanding on the part of viewers that bisexual desires and perspectives exist is necessary. That the growth of bisexual visibility during the 1980s and 1990s occurred primarily *within* gay and lesbian movements[12] suggests that gay- and lesbian-themed films are appropriate textual sources for bisexual elements that address spectators on the fence. Paradoxically, because the term "bisexual" historically has been used to denote gay and/or lesbian sexuality as well as bisexuality, the meaning(s) of bisexuality(ies) are subject to both a surplus and a surfeit of visibility, and the films I analyze are no exception. In *The Crying Game*, for example, the bisexual character Jody can be identified as such only after his death. In *Three of Hearts*, Ellen is displaced from her central position in the triangulated narrative by the straight male character's action subplot, and, in *The Hunger*, bisexual desire is conflated with vampirism, a common device for representing lesbian desire in horror films.

The mainstreaming of sexual deviance, including bisexuality, is a double-edged sword; film narratives that treat homosexuality, lesbianism, and bisexuality are subject to certain generic constraints of "normalization." They often reiterate narrative traditions which speak to viewers' investment in monosexuality and make it difficult, although not necessarily impossible, for readers to deviate from the familiar rhetoric of romantic coupling.

Queer Couplings

One narrative tradition that poses problems for alternative representations of sexuality is the device of coupling. Virginia Wexman's recent study of Hollywood cinema points to the ways romantic coupling on screen has both reflected and shaped norms regarding marriage, gender, and sexuality.[13] Conventional coupled romance narratives, whether concerned with gay, lesbian, or heterosexual scenarios, make it difficult to recognize or to imagine bisexuality other than as a developmental stage prior to "mature" monogamous monosexuality.

The three films I discuss reconfigure romantic *triangles* in overtly gay, lesbian, and bisexual terms. In the history of Western representations of love, romance, and sexuality, a triangulated structure of desire, according to literary theorist René Girard, constructs the love object.[14] Eve Sedgwick, examining the implications of male homosociality, concludes that, in English literature, the bonds between male rivals are as strong as those between either man and the female love interest.[15] Marjorie Garber observes that erotic triangles are important to examine in terms of positioning, arguing that erotic desire depends upon one's position within the triangle rather than upon essential gender or sexual identities.[16] She stresses the importance of examining "the connections among the 'other' partners that need articulating" (433). In other words, the rivalry, jealousy, and competition that characterize relations between and among certain characters within a triangle generally are construed as involving only similarity and identification, rather than identification *and* desire. Because the triangle offers the possibility for simultaneous desire and identification among its various positions, regardless of the gender of the figures occupying those positions, triangulation often highlights the both/and quality of bisexual desire.

Moreover, romantic coupling and temporal closure are related narrative structures affecting the possibility of representing desires which are not restricted to "one" sexual object or one "type" of sexual object. Coupling signifies completion, wholeness, and stasis and usually suggests a diachronically stable object choice. Temporality is critical. In order to use a visual medium to render "same" and "opposite" sex desires that are not mutually exclusive, two conditions must obtain: either the film must depict multiple, variously sexed partners in particular scenes, or it must suggest an "oscillation" between partners of both sexes. Clearly, neither of these alternatives has been acceptable politically and/or aesthetically in most gay/lesbian films, many of which seek to validate coming out and the ultimate formation of a homosexual union. Furthermore, chronological narrative structures that assign more weight and import to the conclusion—typical of Hollywood film rather than, say, European art cinema—may be less compatible with bisexual reading strategies, which focus on the episodic quality of a nonteleological temporal continuum across which a number of sexual acts, desires, and identities might be expressed.

I have chosen to examine three films in which bisexuality is explicitly represented and in which triangles are crucial to representing bisexuality.[17] Although films which do not attempt queer representations can be read queerly, as Doty demonstrates, it is equally important to investigate recent feature films which present gay, lesbian, and bisexual persons, relationships, and themes in terms of the ways that those films have expanded, and sometimes simultaneously foreclosed, bisexuality as a sexual identity and practice. If, as I have argued here, temporal and narrative conventions are critical to a bisexual reading practice, then gay and lesbian narratives which reinforce notions of coupling and closure may make a bisexual reading as difficult as, or even more difficult than, a more mainstream Hollywood product which involves some form of triangulation.

In *The Crying Game* (Neil Jordan, 1992), *Three of Hearts* (Yurek Bogayevicz, 1992), and *The Hunger* (Tony Scott, 1986), triangulated relationships express complex relations along and between all vertices. Such triangles can remain unresolved when the films' conclusions offer open-ended possibilities for erotic desires. The "third term" produced within a triangulated context—a position sometimes but not always occupied by a bisexual character—becomes a metaphor for and/or agent of structural instability in heterosexual relations rather than operating as merely an obstacle for heterosexual or homosexual characters to "overcome." In addition, when the temporal structures in these films are more ambivalent, less determining, they further undermine the stability of any form of coupling.

Analyzing these films from a bisexual perspective, I focus on romantic coupling and the treatment of temporality as key structural components which gesture beyond monosexualities. In addition to these formal concerns, I examine whether or not the narrative content resolves the tension between identification and desire created in the context of the bisexual triangle. That resolution, when it assumes the form of an opposition between identification and desire (heterosexuality) or a conflation (homosexuality), gives resonance and permanence to monosexual formations and disallows the continual interplay of identifications and desires across sex and gender that characterizes bisexuality.

The additional theoretical challenge bisexualities pose to film studies concerns not the textual politics of contemporary queer cinema but practices of spectatorship themselves. In other words, bisexual readings, invited by triangulated and temporally fluid narrative patterns, are also contingent upon certain practices of spectatorship that, as of yet, have not been clearly articulated within film theory. Below, I briefly outline how bisexuality has been employed by feminist film theorists, who have developed readings of sexuality in cinema to the greatest extent. In feminist film theory, shifting and imprecise terminology regarding bisexuality—particularly the adoption of a Freudian model of a constitutional bisexuality—clouds attempts to develop more complex and nuanced models of spectatorship.

Fencing the Screen

Bisexual reading practices are dynamic processes involving both textual address and a motivated readership. In theories of film spectatorship, this posited interaction encompasses the narratives and images projected upon the screen (highlighted in structural or apparatus approaches) and the audience's activities of and investment in interpreting those images (emphasized in cultural studies and ethnographic approaches).[18] Apparatus models present cinema as a seamless ideological machine, whereas reception studies emphasize readings and responses of historical spectators whose activity of watching is assumed to construct the text's meaning, often in opposition to culturally authorized interpretations. Studies of gay and lesbian film spectatorship, of particular relevance here, often rely implicitly on the assumption that gay and lesbian audience members are uniquely willing and able to read against the grain of mainstream texts to rewrite heterosexual endings or to elucidate homoerotic or homosexual elements which the narrative elides or represses.[19]

In their studies of spectatorship, Judith Mayne, Rob Lapsley, and Michael Westlake conclude that "the relation between text and spectator is better comprehended as a dialectic," arguing that the spectator is both constituted by and constitutes the text.[20] The model of bisexual spectatorship I employ assumes that spectators construct textual meaning, yet also recognizes that a film's narrative and visual structures, while not inescapable, must inform viewer positioning. I am speaking from both sides of the screen—the "fence," as it were, in the field of film studies—to argue that both textual address and social-historical circumstances provide the conditions of possibility for bisexual reading practices. "Fencing" thus refers to my positioning of the film screen in a shifting and indeterminate "both/and" location "in between" social and economic practices of production and reception, not unlike the problematic but sometimes productive positioning of bisexual practices and identities as "in between" heterosexuality and homosexuality. The term also refers to the sport of fencing, the dodging and parrying that all spectators continually engage in, working with and against film's representational conventions to produce meaningful readings. Finally, in its most prosaic form, "fencing" refers to unloading stolen property. I embrace the materialist connotations of this definition and connect that extra-market activity to my understanding of bisexual spectatorial pleasure, a pleasure often stolen from conventional monosexual narratives that, sometimes unwittingly, encourage bisexual readings through their deployment of the romantic triangle.[21]

Bisexing Feminist Film Theory

Feminist film theory asks us not only to read films in terms of narrative structures and visual techniques that privilege heterosexuality and heterosexual difference but also to consider how we read films as spectators marked by our sexes and sexualities. Laura Mulvey's "Visual Pleasure and Narrative Cinema" posits a psychoanalytically inflected masculinized spectator as the ideal object of mainstream Hollywood's enunciative apparatus.[22] Mulvey argues that visual and narrative pleasures are predicated on a heterosexual division of labor which both invites the spectator's identification with male characters and appeals to his need to fetishize women's threatening, castrated bodies. Mulvey characterizes the masculine spectator as one who unproblematically identifies with on-screen men but must disavow the threat implied by the on-screen woman's bodily castration. "A male movie star's glamorous characteristics are thus not those of the erotic object of the gaze, but those of the more perfect, more complete, more powerful ideal ego conceived in the original moment of recognition in front of the mirror. . . . But in psychoanalytic terms, the female figure poses a deeper problem . . . her lack of a penis, implying the threat of castration and hence unpleasure" (34–35).

Mulvey's original model of cinema's all-consuming masculine gaze has been criticized for its apparent assumption of passive spectators in thrall to a pervasive patriarchal ideology and for its neglect of the female spectator.[23] Her ability to imagine an oppositional film practice, however,[24] does suggest that spectators, when presented with alternative modes of filmic representation, will meet that challenge with a heightened awareness of the ideological implications of conventional narrative structures. Mulvey's early theories are relevant to bisexual spectatorship because she begins with a psychoanalytic model of heterosexual difference and assumes that male and female spectators' opportunities for identification with opposite-sex characters and desire for same-sex characters are severely circumscribed.

Whereas Mulvey's original thesis endows the cinematic apparatus with the determinative power to satisfy both narcissistic and scopophilic (identificatory and projective, object-oriented) desires of the masculine spectator, she later recognizes that not all spectators comfortably occupy that position. "In-built patterns of pleasure and identification impose masculinity as point-of-view," she continues to argue in "Afterthoughts on 'Visual Pleasure and Narrative Cinema' Inspired by *Duel in the Sun*," but questions "whether the female spectator is carried along, as it were by the scruff of the text, or whether her pleasure can be more deep-rooted and complex."[25] Describing female spectators' pleasure in identifying with active characters (generally, but not exclusively, male) as "an oscillation between 'passive' femininity and regressive 'masculinity,'" Mulvey relates such trans-sex identification or "transvestism," to women's inability to establish a stable sexual identity (25–28). This association of an unstable bisexuality with women is based upon Freud's analysis of women's unsuccessful repression of their phallic, masculine aspirations; Mulvey here reiterates this "constitutional" model of bisexuality, based itself upon processes of identification rather than desire. That is to say, bisexuality here is figured as an inability to identify fully with either male or female characters, rather than as desire for characters of both sexes, regardless of the spectator's sex or gender identity.

Mulvey's notion of women's trans-sex identification practices has been questioned on the grounds that identification involves denying the differences between the spectator's and the object's bodies. Anne Friedberg notes that "countless films (with monsters, robots, animals) attest [to the fact that] any body offers an opportunity for identificatory investment."[26] Robin Wood considers identification practices in relation to horror films, where, he claims, spectators are simultaneously fascinated with and disgusted by the monster, who embodies social taboos, including homosexuality and bisexuality. Other scholars point to the certainty of spectators' capacity for multiple identifications across sex, race, and species.[27] These capacities may indeed be termed bisexual spectatorship practices, as I am using that term, for they encompass identification and desire—narcissism and scopophilia in Mulvey's Freudian system—without neatly distinguishing between the two or defining them as oppositional.

Tania Modleski discusses women's bisexuality and its implications for male characters' identification with women in Hitchcock films, linking bisexuality to mother-daughter relationships that threaten patriarchal power relations. She implies that women's bisexual nature, rooted in preoedipality, and her consequent alleged tendency to overidentify with other women and with texts, is less a problem for women, as Doane would have it, than it is for patriarchy . . . not only . . . [because] female bisexuality would make women into competitors for "the male preserve," but far more fundamentally because it reminds man of his *own* bisexuality (and thus his resemblance to Norman Bates), a bisexuality that threatens to subvert his "proper" identity, which depends upon his ability to distance woman and make her his property.[28]

Here she suggests that bisexuality is not the exclusive property of on-screen women or female spectators but, nevertheless, is more likely to be repressed by on-screen and spectatorial subjects who define themselves as male, hinting that part of that heterosexual male self-definition is based upon the repression of bisexuality. Here, bisexuality is a metaphor for a masculine/feminine split in the subject that is problematic for male characters who seek to assert a singular and fully masculine identity. Bisexuality for the man, however, as it is for Mulvey, is a question of identifying with the mother rather than of experiencing identifications with and desires for various others, including men and women, transgendered people, and/or androgynes.

Modleski's notion of bisexuality, importantly, is asymmetrical along the male/female axis and, therefore, is implicated in gendered power relations, including those that may govern spectatorship practices: "[A] discussion of bisexuality as it relates to spectatorship ought, then, to be informed by a knowledge of the way male and female responses are rendered asymmetrical by a patriarchal power structure. As Hitchcock films repeatedly demonstrate, the male subject is greatly threatened by bisexuality, though he is at the same time fascinated by it; and it is the woman who pays for this ambivalence—often with her life itself" (10). In Hitchcock's films, men seek to repress the preoedipal identification with the mother, with dire consequences for women. Male characters project their repressed feminine aspect onto women characters, who do the suffering for both of them, a dynamic Modleski calls a "dialectic of identification and dread" (13).

These discussions of bisexual spectatorship rely almost exclusively upon the notion of identification "across" gender. They do not adequately address the question of the relationship between identification and desire, however. From my perspective on the fence, reading a film bisexually has less to do with aligning one's identity with a particular character (on the basis of male/female sex distinctions or on the basis of activity/passivity) and has more to do with the spectatorial difficulty of clearly distinguishing between wanting to "be" a character (Mulvey's ego-ideal) and wanting to "have" a character (scopophilic, fetishistic, erotic possession through the gaze). Reading bisexually recognizes that culturally imposed binary sex and gender differences do not guarantee the "proper" channeling of ego- or object-driven desire for characters or spectators: any character is a potential ego-ideal as well as a sexual object for other characters and for spectators.

In each of the films I analyze, the characters' struggles between identification and desire do not obey heterosexual codification, which is what distin-

guishes them from most gay and lesbian characters, for whom objects of identification and of sexual desire often are as easily differentiated as they are for heterosexual characters. The films do not resolve or contain bisexual desires
through monosexual recuperation, instead resisting the happily-ever-after resolution of heterosexual or homosexual coupling. The couple's romantic status is
either problematized and indefinitely deferred (Fergus-Dil in *The Crying Game*;
Sarah-Miriam in *The Hunger*) or displaced by a cross-sex buddy relationship
that results from bonding over the same love object (Connie-Joe in *Three of
Hearts*). *The Crying Game* and *Three of Hearts* do privilege the couple as unit, but
not heterosexuality or homosexuality per se, and they emphasize the ongoing
importance of triangulated desire. *The Hunger* more explicitly presents the fluidity of triangulated bisexual desire, perhaps because of its peculiar temporal
structure: the "life" expectancy of a vampire.

Desire Deferred: The Crying Game

The Crying Game's central metaphor of fluid identity finds geographical and textual resonance in the water crossings between Ireland and England and in the
scorpion and frog fable. This parable about trust and true nature which Jody
tells to Fergus, who retells it to Dil in the film's conclusion, underscores the
danger of rigid adherence to an essential, unchanging identity. The scorpion
destroys itself and the frog because the scorpion is locked into its "natural" role
as destroyer. The untrustworthy character of the scorpion also hints at the
shifting and duplicitous nature of political and romantic triangles; in this film,
being and seeming are often at odds in both political and sexual terms. The environment of political intrigue associated with IRA terrorism resonates with the
"hermeneutic of passing"[29] Marjorie Garber identifies in *M. Butterfly*; she observes that "*passing* is what *acting* is, and what *treason* is" (143). The act of passing itself, undertaken at various points by all of the primary characters in the
film, introduces triangulation in the sense that triangles are formed among
(1) the persona a character adopts; (2) the person he or she "really" is in the text
or subtext of the film; and (3) the character or spectator toward whom the performance is directed. Passing in this film is also a practice of fluid identity: characters are engaged in both passing *as* and passing *between*.

    The film's romantic triangles are structured by a series of looks, all in-
volving Fergus, the self-sacrificing hero ostensibly at the center of the narrative.
Several romantic configurations express Fergus's heterosexual, homosocial, and
homoerotic capacities but also complicate his attempt to differentiate between
identification and desire. Fergus struggles with his desire to have (Jody) and his
desire to be (Jody). In Lacanian terms, these desires—to have and to be—are associated with the phallus, the imaginary signifier par excellence. A bisexual
reading of this film recognizes that, in fact, Jody occupies the paradoxically absent center of the film, for it is Jody, a black bisexual man, who occupies the untenable position of the phallus (an object no one can be or have). Clearly, the

film's phallic rhetoric is racially inflected, with implications for its representation of masculinity: Fergus holds Jody's penis while the latter urinates, and Fergus, along with spectators, witnesses Dil's unveiling of her/his penis. Fergus's sexuality is therefore constructed in relation to a black phallus, traditionally a racist signifier of hypermasculinity, whose various manifestations in this film, however, serve to undermine the equation of black male bodies with excessive heterosexual desire.[30]

Throughout the film, Fergus's involvement with actual sex partners (Jude and Dil) is mediated by Jody, whose positioning as a "third term" defines his status as an object of both identification and desire for Fergus. In the opening sequence, Jude entices Jody into a truncated sexual liaison while Fergus watches; until Jody's capture it is unclear whether Fergus is a jealous lover or disapproving onlooker.[31] This first triangle (Jody-Jude-Fergus) emphasizes parallels between Jody and Fergus as well as their competition for Jude: when Jude complains about her role as sexual bait for the black British soldier, for example, she tells Fergus that she was able to carry out the distasteful task because she pretended that Jody was Fergus.

During Jody's incarceration, Jody and Fergus look at the photograph of Dil that Jody carries with him, a moment in which Dil supplants Jude as the object of their sexual interest. As they both look at Jude at the carnival and at Dil in the IRA hideout, Fergus and Jody forge an identification through their gazes. In these instances of visual triangulation, the structure of jealousy and competition traditionally associated with romantic triangles is recast in the more ambiguous terms of the homosocial/sexual relation between Jody and Fergus—also dependent upon gazes. Jody asserts his ability to look despite the fact that he is objectified and dehumanized by his captors and is the constant object of Fergus's gaze. "You're the handsome one," Jody tells Fergus, his words muffled by the hood over his face. Frann Michel writes that the connection between Jody and Fergus is "part kinship, part antagonism, part eroticism,"[32] which also suggests their joint resistance to Jude, the increasingly cruel and crude female outsider. The ensuing narrative maintains a delicate balance between Fergus's (homosexual) desire for Jody and his (homosocial) desire to be Jody. Despite his growing attachment to Dil, Fergus's identification with Jody does not eclipse his desire for Jody. Fergus's identification with and desire for Jody are evidenced by his dreams of Jody during sex with Dil, his mimicry of the cricket game (Jody's game) he observes from his work site, his desire to take care of Dil, and his decision to disguise Dil in Jody's cricket clothes.

The canted angle and figure placement in the scene where Jody and Fergus look at the photograph literally resituate the vertices of the initial romantic triangle; the camerawork is the visual corollary to the narrative's reconfiguration of romance, as Dil becomes the object of Jody's and Fergus's gazes. Fergus mirrors Dil's place in the photograph; he stands over Jody just as Dil leans over Jody in the photograph. The composition produces a multiplicitous reading of Fergus as identifying with and desiring both Jody and Dil. The figure placement can be read as indicating Fergus's desire to occupy Dil's position in relation to Jody or as foreshadowing Fergus's assumption of Jody's position in relation to Dil.

Yet identifying with and desiring Jody are dangerous propositions, given the difficulty most characters, including Fergus, have in "reading" Jody's various identities "properly." A West Indian from Tottenham, Jody's political, national, and sexual identities are the most fluid of all the characters and the most disturbing in terms of monosexual coherence and narrative closure. Jody stands for the British colonial presence in Ireland, but neither his national nor sexual identity is capable of being recuperated by traditional definitions of race, citizenship, or monosexual orientation. Jody plays cricket and appears to be an assimilated colonial, yet his usurpation of the sport of the colonizer—like the costumes he dons as soldier and cricket player—can be read through Homi Bhabha's concept of mimicry, a "double vision which in disclosing the ambivalence of colonial discourse also disrupts its authority."[33] It is appropriate, then, that Jody's cricket pitch is the "googli," roughly equivalent to a knuckleball in American baseball; his pitches are never what they appear to be. His comments to Fergus about the treatment of black people in England and Ireland—a discussion in which Fergus likens his status as an Irishman to Jody's as a black man—suggest that Jody is well aware of his impossible location in a world demarcated by strict definitions of race and nation. A British subject and soldier, he is nevertheless despised, called a "nigger" in Ireland. This "fenced" national identity—partly British, partly "West Indian"—parallels Jody's sexual ambidexterity, which we learn about only after his death.

We first encounter Jody in the context of a sexual liaison with Jude and as a devoted lover of Dil, whom we are encouraged to assume is a woman. Yet Jody must be described—in retrospect—as neither exclusively heterosexual nor homosexual, but bisexual. He establishes a strong homosocial/sexual bond with Fergus, is involved in a relationship with Dil, a transsexual,[34] and apparently looks forward to a sexual encounter with Jude. The implicit gender ambiguity of Jody's name, as well as Jude's, suggests that both figures pose a challenge to strict categories of gender and sexual identity: Jude through her increasing association with unfeeling "masculine" violence, Jody through his nonexclusive sexual desire. Yet Jody's bisexuality is absent from the film in the present tense—deferred until the unmasking of Dil's penis in a scene which privileges Fergus's visceral and negative reaction.

Jody and Jude are violently eliminated from the ever-shifting romantic triangle, the former in a tragically inevitable "accident" of colonial military might, the latter in an equally inevitable confrontation with Dil that the film constructs as anything but tragic. The blame for Jody's death is displaced onto Jude, whose transformation into a high-tech hit woman and femme fatale makes that displacement seem acceptable. Even dressed in Jody's clothes, Dil is more woman than Jude, because Dil suspects that it takes "tits" and "ass," not violent coercion, to secure the affections of Jody and Fergus. Dil's performance as a woman in this predominantly male environment may thus require the elimination of Jude, the biological woman whose shifting identity nevertheless maintains consistency in terms of her excessive violence. In this film, clothes do not "make the man" or woman, for Jude's transformation is more style than substance.

Fergus less frequently fantasizes about Jody and ultimately assumes his persona as imprisoned storyteller, suggesting that Fergus's identification with Jody has come to overshadow his desire for Jody. Fergus's incarceration prevents his full assumption of Jody's position in relation to Dil, however. The all-male prison environment in which Fergus resides, with its implicit overtones of homosexuality, emphasizes the gender distinction between Fergus and Dil and situates the two as a couple but does not resolve Fergus's sexuality in terms of a "true" hetero- or homosexuality. As Jonathan Romney puts it: "Fergus' revelation is not that he is 'really' homosexual, but that sexuality must adapt to the demands of love in a loveless world."[35]

Thus the narrative skirts both a conventional romantic heterosexual resolution and a gay coming out saga and provides a deferred fantasy of coupling that is detached from monosexuality and remains triangular. Fergus becomes Jody, yet his desire for Jody has not been quelled by the violence that follows in the wake of his makeover of Dil in Jody's image.[36] Fergus becomes Jody, but with a difference; he cannot act on his desire(s) for Dil, for Jody, or for anyone else, a situation that foregrounds certain questions pertaining to the nature of desire when it is not "acted out" in sexual terms. His desire for Jody may be expressed *through* his identification with Jody, not in opposition to it, as a prisoner retelling the frog-scorpion story. The deferral of consummation is manifested in the glass barrier between Fergus and Dil, a visually permeable structure that David Lugowski takes issue with: "The film clearly wants to play against the notion that 'biology is destiny,' and yet the social discourse surrounding Fergus's relationship with Dil is not fully explored. The result is that the film's coda . . . is a little too pat, leaving one to wonder about the significance of the glass barrier between the two men."[37]

This deferral of sexual consummation resists the "happily ever after" formula, a resistance ironically underscored by Lyle Lovett's rendition of "Stand by Your Man," a song which does double duty in describing both Dil's and Fergus's positions. The glass barrier is a transparent body much less fluid and more stringently policed than the Irish sea; yet it stands for the fluid, undecidable third term that structures the film's political and sexual aesthetic. In Fergus's relationship with Dil, that vertex is variously occupied by Jody, by Jude, by Dil's penis, and by the British state. This representational triangularity is, like the film screen itself, a structure in which, fencelike, identification and desire meet but do not cancel each other out.

And Buddy Makes Three: Three of Hearts

In *Three of Hearts*, issues of triangulation and temporality pervade a film about love stories that ultimately displaces romantic love in favor of coupled friendship. The break-up of a relationship between a lesbian and a bisexual woman gives rise to a triangulated relationship among the two women, Connie and Ellen, and Joe, the man Connie hires to break Ellen's heart so that she will return to Connie. Underlying this master plan is the assumption of a symmetrical and oscillating serially monogamous bisexuality (arguably, the least threatening enactment of bisexuality). The plan assumes that Ellen will reject men in general and return to women in general, and Connie in particular, after Joe breaks her heart. Joe and Ellen fall in love, but when Ellen learns that Connie and Joe have conspired against her, she rejects them both.

The relationship between Connie and Ellen ends in the second scene of the film, and their romance is presented only in the past tense, through videos that Connie watches obsessively. This representational device reverses the traditional associations of videotape with immediacy,[38] for although the tapes transmit the spontaneity and intimacy of Connie and Ellen's relationship, their use in the narrative highlights a tearful Connie's obsessive postmortem inability to relinquish the romance. Douglas Keller observes that the film is "a quasi-lesbian romance for the '90s without any lesbian sex and without any in-depth examination of a lesbian relationship in the '90s."[39] Lucy Richer is more direct on this point: "[t]he film lacks the courage of its convictions, shy to show girls snogging."[40] One may reasonably ask whether the romance itself is lesbian if Ellen is bisexual; often, bisexual women "disappear" when they are sexually involved with women, only to reappear as bisexual when they take up with male lovers.

The temporal structure of the film thus supports the notion of serial bisexual monogamy but gives us the present tense of Joe and Ellen's sexual coupling and Joe and Connie's friendly coupling. The lesbian-bisexual relationship is distinctly relegated to history, while the buddy relationship unfolds in "real time." After their second date, Ellen explains to Joe that she and Connie "used to be a couple." The temporal displacement of the women's relationship clears the way for Ellen's complete immersion in a sexual and romantic relationship with Joe and serves to align viewer sympathy with the "real-time" relationships between Ellen and Joe and, especially, between Connie and Joe.

The film's heart may be in the right place in terms of its attempt to depict a bisexual woman's plight, but the narrative's movement undermines the liberal attempt to embrace all sexual identities. For example, in the scene in which Ellen and her sister discuss Ellen's relationship with Connie, Ellen refuses her sister's reading of the relationship as a manipulation on Connie's part. "I loved Connie and she loved me," she states. Yet Ellen's desires are represented as unstable; her rejection of Connie in the opening of the movie is not attributed to anything specific in their relationship except that she "needs space." Furthermore, she is immediately and completely vulnerable to Joe, who poses as a student in her poetry class at NYU, and his initially bungling attempts at sincerity. The suspense, and, therefore, narrative interest, is carried by Ellen's developing sexual relationship with Joe, because it is unclear whether her desire for him is strong enough to overcome his betrayal. Ellen is most important as the third term which establishes a friendship between Connie and Joe, and Joe assumes the central location in the film as the subplot of his dangerous affiliation with a criminal underworld, and Connie's attempts to help him, takes center stage.

Joe mediates Connie and Ellen's relationship throughout the film. Edmond Grant writes that reducing the women's relationship to "near-subliminal status," is "a disservice to the gay characters, making [the film] simply another nimble variation on the old Hollywood three-way love affair. Which leaves us with the prospect of a movie centered around the third point of the triangle, a dimwitted male prostitute."[41] While the triangle involves a lesbian, a bisexual woman, and a straight man, and offers possibilities for sexual multiplicity—for example, a more complicated investigation of Joe's gender and sexuality, given his commodified and objectified status as a prostitute—this film revolves around Joe's heterosexuality and serial monogamy. Joe's buddy relationship with Connie, and his initiation into lesbian culture, develops through bonding activities such as playing pool and brushing their teeth before bed.

The resolution of the film secures the coupling of Joe and Connie as buddies who share a (lost) love object while it rejects any conclusive sexual relationship for Ellen. Thus, the relationship of identification forged between Connie and Joe, and furthered by scenes in which they look at photographs or videos of Ellen is strengthened by the failure of their relationships with Ellen. The Connie-Joe friendship is minimally tinged with the prospect of sexual desire when Joe demonstrates his supposed talent for seducing "any woman any time." He compliments an extremely vulnerable and appreciative Connie on her appearance in one of their buddied bedroom scenes. That she falls for his performance is meant to suggest that no woman, not even a lesbian, could be immune to the pleasures of his male attention, rather than that Connie might explore her sexuality with a man.

While it might seem that Ellen's departure in the final scene limits the potential for a bisexual reading of, or pleasure in, this film, Ellen's single status at the end of the film, in fact, prevents her joint desires for men and women from collapsing conveniently into a single relationship and, therefore, staves off an implicit reimposition of monosexuality. The coupling in *Three of Hearts*, as in *The Crying Game*, does not secure heterosexuality but instead suggests the importance of a coupled *friendship* over (heterosexual, homosexual, or bisexual) romance. The open-endedness of the conclusion resists the codification of Ellen's sexuality as dependent upon an individual object choice and also resists the overarching celebration of romance to the exclusion of alternative couplings, such as that between Joe and Connie.

Lacking the structural and thematic complexity of *The Crying Game* or the polymorphous perversity of *The Hunger*, *Three of Hearts* nevertheless provides an excellent example of mainstream films that attempt to offer viewers alternatives to heterosexuality and coupling, and thus are capable of calling forth bisexual readings that focus on third terms and temporal fluidity. But ultimately many of these films are less imaginative and subversive than they might be. The relationship between Connie and Joe, for example, is predicated on their shared attraction to Ellen, confirming the stereotypical view of lesbians as heterosexual men in women's bodies. Furthermore, the both/andness of bisexual desire is circumscribed by the rigidly serialized nature of the romantic involvements.

Timeless Sex, Regular Feedings: The Hunger

In Tony Scott's *The Hunger*, the narrative's open-ended temporal organization and refusal of definitive monosexual coupling are manifested in the figure of the vampire through her/his desire for companionship, need for human blood, and status as the undead. In the opening scene, shots alternate between an ape in captivity and the lead singer in a band playing at the gothic-themed nightclub frequented by vampires Miriam Blaylock and her husband, John. This sequence introduces the visual and thematic parallels the film makes between the human and inhuman, parallels which subvert distinctions between human and ape, dead and undead, vampire and victim. Cross-cutting between the singer, intoning "Bela Lugosi's dead . . . undead . . undead" from behind a mesh screen on stage, and the caged ape, the experimental captive of doctors investigating aging, also brings to the foreground the importance of pleasure in identificatory looking and the way in which such looking implies control.

Vision is central to the vampires' hunt: initial close-ups of Miriam and John at the club depict their eyes shrouded in sunglasses as they watch an exhibitionist male-female couple dance. Miriam, John, and their prey—who resemble Miriam and John physically—form a group that is associated with both sexuality and bloodlust. This encounter sets the stage for the film's rendering of the vampires' polymorphous mesh of desire for and identification with their victims. John and Miriam take the couple home, nonverbally promising seduction, as the editing emphasizes the similarities between Miriam and the woman. In particular, matches on action associate Miriam's gestures with that of the woman: one lights a cigarette, the other takes a drag from her own cigarette; as the woman dances in front of a white screen, Miriam's shadow occupies the blank half of the screen. Furthermore, this anonymous female victim serves as a visual mediator between the two women protagonists (Miriam Blaylock and Sarah Roberts). The woman's short red hair and her gesture of running her hands through it foreshadow the hair color and nervous habit of Sarah Roberts, a doctor researching the aging process, who becomes Miriam's lover and victim.

By drawing these parallels, the film raises the question of Miriam's identification with, desire for, and oral incorporation of her victims. Diana Fuss has remarked upon the oral/anal incorporation of the "other" as a trope of gay male sexuality in *The Silence of the Lambs*.[42] In *The Hunger*, oral eroticism and violence suggest the powerful identification between vampire and victim and emphasize the shared bloodlust of Miriam and Susan, who are shown with bloody mouths in several scenes. The counterpart "feeding" shot for John is early on, where his lips are covered in the lipstick of the first female victim, signifying his oral insatiability, sexual ambiguity, and identification with female vampires and victims.[43] The male and female vampires feed on humans of both sexes for physical sustenance; furthermore, Miriam chooses certain humans (John, Sarah) to make over into vampire companions. As she injects some of her own blood into their veins, she makes her victim-lovers "a part of her": parts that will never die, but which must eventually age into decrepitude.

Precisely because the vampire companions Miriam creates cannot maintain their vitality forever, she must replace them approximately every two hundred years.[44] But Miriam's choice of companion depends not only upon her sexual desire but also upon her capacity for identification and hopes for companionship. John suspects that Miriam plans to replace him with Alice, the child who comes to their house to play the violin. During his rapid deterioration, John kills young Alice, an easy target for a decaying vampire, thus obliterating by incorporation the triangle formed by Miriam, John, and Alice when the three play music together.

Miriam's previous lovers have been men and women. She seems to have relied upon one primary companion at a time—another example of serial bisexual monogamy—yet also forms triangles, like that between herself, John, and Alice, when she senses the literal need for new blood. Miriam's seduction of Sarah makes her a vampire, arguably one of Miriam's "children" (she has created them),[45] and disrupts Sarah's relationship with her male lover. After having sex with Miriam, Sarah envisions Miriam reflected in a mirror that should be reflecting her male lover, first visually and then physically replacing him with Miriam. Sarah finally kills him for his blood, a reversal of the trend toward coupled heterosexual recuperation Andrea Weiss observes. In other words, although these bisexual triangles eliminate male figures (John and Sarah's boyfriend), paving the way for exclusively lesbian relationships, they also represent dyadic relations, such as that between Sarah and Miriam, as more unstable than triangular structures. Feeding and dyadic stability require the existence *and* annihilation of the third term, as in the opening scene where "seducing" and feeding upon the anonymous couple satiates Miriam and John.

When Sarah learns she has become a vampire, less herself and more Miriam, she attempts to kill herself, and thus to weaken Miriam's power. But Sarah survives, usurping Miriam's position at the film's conclusion as the "matriarchal" vampire. In the final scene, Miriam, who has physically deteriorated because of Sarah's attempted suicide, is confined to a coffin secured with chains and encircled by a fence. Sarah is shown with a young couple, a man and a woman. Although she kisses the young woman, suggesting a preference, there is no clear implication that either must be sacrificed—only that some human(s) ultimately will become Sarah's victim(s) and/or lover(s). In fact, because triangles have been represented as at least as stable, if not more stable than, couplings, and because it is unclear exactly how long vampires live and in what physical condition, the conclusion is unresolved on several counts. The temporal pattern of vampire existence, stretching through the centuries, disrupts linear time measured in human terms, and the final bisexual triangle invites a bisexual reading wherein same and opposite sex desires need not supplant one another but may oscillate over time or coexist simultaneously.

The narrative revolves around the bisexual woman vampire whose couplings with her victim-lovers are secured only by the repeated incorporation of the third term—another victim who is perhaps also a lover. Furthermore, her knowledge that her human-cum-vampire companions must eventually age and deteriorate forces her to look for a third party. Miriam seeks companions for their erotic and identificatory potential; in addition, she must make her lovers over in her own image—make them parts of her—in order to coerce or secure their companionship and her continued existence.

The polymorphous vampire, whose sexual and sensual appetites wed desire and identification, may be the quintessential representational figure of bisexuality in the 1980s and 1990s, evidenced not only by *The Hunger* but also in Anne Rice's vampire chronicles.[46] The vampire's peculiar physiognomy permits an exploration of sexuality beyond gender and sex, because desire becomes an all-pervasive rhythm of sex, blood, and satiation rather than courtship, coupling, and conclusion.

Conclusion?

In these film readings I have attempted to account for the various fences that are critical to theorizing cinematic bisexualities: the fence constructed by writers, directors, and producers who attempt to garner a mass audience and also investigate alternatives to heterosexuality; the fence of spectatorship theory in film studies, which forces a recognition that both sociohistorical events and textual rhetoric inform spectatorship; and the fence of bisexual representation, an ambiguous and often undecidable location where identification meets desire. Rather than focus on whether or not these films represent bisexual men and women in stereotypical ways, I find it more useful to consider what the requirements are for anyone to perform a bisexual reading of narrative films. My conclusions with regard to textual issues are that temporality (whether a final coupling is presented at all or is presented as permanent) and coupling (whether the coexistence of same and opposite sex desire in a single individual can be suggested, or if a final choice reflects a stable monosexual orientation) are key facets of bisexual narrative structure. I have argued that the deployment of triangulation, temporality, and closure is as important to representational politics as are individual characters or sexual stereotyping.

Furthermore, I have argued that reading films bisexually demands a more nuanced approach to the issue of identification, in terms of spectators' and characters' multiple sexual and identificatory investments. In order to perform a bisexual reading, one must relinquish monosexual structures of looking which deem either same or opposite sex characters the appropriate pool from which to draw from for either identification or sexual objectification.

Notes

1. I use the problematic concepts of "same" and "opposite" sex desire, and the coexistence of these desires, as part of my working definition of bisexuality for the purposes of this article. I am aware of the limitations this model imposes on theorizing sexualities "beyond" binary notions of male and female. I am also convinced, however, that contemporary bisexualities are constructed in light of and in spite of cultural practices that define subjects as male and female and normalize heterosexual difference as complementarity. I am suggesting that a male or female or multiply gendered subject may construct her/his/its/their sexual object choice as "both/and" instead of "either/or." This definition of bisexuality departs from the "constitutional" model employed by film critics such as Robin Wood, in *Hollywood From Vietnam to Reagan* (New York: Columbia University Press, 1986) and Dennis Bingham, in *Acting Male: Masculinities in the Films of James Stewart, Jack Nicholson, and Clint Eastwood* (New Brunswick: Rutgers University Press, 1994), which posits that every individual is composed of masculine and feminine aspects.

2. Andrea Weiss, *Vampires and Violets: Lesbians in Film* (New York: Penguin, 1992), 103.

3. Sue George, in *Women and Bisexuality* (London: Scarlet Press, 1993), discusses the frequent characterization of bisexuality as "a dangerous stage" and attributes this formulation to both Freud and Kinsey (28–33). Jay P. Paul too notes the tendency to see bisexuality as a stage. "Bisexuality: Reassessing Our Paradigms of Sexuality," in *Two Lives to Lead: Bisexuality in Men and Women*, ed. Fritz Klein and Timothy Wolf (New York: Harrington Park Press, 1985), 22. Also see Judith Roof's *A Lure of Knowledge: Lesbian Sexuality and Theory* (New York: Columbia University Press, 1991) for a discussion of film pornography and its treatment of lesbian sex as an intermediate location on the path to heterosexuality.

   The bisexual woman in the two examples Weiss cites is positioned as the child in the primal triangle of Freud's family romance: she will attain hetero/monosexuality through the repression of her narcissism/desire for her mother and channel her libido toward her father, her proper heterosexual object. Freud theorized a preoedipal bisexuality that has particular repercussions for women, who must eventually relinquish their desire for the first object, the mother. He also held that there was a conflict between identification and object cathexis, a distinction which I question in my analysis of bisexual spectatorship. I characterize a bisexual viewing practice as one which refuses to "choose" between identification and sexual desire.

4. Alexander Doty, *Making Things Perfectly Queer: Interpreting Mass Culture* (Minneapolis: University of Minnesota Press, 1993).

5. See David Bordwell, Janet Staiger, and Kristin Thompson's *Classical Hollywood Cinema: Film Style and Mode of Production to 1960* (New York: Columbia, 1985), where they discuss the ubiquity of goal-oriented heterosexual love in classical Hollywood cinema. In their nonrandom sample of one hundred films, "ninety-five involved romance in at least one line of action, while eighty-five made that the principal line of action" (16).

6. See Jackie Stacey, *Star-Gazing. Hollywood Cinema and Female Spectatorship* (New York: Routledge, 1994) and Teresa de Lauretis, *The Practice of Love: Lesbian Sexuality and Perverse Desire* (Bloomington: Indiana University Press, 1994) for two different viewpoints on the relation between identification and desire in cinema

spectatorship. De Lauretis views Stacey's more fluid conceptualization of desire and identification as a problematic de-eroticization of lesbian desire. Stacey remarks that she seeks not to de-eroticize desire but to eroticize identification (29).

7. Wood, *Hollywood from Vietnam to Reagan*, 3.

8. Parker Tyler, *Screening the Sexes: Homosexuality in the Movies* (New York: Da Capo Press, 1993 [1973]), xxiii, xix, xx.

9. Danae Clark, "Commodity Lesbianism," *Camera Obscura* 25–26 (Jan./May 1991): 181–201.

10. Lucy Richer, *"Three of Hearts," Sight and Sound* 3 (August 1993): 54.

11. In *Bi Any Other Name: Bisexual People Speak Out* (Boston: Alyson Publications, 1991), Loraine Hutchins and Lani Ka'ahumanu describe bisexual identity as "individuals of either sex who are attracted to both sexes" (2), and this is the definition of bisexual identity I am using here. I distinguish between bisexual identity and bisexual spectatorship practices: the latter refers to the activity of viewing by spectators, regardless of gender or sexual identity, which acknowledges that same and opposite sex desire are not mutually exclusive.

12. I use these terms intentionally, because, until very recently, queer movements have been organized according to gay and lesbian agendas, despite the presence and work of bisexuals and transgendered people. See Michael du Plessis's "Blatantly Bisexual" in this volume for a discussion of the politics surrounding such naming practices.

    Amanda Udis-Kessler's "Identity/Politics: A History of the Bisexual Movement," presented at "In/Queery/Theory/Deed," University of Iowa, November 18, 1994, provides an excellent account of bisexual activism in relation to gay and lesbian organizing. An earlier version of that paper appears in *Bisexual Politics: Theories, Queries, and Visions*, ed. Naomi Tucker (Binghamton, N.Y.: Haworth Press), 1996.

13. See Virginia Wexman's *Creating the Couple: Love, Marriage, and Hollywood Performance* (Princeton: Princeton University Press, 1993). Wexman's final chapter, "Destabilization of Gender Norms and Acting as Performance," is ostensibly an account of the breakdown of traditional coupling. It appears in the book's epilogue which is itself entitled "Beyond the Couple." But Wexman's choice of three exemplary films is disappointing. Apparently chosen for their deployment of particular performance styles (improvisational, absurdist, and Brechtian) are Robert Altman's *Nashville* (1975), David Mamet's *House of Games* (1987), and Spike Lee's *Do the Right Thing* (1989), all films that problematize marriage, but not the naturalization of heterosexual coupling.

14. René Girard, *Desire, Deceit, and the Novel: Self and Other in Literary Structure*, trans. Yvonne Freccero (Baltimore: Johns Hopkins University Press, 1990).

15. Eve Kosofsky Sedgwick, *Between Men: English Literature and Male Homosocial Desire* (New York: Columbia University Press, 1985).

16. Marjorie Garber, *Vice Versa: Bisexuality and the Eroticism of Everyday Life* (New York: Simon and Schuster, 1995).

17. In *Now You See It: Studies on Lesbian and Gay Film* (London and New York: Routledge, 1990), Richard Dyer discusses gay and lesbian films prior to 1980, a date he admits is somewhat arbitrary (2), and points to the proliferation of gay and lesbian filmmaking since 1980. In that study, he, too, is interested in "the deliberate, overt and owned expression of [gay/lesbian] feelings and perceptions in film" (1).

18. See Judith Mayne's *Cinema and Spectatorship* (New York: Routledge, 1994) for a discussion of models of spectatorship in historical and theoretical perspective.

19. See Elizabeth Ellsworth, "Illicit Pleasures: Feminist Spectators and *Personal Best*," *Wide Angle* 8 (2): 45–56 and Richard Meyer, "Rock Hudson's Body" in *Inside Out: Lesbian Theories, Gay Theories*, ed. Diana Fuss (New York: Routledge, 1991), 259–88 as examples of how spectators, including film critics, read against the grain in terms of film narrative and star persona.

20. Rob Lapsley and Michael Westlake, "From *Casablanca* to *Pretty Woman:* The Politics of Romance," in *Contemporary Film Theory*, ed. Anthony Easthope (London: Longman, 1993), 190–91 and Judith Mayne, *Cinema and Spectatorship*, 43, 76, and chapter 4.

21. I am arguing that triangulation triggers bisexual connotations. Investigating the use of the romantic triangle in films which are not explicitly representing alternatives to monosexuality may also prove fruitful but is beyond the scope of this essay.

22. Laura Mulvey, "Visual Pleasure and Narrative Cinema," in *Issues in Feminist Film Criticism*, ed. Patricia Erens (Bloomington: Indiana University Press, 1990 [1975]), 28–40.

23. See D. N. Rodowick, "The Difficulty of Difference," *Wide Angle* 5 (1): 4–16.

24. Mulvey, "Visual Pleasure," 39.

25. Laura Mulvey, "Afterthoughts on 'Visual Pleasure and Narrative Cinema' Inspired by *Duel in the Sun*," *Psychoanalysis and Cinema*, ed. E. Ann Kaplan (New York: Routledge, 1990), 24–35.

26. Anne Friedberg, "A Denial of Difference: Theories of Cinematic Identification," in *Psychoanalysis and Cinema*, 42.

27. Janet Bergstrom, "Enunication and Sexual Difference (Part One)," *Camera Obscura* 3–4 (Summer 1979): 33–69 and Nick Browne, "The Spectator-in-the-Text: The Rhetoric of Stagecoach," in *Movies and Methods* vol. 2, ed. Bill Nichols (Berkeley: University of California Press, 1985), 458–75. In *Hollywood from Vietnam to Reagan*, Robin Wood discusses bisexuality in the horror film genre in terms of the monster's embodiment of social taboos and the spectator's multiple identifications with both the monster and her/his victims (92).

28. Tania Modleski, *The Women Who Knew Too Much: Hitchcock and Feminist Theory* (New York: Routledge, 1988), 8.

29. Marjorie Garber, "The Occidental Tourist: *M. Butterfly* and the Scandal of Transvestism," in *Nationalisms and Sexualities*, ed. Andrew Parker, Mary Russo, Doris Sommer, and Patricia Yeager (New York: Routledge, 1992), 121–46.

30. The scene in which Jody is beaten by Jude and bleeds from his mouth further suggests that his phallic status is a "both/and" one: the only visible parts of his anatomy are his bleeding lips, a signifier of female genitalia.

31. Another of the film's implicit ironies is the possibility that Jody has been targeted by the IRA as the soldier most likely to fall into their sexual trap *because* he is a black man.

32. Frann Michel, "Racial and Sexual Politics in *The Crying Game*," *Cineaste* 20 (1) (1993): 30.

33. Homi Bhabha, "Of Mimicry and Man: The Ambivalence of Colonial Discourse," *October* 28: 129.

34. Although biologically a man, a fact which the film foregrounds to the point of the spectacular, Dil dresses and, importantly, lives as a woman, which distinguishes the character from the traditional transvestite. See Marjorie Garber's, *Vested Interests: Cross-Dressing and Cultural Anxiety* (New York: Routledge, 1992), particularly chapter 6, "Breaking the Code: Transvestism and Gay Identity."

35. Jonathan Romney, *"The Crying Game," Sight and Sound* 2 (November 1992): 40.

36. An ironic reference to Hitchcock's *Vertigo* may be at work here. Fergus is successful at making his "woman" over (into a man), whereas Scottie Ferguson was not (Gavin Elster got there first).

37. David Lugowski, "Genre Conventions and Visual Style in *The Crying Game,*" *Cineaste* 20 (1) (1993): 34.

38. See, for example, Timothy Shary's "Present Personal Truths: The Alternative Phenomenology of Video in *I've Heard the Mermaids Singing," Wide Angle* 15.3 (July 1993): 37–55. Shary argues that video images, when used in a film, call up cultural associations with live news broadcasts, specifically, with the simultaneity of filming and transmitting images that video technology permits and with the medium's ability to capture reality (37–38, 41–42). The association of video with immediacy and real time in *I've Heard the Mermaids Singing* is largely due to Polly's first-person narration and the fact that her video camera can only broadcast live images (46–47), which differs significantly from the use of videotape as visual archive in *Three of Hearts*.

39. Douglas Keller, "Only Two of Three Hearts Portrayed Convincingly," *Tech* 113 (25) (April 30, 1993): 7.

40. Richer, *"Three of Hearts,"* 54.

41. Edmond Grant, *"Three of Hearts," Films in Review* 44 (July/August 1993): 264.

42. Diana Fuss, "Monsters of Perversion: Jeffrey Dahmer and *The Silence of the Lambs,*" in *Media Spectacles,* ed. Marjorie Garber, Jann Matlock, and Rebecca L. Walkowitz (New York: Routledge, 1993), 181–205.

43. Certainly Scott's casting of rock star David Bowie in the role of the husband also calls forth associations with bisexuality, because of Bowie's ambiguous sexual persona. The lipstick traces and John's apparent obsession with his appearance create further references to Bowie's "stage" personae. A number of star biographies document Bowie's contradictory public statements about his sexuality, including Peter and Leni Gillman, *Alias David Bowie: A Biography* (New York: Holt, 1987).

44. This time span is suggested in John's flashbacks to his initial encounter with Miriam, where they are both playing musical instruments in costumes that suggest the late eighteenth or early nineteenth century.

45. See Barbara Creed's *The Monstrous Feminine: Film, Feminism, Psychoanalysis* (New York: Routledge, 1993), where she argues that Miriam is associated with the devouring "archaic" mother.

46. See Rice's "Vampire Chronicles," including *Interview with the Vampire* (New York: Knopf, 1976), *The Vampire Lestat* (New York: Ballantine Books, 1985), *Queen of the Damned* (New York: Knopf, 1988), and *The Tale of the Body Thief* (New York: Knopf, 1992). Not surprisingly, a number of difficulties have plagued the translation of Rice's polymorphous, polysexual literary vampires into film.

Questions for Reflection, Discussion, and Writing

1. In what ways does Pramaggiore claim that her identification as a bisexual woman enables her to interpret and view both "'same' and 'opposite' sex desires"? In what ways does Pramaggiore suggest that she is speaking from "both sides of the screen" (279)?

2. On what basis did Pramaggiore claim she chose to examine *Three of Hearts, The Crying Game* and *The Hunger?* What techniques does she suggest that the producers of the three films used to convey or suggest bisexuality?

3. What themes are recurrent in Pramaggiore's analyses of each of the films? In what ways are they different (stylistically and contextually) in their representations of or allusions to, bisexuality?

4. According to Pramaggiore, her purpose is to "consider what the requirements are for anyone to perform a bisexual reading of narrative films." What are those requirements, and in what ways does she suggest they are represented in the three films?

Related Reading

Elizabeth Reba Wise, "Bisexuality, *The Rocky Horror Picture Show*, and Me" in *Bi Any Other Name: Bisexual People Speak Out.* Loraine Hutchins and Lani Ka'ahumanu, Eds. Boston: Alyson Publications. 1991. 134–139.

Chris Cagle, "Rough Trade: Taxonomy in Postwar America" in *RePresenting Bisexualities: Subjects and Cultures of Fluid Desire.* Donald E. Hall and Maria Pramaggiore, Eds. NY: NYUP. 1996. 234–252.

Annalee Newitz and Jillian Sandell, "Bisexuality and How To Use It: Toward A Coalitional Identity Politics" in *Bad Subjects: Political Education for Everyday Life.* Michael Berube and Janet Lyon, Eds. NY: NYUP. 1998. 89–99.

Alexander Doty, "Everyone's Here For Love: Bisexuality and *Gentlemen Prefer Blondes*" in *Flaming Closets: Queering the Film Canon.* NY: Routledge. 2000. 131–153.

Film

Sunday, Bloody Sunday (1971). John Schlesinger. 110 m.
The Hunger (1986). Tony Scott. 97 m.
The Crying Game (1992). Neil Jordan. 112 m.
Three of Hearts (1993). Yurek Bogayevicz. 102 m.
Chasing Amy (1997). Kevin Smith. 111 m.

Special Topics

Queer vampire films: the other, the irresistible sexual consummation, the perpetual status as an outsider from the "normal" world, bisexual seductions *de rigueur.* And why are so many of them about lesbians?

Film

The Vampire Lovers (1970). Roy Ward Baker. 88 m.
Dracula (1931). Tod Browning. 75 m.
Vampyr (1932). Theodor Dreyer. 73 m.

Dracula's Daughter (1936). Lambert Hillyer. 70 m.
Twins of Evil (1971). John Hough. 85 m.
Interview With the Vampire (1994). Neil Jordan. 122 m.
Daughters of Darkness (1970). Harry Kumel. 87 m.
Lust For A Vampire (1971). Jimmy Sangster. 95 m.
The Hunger (1986). Tony Scott. 97 m.
Blood and Roses (1960). Roger Vadim. 74 m.

Reading

Sue-Ellen Case, "Tracking the Vampire." *differences 3.2* (Summer 1991): 1–20.

Christopher Craft, "'Kiss Me With Those Red Lips': Gender and Inversion in Bram Stoker's *Dracula*" in *Speaking of Gender*. Elaine Showalter, Ed. NY: Routledge. 1989. 216–242.

Richard Dyer, "Children of the Night: Vampirism as Homosexuality, Homosexuality as Vampirism" in *Sweet Dreams: Sexuality, Gender and Popular Fiction*. Susannah Radstone, Ed. London: Lawrence and Wishart. 1988. 47–72.

Ellis Hanson, "Undead" in *Inside/Out: Lesbian Theories, Gay Theories*. Diana Fuss, Ed. NY: Routledge. 1991. 324–340.

Ellis Hanson, "Lesbians Who Bite" in *Out Takes: Essays on Queer Theory and Film.*" Ellis Hanson, Ed. Durham: Duke UP. 1999. 183–222.

Andrea Weiss, "The Vampire Lovers" in *Vampires and Violets: Lesbians in Film*. NY: Penguin. 1992. 84–108.

Bonnie Zimmerman, "*Daughters of Darkness:* Lesbian Vampires." *Jump Cut 24/25* (1981): 23–24.

Transgender Mirrors: Queering Sexual Difference

Chris Straayer

Since the invention of homosexuality more than a century ago, professional and lay "audiences" alike have situated gender as its primary marker—as both what marks it and what it marks. From Weimar Germany's "third sex" to second-wave feminism's "lesbian-woman," gay men and lesbians have been measured in terms of their femininity and masculinity, which then have laid claims on their femaleness and maleness. Although gender displaced sexual orientation in these crude schemes, it also provided a primary visual semiotics through which queers communicated their sexualities. The present essay also reverses the signifying chain: rather than an en-gendering look at queerness, I take a queering look at gender.[1]

While they are often characterized as distinct traits, gender and sexual orientation are not entities that can be plucked from or implanted in a person. Outside the social event known as "self," they do not exist. Neither are they uniform from self to self. Gender and sexual orientation come into "being" within individual-cultural complexes that variably form and incorporate them. (The concepts of transgender and homosexual identities, born from oppression as well as resistance, always remain most suitable to the oppressors' dehumanizing mode of thought.) Transgendered people and gays and lesbians are fighting and delighting on multiple fronts simultaneously.

In this essay, I will discuss two independent video documentaries: *Juggling Gender* (Tami Gold 1992), which profiles Jennifer Miller, a bearded lesbian; and *OUTLAW* (Alisa Lebow 1994) which profiles Leslie Feinberg, a transgendered lesbian. These works dispute binary sex and the sex-gender matrix. Because feminism has enacted the most intensive investigation of gender, it offers an appropriate starting point for discussion. While I understand that feminism is not a static and impermeably bounded discipline, I nevertheless find its paradigm of sexual difference inadequate to certain questions about identity raised by *Juggling Gender* and *OUTLAW*.

In writing about independent documentary, I am less concerned with the distinction between representation and reality (the issue of document) than with the competition between different representations to define "reality" (the issue of independence). I take as a given that the documentaries I discuss are instances of discourse rather than windows on reality. Nevertheless, I also assume that the producers and subjects enacting such discourse are communicating with real purpose. Although both mainstream and independent documentaries are mediated, they are differently mediated at the institutional level. Independent productions avoid much of the gatekeeping and censorship of corporate financing entities and exhibition venues.

As I see it, the problem of mistaking representation for reality is now most salient not at the level of the viewership, but in the claim made by dominant ideology on representation itself. I focus on *independent* media production because it dearticulates the "insider" perspective that too often imbues mainstream media as well as contemporary theory. These video profiles in particular represent "outsider" experiences by foregrounding otherwise marginalized voices. Acknowledging the existence of such voices exposes the self-serving conflation of center with all, mainstream with society. I am not suggesting that independent media's sanctioned charge should be to accurately represent reality or even potential reality. Rather, I am looking at these specific videos as counterdominant discourses that *produce* countermeanings. I value them not only for their difference from mainstream representations but also for the important contributions they offer to theorizations of subjectivity. Again and again, "outsider" representations reveal the inadequacy of dominant ideology—sometimes through wrenching testimony.

Juggling Gender is a portrait of Jennifer Miller, a woman in her early thirties who began to develop a beard in late adolescence. Although beards do not uniformly occupy a sex-defining position across different races and cultures, they do in Miller's family and culture.[2] As her beard thickened, Miller became increasingly estranged from her family. Her grandmother urged her to undergo electrolysis, but Miller experienced the process as an extremely painful mutilation; further, having come out in the lesbian-feminist era and then undergoing electrolysis made Miller feel like a traitor to herself and her cause. If lesbian feminism's aesthetic of natural womanness encouraged letting one's leg and underarm hair grow, why not facial hair too? In lesbian bars and other women-only spaces, however, many women have resented the confusion Miller's appearance can cause. They never expected to mistake a "natural" woman for a man. Ironically, it was cultural feminism's endorsement of essential womanhood that enabled Miller to challenge the codification of sexual difference.

Miller describes how having a full beard has altered her gender, which is formed not only from who she is and how she behaves but also by her interactions with society. She would like the term *woman* to include her; however, after years of also being treated like a man, she thinks of herself as not just woman. Her experiences on the street have widened her construction to incorporate sometimes being man.[3]

Against earlier plans for college and professional life, Miller helped create a feminist circus where her "freak" status is acceptable. In the circus, she juggles, bearded and bare-breasted, foregrounding her sexual discontinuity. She eats fire, lies on a bed of nails, and performs other circus acts to make explicit society's ostracizing gaze at her. Performing as a Coney Island sideshow, she reminds the audience that many women have beards, that nonbearded femininity is constructed via shaving and electrolysis. "Women have the potential to have beards," she challenges them, "if only they would reach out." Unlike the women in the audience, however, Miller *is* the bearded lady, constructed as such by their look *at* her.

At the end of *Juggling Gender*, Miller is shown at a lesbian and gay pride march performing "faggot" drag. As she notes, there are as yet no codes for performing a bearded lesbian gender. Faggot behavior, she explains, is a response to being looked at, a situation to which she relates. Suddenly the camera pans back and forth between Miller and a drag queen sticking out their tongues to mime each other.

Miller's life as a bearded lesbian combines two discourses that elsewhere have produced altercation—cultural feminism and gay male drag. Many feminists, including many lesbian feminists, have read gay male drag as misogynous, even as they criticize the trappings of femininity for women. The fact that gay drag was read as a criticism of women themselves (rather than a parody of the masquerade)[4] illustrates the lasting power of reactionary codes even as they are deconstructed. In the present semiotic system, it *is* difficult to undo the collapse of woman with feminine masquerade. But Jennifer Miller's decision to let her beard grow exposes the *complicity* of many women in *maintaining* a system in which a beard is an essential definer of sex. Although under severe ideological pressure that would naturalize and thus strongly determine it, most women *consciously* choose electrolysis. If women are essentially different from men, this difference is certainly not attributable to a lack of facial hair. An essentialist position that also claims the accoutrements of masquerade or relies on the reconstruction of bodies is questionable. On the other hand, if one is constructed in the meaning that one's signs have to others, is not the presence or absence of accoutrements and facial hair an important producer of gender?

Miller's performance demonstrates how essentialist and constructionist discourses can lead into each other. Allowing her beard to grow is a direct extension of her cultural feminist training; but in so doing Miller belies the essentialism on which cultural feminism is based. In taking cultural feminism's tenet of "naturalness" to its logical conclusion, Miller risks exclusion from that very community, because to that community, as to mainstream society, she risks appearing to "be" a man.

Jennifer Miller is not the only character in *Juggling Gender*, for videomaking is also a means of performing. Offscreen but verbally present, the videomaker Tami Gold narrates her experience of making the tape. Gold initially explores her identity as a feminist, but her contact with Miller causes her to question gender itself. "What is a woman?" she asks. By including herself in the video as a thinking and learning presence, Gold suggests a responsible viewing mode for us. Our similarity to and difference from Coney Island audiences become clearer as Gold situates us to hear and consider what Miller is saying. Like Gold herself, we stare at Miller's image, but the tape infuses this voyeurism with a keen awareness of Jennifer Miller's subjectivity. Rather than hiding Miller's body and shying away from her "freakish" self-presentations, Gold contextualizes such images with Miller's testimony. Gold not only constructs Miller's image but also constructs herself as our surrogate. As such she encourages self-critical, intellectually engaged, and informed looking.

Endocrinology, psychoanalysis, and object relations are among the dominant discourses that define gender identity. Although many factors distinguish these theories, they all understand gender as basically fixed. Recent endocrinology research looks to the fetal environment for the determination of a core gender identity; psychoanalysis looks to the oedipal stage up to approximately age five and only secondarily to adolescence; object relations theory looks to the preoedipal mother-child relation in very early childhood. Many feminist theorists who assert the construction of gender follow object relations to understand sex attribution as the primary determinant of gender. I agree that sex attribution is influential, but, taking Jennifer Miller's gender juggling as a case in point, I neither locate it exclusively in early childhood nor understand it as fixed. Gender formation is constantly in process; rather than being a root of oneself, it continues throughout life via interactions with others. Not only one's mother is a gender mirror, but also everyone else one meets in life. The process of sex attribution (that is, gendering) does not stop at birth. For most people, complicity with binary gender semiotics (sex role stereotypes, conventional clothing, and so on) allows social interaction to reinforce birthtime sex attribution and thus gender. For others, voluntary or involuntary non-conformity causes radical disruptions and contradictions.

Wearing a beard, Jennifer Miller crosses the semiotic boundary between female and male and thus alters the basis upon which others construct her gender. This circular, interactive formation raises complex issues about "self." Obviously, had Miller concealed her beard, as other women have, her gender identity today would be different than it is—not because gender resides in biology (which can be controlled), but because of (a different) cultural production. A person, then, is simultaneously the producer of a persona and the product of the way(s) others read (and project into) that persona (and its failings).

Although Jennifer Miller is "out" as a lesbian in *Juggling Gender*, the tape produces meaning for the most part via its feminist voice.[5] Gold underlines the tape's feminist parameters by replacing the disembodied male authority of voice-of-God documentaries with cinema verité segments, performance, interviews, and attributable, subjective voice-overs by Miller and herself. She identifies herself as a continuing feminist even as her (particular) feminist perspective and assumptions are challenged by Miller. Miller also identifies as a feminist even though some feminists reject her. More importantly, Miller is portrayed as neither hero nor outlaw, for both positions would support an all-or-nothing mode of thinking. Instead she is cast as a noncomplicit survivor, which is why she impresses many audiences as a role model.[6] As such, she variously identifies as a woman and passes as a man.

Miller expresses "contradictory" positions throughout *Juggling Gender*: at times she asserts that she *is* still a woman (despite mistaken interpretations by strangers), but she also clearly insists that her gender is no longer reducible to *woman*. In my analysis here, I do not claim direct access to Jennifer Miller, Tami Gold, or *Juggling Gender*. Instead, I am elaborating on *my reading* of the tape. My own theorization of gender dismisses any prediscursive nature/body that would fix gender. I understand both gender and sex as "knowable" and negotiable only through convention. Like Gold and Miller, who are feminists challenging feminism, *Juggling Gender* pressures feminism rather than attacks it.

In 1970, at the Second Congress to Unite Women, the "lavender menace" disrupted scheduled events with a staged coming out that confronted straight feminists with their heterosexism and homophobia. Ironically, while denaturalizing the gathering's assumed unity, the action ultimately functioned to unite heterosexual women and lesbians via a circulated position paper from the Radicalesbians entitled "The Woman Identified Woman." In this short paper, the authors concisely argued that straight feminists should, like lesbians, channel their nurturance toward other women. In this way, they posited lesbianism as a feminist practice and feminism as the defining characteristic of lesbianism. The paper began, "What is a lesbian? A lesbian is the rage of all women condensed to the point of explosion." The Radicalesbians suggested that the straight versus lesbian split in the women's movement was attributable to patriarchal oppression on two counts: first, lesbianism, as distinct from heterosexuality, was the result of women's struggle for self-growth; and second, accusations of lesbianism were used by men to keep straight women in subservient roles. The paper called for straight women to lose their defensiveness by refusing to consider lesbianism as negative and to replace their internalized sexism with a commitment to women:

> It must be understood that what is crucial is that women begin disengaging from male-defined response patterns. In the privacy of our own psyches, we must cut those cords to the core. For irrespective of where our love and sexual energies flow, if we are male identified in our heads, we cannot realize our autonomy as human beings. . . .
>
> Only women can give each other a new sense of self. That identity we have to develop with reference to ourselves and not in relation to men. This consciousness is the revolutionary force from which all else will follow, for ours is an organic revolution. For this we must be available and supportive to one another, give our commitment and our love, give the emotional support necessary to sustain this movement. Our energies must flow toward our sisters, not backward toward our oppressors.[7]

Terralee Bensinger has argued that this document sacrificed lesbian sexuality to the politics of sexual difference.[8] One can readily see its contribution to a lesbian continuum where feminist mutuality (aka sisterhood) rather than sexuality defines the term *lesbian*. From a different perspective, Eve Kosofsky Sedgwick has described the document as "a stunningly efficacious coup of feminist redefinition" that provided a rare shift in the understanding of lesbianism, from a model of gender inversion to one of gender separatism.[9] I would like to briefly highlight what I see to be a related and equally important negotiation in the document, between two modes of identity.

Cultural feminism seems an essentialist discourse par excellence. Inverting the sexual hierarchy without disturbing sexual binarism, it valorizes female over male characteristics. Cultural feminism appropriates men's association of women with nature as the model for a better world. Extrapolated from women's birthing capacity, nurturance becomes a gender-defining principle.[10] In "The Woman Identified Woman," the Radicalesbians were able to turn the accusation of male-identification (previously directed at lesbians, who, because of their attraction to women, were assumed to be like men—that is, not real women) back on straight feminists by asserting the source of identity to be relational rather than integral. Directed at lesbians, the accusation of male identification posits a condition of self (virilization); directed at straight women, it posits a condition of (nonfeminist) allegiance. Viewed through this lesbian-feminist lens that understands identity through relations, personal relations with men jeopardize straight women's gender identity, while lesbians' female gender is secured by their romantic relationships. In this sense, sexual practice is not to-tally absent from the document's scene. In fact, object choice now determines gender via a schematic directly opposed to the assumption of heterogender that previously cast lesbians as "wannabe" men. Rather than basing *feminist* identity on what one is, the privileged ethic of nurturance was deployed to relocate such identity in how and toward whom one directs one's energy. This is a significant shift in terms. Unlike the gender essentialism on which female identity is based, feminist identity (the woman identified woman) is based on relational behavior. Further, such behavior ironically is attributed to natural womanness.

Although situated somewhat differently, Jennifer Miller's gender identity is also relations-based. Treated like a man, she becomes manlike. It is not her beard but rather people's reactions to its mark that have altered her gender. Those who see her as a man (as well as those who see her as a woman, or as a bearded woman) help mold her gender. Their gaze is her gender mirror. Like their gaze, her gender is both multifaceted and culturally specific; thus it dis-rupts unified concepts of gender. Unlike both cultural feminists and the Radi-calesbians, Miller wants the category of women to expand to include her "virilization."

Elizabeth Grosz's book *Volatile Bodies* is a project against the dualism of mind versus body. Describing the body as a sociohistorical product that func-tions interactively,[11] Grosz implants corporeality in the theorization of subjec-tivity. The material textures of bodies, rather than being blank pages waiting for cultural inscription, participate in and affect such inscriptions. This would seem to support Jennifer Miller's account of her gender formation.

In her final chapter, "Sexed Bodies," Grosz uses the work of Mary Douglas, Julia Kristeva, Luce Irigaray, and Iris Young to scrutinize how, in Western culture, bodily fluids that "attest to the permeability of the body"[12] are assigned to the feminine. Orifices and leakage threaten a masculine order that relies on a notion of self as closed entity. A production of otherness thus under-lies man's projection of the body itself onto woman, which seeks to eliminate his own pervious status and claim for him alone the supposedly more neutral, less situated mind. "Women, insofar as they are human, have the same degree of solidity, occupy the same genus, as men, yet insofar as they are women, they are represented and live themselves as seepage, liquidity."[13] Patriarchal dis-course does not describe subject formation as relational but rather as the ascen-sion to a bounded, phallic self.

While Grosz challenges the mind-body dualism and presses that chal-lenge against the "mechanics of solids" that inscribes and supports male subjec-tivity,[14] she generally preserves the dualism of sexual difference. She deontologizes sex, but culturally produced sexual difference remains essential to her argument. Although she alludes to hermaphroditic bodies and more than two sexes, she ultimately posits "the irreducible specificity of women's bodies."[15] One instance of specificity is menstruation, notable for its difference from the excretory functions mastered during toilet training. Appearing during female adolescence, it is the reemergence of the out of control body, the dirty. Menstruation thus is seen as *significantly* different from the flows shared by male and female bodies. In a footnote Grosz writes: "I am not advocating a naturalist or even a universalist attribute. Nonetheless, it is also true that all women, whatever the details of their physiology and fertility, are culturally understood in terms of these bodily flows [menstruation and lactation]."[16] Although it is conventionally marked, sexual difference remains salient.

This may be so, but it is disappointing that Grosz does not more aggressively apply her theorization of corporeal experience to affirm and explore more varied subjectivities arising from further elaborated bodily specificities. In a discussion about gay men's sexual practices, she does suggest embraced permeability as a possible component of male sensibility. Nevertheless, she ultimately remains primarily concerned with the generalities of two sexes:

> There will always remain a kind of outsideness or alienness of the experiences and lived reality of each sex for the other. Men, contrary to the fantasy of the transsexual, can never, even with surgical intervention, feel or experience what it is like to be, to live, as women. At best the transsexual can live out his fantasy of femininity—a fantasy that in itself is usually disappointed with the rather crude transformations effected by surgical and chemical intervention. The transsexual may look like a woman but can never feel like or be a woman.[17]

But if a transsexual looks like a woman, will she not also be culturally understood/treated/formed in terms of menstrual flow (despite its absence)? Grosz does not extend her discussion toward the question of how a transsexual's changed corporeality and appearance *do* affect subjectivity. The strength of Grosz's work is that it asserts that the experience of one's body (including one's relation to cultural meanings of one's sex) contributes to the formation of subjectivity. From this she rightly concludes that one's previously sexed life experience and subjectivity do not simply drop away with a sex change. However, does the influence of bodily and relational experiences suddenly halt with a sex change? What might Grosz's investigation of corporeal experience throughout her book offer to understanding how subject formation continues as bodily changes occur, whether via sex change or menopause? My pointing to an interplay of representation, perception, and experience with regard to subject formation allows that the (changing) body can influence subjectivity without discounting contrary gender identifications. To my mind, Grosz stops short of the potential her own work suggests.

We might ask, Is sexual difference not only productive for but necessary to feminism? Does "this gulf, this irremediable distance" between the sexes, as Grosz puts it,[18] prevent a fluidity of sex? Is feminism itself dependent on a "mechanics of solids" to postulate subjectivity?

Jennifer Miller's beard arrived on her with discursive valence. After all, it is a secondary sex characteristic. As such, it was supposed to (but did not) support an already sexed subjectivity, a sexual identity. A beard is supposed to be a reward at the end of horrifying *male* adolescence, a solidification after that messy stage of bodily transformations. Secondary sex characteristics are conceptualized as the final confirmations, not complications, of one's sex. They are *supposed* to offer relief after prolonged worries about whether our childish bodies will deliver the "appropriate" sexes or ultimately expose us as "freaks."

We patrol gender expressly because our claim to normality (that is, conventional humanness) has been made to rely on it. Not to be one's true sex is a crime against the law of pure difference. Mary Douglas's definition of dirt as that which is (culturally determined to be) out of place describes Jennifer Miller's beard. Hair is a waste product of our bodies, like urine, menstrual blood, and toenails. A man's beard, evidence of "masculine" flow, is best kept shaved or trimmed into a sculpture. A bearded woman, evidence of flow across sexual difference, is cultural feminism's abject.

In *Bodies That Matter*, Judith Butler analyzes how "properly" gendered bodies are materialized through heterosexual norms and how such formation of heterosexual subjects relies on foreclosures that produce homosexuality and gender inversion as abject: "The abject designates here precisely those 'unlivable' and 'uninhabitable' zones of social life which are nevertheless densely populated by those who do not enjoy the status of subject, but whose living under the sign of 'unlivable' is required to circumscribe the domain of the subject."[19] Constraints generate both sanctioned and unsanctioned positions but uphold the former via a logic that repudiates the latter. Such a normative scheme would understand Jennifer Miller as having failed to materialize as a (human) subject. Instead, her deformation serves as the constitutive "outside" by which normality is constituted and regulatory norms are fortified.[20] Her abject status locates her outside subjecthood. She is alive but not fully human.

The underlying problems in this operation, which affect all gay and lesbian and transgendered "subjects," are an Althusserian-influenced totalizing of ideology[21] and an overwillingness in Lacanian psychoanalysis to relegate irregular subjects to the "unrepresentable," a zone lacking symbolization and hence subjects. This is to mistake dominant ideology for all symbolization and to assume that what is unrepresented is unrepresentable. By contrast, Jennifer Miller does not experience herself as abject, and she obviously claims subjecthood. She has not undergone a "psychotic dissolution" simply because she is no longer one-sex-identified. Nor does *she* see herself as the "living prospect of death."[22]

Despite her valuable identification of regulatory regimes that construct abjection, Butler details this operation *rhetorically* from an "inside" perspective. This limits the "imagination" of her theorization and contributes to the naturalization of a particular standpoint, which is then allowed to define abjection. Certainly, it can be argued that no person can exist totally outside dominant ideology, and therefore that the dominant ideology's abject is uninhabitable. However, given the coexistence of "other" discourses that rearticulate dominant terms from "other" positions (that dominant ideology would assign to the abject), a particular subject materialization may be considerably more complex than such a regulating discourse would suggest. Part of what dominant ideology expels via assignment to *its* abject is, in fact, *formative* counterdiscourse.[23]

Butler opposes (theoretically speaking) any claim to coherent identity.[24] Following Laplanche and Pontalis's theorization of fantasy as the staging and dispersion of the subject, in which the subject cannot be assigned to any one position, Butler asserts that the normative subject is produced not by the refusal to identify with the other, but rather through *identification with* an abject other.[25]

> A radical refusal to identify with a given position suggests that on some level an identification has already taken place, an identification that is made and disavowed, a disavowed identification whose symptomatic appearance is the insistence on, the overdetermination of, the identification by which gay and lesbian subjects come to signify in public discourse.[26]

Likewise, Butler is careful to qualify the subversive potential of gender performativity. One cannot simply take on gender like one chooses clothing; this would imply a subject prior to gender. Rather, it is repetition in gender that forms the subject. Butler credits subversive rearticulation of the symbolic to the return of figures once repudiated (to the imaginary); this establishes a process of resignification rather than opposition and attributes contestation to the process of signification that inadvertently enables what it attempts to restrict.[27] Although Butler allows for inexact repetitions, she is opposed to attributing any amendments to personal choice or deliberation:

> The practice by which gendering occurs, the embodying of norms, is a compulsory practice, a forcible production, but not for that reason fully determining. To the extent that gender is an assignment, it is an assignment which is never quite carried out according to expectation, whose addressee never quite inhabits the ideal s/he is compelled to approximate. Moreover, this embodying is a repeated process. And one might construe repetition as precisely that which *undermines* the conceit of voluntarist mastery designated by the subject in language."[28]

Butler's work is outstanding for its deconstructions of identity and "natural" gender. However, her elucidation here seems more useful for understanding women's attempts to live up to an ideal—that is, their complicity with the maintenance of sexual difference—than for understanding feminist rejections of the ideal. For example, it better accounts for electrolysis as gender performativity ("the tacit cruelties that sustain coherent identity, cruelties that include self-cruelty")[29] than for Miller's refusal of electrolysis. It better explicates women's assumption of dominant norms for purposes of self-hatred than Miller's unconventional strength. Jennifer Miller's gendering cannot be explained simply as a failure to repeat. Certainly, the development of a beard on her body misses its conventional assignment; however, is not her decision to let the beard grow a choice (even if it is derived from a feminist ideology), and the subsequent (re)gendering (via the responses of others to her body) a result of her deliberate action (or inaction)? Does not Miller's bodily utterance alter the language of gender to some extent? Does not Gold's videotape reveal the boundary between symbolization and the "unrepresentable" real to be always in practice a fiction produced from a particular (dominant yet limited) point of view?

What I am suggesting by my discussion of Jennifer Miller in *Juggling Gender* is a salient temporality in subject formation. If indeed the subject is always a subject-in-process, then at any one point she is formed, being formed, and forming. Does not her formedness grant some subjectivity (however provisional), which she exercises even as cultural norms continue to interpellate her? My insistence on taking up marginal rather than (exclusively) dominant perspectives in theorizing subjectivity opens the way for *appreciating* a difference between a *failure* to repeat and a *refusal* to repeat.

In *OUTLAW* Leslie Feinberg, a transgender lesbian, describes her life as an everyday struggle. Feinberg is interviewed in a variety of meaningful settings. At the Pyramid Club, she refers to the female impersonators as sisters. At Liberty State Park in New Jersey, she criticizes people who assume the right to stare. At the Hudson piers, a Manhattan site notorious for transgenderist (and gay) gatherings and bashings, she explains that any place where transgenderists go becomes dangerous (for them). In her backyard, she explains that, to her, *butch* means butch on the street, an act of courage that earns one the right to engage in whatever acts she wants to in bed. At the gym, surrounded by workout machines and mirrors, she describes her self-image as a combination of how she sees herself and how the world sees her. In choosing the gym as an interview setting, Feinberg contributed to her media construction in a way transgenderists seldom are allowed to do. Rather than simply exposing the transgendered body for spectacle, Feinberg retains her subject position in an environment symbolic of self-empowerment.

Feinberg's testimony is solemn throughout *OUTLAW*. Only at rare moments does her enjoyment of life break through: in her exquisite "men's" suits, in scenes with her lover repotting plants and watching a home movie. When clips from *The Rocky Horror Picture Show* suggest a reprieve from her testimony of constant oppression, Feinberg reminds us that a mere movie is not going to liberate Eighth Street (in New York City, where the film was then playing midnights) from transgender bashing. Elsewhere, when Feinberg speaks of transgenderists reclaiming their histories, her smile is undercut by an edit to helicopters flying overhead in formation.

The pleasure in viewing *OUTLAW* derives from the complex collaboration of Feinberg's discourse and Alisa Lebow's disquisition. Using music (Danny Galton's "Funky Momma," for example), intertitles ("Suit and Tie Optional," for example), and extradiegetic imagery (a woman bodybuilder, for example), Lebow both underlines and adds ambiguity to Feinberg's analysis of transgender oppression. At one point Feinberg expresses disapproval and impatience with people who compare their childhood gender crossings with her lived experience. Such linkages erase the actual repression she risks when, for instance, she uses a public washroom. Lebow's inclusion of footage from the film *Yentl* at this point in the tape both demonstrates how transgenderism is often trivialized and also implies a continuum from feminist cross-dressing to transgenderism, which offers a conduit for viewer identification.

Lebow's videomaking is most aggressive when she re-presents a scene of Feinberg appearing on the *Joan Rivers Show*, where Feinberg proclaims the need for transgenderists to name and speak for themselves. Through skillful editing, Lebow becomes Feinberg's co-conspirator. "I'm so sick of being psychologized. I'm so sick of being studied like a butterfly pinned to the wall," says Feinberg in voice-over as the face of a token authority figure, clinical sexologist Roger E. Peo, Ph.D., appears on the screen. Then Lebow audiocuts to sync sound as Peo begins, "I'm not in a position to judge and say this person should do this thing or that thing. What I try to do is . . ." On the original broadcast, the authority no doubt went on to state his opinion, but in the Lebow/Feinberg version his appraisal is excised. Smoothly but decisively, Lebow interrupts him with an audio-visual cut to Feinberg, who continues, now in sync sound: "All our lives, we've always seen ourselves refracted through other people's prisms. We're always hearing people analyze us, describe what our feelings are, what our thoughts are. How about talking about why Jesse Helms needs some therapy?"

OUTLAW begins with a discussion of Joan of Arc and ends with a dedication to Brandon Teena and Marsha P. Johnson. Brandon Teena (born Teena Brandon but living as a male) was raped by two young men on Christmas Eve 1993 in Nebraska. Although Teena's face was injured and a hospital test confirmed recent vaginal penetration, his attackers were released after questioning. No arrests were made. One week later, on New Year's Eve, the same young men allegedly killed Teena. Martha Johnson, a drag queen veteran of the Stonewall rebellion, was found dead in the Hudson River (off the piers) after the 1992 New York City gay pride march. Although there were signs of resistance, Johnson's death was declared a suicide after a perfunctory police investigation. In addition to the outsider status guaranteed by their transgenderism, Teena and Johnson were working-class people. Like Feinberg, they lacked the protection of class privilege experienced by more acclaimed historical cross-dressers such as Radclyffe Hall, George Sand, and Gertrude Stein. It is significant to Feinberg that the powerful and persecuted Joan of Arc, who not only sported men's clothes but also passed as a man, was a peasant. That Feinberg could not know this as a child is a culpable suppression of (transgender) evidence. Gender and class are inseparable in all of these people and their expressions; we cannot know the meanings of their different transgenders without also knowing their class situations.

While claiming both transgenderism and homosexuality, Feinberg is careful to distinguish between them. During her interview at the Pyramid Club, she draws two intersecting circles on a blackboard and indicates her own position: within the intersection. *OUTLAW* reminds us that much of the violence enacted against gays and lesbians actually is directed at transgenderism.[30] Of course, as I remarked at the beginning of this essay, gender and sexual orientation have been intertwined historically by sexological discourse and homosexual appropriation of such discourse for self-coding. Transgenderism is attacked partly because it reads as homosexuality and vice versa. It is therefore important neither to collapse homosexuality and transgenderism nor to overlook their specific imbrications.

Eve Kosofsky Sedgwick argues in "How to Bring Your Kids Up Gay" that neither an essentialist nor a constructionist position guarantees safety for homosexual subjectivity. She locates a shift during the 1970s and 1980s from pathologizing adult homosexuality to pathologizing childhood gender crossing. The 1980 edition of the American Psychiatric Association's *Diagnostic and Statistical Manual* was both the first not to contain an entry for "Homosexuality" and the first to contain the entry "Gender Identity Disorder of Childhood." To Sedgwick, this *preventive* measure expresses the rage of parents, professionals, society at large, and even gays and lesbians at sissy boys and, to a lesser extent, butch girls. Ironically, she points out, the new psychoanalytic move to pathologize gender disorder while depathologizing sexual orientation is based on the recent theoretical move to distinguish gender and sex orientation (for example, the gender constructionist approaches of John Money and Robert Stoller).[31] This makes it clear that the attempt by some homosexuals to pry apart gender and sexual orientation not only is inadequate but can fuel a reactionary discourse against those among us who cross gender. Therefore, any rejection of masculinity in lesbians or metaphoric feminization of the term *lesbian* warrants extreme caution.

Juggling Gender and *OUTLAW* re-present voices that contest the borders generally assumed to dominate symbolization and subject formation and problematize theory that situates its rhetorical point of view strictly within those borders. I understand gender and gender formation to be more flexible than the paradigm sexual binarism produces and to be continually influenced by social experience. By focusing on independent media, I call attention to alternative representations as well as alternative subjects.

Notes

1. This essay draws on two excerpts from my book *Deviant Eyes, Deviant Bodies: Sexual Re-Orientations in Film and Video* (New York: Columbia University Press, 1996). The videos discussed, *Juggling Gender* and *OUTLAW*, are distributed by Women Make Movies, 462 Broadway, Suite 500D, New York, NY 10013; telephone 212-925-0606; fax 212-925-2052; E-mail distdept@wmm.com.

2. For a wide-ranging discussion of differently sexed and gendered cultures, see Gilbert Herdt, ed., *Third Sex, Third Gender* (New York: Zone, 1994).

3. In *Juggling Gender*, gender often refers also to sex. Because of Miller's being perceived as one of the male sex, her constructed gender-sex expands beyond womanness.

4. Mary Ann Doane, drawing on Joan Riviere, has argued that womanliness *is* the masquerade of femininity ("Film and the Masquerade: Theorizing the Female Spectator," in *Femmes Fatales: Feminism, Film Theory, Psychoanalysis* [New York:

Routledge, 1991], 17–32). I complicate this in chapter 5 of *Deviant Eyes, Deviant Bodies*.

5. The video foregrounds feminism over lesbianism. The extent to which the absence of lesbian sexuality is a by-product of the tape's focus, necessary for its feminist efficacy, and/or a self-conscious avoidance of the dangerous terrain of gender inversion explanations of homosexuality is difficult to determine.

6. The function of role model is important here because, as Judith Butler argues, the performative utterance has no valence unless it is repeated (*Bodies That Matter: On the Discursive Limits of "Sex"* [New York: Routledge, 1993], 107). Ultimately, Miller's rearticulation "exposes the norm itself as a privileged interpretation" (*Bodies*, 108) and serves as a model for *not* citing, *not* repeating assumed symbolic categories. In this way, I question the precision and efficacy of using the term *citation* (or *repetition*) to refer to both complicit and subversive acts.

7. Radicalesbians, "The Woman Identified Woman," in *Radical Feminism*, ed. Anne Koedt, Ellen Levine, and Anita Rapone (New York: Quandrangle, 1973), 166.

8. Terralee Bensinger, "Lesbian Pornography: The Re/Making of (a) Community," *Discourse* 15.1 (1992): 74.

9. Eve Kosofsky Sedgwick, *Epistemology of the Closet* (Berkeley: University of California Press, 1990), 84, 88.

10. See Alice Echols, *Daring to Be Bad: Radical Feminism in America 1967–1975* (Minneapolis: University of Minnesota Press, 1989); Alison M. Jagger, *Feminist Politics and Human Nature* (Totowa, N.J.: Rowman and Allanheld, 1983); and my discussion of motherhood in chapter 5 of *Deviant Eyes, Deviant Bodies*.

11. Elizabeth Grosz, *Volatile Bodies: Toward a Corporeal Feminism* (Bloomington: Indiana University Press, 1994), x, xi.

12. Ibid., 193.

13. Ibid., 203.

14. Ibid., 204.

15. Ibid., 207.

16. Ibid., 228 n17.

17. Ibid., 207.

18. Ibid., 208.

19. Butler, *Bodies*, 3.

20. Ibid., 16.

21. The continued deployment of the repressive state apparatus should remind us that the ideological state apparatus is not as totalizing as it would have us believe.

22. See Butler, *Bodies*, 98: "The breaking of certain taboos brings on the spectre of psychosis, but to what extent can we understand 'psychosis' as relative to the very prohibitions that guard against it? In other words, what precise cultural possibilities threaten the subject with a psychotic dissolution, marking the boundaries of livable being? To what extent is the fantasy of psychotic dissolution itself the effect of a certain prohibition against those sexual possibilities which abrogate the heterosexual contract? Under what conditions and under the sway of what regulatory schemes does homosexuality itself appear as the living prospect of death?"

23. For clarification, I want to stress that I am not taking up an imagined "other" position with respect to Butler. I am not promoting a humanist view of free will and individuality. I agree with Butler that language constrains subject formation. Nevertheless, I think that theoretical investigation should include the choice and responsibility within these limitations. To think of culture as *all* determining is

neither accurate nor productive. Butler *asks:* "Does not the refusal to concur with the abjection of homosexuality necessitate a critical rethinking of the psychoanalytic economy of sex?" (*Bodies*, 97). Butler's focus here is sexual orientation, but I think she produces the same question regarding gender.

24. This includes those claims from the homosexual abject, whether gay, lesbian, sissy, butch, or femme (Butler, *Bodies*, 113). As she states, "Heterosexuality does not have a monopoly on exclusionary logics" (*Bodies*, 112).

25. Butler, *Bodies*, 267, 112.

26. Ibid., 113.

27. Ibid., 109.

28. Ibid., 231; emphasis in the original.

29. Ibid., 115.

30. Such violence is also directed at transgenderism among heterosexuals.

31. Eve Kosofsky Sedgwick, *Tendencies* (Durham, N.C.: Duke University Press, 1993), 154–64.

Questions for Reflection, Discussion, and Writing

1. What does Straayer claim about why independent documentaries are valuable as "instances of discourse rather than windows on reality"? In what ways does Straayer argue that they are "differently mediated" than mainstream documentaries?

2. In the documentary *Juggling Gender*, Jennifer Miller refuses to alter her facial hair. What reasons are offered? What do these reasons and her refusal to remove or alter her facial hair suggest about mainstream and lesbian understandings of "woman," "beauty," and "gender" according to Straayer?

3. What connection does Straayer establish between Miller's refusal to shave her beard and Miller's self-concept? How does Gold, as producer, help to construct our understandings of that meaning, according to Straayer?

4. By juggling in a feminist circus, Miller invites the audience's gaze. What interpretation does Straayer offer this use of "the gaze?"

5. According to Straayer, in what "important" ways is Alisa Lebow's documentary *OUTLAW* different from more mainstream renderings of transgendered people? What techniques does Straayer suggest Lebow employs to enable Feinberg to retain her subject position?

6. In what ways does Lebow contextualize Feinberg's testimony—historically, rhetorically, and intellectually—and in so doing, challenge mainstream appropriation in the form of "the gaze?"

Related Reading

Pamela Robertson, "Home and Away: Friends of Dorothy on the Road in Oz" in *The Road Movie Book*. Steven Cohan and Ina Rae Hark, Eds. NY: Routledge. 1997. 271–286.

Sharon Willis, "Race on the Road: Crossover Dreams" in *The Road Movie Book*. Steven Cohan and Ina Rae Hark, Eds. NY: Routledge. 1997. 287–306.

Anne Ciecko, "Transgender, Transgenre, and the Transnational: Sally Potter's *Orlando.*" *Velvet Light Trap 41* (1998 Spring): 19–34.

Film

Adventures of Priscilla, Queen of the Desert (1994). Stephan Elliott. 102 m.
Juggling Gender (1992). Tami Gold. 27 m.
To Wong Foo, Thanks For Everything, Julie Newmar (1995). Beeban Kidron. 108 m.
Outlaw (1994). Alisa Lebow. 26 m.
The Crying Game (1992). Neil Jordan. 112 m.
Orlando (1993), Sally Potter. 93 m.

Special Topics

Neil Jordan's 1992 *The Crying Game* (112 m.) inspired critical response in the areas of Nation and Post-Colonial Studies, Gender, Identity, and Performance, and Textual Studies (literature and film). It raises essential issues about the intersections of race, gender, political oppression, desire, nation, and revolution. This film is also entirely relevant and applicable to transgender studies.

Irish, Nation and Post-Colonial Studies

Nicholas Daly, "Post-Colonial Carnival (?): Neil Jordan's *The Crying Game*" in *Borderlands: Negotiating Boundaries in Post-Colonial Writing*. Monika Reif-Hulser, Ed. Amsterdam: Rodopl. 1999. 215–225.

Leslie Gerber, "The Virtuous Terrorist: Stanley Hauerwas and *The Crying Game.*" *Cross Currents 43.2* (1993 Summer): 230–234.

Maureen S.G. Hawkins, "Women, 'Queers,' Love, and Politics: *The Crying Game* as a Corrective Adaptation of/Reply to The Hostage" in *Representing Ireland: Gender Class, Nationality*. Susan Shaw Sailer, Ed. Gainesville, FL: UP of Florida. 1997. 194–212.

Rosemary Hennessy, "Ambivalence as Alibi: On the Historical Materiality of Late Capitalist Myth in *The Crying Game* and Cultural Theory" in *On Your Left: The New Historical Materialism*. Ann Kibbey, et al, Eds. NY: NYUP. 1996. 1–34.

Katrina Irving, "EU-Phoria? Irish National Identity, European Union, and *The Crying Game*" in *Writing New Identities: Gender, Nation, and Immigration in Contemporary Europe*. Gisela Brinker-Gabler and Sidonie Smith, Eds. Minneapolis: U of Minnesota P. 1997. 295–314.

Ella Rantonen, "A Game of Chess: Race, Gender and Nation in Neil Jordan's *The Crying Game*" in *Postcolonialism and Cultural Resistance*. Jopi Nyman, John Stotesbury, Eds. Joensuu, Finland: Faculty of Humanities, University of Joensuu. 1999. 192–204.

Gender, Identity, and Performance

Jack Boozer, Jr. "Bending Phallic Patriarchy in *The Crying Game*." *Journal of Popular Film & Television 22.4* (1995 Winter): 172–179.

Jonathan Crewe, "In the Field of Dreams: Transvestism in *Twelfth Night* and *The Crying Game*." *Representations 50* (1995 Spring): 101–121.

Shantanu DuttaAhmed, "'I Thought You Knew!': Performing the Penis, the Phallus, and Otherness in Neil Jordan's *The Crying Game*." *Film Criticism 23.1* (1998 Fall): 61–73.

Sarah Edge, "'Women Are Trouble, Did You Know That Fergus?': Neil Jordan's *The Crying Game*." *Feminist Review 50* (1995): 173–186.

Kristin Handler, "Sexing *The Crying Game:* Difference, Identity, Ethics." *Film Quarterly 47.3* (1994 Spring): 31–42.

Joy James, "Black Femmes Fatales and Sexual Abuse in Progressive 'White' Cinema: Neil Jordan's *Mona Lisa* and *The Crying Game*." *Camera Obscura 36* (1995 September): 33–46.

Aspasia Kotsopoulos and Josephine Mills, "Gender, Genre and 'Postfeminism': *The Crying Game*." *Jump Cut: A Review of Contemporary Media 39* (1994): 15–24.

Susan Lurie, "Performativity in Disguise: Ideology and the Denaturalization of Identity in Theory and *The Crying Game*." *Velvet Light Trap 43* (1999): 51–62.

Frann Michel, "Racial and Sexual Politics in *The Crying Game*." *Cineaste 20.1* (1993): 30, 32, 34.

Bronwyn Morkham, "From Parody to Politics: Bodily Inscriptions and Performative Subversions in *The Crying Game*." *Critical Inqueeries 1.1* (1995 September): 47–68.

Amy Zilliax, "The Scorpion and the Frog: Agency and Identity in Neil Jordan's *The Crying Game*." *Camera Obscura 35* (1995 May): 25–51.

Textual Studies

Peter N. Chumo II, "*The Crying Game*, Hitchcockian Romance, and the Quest for Identity." *Literature-Film Quarterly 23.4* (1995): 247–253.

John Hill, "Crossing the Water: Hybridity and Ethics in *The Crying Game*." *Textual Practice 12.1* (1998 Spring): 89–100.

David Lugowski, "Genre Conventions and Visual Style in *The Crying Game*." *Cineaste 20.1* (1993): 31, 33, 35.

Special Topics

Jennie Livingston's documentary *Paris Is Burning* (1990, 71 m.) set off a maelstrom of critical conversation: her narrative about the lives of African American and Latino men in Harlem's drag ball culture raised sometimes conflicting perspectives on the issues of class, white privilege, racialized subjects and the aesthetics of otherness. Critics such as Judith Butler located in drag's self-conscious play(ing) with gender an ideal metaphor to illustrate the permeability of sex and gender distinctions. Drag was queer. But it was also, in the film, raced and classed, with a sometimes none too definite distinction be-tween those subjects who represented as transvestites, and those who identified as trans-gender. Using any of the film/readings below in conjunction with a screening of the film can constitute a separate unit in itself.

Film

Voguing: The Message (1989). Jack Walworth, David Bronstein & Dorothy Low. 13 m.

Reading

Lisa Henderson, "Paris is Burning and Academic Conservatism." *Journal of Communica-tion 42.2* (1992): 113–122.

Ilsa J. Bick, "To Be Real: Shame, Envy, and the Reflections of Self in Masquerade." *Discourse: Journal for Theoretical Studies in Media & Culture. 15.2* (1992–1993): 80–93.

Peggy Phelan, "Crisscrossing Cultures" in *Crossing the Stage" Controversies on Cross-Dressing.* Lesley Ferris, Ed. NY: Routledge. 1993. 155–170.

Jackie Goldsby, "Queens of Language: *Paris Is Burning*" in *Queer Looks: Perspective on Lesbian and Gay Film and Video.* Martha Gever, John Greyson and Pratibha Par-mar, Eds. NY: Routledge. 1993. 108–115.

Gabriel Gomez, "Homocolonialism: Looking for Latinos in *Apartment Zero* and *Paris Is Burning.*" *Post Script: Essays in Film & the Humanities 14.1* 1–2 (1994–95): 117–124.

Judith Butler, "Gender Is Burning: Questions of Appropriation and Subversion" in *Dangerous Liaisons: Gender, Nation, and Postcolonial Perspectives.* Anne McClintock, aamir Mufti and Ella Shohat, Eds. U of Minnesota P. 1997. 381–395.

Christian A. Gregory, "Performative Transformation of the Public Queer in *Paris Is Burning.*" *Film Criticism 23.1* (1998): 18–37.

Caryl Flinn, "Containing Fire: Performance in *Paris Is Burning*" in *Documenting the Doc-umentary: Close Readings of Documentary Film and Video.* Barry Keith Grant and Jeanette Sloniowiski, Eds. Detroit, MI.: Wayne State UP. 1998. 429–445.

Phillip Brian Harper, "The Subversive Edge: *Paris Is Burning,* Social Critique, and the Limits of Subjective Agency" *in Private Affairs: Critical Ventures in the Culture of Social Relations.* NY: NYUP. 1999. 33–59.

Queer Fictions of the Past

One of the alterations postmodern thought has brought into the discipline of history is a shift from emphasizing the objective in an historical account to an awareness of the subjectivity of *all* historical accounts, and an attunement to their qualities as texts not all that different from fiction. Though history concerns itself with documents, facts, and events from an historical rather a fictional past, it is also true that any given historical account begins in a certain place, emphasizes some chief actors and characters and ignores others, recounts a select group of events, and ends at an arbitrarily chosen point, similar to the ways fictions operate. Histories, in other words, are fictions of a sort when we think of them as texts constructed to tell a specific story.

Such reconstruction has been especially important for queer histories. In the first place, much of gay and lesbian history has been ignored and suppressed throughout the twentieth century until recently. Redefinitions of what constitute acceptable subjects and investigations have expanded considerably in recent decades, much to the benefit of queers, women, people of color, and the working poor. Queer theory, moreover, has opened up the field of sexual history by allowing researchers and writers to look beyond the categories of gay and lesbian which, as Foucault and others argue, are late nineteenth- and twentieth-century constructions. Queer constructions, those that do not adhere to the normative sexual and gender expectations of a given society, can now be investigated, described, and analyzed free from the obligation to locate a gay or lesbian identity across historical periods. Nor should we assume that, *a priori*, social opprobrium necessarily exists regarding same sex affiliations in earlier periods as it does in twentieth-century societies which have inherited the scientific categories of sexual behavior and deviance created in a nineteenth-century world and outlined by Foucault in his *History of Sexuality*.

The content of the queer histories in this section is as important as is critical reflection about how these particular histories are conveyed. Who are the main characters in these texts? What evidence and events illustrate their stories? What is each historian claiming about a particular time and place? Is the essay's argument effective? Why or why not? History is the collectivity of the stories we tell about the past. Think about what kinds of queer pasts you encounter in these essays, and ponder their effects on, as well as their relevance to, the queer present in which we live today.

■

Boys' Own Stories and New Spellings of My Name: Coming Out and Other Myths of Queer Positionality

Robert McRuer

Myths of Queer Positionality

In *The Beautiful Room Is Empty*, Edmund White's nameless narrator envisions a day when gay people will claim the right to define themselves: "Then I caught myself foolishly imagining that gays might someday constitute a community rather than a diagnosis" (226). This exhilarating thought comes to White's protagonist as he finds himself in the middle of an uprising at the Stonewall Inn Bar in Greenwich Village on the night of June 27, 1969. Drawing on Civil Rights rhetoric, the protagonist and his friends reclaim and reposition their own experiences with chants such as "Gay is good" and "We're the Pink Panthers" (226).[1]

Although White's account is fictional, the riots outside the Stonewall Inn are generally considered the beginning of the contemporary gay liberation movement. They did indeed usher in a decade of redefinition by lesbian and gay communities. Within weeks, the Gay Liberation Front (GLF) had formed, employing the slogan "Out of the Closets and into the Streets!" Within a year, the Radicalesbians, influenced by both gay liberation and the women's movement, had presented feminists with the "woman-identified woman," a position that they hoped would facilitate the formation of challenging, politicized coalitions among women. By 1974, activists had successfully removed homosexuality from the American Psychiatric Association's (APA's) list of mental disorders. In short, the new names and identities embraced by White's protagonist and his friends were high on the agenda for early gay liberationists.[2]

These newly available gay and lesbian identities were claimed and pro-claimed through the act of "coming out." This act provided lesbians and gay men with positions that could serve as starting points for the radical political ac-tion the early gay liberationists believed was necessary to reconfigure the sys-tems of capitalism and patriarchy responsible for gay and lesbian oppression. Indeed, the very slogan of the gay liberationists (and the title of a 1972 essay by Allen Young), "Out of the Closets, into the Streets," suggests not simply that one claims a position ("out of the closet") but that one moves from that position to effect radical social change. Young writes, "Of course, we want to 'come out.'. . . But the movement for a new definition of sexuality does not; and can-not, end there. . . . The revolutionary goals of gay liberation, including the elimination of capitalism, imperialism and racism, are premised on the termina-tion of the system of male supremacy" (10). Similarly, "woman-identification," according to the Radicalesbians, could be "develop[ed] with reference to our-selves, and not in relation to men. This consciousness is the revolutionary force from which all else will follow" (Radicalesbians, 176). Like the identity posi-tions (pro)claimed by all the so-called new social movements, the identities into which gay and lesbian activists "came out" were collective identities meant to generate radical social change based on new and different ways of understand-ing the world.[3]

Coming out generally does not have the same radical edge for the new generation of queer activists, or for the writers of the Queer Renaissance, that it had for their gay liberationist forebears. On the contrary: coming out, along with its product—one's "coming-out story"—has been thoroughly critiqued by many contemporary lesbian and gay writers. In particular, theorists have cri-tiqued coming-out stories for their emphasis on the "discovery" of an individual and essential gay identity, unmarked by other categories of difference, such as race or class. This chapter briefly surveys these and other criticisms but simul-taneously attempts to lay the theoretical groundwork for a reclamation of com-ing out's radical potential. Specifically, through readings of Edmund White's *A Boy's Own Story* and Audre Lorde's *Zami: A New Spelling of My Name*, I consider whether a feminist-informed and antiracist analysis might redefine the parame-ters of the coming-out story, shaping it into a myth of what I call "queer (op)positionality."

Through the term *(op)positionality*, I intend to invoke the "opposition" to established and oppressive systems of power that was voiced by the GLF, the Radicalesbians, and members of all the new social movements, and that has been rearticulated in the contemporary Queer Renaissance. I also intend to in-voke "positionality" theory (or "standpoint epistemology") as it has evolved in recent feminist writing. Standpoint theorists, often explicitly citing both the strengths and the weaknesses of the social movements of the 1960s and early 1970s, argue for a nonessentialized "position" from which to forge coalition-based political action.[4] Linda Alcoff, for example, argues, "If we combine the concept of identity politics with a conception of the subject as positionality, we can conceive of the subject as nonessentialized and emergent from a historical experience and yet retain our political ability to take gender as an important point of departure" (433). As Alcoff sees it, this new position is both fluid and relational: "being a 'woman' is to take up a position within a moving historical context and to be able to choose what we make of this position and how we alter this context," so that "women can themselves articulate a set of interests and ground a feminist politics" (435).

Similarly, Donna Haraway's feminist redefinition of "objectivity" argues for an openly acknowledged, although partial, position or perspective. Haraway writes, "Feminist objectivity is about limited location and situated knowledge, not about transcendence and splitting of subject and object" (190). This *partial* perspective is necessitated since, not unlike Edmund White's narrator in *The Beautiful Room Is Empty*, with his concern about psychiatric diagnoses, Haraway confesses that she has occasional paranoid fantasies about so-called *impartial*, "objective" discourses that appropriate "embodied others" as "objects" of knowledge:

> Academic and activist feminist enquiry has repeatedly tried to come to terms with the question of what *we* might mean by the curious and inescapable term "objectivity." We have used a lot of toxic ink and trees processed into paper decrying what *they* have meant and how it hurts *us*. The imagined "they" constitute a kind of invisible conspiracy of masculinist scientists and philosophers replete with grants and laboratories; and the imagined "we" are the embodied others, who are not allowed *not* to have a body. (183)

Because of these fears, Haraway's redefinition of "objectivity," like the rhetoric of gay liberation, gives preference to other ways of seeing, particularly those ways of seeing that emerge from what she calls the "standpoints of the subjugated." She writes, "'Subjugated' standpoints are preferred because they seem to promise more adequate, sustained, objective, transforming accounts of the world" (191). Such standpoints are actually *more* "objective" because they do not claim to see, simultaneously, "everything from nowhere" (189) or "to be," as Richard Dyer puts it in his analysis of the social construction of whiteness, "everything and nothing" (Dyer, 45). Such standpoints are more "transforming" because a coalition politics that emphasizes working together across difference is fundamental to what theorists of positionality envision. Indeed, this model would not have been shaped in the first place if feminists of color had not called for a more rigorous analysis of the differences within feminism and for an ongoing interrogation of the ways in which feminist concerns overlap with the concerns of other groups. Both Haraway and Alcoff, consequently, place race as well as gender at the center of their analyses: to Haraway, the category "women of color" "marks out a self-consciously constructed space that cannot affirm the capacity to act on the basis of natural identification, but only on the basis of conscious coalition, of affinity, of political kinship" (Haraway, 156); to Alcoff, positionality theory "can be readily intuited by people of mixed races and cultures who have had to choose in some sense their identity" (Alcoff, 432).

Other theorists, recognizing the value of such coalition-based and self-reflexive positionality, have attempted to link gay male and feminist standpoint theory. Earl Jackson, Jr., for one, begins his study of Robert Glück by acknowledging, "One of the most important things gay men can learn from feminist and lesbian-feminist discursive practices is how to read and write from responsibly identified positions" (112). Nevertheless, there are drawbacks to any attempt to link, specifically, *coming out* to feminist theories of positionality; these drawbacks become evident from the critiques of coming out I alluded to earlier. The position "out of the closet," much more than the "standpoint" of recent feminist theory, has become in the past two decades a mandated and delimited position, for both men and women. In the process of forging the imperative to come out, unfortunately, some lesbian and gay communities lost the sense that coming out was, as feminist theorists now argue about the feminist standpoint, only a beginning point from which to launch political action. The collective rallying cry "Out of the Closets, into the Streets" quickly became the demand that individuals simply "Come out of the closet." Assimilation, rather than transformation, became the goal; increased visibility, it was thought, would lead to gay civil rights and acceptance into mainstream society. Martin Duberman explains that the Gay Activists Alliance emerged

> as a breakaway alternative to the Gay Liberation Front, and would shortly supercede it. . . . Whereas GLF had argued that sexual liberation had to be fought for in conjunction with a variety of other social reforms and in alliance with other oppressed minorities, GAA believed in a single-minded concentration on gay civil rights and eschewed "romantic" excursions into revolutionary ideology. (*Cures*, 213–14)[5]

Maintaining the GLF's insistence that gay men and lesbians speak up but abandoning their politics of alliance, the GAA redirected the movement and circumscribed the meaning of coming out.

In addition to the dangers of quietism, coming out as a focus for gay and lesbian theory could also underwrite an apolitical essentialism. The narrowing of vision Duberman recounts could, and often does, narrow even further, so that coming out comes to signify solely the assertion of one's (supposedly long-repressed) identity. This model of coming out, by itself, exhibits little concern for how lesbian or gay identities are socially constituted, for how they are intersected by other arenas of difference, or for what sort of collective political action might develop from an assertion of one's gay or lesbian identity. Coming out here becomes a suspiciously white and middle-class move toward "self-respect," not revolutionary social change, and many contemporary coming-out narratives might be seen as products of this shift toward individualism and essentialism. To be fair, however, John D'Emilio writes, in reference to the early gay liberationists:

For a gay man or lesbian of that time, I don't think that it was possible to experience anything of comparable intensity. In a psychological sense it was an act of
"revolutionary" import. No manner of political analysis could convince someone
who had come out that he or she wasn't turning the world inside out and upside
down. (*Making Trouble*, 249)

Still, D'Emilio's comment is less a trumpeting of the benefits of coming
out than it is a note of caution. He is attempting to contextualize, but also look
critically at, the psychological empowerment that coming out could bring:
"Only later, as the movement matured, would it become clear that coming out
was a first step only. An openly gay banker is still a banker" (*Making Trouble*,
249). By the end of the 1970s and throughout the 1980s, many lesbians and gay
men no longer had the sense that coming out was a first step only. Coming out
came to have one meaning, across all social locations: announcing one's homosexuality. The act no longer necessarily carried the sense that lesbians and gays
should collectively move to *new* locations; one could come out, and stay out,
anywhere. Although "coming out conservative" would have been a logical impossibility to members of the GLF, by 1992, because of the ways in which the
act had been redefined as the assertion of one's essential, no longer repressed
identity, it was the title of a popular book about Marvin Liebman, a formerly
closeted anticommunist and conservative activist.

In a slightly different vein, Haraway, too, stresses that essentialism in its
many guises is a pitfall for feminist theories of positionality, especially those,
like hers, that foreground the "standpoints of the subjugated": "But here lies a
serious danger of romanticizing and/or appropriating the vision of the less powerful while claiming to see from their positions. . . . A commitment to mobile
positioning and to passionate detachment is dependent on the impossibility of
innocent 'identity' politics" (191–92). Haraway's disclaimers suggest that these
essentializing tendencies might not engulf feminist theories of positionality, as
long as "situating knowledge" entails continually and collectively *re*positioning
identity: "The knowing self is partial in all its guises, never finished, whole, simply there and original; it is always constructed and stitched together imperfectly, and *therefore* able to join with another, to see together without claiming
to be another" (193).

An "innocent identity politics," however, has already engulfed the coming-
out narrative, according to many lesbian and gay critics. Diana Fuss sees even in
the Radicalesbians a "tension between the notions of 'developing' an identity
and 'finding' an identity" that "points to a more general confusion over the very
definition of 'identity' and the precise signification of 'lesbian'" (*Essentially
Speaking*, 100). Biddy Martin discusses how, by the end of the 1970s, the imperative to come out is evolving into a predictable (and white) narrative, and how
many coming-out stories "are tautological insofar as they describe a process of
coming to know something that has always been true, a truth to which the author has returned" (89). Jeffrey Minson takes this accusation of tautology a step
further, suggesting that "far from constituting a break from a repressive, closet-

ted past, coming out might be situated as the latest in a long line of organised rituals of confession. . . . Sexual avowal therefore is a mode of social regimentation" (37). In Minson's ominous scenario, coming out simply reproduces and undergirds the homophobic notion that homosexuality wholly explains a lesbian or gay person's identity.

Finally, although Fuss's, Martin's, and Minson's criticisms might also be leveled at some feminist theories of positionality, coming out may be problematic for a unique, more mundane reason: the imperative "Come out!" is by now, for many, a worn-out refrain. "National Coming Out Day" is at this point televised yearly on *The Oprah Winfrey Show*, and encouragement, such as the exhortation in my own campus newspaper to "come out, wherever you are, and friends won't turn away" (Behrens, 19), often sounds like pandering for heterosexual "compassion." Since coming out, according to this mainstream model, is virtually synonymous with a call to "respect yourself," many gay and lesbian people are understandably bored or irritated with this focus on coming out and its product, the coming-out narrative.[6] For example, David Van Leer insists that for White, coming out is "the quintessential gay experience"; but in a review of *The Faber Book of Gay Short Stories*, which White edited, Van Leer suggests that, in its "preoccupation with the opinion of others," coming out "sometimes looks like a bid for heterosexual sympathy, even for absolution" (50). Sarah Schulman states more forcefully, "The coming out story should be permanently laid to rest. . . . It was a defining stage we had to go through, but it doesn't help us develop a literature true to our experience" (qtd. in Fries, 8).

Although I have no doubt that "we" will never construct a literature "true to our experience," since that "experience" is multiple and that "truth" is always socially constituted and continually shifting, I am nonetheless sympathetic with Schulman's frustration over the primacy given the coming-out narrative, especially when this focus comes at the expense of attention to other queer stories. Richard Hall, in a review of White's *The Beautiful Room Is Empty*, is more tentative than Schulman, suggesting, "Not that the coming-out novel in its pristine liberationist form is dead. Maybe it's just weary. . . . Here is another coming-up-and-out story, taking the narrator into adolescence and young manhood. . ." (27). Although Hall feels White's novel is told with "wit, humor and aphoristic elegance" (27), his reservations about the coming-out novel are standard fare these days in reviews of contemporary lesbian and gay literature.[7]

Thus, despite a possible affinity with recent feminist theory, as a myth of "queer positionality," coming out can be read as a worn-out concept. In the remainder of this chapter I explore more thoroughly why this is the case, but I also use the insights offered by feminist positionality theory to present an analysis that considers ways to revise or reclaim the coming-out story. Myths of queer positionality/identity need not be hopelessly lost on teleological journeys toward essential wholeness; "noninnocent" myths of queer positionality can be shaped in a queer world that is about "lived social and bodily realities [and] in which people are not afraid . . . of permanently partial identities and contradictory standpoints," as in the cyborg world Haraway envisions and argues for

(154). *A Boy's Own Story* and *Zami: A New Spelling of My Name* were both published in 1982, when the cultural phenomenon I call "the Queer Renaissance"
had only just begun. Through an examination of these two very different
coming-out stories, I want to flaunt the ways coming out has been reinvented in
the Queer Renaissance as a myth of queer (op)positionality.[8]

Queer Oppositionality/Queer Apositionality

Edmund White's *A Boy's Own Story* is the first novel in a planned three-novel
series. In each text, White traces the development of his nameless, faceless narrator. *A Boy's Own Story* focuses on this development during the 1950s; *The
Beautiful Room Is Empty*, on this development during the 1960s. The novel as
yet unfinished (*The Farewell Symphony*) will carry the protagonist through the
1970s and 1980s.

   The "invisibility" used as a mechanism in these texts works as a metaphor
for the pain the protagonist goes through as a gay youth in heterosexist America. Ed Cohen writes that

> the structuring stories we commonly use in order to make sense of our daily lives
> provide us with very few plots that do not emplot us in normative versions of gen-
> der and sexuality. . . . [These normative narratives] have special consequences for
> those of us whose movements appear to transgress the possibilities of such accept-
> able representations, effectively rendering us "unrepresentable." ("Constructing
> Gender," 545)

Thus, like many other gay men and lesbians, White's protagonist feels that
none of the people around him knows who he "really" is, and that he must consequently wear a (heterosexual) mask. The young narrator of *A Boy's Own Story*
muses, "What if I could write about my life exactly as it was? What if I could
show it in all its density and tedium and its concealed passion . . . ?" (41). The
point is, however, that he cannot, given the normative versions of gender and
sexuality available to him, and hence invisibility works to underscore that the
narrator is forced to "live a lie" at the same time as it works to stress more generally the pain and isolation of being marginalized in and by American society.
Like the narrator of Ralph Ellison's *Invisible Man*, White's protagonist might
say, "I am invisible . . . because people refuse to see me" (Ellison, 3).

   I mention Ellison at this point because White's use of the trope of invisibility in *A Boy's Own Story* and elsewhere is not unlike Ellison's use of the same
trope in his 1952 novel: both writers use invisibility to comment on the exclusionary logic at the heart of American culture. Perhaps not surprisingly, then,
White's narrators often see parallels between their experiences and the experiences of African Americans in the United States. In *A Boy's Own Story*, for example, the narrator finds himself pressured by his friends to accompany them to
a whorehouse staffed by two black women and one white woman. As the protagonist sits in the waiting room, one of the black prostitutes engages him in

conversation. The narrator admits, "I felt sorry for her. I thought she might really need my ten dollars. After all this was Saturday night, and yet she didn't have any customers. Somehow I equated her fatness, her blackness, her unpopularity with my own outcast status" (183). White's narrator goes on to imagine a marriage between the two, "she a Negro whore and I her little protector. . . . If this fantasy kept me a pariah by exchanging homosexuality for miscegenation, it also gave me a sacrifice to make and a companion to cherish. I would educate and protect her" (183). Since both characters are invisible "outcasts," White's narrator imagines that they might more effectively face the world together.

The identifications here and elsewhere in White with African American (and with "fat" and "unpopular") identity, however, are suspect for several reasons, and my main argument in this section is that the construction of sexuality in *A Boy's Own Story* is in tension with the construction of race in ways that forestall the possibility that the story might serve as a myth of queer (op)positionality. Although the novel is in some ways "oppositional," I argue that any "oppositionality" is ultimately undercut by the "apositionality," or invisibility, of whiteness in the text. It is not White's own story, necessarily, that produces this tension: by 1982, the standard coming-out story, with its single-minded focus on the discovery of one's essential identity, required such apositionality. The remainder of this section shows how white apositionality fixes *A Boy's Own Story* as a representative—or *the* representative—coming-out story and considers what ramifications the effacement of whiteness has for contemporary gay male writing generally. In the next section, however, I turn to an analysis of the ways in which Audre Lorde reconceives the coming-out story as a fluid and relational myth of queer (op)positionality.

Initially, White's novel may be read as "oppositional" for its disruption of linear models of sexual development in which heterosexuality is both the ultimate goal and the mark of maturity. This disruption of heterosexual telos is underscored by the very form of the text, which represents the protagonist's story in a nonlinear fashion (he is fifteen in the first chapter, seven at the beginning of the third, fifteen again by the end of the sixth, and so on).[9] Yet, despite this "opposition" to heterosexual telos, White's novel nonetheless teleologically represents his protagonist's coming to a racially unmarked gay consciousness. Although overt acts of coming out into this new gay consciousness are deemphasized in the text (the narrator confesses to a friend that he is gay only once, offhandedly [88]), it is still clear throughout *A Boy's Own Story* that homosexuality is precisely and primarily what White's nameless narrator must confront. Indeed, he uses a homosexual encounter with and betrayal of a "straight" teacher at the very end of the novel to confront this identity, which, he says, is "at once my essence and also an attribute I was totally unfamiliar with . . . this sexual allure so foreign to my understanding yet so central to my being" (198). In the end, the betrayal of his teacher finally allows White's narrator to work through the contradiction inherent in his "impossible desire to love a man but not to be a homosexual" (218). Thus, although *A Boy's Own Story* certainly disrupts the cultural mandate to develop heterosexually, it also institutes a coming-out narrative as necessary for understanding one's (essential) gay identity. In fact, White later asserted that the novel "succeeded partly because it seemed to fill an empty niche in the contemporary publishing ecology, the slot of the coming-out novel" (*Burning Library*, 372).

White's discussion of niches and slots implies that *A Boy's Own Story* was an easy fit; the publishing world was ready for a novel with a unitary focus on coming out. I would argue, however, that at the time the "contemporary publishing ecology" could provide a home for White's novel only on two, unspoken conditions. First, gay identity had to be understood, as it is in *A Boy's Own Story*, as an "essence . . . central to [one's] being." Such an understanding is what enabled the empty niche to be filled so exactly. Second, gay identity could not be explicitly intersected by other facets of identity, such as gender or race: in other words, this "gay" slot was white and male, although not *openly* white and male. Lisa Duggan's comments suggest that these two points are, in fact, interrelated: "*Any* gay politics based on the primacy of sexual identity defined as unitary and 'essential' . . . ultimately represents the view from the subject position '20th-century Western white gay male'" ("Making It Perfectly Queer," 18). Duggan outs the subject position as white and male, however; generally, such representations are advanced without being explicitly marked as such. And indeed, in *A Boy's Own Story*, a unitary, essential gay subject position is achieved through the mechanism of invisibility.

The mechanism of invisibility in White's novel is not intentionally deployed to cover the main character's gender and race; White's narrator is "invisible" throughout the novel precisely because homosexuality is an identity that he cannot openly embrace. Yet the construction of sexuality here inadvertently colludes with hegemonic constructions of whiteness, which maintains its power precisely to the extent that it is able to remain hidden from view. As Richard Dyer argues, "White power secures its dominance by seeming not to be anything in particular" (44). What this effects in *A Boy's Own Story* is contradictory: on the one hand, the story is one of marginalization and oppression; on the other hand, the story is *representative*. White himself recently gave voice to this contradiction, insisting, "When I was growing up, I felt I was a totally freaky person . . . and then later I came to realize that my life, which I had thought was the most *exceptional* imaginable, was actually the most *representative*. All I needed to do was to say what I went through in order to say what gay people went through in their evolution toward freedom" (in Avena, 224). In the end, even White's title conveys this dual sense of the exceptional and the representative, suggesting that this "boy's own story" is as much about any (gay) boy as about White's specific protagonist. Indeed, I was struck, when I attempted to teach one of White's texts, by a student's response to my very first question, "Why do you think White chooses not to give his narrator a name or face?" A Filipino American student of mine responded, "So we can put ourselves into the story?"

My student was not "wrong" to identify with White's protagonist; he is, in fact, like White's narrator, a gay man living in a homophobic society. Yet the interrogative inflection my student gave to his response suggests that he suspected his resolution to my question might be a bit problematic. For White's character is not simply a representative "Everyboy": his mother and he play games with the classical radio station, guessing whether the composer is Haydn, Mozart, or early Beethoven (80); a (black female) maid, a (white male) therapist, and a private school are all part of his childhood; and he admits, however ironically, "Even as I made much of my present miseries I was cautiously planning my bourgeois future" (178). In short, aspects of the protagonist's identity can be read as race-and class-coded, despite his "invisible" gay identity. Indeed, his gay identity is rendered representative precisely because the "naturalness" of his racial identity is maintained through White's "god-trick" of "invisibility."[10]

The term *god-trick* is Haraway's, and she uses it to refer to seemingly innocent perspectives that claim to see the world more comprehensively while actually "being nowhere" (191). This may seem to be an unfair charge to level at White's story of gay development, but it is harder to dismiss in the context of Dyer's analysis of whiteness. Dyer suggests that

> white people . . . are difficult, if not impossible, to analyse *qua* white. The subject seems to fall apart in your hands as soon as you begin. Any instance of white representation is always immediately something more specific—*Brief Encounter* is not about white people, it is about English middle-class people; *The Godfather* is not about white people, it is about Italian-American people; but *The Color Purple* is about black people, before it is about poor, southern US people. (46)

Similarly, *A Boy's Own Story* is not about white people, it is about gay people; but *Zami* is the autobiography of a black lesbian, not of the gay community more generally. *A Boy's Own Story* posits a seemingly innocent perspective that implicitly claims to see gay identity more comprehensively, but it is able to do so because white identity is nowhere to be seen.

The very landscape of *A Boy's Own Story* underwrites white apositionality. The story takes place, alternately, in Illinois, Michigan, and Ohio. This is not Toni Morrison's Ohio, however, in which racial divisions are graphically (and in *Sula*, geographically) represented. Like the protagonist, the various settings for the novel are unmarked: a "boy's own story" presumably takes place in Anywhere, U.S.A. David Bergman argues that "the importance of Cincinnati . . . cannot be underestimated in White's fiction," but it is Bergman, not White, who actually names the "Queen City" that plays such a "prominent role in [White's] autobiographical novel *A Boy's Own Story*" ("Edmund White," 387). Of course, the Midwest has long had a reputation for being the blank "nonregion" of the United States, the land—as in Don DeLillo's *White Noise*—of supermarkets, station wagons, and "an expressway beyond the backyard." (DeLillo, 4). This unmarked regional identity, however, does not preclude White in his novel from marking *other* parts of the country regionally: the protagonist and his sister make fun of "hillbillies" from Kentucky (73), and the protagonist himself dreams of escaping to the "charm" and sophistication of New York City (52–57).

As in DeLillo, certainly, the blankness of White's Midwest might be read as simply a metaphor for the region's supposed cultural sterility. This interpretation would elide, however, the ways in which regional blankness underwrites racial invisibility in *A Boy's Own Story*. Like Kentuckians and New Yorkers, African Americans in White's Cincinnati are embodied as such, and throughout this text, it is the location of regional and racial identity in embodied "others" that enables the protagonist *not* to have a regional and racial identity of his own. This disembodiment, in turn, ensures that the protagonist's coming-out story can be read as representative. The "other," marked identities allow White's narrator to negotiate a problematic sleight of hand: while he effaces differences of race and region, he simultaneously appropriates representative "outcast" status for himself.

In *Playing in the Dark: Whiteness and the American Literary Imagination*, Toni Morrison argues that white American writers have often used their African American characters to perform such sleights of hand. Morrison's study emerges from her interest "in the way black people ignite critical moments of discovery or change or emphasis in literature not written by them" (viii). Insisting that an understanding of American literature is incomplete without an understanding of the central role an African American presence has played in the American literary imagination, she concludes, "What became transparent were the self-evident ways that [white] Americans choose to talk about themselves through and within a sometimes allegorical, sometimes metaphorical, but always choked representation of an Africanist presence" (17). In *A Boy's Own Story*, this metaphorical process begins in the second chapter. At first, the chapter might be read as starkly exposing the mechanisms of power that enable and ensure white privilege: the unmarked and privileged white identity is depicted here as depending for its very existence on the labor of a marked and African American identity. The protagonist admits:

> As a little boy, I'd thought of our house . . . as the place God had meant us to own, but now I knew in a vague way that its seclusion and ease had been artificial and that it had strenuously excluded the city at the same time we depended on the city for food, money, comfort, help, even pleasure. The black maids were the representatives of the city I'd grown up among. I'd never wanted anything from them— nothing except their love. To win it, or at least to ward off their silent, sighing resentment, I'd learned how to make my own bed and cook my own breakfast. But nothing I could do seemed to make up to them for the terrible loss they'd endured. (36)

Although he realizes his knowledge is "vague," White's protagonist is able to recognize here that race and geography shape subjectivity, including his own.

Events later in the chapter corroborate the possibility that, at least initially, the narrator is gaining insight into the unequal distribution of power and wealth. When their maid's daughter survives a bloody fight and needs help, the protagonist's father takes him along on a journey to her home in the "dangerous" section of town. This journey forces the protagonist to confront the poverty of the African American section of their town:

> That had been another city—Blanche's two rooms, scrupulously clean in contrast to the squalor of the halls, her parrot squawking under the tea towel draped over the cage, the chromo of a sad Jesus pointing to his exposed, juicy heart as though he were a free-clinic patient with a troubling symptom, the filched wedding photo of my father and stepmother in a nest of crepe-paper flowers, the bloody sheet torn into strips that had been wildly clawed off and hurled onto the flowered congoleum floor. (50)

Nonetheless, the wedding photo "filched" by Blanche from her white employer is the first sign, I think, of what Morrison might label the "choked representation" in this scene. White specifically chokes, or checks, the "silent, sighing [and potentially threatening] resentment" of "the black maids" through the representation of Blanche's shrine, which certainly suggests anything but resentment. Moreover, the identification of an/other city is already appropriated by the end of the chapter to facilitate the protagonist's *own* developing sense of self. The very use of the name Blanche foreshadows the possibility that this scene could be as much about "White" as it is about the maid herself.[11] And indeed, when he is considering running away to New York City, the protagonist appropriates—without reference to Blanche herself—the rhetoric he had earlier used to identify her: "I'd go hungry! The boardinghouse room with the toilet down the hall, blood on the linoleum, Christ in a chromo, crepe-paper flowers . . ." (56). In this entire section, difference is not so much "exposed" and challenged as it is safely contained—in White's Cincinnati, in this section of his novel, and, ultimately, in his own "outcast" protagonist.

This is White's second chapter, and racial difference becomes a crucial factor only once more in the novel: when White's protagonist and his friends, in the final chapter, visit the whorehouse. Despite the reemergence of race, though, the relations of power that determine and maintain white dominance remain safely behind in chapter 2. What was earlier an identification *of* racial difference and discrimination becomes, at the whorehouse, an identification *with* racial difference (White's protagonist, as I mentioned earlier, equates the woman's situation with his own). It is precisely the "invisibility" of the protagonist's racial identity (as well as the "blankness" of the regional scene upon which all of this is played out) that allows for this slippage and appropriation to go unnoticed. Since the narrator's regional and racialized body is invisible, he can safely appropriate "other" identities for his own limited—I would not necessarily call them "queer"—uses. Thus the blankness of the Midwestern landscape and the invisibility of whiteness in *A Boy's Own Story* are more than simply metaphors for cultural sterility. Unmarked and dislocated racial and regional identities are exactly what enable this to be a "representative" story about *gay* people, rather than about white Midwesterners.

Hence queer (op)positionality in *A Boy's Own Story* is choked by white apositionality. As I suggested, this is as much a function of how the coming-out story had evolved as it is of White's particular novel. However, in some other contexts, the ways in which the identity "Edmund White" is constructed replicates this pattern. For example, after White edited an anthology of gay fiction (*The Faber Book of Gay Short Fiction*) that included only one black writer (James Baldwin) and no women, the controversy was reported in a publication no less mainstream than *USA Today*. In the article, Kent Fordyce explicitly spells out the tension between sexuality and race: "I think Faber flubbed the title. . . . I think it should be 'Edmund White's Anthology of White Short Story Writers'" (qtd. in C. Wilson, 8D). *The book isn't about white people*, White himself seems to be saying when he explains, "[I] read dozens of stories by dozens of gay black writers and I didn't find anything too suitable. And I thought it was wrong to include them just because they were black" (qtd. in C. Wilson, 8D).

His dismissal of race notwithstanding, in the foreword to *The Faber Book*, White continues to appropriate racial identity for its comparative value: "Do gays really constitute something like an ethnic minority? Does an author's sexuality represent a more crucial part of his identity than his social class, generation, race or regional origins?" (xvii). White's persistent blindness to race (and to other arenas of difference) except when he is appropriating it to talk about his own oppression is surely what led Essex Hemphill to signify on White in his own introduction to *Brother to Brother: New Writings by Black Gay Men:* "When black gay men approached the gay community to participate in the struggle for acceptance and to forge bonds of brotherhood . . . we discovered that the beautiful rhetoric was empty" (xix).

In *Essentially Speaking: Feminism, Nature and Difference*, Diana Fuss admits to implying throughout that "the adherence to essentialism is a measure of the degree to which a particular political group has been culturally oppressed" (98). And yet, in her chapter on lesbian and gay identity politics, Fuss spends only a page early on "exposing" the "essentialism" of the Combahee River Collective, Cherríe Moraga and Barbara Smith (99). Although Audre Lorde is mentioned in passing in an earlier chapter (44), no other openly gay or lesbian writers of color are engaged in the chapter on identity politics, or in the entire book, for that matter. To me, this hardly provides enough material to justify a sweeping statement the logical conclusion of which would be that lesbians of color are the *most* essentialist of all. In fact, in contrast to Fuss, I would propose that those who are oppressed in only one facet of their identity often stand the most to gain from essentialism.[12] As White writes in introducing his anthology of (white) gay short story writers, "Most gay men believe they did not choose to be homosexual, that this orientation was imposed on them, although whether by nature or nurture they have no way of knowing" (ix). White does not and need not necessarily speak for all white gay men here, but as in *A Boy's Own Story*, coming out into an essential and essentially oppressed gay identity is exactly what allows White to mask white and male power and to assume a voice that purports to speak for "most gay men."

The subordination of racial identity to an unmarked (white) gay identity has ramifications far beyond White's texts. It is evident in some recent criticism of gay male fiction that likewise tends not to notice the apositionality of White and whiteness. David Bergman, in his study of gay self-representation in American literature, *Gaiety Transfigured*, examines Baldwin in one chapter on "The Agony of Gay Black Literature," while White and other whites provide the material for the next chapter on "Alternative Service: Families in Recent American Gay Fiction." Yet under what discursive regime can Baldwin be understood as *not* about "family"? Indeed, I have a hard time thinking of many twentieth-century American writers more interested in exploring the family than James Baldwin. Nonetheless, Bergman positions White under the sign *family*, while Baldwin is positioned and contained under the sign *race*.

Bergman explains, in the introduction to *Gaiety Transfigured*, that he added a chapter on "race and homosexuality" only after the "excellent suggestions" of Robert K. Martin (24), and he also concedes, "I felt some . . . reluctance when I began to explore black gay literature, namely, that as a white man I would fail to grasp the subtle—and not so subtle—differences between the black and gay experiences" (13). Although he admits that it was a challenge, he reports that he now feels "a greater sympathy with the gayness of black men than many heterosexual blacks have expressed" (13). In short, Bergman may not feel competent to write much about black gays, but he is certainly competent to make sweeping dismissals of "many" black heterosexuals. Bergman's naive oversensitivity to the positionality of blacks and his reinscription of White/white apositionality result in a chapter on "family" in which he examines without critical comment such questionable scenes from contemporary gay fiction as Andrew Holleran's description of two white men in Union Square observing a "cocoa-colored youth" whom they feel they have a right to "have" (*Gaiety Transfigured*, 188) and White's narrator's own fantasy of an expatriate white gay friend living as a "garden god" among a tribe in Mexico (*Gaiety Transfigured*, 199).

Baldwin's ghettoization under the sign *race* here connects, moreover, to the ways in which "race" is contained in the larger narrative that some critics, including Bergman, are beginning to tell us about post-Stonewall gay male literature. Around 1978 (or so the story goes), gay literature began to come of age. Since 1978, Bergman explains, "when Edmund White's *Nocturnes for the King of Naples*, Larry Kramer's *Faggots*, and Andrew Holleran's *Dancer from the Dance* gained critical and commercial success—gay books have become a regular and increasingly large portion of trade publishers' lists" (*Gaiety Transfigured*, 9–10). This version of the story is underwritten by White: "It wasn't until 1978 that three gay novels came out: Larry Kramer's *Faggots*; *Dancer from the Dance*, by Andrew Holleran; and my *Nocturnes for the King of Naples*. Those three books gave the impression of a new wave, of a new movement coming along" (in Bonetti, 95). White modestly appends a disclaimer—"Mine was probably the least important of those three, as a publishing event" (in Bonetti, 95)—but just as for Bergman, 1978 is the banner year for White, the turning point for post-Stonewall gay male literature. As White asserts elsewhere, "Gay male fiction was suddenly on the map" ("On the Line," xii).

Yet where was Baldwin during all of this critical and commercial success? Although Baldwin was never wholly comfortable with the term *gay*, his most comprehensive study of *black* gay desire is nonetheless a product of exactly this period. *Just Above My Head* was published in 1979, but portions of the novel had begun to appear in that "banner year," 1978. My objection here could certainly be qualified (Baldwin was nearing the end of his career, whereas the three white authors were at the beginning of theirs; and *Just Above My Head* first began to appear in *Penthouse*, hardly the premier gay venue), but this has not kept some critics from telling the White/Bergman "banner year" story otherwise. Joseph Beam, for example, in his introduction to *In the Life: A Black Gay Anthology*, positions Baldwin's novel as one of the few landmarks: "More and more each day, as I looked around the well-stocked shelves of Giovanni's Room, Philadelphia's gay, lesbian, and feminist bookstore where I worked, I wondered where was the work of Black gay men. . . . How many times could I reread Baldwin's *Just Above My Head* and Yulisa Amadu Maddy's *No Past, No Present, No Future?*" (14). The year 1978 may have been commercially successful for some gay writers, but the narrative that Bergman, White, and others tell depends on a unitary notion of what "gay" literature is. In contrast, for Beam gay literature was not necessarily "on the map," since so much territory still remained uncharted. Baldwin and Maddy, however, not White, Holleran, and Kramer, provide Beam with a place to begin the journey.

Like Beam, Emmanuel Nelson, in his preface to *Contemporary Gay American Novelists: A Bio-Bibliographical Critical Sourcebook*, makes Baldwin (and John Rechy) central to his own coming-of-age as well as to the story we might tell ourselves about contemporary gay literature. In contrast to the deracinated narratives Bergman and White provide, Nelson's narrative begins with the overbearing presence of "whiteness":

> Barely twenty years old, I had just arrived in the United States from India to work toward a doctorate in twentieth-century American literature. Before long I grew uncomfortable and impatient with a good deal of American literature that was the staple of my graduate courses: the works of white, straight authors. . . . The exclusive focus on white writers . . . was tiresome and frustrating. (xi)

Gay literature provided Nelson with alternatives. "Gay literature," however, signifies much differently for Nelson than it does for Bergman and White:

> It was then that I started to discover, on my own, those literary territories whose existence was either unacknowledged or derisively dismissed in the classrooms. . . .

I began to seek reflections of my own realities within the ethnic and gay spaces of American literature. In particular, I was drawn to the works of James Baldwin and John Rechy. I was drawn to Baldwin because of his elegant prose, his expansive humanity, his sharp challenges to the logic of racism, and his uncompromising deconstructions of conventional sexual assumptions. I was drawn to Rechy because of his authentic style and his rebellious stance; moreover, I imagined an affinity with his dark, Latino protagonists and their familiar and frantic journeys through the anarchic sexual underworlds. That Baldwin and Rechy were, like me, ethnic as well as sexual outsiders in American culture made their perspectives recognizable; their voices and visions became reassuring, even liberating. Their widely different styles of managing their competing ethnocultural and homosexual subjectivities offered me potential models to reconcile the conflicting claims of my own multiple identities. Above all, Baldwin and Rechy enabled me to rediscover American literature. (xi–xii)

Of course, there is more than a little irony in this alternative narrative, in which a scholar from India "rediscovers" America and its literature. In contrast to the "discoverer" of America who came to this continent and saw "Indians," Nelson comes to America, looks around at its literature, and sees nothing but white folks. By putting a face to the unmarked (white) "American" identity of his graduate studies ("I grew uncomfortable and impatient with . . . the works of white, straight authors. . . . The exclusive focus on white writers . . . was tiresome and frustrating"), Nelson is able to resist and move beyond the hegemonic narrative being told not only about contemporary gay literature but about American literature more generally.

"One of the signs of the times is that we really don't know what 'white' is," Kobena Mercer writes ("Skin Head Sex Thing," 204). Whiteness, after all, maintains its hegemony by passing itself off as no-thing. As *A Boy's Own Story* and some recent gay male criticism indicate, whiteness is apositionality; it denies "the stakes in location, embodiment, and partial perspective [and makes] it impossible to see well" (Haraway, 191). "Every gay man has polished his story through repetition," White writes in the foreword to *The Faber Book*, "and much gay fiction is a version of this first tale" (ix). Perhaps. Yet White's celebration of the coming-out story as the original gay tale obscures the ways in which the coming-out story positions some gay people as more "polished" or representative than others. In *A Boy's Own Story* and *The Faber Book*, White disavows the appropriations and erasures that enable him to transform *his* story into "a boy's own." Denying its own racial situatedness, White's coming-out novel fails as a "noninnocent" myth of queer (op)positionality. Like the texts Biddy Martin examines, White's understanding of the "story" "reproduces the demand that women [and men] of color . . . abandon their histories, the histories of their communities, their complex locations and selves, in the name of a [gay] unity that barely masks its white, middle class cultural reference/referent" (Martin, 93). The Queer Renaissance requires another myth of queer positionality, one that *re*names "gay unity" by continually reimagining and relocating the complexity of queer histories, communities, and selves.

An/other Myth of Queer Positionality

Audre Lorde's *Zami: A New Spelling of My Name* is set in roughly the same time as Edmund White's *A Boy's Own Story*. At about the same time that White's protagonist is learning the difference between Mozart and Haydn, Audre, the persona at the center of what Lorde calls her "biomythography," goes to Washington, D.C., to celebrate her graduation from the eighth grade. Stopping at a Breyer's ice-cream and soda fountain, Audre and her family are told they can get their dessert to "take out," but they cannot eat the ice cream on the premises. The bitter episode ends with Audre thinking, "The waitress was white, and the counter was white, and the ice cream I never ate in Washington, D.C. that summer I left my childhood was white, and the white heat and the white pavement and the white stone monuments . . . made me sick to my stomach for the whole rest of that trip and it wasn't much of a graduation present after all" (71). In stark contrast to *A Boy's Own Story*, the mechanisms of white power are all too visible in *Zami*.

Clearly, despite nominal similarities (the 1950s setting, the 1982 publication date, the autobiographical elements, homosexuality), *A Boy's Own Story* and *Zami* are extremely different texts. Their publication history reflects their difference as well: whereas White's novel was published in hardcover by E. P. Dutton and in paperback by Plume, both divisions of New American Library, *Zami* was rejected by a dozen or more mainstream publishing houses, including, as Barbara Smith reports, a house known for publishing gay titles ("Truth That Never Hurts," 123). Smith explains, "The white male editor at that supposedly sympathetic house returned the manuscript saying, 'If only you were just one,' Black or lesbian" (123). So much for the "empty niche in the contemporary publishing ecology" in 1982, the "slot" waiting to be filled by the coming-out novel! To my knowledge, Lorde was never interviewed by *USA Today*.

Zami was eventually published by Persephone Press and the Crossing Press Feminist Series, and Donna Haraway, Katie King, and others have already noted *Zami's* importance for feminist theory. Haraway includes *Zami* in her discussion of "feminist cyborg stories," which "have the task of recoding communication and intelligence to subvert command and control" (175). King is more specific, suggesting:

> It is in this currently contested time/place [the lesbian bar of the 1950s] where "the passing dreams of choice" are mobilized that Lorde looks for the secrets of the making of her personal identity; the passing dreams of choice, where sexual identity is neither an existential decision nor biochemically/psychoanalytically programmed, but instead produced in the fields of difference individually *and* collectively. (332)

In this section, taking Haraway's and King's observations as a starting point, I suggest further that, in these "fields of difference" where sexual identity is "produced . . . individually *and* collectively," *Zami* also allows for a "recoding" of the coming-out story, a recoding along the lines of what I call "queer (op)po-sitionality." In *Zami*, coming out can be seen as an/other myth of queer posi-tionality—not because Lorde makes, as White does in *A Boy's Own Story*, an attempt to construct her protagonist into an alienated, marked "other" but rather because *Zami* is concerned, as King notes, with collective identity. A hu-manist, unified self is not Lorde's objective, but rather a definition of "self" as defined in and through others, particularly those "who work together as friends and lovers" (Lorde, *Zami*, 255).

Already this goes against White's objectives in *A Boy's Own Story*, which ends, after all, with a betrayal that enables the protagonist to self-define *as against* a lover. Moreover, Lorde's biomythography improves on Linda Alcoff's theory of positionality, which fears that "post-structuralism's negation of the authority of the subject coincides nicely with classical liberal views that human particularities are irrelevant" (Alcoff, 420). Indeed, the fiction of identity Lorde constructs in *Zami* goes beyond the poststructuralism Alcoff fears, since a nega-tion of the authority of the subject underscores here the *relevance* of human par-ticularities. Taking its protagonist through approximately two decades of development, *Zami* is framed by a prologue and an epilogue that are medita-tions on the *particular* women Audre has loved. In the prologue, Lorde poses the question "*To whom do I owe the woman I have become?*" (4) and proceeds to answer it by naming and describing those who have shaped her identity. Lorde concludes the prologue by apostrophizing:

> To the battalion of arms where I often retreated for shelter and sometimes found it. To the others who helped, pushing me into the merciless sun—I, coming out blackened and whole.
>
> *To the journeywoman pieces of myself.*
> *Becoming.*
> *Afrekete.* (5)

Of course, the penultimate stanza of the prologue might read like another teleological myth of essential wholeness, but Lorde immediately undercuts this with fragmentation and open-endedness ("pieces of myself," "becoming"). Moreover, even the "wholeness" into which Lorde "comes out" here is unlike the myth of identity represented in White. Particular "others" have helped forge this identity, and the metonymic reference to baking underscores Lorde's emphasis on the construction, not the preexistence, of identity.

Zami constructed a collective "new spelling of my name" that was subse-quently taken up and reshaped by other readers and writers in the Queer Re-naissance. Lorde promoted a similar identity in her *Chosen Poems—Old and New*, which were also published in 1982. The rest of this section first overviews exactly how identity is reinvented in these two texts. Then, after examining the ways in which both Lorde and White have responded to being cast, in various contexts, as "representative," I conclude by reconnecting *Zami* to Stonewall and the myths of queer (op)positionality with which I began.

In the body of the text of *Zami*, Audre has a number of "friends and lovers," black and white, beginning with Genevieve, a friend who commits suicide while the two are still in high school. Both in her biomythography and elsewhere, Lorde stresses how important this event was for her. *"Yes, I see Gennie often,"* she acknowledged in an interview twenty-five years after the suicide. "I'll never forget what it is to see young waste and how painful it is. And I never got over wanting to help so that it would not happen again" (in Cornwell, 43). In *Zami*, the placement of the suicide in the text makes it appear that the event inaugurates Audre into an identity separate from others; after the chapter detailing Gennie's suicide concludes, the next chapter opens, "Two weeks after I graduated from high school, I moved out of my parents' home" (103).

The separation from home and parents, however, does not mark the end of Audre's development; on the contrary, this emergence into a separate identity initiates a cycle of desire that takes Audre through a series of lovers over the course of the text. Although after Gennie's suicide, the protagonist *"decided that I would never love anybody else again for the rest of my life"* (141), she admits the loss of the wholeness she felt with Gennie was actually the commencement, not the end, of desire: "It is the last dream of children, to be forever untouched" (141). That this loss was a commencement is underscored by the fact that, in the text, Lorde positions the admission that after Gennie she "would never love anybody else again" *after* she details Audre's first sexual affair with *another* woman, Ginger. Ginger helps Audre recognize that her earlier resolve to separate from others was both misguided and untrue to what she had learned from and with Gennie. After this affair, Genevieve is not often invoked in *Zami*; in fact, Audre is caught off guard at one point when she mentions the girl to a lover: "I surprised myself; usually I never talked about Gennie" (185). In general, the formation of Audre's identity and her explorations of desire proceed without explicit reference to Genevieve.

Near the end of the text, however, Audre meets Afrekete ("Kitty") at a party for black women. When the two women arrive at Afrekete's apartment, Audre notes they are "in Gennie's old neighborhood" (247). Indeed, the two are in Gennie's old neighborhood in more than one sense: Afrekete is Audre's final lover in *Zami*, and she provides a fitting conclusion/nonconclusion to the problematics of identity and desire that commenced with the loss of Gennie. On one level, the nickname Kitty recalls Audre herself, since—as AnnLouise Keating points out—Ginger had repeatedly labeled Audre the "slick kitty from the city" (Keating, 29). This is only the first link in a chain of associations, however; the identity of this final lover is highly unstable and merges freely with others. Not only does the epilogue explain what the prologue did not—that Afrekete is the name of a goddess and of a *"mischievous linguist, trickster, best-beloved, whom we must all become"* (255)—but even as Audre and Kitty make love, the scene shifts seamlessly from the present to memories of Genevieve, so that the identity of the first lover reemerges in the identity of the last. Afrekete thus completes a circle for Audre/Lorde, bringing her to the point where she can write that her "life had become increasingly a bridge and field of women" (255). In other words, whether she understands her life linearly or circularly, as a bridge over which she crosses or as a field that surrounds her on all sides, connections between women are what give that life its shape. Furthermore, in the epilogue, although "human particularities" (women's roles and names, both "real" and mythical) are present, "Audre," in her specificity as a named, individual subject, is not. In fact, the "new spelling of my name" envisioned in the title is finally explained in the epilogue, and it turns out not to be about individuality at all: "*Zami. A Carriacou name for women who work together as friends and lovers*" (255).

Alcoff wants to reclaim an "identity," fictional though it may be, from which women can construct a feminist politics (435). The queer position *Zami* establishes, however, disclaims Lorde's individual identity. Earlier in the text, Audre realizes that, for her, the passage "beyond childhood" entails recognizing herself as "a woman connecting with other women in an intricate, complex, and ever-widening network of exchanging strengths" (175). Others have thus authored "Zami," this new identity, with her. Sagri Dhairyam argues, "*Zami* . . . calls itself 'biomythography,' a description which explicitly . . . recognizes the tactical uses of fictional identity, but refuses to grant the author primacy over the textuality of her life" (231). In the end, this refusal to grant primacy to any concept of the supposedly individual author ensures that, in *Zami*, fictional identity and *nonidentity* alike construct "the very house of difference rather than the security of any one particular difference" (*Zami*, 226).

At the same time, this is not some White/white "god-trick" that disavows its own situatedness. It may be impossible to read "Audre" as a self-identical, unified individual, but the identities "black," "lesbian," and "woman" are all present in the identity "Zami."[13] In a sense, Lorde's persona comes out into a fiction of nonidentity not unlike what Trinh T. Minh-ha envisions:

> A critical difference from myself means that I am not *i*, am within and without i. I/i can be I or i, you and me both involved. . . . "I" is, therefore, not a unified subject, a fixed identity, or that solid mass covered with layers of superficialities one has gradually to peel off before one can see its true face. "I" is, itself, *infinite layers*. Its complexity can hardly be conveyed through such typographic conventions as I, i, or I/i. Thus, I/i am compelled by the will to say/unsay, to resort to the entire gamut of personal pronouns to stay near this fleeing *and* static essence of Not-I. (90, 94)

This, it seems to me, is queer (op)positionality at its best: an effacement of, and in-your-face-ment to, the liberal humanist God/man/subject, with its notions of separation, individualism, and fixity.

As much as *Zami* works as a realization of Trinh's unstable i/I/Not-I, it also, *pace* Alcoff, maintains in its very self-definition a commitment to feminist political action; these are, after all, women actively *working* and *loving* together.

Zami constructs a nonessentialized identity position from which to forge a coalition-based, and oppositional, politics. In fact, King and Haraway both position *Zami* as an example of Chela Sandoval's "oppositional consciousness" (K. King, 338; Haraway, 174). Sandoval herself explains that the notion of oppositional consciousness provides feminists with a new, more fluid definition of "unity": "These constantly speaking differences stand at the crux of another, mutant unity . . . mobilized in a location heretofore unrecognized. . . . This connection is a mobile unity, constantly weaving and reweaving an interaction of differences into coalition" (18). The act of reading *Zami* stands as a figure for the "weaving and reweaving . . . of differences into coalition": since the "new spelling of my name" in Lorde's biomythography is not defined until the epilogue, one must read the entire text, with all of its "constantly speaking differences" and "location[s] heretofore unrecognized," before one can begin to understand that new spelling.

Zami does not end with the epilogue, however. Indeed, there is a sense in which Lorde's biomythography cannot end, even with her death. By remembering the identities envisioned in *Zami*, readers have attested to its ongoing vitality and success at achieving an/other, mutant, mobile unity. The editors of *Afrekete: An Anthology of Black Lesbian Writing*, for instance—Catherine E. McKinley and L. Joyce Delaney—frame their collection with selections from Audre Lorde. The first selection, "Tar Beach," is the excerpt from *Zami* wherein Audre is transformed through her encounter with Afrekete. The final selection, "Today Is Not the Day," is a poem in which Lorde calls on Afrekete and resolves to continue working and loving in the face of mounting challenges (particularly cancer). Afrekete and *Zami*, then, both set the stage for the explorations of identity furthered by this anthology and sustain the writer(s) through the process.

In her introduction to *Afrekete*, McKinley explains, "This is a story at once familiar and new. You may find yourself in it" (xii). McKinley goes on to detail her own experience of first reading *Zami* and explains how and why Lorde's text provides the writers included with a useful myth of positionality:

> Afrekete, in *Zami*, is Audre's last embrace. Afrekete is a child of the South, a migrant to Harlem. She is someone you may know. She is both wonderfully common and of the substance from which myths are spun: 'round the way girl, early banjee, roots daughter, blues singer. . . . AFREKETE is many women. With contradictory selves. And while AFREKETE troubles identity politics—her vision stretches much wider. (xiii–xv)

Afrekete, then, is both ancient and new; she is mythological, historical, and visionary. With this contradictory and impetuous figure as their muse, the contributors to *Afrekete*, according to McKinley, are committed to shaping new visions, selves, and communities:

> The contributors and these editors identify as lesbian, gay, zamis, dykes, queers, Black, African, African-American, biracial—and often may use these terms and

others interchangeably. And while sexuality, or race for that matter, is and is not always at the center of their work, both deeply inform the writer's vision. The work featured is written in a range of styles, a breadth of aesthetics reflecting the birthing and meshing of seemingly disparate artistic sensibilities and traditions: Black and queer, as well as others. (xvi)

Many other readers have similarly reinvented themselves and their communities because of the queer identities posited in and by Lorde and *Zami*.[14]

Lorde's *Chosen Poems—Old and New* were published in the same year as her biomythography, and the narrative she constructs about her life in this collection of poetry is similar to the narrative she constructs in *Zami*, in the sense that both texts posit a shifting positionality and a self ultimately defined in and through others. The volume opens with four poems depicting the poet's attempt to come to terms with Genevieve's death. In "Memorial II," the poet approaches her mirror and sees not her own face but Gennie's. Despite this merging of the two girls' identities, however, "Memorial II" also represents the poet's attempt to recognize that she does indeed have an identity that is separate from Genevieve's. By the last stanza, the speaker acknowledges that any vision of Genevieve in the poet's mirror can only be a fantasy. In this early poem, the poet must recognize herself, as she gazes into her mirror, as a subject separate from Gennie; for if Genevieve were to see her again, she would not recognize the young woman the poet has become: "Are you seeking the shape of a girl / I have grown less and less / to resemble" (5). Although the separation from Gennie is painful and difficult—at the end the poet laments that "your eyes / are blinding me / Genevieve" (5)—it is, at this point, nonetheless inevitable.

"Memorial II," then, with its emphasis on the formation of an individual identity, might allow for a reading of identity that is opposed to the collective identity represented in the epilogue to *Zami*. Yet, as in *Zami*, this assumption of a separate identity in *Chosen Poems* is only the beginning of the story. The poet's new, autonomous identity never quite seems to fit. In "Change of Season," for example, she complains, "Am I to be cursed forever with becoming / somebody else on the way to myself?" (40). Beyond this, the figure of Gennie and that original loss continue to haunt "Change of Season" and many other poems: "I was so terribly sure I would come to april / with my first love who died on a sunday morning / poisoned and wondering / was summer ever coming" (41). "Memorial III: From a Phone Booth on Broadway" shows how easily the poet's supposedly stable world is thrown into disarray by the memory of that loss:

> you will blossom back into sound
> you will answer
> must answer
> answer me answer me
> answer goddammit
> answer
>   please . . . (89)

In short, the death of Gennie in *Chosen Poems* provokes the poet's assumption of a separate identity, but with all the insecurities and instabilities specific to a poststructuralist account of the subject incompletely sutured into an identity. In *Chosen Poems* and *Zami* alike, however, inauguration into identity for the poet is much more than this: inauguration into identity is simultaneously inauguration into a social system dependent on racism, sexism, and homophobia, and hence into a system intent on defining and controlling all that is black, female, and queer. "Good Mirrors Are Not Cheap" captures the lack of control the poet feels because the cultural context in which she finds herself allows only for deceitful, masked representations of her identity:

> down the street
> a glassmaker is grinning
> turning out new mirrors that lie
> selling us
> new clowns
> at cut rate. (44)

Lorde is thus caught, in *Chosen Poems*, in the paradox of recognizing the instability of any subject position and yet desperately needing to articulate an identity that has been systematically distorted. Gennie's suicide itself, in both *Chosen Poems* and *Zami*, illustrates this central paradox. In *Zami*, before detailing in prose the events surrounding Gennie's death, Lorde includes a poem that foregrounds the ways in which the event is simultaneously an effacement and an assumption of identity:

> But we wept at the sight of two men standing alone
> flat on the sky, alone,
> shoveling earth as a blanket
> to keep the young blood down.
> For we saw ourselves in the dark warm mother-blanket
> saw ourselves deep in the earth's breast-swelling—
> no longer young—
> and knew ourselves for the first time
> dead and alone. (97)

We "knew ourselves for the first time / dead and alone": obliteration of identity and assumption of identity come together in the same moment. All of this, at the same time, occurs in an oppressive system intent on "keep[ing] the young blood down."

In "Need: A Choral of Black Women's Voices," the final entry in *Chosen Poems* and one newly written for Lorde's collection, the poet further probes this paradox, reproducing on a more urgent level the exploration of identity/non-identity found in the epilogue to *Zami*. Coming together with others is never easy (in fact, another selection in *Chosen Poems* poses the insistent question

"Who Said It Was Simple" [49]), but from the title of "Need" on, Lorde implies that a collective voice is necessary for survival.

"Need" opens by giving voice to that which has been silenced and by making visible that which would otherwise be effaced:

> This woman is Black
> so her blood is shed into silence
> this woman is Black
> so her death falls to the earth
> like the dripping of birds
> to be washed away with silence and rain. (111)

The poem has three speakers, "I," "P.C.," and "B.J.G.," the latter two representing the voices of Patricia Cowan and Bobbie Jean Graham, two women murdered in Detroit and Boston in 1978 and 1979, respectively. As in *Zami*, naming is a central preoccupation in "Need." After P.C. and B.J.G. describe their violent deaths, the "I" of the poem rages, "I do not even know all their names. / My sisters deaths are not noteworthy / nor threatening enough to decorate the evening news . . . blood blood of my sisters fallen in this bloody war / with no names no medals no exchange of prisoners" (112). The three voices weave in and out in this prolonged meditation on violence and oppression, until the final stanza of the poem, when the "I" transforms into an "All": " '*We cannot live without our lives.*' / '*We cannot live without our lives*' " (115). A note explains that the italicized quotation is from a poem by Barbara Deming. The words are therefore Lorde's and not Lorde's, and the individual identities of Lorde/I/Patricia Cowan/Bobbie Jean Graham/Barbara Deming, along with all the women named and not named in *Chosen Poems*, coalesce, as they do in the epilogue to *Zami*, into a collective and threatening identity that depends for its existence on the foregrounded yet constantly shifting positionality of the identity "black"/"lesbian"/"woman." The poem, once again, belies any notion of an essentialized self existing apart from others, and indeed, in the face of such violence and destruction, such separation seems not only unproductive but absurd.

"Need" itself is a particularly useful example of the ways in which Lorde comes out into a myth of collective identity. Lorde's *Chosen Poems—Old and New* was originally published by W. W. Norton and Company. "Need," however, was reissued as a pamphlet in 1990 by Kitchen Table: Women of Color Press as part of their Freedom Organizing Series. In the preface to this new, revised version of *Need*, Lorde traces the poem's genealogy. As 1978 was for white gay men, 1979 is a "banner year" for black and Latina lesbians. The latter banner year, however, looks significantly different from the former:

"Need" was first written in 1979 after 12 Black women were killed in the Boston area within four months. In a grassroots movement spearheaded by Black and Latina Lesbians, Women of Color in the area rallied. . . . My lasting image of that spring, beyond the sick sadness and anger and worry, was of women whom I knew, loved, and trembled for: Bar-

bara Smith, Demita Frazier, Margo Okazawa-Rey, and women whose names were unknown to me, leading a march through the streets of Boston behind a broad banner
stitched with a line from Barbara Deming: "WE CANNOT LIVE WITHOUT OUR LIVES." (3)

    Lorde again attributes the words to Barbara Deming, but the
identity/nonidentity articulated in *Need* and in Lorde's genealogy of "Need"
belies any unified authorial consciousness. Instead, the identity is an example of
Haraway's "contradictory" standpoint, which gains its strength precisely because authorial consciousness is "permanently partial." Deming does not, therefore, become so much the "source" here as another element in the collective
and shifting identity into which the women behind the banner come out. This
collective identity is a powerful and threatening one, made more so by its lack
of fixity. Indeed, the (re)issuance of *Need* reaffirms and deploys that lack of fixity: each pamphlet includes a button with the line "We Cannot Live without
Our Lives" printed on top of the pan-African colors and beside the symbol for
female. Neither Lorde nor Kitchen Table makes any attempt here to suture,
within the reissued text, the identity being articulated; on the contrary, the button and a "Resources for Organizing" section that follows the poem encourage
women (and apparently, men) reading the text to join and hence continually reshape this collective identity. Lorde herself, in fact, traces the 1990 revisions of
the poem to the ways in which others had used and reshaped it since its publication: "Alterations in the text since the poem was originally published are a result
of hearing the poem read aloud several times by groups of women" (*Need*, 3)[15]
    The Kitchen Table version of *Need* seems at least to allow for male inclu-
sion: the "Resources for Organizing" section that follows the poem includes the
addresses for organizations such as NCBLG: The National Coalition of Black
Lesbians and Gays, the National Black Men's Health Network, Men Stopping
Rape, and the Oakland Men's Project (*Need*, 16–17). Identity, as Lorde constructs
it in *Zami*, *Need*, and elsewhere, however, while not exclusionary, does not always
simplistically include men or white people; connection is not necessarily easy or
automatic. Hence "Zami" is *an* "other myth of queer positionality," *not the* necessary corrective to versions of coming out such as White's. As Elizabeth Alexander
notes," 'A' new spelling (as opposed to 'the') means there is probably more to
come" (704). In the Queer Renaissance, there have indeed been many more "new
spellings," as subsequent chapters of this book will demonstrate.
    However, Lorde often does connect with men—particularly men of
color/gay men—throughout her work. In fact, one of Lorde's earliest uses of
the phrase that would become the subtitle to *Zami* occurs in a poem from the
late *1970s* to "Brother Alvin," a boy from Lorde's second-grade class who suddenly died of tuberculosis:

> I search through the index
> of each new book
> on magic

> hoping to find some new spelling
> of your name. (*The Black Unicorn*, 54)

A more recent and particularly poignant example of connection with a man comes in her poem to the late Joe Beam. In "Dear Joe," Lorde uses as an epigraph words from "Sister, Morning Is a Time for Miracles" (*Chosen Poems*, 109–10). The words that had signified Lorde's attempt to connect with another woman, her sister, are here re-signified in her memorial to Beam: "if you have ever tried to reach me / and I could not hear you / these words are in place of the dead air / still between us" ("Dear Joe," 47). "Zami," then, may signify "women working together as friends and lovers," but the new ways of spelling identity that Lorde envisions do not preclude working with and loving others.[16]

As *Need*, "Brother Alvin," and "Dear Joe" illustrate, and as with White in and out of *A Boy's Own Story*, the construction of identity in *Zami* connects to the construction of "Audre Lorde" in other contexts. I should note before continuing, however, that my earlier account of White as the one of these two authors more likely to be published by houses such as New American Library, while Lorde is consigned to lesser-known houses such as Persephone or Crossing Press, was somewhat unfair. White's publication history, like Lorde's, has at times been rocky, and Lorde has indeed been published by both small feminist presses and mainstream houses such as Norton.[17] Both authors are therefore made available for representation in a variety of contexts. I do not want to institute an argument in this chapter that implies too much about either White's or Lorde's canonical or precanonical status: for example, that White is "more canonical" than Lorde because he is oppressed in only one facet of his identity and is hence closer to what Lorde called the "mythical norm" of American society (*Sister Outsider*, 116). The "canonicity" of either author is actually quite difficult to assess, and not only because both are contemporary authors. It would appear that both White and Lorde are fairly canonical, but in two different contexts. Although *Time* magazine declared White "America's most influential gay writer" (L. Schulman, 58), it is Lorde who is more likely to be taught in college classrooms or to be the subject of scholarly articles. The MLA (Modern Language Association) Bibliography, for instance, lists forty entries for Lorde between 1981 and 1994 and twelve for White. Ten of White's entries, however, are articles he himself has written, compared to only four such articles for Lorde: Of Lorde's forty entries, moreover, seven are dissertations, underscoring her importance to the generation of scholars who will be shaping the academy over the next few decades.

Lorde's burgeoning academic reputation is highly contestable, of course; other contemporary writers, such as Toni Morrison and Thomas Pynchon, have garnered much more attention during the same time period (Morrison; 329 MLA Bibliography entries; Pynchon, 514 entries). Nonetheless, Lorde is better known than White in academe (in part because of women's studies departments and academic feminism), while White, in contrast, is becoming ensconced as the gay author mainstream readers need to know. The Quality Paperback Book Club (QPB), for example, "proud to announce the launch of Triangle Classics, a series of landmark books illuminating the gay and lesbian experience," initially included one writer from the 1980s in their new series: Edmund White. The flyer for the series declares that QPB's edition "brings together Edmund White's landmark novels of coming-of-age and coming out," that is, *A Boy's Own Story* and *The Beautiful Room Is Empty*. The series included one black author, James Baldwin; but significantly, the Baldwin novel included, *Giovanni's Room*, is about white Europeans.[18]

If, as Richard Ohmann suggests, contemporary canon formation is the result of "both large sales . . . and the right kind of critical attention" (384), then it would seem that White is cornering the market on one necessary qualification and Lorde on the other. Michael Bérubé complicates Ohmann's thesis, suggesting that "we are no longer confronting Ohmann's mid-1970s landscape" and that academic critics "now represent contemporary writers to different audiences from those of the nonspecialist press" (31). To Bérubé, then, the Toni Morrison of academic criticism is not the same as the Toni Morrison of nonacademic journals and reviews; indeed, there is a competition between members of these two groups for what "Toni Morrison" will signify. In contemporary lesbian and gay writing, this competition, I would argue, is conducted not so much over individual authors as over the very sign *gay/lesbian literature*, and moreover, this competition tends to be split along gender lines. Hence, and very generally, the contemporary "gay(/lesbian) literature" represented in nonacademic journals and reviews is not the same contemporary "lesbian(/gay) literature" of academic criticism.

Consider, for instance, the very different observations of Ed Cohen, a professor of English at Rutgers University, and Victoria Brownworth, a lesbian journalist and fiction writer. Cohen justifies his focus on gay men in his essay on "Constructing Gender," in *The Columbia History of the American Novel*, in this way:

> If I focus now on the former [gay male writing] rather than the latter [writings by women of color/lesbians, which he acknowledges have also been important to his intellectual development] it is because I know that in a volume like this one it is likely that the works of women of many races and ethnicities will have been addressed heretofore, while the works of men who are exploring the possibilities for sexual and emotional intimacies with other men will most probably remain eccentric. (557)

In contrast, Brownworth insists:

> Unlike gay men . . . lesbians have not been part of the big queer book boom of the last few years. We haven't received the same advances as our gay male counterparts. So while there may be more lesbian writers than ever before, few of us are making a living by writing alone—most of us supplement our income with teaching or lecturing. For lesbians there's no money in being a writer. (49)

Lesbian writers and readers have witnessed a few major "publishing events" over the past few years (most notably Dorothy Allison's *Bastard out of Carolina*, which was a finalist for the National Book Award), but some have claimed that these events were made possible because the lesbian content was not always explicit in such books.

This is not to argue, by any means, that academic criticism is somehow inherently more progressive because lesbians are on top; on the contrary, in both arenas, the uses to which the winner of the gendered competition might be put are more important than who, specifically, wins. Publishers take advantage of White's purchase *outside* the academy, for example, to market his texts. The cover of White's 1978 novel *Nocturnes for the King of Naples* includes *Newsweek's* assessment of the author, which is identical to that of *Time* magazine: "White is unquestionably the foremost American gay novelist." *Inside* the academy, in contrast, Lorde is able to cash in on a desire for "difference" that can be, nonetheless, safely contained. Anna Wilson, discussing Lorde's increasing canonization in the academy, argues:

> For feminist academia Lorde is particularly effective as a token: since she is Black, lesbian and a mother, her work compactly represents that generally repressed matter towards which white feminists wish to make a gesture of inclusion—but since Lorde conveniently represents so much at once, she can be included without her presence threatening the overall balance of the white majority vision. (77)

Certainly, the majority vision in literary studies, if not in feminist academia, is also heterosexual, or at least heterosexualized. Thus, in literary studies, Lorde can "conveniently represent," along with other "differences," a homosexuality that nonetheless does not threaten to disrupt the straight narrative.

Of course, according to Ohmann's thesis, openly lesbian and gay literature will never be canonized, since the two necessary ingredients of canon formation are not really coalescing for any individual author. I have already mentioned Bérubé's complication of Ohmann, but I include here a third, mediating context that emerged during, and even before, the Queer Renaissance and that particularly complicates the canonicity question for queers: the gay and lesbian marketplace. Lorde and White may not be "canonical" in quite the same way as other contemporary writers are, but because of the existence of a community-based marketplace, as White himself points out, "even quite celebrated heterosexual authors—watching their books go out of print or out of stock—might well envy the longevity of books written by lesbians and gay men" ("Twenty Years On," 4). Lesbian and gay bookstores, literary reviews, award ceremonies, and the like ensure that canonization is an extremely complex affair for openly gay and lesbian writers. In this third context, the community context, White and Lorde are both among the most canonical of contemporary writers.

Thus both Edmund White and Audre Lorde are positioned by others, in various ways, as "representative," and as representative of overlapping and competing constituencies with varying degrees of access to the "center." Each author, however, responds differently to the ways in which he or she has been represented by others, and in general, White's and Lorde's responses parallel the ways in which each constructs identity within the texts I have been examining. In 1990, when Lorde was presented with the second annual Bill Whitehead Memorial Award, in recognition of outstanding contributions to lesbian and gay literature, she informed the audience, "One award will not counterbalance a continuing invisibility of Lesbian and Gay writers of color" ("What Is at Stake," 66). Using her individual location to emphasize how her identity had been shaped in and through others, Lorde went on to explain that the best way to honor her was to honor those she had loved and worked with: "If this group wishes to truly honor my work, built upon the creative use of differences for all our survivals, then I charge you, as a group, to include and further expose the work of new Lesbian and Gay writers of color within the coming year, and to report on what has been done at next year's award ceremony" ("What Is at Stake," 66).[19] In contrast, Edmund White, the recipient of the first annual Bill Whitehead Memorial Award in 1989, concluded his speech with the reflection, "Oddly enough, what literature has always taught us is that only in tracing our individuality can we become universal" ("Twenty Years On," 5). "We," "our," and "us," of course, signify quite differently in White's speech from how "our" signifies in Lorde's "creative use of differences for all our survivals." Despite his stress on "the recording of our differences" in gay and lesbian literature, when White himself acknowledges that "it has struck me as no coincidence that many of the most original writers of this century have been gay" (5), the list he produces in support of this claim includes no people of color.[20]

Then I caught myself foolishly imagining that gays might someday constitute a community rather than a diagnosis. White's protagonist's thoughts during the Stonewall Riots, with which I began this chapter, apparently contradict the points I have been making about White/white apositionality and appear to participate in a more productive myth of identity, akin to those articulated in *Zami* and "Need." This moment of potentiality in *The Beautiful Room Is Empty*, however, is trumped by the novel's notorious ending:

> I stayed over at Lou's [one of the nameless narrator's friends]. We hugged each other in bed like brothers, but we were too excited to sleep. We rushed down to buy the morning papers to see how the Stonewall Uprising had been described. "It's really our Bastille Day," Lou said. But we couldn't find a single mention in the press of the turning point of our lives." (227–28)

At the end of *The Beautiful Room Is Empty*, bittersweet isolation and invisibility triumph over the possibility of community.[21]

Yet the story of Stonewall has been told otherwise. Martin Duberman's historical overview, *Stonewall*, interweaves the stories of six people who were active in lesbian and gay communities during the time of the Stonewall Riots. Craig Rodwell was one of the men actually present when the riots broke out, and Duberman details his reaction: "Craig dashed to a nearby phone booth. Ever conscious of the need for publicity—for *visibility*—and realizing that a critical moment had arrived, he called all three daily papers, the *Times*, the *Post*, and the *News*, and alerted them that 'a major story was breaking.' Then he ran to his apartment a few blocks away to get his camera" (*Stonewall*, 198; emphasis mine). Rodwell's photographs never came out, but Duberman's "day after" is nonetheless not characterized by the existential alienation White's protagonist and his friend feel:

> Word of the confrontation spread through the gay grapevine all day Saturday. Moreover, all three of the dailies wrote about the riot (the *News* put the story on page one), and local television and radio reported it as well. The extensive coverage brought out the crowds, just as Craig had predicted (and had worked to achieve). All day Saturday, curious knots of people gathered outside the bar to gape at the damage and warily celebrate the fact that, for once, cops, not gays, had been routed. (*Stonewall*, 202)

At Stonewall and in *Stonewall*, gay men and lesbians "come out" into a myth of collective identity, and the ramifications of that collective act are still being felt today.

During high school, the protagonist of *A Boy's Own Story* and Tommy, his current obsession, go slumming: "He and I had trekked more than once downtown . . . to listen, frightened and transported, to a big black Lesbian with a crew cut moan her way through the blues" (120–21). Of course, this exoticization of the "big black Lesbian" is only a minor incident for the narrator, unconnected to the larger project of coming out into his own, individual, gay consciousness. And yet the black lesbian singing the blues in *A Boy's Own Story* is not as out of place as she might at first appear. Teleological and essential (white) "boys' own stories" at this point offer feminism and queer politics little in the way of queer (op)positionality. Like the protagonist of Lorde's *Zami*, whose "heart ached and ached for something [she] could not name" (85), the blues singer in White's novel needs an/other myth of queer positionality. Coming out into an essential wholeness may be the myth that lesbians and gay men are told they must embrace, but as Audre's teacher declares early on, when the young protagonist of *Zami* refuses to take dictation in the same manner as the rest of the class, Audre is "a young lady who does not want to do as she is told" (26). Lorde responds instead with a nonessentialized, non-self-identical "new spelling of my name" in *Zami*, and only through this new construction is she able to envision a queer and powerful community of women, whose new identities are permanently partial and whose coalitions are conscious.

Notes to Chapter 1

1. John D'Emilio explains that homophile activists adopted the slogan "Gay is Good" in 1968 (*Making Trouble*, 239). Barry Adam notes that Franklin Kameny of

the Mattachine Society of Washington, D.C., had used the phrase as early as 1964: "In [the] face of the MSNY [Mattachine Society of New York] president's traditional homophile contention that 'we must lose the label of homosexual organizations,' Kameny asserted simply that 'gay is good!'" (71). Kameny was consciously referencing African American rhetoric, such as the slogan "Black is Beautiful." For a discussion of the influence on the early gay movement of the rhetoric of African American and Latino groups such as the Black Panthers and the Young Lords, see D'Emilio, *Making Trouble*, 240–41. On Stonewall generally, see Duberman, *Stonewall*.

2. See the essays included in Jay and Young. On the GLF, see D'Emilio, *Sexual Politics*, 233–35, and *Making Trouble*, 239–46; Adam, 73–89; Kissack. Adam specifically recounts the GLF and GAA (Gay Activists Alliance) zaps that helped pave the way for the APA shift (81–82). On the Radicalesbians, see Echols, 215–17, 232; Kissack, 121–23. The construction of the woman-identified woman enabled heterosexual feminists to identify more fully with their lesbian sisters, but it was, in many ways, a conservative move. Alice Echols argues that it was "designed to assuage heterosexual feminists' fears about lesbianism" (215); consequently, it ended up desexualizing lesbianism. Still, despite its evasion of "the knotty problem of sexuality," the construction at least temporarily "redefined lesbianism as the quintessential act of political solidarity with other women" (Echols, 217).

3. I have already mentioned the re-presentation of Civil Rights rhetoric in Edmund White's fictional account of Stonewall. The name Gay Liberation Front itself was meant to give tribute to the liberation struggles in Vietnam and Algeria (Duberman, *Stonewall*, 217).

4. For a good overview of feminist standpoint epistemology, as well as an "archeology of standpoint theory" (76), see Sandra Harding. Harding explains that feminist standpoint theory emerges from an engagement with Marxism (53–54). On this point, see Haraway, 186–87. By translating standpoint theory to a queer context, I am trying to further coalition building among theorists; like Harding, I recognize that "even though standpoint arguments are most fully articulated as such in feminist writings, they appear in the scientific projects of all the new social movements" (54). Echols's overview of radical feminism demonstrates that the boundaries between the different groups engaging in this self-reflexive constructionism were often blurred.

5. On this shift, see also D'Emilio, "Foreword," xxiv–xxviii, and *Making Trouble*, 239–51.

6. I am grateful to Steve Amarnick for helping me sort out some of the issues I am working with here. I am not dismissing the psychological importance of coming out, nor am I denying that Oprah Winfrey's sensitivity to coming out is empowering to thousands of gay and lesbian individuals. Rather, I am suggesting that the "coming out equals self-respect" model alone can be equally disempowering for the gay and lesbian *movement*, and for the many other lesbian and gay people who too infrequently see themselves represented in any other way.

7. For a counterexample, see John Preston. The very fact that Preston can say, "I always shake my head in disbelief when I read critics who think the coming out novel is just a stage we're going through" (39), suggests that many critics have expressed their reservations about the genre. Indeed, Preston's article is in the same issue of *Lambda Book Report* that includes Sarah Schulman's derisive comments about the coming-out story (see Fries). In his introduction to the most recent edi-

tion of *A Boy's Own Story*, White himself notes the reservation that have been expressed about the genre: "Now [1994] there's an excess of coming-out novels, and critics talk of creating a ban against any further ones" ("On the Line," xv).

8. Neither White nor Lorde has necessarily identified with the concept of "queer" as it is deployed in this chapter and throughout this study, although White has begun to use the term *queer* more frequently, generally as a synonym for gay men and lesbians. See White, "The Personal Is Political: Queer Fiction and Criticism," in *The Burning Library*, 367–77. The work of Lorde (and other women of color) in the early 1980s, however, helped usher in the queer theory and activism of the later 1980s by facilitating the emergence of the disruptive identities that are at the center of the Queer Renaissance— identities that are not fixed in advance but are rather constantly reshaped in interaction with other identities. See chapter 3 for a fuller consideration of these issues in relation to Gloria Anzaldúa and the 1981 publication of *This Bridge Called My Back;* see my introduction for a consideration of these issues in relation to my own use of the term *queer*. Some of Lorde's readers, of course, do identify with the term *queer* and deploy it in various ways, as my discussion of *Afrekete: An Anthology of Black Lesbian Writing* later in this chapter highlights. For another reading of *Zami* through and as feminist positionality theory, see Carlston, 226, 231–32, 236. On positionality theory in relation to Lorde's 1986 collection of poetry *Our Dead Behind Us*, see Hull, 155; 159.

9. My thoughts on the ways in which *A Boy's Own Story* disrupts heterosexist understandings of linear sexual development are indebted to Kenneth Kidd.

10. White himself has at other times disavowed the possibility that *A Boy's Own Story* might be somehow representative; he writes, "The novel is not a political tract, nor is it meant to be representative or typical" ("On the Line," xii). My larger point here, however, is that the invisibility of whiteness allows for *A Boy's Own Story* to be cast as representative regardless of White's (clearly contradictory) intentions. The packaging of the novel underscores this: in spite of White's disavowal, a blurb on the back cover from the *New York Times's* Christopher Lehmann-Haupt announces, "It is any boy's story. . . . For all I know, it may be any girl's story as well." The Plume paperback has gone through at least three cover designs since 1982, each utilizing a photograph of a different young (white) boy.

11. I am grateful to Michael Thurston for pointing out this connection to me.

12. Barbara Smith has made a similar point (Bulkin, Smith, and Pratt, 75–76).

13. This interpretation attempts to resist what Sagri Dhairyam points out about critical responses to Lorde's poetry: "The relational, shifting points of the politics of identity enacted by and through Lorde's poems are stilled by their recuperation into canons of feminine or lesbian identity" (243). Nonetheless, I have framed this interpretation in a chapter about "coming out," and this, coupled with my own gay male location, might still the "shifting points of the politics of identity" yet again, recuperating Lorde, this time, into a rapidly expanding canon of "queer theory." This tension within "queerness," which I discuss at greater length in chapter 3, is unavoidable, but I hope that a negotiation of the tension will fuel, rather than forestall, the work of queer theory.

14. Lorde's work has influenced the shaping and reshaping of so many readers, writers, and communities that it would be impossible to compile a comprehensive list of the locations where such reinvention has occurred. *Celebrate the Life and Legacy of Audre Lorde*, a booklet distributed for Lorde's memorial service in New York City on January 18, 1993, particularly attests to the scope of her vision and influ-

ence. *Celebrate the Life and Legacy* includes tributes from, among many others, Palestinian feminists, groups fighting for Hawaiian independence, the Organization of Women Writers of Africa, and Men of All Colors Together. I am grateful to Steve Amarnick for sending me a copy of this document.

15. In 1992 a revised edition of *Chosen Poems—Old and New* was published as *Undersong*. In that collection, Lorde reiterated her commitment to revision: "The process of revision is, I believe, crucial to the integrity and lasting power of a poem. The problem in reworking any poem is always when to let go of it, refusing to give in to the desire to have that particular poem *do it all*, say it all, become the mythical, unattainable Universal Poem" (xiii).

16. For white gay male creative work that is more self-reflexive about whiteness or about positionality, respectively, see Allan Gurganus's 1990 collection of stories *White People* and Tom Joslin and Peter Friedman's 1993 film *Silverlake Life: The View from Here*. Gurganus's stories explore both gay and nongay white life in North Carolina, and Joslin and Friedman's film is a collective effort (often depending on who had the strength to work the camera) at documenting Joslin's and his lover Mark Massi's deaths from AIDS. The position from which the camera "sees" is repeatedly foregrounded and complicated. For a discussion of embodied and communal identity in the work of another white gay male author, Robert Glück, see Jackson. See also Crimp, "Right On, Girlfriend!" and my discussion of Tony Kushner and "queer perestroika" in chapter 4, for considerations of the sort of collective identity I discuss throughout this chapter.

17. Jewelle Gomez notes, significantly, that "commercial companies . . . would publish Audre's poems but could not bring themselves to publish the more explicit ideas of her essays" (7). On White's sometimes rocky experiences with publishers, see Bonetti, 101–2.

18. I am grateful to Stacy Alaimo for calling my attention to this series. The Book-of-the-Month Club instituted a similar series with fewer authors but initially—the same problems: included are Baldwin (*Giovanni's Room*), White (*A Boy's Own Story* and *The Beautiful Room Is Empty* ["available here in one exclusive volume"]), and Rita Mae Brown (*Rubyfruit Jungle*, published in 1973). After Lorde's death in 1992, however, an "exclusive three-in-one volume" of *Zami, Sister Outsider*, and *Undersong* was the first new addition to the Book-of-the Month Club series. This addition highlights the difficulty of making overly hasty generalizations about either White's or Lorde's canonicity. Also, I should note that, despite mainstream attempts to cast White as "America's most influential gay writer," such attempts have hardly garnered him nationwide fame. White has found such fame instead in European countries: in France, White is considered by many to be the most important American writer since Henry James, and in England, as he himself explains, *A Boy's Own Story* "made me so well known that English fans are always astonished to learn that most Americans don't know who I am" ("On the Line," xix).

19. Since, at the time of this award, Lorde was in Berlin undergoing treatment for the cancer she had been battling for more than a decade (and which eventually took her life), Jewelle Gomez, another black lesbian writer, delivered Lorde's speech. The "I" of Lorde's speech is thus destabilized in a way similar to that of the "I" in "Need," discussed above.

20. White's "greatest hit" list is as follows: among non-American writers, "Marcel Proust, Virginia Woolf, Colette, Jean Genet, Thomas Mann, Christopher Isher-

wood, Ronald Firbank," and among Americans, "Elizabeth Bishop, James Merrill, and John Ashbery" ("Twenty Years On," 5). Overall, I might add, White's 1989 acceptance speech is about two and a half times longer than Lorde's 1990 speech.

21. Such bittersweet isolation is conveyed by the very title of White's novel: "*The Beautiful Room Is Empty* . . . takes its title from one of Kafka's letters alluding to the unfortunate inability of two people (or perhaps two psyches) to inhabit a single space" (Radel, 184). White's beautiful and empty room contrasts significantly with Lorde's "house of difference," where cohabitation, though never easy, is both possible and necessary for survival.

Questions for Reflection, Discussion, and Writing

1. What goals did "coming out" narratives serve, according to McRuer? What dangers does McRuer currently associate with "coming out" narratives?

2. In what ways might "coming out" narratives be antithetical to "transformation," according to the argument presented by McRuer? What current authors, historical groups and public figures does McRuer identify to articulate the arguments and belief systems that both support and critique the "coming out narrative"?

3. How does McRuer use the "myth of queer positionality" to critique White's portrayal of race and class in *A Boy's Own Story?* What techniques and social attitudes does McRuer suggest enable White's subscription to "normativity" to go unchallenged and celebrated in the mainstream press?

4. McRuer claims that many anthologies of gay writings are disproportionately white. To what factors does McRuer attribute the lack of gay black authors like James Baldwin in favor of gay white authors like White?

5. How does Audre Lorde's *Zami: A New Spelling of My Name* allow for "a 'recoding' of the coming-out story . . . along the lines of . . . 'queer (op)positionality,' " according to McRuer?

6. What about lesbian and other minority experiences does McRuer suggest a term like "Afrekete" indicates?

7. What does the gay and lesbian community need to do in order to realize the dream articulated by White's protagonist, according to McRuer?

Related Reading

Lee Edelman, "Homographesis." *The Yale Journal of Criticism 3.1* (Fall 1989): 189–207.

Claude J. Summers, *Gay Fictions Wilde to Stonewall: Studies in a Male Homosexual Literary Tradition*, NY: Continuum 1990.

David Bergman, *Gaiety Transfigured: Gay Self-Representation in American Literature*. Madison: U of Wisconsin Press. 1991.

James Levin, *The Gay Novel in America*. NY: Garland Publishing. 1991.

Arthur Flannigan-Saint-Subin, "The Mark of Sexual Preference in the Interpretation of Texts: Preface to a Homosexual Reading." *Journal of Homosexuality 24*. 1–2 (July–August 1992): 65–88.

Gregory W. Bredbeck, "The New Queer Narrative: Intervention and Critique." *Textual Practice* 9.3 (1995): 477–502.

Michael Trask, "Merging with the Masses: The Queer Identity Politics of Leftist Modernism." *differences: A Journal of Feminist Cultural Studies* 8.1 (1996): 94–131.

Eve Kosofsky Sedgwick, Ed. *Novel Gazing: Queer Readings in Fiction.* Durham, NC: Duke UP. 1997.

Reed Woodhouse, *Unlimited Embrace: A Canon of Gay Fiction 1945–1995.* Amherst, MA: U of Massachusetts P. 1998.

Mark D. Hawthorne, *Making it Ours: Queering the Canon.* New Orleans, UP of the South. 1998.

Walter Holland, "The Calamus Root: A Study of American Gay Poetry Since World War II." *Journal of Homosexuality 34.* 3–4 (March 1998): 5–25.

Samuel R. Delaney, *Shorter Views: Queer Thoughts & The Politics of the Paraliterary.* Hanover, NH: UP of New England. 1999.

Marilee Lindemann, "Who's Afraid of the Big Bad Witch? Queer Studies in American Literature." *American Literary History 12.4* (Winter 2000): 757–770.

Richard Canning, Ed. *Gay Fiction Speaks: Conversations with Gay Novelists.* NY: Columbia UP. 2000.

Claude J. Summers, *The Gay and Lesbian Literary Heritage.* New York: Routledge. 2002.

John Emil Vincent, *Queer Lyrics: Difficulty and Closure in American Poetry.* New York: Palgrave. 2002.

A.B. Christa Schwartz, *Gay Voices of the Harlem Renaissance.* Bloomington: Indiana UP. 2003.

Special Topics

McRuer features the work of Audre Lorde and Edmund White in his essay, and students will appreciate its arguments more if they are assigned to read either of these authors in conjunction.

Reading

Audre Lorde, *Uses of the Erotic: The Erotic as Power.* Brooklyn, NY: Out & Out Books. 1978.

———, Zami: *A New Spelling of My Name.* CA: The Crossing Press. 1982.

———, *Chosen Poems, Old and New.* NY: W.W. Norton. 1982.

———, *Sister Outsider: Essays and Speeches:* Trumansberg, NY: Crossing Press. 1984.

Karla Hammond, "Audre Lorde: Interview:" *Denver Quarterly 16.1* (1981): 10–27.

"Revolutionary Hope: A Conversation between James Baldwin and Audre Lorde." *Essence* (1984): 72–45.

Sharon Patricia Holland, "'Which Me Will Survive?': Audre Lorde and the Development of a Black Feminist Ideology." *Critical Matrix: the Princeton Journal of Women, Gender, & Culture. Special Issue 1* (1988): 1–30.

Ruth Ginzburg, "Audre Lorde's (Nonessentialist) Lesbian Eros." *Hypatia 7.4* (1992): 73–90.

Cheryl Kader, "'The Very House of Difference': Zami, Audre Lorde's Lesbian-Centered Text." *The Journal of Homosexuality 26.1* (Aug–Sept 1993): 181–194.

Kara Provost, "Becoming Afrekete: The Trickster in the Work of Audre Lorde." *MELUS 20.4* (1995 Winter): 45–59.

AnaLouise Keating, *Women Reading, Women Writing: Self-Invention in Paula Gunn Allen, Gloria Anzaldúa and Audre Lorde.* Philadelphia, PN: Temple UP. 1996.

Film

The Body of a Poet: A Tribute to Audre Lorde (1995). Sonali Fernando. 29 m.

Edmund White, *States of Desire: Travels in Gay America.* NY: Dutton. 1980.

———, *A Boy's Own Story.* NY: Dutton. 1982.

———, *The Burning Library: Essays.* David Bergman, Ed. NY: Alfred A. Knopf. 1994.

———, *The Farewell Symphony: A Novel.* NY: Alfred A. Knopf. 1997.

———, *The Married Man.* NY: Alfred A. Knopf. 2000.

Adam Block, "Interview with Edmund White." *Out/Look 3.2* (Fall 1990): 56–62.

Nicholas F. Radel, "Self as Other: The Politics of Identity in the Works of Edmund White" in *Queer Words, Queer Images: Communication and the Construction of Homosexuality.* R. Jeffrey Ringer, Ed. NY: NYUP. 1994. 175–192.

Edmund White, "Edmund White Speaks with Edmund White." *The Review of Contemporary Fiction 16.3* (1996): 13–30.

Robert D. Fulk, "Greece and Homosexual Identity in Edmund White's 'An Oracle'." *College Literature 24.1* (February 1997): 225–239.

Queer Fictions of Stonewall

Scott Bravmann

> *"Stonewall" is the emblematic event in modern lesbian and gay history.*
> (Martin Duberman)[1]

In indication of the scope and depth of their importance to queer historical subjects, the Stonewall riots have been referred to as "[a] sort of lavender Bastille Day"; "the official start of the gay liberation movement"; "our Verdun—they shall not pass and all that"; and, in a campy play on that more famous opening salvo two centuries before, as "the hairpin drop heard round the world"; as well as, in numerous accounts, the beginning of the "modern" gay and lesbian movement.[2] Indeed, it is the significance of "Stonewall" as a symbol—as *"the* emblematic event"—for a wide range of gay and lesbian political, social, and cultural practices that has occasioned this chapter, for these multiple practices refuse any facile, consistent, or coherent summing up, even as they call for critical analysis. There exists, I want to suggest, a very deep and basic paradox for gay and lesbian communities in relation to those several nights' events, and it is a paradox that powerfully reiterates the themes of identity and difference framing, motivating, and traversing this book's project of queer cultural studies of history. Regarded as the catalytic event in the formation of gay militancy, "Stonewall" is also seen as, on the one hand, a unifying encapsulation of the diversity within queer heterosociality and, on the other hand, a moment of rupture "authentically" rooted in the experiences and actions of men and (some) women marginalized in gay politics as people of color, as drag queens, as butch dykes, as street people, as counterculturalists.

Queer fictions of Stonewall—the meanings "we" attach to or find in the riots, the sense "we" make of them—are not isolated social/cultural texts about some *singular* essence and autonomy of gay and lesbian identity, community, and history. Rather, these sense-making projects locate the riots in the larger historical field whose own contours they (implicitly) map as well. Literally through annual public celebrations that bring "the community" "together," and symbolically through various naming strategies and institutional structures, representations of Stonewall help to assert the queer nation of the late-twentieth century. Despite their shared point of departure, however, queer fictions of Stonewall draw on open-ended representational possibilities that also suggest the problematic and contested nature of claims about community and identity. Like the widespread currency of models of Greek antiquity in certain gay and lesbian historical representations that I engaged in the previous chapter, queer fictions of Stonewall also need to be taken up as subjects of social, cultural, and political analysis in the historical construction of lesbian and gay identities and differences, of queer fictions of the present. Several areas (again those made visible around race and gender and also, in this case, political practice broadly construed) usefully highlight the paradoxical character of those investments in Stonewall. Before turning to the principal analysis proposed for this chapter, however, I want to begin with a relatively extensive discussion of Martin Duberman's recent book *Stonewall*, the first full-length study of the riots, the political and cultural context in which they occurred, and their immediate aftermath in New York City.

Reading *Stonewall*

In the preface to his book, Duberman points out that "'Stonewall' has become an empowering symbol of *global* proportions."[3] He continues, however, with a critical observation that decisively informs the nearly 300 pages that follow, and especially the middle section of the book called "1969" (pp. 169–212):

> Remarkably—since 1994 marks the twenty-fifth anniversary of the Stonewall riots—the *actual* story of the upheaval has never been told *completely,* or been *well understood.* We have been trading the same few tales about the riots from the same few accounts—trading them for so long that they have transmogrified into *simplistic myth.* (p. xv, emphasis added)

Suggesting that his book will tell the whole story, Duberman undertakes the "overdue" project of "grounding the symbolic Stonewall in empirical reality and placing the events of 1969 in historical context" (p. xv). The book's epigraph—an excerpt from Clifford Geertz's *The Interpretation of Culture* that not only situates becoming human in the paradoxical process of "becoming individual . . . under the guidance of cultural patterns" but also urges us to investigate "detail" in order to get beyond "misleading tags" and "empty similarities"—anticipates the way Duberman pursues this task. "In attempting to [ground the riots in reality and to contextualize them]," Duberman explains in his preface,

> I felt it was important *not* to homogenize experience to the point where individual voices are lost sight of. My intention was to embrace precisely what most contemporary historians have discarded: the ancient, essential enterprise of *telling human stories.* (pp. xv–xvi, emphasis in original)

This approach explains the "unconventional narrative strategy in the opening sections of the book" which recreate "half a dozen lives with a particularity that conforms to no interpretive category but only to their own idiosyncratic rhythms" (p. xvi).

Duberman is also careful, however, to place his book within the context of professional historiography because "gay men and lesbians—so long denied any history—have a special need and claim on historical writing that is at once accurate *and* accessible" (p. xvii). The book's structure and development tie these concerns about accessibility and accuracy closely together, a connection that demands its reader's critical engagement. Though Duberman deliberately focuses on "individual lives" in order "to make past experience more directly accessible than is common in a work of history," his project is "decidedly not designed as 'popularized' history—by which is usually meant the slighting of historical research or the compromising of historical accuracy" (p. xvii). Indeed, the extensive footnotes to virtually all of the written text of *Stonewall* attest to Duberman's "[diligent search] for previously unknown or unused primary source materials" and suggest his "[scrupulous adherence] to scholarly criteria for evaluating evidence" (p. xvii). Aware of the potential for certain kinds of professional objections to his method of historical representation, Duberman acknowledges the grounds for such criticism:

> My emphasis on personality might legitimately be called novelistic but, in contrast to the novelist, I have *tried* to restrict invention and remain faithful to known historical fact. (p. xvii, emphasis added)

It is precisely this fact–invention distinction that motivates Duberman's research: recognizing that such a "grounding" and "context[ualizing]" are "overdue," Duberman sets out to tell "completely" "the actual story of the upheaval" set off by the police raid on the Stonewall Inn (p. xv). His particular mode of historical representation—"the focus on individuals and on narrative"—is explicitly an attempt to "increase the ability of readers to *identify* . . . with experiences *different* from, but *comparable* to, their own" (p. xvii, emphasis added).

Duberman's preface raises two important points in relation to the questions pertaining to historical representation that form this book's second principal axis of investigation. Though Duberman studiously tries to offer a full accounting of the real story of the riots, I want to suggest that his book is ultimately unable to escape its opening sentence: "'Stonewall' is *the* emblematic event in modern lesbian and gay history." For, as the diacritical marking of the bar's name reminds us, no matter what kind of history is being recounted or, to put it another way, what version of "the ancient, essential enterprise of *telling human stories*" is being employed, "Stonewall" always already means more in gay and lesbian historical imaginations than a mere bar, a routine police raid, and even the exceptional riots of several nights' duration that followed the raid. In contemporary gay and lesbian cultures, "Stonewall" signifies much beyond the "empirical reality" and "historical context" of 1969, though precisely what it signifies has always been a site of contestation. The current value of the "events," even—or especially—to the degree of the urgency of their narration as a complete and actual story, is precisely their mythic proportions, their non-actualness, their partiality.

In spite of the ostensibly objective, unchanging, and universal appeal of "empirical reality" and "historical context," Duberman's account contains a barely concealed wish for diversity in gay and lesbian historical representations, a diversity that is partially belied by the story he tells. Yet Duberman's account leaves unasked and thus unanswered the question of whose reality he is writing about and whose context he is placing those events in. Though he points out that "[n]o group of six could possibly represent the many pathways of gay and lesbian existence" (p. xvi), Duberman maintains that:

> they can suggest some of the significant childhood experiences, adult coping strategies, social and political activities, values, perceptions and concerns *that centrally characterized the Stonewall generation.*   (p. xvii, emphasis added)

Neglected in this construction of "reality" and "context" are questions of how and when "Stonewall" has been located within "other" historical accounts, trajectories, ruptures, projects, and locations. Not only do we need to regard the multiple and different histories that inform our locations in the world as integral to the construction of our "reality" and "context" but also how (dominant) representations of "reality" and "context" construct silences, gaps, and discontinuities.

The latter third of Duberman's book recounts the riots' effects on his six narrators, gay and women's liberation politics in New York City, and the organizational efforts behind the first anniversary march (pp. 215–280). With less than one-fifth of its pages devoted to the entire year of 1969, and less still to the riots themselves, however, how much of his book is really about the narrowly construed notion of "Stonewall"—a "Stonewall" stripped of its mythology—that Duberman wants to articulate? How much, on the other hand, is about efforts then and now to articulate a political movement grounded in a spontaneous "nay-saying" that evokes both an innocence and a collective consciousness? These questions are related to questions that might be asked about the way Duberman presents his account. Duberman's oral history method of *"telling human stories"* places him as the (invisible) transmitter and editor of his subjects' voices but not their source, and he acknowledges that his "greatest debt is to the six people who trusted me to tell their stories and endured the multiple taping sessions which made that possible" (p. xi). Yet, although those interviews are "the source of most of the quotations" in the text, he "could not surrender to [his six subjects] the authorial responsibility to interpret the evidence" (p. xi). To have surrendered this responsibility would not only have compromised his "adhere[nce] to scholarly criteria for evaluating evidence" (p. xvii) but it would, in effect, also have inserted his account back into the realm of popular memory or mythology from which Duberman set out to rescue representations of Stonewall in the first place.[4]

Although I agree with Duberman about the urgency of providing lesbians and gay men with "access" to the past, I want to take issue with his project as well. Duberman's reliance on "an unconventional narrative strategy" (p. xvi), his refusal to "[conform] to [any] interpretive category" (p. xvi), his "belief in democracy: the importance of the individual, the commonality of life" (p. xvi), his attempt to "restrict invention and [to] remain faithful to known historical fact" (p. xvii), and finally his appeal to "individual experience" (p. xvi) and "lively human representation" (p. xvii) as antidotes to the "simplistic myth" (p. xv) of the riots that continues to circulate through gay and lesbian networks calls for critical investigation. Such a reevaluation is especially urgent in light of the recent philosophical, tropological, and political critiques of historiography discussed in chapter 2, the peculiarities oral sources present for historiography, and the problematic use of "experience" as historical evidence. I want to dwell briefly on these latter two points.

For his part, Duberman makes a paradoxical appeal to narrative and experience. On the one hand, in an oddly mixed metaphor, he tells us he wants to prevent "individual voices [from being] lost sight of" without, on the other hand, "foreclos[ing] speculation about patterns of behavior" (p. xvi). Duberman insists that the life stories of his subjects offered in the opening sections of his book are recreated "with a particularity that conforms to no interpretive category but only to their own idiosyncratic rhythms" (p. xvi), yet he makes no particular or explicit claim about the mode of interpretation he uses in the latter

half of the book, except that he "ha[s] tried to remain faithful to known historical fact" and has "scrupulously adhered to scholarly criteria for evaluating evidence" (p. xvii). Even if we allow Duberman the possibility of an unmediated
historical representation in which he merely collects, organizes, and edits the
life stories of his subjects, it remains questionable whether his six narrators told
their stories without using "interpretive categories"—consciously or unconsciously. Indeed, as Alessandro Portelli reminds us, it is precisely narrators' desires, imaginations, and reconstructions—*their interests*—that make oral history
a valuable, and unique, way of producing knowledge about the past. Accordingly, however, because "[o]ral sources are *narrative* sources . . . the analysis of
oral history materials must avail itself of some of the general categories developed in the theory of literature" such as those that address "the velocity of narration," and also "distance," "perspective," and "distinctions between narrative
genres."[5] In other words, the "idiosyncratic rhythms" of Duberman's narrators'
stories both contribute to our understanding of how "Stonewall" animates particular lives *and* suggest the need for thinking critically about them in terms of
the "novelistic" against which Duberman contrasts his account (p. xvii).

Yet Duberman's book does reveal, to reiterate Portelli's remarks on "the
unique and precious element" of oral history, not just what his six subjects and a
larger group of gay activists "did, but what they wanted to do, what they believed they were doing, what they now think they did." This suggestion has important implications for reading the allegedly complete, empirically grounded,
and historically contextualized account of the riots *Stonewall* promises. Though
the events themselves are recounted in substantial detail, it is ultimately Duberman's narrators and his written account of their stories that construct the events
surrounding Stonewall as "facts" by locating those specific events in larger webs
of socially mediated individual and collective meaning. As Joan Scott explains,
experience occurs within discourse rather than in "a realm of reality outside discourse" and, because of the shared nature of discourse, "experience is collective
as well as individual."[6] Such is the case not only with *Stonewall* the text but also
with the text of Stonewall, "the symbolic 'Stonewall'" that Duberman seeks to
ground and contextualize. These discourse-defined textualizations, in other
words, are both interpretations and something to be interpreted.

In ways consistent with Scott's notion of agency—one in which subjects
"are not unified, autonomous individuals exercising free will, but rather subjects
whose agency is created through situations and statuses conferred on them"
(p. 409)—Duberman's account shows how his subjects' sense of the (potential)
significance of the riots worked differentially to construct those events as
"facts" depending on the locations from which their choices were enabled,
though his own narrative, in Scott's words, "reif[ies] agency as an inherent attribute of individuals" (p. 399). Moreover, Duberman's subjects' subsequent
narration of events, and their roles in them, occurred only after the significant
interval of nearly twenty-five years in which the riots have become legendary,

invested with political significance, and as Duberman himself acknowledges "transmogrified into . . . myth" (p. xv).

Possessing a hard-to-come-by political savvy, both Craig Rodwell and Jim Fouratt, two of Duberman's narrators, immediately sought to expand the impact of the riot beyond a brief encounter with and resistance to the police. Rodwell, a white radical member of the New York Mattachine Society and owner of the Oscar Wilde Memorial Bookstore, "[e]ver conscious of the need for publicity—for visibility—" ran to a pay phone close by to alert New York's three dailies "that 'a major news story was breaking'" (p. 198). Jim Fouratt, a white former priest, an actor, and "a major spokesperson for the countercultural Yippie movement" (p. xx), "also dashed to the phones—to call his straight radical-left friends, to tell them 'people were fighting the cops—it was just like Newark,'" though he was unsuccessful in getting them to "lend their support" to his cause (p. 198). On the day following the raid, while Sylvia Rivera, a Puerto Rican hustler and founder of Street Transvestite Action Revolutionaries, walked about "setting garbage cans on fire, venting her anger" (p. 202). Rodwell "channeled [his excitement] according to his own temperament—by jump-starting some organizational work" (p. 203). In contrast to Rivera's frustration and racial and class disenfranchisement, Rodwell's sophisticated ability to articulate himself and his political and business experience, as well as his racially linked upward class mobility and his charismatic leadership skills, might well have provided both the vision and sense of entitlement that allowed him to see that "[w]hat was needed . . . was a leaflet, *some crystallizing statement* of what had happened and why, complete with a set of demands for the future" (p. 203, emphasis added). Though his immediate plans for such a statement were overtaken by the party-like atmosphere in the street in front of the Stonewall Inn that evening, Rodwell ultimately did act on the question he posed to himself at the time: "Didn't the events at Stonewall themselves require commemoration?" (p. 211), a rhetorical question that anticipates the symbolization that has constructed those events as emblematic "in modern lesbian and gay history."

In the same street scene in front of the bar that distracted Rodwell (including a media, police, and gay presence), Duberman writes, "'stars' from the previous night's confrontation reappeared to pose campily for photographs" (p. 203). Yet, this notion of "stars" posing to be photographed belies the ostensibly unmediated "truth" of mass media's photographic representation of the "news" and raises questions about who was photographed: who wanted to be photographed, who could "afford" such possible publicity, whom did the photographers target as suitable or "representative" subjects, what was their role in or relationship to the riots? Furthermore, it was not until Sunday that word of the riots reached Karla Jay, one of Duberman's two female narrators (neither of whom was part of the Stonewall crowd). Jay "tried [unsuccessfully] to get Redstockings [a New York-based radical feminist group] to issue some sort of sympathetic statement" (p. 207), an effort towards articulating a coalition politics that was dependent on Jay's analysis and interpretation of the events.[7] Jay's coalition-oriented political desires are echoed in her subsequent interest in the formation of "a Gay Liberation Front—men *and* women working together to produce broad social change" which developed out of what she initially saw as "'the little penny-ante thing' going on at Stonewall" (p. 219).

Departing from the threads loosened in my reading of Duberman's project in *Stonewall,* the remainder of this chapter focuses on racial, gender, and political difference in relation to the emblematic and the symbolic dimensions of Stonewall in post-Stonewall lesbian and gay political cultures.

Race Matters

Despite its invisibility in the naming of the problematic subjects of lesbian and gay studies, cultures, and communities, race has been a central organizing principle in and across all of these overlapping domains. To whatever extent that queer identity exerts a centripetal force drawing "us" together towards some fictive or imagined center, it does so only against, even necessarily in tandem with, the centrifugal force of racial formations that ceaselessly pull "us" apart, moving us outward and away from each other towards other locations that mark our complexly racially divided societies. Yet, these forces must not be seen in mutually exclusive terms, as contradictory opposites, but rather as conceptual fictions that frame, inform, and overlap each other. In representations and analyses of Stonewall, race matters—the race of the rioters, the location of the riots at the tail-end of a decade defined by racial struggles, the complex racial makeup of New York City, the ways the police and the press dealt with the riots, the view of the riots as a point of rupture, and the organizations that quickly emerged after the riots—have received only minimal critical attention. But precisely because race matters, these racial dynamics bear importantly on how we understand the riots.

The week following the riots, *The Village Voice* published two front-page stories covering them: Lucian Truscott IV's "view from outside" and Howard Smith's "view from inside."[8] Accompanying these news accounts were two photographs of the post-riot scene taken by *Voice* photographer Fred McDarrah, the one of "some graffiti" in block letters reading "gay prohibition corrupt$ cop$, feed$ mafia," the other a nighttime shot of thirteen young men in front of the boarded-up, graffiti-covered bar, its caption reading simply "in front of the Stonewall." Though obviously staged for the camera rather than a "live-action" shot, the latter photograph provides the closest approximation of an on-the-scene visual image of the riots, its campily posed subjects continuing to garner anonymous fame with recent republications of the picture.[9] While it is perhaps difficult to use this visual text to ascertain "who was there," we can productively juxtapose it to the verbal texts on the riots. Such a juxtaposition reveals a pronounced disjunction between what the photograph shows us and what the written accounts tell us, even suggesting some of the different ways the two kinds of texts, verbal and visual, are mediated by and read through framing conventions.

Although this photograph shows a racially mixed group of young men (only one of whom is in drag), the print media accounts of the riots are (virtually) silent on the question of race. The literal visibility of men of color and the harmonious racial integration suggested by the camaraderie in McDarrah's photograph are paralleled by the unreadability in the written texts of these two ways that race matters. In contrast to the press coverage of the (admittedly much larger) "race" riots of a few years earlier (e.g. Watts, Chicago) in which the ("Negro") race of the participants is remarked in almost every paragraph and the uncontained "spread" of violence to "white areas" as "youths run wild" informs the journalistic analysis, the written text accounts of the Stonewall riots suggest, perhaps not without *some* reason, that they were racially neutral.[10] In a sense, the *Voice's* headline "Gay Power Comes to Sheridan Square" reflects/constructs the social dynamics at play, something which is even revealed in the *New York Times's* much more coded "4 Policemen Hurt in 'Village' Raid" and "Police Again Rout 'Village' Youths," where Greenwich Village is understood not purely as a way to pinpoint the location of the specific crime (allegedly operating a bar without a liquor license) within metropolitan New York but also as a metaphor for deviant sexuality.[11] Whereas Watts and Chicago's South Side have been racially defined (meaning black) in media representations, Greenwich Village has been sexually defined throughout the twentieth century.[12] This apparent racial neutrality of the riots, however, might also be regarded as the absence of racial analysis in recountings of them, an analysis in which racial and sexual dynamics are addressed simultaneously. This absence is, in other words, a veil which obscures racial differences and racial *meanings* under the unifying category of homosexuality.

The differences in the legibility of "race" in the two media representations suggest ways in which what Duberman calls Stonewall's resonance "with *images* of insurgency and self-realization" (p. xv, emphasis added) might begin to look (to retain his mixed metaphor) more like dissonance. As a visual reminder of a particular moment in gay politics, a documentary image of "*the* emblematic event in modern lesbian and gay history," McDarrah's photograph is also an enigma, an anomaly which only temporarily disrupts the connection between pre- and post-Stonewall photographic representations of gay and lesbian political activism. On this enigmatic rather than emblematic reading, McDarrah's *Voice* photograph provokes consideration of, on the one hand, how narratives of queer history are racialized and, on the other, how critical attention to racial specificity and (feigned) racial neutrality erodes under the weight of "gay identity" politics or emerges in light of complex current concerns. Although photographs from the homophile era of the mid-1960s and those from the Gay Liberation era of the early 1970s reveal that activists dressed, embraced, and presented themselves in markedly different ways, they just as clearly reveal a

continuity across that emblematic/enigmatic point of rupture—the overwhelming, not to say exclusive, whiteness of the groups.[13] Indeed, however stunning
the discontinuities between the earlier and later styles of gay and lesbian self-
representations in contexts specifically intended as *political* appear to be, these
differences are remarkable in part because of the constricted range of what—
more precisely, *who*—is visible within the documentary photographic field.

Interestingly, except for Duberman's passing reference to "'stars' from the
previous night's confrontation [who] reappeared to pose campily for photographs" (p. 203), McDarrah's visual text is conspicuously absent from the secondary literature's discussions of the riots. Their slighting of this valuable text,
however, is puzzling, even acutely problematic, since it is this one image which
provides the most—indeed, the *only*—compelling documentary evidence for
their claims regarding the racial makeup of the bar's clientele and the rioters.
Relying exclusively on the *New York Times*, the *Village Voice*, and the New York
Mattachine Society *Newsletter*, for instance, John D'Emilio and Lillian Faderman make statements about the patrons and rioters which can only be (specula-
tively) supported by this singular photograph or by unacknowledged
extra-textual information such as interviews, written eye-witness accounts, or
hearsay.

In his groundbreaking *Sexual Politics, Sexual Communities*, D'Emilio writes:

> Patrons of the Stonewall tended to be young and nonwhite . . . Rioting continued
> far into the night, with Puerto Rican transvestites and young street people leading
> charges against rows of uniformed police officers and then withdrawing to re-
> group in Village alleys and side streets.[14]

For its part, Faderman's brief discussion of the riots in her survey of US lesbian
history states:

> The two hundred working-class patrons—drag queens, third world gay men, and
> a handful of butch lesbians—congregated in front of the Stonewall and . . . com-
> menced to stage a riot.[15]

Even more thorough secondary accounts—such as Duberman's book which relies extensively on oral sources and a larger number of published texts—barely
corroborate D'Emilio's and Faderman's "hunches" that the Stonewall Inn's
clientele and the rioters themselves were "nonwhite," "Puerto Rican," and
"third world gay men." Other secondary literature mentions only "street
queens," "drag queens, dykes, street people, and bar boys," "dykes, straights,
kids, hippies, leather queens," "drag queens" and "sequined gays," "'dope-
smokers,' 'acid heads,' or 'speed-freaks,'" "flamboyant homosexual cross
dressers,"and "a particularly unconventional group of homosexuals," "blatant
queens—in full drag," and "transvestites." Race is not a factor in any of these
descriptions of the rioters.[16] (It is, at any rate, notoriously difficult to ascertain
racial proportions from impressionistic accounts; while not utterly unreliable,

such estimates are likely to be inflated or deflated by individual racial biases, anxieties, projections, feelings of invisibility, or desires for racial harmony.)

Writing around Stonewall's twentieth anniversary, Mark Haile reminds us that "[i]n the retelling of the tale [of the riots], history has become myth and desperation is remembered as romance." He points to the larger context of (official) American historical representations in which "[c]hanges and omissions, whether accidental or intentional, are nothing new . . . when it concerns people of color, gays, or women" to frame his revised "truth about Stonewall." In this revision, Haile specifically identifies "drag queens, hustlers, jailbait juveniles, and gay men and lesbians of color" as "the key players who started it all."[17] What I am interested in remarking here, however, pertains less to positivist notions of a singular "truth" of these assertions than to how various *truths* about the riots circulate among "us" in (de)racialized forms. For, despite Haile's perceptive and crucial observation regarding historical changes and omissions, the Stonewall riots have in fact *become* uniquely racialized in queer fictions of the past: while the first decade's reporting, commentary, and analysis ignored questions of race, over the course of the 1980s (at least since the publication of D'Emilio's book in 1983) people of color have been written into accounts of the riots, perhaps rightly recentering them in narratives of an event which they started and sustained.

Regardless of the veracity of claims that the clientele of the bar "tended to be . . . nonwhite" and that the rioters were "third world gay men," however, it remains of equal (greater?) moment that other aspects of gay and lesbian political history—that is, those that are regarded as pertaining to all of "us"—have been left substantially unmarked in racial terms. Where D'Emilio and Faderman, for instance, remark the race(s) of gay and lesbian activists, they do so principally to draw attention to separate organizations of people of color.[18] Unlike such groups as Gay American Indians, Third World Gay Revolution, UNIDOS, and Asian Lesbians of the East Coast, both such pre-Stonewall homophile groups as the Daughters of Bilitis and the Society for Individual Rights and such post-Stonewall gay organizations as the Gay Liberation Front and the Gay Activists Alliance were racially unmarked, ostensibly racially neutral, in principle perhaps even racially integrated. In fact, however, precisely like American society as a whole, racial segregation was (and has been) the norm defining the composition of such "open," "general," "non-separatist," and "racially unmarked" activities.

It is here, I would like to suggest, that we might begin better to understand how race matters to Stonewall's troubling importance as an emblem for gay and lesbian communities. Whether historically accurate or not, those recountings of the riots which have placed Puerto Ricans, blacks, and other people of color at the very center of "*the* emblematic event in modern lesbian and gay history" render Stonewall's ability to signify "us" fairly remarkable. To put it somewhat differently, just as the riots were a response to the urgent crisis in political representation facing gays and lesbians at the time, these racially marked queer fictions of Stonewall are emblems of the crisis in historical representation attendant on gay and lesbian identity-based politics, for their placement of race matters directly in the middle of narratives of the past disrupts comic readings of unity across difference. The cultural history of the riots, the multiple ways they were seized upon, and their continued transformations as a symbol in the decades that followed, in other words, necessarily make a substantially different sort of sense when the abiding racial dissonance in queer contexts is held in focus.

I want to return to McDarrah's photograph—that uniquely valuable and enigmatic visual text of the riots—to address (briefly and somewhat polemically) the particular question of how men of color function in resolving these crises in political and historical representation. From one perspective, the apparent integration and harmony of this image might seem to portend a reconciliation of the tensions of racial differences, suggesting their ultimate dissolution as significant and meaningful aspects of queer identity. In a sense, this singular photograph provides an alternate picture of what gay identity politics might, and did, look like. Regarding the image this way inscribes gay and lesbian history—or at least its "emblematic event"—with a vivid instance of multiculturalism that could itself serve as a model for community.

As much as it posits an alternative to racial segregation, however, this vision also helps sustain a false sense of racial cooperation and simply displaces critical reflections on race matters. By (falsely) grounding the ostensible origins of contemporary queer politics in an already present resolution of racial differences, tensions, and segregation, the previous and subsequent white-dominated political organizations can be regarded—even criticized—as unauthentic, as merely historical aberrations for their failure to reconcile queer differences. It is, on this reading, not Stonewall—or the posed photographic image of the post-riot scene—that is an enigma visually challenging segregated racial representations in gay and lesbian political history; rather, it is that very history itself that is enigmatic. In addition to the false sense of racial cooperation that promises the security of an untroubled "us," (re)populating the riots with "racial minorities" disturbingly parallels the expendability of men of color evidenced in other violent conflicts staged for "the general good," such as the (undeclared) war in Vietnam which was concurrent with Stonewall.

At any rate, this provocatively problematic visual text of "*the* emblematic event in modern lesbian and gay history" consists of thirteen men and no women.

Gender Trouble: "Were There Lesbians at Stonewall?"[19]

As much as the Stonewall Inn meticulously described by Duberman was an "oasis" in an indifferent, uninviting, even hostile world (p. 182), so too were the atmosphere and clientele of this oasis decidedly male: "[v]ery few women ever appeared in Stonewall" (p. 190). One lesbian quoted by Duberman who occasionally went to the Stonewall in the company of gay male friends "recalls that she 'felt like a visitor.'" On her assessment, "[t]here didn't seem to be hostility" between the predominantly gay male crowd and the few lesbians at the bar, "but there didn't seem to be camaraderie" either (p. 190). In contrast to this unnamed woman's account of the gender dynamics at the bar as a relative indifference between the many male patrons and the few female "visitors," Richard Savin, an "eyewitness" to the riots profiled in a recent article in the *Advocate*, insists that most of the lesbians at the bar on the night of the raid were helping the police. "The women were used to keeping us in line" as bouncers at the door, he explains, "and they didn't see this riot as a political statement. To them it was just a barroom brawl, and they were just doing their jobs."[20] Possibly distorted by his poorly concealed misogyny, Savin's claim appears to be of dubious accuracy or validity when read against Duberman's account in which all the bouncers are male: Ed Murphy, "Bobby Shades," Frank Esselourne (p. 187), and "Sascha L., who in 1969 briefly worked the door at the Stonewall alongside Murphy" (p. 182). Just past the door, "the [all male] Junior Achievement Mafia Team" (p. 187) staffed a table where one paid to get into the bar itself. (One woman, Dawn Hampton, did work the hatcheck [p. 181].)

As reported in Duberman's oral history, however, Karla Jay's initial attitude towards "the 'little penny-ante thing' going on at the Stonewall" partially reflects Savin's understanding of how lesbians viewed the "barroom brawl." To Jay, Duberman writes, the rioting "was just another all-male squabble with the prize nothing more than the right to lead an unhampered bar life . . . She had never been taken with the bar crowd, gay or lesbian, and this unsavory bunch seemed to [her] to have *stumbled* into rebellion" (pp. 219, 208). Although certain that the *real* revolution was nearing, Jay nonetheless doubted whether "the Stonewall riots represented its imminent arrival" (p. 208). She did, however, revise her assessment of the riots on hearing of the plans to form a Gay Liberation Front. Jay's change of heart both gives cause to ponder precisely how queer heterosocial relations have constructed Stonewall as emblematic in *gay and lesbian* history and anticipates the differences and (mis)alliances "across" gender that are marked and masked by such understandings of Stonewall's significance.

Over the same twenty-five years that the presence of black and Puerto Rican gay men has been alternately evacuated from or located centrally within queer fictions of Stonewall, a process of historical revision has also sought to reconstruct Stonewall as an event equally populated by and relevant to gay men *and* lesbians. A decade and a half ago, on the eve of the tenth anniversary of the riots, Maida Tilchen recognized this reconstruction as a "mythology." Was Stonewall, Tilchen asked in 1979, "the beginning of gay liberation for both men and women, or is it just another case of women being carried along in historical reports despite what they did or didn't do?"[21] One popular, though disputed, version of the riots locates *the* incendiary moment in the actions of a single lesbian. This particular queer fiction of Stonewall is so momentous that Elizabeth Kennedy and Madeline Davis make explicit reference to it in *Boots of Leather, Slippers of Gold*, an oral history-based study of butch and femme identities in the working-class lesbian community in Buffalo, New York, from the mid-1930s to the 1960s.

> In *lesbian and gay* mythology the first person to take a swing at the police in the Stonewall Riots, thereby igniting the street battle, was a lesbian. Assigning a rough and tough lesbian a primary role in the launching of gay liberation is completely in keeping with her character. Her fighting back would not be the isolated act of an angry individual but would have been an integral part of her culture.[22]

This "lesbian theory," as Maria De La O points out, reaches as far back as the *Village Voice* coverage of the riots which identifies "a dyke" as the first person to "put up a struggle."[23] Although doubts persist about whether a lesbian "started" the riot, De La O maintains, "there is no doubt that women were fighting alongside their 'gay brothers' on that hot summer night in 1969."[24] A striking commonality in these speculative, contested, even normative reconstructions of the riots recognizing lesbians' "involvement" in them, however, is still the preponderance of men: the Stonewall riots were as decidedly male as the bar itself.

In the same issue of the Boston-based *Gay Community News* as Tilchen's article, the staff of the collectively run weekly paper also recognized the "inadequacies" of existing representations of the past and editorialized the need for a co-gendered revision of queer fictions of Stonewall in order to enable future politics:

> We have a romantic vision and see ourselves fighting together towards common goals . . . Stonewall *must come to mean* lesbians and gay men fighting back against oppression, passionately and *together*.[25]

This imperative to invest Stonewall with a spirit of gay and lesbian cooperation articulates an explicitly figurative understanding of the riots as a symbol that draws on then-current emergent political practices. Prior to 1979, the editorial suggests, Stonewall did not yet resonate with such a spirit of cooperation, although it could—even should—do so. The future-oriented posture of this assertion is at least a partial call to move away from the highly separate gay male and lesbian movements that characterized the 1970s at a time when each of these movements was equally challenged by the powerful emergence of the New Right's explicit homophobia and to revitalize the immediate post-Stonewall activity that appealed to Karla Jay —"men *and* women working together to produce broad social change." While the *Gay Community News* editorial is perhaps overly ambitious in its belief in the malleability of history in order to meet current or future needs, it does remark the close configuration between knowledge and interest.

Revitalizing the Stonewall riots along an axis that connects the past to the future through the "interests" of the present, however, begs the question posed by Tilchen: "is [Stonewall] just another case of women being carried along in historical reports despite what they did or didn't do?" The point is more complex than a face-value reading of De La O's claim that there is no "doubt that women took up Stonewall as a rallying cry for a more activist-oriented fight for gay and lesbian liberation."[26] Indeed, lesbians have consistently noted their ambivalence towards the significance of Stonewall, as is suggested by Victoria Brownsworth's critique of Stonewall 25, the series of events held in New York City to commemorate the riots' twenty-fifth anniversary.

> The celebration of Stonewall is, for many lesbians, somewhat bittersweet because it is symbolic of the real divergence between lesbians and gay men in the struggle for queer civil rights . . . The simple fact that we, as a queer community, date our struggle for civil rights from the night of the riots at the Stonewall Inn in Greenwich Village is indicative of [the] exclusion [of lesbians from both the pre-Stonewall "gay" world and the post-Stonewall world of queer politics].[27]

Although in speaking of "a queer community" in the singular Brownsworth displaces a central aspect of the problem she articulates ("the real divergence between lesbians and gay men"), her critical observation nonetheless enables us to reframe the literal and figurative relationship between lesbians and Stonewall—between doubts about the literal presence of lesbians at Stonewall and the figurative force of queer fictions of Stonewall to pull lesbians into accounts of a past from which they might very well have been absent.

Important documents of the gay liberation and lesbian-feminist movements not only demonstrate the divergence between them but also raise fundamental questions about the relevance of Stonewall to the textual articulation of lesbian-feminism, especially in the years immediately after the riots. While most, if not all, gay male texts from this period refer to, invoke, or analyze the riots (at least briefly), as a whole lesbian-feminist texts are much less attentive to them. Several of the earliest post-Stonewall lesbian-liberationist texts, however, did position the riots as transformative for lesbians. In *Sappho Was a Right-On Woman*, Sidney Abbott and Barbara Love wrote in 1972, "[t]he effects [of the riots] were far-reaching and permanent *for Lesbians as for their gay brothers*."[28] Two years later, Dolores Klaich suggested in Woman+Woman that for lesbians in the gay liberation and women's movement "[n]othing has been the same since" Stonewall.[29] Yet, a far larger number of lesbian-feminist texts throughout the 1970s are silent on the issue; "Stonewall" is conspicuous principally by its absence from the majority of lesbian-feminist writings from the period. Although texts such as *Sappho Was a Right-On Woman*, Woman+Woman, and the lesbian contributions to co-gendered gay liberationist volumes such as Karla Jay and Allen Young's anthology *Out of the Closets* do consider Stonewall, they reiterate the split between the gay and lesbian-feminist movements as effectively as they suture across it. When they were not developing an explicitly autonomous discourse and politics, lesbian-feminist texts of the period were much more in dialogue or argument with the women's movement than they were with the gay liberation and later gay rights movements of the 1970s, including the significance of Stonewall.[30]

Even quite recent attempts to retain and specify the uncomfortable positioning of lesbians in relation to both the women's and the gay liberation movements, however, have (inadvertently) reiterated Stonewall's significance. Questioning whether "the gay/lesbian bar" is "a theoretical joint," Teresa de Lauretis returns to textual and historical differences between gay men and lesbians to resist the elision of differences effected "by the discursive coupling of th[e] two terms in the politically correct phrase 'lesbian and gay.' "[31] Her temporal marker of a key aspect of these differences, however, is rather telling, for it hypostatizes the events of Stonewall, whose "history" it should be interrogating. "Since the late 60s, *practically since Stonewall*," de Lauretis argues, "North American lesbians have been more or less painfully divided between an allegiance to the women's movement . . . and an allegiance to the gay liberation movement" (pp. vii–viii, emphasis added). Yet, because the riots occurred with only six months left in the decade, there is no *literal* difference between the phrases "since the late 60s" and "practically since Stonewall." Rather, the difference between them is figurative. While the former phrase references a specific point in time and, perhaps, a general sense of revolutionary political possibility, the precision of the latter phrasing is not temporal but rhetorical. The second phrase's purchase in current contexts is afforded by Stonewall's wealth of cultural capital and takes for granted, rather than decenters, Stonewall's emblematic status in the construction of a "queer common sense" that resonates across unresolved lines of social differentiation.

The construction of such a common sense is anticipated and called for by the *Gay Community News* editorial on Stonewall's tenth anniversary. Consistently emphatic and hortatory, the editorial is both reflective ("we must examine our culture") and prescriptive ("Stonewall must come to mean lesbians and gay men fighting back . . . together"). These reflective and prescriptive strains of the editorial, however, are framed by a rhetorical construction of Stonewall as a point of condensation, even an originary moment, for gay and lesbian resistance: "Stonewall," the editorial states in its opening sentence, "means fighting back," something that "gay people have begun" doing "[i]n the past ten years." Besides being historically myopic, these rhetorical positionings of Stonewall as both a unifying and originary historical moment from which the present logically and coherently followed have implications for how the past is reinterpreted for the future.

Although it acknowledges in general the varieties of who "we" are ("a nation across lines of gender and color and language and class"), the editorial's un-selfcritical use of the first person plural nonetheless constructs an undifferentiated "us" who "have a romantic vision and see ourselves fighting together toward common goals." Not only the references to then-immediate political crises—the successful effort in Dade County, Florida, to overturn civil rights protections based on sexual orientation; the unsuccessful Briggs Initiative, which sought to prevent gay men and lesbians from teaching in California's public schools; and the mockery of justice in the trial of Dan White, who assassinated San Francisco Supervisor Harvey Milk and Mayor George Moscone—but also the explicit call for a re-visioning of the Stonewall riots, seek to position "us" in relation to (unspecified longer-term) "common goals." This loosely pluralist identity-based political positioning, however, was not new in 1979. Precedents for it appeared throughout the 1970s at rallies and other political events and formed one of the core projects—and principal tensions—of the homophile organizations during the 1950s and 1960s.

Queer fictions of Stonewall create various versions of "us" by defining and refining the past. The powerful "common-sense" fiction that "we" share at least some common goals—goals that are symbolically represented by the resistance during the riots—is one centrally problematic way Stonewall erases and creates historical memory, in regard to relations between gay men and lesbians as well as racial and political differences. The period right after the riots—that period of men and women working together that interested Karla Jay—is especially salient in such reinscriptions. De La O, for instance, reflects favorably on "the cooperation among men and women at the riot and in the next couple of years of the GLF."[32] But this fabled cooperation in the early 1970s, though not nonexistent, was far from complete. Part of the project of regarding "Stonewall" must continually return to this point, particularly as a lens to focus on the ostensible cooperation and community among lesbians and gay men in the present. The point is not that queer heterosociality does not include or enable cooperative interactions across difference. Rather, these cooperative moments are (often) limited, partial, and tense, and it is precisely *in* those limitations and tensions that queer heterosociality consists.

Stonewall Was a Riot

"To remember Stonewall," J. E. Freeman writes in a vaguely poetic reminiscence on the riots published on the eve of their twenty-fifth anniversary,

> one must remember its context. Its moment in time. It was a time of politics. A time of demonstrations, awareness and idealism. It was a time to march on Washington. On the Pentagon. On the convention in Chicago.[33]

Urban disturbances of this sort were apparently so ordinary during this time of politics that when asked by her out-of-town companions what was going on as they neared Sheridan Square across from the Stonewall Inn on the first night of the riots, Martha Shelley, an increasingly radical officer of the New York chapter of the Daughters of Bilitis and soon-to-be gay liberationist, answered matter-of-factly, "Oh, it's a riot. These things happen in New York all the time."[34] Seeking to disabuse his readers of the notion that the first night's rioting was "a spontaneous outpouring of anger that changed the course of history," John D'Emilio also insists on the importance of the circumstances surrounding Stonewall, of "its moorings in time and place." "Yes," he acknowledges, "the riot was unplanned, impulsive, and unrehearsed—three common meanings of 'spontaneous'—but it was also rooted in a specific context that shaped the experience and consciousness of the participants."[35]

By the same token, however familiar these practices might have been to the bar's patrons, the Stonewall riots were tame in relation to the scope of protests, riots, and police brutality that would also have been familiar from elsewhere. Indeed, compared to attacks on civil rights activists, the Tlatelolco massacre in Mexico City, the events at the Sorbonne in May 1968, and the Columbia University strike, the level of violence surrounding the events at the Stonewall was low. "Yet," as Paul Berman points out in a review essay of several recent works in gay and lesbian historiography, "those June and July '69 crowds in Greenwich Village were furious even so. And their fury had an odd quality: *it didn't fade.*"[36] Though perhaps the fury did not fade, gay and lesbian liberation organizations were unable to sustain their original impulse and energy. In the less hospitable environment of the 1970s, as D'Emilio observes, radical gay liberation groups, "were being replaced by other kinds of gay and lesbian organizations," ones that were not only more narrowly focused but were also increasingly defined by the sharp divisions between men and women during the course of "the gendered seventies."[37]

Because both the specific modes of gay and lesbian politics and the larger context in which they were situated changed so quickly, and have continued to change in the nearly thirty years since the riots, it is difficult to construe the multiple meanings Stonewall still holds for gay men and lesbians simply in terms of the radicalism in which the riots were situated. Without either mourning the loss of such "a time of politics" or waxing nostalgic on the idealism of the times, it is important to ponder why "Stonewall" is still what Duberman calls "*the* emblematic event in modern lesbian and gay history." What is the "meaning" of a late-1960s riot in relation to current gay and lesbian contexts? The beginning of an answer to this question is suggested by the legacy of the gay liberation movement.

While Gay Liberation Fronts and similar groups clearly failed to sustain their radical activism beyond the early to mid-1970s, to focus on this "failure" is both to neglect the achievements those often loose-knit organizations did make and to construe politics—even radical politics—rather narrowly. Gay liberation's legacy includes a vast revisioning of the place and meaning of homosexuality in American society, with important implications for queer historical subjects, popular culture, and various state apparatuses. In particular, post-Stonewall activists created a new language of gay pride and a huge array of political, social, and cultural institutions that effectively brought people together and helped make the movement and the urban communities they were based in.

Central to this revisioning was the transformation of the meaning of "coming out" wrought by gay liberationists. "Before Stonewall," D'Emilio writes,

> the phrase had signified the acknowledgment of one's sexuality to others in the gay world; after Stonewall, it meant the public affirmation of homosexual identity. This revised form of coming out became . . . the quintessential expression of sixties cultural radicalism. It was "doing your own thing" with a vengeance; it embodied the insight that "The personal is political" as no other single act could.[38]

By thus "flesh[ing] out the implications of the riot," gay liberationists "ensured [that Stonewall] would become the symbol of a new militance" (p. 245). Accordingly, on D'Emilio's reading, it is through "the magic of coming out" (p. 248) that the Stonewall riots have maintained—even achieved—their emblematic status in gay and lesbian history. This connection between the riots and the transformed meaning of coming out (both of which have dangerous and exhilarating aspects) explains why, as Duberman puts it, "[t]oday the word [Stonewall] resonates with images of insurgency *and self-realization* and occupies a central place in the iconography of lesbian and gay *awareness*."[39] Although the earlier militance is still present in the form of "images of insurgency," Duberman points as well to how contemporary understandings of Stonewall have worked their alchemy on individuals, effecting a curious kind of self-knowledge that is also a knowledge of a collectivity. "The 1969 riots," Duberman states, "are now generally taken to mark . . . that moment in time when gays and lesbians recognized all at once their mistreatment *and* their solidarity" (p. xv, emphasis added).

Contesting the distinctions between the personal and the political has been the central tenet of gay and lesbian identity politics since Stonewall. Yet, as Diana Fuss cogently argues in the chapter on lesbian and gay theory in her book *Essentially Speaking*, the equation of the personal with the political is doubly damaging. While Fuss cautions us against "los[ing] sight of the historical importance of a slogan which galvanized and energized an entire political movement," she pointedly remarks that "attributing political significance to every personal action" quickly voids the political "of any meaning or specificity at all, and . . . paradoxically depersonalize[s]" the personal. Fuss states her position more emphatically a few lines later: "simply *being* gay or lesbian is not sufficient to constitute political activism."[40] Fuss's polemical point also resonates with D'Emilio's assessment of the historically important process. "Only later, as the movement matured," D'Emilio writes, "would it become clear that coming out was a first step only. An openly gay banker is still a banker."[41] Both Fuss's criticism of conflating the political with the personal and D'Emilio's observation on the limited political efficacy of coming out direct us to the equivocal "meaning" of the political at the nexus of several persistent modes of self-representation in lesbian and gay communities; from several of these perspectives, the politics of being gay or lesbian might be actively participating in a movement for liberation or reform, having an identity-based personal politics, or living a certain lifestyle. Less about the events themselves or "the actual story of the upheaval" that Duberman seeks to recount than about the meanings attributed to the riots, the disputes about Stonewall are reiterated in the ambiguity of the "political" in lesbian and gay movements, communities, and cultures.

In the postwar period, bars have been important meeting places, community institutions, and sites of resistance that have helped to forge public and collective (albeit problematic and tension-fraught) gay and lesbian identities.[42] This public and collective identity was clearly an important part of the context framing the Stonewall riots. As Duberman remarks, although it had its critics, including his narrators Craig Rodwell and Jim Fouratt, the Stonewall Inn was "the most popular gay bar in Greenwich Village" when the riots occurred.

> Many saw it as an oasis, a safe retreat from the harassment of everyday life, a place less susceptible to police raids than other gay bars and one that drew a magical mix of patrons ranging from tweedy East Siders to street queens. It was also the only gay male bar in New York where dancing was permitted[43]

Yet the attention to the public and collective aspects of gay bar life deflects attention away from the bar's location within the "private" sphere of the marketplace based on economic self-interest and commodity culture (and in the case of the Stonewall Inn, the collusion of the mafia and the police). More importantly, to the extent that they help to contain gay life in commercial enterprises, bars problematically reprivatize gay identities within what one commentator has called "the colossal closet."[44]

The commercial gay subculture of the 1970s, much vaster than its lesbian counterpart and less politicized than many other aspects of lesbian-feminist subcultures, is replete with consumerist, reprivatizing, and depoliticizing impulses. Yet the growth of this commercial scene during the 1970s had a positive impact on the lives of many gay men, providing them opportunities to escape the pervasive homophobia and heterosexism they experienced outside the gay ghettos. There has also been an important relationship between the proliferation of commercial venues and the growth of a political movement. As Dennis Altman puts it:

> the victories of the movement help provide a climate in which bars and suchlike can flourish, while the growth of a commercial world can provide the beginnings of a sense of community that the movement can in turn mobilise.[45]

D'Emilio identifies this dialectical relationship more sharply. "[T]he absence of overt politicization" in the gay male subculture of the 1970s, he argues, "can be attributed in part to the success, in its own narrow terms, of reformist politics. Since the sexual subculture had been the location where gay men most acutely experienced both their gayness and their vulnerability," the reform movement's success in reducing harassment by the police "seemed incontrovertible evidence that they were free." Once gay men "could be open about their 'lifestyle' on the streets of the burgeoning gay neighborhoods suddenly visible in large American cities after the mid-1970s," the concerns of activists "seemed like the ravings of grim politicos who just didn't know how to have fun." In an unexplicit reference to the future that echoes Altman's assessment of the political potential of the commercial world, D'Emilio contends that "though it was not apparent at the time, the commercialized subculture was . . . the seedbed for a consciousness that would be susceptible to political mobilization."[46]

On this somewhat generous reading of it, the commercialized gay subculture is much like the post-Stonewall conception of coming out. Rather than purely public or political in their own right, both the disclosure made by coming out and the commercial gay subculture function as gateways or interfaces between private and public worlds, between the personal and the political.[47] More than suggesting merely a permeable or unfixed boundary between them, however, gay and lesbian identity politics rooted in and animated by subcultural expressions are part of the larger process of democratization that has begun to unsettle the public–private distinction and to politicize social relations.

Thus, not only has the political context changed since Stonewall, but there has also occurred a change in the nature and meaning of politics itself as a result of the politicization of social relations. By displacing the demarcation between the private and the public, as Ernesto Laclau and Chantal Mouffe argue in their influential book *Hegemony and Socialist Strategy*, this politicization "has . . . exploded . . . the idea and the reality itself of a unique space of constitution of the political."[48] For this reason, to identify Stonewall's "moment in time" as "a time of politics" reifies the political—as if the meanings, goals, and processes of "politics" were stagnant, universal, always the same—and evacuates the political from present contexts. In order to avoid reified, obfuscating, and ultimately disempowering conceptions of the political, therefore, we need to historicize "politics." As Fuss cautions, however, such a project "should not lead us on a quest to locate the 'true' identity of politics." Politics, she continues, "is irreducibly cast in the plural. That politics linguistically connotes difference . . . immeasurably frustrates our attempts to locate and anatomize the identity of politics."[49]

Part of Fuss's own interest in theorizing politics is to resist conflating the personal and the political so that "[s]exual desire [does not become] invested with macropolitical significance." Retaining the distinction between the personal and the political, Fuss argues, serves to prevent "a telescoping of goals, a limiting of revolutionary activity to the project of self-discovery and personal transformation." Yet despite the rhetorical clarity of her distinction between the personal and the political, Fuss's argument slips on the equation of the "social" with the political. "Initially," she writes, "'the personal is political' operated as a gravitational point for attracting attention to minority group concerns" that originated in "concrete social oppression." At some subsequent time (presumably "now," given the shift in verb tense), however, "'[t]he personal is political' re-privatizes *social* experience" (p. 101, emphasis added). In Fuss's argument "the social" can (even, must) occupy only one location in the dichotomy between the public and the private. Against this understanding, which itself does nothing to frustrate our search for the identity of politics, Laclau and Mouffe's recognition of the social as the third term that destabilizes the hegemonic distinction between the personal and the political offers a more promising, and complex, way to approach queer transformations of the public sphere. What Fuss's position does allow, however, is an historicizing approach to identity politics that would, for instance, recognize the no longer novel, though perhaps still personally transforming, aspects of coming out, of taking what D'Emilio calls "a first step only."

The tensions between these two perspectives on the social are reflected in the precarious balance between gay and lesbian subcultures and gay and lesbian movements, between the resilient redefinitions of politics located in the politicization of the social itself and the relatively passive sense of the political in a "politics" of mere visibility. As D'Emilio stresses, however, this precarious balance is central rather than incidental to the articulation of the political in gay and lesbian contexts.

> The history of lesbian and gay politics is as much the history of the creation and elaboration of a self-conscious community and culture as it is the story of a social movement . . . The structure of the community marks the terrain on which the movement can operate, and the actions of the movement are continually reshaping the life of the community.[50]

To say, however, as one observer rather glibly pronounced in anticipation of Stonewall 25, "[t]his is the gay gift: politics as party,"[51] might be a catchy one-line quip about gay people's unique contribution to the politicization of social relations, but its failure to distinguish between "politics" and "party" naively treats a point of abiding significance to considerations of political organizing, the analysis of social movements, and an understanding of cultural politics. The steady growth and continued strength of the lesbian and gay movement through the 1980s and 1990s while other movements on "the left" have experienced, in D'Emilio's words, "a widespread sense of retrenchment, of losing ground, of being under siege" cannot be understood simply in terms of a conflation of social change with socializing, of reducing gay politics to a party.[52] Nonetheless, there exists a need to reconsider the vitality of the gay and lesbian movement, particularly in terms of the social terrain on which the movement operates.

Regarding the latter point, I want to pause briefly to echo a certain degree of critical skepticism towards the recent Stonewall 25 events in New York City. Anticipating that it would be yet "another weekend lost," Mary Breslauer wrote in the *Advocate*, "Stonewall 25 will be a massive reaffirmation of who we are. But it also graphically symbolizes our inability to organize en masse for anything but a party."[53] While on the one hand Breslauer's pessimism reiterates the naive, historically inaccurate, and ultimately homophobic reading of "the gay gift" that conflates lesbian and gay politics with an endless party, it does on the other hand point to the need to be wary of uncritically accepting huge public gatherings of gay men and lesbians as effective, viable forms of political activism simply because they make "us" "visible" to those who need to see "us" and make "us" feel good about who "we" "are." At the very least, one might wonder how one million people and the hundreds of millions of dollars they collectively spent to be in New York might have been put to use differently in this age of a socially constructed scarcity of resources.

Of course, part of the "queer money" spent during that long weekend was "reinvested" in the "community," either through purchases made at gay- and/or lesbian-owned businesses or through the donation to charity of the proceeds raised at various of the parties and so forth celebrating Stonewall. Consider the following, for instance. The cover of the Stonewall 25 and Gay Games "special supplement to *Out* magazine," by far the most successful of several relatively new slick "lifestyle" gay and lesbian publications to appear in the last several years, beckoned its readers with attractive and alluring promises of a chic and fulfilling fantasy vacation during what the attached advance-ticket order form proudly boasted would be an "historical week of events."

> This June 18–26, come to New York City for Stonewall 25, Gay Games IV, and the events of Out in New York '94. See stars and celebrities! Dive into parties and concerts. Help raise $$ for AIDS.

Although all proceeds from the dozen and a half "Out in New York '94"-sponsored events benefitted "AIDS organizations nationwide," the cynic might read the promotional materials themselves as identifying this distribution of the profits as an incidental or serendipitous, rather than integral and planned, outcome. In addition, labelling a series of cocktail parties, concerts, and balls—even if they are fundraisers for important organizations—an "historical week of events" is itself a naive assessment that reflects both a failure to grasp the extent to which such social events are already institutionalized in gay and lesbian urban subcultures throughout the USA and an inability to differentiate between a busy week of attending expensive social gatherings and three days of rioting in the face of a large and hostile police presence.

As the most salient reminders of this emblematic event in gay and lesbian history, the annual parades, celebrations, and marches commemorating Stonewall locate the riots at the center of a collective, albeit temporary and partial, post-Stonewall gay-and-lesbian identity. Paradoxically, however, gay and lesbian freedom day parades also make visible myriad queer differences, ranging from relatively benign lifestyle choices to much more entrenched, overdetermined, and poignant differences having to do with historically constructed inequalities in social relations. As Richard Herrell observes in regard to the Chicago parade:

> the gay and lesbian parade today uses a society-wide system of heterogeneity in religion, politics, sports teams, musical organizations, and other interests to claim an

essential similarity. It says to Chicago, "We as gay people are fundamentally different among ourselves and that's why—and how—we're just like you."[54]

On this analysis, differences between and among queer historical subjects become visible in proportion to the degree that various gay and lesbian individuals, communities, and organizations participate in these annual commemorations.
And, the more fully visible those differences become, the more completely gay
and lesbian people can show ourselves to be just like heterosexuals.

In terms of Herrell's assessment of this paradoxical spectacle of identity
and difference, the multiple differences between and among queer historical
subjects are rendered equivalent, reduced to no more significance than their
share of the whole. In other words, as simply mirroring "a society-wide heterogeneity" in which all differences are seen as "interests," the mere act of making
queer heterosocial differences visible becomes sufficient, being itself a minimal-
ist sort of participatory democratic practice. By conflating all differences to an
essential similarity, however, this understanding equates categories of differences such as race and gender with a hobby, one's favorite bar, or the college
one might have attended. In such a reading of the multiple differences among
queer historical subjects, challenges to racism, sexism, and particular kinds of
political practice are robbed of their ability to make critical interventions into
specific historical relations and concrete social circumstances. Since every one
of us is "different" according to this framework, certain, any, or all differences
no longer matter because the specificity of differences that reflect social and
historical processes of privilege, subordination, allegiances, alienation, resistance, and so forth is evacuated, leaving these differences undifferentiated from
merely personal preferences and individual character traits.

This liberal-pluralist model invests visibility with a deep significance,
ironically "transcending" the very differences it attempts to make visible. The
multiplication of differences among queer historical subjects, which has made
important inroads against the persistent fiction of a unified and stable gay and
lesbian community, has turned towards the increased visibility of various categories of differences as the one political goal shared by all groups. Thus, as
Martha Gever has pointed out in commenting on the divergent strategies in
cinematic representations of lesbian history, "[v]isibility itself now constitutes
the basis for a sense of interests shared across groups that have little in common otherwise."[55] Such efforts towards making visible multiple differences can
be seen as reviving and revising the post-Stonewall meaning of coming out. In
so doing, visibility itself becomes a new, if slippery and decentered, queer common sense indirectly framed in terms of the symbolic dimensions of Stonewall,
using the annual celebrations of the riots and their legacies as staging grounds
for the many differences among queer historical subjects. The reduction of advocacy in the public realm to (the not always so simple) task of achieving visibility, however, is ultimately a deeply unsatisfactory understanding of
Stonewall as an emblem. By rendering all differences equivalent, the politics of

visibility betrays the deep significance of queer historical practices that reread, reframe, and refuse various constructions of the present moment. Not only does its strategy of equating queer historical subjects with heterosexual subjects retreat from the very necessary processes of historicizing the social constructions of sexual differences, but it also implicitly articulates a consensus model of American society in which social, political, and historical struggles are recontained and curtailed.

Coda

Finally, I want to suggest that one of the primary meanings attached to the riots—perhaps *the* queer fiction of Stonewall—is the structuring of those events in a way that reiterates a larger tale of triumph over adversity and the reconciliation of differences and, thus, echoes the themes of a comic mode of emplotment in literary and dramatic works.[56] Such a comic plot structure, for instance, underlies Duberman's historical account of the riots. In spite of the conflicts, challenges, and disappointments written into *Stonewall*'s "actual story of the upheaval," the book ends with the commemorative marches in New York and Los Angeles on the first anniversary of the riots, festive occasions reconciling differences and promising a new secular order. Duberman's six subjects, we read in the book's final paragraph,

> were all, in their own ways, euphoric, just as, in their own ways, they had all somehow come through, had managed to arrive at this unimaginable coming together, this testimony to a difficult past surmounted and a potentially better future in view.[57]

Although Duberman is careful not to evoke an image of "[t]he decades preceding Stonewall . . . as some vast neolithic wasteland" (p. xv), his decision to end the book when and how he does provides a particular kind of meaning to or interpretation of the Stonewall riots. Through a comic emplotment, *Stonewall* explains those events as crucial moments in a narrative of gay redemption and restates the mythic importance of the riots as "*the* emblematic event in modern lesbian and gay history."

The undeniable significance of the riots and their annual commemoration notwithstanding, however, there are also compelling reasons to regard Stonewall differently, to tell or interpret the story in a different mode. While understanding the Stonewall riots through a comic emplotment allows us to read them as a story of progress that promises a harmonious resolution of gay differences and the problems gay people face in a heterosexist society, an alternative emplotment of Stonewall—for instance, one identifiable as archetypically "tragic"—might allow us to explore more fully the loss of "our unity for the rest of our lives," as Duberman's narrator Sylvia Rivera thought it might be (p. 246). Such a tragic emplotment would suggest that festive occasions of triumph and reconciliation are false or illusory ones and would indicate much deeper divisions among "us" than previously imagined. Certainly, "the unimaginable coming together" of the first year's anniversary march is only one way of reading the political differences between the Gay Liberation Front and the Gay Activists Alliance, the tensions between gay men and lesbians, and the still underexplored relationships among white and Third World activists, to mention only several of these divisions.[58]

Because post-Stonewall gay and lesbian movements have been organized around the teleological premise of progress and liberation, pursuing a narrative of emancipation, of coming out, perhaps they can only make sense in a comic mode. In a sense, because there was a gay liberation movement which—in its new, militant, and unapologetic form—followed directly on the heels of the riots, the story of Stonewall had to be emplotted as a comedy (though not from a homophobic or reactionary perspective). But, however inevitable or necessary a comic emplotment of the riots and their aftermath might seem, I want to propose rethinking that premise, particularly in light of the multiple critiques of identity politics and movements organized around identity whose emphasis on difference, antagonism, and social inequality upset the possibility that, even in "triumphant" moments, some collective "we" have surmounted "the same" difficult past. Within the logic of such comic emplotments, commemorations of Stonewall offer a sense of stability, resolution, and narrative closure that masks crucial instabilities, dissolutions, and ruptures in gay and lesbian social, cultural, and political practices. While annual public celebrations of the riots and various institutional structures claiming Stonewall's legacy for themselves help to assert the queer nation of the late twentieth century, the highly salient points of social rupture in gay and lesbian political practices that disappear in comic readings of Stonewall persist nearly three decades after the riots. For this reason, we would do better to look at how these differences inform the multiple contests for meaning invoked and evoked in representations of and claims to the Stonewall riots.

Because the significance queer historical subjects find in the riots is always informed by the fact that most of us have no literal connection to them, the questions of identity, difference, and representation raised by the symbolic and figurative dimensions of Stonewall concern the ability to imagine communities, to see individuals and collectivities in relation to each other. Despite—one could say because of—their partiality, queer fictions of Stonewall allow us to reconsider the collective queer heterosocial differences among gay men and lesbians as problematic subjects in history. Indeed, it is the particularly public nature of the annual parades commemorating Stonewall that makes them especially well suited to the task of *re*forming the world. Furthermore, the unresolved debates about the meaning of the riots are themselves concerned with the public sphere, including the question of equal access to public spaces and those spaces defined as queer. In this way, these debates are fundamentally about the articulation and possibility of community across multiple differences. Finally, then, although they indicate a lack of consensus on who or what gay and lesbian people are and even highlight the anti-community aspects of the differences between and among queer historical subjects, queer fictions of Stonewall are also important social/cultural texts in the reconstruction and reiteration of the sexual differences of lesbian and gay sexualities from normative heterosexuality.

Notes

1. Martin Duberman, *Stonewall* (New York: Dutton, 1993), p. xv.
2. Respectively, the first four quotations are taken from Chris Adams, "Birth of Defiance," review of Martin Duberman, *Stonewall*, in the *San Francisco Chronicle*, review section (June 20, 1993), p. 1; Diana Walsh, "250,000 Watch S.F. Gay March, a Parade of Firsts," *San Francisco Examiner* (July 1, 1991), p. A-10; an unnamed witness to the riot quoted in Donn Teal, *The Gay Militants* (New York: Stein and Day, 1971), p. 20; and [Dick Leitsch], "The Hairpin Drop Heard Round the World," supplemental leaflet to *New York Mattachine Newsletter* (July, 1969). The rather odd term "modern" to describe gay and lesbian history since Stonewall is used with such frequency that it would be impossible to list all of its occurrences, but see Duberman, *Stonewall*, p. xv.
3. Duberman, *Stonewall*, p. xv, emphasis added.
4. Duberman's style is also informed by the trope of the historian as visual artist engaged in portraiture, drawing, and painting (p. xvi). In other words, Duberman's *Stonewall* is informed by both a verbal style and a visual metaphor that draws on realist models of historical representation which purport merely to describe or to make visible the events of the past in small and precise detail and to offer them as literal, unmediated, and true "images" of what happened.
5. Alessandro Portelli, "The Peculiarities of Oral History," *History Workshop*, 12 (autumn 1981), pp. 98–99.
6. Joan W. Scott, "The Evidence of Experience," in *The Lesbian and Gay Studies Reader*, ed. Henry Abelove, Michèlle Aina Barale, and David M. Halperin (New York: Routledge, 1993), pp. 399, 407, 409
7. On Redstockings, see Alice Echols, *Daring to Be Bad: Radical Feminism in America, 1967–1975* (Minneapolis: University of Minnesota Press, 1989), pp. 139–158.
8. Howard Smith, "Full Moon over the Stonewall," *Village Voice* (July 3, 1969), pp. 1, 25, 29 and Lucian Truscott IV, "Gay Power Comes to Sheridan Square," *The Village Voice* (July 3, 1969), pp. 1, 18.
9. The photograph has recently been reprinted opposite Sara Hart, "Stonewall 25," *Ten Percent* (June, 1994), p. 47; in Fred W. McDarrah and Timothy S. McDarrah, *Gay Pride: Photographs from Stonewall to Today* (Chicago: A Capella, 1994), on the front cover and opposite p. 1; and in the *Village Voice* (November 14, 1995), p. 41 as part of their forty-year retrospective. An alternate image of this scene appears in *Gay Pride*, p. xxiii.
10. Exemplary, though not unique, are the following: "New Negro Riots Erupt on Coast; 3 Reported Shot," *New York Times* (August 13, 1965), p. 1; "2,000 Troops Enter Los Angeles on Third Day of Negro Rioting; 4 Die as Fires and Looting Grow," *New York Times* (August 14, 1965), p. 1; and "2,000 Guardsmen on Chicago Alert," *New York Times* (August 15, 1965), p. 1.

11. "4 Policemen Hurt in 'Village' Raid," *New York Times* (June 29, 1969), p. 33; "Police Again Rout 'Village' Youths," *New York Times* (June 30, 1969), p. 22.

12. A more explicit marking of this racial—sexual dichotomy is reflected in a police officer's comment overheard by a New York Mattachine Society member: "I like nigger riots better because there's more action, but you can't beat up a fairy. They ain't mean like blacks; they're sick" (quoted in [Leitsch], "The Hairpin Drop Heard Round the World," p. 23). Jim Fouratt also argued along these lines, noting that "[n]ot one straight radical group showed up at Stonewall. *If* it had been a *black* demonstration they'd have been there" (quoted in Duberman, *Stonewall*, p. 211, emphasis added). On Greenwich Village, see George Chauncey, *Gay New York: Gender, Urban Culture, and the Making of the Gay Male World, 1890–1940* (New York: Basic Books, 1994), esp. pp. 228–244 and Ellen Kay Trimberger, "Feminism, Men, and Modern Love: Greenwich Village, 1900–1925," in *Powers of Desire: The Politics of Sexuality*, ed. Ann Snitow, Christine Stansell, and Sharon Thompson (New York: Monthly Review Press, 1983), pp. 131–152.

13. Consider, in particular, the following pictures reprinted in Duberman, *Stonewall*: the 1965 ECHO convention; the May 21, 1965, picket in front of the White House; and the Gay Liberation Front poster.

14. John D'Emilio, *Sexual Politics, Sexual Communities: The Making of a Homosexual Minority in the United States 1940–1970* (Chicago: University of Chicago Press, 1983), pp. 231, 232. In more recent writings, D'Emilio vacillates on the relative numbers of men of color involved in the riots and leaves white participants unmarked. Citing no sources in either instance he maintains, "[y]oung gay men of color as *many* of the [patrons of the Stonewall] were, they could not have been immune to the rhetoric and politics of groups such as the Black Panthers and the Young Lords" ("After Stonewall," pp. 240–241, emphasis added) and "*some* of [the rioters] were young men of color whose home communities were permeated by radical politics" (John D'Emilio, "Foreword," in *Out of the Closets: Voices of Gay Liberation*, ed. Karla Jay and Allen Young, reprint edition [New York: New York University Press, 1992], p. xix, emphasis added).

15. Lillian Faderman, *Odd Girls and Twilight Lovers: A History of Lesbian Life in Twentieth-Century America* (New York, Columbia University Press, 1991), p. 194.

16. Sidney Abbott and Barbara Love, *Sappho Was a Right-On Woman: A Liberated View of Lesbianism* (New York: Stein and Day, 1972), p. 159; Barry Adam, *The Rise of a Gay and Lesbian Movement* (Boston: Twayne, 1987), p. 75; Sam Binkley, "'I'm Sorry I Threw Bricks at Stonewall!': A Faghag's Historical Commentary: Excerpts from an Interview with Penny Arcade," *Found Object*, 4 (fall 1994), p. 127; Mike Long, "The Night the Girls Said No!" *San Francisco Sentinel* (June 22, 1989), p. 2; Toby Marotta, *The Politics of Homosexuality* (Boston: Houghton Mifflin Company, 1981), pp. 71, 74; Cindy Stein, "Stonewall Nation 69–79: What Really Happened, Anyhow?" *Gay Community News* (June 23, 1979), p. 9; Teal, *The Gay Militants*, p. 18; Allen Young, "Out of the Closets, Into the Streets," in *Out of the Closets*, p. 25.

17. Mark Haile, "The Truth about Stonewall," *BLK*, 7 (June, 1989), p. 8.

18. John D'Emilio, "After Stonewall," in *Making Trouble: Essays on Gay History, Politics, and the University* (New York: Routledge, 1992), p. 261; Faderman, *Odd Girls and Twilight Lovers*, pp. 284–288.

19. Maida Tilchen, "Mythologizing Stonewall," *Gay Community News* (June 23, 1979), p. 16.

20. Robert L. Pela, "Stonewall's Eyewitnesses," *The Advocate* (May 3, 1994), p. 52.
21. Tilchen, "Mythologizing Stonewall," p. 16.
22. Elizabeth Lapovsky Kennedy and Madeline D. Davis, *Boots of Leather, Slippers of Gold: The History of a Lesbian Community* (New York: Routledge, 1993), p. 378, emphasis added.
23. Truscott, "Gay Power Comes to Sheridan Square," p. 1.
24. Maria De La O, "Stonewall: The Queer Revolution Twenty Years Later," *Deneuve* (June, 1994), p. 30; see Duberman's discussion of the persistent doubts about whether a lesbian "started" the riots (*Stonewall*, pp. 196ff.).
25. Editorial, "A Stonewall Nation," *Gay Community News* (June 23, 1979), p. 4, emphasis added.
26. De La O, "Stonewall," p. 30; John D'Emilio argues that "Stonewall was the catalyst that allowed gay women and men to appropriate to themselves the example, insight, and inspiration of the radical movements of the 1960s—black power, the new left, the counterculture, *and, above all, feminism*—and take a huge step forward toward liberation" ("Dreams Deferred: The Birth and Betrayal of America's First Gay Liberation Movement," in *Making Trouble*, p. 54, emphasis added).
27. Victoria A. Brownsworth, "Stonewall 25: Not a Happy Anniversary for Lesbians," *Deneuve* (June, 1994), p. 38.
28. Abbott and Love, *Sappho Was a Right-On Woman*, p. 159, emphasis added.
29. Dolores Klaich, Woman + Woman (New York: Simon and Schuster, 1974), p. 219.
30. Abbott and Love, *Sappho Was a Right-On Woman;* Dennis Altman, *Homosexual: Oppression and Liberation* (New York: Outerbridge and Dienstfrey, 1971); Ti-Grace Atkinson, *Amazon Odyssey* (New York: Links, 1974); Jay and Young (eds.), *Out of the Closets;* Jill Johnston, *Lesbian Nation: The Feminist Solution* (New York: Simon and Schuster, 1973); Klaich, Woman + Woman; Del Martin and Phyllis Lyon, *Lesbian/Woman* (San Francisco: Glide Foundation, 1972); Nancy Myron and Charlotte Bunch (eds.), *Lesbians and the Women's Movement* (Baltimore, MD: Diana Press, 1975); Len Richmond and Gary Noguera (eds.), *The Gay Liberation Book* (San Francisco: Ramparts Press, 1972); Ruth Simpson, *From the Closets to the Courts* (New York: Viking, 1976); Teal, *The Gay Militants.*
31. Teresa de Lauretis, "Queer Theory: Lesbian and Gay Studies, an Introduction," *differences: A Journal of Feminist Cultural Studies* 3.2 (summer 1991), pp. iv, v.
32. De La O, "Stonewall," p. 31.
33. J. E. Freeman, "I Remember," *San Francisco Examiner Magazine* (June 19, 1994), p. 11.
34. Interview with Martha Shelley in Eric Marcus, *Making History: The Struggle for Gay and Lesbian Equal Rights, 1945–1990, an Oral History* (New York: Harper-Collins, 1992), p. 180.
35. D'Emilio, "After Stonewall," p. 240.
36. Paul Berman, "Democracy and Homosexuality," *The New Republic* (December 20, 1993), p. 24, emphasis added.
37. D'Emilio, "After Stonewall," pp. 245, 246–256.
38. D'Emilio, "After Stonewall," p. 244.
39. Duberman, *Stonewall*, p. xv.
40. Diana Fuss, *Essentially Speaking: Feminism, Nature, and Difference* (New York: Routledge, 1989), p. 101.

41. D'Emilio, "After Stonewall," p. 249.

42. Abbott and Love, *Sappho Was a Right-On Woman*, ch. 3; Allan Bérubé, *Coming Out under Fire: The History of Gay Men and Women in World War Two* (New York: The Free Press, 1990), passim; Donald Webster Cory (pseud.), *The Homosexual in America: A Subjective Approach* (New York: Greenberg, 1951), ch. 11; D'Emilio, *Sexual Politics, Sexual Communities*, p. 32; Faderman, *Odd Girls and Twilight Lovers*, esp. pp. 161–167; Leslie Feinberg, *Stone Butch Blues* (Ithaca, NY: Firebrand Books, 1993), passim; Evelyn Hooker, "Male Homosexuals and their 'Worlds,' " in *Sexual Inversion*, ed. Judd Marmor (New York: Basic Books, 1965), pp. 83–107; Kennedy and Davis, *Boots of Leather, Slippers of Gold*, passim; Audre Lorde, *Zami: A New Spelling of My Name* (Trumansburg, NY: The Crossing Press, 1982), passim; Joan Nestle, "Butch-Femme Relationships: Sexual Courage in the 1950s," in *A Restricted Country* (Ithaca, NY: Firebrand Books, 1987), pp. 100–109; Kenneth E. Read, *Other Voices: The Style of a Male Homosexual Tavern* (Novato, CA: Chandler and Sharp, 1980); and Wayne Sage, "Inside the Colossal Closet," in *Gay Men: The Sociology of Male Homosexuality*, ed. Martin P. Levine (New York: Harper and Row, 1979), pp. 148–163.

43. Duberman, *Stonewall*, p. 182.

44. Sage, "Inside the Colossal Closet."

45. Dennis Altman, "What Changed in the Seventies?" in *Homosexuality: Power and Politics*, ed. Gay Left Collective (London: Allison and Busby, 1980), p. 57.

46. D'Emilio, "After Stonewall," p. 251.

47. This ambiguous status *vis-à-vis* the public is reflected in the transformation of the rallying cry of gay liberationists ten years after Stonewall on the night of the riots at San Francisco's City Hall in protest at the lenient sentence given to Dan White for assassinating Supervisor Harvey Milk and Mayor George Moscone. In recognition of the vastly transformed nature of the gay subculture and in a fairly explicit attempt to equate the closet of the late 1960s with the commercial subculture of the late 1970s, the earlier slogan "Out of the closets, into the streets" became "Out of the bars and into the streets." See Allen Young, "Out of the Closets, Into the Streets" and Randy Shilts, *The Mayor of Castro Street: The Life and Times of Harvey Milk* (New York: St. Martin's Press, 1982), p. 327.

48. Ernesto Laclau and Chantal Mouffe, *Hegemony and Socialist Strategy: Towards a Radical Democratic Politics* (London: Verso, 1985), p. 181.

49. Fuss, *Essentially Speaking*, p. 105.

50. D'Emilio, "After Stonewall," p. 237.

51. Paul Rudnick, "Gaytown, USA," *New York* (June 20, 1994), p. 38.

52. D'Emilio, "After Stonewall," p. 236.

53. Mary Breslauer, "Another Weekend Lost," *The Advocate* (February 22, 1994), p. 5.

54. Richard Herrell, "The Symbolic Strategies of Chicago's Gay and Lesbian Pride Day Parade," in *Gay Culture in America: Essays from the Field*, ed. Gilbert Herdt (Boston: Beacon Press, 1991), p. 245.

55. Martha Gever, "What Becomes a Legend Most?" *GLQ: A Journal of Lesbian and Gay Studies*, 1.2 (May, 1994), p. 210. Rosemary Hennessey has argued that "for those of us caught up in the circuits of late capitalist consumption, the visibility of sexual identity is often a matter of commodification, a process that invariably depends on the lives and labor of invisible others." See her "Queer Visibility in Commodity Culture," *Cultural Critique*, 29 (winter 1994–1995), pp. 31–76; the quotation is on p. 31.

56. On emplotment in general, see Northrop Frye, *The Anatomy of Criticism: Four Essays* (Princeton, NJ: Princeton University Press, 1957); on emplotment and historical explanation, see Hayden White, *Metahistory: The Historical Imagination in Nineteenth-Century Europe* (Baltimore: Johns Hopkins University Press, 1973), esp. pp. 7–11.

57. Duberman, *Stonewall*, p. 280.

58. Although the scope of inclusion is defined by the politics of gay liberation, the writings anthologized in Jay and Young (eds.), *Out of the Closets* suggest some of these acute differences. See also, Terrence Kissack, "Freaking Fag Revolutionaries: New York's Gay Liberation Front, 1969–1971," *Radical History Review* 62 (spring 1995), pp. 104–134.

Questions for Reflection, Discussion, and Writing

1. According to Bravmann, why is Stonewall often understood to be a central facet and moment of "gay and lesbian identity, community and history"? How does Bravmann claim he offers an extensive critique of the representation of Stonewall in Duberman's work?

2. What justification for his methods does Bravmann claim Duberman offers? In what ways does Bravmann critique those methods? What central problem about agency, does Bravmann claim Duberman's use and representations of his research volunteers illustrates?

3. What parallels does Bravmann draw between the ways the media represented race and sexuality during the Stonewall and "race" riots?

4. How did lesbian-feminists represent Stonewall, according to Bravmann? What ongoing ideological "splits" between lesbians and "gay commercial subculture" does Bravmann claim those representations of Stonewall illustrate?

5. Beginning by analyzing Fuss, Bravmann addresses the relationship between the "personal" and the "political." According to Bravmann what gets obscured when events like PRIDE marches or other "queer" celebrations tend to render "all differences equivalent"?

6. According to Bravmann, why do we need readings of Stonewall that differ from the one Duberman offers?

Related Reading

Barry D. Adam, *The Rise of A Gay and Lesbian Movement.* Boston: Twayne Publishers. 1987.

Martin Duberman, *Stonewall.* NY: Dutton. 1993.

Jarrod Hayes, Lauren Kozol and Wayne Marat VanSertima, "Stonewall: A Gift to the World: An Interview with Tony Kushner and Joan Nestle." *Found Object 4* (Fall 1994): 94–107.

Lisa Duggan, "Becoming Visible: The Legacy of Stonewall." *Radical History Review 62* (1995): 188–194.

Eric Orner, "Stonewall Unremembered." *The Harvard Gay & Lesbian Review* 6.3 (Summer 1999): 30–31.

William Scroggie, "Producing Identity: From *The Boys in the Band* to Gay Liberation" in *The Queer Sixties*. Patricia Juliana Smith, Ed. NY: Routledge. 1999. 237–254.

Film

Stonewall (1995). Nigel Finch. 99 m.

A Question of Equality: "Outrage '69" (1995). Arthur Dong. 55 m.

After Stonewall: From the Riots to the Millennium (1999). John Scagliotti. 88 m.

Web Resource

http://www.columbia.edu/cu/libraries/events/sw25/about.html

Historical Explanations and Rationalizations for Transgenderism

Gordene Olga Mackenzie

Individuals who cross-dressed and/or attempted to live in the "opposite" gender role have always existed. However, the medicalization of these individuals only began in the 1800s, when early German and English sexologists began the classification of what they called the "sexual perversions."[1] In the U.S., by the mid-to-late 1800s, moral control over sexual behavior and gender roles shifted from the clergy to the new science of medical psychology. Medical theories of "disease" and "treatment" replaced religious threats of eternal damnation and/or exorcism previously applied to "deviant" sexuality.

Major theories about sex and gender at the turn of the century were derived from Freudian psychoanalysis as well as from attempts by early sexologists to categorize individuals on the basis of their sexual behavior. According to American interpretations, Freud's Oedipal complex, starting with the recognition of the anatomical differences between the sexes, set off the "castration complex" in males and "penis envy" in females, both of which supposedly culminated in a "normal" gender identification, masculinity for males and femininity for females and in heterosexual desire.

In order to understand the role of transsexual ideology in shaping and reflecting clinical and popular gender attitudes in American culture, it is necessary to explore the history of transgender and transsexual ideology and the gender attitudes these beliefs inspired. Here I will use historical sexological categorizations of transgenderists who felt themselves to be members of the "opposite" sex and/or desired to live in the role of the "opposite" gender as precursors of the modern category of transsexuals. These early sexological theories, primarily based on case histories, provide us with a glimpse into the unique historical relationship between transgenderists and their culture.

The term *transsexual* was reportedly first used in the medical literature in 1949 in America by the medical doctor D.O. Cauldwell. Cauldwell used the term "psychopathia transsexualis" to describe the case of a girl who wanted to change her sex. Prior to the 1910 publication of sexologist Magnus Hirschfeld's volume *Transvestism*, there were no separate medical categories or theories about cross-dressers or transgenderists. Rather, these individuals were routinely classified as "inverts," an early term for homosexuals, who at the time were considered with "sexual perverts."

Kenneth Plummer, a scholar who has written extensively about the social construction of homosexuality, demonstrates the historical damage labeling and categorizing have had on lesbians and gays. Plummer observes:

> . . . the categories exist; they are applied . . . to millions of people throughout the world, and indeed are also today applied to large numbers of people throughout history . . . Certainly there is considerable political intent behind the making of such categorizations—to order, control and segregate in the name of benevolence.

> Certainly too these categories have rendered—in the main—whole groups of people devalued, dishonorable or dangerous, and have frequently justified monstrous human atrocities and the denial of human rights. (53)

The same can be said of transgenderists and cross-dressers who have also been victimized and stigmatized by medical labels and categories.

Historically, transgenderists, cross-dressers and transsexuals were embedded within the category of homosexuality. Most early researchers argued that cross-dressing and cross-gender behavior were "symptoms of homosexuality." At the turn of the century, individuals engaging in same-sex relations were viewed with disgust and branded as "criminals against nature," because same-sex acts did not lead to procreation. Part of the categorical confusion is that no real distinction was made between sex and gender. Terms that seem to closely approximate the idea of gender, like "soul," "spirit" and "psyche," were commonly used by early sex researchers in an attempt to explain homosexuality. The lumping together of transgender behavior and homosexuality can be traced to early theories about homosexuality, many of which were really elaborate theories about gender.

In an attempt to explain same-sex attractions, a number of the early sexologists adopted Karl Ulrichs' theories on homosexuality, which confused gender and sexual preference. Ulrichs, a German lawyer and advocate of homosexual rights, in the mid 1800s refuted the dominant belief that same-sex acts were crimes against nature. Basing his theory largely on himself, Ulrichs proposed that male homosexuality was the result of a feminine soul in a male body and that female homosexuality arose from a masculine soul caught in a female body. Based on this hypothesis, Ulrichs argued "love directed towards a man must be a woman's love" and as such must not be considered a crime against nature (Kennedy 105–07).

Ulrichs' theory, based on a heterosexual model, raised many questions, including whether a non-transgendered same-sex partner was considered a homosexual. For Ulrichs, individuals who cross-dressed or expressed the gender role of the "opposite" sex were viewed as expressing their true "spirit," which was defined as a manifestation of homosexuality. Even though his theory was psychologically based, Ulrichs, a product of his time, believed in congenital theories of homosexuality which stressed genetic and/or inherited origins. Here Ulrichs' ideas resemble current popular theories about the origin of homosexuality which stress differences in brain structure.[2]

Ulrichs' "third sex theory," while attempting to liberate homosexuals from legal persecution and social ostracism, ultimately helped blur the lines between homosexuals and cross-gender-identified individuals. In retrospect, Ulrichs' definition of homosexuals as individuals whose biological sex contradicts their gender, (spirit, soul, psyche) is far more descriptive of the plight of transsexuals than homosexuals. "Elizabeth," a 42-year-old, non-surgical male-to-woman transsexual I spoke with in 1986, recalls Ulrichs' theories with her statement:

> I have always had the soul or spirit of a woman. I have felt that I've had to masquerade as a man. When I am with a man sexually, my relationship to him is that of a woman. I was simply born into the wrong body. Nature made a terrible error and it is up to me to correct it. (pers. comm. 1986)

As categories, homosexuality and transsexualism share many historical antecedents. Homosexuality was defined and treated as a medical problem by the psycho-medical model until 1973, when it was deleted from the American Psychiatric Association's *Diagnostic and Statistical Manual of Mental Disorders (DSM III)*. As of this writing, even though it is being challenged, transsexualism is still considered a psycho-medical problem that might be "cured" through surgery (*DSM III Third and Revised [DSM III-R]*). As a result of being medicalized, transsexuals, like homosexuals, have internalized medical labels, causing them to view themselves as sick and deviant. Because of the process of self-stigmatization, theorists like Plummer stress the necessity of viewing transsexualism as a political category, reflective of a repressive society, rather than as a "medical condition" requiring treatment. With the advent of Gay and Lesbian Liberation, many individuals with same-sex sexual and/or political preferences substituted their own terms, "gay" and "lesbian," thereby rejecting the medical label and the associated social stigma of the term "homosexual." As I mentioned earlier, inspired by the use of self-generated labeling as a fight against oppression, some transsexuals and members of the gender community are rejecting the use of the medical term "transsexual," using instead self-generated terms like transgendered, "transgenderist" and "cross-dresser."[3] But there is still a long way to go. The categories of transsexual and homosexual, as well as individual transsexuals, transgenderists and homosexuals have been and to a large degree still are confused by both the general and medical population. It is impossible to think clearly about transsexualism and transgenderism unless we make the distinction that the term *homosexuality* refers to sexual preference as compared to *transsexualism*, and *transgenderism* which refer to gender preference; therefore a transsexual may be lesbian, gay, heterosexual, bisexual or asexual and a lesbian or gay may be masculine, feminine or any combination of the two.

In his 1981 investigation of the category of homosexuality, Plummer raises four questions that can be applied to the categorization of transsexuality. First, he asks what is the nature of the categorization? Second, when and how did the categorization emerge? Third, how is the category conferred on certain people and behaviors? And finally, what is the impact on the people categorized? As Foucault observed, the history of sexuality becomes a history of historical discourses on sexuality. Further, Foucault maintained that discourses on sexuality, in which discourses on gender are included, are an ever-changing and expanding part of a complex growth of social control over individuals exercised through the apparatus of sexuality. Of course, Foucault overlooks the obvious—his own white, male and elite class privilege. As Emma Perez notes in her article, "Sexuality and Discourse: Notes from a Chicano Survivor," "He [Foucault] does not say . . . European white men hold political, social, racial and sexual power over women: and . . . use that power throughout history to control women and to sustain patriarchal power" (166).

Historic and Mythic Accounts of Transgenderists

Throughout history numerous reports of transgender persons attempting to live in the gender role of the "opposite" sex emerge. Among them are members of European royalty, colonial governors in America, Native American healers, and others. Some of the earliest written accounts of transgenderists come from ancient Greece and Rome. Roman Emperor Nero was said to have murdered his pregnant wife by kicking her in the stomach. Arguing that his male ex-slave Sporum bore a remarkable resemblance to his dead wife, Nero ordered that he be changed into a woman.

After an operation probably consisting of penile castration, Nero and Sporum were married. Sporum reportedly was "delighted to be called the mistress, the wife, the Queen of Hiercolces" (Bulliet 79–80). He is alleged "to have offered half of the Roman Empire to the physician who could equip him with female genitalia" (Green and Money 15).

Transsexual desire is also found in ancient Greek and Roman myths. If we examine myth as a collective reflection of our cultural wishes, desires and fears, we can speculate why Sporum offered half of the Roman Empire to the physician who could create female genitals for him. In most ancient Greek and Roman sex-change myths, males are transformed into women as punishment. However, such punishment rarely works because the newly transformed male-to-woman reports much greater sexual pleasure in her new role.

One example is the ancient Greek myth of Tiresias, a Theban soothsayer. According to the myth, Tiresias came upon two snakes mating. He killed the female snake and as punishment was transformed into a woman. When Tiresias remarked that "a woman's pleasure during sexual intercourse was ten to man's one, he was changed back into a man" (Green and Money 13). Such sex-change myths and reports of subsequent superior sexual pleasure also contain a subtext of violence toward that which is female or associated with females. Nero's murder of his wife preceded Sporum's sex change, as did the murder of the female snake precede Tiresias' transformation. An ancient Roman myth follows a similar pattern. In the myth males who pillaged and destroyed Venus' temple were subsequently changed into women. The inscription of power to female genitalia can also be found in historical and contemporary sexological and clinical theories that maintain that female sexual pleasure is much greater than a male's and that female genitals, because of their reproductive potential, represent a power that males envy and also fear.[4]

Perhaps some contemporary analogues to these mythic and historical accounts of female devaluation, followed by male-to-women sex changes, do occur. In America, when the contemporary Women's Movement began naming injustices against women, sex-change surgeons were performing the first widely publicized sex-reassignment surgeries on male-to-women transsexuals at Johns Hopkins University Hospital. In the early 1990s, during the Bush administration when women's rights were being eroded by Supreme Court decisions on abortion, Christian fundamentalists and neo-conservatives pushed for a return to "traditional" roles and "family values," which threatened women's rights. At the same time male-to-woman sex-reassignment surgeries were on the increase.

Not all historical personages who lived in the role of the "opposite" gender desired to have the genitals of the "opposite" sex. In 16th-century France, King Henry III was reportedly content just living in the gender role of a woman. Henry dressed as a woman and requested that he be referred to as "Sa Majeste," which means "Her Majesty" (Green and Money 16).

Perhaps the most famous transgenderist in history was the Chevalier d'Eon, a member of Louis the XV's court in 18th-century France. The Chevalier lived his first 49 years of life as a man and her last 34 years as a woman. The Chevalier undertook several secret missions to Russia as a woman and went undetected. Many believed the Chevalier's true sex to be female. However, an autopsy at death revealed her to be a biologically "normal" male, much to the distress of members of the court that wagered the Chevalier was a female.

Inspired by biographies of the Chevalier, sexologist and sex reformer Havelock Ellis coined the term *Eonist* to describe cross-dressers and transgenderists. However, not all *Eonists* enjoyed the privileged status that the Chevalier d'Eon did. Prior to the domination of the medical view on Western thought, socioeconomically privileged transgenderists and cross-dressers were tolerated as objects of curiosity. Religious and legal condemnation was generally reserved for less economically privileged transgenderists.

Turn of the Century Transgenderists

America at the turn of the century was not a good place to be if you were poor and transgendered. Violence was an all-too-common event in the lives of male-to-women transgenderists unprotected by wealth and status. Female-to-men transgenderists were also victimized. Historian Jonathan Katz observes that at the turn of the century there seemed to be an "irrational horror" that motivated a violent reaction to cross-dressers and transgenderists. Male-to-women transgenderists of the time commonly referred to themselves and each other as "men-women." Female-to-men transgenderists called themselves "women-men" (see Katz). An early 1900s newspaper account reflects the violence confronting transgendered persons. It tells of a man-woman who was found bludgeoned to death, her body salted down, then bent and stuffed in a trunk by her father, a meat packer. A transgenderist who knew the victim remarked:

> In such strange ways a continuous string of both men-women and women-men are being struck down in New York for no other reason than loathing for those born bisexual. And public opinion forbids the publication of the facts of bisexuality, which, if generally known, would put an end to . . . these murders of innocents. (Katz 557)

This account bears a chilling resemblance to the hate crimes occurring almost 100 years later as we near another turn of the century. The term *bisexual* here refers to cross-gender.

From the 16th through the 19th centuries in America, scattered reports of transgenderists can be found in newspapers, legal records, medical journals and in the writings of the early sexologists. Accounts of Native American "berdaches," males who cross-lived as women, routinely appeared in the medical and sexological writings about cross-dressers at the turn of the century. Most accounts were usually derived second-hand from the diaries of Christian missionaries, travelers, and early explorers. Typically they were moralistic and racist diatribes against Native American transgenderists who were branded as "sinful sodomites" and "corrupt men with long hair" who wore women's clothing and performed women's work (see Katz; Williams, *The Spirit and the Flesh*; Roscoe).

Although thought of as deviants by European and American missionaries out to convert and/or destroy them, many Native American transgender persons were revered as sacred in their own societies and were thought to possess exceptional abilities. Author Will Roscoe maintains that because of forced assimilation into the dominant American culture, visible signs of males in women's clothing among Native Americans largely disappeared after World War II. However, he observes that the acceptance of transgender behavior remained. Today, some Native Americans who have been assimilated into the dominant culture define as transsexuals and seek transsexual surgery.

Fewer accounts of female-to-men "amazons," a term anthropologist Walter Williams coined for the female equivalent to "berdache," have been recorded. Paula Gunn Allen, a Native American writer, suggests that fewer accounts of cross-gender women exist because women have always been considered less important than men.

Concerns raised in early America about whether transgenderists were gay or lesbian are still with us and reflect the homophobia transgenderists are confronted with in addition to transgenderphobia. Sodomy was considered a serious crime, punishable by death. Accused sodomites were hanged, suffocated and drowned—torments and executions reminiscent of the witch trials (Katz 861).

While transgenderists and cross-dressers were being routinely tortured and sacrificed, sexologists at the turn of the century began the search for the etiology of cross-gender behavior. Rooted in biological explanations, early sexological theories cracked the door to public tolerance by replacing the image of transgenderists as "criminals" with the image of the transgenderist as "sick" and in need of treatment. Unfortunately some of the treatments were as fatal as the criminal penalties for sodomy.

Most turn-of-the-century sexologists believed that gender was related to the sex organs. Therefore, injuries to the genitals were thought to cause transgender behavior. Sexologist Krafft-Ebing theorized that excessive horseback riding probably caused injury to Native American men's testicles, resulting in transgenderism and impotence since gender and sexual preference were thought to be related to the health of the genitals. Gay men and male-to-women transgenderists were thought of as "failed men," with diseased, injured and/or inadequate genitals. In addition theorists like Krafft-Ebing argued that "failed men" were more like females than males. Of course conversely, "failed" or genitally deficient females were not viewed as being like males. Rather, it was the highly accomplished and independent woman who was thought to be more manlike. Such attitudes suggest how deeply the superiority of males is rooted in Western sex and gender roles.

In 1881, the *Chicago Medical Review* reported that the first Colonial governor of New York, Edward Hyde, also known as Lord Cornbury, frequently appeared in public wearing women's clothing. Opinions among sexologists about Cornbury's behavior varied. Most conservative sexologists, like Krafft-Ebing, who thought the only reason males wore dresses was to attract other males, labeled Cornbury a homosexual. The more progressive sexologists seemed less concerned about sexual preferences and described Cornbury as a person who desired to live in the "opposite" gender role. Krafft-Ebing condemned Cornbury as an amoral homosexual.

> who was apparently affected with moral insanity; was terribly licentious and in spite of his position could not keep from going about the streets in female attire, coquetting with all the prostitutes. (Krafft-Ebing 438)

The diagnosis of "moral insanity" highlights how moral judgments disguised as medical facts were commonly used to condemn cross-dressers and transgenderists.

Captain Robbins, an American commander from Maine who had both a brilliant war record and a desire to dress in fine dresses and gowns, elicited the attention of the major sexologists. Depending on the sexologist's own values, Robbins was categorized as either a homosexual or a cross-dresser. Due to their elite status Governor Cornbury and Captain Robbins were never prosecuted.

Progressive German sexologist, sex reformer, self-defined homosexual and cross-dresser Magnus Hirschfeld expressed shock at Americans' reactions to cross-dressers. On a visit to America in the early 1900s he observed:

> American newspapers report with unusual frequency the arrests of men who dress in women's clothing and women who dress in men's clothing . . . For example, one man who simply could not stop dressing as a woman was finally forced to wear a sign on his waist with the legend: "I am a man." (Katz 77)

Hirschfeld was used to fighting for the rights of cross-dressers and transgenderists. He even successfully petitioned the Berlin police to issue permits allowing transgenderists to cross-dress and/or cross-live (Katz 231). I am unaware of similar political action for transgender rights during this period in America.

In the U.S. cross-dressers and transgenderists were more likely to be stigmatized and tortured. Newspaper accounts reveal in New York, cross-dressers and transgenderists congregated at "Paresis Hall" to cross-dress and socialize. Is it just a coincidence that the name of the hall, Paresis, refers to a disease of the brain caused by syphilis? Perhaps the name of the hall is just a symbol of the social, medical and self stigmatization cross-dressers and transgenderists of the time were forced to endure? The "much hated" members of "Paresis Hall," thought to be "diseased," "insane" and "homosexual," were harassed and finally pushed out by the police (Katz 353).

Early Categories of Transsexuals

Contemporary transsexual researcher David King reminds us that even though transsexualism is a recent conceptualization, it is important to link it to its historical and cultural past in order to better understand the sociocultural and psychological consequences of early categorizations on transgenderists. Many early attempts to categorize transgenderists were inspired by the development of the case study, popularized by Freudian psychoanalysis. At the time most sexologists catalogued the so-called sexual aberrations in a formulaic style under major categories. These categories were substantiated by case studies and accompanied by personal documents, sexological analysis and diagnosis. Cases that today would be defined as "transsexual" were originally classified under the categories of homosexuality, sexual perversions, Eonism, androgyny, psychic hermaphroditism and transvestism. Each of these categories contained subcategories such as cross-dressing, effeminateness, congenital sex inversion, antipathic sexual instinct, uranism, transmutatio sexus, transformation of sex and metamorphosis sexualis. This preponderance of categories within categories reflected the confusion of early sexologists in attempting to understand cross-gender behavior (Krafft-Ebing 302–95).

At the turn of the century a search for the cause of transgenderism and cross-dressing was launched in order to justify medical "treatments," "cures" and "prevention." Conservative theories espoused by most psychoanalysts and sexologists like Krafft-Ebing held that transgenderism and cross-dressing were "symptoms" on the road to insanity and a sexual abnormality. Proponents of this theory felt transgenderism and cross-dressing were deviant and dangerous behaviors that could bring a state of anarchy to established "norms" of heterosexual, monogamous, reproducing behavior. Because of the alleged threat transgenderists and cross-dressers posed to gender bipolarism, they were frequently subjected to popular "treatments" like cold sitz baths and intellectual retraining. Legal penalties for being a transgenderist were much harsher and included instances of cross-dressers being expelled from universities, committed to insane asylums and even put to death (see Katz).

Early Theories of Causation

Sexologists who supported the illness model of transgenderism and cross-dressing thought it was a symptom of homosexuality. Like homosexuality, cross-dressing and transgenderism were believed to result from a congenital, hereditary, or acquired condition. Congenital causes of transgenderism were thought to emanate from endocrinologic, glandular, and/or other physiological abnormalities. Krafft-Ebing staunchly believed that physiological abnormalities led to transgenderism and went to great lengths to prove congenital causes of transgenderism. He performed autopsies on the dead and measured the hips, ears, faces, pelvises, and skulls of the living.

The case of Count Sandor, a female-to-man transgenderist writer married to a female was one case Krafft-Ebing used to validate his theory. He thought that Sandor's "somewhat" masculine appearance might be a clue to a genetic basis for his transgenderism. Like other proponents of congenital theories of transgenderism, Krafft-Ebing seemed obsessed with the sexual preferences of transgenderists and cross-dressers. If they were gay, lesbian or bisexual, they were far more likely to be diagnosed as "sick." Krafft-Ebing categorized Count Sandor as a "congenital sexual invert" and included the following justifications:

> She was 153 centimeters tall, of delicate build, thin but remarkably muscular on the breast and thighs. Her gait in female attire was awkward . . . The hips did not correspond in any way with those of a female, waist wanting . . . The skull slightly oxcephalic, and in all measurements below average . . . Circumference of the head 52 centimeters . . . Pelvis generally narrowed (dwarf pelvis), and of decidedly masculine type . . . labia minora having a cock's-comb-like form and projecting under the labia majora . . . On account of narrowness of pelvis, the direction of the thighs not convergent, as in a woman, but straight.

> The opinion given showed that in S. there was a congenitally abnormal inversion of the sexual instinct, which, indeed, expressed itself, anthropologically, in anomalies of development of the body, depending upon great hereditary taint; further, that the criminal acts of S. had their foundation in her abnormal and irresistible sexuality. (Krafft-Ebing 436–38)

Heredity was another suspected cause of transgenderism that was investigated at the turn of the century. Theories of heredity stressed that the "sexual perversion" of transgenderism and/or cross-dressing was inherited from "insane" parents or relatives. As a precaution against inflicting their "insanity" on their offspring, transgenderists were warned not to marry or have children. Case histories used to validate this theory of transgenderism included lengthy family histories marked by insanity. In support of the heredity theory of transgenderism sexologist Havelock Ellis presented the case of a male-to-woman transgenderist who desired to become a woman. Ellis traced the transgenderist's desire to her father and reported: ". . . it is possible that T.S.'s father had a latent impulse of this kind . . . near the end of his life . . . he endeavored to put on his wife's clothing" (Ellis 110).

It was widely believed that congenital and inherited cases of transgenderism and cross-dressing were incurable. Therefore "prevention" was stressed. Such prevention included advising transgenderists not to masturbate or succumb to homosexual desire. Above all heterosexuality was encouraged! (Krafft-Ebing 450).

If congenital and inherited causes of transgenderism were given a poor prognosis by pioneer sex researchers, acquired cases of transgenderism were given a much better chance of recovery. Acquired causes of transgenderism and cross-dressing included excessive masturbation and/or being seduced by an "invert" and/or transgenderist. Popular remedies for persons "afflicted" with acquired cases of transgenderism included the use of hypnotic suggestion and prescriptions for heterosexual marriage. For cases of "antipathic sexual inversion," a category which included "men in women's garb and women in men's attire" who "psychically consider themselves to belong to the opposite sex," Krafft-Ebing advised hypnosis. Sometimes he prescribed the use of hypnosis in conjunction with hydrotherapy. A male-to-woman transgenderist who Krafft-Ebing believed was suffering from an acquired case of transgenderism was given the following suggestions every two or three days:

1. I abhor onanism, because it makes me weak and miserable.
2. I no longer have inclination toward men; for love for men is against religion, nature and law.
3. I feel an inclination toward woman; for woman is lovely and desirable, and created for man. (Krafft-Ebing 457)

Sexologists generally believed if patients could be rendered "sexually neutral" then medicine would have provided a service to society and the individual. In the early 1900s, Krafft-Ebing's views on transgenderism mellowed a bit. He suggested that patients with "antipathic sexual inversion" were "no worse than drunks" and in most cases did "not need to be confined to an asylum." Contemporary theories about transgenderism and homosexuality which stress hormonal causation can be directly traced to theories of the early sex researchers.

Instead of searching for physiological causes of transgenderism, the early psychoanalysts proposed possible psychological origins for cross-dressing and transgenderism. Delusions brought on by disruptions in the Oedipal complex, such as identification with the "wrong" parent at crucial stages and/or problems with the mother, were thought to be major causes of transgenderism. Wilhelm Stekl, a psychoanalyst and colleague of Freud, argued that separate categories for transgenderists and cross-dressers were unnecessary, since all were really cases of "latent homosexuality." Gutheil, Stekl's assistant, believed that "incest fixation" was the driving motive behind cross-dressing and transgenderism. In the case of Elsa, a female-to-man cross-dresser, Gutheil and Stekl theorized that Elsa became a man in order to identify with her beloved father and brother (Ellis 23).

The only case Freud published relating to transgenderism was "The Schreber Case" in 1911. Freud diagnosed Schreber's "symptom" to be the delusion that he was changing sexes and becoming a woman, "god's wife." Freud argued that Schreber's change-of-sex "fantasy" was related to his repressed homosexuality, delusions and psychosis and was not a case of transgenderism. Lothstein credits Freud's diagnosis of Schreber with alerting contemporary transsexual researchers "to the differential diagnosis between homosexuality and transsexualism" (Lothstein, *Female-to-Male Transsexualism* 54).

Before the 1910 publication of sex reformer Magnus Hirschfeld's *Transvestism: An Investigation into the Erotic Impulse of Disguise*, transgenderism was a sub-category of homosexuality. Hirschfeld, considered the leading expert of his time, argued that transvestism was clearly distinguishable from homosexuality and other groups of sexual "aberrations." The German sexologist, who was an openly gay cross-dresser, suggested that there were five separate categories of cross-dressers or "transvestites." His categories were based on sexual behavior instead of gender and included heterosexual, bisexual, homosexual, narcissistic and asexual transvestites. Although still placing more emphasis on sex instead of gender, Hirschfeld's transvestite categories at least opened the door for new categories of cross-dressers and transgenderists to emerge. Because of Hirschfeld's work, the term *transvestite* became widely used by sex researchers who used it to describe transgenderists, cross-dressers and transsexuals. As a category, transsexualism remained embedded in the category of *transvestite* until the 1960s, when the term *transsexual* first appeared in the *Index Medicus*.

Havelock Ellis, dissatisfied with Hirschfeld's categories of transvestites and psychoanalytic theories of transgenderism, was the first sexologist to make the distinction between individuals who simply enjoy dressing as members of the "opposite" sex and individuals who desire to live as or become members of the "opposite" sex. Ellis argued that Hirschfeld's categories failed to cover the wide spectrum of cross-dressers. Further, Ellis objected to Hirschfeld's sub-title of his book, "The Erotic Impulse of Disguise." Rather, he argued that for some transgenderists, the act of cross-dressing was an "emancipative act" that freed them from their social "disguise." Ellis argued that for those who believed they were born into the "wrong body," the act of cross-dressing confirmed their true self. His new category of "aesthetic inversion," under his category of "Eonism," delineated two types of aesthetic inverts that parallel today's transvestites and cross-dressers and transsexuals and transgenderists. He described the two categories as:

> One, the most common kind, in which the inversion is mainly confined to the sphere of clothing, and the other, less common, but more complete, in which cross-dressing is regarded with comparative indifference but the subject so identifies himself with those of his physical and psychic traits which recall the opposite sex that he feels really to belong to that sex although he has no delusion regarding his anatomical conformation. (Ellis 36)

The "most common kind" refers to transvestites and cross-dressers, while the less common category of aesthetic inversion describes the plight of transsexuals and transgenderists. Years before the development of sex-reassignment surgery, Ellis described the case of a 35-year-old biological male who longed to be a woman. Ellis published her letter expressing a transsexual desire:

> . . . it is as if the soul of a woman had been born in a male body . . . my secret ambition—to dress and live as a lady when I grew up . . . I really desired to be a woman, and not merely dress as one . . . I would undergo an operation if the result would be to give me a beautiful or attractive female form with full womanhood. (76–86)

Although Ellis distinguished the category of transsexuals and transgenderists from other cross-dressers and fought psychoanalytic assertions that cross-dressers were delusional and homosexual, it took almost 40 years before "transsexuals" were recognized as a separate category.

In sum, the category of transsexualism emerged out of the categories of homosexuality, cross-dressing and transvestism. In the late 1800s, as sex became increasingly medicalized, two major beliefs about transgenderists and cross-dressers emerged. The conservative ideology influenced by the writings of Krafft-Ebing and the early psychoanalysts did not make distinctions between types of cross-dressers. Krafft-Ebing viewed transgenderism as a path to moral insanity. The psychoanalysts argued that transgenderists and cross-dressers were really latent homosexuals, plagued by delusions caused by a failure to resolve the Oedipal complex. Advocates of both views sought to medically "cure" cross-dressers and transgenderists.

In comparison, sex reformers like Ellis and Hirschfeld recognized different categories of cross-dressers and transgenderists. Ellis' category of "aesthetic inversion," which emphasized the difference between transvestites and transsexuals, anticipated the modern category of transsexualism. Most significantly, Hirschfeld and Ellis placed less emphasis on "cures" and more emphasis on fighting for legal reform and public tolerance for cross-dressers and transgenderists.

Sex-Change Surgery 1920–1950

New experiments and technology in sex-change surgery from the 1920s through the 1950s helped further differentiate transsexuals from other cross-dressers. The first recorded modern attempt to surgically transform a male into a woman took place in Denmark during the 1920s. Lili Elbe, a male Danish painter, underwent a series of obscure genital operations, including the implantation of female ovaries. Even though Lili Elbe died soon after the operation, the event recorded in a book by Neil Hoyer impacted the consciousness of countless individuals in America who felt trapped in the "wrong body."

Since Ellis' category of "aesthetic inversion" was never widely used, the medical category of transvestite included not only individuals who felt they were members of the "opposite" sex, but also those individuals who wanted to be surgically transformed. As reports of sex-change surgery spread, the cross-gender identified "transvestite" became medically identified with the desire for surgical transformation. The case of Lili Elbe's change of sex published in the 1930s anticipated not only a future surgical "cure," but also a medically dependent relationship for the cross-gender identified transvestite.

The first official scientific sex-change operation reportedly was performed in Germany by Abraham in 1931. This technology was unfortunately used on unconsenting adolescent boys by sadistic Nazi doctors during World War II. One male-to-woman surgical victim desperately and without success tried to get the sex-change operation reversed (see Raymond). Another casualty of the Nazis was Hirschfeld's entire transvestite research records, burned along with his clinic. Hirschfeld himself was severely beaten and left for dead by the Nazis. He escaped to France, only to die while trying to rebuild his sex clinic. Transgender activist Phyllis Randolph Frye maintains that the majority of people who were murdered during the beginning of the Nazi Holocaust while wearing pink triangles were the transgendered of all sexual orientations.

After World War II, castration surgery, thought to "cure" homosexuals and transgenderists, became popular in the Scandinavian countries, particularly in Holland, Denmark and Sweden. U.S. males victimized by social condemnation and threats of violence often traveled abroad seeking castration surgery. Scattered reports of the "*castration cure*" appeared in America after the turn of the century, particularly in St. Louis, Kansas and Chicago. Both Ellis and Hirschfeld warned against castration surgery, claiming it would not inhibit sexual or gender desires. One rationale for performing castration surgery was a belief that transgenderism and homosexuality were inherited conditions. Therefore it was argued that it would keep social "deviants" and "misfits" from procreating. Since gays and transgenderists were thought to be little more than criminals, it is no surprise that "castration surgery" was also routinely used in the Scandinavian countries and to a lesser extent in America as a punishment for sex offenders. Castration, and other genital surgery performed to alter behavior, reinforced the deeply ingrained idea that gender behavior and sexual preference emanated somehow from the sex organs.

McCarthyism, Alfred Kinsey and Transgenderism

American sexologist Alfred Kinsey, though not credited for it, made important contributions to theories of transsexualism and transgenderism. One year before D.O. Cauldwell allegedly coined the term *transsexual*, Kinsey had already used the term *transsexual* in one of his studies. In his 1948 study, *The Sexual Behavior in the Human Male*, Kinsey criticized the use of the term *transsexual* as a synonym for homosexual because it implied that homosexuals were "neither male nor female, but persons of a mixed sex." Few if any critics took notice of Kinsey's observation, which differentiated transgenderists from lesbians and gays. Instead, Kinsey's observation that 37 percent of all the males in his study engaged in a homosexual experience to orgasm set off a bomb in homophobic America, obscuring many of his other findings.

A major reason for the overt public reaction to Kinsey's finding was the social and political climate of the early 1950s. Most Americans in the U.S., fearful after World War II, tried to insulate themselves from the grim realities of the war by reviving outdated, "traditional" sex roles and creating "nuclear" families. The middle class fled to the suburbs and found salvation in consumerism. Meanwhile, a growing McCarthyism exploited this post-war fear and anxiety by creating the image of Communist "enemies" that had not only infiltrated the government but also the family. As the McCarthy hysteria grew, fueled by social and political anxieties, anyone perceived as different became targeted as a possible enemy.

In the early 1950s, the homosexual was targeted by McCarthyism as a "sexually perverted" bogeyman eager to betray the American government and harm the American family. A 1950 *New York Times* news story documents how homosexuals were targeted as the new enemy of America:

> . . . Gabrielson, Republican National Chairman, asserted today that sexual perverts who have infiltrated our Government in recent years were perhaps as dangerous as the actual Communists. (Katz 141)

Homophobic members of the witch-hunt used Kinsey's report that most individuals were not exclusively heterosexual or homosexual but somewhere in between, to create a moral panic. They argued that the homosexual, like the Communist, posed a direct threat to both national and personal security. Foes of the "homosexual menace" tried to portray themselves as good heterosexual Americans. Most didn't even know what constituted a "homosexual." Frantic, they resurrected stereotypes of homosexuals as cross-dressers and transgenderists. As a result, persons suspected of violating mainstream sex or gender roles were targeted. As the most visually blatant, the cross-dresser and transgenderist were used as symbols of homosexuality. As a result, "masculine" appearing and/or acting females, as well as "feminine" appearing and/or acting males, regardless of their sexual preference, became major targets of the hysterical witch-hunt. Many were forced out of their government jobs.

Hate speech originating from Congress and the State department used the stereotype that all lesbians and gays resembled or wanted to be the "opposite" sex. Congressman Miller perpetrated this myth by describing gay males as: ". . . proud queens . . . not ashamed of the trick nature played on them. It is found the cycle of these individuals . . . follows the menstrual period of women" (Katz 154–55). In the same vein, lesbians were also commonly stereotyped as being "masculine": ". . . The mannish women . . . display themselves, strut around in fairy joints . . . on the make for the same girls the he-wolves are chasing" (154). As a result of the witch-hunt, thousands of transgenderists were forced into economic, social and personal ruin. In 1955 the *New York Times* reported 8,008 individuals were separated as "security risks" during the first 16 months of the security program. The records show "5912 individuals . . . dismissed or deemed suspect for reasons unrelated to disloyalty or subversion" and historians assume that the majority were accused of homosexuality (Katz 160).

McCarthyism fueled the raging homophobia in America, collapsing categories of sex and gender in the popular imagination. Kinsey's 1953 study on *The Sexual Behavior in the Human Female*, distinguished like Ellis before him, two types of transvestites. The "partial transvestite," the prototype for today's cross-dresser, was described as a male who on occasion adopted women's clothing and/or a feminine gender role. The second type of transvestite, the "true transvestite," is the blueprint description of the modern transsexual and/or transgenderist. Kinsey described the "true transvestite" as a cross-gender-identified person who desired to live in the opposite gender role full-time. True transvestites, Kinsey argued, were

> persons . . . who try to identify with the opposite sex in their work as well as in their homes, at all times of the day and through all days of the year. (Kinsey, Pomeroy, Martin and Gebhard 679–80)

Like other progressives before him, Kinsey did not think cross-dressers or transgenderists were "sick." He disdained "moral classifications," concentrating instead on whether members of sexual categories were accorded social advantages or disadvantages. Kinsey also pointed out that transvestites existed in almost all societies.

From the 1940s through the early 1950s, Kinsey began to focus his attention on the so-called sexual underworld of transgenderists and cross-dressers. In 1953 Kinsey proposed a wide-scale study of the actual occurrence of transgenderists in the United States. No doubt such a study would have differentiated transvestites and transsexuals and influenced our attitudes and beliefs about gender. To date, no study of this magnitude has been undertaken.

Unfortunately, in 1954, due to pressures from political conservatives and right wing fundamentalist Christian groups, the Rockefeller Foundation, responsible for funding Kinsey's sex clinic for 12 years, withdrew all financial support. It is hard not to draw a parallel between the Nazis' destruction of Hirschfeld's sex clinic and the end of Kinsey's research caused by conservatives and right wing fundamentalist Christian groups. An associate of Kinsey's, C.A. Tripp, commenting on the withdrawal of the $50,000 a year from Kinsey's research by the Foundation, reveals how they not only gave in to right wing fundamentalist pressure groups but also bought them off. Tripp charges:

> At the same time, as if by some combination of apology and bribery the Foundation quieted one of the noisiest groups of critics . . . by making it one of the largest grants in its history—$525,000 to . . . Union Theological Seminary, to aid in the development of vital religious leadership. (Tripp 233)

Transsexuals, the U.S. and the 1950s

Transsexualism and transgenderism were introduced into American consciousness in the 1950s by two significant events. The first was Christine Jorgenson's return home to America after her "sex-change" surgery in Denmark. Not only was Jorgenson America's first publicly recognized transsexual, her story was also the most news-covered event of 1953. Secondly, Harry Benjamin, considered the American father of transsexualism, had his transsexual research generously funded by the Erikson Foundation. Newspapers and magazines were filled with photos and accounts of Jorgenson's story. The popular headline, "Ex

G.I. George Jorgenson returns home as blonde bombshell, Christine Jorgenson" was circulated around the world. Even though Jorgenson was referred to as a "transvestite with sex-change surgery," the new category of transsexualism was about to emerge.

The same year that Jorgenson became a media sensation, endocrinologist Harry Benjamin presented a paper on transsexualism at a major American medical conference. He used the term *transsexual* to describe individuals who felt "trapped in the wrong" body. Although the term caught the attention of some members of the medical establishment, ultimately it was the media's popularization of the word *transsexual* that not only encouraged the widespread medical use of the term but also forever implanted it in the American consciousness. Jorgenson and Benjamin paved the way for the emergence of transsexualism not only as a distinct category, but also as a distinct identity. The 1950s marked the beginning of America's public and medical recognition of individuals who felt they were members of the "opposite" sex as a distinct category separate from other categories of cross-dressers.

Contemporary Categories Confused with Transsexualism

In the 1950s through the 1960s transsexualism was presented to the American public as a medical condition requiring treatment. Jorgenson's condition was explained by her doctors as a "hormonal problem." However, there is little evidence to back this diagnosis; rather, evidence suggests her physicians used the hormonal argument as a means of encouraging her social acceptance. Defining transsexualism as an illness served to elicit some public sympathy and curiosity. But it also reinforced in post-McCarthy America the myth that any gay male putting on a dress or acting "feminine" was a homosexual who really wanted to be a woman, implying surgery could cure homosexuals.

One way the U.S. and other countries have controlled so-called gender deviants is to categorize them. Doing so creates hierarchies of behavior under which individuals are classified and labeled. Although this approach may be useful from a diagnostic standpoint, i.e., for insurance purposes, it does not help most individuals understand themselves any better. The process of defining behavior in most cases operates more to confine behavior by relegating it to narrow categories. For example, in *DSM III* and *DSM III-R* transsexuals are distinguished from the category of transvestites on the basis of their desire for sex-reassignment surgery.

What happens when a transvestite decides to have surgery? Does it imply that he or she must adopt all the "symptoms" of transsexualism in order to be considered a serious candidate for surgery? As Anne Bolin suggests, strictly defined and enforced categories of behavior inhibit individuals from expressing or revealing behavior that is not included in specific categories. In the area of cross-dressing, it is simplistic to assume that all behavior will fit neatly into one category without overlap.

In my own research, I have encountered life-long transvestites, drag-queens, cross-dressers and transgenderists who sometimes cross gender lines into transsexualism. This is not to imply that a transsexual is lurking in the heart of every drag-queen, cross-dresser and transgendered person, but that in some cases cross-gender feelings may expand or change beyond the bounds of one category. I suggest that we view gender as a mercurial construct at the mercy of sociopolitical ideologies. As such, gender is always in a state of negotiation between the individual and society. America's dominant gender attitudes toward cross-dressers and transgenderists are heavily influenced by religious, psychological, and popular culture gender ideologies. As products of enculturation, cross-dressers and transgenderists often regard their own behavior as "sick" and "deviant" and experience great conflict, guilt and self-hate. Instead of locking individuals into narrow categories, it may be more useful to delineate the degrees of cross-gender-identity individuals are experiencing, as well as the social, psychological and political impact of their behavior. Although the category of *transsexual* signifies an individual with a cross-gender identity who desires or has had some medical intervention, numerous other categories and groups of individuals are confused with transsexuals.

Some of the biological conditions confused with transsexualism include "hermaphroditism" and "intersexed individuals." True hermaphrodites are rare. Most cases of hermaphroditism consist of individuals who are born with combinations of male and female genitals and/or secondary sex characteristics. Usually one sex is more dominant. The ancient Greeks and other cultures considered the hermaphrodite to be a sacred symbol. However, real infant hermaphrodites in most ancient western societies were routinely eliminated. Navajos in the Southwestern U.S. were an exception in their reverence toward the "Nadle," their male-to-women transgenderists, who they maintained were really hermaphrodites.[5]

Intersexed individuals are usually born sexually ambiguous at birth due to hormonal, gonadal, chromosomal, and/or genital contradictions. Some intersexed persons develop secondary sex characteristics of the "opposite" sex during puberty. In the U.S. transsexual surgery was developed from surgical techniques used on intersexed persons, who in some cases were raised as the "wrong" gender and after puberty had surgery to coincide with the gender of rearing.

Besides biological conditions, sexual preference is also commonly confused with transsexualism, particularly homosexuality and bisexuality. *Homosexual* refers to individuals with a sexual and/or political preference for members of the same sex. Many individuals with same-sex preferences refer to themselves as *gays* and *lesbians*, instead of the medically derived term "homosexuals." Like transsexualism, today, homosexuality was once thought to be an illness. Unlike transsexualism, homosexuality was deleted from *DSM III* in 1973.

Bisexuals are individuals whose sexual preference includes males and females. Generally the desire for one sex is greater at particular times. Freud and others maintain that we are all basically bisexual.

In addition to biological conditions and sexual preferences confused with transsexualism, there is also a preponderance of media-created terms that have been used to describe cross-dressers and transgenderists. Some of the more common terms, though not all-inclusive, are *gender chameleons, gender blenders* and *gender fuckers*. These terms are usually applied to persons in popular culture whose appearances incorporate the "other" gender in some way. In *Gender Chameleons* Steven Simels illustrates how frequently heavy metal male rock icons appear in full "feminine" make-up and hair-dos. However, as a defense against being labeled "feminine" males they usually accent their "drag" attire with a "kick-ass" attitude. This image combines a "feminine" exterior with a "masculine" interior for maximum commercial appeal. The popular Seattle band, Nirvana, appear in house dresses (grunge drag) and proceed to trash the set in their 1993 award-winning music video "In Bloom." During the 1993 MTV music video awards ceremony, lead singer Kurt Cobain, when accepting an award for the music video, unzipped his pants and grabbed his penis, an affirmation of his "masculinity." Female rock and pop stars also incorporate degrees of gender-crossing into their public performances. Among the most notable at present is Madonna, known for combining elements of masculinity and femininity into her performances in order to push the audience's emotional buttons. Most recently she appeared in drag in a racist and sexist opening act "The Girlie Show" for MTV's 1993 video awards ceremony.

Gender terms, ranging from *flaming faggot, radical* fair (sic), *butch, femme* and *diesel dike*, evolved in the gay and lesbian communities to the more general term *androgyny*, all describe individuals expressing and experimenting with various psychological and physical representations of gender. *Androgynous* refers to the psychological blending of culturally conditioned "masculine" and "feminine" traits. In the early stages of the contemporary Women's Movement, it was used as a concept implying movement toward equality, but was later discarded by feminists who complained it merely reinforced the bipolar gender system (see Heilburn).

However, since the late 1970s the media has picked up on the term "androgyny," using it to describe individuals who blend cultural stereotypes of masculinity and femininity in their appearance. Entertainers dubbed by the media as androgynous in the mid 1980s through the early 1990s included Michael Jackson, David Bowie, Annie Lennox, Boy George, Prince, Grace Jones, Stephen Tyler, Axle Rose, and Madonna. Two of the more recent additions to the pantheon of media dubbed androgyny is k.d. lang who plays with images of male and female drag, much to the delight of her audiences and "supermodel" pop star RuPaul. Carl Jung's ideas about psychological archetypes, recycled in the 1960s and early 1970s, asserted that within every female is a man, referred to as the *animus* and within every male is a woman referred to as the *anima*. Jungian analysts suggest that these largely unconscious psychological constructs must be incorporated into the conscious mind in order for the individual to become a "whole," or well-integrated person.

Like the idealized androgyne, the Native American transgenderist is said to incorporate both "masculine" and "feminine" traits (see Williams, *The Spirit and the Flesh;* Roscoe). Anthropologists commonly use the term *berdache* to describe Native American males who choose to incorporate feminine traits and/or live in the role of a woman. Some current and past Native American cultures not only accept but revere transgendered male-women as sacred. Williams proposed the term "amazon" be applied to describe the less visible Native American females who reject traditional "feminine" roles and choose to live in the "opposite" gender.[6]

Transgenderists exist in most societies from the Siberian shamans to the Arab Xaniths, to the Hawaiian "mahus" and the Native American "berdaches" and "amazons." Unlike contemporary American drag-queens, cross-dressers, transgenderists and transsexuals who are frequently objects of scorn and attack, transgender persons in other cultures were and are often thought to possess magical powers. Some occupy the role of healers or shamans. Sometimes the gender role is a transitory one, as in the Omani who live on the Arabian peninsula. Transgender Omani males often dress and act as women when young. Sometimes they engage in prostitution with males in order to save money to marry females. In later life, some return to a transgender role. Some societies, such as the Hawaiians, allow only one or two males to occupy the "sacred" transgender position of the *mahu* (see Archer; Kellis).

Drag-Queens

In contemporary America, the two categories most related to and confused with transsexuals are drag-queens and transvestites. The drag-queen is probably the most recognized cross-dresser in America. Drag-queens became particularly visible in America during World War II when enlisted men in dresses, make-up, heels and wigs were paid to entertain the troops. Drag, the dressing up to varying degrees and/or incorporating the gestures of the "opposite" sex, has been traced back to ancient Greece and played an important role in rites of passage. Mircea Eliade documents that, on the wedding night, brides and grooms in ancient Greece switched clothing before consummating their marriage.

In America, the stereotypical drag-queen is a male acting or performing in varying degrees as a woman. Such drag often includes "big hair," a huge bosom, tons of make-up, flashy clothing, high heels, exaggerated gestures, voice alteration and extreme verbal agility and wit. Drag might also include cosmetic surgery, hormones, and/or electrolysis. Unlike the male-to-woman transsexual, the goal of most drag-queens is not to become a woman, but to impersonate a woman. Drag-kings, females who impersonate males, have just started to receive media attention. Some of the better known entertainers who incorporated drag into their performances included Judy Garland, Lily Tomlin and Judy Tenuta, known for her great Elvis impersonation. Popular drag in America ranges from amateur lip-sync impersonations in gay bars to professional female impersonators playing the straight clubs, to political camp.

Drag in the U.S. is usually associated with entertainment and/or comedy. Because it can potentially threaten traditional sex and gender roles, a crucial aspect of many male drag shows playing to mainstream audiences is to demonstrate their maleness, usually accomplished by pulling off a wig or exposing a male chest. Although viewed as threatening and thrilling to mainstream audiences, drag-queens and kings often exist peripherally within the gay and lesbian subculture and are treated with ambivalence. Queens are frequently judged harshly by gay males who accuse them of resurrecting the stereotype that all gay males are effeminate and really desire to be women and by women who feel drag is insulting to women for reinforcing stereotypes. Similar charges have been hurled at drag-kings and butch lesbians by the lesbian community.[7] As stated earlier, gay males dressed as women trying to attract men occupy a precarious position.

Gay folklorist Joseph Goodwin describes the loneliness that plagues drag-queens in contemporary America: "Gay men don't want us because we look real, and straight men don't want us because we aren't real" (Goodwin 59). "Cheri," a 28-year-old, local, well-known drag-queen who works at *glam drag*, a term meaning outdoing females at the glamour game and being concerned with the creation of the external appearance over the content of the act, lamented that most gay males didn't understand her. She observed that as a gay male dressed as a woman, trying to attract a gay male, she occupied a precarious position. Cheri shared her dilemma:

> I really have problems with the gay men I pick up while doing drag shows at the gay bars. I always tell them that when I'm in drag that I'm creating an illusion. What they see is not what they get. Externally they see the illusion of Cher or Marilyn, but they don't see the foam rubber breasts duct taped to my chest, or the eight pair of panty hose with padding, or the pounds of make-up, or the fake eyelashes. When I greet them at my door dressed as a male they are disappointed. I want to be with a male as a man, not as a woman. (pers. comm. 1989)

In *Female Impersonators in America* Esther Newton argues that, because of the double social stigma of being gay and a drag-queen, most queens are relegated to a state of economic powerlessness. For many, the only "power" they feel is when performing.

A more aggressive and political form of drag is "camp." In camp, instead of relying solely on how one looks, humor is used as a weapon against sex and gender oppression. The Stonewall Riots of 1969, which ushered in the Gay and Lesbian Liberation Movement, were led by angry and campy drag-queens and lesbian butches, sick and tired of continual police harassment against themselves and their gay and lesbian bars. In *Persistent Desire* Joan Nestle points out that in New York and other cities it was not uncommon for cross-dressers to be arrested, brutalized, and sometimes raped for not wearing two or three pieces of clothing that were considered "appropriate" to their biological sex.

Joseph Goodwin calls *camp* an aggressive form of drag that "provides a way for the colonized to defy enforced sex and gender roles." Most significantly, on a political level, camp suggests that if males can pass as women and females as men, then gender may be an artificial category. Amber, a British drag-queen who does camp, underscores this point in her assertion that:

> People should realize that the female image, like the male image is something that has been created. It's not a natural thing. When you're born you don't pop out wearing make-up and a dress do you, or a man's suit? (Kirk and Heath 134)

Other terms related to drag are she-males and female impersonators. She-males are biological males who usually undergo differing degrees of electrolysis, breast implants, and/or other cosmetic surgery in order to appear more "feminine." Most stop short of sex-reassignment surgery, preferring to retain their penises. In street slang they are referred to as "hormone queens" because they take female hormones. Their existence is often more tenuous than glam and camp queens in the gay and lesbian community. Part of this tenuousness is because a number of she-males work as professional prostitutes. There are also class distinctions among female impersonators.

As anthropologist Esther Newton notes, most amateur queens are looked down on by the "pros," because of their excessive, loud appearances and life styles. Some of the professional impersonators in Newton's 1979 study called amateur queens "street fairies." Another difference between professional and amateur female impersonators is that the "pros" usually only dress while performing.

Transvestites

The cross-dressing and sometimes cross-gender-identified group most frequently confused with the category of transsexuals and perhaps their closest kin are transvestites. Since transvestism is a medically derived term, many members of the gender community prefer the term *cross-dresser* which is less stigmatizing. The *DSM III-R* diagnostic criteria for *transvestic fetishism* include:

> Over a period of at least six months, in a heterosexual male, recurrent intense sexual urges and sexually arousing fantasies involving cross-dressing.

> The person has acted on these urges, or is markedly distressed by them. (*DSM III-R 164*)

While this definition stereotypes transvestites as sick, fetishistic, heterosexual and male, a different interpretation of cross-dressing behavior is offered by transvestites themselves. Most male transvestites maintain that they cross-dress in order to relax and gain relief from the demanding male role and/or to express their feminine self. A large number also state that they cross-dress initially for erotic purposes. A major concern among most clinical researchers of transvestism focuses on their heterosexuality. This consensus among clinicians and some Tri-Ess (a national transvestite, cross-dresser organization) members is contrary to my findings. My research, gathered from over 100 local male transvestites and cross-dressers ranging in age from 25 to 58, indicated sexual preferences ranging across heterosexual, bisexual, asexual and gay and lesbian lines. However, most transvestites in the early stages of coming-out assert that they are strictly heterosexuals. Yet, some later report having fantasies of being with a male when dressed as a woman.

The idea that most transvestites are heterosexual has long been promoted by the "grand dame of transvestitism," Virginia Prince. Prince, a biochemist and self-defined heterosexual transvestite, launched a public relations campaign in the early 1960s in order to educate professionals and the general public about transvestism. One of Prince's motives was to make the transvestite more socially acceptable in the aftermath of McCarthy's homosexual propaganda campaign of the 1950s. In the 1970s, Prince described and defined the heterosexual transvestite as a "femmiphile," a "lover of the feminine." Prince differentiated reasons for cross-dressing among drag-queens and transvestites. She stressed that drag-queens dress to attract other males, while femmiphiles dress to express their inner feminine selves. Some cross-dressers accuse Prince of ignoring the erotic components of cross-dressing in her writings. Instead, Prince maintains, she focuses on clothing as a manifestation of an inner state and she suggests:

> As long as we wear the uniform of one gender—clothing etc . . . we can only experience that half of the possible world that is appropriate to that gender. But when we change clothes . . . we can experience a whole new, previously unknown way of seeing and experiencing our world. ("Sexual vs. Genderal Identity" 89)

As the matriarch of cross-dressers and transgenderists, in the 1960s, Prince founded an organization for the expression of the "feminine" self, now known as Tri-Ess. Today, as a large national organization, Tri-Ess provides a safe environment where heterosexual cross-dressers can dress and socialize with other cross-dressers and their partners. In addition to Tri-Ess, numerous other groups for transgenderists, cross-dressers and transsexuals exist locally, nationally and internationally. *Tapestry*, a magazine written for and by cross-dressers and transgenderists, lists over 200 national cross-dresser and transgender groups. Organizations for cross-dressers also exist world-wide in countries including New Zealand, England, France, Canada, Australia, Japan and Egypt. Many of the U.S. groups sponsor nationwide social and educational activities for cross-dressers and friends of the gender community. One such activity, and the most attended annual "Texas 'T' Party" includes presentations of new research from the psycho-medical and academic communities, seminars for partners of cross-dressers, tips on how to pass, a safe environment to dress and be real in, political forums, and lots of entertainment. Jessa B., a local transgenderist who attended the 1991 "T" Party, reported the most important aspect of the event for her was the complete "atmosphere of acceptance where we were free to be ourselves" (pers. comm. 1991). Numerous events in the U.S., sponsored by the gender community, for and about cross-dressing, transgenderism and transsexualism from the "Fantasia Fair" to the International Gender Education Foundation's annual conference to The First International Conference on Transgender Law, all provide information, acceptance, and forums for new ideas for participants. As the featured speaker of the 1993 Texas "T" Party I was thrilled to see the level of political activism among many of the participants as well as the level of healthy individuals, many of whom were freed from "the closet" for a few days.

Unfortunately, many researchers investigating cross-dressing and transvestism ignore these growing social networks and continue to concentrate instead on the etiology of transvestism, hoping to find a "cure." Most psychological and medical studies about transvestism, though sparse, blame the mother or argue that transvestites were forcibly dressed at an early age. Evidence supporting the "forced to dress" theory advanced by Robert Stoller is very weak, reflecting more, perhaps, an internalized fantasy based on cultural taboos. This fantasy can be found in mass-produced as well as self-authored cross-dressing literature.

Another issue frequently ignored or trivialized by gender researchers is the existence of the female transvestite or cross-dresser. Few case studies of the female-to-man transvestite are documented. Most researchers contend it is generally an exclusively male phenomenon. Reasons usually cited for this assumption include that it is socially acceptable and even fashionable for a female to wear men's clothing; women's clothing is taboo for males; and finally, that women's clothing is highly eroticized in contemporary American culture. Although these issues are important, we must be careful to avoid a male-bias, which regards female behavior as unimportant. This bias can occur if one accepts dated cultural sex stereotypes, such as the idea that females are not as sexual or are not as easily aroused by visual stimuli as males are. Yet one of the self-defined female transvestites I know, "Mackie," observed that she became highly aroused while wearing Calvin Klein jockey shorts. But we must not become bogged down in psycho-medical definitions of transvestites. Looking only for patterns of arousal may obscure other important sociocultural aspects of transvestism and cross-dressing.

My research, largely drawn from the Albuquerque gender community and from numerous national contacts, confirms that there is a wide variation of behavior found among transvestites and cross-dressers. It is impossible and highly erroneous to say all transvestites are alike. However, there are a few characteristics many share. For most, cross-dressing began at an early age (5–9) with a relative's clothing and it was done in secret. At puberty most transvestites developed a strong masturbatory and erotic response to being cross-dressed. This erotic connection between the clothing and orgasm has led the medical model to view transvestites as 'fetishistic.' One of the difficulties involved in studying transvestites' behavior is that until recently, most of it was done in secret for fear of stigmatization. It is estimated that only a small proportion of cross-dressers join support or social groups.

The diagnostic criterion used in defining transvestism as sexually arousing fails to note that there are many arousing stimuli for most female and male adolescents. A more interesting aspect of cross-dressing may be that the more individuals cross-dress, the more likely they are to develop their cross-gender identities and their desire to cross-live. This may in part be due to finding an accepting environment in which to express the "true" self. Often the growing cross-gender identity is signified by the adoption of a cross-gender name. Cross-dressing among transvestites varies in frequency and amount. Members of the Albuquerque cross-dressers support group report dressing anywhere from twice a year to daily. Some members wear only women's lingerie or men's jockey shorts under their clothing, while others work hard to pass as members of the "other" gender. Some male transvestites and cross-dressers maintain they will never give up their "masculine" selves and view their "femme" personalities as occasional escapes from the rigid male role. Yet over a period of years, as their femme persona develops, many transvestites and cross-dressers attempt to live full-time in the "opposite" gender role.

Psychologist Richard Docter labels transvestites who desire to live more and more in the cross-gender role "marginal transvestites," who, he theorizes, will eventually become "secondary transsexuals." Docter has also begun to use the term *transgenderist*, originally coined by Virginia Prince, to describe those who choose to live in the "opposite" gender role full-time without surgery. Docter uses *transgenderist* to describe cross-dressers who desire only rarely to live in the gender congruent with their biological sex. What is disturbing here is that a self-generated term among transvestites is being used as a medically stigmatizing term.

Large numbers of cross-dressers are coming out of the closet nationwide in cross-dresser groups. As of this writing, Albuquerque has two such groups. The Albuquerque cross-dresser and transgenderist support group is open to all cross-dressers, transsexuals and transgenderists, regardless of their sexual preferences and "Fiesta" a local chapter of Tri-Ess started in Albuquerque in 1988. Fiesta is primarily a social group for heterosexual transvestites and their partners.

Although there are no exact numbers of how many cross-dressers exist, when the Albuquerque cross-dressers support group ran a one-day ad in the local newspaper classifieds advertising the group, the community center where the meetings are held reported over 60 phone calls in one day. "Ricky," a former member of the group who has since moved to another state, related the following incident as a measure of how many cross-dressers and transgenderists there might be in contemporary American society:

> I was out playing golf with some of the guys I work with, when I stepped into a hole and broke my leg. In the ambulance on the way to the hospital all I could think about was being caught in 'female' underclothes . . . As the doctor cut through my trousers, exposing my black panties, he laughed and shook his head and said "you too?" (pers. comm. 1987)

Ricky interpreted the doctor's comment to mean that he was also a cross-dresser.

The most recent research on transvestism and cross-dressing to emerge from the psycho-medical model is Richard Docter's 1988 study on Tri-Ess members, in which he concludes that most transvestites and cross-dressers are heterosexual married men who experience gender envy because of social taboos prohibiting their dressing in women's clothing. Docter suggests that cross-dressing creates an altered state of consciousness that reinforces subsequent episodes of dressing, ultimately leading to a slow development of a female personality that in some cases completely "overthrows" the male personality, leading to secondary transsexualism.

In analyzing Docter's conclusions on a sociocultural level, we must question the way he uses the term *secondary transsexualism*. Within the context of his work, secondary transsexualism is presented like a dread disease that transvestites might catch if they develop their feminine gender identities too much. This suggests a hierarchical ranking in which being a transvestite is valued more than being a transsexual! Docter's insistence that most transvestites are heterosexual men is also suspect. Why is this aspect so important? Because of the fact that his population was drawn from Tri-Ess groups, which limit membership to heterosexual cross-dressers, his conclusion should come as no surprise.

I discussed Docter's findings with members of the local support group, which includes two individuals who participated in his study. Both expressed dismay with his findings. One member, Jerry, a 50-year-old male-to-woman cross-dresser from California, questioned Docter's assertion that cross-dressing produces an altered state of consciousness. Jerry stated that:

> I'm sick of the psycho-babble. Anything can produce an altered state of consciousness. It's a catch-all term. The bottom line of why I cross-dress is because it's fun. Period. (pers. comm. 1990)

This comment was followed by laughter, as other group members confirmed Jerry's comment and added "we dress to express who we really are, instead of who we are told to be" (pers. comm. 1990).

Transgenderism

Often we lose sight of the individual with clinical categorizations and rigid definitions. Historically, categories of sex and gender have operated on two levels. First, as Foucault and Plummer suggest, they have stigmatized, dehumanized, condemned and justified the barbaric torture of whole groups of people as "sick" and "deviant" simply because they did not conform to the status quo. Second, as gay activist Jefferey Escoffier asserts, the categories and definitions also helped mobilize and organize stigmatized groups to fight further stigmatizing, medicalizing, and stereotyping of their behavior. Ultimately, some of these stigmatized minorities have formed social movements, like Gay and Lesbian Liberation, to demand their civil rights. Most individuals identified with the different categories I have listed express the desire to have the freedom to explore their sex or gender roles. Being guided by everyone else's definitions of who they are does not allow this. As some members of the gender community observe, it is time to stop letting everyone from psychological and medical "experts" to television talk show hosts define us.

No doubt the most important categorization and labeling is self-generated. Empowering instead of disabling, Virginia Prince's term *transgenderist* accomplishes this. Members of the gender community first used it to define individuals who courageously cross socially defined gender borders full-time, although it is sometimes also applied to part-time gender-crossers. Members of the gender community also use the term *cross-dresser* as a non-stigmatizing and all inclusive term which unites members of the gender community. Such terms inspire the courage to be. Most recently Phyllis Randolph Frye, an inspiring transgendered activist, has suggested that transgendered be an umbrella term that includes transsexualism. However, there have been, should be and will continue to be struggles against allowing others to label and define transgenderists and their reality. Perhaps the category producing the most battle scars is the medical category of transsexualism. In the case of transsexuals who have been diagnosed and categorized, once surgically reassigned they cannot turn back. Much of the medical and legal pressure for sex-reassignment surgery is based on the persistent American belief that somehow gender emanates from the genitals.

Notes

1. Sexual perversion seems to include anything deviating from monogamous, heterosexual, reproducing couples.
2. For more information on LaVey's theories see "The Way We Wear Out Genes: Could a Cluster of Brain Cells Be the Cause of Homosexuality" by Robert Massa in *The Village Voice*, Dec. 24, 1991.
3. This is most evident in Phyllis Frye's definition of *transgendered* community which she noted includes transvestites, passing women, female and male impersonators pre-, non and post-operative transsexuals and "females-to-male." See transcript of speech given by Frye for March on Washington April 25, 1993. Recently Richard Docter has attempted to medicalize Prince's term "transgenderist" (see Docter 1988). Most recently, Prince has suggested the term "bigenderist" as a more accurate term to describe transgenderists and cross-dressers. Prince's new label has at this point not caught on in the gender community.
4. For an enlightened and different perspective see Jessa Bryan's "Hermaphrodite's Love" in which she rewrites Ovid's myth of Hermaphrodite so it becomes "A

coming together of male and female," a positive transformation. In *Chrysalis Quarterly* no. 6, 1993.

5. There is no supporting evidence that nadles were actual hermaphrodites.
6. For further discussion of Native American female-to-man transgenderist, see Evelyn Blackwood "Sexuality and Gender in Certain Native American Tribes: The Case of Cross-Gender Females" in *Signs* 10, #1, 1984 and Yudkin 1978, Williams 1986 and Roscoe 1991.
7. For more details on this see Joan Nestle 1992 and Keith Clark 1993.

Questions for Reflection, Discussion, and Writing

1. In what ways were turn of the century theories different from prior explanations of people we today call "transgenderists, cross-dressers, and transsexuals"?
2. In what ways does MacKenzie link transgenderism to issues of class in America at the turn of the century?
3. In what ways were the causes and cures of transgenderism different according to the theories posed by Krafft-Ebing, Magnus Hirschfeld, and Havelock Ellis? What were some policitical and social implications of those differences, according to MacKenzie?
4. What political and social forces tended to obscure Alfred Kinsey's claims in his 1948 study *The Sexual Behavior in the Human Male*? To what causes did Kinsey attribute cross-dressing and transgenderism?
5. Who was Christine Jorgenson, and what did her return from Denmark signify, according to MacKenzie? How was she "explained" to the American public by her doctors, and what strategies were used to elicit sympathy? As a result, what myths were also reinforced?
6. What distinctions among terms does MacKenzie outline? What criteria does she use to justify those categorizations?
7. What forces does MacKenzie suggest maintain gender binaries? In what ways do those binaries create and reinforce damaging messages for transgenderists in particular?

Related Reading

Earl Lind, *Autobiography of an Androgyne* (1922). NY: Arno Press. 1975.

———(as Ralph Werther), *The Female-Impersonators* (1922). NY: Arno Press. 1975.

Mario Martino, *Emergence: A Transsexual Autobiography*. NY: Crown. 1977.

Louis Sullivan, *From Female to Male: The Life of Jack Bee Garland*. Boston: Alyson. 1990.

Sandy Stone, "The Empire Strikes Back: A Posttranssexual Manifesto" in *Body Guards: The Cultural Politics of Gender Ambiguity*. NY: Routledge. 1991. 280–304.

Judith Shapiro, "Transexualism: Relfections on the Persistence of Gender and the Mutability of Sex" in *Body Guards: The Cultural Politics of Gender Ambiguity*. NY: Routledge. 1991. 280–304.

Anne Bolin, "Transcending and Transgendering: Male-to-Female Transsexuals, Dichotomy and Diversity" in *Third Sex, Third Gender: Beyond Sexual Dimorphism in Culture and History.* Gilbert Herdt, Ed. NY: Zone Books. 1994. 447–486.

Kate Bornstein, *Gender Outlaw: On Men, Women, and the Rest of Us.* NY: Vintage. 1995.

Bernice L. Hausman, *Changing Sex: Transsexualism, Technology, and the Idea of Gender.* Durham, NC: Duke UP. 1995.

Leslie Feinberg, *Transgender Warriors.* Boston: Beacon Press. 1996.

Dwight B. Billings and Thomas Urban, "The Socio-Medical Construction of Transsexualism: An Interpretation and Critique" in *Blending Genders: Social Aspects of Cross-Dressing and Sex-Changing.* London: Routledge. 1996. 99–115.

ki namaste, "Tragic Misreadings': Queer Theory's Erasure of Transgender Subjectivity" in *Queer Studies: A Lesbian, Gay, Bisexual, and Transgender Anthology.* Brett Beemyn and Mickey Eliason, Eds. NY: NYUP. 1996. 183–203.

Mildred L. Brown, *True Selves: Understanding Transsexualism,* San Francisco, CA: Jossey-Bass. 1996.

Phyllis Burke, *Gender Shock: Exploding the Myths of Male and Female.* NY: Anchor Books. 1996.

Riki Anne Wilchins, *Read My Lips: Sexual Subversion and the End of Gender.* Ithaca, NY: Firebrand Books. 1997.

Suzanne Kessler, "Creating Good-Looking Genitals in the Service of Gender" in *A Queer World.* Martin Duberman, Ed. 1997. 153–173.

Bruce Bagemihl, "Surrogate Phonology and Transsexual Faggotry: A Linguistic Approach for Uncoupling Sexual Orientation from Gender Identity" in *Queerly Phrased: Language, Gender, and Sexuality.* Anna Livia and Kira Hall, Eds. Oxford: Oxford UP. 1997. 380–401.

Dallas Denny, "Transgender: Some Historical, Cross-Cultural, and Contemporary Models and Methods of Coping and Treatment" in *Gender Blending.* Bonnie Bollough, Vern Bullough, and James Elias, Eds. Amherst, NY: Prometheus Books. 1997. 33–47.

Virginia Prince, "Seventy Years in the Trenches of the Gender Wars" in *Gender Blending.* Bonnie Bollough, Vern Bullough, and James Elias, Eds. Amherst, NY: Prometheus Books. 1997. 469–476.

Joanne Meyerowitz, "Sex Change and the Popular Press: Historical Notes on Transexuality in the United States, 1930–1955." *GLQ 4.2* (1998): 159–187.

Leslie Feinberg, *TransLiberation: Beyond Pink or Blue.* Boston: Beacon. 1998.

Patricia Elliot and Katrina Roen, "Transgenderism and the Question of Embodiment: Promising Queer Politics?" *GLQ 4.2* (1998): 231–261.

Deidre McCkosky, *Crossing: A Memoir.* Chicago: U of Chicago P. 1999.

Ian Fried, "It's A Long Journey, So Bring an Extra Set of Clothes" in *Out & About On Campus: Personal Accounts by Lesbian, Gay, Bisexual & Transgendered Students.* Kim Howard and Annie Stevens, Eds. Los Angeles, CA: Alyson Publications. 2000. 244–255.

Vivian K. Namaste, *Unvisible Lives: The Erasure of Transsexual and Transgendered People.* Chicago: U of Chicago P. 2000.

Alan Sinfield, "Transgender and Les/Bi/Gay Identities" in *Territories of Desire in Queer Culture: Refiguring Contemporary Boundaries*. David Alderson and Linda Anderson, Eds. Manchester, England: Manchester UP. 2000. 150–165.

Morgan Holmes, "Queer Cut Bodies" in *Queer Frontiers: Millennial Geographies, Genders, and Generations*. Joseph A. Boone, et al, Eds. Madison: U of Wisconsin P. 2000. 84–110.

Jill St. Jacques, "Embodying a Transsexual Alphabet" in *Queer Frontiers: Millennial Geographies, Genders, and Generations*. Joseph A. Boone, et al., Eds. Madison: U of Wisconsin P. 2000. 111–123.

Anne Fausto-Sterling, *Sexing the Body: Gender Politics and the Construction of Sexuality*. NY: Basic Books. 2000.

Aleshia Brevard, *The Woman I Was Not Born To Be: A Transsexual Journey*. Philadelphia: Temple UP. 2001.

Reg McKay, *None So Pretty: The Sexing of Rebecca Pine*. NY: Routledge. 2001.

Film

Metamorphosis: Man into Woman (1990). Lisa Leeman. 58 m.

The Blank Point: What is Transsexualism? (1991). Xiao-Yen Wang. 58 m.

Adventures in the Gender Trade (1993). Susan Marenco. 40m.

A Transsexual Journey (1995). Behzad Sedghi. 44 m.

Different For Girls (1996). Richard Spence. 101 m.

Web Resource

http://www.pridelinks.com/Groups_and_Identity/Transgender_and_Transexual

Special Topics

In 1952, after word leaked to the American press from Copenhagen, Christine Jorgensen (neé George William Jorgensen) became famous as the first person whose sex reassignment surgery made world headlines. Students may wish to research accounts from the time and compare them to contemporary understandings of transgenderism and transsexualism. What has changed in our attitudes, descriptions, characterizations, political consciousness, and understanding about this issue in fifty years? What hasn't changed? Where do we need to go from here?

Reading

Christine Jorgensen, *Christine Jorgensen: A Personal Autobiography*. NY: Bantam Books. 1968.

David Harley Serlin, "Christine Jorgensen and the Cold War Closet." *Radical History Review* 62 (Spring 1995): 136–165.

Linda Heidenreich, "A Historical Perspective of Christine Jorgensen and the Develop-
    ment of an Identity" in *Gender Blending*. Bonnie Bollough, Vern Bullough, and
    James Elias, Eds. Amherst, NY: Prometheus Books. 1997. 267–276.

Film

The Christine Jorgensen Story (1970). John Carpenter. 89 m.

Trade, Wolves, and the
Boundaries of Normal Manhood

Geoge Chauncey

The most striking difference between the dominant sexual culture of the early
twentieth century and that of our own era is the degree to which the earlier culture permitted men to engage in sexual relations with other men, often on a
regular basis, without requiring them to regard themselves—or to be regarded
by others—as gay. If sexual abnormality was defined in different terms in prewar culture, then so, too, necessarily, was sexual normality. The centrality of
the fairy to the popular representation of sexual abnormality allowed other men
to engage in casual sexual relations with other men, with boys, and, above all,
with the fairies themselves without imagining that they themselves were abnormal. Many men alternated between male and female sexual partners without believing that interest in one precluded interest in the other, or that their
occasional recourse to male sexual partners, in particular, indicated an abnormal, "homosexual," or even "bisexual" disposition, for they neither understood
nor organized their sexual practices along a hetero—homosexual axis.

    This sexual ideology, far more than the other erotic systems with which it
coexisted, predominated in working-class culture. It had particular efficacy in
organizing the sexual practices of men in the social milieu in which it might be
least expected: in the highly aggressive and quintessentially "masculine" subculture of young and usually unmarried sailors, common laborers, hoboes, and
other transient workers, who were a ubiquitous presence in early-twentieth-
century American cities. After demonstrating how widely it was assumed that
"normal" men could engage in sexual relations with other men and the role of
this sexual ideology in organizing the sexual world of "rough" working-class
men, this chapter explores the basis of that ideology in working-class gender
ideology and in the deeper logic of the association of fairies with prostitutes.
For the complex conventions governing the social interactions of fairies and

normal workingmen established the terms of their sexual relations as well, and reveal much about the organization of gender, sex, and sexuality in working-class culture.

The Sisters and Their Men: Trade and the Conceptualization of Male Sexual Relations in Working-Class Culture

The strongest evidence that the relationship between "men" and fairies was represented symbolically as a male–female relationship and that gender behavior rather than homosexual behavior per se was the primary determinant of a man's classification as a fairy was that it enabled other men to engage in sexual activity with the fairies—and even to express publicly a strong interest in such contacts—without risking stigmatization and the undermining of their status as "normal." So long as they maintained a masculine demeanor and played (or claimed to play) only the "masculine," or insertive, role in the sexual encounter—so long, that is, as they eschewed the style of the fairy and did not allow their bodies to be sexually penetrated—neither they, the fairies, nor the working-class public considered *them* to be queer. Thus a private investigator reported in 1927 that a Mr. Farley, owner of a newsstand in the basement of the Times Square Building at Forty-second Street and Broadway, complained to him that "whenever the fleet comes into town, every sailor who wants his d— licked comes to the Times Square Building. It seems to be common knowledge among the sailors that the Times Square Building is the place to go if they want to meet any fairies." He was unhappy about the commotion so many unruly sailors caused around his newsstand and disapproved of their actions. In no way, however, did he indicate that he thought the sailors looking for sex with the fairies were themselves fairies or otherwise different from most sailors. The investigator himself observed "two sailors . . . in the company of three men who were acting in an effeminate manner." He labeled the effeminate men "fairies" even though it was the sailors who were "making overtures to these men to go to their apartments [and the men] declined to go."[1]

Even men working for state policing agencies categorized men in these terms. New York State Liquor Authority agents investigating a sailors' bar in Brooklyn in October 1938 reported that shortly after midnight, "several males who were apparently 'fags' enter[ed] the premises in groups of twos and threes." They later observed "sailors leaving with some girls, and some men in uniform leaving with the fags." To make it clear that they thought the sailors were leaving with the fags for the same sexual reason that other sailors left with female prostitutes, they added: "In particular it was observed that two marines left with two of the fags and remained in the dark street under the railroad trestle." The investigators did not regard the marines who left with the "fags" as "fags" themselves, nor did they otherwise question the marines' status as men. Indeed, their final report recommended that the state close the bar precisely because it "permitt[ed] prostitutes to congregate with male customers . . . [and] permitt[ed] 'fags' to congregate on the premises and solicit males for immoral purposes."[2] They gave no indication that they found it shocking or unusual that the "fags" should have as much success picking up sailors as female prostitutes did. On the contrary, they regarded the sailors' response to the solicitations of "fags" as no different in kind from their responses to those of female prostitutes.

The acceptance of men's relations with fairies as proper manifestations of the male quest for pleasure and power was indicated even more strikingly by the structure of male prostitution in the late nineteenth and early twentieth centuries. By the 1910s and 1920s, it was increasingly common for both gay- and straight-identified men to sell sexual services to gay-identified men. But at the turn of the century the predominant form of male prostitution seems to have involved fairies selling sex to men who, despite the declaration of desire made by their willingness to pay for the encounters, identified themselves as normal. Indeed, while the term *fairy* generally denoted any flamboyantly effeminate homosexual man (whose self-presentation resembled that of a female prostitute), numerous references in the early twentieth century make it clear that the word was sometimes used specifically to denote men who actually worked as prostitutes selling sexual services to "normal" men.[3] Fairies still appeared in this role in several novels published in the 1930s about New York–based homosexual characters. One 1933 novel, for instance, referred to "the street corner 'fairy' of Times Square" as a "street-walker," invariably "rouged, lisping, [and] mincing." And in Kennilworth Bruce's *Goldie*, also published in 1933, a working-class youth from New Jersey explained "the ways and wiles of the twilight world in New York" to the protagonist, whom the youth had identified as a fairy: "He told him about the 'fairies' and the 'wolves' that frequent the streets of New York . . . around the Times Square section. . . . 'The fairies pull down big dough, too. . . . There's the actors and musicians when the shows break; there's the gamblers and guys with small-time rackets; and there's the highbrow sots when they leave the speakeasies in the wee hours. Fairies work up a regular trade."[4]

Numerous accounts of turn-of-the-century homosexual prostitution confirm that it commonly involved men paying fairies for sex, while still considering themselves to be the "men" in the encounter. This, after all, was the premise of the Lower East Side resorts, such as Paresis Hall and the Slide, where female prostitutes also gathered and where many of the fairies were not only called "male prostitutes" but (in the language of the day) "sat for company," having the men who joined their tables buy them drinks, just as female prostitutes did. Significantly, in prostitutes' slang a "slide" denoted an "establishment where male homosexuals dress[ed] as women and solicit[ed] men," a meaning apparently known to the officials involved in a state investigation of police corruption in 1894. A Captain Ryan testified he had "closed up every disorderly-house, every gambling-house and policy office, and every slide and dives [sic] in the precinct [within] three months [of taking command]." When asked if he were sure he knew what a slide was, he reminded his questioner that "we had one of the most notorious slides in the world in Bleecker Street when I had command of that precinct." His comment both confirms the fame of the Slide, which he had shut down in 1892, and suggests that the resort's management had deliberately used the slang term in naming the club in order to announce its character (even though, in fact, the fairies there did not dress as women).[5] Moreover, the very existence of the slang term suggests that other such resorts existed, as indeed they did.

There were also brothels where men could meet fairies more privately, as the Reverend Charles Parkhurst discovered in 1892 when he took his famous tour of New York's underworld (his own form of slumming) to gather evidence for his assault on Tammany Hall corruption. His guide took him to a brothel on West Third Street, the Golden Rule Pleasure Club, where the basement was divided into cubicles, each occupied by "a youth, whose face was painted, eyebrows blackened, and whose airs were those of a young girl, . . . [who] talked in a high falsetto voice, and called the others by women's names," each youth waiting for a man to hire his services.[6] It should be remembered that neither the fairies at the Slide nor those at the Pleasure Club were dressed as women; no customer seeking their services could have mistaken them for "normal" women.

This pattern was not restricted to such brothels and saloons. Fairy prostitutes, usually dressed as men but using their hair, makeup, and demeanor to signal their character, worked along the Bowery, Riverside Drive, Fourteenth Street, and Forty-second Street, and in Bryant Park and Prospect Park, as well as in the back rooms of saloons on Elizabeth Street and Third Avenue. . . . One fairy, for instance, a female impersonator from a poor neighborhood in Brooklyn where he was known as Loop-the-loop, a suggestive play on the name of a popular ride at Coney Island, reported to a doctor in 1906 that he regularly plied his trade "chiefly for the money there is in it." Loop-the-loop often worked in his neighborhood as well as in Prospect Park, where, he reported, he and the other prostitutes paid off the patrolmen so that they could wear dresses. His efforts at female impersonation would not have persuaded any of his clients that they were having sex with a woman, given the inartfulness of his costume and the heavy growth of hair on his legs and arms (he complained of the hair himself, but added that "most of the boys don't mind it").[7] But his costume and demeanor, like those of the fairies at Paresis Hall, *did* signify to "the boys" that he was not a normal man, either, but rather a third-sexer, with whom they could have sex without complicating their understanding of their own sexual character.

The relationship between a fairy prostitute and his male customers emblematized the central model governing the interpretation of male–male sexual relationships. The term *trade* originally referred to the customer of a fairy prostitute, a meaning analogous to and derived from its usage in the slang of female prostitutes; by the 1910s, it referred to any "straight" man who responded to a gay man's advances. As one fairy put it in 1919, a man was trade if he "would stand to have 'queer' persons fool around [with] him in any way, shape or manner."[8] *Trade* was also increasingly used in the middle third of the century to refer to straight-identified men who worked as prostitutes serving gay-identified men, reversing the dynamic of economic exchange and desire implied by the original meaning. Thus the term *trade* sometimes referred specifically to "straight" male prostitutes, but it also continued to be used to refer to "straight" men who had sex with queers or fairies for pleasure rather than money. The sailors eagerly seeking the sexual services of fairies at the Times Square Building, like those who left the Happy Hour Bar & Grill with the "fags," were considered trade, whether or not money was part of the transaction. So long as the men abided by the conventions of masculinity, they ran little risk of undermining their status as "normal" men.[9]

Although it is impossible to determine just how common such interactions were in the early twentieth century or precisely how many men were prepared to engage in homosexual behavior on these or any other terms, Alfred Kinsey's research suggests that the number may have been large. Published in 1948, *Sexual Behavior in the Human Male* was based on the sexual life histories Kinsey and his associates gathered from men in the 1930s and 1940s, and thus offers an overview of sexual patterns among men in the half-century preceding World War II. Although most recent commentary on the Kinsey Report has focused on (and criticized) its supposed estimate that 10 percent of the population were homosexuals, Kinsey himself never made such an estimate and argued explicitly that such estimates could not be based on his findings. His research is much more helpful if used, as Kinsey intended, to examine the extent of occasional homosexual behavior among men who may or may not have identified themselves as "homosexual." Only 4 percent of the men he interviewed reported having been exclusively homosexual in their behavior throughout their lives, but 37 percent acknowledged having engaged in at least one postadolescent homosexual encounter to the point of orgasm, and fully a quarter of them acknowledged having had "more than incidental homosexual experience or reactions" for at least three years between the ages sixteen and fifty-five.* Clearly some cultural mechanism was at work that allowed men to engage in sexual relations with other men without thinking of themselves as abnormal.

Kinsey's own remarks about the proper interpretation of his findings suggest the prevalence at the time of the interpretation of homosexual relations outlined here. They indicate that many of the men he interviewed believed

---

*Alfred Kinsey, Wardell Pomeroy, and Clyde Martin, *Sexual Behavior in the Human Male* (Philadelphia: W. B. Saunders, 1948), 650–51. Kinsey's statistical methods were subject to criticism almost from the moment of their publication, and this criticism has mounted in recent years in the wake of several new studies that have produced lower estimates of the incidence of homosexual behavior. It is not necessary to defend Kinsey's sampling methodology or to assert the infallibility of his estimates, however, to object on historical grounds to the effort by recent critics to prove Kinsey was "wrong" by contrasting his figures with the lower figures produced in recent studies. The fact that a

their sexual activity with other men did not mean they were homosexual so long as they restricted that behavior to the "masculine" role. (Indeed, his commentary is probably more useful to historical analysis than his statistical claims.) He presumably singled out for comment those notions that his interviews had revealed to be particularly widespread in the culture. His comments are not now generally noted, since the hetero–homosexual binarism has become hegemonic and the ideas against which he argued no longer have credibility. But it is significant that in the 1940s he still believed he needed to take special care to dispute interpretations of homosexual relations that regarded only one of the men involved in them as "genuinely homosexual" (and possibly not genuinely a man) and the other as not homosexual at all. It was absurd to believe, he argued, that "individuals engaging in homosexual activity are neither male nor female, but persons of mixed sex," or that "inversion [by which he meant a man playing the roles culturally ascribed to women] is an invariable accompaniment of homosexuality."[10] Equally untenable (and, apparently, common), he thought, were the claims of men who allowed themselves to be fellated but never performed fellation on other men that they were really "heterosexual," and the popular belief that "the active male in an anal relation is essentially heterosexual in his behavior, and [only] the passive male . . . homosexual."[11]

To argue that the fairy and his man emblematized the dominant conceptual schema by which homosexual relations were understood is not to argue, however, that it was the only schema or that all men were equally prepared to engage in sexual relations with other men on those terms. The image of the fairy was so powerful culturally that it influenced the self-understanding of all sexually active men, but men socialized into different class and ethnic systems of gender, family life, and sexual mores nonetheless tended to understand and organize their sexual practices in significantly different ways. Several sexual cultures coexisted in New York's divergent neighborhoods, and the social locus of the sexual culture just described needs to be specified more precisely. As the next chapter will show, middle-class Anglo-American men were less likely to accept the fairy-trade interpretive schema Kinsey reported, and even their limited acceptance of it declined during the first half of the century. It was, above all, a working-class way of making sense of sexual relations.

---

certain percentage of the population engaged in homosexual practices in the 1990s does not mean that the same percentage did so fifty years earlier, when Kinsey conducted his study. It is precisely the argument of this book that such practices are culturally organized and subject to change, and that the prewar sexual regime would have made it easier for men to engage in casual homosexual behavior in the 1930s than in the 1980s, when such behavior would ineluctably mark them as homosexual. Kinsey's methodology makes his precise statistical claims unreliable, but the fact that they are higher than those produced by recent studies does not by itself demonstrate they are wrong. Moreover, Kinsey's study had the merit of trying to measure the incidence of homosexual activity rather than presuming that there was a clearly defined population of "homosexuals" whose size he could measure. Even if Kinsey's study overestimated the incidence of homosexual activity twofold or threefold, his numbers are still astonishingly high.

Among working-class men there were also ethnic differences in the social organization and tolerance of homosexual relations. Unfortunately, the evidence is too fragmentary to support a carefully delineated or "definitive" characterization of the predominant sexual culture of any of the city's immigrant or ethnic groups, and, in any case, no single sexual culture existed in any such group since each of them was divided internally along lines of gender, class, and regional origin. Nonetheless, the limited evidence available suggests that African-Americans and Irish and Italian immigrants interacted with "fairies" more extensively than Jewish immigrants did, and that they were more likely to engage in homosexual activity organized in different terms as well. Certainly, many Anglo-American, Jewish, and African-American gay men thought that "straight" Italian and Irish men were more likely to respond to their sexual advances than straight Jewish men were, and police records tend to support the conclusions of gay folklore.[12]

The contrast between Italians and Jews, the two newest and largest groups of immigrants in New York at the turn of the century, is particularly striking. A 1921 study of men arrested for homosexual "disorderly conduct," for instance, reported that "the Italians lead" in the number of arrests; at a time when the numbers of Italians and Jews in New York were roughly equal, almost twice as many Italians were arrested on homosexual charges.[13] More significant is that turn-of-the-century investigators found a more institutionalized fairy subculture in Italian neighborhoods than in Jewish ones. The Italian neighborhood of the Lower East Side had numerous saloons where fairies gathered interspersed among the saloons where female prostitutes worked. In 1908, Vito Lorenzo's saloon, located at 207 Canal Street (near Baxter), was charged by the police with being a "fairy place."[14] In 1901, agents conducting a systematic survey of "vice conditions" on the Lower East Side found male prostitutes working in two Italian saloons on the block of Elizabeth Street between Hester and Grand, the same block where the Hotel Zaza's manager hired rooms to female prostitutes who stood at the windows in "loose dresses and call[ed] the men upstairs."[15] One investigator noted that the Union Hall saloon was crowded with old Italian men and several young fairies on the night of March 5; a few doors up the street, at 97 Elizabeth, stood a saloon where the fairies, aged fourteen to sixteen, could "do their business right in [the] back room." A month later the same saloon was said to have "5 boys known as [*finocchio*, or fairies] about 17 to 25 years of age."[16]

Strikingly, the same investigators found no such open "fairy resorts" in the Lower East Side's Jewish section, located just a few blocks to the east, even though they discovered numerous tenements and street corners where female prostitutes worked. The police periodically discovered men soliciting other men in a less organized fashion in the Jewish neighborhood's streets, tenements, and even synagogues, to be sure. Two policemen, for instance, arrested a twenty-two-year-old Jewish immigrant for soliciting men from the window of 186 Suffolk Street, at Houston, in 1900.[17] But they arrested far fewer Jews than Italians on such charges, and the sites of homosexual rendezvous were less stable and commercialized, less well known, and thus, presumably, less tolerated in the Jewish neighborhood than in the Italian.

It is difficult to assess the reasons for the apparent differences in the social organization of and larger community's tolerance of male homosexual relations in Italian versus Jewish immigrant enclaves, particularly given the absence of more extensive ethnographic studies of the overall sexual culture of either group. But three interrelated factors seem particularly crucial: the sexual cultures the Jews and Italians brought with them to the States from Europe, the different circumstances of their immigration, and the ways gender relations were organized in their communities.

The sexual cultures of immigrants in the United States were clearly shaped in large part by the gender and sexual cultures of their homelands, each of which was, in turn, significantly differentiated internally along regional and class lines. Northern Italians brought to the United States a set of cultural assumptions about sex different from those of Sicilians, for instance; middle-class Italians were likely to organize gender relations differently from peasants or workers.*

Although both Catholic and Jewish religious authorities condemned homosexual relations, Catholic teaching, especially, focused on the moral dangers posed by sexual contact between men and women to such a degree that it may implicitly have made sexual contact between men seem relatively harmless. One man who grew up in an Italian neighborhood recalled that "homosexuality just wasn't regarded as a mortal sin, it wasn't seen as that bad." Perhaps more significant is that immigrant Italians were well known for their rejection of church teaching on a wide range of moral matters, and the anti-gay religious injunction was much less effective among them than among Jewish men. Kinsey singled out Orthodox Jewish men for their "phenomenally low" rates of homosexual activity.[18]

By the late nineteenth century, southern Italian men had a reputation in northern Italy and in the northern European gay world for their supposed willingness to engage in homosexual relations. Although this reputation doubtless resulted in part from the propensity of dominant cultural groups to try to differentiate and stigmatize subordinate groups by attributing "immoral" or "bizarre" sexual practices to them, considerable evidence nonetheless suggests that such practices were both more common and more accepted in southern Italy than in the north. Numerous British and German gay men traveled to

---

*Unfortunately, no ethnographic studies have been made of the social organization of homosexual relations in southern Italy or the Jewish Pale of Settlement in Russia at the turn of the century, for example, that might shed light on the behavior of immigrants from those regions. As a result, my comments here must remain highly tentative and can only suggest directions for future research by historians of Europe as well as of American immigrants. Such research would not only help us understand the social organization and cultural meaning of same-sex relations in those cultures, but would also offer a revealing new vantage point for thinking more generally about gender relations in each group.

southern Italy at the turn of the century in search of a more tolerant climate; forty years later, during World War II, many gay American soldiers were startled to discover the frequency and overtness of homosexual solicitation there. On the basis of his own observations during a research trip to Europe in 1955 and the reports he received from several of his most trusted informants, Alfred Kinsey also concluded that southern Italian men were considerably more open to homosexual relations than northern Europeans were. Many Italian youths adopted an instrumental attitude toward their bodies before marriage and did not consider it shameful to use them to secure cash or advancement, observers reported, and even many married men were willing to engage in homosexual relations so long as they took the "manly part." Only the adult male who took the "woman's part" was stigmatized.

The patterns of homosexual behavior noted in Sicily appear to have persisted in modified form in the Italian enclaves on the Lower East Side, in Greenwich Village, and in East Harlem. Although more research would need to be done to substantiate the point, it seems likely that an important part of the homosexual culture of fairies and their sex partners visible in turn-of-the-century New York represented the flowering in this country of a transplanted Mediterranean sexual culture.[19]

The relative acceptance of homosexual relations in Italian immigrant communities was related as well to the demographics of Italian immigration to the United States, which were strikingly different from those of eastern European Jews. Given the escalation of anti-Semitic violence and the draconian restrictions placed on Jewish economic and social activities in eastern Europe in the late nineteenth century, most Jewish immigrants to New York had decided to leave their villages for good with as many of their family members as possible. But the great majority of the city's Italian immigrants were single men or married men unaccompanied by their families who planned to return to Italy after earning funds to invest there. Eighty percent of the Italians who entered the United States from 1880 to 1910 were males, and the great majority of them were in their prime working years, from fourteen to forty-four years old. So many of them came to work on a seasonal basis or for only a year or two that 43 Italians left the United States for every 100 who arrived in the mid-1890s, and 73 left for every 100 who arrived in the peak immigration years of 1907–11. By contrast, only 21,000 Jews left the United States in 1908–12, while 295,000 arrived; 42 percent of Jewish immigrants were females in the 1890s—twice the proportion of Italian females—and a quarter were children under fourteen, compared to only 11 percent of the Italians.[20] Italian men may have been more responsive to homosexual overtures than Jewish men in part simply because far fewer of them were living with their wives.

Italian men also tended to have less contact with women than Jewish men did because of the greater gender segregation of Italian neighborhoods, a cultural difference only accentuated by the demographics of southern Italian immigration. Not only did more Jewish men live with their families, they centered their social lives in their apartments as well as in their synagogues, union halls, and other communal meeting places. Young Jewish men and women had their own gender-segregated groups and young women bore heavy responsibilities at home, but they were also likely to socialize in mixed-gender groups and at the dance halls, movie theaters, and other commercial amusements that abounded in their neighborhoods. Although they expected to be asked for permission, Jewish parents tended to allow their daughters to go to dances or take walks with young men. The high degree of interaction between young Jewish men and women stood in sharp contrast to the gender segregation of Italian neighborhoods, as many contemporary observers noted. The social investigator Sophonisba Breckinridge commented in 1921, "Most immigrant parents, except those from southern Italy, recognize the impossibility of maintaining the old rules of chaperonage and guardianship of the girls . . . [but] Italian parents . . . try to guard their girls almost as closely as they did in Italy."[21]

Although many Italian men in New York also lived with their families and many others boarded with families, a large number of them lived in rooming houses, where they organized surrogate, all-male families with other Italian men. Even those men who boarded with families spent much of their time outside their cramped accommodations, in the neighborhood's streets, poolrooms, and saloons; young men living with their parents spent most of their time in similar locales. As the historian Robert Orsi notes, "Men significantly outnumbered women in the first decades of Italian Harlem . . . [and] they lived in a largely male world."[22]

In this all-male social world, clubs or "gangs" of various sorts formed, usually with loosely defined memberships that fluctuated as people moved in and out of the neighborhood. Walking down four short blocks of Mulberry Street, the chief thoroughfare of the Italian Lower East Side, around 1920, John Mariano counted signs announcing the existence of at least thirty such clubs, each of them drawing young men from the immediate neighborhood, often a single block. He described the members of one of them as American-born truckers, dockworkers, and the like, who ranged in age from twenty to thirty. Employed irregularly in seasonal labor markets that made it impossible for most of them to establish even a modicum of economic security, they prided themselves on their rejection of the unrealizable "American" work ethic. "When they desire to be facetious," he noted disapprovingly, "they call themselves 'the Sons of Rest.'" Not only were two-thirds of these men in their twenties unmarried, but the third who were married nonetheless spent a great deal of their leisure time in the all-male group.[23]

The Bachelor Subculture

As men who (whether married or not) spent most of their time in a largely male social world, these first- and second-generation Italian immigrants were prototypical members of what several historians and sociologists have rather ambiguously termed a "bachelor subculture." This subculture was the primary locus of the sexual dyad of fairies and trade, and its dynamics help explain the sexual culture not only of Italian immigrants but also of many Irish, African-American, and Anglo-American working-class men. The bachelor subculture played a significant (though relatively little studied) role in American cities from the mid-nineteenth century until the mid-twentieth, when about 40 percent of the men over fifteen years old were unmarried at any given time. It was really a series of distinct but overlapping subcultures centered in the poolrooms and saloons where many workingmen spent their time, in the cellar clubrooms and streets where gangs of boys and young men were a ubiquitous presence, and in the lodging houses that crowded the Bowery and the waterfront.* It was a highly gender-segregated social world of young, unmarried, and often transient laborers, seamen, and the like, the "rough" working-class men, that is, whom we have already seen at the Times Square newsstand and the Brooklyn sailors' bar and whom Ralph Werther, for one, identified as particularly receptive to his advances.

Many of the young men of the bachelor subculture would later go on to marry. Many were immigrants (such as the Italians) planning to work in the States only a short while before returning to their families in Europe. The Irish contributed disproportionate numbers of men to this subculture as well. Irish-American men, like their compatriots in Ireland itself, tended to marry only in their early thirties, if at all, and much of their social life was consequentially organized around all-male groups. Indeed, the high rates of lifelong bachelorhood among the Irish provoked periodic discussions in the Irish and Catholic press of the danger of Irish "race suicide."[24] The bachelor subculture also included native-born Anglo-Americans who either had not yet married or planned never to do so, as well as immigrants who had left home precisely in order to escape the pressure to marry. It also included married men from many backgrounds who chose to spend most of their time in the company of other men and moved regularly between the bachelor world of "rough" workingmen and the more family-oriented world of "respectable" workingmen.

---

*These men have received remarkably little attention in recent studies of immigration and working-class culture. In response to an older historiographical and sociological tradition that viewed social "disorganization" and instability as the inevitable consequences of immigration, a generation of historians has sought to document the social cohesiveness of the extended kinship systems of immigrants and their central role in organizing migratory networks and settlement patterns. In response to older studies that made universal claims about the process of immigration on the basis of men's experience alone, a generation of historians has offered a finely nuanced analysis of the role of women and families in immigration. These studies have corrected and deepened our understanding of immigration in significant ways, but an inadvertent consequence of their focus has been to ignore the ubiquitous presence of unattached men in immigrant neighborhoods and to limit inquiry into the social worlds they created. Although such men often migrated to the United States to serve the interests of a larger family-oriented and family-determined economic strategy (to raise capital for investment in land in southern Italy, for instance), once in this country many of them moved in an all-male world.

The working-class bachelor subculture drew heavily from three some-times overlapping occupational cultures: sailors, merchant marines, and other seamen; transient workers who spent time in the city between stints in the countryside as agricultural laborers, lumberjacks, construction workers, and ice cutters; and common laborers based in New York, who worked on the water-front, in construction, and in other heavy manual-labor jobs. The highly irreg-ular and unpredictable work of many of them on shipboard, in agriculture, or in construction often took them out of the city on a seasonal basis and made it dif-ficult for them to support or maintain regular ties with a family. The native-born among them, especially, were part of the immense army of migrant laborers, usually known as hoboes or tramps, who constituted a significant part of the American workforce in the decades before the 1920s.

The sailor, seen as young and manly, unattached, and unconstrained by conventional morality, epitomized the bachelor subculture in the gay cultural imagination. He served for generations as the central masculine icon in gay fig-ure pornography, as the paintings of Charles Demuth and Paul Cadmus from the early decades of the century and the photographs produced by gay pornog-raphers in its middle decades attest.[25] But as the records of anti-vice investiga-tors show, his role in the gay subculture was not simply an object of fantasy. He was a central figure in the subculture, and his haunts became the haunts of gay men as well. He was, however, usually not "of" that culture, since he typically declined to identify himself as other than normal and in sexual encounters al-most always took the role of the "man."

The members of the bachelor subculture were a ubiquitous presence in New York in 1900, when two of every five men in Manhattan aged fifteen years or older were unmarried. They were especially evident in parts of Harlem, in the Italian and Irish districts, along the bustling waterfront, and along the Bow-ery, long known as the "main stem," or center, of the city's "Hobohemia." Their world began to disappear in the 1920s, when the sex ratios of immigrant communities started to stabilize after the strict new federal immigration laws passed in that decade made it difficult for immigrant workers to enter the United States for brief periods of work. The number of seamen in the city began to decline as New York's port declined, and the number of transient workers (or hoboes) dropped throughout the country in the 1920s, as economic and technological developments, such as refrigeration, the mechanization of agricultural production, and the expansion of auto transport, reduced the need for them.[26] The men of the working-class bachelor subculture continued to play a significant role in the city's life throughout the half-century before World War II, however, and it was in their social world that the interaction of fairies and trade took its most visible and highly developed form.

The bachelor subculture, as several historians have shown, shared many of the characteristics of working-class male culture as a whole, but it also had certain distinctive elements that made it particularly amenable to the presence of fairies.[27] The dominant working-class ideology made the ability and willingness to undertake the responsibility of supporting a family two of the defining characteristics of both manliness and male "respectability." But many of the men of the bachelor subculture, either because their irregular and poorly paid work made supporting a family difficult or because they had deliberately chosen to avoid such family encumbrances, forged an alternative definition of manliness that was predicated on a rejection of family obligations. Although many of the men would eventually marry, they tended to remain isolated from women and hostile to the constraints of marriage during the many years they were involved in the bachelor subculture. (They were also considerably more open to advances of fairies before their marriages; Ralph Werther, for instance, noted that most of his young Italian and Irish sex partners went on to marry women.)[28] Indeed, not only their disengagement from the conventions of family life and domesticity but their decided rejection of them were central elements of their culture; they were considered "rough" not simply because many of them rejected family life per se, but more precisely because they scorned the manners associated with the domesticating and moralizing influence of women.

Some of the descriptions of "rough" working-class life provided by hostile middle-class observers in the 1900s and 1910s suggest the extent to which the observers considered the rejection of the feminine domestication of male behavior, the casual mingling of men and fairies, and open displays of homosexuality to be characteristic of such life. An agent investigating the Subway Cabaret on East Fourteenth Street for a moral-reform society in 1917 cited such mingling, along with men refusing to doff their hats (a sign of their lack of domestication), in order to illustrate the "lowergrade" character of the place to his supervisor:

> For instance, at one table one sees three or four tough looking fellows . . . who have to be requested to keep their hats off. At another table one sees a sailor, sitting drinking with two other fellows in civilian clothes, the sailor with his arm around the other fellows neck. The proprietor had to make the sailor behave himself. The sailor was constantly going out with one of the other fellows to the lavatory. I went out also a couple of times but they would just stand there and talk while I was there, and thus I was cheated out of witnessing a little homosexuality.[29]

Embodying a rejection of domesticity and of bourgeois acquisitivism alike, the bachelor subculture was based on a shared code of manliness and an ethic of male solidarity. The solidarity it celebrated was expressed in the everyday ties built at work on the waterfront or in construction; it was symbolized by the rituals of saloon conviviality that expressed mutual regard and reciprocity, perhaps most commonly through the custom of treating one's fellows to rounds of drinks. A man's "manliness" was signaled in part by his participation in such rituals and by his behavior on the job, but it was demonstrated as well by his besting of other men in contests of strength and skill in all-male arenas such as the boxing ring, poolroom, and gambling den. Sexual prowess with women was another important sign of manliness, but such prowess was significant not only as an indication of a man's ability to dominate women but also as evidence of his *relative* virility compared to other men's; manliness in this world was confirmed by other men and in relation to other men, not by women.[30]

The way the men in this social milieu constructed their manliness allowed other men to construct themselves as something other than men. The men in this culture regarded manhood as a hard-won accomplishment, not a given, and as a continuum, not an absolute value or characteristic. Even as they celebrated their masculine camaraderie and commitment to fraternity, they constantly had to prove their manhood and often sought to demonstrate that they were more manly than their rivals. To be called a "man" or a "regular guy" was both the highest compliment in this world and the most common. But the very repetitiveness of such praise implied that men were in danger of being called something else: unmanly, a mollycoddle, a sissy, even a pansy. Whereas manhood could be achieved, it could also be lost; it was not simply a quality that resulted naturally and inevitably from one's sex. The calculated character of the everyday rituals of male sociability, solidarity, and competition by which men enacted their manliness and demonstrated their relative virility suggests the remarkable degree to which they regarded their manliness as a kind of ongoing performance, to use Erving Goffman and Judith Butler's term. It also reveals the degree to which relations in this all-male environment were gendered.[31] It was both this self-consciousness about the performativity of gender and the gendering of relations among men that allowed some males to turn themselves into "she-men," so long as they did not question other men's status as men, and allowed other males to confirm their own "he-manliness" by subordinating them. The very theatricality of the fairies' style not only emphasized the performative character of gender but evoked an aura of liminality reminiscent of carnivals at which the normal constraints on men's behavior were suspended, making it easier for men to interact with them without considering it consequential.[32]

One of the reasons fairies were tolerated by tough working-class men and often had remarkably easygoing relations with them was the care they took to confirm rather than question the latter's manliness. Fairies related to men as if they themselves were women—though often the "tough" women who dared venture into the social spaces dominated by tough men—and they did so in a manner that confirmed the complex social conventions of gender deference, inequality, and power characteristic of gender relations in that culture. But some gangs of men regarded fairies, like women, as fair game for sexual exploitation. Sexually using a fairy not only could be construed and legitimized as a "normal" sexual act but could actually provide some of the same enhancement of social status that mastering a woman did.

That this dynamic sometimes influenced the meaning ascribed to homosexual encounters is suggested by the experience of one Italian youth around 1920. He was sexually active with other men (almost always, he said, "act[ing] as a woman"), but he tried to protect his reputation by developing a conventionally masculine style in the other spheres of his life. He did not carry himself as a fairy and sought to establish his masculinity with the other youths he met at a neighborhood gymnasium by deliberately "talk[ing] about women" with them. Participating in the collective sexualization and objectification of women was one of the rituals by which he established himself as a man. At the gym he met a twenty-five-year-old boxer to whom he was attracted, and he eventually agreed to let the boxer, who had sensed his interest, anally penetrate him. To the boy's horror, the boxer promptly went to the gym and told everyone what he had done; the boy, humiliated, concluded he could never go there again.[33] A man who allowed himself to be used sexually as a woman, then, risked forfeiting his masculine status, even if he were otherwise conventionally masculine; in this case, the boy's shame clearly derived from his perception that he had been made a fairy in the eyes of his comrades. The story also illustrates the belief among men in this world that so long as they played the "man's" role, they remained men. The most striking aspect of the story is the confidence the boxer felt that reporting the encounter would not endanger his status among his friends, that, indeed, having sexually subordinated the boy would enhance it. If a man risked forfeiting his masculine status by being sexually passive, he could also establish it by playing the dominant role in an encounter with another man. Sexual penetration symbolized one man's power over another.

Men's sexual relations with fairies were also fundamentally influenced by the character of their sexual relations with women, particularly the prostitutes and other "tough girls" who were the only women with whom many men in the bachelor subculture interacted. The very social organization and meaning of their sexual relations with women made it relatively unobjectionable for them to substitute fairies when such women could not be found. Numerous reports by undercover agents investigating female prostitution in the early decades of the century make it clear that in those social milieus dominated by young, single laborers and seamen, it was understood that men in search of women sexual partners might be willing to make just that substitution. It was not thought that all men *would*, but it was not considered remarkable when any man *did*.

One evening in the fall of 1927 two agents in search of female prostitutes were taken by a sailor to an Italian restaurant on West Seventeenth Street, where sailors and "hardened neighborhood girls" congregated. After failing to lure any of the women away from the sailors (but, presumably, having succeeded in demonstrating their sexual interest in women), they asked their waitress if she knew where they could find a "sporting girl." The woman said she did not, but immediately added that "there is a fairy [who] comes in here," and called him over. One might expect that the fairy was pimping for female prostitutes, but the agents' response indicates they believed they were being offered the fairy in place of a prostitute. Quickly taking advantage of the unexpected opportunity, they "tried to make an appointment with [him] . . . and [made] an effort . . . to learn where he resided or took his trade." The fairy begged off, citing a previous appointment.[34] The fairy's disinclination to cooperate meant that the agents—and we—learned nothing more of his life, but the fact that the waitress referred the agents to him in the first place tells us much about the understanding of male sexuality she had developed while working in a milieu dominated by sailors and Italian laborers. It evidently seemed plausible—even likely—to her that a man anxious for sexual satisfaction would accept it from a fairy if a woman were unavailable.

The Italian waitress was not the only one who believed this. The general secretary of the city's major anti-prostitution society warned in 1918 that opponents of his anti-prostitution campaign might use the "apparent increase of male perversion" during World War I as "evidence to sustain their argument that vice driven out of one form will appear in another."[35] (The campaign is discussed in chapter 5.) His fear that such reasoning would seem plausible was well founded. One of his own investigators had used it to explain the homosexual liaisons he had observed on the streets surrounding the Brooklyn Navy Yard late one summer night in 1917, when no women were to be found:

> The streets and corners were crowded with the sailors all of whom were on a sharp lookout for girls. . . . It seemed to me that the sailors were sex mad. A number of these sailors were with other men walking arm in arm and on one dark street I saw a sailor and a man kissing each other. . . . It looked like an exhibition of mail [sic] perversion showing itself in the absence of girls or the difficulty of finding them. Some of the sailors told me that they might be able to get a girl if they went 'up-town' but it was too far up and they were too drunk to go way up there.[36]

The belief that fairies could be substituted for female prostitutes—and were virtually interchangeable with them—was particularly prevalent among men in the bachelor subculture whose opportunities for meeting "respectable" women were limited by the moral codes, gender segregation, or unbalanced sex ratios of their ethnic cultures. Indeed, many of these men found the sexual services of fairies to be both easier and cheaper to secure than those of women. They could be found around the Navy Yard and along the waterfront, on well-known streets and in many saloons frequented by sailors and workingmen, and even in many subway washrooms, where a man could find quick release on the way home from work merely by presenting himself. A finely calibrated map of the sexual geography of the neighborhood was usually part of men's gender-specific "local knowledge." Many workingmen knew precisely where to go to find fairies with whom, if they chose, they need not exchange a word to make their wishes clear.[37]

Still, the relative accessibility of fairies to men isolated from women hardly explains the latter's willingness to turn to them. After all, thousands of women were working as prostitutes in the city, and workingmen often *did* have recourse to them; the immense number of single men in the city with few other means of meeting women supported the business of prostitution on a scale that would never be repeated after the 1920s.[38] If men had risked being stigmatized as queer on the basis of a single homosexual encounter, most of them would have sought sex exclusively with such women.

But the very character of their sexual relations with prostitutes and other "tough" women made it possible for them to turn to fairies as well. The moral codes governing the sexual practices of many men in the bachelor subculture (as in the larger culture of men) divided the world into "pure women," with whom men did not expect sexual contact until after marriage, and "impure women" or "whores," whom men felt free to pursue aggressively for sexual purposes.[39] In the eyes of such men, the simple willingness of a woman to enter the saloons, poolrooms, and other social spaces they dominated was a sign that she was a prostitute. In a culture in which men regarded themselves as highly lustful creatures whose health would be impaired if their explosive sexual needs did not find release (or, as they usually termed it, "relief" or "satisfaction"),[40] a phallocentric economy of sexual pleasure governed relations with such women. Sex was something a man did *to* them, not *with* them: a man's phallic dominance and "satisfaction" were his paramount concern. A man might have a close romantic relationship with one woman, whom he hoped to marry and treated with affection and respect, but still feel free to use a prostitute to satisfy his immediate sexual needs. Few men would ever even imagine substituting a fairy for their beloved (although they might develop feelings of affection for some fairies, just as they did for some prostitutes, and might even find it easier to relate to fairies than to prostitutes because they found it easier to relate to men than to women).* But many men did find it relatively easy to substitute a fairy for a prostitute, since both offered immediate sexual satisfaction, as well as the pleasures and amusements of bawdy "female" companionship. In a world in which "every woman is just another place to enter," as one Italian teenager described the attitude of men at his neighborhood pool hall in 1930, the body to enter did not necessarily have to be a woman's.[42]

Gang rapes and other phallocentric sexual practices highlighted the cultural logic that allowed men to substitute fairies for women as objects of sexual penetration. Loop-the-loop, the fairy prostitute mentioned previously, reported to a doctor in 1906 that on a single day he had had sex with "no fewer than twenty-three men . . . one immediately after the other . . . in a room in Brooklyn."[43] His boast is more plausible than it may at first seem, for he would have engaged in a well-established practice when he had sex with a line of men, even if he exaggerated the number. "Line-ups," in which men ("anywhere from three to seventeen," by one account from an Italian neighborhood in the late 1920s) formed a queue to have intercourse, one after another, with a single woman, were not uncommon. Some line-ups constituted nothing less than gang rapes

---

*Will Finch, a middle-class gay man who had pursued and constantly associated with straight working-class men since the 1930s, believed that the homosocial character of "rough" working-class culture gave gay men an advantage over women in one respect: *"We* can be *buddies* of men, whereas a woman never can." For most of the unmarried working-class men he knew, women were for sex, men for "companionship," a situation, Finch thought, comparable to that in classical Greece. One of his sex partners, whom Finch wryly christened "the voice of the urban proletariat," had commented, typically enough, "that he is not at ease with a girl socially and intellectually and emotionally, but only with other males. But girls are lots of fun to fuck."[41]

(in which the women "were the victims of a planned scheme on the part of the men," according to the same account). In a smaller number of cases, the women had enough control of the situation to stop it when they chose and to charge the men for the encounter. Every line-up allowed men to find sexual satisfaction and to enact their solidarity with other men by establishing their collective difference from and dominance of the woman they used. In a similar manner, groups of young men and boys sometimes forced younger boys to provide them with sexual "relief," either by submitting to anal penetration, or, when the number of boys was too large, by masturbating the older boys, one after another.[44] The very structure of such encounters and the interchangeability of fairies, women, and boys in them highlights the degree to which men were simply using the body of the fairy and sometimes the body of a boy, just as they might use the body of a woman, as a vehicle for phallic satisfaction and manly solidarity.

The phallocentric presumption that a man's sexual satisfaction was more significant than the gender or character of the person who provided that satisfaction allowed gay men to make certain arguments in their approach to "normal" men that would seem utterly incredible in the absence of that presumption. Most commonly, gay men simply offered to perform certain sexual acts, especially fellation, which many straight men enjoyed but many women (even many prostitutes) were loath to perform. In such cases it was the particular phallocentric pleasure, rather than the gender of the person providing the pleasure, that men found appealing, although fairies, who were commonly called "cocksuckers," were especially known for this service, in part because so many women refused to provide it. As one gay man observed of the Irish and Italian young men from South Brooklyn with whom he associated in the 1940s and 1950s, they "do not (necessarily) despise fellators—including these 'nice' Brooklyn boys. Or especially they. They find the fellator desirable. . . . The same with sailors."[45] But even though men found the queer man's services desirable, they also believed that a man lost status if he fellated another man. This was not simply a matter of his losing gender status, however, for women also lost status by performing fellation, which is one reason so many women refused to do it. The act itself—a nonreproductive sexual act whether performed by man or woman and thus "unnatural" by the tenets of a reproductively oriented sexual ideology—was considered perverted for men and women alike to do. Its transgressive character was, indeed, part of its appeal, whether performed by men or women.

Some gay men interested in sex with "straight" men also portrayed themselves as less dangerous than women by arguing that there was no chance they would infect the men with the venereal diseases women were thought to carry. Their success with this remarkable line becomes more understandable when one considers the focus of the highly publicized education campaigns launched to curb venereal disease during World War I. The campaigns, controlled by officials concerned with preserving the sexual morality of young men from rural homes as much as with protecting their health, had tried both to heighten men's fear of venereal disease and to use that fear to persuade them to shun contact with prostitutes or the other "loose" women they might encounter in the nation's port cities and training camps. Some educational materials explained that condoms could protect men from venereal disease (and a measure of their success was that condoms came to be called "protectors" in the slang of the 1920s). But most leaflets and posters identified sex with a woman, rather than sex without a condom, as the source of venereal disease.[46] Ironically, one quite unintentional effect of such moralistic campaigns was to reinforce the traditional belief among men that they could catch syphilis or gonorrhea *only* from female prostitutes or other women, whereas sexual contacts with another man were safe—a misconception men interested in seducing other men were quick to seize upon. An investigator posing as a seaman recounted the following conversation with a thirty-year-old Swede employed by the United Fruit Line, in a waterfront cafeteria's washroom in 1931:

> I was about to leave and he said "It smells like a c . . . house. Did you have a woman lately?" I said "No, I am looking for one. Do you know a place?" He said "Wouldn't it be much safer to have it blown?" I said "Do you know a woman who would do that?" He said "Why do you want a woman, they are not safe." I said, "I want only a woman." He then took hold of my arm and said, "Let's get inside. I'll do it for you."[47]

This view was shared by the police as well. A crackdown on homosexual activity after World War I came to an end, in part, because the chief of the vice squad grew concerned that the campaign had diverted too much attention from the squad's efforts against prostitutes, who, he apparently feared, posed a medical, as well as moral, danger to their customers, and through them to their families. Telling his men that "one prostitute was more dangerous than five degenerates," he ordered them to give more attention to the former, a shift in priorities soon reflected in the squad's arrest statistics.[48] Concern about the relative health risk posed by sexual relations with fairies and prostitutes was possible only because it was pre-supposed that men could substitute fairies for women without undermining their masculine status. Indeed, men's ability to calculate the relative rewards and risks involved in each kind of encounter provides the most powerful evidence possible that the hetero-homosexual axis did not govern their thinking about sexual practices. In the right circumstances, almost any man might choose to experiment with the queer pleasures of sex with a fairy.

Husbands, Wolves, and Punks

If every workingman was thought to have the capacity to respond to the advances of a fairy, it was nonetheless the case, as gay men themselves realized, that some men were more interested in sexual contacts with fairies and boys than others were. And although some men treated fairies in the same way they treated prostitutes, not every relationship between a man and a fairy was brief, coercive, or loveless, nor did all men orchestrate the relationships in a way that established their distance from the fairies. Some men sought love and even marriage with fairies, and others at least made no bones about their sexual preference for them. Parker Tyler found many of the Italian men who lived in the Village to be responsive to his charms, for instance, but in his 1929 account of his interaction with the cameramen in a Village speakeasy, he regarded the one who seemed the most anxious about the meeting and who made the most earnest entreaties *to him* as a more distinctive character: a "wolf."

Such men, known as "husbands," "wolves," and "jockers" (terms sometimes used interchangeably, sometimes for different groups of men in different social milieus), occupied an ambiguous position in the sexual culture of the early twentieth-century. They abided by the conventions of masculinity and yet exhibited a decided preference for male sexual partners. From a late-twentieth-century perspective they might be regarded as homosexuals more easily than the men just described, since they engaged in homosexual activity on a more exclusive basis than most men who were trade. But the fact that neither they nor their peers regarded them as queer, even if they sometimes regarded them as *different* from other "normal" men, highlights the degree to which gender status superseded homosexual interest as the basis of sexual classification in working-class culture.

Some men involved in marriages with fairies were so confident of their status as "normal" men that they readily acknowledged their relationships to others. One such man, a band musician, told a doctor in 1906 that he did not limit himself to brief, anonymous, and infrequent sexual encounters with other men, but considered himself the "husband" of a fairy (the prostitute Loop-the-loop), with whom he was involved in an ongoing relationship. He "apparently [did] not care an iota," Dr. Shufeldt reported, "whether I was aware of his sex relations with [the fairy] or not," an impression strengthened by the man's willingness to confide to the doctor, man to man as it were, that Loop-the-loop was "the most passionate mortal he had ever heard of, and one of the most difficult to satisfy." Given the doctor's middle-class and professional background, his response to the man was ambivalent. By remarking on the man's nonchalance, the doctor implied that he, in contrast to his subject, considered the arrangement noteworthy and somewhat objectionable. He also expressed his "surprise [that] he was an intelligent young man," although his surprise was probably due at least in part to the fact that he would have predicted a less respectable husband for the fairy, whom he considered "very uncouth." But he did not feel compelled to comment directly on the man's sexual character, and clearly did not regard him in the same terms as he regarded the fairy. The relationship reproduced the conventions of a highly role-differentiated marriage between a man and a woman, and the "husband," since he played the conventional masculine role, even though with a wife who was anatomically male, did not seem so "abnormal."[49]

The male partners of men such as the musician were not always fairies, nor were the relationships always so close. Indeed, some sexual relationships were organized on the basis of a power and status hierarchy dictated by age rather than by gender (although that age hierarchy was sometimes thematized as one of gender) and sometimes took on a more coercive edge. Known as "active pederasts" or, most commonly, "wolves," the term Tyler used, such men acknowledged having a particular predilection for playing the "man's role" in sex with fairies and, more typically, youths, the latter usually referred to as "punks." *Punk* generally denoted a physically slighter youth who let himself be used sexually by an older and more powerful man, the wolf, in exchange for money, protection, or other forms of support.

The punk's sexual character was ambiguous: he was often neither homosexually interested nor effeminate himself, but was sometimes equated with women because of his youth and his subordination to the older man. He was regarded by some men as simply a young homosexual, by others as the victim of an aggressive older man, and by still others as someone whose sexual subordination was merely an aspect of his general subordination to a dominant older man.[50] In a west Pennsylvania prison in 1892, for instance, an older prisoner explained the meaning of *punk* to the anarchist Alexander Berkman in the following manner: "Ever read Billy Shakespeare? Know the place, 'He's neither man nor woman; he's punk.' Well, Billy knew. A punk's a boy that'll . . . give himself to a man. . . . It's done in every prison, an' on th' road [by which he meant among hoboes], everywhere." This may have been the original derogatory meaning of *punk*, which only later passed into underworld and then more general slang as an epithetic diminutive without specifically sexual connotations.[51]

The erotic system of wolves and punks was particularly widespread (and tended to take somewhat different form) among three groups of men who were exceptionally disengaged from the family and neighborhood systems that regulated normative sexuality: seamen, prisoners, and the immense number of transient workers (or hoboes) who passed through American cities before the 1920s. That the wolves regarded themselves as something other than queer attests both to the absence of a sharp hetero–homosexual binarism in their culture, which would inevitably have classified them as homosexual, and to the centrality instead of effeminacy to the definition of sexual abnormality among workingmen. Their behavior in prison or on shipboard could be dismissed as a product of the situation (the absence of women) rather than of predisposition (a preference for boys or fairies), but such explanations became implausible when the behavior persisted in settings where women were available. Wolves combined homosexual interest with a marked masculinity. None of them behaved effeminately or took feminine nicknames, and few played the "woman's part" in sexual relations—and then only secretly. On the contrary, their very appellation, *wolf*, evoked the image of the predatory man-about-town intent on seducing young women, and their masculine dominance over punks was further emphasized by the fact that the latter were also referred to as *lambs* and *kids*.

Wolves generally did not seek sexual encounters with other "men," in which they might have been forced into sexual roles that would have compromised their own masculine identification, but only with punks or fairies, males ascribed lower status because of their youth or effeminacy.[52]

Thus a seaman blithely explained to an undercover agent whom he met on the lower Manhattan waterfront in 1931 that he liked sex with "fairies or c . . . s . . . . . .," particularly fifteen- and sixteen-year-old boys he called "punks." "I had one of those punks living with me at the [Seamen's Church] Institute for quite some time," the man bragged. "He was a young kid about 15 years old, [and] pretty." The fact that he found a boy attractive, regularly had sex with him, and supported him financially did not make the older man, in his own mind or in the opinion of the investigator, a fairy or queer. Critical to both was the fact that, in the seaman's version of the relationship, the boy "satisfied me the same as a woman." At the same time, the seaman appears to have believed that some men—possibly including the investigator—were more likely than others to take an interest in punks; he mentioned his relations with the punks only after learning that the investigator had not visited the "sporting houses" (tenement brothels) that he had previously shown him.[53] Indeed, their interaction suggests that having recourse to a punk or fairy did not have the same reputability in this milieu that going to a prostitute did. When the seaman introduced the agent to a punk prostitute, the agent was able to put off meeting with him by indicating he did not want to make an appointment in front of his friend. This concern evidently seemed plausible to the boy, who accepted the excuse but assured the agent that he could find him anytime around the Seamen's Church Institute.[54] Nonetheless, the seaman's willingness to boast about his relationship with a punk to a man he barely knew suggests that he did not expect to lose much, if any, status because of it. If one man might be reticent about admitting such interests (as he might be about any sexual matter), they were acceptable enough that another man could take pride in commenting on them.

The seaman's interest in punks and fairies was not unusual, nor were such interactions kept carefully hidden. The investigator accompanied the man to Battery Park, whose benches were filled with young men waiting to be picked up by sailors. The punk to whom the seaman introduced him, a sixteen-year-old named Julius, assumed he wanted a rendezvous and immediately offered to find a room in a lodging house in Chatham Square. He also offered a straightforward account of his prices: along with the room, which cost a dollar, he charged 50 cents for oral sex and 75 cents for anal sex. The investigator frequently saw punks and fairies talking with seamen at the Institute, in nearby lunchrooms, and in the park; on one occasion a seaman identified fifteen male prostitutes in the park, sitting "on separate benches, always leaving room for a [man] to sit down."[55] Although the openness and even the existence of such men was news to the investigator, it must have been common knowledge among workers and residents of the waterfront.

Long-term relationships or "marriages" between wolves and punks seem to have been even more common among hoboes, although precisely how many hoboes participated in such relationships is, of course, impossible to determine. A study of a hundred "vagrants" in New York City in 1916 identified a quarter of them as "perverts"; studies conducted in other cities produced lower figures, although any such estimates need to be regarded with suspicion.[56] The prevalence of homosexual relations was so "generally assumed to be true among hoboes," wrote the sociologist and former hobo Nels Anderson in a 1931 hobo handbook, "that whenever a man travels around with a lad he is apt to be labeled a 'jocker' or a 'wolf' and the road kid is called his 'punk,' 'preshun,' or 'lamb.' It has become so that it is very difficult for a good hobo to enjoy the services of an apprentice."[57]

As Anderson's comment suggests, partnerships between older and younger men on the road were common, and while they were presumed to have a sexual element, many did not. In both sexual and nonsexual partnerships, the older man usually took responsibility for teaching his apprentice the arts of the road as well as providing for his material needs. The younger man performed a host of services for his mentor, including shaving him, and also contributed to their supply of cash. In many respects their relationship reproduced the sexual roles, division of labor, and conventions of mutual dependence that were characteristic of husbands and wives in the dominant culture. In his classic 1923 sociological study of hoboes, Anderson noted that "it is not uncommon to hear a boy who is seen traveling with an older man spoken of as the 'wife' or 'woman.'"[58] As with heterosexual marriages, the quality of the partnerships varied widely: some were brutal and coercive, others were close and affectionate, and still others simply instrumental.

The character of such relationships needs to be explored more fully by historians, but it seems likely that the widespread existence of hobo partnerships made it easier for men in sexual relationships to fit into the social world that took shape in rural hobo camps and in urban "hobohemias," the districts, such as the Bowery, where many transient workers spent the winter. Some men doubtless entered into such relationships only because of the circumstances in which they found themselves, but other men must have sought out such circumstances precisely because they made it possible for them to engage in homosexual intimacies.*

Another locus of relations between wolves and punks, the New York City Jail on Welfare Island, deserves scrutiny because the organization of sexual relations in it illuminates the boundaries drawn between different kinds of men

---

*Indeed, homosexual relationships appear to have been so widespread among seamen and hoboes that historians need to recognize the desire to live in a social milieu in which such relationships were relatively common and accepted—or to escape the pressure to marry in a more family-oriented milieu—as one of the motives that sent men on the road or to sea. More work needs to be done on the patterns of same-sex relations in all-male work settings where "hoboes" and other transient laborers worked, such as lumber camps, cattle ranges, and many mining camps.[59]

who engaged in homosexual practices. Although the homosexual world that took shape among prisoners was a peculiar one, it was not so exceptional as is often thought. Nor does the culturally blind concept of "situational homosexuality" offer an adequate framework for analyzing that world. In a remarkable study of homosexual relations in an American prison in the 1970s, Wayne S. Wooden and Jay Parker showed that the social organization of such relations varied among Chicanos, African-Americans, and Euro-Americans. Men did not react to being deprived of other sexual contacts by engaging in homosexual practices in a spontaneous and unstructured way, but organized those relations in accordance with the sexual norms they brought to the prison from their own cultures.[60] Similarly, the homosexual world that evolved in the New York City Jail in the early twentieth century, rather than being a singular world cut off from wider cultural patterns, was profoundly shaped by those patterns. It drew especially on the patterns of the bachelor subculture, whose members, as the men least socialized into the dominant social order, were disproportionately represented in the jail.

The dominant pre–World War II conceptualizations of homosexuality were inscribed in the spatial organization of prisons and in the everyday interactions of prisoners. The central position of the fairy in the dominant cultural conception of homosexuality was signaled by the decision of prison authorities not only to segregate homosexual prisoners from other men but to classify as "homosexuals" only those men who exhibited the typical markers of effeminacy. It is not clear when this policy was initiated, but it had become a well-established practice by the 1910s. All prisoners who had been convicted of homosexual solicitation or transvestism were incarcerated in this unit, of course, but the majority of inmates identified as "perverts" had been convicted of drug use or other nonsexual offenses; the authorities segregated any man whose dress or mannerisms suggested he might be homosexual. Segregation from the other prisoners was complete. "Fags" were confined to the prison's South Annex, the most isolated and secure section of the prison; they ate separately, saw movies separately, and worked in separate work gangs, which were assigned "women's work" in the prison laundry and in the warden's home. Within the South Annex (which many prisoners called the Fag Annex), men were informally allowed to wear long hair, wigs, makeshift dresses, and homemade rouge and lipstick. Guards and other prisoners alike usually referred to them by their camp names—"Greta Garbo," "Lillian Russell," "Broadway Rose"—and at Christmas the South Annex inmates staged a bawdy show called the "Fag Follies" for a select audience of guards and well-connected prisoners. Normally the only contact between the "fags" and other prisoners came when the former were marched past the latter on their way to the mess hall.[61]

If the basis on which the authorities segregated homosexual prisoners confirms how widely the fairy was regarded as a distinct social type, the reasons they gave for segregating them confirm how widely it was believed that any man might be attracted to a fairy. Most authorities did not think that men isolated from women would randomly engage in homosexual behavior, but they did assume that such men would be susceptible to the fairies. When a new administrator took over the jail in 1934 he announced that he would force the fairies with long hair to get "military hair cuts," in order, he explained to the press in a revealing comment, to "cut down their attractiveness."[62] Although most prison authorities found inmates' having sex with fairies to be reprehensible, they hardly considered it unusual. Indeed, their fear was not just that fairies would induce other men to engage in homosexual practices but that rivalries between men for a fairy's attentions would escalate into violent confrontations. "Perverts, frank and under cover, stimulate tortured men to indulge in perversion, often by direct solicitation," one prison doctor and reform advocate warned in 1934. "The constitutional type, the one the man in the street recognizes under the optimistic title of 'fairy,' should be segregated in colonies, such as now utilized for mental defectives; only in this way can their moral leprosy be prevented from spreading."[63]

Prison officials generally refused to acknowledge the existence of homosexual activity in their prisons, but reformers brought it to the attention of the public in 1934. Shortly after the newly elected mayor, Fiorello La Guardia, appointed his own commissioner of corrections, Austin H. MacCormick, the commissioner conducted a raid of Welfare Island. His purpose was both to seize control of the prison from the crime-boss inmates who exercised effective suzerainty within it—running numbers rackets, selling liquor, and leading as luxurious a life as prison conditions would allow—and to discredit both the old prison administration that had allowed such conditions to develop and the Tammany Hall mayoral administration preceding La Guardia's.[64] The raid produced sensational newspaper stories that destroyed the credibility of the old administration. Some of the most lurid stories concerned the homosexual segregation unit. The new administrators used the "freedoms" granted homosexuals as well as gang lords to attack the old administration; when they invited the press to tour the prison on the day of the raid, they pointed to the spectacle of homosexual depravity to demonstrate the depths to which the prison had sunk.

The *New York Herald Tribune* cooperated fully in the effort. It described the scene witnessed by the crusading commissioner on the day of the raid when the "sex perverts" entered the mess hall: "These men appeared for lunch, some of them heavily rouged, their eye brows painted, their lips red, hair in some instances hanging to the shoulder, and in most cases hips swinging and hands fluttering. . . . Mr. MacCormick [said] he could see no reason 'for permitting them to flaunt themselves in front of the rest of the prisoners in this way,' " and he "intimated" that this was "but a slight example of the liberties this group had previously had in the prison." The *Daily Mirror* offered a fuller account of their "liberties" when it noted they "had been permitted by the prison bosses to roam the Island, visiting various buildings and cell-tiers 'in drag'—or female costume," although even it only hinted at the sordid purpose of their visits. When the raiding party entered the South Annex, the *Herald Tribune* continued, it was "greeted by cries and howls in high falsetto voices. . . . Inside the cells were found every conceivable article of women's wearing apparel. Dozens of compacts, powder puffs, and various types of perfume were found, while silk step-ins, nightgowns and other bits of negligee were strewn about the cells." The paper also described the dramatic scene as "one man . . . clung desperately to a set of false eyelashes, which he did not want disturbed," in an apparent effort to turn the confiscation of the false eyelashes into a symbol of the reformers' struggle to restore order to the New York City Jail.[65] The sensational news arti-cles were soon followed by a flurry of more "authoritative" studies by prison doctors and reformers with titles like *Sex in Prison* and *Revelations of a Prison Doctor.*[66]

The segregation of "fags" hardly put an end to homosexual liaisons in the city jail, though. As numerous reformers and prisoners themselves testified, the jail was the quintessential home of the "wolf" and the "punk," and the treat-ment accorded the wolf by inmates and prison authorities alike attests to the de-gree to which he was regarded as a "normal" man. The wolf's behavior led him to lose little status among other prisoners; if anything, he gained stature in many men's eyes because of his ability to coerce or attract a punk. Prison au-thorities did not try to segregate the highly masculine and aggressive older wolves by confining them in the "degenerate" unit in which they segregated the effeminate fairies, primarily because they did not think it was possible to distin-guish wolves from other prisoners.

Whether the wolf could be distinguished from the other inmates was sub-ject to debate. Some prison reformers, such as Thomas Mott Osborne, thought that " 'wolves,' who by nature or practice prefer unnatural to what we may call natural vice," should be distinguished from other homosexually active men "who have no liking for unnatural vice [and] outside of prison would never be guilty of it." Several reformers recommended that wolves be segregated from vulnerable youths.[67] But most prisoners, like the prison authorities, seem to have regarded the wolves as little different from other men; their sexual behav-ior may have represented a moral failure, but it did not distinguish them from other men as the fairy's gender status did. As one prisoner wrote in 1933, "The 'wolf' (active sodomist), as I have hinted before, is not considered by the aver-age inmate to be 'queer' in the sense that the oral copulist, male or female, is so considered. While his conduct is felt to be in some measure depraved, it is con-duct which many a prisoner knows that he himself might resort to under certain special circumstances." The "special circumstances" he envisioned were not so special after all and presumed that any prisoner might be attracted to a youth. "If the prisoner can find a good-looking boy, and the opportunity, and is suffi-ciently 'hard up' for sexual satisfaction," he explained, "he will not usually dis-dain to make use of him for purposes of relief."[68] The line between the wolf and the normal man, like that between the culture of the prison and culture of the streets, was a fine one indeed.

The ability of many workingmen to alternate between male and female sexual partners provides powerful evidence that the hetero–homosexual axis—the di-chotomy between the "homosexual" and the "heterosexual"—governed neither their thinking about sexuality nor their sexual practices. While fairies, trade, wolves, and punks all engaged in what we would define as homosexual behavior, they and the people who observed them were careful to draw distinctions between different modes of such behavior: between "feminine" and "masculine" behavior, between "passive" and "active" roles, between desire for sex with a man and desire for sex. The organization of the relationships between fairies or punks and their husbands, trade, wolves, and customers (sometimes overlapping groupings of men) serves to highlight the cultural presumption that the men in such relationships were defined by their *differences*—manifested in their different sexual roles or their differently gendered modes of self-presentation—rather than by their *similarities*—their shared "homosexuality." Even evidence of persistent and exclusive interest in sexual relations with another man did not necessarily put a man in the same category as his partner. The band musician's marriage to Loop-the-loop did not turn him into a fairy, after all, but into the husband of a fairy. While today we might regard all of them equally as "homosexuals," they recognized no "homosexual" category in which they all could be placed. In the very different sexual culture that predominated at the turn of the century, they understood themselves—and were regarded by others—as fundamentally different kinds of people. To classify their behavior and identities using the simple polarities of "homosexual" and "heterosexual" would be to misunderstand the complexity of their sexual system, the realities of their lived experience.

As this chapter's ethnography of sexual practices and identities demonstrates, men did not just use different categories to think about a sexuality that, despite appearances, was fundamentally the same as that of men today, for those different cultural categories governed and were manifest in men's everyday social practices. Even in the terms of the late-twentieth-century hetero-homosexual axis, in other words, it would be difficult to argue that the "normal" men who had sex with fairies were *really* homosexuals, for that would leave inexplicable their determined pursuit of women sexual partners. But neither could they plausibly be regarded as heterosexuals, for heterosexuals would have been incapable of responding sexually to another male. Nor were they bisexuals, for that would have required them to be attracted to both women as women and men as *men*. They were, rather, men who were attracted to womanlike men or interested in sexual activity defined not by the gender of their partner but by the kind of bodily pleasures that partner could provide.

Not all men in working-class New York had the same degree of interest in sex with a fairy (and many had none at all), just as not all men had the same degree of interest in sex with a dark-skinned woman or a middle-aged woman or a blue-eyed woman. But almost all workingmen—from the liquor authority agents who watched "fags" trying to pick up sailors at the Happy Hour Bar to the newsstand owner who watched sailors trying to pick up fairies at the Times Square Building—considered it unremarkable that a man might go with a fairy and as little revelatory about his sexual identity as his preference for one kind of woman over another. A man's occasional recourse to fairies did not prove he had homosexual desire for another man, as today's hetero–homosexual binarism would insist, but only that he was interested in the forms of phallic pleasure a fairy could provide as well as a female prostitute could. Men's identities and reputations simply did not depend on a sexuality defined by the anatomical sex of their sexual partners. Just as the abnormality of the fairy depended on his violation of gender conventions, rather than his homosexual practices alone, the normality of other men depended on their conformity to those conventions rather than on an eschewal of homosexual practices which those conventions did not require. Heterosexuality had not become a precondition of gender normativity in early-twentieth-century working-class culture. Men had to be many things in order to achieve the status of normal men, but being "heterosexual" was not one of them.

Notes

1. Report on Times Square Building by J. K., May 2, 1927, COF. "D—" in the original.
2. *Happy Hour Bar & Grill, Inc.*, v. *Bruckman, et al.*, 256 A.D. 1074 (2nd Dep't 1939), reports on the Happy Hour Bar & Grill by investigators Tierney and Kirschenbaum, dated Oct. 10 and Oct. 17, 1938, contained in Record on Review, 47–48, 56.
3. E. S. Shepherd, for example, specifically referred to "fairies" as "the male prostitute of the streets" in "Contribution to the Study of Intermediacy," *American Journal of Urology and Sexology* 14 (1918): 245.
4. Richard Meeker, *Better Angel* (New York: Greenberg, 1933), 259; Kennilworth, Bruce, *Goldie* (New York: William Godwin, 1933), 105.
5. Gershon Legman, "The Language of Homosexuality: An American Glossary," in George W. Henry, *Sex Variants* (New York: Paul B. Hoeber, 1941), vol. 2, appendix VII, 1176, quoting a study of prostitutes' slang; *Report and Proceedings of the [Lexow] Senate Committee appointed to investigate the Police Department of the City of New York* (Albany: J. B. Lyon, 1895), Captain Ryan testimony, 5591.
6. Charles W. Gardner, *The Doctor and the Devil; or, the Midnight Adventures of Dr. Parkhurst* (New York: Gardner & Co., 1894), 52.
7. R. W. Shufeldt, M.D., "Biography of a Passive Pederast," *American Journal of Urology and Sexology* 13 (1917): 451–60. Although the interview was reported in 1917, it took place in 1906. "Looping the loop" had become a generic slang expression for such amusement park rides in the 1900s; see Jane Addams's reference to "looping the loop" in *The Spirit of Youth and the City Streets* (New York: Macmillan, 1909), 69, as quoted in John F. Kasson, *Amusing the Million: Coney Island at the Turn of the Century* (New York: Hill and Wang, 1978), 100, who also discusses the ride on pp. 81–82.
8. Quoted in George Chauncey, "Christian Brotherhood or Sexual Perversion? Homosexual Identities and the Construction of Sexual Boundaries in the World War I Era," *Journal of Social History* 19 (1985): 195. The sailor was questioned at the Newport, Rhode Island, naval training station, but had spent time in New York and was involved in a gay world not far removed from that of the city.

9. R. E. Fay, C. F. Turner, A. D. Klassen, and J. H. Gagnon, "Prevalence and Patterns of Same-Gender Sexual Contact Among Men," *Science* 243 (1989): 343–48; S. M. Rogers and C. F. Turner, "Male-Male Sexual Contact in the USA: Findings from Five Sample Surveys, 1970–1990," *Journal of Sex Research* 28 (1991): 491–519; J. O. G. Billy, K. Panfer, W. R. Grady, and D. H. Klepinger, "The Sexual Behavior of Men in the United States," *Family Planning Perspectives* 25 (1993): 52–60.

10. Alfred Kinsey, Wardell Pomeroy, and Clyde Martin, *Sexual Behavior in the Human Male* (Philadelphia: W. B. Saunders, 1948), 612, 614.

11. Ibid., 616.

12. The reputation of Italian men for trade in the gay world was noted by Frank Burton, Bruce Nugent, and Sebastian Risicato in interviews; see also the role of Italian men in Charles Henri Ford and Parker Tyler, *The Young and Evil* (Paris: Obelisk Press, 1933), which was based on Tyler's experiences in the Village, where he regularly encountered "straight" Italian men interested in sex with men. On Irish men, see the discussion of Charles Tomlinson Griffes and policemen in the following chapter. I have been unable to locate sufficient evidence concerning the sexual cultures of other immigrant groups in New York to propose even a tentative analysis of them. New York City's small Chinatown community, for instance, consisted almost entirely of bachelors as a result of restrictive immigration policies. While slender oral history evidence hints at homosexual activity among some of the bachelors, there is not a single gay-related reference (and virtually no reference of any kind) to Chinese men in the records of the Committee of Fourteen and Committee of Fifteen I have examined. The single sodomy case I have found concerns an unmarried twenty-four-year-old Chinese laundryman, who allegedly forced sex on two Jewish boys he enticed into the premises of a laundry on East Broadway one evening in 1898. He was acquitted, and the DAP case file contains no additional information (*People* v. *Ong*, DAP 22,086 [CGS 1898]).

13. Frederick H. Whitin, "Sexual Perversion Cases in New York City Courts, 1916–1921," bulletin 1480, Nov. 12, 1921, box 88, COF. My review of the backgrounds of the two hundred men arrested by the police (with the assistance of the Society for the Suppression of Vice) for degenerate disorderly conduct in 1920–21 suggests that almost twice as many Italians than Jews were arrested (see the elevenpage list, untitled, in "Homosexuality" folder, box 63, COF). Religious and national backgrounds for most (but not all) of the men arrested were supplied in the records of the Society itself, volumes 3–5 (SSV). These figures, of course, may reveal as much about the enforcement priorities of the police as about the actual incidence of homosexual conduct. I include them, however, as one piece of evidence for the pattern of ethnic differences suggested more conclusively by the greater visibility and institutionalization of gay life in the Italian than Jewish Lower East Side.

14. 207 Canal St. report, "Court of Special Sessions [cases]," box 65, COF. A judge ultimately refused to close the saloon on the basis of "disorderly conversation" alone.

15. Report of J. R., Mar. 22, 1901, box 7, Committee of Fifteen papers, NYPL.

16. Report of H. S. Conklin, Mar. 5, 1901, box 5; report of Salomon and Robinson, February 1901, box 7, Committee of Fifteen papers, NYPL. According to the typed transcript of the investigators' notes cited here, the five boys were known as

"faniss," by which they may have meant "finocchio," the Italian-American term for fennel, used in the production of licorice, which Italian-Americans used synonymously with the English term cocksucker. (This presumably was the origin of the name of Finocchio's, a famous club in San Francisco featuring a female-impersonation act in the 1940s and 1950s.) Other investigators' reports refer to such men as "fairies," as well as "perverts" and, most commonly, "cock suckers." "Pansy" did not become a common term for gay men until the 1920s.

17. Report of Captain Titus [to the Mayor], Dec. 20, 1900, box 9, Van Wyck papers, Mayors' Papers, NYMA. The same report notes that the police investigated rumors that 138 Chrystie St. was a disorderly house, but does not indicate what kind of "disorder" was said to occur there. I am indebted to Timothy Gilfoyle for this reference.

18. Kinsey, *Sexual Behavior*, 483. On Italian immigrants' response to church teachings, see Robert Orsi, *The Madonna of 115th Street: Faith and Community in Italian Harlem, 1880–1950* (New Haven, Conn.: Yale University Press, 1985), xvi–xviii, 219–21; Gary R. Mormino and George E. Pozzetta, *The Immigrant World of Ybor City: Italians and Their Latin Neighbors in Tampa, 1885–1985* (Urbana: University of Illinois Press, 1987), 210–32.

19. Kinsey also noted that many sexologists in Italy itself considered southern Italy "the most homosexual place in the world," although he continued to believe that homosexual behavior was more widespread in several countries in the Middle and Far East. See Wardell Pomeroy, *Dr. Kinsey and the Institute for Sex Research* (New Haven, Conn.: Yale University Press, 1972), 423–27. On the general openness of Italian men to sexual contracts with men, see also the letters from one of Kinsey's informants reprinted in Martin Duberman, *About Time: Exploring the Gay Past* (New York: Gay Presses of New York, 1986), 173–77. For one gay veteran's view of homosexual life in Italy, see John Hope Burns's postwar novel, *The Gallery* (New York: Harper, 1947). On instrumentalist approaches to the body, see Pierre Bourdieu's observations in "Sport and Social Class," *Social Science Information* 17 (1978): 819–40. Bourdieu argues that such attitudes are more characteristic of (French) working-class men than middle-class men, but unfortunately does not historicize that assessment. Although the homosexual culture on the Lower East Side bears a remarkable resemblance in many respects to the limited accounts we have of Mediterranean sexual patterns, the subtle variations in those patterns, both within the Mediterranean basin and between Europe and the United States, need to be studied with care. "Mediterranean" cultures are often represented as more homogeneous in such matters than they actually are. On the dangers of such homogenization, see, for example, Michael Herzfeld, "The Horns of the Mediterraneanist Dilemma," *American Ethnologist* 11 (1984): 439–54. See also John J. Winkler, *Constraints of Desire* (New York: Routledge, 1990).

20. On the different demographic patterns of Italian and Jewish immigration to New York, see Thomas Kessner, *The Golden Door: Italian and Jewish Immigrant Mobility in New York City* (New York: Oxford University Press, 1977), 26–32. On the unusually large number of single men who immigrated to the United States from Italy, see also Dino Cinel, *From Italy to San Francisco: The Immigrant Experience* (Stanford, Calif.: Stanford University Press, 1982), 162–72. For an analytic overview of the circumstances in Europe and the Americas that resulted in European emigration and of the significance of family networks to migration, see John

Bodnar, *The Transplanted: A History of Immigrants in Urban America* (Bloomington: Indiana University Press, 1985), 1–84. Numerous historians have studied Italian and Jewish immigration to New York. See, for example, Moses Rischin, *The Promised City: New York's Jews, 1870–1914* (Cambridge, Mass.: Harvard University Press, 1962); Irving Howe, *World of Our Fathers* (New York: Harcourt Brace Jovanovich, 1976); Donna R. Gabaccia, *From Sicily to Elizabeth Street: Housing and Social Change Among Italian Immigrants* (Albany: State University of New York Press, 1984); as well as the other studies cited elsewhere in this section.

21. Sophonisba Breckinridge, *New Homes for Old* (New York: Harper, 1921), 176–77. See also Susan A. Glenn, *Daughters of the Shtetl: Life and Labor in the Immigrant Generation* (Ithaca, N.Y.: Cornell University Press, 1990), 81–82, 159–66, 162, 215–16. On the greater degree of social interaction between men and women in Jewish than Italian neighborhoods, see also Kathy Peiss, *Cheap Amusements: Working Women and Leisure in Turn-of-the-Century New York* (Philadelphia: Temple University Press, 1986), 30, 68; Elizabeth Ewen, *Immigrant Women in the Land of Dollars: Life and Culture on the Lower East Side, 1890–1925* (New York: Monthly Review Press, 1985), 210–11; Elinor Lerner, "Family Structure, Occupational Patterns, and Support for Women's Suffrage," in *Women in Culture and Politics: A Century of Change*, ed. Judith Friedlander et al. (Bloomington: Indiana University Press, 1986); Gabaccia, *From Sicily*, 97.

22. Orsi, *The Madonna of 115th Street*, 21, 115–17, 135–43. On living arrangements, see Kessner, *The Golden Door*, 99–101; and Gabaccia, *From Sicily*, ch. 5–6. On the use of leisure time, see Perry R. Duis, *The Saloon: Public Drinking in Chicago and Boston, 1880–1920* (Urbana: University of Illinois Press, 1983), 146–48, Louise C. Odencrantz, *Italian Women in Industry: A Study of Conditions in New York* (New York: Russell Sage), 203–5, who noted that in such families "the mother had no recreation and [even] the father took his alone" (203), and Gabaccia, *From Sicily*, 97.

23. John H. Mariano, *The Second Generation of Italians in New York City* (Boston: Christopher Publishing, 1921), 140–43. For a fine analysis of such social clubs and gangs, see Leonard H. Ellis, "Men Among Men: An Exploration of All-Male Relationships in Victorian America" (Ph.D. diss., Columbia University, 1982), 1–60. Ellis assumes too readily that boys usually left such gangs for poolrooms and saloons once they reached the age of sixteen or eighteen, but he offers a thoughtful analysis of the role of all three such neighborhood-based all-male social groupings and spaces in the everyday lives of late-nineteenth-century men.

24. For a fascinating analysis of the origins and social organization of the Irish bachelor culture, see Richard Stivers, *A Hair of the Dog: Irish Drinking and American Stereotype* (University Park: Pennsylvania State University Press, 1976). For evidence of the concern the high rates of bachelorhood and spinsterhood provoked among Irish and Catholic leaders, see the articles cited by Stivers: James Walsh, "Catholic Bachelors and Old Maids," *America*, Aug. 12, 1922, 389–90; idem, "The Disappearing Irish in America," *America*, May 1, 1926, 56–57; idem, "Shy Irish Bachelors," *America*, Mar. 29 1930, 592–93; M. V. Kelly, "The Suicide of the Irish Race," *America*, Nov. 17 and 24, 1928, 128–29, 155–56.

25. The paintings by Cadmus and Demuth of sailors in homoerotic situations appear in many of the catalogs of their work. In addition to the Cadmus painting reproduced at the beginning of this chapter, see the paintings reproduced in the catalog for the Demuth retrospective at the Whitney Museum of American Art, *Charles*

Demuth (New York: Abrams, 1987). For later pornographers, see almost any issue of *Tomorrow's Man, VIM, Physique Pictorial,* and the other gay-oriented "physique magazines" published in the 1940s–1960s.

26. On the decline of the transient workforce, see Nels Anderson, *Men on the Move* (Chicago: University of Chicago Press, 1940), 2–5, 12.

27. There were also ethnic, occupational, and generational differences among he men in the various male subcultures that collectively constituted the "bachelor subculture," but most of them shared its distinctive characteristics to some degree.

28. Ralph Werther, *Autobiography of an Androgyne* (New York: Medico-Legal Journal, 1918), 83–84, 88.

29. Report on the Subway Cabaret, Fourteenth St. near Fourth Ave., 10 P.M., Jan. 12, 1917, COF.

30. On the importance of what he calls "masculine conviviality" to such men, the character of the bachelor subculture, and the relationship between the culture of the "rough" working class and the respectable, see David Montgomery, *The Fall of the House of Labor: The Workplace, the State, and American Labor Activism, 1865–1925* (Cambridge: Cambridge University Press, 1987), 87–92; Roy Rosenzweig, *Eight Hours for What We Will: Workers and Leisure in an Industrial City, 1870–1920* (New York: Cambridge University Press, 1983), 57–64, 74–81; Elliott J. Gorn, *The Manly Art: Bare-Knuckle Prize Fighting in America* (Ithaca, N.Y.: Cornell University Press, 1986), 129–45, especially 140–45; Ned Polsky, *Hustlers, Beats, and Others* (Chicago: Aldine, 1967), 31–37, 90, 105, 109–10; Ellis, "Men Among Men," 1–60; and Peter Bailey, " 'Will the Real Bill Banks Please Stand Up?' Towards a Role Analysis of Mid-Victorian Working-Class Respectability," in *Expanding the Past: Essays from the Journal of Social History,* ed. Peter N. Stearns (New York: New York University Press, 1988), 73–90.

31. For two distinct perspectives on the performativity of everyday life, see Erving Goffman's classic study, *The Presentation of Self in Everyday Life* (Garden City, N.Y.: Doubleday, 1959); and Judith Butler's splendid *Gender Trouble: Feminism and the Subversion of Identity* (New York: Routledge, 1990).

32. On the carnival, see Peter Stallybrass and Allon White, *The Politics and Poetics of Transgression* (Ithaca, N.Y.: Cornell University Press, 1986).

33. Antonio L., quoted in Henry, *Sex Variants,* 420.

34. Report on Italian Restaurant, 207 W. 17th St., Oct. 6, 1927, box 36, COF.

35. Frederick H. Whitin to Captain T. N. Pfeiffer, War and Navy Departments Commission, Washington, Apr. 3, 1918, box 25, COF.

36. J. A. S., Conditions about the Brooklyn Navy Yard, June 6, 1917, box 25, COF. See also, for example, Harry Benjamin's 1931 article arguing that "the suppression of prostitution [in New York] has probably increased and favored homosexual tendencies and practices" (" 'For the Sake of Morality,' " *Medical Journal and Record* 133: 380–82).

37. For more on the sexual mapping of the city, see chapter 7.

38. On the magnitude of the business of prostitution in nineteenth- and early-twentieth-century New York City, and its decline after the 1910s, see Timothy J. Gilfoyle, *City of Eros: New York City, Prostitution, and the Commercialization of Sex, 1790–1920* (New York: Norton, 1992).

39. Kinsey, *Sexual Behavior,* 38; William Foote Whyte, "A Slum Sex Code," *American Journal of Sociology* 49 (1943): 24–31.

40. On the belief that men had to have regular orgasms to maintain their health, see Charles Rosenberg, "Sexuality, Class, and Role in Nineteenth-Century America," in *The American Man*, ed. Elizabeth H. Pleck and Joseph H. Pleck (Englewood Cliffs, N.J.: Prentice-Hall, 1980), 230–32, and E. Anthony Rotundo, *American Manhood: Transformations in Masculinity from the Revolution to the Modern Era* (New York: Basic Books, 1993), 121–22. Both accounts focus on the nineteenth century, but it is clear that the belief persisted into the twentieth. For examples of the term *satisfaction* used casually to mean orgasm, see, for example, Salvatore N., quoted in Henry, *Sex Variants*, 176; Victor F. Nelson, *Prison Days and Nights* (Boston: Little, Brown, 1933), 157–58.

41. Finch diary. Aug. 8, 1949, KIL.

42. "Social Contagion in the Pool-room," 14–15, in Frederic M. Thrasher, "The Use of the Superior Boy in Research," BSH, box 11, folder 229 ("NYU Boys Club Study, 1930"), microfilm reel 6.

43. Shufeldt, "Biography of a Passive Pederast," 457.

44. "Sex Practices and Stimuli," 12–13, in Thrasher.

45. Finch diary, Jan. 3, 1951. Committee of Fourteen investigators regularly reported that even prostitutes were unwilling to engage in oral sex; see, for example, the reports on 269 1/2 W. 22nd St., May 26, 1927; tenement, 756 Eighth Ave., Dec. 4, 1928; tenement, 2544 Eighth Ave., June 21, 1928; Navarre Hotel, Seventh Ave. and 38th St., Mar. 16, 1928, box 36, COF. Not all women rejected such requests, however; see the reports on tenement, 954 Eighth Ave., Sept. 20, 1927 ("I don't make a practice of it, but if you want it, I'll accommodate you"); tenement, 42 W. 46th St., July 22, 1927; and B & G Sandwich Shop, 140 Fulton St., Dec. 19, 1927 (the woman there said "the only way I do it is the French way," explaining that she did not want to risk pregnancy), all in the same file.

46. Allan M. Brandt, *No Magic Bullet: A Social History of Venereal Disease in the United States Since 1880* (New York: Oxford University Press, 1985), ch. 2–3, provides the best account of such campaigns. On men's fear of catching a disease from a prostitute, see, for example, Report on Maxim's, 108 W. 38th St., Sept. 25, 1916, box 31, COF. In significant respects such campaigns prefigured the AIDS education campaigns of the early 1980s, which often identified sex with a gay man or an IV-drug user, rather than sex without a condom, as the source of AIDS. Such campaigns led many people to fear that the most casual contact with certain categories of people was unsafe, while reassuring them, with deadly inaccuracy, of the safety of the most intimate contact with other categories of people.

47. Report on Hanover Lunch, 2 South St., June 12, 1931, box 35, COF. Gene Harwood and Frank Burton, in discussing their memories of the 1920s and 1930s in an interview with the author, also pointed to men's fear of getting venereal diseases from women as a reason for their willingness to have sex with gay men. The sociologist Nels Anderson also reported that hoboes argued they were less likely to catch a venereal disease from homosexual than from heterosexual intercourse (*The Hobo: The Sociology of the Homeless Man* [Chicago: University of Chicago Press, 1923], 134, 147–48), a view shared by the Chicago Vice Commission in its 1911 report, *The Social Evil in Chicago*, 296–97, cited in Anderson, 148. See also Samuel Kahn, *Mentality and Homosexuality* (Boston: Meador, 1937), 50–51. For indications that this belief was of long standing, see Randolph Trumbach, "The Birth of the Queen: Sodomy and the Emergence of Gender Equality in Modern

Culture, 1660–1750," in *Hidden from History: Reclaiming the Gay and Lesbian Past*, ed. Martin Duberman, Martha Vicinus, and George Chauncey (New York: New American Library, 1989), 129–40.

48. Bulletin 1504, Mar. 24, 1922, box 88, COF.

49. Shufeldt, "Biography of a Passive Pederast," 459, 456.

50. Will Finch thought the latter, although he sometimes substituted the older Navy word *pogue* for the more generally used *punk*. As he commented of one young Norwegian sailor, an older sailor's "boy" who nonetheless ended up in bed with Finch one summer night in 1946 and made it clear he expected Finch to anally penetrate (or "brown") him: "I decided that he was either queer and *liked* to be browned or the big guy's pogue and *expected* to be browned" (Finch diary, July 4, 1946). On the widespread use of *pogue* by sailors in the World War I era to mean a man who desired to be browned, see Chauncey, "Christian Brotherhood or Sexual Perversion?" especially 192, 196. The evidence suggests that the young men to whom the term was applied fell into all three camps.

51. Alexander Berkman, *Prison Memoirs of an Anarchist* (New York: Mother Earth Publishing Association, 1912), 170, 172. Joseph F. Fishman, the first federal Inspector of Prisons and, in the late 1920s, the Deputy Commissioner of the New York City Department of Corrections, used the word *wolf* for the aggressive party in homosexual encounters in his description of prison homosexuality among non-homosexuals, in *Sex in Prison* (New York: National Library Press, 1934), 152, as did his critic, Louis Berg, *Revelations of a Prison Doctor* (New York: Milton, Balch, 1934), 120, 142. For evidence of the use of such terms among hoboes in the 1910s–1930s, see Anderson, *The Hobo*, 99, 101, 103, 144–48 (*wolf, jocker, lamb, kid, wife,* and *punk*), and *Broadway Brevities*, Nov. 9, 1931, 10. In the novel *Goldie*, a sailor approached the protagonist, who was hustling on Times Square, called himself "the slickest wolf in ther navy," and added, in reference to the hustler, "I guess I ought ter know a regular punk when I sees one" (116). The terms were also used in Los Angeles by the 1920s, according to Aaron J. Rosanoff, "Human Sexuality, Normal and Abnormal, from a Psychiatric Standpoint," *Urologic and Cutaneous Review* (1929), 528. *Punk* was also widely used in the criminal underworld beyond the prison walls, specifically to refer to the underlings in a criminal gang and more generally as an epithet; see, for example, its use in Cornelius Willemse, *Behind the Green Lights* (New York, 1931), 336–37. On the term's diffusion into general slang, see Legman, "The Language of Homosexuality," 1174. The terms were still used with similar sexual meanings in prisons in the 1970s; see Wayne S. Wooden and Jay Parker, *Men Behind Bars: Sexual Exploitation in Prison* (New York: Da Capo, 1982).

52. The distinction between "wolves" and homosexuals (or "queers") persisted. One hustler picked up in 1949 by a conventionally masculine queer, Will Finch, queried whether he were " 'just queer or a wolf,' " adding that there was "no use in 'getting up there and finding out it's no use,' " which Finch took to mean that "he won't be pedicated" (Finch diary, May 20, 1949). The hustler, in other words, insisted on remaining the man in the encounter, which he could do if he were sexually serviced by a queer, and refused to be feminized by being pedicated by a wolf. Finch's response, that he was "not a wolf—unless [the hustler] wants me to be," suggests that, at least by the postwar period, *wolf* described a sexual role as much as a social or characterological "type."

53. Report on the Seamen's Church Institute and vicinity, July 15 and 16, 1931, COF.

54. Reports on the Seamen's Church Institute and vicinity, May 27, June 22, July 2, and July 15 and 16, 1931, COF.
55. Ibid.
56. Rev. Frank Charles Laubach, "Why There Are Vagrants: Based upon an Examination of One Hundred Men" (Ph.D. diss., Columbia University, 1916), 13–14, reported that twenty-four of the hundred men were perverts. A 1935 survey of ninety men housed in a Chicago shelter for the homeless noted that "7 percent stated they were engaging in homosexual practices" (Edwin J. Sutherland and Harvey J. Locke, *Twenty Thousand Homeless Men: A Study of Unemployed Men in the Chicago Shelters* [Chicago: Lippincott, 1936], 131). The 7 percent figure is almost surely low: not only does it report the number of men who "stated" they were homosexually active, something many such men would doubtless deny to people surveying them in a homeless shelter, but the figure was produced during the Depression, when a more diverse group of men had been made homeless.
57. Dean Stiff [pseudonym of Nels Anderson], *The Milk and Honey Route: A Handbook for Hobos* (New York: Vanguard Press, 1931), 161.
58. Anderson, *The Hobo*. 145.
59. Important early efforts to investigate such social worlds from this perspective include Susan Lee Johnson's " 'The Gold She Gathered': Difference, Domination, and California's Southern Mines, 1848–1853" (Ph.D. diss., Yale University, 1993); B. R. Burg, *Sodomy and the Pirate Tradition: English Sea Rovers in the Seventeenth-Century Caribbean* (New York: New York University Press, 1984); Chad Heap, "The Melting Pot of Trampdom," unpublished seminar paper, University of Chicago, 1993.
60. Wooden and Parker, *Men Behind Bars*.
61. Berg, *Revelations of a Prison Doctor*, 137, 152–61; Kahn, *Mentality and Homosexuality*, 23–24, 129; see also Perry M. Lichtenstein, "The 'Fairy' and the Lady Lover," *Medical Review of Reviews* 27 (1921): 369–74.
62. *New York Herald Tribune*, Jan. 27, 1934, 2.
63. Berg, *Revelations of a Prison Doctor*, 161–63.
64. The raid has not received much attention from historians, but for La Guardia's appointment of Austin H. MacCormick as Commissioner of Corrections and his insistence that the Tammany influence be driven from the Corrections Department, see Lowell M. Limpus and Burr W. Leyson, *This Man La Guardia* (New York: Dutton, 1938), 378, 381, and Thomas Kessner, *Fiorello H. La Guardia and the Making of Modern New York* (New York: McGraw-Hill, 1989), ch. 8.
65. "M'Cormick Raids Welfare Island, Smashes Gangster Rule of Prison; Warden Relieved, Deputy Seized: Commissioner Discovers Top Notch Thugs Living at Ease in Hospital . . . Private Section Housing Degenerates Revealed in 'World's Worst' Bastille; Flare-Up Feared," *New York Herald Tribune*, Jan. 25, 1934, 1, 9; "McCann Admits 'Convict Rule,' " *Daily Mirror*, Jan. 26, 1934, 10. In yet another article in the same issue, "Welfare Milk Racket Bared," 3, the paper asked "why 'Greta Garbo,' alias 'Top and Bottom,' the drug-eaten former U.S. Navy gob, wears his hair to his waist." The *New York Times* also gave the prison raid extensive coverage. Although it paid less attention to the most scandalous elements, even it described the "altogether different line of contraband" found in the homosexual cell block, including "rouge, powder, mascara, perfume, even a woman's wig," and went on to describe how "several of the inmates of this cell block af-

fected long hair. Silk undergarments were found in the cells" ("Welfare Island Raid Bares Gangster Rule Over Prison; Weapons, Narcotics Found . . . Vice Carried on Openly," Jan. 25, 1934, 3).

66. In addition to the studies already cited, see Joseph F. Fishman, *Sex in Prison: Revealing Sex Conditions in American Prisons* (New York: National Library Press, 1934). The growth of interest in homosexuality in prisons may account for the publication of Samuel Kahn's study, *Mentality and Homosexuality*, in 1937, even though it had been written more than a decade earlier.

67. Thomas Mott Osborne, *Prisons and Common Sense* (Philadelphia: Lippincott, 1924), 89–90. He also recognized a third category: "the degenerates, whose dual nature [combining male and female elements] has been a problem to the psychologist since the days of ancient Greece."

68. Nelson, *Prison Days and Nights*, 157–58. Note the assumption that male and female fellators were equally anomalous and virtually interchangeable.

Questions for Reflection, Discussion, and Writing

1. As a result of the absence of the hetero–homosexual binary that characterizes our era, what was true about sex between some working-class men in the early twentieth century, according to Chauncey?

2. What did the label "fairy" indicate, who tended to be labeled a "fairy," and how did men who engaged in sex with other men avoid being labeled one?

3. What do Kinsey's findings in *Sexual Behavior in the Human Male* indicate, and in what ways does Chauncey suggest that Kinsey's findings on the male "homosexual" should be understood?

4. What differences between Jewish and Italian subcultures may have supported sex between men, according to Chauncey? What evidence does he offer to support that theory?

5. What did the act of fellatio indicate, according to Chauncey? What underlying socio-cultural beliefs supported ideas about fellatio?

6. What was the relation between "wolves" and "punks"? What did each term indicate?

7. According to Chauncey, why did men who had sex with other men at the turn of the century not all fit under one category that today we might call "homosexual"?

Related Reading

John D'Emilio, *Sexual Politics, Sexual Communities: The Making of a Homosexual Minority in the United States, 1940-1970.* Chicago, IL: U of Chicago P. 1983.

Eric Marcus, *Making History: The Struggle for Lesbian and Gay Equal Right, 1945–1990.* NY: Harper Collins. 1992.

Joseph A. Boone, "Queer Sites in Modernism: Harlem/The Left Bank/Greenwich Village" in *The Geography of Identity.* Patricia Yarger, Ed. Ann Arbor, MI: U of Michigan P. 1996. 243–72.

Charles Kaiser, *Gay Metropolis, 1940–1960.* Boston: Houghton Mifflin. 1997.

Sherrie A. Inness, "Who's Afraid of Stephen Gordon, & The Lesbian in the United States Popular Imagination" in *The Lesbian Menace: Ideology, Identity, and the Representation of Lesbian Life*. Amherst, MA: University of Massachusetts Press. 1997. 13–32

Robert J. Cooper, *Homosexuality in Cold War America: Resistance and the Crisis of Masculinity*. Durham, NC: Duke UP. 1997.

Steven Maynard, " 'Horrible Temptations': Sex, Men, and Working-Class Male Youth in Urban Ontario, 1890–1935." *Canadian Historical Review* 78 (June 1997): 191–235.

___, "Queer Musings on Masculinity and History." *Labour/Le Travail* 42 (1998): 183–197.

David Higgs, Ed., *Queer Sites: Gay Urban Histories Since 1600*. NY: Routledge. 1999.

Marc Stein, *City of Sisterly and Brotherly Loves: Lesbian and Gay Philadelphia, 1945–1972*. Chicago, IL: U of Chicago P. 2000.

Matthew Basso, Laura McCall and Dee Garceau, Eds., *Across the Great Divide: Cultures of Manhood in the American West*. NY: Routledge. 2001.

Special Topics

No one defined for the twentieth century the delicate boundaries of the masculine "normal" and the "abnormal" more than Oscar Wilde. His three trials in 1895 and his ultimate conviction on the charges of "gross indecency with a male person" turned Wilde into a transatlantic example of non-normative male sexuality, based upon a fluidity and sense of self-constructedness in the Wildean persona. Students may wish to further research this important and fascinating character.

Reading

Neil Bartlett, *Who Was That Man? A Present for Mr. Oscar Wilde*. London: Serpent's Tail. 1988.

Jeffrey Weeks, "Inverts, Perverts, and Mary-Annes: Male Prostitution and the Regulation of Homosexuality in England in the Nineteenth and Early Twentieth Centuries" in *Hidden from History: Reclaiming the Gay & Lesbian Past*. Martin Duberman, Martha Vicinus and George Chauncey, Jr., Eds. NY: NAL. 1989. 195–211.

Eve Kosofsky Sedgwick, "Some Binarisms (II): Wilde, Nietzsche, and the Sentimental Relations of the Male Body" in *Epistemology of the Closet*. Berkeley: University of California Press. 1990. 131–181.

Lawrence Danson, "Oscar Wilde, W.H., and the Unspoken Name of Love." *ELH* 58.4 (Winter 1991): 79–100.

Kevin R. Kopelson, "Wilde's Love-Deaths." *The Yale Journal of Criticism* 5.3 (Fall 1992): 31–60.

Seth Koven, "From Rough Lads to Hooligans: Boy Life, National Culture and Social Reform" in *Nationalisms and Sexualities*. Andrew Parker, Mary Russo, et al., Eds. NY: Routledge. 1992. 365–391.

Jonathan Dollimore, "Different Desires: Subjectivity and Transgression in Wilde and Gide" in *The Lesbian and Gay Studies Reader*. Henry Abelove, Michèle Aina Barale and David M. Halperin, Eds. NY: Routledge. 1993. 626–641.

Ed Cohen, *Talk on the Wilde Side: Toward A Genealogy of a Discourse on Male Sexualities.* NY: Routledge. 1993.

Gert Hekma, " 'A Female Soul in a Male Body': Sexual Inversion as Gender Inversion in Nineteenth-Century Sexology" in *Third Sex, Third Gender: Beyond Sexual Dimorphism in Culture and History.* Gilbert Herdt, Ed. NY: Zone Books. 1994. 213–239.

Christopher Lane, "Framing Fears, Reading Designs: The Homosexual Art of Painting in James, Wilde, and Beerbohm." *ELH* 61.4 (Winter 1994): 23–54.

Alan Sinfield, *The Wilde Century: Effeminacy, Oscar Wilde and the Queer Moment.* NY: Columbia UP. 1994.

_____, " 'Effeminacy' and 'Femininity': Sexual Politics in Wilde's Comedies." *Modern Drama* 37.1 (1994): 34–52.

Christopher Craft, *Another Kind of Love: Male Homosexual Desire in English Discourse, 1850–1920.* Berkeley, CA: U of California P. 1994.

Joseph Bristow, *Effeminate England: Homoerotic Writing After 1885.* NY: Columbia UP. 1995.

Jeffrey Nunokawa, "The Disappearance of the Homosexual in *The Picture of Dorian Gray*" in *Professions of Desire: Lesbian and Gay Studies in Literature.* George S. Haggerty and Bonnie Zimmerman, Eds. NY: MLA. 1995. 183–190.

Eve Kosofsky Sedgwick, "Tales of the Avunculate: Queer Tutelage in *The Importance of Being Earnest*" in *Professions of Desire: Lesbian and Gay Studies in Literature.* George S. Haggerty and Bonnie Zimmerman, Eds. NY: MLA. 1995. 191–209.

David Schulz, "Redressing Oscar: Performance and the Trials of Oscar Wilde." *The Drama Review: A Journal of Performance Studies* 40.2 (1996): 37–59.

Jeffrey Nunokawa, "The Importance of being Bored: The Dividends of Ennui in The Portrait of Dorian Gray." *Studies in the Novel* 28.3 (Fall 1996): 357–371.

David Hugh, *On Queer Street: A Social History of British Homosexuality, 1895–1995.* London: HarperCollins. 1997.

Joseph Bristow, " 'A Complex Multiform Creature': Wilde's Sexual Identities" in *The Cambridge Companion to Oscar Wilde.* Peter Raby, Ed. Cambridge, England: Cambridge UP. 1997. 195–218.

Edward S. Brinkley, "Homosexuality as (Anti)Illness: Oscar Wilde's *The Picture of Dorian Gray* and Gabriele D'Annunzio's *Il Piacere.*" *Studies in Twentieth Century Literature* 22.1 (Winter 1998): 61–82.

Don Gorton, "Wilde Paid for Henry VIII's Sins." *The Harvard Gay & Lesbian Review* 6.4 (Fall 1999): 24–28.

Chris White, Ed., *Nineteenth-Century Writings on Homosexuality.* NY: Routledge. 1999.

Rick Whitaker, "Taming the Wilde Frontier." *The Harvard Gay & Lesbian Review* 7.4 (Fall 2000): 37–39.

Film

The Picture of Dorian Gray (1945). Albert Lewin. 110 m.
The Importance of Being Earnest (1952). Anthony Asquith. 95 m.
Forbidden Passion (1976). Henry Herbert. 120 m.

Ballad of Reading Gaol (1988). Richard Kwietniowski. 12 m.
Wilde (1998). Brian Gilbert. 115 m.

Web Resource

http://classiclit.about.com/cs/wildeoscar

Sex Before Sexuality:
Pederasty, Politics, and Power
in Classical Athens

David M. Halperin

The sexual practices and institutions of the classical Greeks, along with the en-
during prestige that in modern times has traditionally surrounded their achievements, have long made them a kind of rallying point for lesbians and gay men of
the educated classes, to whom they have seemed to offer an ideological weapon
in the struggle for dignity and social acceptance. Recent scholarly attempts to bring
the Greeks within the purview of the emerging "history of sexuality" have also focused on "Greek homosexuality." Against this background, David M. Halperin
argues that in fact the Greek record confronts us with a radically unfamiliar set of
values, behaviors, and social practices. These, Halperin further argues, expose the
purely conventional character of our own social and sexual experiences, including,
most notably, "sexuality," conceived as an autonomous dimension of human life,
and "heterosexuality" and "homosexuality," understood as the fundamental organizing principles of sexual object-choice. According to Halperin, "heterosexuality" and "homosexuality" do not properly name eternal aspects of the human
psyche but represent, instead, a distinctively modern cultural production alien to
the experience of the ancient Greeks. The study of the cultural articulation of
sexual desire in classical Athens therefore calls into question the stability of the
concept of "sexuality" as a category of historical analysis.

I

In 1992, when the patriots among us will be celebrating the five hundredth anniversary of the discovery of America by Christopher Columbus, our cultural
historians may wish to mark the centenary of an intellectual landfall of almost

equal importance for the conceptual geography of the human sciences: the invention of homosexuality by Charles Gilbert Chaddock. Though he may never rank with Columbus in the annals of individual achievement, Chaddock would hardly seem to merit the obscurity that has surrounded him throughout the past hundred years. An early translator of Krafft-Ebing's *Psychopathia sexualis*, Chaddock is credited by the *Oxford English Dictionary*[1] with having introduced "homo-sexuality" into the English language in 1892, in order to render a German cognate twenty years its senior.[2] Homosexuality, for better or for worse, has been with us ever since.

Before 1892 there was no homosexuality, only sexual inversion. But, as George Chauncey, Jr., has demonstrated:

> Sexual inversion, the term used most commonly in the nineteenth century, did not denote the same conceptual phenomenon as homosexuality. "Sexual inversion" referred to a broad range of deviant gender behavior, of which homosexual desire was only a logical but indistinct aspect, while "homosexuality" focused on the narrower issue of sexual object choice. The differentiation of homosexual desire from "deviant" gender behavior at the turn of the century reflects a major reconceptualization of the nature of human sexuality, its relation to gender, and its role in one's social definition.[3]

Throughout the nineteenth century, in other words, sexual preference for a person of one's own sex was not clearly distinguished from other sorts of nonconformity to one's culturally defined sex role: Deviant objectchoice was viewed as merely one of a number of pathological symptoms exhibited by those who reversed, or "inverted," their proper sex roles by adopting a masculine or a feminine style at variance with what was deemed natural and appropriate to their anatomical sex. Political aspirations in women and (at least according to one expert writing as late as 1920) a fondness for cats in men were manifestations of a pathological condition, a kind of psychological hermaphroditism tellingly but not essentially expressed by the preference for a "normal" member of one's own sex as a sexual partner.[4]

This outlook on the matter seems to have been shared by the scientists and by their unfortunate subjects alike: Inversion was not merely a medical rubric, then, but a category of lived experience. Karl Heinrich Ulrichs, for example, an outspoken advocate for the freedom of sexual choice and the founder, as early as 1862, of the cult of Uranism (based on Pausanias's praise of Uranian, or "heavenly," pederasty in Plato's *Symposium*), described his own condition as that of an *anima muliebris virili corpore inclusa*—a woman's soul confined by a man's body. That sexual object-choice might be wholly independent of such "secondary" characteristics as masculinity or femininity never seems to have occurred to anyone until Havelock Ellis waged a campaign to isolate object-choice from role-playing and, concurrently, Freud, in his classic analysis of a

Note: Originally published, in different form, as "One Hundred Years of Homosexuality" in *The Mêtis of the Greeks*, ed. Milad Doueihi, *Diacritics*, 16, no. 2 (Summer 1986): 34–45.

drive in the *Three Essays* (1905), clearly distinguished in the case of the libido between the sexual "object" and the sexual "aim."[5]

The conceptual isolation of sexuality per se from questions of masculinity and femininity made possible a new taxonomy of sexual behaviors and psychologies based entirely on the anatomical sex of the persons engaged in a sexual act (same sex vs. different sex); it thereby obliterated a number of distinctions that had traditionally operated within earlier discourses pertaining to same-sex sexual contacts and that had radically differentiated active from passive sexual partners, normal from abnormal (or conventional from unconventional) sexual roles, masculine from feminine styles, and pederasty from lesbianism: All such behaviors were now to be classed alike and placed under the same heading.[6] Sexual identity was thus polarized around a central opposition defined by the binary play of sameness and difference in the sexes of the sexual partners; people belonged henceforward to one or the other of two exclusive categories, and much ingenuity was lavished on the multiplication of techniques for deciphering what a person's sexual orientation "really" was—independent, that is, of beguiling appearances.[7] Founded on positive, ascertainable, and objective behavioral phenomena—on the facts of who had sex with whom—the new sexual taxonomy could lay claim to a descriptive, trans-historical validity. And so it crossed the "threshold of scientificity"[8] and was enshrined as a working concept in the social sciences[9]

A scientific advance of such magnitude naturally demanded to be crowned by the creation of a new technical vocabulary, but, unfortunately, no objective, value-free words readily lent themselves to the enterprise. In 1891, just one year before the inauguration of "homosexuality," John Addington Symonds could still complain that "The accomplished languages of Europe in the nineteenth century supply no terms for this persistent feature of human psychology, without importing some implication of disgust, disgrace, vituperation."[10] A number of linguistic candidates were quickly put forward to make good this lack, and "homosexuality" (despite scattered protests over the years) gradually managed to fix its social-scientistic signature upon the new conceptual dispensation. The word itself, as Havelock Ellis noted, is a barbarous neologism sprung from a monstrous mingling of Greek and Latin stock,[11] as such, it belongs to a rapidly growing lexical breed most prominently represented by the hybrid names given to other recent inventions—names whose mere enumeration suffices to conjure up the precise historical era responsible for producing them: e.g., "automobile," "television."

Unlike the language of technology, however, the new terminology for describing sexual behavior was slow to take root in the culture at large. In his posthumous autobiographical memoir, *My Father and Myself* (1968), J. R. Ackerley recalls how mystified he was when, about 1918, a Swiss friend asked him, "Are you homo or hetero?": "I had never heard either term before," he writes. Similarly, T. C. Worsley observes in his own memoir, *Flannelled Fool* (1966), that in 1929 "The word [homosexual], in any case, was not in general use, as it is now. Then it was still a technical term, the implications of which I was not entirely aware of."[12] These two memoirists, moreover, were not intellectually deficient men: At the respective times of their recorded bewilderment, Ackerley was shortly about to be, and Worsley already had been, educated at Cambridge. Nor was such innocence limited—in this one instance, at least—to the holders of university degrees: The British sociologist John Marshall, whose survey presumably draws on more popular sources, testifies that "a number of the elderly men I interviewed had never heard the term 'homosexual' until the 1950s."[13] The *Oxford English Dictionary*, originally published in 1933, is also ignorant of (if not willfully blind to) "homosexuality"; the word appears for the first time in the *OED*'s 1976 three-volume Supplement.[14]

It is not exactly my intention to argue that homosexuality, as we commonly understand it today, didn't exist before 1892. How, indeed, could it have failed to exist? The very word displays a most workmanlike and scientific indifference to cultural and environmental factors, looking only to the sexes of the persons engaged in the sexual act. Moreover, if homosexuality didn't exist before 1892, heterosexuality couldn't have existed either (it came into being, in fact, like Eve from Adam's rib, eight years later),[15] and without heterosexuality, where would all of us be right now?

The comparatively recent genesis of heterosexuality—strictly speaking, a twentieth-century affair—should provide a clue to the profundity of the cultural issues over which, hitherto, I have been so lightly skating. How is it possible that until the year 1900 there was not a precise, value-free, scientific term available to speakers of the English language for designating what we would now regard, in retrospect, as the mode of sexual behavior favored by the vast majority of people in our culture? Any answer to that question—which, in its broadest dimensions, I shall leave for the intellectual heirs of Michel Foucault to settle—must direct our attention to the inescapable historicity of even the most innocent, unassuming, and seemingly objective of cultural representations. Although a blandly descriptive, rigorously clinical term like "homosexuality" would appear to be unobjectionable as a taxonomic device, it carries with it a heavy complement of ideological baggage and has, in fact, proved a significant obstacle to understanding the distinctive features of sexual life in the ancient world.[16] It may well be that homosexuality properly speaking has no history of its own much before the beginning of our century. For, as John Boswell remarks, "If the categories 'homosexual/heterosexual' and 'gay/straight' are the inventions of particular societies rather than real aspects of the human psyche, there is no gay history."[17]

II

Of course, if we are to believe Foucault, there are basic historical and cultural factors that prohibit the easy application of the concept of homosexuality to persons living in premodern societies. For homosexuality presupposes sexuality:

It implies the existence of a separate, sexual domain within the larger field of man's psychophysical nature and it requires the conceptual demarcation and isolation of that domain from other, more traditional, territories of personal and social life that cut across it, such as carnality, venery, libertinism, virility, passion, amorousness, eroticism, intimacy, love, affection, appetite, and desire—to name but a few. The invention of homosexuality therefore had to await, in the first place, the eighteenth-century discovery and definition of sexuality as the total ensemble of physiological and psychological mechanisms governing the individual's genital functions and the concomitant identification of that ensemble with a specially developed part of the brain and nervous system; it had also to await, in the second place, the early-nineteenth-century interpretation of sexuality as a singular "instinct" or "drive," a mute force that shapes our conscious life according to its own unassailable logic and thereby determines, at least in part, the character and personality of each one of us.[18]

Before the scientific construction of "sexuality" as a positive, distinct, and constitutive feature of individual human beings—an autonomous system within the physiological and psychological economy of the human organism—a person's sexual *acts* could be individually evaluated and categorized, but there was no conceptual apparatus available for identifying a person's fixed and determinate sexual *orientation*, much less for assessing and classifying it.[19] That human beings differ, often markedly, from one another in their sexual tastes in a great variety of ways (of which the liking for a sexual partner of a specific sex is only one, and not necessarily the most significant one) is an unexceptionable and, indeed, an ancient observation,[20] but it is not immediately evident that differences in sexual preference are by their very nature more revealing about the temperament of individual human beings, more significant determinants of personal identity, than, for example, differences in dietary preference.[21] And yet, it would never occur to us to refer a person's dietary object-choice to some innate, characterological disposition or to see in his or her strongly expressed and even unvarying preference for the white meat of chicken the symptom of a profound psychophysical orientation, leading us to identify him or her in contexts quite removed from that of the eating of food as, say, a "pectoriphage" or a "stethovore" (to continue the practice of combining Greek and Latin roots); nor would we be likely to inquire further, making nicer discriminations according to whether an individual's predilection for chicken breasts expressed itself in a tendency to eat them quickly or slowly, seldom or often, alone or in company, under normal circumstances or only in periods of great stress, with a clear or a guilty conscience ("ego-dystonic pectoriphagia"), beginning in earliest childhood or originating with a gastronomic trauma suffered in adolescence.[22] If such questions did occur to us, moreover, I very much doubt whether we would turn to the academic disciplines of anatomy, neurology, clinical psychology, or genetics in the hope of obtaining a clear causal solution to them. That is because (1) we regard the liking for certain foods as a matter of taste; (2) we currently lack a theory of taste; and (3) in the absence of a theory we do not normally subject our behavior to intense scientific or etiological scrutiny.

In the same way, it never occurred to premodern cultures to ascribe a person's sexual tastes to some positive, structural, or constitutive feature of his or her personality. Just as we tend to assume that human beings are not individuated at the level of dietary preference and that we all, despite many pronounced and frankly acknowledged differences from one another in dietary habits, share the same fundamental set of alimentary appetites, and hence the same "dieticity" or "edility," so most premodern and non-Western cultures, despite an awareness of the range of possible variations in human sexual behavior, refuse to individuate human beings at the level of sexual preference and assume, instead, that we all share the same fundamental set of sexual appetites, the same "sexuality." For most of the world's inhabitants, in other words, "sexuality" is no more a fact of life than "dieticity." Far from being a necessary or intrinsic constituent of the eternal grammar of human subjectivity, "sexuality" seems to be a uniquely modern, Western, even bourgeois production—one of those cultural fictions that in every society give human beings access to themselves as meaningful actors in their world, and that are thereby objectivated.

At any rate, positivism dies hard, and sexual essentialism (the belief in fixed sexual essences) dies even harder. Not everyone will welcome a neohistoricist critique of "sexuality." John Boswell, for example, has argued reasonably enough that any debate over the existence of universals in human culture must distinguish between the respective modes of being proper to words, concepts, and experiences: According to this line of reasoning, the ancients experienced gravity even though they lacked both the term and the concept; similarly, Boswell claims that the "manifest and stated purpose" of Aristophanes' famous myth in Plato's *Symposium* "is to explain why humans are divided into groups of predominantly homosexual or heterosexual interest," and so this text, along with a number of others, vouches for the existence of homosexuality as an ancient (if not a universal) category of human experience—however newfangled the word for it may be.[23] Now the speech of Plato's Aristophanes would seem indeed to be a *locus classicus* for the differentiation of homo from heterosexuality, because Aristophanes' taxonomy of human beings features a distinction between those who desire a sexual partner of the same sex as themselves and those who desire a sexual partner of a different sex. The Platonic passage alone, then, would seem to offer sufficient warrant for positing an ancient concept, if not an ancient experience, of homosexuality. But closer examination reveals that Aristophanes stops short of deriving a distinction between homo- and heterosexuality from his own myth just when the logic of his analysis would seem to have driven him ineluctably to it. That omission is telling—and it is worth considering in greater detail.

According to Aristophanes, human beings were originally round, eight-limbed creatures, with two faces and two sets of genitals—both front and back—and three sexes (male, female, and androgyne). These ancestors of ours were powerful and ambitious; in order to put them in their place, Zeus had them cut in two, their skin stretched over the exposed flesh and tied at the navel, and their heads rotated so as to keep that physical reminder of their dar-

ing and its consequences constantly before their eyes. The severed halves of
each former individual, once reunited, clung to one another so desperately and
concerned themselves so little with their survival as separate entities that they
began to perish for lack of sustenance; those who outlived their mates sought
out persons belonging to the same sex as their lost complements and repeated
their embraces in a foredoomed attempt to recover their original unity. Zeus at
length took pity on them, moved their genitals to the side their bodies now
faced, and invented sexual intercourse, so that the bereaved creatures might at
least put a temporary terminus to their longing and devote their attention to
other, more important (if less pressing) matters. Aristophanes extracts from this
story a genetic explanation of observable differences among human beings with
respect to sexual object-choice and preferred style of life: males who desire females are descended from an original androgyne (adulterers come from this
species), whereas males descended from an original male "pursue their own
kind, and would prefer to remain single and spend their entire lives with one
another, since by nature they have no interest in marriage and procreation but
are compelled to engage in them by social custom" (191e–192b, quoted selectively). Boswell, understandably, interprets this to mean that, according to
Plato's Aristophanes, homosexual and heterosexual interests are "both exclusive
and innate."[24]

But that, significantly, is not quite the way Aristophanes sees it. The conclusions that he draws from his own myth help to illustrate the lengths to which
classical Athenians were willing to go in order to avoid conceptualizing sexual
behaviors according to a binary opposition between different- and same-sex
sexual contacts. First of all, Aristophanes' myth generates not two but at least
three distinct "sexualities" (males attracted to males, females attracted to females, and—consigned alike to a single classification, evidently—males attracted to females as well as females attracted to males). Moreover, there is not
the slightest suggestion in anything Aristophanes says that the sexual acts or
preferences of persons descended from an original female are in any way similar
to, let alone congruent or isomorphic with, the sexual acts or preferences of
those descended from an original male;[25] hence, nothing in the text allows us to
suspect the existence of even an implicit category to which males who desire
males and females who desire females *both* belong in contradistinction to some
other category containing males and females who desire one another.[26] On the
contrary, one consequence of the myth is to make the sexual desire of every
human being *formally identical* to that of every other: We are all looking for the
same thing in a sexual partner, according to Plato's Aristophanes—namely, a
symbolic substitute for an originary object once loved and subsequently lost in
an archaic trauma. In that respect we all share the same "sexuality"—which is to
say that, despite the differences in our personal preferences or tastes, we are not
individuated at the level of our sexual being.

Second, and equally important, Aristophanes' account features a crucial
distinction *within* the category of males who are attracted to males, an infra-

structural detail missing from his description of each of the other two categories: "while they are still boys [i.e., pubescent or preadult],[27] they are fond of men, and enjoy lying down together with them and twining their limbs about them, . . . but when they become men they are lovers of boys. . . . Such a man is a pederast and philerast [i.e., fond of or responsive to adult male lovers]"[28] at *different stages of his life* (*Symposium* 191e–192b, quoted selectively). Contrary to the clear implications of the myth, in other words, and unlike the people comprehended by the first two categories, those descended from an original male are *not* attracted to one another *without qualification;* rather, they desire boys when they are men and they take a certain (nonsexual) pleasure in physical contact with men when they are boys.[29] Now since—as the foregoing passage suggests—the classical Athenians sharply distinguished the roles of pederast and philerast, relegating them not only to different age-classes but virtually to different "sexualities,"[30] what Aristophanes is describing here is not a single, homogeneous sexual orientation common to all those who descend from an original male but rather a set of distinct and incommensurable behaviors that such persons exhibit in different periods of their lives; although his genetic explanation of the diversity of sexual object-choice among human beings would seem to require that there be some adult males who are sexually attracted to other adult males, Aristophanes appears to be wholly unaware of such a possibility, and in any case he has left no room for it in his taxonomic scheme.[31] That omission is all the more unexpected because, as Boswell himself has pointed out (in response to the present argument), the archetypal pairs of lovers from whom all homoerotically inclined males are supposed to descend must themselves have been the same age as one another, inasmuch as they were originally halves of the same being.[32] No age-matched couples figure among their latter-day offspring, however: The social reality described by Aristophanes features an erotic asymmetry absent from the mythical paradigm used to generate it. In the world of contemporary Athenian actuality—at least, as Aristophanes portrays it—reciprocal erotic desire among males is unknown.[33] Those who descend from an original male are not defined as male homosexuals but as willing boys when they are young and as lovers of youths when they are old. Contrary to Boswell's reading of the passage, then, neither the concept nor the experience of "homosexuality" is known to Plato's Aristophanes.

A similar conclusion can be drawn from careful examination of the other document from antiquity that might seem to vouch for the existence both of homosexuality as an indigenous category and of homosexuals as a native species. Unlike the myth of Plato's Aristophanes, a famous and much-excerpted passage from a classic work of Greek prose, the document to which I refer is little known and almost entirely neglected by modern historians of "sexuality";[34] its date is late, its text is corrupt, and, far from being a self-conscious literary artifact, it forms part of a Roman technical treatise. But despite its distance from Plato in time, in style, in language, and in intent, it displays the same remarkable innocence of modern sexual categories, and I have chosen to discuss it here partly in order to show what can be learned about the ancient world from texts that lie outside the received canon of classical authors. Let us turn, then, to the ninth chapter in the Fourth Book of *De morbis chronicis*, a mid-fifth-century A.D. Latin translation and adaptation by the African writer Caelius Aurelianus of a now largely lost work on chronic diseases by the Greek physician Soranus, who practiced and taught in Rome during the early part of the second century A.D.

The topic of this chapter is *molles* (*malthakoi* in Greek)—that is, "soft" or unmasculine men who depart from the cultural norm of manliness insofar as they actively desire to be subjected by other men to a "feminine" (i.e., receptive) role in sexual intercourse. Caelius begins with an implicit defense of his own unimpeachable masculinity by noting how difficult it is to believe that such people actually exist;[35] he then goes on to observe that the cause of their affliction is not natural (that is, organic) but is rather their own excessive desire, which—in a desperate and foredoomed attempt to satisfy itself—drives out their sense of shame and forcibly converts parts of their bodies to sexual uses not intended by nature. These men willingly adopt the dress, gait, and other characteristics of women, thereby confirming that they suffer not from a bodily disease but from a mental (or moral) defect. After some further arguments in support of that point, Caelius draws an interesting comparison: "For just as the women called *tribades* [in Greek], because they practise both kinds of sex, are more eager to have sexual intercourse with women than with men and pursue women with an almost masculine jealousy . . . so they too [i.e., the *molles*] are afflicted by a mental disease" (132–133). The mental disease in question, which strikes both men and women alike and is defined as a perversion of sexual desire, would certainly seem to be nothing other than homosexuality as it is often understood today.

Several considerations combine to prohibit that interpretation, however. First of all, what Caelius treats as a pathological phenomenon is not the desire on the part of either men or women for sexual contact with a person of the same sex; quite the contrary: Elsewhere, in discussing the treatment of satyriasis (a state of abnormally elevated sexual desire accompanied by itching or tension in the genitals), he issues the following advice to people who suffer from it (*De morbis acutis*, 3.18.180–181).[36]

> Do not admit visitors and particularly young women and boys. For the attractiveness of such visitors would again kindle the feeling of desire in the patient. Indeed, *even healthy persons*, seeing them, would in many cases seek sexual gratification, stimulated by the tension produced in the parts [i.e., in their own genitals].[37]

There is nothing medically problematical, then, about a desire on the part of males to obtain sexual pleasure from contact with males; what is of concern to Caelius,[38] as well as to other ancient moralists,[39] is the male desire to be sexually penetrated by males, for such a desire represents the voluntary abandonment of a "masculine" identity in favor of a "feminine" one. It is sex-role reversal, or *gender deviance*, that is problematized here and that also furnishes part of the basis for Caelius's comparison of *molles* to *tribades*, who assume a "masculine" role in their relations with other women and actively "pursue women with an almost *masculine* jealousy." Indeed, the "soft"—that is, sexually submissive—man, possessed of a shocking and paradoxical desire to surrender his masculine autonomy and precedence, is monstrous precisely because he seems to have "a woman's soul confined by a man's body" and thus to violate the deeply felt and somewhat anxiously defended sense of congruence on the part of the ancients between gender, sexual practices, and social identity.[40]

Second, the ground of the similitude between Caelius's *molles* and *tribades* is not that they are both homosexual but rather that they are both *bi*sexual (in our terms). The *tribades* "are *more* eager to have sexual intercourse with women *than with men*" and "practise both kinds of sex"—that is, they have sex with both men and women.[41] As for the *molles,* Caelius's earlier remarks about their extra-ordinarily intense sexual desire implies that they turn to receptive sex because, although they try, they are not able to satisfy themselves by means of more conventionally masculine sorts of sexual activity, including insertive sex with women,[42] far from having desires that are structured differently from those of normal folk, these gender-deviants desire sexual pleasure just as most people do, but they have such strong and intense desires that they are driven to devise some unusual and disreputable (though ultimately futile) means of gratifying them. That diagnosis becomes explicit at the conclusion of the chapter when Caelius explains why the disease responsible for turning men into *molles* is the only chronic disease that becomes stronger as the body grows older (137).

> For in other years when the body is still strong and can perform the normal functions of love, the sexual desire [of these persons] assumes a dual aspect, in which the soul is excited sometimes while playing a passive and sometimes while playing an active role. But in the case of old men who have lost their virile powers, all their sexual desire is turned in the opposite direction and consequently exerts a stronger demand for the feminine role in love. In fact, many infer that this is the reason why boys too are victims of this affliction. For, like old men, they do not possess virile powers; that is, they have not yet attained those powers which have already deserted the aged.[43]

"Soft" or unmasculine men, far from being a fixed and determinate sexual species, are evidently either men who once experienced an orthodoxly masculine sexual desire in the past or who will eventually experience such a desire in the future. They may well be men with a constitutional tendency to gender-deviance, according to Caelius, but they are not homosexuals. Moreover, all the other ancient texts known to me that place in the same category both males who enjoy sexual contact with males and females who enjoy sexual contact with females display one or the other of the two taxonomic strategies employed by Caelius Aurelianus: If such men and women are classified alike, it is either because they are both held to *reverse* their proper sex roles and to adopt the sexual styles, postures, and modes of copulation conventionally associated with the opposite sex or because they are both held to *alternate* between the personal characteristics and sexual practices proper, respectively, to men and to women.[44] No category of homosexuality, defined in such a way as to contain men and women alike, is indigenous to the ancient world.

No scruple need prevent *us*, to be sure, from qualifying as "homosexual" any person who seeks sexual contact with another person of the name sex, whether male or female. But the issue before us isn't whether or not we can accurately apply our concept of homosexuality to the ancients—whether or not, that is, we can discover in the historical record of classical antiquity evidence of behaviors or psychologies that are amenable to classification in our own terms (obviously, we can, given the supposedly descriptive and trans-historical nature of those terms); the issue isn't even whether or not the ancients were able to express within the terms provided by their own conceptual schemes an experience of something approximating to homosexuality as we understand it today.[45] The real issue confronting any cultural historian of antiquity, and any critic of contemporary culture, is, first of all, how to recover the terms in which the experiences of individuals belonging to past societies were actually constituted and, second, how to measure and assess the differences between those terms and the ones we currently employ. For, as this very controversy over the scope and applicability of sexual categories illustrates, concepts in the human sciences—unlike in this respect, perhaps, concepts in the natural sciences (such as gravity)—do not merely describe reality but, at least partly, constitute it.[46] What this implies about the issue before us may sound paradoxical, but it is, I believe, profound—or, at least, worth pondering: Although there have been, in many different times and places (including classical Athens), persons who sought sexual contact with other persons of the same sex as themselves, it is only within the last hundred years or so that such persons (or some portion of them) have been homosexuals.

Instead of attempting to trace the history of "homosexuality" as if it were a *thing*, therefore, we might more profitably analyze how the significance of same-sex sexual contacts has been variously constructed over time by members of human living groups. Such an analysis will probably lead us into a plurality of only partly overlapping social and conceptual territories, a series of cultural formations that vary as their constituents change, combine in different sequences, or compose new patterns. In the following paragraphs I shall attempt to draw a very crude outline of the cultural formation underlying the classical Athenian institution of pederasty, an outline whose details will have to be filled in at some later point if this aspect of ancient Greek social relations is ever to be understood historically.

III

The attitudes and behaviors publicly displayed by the citizens of Athens (to whom the surviving evidence for the classical period effectively restricts our power to generalize) tend to portray sex not as a collective enterprise in which two or more persons jointly engage but rather as an action performed by one person upon another. The foregoing statement does not purport to describe positively what the experience of sex was "really" like for all members of Athenian society but to indicate how sex is *represented* by those utterances and actions of free adult males that were intended to be overheard and witnessed by other free adult males.[47] Sex, as it is constituted by this public, masculine discourse, is either act or impact: It is not knit up in a web of mutuality, not something one invariably has *with* someone. Even the verb *aphrodisiazein*, meaning "to have sex" or "to take active sexual pleasure," is carefully differentiated into an active and a passive form; the active form occurs, tellingly, in a late antique list (that we nonetheless have good reason to consider representative for ancient Mediterranean culture, rather than eccentric to it)[48] of acts that "do not regard one's neighbors but only the subjects themselves and are not done in regard to or through others: namely, speaking, singing, dancing, fist-fighting, competing, hanging oneself, dying, being crucified, diving, finding a treasure, having sex, vomiting, moving one's bowels, sleeping, laughing, crying, talking to the gods, and the like."[49] As John J. Winkler, in a commentary on this passage, observes, "It is not that second parties are not present at some of these events (speaking, boxing, competing, having sex, being crucified, flattering one's favorite divinity), but that their successful achievement does not depend on the cooperation, much less the benefit, of a second party."[50]

Not only is sex in classical Athens not intrinsically relational or collaborative in character; it is, further, a deeply polarizing experience: It serves to divide, to classify, and to distribute its participants into distinct and radically dissimilar categories. Sex possesses this valence, apparently, because it is conceived to center essentially on, and to define itself around, an asymmetrical gesture, that of the penetration of the body of one person by the body—and, specifically, by the phallus[51]—of another. Phallic penetration, moreover, is construed as sexual "activity"; even if a sexual act does not involve physical penetration, it still remains polarized by the distribution of phallic pleasure: The partner whose pleasure is promoted is considered "active," while the partner who puts his or her body *at the service* of another's pleasure is deemed "passive"—read "penetrated," in the culture's unself-conscious ideological shorthand. Sexual penetration, and sexual "activity" in general, are, in other words, thematized as domination: The relation between the "active" and the "passive" sexual partner is thought of as the same kind of relation as that obtaining between social superior and social inferior, between master and servant.[52] "Active" and "passive" sexual roles are therefore necessarily isomorphic with superordinate and subordinate social status; hence, an adult, male citizen of Athens can have legitimate sexual relations only with statutory minors (his inferiors not in age but in social and political status): The proper targets of his sexual desire include, specifically, women, boys, foreigners, and slaves—all of them persons who do not enjoy the same legal and political rights and privileges that he does.[53] Furthermore, what a citizen does in bed reflects the differential in status that distinguishes him from his sexual partner: The citizen's superior prestige and authority express themselves by his sexual precedence—by his power to initiate a sexual act, his right to obtain pleasure from it, and his assumption of an "active" sexual role. What Paul Veyne has said about the Romans can apply equally well to the classical Athenians: They were indeed puritans when it came to sex, but (unlike modern bourgeois Westerners) they were not puritans about conjugality and reproduction; rather, like many Mediterranean peoples, they were puritans about virility.[54]

The very enterprise of inquiring into ancient Greek "sexuality," then, necessarily obscures the nature of the phenomenon it is designed to elucidate because it effectively isolates sexual norms from social practices and thereby conceals the strict sociological correspondences between them. In classical Athens sex, as we have seen, was not simply a private quest for mutual pleasure that absorbed, if only temporarily, the social identities of its participants. Sex was a manifestation of public status, a declaration of social identity; it did not so much express an individual's unique "sexuality" as it served to position social actors in the places assigned to them (by virtue of their political standing) in the hierarchical structure of the Athenian polity. Instead of reflecting the peculiar sexual orientation of individual Athenians, the sexual protocols of classical Athens reflected a marked division in the social organization of the city-state between a superordinate group, composed of citizens, and a subordinate group, composed of noncitizens; sex between members of the first group was practically inconceivable, whereas sex between a member of the first group and a member of the second group mirrored in the minute details of its hierarchical arrangement the relation of structured inequality that governed their wider social interaction. Far from being interpreted as an expression of commonality, as a sign of some shared sexual status or orientation, sex between social superordinate and subordinate served, at least in part, to articulate the social distance between them. To assimilate both the senior and the junior partner in a pederastic relationship to the same "sexuality," for example, would therefore have struck a classical Athenian as no less bizarre than to classify a burglar as an "active criminal," his victim as a "passive criminal," and the two of them alike as partners in crime[55] (burglary—like sex, as the Greeks understood it—is, after all, a "nonrelational" act). The sexual identities of the ancient Greeks—their experiences of themselves as sexual actors and as desiring human beings—were hardly autonomous; quite the contrary: They were inseparable from, if not determined by, their social identities, their outward, public standing. Indeed, the classical Greek record strongly supports the conclusion drawn (from a quite different body of evidence) by the French anthropologist Maurice Godelier: "It is not sexuality which haunts society, but society which haunts the body's sexuality."[56]

In classical Athens, then, sexual partners came in two different kinds—not male and female but active and passive, dominant and submissive.[57] The relevant features of a sexual object were not so much determined by a physical typology of genders as by the social articulation of power. That is why the currently fashionable distinction between homosexuality and heterosexuality had no meaning for the classical Athenians: There were not, so far as they knew, two different kinds of "sexuality," two differently structured psychosexual states or modes of affective orientation, but a single form of sexual experience, which all free adult males shared—making due allowance for variations in individual tastes, as one might make for individual palates. Thus, in the Third Dithyramb by the classical poet Bacchylides, the Athenian hero Theseus, voyaging to Crete among the seven youths and seven maidens destined for the Minotaur and defending one of the maidens from the sexual advances of the libidinous Cretan commander, warns him vehemently against molesting *any one* of the Athenian youths (*tin' êitheôn:* 43)—that is, any girl *or boy.* Conversely, the antiquarian *littérateur* Athenaeus, writing six or seven hundred years later, is amazed that Polycrates, the tyrant of Samos in the sixth century B.C., did not send for any boys *or women* along with the other luxury articles he imported to Samos for his personal use during his reign, "despite his passion for relations with males" (12.540c–e).[58] Now *both* the notion that an act of heterosexual aggression in itself makes the aggressor suspect of homosexual tendencies *and* the mirror-opposite notion that a person with marked homosexual tendencies is bound to hanker after heterosexual contacts are nonsensical to us, associating as we do sexual object-choice with a determinate kind of "sexuality," a fixed sexual nature, but it would be a monumental task indeed to enumerate all the ancient documents in which the alternative "boy or woman" occurs with perfect nonchalance in an erotic context, as if the two were functionally interchangeable.[59] Scholars sometimes describe this cultural formation as a bisexuality of penetration[60] or as a heterosexuality indifferent to its object,[61] but I think it would be more accurate to describe it as a single, undifferentiated phallic "sexuality" of penetration and domination, a socio-sexual discourse whose basic terms are phallus and non-phallus.[62]

If there is a lesson that historians should draw from this picture of ancient sexual attitudes and behaviors, it is that we need to de-center *sexuality* from the focus of the interpretation of sexual experience. Just because modern bourgeois Westerners are so obsessed with sexuality, so convinced that it holds the key to the hermeneutics of the self (and hence to social psychology as an object of historical study), we ought not therefore to conclude that everyone has always considered sexuality a basic and irreducible element in, or a central feature of, human life. On the contrary, if the sketch I have offered is accurate, it seems that many ancients conceived of "sexuality" in nonsexual terms: What was fundamental to their experience of sex was not anything *we* would regard as essentially sexual; rather, it was something essentially social—namely, the modality of power relations that informed and structured the sexual act. Instead of viewing public and political life as a dramatization of individual sexual psychology, as we often tend to do, they saw sexual behavior as an expression of the dominant themes in contemporary social relations. When Artemidorus, a master dream analyst who lived and wrote in the second century A.D., came to address the meaning of sexual dreams, for example, he almost never presumed that such dreams were *really* about sex: They were about the rise and fall of the dreamer's public fortunes, the vicissitudes of his domestic economy.[63] If a man dreams of having sex with his mother, according to Artemidorus, his dream signifies nothing in particular about his own sexual psychology, his fantasy life, or the history of his relations with his parents; it may signify—depending on the family's circumstances at the time, the sexual postures of the partners in the dream, and the mode of penetration—that the dreamer will be successful in politics, that he will go into exile or return from exile, that he will win his lawsuit, obtain a rich harvest from his lands, or change professions, among many other things (1.79). Artemidorus' system of dream interpretation begs to be compared to the indigenous dream lore of certain Amazonian tribes, equally innocent of "sexuality," who (despite their quite different socio-sexual systems) also believe in the predictive value of dreams and similarly reverse what modern bourgeois Westerners take to be the natural flow of signification in dreams (i.e., from what is public and social to what is private and sexual): in both Kagwahiv and Mehinaku culture, for example, dreaming about the female genitalia portends a wound; dreamt wounds do not symbolize the female genitalia.[64]

To discover and to write the history of sexuality has long seemed to many a sufficiently radical undertaking in itself, inasmuch as its effect (if not the intention behind it) is to call into question the very naturalness of what we currently take to be essential to our individual natures. But in the course of implementing that ostensibly radical project many historians of sexuality seem to have reversed—perhaps unwittingly—its radical design: By preserving "sexuality" as a stable category of historical analysis not only have they not denaturalized it but, on the contrary, they have newly idealized it.[65] To the extent, in fact, that histories of "sexuality" succeed in concerning themselves with *sexuality*, to just that extent are they doomed to fail as *histories* (Foucault himself taught us that much), unless they also include as an integral part of their proper enterprise the task of demonstrating the historicity, conditions of emergence, modes of construction, and ideological contingencies of the very categories of analysis that undergird their own practice.[66] Instead of concentrating our attention specifically on the history of sexuality, then, we need to define and refine a new, and radical, historical sociology of psychology, an intellectual discipline designed to analyze the cultural poetics of desire, by which I mean the processes whereby sexual desires are constructed, mass-produced, and distributed among the various members of human living-groups.[67] We must train ourselves to recognize conventions of feeling as well as conventions of behavior and to interpret the intricate texture of personal life as an artefact, as the determinate outcome, of a complex and arbitrary constellation of cultural processes. We must, in short, be willing to admit that what seem to be our most inward, authentic, and private experiences are actually, in Adrienne Rich's admirable phrase, "shared, unnecessary/and political."[68]

Notes

1. Wrongly, no doubt: The same entry in the *OED* records the use of the word by J. A. Symonds in a letter of the same year, and so it is most unlikely that Chaddock alone is responsible for its English coinage. See R. W. Burchfield, ed., *A Supplement to the Oxford English Dictionary* (Oxford. 1976), 2:136, s.v. homosexuality.

2. The terms "homosexual" and "homosexuality" appeared in print for the first time in 1869 in two anonymous pamphlets published in Leipzig and composed, apparently, by Karl Maria Kertbeny. Kertbeny (né Benkert) was an Austro-Hungarian translator and *littérateur* of Bavarian extraction, not a physician (as Magnus Hirschfeld and Havelock Ellis—misled by false clues planted in those pamphlets by Kertbeny himself—maintained); he wrote in German under his acquired Hungarian surname and claimed (rather unconvincingly) in the second of the two tracts under discussion not to share the sexual tastes denominated by his own ingenious neologism. For the most reliable accounts of Kertbeny and his invention, see Manfred Herzer, "Kertbeny and the Nameless Love," *Journal of Homosexuality*, 12.1 (1985): 1–26, and, now, Hubert Kennedy, *Ulrichs: The Life and Works of Karl Henrich Ulrichs, Pioneer of the Modern Gay Movement* (Boston, 1988). pp. 149–56. See also John Lauritsen and David Thorstad, *The Early Homosexual Rights Movement (1864–1935)* (New York: Times Change Press, 1974), pp. 6–8; Jean-Claude Féray, "Une histoire critique du mot homosexualité," *Arcadie* 28, nos. 325–28 (1981): 11–21, 115–24, 171–81, 246–58; Wayne Dynes, *Homolexis: A Historical and Cultural Lexicon of Homosexuality*, Gai Saber Monograph No. 4 (New York: Gay Academic Union, 1985), p. 67, who notes that Kertbeny's term "might have gone unnoticed had not [Kertbeny's friend] Gustav Jaeger popularized it in the second edition of his *Entdeckung der Seele* (1880)." The earlier of Kertbeny's two pamphlets is reprinted in the *Jahrbuch für sexuelle Zwischenstufen* 7 (1905): 1–66.

3. George Chauncey, Jr., "From Sexual Inversion to Homosexuality: Medicine and the Changing Conceptualization of Female Deviance," in *Homosexuality: Sacrilege, Vision, Politics*, ed. Robert Boyers and George Steiner = *Salmagundi* 58–59 (1982–83): 114–46 (quotation on p. 116). Cf. Michel Foucault, *The History of Sexuality, Volume I: An Introduction*, trans. Robert Hurley (New York, 1978), pp. 37–38; Féray "Une histoire," esp. pp. 16–17, 246–56; Jeffrey Weeks, "Discourse, Desire and Sexual Deviance: Some Problems in a History of Homosexuality," in *The Making of the Modern Homosexual*, ed. Kenneth Plummer (London: Hutchinson, 1981), pp. 76–111, esp. 82ff.; John Marshall, "Pansies, Perverts and Macho Men: Changing Conceptions of Male Homosexuality," in *The Making of the Modern Homosexual*, pp. 133–54; Arnold I. Davidson, "Closing Up the Corpses: Diseases of Sexuality and the Emergence of the Psychiatric Style of Reasoning," in *Reason, Language and Method: Essays in Honour of Hilary Putnam*, ed. George Boolos (Cambridge, forthcoming). To be sure, the formal introduction of "inversion" as a clinical term (by Arrigo Tamassia, "Sull' inversione dell' istinto sessuale," *Rivista sperimentale di freniatria e di medicina legale* 4 [1878]: 97–117: the earliest published use of "inversion" that Havelock Ellis, *Sexual Inversion = Studies in the Psychology of Sex*, vol. 2, 3d ed. [Philadelphia, 1922]: 3, was able to discover) occurred a decade *after* Kertbeny's coinage of "homosexuality," but Ellis suspected the word of being considerably

older: It seems to have been well established by the 1870s, at any rate, and it was certainly a common designation throughout the 1880s. "Homosexuality," by contrast, did not begin to achieve currency in Europe until the Eulenburg affair of 1907–1908 (see Féray, "Une histoire," pp. 116–22), and even thereafter it was slow in gaining ascendancy. The main point, in any case, is that "inversion," defined as it is by reference to gender deviance, represents an age-old outlook, whereas "homosexuality" marks a sharp break with traditional ways of thinking.

4. Chauncey, "From Sexual Inversion to Homosexuality," esp. pp. 117–22, citing W. C. Rivers, "A New Male Homosexual Trait (?)," *Alienist and Neurologist* 41 (1920): 22–27; the persistence of this outlook in the United States, along with some of its practical (military, legal, and ecclesiastical) applications, has now been documented by Chauncey, "Christian Brotherhood or Sexual Perversion? Homosexual Identities and the Construction of Sexual Boundaries in the World War One Era," *Journal of Social History* 19 (1985): 189–211 (reprinted in this volume), in a study of the role-specific morality that once governed sexual attitudes and practices among members of the United States Navy. For even more recent expressions of the traditional outlook in Great Britain, see the citations discussed by Marshall, "Pansies, Perverts, and Macho Men," pp. 149–52. Cf., also, Albert J. Reiss, Jr., "The Social Integration of Queers and Peers," *Social Problems* 9 (1961/62): 102–20, with references to earlier work; John H. Gagnon and William Simon, *Sexual Conduct: The Social Sources of Human Sexuality* (Chicago, 1973), 240–51; and, esp., Jack H. Abbott, "On 'Women,'" *New York Review of Books*, 28, no. 10 (June 11, 1981): 17. The classic statement of the "inversion" thesis is the opening chapter of Proust's *Sodom and Gomorrah:* see Marcel Proust, *À la recherche du temps perdu*, ed. Pierre Clarac and André Ferré (Paris, 1954), 2: 601–32, esp. 614–15, 620–22; *Remembrance of Things Past*, trans. C. K. Scott Moncrieff and Terence Kilmartin (New York, 1981), 2: 623–56, esp. 637–38, 643–45.

5. See Chauncey, "From Sexual Inversion to Homosexuality," pp. 122–25; Marshall, "Pansies, Perverts and Macho Men," pp. 137–53; Arnold I. Davidson, "How to Do the History of Psychoanalysis: A Reading of Freud's *Three Essays on the Theory of Sexuality*," in *The Trial(s) of Psychoanalysis*, ed. Françoise Meltzer, *Critical Inquiry* 13 (1986/87): 252–77, esp. 258–71; Jerome Neu, "Freud and Perversion," in *Sexuality and Medicine*, ed. Earl E. Shelp, Philosophy and Medicine, 22–23 (D. Reidel: Dordrecht, 1987), 1:153–84, esp. 153ff. For the modern distinction between "inversion" (i.e., sex-role reversal) and "homosexuality," see C. A. Tripp, *The Homosexual Matrix* (New York, 1975), 22–35.

6. For the lack of congruence between traditional and modern sexual categories, cf. Gilbert H. Herdt, ed., *Ritualized Homosexuality in Melanesia* (Berkeley, 1984), pp. viii-x; Giami De Martino and Arno Schmitt, *Kleine Schriften zu zwischenmännlicher Sexualität und Erotik in der muslimischen Gesellschaft* (Berlin: author, 1985), esp. pp. 3–10. The new scientific conceptualization of homosexuality reflects, to be sure, a much older habit of mind, distinctive to northern and northwestern Europe since the Renaissance, whereby sexual acts are categorized not according to the modality of sexual or social roles assumed by the sexual partners but rather according to the anatomical sex of the persons engaged in them: see Randolph Trumbach, "London's Sodomites: Homosexual Behavior and Western Culture in the 18th Century," *Journal of Social History* 11 (1977): 1–33, esp. 2–9, with notes. This habit of mind seems to have been shaped, in its turn, by the same aggregate of cultural

factors responsible for the much older division, accentuated during the Renaissance, between European and Mediterranean marriage-patterns; northern and northwestern Europe typically exhibits a pattern of marriage between mature coevals, a bilateral kinship system, neolocal marriage, and a mobile labor force, whereas Mediterranean societies are characterized by late male and early female marriage, patrilineal kinship organization, patrivirilocal marriage, and inhibited circulation of labor: see R. M. Smith, " 'The People of Tuscany and their Families in the Fifteenth Century: Medieval or Mediterranean?' " *Journal of Family History* 6 (1981): 107–28; recent work has produced evidence for the antiquity of the Mediterranean marriage-pattern: see M. K. Hopkins, "The Age of Roman Girls at Marriage," *Population Studies* 18 (1964/65): 309–27; Richard P. Saller, "Men's Age at Marriage and Its Consequences in the Roman Family," *Classical Philology* 82 (1987): 21–34, esp. 30; Martha T. Roth, "Age at Marriage and the Household: A Study of Neo-Babylonian and Neo-Assyrian Forms," *Comparative Studies in Society and History* 29 (1987): 715–47.

7. E.g., K. Freund, "A Laboratory Method for Diagnosing Predominance of Homo- or Hetero-Erotic Interest in the Male," *Behavior Research and Therapy* 1 (1963–64): 85–93; N. McConaghy, "Penile Volume Change to Moving Pictures of Male and Female Nudes in Heterosexual and Homosexual Males," *Behavior Research and Therapy* 5 (1967): 43–48. For a partial, and critical, review of the literature on testing procedures, see Bernard F. Riess, "Psychological Tests in Homosexuality," in *Homosexual Behavior: A Modern Reappraisal*, ed. Judd Marmor (New York, 1981), pp. 296–311. Compare the parallel tendency in the same period to determine the "true sex" of hermaphrodites: see Michel Foucault's introduction to *Herculine Barbin, Being the Recently Discovered Memoirs of a Nineteenth-Century French Hermaphrodite*, trans. Richard McDougall (New York, 1980), esp. pp. vii-xi.

8. See Foucault, *The Archaeology of Knowledge and the Discourse on Language*, trans. A. M. Sheridan Smith (New York, 1972), p. 190, for the introduction of this concept; for its application to the history of sexual categories, see Arnold I. Davidson, "Sex and the Emergence of Sexuality," *Critical Inquiry* 14 (1987/88): 16–48, esp. 48.

9. On the emergence of the concept of homosexuality, see Jeffrey Weeks, "'Sins and Diseases': Some Notes on Homosexuality in the Nineteenth Century," *History Workshop* 1 (1976): 211–19, and *Sex, Politics and Society: The Regulation of Sexuality since 1800* (London, 1981), esp. pp. 96–121; also, Marshall, "Pansies, Perverts and Macho Men." For a lucid discussion of the sociological implications, see Mary McIntosh, "The Homosexual Role," *Social Problems* 16 (1968/69): 182–92, who also examines some of the quasi-theological refinements ("bisexuality," "latent homosexuality," "pseudohomosexuality") that have been added to this intellectual structure in order to buttress its central concept.

10. *A Problem in Modern Ethics*, quoted by Jeffrey Weeks, *Coming Out: Homosexual Politics in Britain, from the Nineteenth Century to the Present* (London, 1977), p. 1.

11. While condemning "homosexuality" as "a bastard term compounded of Greek and Latin elements" (p. 2), Ellis acknowledged that its classical etymology facilitated its diffusion throughout the European languages; moreover, by consenting to employ it himself, Ellis helped further to popularize it. On the philological advantages and disadvantages of "homosexuality," see Féray, "Une histoire," pp. 174–76.

12. This passage, along with others in a similar vein, has been well discussed by Marshall.

13. Marshall, "Pansies, Perverts and Macho Men," p. 148, who goes on to quote the following passage from the preface to a recent survey by D. J. West, *Homosexuality Reassessed* (London, 1977), p. vii: "A generation ago the word homosexuality was best avoided in polite conversation, or referred to in muted terms appropriate to a dreaded and scarcely mentionable disease. Even some well-educated people were hazy about exactly what it meant." Note, however, that Edward Westermarck, writing for a scholarly audience in *The Origin and Development of the Moral Ideas*, could allude to "what is nowadays commonly called homosexual love" (2:456) as early as 1908. Westermarck's testimony has escaped the *OED* Supplement, which simply records that in 1914 George Bernard Shaw felt free to use the word "homosexual" adjectivally in the *New Statesman* without further explanations and that the adjective reappears in *Blackwood's Magazine* in 1921 as well as in Robert Graves's *Good-bye to All That* in 1929. The French version of "homosexuality," by contrast, showed up in the *Larousse mensuel illustré* as early as December 1907 (according to Féray, "Une histoire," p. 172).

14. The earliest literary occurrence of the German loan-word "homosexualist," of which the *OED* is similarly ignorant, took place only in 1925, to the best of my knowledge, and it illustrates the novelty that evidently still attached to the term: In Aldous Huxley's *Those Barren Leaves* we find the following exchange between a thoroughly modern aunt and her up-to-date niece, who are discussing a mutual acquaintance.

> "I sometimes doubt," [Aunt Lilian] said, "whether he takes any interest in women at all. Fundamentally, unconsciously, I believe he's a homosexualist."
> "Perhaps," said Irene gravely. She knew her Havelock Ellis [Part III, Chapter 11].

(The earliest occurrence of "homosexualist" cited in the *OED* Supplement dates from 1931.)

15. According, once again, to the dubious testimony of the *OED*'s 1976 Supplement, 2:85, s.v. heterosexuality. (Note that Kertbeny, the coiner of the term "homosexual," opposed it not to "heterosexual" but to *normalsexual*: Féray "Une histoire," p. 171.) On the dependence of "heterosexuality" on "homosexuality," see ibid., pp. 171–72; Harold Beaver, "Homosexual Signs (*In Memory of Roland Barthes*)," *Critical Inquiry* 8 (1981/82): 99–119, esp. 115–16.

16. Some doubts about the applicability of the modern concept of homosexuality to ancient varieties of sexual experience have been voiced by George Devereux, "Greek Pseudo-Homosexuality and the 'Greek Miracle,' " *Symbolae Osloenses* 42 (1968): 69–92, esp. 71–76; W. Thomas MacCary, *Childlike Achilles: Ontogeny and Phylogeny in the ILIAD* (New York, 1982), pp. 178–85; Bernard Sergent, *Homosexuality in Greek Myth*, trans. Arthur Goldhammer (Boston, 1986), pp. 46–47.

17. John Boswell, "Revolutions, Universals and Sexual Categories," *Salmagundi* 58–59 (1982–83): 89–113. esp. 20 (as reprinted in this volume). Boswell himself, however, argues for the contrary position, which has been most baldly stated by Vern L. Bullough, *Homosexuality: A History* (New York, 1979), pp. 2, 62: "Homosexuality has always been with us; it has been a constant in history, and its presence is clear." Opponents of the view advocated by Boswell and Bullough can be found in

Guy Hocquenghem, *Homosexual Desire*, trans. Daniella Dangoor (London, 1978), esp. pp. 36–37; Paul Veyne, "La famille et l'amour sous le Haut-Empire romain," *Annales (E.S.C.)* 33 (1978): 35–63, esp. 52; Robert A. Padgug, "Sexual Matters: On Conceptualizing Sexuality in History," *Radical History Review* 20 (1979): 3–23 (reprinted in this volume); Weeks, *Sex, Politics and Society*, esp. pp. 96–121; Alan Bray, *Homosexuality in Renaissance England* (London: Gay Men's Press, 1982), esp. pp. 8–9, 13–32; Gayle Rubin, "Thinking Sex: Notes for a Radical Theory of the Politics of Sexuality," in *Pleasure and Danger: Exploring Female Sexuality*, ed. Carole S. Vance (Boston, 1984), pp. 267–319, esp. 285–86; De Martino and Schmitt, *Kleine Schriften;* Davidson, "Sex and the Emergence of Sexuality"; and, most pertinently, the essays collected in Plummer, ed., *The Making of the Modern Homosexual*. Additional fuel for the fires of historicism can be found in the writings of those who attempt to relate the rise of homosexuality to the rise of capitalism: see Hocquenghem; Jeffrey Weeks, "Capitalism and the Organisation of Sex," in *Homosexuality: Power & Politics*, ed. Gay Left Collective (London, 1980), pp. 11–20; Dennis Altman, *The Homosexualization of America* (New York, 1982), esp. pp. 79–107; John D'Emilio, "Capitalism and Gay Identity," in *Powers of Desire: The Politics of Sexuality*, ed. Ann Snitow, Christine Stansell, and Sharon Thompson (New York, 1983), pp. 100–13; Barry D. Adam, "Structural Foundations of the Gay World," *Comparative Studies in Society and History* 27 (1985): 658–71.

18. See Foucault, *The History of Sexuality*, pp. 68–69, and *The Use of Pleasure*, The History of Sexuality, vol. 2., trans. Robert Hurley (New York, 1985), pp. 35–52; Weeks, "Capitalism and the Organisation of Sex," p. 13 (paraphrasing Foucault:) "Our culture has developed a notion of sexuality linked to reproduction and genitality and to 'deviations' from these. . . ."; Féray, "Une histoire," pp. 247–51; Davidson. "How to Do the History of Psychoanalysis," pp. 258–62; Thomas Laqueur, "Orgasm, Generation, and the Politics of Reproductive Biology," in *Sexuality and the Social Body in the Nineteenth Century*, ed. Catherine Gallagher and Thomas Laqueur, *Representations* 14 (Spring 1986): 1–41. The biological conceptualization of "sexuality" as an instinct is neatly disposed of by Tripp, *The Homosexual Matrix*, pp. 10–21.

19. See Foucault, *The History of Sexuality*, p. 43: "As defined by the ancient civil or canonical codes, sodomy was a category of forbidden acts; their perpetrator was nothing more than the juridical subject of them. The nineteenth-century homosexual became a personage, a past, a case history, and a childhood, in addition to being a type of life, a life form, and a morphology, with an indiscreet anatomy and possibly a mysterious physiology. Nothing that went into his total composition was unaffected by his sexuality. It was everywhere present in him: at the root of all his actions because it was their insidious and indefinitely active principle; written immodestly on his face and body because it was a secret that always gave itself away. It was consubstantial with him, less as a habitual sin than as a singular nature." Cf. Trumbach, "London's Sodomites," p. 9; Weeks, *Coming Out*, p. 12; Richard Sennett, *The Fall of Public Man* (New York, 1977), pp. 6–8; Padgug, "Sexual Matters," pp. 59–60; Féray, "Une histoire," pp. 246–47; Alain Schnapp, "Une autre image de l'homosexualité en Grèce ancienne," *Le Débat* 10 (March 1981): 107–17, esp. 116 (speaking of Attic vase-paintings): "One does not paint acts that characterize persons so much as behaviors that distinguish groups"; Pierre J. Payer, *Sex and the Penitentials: The Development of a Sexual Code 550–1150* (Toronto, 1984), pp. 40–44, esp. 40–41: "There is no word in general usage in the

penitentials for homosexuality as a category. . . . Furthermore, the distinction between homosexual acts and people who might be called homosexuals does not seem to be operative in these manuals. . . ."

20. For ancient expressions by males of a sexual preference for males, see, e.g., Theognis, 1367–68; Euripides, *Cyclops* 583–84; Xenophon, *Anabasis* 7.4.7–8; Aeschines, *Against Timarchus* 41, 195; the fragment of Seleucus quoted by Athenaeus, 15.697de (= J. U. Powell, ed., *Collectanea Alexandrina* [Oxford, 1925], p. 176); an anonymous dramatic fragment cited by Plutarch, *Amatorius* 766f–767a (= August Nauck, ed., *Tragicorum Graecorum Fragmenta*, 2d ed. [Leipzig, 1926], p. 906, #355 [also in Kock, *Com. Att. Fr.*, 3:467, #360]); Athenaeus, 12.540e, 13.601e and ff.; Achilles Tatius, 2.35.2–3; pseudo-Lucian *Erôes* 9–10; Firmicus Maternus, *Mathesis* 7.15.1–2; and a number of epigrams by various hands contained in the *Palatine Anthology:* V, 19, 65, 116, 208, 277, 278; XI, 216; XII 7, 17, 87, 145, 192, 198, and *passim.* See, generally, K. J. Dover, *Greek Homosexuality* (London, 1978), pp. 62–63; Boswell, "Revolutions, Universals, and Sexual Categories," pp. 98–101; John J. Winkler, "Unnatural Acts: Erotic Protocols in Artemidorus' Dream Analysis," in *The Constraints of Desire: The Anthropology of Sex and Gender in Ancient Greece* (New York, 1989).

21. Foucault, *The Use of Pleasure*, pp. 51–52, remarks that it would be interesting to determine exactly when in the evolving course of Western cultural history sex became more morally problematic than eating; he seems to think that sex won out only at the turn of the eighteenth century, after a long period of relative equilibrium during the middle ages: see, also, *The Use of Pleasure*, p. 10; "On the Genealogy of Ethics: An Overview of Work in Progress," in Hubert L. Dreyfus and Paul Rabinow, *Michel Foucault: Beyond Structuralism and Hermeneutics*, 2d ed. (Chicago, 1983), pp. 229–52, esp. 229; *The Care of the Self*, The History of Sexuality, vol. 3, trans. Robert Hurley (New York, 1986), p. 143. For a discussion of Foucault's approach to "the history of sexuality," see my review of the original French edition of *The Use of Pleasure:* "Sexual Ethics and Technologies of the Self in Classical Greece," *American Journal of Philology* 107 (1986): 274–86, where I observe that the evidence newly assembled by Caroline Walker Bynum, *Holy Feast and Holy Fast: The Religious Significance of Food to Medieval Women* (Berkeley, 1987), suggests that moral evolution may not have been quite such a continuously linear affair as Foucault appears to imagine. (See, also, note 22.)

22. See, however, Stephen Nissenbaum, *Sex, Diet, and Debility in Jacksonian America: Sylvester Graham and Health Reform*, Contributions in Medical History, vol. 4 (Westport, Conn.: 1980), for an example from relatively recent history of the possible linkage between sexual and dietary morality. Hilary Putnam, *Reason, Truth and History* (Cambridge, 1981), pp. 150–55, in the course of analyzing the various criteria by which we judge matters of taste to be "subjective," argues that we are right to consider sexual preferences more thoroughly constitutive of the human personality than dietary preferences, but his argument remains circumscribed, as Putnam himself emphasizes, by highly culture-specific assumptions about sex, food, and personhood.

23. Boswell, "Revolutions, Universals, and Sexual Categories," pp. 21–27. Bullough, *Homosexuality*, p. 3, similarly appeals to Aristophanes's myth as "one of the earliest explanations" of homosexuality.

24. Boswell, "Revolutions, Universals, and Sexual Categories," p. 25; cf. Auguste Valensin, "Platon et la théorie de l'amour," *Études* 281 (1954): 32–45, esp. 37.

25. Something like this point is implicit in Luc Brisson, "Bisexualité et médiation en Grèce ancienne," *Nouvelle revue de psychanalyse* 7 (1973): 27–48, esp. 42–43; see also Neu, "Freud and Perversions," p. 177, n. 1. My own (somewhat different) reading of Aristophanes' speech is set forth in greater detail in "Platonic *Erôs* and What Men Call Love," *Ancient Philosophy* 5 (1985): 161–204, esp. 167–70; I have reproduced some of my earlier formulations here.

26. To be sure, a certain symmetry does obtain between the groups composed, respectively, of those making a homosexual and those making a heterosexual object-choice: Each of them is constituted by Aristophanes in such a way as to contain both males and females in their dual capacities as subjects and objects of erotic desire. Aristophanes does nothing to highlight this symmetry, however, and it may be doubted whether it should figure in our interpretation of the passage.

27. The term "boy" (*pais* in Greek) refers by convention to the junior partner in a pederastic relationship, or to one who plays that role, regardless of his actual age; youths are customarily supposed to be desirable between the onset of puberty and the arrival of the beard: see Dover, *Greek Homosexuality*, pp. 16, 85–87; Félix Buffière, *Eros adolescent: la pédérastie dans la Grèce antique* (Paris, 1980), pp. 605–14; N. M. Kay, *Martial Book XI: A Commentary* (London, 1985), pp. 120–21.

28. On the meaning of the term "philerast," see Elaine Fantham, "*Zêlotypia*: A Brief Excursion into Sex, Violence, and Literary History," *Phoenix* 40 (1986): 45–57, esp. 48, n. 10.

29. For an explication of what is meant by "a certain (nonsexual) pleasure in physical contact with men," see note 33.

30. See Dover, *Greek Homosexuality*, esp. pp. 73–109; a general survey of this issue together with the scholarship on it can be found in my essay, "Plato and Erotic Reciprocity," *Classical Antiquity* 5 (1986): 60–80.

31. Nor does Aristophanes make any allowance in his myth for what was perhaps the most widely shared sexual taste among his fellow Athenian citizens—namely, an undifferentiated liking for good-looking women and boys (that is, a sexual preference not defined by an exclusively gender-specific sexual object-choice). Such a lacuna should warn us not to treat Aristophanes' myth as a simple description or reflection of contemporary experience.

32. Public lecture delivered at Brown University, 21 February 1987.

33. In "Plato and Erotic Reciprocity," I have argued that—in this one respect, at least—the picture drawn by Plato's Aristophanes, *if* taken to represent *the moral conventions* governing sexual behavior in classical Athens rather than the reality of sexual behavior itself—is historically accurate. To be sure, the pederastic ethos of classical Athens did not prohibit a willing boy from responding enthusiastically to his lover's physical attentions: Aristophanes himself maintains that a philerast both "enjoys" and "welcomes" (*khairein, aspazesthai*: 191e–192b) his lover's embraces. But that ethos did stipulate that whatever enthusiasm a boy exhibited for sexual contact with his lover sprang from sources other than sexual desire. The distinction between "welcoming" and "desiring" a lover's caresses, as it applies to the motives for a boy's willingness, spelled the difference between decency and degeneracy; that distinction is worth emphasizing here because the failure of modern interpreters to observe it has led to considerable misunderstanding (as when historians of sexuality, for example, misreading the frequent depictions on Attic blackfigure pottery of a boy leaping into his lover's arms, take those paintings to be evidence for the strength of the junior partner's sexual desire). A very few

Greek documents seem truly ambiguous on this point, and I have reviewed their testimony in some detail in the notes to "Plato and Erotic Reciprocity": see, esp. p. 64, nn. 10 and 11; p. 66, n. 14.

34. The notable exceptions are Bullough, *Homosexuality*, pp. 3–5, who cites it as evidence for the supposed universality of homosexuality in human history, and John Boswell, *Christianity, Social Tolerance, and Homosexuality: Gay People in Western Europe from the Beginning of the Christian Era to the Fourteenth Century* (Chicago, 1980), pp. 53n, 75n.

35. See P. H. Schrijvers, *Eine medizinische Erklärung der männlichen Homosexualität aus der Antike (Caelius Aurelianus DE MORBIS CHRONICIS IV 9)* (Amsterdam: B. R. Grüner, 1985), p. 11.

36. I have borrowed this entire argument from Schrijvers, pp. 7–8; the same point had been made earlier by Boswell, p. 53, n. 33.

37. Translation, with emphasis added, by I. E. Drabkin, ed. and trans., *Caelius Aurelianus: ON ACUTE DISEASES and ON CHRONIC DISEASES* (Chicago, 1950), p. 413.

38. As the chapter title, "De mollibus *sive subactis*," implies.

39. See, esp., the pseudo-Aristotelian *Problemata* 4.26, well discussed by Dover, *Greek Homosexuality*, pp. 168–70; by Boswell, *Christianity*, p. 53; and by Winkler, "Unnatural Acts"; generally, Foucault, *The Use of Pleasure*, pp. 204–14.

40. Compare Aeschines, *Against Timarchus* 185: Timarchus is "a man who is male in body but has committed a woman's transgressions" and has thereby "outraged himself contrary to nature" (discussed by Dover, *Greek Homosexuality*, pp. 60–68). On the ancient figure of the *kinaidos*, or *cinaedus*, the man who actively desires to submit himself passively to the sexual uses of other men, see the essays by John J. Winkler and by Maud W. Gleason in *Before Sexuality: The Construction of Erotic Experience in the Ancient Greek World*, ed. Halperin, Winkler, and Froma I. Zeitlin (Princeton, 1989). Davidson, "Sex and the Emergence of Sexuality," p. 22, is therefore quite wrong to claim that "Before the second half of the nineteenth century persons of a determinate anatomical sex could not be thought to be really, that is, psychologically, of the opposite sex."

41. The Latin phrase *quod utranque Venerem exerceant* is so interpreted by Drabkin, *Caelius Aurelianus*, p. 901n., and by Schrijvers, *Eine medizinische Erklärung*, 32–33, who secures this reading by citing Ovid, *Metamorphoses* 3.323, where Teiresias, who had been both a man and a woman, is described as being learned in the field of *Venus utraque*. Compare Petronius, *Satyricon* 43.8: *omnis minervae homo*.

42. I follow, once again, the insightful commentary by Schrijvers, p. 15.

43. I quote from the translation by Drabkin, p. 905, which is based on his plausible, but nonetheless speculative, reconstruction (accepted by Schrijvers, p. 50) of a desperately corrupt text.

44. Anon., *De physiognomonia* 85 (vol. ii, p. 114.5–14 Förster); Vettius Valens, 2.16 (p. 76.3–8 Kroll); Clement of Alexandria, *Paedagogus* 3.21.3; Firmicus Maternus, *Mathesis* 6.30.15–16 and 7.25.3–23 (esp. 7.25.5).

45. Thus, Boswell, "Revolutions, Universals, and Sexual Categories," argues that the term "pederast," at least as it is applied to Gnathon by Longus in *Daphnis and Chloe* 4.11, is "obviously a conventional term for 'homosexual' " (p. 478n.10) and he would presumably place a similar construction on *paiderastês* and *philerastês* in the myth of Plato's Aristophanes, dismissing my interpretation as a terminological

quibble or as a misguided attempt to reify lexical entities into categories of experience.

46. For a philosophical defense and qualification of this claim (and of other, similarly "constructionist," claims), see Ian Hacking, "Making Up People," in *Reconstructing Individualism: Autonomy, Individuality, and the Self in Western Thought*, ed. Thomas C. Heller, Morton Sosna, and David E. Wellbery, with Arnold I. Davidson, Ann Swidler, and Ian Watt (Stanford, 1986), pp. 222–36, 347–48.

47. On the characteristic failure of "culturally dominant ideologies" actually to dominate all sectors of a society, and for a demonstration of their greater pertinence to the dominant than to the dominated classes, see Nicholas Abercrombie, Stephen Hill, and Bryan S. Turner, *The Dominant Ideology Thesis* (London, 1980), esp. pp. 70–127.

48. See Winkler, "Unnatural Acts."

49. Artemidorus, *Oneirocritica* 1.2 (pp. 8.21–9.4 Pack).

50. Winkler, "Unnatural Acts."

51. I say "phallus" rather than "penis" because (1) what qualifies as a phallus in this discursive system does not always turn out to be a penis (see note 62) and (2) even when phallus and penis have the same extension, or reference, they still do not have the same intention, or meaning: "Phallus" betokens not a specific item of the male anatomy *simpliciter* but that same item *taken under the description* of a cultural signifier; (3) hence, the meaning of "phallus" is ultimately determined by its function in the larger socio-sexual discourse: i.e., it is that which penetrates, that which enables its possessor to play an "active" sexual role, and so forth: see Gayle Rubin, "The Traffic in Women: Notes on the 'Political Economy' of Sex," in *Toward an Anthropology of Women*, ed. Rayna R. Reiter (New York, 1975), pp. 157–210, esp. 190–92.

52. Foucault, *The Use of Pleasure*, p. 215.

53. In order to avoid misunderstanding, I should emphasize that by calling all persons belonging to these four groups "statutory minors," I do not wish either to suggest that they enjoyed the *same* status as one another or to obscure the many differences in status that could obtain between members of a single group—e.g., between a wife and a courtesan—differences that may not have been perfectly isomorphic with the legitimate modes of their sexual use. Nonetheless, what is striking about Athenian social usage is the tendency to collapse such distinctions as did indeed obtain between different categories of social subordinates and to create a single opposition between them all, *en masse*, and the class of adult male citizens. On this point, see Mark Golden, "*Pais*, 'Child' and 'Slave,' " *L'Antiquité classique* 54 (1985): 91–104, esp. 101 and 102, n. 38.

54. Veyne, "La famille et l'amour," p. 55, and "Homosexuality in Ancient Rome," in *Western Sexuality: Practice and Precept in Past and Present Times*, ed. Philippe Ariès and André Béjin, trans. Anthony Forster (Oxford, 1985), pp. 26–35. Cf. Alan Dundes, Jerry W. Leach, and Bora Özkök, "The Strategy of Turkish Boys' Verbal Dueling Rhymes," *Journal of American Folklore* 83 (1970): 325–49, supplemented and qualified by Mark Glazer, "On Verbal Dueling Among Turkish Boys," *Journal of American Folklore* 89 (1976): 87–89; J. M. Carrier, "Mexican Male Bisexuality," in *Bisexualities: Theory and Research*, ed. Fritz Klein and Timothy J. Wolf = *Journal of Homosexuality* 11.1–2 (1985): 75–85; De Martino and Schmitt, *Kleine Schriften*, esp. pp. 3–22; Michael Herzfeld, *The Poetics of Manhood: Contest and Identity in a Cretan Mountain Village* (Princeton, 1985).

55. I have borrowed this analogy from Arno Schmitt, who uses it to convey what the modern sexual categories would look like from a traditional Islamic perspective: see De Martino and Schmitt, *Kleine Schriften*, p. 19.

56. Maurice Godelier, "The Origins of Male Domination," *New Left Review* 127 (May–June 1981): 3–17 (quotation on p. 17); see, also, Godelier, "Le sexe comme fondement ultime de l'ordre social et cosmique chez les Baruya de Nouvelle-Guinée. Mythe et réalité," in *Sexualité et pouvoir*, ed. Armando Verdiglione (Paris, 1976), pp. 268–306, esp. 295–96.

57. The same point is made, in the course of an otherwise unenlightening (from the specialist's point of view) survey of Greek social relations, by Bernard I. Murstein, *Love, Sex, and Marriage through the Ages* (New York, 1974), p. 58.

58. Cf. Padgug, "Sexual Matters," p. 3.

59. See Dover, *Greek Homosexuality*, pp. 63–67, for an extensive, but partial, list.

60. "Une bisexualité de sabrage": Veyne, "La famille et l'amour," pp. 50–55; cf. the critique by Ramsay MacMullen, "Roman Attitudes to Greek Love," *Historia* 32 (1983): 484–502. Other scholars who describe the ancient behavioral phenomenon as "bisexuality" include Brisson, "Bisexualité"; Schnapp, "Une autre image," esp. pp. 116–17; Hans Kelsen, "Platonic Love," trans. George B. Wilbur, *American Imago* 3 (1942): 3–110, esp. 40–41; Lawrence Stone, "Sex in the West," *The New Republic*, July 8, 1985, pp. 25–37, esp. 30–32 (with doubts). *Contra*, Padgug, "Sexual Matters," p. 59: "to speak, as is common, of the Greeks as 'bisexual' is illegitimate as well, since that merely adds a new, intermediate category, whereas it was precisely the categories themselves which had no meaning in antiquity."

61. Cf. T. M. Robinson, review of Dover, *Greek Homosexuality*, in *Phoenix* 35 (1981): 160–63, esp. 162: "The reason why a heterosexual majority might have looked with a tolerant eye on 'active' homosexual practice among the minority, and even in some measure within their own group [!], . . . is predictably a sexist one: to the heterosexual majority, to whom (in a man's universe) the 'good' woman is *kata physin* [i.e., naturally] passive, obedient, and submissive, the 'role' of the 'active' homosexual will be tolerable precisely because his goings-on can, without too much difficulty, be equated with the 'role' of the male *hetero*sexual, i.e., to dominate and subdue; what the two have in common is greater than what divides them." But this seems to me to beg the very question that the distinction between heterosexuality and homosexuality is supposedly designed to solve.

62. By "phallus" I mean a culturally constructed signifier of social power: for the terminology, see note 51. I call Greek sexuality phallic because (1) sexual contacts are polarized around phallic action—i.e., they are defined by who has the phallus and by what is done with it; (2) sexual pleasures other than phallic pleasures do not count in categorizing sexual contacts; (3) in order for a contact to qualify as sexual, one—and no more than one—of the two partners is required to have a phallus (boys are treated in pederastic contexts as essentially un-phallused [see Martial, 11.22; but cf. *Palatine Anthology* XII: 3, 7, 197, 207, 216, 222, 242] and tend to be assimilated to women; in the case of sex between women, one partner—the "tribad"—is assumed to possess a phallus-equivalent [an over-developed clitoris] and to penetrate the other: Sources for the ancient conceptualization of the tribad—no complete modern study of this fascinating and long-lived fictional type, which survived into the early decades of the twentieth century, is known to

me—have been assembled by Friedrich Karl Forberg, *Manual of Classical Erotology*, trans. Julian Smithson [Manchester, 1884; repr. New York, 1966], 2:108–67; Gaston Vorberg, *Glossarium eroticum* [Hanau, 1965] pp. 654–55; Werner A. Krenkel, "Masturbation in der Antike," *Wissenschaftliche Zeitschrift der Wilhelm-Pieck-Universität Rostock* 28 [1979]: 159–78, esp. 171; see, now, Judith P. Hallett, "Female Homoeroticism and the Denial of Roman Reality in Latin Literature," *Yale Journal of Criticism*, 3.1 [1989], forthcoming).

63. Foucault, *The Care of the Self*, pp. 3–36, esp. 26–34; S. R. F. Price, "The Future of Dreams: From Freud to Artemidorus," *Past and Present* 113 (November, 1986): 3–37, abridged in *Before Sexuality*.

64. See Waud H. Kracke, "Dreaming in Kagwahiv: Dream Beliefs and Their Psychic Uses in an Amazonian Indian Culture," *The Psychoanalytic Study of Society* 8 (1979): 119–71, esp. 130–32, 163 (on the predictive value of dreams) and 130–31, 142–45, 163–64, 168 (on the reversal of the Freudian direction of signification—which Kracke takes to be a culturally constituted defense mechanism and which he accordingly undervalues); Thomas Gregor, "'Far, Far Away My Shadow Wandered . . .': The Dream Symbolism and Dream Theories of the Mehinaku Indians of Brazil," *American Ethnologist* 8 (1981): 709–20, esp. 712–13 (on predictive value) and 714 (on the reversal of signification), largely recapitulated in Thomas Gregor, *Anxious Pleasures: The Sexual Lives of an Amazonian People* (Chicago, 1985), pp. 152–61, esp. 153.

65. Cf. Davidson, "Sex and the Emergence of Sexuality," p. 16.

66. Cf. Padgug, "Sexual Matters," p. 55: "In any approach that takes as predetermined and universal the categories of sexuality, real history disappears."

67. My conclusion coincides exactly with that of Jeffrey Weeks, "Discourse, Desire and Sexual Deviance," p. 111: "Social processes construct subjectivities not just as 'categories' but at the level of individual desires. This perception . . . should be the starting point for future social and historical studies of 'homosexuality' and indeed of 'sexuality' in general." Stephen Greenblatt, "Fiction and Friction," in *Reconstructing Individualism*, ed. Heller, Sosna, and Wellbury, pp. 30–52, 329–32, esp. 34, makes a similar point; arguing that "a culture's sexual discourse plays a critical role in shaping individuality," he goes on to say, "it does so by helping to implant in each person an internalized set of dispositions and orientations that governs individual improvisations."

68. "Translations" (1972), lines 32–33, in Adrienne Rich, *Diving into the Wreck: Poems 1971–1972* (New York, 1973), pp. 40–41 (quotation on p. 41).

Questions for Reflection, Discussion, and Writing

1. What sociocultural and linguistic factors contributed to the "invention" of both homosexuality and heterosexuality, according to Halperin? What historical figures does he name as figuring prominently in that invention?

2. What does John Boswell claim about historical notions of homosexuality, according to Halperin? How does Halperin critique that argument?

3. How does Halperin use a dietary metaphor to explain the differences in belief systems about sexuality between premodern and current cultures?

4. What textual evidence from Greek texts does Halperin offer to support his claim that homosexuality is a modern invention? What rationale does he offer for the texts he has chosen?

5. What distinctions about social status, masculinity and the nature of sexual desire does Halperin articulate in his analysis of premodern and present political and social systems? What does he claim one who attempts to compare ancient and modern notions of sexuality needs to understand about language and the terms used to reference sexuality?

6. What did sex signify in ancient Athens, according to Halperin? What roles were available for various members of Athenian culture?

Related Reading

David M. Halperin, *One Hundred Years of Homosexuality and Other Essays on Greek Love.* NY: Routledge. 1990.

John J. Winkler, *The Constraints of Desire: The Anthropology of Sex and Gender in Ancient Greece.* NY: Routledge. 1990.

David M. Halperin, John J. Winkler and Froma I. Zeitlin, Eds. *Before Sexuality: The Construction of Erotic Experience in the Ancient Greek World.* Princeton, NJ: Princeton UP. 1990.

Keith DeVries, "The 'Frigid Eromenoi' and Their Wooers Revisited: A Closer Look at Greek Homosexuality in Vase Painting" in *Queer Representations: Reading Lives, Reading Cultures.* Martin Duberman, Ed. NY: NYUP. 1997. 14.24.

William A. Percy III, "Paederasty in the Western Mind." *The Harvard Gay & Lesbian Review* 6.4 (Fall 1999): 16–19.

Special Topics

"Sapphic" has been, for at least two hundred years or more, a term used to denote lesbianism. This term, of course, is derived from the 6th-century B.C.E. Greek lyric poet, Sappho, who lived on the isle of Lesbos. Students may wish to read the seven fragments of Sappho's poetry that remain, as well as one or more of the recommended critical and historical essays below. Given the argument Halperin makes in his essay, can you read lesbianism in Sappho's poetry? Why or why not? Why is this category a complicated one in the study of Greek antiquity?

Reading

Archilochos, Sappho, Alkman: Three Lyric Poets of the Seventh Century B.C. Guy Davenport, Trans. Berkeley, CA: U of California P. 1980.

Eva Stehle Stigers, "Sappho's Private World" in Helene P. Foley, Ed., *Reflections of Women in Antiquity.* NY: Gordon and Breach Science Publishers. 1981. 45–61.

Joan DeJean, "Fictions of Sappho." *Critical Inquiry* 13.4 (Summer 1987): 787–805.

John J. Winkler, "Double Consciousness in Sappho's Lyrics" in *The Lesbian and Gay Studies Reader*. Henry Abelove, Michèle Aina Barale and David M. Halperin, Eds. NY: Routledge. 1993. 577–594.

Page DuBois, *Sappho Is Burning*. Chicago, IL: U of Chicago P. 1995.

Ellen Greene, Ed., *Re-Reading Sappho: Reception and Transmission*. Berkeley, CA: U of California P. 1996.

Jane McIntosh Snyder, *Lesbian Desire in the Lyrics of Sappho*. NY: Columbia UP. 1997.

Margaret Reynolds, Ed. *The Sappho Companion*. New York: Palgrave. 2002.

SECTION SEVEN

Queer Theories/Social Realities

How queer theory operates within the political arena is still in process and under scrutiny. Some activists have been dismissive of the critique queer theory brings to politics. They argue that such a deconstructive focus on what is normative is counterintuitive to the way the political world operates because what is normative is so socially powerful and even hegemonic. It makes more sense, from this position, to work to be included within what is normative rather than to fight the concept and the social practice of normal itself. It is also true that many gains have been made through the coalitions built upon gay and lesbian identity politics, so it is understandable that some people would be unnerved by, and even hostile to, the collapse of identity categories that queer theory seems to endorse.

As a consequence, much of the political thrust of the gay and lesbian rights movement has been to seek inclusion within the social and economic privileges reserved for a heterosexual majority (such as gay marriage, social security and retirement benefits for partners, nondiscrimination enforcement in employment, housing, and the military). Yet certain applications of queer theory, including many of those contained in this section, might instead contest the very arrangement of social privileges upon which these "rights" are based. Arguing that what frequently falls under the regime of the normative also, *a priori*, involves the oppression of others through institutionalized systems of discrimination based on race, on class, and on gender, some queer authors and activists have called for an increasingly radical and radicalized politics of queer. Central to this conception is coalition building, so that queers make contact with, and support actively, the rights of other groups who suffer also under systems in which the norm is protected so unconsciously and so ferociously.

Such a queerly informed politics would, for instance, question through historical analysis the institution of marriage as an economic exchange between men of women and property, and in so doing would attempt to undermine the forces which normalize marriage in society. Similarly, rather than fight for inclusion within laws that privilege married couples (such as health and retirement benefits), queer theory would question why such rights are reserved exclusively for couples rather than for individuals, and it would deconstruct the normalizing regime of sexual partnerships endorsed by the state embedded in such laws.

Other essays throughout this section question what our active participation in capitalism as consumers and as producers is and ought to be. Others turn their attention to the issues faced by queer youth, themselves right in the midst of an age-appropriate search for an identity that feels wearable. What does queer theory and its challenge to identity as we know it have to say to these young people? What we can and want to fight for, how we manage or don't to get along within a community of increasing breadth, what models of behavior, of hope, of wisdom can and do we offer queer youth, these are the pressing questions of this section and of our times.

Spirit and Passion

Carmen Vazquez

I continue to search for passion in my reason, to understand my journey, to understand why I move and leave the ones I love only to miss and seek them again, to come back to the same place that is now different because she wears a new perfume and there is in her a new yearning. I was looking for the yearning.

Yearning belongs to the spirit. Spirit is what we can't know yet about ourselves. Spirit lives in the impossibly sweet smell of honeysuckle in summer heat. Spirit brings a white rose blooming on a cold November day. Spirit soars on salted ocean air and stays in my lover's hair. Spirit imagines the sinews of her back and thighs for me when she isn't here. Spirit saunters with me and Marcie over the Brooklyn Bridge, and from its highest point we see Manhattan, glittering phallic splendor of lights and steel, rising in triumph before us. Spirit is what I hope for and dream about. Spirit is what I lose myself for and in.

The trouble is, when a lesbian speaks of spirit, she is suspect. This is because it used to be that lesbians and people like us were not named, our presence invisible, our yearning forbidden, our spirit denied. We were She-devils and witches, warlocks and madmen. When we dared embrace our desire, we were no more than silent snow whispering down frosted lamplights outside my window, every flake visible in a midnight moment that is beautiful because it will never come again, not the same way, not the same snowflakes, not the same lamplight. But we never dared dream of morning. The flakes died on the ground.

The modern lesbian, gay, bisexual, and transgender movement misses this point. We forget how we were once unnamed and how young we are, how few are the years we have had to reflect on our experience, and how unique a gift we are to the collective human spirit. We forget that it is lesbians and gay men who have embraced the pleasure of sexual desire and the power of love freely chosen without the justification of reproduction. We forget that over and over again we have created family and community among ourselves without acknowledgement from the state or institutional religion. We forget that it is lesbians and gay men who have refused to submit to the sexual constrictions of gender.

This is what I know: Sexuality is not simply what we do, it is who we are. Morality defines behavior as good or bad depending on a set of values commonly shared among a people. Our society has invented morality as a shield against passion and greed and lawlessness. We have woven stories and myths of what is decent and necessary for the preservation of the common good and the betterment of humanity. Morality changes because humanity evolves, and our evolution is not ever a linear forward progression. If it were, the excess of political and social power we have termed fascism would not have happened sixty years ago. It would not still threaten us today.

But sexuality is not a function of morality. Sexuality is an expression of passion and spirit, as unique to each of us as the snowflakes outside my window. As an expression of self, it cannot be good or bad. It can be delicious or boorish, but it cannot be good or bad. Christian right-wing ideologues are lying when they paint us as evil, and they know it. They know that what is forbidden is not desire but its satisfaction. They know that a culture that has become completely eroticized thrives on appetite. They know you can wear Calvin Klein's Escape, but you can't escape Calvin Klein—cannot avoid the constant bombardment of images designed to keep us in a constant state of desire.

We keep muddling our response because, in our haste to become "accepted" by mainstream culture, we think we have to downplay our desire. We think spirit must be placed outside our passion. We are wrong. Our passion is our spirit. We can name and give voice to what the Right accepts as commercial necessity but denies as immoral—the pleasure of desire divorced from reproduction. It is our gift to humanity.

The Catholic Church was the home of my spirit for a long time in my life, but it wasn't my first home. My first home was in Vega Alta, Puerto Rico. It was a country home, high up in hills filled with the sweetness of *azucenas* and oranges and mangoes. I lived in a house built on wood beams with a porch all around that saved me from the flaming sun of noon. I used to sleep underneath that porch in the afternoons and breathe in the coolness of the earth. At night, I sat in my grandmother's lap on her rocker, overwhelmed by her softness and the talcum that smelled of roses on her neck. When the silver moon rose big as the sun just beyond my reach before I went to sleep, I used to think that big moon was Los Nueva Yores, where my mother and father had gone to make a new life and be rich and have *electricidad* and a car.

That's how I first got to be lonely. My mother left me to go to New York to make money and be with my father, and I got to stay with Pepita and Nito, my grandparents. I would get up in the still night-wet, cool morning that was just turning blue-gray to get milk from the cow with my Uncle Hernan, when the coqui had quit their "*coqui coqui coqui*" shrill and the birds weren't singing. It was *callaito, callao.* It was very, very still *en la mañanita* when I went for the milk from that cow. She had no name. She was just a cow.

I was sitting on the kitchen porch one of those wet mornings waiting for my Uncle Hernan to pick me up so we could get the milk from the cow when I saw my grandma Pepita. I called her Mami. I saw Mami Pepita's room. I could see Mami Pepita and Nito in the room, in there in the bed under the mosquito net. It was all a white light, except under the mosquito net were shadows. But it was them. They were fighting, I knew it. I saw them in their shadows, and then I heard Mami Pepita screaming, and I saw Nito's arm go up, a huge tree shadow on that mosquito net, and then the tree arm came crashing down on Mami Pepita's face, came up and down and up and down again, smashing her screaming whimpers into the bed. I saw her and heard her cry out once more, and then she was just a flat shadow on the bed, and then Nito screamed real hard, so hard I thought he was dying and killing Mami Pepita. But he wasn't because I saw him come out of the bedroom and smoke a cigarette on the porch.

Now the blue-gray light was getting lighter, and I could hardly breathe in my crouch on the porch, but I knew I was crying because I could feel the hot on my face, but I didn't dare move. I just stayed like that for a long time. I missed my mother, my Mami Carmin, very much. Then Hernan came to get me so we could get milk from the cow. I wanted to tell him about Nito hurting Pepita, but nothing came out of my mouth. I didn't know what to say to him. There was only dryness in my mouth. Then all of my body hurt, and I cried like my baby cousin, sobbing and screaming with no words. Hernan held me until I could tell him that Mami Pepita wouldn't hold me on the porch anymore at night. He hushed and stroked me and told me that wasn't true. Then he took me to milk the cow and when we were done we took the warm milk to the kitchen for Mami Pepita to make *café* like she always did, but she wasn't there. Hernan took me to her room, where we found her, crying. She took me in the bed with her, and I stayed there next to her until the sun rose hot. Then she asked me to bring her slippers, and we went to the kitchen.

This is a memory of misogyny and violence, of lush beauty and inno- cence. I have other memories of mothers wailing, beating dirt and devil spirits out of threadbare clothes down by the river shore on rocks smoothed and bleached by decades of wash days. I have memories of soft soap water and wrin- kled hands that fingered rosary beads, dug out *yautias* from the earth, and soothed the fevered sweating foreheads of little children and grown men. The mothers said to me: "It is the flesh, not the spirit that will die. Oh, Jesus, save her from the evil of the flesh." I watched the mothers lift white lace veils over their old heads with the parched skin of their hands. I watched the cracked and yellowed fingernails on their bent fingers make the sign of the cross. I watched those hands, trembling, light a row of candles to the holy Virgin Mary who crushed the snake and brought forth our salvation, the Word incarnate, Jesus, son of God. I prayed I would not be evil. But I didn't know what evil meant. I understood *la carne*, the flesh, my body. I prayed my body would not be evil.

The strain of social discourse that insists on the "immorality of homosexuality" is actually an old voice that condemns all sexuality not related to procreation. The separation of pleasure, sexual desire, and its satisfaction from reproduction, however, is well over a hundred years old. Why then, does the voice of the religious right and their insistence on moralizing sexuality hold such sway? Why does a secular democratic government allow such blatantly religious viewpoints to remain or become social policy or law? Why is sexuality as morality, a religious minority point of view, so powerfully the voice of the State? The answer is not a moral one. It is political and economic. Sexuality as a tool for power and control is older than the concepts of homosexuality or heterosexuality. It is older than the United States itself. If you can control a people sexually, you can control them absolutely. You can declare a war on drugs while letting the streets fill with crack and heroin. You can sell a woman ten shades of Revlon lipstick and then tell her what to do with her body when the sexy lady gets pregnant. You can condemn pornography and wink at Navy men "buying" women at their ports of call.

In our individual and personal lives, political and religious strings on our desire are not what we first remember. My first memory of sensuality is the soft sheen of black that was my mother's hair as she brushed it, stroke after stroke, in the blue and amber haze of a lamp fueled by kerosene. I was three. My first memory of desire was Judy, the German girl on Fifth Street in New York whose new perm I mocked as I walked by her, but whom I wanted to be near, sit near, touch in the private place when we played in the backyard under the fire escape. I was six. My first memory of ecstasy was in St. Joseph's Church on Morningside and 125th Street in Harlem, New York, when, in the midst of incense and the chanting of a choir and the longing for what God might be, I sat transfixed and unmoving on a church pew, lost in a never-ending stream of stars in the blackness of the universe. I was eight.

The sensuality, desire, and spirit life of the child are those of the woman. Their essence has not changed. Only my consciousness of them and my will to seek them over and over again are different.

Why, then, are my sensuality, desire, and spirit at the center of a national debate? Am I that important to the economy of this nation? To the nation's security? Do I affect the rate of crime? Will there be more homeless people if I am allowed to live freely? Will the air be less clean? Will more fish die in the rivers? Will more husbands rape their wives?

There are no answers to my questions because the questions are unrelated to the truth of why Mr. Buchanan and Mr. Sheldon and Mr. Robertson and Mr. Gingrich and all the other Mr.'s and their Mrs.'s are so determined to bring the full force of the state to bear on my body. There is one kind of state-sanctioned sexuality and one only: heterosexual sex in marriage for the purpose of procreation. There is one kind of state-sanctioned family wrought into the consciousness of each and every one of us: father, mother, the offspring of both, and their blood kin. In the United States, those images have historically been what is called "white." It is almost impossible to think of a "traditional American" family and not conjure this image. This Christian social construct as the ideal (it has never been the only reality for rural and urban poor people) represents a social contract that the state enforces in the interests of "traditional values," a poorly disguised code for "white" people with enough economic and social clout to influence and control the workings of government and its considerable force.

I mix up my childhood memories with the politics of queer oppression because, despite our numerous protests to the contrary, I believe there is such a thing as a "Gay" sensibility, forged in the contradiction of growing up gay and with our feet on the ground, with a job and a roof over our heads, with some semblance of trying to live without fear, and with some shred of pride in the midst of hatred and violence and the spewing of "abomination" and "immoral" and "child molesters" that makes us want to run as far as possible from the truth of who we are even when we're at the front of the Gay Rights March.

The modern lesbian and gay movement is ill-equipped to defend itself because it insists on denying the very difference that might help us understand the essence of our historic origins as a self-identified group and the basis for our oppression and continued persecution: our sexuality. Our experience of a different sexuality informs our sense of self, our spirit and passion, our art, our view of the world, our creation of family and community, and above all, our perpetual status as outsiders in a Christian state. Our sexuality and the shape of our desire are also informed by our race, our class histories and present economic circumstances, and our status as citizens or noncitizens.

The heterosexual nuclear family is the ideal we are all socialized to aspire to. Some of us believe we should be like that or that we should at least be granted the benefits and protections accorded to people who are like that. Well, yes, we should be accorded the rights and benefits accorded to heterosexuals. But we should have those rights because we breathe. We have a right to health care and shelter and equal opportunity for an education and to work; we have a right to love—because we exist. Our relationship to another human being and the form of our desire, the expression of our love and spirit, cannot and must not be reason to bestow or deny anyone the rights and benefits of living in a democracy.

I have been a lesbian and gay rights activist for the last eighteen years. Despite the racism of so many of my colleagues and because of the generosity of so many, I have been able to hold on to the different threads that I have woven into what I call my self, my identity—my Puerto Rican self, my butch self, my socialist self. In this historic moment of right-wing political ascendance, however, I am profoundly saddened by the barrenness of spirit, by the emptiness of "gay speak" that refuses over and over again to listen and give credence to the voices within our own movement and to the many, many people outside our movement whose experiences might allow us to understand what being treated as though you had no soul feels like. Among the most clipped and nonsensical of the "gay speak" jargon I hear is the *"we are just like everybody else"* soundbite we love to mouth on talk shows and at the first hint of controversy.

What does that mean? Which "everybody else"?

I think "everybody" in gay speak is meant to have us believe that we will be free if we just act "normal," if we can prove to the abstract "everybody" that is America that we are just the same as they are. Gay folks who want to be part of the "everybody" desperately claim that we are not messy, not poor, not addicted, not shot through our hearts or brains by random gunfire, not promiscuous or "obsessed by sex," not into leather or sex roles of any kind, not making a living with our bodies, not traveling on Greyhound buses to the underbellies of U.S. cities or to dusty towns without hope.

No. "Everybody" in gay speak is actually Norman Rockwell. The middle- and upper-class distortions that are the requisite public image of the modern lesbian and gay movement preclude any genuine reflection on the nature of queerness as something that, when freely expressed, can only be considered social rebellion against prescribed state sexuality, appropriate male and female gender roles, and the prevailing legal and dominant social definition of family. You can't be queer and like "everybody" else, because heterosexuality is to other expressions of sexuality what whiteness is to "race." It is the normative standard against which everything else is "other." The heterosexual standard needs no definition of its own, and it bestows upon those that adhere to it legal protections and social privileges denied the rest of us.

I am without borders, at least without the "normal" ones. I know what they are. I can't live within them. I never have. I have wanted to be great. Not good. Great. Better than good. Better than myself yesterday or even this morning. I get up, like everybody, and repeat routines, rituals of comfort. I put on the water and milk to heat for coffee. I feed the kitties. I turn on *The Today Show* and smile at Katie and Bryant and the snake line of people waiting their turn to wave hello to America in the morning. When the milk is done and the coffee and sugar are in it and stirred to perfect sweetness, I smoke my first Export "A" and then think about this day, the letters and memos and phone calls, the words to tell Marcie I need and love her, my sister's baffled life and disease I can't understand because every few months it's a different one or a compounded one. I wonder if my brother is still working. I feel my body waking up to caffeine and nicotine *(I know it's bad)* and myself spreading around the middle of me for lack of the exercise I don't do once again.

All the while I am putting on my Calvin Klein briefs and my white tab-collar shirt and Urban Canvas tie and my Roma Uomo scent, I know I am butch. I put on the coat and scarf and close the door behind me, leaving the kitties to jazz. I walk down the stairs and pick up the *New York Times* from the stoop on my brownstone on Henry Street. For a moment, I will feel like everybody else in Brooklyn. But I won't be. I will be my butch self smiling good morning to the old Italian man standing in front of the brownstone two houses down, his shoulders bent and eyes watering from the cold air under his black cap, with smoke rising blue from his morning cigarette. I watch him adjust to my tie and my Roma Uomo scent, smiling my good morning back to me in his discomfort and the odd pleasure of experiencing a woman greeting him man to man. I love the moment with him and walk on.

The parameters of "normal" fall apart every morning for millions of queers in the United States. This is true whether we drive buses or march into law firms or city halls or enter medical practices or answer the phones or sweep the entryways to our community centers or organize unions. Individual and collective liberation requires that we understand and consciously be who we are as much of the time as we can stand. It also requires that we be conscious of who else is standing there with us and who won't fall back in fear when "normal" falls apart.

Upper-class aspirations—or the promise of their comfort—require a dulling of that consciousness, a thwarting of the desire to be great by being exactly who you are. In addition to what you earn or own, "class" has also come to mean acting white and straight and pretentious regardless of your skin color or your language or what's underneath your skin in the explosions of desire and tenderness and fury and fear that we call sex.

None of this should be construed as an assault on the middle class or the United States or things American. I am, in fact, more of a patriot than the new or old Republicans. I actually believe in the Constitution. I hold out for the promise, still to be realized, of equality and freedom for all people living in this land. I do not, however, believe individual freedom or equality of opportunity are attainable for people of color or lesbians and gay men without radical change in the values, family definitions, and economic systems we live under. My detractors would say we have achieved those changes. They would be lying or ignoring history. With the significant exception of the constitutional amendments that enfranchised Black men and, later, women, there have been no radical and sustained changes in the values, family definitions, and economic systems of the U.S. since the end of slavery.

I haven't ever believed that we could leapfrog from the anonymity of the "love that dared not speak its name" or the pathologizing of homosexuality without the legal strategies and cultural adaptations that would make it possible for us to be heard and seen by people who have been well trained in how to loathe and fear us. Seeking common ground is a tactical necessity in the struggle for civil rights, and it would be foolish to argue against it. What I have tried to argue for a very long time is that those tactical and strategic efforts alone would not be sufficient to undo the fundamental character of heterosexism and racism and sexism in our society. I have tried to argue that the racism, sexism, and lack of class analysis internal to our movement leaves us ill-prepared to defend ourselves against the erosion of whatever civil rights we may have carved out for ourselves when the backlash comes. Well, the backlash is here in all its fury and, for the most part, mainstream queers still think I'm a cuckoo lefty who just doesn't get the "reality" of what it takes to create political change in the United States. I'm left to wonder, am I really off-base here? Is my language truly inaccessible or excessively Left and archaic? Or have I missed a crucial piece of the organizing puzzle?

All of the above could be true. I think what is most true is that I have missed a crucial piece of the organizing puzzle. *There is a Left to this movement, and there is a Right.* We have different goals and different processes. An understanding of class and class privilege and their relationship to any system of oppression is the only bridge we queers have to build on in our efforts to forge relationships of solidarity and respect with other oppressed people. Drop the class piece, and we have no basis for understanding the wedge created by the right wing (both internal and external to our movement) between us and communities of color. We have no basis for understanding the welfare war or the immigrant war or the teenage pregnancy war or the reproductive rights war. And, by and large, we have dropped the class piece.

Sometimes, *we are the Right.* Until some of us are willing to make that distinction, our ability to cohere a progressive lesbian, gay, bisexual, and transgender agenda capable of working with other progressive movements in this country will be extremely limited. We need a class analysis that can illuminate the role and persistence of heterosexuality in western, advanced-capitalist culture, and the emergence of homosexual identity, culture, and community as a logical response to the changing exigencies of the family. Because that analysis is not going to come from the Right in our movement, we also need an identified Left in our movement.

It will be pointed out, correctly, that such an analysis already exists in the work of people like Barbara Smith and Mab Segrest and John D'Emilio and many, many others in our movement. What exists as queer left theory, however, remains that—queer left theory. We are challenged by how to make such theory an organizing principle. We are challenged by how to make our theory make sense and become a point of unity with people who completely repudiate the Right because they know their lives depend on their ability to resist the Right and its political ascendance. We are challenged by the terrible confusion of trying to simultaneously create and defend a relatively new identity in a culture and economic system that is very good at absorbing social unrest and political dissent and eventually turning them into marketable commodities. We are challenged by our unwillingness or inability to let our sexuality and desire be at the very center of our popular movement—even if we are of the Left. We say people just can't handle that, the sex thing. We make it too rarefied a field of thought and political resistance for poor folk and colored folk to take kindly to. We buy the race and class lie that poor and colored folk are too unsophisticated to hear the truth of who we are and love us that way. When we have tried, we have never been turned away, not if we were honest.

In a society that exalts enforced heterosexuality, queer liberation is not possible without prolonged cultural struggle (in educational systems, media, and the arts) to change the value assigned to "traditional" male and female roles and to change sex into something human beings engage in for pleasure and spiritual communion rather than for procreation only. In a society that values economic profit above the individual and communal needs of its citizens, a queer "mainstreaming" strategy leaves those of us who happen to be female, of color, working-class, or poor still knocking on the door of a freedom that can't be realized without a conscious redistribution of wealth—something that requires the political muscle and sinew of a broad-based political movement and party that don't exist yet.

This is not theory. This is my life.

My full participation in a democratic society should not require that I wear a dress, act white, fuck a man, or remain mute in the face of the obscene redistribution of wealth upward that is leaving one U.S. working-class community after another feeling hopeless, alienated, and furious. But, in fact, such are the requirements for accommodation and success if you are female in the United States. I have no use for an accommodation requiring me to jettison the spirit and passion of my ancestors or the liberation of spirit I can only experience when I am free to love and desire as I choose. A lesbian and gay movement strategically focused on assimilation into the status quo leaves huge pieces of my soul in prison. It isn't enough.

I believe we need a broader audience for alliance. I believe we need to speak with and touch the people who have been left adrift by current economic policies: with African Americans who still live under the burden of a slave-era-imposed sexuality as sexual "predatory" males and "promiscuous" females; with Latinos who can't find work above the minimum wage even when jobs are *available*, but get plenty of fanfare as "hot and sexy" people whose homelands we should vacation in; with Asian Pacific Islander people whose relatives are sold to G.I.s every day for sex.

We needn't bother with engaging Newt Gingrich or Bob Dole or even Bill Clinton in a dialogue about whether we are born gay or choose it. They don't care.

Rather, the dialogue we should engage in is with other people who know what it is to have their lives threatened and their homes burned and their livelihood denied because of who they are. The fact that who we are is ultimately tied to our erotic desire for people of our own gender changes none of the circumstances or experiences of bigotry; it changes none of the feelings of it. We need to learn to speak the truth of that experience to the majority of people who can actually understand it. We need to find ways of speaking to poor and working-class Americans because that's who the majority of us are connected to by blood, by class, and by spirit.

If we are serious about creating a broader audience for alliance, the dialogue we must engage in with our sisters and brothers of color, the dialogue we must engage in with organized labor and unorganized civil service workers, college students, and the people in welfare waiting rooms, is about the truth of who we are, the whole truth. The sex part and the race part and the class part and the gender part.

The dialogue about racism in the United States must be about more than whether or not we will use offensive language; it must also be about how together, white people and people of color, we will end the subjugation by political and economic force of white people over people of color. So, too, must the dialogue be about more than whether we were born gay or chose it and how we are alike or unlike everybody else. The dialogue must instead be about how we will choose to be subject and object in our sexual lives, how we will be free.

In our hurry to win legal and legislative battles, we must not forsake the spirit in us that keeps longing for a freedom that laws alone can never give us. The language and image, the strategies and tactics, the song and spirit of our movement should have more in common with the people still working to end racism and economic injustice in our country than with those espousing the notion that thirty years of affirmative action have somehow given African Americans and other people of color in this country "equal" opportunity. It should, because, like ours, these are struggles for dignity and hope, for the right to choose where we live and whom we love, for the right to choose work commensurate with our capacities—not our color or our gender or our sexual orientation or our bank statement.

The challenge of realizing liberation for lesbian, gay, bisexual, and transgendered people requires that we look beyond the next election. It is a challenge to transform ourselves and our society, to claim our passion as our spirit, to reclaim the Left and, in the process, to reclaim our souls.

Snowflakes don't really die when they fall on the ground. They melt and evaporate and come back to us again in a spring rain or a summer storm. So do we return in the life of two-spirit people, in the men and women who fought fascism in a military that rejected them and still does, in the life of UPS drivers who press their uniforms every day and come out just a little at a time, in the lives of African Americans who stood up to the dogs and water hoses and gunfire for racial equality even as their ministers railed against the abomination of homosexuality. We return in the lives of young queers today who demand and deserve a life of joy and dignity in an intergenerational community. We will return until we are free.

Questions for Reflection, Discussion, and Writing

1. What critique of the modern lesbian, gay, bisexual, and transgender movement does Vazquez offer? What reasons does she offer to support her critique?
2. What purpose does morality serve, and what forces maintain current understandings of it? In what ways do current notions of morality both sustain and cripple expressions of sexuality?
3. How does Vazquez mix her memories with politics to support her claims about sexuality?
4. Within the context of Vazquez's article, who is "everybody" and what does she claim constitutes "normal"? What forces authorize those terms, and which people and which groups are excluded from and by such terms?
5. What does Vazquez suggest that queers need to recognize and to do in order to create progressive and viable political and social alliances? What roles do spirit and passion play in forging that alliance?

Writing Assignment

Write an essay in which you both explore and reflect upon your current ideas about sexuality and morality, spirit, and passion. Like Vazquez, you might consider your earliest memories and the ways they do or don't inform your current perspective. Contemplate the terms you would use to describe yourself as a sexual being. As you do so, think about the ways your ideas about sexuality and morality, spirit and passion have been influenced by the communities and organizations to which you currently belong. Who is included and excluded from those communities and why? Do you see any places where alliances and coalitions might be formed between those communities? Why?

Related Reading

Dennis Altman, "My America and Yours: A Letter to US Activists." *Out/Look* 2.4 (Spring 1990): 62–65.

Amber Hollibaugh, "Writers As Activists." *Out/Look* 3.2 (Fall 1990): 69–72.

Matthew Rees, "Homocons." *New Republic*, June 8, 1992. 30–31.

Lisa Duggan, "Queering the State." *Social Text 39* (Summer 1994): 1–14.

Nicola Field, "Cultural Activism" in *Over the Rainbow: Money, Class and Homophobia.* London: Pluto Press. 1995. 120–132.

Scott Tucker, "There's No Place Like Home: Straight Supremacy, Queer Resistance, and Equality of Kinship." *The Queer Question: Essays on Desire and Democracy.* Boston, MA: South End Press. 1997. 202–246.

Mary F. Rogers and Phillip B. Lott, "Backlash, The Matrix of Domination, and Log Cabin Republicans." *Sociological Quarterly 38.3* (1997): 497–512.

Donna Minkowitz, *Ferocious Romance: What My Encounters With the Right Taught Me About Sex, God, and Fury.* NY: The Free Press. 1998.

Mab Segrest, "Race and the Invisible Dyke" In *Dangerous Liaisons: Blacks, Gays, and the Struggle for Equality.* Eric Brandt, Ed. NY: The New Press. 1999. 45–56.

Margaret Davies, "Queer Property, Queer Persons: Self-Ownership and Beyond." *Social & Legal Studies 8.3* (1999): 327–352.

Alliances and Coalitions: Nonidentity Politics

Shane Phelan

The vertiginous appeal of poststructuralist theories is due precisely to the rejection of the move in which philosophy is separated from and privileged over politics. As Gayatri Spivak puts it, "deconstruction teaches one to question all transcendental idealisms." In so doing, it does not provide a new idealism, a new metanarrative, but "is always different from itself, always defers itself. It is neither a constitutive nor, of course, a regulative norm."[1] The space once occupied by the metanarratives that regulate our knowledge becomes an open field for politics, a politics that knows itself to be such and so empowers its practitioners more democratically than do academic discourses of "truth."

Any real transformation of the social and political landscape will require lesbians to form coalitions and alliances with nonlesbians. This common action cannot be simply the strategic alignment of diverse groups over a single issue, nor can it mean finding the real unity behind our apparently diverse struggles. It means living in tension with the fact that humans share important needs, desires, hopes, and fears, but we do not share every important thing, or agree on the nature of those we do share. It means that we have long-term interests in helping one another to be heard *in the language that we each speak* rather than by simply convincing those in power that we are really part of their whole. This is the stance of radical democracy. Such a stance enables us to join with others to fight our oppression and theirs without having to find the thread of the grand theory that connects us.

Lesbians have been denied the right to be heard, not simply by forced silence, but also by having our phrases deprived of authority. So the first need for our politics is the guarantee that we will be heard. As Sandra Harding has said, "the right to define the categories through which one is to see the world and to be seen by it is a fundamental political right."[2] This right cannot be achieved, however, by isolating ourselves and our discourse from others; to do so will serve only to perpetuate public silence. We must enter the arena of public discourse without vanishing, though also without falling into essentializing or naturalizing narratives of lesbian existence.

In this chapter I will look at what sorts of alliances are viable and necessary for lesbians in the 1990s and beyond. Successful alliance requires rethinking our assumptions about *everyone's* identity and sexuality, and also about politics. Interest-group pluralism rests on assumptions about natural identities and memberships that are barriers to politics. Further, the pluralist conception of justice in distributive terms, and of our claims as ones of private interest, implicitly opposed to a common good, makes justice alternately unachievable and limited.[3] It thus blocks discussion and debate, and occludes the social foundations of ideas that are needed for critical thought. Interest-group pluralism is also the culprit behind the idea that these many memberships (Black, female, class, and the like) conflict within us; we are trained to think of these as memberships in interest groups, and so the political question becomes, to which group do I give primary allegiance? If we get past interest-group pluralism, however, the questions open up. Who are we? What do we have in common? What might justice be among a diverse people?

"Postmodern" politics means that as we enter public discourse we do so, not as "Lesbians" with a fixed, eternal identity, but as lesbians, people occupying provisional subject positions in heterosexual society. As such, we must acknowledge that speaking and being heard does not mean simply drawing on our "experience" in an unmediated way but means articulating our lives, interpreting and reinterpreting them in ways that link us to others. Coalitions of the future will require us to maintain the subject position of lesbians and our belief in our voices with the growing awareness that our own subjectivity is part of the terrain of possible change. To paraphrase Foucault, "we must insist on *becoming* [lesbian], rather than persist in defining ourselves as such."[4] Thus, the problem for coalition politics is not "What do we share?" but rather "What *might* we share as we develop our identities through the process of coalition?" Coalition cannot be simply the strategic alignment of diverse groups over a single issue, nor can coalition mean finding the real unity behind our apparently diverse struggles. Our politics must be informed by affinity rather than identity, not simply because we are not all alike, but because we each embody multiple, often conflicting, identities and locations.[5]

Interest in the House of Difference

Most discussions of coalition presume an interest-group model of politics. The model assumes that each group is self-contained, and thus does an injustice to many of their members; for example, separating "Blacks" from "women" renders Black women invisible.[6] The possibility of this oversight rests on the rela-

tive privilege of those making the assumptions. When the constructors are
WASP middle-class heterosexual men, it is easy to neglect the overlaps between
class, race, sexuality, gender, and other "interests." It was easy to talk of
"Italian-Americans" as a cohesive group, especially when women of each group
were overlooked or defined by the men of that group.[7] Similarly, it is possible
for white lesbians to privilege "lesbian" as a coherent category, so long as our
daily lives do not force us to notice our overlapping membership as whites.

Many gay men have insisted that lesbians are gay, just as "Blacks" are both
male and female. And indeed, many women refer to themselves as "gay
women." We should not confuse the English grammar with social structures of
equality, however. The nonneutral generic male extends to the nongeneric gay;
if "gay" refers to a "social identity and consciousness," as Mark Thompson asserts, then in a gendered society that identity and consciousness will be profoundly gender marked.[8] Denial of this reality by means of a generic "gay" is
unavoidably sexist, reinforcing the invisibility of women.

As an example of the construction of interest and identity as monolithic
and natural, we can use the best-selling book on gay politics *After the Ball*. This
book was written by two white male Harvard graduates, Marshall Kirk and
Hunter Madsen, currently working at high-prestige, high-income jobs. They
propose a "marketing strategy" to overcome homophobia in the United States.
This strategy includes advertisements that plant the idea that gays and lesbians
are "just like everyone else." This is not just strategic; they believe that

> when treated with respect and friendship, we're as happy and psychologically well
> adjusted as they are. . . . We look, feel, and act just as they do; we're hard-working,
> conscientious Americans with love lives exactly like their own.[9]

This is a fascinating statement because it follows a hundred pages of castigation
of gay male sexual, political, and personal behavior. Kirk and Madsen continually contrast the pathology of gay life to the nice, normal picture of heterosexuality. They manage this dissonance by separating the "bad gays" from the "good
gays," claiming that "good gays" are just like heterosexuals. They experience
themselves as just like their straight friends, and so they are embarrassed by the
"deviants."

There is much to take exception with in this book, and much to think
about. For one thing, these two men subsume lesbians into the category of
"gay" with remarkable ease. Although they occasionally acknowledge that lesbians do not have the proclivity for casual sex that gay men do (a difference of
which they approve) and that we face some problems as women, the bulk of the
book makes no distinction between gays and lesbians. This erasure is not simply
sexist but reflects these authors' ability to see gayness as a singular distinguishing mark in their lives. Were it not for their "sexual orientation," they would be
just like their (white?) heterosexual friends and fellow Harvard graduates. Thus
"gayness" appears to them as a discrete identifier, and the "gay" they are discussing emerges as male, white, and middle- (or upper-) class.

Because of this view, their aims are narrow. Kirk and Madsen seek simply to end antigay prejudice, to get equal rights (such as formal marriages) with heterosexuals, and, eventually, just to fit in like everyone else. They have no problem with any other structures of oppression in the United States, and so they urge "gays" not to distract themselves from the fight for gays by "admixture with superfluous issues that might further upset or distract ordinary Americans."[10] Included in the list of "superfluous" or "utterly extraneous" causes are racial justice, feminism, environmentalism, and others. They disdain the Rainbow Coalition concept as a distraction.

What is a lesbian to make of this? What is a Chicana (or Black, or Asian, or Native American, or poor, or . . .) lesbian to think? Kirk and Madsen are telling us not simply that feminism is not equivalent to lesbianism, but that feminism is dangerous to the cause of gay rights. Discussions of race or class are divisive.

Imagine the response of Audre Lorde. In *Zami: A New Spelling of My Name*, Lorde describes her position as a Black lesbian among lesbians in Greenwich Village:

> Being women together was not enough. We were different. Being gay-girls together was not enough. We were different. Being Black together was not enough. We were different. Being Black women together was not enough. We were different. Being Black dykes together was not enough. We were different. . . . It was a while before we came to realize that our place was the very house of difference rather than any one particular difference.[11]

Within the "house of difference," Kirk and Madsen's advice is inadequate. And not only Black lesbians dwell in that house; the differences were differences among that progressively more narrowly defined group, inseparable from the individuality of its members. From this perspective, Kirk and Madsen's prescription is both politically naive and theoretically incoherent. It rests on the idea of gayness as a discrete identifier, in the manner of interest-group liberalism, and reduces that identifier to whom we have sex with. It then colonizes all those who have or would like to have sex with members of the same sex as "gays," and tells them to address that in isolation from the rest of their lives. Their aim is to "keep the message focused," but the effect is to isolate white bourgeois gay men from any potential allies other than straight white men. Just as the phrase "as a woman" has been discredited in feminism as "the Trojan horse of feminist ethnocentrism,"[12] we cannot rest with "as a gay" or "as a lesbian"; we need to produce public spaces to discuss what these words can mean, and we need to recognize their insufficiency in fully capturing the nature of our sexualities.

Kirk and Madsen provide us with an example of how a simple white identity politics can fail. Although they have many good suggestions for media campaigns to convince heterosexuals that we are "just like them," they fail to provide any reason for the majority of lesbians or queers of color to work with them. Theirs is a pre-Stonewall, prefeminism politics. (They state that "the gay revolution has failed," that post-Stonewall gay activism has been a "disaster," though the legal and social advances of lesbians and gays in the last two decades, when compared with the advances under homophile organizations, are staggering.)

The narrowness of this prescription rests on the assumption of a clear "gay interest." As we saw earlier, this is a problematic notion. Even if we could/can posit a discrete "gay interest," though, there is no entailment between such an interest and the rejection of coalition. One could assume such an interest and still advocate coalition politics. The motivation of such a politics would be a quid-pro-quo understanding: I'll protect you from "them" if you protect me. I'll support racial or class advances if you support feminism and lesbian rights.

Such conceptions of coalition have their basis in several assumptions of mainstream political science and white American life. First is the assumption of identifiable groups and corresponding interests, as discussed above. Next is the assumption of self-interest as the basis of political action, with its embedded assumptions about the nature of the self. These assumptions present persons as individualist satisfaction-maximizers, whose satisfaction may or may not arise from others' satisfaction or welfare. The language of individualism makes it difficult to discuss or conceive of rationales for coalition that are not essentialist, but the job is not impossible.[13]

The first break in the smooth surface of this presentation occurs with the recognition by early pluralists that persons possess (note the possessive) characteristics that will strongly influence their interests.[14] In pluralist theory, the "characteristics" of social actors are not simple possessions, but place them in social groups. Nonetheless, the interest paradigm remains, for these groups will have interests that are identifiable and separable; "blacks' interest" will be different from and unrelated to "lesbians' interest" and so forth.

This model collapses in the face of specific thinking about our lives. "Overlapping" memberships in various social groups may cause some people to hold "several agendas" for change at once: Black lesbians will have an agenda on the basis of race, on gender, and on sexuality. Thus for some, coalitions will be the only way to do justice to their concerns, their "interests." Even so, this argument still remains in the realm of essentialist thinking about social groups. It conceives of "Blacks" and "lesbians" as distinct and uniform groups; the anomaly of Black lesbians is precisely that they do not fit the modal version of either group. From an essentialist viewpoint, Black lesbians become "bridges" between groups that are otherwise coherent. But none of these groupings is "natural." *All* are the result of particular historical discourses about race, sexuality, and gender. The coherence and unity of the category of "Blacks," "whites," "lesbians," and so on is a politicohistorical event, not a logical or a natural one.[15]

Once we see that social formations and memberships are not naturally given but are invented or imagined, we can see the bonds between us. These bonds are not ones of mutual affection or concern, not ones of nature, but are the creation of systems of discursive power and hegemony that tell us who we are and where we fit. This recognition in turn forces us to rethink common action. If common action is not (or not exclusively) jostling for one's (pregiven) interest against others who would deny it, what is it? If our group memberships are provisional because those groups are provisional entities/concepts, how do we know whom to work with?

Local Politics

A lesbian politics that is not based on the authenticity of personal experience or subjectivity should not be confused with one that refuses consciousness or social location.[16] On the contrary, it has been part of the ideological function of the subject to remove people from their social locations and present them as equal, autonomous agents, when in fact they are unequal and usually dominated. And try as we might, we have not been able to provide a reformulation of the subject that would eliminate this ideological function and enable us to base claims on our actual, concrete, specific lives.

The answer to this difficulty is not to make the universal "truly" so, as has been the strategy of thinkers and activists for two centuries. Rather, it is to acknowledge that there is no true universal, that justice and freedom do not consist in inclusion per se, but require attention to the specific voice(s) or language(s) in which we speak and what we are saying. The association of justice with a metanarrative of universal principles and structures must give way to a more modest and contextual practice, though we need not be led to abandon "justice" entirely.

If we challenge the grand narratives of race, class, gender, and sexuality in favor of more local and specific analyses, we find that our allies are everywhere. Local politics, and the theories that sustain them, privilege no one axis of oppression. Instead, the space is opened simultaneously for a multiplicity of claims and struggles. Without a theory to tell us what and who belongs where, we have to begin to talk and listen, to endure conflict and welcome shared achievements.

The politics that I am calling for is "local" in two senses. In its first, "postmodern" sense, it is a politics that eschews universal narratives of oppression that base all oppressions on one "most basic" one, that posit the same mechanisms of oppression in all times and places, or that prescribe unitary or homogeneous ideals for all times and places. The rejection of these narratives has, as we have seen, engendered great anxiety on the part of those who see in these forms of narrative the only secure source of critique. The second sense in which my recommended politics is local deals with that issue. In this sense, local politics is a return to the original formulation of identity politics. As described by the Combahee River Collective, identity politics is a practice that resists political agendas given by others and works for those issues that stem from our own experiences and identities. Valuing local politics restores the theoretical priority of seeing the obvious, the injustice that is in front of our noses, rather than explaining or denying or postponing work on it. Local politics is identity politics, but a deessentialized identity politics. It is an identity politics in which we come to know, and come to fashion, the issues that are relevant to us. Such a politics does not require that we become provincial or self-centered. It does require us to notice and address the hunger and violence and exploitation at home as well as that faced far away by people who can never catch us in their eyes.

The privileging of experience in theory has been one of the central targets of feminist challenge and deconstruction. It might be feared that this local politics is a return to such a privilege. The politics I am proposing here is unlike that earlier theory in that the experience I am recommending as the basis for politics is the experience of a postmodern self. This self, aware of its own contradictory and ongoing construction, is a more humble self than that of modern theories. It is a self that knows itself to be product as well as initiator of local politics, and thus possessed of only incomplete knowledge. That we must act is certain; that we do so without full knowledge or understanding of our circumstances is equally so.

Beneath the fear of or skepticism about local politics lies the image of politics inherited from modern revolutions. In this image, real change is effected by massive popular uprising, seemingly as one, with one clear voice. The aim of the uprising is the seizure of power. This image haunts our discussions of "reform versus revolution," in which we have to choose between reform (when "they" retain power while "we" get some crumbs) and revolution (when "we" have power to realize "our" total goals of social reorganization). The statism of this model is obvious. The theoretical challenge to this model, launched perhaps most provocatively by Michel Foucault, broadens our vision beyond the state and its apparatuses to the more "social" minutiae in which power increasingly resides in the modern Western countries. This "micropower" requires not a totalizing theoretical umbrella to connect it to other micropowers and ultimately to the macropower of the state, but resistance. "Revolution" becomes the post-factum label by which we designate an enormity of confrontations, rearticulations, and reconfigurations of power, rather than the a priori designation of certain types of political action. On the other hand, Kirk and Madsen basically invite us to join dominant U.S. culture on its terms. Their "reformism" is the other side of the longing for revolution, daring nothing.

But we know of other possibilities. The work of thinkers such as Laclau and Mouffe converges (nonasymptotically) with that of multi-culturalist writers and activists. The reminder that the social is an open field admitting of partial closures and linkages rather than a total system or structure can encourage us to envision new structures, new alliances and linkages. The work ahead of us is not simply public relations, overcoming "prejudice" so that we can be like "everyone else" (whoever they are), nor is it the institution of a comprehensive system of just relations. It is the patient simultaneous work of entry into and subversion of a social field that denies lesbian existence while presenting hypostatized images of "the lesbian." "Local" politics is participatory politics, perhaps modest in each particular location, but forming in the end a situation discretely different than the one(s) preceding it. Reforms become reformation, re-forming the sociopolitical terrain.

The most prominent recent example of the accumulation of reforms into revolution is the collapse of the Soviet Union. Until his ouster Mikhail Gorbachev oversaw the destruction of the Soviet empire and eventually of the USSR itself. Since Gorbachev's downfall Boris Yeltsin has aimed at the construction of a capitalist state, but the results of that plan are far from certain. Yet none of these changes was announced as such in 1985, and they are not the result of a blueprint hiding in the Kremlin. The shifts in Eastern Europe were unanticipated by those who focused their analysis on the structures labeled as central. The resurgence of nationalism and anti-Semitism and the decline in the moral authority of the churches confound most of the Western expectations for post-USSR Europe. The narrative of Marxism-Leninism assured us that nationalism and anti-Semitism would be erased (though there were always signs to the contrary), and the prominent adversarial role of the churches before the collapse led to beliefs that when they could, Eastern European Christians would flock to church and listen to their clergy. What is now evident is that Eastern Europe changed before "the collapse" in ways that fostered the destruction of Soviet hegemony but that do not lead it simply to capitalism or to harmony. The end of history is not yet upon us.

Another, more pertinent example is the long gradual growth of the structures needed before a "lesbian and gay movement" could develop. The Stonewall riots had a context in years of growing visibility and in the civil rights, feminist, and antiwar movements.[17] The work that made later events possible was "local politics": putting out newsletters, meeting to discuss issues of common concern, working to provide safe environments. These seemingly small acts provided the "free spaces" necessary for lesbians and gay men to learn the practices and the confidence necessary for effective political action.[18]

I thus agree with Kirk and Madsen that lesbians and gays must fight for basic civil rights and for the privileges currently reserved to heterosexuals, but I do not agree with their reassurances to heterosexuals about the limited impact of full equality. Marriage and military service are pedestrian, assimilationist goals, but their achievement would require a full-scale rethinking of these institutions. Citizenship for lesbians and gays would dislocate (which is not to say completely eliminate) the assumptions about heterosexual masculinity that currently drape the figure of the citizen. Domestic bliss would never be the same if lesbians were fully incorporated into the range of possible images. Would these changes be "revolutionary"? I think that is an inhibiting, constraining question. It amounts to checking our desires and our ability to struggle against an abstract list of possibilities. A better question to ask is, What would this change mean for the lives of those who want it and of those who care about them? This question will admit only of more modest, more specific answers, and that is its virtue.

Alliances beyond Identity

Lesbians engage in politics whenever they become visible as lesbians, as they challenge assumptions about heterosexuality. Visibility as lesbians serves to weaken charges of isolation from other politics. Active, visible participation in organizations that do not have lesbians as their main concern builds bridges with others who may not have been allies before. Work on "lesbian issues" is vital as well, but it need not be based on constructions of identity that isolate those issues from other causes. Refusing that isolation and the constructions that foster it provides the resiliency that is needed for continual struggle.

Lesbians are involved in every struggle, sometimes on sides I would not choose. Before it is an identity, lesbianism is a characteristic of many diverse people. Audre Lorde's powerful response to the charge that Black lesbians don't support Black struggle is a documentation of her presence, a Black lesbian presence, in all the struggles that supposedly did not involve gender or sexuality.[19] Lesbians active in antiracist work, in work against violence against women or U.S. imperialism or AIDS or for economic justice, all remain lesbian, as do their Republican, antifeminist, or militarist sisters. All belie a monolithic politics of unitary subjectivity.

This is not news, but this fact has historically been explained on the basis of oppressions that share the same root and the same oppressor—white, straight, bourgeois men versus everybody else—and the false consciousness of those who deny the connections. This line of argument is counterproductive, for it does not prepare us for the inevitable contradictions and conflicts among and within members of these various groups. A postmodern coalitional politics can avoid this by recognizing that such conflicts are inevitable, and that they are not cause for despair but grounds for continued rearticulation, new narratives of political structures and change. As a more modest politics, it reduces the invitation to despair and burnout that is such a chronic problem among opponents of the established order(s).

In this project, the issue is not whom to work with, but how to work with them; or it is both. If politics is a matter of negotiating identities and discourses as much as distribution of goods, then we cannot assume that the people we work with will remain the same (or that we will, for that matter). I do not mean by this that we will work with "different" people, but that identities will change as a result of our politics.

As an example, consider the status of mixed-blood Lakota Sioux before and after the events at Wounded Knee in 1973. Before the American Indian Movement challenged the power not only of the Bureau of Indian Affairs but also of the existing tribal leadership, mixed-bloods were not considered, and did not consider themselves, "really Sioux." In the wake of the siege at Wounded Knee, the turn toward indigenous spirituality to heal the community drew in many mixed-blood people, and now many identify themselves as Lakota rather than white or mixed.[20] Here, outsiders have become insiders.

On the other hand, sometimes insiders become outsiders. The construction of sexual categories in the nineteenth century formed whole groups of people who were no longer fully in their regional, political, social, or religious communities. There was now an "us," implicitly or explicitly heterosexual, and there were "homosexuals," who were no longer really "Americans" or "men" or "women" or "white" or "Black" or. . . . Suddenly, "homosexual men and women" were a group, and have been trying to act politically on the basis of that ascribed commonality for one hundred years. The great advantage of the lesbian feminist articulation of lesbians as women is that lesbians *like* women, and so are more likely to work well with women. Of course, not all lesbians like women, any more than all heterosexual women "like" men, but those lesbians who do not like women are, I suspect, even less likely to like gay men.

Lesbians have been divided between those who would or could work with men and those who would or could not, or between those who interpreted lesbianism as homosexuality and have based their political work on that interpretation and those who have treated it as feminism in practice, distinct from male love of men. I am strongly sympathetic to those who refuse common ground with gay men (especially white middle-class gay men); my own history of such work is disappointing and frustrating, fraught with sexism and misogyny. Nonetheless, lesbians do have a common cause with gay men, like it or not; however we interpret our lives, the hegemonic social and legal interpretation of lesbianism oppresses lesbians as "homosexuals," and thus provides a ground for common struggle.

We must recognize, though, and must keep reminding gay men, that the hegemonic interpretation is not necessarily everyone's. Kirk and Madsen are among the few gay writers to acknowledge the difficulties of this particular alliance:

> Indeed, all that gays and lesbians really share in common is their oppression at the hands of straights and their relative sexual indifference toward each other. Paradoxically, *gay men and women are forced into political intimacy with one another precisely because they don't wish to be sexually intimate*; and what situation could be more awkward than that?[21]

In working with gay men, feminist lesbians must not eschew feminism or tolerate misogyny. It does not serve any purpose to sacrifice central aspects of our selves. We cannot afford simply to leave, however. Bernice Johnson Reagon reminds us that, while we all like to build little "barred rooms" of sameness and comfort, we cannot remain within them all the time. At some point, "the door of the room will just be painted red and then when those who call the shots get ready to clean house, they have easy access to you."[22]

One way to avoid the "red door" problem is to engage in a diversionary "politics" that continually deconstructs or refuses the categories on which contemporary oppressions are based. This, indeed, is the strategy most commonly associated with postmodernism by both enemies and sympathizers. Though this deconstruction is crucial work for the long run, in the short run it is a mistake. It is a mistake first for the reasons Reagon describes. Voters in Colorado, or homophobes with baseball bats, will not be persuaded by discussions of gender ambiguity; such talk will exacerbate their anxiety. Telling them that I am not "really" a lesbian is different from saying it to readers of *Signs*; what the second audience can understand as deconstruction becomes before the first audience simply a return to the closet.

There is another way for postmodern lesbians to address the red door, however. It involves coalitions that are based not on stable identities, but on the recognition that some social signifiers presently embody and transmit relations of oppression. One's relationship to those signifiers need not be settled once and for all for them to be important constituents of one's life and politics. I may insist on my lesbian identity not because I believe myself to be "really" lesbian, but because my relationship to that category (whatever that relationship may be) importantly structures my life.

This brings us to the second mistake of a thoroughly deconstructed vision of politics. In writing about such a politics, it is easy to celebrate fractured identities and ambiguities. In doing the daily work of politics, these breaks and sutures are the source of deep pain and fear as well as joy. More "political" (or less privileged?) writers such as Anzaldúa and Alarcón describe this pain and fear vividly. The messiness so often cheered by contemporary theorists must be granted its due. The leap from theoretical understanding to visceral reaction is a huge one, fraught with danger and anxiety. If postmodern political theorists do not acknowledge this problem, we will be doomed to irrelevance. Becoming coalitional citizens is every bit as painful as becoming lesbians has been for most of us in (hetero)sexist societies. We need to continue to articulate a common political agenda that does not naturalize our alliance, that does not insist that gay men be feminist but that does ensure that our work together will not violate feminist commitments held by participants, and this continued articulation will be nothing short of infuriating.

Queer—A Coalitional Identity?

"Queer" politics is often presented as this articulation of a coalitional identity. Queer theory and politics are products of the 1980s. This new identity had several sources. First, the feminist sex wars exhausted many lesbians and led them to seek new locations. Second, the rising demands of bisexuals for inclusion in gay and lesbian communities and organizations invited a new analysis of the relationship between politics and sexuality. Third, AIDS introduced new patterns of relationships between men and women and provided a basis for alliances. Last, the ascendancy of poststructuralism provided a terrain for queer theory in the academy.

Arlene Stein has done a fine job of narrating the exhaustion of the sex wars.[23] In opposition to lesbian feminists who saw women as inherently life-affirming, gentle, and egalitarian, the prosex lesbians asserted the reality and the value of practices such as pornography, role playing (in and out of bed), and s/m. As a result of the split among lesbians, these "sex radicals" found themselves more often in alliance with nonlesbian "sexual minorities" than with lesbian feminists, and they developed analyses that articulated those alliances. This new articulation is most visible in Gayle Rubin's presentation at the 1982 Barnard conference. "Queer" has eventually become the umbrella that (sometimes) covers all of Rubin's dancing partners.

Inclusion of bisexuals forced another challenge to both gay and lesbian feminist constellations. The easy answer is simply to expand the shopping list—at my campus, the erstwhile Gay and Lesbian Student Union is now the Lesbian, Bisexual, and Gay Alliance—but this doesn't really appreciate the challenge of bisexuality. Bisexuals challenge both the popular view of heterosexuality/homosexuality—that everyone is one or the other—and the lesbian feminist portrayal of the tight linkage between sexuality and politics in which bisexual women are "unreliable" allies because they desire sex with men (whether they ever do it or not). More fundamentally, bisexuals have worked to challenge the automatic equivalence of desire and act, as women such as Robyn Ochs have insisted that they are bisexual even if they live their whole lives with women. By their insistence, they introduce another other, not at the margin but at the heart of lesbian theory.[24]

The third, and perhaps most important, shift was that produced by AIDS. The "crisis of AIDS" consists both in the devastation of the human immunodeficiency virus and in the renewed attacks from homophobes and bigots. Ironically, it may have been these attacks that led to an increased identification between lesbians and gay men, and mushrooming political power. While gay men were dying of AIDS, the sexism of popular discourse discussed "gays" without reference to sex, thereby leaving many heterosexuals equally afraid of lesbians and gay men. Forced again into a common defensive position, lesbians and gays rediscovered common cause in the 1980s. A more dubious foundation for this new alliance lay in the illness itself; the new position of white gay men as victims, as brothers needing help rather than oppressors, made them more appealing to many lesbians.

Finally, we should not overlook the importance in the academy of poststructuralist theories. Theories that focus on the role of language in the construction of the social, that emphasize the historical contingency of even those categories of identity that we consider most "personal," provided an opening for thinking about those who have been called lesbian and gay. Specifically, it allowed for new, postliberal arguments about our place in predominantly heterosexual societies. These arguments have not focused on our similarity to heterosexuals or our common humanity as a ground for rights, but have worked to displace certainty about the division between straight and queer and have thus called into question the very grounds of heterosexism. These theories carry a potential for social transformation that far exceeds the practice of liberal inclusion, but their esotericism also has limited their usefulness in practical battles for hegemony. Most of our political/legal successes have relied on liberal reasoning, and discussions about social constructionism have remained within the academy.

"Queers" are, by and large, younger than gays and lesbians. Many of them do not even know about the battles among lesbians or between gays and lesbians. They are on a path that follows a different geography than the route of their older sisters and brothers, a post-modern landscape sculpted by performance art, by punk rock and its descendants, by Madonna and multiculturalism, and by Reagan and Bush. They are unafraid of camp, or of "roles" that do not mean what they once did but do not mean nothing. They have a sense of humor unlike that of "gays" or "lesbians." The 1993 March on Washington exemplified much of this: although the march was organized along "political" lines, issues of justice and equity and inclusion and dignity, the marchers were much more diverse and hilarious. "We're here; we're gay; can Bill come out and play?" in front of the White House has a very different tone from "Hey, hey, ho, ho, homophobia's got to go!" I was raised on anger, but I was delighted in D.C.

In a deeper way, though, "queers" have not transcended any of the challenges facing "lesbians" or "gays." There are several angles to this. First, who is queer? To many, "queer" is simply a new label for "lesbian and gay." Among these, there is a split between those who use "queer" simply as a convenient shorthand and those who imply a nationalist politics. This second usage provides nothing new, and recycles much that is better left to decompose. Whereas the shorthand usage is a matter of claiming a word that was used against us, the nationalist version of "queer" reanimates the problems of lesbian feminism in its cultural feminist versions without resolving them.

For others, "queer" moves beyond "lesbian and gay" to encompass bisexuals, transgendered people, and other sexual minorities. This is the move toward a coalitional identity. In Lisa Duggan's words, this usage points toward a "new community" that is "unified only by a shared dissent from the dominant organization of sex and gender."[25] "Dissent from the dominant organization of sex and gender" does not, however, guarantee a feminist position. The feminist heritage of "lesbians" is crucial if queers are to avoid the pitfalls of "gay" (white male) politics. Though Queer Nation chapters worked consciously at being nonsexist and nonracist, the later battles within chapters demonstrated that nirvana had not yet been achieved. All of these understandings of queer must be challenged to deny the colonization of lesbians and people of color that occurs within "gay" politics.

The tension between nationalism and its most thoroughgoing deconstruction lies latent in queerdom. Self-described queers include both those who see queerness as a cross-cultural and transhistorical "natural" identity or position and those who use "queer" to designate a liminal position within the contingent sexual and gender frontiers of contemporary capitalist societies. This tension is not to be resolved by the ceding of one side to the other, but must remain a field of contestation. To the extent that queers become nationalist, they will ignore or lose patience with those among them who do not fit their idea of the nation. This dynamic in nationalism will always limit its political usefulness.

The only fruitful nationalism is one that has at its heart the idea of the nonnation—the nation of nonidentity, formed not by any shared attribute but by a conscious weaving of threads between tattered fabrics. And at that point, why speak of nations? Alliances are not nations, and need not be to be strong.

"Queer" does not guarantee a better alliance politics than "gay" or "lesbian" have. The larger notion of queer as encompassing all sexual minorities does not eliminate this problem but reinscribes it in the heart of the queer. The alliance with (heterosexual or homosexual) sadomasochists, fetishists, and pedophiles that is adumbrated in this usage does not enlarge the field of alliance but simply shifts the privilege within it. When others are faced with a "nation" that they do not recognize or desire, they will simply leave. The hegemonic inscription of the queer as *the* sexual minority will then amount to an exclusionary colonization of those who refuse their membership.

Character and Coalition

In the end, identity politics will always be either a nationalist politics or a "practical politics of the open end.[26] Doing a better identity politics does not mean finding the best definition of our identities so as to eliminate problems of membership and goals; it means continual shuffling between the need for categories and the recognition of their incompleteness. No one can decide simply on the basis of identity—any identity—whom any of us will be able to work with. Simple versions of identity politics, in which we know who and what we are and we know by people's identifications whether they are trustworthy, are inadequate. The contingency and multiplicity of agendas furthers this indeterminacy. Because lesbians, gays, and queers differ in their political aims among themselves as well as between groups, the ground for common action cannot be "identity" but must be shared commitments; it must be sympathy and affinity rather than identity. Sympathy and affinity need not be total to be real and effective. They do, however, require a self-consciousness about one's actions and allegiances that is often taken for granted in identity politics. If identity is not sufficient ground for trust or political agreement, but abstract principles in the manner of liberalism or Marxism are not sufficient either, then we need to get specific with one another about what we value and what we will do to realize that value.

What does this specificity look like in action? When I, a white middle-class lesbian with a Jewish mother and Christian father, talk with my male, Jewish, straight, working-class friend, our conversations take time. They take time because we often need to stop and "mark," or note, where a gap between us is due to cultural differences. Sometimes it is relevant that my father was alcoholic, or that his grandparents were present in his life, or that he "is straight" or that I am not, or that he went to Yale and I to a state school. Knowing those things helps us to move through some sources of pain and fear to places where we can see some shared goals and struggles. Other times, however, these facts are less helpful. Even when we get through all the descriptors we can find—astrological, Jungian types, Greek versus Hebrew, as well as the aforementioned—we still find that we are not "just alike under the skin." Each of us is unique. Our friendship could not be transplanted onto our other family members, nor could our political goals or intellectual concerns. Only a very specific focus allows for this dual necessity, for the combination of structural analysis and stubborn individuality; not transcendence of our context, but forever living with the remainder, the unique, the unassimilable.

In a larger political framework, getting specific helps us to locate our allies at particular points, for particular struggles. Paying close attention to our particular social locations forces us to go beyond simple counting of the categories. Our lives are not lived as chunks; though we can certainly specify in some instances structural conditions and inequalities that produce results, most of the time we just live, all of our elements jostling together. Our identities are those jostling, shifting elements. Our politics must account for this complexity. I may work with gay men because we are both targets of a larger hegemonic culture. When I do such work, I do not experience the euphoria of community. I am often frustrated and disgusted. But it is necessary nonetheless, because heterosexism and homophobia structure my existence inescapably. When I work with women of other racial or ethnic identifications, I do so not out of "compassion" for them, or to assuage my guilt. I do so, first, because injustice is not segmentable, but spreads beyond garden borders laid down for it. I do so, second, because I value them in spite of my own racism. That value is not just the value of "difference," of the sort we see on the "ethnic days" in cities where groups gather to dance and sing and eat before returning to being Anglo. I value specific different voices because they intersect with my own, creating a world. There are other different voices that I do not value and do my best not to support: Nazis, white supremacists, antifeminists, corporate polluters, and many others. And then there are people in neither camp: those who, though racist, sexist, classist, or heterosexist, share concerns and try to overcome their pasts and presents as I try to overcome my own.

The question to ask about "allies," then, is not whether they are "really" allies, but how to *make* them allies. While narrow identity politics is framed in terms of the identity checklist for allies, a larger identity politics will ask instead about character. Identity politics, as a politics arising out of the specific oppressions faced by each of us, need not result in a politics shared only by others sharing those oppressions—indeed, it cannot, for that sharing will always be tested as we dwell together in the house of difference. The questions to ask are not whether we share a given position but whether we share a commitment to improve it, and whether we can commit to the pain of embarrassment and confrontation as we disagree. As Samuel Delany puts it,

> Gay men and gay women may well express solidarity with each other. But in the day to day working out of the reality of liberation, the biggest help we can give each other is a clear and active recognition of the extent and nature of the differ-

ent contexts and a rich and working sympathy for the different priorities these contexts (for want of a better term) engender.[27]

The question is whether we can *decide* to be allies, and whether we have the strength to follow through on that decision. Unless these questions are addressed, no theory and no identity will provide a satisfactory result. With positive answers to them, we can forge the bonds between specificities to create a fence against oppression. These very local links can provide the ground for the strength needed to address structures that currently appear insurmountable.

Thus comes about the relevance to political theory both of ethics and of a certain aesthetics of the self. Ethics, treated not as simple rules but as guidelines and starting points for choice, and aesthetics, as the conscious fashioning of character, are both required if politics is to change and produce anything of lasting value. If we fail to address questions of character, formulations of identity will never produce change. Character is not a static entity on which we will be judged by some distant god; character is one name for the processes of the self. Those processes are inseparable from the processes of politics.

Let us say that a political group is "captured" by a driven, committed activist. This person may fight hard for lesbians and/or gays and/or queers, and so is deserving of some praise. While that person is working, she arrogates all power to herself, purports to speak for her organization, alienates other groups, and is unable to listen to criticism. After a while, she may find that she is alone: membership has dwindled, and no one seems to want to work with that group. She castigates the community for their apathy, further alienating everyone. Eventually, she is treated by heterosexuals as a brave fighter, a hero, while no lesbians will have anything to do with her and no real change has been made.

This is a failure of character, on the part of the activist and on the part of those around her. The activist has clearly destroyed that which she aimed to build. Those around her have failed as well, unless they have built an alternative organization that can do the work of the other. Allowing ourselves to abandon the field to the obnoxious activist makes us accomplices. These failures are not failures of theory or of ideology, of misplaced identity. They are failures of political process, and those failures are inseparable from arrogance, cowardice, denial, laziness. Better theory will not bring that organization, or that struggle, back to life. Political action will, and the success of that action relies on the ability of actors to act together. Character is not a "personal" issue, nor is it one to be reserved for right-wing Christians. It is not "the" most important issue, but it is a crucial one if any politics committed to justice is to move toward its professed goals.

Where will this character come from? Basically, from practice. Those looking for allies must begin by volunteering to become allies, developing a commitment to challenge oppression in ourselves and in others. Middle-class and wealthy lesbians must work to learn about and support working-class and poor people's lives and struggles. Men who want to be allies must become knowledgeable and become willing to learn from women. And so on. Alliances are not a matter of harmony and univocity. The distinction between coalitions and alliances is not one of unity or even of durability (though I think there are reasons to expect greater durability from alliances), but of motive and purpose. Recognition of the publicity, the "inter esse" of interest, requires the self-extension of each person toward others. While Nancy points out the incompleteness and instability of being-in-common, he also reminds us of its inevitability, of the necessity of such being-in-common for any individual being. This awareness must be developed into a conscious commitment to the welfare of others, both in general and in each person we meet. This is a form of love. It is a love of the world, a love of democracy, a love of others as inseparably part of the community within which we live. As an activity based on conscious commitment rather than a feeling, love can be chosen and it can be refused. Love need not entail self-negation, but it does require a willingness to "go under," to suffer the small deaths of humility and pain and self-examination. Just as love does not come from others unless we offer it to them, so allies will develop as we ally ourselves with their causes. And as we increasingly open our eyes and hearts, we will help to create those fences against oppression by modeling decency. Without decency and love, bringing us toward one another without requiring sameness, our rhetorical and heartfelt commitments to others will continually be frustrated in the face of ineluctable difference.

The "postmodern" awareness of the incompleteness of any narrative, of the instability of identities and of social topologies, is the opening from modern arrogance to such humility. It requires not only theoretical elegance and acuity but profound interrogation and transformation of oneself. Although not all arrogance is modern, surely the postmodern, "that which denies itself the solace of good forms, the consensus of a taste which would make it possible to share collectively the nostalgia for the unattainable,"[28] that which confronts the abyss of responsibility and choice, is inconsistent with arrogance of any sort. Faced with such an awareness, bereft of models that justify theoretical imperialism on anyone's part, we are forced to confront one another, to build a ground together instead of finding one and inviting others to sit on it.

Getting specific can help us to find the points of connection that enable us to talk to one another at all, as well as the points that keep us apart. If politics is about negotiation, I would rather negotiate with words than with bombs or guns. If democratic politics is about masses, about numbers and majorities, then all of us who share some fragmented parts of a common dream need to develop the ability to talk to each other. This cannot be done by ignoring differences; it must come by moving through and with them. Our politics, disappointingly enough, must consist of continued patient and impatient struggle with ourselves and those "within" and "without" our "communities" who seek to fix us (in the many senses of that term). We can afford neither simple assimilation into mainstream politics nor total withdrawal in search of the authentic community—or we must demand the right to both. We have to stand where we are, acknowledging the contradictions and forging the links between ourselves and other marginal citizens of the world, resisting the temptation to cloak crucial differences with the cloak of universality while also refusing to harden those differences into identities that cannot be crossed. The promise of getting specific is the promise of theorizing, which is to say discussing and working on, the possibility of such a politics.

Notes

1. Gayatri Spivak, *In Other Worlds: Essays in Cultural Politics* (New York: Routledge, 1988), 103.
2. Sandra Harding, *Whose Science? Whose Knowledge? Thinking From Women's Lives* (Ithaca, N.Y.: Cornell University Press, 1991), 252.
3. On justice as distributive, see Iris Marion Young, *Justice and the Politics of Difference* (Princeton, N.J.: Princeton University Press, 1990).
4. Michel Foucault, "Friendship as a Way of Life," in *Foucault Live*, trans. John Johnston, ed. Sylvère Lotringer (New York: Semiotext(e), 1989), 203–9.
5. Donna Haraway, "A Manifesto for Cyborgs," in *Feminism/Postmodernism*, ed. Linda J. Nicholson (New York and London: Routledge, 1990), 197.
6. This is the point of the title of the landmark text in Black women's studies, *All the Women Are White, All the Blacks Are Men, but Some of Us Are Brave*, ed. Gloria T. Hull, Patricia Bell Scott, and Barbara Smith (New York: The Feminist Press, 1982). For an extensive discussion of this point, see Kimberle Crenshaw, "Demarginalizing the Intersection of Race and Sex: A Black Feminist Critique of Antidiscrimination Doctrine, Feminist Theory and Antiracist Politics," in *Feminist Legal Theory: Foundations*, ed. D. Kelly Weisberg (Philadelphia: Temple University Press, 1993), 383–95.
7. See Ozick's comment in chap. 5.
8. Mark Thompson, introduction to *Gay Spirit: Myth and Meaning*, ed. Mark Thompson (New York: St. Martin's Press, 1987), xi.
9. Marshall Kirk and Hunter Madsen, *After the Ball: How America Will Conquer Its Fear and Hatred of Gays in the 90s* (New York: Penguin Books, 1989), 379.
10. Ibid., 180.
11. Audre Lorde, *Zami: A New Spelling of My Name (A Biomythography)* (Trumansburg, N.Y.: The Crossing Press, 1982), 226.
12. Elizabeth V. Spelman, *Inessential Woman: Problems of Exclusion in Feminist Thought* (Boston: Beacon Press, 1988), 13.
13. On individualism as a language that inhibits public discourse among white U.S. citizens, see Robert Bellah et al., *Habits of the Heart* (Berkeley and Los Angeles: University of California Press, 1985).
14. See Kirstie McClure, "Postmodernity and the Subject of Rights," paper delivered at the meetings of the Western Political Science Association, Newport Beach, California, March 1990.
15. For a discussion of social formations as historically specific and "imagined," see Benedict Anderson, *Imagined Communities: Reflections on the Origins and Spread of Nationalism* (London: Verso, 1983). The most impressive example of personal

recognition and exploration of these bonds by a white person remains Minnie Bruce Pratt's essay "Identity: Blood Skin Heart," in Minnie Bruce Pratt, Barbara Smith, and Elly Bulkin, *Yours in Struggle: Three Feminist Perspectives on Anti-Semitism and Racism* (Brooklyn, N.Y.: Long Haul Press, 1984). Rather than discuss that work here, I recommend that every reader of this book drop everything and read it!

16. See Joan W. Scott, "Experience," in *Feminists Theorize the Political*, ed. Judith Butler and Joan W. Scott (New York: Routledge, 1992), 22–40.

17. See John D'Emilio, *Sexual Politics, Sexual Communities: The Making of a Homosexual Minority in the United States, 1940–1970* (Chicago: University of Chicago Press, 1983).

18. See Sara M. Evans and Harry C. Boyte, *Free Spaces: The Sources of Democratic Change in America*, 2d ed. (Chicago: University of Chicago Press, 1992).

19. Audra Lorde, "I Am Your Sister: Black Women Organizing across Sexualities," in *A Burst of Light* (Ithaca, N.Y.: Firebrand Books, 1988), 19–26.

20. This description relies on Milo Yellow Hair's documentary, *In the Spirit of Crazy Horse*, which describes the struggles of the Sioux from the 1860s to the present.

21. Kirk and Madsen, *After the Ball*, 257; emphasis in original.

22. Bernice Johnson Reagon, "Coalition Politics: Turning the Century" in *Home Girls: A Black Feminist Anthology*, ed. Barbara Smith (New York: Kitchen Table, Women of Color Press, 1983), 358.

23. Arlene Stein, "Sisters and Queers: The Decentering of Lesbian Feminism," *Socialist Review* 22, no. 1 (1992): 33–55.

24. See Stacey Young, "Bisexual Theory and the Postmodern Dilemma; or, What's in a Name?," paper presented at the fifth annual Lesbian and Gay Studies Conference, Rutgers University, November 1991.

25. Lisa Duggan, "Making It Perfectly Queer," *Socialist Review* 22, no. 1 (January-March 1992): 20.

26. See Gayatri Chakravorty Spivak, "The Practical Politics of the Open End," in *The Post-Colonial Critic: Interviews, Strategies, Dialogues* (New York and London: Routledge, 1990), 95–112.

27. Samuel Delany, introduction to *Uranian Worlds: A Reader's Guide to Alternative Sexuality in Science Fiction and Fantasy*, ed. Eric Garber and Lyn Paleo, 2d ed. (Boston: Hall, 1990), xix.

28. Jean-François Lyotard, *The Postmodern Condition: A Report on Knowledge* (Minneapolis: University of Minnesota Press, 1984), 81.

Questions for Reflection, Discussion, and Writing

1. According to Phelan, in what ways does postmodern theory decenter the idea of a fixed identity? By extension, how does a lesbian identity function to divide individuals from one another? Similarly, how can identity politics promote division and elide differences among other groups? What examples does she present to support her contention that identity politics create division?

2. In what ways does the concept of a local politics offer solutions for Phelan? What does a theory of local politics entail? What are some of its potential pitfalls? What sorts of alliances can help to sustain such a local politics?

3. Phelan argues that to posit "white bourgeois men" as *the* oppressor in opposition to everyone else is counterproductive because "it does not prepare us for the inevitable contradictions and conflicts among and within members" who are trying to form an alliance. What is Phelan's strategy for addressing this issue? How would you characterize its political choices and beliefs?

4. What three historical markers does Phelan present which help to conceive of queer as a form of coalitional identity?

5. Why, according to Phelan, is it important to "get specific"?

Related Reading

Bernice Johnson Reagon, "Coalition Politics: Turning the Century" in *Home Girls*. Barbara Smith, Ed. Brooklyn, NY: Kitchen Table Women of Color Press. 1983. 356–368.

Gloria Anzaldúa, "Bridge, Drawbridge, Sandbar or Island: Lesbians of Color *Hacienda Alianzas*" in *Bridges of Power: Women's Multicultural Alliances*. Philadelphia: New Society. 1990. 216–231.

Richard Goldstein, Welcome to the Safetydrome." *Village Voice*, June 30, 1992. 39.

Scott Tucker, "'Queerer Than We Imagine': A Defense of Identity and Solidarity" in *The Queer Question: Essays on Desire and Democracy*. Boston, MA: South End Press. 1997. 59–78.

Harvard Educational Review, "Cornel West on Heterosexism and Transformation: An Interview" in *Dangerous Liaisons: Blacks, Gays, and the Struggle for Equality*. Eric Brandt, Ed. NY: The New Press. 1999. 290–305.

Shane Phelan, *Sexual Strangers: Gays, Lesbians, and Dilemmas of Citizenship*. Philadelphia: Temple UP. 2000.

Max H. Kirsch, "From culture to action" in *Queer Theory and Social Change*. NY: Routledge. 2000. 97–112.

Maurianne Adams, et al., Eds. *Readings for Diversity and Social Justice*. NY: Routledge. 2000.

John D'Emilio, William B. Turner and Urvashi Vaid, *Creating Change: Sexuality, Public Policy, and Civil Rights*. New York: St. Martin's. 2000.

Social Activism

What sorts of new political coalitions and alliances could be forged on your college or university campus? Think carefully about what you might want to accomplish by forging such alliances. Do you simply need to increase friendly contact and offer to help one another, or are there more pressing issues that need to be addressed immediately by forming a broad-based coalition? When you have your goal, you can then begin planning a strategy for implementation. Be certain to approach your targeted alliance groups in all interactions as equal political partners rather than as part of an agenda, however well-meaning it may be.

Film

The March on Washington (1993). John Scagliotti. 30 m.
Kamikaze Summer (1996). Chris Collins. 60 m.
When Democracy Works (1997). Catherine Gund. 30 m.

■

Queer Visibility
in Commodity Culture

Rosemary Hennessy

For a lesbian and gay political project that has had to combat the heteronormative tyranny of the empirical in order to claim a public existence at all, how visibility is conceptualized matters. Like "queer," "visibility" is a struggle term in
gay and lesbian circles now—for some simply a matter of display, for others the
effect of discourses or of complex social conditions. In the essay that follows I
will try to show that for those of us caught up in the circuits of late capitalist
consumption, the visibility of sexual identity is often a matter of commodification, a process that invariably depends on the lives and labor of invisible others.

This argument needs to be prefaced, however, with several acknowledgements and qualifications. First of all, the increasing cultural representation of
homosexual concerns as well as the recent queering of sex gender identities undoubtedly have had important positive effects. Cultural visibility can prepare
the ground for gay civil rights protection; affirmative images of lesbians and
gays in the mainstream media, like the growing legitimation of lesbian and gay
studies in the academy, can be empowering for those of us who have lived most
of our lives with no validation at all from the dominant culture. These changes
in lesbian and gay visibility are in great measure the effect of the relentless organizing efforts of lesbians and gay men. In the past decade alone groups like
the National Gay and Lesbian Task Force, the Human Rights Campaign Fund,
GLADD, and ACT-UP have fought ardently against the cultural abjection and
civic eradication of homosexuals. Like other gay and lesbian academics now
who are able to teach and write more safely about our history, I am deeply indebted to those who have risked their lives and careers on the front lines to

Rosemary Hennessy, "Queer Visibility in Commodity Culture" originally published in *Cultural
Critique 29* (Winter 1994–95): 31–76. Copyright © 1995 by the Regents of the University of Minnesota. Reprinted by permission of the University of Minnesota Press.

make gay and lesbian studies a viable and legitimate intellectual concern. Without their efforts my work would not be possible.

But the new degree of homosexual visibility in the United States and the very existence of a queer counterdiscourse also need to be considered critically in relation to capital's insidious and relentless expansion. Not only is much recent gay visibility aimed at producing new and potentially lucrative markets, but as in most marketing strategies, money, not liberation, is the bottom line.[1] In her analysis of the commodification of lesbians, Danae Clark has observed that the intensified marketing of lesbian images is less indicative of a growing acceptance of homosexuality than of capitalism's appropriation of gay "styles" for mainstream audiences. Visibility in commodity culture is in this sense a limited victory for gays who are welcome to be visible as consumer subjects but not as social subjects (Clark 1991, 192). The increasing circulation of gay and lesbian images in consumer culture has the effect of consolidating an imaginary, class-specific gay subjectivity for both straight and gay audiences. This process is not limited to the spheres of knowledge promoted by popular culture and retail advertising but also infiltrates the production of subjectivities in academic and activist work.

Because so much of lesbian and gay studies and queer theory has all but ignored the historical relationship between (homo)sexuality and capitalism, however, one of the dangers of an analysis that sets out to address the connection between the processes of commodification and the formation of lesbian and gay identities is that it risks being misread. Drawing attention to the operations of commodity capitalism on lesbian, gay, and queer knowledges can be misconstrued to mean—*as I certainly do not*—that the material processes of commodification are only economic, that they are all determining, and impossible to oppose. As I understand it, the materiality of social life consists of an ensemble of human practices whose complex interdeterminate relations to one another vary historically. These practices include economic divisions of labor and wealth, political arrangements of state and nation, and ideological organizations of meaning-making and value. Although capitalism is a mode of production characterized by the economic practice of extracting surplus value through commodity exchange, the processes of commodification pervade all social structures. In certain social formations under late capitalism, information has become so much the structure in dominance that language, discourse, or cultural practice is often taken to be the only arena of social life. The challenge for social theory now is to queer-y the reigning Foucauldian materialism that reduces the social to culture or discourse and to refute misreadings of postmodern historical materialism as advocating a return to economic determinism. To examine the historical relations between homosexuality and commodification as they operate at all levels of capitalist societies does not mean dismissing the materiality of discourse and the ways culture constructs subjectivities, reproduces power relations, and foments resistance—quite the contrary. Postmodern historical materialist critiques of sexuality are postmodern to the extent that they participate in postmodernity's historical and critical remapping of social relations, but at the same time they maintain that sexuality is a material practice that shapes and is shaped by social totalities like capitalism, patriarchy, and imperialism as they manifest themselves differently across social formations and within specific historical conjunctures. As social practice, sexuality includes lesbian, gay, and queer resistance movements that have built social and political networks, often by way of capitalist commercial venues. That academic gay studies and queer theory have not very rigorously enquired into the relations between sexuality and capitalism is indicative of the retreat from historical materialism in social and cultural theory in the past decade. But I think it also suggests the particular class interests that have increasingly come to define lesbian and gay studies.

Although I have been using the words "queer" and "lesbian and gay" as if they were interchangeable, these are in fact contentious terms, signifying identity and political struggle from very different starting points. The now more traditional phrase "lesbian and gay" assumes a polarized division between hetero- and homo-sexuality and signals discrete and asymmetrically gendered identities. The more fluid and ambiguous term "queer" has recently begun to displace "lesbian and gay" in several areas of urban industrialized culture—under the signature of "queer theory" in the realm of cultural studies, in avant-garde gay and lesbian subcultures, and in new forms of radical sexual political activism. Lending a new elasticity to the categories "lesbian and gay," queer embraces the proliferation of sexualities (bisexual, transvestite, and pre- and post-op transsexual, to name a few) and the compounding of outcast positions along racial, ethnic, and class as well as sexual lines—none of which is acknowledged by the neat binary division between hetero and homosexual. In other words, "queer" not only troubles the gender asymmetry implied by the phrase "lesbian and gay," but potentially includes "deviants" and "perverts" who may traverse or confuse hetero/homo divisions and exceed or complicate conventional delineations of sexual identity and normative practice. "Queer" often professes to define a critical standpoint that makes visible how heteronormative attempts to fix sexual identities tend to fail often because they are overdetermined by other issues and conflicts—over race or national identity, for example. To the extent that queer tends to advance a subjectivity that is primarily sexual, it can threaten to erase the intersections of sexuality with class as well as the gender and racial histories that still situate queer men and women differently. In this respect queer is, as Judith Butler indicates, a "site of collective contestation" (1993, 228) that is only partially adequate to the collectivity it historically represents.

While in this essay I may string together the terms "lesbian and gay" and "queer," then, this is not in order to conflate them but to indicate that both expressions are being used to name homosexual identities now, even if in contesting ways. To the extent that my analysis focuses primarily on "queer" issues this is because they are increasingly shaping postmodern reconfigurations of gay and lesbian cultural study and politics. Even though many formulations of queer theory and identity are to my mind limited, it does not follow that the viability of "queer" as a sign of collective history and action is to be dismissed. Instead I would argue for a renarration of queer critique as enquiry into the ensemble of social processes—systems of exploitation and regimes of state and cultural power—through which sexualities are produced. I agree with Butler that the two dimensions of queering—the historical enquiry into the formation of homosexualities it signifies and the deformative and misappropriative power the term enjoys—are both constitutive (Butler 1993, 229). But I would add that these dimensions of queer praxis need to be marshaled as forces for collective and transformative social intervention.

Queer Theory and/as Politics

Most well known in political circles from the activities of Queer Nation, "queer" has recently begun to circulate more widely in public and academic writings, the sign of an unsettling critical confrontation with heteronormativity, a distinctly postmodern rescripting of identity, politics, and cultural critique. Although queer academic theory and queer street politics have their discrete features and histories, both participate in the general transformation of identities occurring in Western democracies now as new conceptions of cultural representation are being tested against the political and economic arrangements of a "New World Order"—postcolonial, post-Cold War, postindustrial. The emergence of queer counterdiscourses has been enabled by postmodern reconfigurations of subjectivity as more flexible and ambivalent and by shifting political pressures within the gay community. Among them are the new forms of political alliance between gay men and lesbians yielded by activist responses to the spectacle and devastation of AIDS and to a lesser extent by challenges to gay politics from radical race movements in the 1970s and 1980s. In troubling the traditional gay-versus-straight classification, "queer" draws upon postmodern critiques of identity as stable, coherent, and embodied. Queer knowledges upset traditional identity politics by foregrounding the ways contested issues of sexuality involve concerns that, as Michael Warner puts it, are not captured by the languages designed to name them (1993, xv). By targeting heteronormativity rather than heterosexuality, queer theory and activism also acknowledge that heterosexuality is an institution that organizes more than just the sexual: it is socially pervasive, underlying myriad taken-for-granted norms that shape what can be seen, said, and valued. Adopting the term that has been used to cast out and exclude sexual deviants is a gesture of rebellion against the pressure to be invisible or apologetically different. It is an "in-your-face" rejection of the "proper" response to heteronormativity from a stance that purports to be both antiassimilationist and antiseparatist. Like lesbian-feminism and the gay liberation movement, the queer critique of heteronormativity is intensely and aggressively concerned with issues of visibility. Chants like "We're here, we're queer, get used to it" and actions like Queers Bash Back, Queer Nights Out, Queer Kiss-Ins and Mall Zaps are aimed at making visible those identities that the ubiquitous heteronormative culture would erase. Politically the aim of queer visibility actions is not to include queers in the cultural dominant but continually to pressure and disclose the heteronormative.

Although their often distinct institutional positions situate queer theorists and activists differently in relation to the professional managerial class and the regimes of power/knowledge they help organize, ideologically these contrasts are less neat than is often acknowledged. Both queer activists and theorists employ some of the same counterdiscourses to expand and complicate the parameters of sexuality; both set out to challenge empiricist notions of identity as grounded in an embodied or empirical visibility; and both recast identity as a version of performance: as drag, masquerade, or signifying play. Across the promotion of more permeable and fluid identities in both queer theory and activism, however, visibility is still fetishized to the extent that it conceals the social relations new urban gay and queer identities depend on. The watchwords of queer praxis in both arenas are "make trouble and have fun" (Berube and Escoffier 1991, 15). But often trouble-making takes the form of a cultural politics that relies on concepts of the social, of resistance, and of pleasure that keep invisible the violent social relations new urban identities depend on.

In order to examine some of these concepts and their consequences I want to look more closely at academic and activist knowledges, beginning with three academic theorists whose writings are shaping the new queer theory and whose reputations now rest on their work in this area: Judith Butler, Diana Fuss, and Teresa de Lauretis. All three articulate a version of cultural studies with loose affiliations to poststructuralism. All three offer critiques of heteronormativity that, to paraphrase de Lauretis, are interested in altering the standard of vision, the frame of reference of visibility, of what can be seen and known (1991, 224). And all three are concerned to varying degrees with the invisibility of lesbians in culture.

Judith Butler's *Gender Trouble* (1990a) offers one of the most incisive and widely read critiques of heterosexuality. Against what she calls "the metaphysics of substance" or empiricist and humanist conceptions of the subject, Butler launches a rearticulation of gender identity aimed at making visible the ways in which the fiction of a coherent person depends on a heterosexual matrix. How we see sex and gender is for Butler a function of discourses which set the limits to our ways of seeing. From Butler's postmodern vantage point, the seeming internal coherence of the person is not natural but rather the consequence of certain regulatory practices which "govern culturally intelligible notions of identity" (1990a, 16–17). Identity, then, is not a matter of a person's experience, self-expression, or visible features but of "socially instituted and maintained norms of intelligibility." Intelligible genders are those that inaugurate and maintain "relations of coherence and continuity among sex, gender, sexual practice and desire." In this sense gender intelligibility depends on certain pre-suppositions which the dominant knowledges safeguard or keep invisible. Chief among them is the heterosexual "matrix of intelligibility" that produces "discrete and asymmetrical oppositions between 'masculine' and 'feminine,' where these are understood to be expressive attributes of 'male' and 'female.' " All sexual practices in which gender does not follow from sex, and desire does not follow from either sex or gender thereby become either invisible or perverse (Butler 1990a, 17).

Despite the efforts to safeguard these presuppositions, the fiction of a coherent identity is inevitably vulnerable to exposure as a representation, and it is the deliberate enactment of this fiction as a fiction, and not some utopian sexuality outside or free from heterosexual constructs, that for Butler serves as the site of resistance to heterosexuality. She argues that if sex is released from its naturalized meanings it can make gender trouble—subverting and displacing reified notions of gender that support heterosexual power. This process can only occur *within* the terms set by the culture, however, through parodic repetitions like drag that expose the heterosexual matrix as a fabrication and sex as "a performatively enacted signification" (Butler 1990a, 33). Drag for Butler is not merely a matter of clothing or cross-dressing. It is a discursive practice that discloses the fabrication of identity through parodic repetitions of the heterosexual gender system. As parody, drag belies the myth of a stable self preexisting cultural codes or signifying systems. Against the dominant reading of drag as a failed imitation of the "real thing," Butler posits it as a subversive act. By turning a supposed "bad copy" of heterosexuality (butch and femme, for example) against a way of thinking that posits heterosexuality as the "real thing," drag exposes this pseudo-original as itself a "copy" or representation. It follows for Butler that lesbian or gay identity is inevitably drag, a performance that plays up the indeterminacy of identity and for this reason can be seized upon for political resistance.[2]

According to Butler, then, visibility is not a matter of detecting or displaying empirical bodies but of knowledges—discourses, significations, modes of intelligibility—by which identity is constituted. In this sense her work is clearly a postmodern critique of identity, identity politics, and positivist notions of the visible. Her analysis of sexuality and gender undoubtedly has a strong social dimension: she speaks to and out of feminism and understands the processes that construct sexuality and gender as political. For Butler heterosexuality is a regime of power and discipline that affects people's lives. But her reconceptualization of the experiential and embodied self as only a *discursive* construct is a strategy that safeguards some presuppositions of its own.

One such presupposition is that the social is equivalent to the cultural. Throughout her work, Butler's approach to the problem of identity begins with the premise that identity is only a matter of representation, of the discourses by which subjects come to be established. This notion of the discursively constructed subject is heavily indebted to Foucault, and it is Foucault's problematic concept of materialism and of discursive practices that troubles Butler's analysis as well. While Foucault understands the materiality of the social to be comprised of both discursive and nondiscursive practices, he never explains the material connection between them. Furthermore, most of his attention is invariably devoted to discursive practices.[3] This social logic of non-correspondence appears in Butler's analysis, too, and is most explicit in her explanation of materialism in *Bodies That Matter* (1993). In her own words, this new book is a "poststructuralist rewriting of discursive performativity as it operates in the materialization of sex" (Butler 1993, 12). This poststructuralist reading of materiality begins with the premise that matter is never simply given but always materialized. But what constitutes this materializing is one domain of social production only—the regulatory practices, norms, and discourses that constitute ideology (Butler 1993, 10). Butler's version of materiality is directed against notions of the body and of sex common among constructionists who still maintain them to be in some ways "matter" in the sense of a constitutive "outside" that exceeds the boundaries of discourse. But by explaining materiality so exclusively in terms of discursive practices, Butler effectively conflates the materiality of the social into culture. While she frequently refers to heterosexuality as an institution or a norm, she never explains the material differences or relations between institutions and normative discourses. Are they one and the same? Do institutions like the family, the military, or schools organize and rely on more than discourses: aspects of life like labor and wealth, or social resources like health and health care, the distribution of food and shelter? All of these aspects of social life are, of course, discursively mediated and regulated, but at the same time their materiality is not simply discursive.

I am not disputing that the insidious dictates of heterosexuality operate through the discourses of culture, but surely they organize and help shape other features of social life as well. While political and economic practices are always made intelligible and shaped by our ways of making sense of them, reducing materiality to discourse alone has the effect of obscuring much of social life. The ways of making sense of sexuality that are dispersed through institutions like the military, churches, or the media also depend on and condition divisions of labor and are affected by the operations of particular state and national formations. The proposal to lift the ban on gays in the US military, for instance, threatens to disclose the fiction of heterosexual coherence. But the discourses of identity and sexual citizenship that organize this proposal have only become possible under certain historical conditions, among them changes in the place of the United States in global politics after the Cold War and in the sexual division of labor that has enabled a more flexible patriarchal gender ideology in multinational capitalist economies.

Given Butler's reduction of the social to discourses, it is not surprising that she understands history in very local, limited terms, a feature of her work that is in keeping with its poststructuralist roots. For example, at one point she admits that gender parody in itself is not subversive, rather its meaning depends on "a context and reception in which subversive confusions can be fostered" (Butler 1990a, 139). She quickly passes over the problem of historical "context" (it appears in one of her frequent series of rhetorical questions). But it is, I think, a crucial issue for queer politics now. What does it mean to say that what can be seen as parodic and what gender parody makes visible depend on a context in which subversive confusions can be fostered? What exactly is meant by "context" here?

As Butler uses it, context would seem to be a crucial feature of the meaning-making process: its contingent foundation serves as a backdrop of sorts linking one discursive practice—drag, for example—to others; through these links, presumably, meaning is produced. But considering historical context is quite different from historicizing. Historicizing does not establish connections only in this local scene of reception—between one discursive practice and another—nor does it leave unaddressed the relationship between the discursive and the nondiscursive. Historicizing starts by acknowledging that the continuation of social life depends on its (re)production in various spheres. As a mode of reading, it traces connections between and among these spheres at several levels of analysis—connecting particular conjunctural arrangements in a social formation to more far-reaching ones. To historicize the meaning of drag among the urban middle class in the United States at the turn of the twenty-first century would be to link it as a discursive practice to the social relations that make it possible and in so doing situate practices specific to a particular social formation in the United States within the larger frame of late capitalism's geopolitics and multinational economy. Butler's presupposed concept of the social displaces analysis of social totalities like capitalism and patriarchy, however, in favor of an exclusive emphasis on the specific and the local (à la Foucault). In so doing she confines history to a very limited frame whose unspoken "context" has a very specific address: the new bourgeois professional class.

This historical address is most evident in her earlier conceptions of drag as subversive political practice. For Butler, drag challenges the notion of identity implicit in "coming out," the act of making visible one's homosexuality. In her essay "Imitation and Gender Insubordination" (1991), she argues that coming out is a process one can never completely achieve. No homosexual is ever entirely "out" because identity, always undermined by the disruptive operations of the unconscious and of signification, can never be fully disclosed. This means that any avowal of the "fact" of one's homosexual (or heterosexual) identity is itself a fiction. Performative activities like drag play up the precarious fabrication of a coherent and internal sexual identity by putting on display the made-up (in)congruity of sex, gender, and desire. In her essay, "Performative Acts and Gender Constitution" (1990b), Butler acknowledges these social limitations on signification—"one is compelled to live in a world in which genders constitute univocal signifiers, in which gender is stabilized, polarized, rendered discrete and intractable" and where performing one's gender wrong initiates a set of punishments (1990b, 279). But here, as elsewhere, the critical force of Butler's commentary denaturalizes reified versions of sexuality by addressing them as discursively constructed rather than considering why they are historically secured as they are. Even though Butler concedes that the subversiveness of gender parody depends on the historical context in which it is received, most of her earlier analysis assumes that *anyone* might participate in exposing the fiction of sexual identity.

But of course, they cannot. One reason is that, unfortunately, societies are still organized so that meaning is taken to be anchored in referents or signifieds; "lesbian" and "gay" are often read as referring to authentic identities, either benign or malevolent perversions of a naturalized norm. To date, the indeterminate meanings Butler assigns these words are not shared by all. Gay bashings, at times with murderous outcomes, indicate that the insistence of the signified in the symbolic order continues to organize social life, as does the military's latest "don't ask, don't tell" policy. And in both cases the disclosure of the identity "homosexual" has definite consequences for people's lives. A book like Leslie Feinberg's *Stone Butch Blues* (1993) or a film like Jennie Livingston's *Paris Is Burning*, both of which document the ways "gender parody" often blurs into "passing," each demonstrates the powerful hold on lesbian and gay imaginations of the notion that sex should align with gender. For many lesbians and gays who have not had the social resources or mobility to insulate themselves from heteronormativity's insistence that sex equals gender, drag has been not so much playful subversion as a painful yearning for authenticity, occasionally with brutally violent results.

In *Bodies That Matter* (1993) Butler addresses some of the ways Livingston's documentary of the Harlem balls in *Paris Is Burning* tests her own earlier arguments on performative subversion and the contextual boundaries of drag. As Butler reads their representation in *Paris Is Burning*, drag balls are highly qualified social practices that can both denaturalize and re-idealize gender norms. Furthermore, the murder of Venus Xtravaganza by one of her clients (for whom the discovery that Venus had male genitals is perhaps not at all a playful subversion of gender identity) dramatizes the limits of gender parody. In other words, as she puts it, "there is passing and then there is passing" (Butler 1993, 130). Unlike Willie Ninja who "makes it" as a gay man into the mainstream of celebrity glamor, Venus is ultimately treated the way women of color are treated. Butler's reading of the film acknowledges the insistence of the signified in the symbolic order—Venus dies, she tells us, because the possibilities for resignifying sex and race which the drag balls represent are eradicated by the symbolic. Her death "testifies to a tragic misreading of the social map of power" (Butler 1993, 131) and suggests that the resignification of the symbolic order along with the phantasmic idealizations that drag enacts do have their refusals and their consequences.

There are moments in this essay when Butler hints that the social map of power, while discursive, also includes more than the symbolic order—for example, when she refers to the situation of the numbers of poor black women that the balls' idealizations deny, or when she indicates that the balls' phantasmic excess constitutes the site of women "not only as marketable goods within an erotic economy of exchange, but as goods which, as it were, are also privileged consumers with access to wealth and social privilege and protection" (Butler 1993, 132). But for the most part, here, too, the materiality of social life is ultimately and insistently confined to the ideological. While she makes use of concepts like "ideology" and "hegemony" in this essay conceptually to relate discourse, subjectivity, and power, the systemic connections among ideology, state, and labor in the historical materialist theories of Althusser and Gramsci are dropped out. The result is that important links among social contradictions that materially affect people's lives—uneven and complex though they may be—remain unexplained. I am thinking here especially of connections between the continual effort (and failure) of the heterosexual imaginary to police identities and the racialized gendered division of labor Butler alludes to earlier.

To sum up, my reading of Butler's work suggests several points about the materiality of sexuality that are politically important to queer theory and politics. First of all, if the materiality of social life is taken to be an ensemble of economic, political, and ideological production, we can still acknowledge that the coherent sex/gender identities heterosexuality secures may be fabrications always in need of repair, but their fragility can be seen not as the property of some restlessness in language itself but as the effect of social struggle. Second, the meanings that are taken to be "real" are so because they help secure a certain social order, an order that is naturalized as the way things are or should be and that "illegitimate" meanings to some degree threaten. Because it is the social order—the distribution of wealth, of resources, and power—that is at stake in the struggle over meanings, a politics that contests the prevailing constructions of sexual identity and that aims to disrupt the regimes they support will need to address more than discourse. Third, the naturalized version of sexual identity that currently dominates in the United States as well as the oppositional versions that contest it are conditioned by more than just their local contexts of reception. Any specific situation is made possible and affected by dimensions of social life that exceed it. A social practice like drag, then, needs to be analyzed at several levels: in terms of the conjunctural situation—whether you are looking at what drag means when walking a ball in Harlem or turning a trick in the Village, performing in a Hasty Pudding revue at Harvard or hoping to pass in Pocatello; in terms of its place in the social formation—whether this local scene occurs in an urban or rural area, in the United States, Germany, Nicaragua, or India, at the turn of the twentieth or of the twenty-first century; and in terms of the global relations that this situation is tied to—how even the option of drag as a flexible sexual identity depends on the availability not only of certain discourses of sexuality, aesthetics, style, and glamor but also of a circuit of commodity production, exchange, and consumption specific to industrialized economies. Recognizing that signs are sites of social struggle, then, ultimately leads us to enquire into the social conditions that enable and perhaps even foster the slipping and sliding of signification. Is the subversiveness of a self-consciously performative identity like drag at risk if we enquire into certain other social relations—the relations of labor, for instance—that help enable it? What is the consequence of a theory that does not allow this kind of question?

I want to suggest that one consequence is the risk of promoting an up-dated, postmodern, reinscription of the bourgeois subject's fetishized identity. Alienation of any aspect of human life from the network of social relations that make it possible constitutes the very basis of fetishization. By limiting her conception of the social to the discursive, Butler unhinges identity from the other material relations that shape it. Her performative identity recasts bourgeois humanist individuality as a more fluid and indeterminate series of subversive bodily acts, but this postmodern subject is severed from the collective historical processes and struggles through which identities are produced and circulate. Moreover, in confining her analysis of the inflection of sexuality by racial, national, or class difference to specific historical contexts, she forecloses the possibility of marshaling collectivities for social transformation across differences in historical positioning.

This postmodern fetishizing of sexual identity also characterizes the recent essays of Diana Fuss and Teresa de Lauretis. While their projects are distinct and differently nuanced, they share an ideological affiliation in that the subjects their work constructs are in many ways much the same. Unlike Butler, both Fuss and de Lauretis reference commodity culture in the cultural forms their essays target—advertising and film—and, significantly, de Lauretis occasionally explicitly mentions the commodity. For some readers Fuss's emphatic psychoanalytic approach and de Lauretis's more insistently political feminist analysis might seem to distinguish their theoretical frameworks both from Butler's and from one another's. But it is precisely these differences that I want to question.

In "Fashion and the Homospectatorial Look" (1992) Diana Fuss is concerned with relations of looking that structure fashion photography, in particular the tension between the ideological project to invite viewers to identify with properly heterosexual positions and the surface structure of the fashion photo which presents eroticized images of the female body for consumption by a female audience (1992, 713). Her essay sets out to decode this tension, which Fuss formulates in terms of the "restless operations of identification" (1992, 716). Drawing primarily on psychoanalytic theories of subjectivity (Freud, Lacan, Kristeva), Fuss explains this restlessness of identity as an effect of the subject's entry into the symbolic and its subjugation to the law of the father, a law which mitigates against return to an always irretrievable presymbolic unity. Fuss argues that by persistently representing the female body "in pieces" (showing only a woman's legs, hands, arms, face . . .), fashion photography reminds the woman spectator of her fetishization. But unlike Marx who takes fetishization to be the concealment of a postive network of social relations, Fuss understands fetishization as Freud does, that is, as a lack (castration). For Freud fetishization is the effect of a failed resolution to the Oedipal romance whereby the child disavows his knowledge that the mother does not have a penis by substituting other body parts (a leg, a hand, a foot) for it. Through their fixation on women's body parts, Fuss argues, fashion photos dramatize the role woman plays in the disavowal of the mother's castration, at the same time the fragmented body serves as substitute for the missing maternal phallus (1992, 720). Fashion fetishism is in this sense an effort to compensate for the "divisions and separations upon which subjectivity is based" (Fuss 1992, 721). At the same time, it also points to some of the mechanisms of primary identification, in particular the "fundamental female homosexuality in the daughter's pre-Oedipal identification with the mother" (Fuss 1992, 721). The fascination of fashion photography with repeated close-ups of a woman's face, Fuss argues, entails the ambivalent disavowal—denial and recognition—of the source of pain and pleasure invoked by the potential restitution of this lost object for an always imperfectly Oedipalized woman.

The Freudian concept of the fetish Fuss appropriates might be read as itself a symptom of capitalism's fetishizing of social relations in that it condenses into the nuclear family circle and onto a psychically charged object—the phallus—the more extensive network of historical and social relations the bourgeois family and the father's position within it entail.[4] Fuss fetishizes identity in the sense that she imagines it only in terms of atomized parts of social life—a class-specific formation of the family and the processes of signification in the sphere of cultural representation. Her concepts of vision and the look participate in this economy of fetishization in that visibility is divorced from the *social* relations that make it possible and understood to be only a matter of *cultural* construction: "If subjects look differently," she asserts, "it is only the enculturating mechanisms of the look that instantiate and regulate these differences in the first place" (Fuss 1992, 736–37).

Like Butler's theory, her analysis is not aimed at claiming lesbian or gay identity as a resistant state of being in its own right, but instead sets out to queer-y the dominant sexual symbolic order by exposing the ways it is continually disrupted by the homospectatorial gaze. Heterosexuality is not an original or pure identity; its coherence is only secured by at once calling attention to and disavowing its "abject, interiorized, and ghostly other, homosexuality" (Fuss 1992, 732). For her, too, identity is postmodern in its incoherence and social in its constructedness, but because it is consistently framed in terms of the individual psyche and its history, the subject for Fuss is ultimately an updated version of the bourgeois individual. This individual, moreover, constitutes the historical frame for the images of fashion photography that "tell us as much about the subject's current history as they do about her already shadowy prehistory, perhaps even more" (Fuss 1992, 734). The "perhaps even more" is significant here because it is this individualized "prehistory," a story of lost origins and mother–daughter bonds, that Fuss emphasizes. Indeed it constitutes the basis for the homospectatorial look. Although she insists that the lesbian looks coded by fashion photography "radically de-essentialize conventional notions of identity" (Fuss 1992, 736), contradictorily, an essentially gendered and embodied spectatorial encounter between infant and mother anchors the "history" that constitutes the fashion text's foundational reference point. If history is localized in Judith Butler's queer theory, then, it is even more narrowly circumscribed in Fuss's reading of fashion ads, where it is reduced to an individual's presocial relationship to the mythic mother's face (Fuss 1992, 722).

Locating the basis for identity in a space/time outside history—in memories of an archaic choric union between mother and child—has the effect of masquerading bourgeois individualism's universal subject—with all of the political baggage it carries—in postmodern drag. Like Butler, Fuss admits history makes a difference to meaning: "more work needs to be done on how spectators from different gendered, racial, ethnic, economic, national and historical backgrounds might appropriate or resist these images" (Fuss 1992, 736). But the recognition of sexuality's differential historical context so late in her essay echoes the familiar liberal gesture. Premised on a notion of history as "background," this assertion thematizes difference by encapsulating the subject in individualized cultural slots, while the social struggles over difference that foment the "restless operations of identity" remain safely out of view.

Teresa de Lauretis's essay "Film and the Visible," originally presented at the 1991 conference How Do I Look: Queer Film and Video shares many of the features of Butler's and Fuss's analyses. While she, too, draws upon psychoanalysis as well as a loosely Foucauldian analytic, her work is, I think, generally taken to be more "social" in its approach, and she at times situates it as such against a more textual analysis. Her purported objective in this essay is indeed "not to do a textual analysis" but to "put into discourse" the terms of an autonomous form of lesbian sexuality and desire in relation to film. While there are films about lesbians that may offer positive images, she argues, they do not necessarily produce new ways of seeing or new inscriptions of the lesbian subject (de Lauretis 1991, 224). De Lauretis presents Sheila McLaughlin's film *She Must Be Seeing Things* as an exemplary alternative because it offers spectators a new position for looking—the place of a woman who desires another woman. While the effort to articulate the dynamics of a specifically lesbian sexuality links de Lauretis's work with Diana Fuss's essay, unlike Fuss, she renounces formulations of lesbian sexuality founded in the mother–child dyad. At the same time, for de Lauretis lesbian sexuality is neither contingent with heterosexual female sexuality nor independent of the Oedipal fantasy structure. However, the presuppositions on which these two assertions rest belie her antitextualist stance and link her "new subjectivity" with other fetishized queer identities in the poststructuralist strand of cultural studies.

De Lauretis reads McLaughlin's film as a tale of two women who are lovers and image makers. One (Jo) literally makes movies and the other (Agatha) does so more figuratively in the fantasies she fabricates about her lover. The film demonstrates the ways a pervasive heterosexuality structures the relations of looking for both women; at the same time, the two women's butch/femme role-playing flaunts its (in)congruence with heterosexual positions by marking these roles *as* performances. De Lauretis contends that this role-playing is always at one remove from the heterosexual paradigm, and it is the space of this "remove" that constitutes for her the "excess" of the lesbian subject position. As in Butler's similar argument about performative identities, however, lesbian excess is fundamentally and exclusively a matter of cultural representation. This partial frame of reference for the social is compounded by de Lauretis's reading of Jo's film-within-the-film as a lesbian revision of the psychoanalytic Oedipal drama. Although she reads the interpolated film as a skewed rewriting of the primal scene from the perspective of a woman desiring another woman, de Lauretis's endorsement of this origin story has the effect of equating generic lesbian identity with a very specific bourgeois construction, founded in highly individualized notions of fantasy, eroticism, scopophilia, and romance.

That the narrow limits of her conception of the subject are ultimately the effect of the historical position from which she is reading comes clear in the audience discussion of her essay included in the collection. The first question from the audience addresses a gap in de Lauretis's text—one might even call it an "excess"—that is, her erasure of the film's treatment of racial difference. Her response to this question reveals the fascination with form that underlies de Lauretis's way of reading. Although she may seem more "social" in her orientation, like Fuss and Butler, she, too, fetishizes meaning by cutting it off from the social and historical forces that make texts intelligible. In defense of her omission of any discussion of race, de Lauretis argues that she has "concluded that the film *intentionally focuses on other aspects of their relationship* [emphasis added]" (1991, 268). Despite her initial disclaimers to the contrary, meaning for de Lauretis here seems to be firmly rooted in the text. Indeed throughout the essay she defines the "new position of seeing" McLaughlin's film offers the viewer by reference to the various textual devices that comprise it—the film's reframing of the Oedipal scenario, its structuring of the spectator's look, its title, and its campy use of masquerade, cross-dressing, and Hollywood spectacle. The audience's insistent return to the problem of racial difference can be read as resistance both to this formalist approach to visibility and to the generic lesbian subject it offers.

While de Lauretis insists that race "is not represented as an issue in this film" (1991, 268), clearly for her audience this is not the case. Their questions suggest the need for another way of understanding meaning, not as textual but as historical—the effect of the ways of knowing that spectators/readers bring to a text, ways of making sense that are enabled and conditioned by their different social positions. For some viewers this film may not deal with Freud or Oedipus, show Agatha sharing a common fantasy with Jo, or any number of the things de Lauretis sees in it, but it may deal with a black Latina who is also a lesbian and a lawyer in love with a white woman. The "visibility" of these issues is not a matter of what is empirically "there" or of what the film intends, but of the frames of knowing that make certain meanings "seeable." From this vantage point, a text's very limited "dealing" or "not dealing" with a particular social category can be used to make available another possible telling of its tale, one that might begin to enquire into the historical limits of any particular construction of social reality.[5] At the very least the problem of Agatha as a Brazilian Latina pressures de Lauretis's closing assertion that *She Must Be Seeing Things* "locates itself historically and politically in the North American lesbian community" (1991, 263).

In another essay, "Sexual Indifference and Lesbian Representation,"[6] de Lauretis acknowledges that lesbian identity is affected by the operation of "interlocking systems of gender, sexual, racial, class and other, more local categories of social stratification" (1993, 148). However, the conception of the social hinted at here and the notion of community it entails are somewhat different from those offered above. For in this essay de Lauretis uses Audre Lorde's image of the "house of difference" ("our place was the very house of difference rather than the security of any one particular difference") to define a social life that is not pluralistic, and a community that is not confined to North America, but (in de Lauretis's words) "at once global and local—global in its inclusive and macro-political strategies, and local in its specific, micro-political practices" (1993, 148). If taken seriously, the social and historical frame to which de Lauretis alludes briefly here would radically recast the fetishized conception of identity that leads her to suggest that in order to address the issue of race we would need to "see a film made by or about lesbians of color" (1993, 269). But even in her allusion to a more systemic mode of reading the connection between sexuality and divisions of labor remains entirely invisible, an excess whose traces are hinted only in passing references to the commodity. What would it mean to understand the formation of queer identities in a social logic that did not suppress this other story?

While queer theorists generally have not elaborated the answer, two of de Lauretis's brief remarks on commodification provide glimpses of this unexplored way of seeing. One of them appears in a fleeting comment on Jill Dolan's contention that "desire is not necessarily a fixed, male-owned commodity, but can be exchanged, with a much different meaning, between women," an assertion de Lauretis reads as either "the ultimate camp representation" or "rather disturbing. For unfortunately—or fortunately as the case may be—commodity exchange does have the same meaning between women as between men by definition—that is by Marx's definition of the structure of capital" (1993, 152). The other appears in her argument that the critique of heterosexuality in films like *The Kiss of the Spider Woman* and *The Color Purple* is "suppressed and rendered invisible by the film's compliance with the apparatus of commercial cinema and its institutional drive to, precisely, commodity exchange" (de Lauretis 1993, 153). Both of these remarks suggest an order of (in)visibility that queer theory's critique of heterosexuality does not explore. What is the connection between the ways commodity exchange renders certain social relations (in)visible and the way of looking that structure heteronormativity or even queer theory? Do fetishized versions of identity in queer theory comply with the institutional drive to commodity exchange in the academy?

Queer Nationalism: The Avant-Garde Goes SHOPping

If academic queer theory for the most part ignores the relationship between sexuality and commodification, groups like Queer Nation do not. Founded in New York city in 1990 by a small group of activists frustrated by ACT-UP's exclusive focus on AIDS, Queer Nation has grown into a loosely organized collection of local chapters stretching across the United States.[7] The list of affinity groups comprising Queer Nation is too long and too variable to list here; included among them are the Suburban Homosexual Outreach Program (SHOP), Queers Undertaking Exquisite and Symbolic Transformation (QUEST), and United Colors which focuses on the experiences of queers of color.[8] Queer Nation is less committed to ACT-UP's strategies of direct action through civil disobedience than to creating awareness and increasing queer visibility. Often representing their tactics as explicitly postmodern, Queer Nation shares many of the presuppositions of queer theory: deconstructing the homo/hetero binary in favor of a more indeterminate sexual identity; targeting a pervasive heteronormativity by miming it with a campy inflection; employing a performative politics that associates identity less with interiority than with the public spectacle of consumer culture.

The signifier "nation" signals a commitment to disrupting the often invisible links between nationhood and public sexual discourse as well as transforming the public spaces in which a (hetero) sexualized national imaginary is constructed in people's everyday lives—in shopping malls, bars, advertising, and the media. In seizing the public space as a "zone of political pedagogy," Queer Nation, like ACT-UP, advances some useful ways of thinking about pedagogy as a public political practice.[9] My concern here, however, is with how their antiassimilationist politics understands and makes use of the commodity as part of a campaign for gay visibility.

For Queer Nation, visibility is a crucial requirement if gays are to have a safe public existence. To this end they reterritorialize various public spaces through an assortment of strategies like the policing of neighbourhoods by Pink Panthers dressed in "Bash Back" T-shirts or Queer Nights Out and Kiss-Ins where groups of gay couples invade straight bars or other public spaces and scandalously make out (Berlant and Freeman 1992, 160–63). In its most "postmodern moments" Queer Nation uses the hyperspaces of commodity consumption as sites for political intervention. Queer Nation is not interested in marketing positive images of gays and lesbians so much as inhabiting and subverting consumer pleasure in commodities in order to "reveal to the consumer desires he/she didn't know he/she had" (Berlant and Freeman 1992, 164). Tactics like producing Queer Bart Simpson T-shirts or rewriting the trademarks of corporations that appropriate gay street styles (changing the "p" in GAP ads to "y") are meant to demonstrate "that the commodity is a central means by which individuals tap into the collective experience of public desire" and to disrupt the heterosexual presupposition on which that desire rests (Berlant and Freeman 1992, 164). To this end, the Queer Shopping Network of New York and the Suburban Homosexual Outreach Program (SHOP) of San Francisco stage mall visibility actions. By parading into suburban shopping spaces dressed in full gay regalia, holding hands, or handing out flyers, they insert gay spectacle into the centers of straight consumption. Berlant and Freeman argue that the queer mall spectacle addresses "the consumer's own 'perverse' desire to experience a different body and offers *itself* as the most stylish of the many attitudes on sale at the mall" (1992, 164).

If in postmodern consumer culture the commodity is a central means by which desire is organized, how are Queer Nation's visibility actions disrupting this process? I want to suggest that while Queer Nation's tactics attend to the commodity, the framework in which the commodity is understood is similar to the informing framework of much queer theory. It is, in short, a cultural one in which the commodity is reduced to an ideological icon. Like queer theory, Queer Nation tends to focus so exclusively on the construction of meanings, on forging an oppositional practice that "disrupts the *semiotic* boundaries between gay and straight [emphasis added]" (Berlant and Freeman 1992, 168), that social change is reduced to the arena of cultural representation. Condensed into a cultural signifier, the commodity remains securely fetishized. Infusing consumer space with a gay sensibility may queer-y commodities, but "making queer good by making goods queer" (Berlant and Freeman 1992, 168) is hardly antiassimilationist politics! If the aim of mall visibility actions is to make the pleasures of consumption available to gays, too, and to commodify queer identity as "the most stylish of the many attitudes on sale at the mall," then inclusion seems to be precisely the point. Disclosing the invisible heterosexual meanings invested in commodities, I am suggesting, is a very limited strategy of resistance, one that ultimately nourishes the commodity's gravitation toward the new, the exotic, the spectacular.

As in queer theory, many of the activities of Queer Nation take visibility at face value and in so doing short-circuit the historicity of visibility concealed in the logic of the commodity. In *Capital* Marx demonstrates that this sort of "oversight" is very much a part of the commodity's secret and its magic: "A commodity appears at first sight an extremely obvious, trivial thing. But its analysis brings out that it is a very strange thing, abounding in metaphysical subtleties and theological niceties." Marx's "analysis" of the commodity explains this "first sight" as a fiction, not in the sense that it is false or merely a copy of a copy but in the sense that it confuses the seeable with the visible. The visible for Marx is not an empirical but an historical effect. Indeed, it might be said that much of Marx's critique of the commodity redefines the nature of vision by establishing the connection between visibility and history.[10] In *Capital* Marx demonstrates that the value of a commodity is material, not in the sense of its being made of physical matter but in the sense that it is socially produced through human labor and the extraction of surplus value in exchange. Although the value of commodities is materially embodied in them, it is not visible in the objects themselves as a physical property. The illusion that value resides in objects rather than in the social relations between individuals and objects Marx calls commodity fetishism. When the commodity is fetishized, the labor that has gone into its production is rendered invisible. Commodity fetishism entails the misrecognition of a structural effect as an immediate property of one of its elements, as if this property belonged to it outside of its relation to other elements (Zizek 1989, 24). This fetishizing is enhanced and encouraged under late capitalism when the spheres of commodity production and consumption are so often widely separated.

Any argument for the continued pertinence of Marx's theory of the commodity risks being misread as a reductive "return" to orthodox Marxism. While a more extensive engagement with contemporary rewritings of Marxian commodity theory, Baudrillard especially, is necessary to forestall such a misreading, they are beyond the scope of this essay. Certainly Marx was not theorizing commodity fetishism from the vantage point of late capitalism's flexible production and burgeoning information technologies and their effects on identities and cultures. Nonetheless, because his reading of the commodity invites us to begin by seeing consciousness, state, and political economy as interlinked historical and material forces by which social life is made and remade, it is to my mind a more politically useful critical framework for understanding and combating the commodification of identities than a political economy of the sign. When the commodity is dealt with merely as a matter of signification, meaning, or identities, only one of the elements of its production—the process of image-making it relies on—is made visible. The exploitation of human labor on which the commodity's appearance as an object depends remains out of sight. Changing the Bart Simpson logo on a T-shirt to "Queer Bart" may disrupt normative conceptions of sexuality that infuse the circulation of commodities in consumer culture, but it offers a very limited view of the social relations commodities rely on, and to this extent it reinforces their fetishization.

Queer-y-ing the Avant-Garde

Some of the problems in queer theory and politics I address above are reminiscent of the contradictions that have punctuated the history of the avant-grade in the West over the past hundred years. It is a history worth examining because the modes of reading in cultural studies and queer intellectual activity now are in the process of repeating it. The genealogy of the concept of the avant-garde in radical political thought dates from the 1790s when it signaled the progressive romantic notion of art as an instrument for social revolution (Calinescue 1987). Early twentieth-century avant-garde movements, provoked by the enormous social upheavals of World War I and the 1917 Revolution, promoted a critical rejection of bourgeois culture. Like the aesthetes at the turn of the twentieth century, the avant-garde reacted to the increasing fragmentation of social life in industrialized society. But while aestheticism responded to the commercialization of art and its separation from life by substituting reflexive exploration of its own processes of creation for social relevance, the avant-garde attempted to reintegrate art into meaningful human activity by leading it back to social praxis (Burger 1984). As Raymond Williams has pointed out, there were innumerable variations on avant-garde complaints against the bourgeoisie—often articulating quite antithetical political positions—depending on the social and political structures of the countries in which these movements were active (1989, 54). Despite these variations, like queer theory and activism, avant-garde movements—among them Dada, Surrealism Italian Futurism, the German Bauhaus, and Russian Constructionism—attacked the philosophical and political assumptions presupposed in the reigning bourgeois realist conceptions of representation and visibility. Like Queer Nation, Dada was a broad and disparate movement, crossing national boundaries as well as the ideological divisions between art, politics, and daily life. It, too, found expression in a variety of media: poetry, performance, painting, the cinema, and montage. Attacking the cultural, political and moral values on which the dominant social order relied, it set out to "shock the bourgeoisie" (Plant 1992, 40–41). The Surrealists, many of whom had participated in the Dadaist movement in France, rejected Dada's shock tactics and its purely negative approach and aimed instead to try to make use of Freud's theory of the unconscious in order to unleash the pleasures trapped in experience and unfulfilled by a social system dependent on rationality and the accumulation of capital (Plant 1992, 49). Convinced that the union of art and life, of the individual and the world, was "possible only with the end of capitalism and the dawn of a new ludic age," nonetheless, like other avant-garde movements, their experiments were pursued mainly in the cultural domain (Plant 1992, 52).

The Situationist International (SI) movement that surfaced in France in the late 1950s and lasted through 1972 is an interesting example of a political project that attempted to reclaim the revolutionary potential of the avant-garde and supersede the limitations of its cultural politics. The Situationists acknowledged the historical importance of their avant-garde antecedents' efforts as an effective means of struggle against the bourgeoisie, but were also critical of their failure to develop that spirit of revolt into a coherent critique. Consequently, they set out to transcend the distinction between revolutionary politics and cultural criticism once and for all, and in some respects went further than their predecessors in doing so (Plant 1992, 55–56).[11] Several of their strategies for disrupting the spectacular organization of everyday life in commodity culture share much in common with those of queer activism.

The tactic of *detournement*, for instance, is one—that is, the rearrangement of a preexisting text like an advertisement to form a new and critical ensemble. The SI's critique of consumer society, its political agitation in commodity culture, and efforts to form an international collective had both a revolutionary and a ludic dimension. Sorting out the contradictions in their vision and accounting for the failures in their attempt to revamp the avant-garde might be a useful project for queer intellectuals to pursue and learn from.

Historically, the dissolution of the more revolutionary aspirations and activities of the early avant-garde movements cannot be separated from political forces like Stalinism and Nazism that were responsible for the suppression of their potential oppositional force by the middle of the twentieth century. But their critical edge was also blunted by their own participation in the increasing commodification of social life by retreating to cultural experimentation as their principal political forum. That the term "avant-garde" now connotes primarily, even exclusively, artistic innovation is in this regard symptomatic. Seen from this vantage point, the distinction between the direction the avant-garde finally pursued and aestheticism seems less dramatic—as does the distinction in contemporary theory between poststructuralism's fixation on representation and more recent formulations of social postmodernism. Many of the aesthetic features of the avant-garde reverberate in this more worldly "social postmodernism": a tendency toward formalist modes of reading, a focus on performance and aesthetic experimentation, an idealist retreat to mythic/psychic spirituality, and the disparity between a professed agenda for broad social change and a practice focused exclusively on cultural politics. One way to begin to understand this gravitation toward cultural politics in the history of the avant-garde is to consider it in relation to the more general aestheticization of everyday life in consumer capitalism.

At the same time oppositional intellectuals struggle against the separation of art from daily life, capitalism's need for expanding markets has in its own way promoted the integration of art and life—but in accordance with the requirements of commodity exchange. The aestheticization of daily life is one consequence of this process. By "the aestheticization of daily life" I mean the intensified integration of cultural and commodity production under late capitalism by way of the rapid flow of images and signs that saturate myriad everyday activities, continuously working and reworking desires by inviting them to take the forms dictated by the commodity market. Advertising epitomizes this process and is its primary promoter. Along with computer technology, advertising permeates the fabric of daily life with an infinity of visual spectacles, codes, signs, and information bits. In so doing it has helped erase the boundary between the real and the image, an insertion of artifice into the heart of reality, an act for which Baudrillard has coined the term "simulation."

One effect of the aestheticization of daily life in industrial capitalism is that the social relations on which cultural production depends are even further mystified. The aestheticization of everyday life encourages the pursuit of new tastes and sensations as pleasures in themselves while concealing or back-grounding the labor that has gone into making them possible. In keeping with the aesthetic emphasis on cultural forms, "style" becomes an increasingly crucial marker of social value and identity. While the term has a more restricted sociological meaning in reference to specific status groups, "lifestyle" as a way of making sense of social relations crystallized in the 1980s in the United States as new forms of middle-class professionalism became the focal point for heightened involvement in consumption and the promotion of cosmopolitanism (Clarke 1991, 67–68).[12] The concept of identity as "lifestyle" serves to manipulate a system of equivalences that structures the connection between the economic functions of the new middle class and their cultural formation (Clarke 1991, 68). The economic remaking of the middle class depends on the rising significance of the sphere of circulation and consumption and the invisible though persistent extraction of surplus value through exploited human labor. Although their cultural formation is increasingly flexible, "middle-class identities" continue to be organized by gender and racial hierarchies as well as by a residual individualism. "Lifestyle" obscures these social hierarchies by promoting individuality and self-expression but also a more porous conception of the self as a "fashioned" identity. Advertising, especially, champions a highly coded self-consciousness of the stylized construction of almost every aspect of one's everyday life: one's body, clothes, speech, leisure activities, eating, drinking, and sexual preferences. All are regarded as indicators of individuality and style, and all can be acquired with a few purchases (Featherstone 1991, 83; Goldman 1992). Reconfiguring identities in terms of "lifestyles" serves in some ways, then, as a linchpin between the coherent individual and a more porous postmodern one. "Lifestyle" consumer culture promotes a way of thinking about identity as malleable because open to more and more consumer choices rather than shaped by moral codes or rules. In this way "lifestyle" identities can seem to endorse the breakup of old hierarchies in favor of the rights of individuals to enjoy new pleasures without moral censure. While the coherent individual has not been displaced, increasingly new urban lifestyles promise a de-centering of identity by way of consumer practices which announce that styles of life that can be purchased in clothes, leisure activities, household items, and bodily dispositions all dissolve fixed status groups. Concern with the stylization of life suggests that practices of consumption are not merely a matter of economic exchange but also affect the formation of sensibilities and tastes that in turn support more flexible subjectivities. At the same time, the capacity for hyper-consumption promoted by appeals to lifestyle as well as the constituent features of various "lifestyles" are class specific. For example, in the 1980s in the United States the class-boundedness of stylization became evident in the polarization of the mass market into "upscale" and "downscale," as middle-class consumers scrambled to shore up symbolic capital through stylized marks of distinction: shopping at Bloomingdale's or Neiman Marcus as opposed to K-Mart; buying imported or chic brand name foods (Beck's or Corona rather than Miller and

Budweiser) or appliances (Kitchen Aid or Braun versus Sears' Kenmore) (Ehrenreich 1989, 228).

Aestheticization in consumer culture is supported by philosophies of the subject in postmodern theory that for all of their "social" dimensions nonetheless pose art—not social change—as the goal of a new ethics. In one of his last interviews, for instance, Michel Foucault protests,

> But couldn't everyone's life become a work of art? Why should the lamp or the house be an object, but not our life? . . . From the idea that the self is not given to us, I think that there is only one practical consequence: we have to create ourselves as a work of art (1983, 236–37).

The aestheticized technology of the self here, and in Foucault's later writings generally, is taken straight from Nietzsche's exhortation to "give style to one's character—a great and rare art!" (1974, 290).[13] Queer theory and activism's conception of identities as performative significations anchored in individual psychic histories is not very far from this notion of identity as self-fashioning. For here, too, visibility is theatrical, a spectacle that shows up the always precarious stylization of identity. Foucault's equation of lamp, house, and life as "created" objects elides the different social relations that go into their making by securing them in individual creation. But the answer to why everyone's life couldn't become a work of art could take us somewhere else, to another story, one that makes visible the contradictory social relations the aestheticization of social life conceals. For even as the regime of simulation invites us to conflate style and life, some people's lives are not very artful or stylish, circumscribed as they are by limited access to social resources. How might the woman earning $50 a week for 60 hours of work operating a sewing machine in a sweatshop in the South Bronx or the exhausted migrant worker in the San Joaquin valley harvesting tomatoes for 12 hours a day at two dollars an hour make their lives an art? How artful was the life of Venus Xtravaganza, forced to support herself as a prostitute until she was murdered? Unless "art" is so re-understood as to be disconnected from individual creation or choice and linked to a strategy for changing the conditions that allow so many to suffer an exploited existence, making one's life an art is an intelligible possibility only for the leisured class and their new yuppie heirs. When queer theory reconfigures gender identity as a "style of the flesh" (Butler 1990a, 139), to use Judith Butler's phrasing, or as "the most stylish of the many attitudes on sale in the mall" (Berlant and Freeman 1992, 167), it is taking part in the postmodern aestheticization of daily life.

In the Life(style): Postmodern (Homo)sexual Subjects

It is not accidental that homosexuals have been most conspicuous in the primary domains of the spectacle: fashion and entertainment. In 1993 no fewer than five national straight news and fashion magazines carried positive cover stories on lesbians and gays. One of the most notable among them was the cover of *New York Magazine*'s May 1993 issue which featured a dashingly seductive close-up of k. d. lang dressed in drag next to the words "Lesbian chic: the bold, brave world of gay women." Every imaginable facet of gay and lesbian life—drag, transsexuality, gay teens, gay parents—has been featured on daytime talk shows. The *New York Time*'s recently inaugurated "Styles of the Times" section now includes along with the engagement and marriage announcements regular features on gay and lesbian issues, here explicitly figured as one of many life "styles." The drag queens Ru Paul and Lady Bunny have both been profiled in "Styles of the Times," and in 1993 the front page of the section carried full page stories on the Harlem balls and gay youth.

Gays and lesbians have been more visible than ever in arts and entertainment, despite the industry's still deeply entrenched investment in heteronormativity. Tony Kushner's "joyously, unapologetically, fabulously gay" *Angels in America* won the Pulitzer Prize in 1993 and was nominated for nine Tony Awards. The list of commercial film and video productions on gay subjects grows monthly and includes such notables as Neil Jordan's transvestite love story, *The Crying Game*; Sally Potter's film version of Virginia Woolf's transsexual, *Orlando*; Jonathan Demme's AIDS courtroom drama, *Philadelphia*; Barbara Streisand's film production of Larry Kramer's *The Normal Heart*; HBO's adaptation of Randy Shilts's AIDS exposé *And the Band Played On*. While the movie industry still fears a subject it wouldn't touch five years ago, it goes where the money is, and so far in the 1990s "gay" is becoming a warmer if not a hot commodity.

Nowhere is gay more in vogue than in fashion, where homoerotic imagery is the epitome of postmodern chic. Magazines firmly situated in the middle-class mainstream like *Details*, *Esquire*, *GQ*, or *Mademoiselle* have all recently carried stories addressing some aspect of gay life and/as fashion, and it is here that gay and lesbian visibility blurs readily into a queer gender-bending aesthetic. The June 1993 issue of *Details*, for example, featured a story on couples that included one gay and one lesbian couple; another story offered a gay man's perspective on lifting the ban on gays in the military (including a graphic account of his one-night stand with a marine who is "not gay") and a favorable review by gay novelist David Leavitt of Michelangelo Signorile's *Queer in America* (1993). The first volume of *Esquire*'s new fashion magazine, *Esquire Gentleman*, carried a feature on "The Gay Factor in Fashion" that declared "Just about everyone dresses a little gay these days . . . It is now a marketing given that gay sensibility sells to both gay and straight" (Martin 1993, 140). *Esquire*'s regular June 1993 issue included a review of Potter's *Orlando* as well as a short story by Lynn Darling entitled "Single White Male Seeks Clue."

Darling's story is a symptomatic example of the incorporation of a queer aesthetic into the gender structure of postmodern patriarchy. "It's not easy to be the scion of a dying WASP culture," the cover blurb announces, "when women have more confidence, gay men have more style, and everyone seems to have the right to be angry with you." This is a tale of young urban professional manhood in crisis, a crisis managed through nostalgic detours into the "now vanished set of certainties" preserved in the world of boxing. As the story draws to a close, John Talbot, the single white male of the title, and his girlfriend look out of their hotel room and find in their view a gay couple "dry-humping" on a penthouse roof right below them. "Talbot was tempted to say something snide, but he checked himself. In fact, it was really sweet, he decided, and in his happiness he saw them suddenly as fellow travellers in the community of desire" (Darling 1993, 104). Talbot's inclusion of gays in the diverse community of "fellow travellers" offers an interesting rearticulation of Cold War moral and political discourses that once made all homosexuals out to be communists. Here gays are included in an elastic community of pleasure seekers and a tentatively more pliant heterosexual sex/gender system.

As Talbot's story suggests, the once-rigid links between sex, gender, and sexual desire that the invisible heterosexual matrix so firmly secured in bourgeois culture have become more flexible as the gendered divisions of labor among the middle class in industrialized countries have shifted. While these more accommodating gender codes are not pervasive, they have begun to take hold among the young urban middle class particularly. There are hints, for instance, that wearing a skirt, a fashion choice once absolutely taboo for men because it signified femaleness and femininity, is now more allowed because the gender system's heteronormative regime is loosening. The designers Betsy Johnson, Matsuda, Donna Karan, and Jean Paul Gaultier all have featured skirts on men in their spring and fall shows for the last few years. Some rock stars (among them Axl Rose of *Guns N Roses*) have worn skirts on stage. But skirts for men are also infiltrating more mundane culture. The fashion pages of my conservative local newspaper feature sarongs for men, and my fifteen-year-old daughter reports that at the two-week co-ed camp she attended in the summer of 1993 at least one of the male counselors wore a mid-calf khaki skirt almost every day.

As middle-class women have been drawn into the professional work force to occupy positions once reserved for men, many of them are now literally "wearing the pants" in the family, often as single heads of household, many of them lesbians and/or mothers. The "new man," like Talbot, has managed the crisis of "not having a clue" where he fits anymore by relinquishing many of the former markers of machismo: he expects women of his class to work outside the home and professes to support their professional ambitions, he "helps out" with the housework and the kids, boasts one or two gay friends, may occasionally wear pink, and perhaps even sports an earring. Men of Talbot's class might also read magazines like *GQ* or *Esquire* where the notion of the "gender fuck" that queer activists and theorists have presented as subversive cultural critique circulates as radical chic—in essays like David Kamp's piece on "The Straight Queer" (1993) detailing the appropriation of gay codes by hip heteros or in spoofs like "Viva Straight Camp" that parody ultra-straight gender codes by showing up their constructedness (Powers 1993).

Much like queer theory, the appropriation of gay cultural codes in the cosmopolitan revamping of gender displays the arbitrariness of bourgeois patriarchy's gender system and helps to reconfigure it in a more postmodern mode where the links between gender and sexuality are looser, where homosexuals are welcome, even constituting the vanguard, and where the appropriation of their parody of authentic sex and gender identities is quite compatible with the aestheticization of everyday life into postmodern lifestyles. In itself, of course, this limited assimilation of gays into mainstream middle-class culture does not disrupt postmodern patriarchy and its intersection with capitalism; indeed it is in some ways quite integral to it.

Because patriarchy has become a buzzword in some postmodern/queer circles, I should explain what I mean by it here. I understand patriarchy to be a concept that explains the systematic gendered organization of all areas of social life—economic, political, and ideological—such that more social resources, power, and value accrue to men as a group at the expense of women as a group. In this sense, patriarchy is social, not merely cultural, and the privilege it accords some at the expense of others affects more than the making of meaning. Many poststructuralist critiques rightly target "the notion that the oppression of women has some singular form discernible in the universal or hegemonic structure of patriarchy or masculine domination" and remind us that any sort of monolithic theory of THE patriarchy fails to account for the workings of gender oppression in the concrete cultural contexts in which it exists (Butler 1990, 3). But often they also reduce patriarchy to contingent cultural forms or dismiss it as a viable concept altogether. Like capitalism, patriarchy is a politically urgent concept because it allows us to analyze and explain social hierarchies by which gender, sexuality, and their racial articulations are organized. Patriarchy is a variable and historical social totality in that its particular forms for organizing social relations like work, citizenship, reproduction, ownership, pleasure, or identity have had a persistent effect on heterogendered[14] structures in dominance at the same time these structures vary and are the sites of social struggle.

Some patriarchal formations entail kinship alliances ruled by fathers, although in industrialized countries this form of patriarchy has been unevenly and gradually displaced as the ruling paradigm by bourgeois patriarchy. In bourgeois patriarchy, kinship alliances are subordinate to a social organization split between public wage economy and unpaid domestic production, both regulated by the ideology of possessive individualism. In advanced capitalist countries, public or postmodern patriarchy has recently begun to emerge as the prevailing form. It is characterized by the hyperdevelopment of consumption and the joint wage-earner family, the relative transfer of power from husbands to professionals in the welfare state, the rise of single-mother-headed and other alternative households, and sexualized consumerism (Ferguson 1989, 110). While any one patriarchal formation may dominate, it often coexists with other contesting or residual forms. Policy debates like the current controversy over lifting the ban on gays in the US military as well as cultural narratives of various sorts (films like *A Few Good Men*, *Jungle Fever*, or *The Firm*, for instance) can be read as articulations of the struggle between bourgeois patriarchal formations and their accompanying moral ideologies and postmodern patriarchy's newer forms of family, gender, sexuality, and work.

Finally, patriarchy is differential. This means that while all women as a group are positioned the same (as subordinate or other) in relation to men, they are positioned differently in relation to each other and at times in relation to men in subaltern groups. Some women have access to resources—a professional job, an urban condo, a cleaning lady, a vacation home, a fancy car—that are only possible because of the work of other women and men who do not have these resources. Because patriarchy functions in concert with a racial system of white supremacy, disproportionate numbers of people of color, men and women alike, have historically occupied these exploited, under-resourced social positions. That more women than men fill the ranks of the impoverished speaks loudly to the ways class exploitation is reinforced by patriarchal structures. Similarly, some men have more patriarchal power than others, sometimes power over and at the expense of other men. This difference means that not all men benefit the same from patriarchy. Because the division of labor in general is racialized at the same time race is not necessarily congruent with class, the cultural capital people of color might gain on entry into any class can be canceled out or undermined by the operations of racism. Consequently, the white gay psychiatrist or lawyer is not in the same patriarchal position as his white straight colleagues nor is he in the same patriarchal position as a black gay man of the same class. Some women, lesbians among them, can claim patriarchal power over other women and men by virtue of their institutional privilege. For instance, women, lesbians included, in administrative or managerial positions can make use of their institutional positions to wield power over men and other women who work for them or are affected by the policies they draft. But even women who benefit from patriarchy in some areas of their lives are disadvantaged in a society that systematically accords men power over women. The pervasiveness of rape and wife-battering across classes and races and the general invisibility of lesbians in the culture demonstrate the systematic persistence of patriarchy despite the claims of a postmodern cosmopolitanism that gender hierarchies no longer operate or are readily subverted.

In positing male and female as distinct and opposite sexes that are naturally attracted to one another, heterosexuality is integral to patriarchy. Woman's position as subordinate other, as (sexual) property, and as exploited laborer depends on a heterosexual matrix in which woman is taken to be man's opposite; his control over social resources, his clear thinking, strength, and sexual prowess depend on her being less able, less rational, and never virile. As a pervasive institution within other institutions (state, education, church, media), heterosexuality helps guarantee patriarchal regulation of women's bodies, labor, and desires. Queer critiques of heterosexuality have often not acknowledged—in fact they often disavow—the relationship between heterosexuality and patriarchy. But the struggles of lesbians in groups like Queer Nation and other gay political organizations are testimony that gender hierarchies persist between men and women even when both are fighting against heterosexuality as a regime of power (Maggenti 1991).

The gender flexibility of postmodern patriarchy is pernicious because it casts the illusion that patriarchy has disappeared. But behind this facade corporate interests are delighting in the discovery of new markets. Among the most promising are gays and lesbians in the new professional/managerial class. Among them are "lifestyle lesbians" like the Bay area vice president of a lesbian-owned business group who announced, "Here I am, this funny, warm person that you like and I happen to be a lesbian. I am bourgeois. I have a house in the suburbs. I drive a Saab" (Stewart 1991, 56). Given the increased "visibility" of this sort of gay consumer, "tolerance of gays makes sense" (Tobias 1992). Increasingly marketers of mainstream products from books to beer are aiming ads specifically at gay men and lesbians; *Fortune* magazine contends "it's a wonderful market niche, the only question is how to reach it" (Stewart 1991). Reaching it has so far involved manufacturing the image of a certain class-specific lesbian and gay consumer population. "Visibility is what it is all about," says David Ehrlich of Overlooked Opinions (Gluckman and Reed 1993, 16). These stereotypes of wealthy freespending gay consumers play well with advertisers and are useful to corporations because they make the gay market seem potentially lucrative; they cultivate a narrow but widely accepted definition of gay identity as a marketing tool and help to integrate gay people *as* gay people into a new marketing niche (Gluckman and Reed 1993, 17, 18). But if gay visibility is a good business prospect, as some companies argue, the question gay critics need to ask is "for whom?" Who profits from these new markets?

Out of Sight, Out of Mind

Commodification structures much more than the exchange of goods on the market; it affects even as it depends on the knowledges that mediate what and how we see. The commodification of gay styles and identities in the corporate and academic marketplaces is integrally related to the formation of a postmodern gay/queer subjectivity, ambivalently gender coded and in some instances flagrantly repudiating traditional hetero and homo bourgeois culture. Nonetheless, as I have been arguing, to a great extent the construction of a new "homosexual/queer spectacle" perpetuates a class-specific perspective that keeps invisible the capitalist divisions of labor that organize sexuality and in particular lesbian, gay, queer lives. In so doing queer spectacles often participate in a long history of class-regulated visibility.[15] Beginning around the middle of the nineteenth century, the bourgeoisie mediated their experience of the working class through spatial as well as cultural/ideological arrangements. The erection of physical barriers—subway and rail construction and the siting of retail and residential districts—structured the physical arrangement of the city so as to foreclose the trauma of seeing the laboring classes (Kester 1993, 73). This physical regulation of class visibility was also compounded by the consolidation of a characteristically "bourgeois" mode of perception through an array of knowledges, the philosophic and aesthetic chief among them. The notion of an autonomous aesthetic perception, first developed by eighteenth-century philosophers (Kant, Hume, Shaftesbury), whereby perceived objects are abstracted from the social context of their creation, provided the foundation for a way of seeing that has dominated modern culture and aesthetics through the late twentieth century (Kester 1993, 74). This mode of perception reinforces and is indeed historically necessary to commodity exchange and comes to function as a "phenomenological matrix" through which the bourgeoisie confront an array of daily experiences through modes of seeing that erase the differently valued divisions of labor that organize visibility (Kester 1993, 75). In late twentieth-century "postindustrial" societies like the United States, the (in)visibility of class divisions continues to be spatially regulated by urban planning, but it is also reinforced by changes in First World relations of production as industry has been increasingly consigned to sites in "developing countries" outside the United States. Capital has not been significantly dispersed or democratized in "First World" economies as a result, simply transferred to more profitable sectors, the so-called "tertiary" or service sectors: banking, finance, pension funds, etc. (Evans 1993, 43). The escalating domination of the ideological—the proliferation of information technologies, media images, codes—in postindustrial cultures has helped to reconfigure bourgeois modes of perception in First World populations, producing subjects who are more differentiated and less likely to experience capitalism collectively through production relations and more likely to experience it through relations of consumption. As a result, the neat subject/object split of Kantian aesthetics has been troubled and to some degree displaced, even as the invisibility of social relations of labor in corporate and intellectual commodity spectacles persists.

Gay-friendly corporations like Levi-Strauss, for example, reinforce the gender-flexible subjects their advertising campaigns promote through gay window-dressing strategies by way of public relations programs that boast of their progressive corporate policies for lesbians and gays. Levi-Strauss gives health insurance benefits to unmarried domestic partners of their employees, has created a supportive environment for employees who test HIV positive, and has a Lesbian and Gay Employees Association. Members of this association prepared a video for the company to use in its diversity training in which they, their parents, and their managers openly discuss their relationships (Stewart 1991, 50). But Levi-Strauss's workers in the sweatshops of Saipan who live in cramped and crowded barracks and earn as little as $2.15 an hour remain largely invisible. Although Levi-Strauss ended its contracts last year with the island's largest clothes maker after an investigation by the company found evidence of unsatisfactory treatment of workers in his factories, they still continue to make shirts at five plants there (Shenon 1993). Meanwhile, back in the

United States, Levi-Strauss closed its San Antonio plant in 1990, laying off 1,150 workers, 92 percent of them Latino and 86 percent of them women, and moved its operations to the Caribbean where it can pay laborers $3.80 a day, roughly half the average hourly wage of the San Antonio workforce (Martinez 1993, 22). Displaying the gay-friendly policies of "progressive" US corporations often deflects attention from the exploitative international division of labor they depend on in the interests of the company's bottom line—profits.[16]

The formation of a gay/queer imaginary in both corporate and academic circles also rests on the suppression of class analysis. There have been all too few books that treat the ways gay history and culture has been stratified along class lines.[17] With several notable exceptions, studies of the relationship between homosexuality and capitalism are remarkably sparse, and extended analyses of lesbian and gay poverty are almost nonexistent.[18] To ask the more pointed question of how the achievement of lesbian and gay visibility by some rests on the invisible labor of others is to expose the unspeakable underside of queer critique.

The consolidation of the professional middle class during the 1980s brought with it an array of social contradictions. The recruitment of more and more women into the workforce bolstered the legitimation of both the professional "New Woman" and of academic feminism. The increasing, albeit uneven and complicated, investiture of lesbians and gays into new forms of sexual citizenship and the relative growth of academic gay studies accompanied and in some ways were enabled by these changes. But these were also decades when the chasm between the very rich and the very poor widened and poverty became more than ever feminized. As the 1990s began, a total of 33 million people in the United States—more than 13.5 percent of the population—were officially living in poverty. While estimates of the numbers of people who are homosexual are notoriously unreliable (ranging from the 1993 Batelle Human Research Center's 1.1 percent to the 1948 Kinsey Report's 10 percent), assuming that somewhere between 1 and 10 percent of the population are homosexual, it would be fair to say that there are between 1.65 and 3.3 million impoverished lesbians and gay men in the United States today.[19]

Most lesbians are leading less glamorous lives than their chic commodity images suggest, and poor lesbians of color are the most invisible and worst off. While the wage gap between women and men has supposedly narrowed in the 1980s—in 1990 women earned 72 percent of what men did—much of this change is due to a drop in men's earnings, while the incomes of women have stayed the same (US Bureau of the Census 1991). Furthermore, the bulk of necessary work at home, by some estimates 70 percent, is still left up to women. In other words, women as a group do more than half of all the work in this country and make less than half of what men do (Abelda, et al. 1988, 52). Of all poor people over 18, 63 percent are women, with 53 percent of poor families headed by women (Macionis 1993, 282). While there is no reliable data available on the numbers of poor who are lesbian or gay, the racialized and gendered division of labor suggests that there are more lesbians than gay men living in poverty and proportionately more of them are people of color.[20] Redressing gay invisibility by promoting images of a seamlessly middle-class gay consumer or by inviting us to see queer identities only in terms of style, textuality, or performative play helps produce imaginary gay/queer subjects that keep invisible the divisions of wealth and labor that these images and knowledges depend on. These commodified perspectives blot from view lesbians, gays, queers who are manual workers, sex workers, unemployed, and imprisoned. About a quarter to a half million homosexual and bisexual youths are thrown out of their homes and subjected to prostitution and violence in the streets (Galst 1992). Severing queer sexuality and homosexuality from the operations of class keeps these lives from view, forecloses consideration of the ways sexual identities are complicated by the priorities imposed by impoverishment, and keeps a queer political agenda from working collectively to address the needs of many whose historical situation is defined in terms of counterdominant sexual practices. That so little work has been done in the academy, even within lesbian and gay studies, to address these populations and the invisible social relations that maintain their marginality and exploitation speaks loudly to the ways a class-specific "bourgeois (homosexual/queer) imaginary" structures our knowledge of sexual identity, pleasure, and emancipation.

Critique-al Visibility

Critique is a political practice and a mode of reading that establishes the intimate links between the visible and the historical by taking as its starting point a systemic understanding of the social. A radical critique of sexuality understands that the visibility of any particular construction of sexuality or sexual identity is historical in that it is shaped by an ensemble of social arrangements. As a way of seeing sexuality, critique insists on making connections between the emergence of a discourse or identity in industrialized social formations and the international division of labor, between sexy commodity images and labor, the spectacle and the sweatshop, style and class. This sort of critique-al intervention into heterosexuality, therefore, does not see sexuality as just the effect of cultural or discursive practice, merely the product of ideology or institutions, but as a regulatory apparatus that spans the organization of social life in the modern world and that works in concert with other social totalities—capitalism, patriarchy, colonialism.

As a political practice, critique acknowledges the importance of "reading" to political activism. Understood broadly as all those ways of making sense that enable one to be conscious, to be literate in the culture's codes, and so to be capable of acting meaningfully in the world, reading is an activity essential to social life. Although they often go unacknowledged, modes of reading are necessary to political activism. Paying attention to how we read and considering its implications and consequences are a key component of any oppositional political work. To ignore this crucial dimension of social struggle is to risk reproducing the very conditions we seek to change. The ways of making sense available in any historical time will tend to support the prevailing social order, but they are also contested. A critical politics joins in and foments this contest not just to reframe how we interpret the world but in order to change it. It is radical in the sense that it does not settle just for a change in the style or form of commodities but demands a change in the invisible social relations that make them possible.

I have tried to show that this way of reading is not just a matter of widening the scope of what we see, but of starting from a different place in how we see. Understanding social life to be "at once global and local" requires that we analyze what presents itself on first sight as obvious in order to show its connection to social structures that often exploit and oppress. While local situations (the commodification of pleasure in suburban malls, for instance) are necessary and important places to disrupt heteronormativity, they do not exist on their own, and we read them as such only at a cost. I am suggesting that a radical sexual politics that is going to be, in Judith Butler's words, "effectively disruptive, truly troubling," needs a way of explaining how the sexual identities we can see are systemically organized. We need a way of understanding visibility that acknowledges both the local situations in which sexuality is made intelligible as well as the ties that bind knowledge and power to commodity production, consumption, and exchange.

The critical way of reading I am proposing in this essay is indeed queer. If it is not very well received now in the academy or in activist circles—and it is not—that may be because in challenging the postmodern fetishizing of social life into discourse, culture, or local contexts, critique puts into crisis the investments of middle-class academics and professionals, queers among us, in the current social order. For this reason it is undoubtedly a risk. Perhaps it is also our best provisional answer to the question "what is to be done?"

Notes

For sharing her many resources and ideas and for her strong readings of various drafts of this essay, I want to thank Chrys Ingraham. I am also indebted to the students in graduate courses I taught in 1993 on the topics of Lesbian and Gay Theory and Critique of Commodity Culture at the University at Albany, SUNY. Their work inspired and challenged me and offered a critical forum for developing many of the arguments I present here.

1. For an astute analysis of the commodification of gay and lesbian culture see Gluckman and Reed 1993.
2. In *Bodies That Matter* (1993) Butler qualifies her earlier position by asserting that drag may not always be unproblematically subversive. Nonetheless, due to the theatrical gender trouble drag incites, it remains for her a commendable practice, perhaps the only viable form of political resistance to heterosexuality's regulatory power.

3. For a more detailed critique of Foucault's concept of discursive practice see Hennessy 1993, 37–46.
4. While the concept of the fetish has been taken up in some recent work in cultural theory (a few of the many recent examples include Adams 1989; Apter 1991; Findlay 1992; Mercer 1989), the relationship between Freud's theory of the fetish and Marx's theory of commodity fetishism has not been very rigorously addressed from a materialist perspective. Most analyses tend to draw upon one theoretical framework or the other, with the Freudian version receiving most attention. Zizek's work on ideology (1989), for example, makes use of Lacanian analysis and poststructuralist reconceptualizations of the social (vis à vis Laclau and Mouffe) to elaborate and extend the post-Marxist return to idealism in cultural theory; his endorsement of the Freudian concept of the fetish as "lack" ignores the possibility that the very notion of castration might be read as the effect of a positive network of (patriarchal) social relations.
5. For a much fuller elaboration of this distinction between the seeable and the visible and its bearing on the reception of film see Zavarzadeh 1991.
6. I have chosen this essay of de Lauretis's for its attention to issues of visibility but also because of its institutional impact which is indicated by its publishing history. Originally appearing in *Theatre Journal* (1988), it has since been reprinted in *Performing Feminisms* (Case 1990) and most recently in *The Lesbian and Gay Studies Reader* (Abelove, et al., 1993). The page numbers used here are from Abelove.
7. For summary-analyses of Queer Nation's history see Baker, et al. 1991; Berlant and Freeman 1992; Berube and Escoffier 1991; Bull 1992; Chee 1991; Duggan 1992; Signorile 1993, 88, 317–18; Smyth 1992. For more critical assessments see Fernandez 1991; Maggenti 1991; Mitchell and Olafimihan 1992; Smith 1993. Since 1992 Queer Nation, like ACT-UP, has been riven by internal strife over whether its focus and political actions should also address issues of racism and sexism; as a result, several local chapters have been dissolved or fragmented.
8. For more extended lists of affinity groups see Berlant and Freeman 1992, 152 n. 3, and Berube and Escoffier 1991, 16.
9. For a more detailed analysis of the concept of nationhood in Queer Nation see Berlant and Freeman 1992.
10. Ann Cvetkovitch's chapter on *Capital* in her study of Victorian sensationalism (1992) offers an incisive reading of the relationship between visibility and the commodity.
11. On the SI see Knabb 1981; Marcus 1989; Plant 1992.
12. On the former connotations of lifestyle see Bourdieu 1984; Sobel 1982; Rojek 1985. On the latter see Ehrenreich 1989; Featherstone 1991.
13. See Callinicos 1989, 62–91 and 168–171, on the connection between poststructuralism and aestheticism, particularly in Foucault. See also Hennessy 1993, 55–59 on the relationship between the aesthetic and the ethical in Foucault.
14. For an elaboration of the concept of "heterogender" and its effects on the disciplining of knowledge see Ingraham 1994.
15. Grant Kester's fine essay (1993) on the imaginary space of postindustrial culture prompted my analysis of the class dimensions of visibility here; the phrase "out of sight, out of mind" is in part a reference to his title.
16. I am grateful to Catherine Sustana for pointing out to me the following detail: Levi-Strauss is owned by Robert Haas, the great-great-grandnephew of the com-

pany founder; when Haas staged a successful leveraged buyout to take the company private in 1985, profits rose by a staggering 31 percent (Sustana 1993).

17. Among the books that address the class dimension of lesbian and gay history and culture are: Bunch 1987; Faderman 1991; Kennedy and Davis 1993; Moraga 1983; Nestle 1987. Essays include D'Emilio 1983a; Franzen 1993; Weston and Rofel 1984.

18. On the relationship between (homo)sexuality and capitalism see Altman 1982; D'Emilio 1983a; Evans 1993. Most of the little work on gay poverty has, not accidentally, focused on lesbians and has circulated mostly in alternative/activist presses. Notable examples include Egerton 1990, Helmbold 1982, Levine 1992.

19. The accuracy of the federally funded Batelle Institute's findings has been questioned for a number of reasons: the study was aimed at addressing behavior related to AIDS, not homosexuality per se; the survey was based on self-reports from men; the interviewers were exclusively women who were not trained in sex research; and the questions about sex with men had a 30 percent non-response rate.

20. According to the US Bureau of the Census (1991) about 30 percent of the poor are black.

References

Abelda, Randy, Elaine McCrate, Edwin Melendez, June Lapidus, and the Center for Popular Economics. 1988. *Mink Coats Don't Trickle Down: The Economic Attack on Women and People of Color*. Boston: South End.

Abelove, Henry, Michele Aina Barale, and David Halperin, eds. 1993. *The Lesbian and Gay Studies Reader*. New York: Routledge.

Adams, Parveen. 1989. "Of Female Bondage." In *Between Feminism and Psychoanalysis*, ed. Teresa Brennan, 247–65. London: Routledge.

Altman, Dennis. 1982. *The Homosexualization of America*. Boston: Beacon Press.

Apter, Emily. 1991. *Feminizing the Fetish: Psychoanalysis and Narrative Obsession in Turn-of-the-Century France*. Ithaca, N. Y.: Cornell University Press.

Baker, James N., Anthony Duignan-Cabrera, Mark Miller, and Michael Mason. 1991. "What Is Queer Nation?" *Newsweek*, 12 Aug. 1991: 24.

Berlant, Lauren, and Elizabeth Freeman. 1992. "Queer Nationality." *boundary 2*, 19(1): 149–80.

Berube, Allan and Jeffrey Escoffier. 1991. "Queer Nation." *Out/Look*, 11: 12–14.

Bourdieu, Pierre. 1984. *Distinction: A Social Critique of the Judgement of Taste*, trans. R. Nice. London: Routledge and Kegan Paul.

Bull, Chris. 1992. "Queer Nation Goes on Hiatus in San Francisco." *Advocate*, 14 Jan. 1992: 24.

Bunch, Charlotte. 1987. *Passionate Politics*. New York: St. Martins.

Burger, Peter. 1984. *Theory of the Avant-Garde*, trans. Michael Shaw. Minneapolis: University of Minnesota Press.

Butler, Judith. 1990a. *Gender Trouble: Feminism and the Subversion of Identity*. New York: Routledge.

1990b. "Performative Acts and Gender Constitution: An Essay in Phenomenology and Feminist Theory." In *Performing Feminisms: Feminist Critical Theory and Theatre*, ed. Sue Ellen Case, 270–82. Baltimore: Johns Hopkins University Press.

1991. "Imitation and Gender Insubordination." In *Inside/Out: Lesbian Theories, Gay Theories*, ed. Diana Fuss. New York: Routledge.

1993. *Bodies That Matter: On the Discursive Limits of "Sex."* New York: Routledge.

Calinescue, Matei. 1987. *Five Faces of Modernity: Modernism, Avant-Garde, Decadence, Kitsch, Postmodernism.* Durham, N. C.: Duke University Press.

Callinicos, Alex. 1989. *Against Postmodernism: A Marxist Critique.* New York: St. Martins.

Case, Sue Ellen, ed. 1990. *Performing Feminisms: Feminist Critical Theory and Theatre.* Baltimore and London: Johns Hopkins University Press.

Chee, Alexander S. 1991. "Queer Nationalism." *Out/Look*, 11 (Winter): 15–19.

Clark, Danae. 1991. "Commodity Lesbianism." *Camera Obscura*, 25–26: 181–201.

Clarke, John. 1991. *Old Times, New Enemies: Essays on Cultural Studies and America.* London: Harper Collins.

Cvetkovich, Ann. 1992. *Mixed Feelings: Feminism, Mass Culture, and Victorian Sensationalism.* New Brunswick, N. J.: Rutgers University Press.

Darling, Lynn. 1993. "Single White Male Seeks Clue." *Esquire*, June 97–104.

De Lauretis, Teresa. 1991. "Film and the Visible." In *How Do I Look?*, ed. Bad Object Choices, 223–76. Seattle: Bay.

1993. "Sexual Indifference and Lesbian Representation." In *The Lesbian and Gay Studies Reader*, ed. Henry Abelove, Michele Barale, and David Halperin, 141–58. New York: Routledge.

D'Emilio, John. 1983a. "Capitalism and Gay Identity." In *Powers of Desire: The Politics of Sexuality*, ed. Ann Snitow, Christine Stansell, and Sharon Thompson, 100–13. New York: Monthly Review.

1983b. *Sexual Politics, Sexual Communities: The Making of a Homosexual Minority in the United States.* Chicago: University of Chicago Press.

Duggan, Lisa. 1992. "Making It Perfectly Queer." *Socialist Review*, 22 (1): 11–31.

Egerton, Jayne. 1990. "Out But Not Down: Lesbians' Experience of Housing." *Feminist Review*, 36 (Autumn): 75–88.

Ehrenreich, Barbara. 1989. *Fear of Falling: The Inner Life of the Middle Class.* New York: Harper.

Evans, David T. 1993. *Sexual Citizenship: The Material Construction of Sexualities.* London: Routledge.

Faderman, Lillian. 1991. *Odd Girls and Twilight Lovers: A History of Lesbian Life in Twentieth-Century America.* New York: Penguin.

Featherstone, Mike. 1991. *Consumer Culture and Postmodernism.* London: Sage.

Feinberg, Leslie. 1993. *Stone Butch Blues.* Ithaca, N. Y.: Firebrand.

Ferguson, Ann. 1989. *Blood at the Root: Motherhood, Sexuality, and Male Dominance.* London: Pandora.

Fernandez, Charles. 1991. "Undocumented Aliens in the Queer Nation." *Out/Look*, Spring: 20–23.

Findlay, Heather. 1992. "Freud's 'Fetishism' and the Lesbian Dildo Debates." *Feminist Studies*, 18.3: 563–79.

Foucault, Michel. 1983. "On the Genealogy of Ethics: An Overview of Work in Progress." In *Michel Foucault: Beyond Structuralism and Hermeneutics*, ed. Herbert Dreyfus and Paul Rabinow, 229–59. Chicago: University of Chicago Press.

1990. *The History of Sexuality*, vol. 1, trans. Robert Hurley. New York: Vintage.

Franzen, Trisha. 1993. "Differences and Identities: Feminism and the Albuquerque Lesbian Community." *Signs*, 18.4 (Summer): 891–906.

Fuss, Diana. 1992. "Fashion and the Homospectatorial Look." *Critical Inquiry*, 18.4: 713–37.

Galst, Liz. 1992. "Throwaway Kids." *Advocate*, 29 December: 54.

Gluckman, Amy and Betsy Reed. 1993. "The Gay Marketing Moment." *Dollars and Sense*, Nov.–Dec.: 16–35.

Goldman, Robert. 1992. *Reading Ads Socially*. New York: Routledge.

Helmbold, Lois Rita. 1982. "Shopping Bag Lesbians." *Common Lives/-Lesbian Lives*, 5 (Fall): 69–71.

Hennessy, Rosemary. 1993. *Materialist Feminism and the Politics of Discourse*. New York: Routledge.

Hooks, Bell. 1992. "Is Paris Burning?" In *Black Looks: Race and Representation*, 145–55. Boston: South End.

Ingraham, Chrys. 1994. "The Heterosexual Imaginary: Feminist Sociology and Theories of Gender." *Sociological Theory*, 12.2: 203–19.

Kamp, David. 1993. "The Straight Queer." *GQ*, July: 94–99.

Kennedy, Elizabeth Lapovsky, and Madeline D. Davis. 1993. *Boots of Leather, Slippers of Gold: The History of A Lesbian Community*. New York: Routledge.

Kester, Grant H. 1993. "Out of Sight Is Out of Mind: The Imaginary Spaces of Postindustrial Culture." *Social Text*, 35 (Summer): 72–92.

Knabb, Ken, ed. 1981. *Situationist International Anthology*. Berkeley: Bureau of Public Secrets.

Levine, Rebecca. 1992. "The Lesbian and Gay Prisoner Project: A Vital Connection." *Gay Community News*, 19.26: 5.

Maciones, John J. 1993 *Sociology*. Englewood Cliffs, N. J.: Prentice Hall.

Maggenti, Maria. 1991. "Women as Queer Nationals." *Out/Look*, 11: 20–23.

Marcus, Greil. 1989. *Lipstick Traces: A Secret History of the Twentieth Century*. Cambridge: Harvard University Press.

Martin, Richard. 1993. "The Gay Factor in Fashion." *Esquire Gentleman*, 13 July: 135.

Martinez, Elizabeth. 1993. "'Levi's, Button Your Fly—Your Greed Is Showing.'" *Z Magazine*, Jan.: 22–27.

Mercer, Kobena. 1989. "Skin Head Sex Thing." In *How Do I Look*, ed. Bad Object Choices, 169–222. Seattle: Bay.

Mitchell, Hugh, and Kayode Olafimihan. 1992. "Living." *Living Marxism*, Nov.: 38–39.

Moraga, Cherrie. 1983. *Loving in the War Years*. Boston: South End.

Nestle, Joan. 1987. *A Restricted Country*. Ithaca, N. Y.: Firebrand.

Nietzsche, Friedrich. 1974. *The Gay Science.* New York: Penguin.

Plant, Sadie. 1992. *The Most Radical Gesture: The Situationist International in a Postmodern Age.* London: Routledge.

Powers, Ann. 1993. "Queer in the Streets, Passing in the Sheets." *Village Voice,* 29 June: 24.

Rojek, Chris. 1985. *Capitalism and Leisure Theory.* London: Tavistock.

Shenon, Philip. 1993. "Saipan Sweatshops Are No American Dream." *New York Times,* 18 July: 1.

Signorile, Michelangelo. 1993. *Queer in America: Sex, the Media, and the Closets of Power.* New York: Random House.

Smith, Barbara. 1993. "Where's the Revolution?" *Nation,* 5 July: 12–16.

Smyth, Cherry. 1992. *Queer Notions.* London: Scarlet.

Sobel, E. 1982. *Lifestyle.* New York: Academic Press.

Stewart, Thomas. 1991. "Gay in Corporate America." *Fortune,* 16 Dec.: 42.

Sustana, Catherine. 1993. "The Production of the Corporate Subject." Conference on Literary/Critical Cultural Studies. University at Albany, SUNY, December.

Tobias, Andrew. 1992. "Three Dollar Bills." *Time,* 23 Mar.

Warner, Michael. 1993. "Introduction." *Fear of A Queer Planet.* Minneapolis, Minn.: University of Minnesota Press.

Weston, Kathleen and Lisa Rofel. 1984. "Sexuality, Class, and Conflict in a Lesbian Workplace." *Signs,* 9.4 (Summer): 623–46.

Williams, Raymond. 1989. *The Politics of Modernism.* London: Verso.

Zavarzadeh, Mas'ud. 1991. *Seeing Films Politically.* Albany, N. Y.: State University of New York Press.

Zizek, Slavoj. 1989. *The Sublime Object of Ideology.* London: Verso.

Questions for Reflection, Discussion, and Writing

1. What argument does Hennessy offer to explain why visibility is an important and often undertheorized aspect of gay, lesbian and queer cultures? How does her argument about visibility provide the background for her claim about the nature of commodity culture and capitalism?

2. How does Hennessy define "queer"? According to her essay, who identifies as queer? How does she challenge the purported "liberatory" nature of queer theory as it currently exists?

3. How does Hennessy critique Butler, Fuss, and de Lauretis? What aspects of their work does she support?

4. What aspects of the labor market and capitalism's workings does our current focus on "lifestyle" as identity (and a function of postmodernism) conceal, according to Hennessy? What does she find problematic about that concealment?

5. What evidence does Hennessy offer to support her claim that the entertainment industry has appropriated lesbian/gay/queer images? According to Hennessy, why and for whom is that appropriation problematic?

6. What relationship exists between patriarchy and heterosexuality, according to Hennessy?

7. What critiques about class and queer academia does Hennessy make? What solutions or suggestions does she offer?

Writing Assignment

Perform a close reading (including textual analysis and cultural critique) of any ad out of a recent, glossy gay magazine such as the *Advocate*, *Out*, or *Curve*. Who is its intended audience? What assumptions does it make of shared values? What is the basis of its appeal: class, sex, lifestyle? Ultimately, this question asks you what is being sold and whether or not you're buying.

Related Reading

John D'Emilio, "Capitalism and Gay Identity" in *The Lesbian and Gay Studies Reader*. Henry Abelove, Michèle Aina Barale and David M. Halperin, Eds. NY: Routledge. 1993. 467–476.

Sue-Ellen Case, "The Student and the Strap: Authority and Seduction in the Class(room)" in *Professions of Desire: Lesbian and Gay Studies in Literature*. George S. Haggerty and Bonnie Zimmerman, Eds. NY: MLA. 1995. 38–46.

Nicola Field, "Identity and the Lifestyle Market" in *Over the Rainbow: Money, Class and Homophobia*. London: Pluto Press. 1995. 50–71.

Lisa Peñaloza, "We're Here, We're Queer, and We're Going Shopping! A Critical Perspective on the Accommodation of Gays and Lesbians in the U.S. Marketplace." *Journal of Homosexuality 31*.1/2 (1996): 9–41.

Sidney Matrix, "Desire and Deviate Nymphos: Performing Inversion(s) as a Lesbian Consumer." *Journal of Homosexuality 31*.1/2 (1996): 71–81.

Anthony Freitas, Susan Kaiser and Tania Hammidi, "Communities, Commodities, Cultural Space, and Style." *Journal of Homosexuality 31*.1/2 (1996): 83–107.

M. Wayne DeLozier and Jason Rodrigue, "Marketing to the Homosexual (Gay) Market: A Profile and Strategy Implications." *Journal of Homosexuality 31*.1/2 (1996): 203–211.

Subodh Bhat, "Some Comments on 'Marketing to the Homosexual (Gay) Market: A Profile and Strategy Implications.'" *Journal of Homosexuality 31*.1/2 (1996): 213–217.

Richard R. Cornwell, "Queer Political Economy: The Social Articulation of Desire" in *Homo Economies: Capitalism, Community, and Lesbian and Gay Life*. Amy Gluckman and Betsy Reed, Eds. NY: Routledge. 1997. 89–122.

M.V. Lee Badgett, "Thinking Homo/Economically" in *A Queer World*. Martin Duberman, Ed. NY: NYUP. 1997. 467–476.

Sean Strub, "The Growth of the Gay and Lesbian Market" in *A Queer World: The Center for Lesbian and Gay Studies Reader*. Martin Duberman, Ed. NY: NYUP. 1997. 514–518.

Amy Gluckman and Betsy Reed, "The Gay Marketing Movement" in *A Queer World: The Center for Lesbian and Gay Studies Reader*. Martin Duberman, Ed. NY: NYUP. 1997. 519–525.

Peter F. Cohen, "'All They Needed': AIDS, Consumption, and the Politics of Class." *Journal of the History of Sexuality 8* (July 1997): 86–115.

Richard R. Cornwall, "Incorporating Social Identities into Economic Theory: How Economics Can Come Out of Its Closet of Individualism" in *A Queer World: The Center for Lesbian and Gay Studies Reader*. Martin Duberman, Ed. NY: NYUP. 1997. 477–501.

Michael Piore, "Economic Identity/Sexual Identity" in *A Queer World: The Center for Lesbian and Gay Studies Reader*. Martin Duberman, Ed. NY: NYUP. 1997. 501–507.

Richard R. Cornwall, "A Primer on Queer Theory for Economists Interested in Social Identities." *Feminist Economics 4.2* (Summer 1998): 73–82.

Katherine Sender, "Selling Sexual Subjectivities: Audiences Respond to Gay Window Advertising." *Critical Studies in Mass Communication 2* (June 1999): 172–196.

Rob Cover, "Queer With Class: Absence of Third World Sweatshop in Lesbian/Gay Discourse and a Rearticulation of Materialist Queer Theory." *Ariel 30.2* (April 1999): 28–48.

Gerald Hunt, *Laboring for Rights: Unions and Sexual Diversity Across Nations*. Philadelphia: Temple UP. 1999.

M.V. Lee Badgett, "The Myth of Gay & Lesbian Affluence." *The Gay & Lesbian Review 7.2* (Spring 2000): 22–25.

Howard Bufford, "Understanding Gay Consumers." *The Gay & Lesbian Review 7.2* (Spring 2000): 26–28.

Max H. Kirsch, "Capitalism and its transgressors" in *Queer Theory and Social Change*. NY: Routledge. 2000. 65–78.

Fred Fejes and Ron Lennon, "Defining the Lesbian/Gay Community? Market Research and the Lesbian/Gay Press." *Journal of Homosexuality 39.1* (2000): 25–42.

Rosemary Hennessy, *Profit and Pleasure: Sexual Identities in Late Capitalism*. NY: Routledge. 2000.

Katherine Sender, "Gay Readers, Consumers, and A Dominant Gay Habitus: 25 Years of the *Advocate* Magazine." *Journal of Communication 51.1* (2001): 73–99.

M.V. Lee Badgett, Money, *Myths, and Change: The Economic Lives of Lesbians and Gay Men*. Chicago, IL: U of Chicago P. 2001.

Teamwork

Lisa Walter
Harvey Mudd College, California

We were ahead by more than 15 points in the middle of the second quarter, ahead so much that we sat eagerly on the bench, waiting to be put into the game. As freshmen, we knew we were about to get some playing time. While the starting five continued to cream our opponents, Julie and her girlfriend entered the gym holding hands. The pair walked along the sideline and up several rows of bleachers to find some seats. Kammi, one of our freshman guards, was sitting next to me on the bench. I saw her eyes follow the couple from the moment they entered the doorway. She leaned toward me and whispered, "Hey, Lisa, look at those two girls over there." She motioned to Julie, unaware I knew her, let alone lived with her. "I can't believe they're doing that in public! Hey, Kelly, look!"

Everyone on the bench turned their heads one by one to look at Julie as the message was passed from one player to the next. A minute later our entire row of women in white and maroon were all blatantly staring at Julie and her girlfriend. I glanced up to see her expression. I think she noticed my team staring, but it didn't seem to bother her. She kept watching the game and talking with her girlfriend. I meekly smiled at my teammates, pretended to laugh it off, and tried to focus on the game.

After we won we all headed into the locker room for the five minutes we were allotted to change before our team meeting.

"Ugh! That's so disgusting!" Kammi said as soon as she was in the door. "I can't believe those two girls came to our game. That's so gross!" Our freshman point guard, Kelly, nodded her head and made a face as if she had just seen someone eat feces.

Stacy, our freshman three-point shooter, said with a provoking smile on her face, "There are lesbians in our gym, Kammi! Lesbians! Lesbians!"

"Well, don't let them in here! I'd die if someone on our team was gay, changing in the same locker room as us. They'd be checking us out," Kammi said with a fierce smirk.

"Luckily, we don't have that problem on this team," Stacy added.

"Yeah, thank God nobody here is like that," Kammi continued. "Damn dykes. They shouldn't even be allowed in the gym. We shouldn't have to deal with that when we're playing."

I dressed as quickly as possible. I was nervous someone on my team would wonder why I didn't join in the conversation and suspect me of watching them change or shower. I was sure one of them would be able to figure out sooner or later that I dated women as well as men. I was also sure that if they knew Julie was my suitemate, it would cause more problems than I was ready to deal with.

Julie was a huge role model for me during my freshman year. Like me, she was half Asian and half white. Like me, she played a varsity sport. And like me, she led an alternative lifestyle. She was a senior and had survived the rigorous academic program at our small technical school.

Our school is unusual in that it sits on the same campus as four other small private colleges. Only 650 students are enrolled at my school. Combined with the other colleges, the five student bodies form the student-run organizations, such as the LGB Student Union and the intercollegiate sports programs. Our varsity women's NCAA Division III basketball team consists of students from three of the five colleges, but I'm the only player from my school.

From the start I was open about my sexuality at my college, just as I'd been in high school. My college has provided an open and supportive atmosphere, but I quickly learned that this wasn't the case at the other schools. Conversations with upperclassmen during freshman orientation and at parties I attended at the other colleges made it clear that gay jokes and homophobic attitudes were prevalent and seemingly acceptable there. I didn't feel safe in this respect when I spent time with students from other colleges—including my teammates—which made being on the team a challenge. During our five-month season of six-day-a-week, two-to-three-hours-a-day practice and game schedules, my teammates and I spent more time with each other than with anyone else.

Julie and her girlfriend attended all our home games that first month my freshman season. And after a month of listening to remarks about them from my teammates, I'd had enough. I finally told them Julie was one of my suitemates, hoping they might stop criticizing her. Instead, it provoked a range of responses.

"How can you live with something like that?" Kammi asked. "I'd move out if I were you. It's not fair that you're stuck living with a lesbian. You should complain because the college shouldn't do that unless you specifically request it."

Kelly, on the other hand, became curious about Julie. "What do they do for sex?" she asked, wanting to know all the details.

"Ask them yourself," I said, feeling annoyed.

By the end of the season my freshman year, no one on my team had figured out my sexuality. None of my teammates knew anyone at my school, so it was easy for me not to disclose anything to them. I was tired, however, of not being able to be myself when hanging out with them. We were spending more and more time together outside of basketball, so things like dating and friends came up in our conversations all the time. I talked only about the men I was dating and left the women out of it.

I came out to two of the more open-minded players on our team at the end of the school year: another post player, Anna, and one of our guards, Christina. They were pretty indifferent about it, and neither brought it up again. I thought that if these two didn't care, maybe the rest of the team wouldn't find it so bad either.

Around the same time, I also started attending LGBSU meetings, where I found support when discussing my team. I was the only Asian person there and one of the slim minority who considered themselves bisexual. I'd hoped to find other Asian students and more bisexuals. I identified strongly with the other ethnic minority students in the LGBSU and the issues they faced: the strong stigmas in their cultures against being anything but straight and the difficulties of finding others with whom to identify. Though no other students in the LGBSU identified as Asian and though I was one of few who identified as bi-sexual, I found a great deal of support through the other members. I listened to several students from each of the five colleges tell their coming-out tales, and the majority of their stories had happy endings. This shed a bit of hope on my situation, so I considered doing what I wanted most, letting my team know who I really am.

During preseason my sophomore year, our college hosted a basketball tournament over Thanksgiving weekend. On the second night of the tourna-ment, Kelly, by then my closest friend, invited one of the men's teams from Virginia to her apartment along with our women's team. The players trickled into her living room in small groups that Saturday evening, and we had a few conversations about our team records and coaches, interspersed with shots of hard alcohol. Everyone had arrived by a quarter to 11, and all of us, slightly in-toxicated, crowded around a coffee table. We had two large bottles of vodka and several liters of Kool-Aid to share among the 20 of us, and we decided to play the drinking game "I Never."

"I Never" goes like this: One person starts out saying, "I never . . . smoked pot," for example. Everyone who has done what the person said takes a drink, while everyone else watches.

My palms were sweating, and I quickly downed a half-and-half vodka and strawberry Kool-Aid and poured another.

The point guard of the men's team from Virginia went first. He paused for a minute to think of something good, something maybe someone in the room had done but that he had never tried. He looked around the room at each of us. "I never . . . kissed someone of the same sex."

No one in the room budged. My eyes passed from one person to the next. This seemed to be a good opportunity to come out, and I could always say later that I was drunk and didn't mean it. I grabbed my Kool-Aid and vodka from the table and took a sip.

Everyone started. My teammates dropped their jaws. But by then I was so drunk, I didn't care what they thought. The next player said, "I've never slept with someone of the same sex." I took another sip, and on it went until people ran out of things to say or I passed out; I don't remember which came first.

The next day my teammates acted as if they had forgotten about the night before, as did I. It wasn't until three days later on a van ride back from a game that one of them got up the courage to ask, "So, do you consider yourself bi?" I nodded, and for the rest of the ride, there was dead silence.

A week later our dorm hosted a party open to students of all five colleges. I volunteered to check IDs and stamp hands during the 11-to-1 shift. Many of my teammates were at the party, and drunk. As things were wrapping up, Stacy, physically supported by two of her friends, came by.

"Lisa, how's it going?" she loudly slurred, tripping over her own foot. I smiled. She looked in the general direction of her friends. "Hey, guys, I'm going to say bye to Lisa." She took a step toward me and landed with her arms flung around my shoulders, simultaneously planting a kiss on my cheek. I braced my arms around her to keep her from falling over. Then she kissed me again on the cheek, this time closer to my mouth.

I looked at her friends, who were intoxicated too, and said, "I'll see you tomorrow, Stacy." She jerked her head from where it was resting on my shoulder and brought her lips close to mine. What the hell was she doing? Images of her telling people how I came on to her when she was drunk at this party flew through my head, and I turned away. She proceeded to kiss my neck as I brought her a step closer to her friends. "Make sure she makes it back to her dorm, OK?" I smiled and handed her over. My shift had just ended, and I went to my dorm room. I never brought it up with her or anyone else on the team.

My teammates began to refer to me as a lesbian, and I found myself correcting them constantly. Anna, Kelly, Janelle, and a few freshmen on the team approached me once and asked, "Does being bi mean that you have an equal preference for both men and women?"

I told them, "For me, it's more like 60-40 in the direction of women."

I tried to be open about my sexuality and told my teammates I'd answer any questions they had. Some of them started asking in confidentiality what it was like to be with a woman, and many told me they had thought about it a lot.

Kelly, in particular, was curious, and her questions were the most explicit. Once she said, "So, you don't have to answer this if you don't want to, but I'm curious . . . does a man's or a woman's cum taste better?" She turned bright red and smiled nervously.

I laughed, drawing a blank. This was a question I hadn't expected anyone to ask. "Well, they're kind of different, you know. I mean, you can't compare them. I guess they're both kind of good." My complexion quickly matched hers.

Questions from teammates became easier to answer, and the context in which they asked them became more and more casual. Frequently we'd be sitting in the locker room and they'd ask me whether certain phrases offended me and about my dating life. Janelle asked me once, in front of our team, "Does it bother the guys you go out with that you've dated women?"

"No, not really. It's fine with them," I said.

Anna followed up with, "Does it bother the women you date that you would still go out with a man?"

"Yeah, most of the lesbians I date have a problem with it, but with bi women it doesn't matter, of course."

The more questions they asked and the more questions I answered honestly, the more comfortable everyone was becoming with my being bisexual.

During winter break my sophomore year, Christina, our starting guard, and I became close. We went out to get frozen yogurt several times and sneaked into the college pool in the middle of the night once. I stayed with her at her apartment for most of the break, since my campus was completely empty and we still had daily practices.

Every time I spent the night at her apartment, we shared a bed in the room of one of her roommates. One night as we lay in bed in the dark, I asked, "Have you ever had sex with a guy?"

"Yes," she hesitantly responded. I was surprised. The other players viewed her as one of the most conservative people on the team, and everyone thought she was still a virgin.

"Have you ever had sex with a woman?"

"Yes, in high school. My best friends found out my senior year and told everyone. I lost all my close friends. It sucked. I didn't tell anyone except my roommate when I got here. That's why I never talk about high school."

"Christina, I can't believe you dealt with all that when you were in high school. You're an incredibly strong person."

I continued to spend the night at her apartment, and we ended up talking more and more the following nights. I told her about my ideas on relationships, how I was going to date whomever I wanted whenever I wanted, regardless of gender, and she liked that image of freedom. She said she wanted to have a relationship with a woman again, that she wanted to be free to live her dating life as she pleased, that she was in love with her best friend who happened to be a woman, that she hated that she couldn't do any of these things because of the conservative attitudes at her school. Christina even told me she didn't really like her boyfriend and went out with him only because he pursued her.

One night I asked her, "Why do you sleep in here?" I was wondering why we'd been sleeping in her roommate's room instead of her room this whole time.

She must have thought I was asking her why she'd been sleeping in the same bed as me instead of her own, because she stuttered and said, "I'm attracted to you, Lisa. I've been attracted to you for a long time. Last school year I told my best friend and asked her if she thought you might feel the same way."

I was speechless. "Wow. That's flattering. Thanks for your honesty. It means a lot. You know I think you're beautiful, Christina."

She laughed in disbelief. We lay silent for half an hour, trying to fall asleep. I laid my hand on her shoulder. Then she reluctantly said, "Do you think it would be bad if. . .we just lie close?"

"I don't think it would be bad, but I'm not sure what you mean by 'bad.'"

We pressed our bodies together, her silhouette fitting snugly against mine, and lay without moving, without breathing. I stroked her shoulder, arm, leg, stomach, and back, and she stroked mine. We stayed up most of the night, still as statues, stomachs churning, minds racing.

The next morning I came back into the room after dressing and apologized for keeping her up. She said, "That's OK. I wanted you to." I lay next to her again and caressed her body. She returned my advances, first touching my shoulder, then arm, then left breast as I slid my hand across her chest. . . .

Christina and I were secretive about the time we spent together those few weeks. Although we never talked about it, I could tell she didn't want anyone on the team to know. The day before everyone returned to campus from winter break, we woke up and lay in bed together as usual before it was time to go to practice. I asked, "So when are you getting back tonight?"

She turned her head away. "Lisa, you can't spend the night here anymore. We can't keep seeing each other like this. My roommates are coming back, and my boyfriend is going to be back soon, and everyone will be around."

I was stunned, but looking back on it I can't say I didn't see it coming. Christina wanted a relationship when her peers weren't around. I was enraged, but I'm not one to argue much or drag things out. I gave her a confused look, glared at her, and said, "All right." I grabbed my stuff and walked out the door.

I dropped by Christina's apartment a few times to say hi, but she didn't seem to want me there, so I reluctantly stopped visiting and calling and eventually stopped telling friends about my wonderful teammate. I resented that she had let us become so close and then cut me off, that she stayed with the boyfriend she didn't like for so long and didn't make an attempt to talk to someone she was interested in.

Practices were weird for the rest of the season. Every time Christina and I had to guard each other, she became nervous and lost the ball. One of the assistant coaches noticed this and asked me what the hell had gotten into her, I shrugged. I was unable to get much support from anyone, unable to channel my thoughts, feelings, and anxieties about the situation. By that time I was actively involved in LGBSU but couldn't get support there because I promised Christina I wouldn't tell anyone about her personal life. I spent every practice the rest of that season trying to ignore her ignoring me.

The team dynamics had become uncomfortable in a number of other ways. In addition to Stacy making a pass at me earlier in the year, Kelly was coming on to me every time she got drunk. Soon I felt like the team's token lesbian. It seemed that everyone on our team who wanted to experiment with a woman tried to do so with me. I guess it was flattering, but when you're looking for a relationship, you don't want to be someone else's science project.

Though some of my teammates were making my life uncomfortable, others were doing the opposite. Teammates who felt close to me began to actively reprimand and correct anyone on the team who dared to make a homophobic comment, whether I was around or not. Anna and Janelle approached me in the locker room before practice one day to tell me about such an incident.

"Lisa, we were hanging out with Heidi yesterday, talking about our team, and then the subject of gay people came up," Anna said in a low voice. "Heidi said she was glad there wasn't anyone on our team who liked women, and I was like, 'What about Lisa?'"

Janelle continued, "So then Heidi said, 'What *about* Lisa?' And we told her you date women. We thought she already knew."

"I thought so too. Maybe it slipped her mind," I said with interest.

"Anyway, she was really homophobic about it. She said she didn't feel comfortable changing in the same room with you anymore and also mentioned that you were still dating men, so according to her you're just experimenting. I got pissed off and told her she needed to be more open-minded or quit the team. After all, she's only a freshman," Janelle said.

Although this sounded harsh, I realized that some individuals on my team respected me and were going to stand by me. I was glad to hear that my lifestyle wasn't only tolerated but also accepted in an environment where this was important to me.

Kammi and Stacy still kept up with their homophobic remarks whenever they saw Julie and her girlfriend and other same-sex couples at our games, regardless of the admonishments they received. Whenever they talked to me about who I was dating, they were interested in hearing only about the men. Some of my teammates tried to avoid the subject of sexuality altogether. I felt like I was in the middle of much of this, so I was happy when the season ended. Stacy, Kammi, and Heidi didn't return to the team the following season for unrelated reasons, and I was relieved to know I'd no longer have to hear their comments.

Just after basketball season started my junior year, a formal dance was held at one of the colleges. My teammates were planning on attending in a group with their dates, and I was dating a woman at the time. They automatically assumed I would bring her with me, and it was no big deal.

The morning after the dance, I showed up to practice bright and early along with the rest of my teammates, all of us feeling a little out of it from drinking the night before. I changed from my sweats into practice gear. As I walked by the full-length mirror in the locker room on the way out, I glanced at my reflection. "Holy shit!" My neck was covered in hickeys of various shades of red and purple. I didn't have any cover-up with me, and practice was starting in two minutes.

Everyone noticed the hickeys the moment they saw me. "Lisa got lucky last night!" one of my teammates called out. Our coaches came into the gym about a minute later. The head coach approached and said, "Hey Lisa, what guy gave you those hickeys?"

"Oh, nobody, Coach," I smiled. Everyone looked at one another and laughed. After practice we went to the locker room to change before going back to our rooms.

Anna said, "Did you hear what Coach said? I can't believe she actually asked you that!" Everyone giggled. Although my coach was clueless about whom I was dating, it was clear that me being bi was no longer a big deal to my teammates.

The following week our team took a day trip to a mall in a neighboring city. Anna and I were supposed to drive. Six of us met in the parking lot, and Christina and I arrived last. The other four had already piled into Anna's car, leaving Christina and me alone. We looked at each other. "Ready to go?" I asked. She nodded and reluctantly got into my car. We hadn't been alone since our last morning together a year prior. I was so nervous that I stalled the car on the way out of the parking lot.

The ride was two hours long, and for the first hour or so we talked about basketball. Then out of nowhere Christina said, "Lisa, I think you're a cool person. And I want you to know I'm sorry about that whole thing last year. I was weirded out by the situation and didn't know what to do. I know I acted strange, and I'm sorry." My stomach cramped. I had come to terms with what had happened between us a year ago and wanted just to be able to talk with her. I was a bit startled she brought it up.

"Don't worry about it," I said. "I didn't know what to do either. I thought you didn't want to talk to me anymore, so I left you alone."

"That wasn't it at all. I think you're an incredible person. I can't be strong like you and do things however I want. You can."

I was amazed at how one awkward moment had evolved into an over-whelming atmosphere of relief. We talked for the rest of the ride and caught up on thoughts and feelings that had stemmed from the previous winter. After that day we were able to talk again. Finally after an entire year, it was no longer awkward to guard her during practice or talk with her alone. She still chose to confide in me about her feelings for other people, and she told me she was still in love with her best friend.

I have one year of college left. Though it's been difficult because I haven't found many other Asian bisexuals. I realize that the experiences accompanying this unique identity have made me stronger. Also, coming out to my basketball team has made a huge difference in the atmosphere on the court and off—from homophobia to tolerance to acceptance to appreciation of our differences. I'm looking forward to our next season.

Questions for Reflection, Discussion, and Writing

1. How does Walter characterize her teammate's reactions to Julie and her girlfriend when they arrive at the game? How does Walter respond to their homophobia? What ideas and thoughts run through her head as a result?

2. How does Walter make her sexuality known? How does she negotiate various responses from her teammates? As a result of publicly recognizing her bisexuality, what sorts of questions do they ask her? How does she react to those questions?

3. In what ways does the LGBSU offer Walter a support system? In what ways does it fall short for her?

4. In telling about her affair with Christina, what ideas about sex and sexuality, privacy and disclosure does Walter raise?

5. At various points during her essay, Walter suggests that there are fundamental differences between lesbianism and bisexuality. Using her essay as evidence, on what do both Walter and her teammates think some of those differences seem to be based? Do you agree?

6. The title of this piece, "Teamwork," can be interpreted in several ways. Offer two or three examples of how "teamwork" is evident in Walter's essay.

Writing Assignment

Using the Walter piece as a model, compose a personal narrative recounting an experience you've had while in college that addresses some aspect or angle of queer experience, including interactions, confrontations, or acts of homophobia you may have witnessed. Strive for honesty, a succinct narrative, self-reflection. Is there a larger issue, conundrum, or contradiction that your experience illustrates?

Related Reading

Anthony D'Augelli, "Homophobia in a University Community: Views of Prospective Resident Assistants." *Journal of College Student Development* 30.6 (1989): 546–552.

———, "Gay Men in College: Identity Processes and Adaptations." *Journal of College Student Development* 32.2 (March 1991): 140–146.

Robert A. Rhoads, *Coming Out in College: The Struggle for a Queer Identity.* Westport, CT: Bergin & Garvey. 1994.

National Gay and Lesbian Task Force, *Lesbian, Gay, Bisexual, and Transgender Campus Organizing: A Comprehensive Manual.* Washington, DC. 1995.

Alali A. Odasuo, "College Newspaper Editors' Perceptions of How Gay and Lesbian Issues Are Covered On Their Campus." *College Student Journal* 30.1 (March 1996): 17–23.

Michele J. Eliason, "A Survey of the Campus Climate for Lesbians, Gay, and Bisexual University Members." *Journal of Psychology & Human Sexuality* 8.4 (1996): 39–58.

Pat Griffin, "The Lesbian Athlete: Unlearning the Culture of the Closet" in *A Queer World: The Center for Lesbian and Gay Studies Reader.* Martin Duberman, Ed. NY: NYUP. 1997. 563–571.

Amy M. Rey and Pamela Reed Gibson, "Beyond High School: Heterosexuals' Self-Reported Anti-Gay/Lesbian Behaviors and Attitudes" in *School Experiences of Gay and Lesbian Youth: The Invisible Minority.* Mary Bierman, et al., Eds. NY: Harrington Park Press. 1997. 65–84.

Tracy J. Dietz and Alan Dettlaff, "The Impact of Membership in a Support Group for Gay, Lesbian and Bisexual Students." *Journal of College Student Psychotherapy 12.1* (1997): 57–72.

Michele J. Eliason, "The Prevalence and Nature of Biphobia in Heterosexual Undergraduate Students." *Archives of Sexual Behavior 26.3* (June 1997): 317–326.

Waldo R. Craig, "Out on Campus: Sexual Orientation and Academic Climate in a University Context." *American Journal of Community Psychology 26.5* (October 1998): 745–774.

Pamela W. Freeman and Shane L. Windmeyer, Eds., *Out on Fraternity Row.* Los Angeles, CA: Alyson Publications. 1998.

Nancy J. Evans and Ellen M. Broido, "Coming Out in College Residence Halls: Negotiation, Meaning Making, Challenges, Supports." *Journal of College Student Development 40.6* (Nov-Dec 1999): 685–668.

Susan Meyer and Alan M. Schwitzer, "Stages of Identity Development Among College Students With Minority Sexual Orientations." *Journal of College Student Psychotherapy 13.4* (1999): 41–65.

Kim Howard and Annie Stevens, Eds., *Out & About On Campus: Personal Accounts by Lesbian, Gay, Bisexual & Transgendered Students.* Los Angeles, CA: Alyson Publications. 2000.

Jonathan J. Mohr and William E. Sedlacek, "Perceived Barriers to Friendship with Lesbians and Gay Men Among University Students." *Journal of College Development 41.1* (Jan-Feb 2000): 70–80.

King-To Yeung and Mindy Stombler, "Gay and Greek: The Identity Paradox of Gay Fraternities." *Social Problems 47.1* (2000): 134–152.

John S. Westfeld, Michael R. Maples, et al., "Gay, Lesbian, and Bisexual College Students: The Relationship Between Sexual Orientation and Depression, Loneliness, and Suicide." *Journal of College Student Psychotherapy 15.3* (2001): 71–82.

Pamela W. Freeman and Shane L. Windmeyer, Eds., *Secret Sisters: Stories of Being Lesbian and Bisexual in a College Fraternity.* Los Angeles, CA: Alyson Publications, 2001.

Film

Out of the Past (1997). Jeff Dupre. 70 m.

Speak Up!: Improving the Lives of Gay, Lesbian, Bisexual and Transgendered Youth (2001). John Kazlauskas. 30 m.

Social Actvism

Speakers Bureaus have been enormously successful instruments to educate high school, college, and university students. Does your home institution have one? If so, invite them to your course, or to another social and/or political group on campus. If not, what would it take to start such a panel series? How would you recruit volunteers? Who in the administration on your campus might help you?

Reading

Gary J. Burkholder and Anne Dineen, "Using Panel Presentations to Increase Awareness of Lesbian and Bisexual People." *Journal of College Student Development* 37.4 (Jul-Aug 1996): 469–470.

Eileen S. Nelson and Shirley L. Krieger, "Changes in Attitudes Toward Homosexuality in College Students: Implementation of a Gay Men and Lesbian Peer Panel." *Journal of Homosexuality* 33.2 (1997): 63–81.

Sasha Grutzeck and Christine A. Gidyck, "The Effects of a Gay and Lesbian Speaker Panel on College Students' Attitudes and Behaviors: The Importance of Context Effects." *Imagination, Cognition & Personality* 17.1 (1997): 65–81.

Beyond Gay Marriage

Michael Warner

"There are no societies which do not regulate sex, and thus all societies create the hope of escaping from such regulations."

—Michel Foucault, 1973

In 1996, debating the so-called Defense of Marriage Act in the House of Representatives, Illinois Republican Henry Hyde delivered what he thought was a clinching argument against same-sex marriage: "People don't think that the traditional marriage ought to be demeaned or trivialized by same-sex unions." Massachusetts Democratic Congressman Barney Frank quickly seized on what seemed a careless phrase. "How does it demean your marriage? If other people are immoral, how does it demean your marriage?" Hyde, who was later forced to admit an adulterous affair even as he came to head the Republican prosecution in the Clinton impeachment, could not manage much of an answer. "It demeans the institution," he said, lamely. "My marriage was never demeaned. The institution of marriage is trivialized by same-sex marriage."

The thing that makes Hyde's remark wrong—not just illogical or pompous—is that it becomes a program not for his own sexuality, but for someone else's. He doesn't just want his marriage to be holy; he wants it to be holy *at the expense of someone else's.* To see gay marriage as "demeaning" is, in his view, a way of seeing "traditional marriage" as more significant. Barney Frank and other marriage advocates have only to expose such thinking to the ridicule it deserves in order to point up its injustice.

But the invidiousness of Hyde's remark is a feature of marriage, not just *straight* marriage. Marriage sanctifies some couples at the expense of others. It is selective legitimacy. This is a necessary implication of the institution, and not just the result of bad motives or the high-toned non sequiturs of Henry Hyde. To a couple that gets married, marriage just looks ennobling, as it does to Hyde. Stand outside it for a second and you see the implication: if you don't have it, you and your relations are less worthy. Without this corollary effect, marriage would not be able to endow anybody's life with significance. The ennobling and the demeaning go together. Marriage does one only by virtue of the other. Marriage, in short, discriminates.

That is one reason why same-sex marriage provokes such powerful outbursts of homophobic feeling in many straight people, when they could just as easily view marriage as the ultimate conformity of gay people to their own norms. They want marriage to remain a privilege, a mark that they are special. Often they are willing to grant all (or nearly all) the benefits of marriage to gay people, as long as they don't have to give up the word "marriage." They need some token, however magical, of superiority. But what about the gay people who want marriage? Would they not in turn derive their sense of pride from the invidious and shaming distinction between the married and the unmarried?

It must be admitted from the outset that there is something unfashionable, and perhaps untimely, about any discussion of marriage as a goal in gay politics. One is apt to feel like the unmannerly wedding guest, gossiping about divorce at the rehearsal dinner. At this point the only people arguing against gay marriage, it seems, are those homophobic dinosaurs—like Hyde, or Senator Jesse Helms, or the feminist philosopher Jean Bethke Elshtain—who still think that marriage is about procreation, or that same-sex marriage somehow threatens to "tear apart America's moral fabric," as Helms put it on the Senate floor. Pope John Paul II is reported to have claimed that same-sex marriage "is a serious threat to the future of the family and society itself." If the arguments against gay marriage are as silly and phobic as this, then naturally marrying will seem to strike deep against bigotry. What purpose could be served by a skeptical discussion of marriage now, given the nature of the opposition?

None at all, says Evan Wolfson, director of the Marriage Project at the Lambda Legal Defense and Education Fund. Wolfson argues that in the wake of *Baehr v. Lewin*—the Hawaii Supreme Court decision that appeared to pave the way for gay marriage—we should "end, or at least suspend, the intracommunity debate over whether to seek marriage. The ship has sailed." He cites the need for a united front against the wave of homophobic state and national initiatives designed to wed marriage indissolubly to heterosexuality. As he also points out, there is ample room for foolishness or hubris when intellectuals ask, at this date, whether or not gay marriage is a worthy political cause. The decision is no longer up to us. The legal system of the United States has its own momentum. The last thing the courts are likely to care about is whether marriage is a good idea from a queer point of view.

There is a kernel of truth in this. One has only to pop the question—for or against gay marriage?—to find oneself at once irrelevant to a process that is no longer a debate, blinded by the urgent temporality of the headline, and suckered into a phony plebiscite. But on this, as on so much else, it may be the courts that will prove to have the narrow view. Within the context that Wolfson takes for granted, dissent is indeed almost unheard. Since the 1993 March on Washington, marriage has come to dominate the political imagination of the national gay movement in the United States. To read the pages of *The Advocate* or *Out* is to receive the impression that gay people hardly care about anything else, other than entertainment. I have no doubt that a large constituency has been formed around this belief. But the commitment is not universally shared, to put it mildly. Gay men, lesbians, and many other unmarried people on the street are just as likely to be made slightly sick by the topic, or perhaps to shrug it off as yet another example of that weird foreign language that people speak in the media world of politics, policy, and punditry.

No one was more surprised by the rise of the gay marriage issue than many veterans of earlier forms of gay activism. To them, marriage seems both less urgent and less agreed upon than such items as HIV and health care, AIDS prevention, the repeal of sodomy laws, antigay violence, job discrimination, immigration, media coverage, military antigay policy, sex inequality, and the saturation of everyday life by heterosexual privilege. Before the election of Bill Clinton in 1992, marriage was scarcely a visible blip on the horizon of queer politics; Paula Ettelbrick and Tom Stoddard's 1989 debate on the issue seemed, at the time, simply theoretical. Many gay activists abroad are equally baffled by the focus on marriage in the United States. To them, at least, it is hardly up to Americans to "suspend the intra-community debate." Both within the United States and abroad, people have tried or discussed an immense array of other options—from common-law marriage and domestic partnership to the disentangling of health and other benefits from matrimony, to the Scandinavian model of a second-tier marriage (identical to straight marriage except for parenting rights), to the French model of legal concubinage, to the newer package of reforms known in France as the *pacte civil de solidarité* (PACS, a "civil solidarity pact" that bestows benefits on households of all kinds, including cohabiting siblings). Given this variety of alternatives, it may well strike many as odd that the question has suddenly been reduced to this: same-sex marriage, pro or con?

The time is ripe to reconsider the issue. The campaign for marriage, never a broad-based movement among gay and lesbian activists, depended for its success on the courts. It was launched by a relatively small number of lawyers, not by a consensus among activists. It remains a project of litigation, though now with the support of the major lesbian and gay organizations. So far the campaign has come up dry. After initial success with the Supreme Court of Hawaii in *Baehr v. Lewin*, advocates of same-sex marriage had reason to be optimistic. The tactic of legal advocacy had apparently worked. But outside the courtroom, the homophobic backlash was building. First, the so-called Defense of Marriage Act was passed by Congress and signed by President Clinton. Then, in November of 1998, a statewide referendum in Hawaii neutralized the *Baehr* decision by allowing the legislature to amend the constitution so as to restrict marriage to heterosexual couples. A similar measure passed in Alaska, and another is on the ballot for California in the year 2000. Moreover, the Hawaii vote was not even close. Though advocates of same-sex marriage had predicted an even battle, the final vote was nearly 70 percent to 30.

Are these merely stumbles in the progress of history? States are codifying restrictions on marriage that had merely been tacit custom before, making new obstacles to marriage reform for the future. Powerful antigay forces have been mobilized around the issue. If reform of marriage was the goal, the tactics of legal advocacy have not worked, and in some ways have made the problem worse. And if a reconsideration of the tactics seems to have been forced by this turn of events, it is also reasonable to reconsider the long-term strategic goal, since debate over the ultimate goals of reform was cut short by the turn to legal advocacy in the first place. "The ship has sailed," Wolfson confidently declared; but now that the ship has run aground, we might ask whether it was headed in the right direction.

How did the shift in an American national agenda come about? What will its consequences be? For whom would marriage be a victory? What would the value of gay marriage be, for example, to sexual dissidents who are not marrying couples? It is at least possible that the worst consequences would fall on those who did not recognize the question of gay marriage as an "intra-community debate" at all, but considered it as something foisted on them by fundamentally alien organizations. (It is no accident that the organizations promoting marriage are defined primarily as advocates for lesbian and gay identity rather than for nonnormative sexual cultures.) Where does the politics of gay marriage lead? What kind of marriage are we talking about, and how might its place in the larger context of state regulations about sexuality be changed? Behind the question of gay marriage as it is posed in the United States, these fundamental questions are not being aired. But they are the questions that count. We cannot wait until American courts have settled the marriage issue before addressing them, not least because the way they are answered will play a large part in determining the meaning and consequences of marriage.

Marriage—Why Not?

Marriage became the dominant issue in lesbian and gay politics in the 1990s, but not before. If marriage is so fundamental to a program of rights, why did gay men and lesbians resist it over the twenty-five-year period of their most defiant activism? The issue had been raised from the beginning. In 1970, riding a burst of radical enthusiasm after Stonewall, the Reverend Troy Perry officiated a ceremony for two lesbians. Under California law at the time, common-law marriage could be formalized by a church ceremony after a couple had lived to-gether for two years. (California law said nothing about the sexes of the couple.) The two women had lived together for just over two years, and so demanded (unsuccessfully, it turned out) that California recognize theirs as an already es-tablished common-law marriage. The same year, a gay male couple in Min-nesota made national headlines by applying for a marriage license. One of the men, Jack Baker, wrote a lengthy rationale for what they had done. Baker em-phasized that marriage was "used by the legal system as a distribution mecha-nism for many rights and privileges" and that as long as the culture considered marriage a right, it was necessary to demand it: "when any minority allows itself to be denied a right that is given to others, it is allowing itself to be relegated to a second-rate position." The mere posing of the issue was a jolt. It made the heterosexuality of marriage visible, to many people, for the first time. It drew attention to the exclusions entailed by marriage, through provisions for inheri-tance, wrongful death actions, tax rates, and the like. And it advanced a claim of equality that had undeniable appeal. Baker's claims seemed scandalous to the straight press. They sparked animated discussions of theory and strategy within the groups that had organized in the wake of Stonewall.

Despite the strength of Baker's reasons, and despite the potent theatrical appeal of the issue, gay and lesbian groups did not pursue marriage as a central part of their strategy over the next twenty years. Why not? Was it simply a mat-ter of lesbian resistance derived from the feminist critique of marriage? Were gay men just too busy snorting poppers at the baths? Was American culture simply not ready for gay marriage? These are the stories now being told by the advocates of same-sex marriage, back in the headlines after more than a quarter century. But we should not discount other explanations. There were, I think, strong and articulate reasons why the gay movement for decades refused to pur-sue the path on which it is now hellbent. They lay at the heart of an ethical vi-sion of queer politics and centered on the need to resist the state regulation of sexuality. Queer thought both before and after Stonewall rested on these prin-ciples:

- It called attention to the mythology by which marriage is idealized.
- It recognized the diversity of sexual and intimate relations as worthy of respect and protection.
- Indeed, it cultivated unprecedented kinds of commonality, intimacy, and public life.
- It resisted any attempt to make the norms of straight culture into the stan-dards by which queer life should be measured.
- It especially resisted the notion that the state should be allowed to accord legitimacy to some kinds of consensual sex but not others, or to confer re-spectability on some people's sexuality but not others.
- It insisted that much of what was taken to be morality, respectability, or decorum was, in practice, a way of regulating sexual pleasures and rela-tions.

- It taught that any self-esteem worth having must not be purchased by a disavowal of sex; it must include esteem for one's sexual relations and pleasures, no matter how despised by others.
- It made itself alert to the invidiousness of any institution, like marriage, that is designed both to reward those inside it and to discipline those outside it: adulterers, prostitutes, divorcees, the promiscuous, single people, unwed parents, those below the age of consent—in short, all those who become, for the purposes of marriage law, queer.
- It insisted that any vision of sexual justice begin by considering the unrecognized dignity of these outcasts, the ways of living they represent, and the hierarchies of abjection that make them secondary, invisible, or deviant.
- It became alert on principle to the danger that those same hierarchies would continue to structure the thought of the gay and lesbian movement itself—whether through "internalized homophobia," ingroup hostility, or simply through the perspective unconsciously embedded in so much of our thought and perception.
- It tried to correct for the tendency of U.S. debates to ignore other societies, on whom they nevertheless have an impact.

These insights and principles are so basic that they found expression equally in the work of academic theorists and untutored activists. They made up the ethical vision I encountered in the writings of 1970s gay activists when I was first coming out, and the same vision later served as the basis for much of the AIDS activist movement. Because of these basic commitments, when gay and lesbian organizations did include the expansion of marriage in their vision of change after Stonewall, they usually contextualized it as part of more sweeping changes designed to ensure that single people and nonstandard households, and not just same-sex couples, would benefit. In 1972, for example, the National Coalition of Gay Organizations called for the "repeal of all legislative provisions that restrict the sex or number of persons entering into a marriage unit and extension of legal benefits of marriage to all persons who cohabit regardless of sex or numbers." They also demanded "elimination of tax inequities victimizing single persons and same-sex couples." This may not have been a focused, detailed reform program, but it showed an insistence that the demands of couples be accompanied by those of the unmarried and of nonstandard households.

Those who now advocate gay marriage have not shown how doing so is consistent with this tradition. They have induced widespread amnesia about it. It is possible, at least in theory, to imagine a politics in which sex-neutral marriage is seen as a step toward the more fundamental goals of sexual justice: not just formal equality before the law, based on a procedural bar to discrimination, but a substantive justice that would target sexual domination, making possible a democratic cultivation of alternative sexualities. (This kind of question was explicitly ruled out of consideration by the *Baehr* court.) The advocates of gay

marriage have not made this case. Many, indeed, have made the opposite case—
that pursuing marriage means abandoning the historical principles of the queer
movement as an antiquated "liberationism." For writers such as Andrew Sullivan, Gabriel Rotello, Michelangelo Signorile, Jonathan Rauch, and Bruce
Bawer, this is part of the appeal of marriage. Others argue, either ingenuously
or disingenuously, that marriage has nothing to do with these historical commitments, that it is not a question of social change or cultural politics at all but
a neutral matter on which each individual must decide. This is the official or
semiofficial position of the major national gay and lesbian organizations: the
National Gay and Lesbian Task Force, the Human Rights Campaign, and
Lambda Legal Defense. Either way, the crucial founding insights behind several decades' worth of gay and lesbian politics are now being forgotten. If the
campaign for marriage requires such a massive repudiation of queer culture's
best insights on intimate relations, sex, and the politics of stigma, then the campaign is doing more harm than marriage could ever be worth. . . .

Marriage Without Cost

A much more benign position on marriage has become the creed of the major
national gay organizations and is fast becoming entrenched as the new common
sense. It is best expressed by Kerry Lobel, executive director of the National
Gay and Lesbian Task Force, in a press release announcing support for gay
marriage: "Marriage is an important personal choice and a basic human right.
Whether gay people decide to get married or not, it should be our choice."
This line of thinking was established by the late Tom Stoddard, who worked
hard to launch both the gay marriage and military service campaigns. He wrote
in *Out/Look* in 1989 that the fundamental issue "is not the desirability of marriage, but rather the desirability of the *right* to marry." Activists, in Stoddard's
view, were obliged to work for as many options as possible for gay people, even
if they disliked marriage in its currently sanctioned form.

   A conception of activism as enlarging the life options of gay men and lesbians has a manifest appeal. And it is undeniable that many gays and lesbians
want to marry. But this way of thinking says nothing about whether pursuing
legal marriage is a good political strategy, about the ethical question of what
marrying does, about state regulation, or about the normativity of marriage. Is
marrying something you do privately, as a personal choice or as an expression
of taste, with no consequences for those who do not marry? Is it a private act, a
mere choice, like an expression of taste?

   That would be true only if marriage were somehow thought to lack the
very privileged relation to legitimacy that makes people desire it in the first
place, or if the meaning of marriage could somehow be specified without reference to the state. As long as people marry, the state will continue to regulate the
sexual lives of those who do not marry. It will continue to refuse to recognize
our intimate relations—including cohabiting partnerships—as having the same

rights or validity as a married couple. It will criminalize our consensual sex. It will stipulate at what age and in what kind of space we can have sex. It will send the police to harass sex workers and cruisers. It will restrict our access to sexually explicit materials. All this and more the state will justify because these sexual relations take place outside of marriage. In the modern era, marriage has become the central legitimating institution by which the state regulates and permeates people's most intimate lives; it is the zone of privacy outside of which sex is unprotected. In this context, to speak of marriage as merely one choice among others is at best naive. It might be more accurately called active mystification. . . .

People might marry for all kinds of reasons. They might want to stick it in the face of the straights. They might want access to health care. They might want a public armature for their own will to sustain a relationship of care. They might have chosen with eyes wide open to embrace a world in which a coupling supported by shared property is the only sign of real belonging and the only publicly recognized context for intimacy. They might simply not trust the relationship to last without third-party assurances. They might think that marriage will relieve their fears of getting old, fat, or undesirable. They might marry for no better reason than that marrying is what one does. Or they might want in-laws. Judge Richard Posner worries, rather extravagantly, that a gay man would marry a succession of AIDS patients in order to collect the life insurance. It's likely enough that people will have many motives and that most will be marked by ambivalence. That's life.

Claudia Card illustrates well the difficulties posed by marriage for queers with nonstandard intimacies when she writes:

> My partner of the past decade is not a domestic partner. She and I form some kind of fairly common social unit which, so far as I know, remains nameless. Along with such namelessness goes a certain invisibility . . . We do not share a domicile (she has her house; I have mine). Nor do we form an economic unit (she pays her bills; I pay mine). Although we certainly have fun together, our relationship is not based simply on fun. We share the sorts of mundane details of daily living that [Richard] Mohr finds constitutive of marriage (often in her house, often in mine). We know a whole lot about each other's lives that the neighbors and our other friends will never know. In times of trouble, we are each other's first line of defense, and in times of need, we are each other's main support. Still, we are not married. Nor do we yearn to marry. Yet if marrying became an option that would legitimate behavior otherwise illegitimate and make available to us social securities that will no doubt become even more important to us as we age, we and many others like us might be pushed into marriage. Marrying under such conditions is not a totally free choice.

This account reminds us that lived intimacies seldom take the form imposed by marriage. It also shows that people are likely to encounter in marriage a mix of constraints and that the meaning of marriage is only partly what they themselves bring to it.

Because the institution of marriage is itself one of the constraints on people's intimate lives, to judge the worthiness of the institution is not to condemn the people in it. But it does mean that marrying should be considered as an ethical problem. It is a public institution, not a private relation, and its meaning and consequences extend far beyond what a marrying couple could intend. The ethical meaning of marrying cannot be simplified to a question of pure motives, conscious choice, or transcendent love. Its ramifications reach as far as the legal force and cultural normativity of the institution. That is a heavy ethical burden to take on, and feminists such as Card have long shown courage in addressing it. No wonder people are so grateful to Wolfson, Lobel, and others who are willing to dismiss the ethics of marriage in such a radical and shallow way.

It is undeniable that the restriction of marriage to heterosexual couples is a potent form of discrimination, regulation, and stigma. But to combat that inequality requires us to think beyond the mere inclusion of gay couples and to recognize that marrying has consequences for the unmarried. Those consequences can be treated, roughly, under the following headings:

- the menu of privileges and prohibitions, incentives and disincentives, directly tied to marriage by the state;
- the material incentives and disincentives tied to marriage in civil society;
- the matrix of state regulations of sexuality of which marriage is the linchpin; and
- the broader cultural normativity of marital status.

Each of these should be challenged, not celebrated, as a condition of same-sex marriage.

The strategic question facing the lawyers is this: should we try to extend benefits and recognition even further beyond conventional marriage, uncoupling them from marital status and making them available to individuals, households, and intimate relations? Or should we claim for ourselves the status of marriage and thereby restrict entitlements and recognition to it? *This is not the decision that is posed to individual lesbians and gay men in the form of a choice to marry.* A poll of gay men or lesbians does not address this issue. We have good reason to be alarmed, given the potential for majoritarianism, when apologists such as Wolfson appeal to a silent majority that favors marriage. You need not argue that gays who marry have chosen to sell out less assimilationist or privileged queers in order to believe that the effect would be to reinforce the material privileges and cultural normativity of marriage. Individual choices to marry are not only rewarded with material benefits and normative recognition, but made from the limited slate of socially supported alternatives. Since the desire to marry is an aspect of the normativity of marriage, it cannot be said to validate the norm, any more than the desire to buy a Coke validates capitalism. Buying commodities sustains the culture of commodities whether the buyers like it or not. That is the power of a system. Just so, marrying consolidates and sustains the normativity of marriage. And it does so despite what may be the best intentions of those who marry. . . .

Notes

81. "The institution of marriage is trivialized by same-sex marriage": The exchange of May 30, 1996, is reproduced in Andrew Sullivan, ed., *Same-Sex Marriage: Pro and Con* (New York: Vintage, 1997), pp. 225–26.

83. What purpose could be served by a skeptical discussion of marriage now, given the nature of the opposition? Jesse Helms's speech on the Senate floor in favor of the Defense of Marriage Act is printed in Robert M. Baird and Stuart E. Rosenbaum, eds., *Same-Sex Marriage: The Moral and Legal Debate* (Amherst: Prometheus Books, 1997), p. 22. Jean Bethke Elshtain's "Against Gay Marriage" appeared in *Commonweal*, October 22, 1991, and is reprinted in Andrew Sullivan, ed., *Same-Sex Marriage: Pro and Con: A Reader* (New York: Vintage, 1997), pp. 57–60. Pope John Paul II is quoted by the *New York Times*, "Pope Deplores Gay Marriage," February 23, 1994.

83. "The ship has sailed": Evan Wolfson, "Crossing the Threshold: Equal Marriage Rights for Lesbians and Gay Men, and the Intra-Community Critique," *New York University Review of Law and Social Change* 21 (1994): 567–615, p. 611. See also Evan Wolfson, "Why We Should Fight for the Freedom to Marry," *Journal of Gay, Lesbian, and Bisexual Identity* 1 (Jan. 1996).

90. "repeal of all legislative provisions . . . victimizing single persons and same-sex couples": quoted in William Eskridge, *The Case for Same-Sex Marriage: From Sexual Liberty to Civilized Commitment* (New York: The Free Press, 1996), p. 54.

91. "Among some gays . . . enemy of more desirable institutions": Robert M. Baird and Stuart E. Rosenbaum, eds., *Same-Sex Marriage: The Moral and Legal Debate* (Amherst: Prometheus Books, 1997), pp. 10–11.

92. "to the extent that same-sex marriage might embolden some couples . . . would seem almost irrelevant": Eskridge, *The Case for Same-Sex Marriage: From Sexual Liberty to Civilized Commitment* (New York: The Free Press, 1996), p. 82.

93. "Whatever gravity gay life may have lacked . . . the value of a committed partner is incalculable": Eskridge, *The Case for Same-Sex Marriage: From Sexual Liberty to Civilized Commitment* (New York: The Free Press, 1996), pp. 58, 74.

95. the fundamental issue "is not the desirability of marriage, but rather the desirability of the right to marry": Tom Stoddard, "Why Gay People Should Seek the Right to Marry," *Out/Look* 6.8 (1990); repr. in Mark Blasius and Shane Phelan, eds., *We Are Everywhere: A Historical Sourcebook of Gay and Lesbian Politics* (New York: Routledge, 1997), quotation on p. 756.

96. "If it is freely chosen . . . the right society has never granted": Evan Wolfson, "Crossing the Threshold," pp. 582–83.

97. "The most important unresolved question . . . can pursue other avenues": Mary C. Dunlap, "The Lesbian and Gay Marriage Debate: A Microcosm of Our Hopes and Troubles in the Nineties," *Law and Sexuality* 1 (1991): 63–96, p. 90.

98. "Whatever the history . . . and, for some, their religious community": Evan Wolfson, "Crossing the Threshold," p. 479.

99. "How could a feminist, out, radical lesbian like myself . . . those who participate in my world": Barbara Cox, "A (Personal) Essay on Same-Sex Marriage," in Baird

and Rosenbaum, *Same-Sex Marriage: The Moral and Legal Debate*, pp. 27–29. This essay was originally a long footnote to an article in the *Wisconsin Law Review*, so the disappearance of the law and the state from Cox's understanding of marriage is especially telling.

101. "The right joining in marriage is the work of the Lord only. . . . we are but witnesses" [Fox] and "Not felon-like law-bound, but wedded in desires" [Clare]: both quoted in Christopher Hill, *Liberty against the Law: Some Seventeenth-Century Controversies* (London: Penguin, 1997), pp. 201–203.

104. "The suggestion that lesbians and gay men . . . the imputation seems wrong, as well as unfair": Evan Wolfson, "Crossing the Threshold," p. 585.

105. "Does everyone who gets married . . . endorse every retrograde aspect of marriage?": Evan Wolfson, "Crossing the Threshold," p. 602.

106. "My partner of the past decade is not a domestic partner . . . Marrying under such conditions is not a totally free choice": Claudia Card, "Against Marriage and Motherhood," *Hypatia* 11.3 (Summer 1996): 1–23, p. 7.

Questions for Reflection, Discussion, and Writing

1. What arguments about why marriage should remain a heterosexual institution are advanced by right-wing and conservative thinkers, according to Warner?

2. What arguments about why the right to marriage should be granted to gays and lesbians are advanced by gay and lesbian groups, according to Warner? Which groups or individuals are currently arguing for "gay marriage" according to Warner?

3. According to Warner, what issues are being obscured or not addressed by and within GLBT communities and individuals as a result of the focus on marriage?

4. What arguments against gay marriage does Warner offer? According to Warner, why is the idea and promotion of gay marriage an anti-queer proposition? What support does he offer for his claims?

5. What is the relationship between the State and marriage, according to Warner?

Writing Assignment

If marriage is *not* the way to proceed with queer rights, then how should queers pursue equality with regard to health, pension and social security benefits? Does Warner provide any answers? What might your strategy be? On what principles and realities is it based?

Related Reading

Thomas B. Stoddard, "Gay Marriage: A Must Or A Bust?" *Out/Look* 2.2 (Fall 1989): 8–9, 10–13.

Paula L. Ettelbrick, "Since When Was Marriage the Path to Liberation?" *Out/Look* 2.2 (Fall 1989): 9, 14–17.

Richard Goldstein, "The Great Gay Marriage Debate." *Village Voice*. January 9, 1996. 24, 29.

Alisa Solomon, "Get Married? Yes, but Not by the State." *Village Voice.* January 9, 1996. 25, 29.

Victoria A. Brownworth, "Tying the Knot or the Hangman's Noose: The Case Against Marriage" in *Too Queer: Essays From A Radical Life.* Ithaca, NY: Firebrand Books. 1996. 129–136.

Ellen Lewin, "'Why in the world would you want to do that?': Claiming Community in Lesbian Commitment Ceremonies" in *Inventing Lesbian Cultures in America.* Ellen Lewin, Ed. Boston: Beacon Press. 1996. 105–130.

Robert Jensen, "The Politics and Ethics of Lesbian and Gay 'Wedding' Announcements in Newspapers. *Howard Journal of Communication* 7.1 (1996): 13–28.

Chai Feldman, "Keep the Sex in Same-Sex Marriage." *The Harvard Gay & Lesbian Review* 4.4 (Fall 1997): 23–25.

Andrew Sulivan, "We're Talking About the Right to Choose." *The Harvard Gay & Lesbian Review* 4.4 (Fall 1997): 25–28.

Evan Wolfson, "How to Win the Freedom to Marry." *The Harvard Gay & Lesbian Review* 4.4 (Fall 1997): 29–30, 32.

Ralph Wedgwood, "What Are We Fighting For?" *The Harvard Gay & Lesbian Review* 4.4 (Fall 1997): 32–33.

Paula Ettelbrick, "Legal Marriage Is Not the Answer." *The Harvard Gay & Lesbian Review* 4.4 (Fall 1997): 34–36.

Michael Shernoff, "Gay Marriage and Gay Widowhood." *The Harvard Gay & Lesbian Review* 4.4 (Fall 1997): 36–37.

Jonathan Rauch, "Who Needs Marriage?" in *Same Sex: Debating the Ethics, Science, and Culture of Homosexuality.* John Corvino, Ed. Lanham, MD: Rowman & Littlefield. 1997. 304–316.

Claudia Card, "Against Marriage" in *Same Sex: Debating the Ethics, Science, and Culture of Homosexuality.* John Corvino, Ed. Lanham, MD: Rowman & Littlefield. 1997. 317–330.

Robert P. Cabaj and David W. Purcell, Eds., *On the Road to Same-Sex Marriage: A Supportive Guide to Psychological, Political, and Legal Issues.* San Francisco, CA: Josey-Bass Publishers. 1998.

Chrys Ingraham, *White Weddings: Romancing Heterosexuality in Popular Culture.* NY: Routledge. 1999.

Richard D. Mohr, "The Stakes in the Gay Marriage Wars." *The Gay & Lesbian Review* 7.3 (Summer 2000): 22–23.

John Corvino, "No Slippery Slope." *The Gay & Lesbian Review* 7.3 (Summer 2000): 37–40.

William N. Eskridge, Jr., *Equality Practice: Civil Unions and the Future of Gay Rights.* NY: Routledge. 2001.

Social Activism

Investigate policy at your educational institution to see what, if any, domestic partnership benefits they have and support. Interview administrators and faculty. Write an article about this subject for your campus newspaper.

CREDITS

SECTION ONE

Page 3, John D'Emilio, "After Stonewall" in *Making Trouble: Essays on Gay History, Politics, and The University*. NY: Routledge. 1992. 237–274. Reprinted by permission of the author.

page 38, Cherry Smyth, excerpt as attached from *Lesbians Talk Queer Notions*. London: Scarlet Press. 1992. 15, 17–19, 20–22, 28–31. Reprinted by permission of Scarlet Press.

Page 51, Lisa Duggan, "Making It Perfectly Queer" in *Socialist Review* 22:1 (1992). 11–31. Reprinted by permission of the author.

Page 67, Eve Kosofsky Sedgwick, excerpt as attached from "Axiomatic" in *Epistomology of the Closet*. Berkeley: University of California Press. 1990. pp. 1–4, 9–11, 17–22, 24–26, 27–31, 51–54. Copyright © 1990 The Regents of the University of California. Reprinted by permission.

Page 83, Ruth Goldman, "Who is That QUEER QUEER? Exploring Norms Around Sexuality, Race, and Class in Queer Theory" in *Queer Studies*. Brett Beemyn and Mickey Eliason, Eds. New York: New York University Press, 1996, pp. 169–182. Reprinted by permission.

SECTION TWO

Page 101, Paula Treichler, "AIDS, Homophobia and Biomedical Discourse: An Epidemic of Signification" in *Aids: Cultural Analysis: Cultural Activism*, Cambridge, MA: MIT Press, 1988, pp. 31–70. Originally published in CULTURAL STUDIES 1–3 (October 1987), 263–305. Reprinted by permission of the author.

Page 138, From a leaflet distributed at an annual gaypride parade in New York, June 1990.

Page 149, Laraine Sommella, "This is about People Dying: The Tactics of Early ACT UP and Lesbian Avengers in New York City" in QUEERS IN SPACE: Communities/Public Spaces/Sites of Resistance. Gordan Brent Ingram, Anne-Marie Bouthillette and Yolanda Retters, Eds. Seattle, Bay Press, 1997, pp. 407–437. Reprinted by permission of Laraine Sommella. "I would like to acknowledge the efforts of Maxine Wolfe and the encouragement of Gordon Brent Ingram, without which this piece would not have been written."

Page 177 Douglas Crimp, "Right On, Girlfriend" in *Fear Of A Queer Planet*, edited by Michael Warner (University of Minnesota Press, 1993), pp. 300–320. Copyright © 1993 by the Regents of the University of Minnesota. Reprinted by permission.

SECTION THREE

Page 199, Samuel R. Delany, "Some Queer Notions about Race" in *Dangerous Liaisons: Blacks, Gays, and the Struggle for Equality*. Eric Brandt, Ed. NY: New Press, 1999, pp. 259–289. Reprinted by permission of Samuel R. Delany.

Page 224, Cherrie Moraga, "Queer Aztlan: The Re-formation of Chicano Tribe," excerpted from *The Last Generation*. Boston: South End Press. 1993. 145–165. Reprinted by permission.

SECTION FOUR

SECTION FIVE

SECTION SIX

SECTION SEVEN